W9-BST-581

Dave Litfin's Expert Handicapping

Dave Litfin's Expert Handicapping

WINNING INSIGHTS INTO BETTING THOROUGHBREDS

by Dave Litfin

LITTLE, BROWN AND COMPANY
BOSTON NEW YORK TORONTO LONDON

Copyright © 1995 by The Daily Racing Form, Inc.

All rights reserved. No part of this book may be reproduced in any form or by any electronic or mechanical means, including information storage and retrieval systems, without permission in writing from the publisher, except by a reviewer who may quote brief passages in a review.

First Edition

The author is grateful for permission to include the following previously published material:

Maiden Stats is compiled and published annually by Bloodstock Research Information Services, Inc., Lexington, Kentucky.

All pedigree and sales statistics published from *Maiden Stats*. Copyright © 1995 by Bloodstock Research Information Services, Inc. Reprinted by permission.

Excerpts from *The Sheets* by Len Ragozin. Reprinted by permission of Len Ragozin.

Excerpts from *The Daily Racing Form*. Copyright © 1995 by The Daily Racing Form, Inc. Reprinted by permission.

Excerpts from *Thoro-graph* performance ratings. Reprinted by permission of Jerry Brown.

Library of Congress Cataloging-in-Publication Data

Litfin, Dave.
[Expert handicapping]
Dave Litfin's expert handicapping : winning insights into betting thoroughbreds / by Dave Litfin.—1st ed.
p. cm.
ISBN 0-316-52781-5
1. Horse racing—Betting. I. Title.
SF331.L58 1995
798.401—dc20 95-8508

10 9 8 7 6 5 4 3 2 1

MV-NY

Published simultaneously in Canada
by Little, Brown & Company (Canada) Limited

Printed in the United States of America

For Robin, who loved me when . . .

CONTENTS

ACKNOWLEDGMENTS

AS DR. BILL QUIRIN wrote in *Handicapping by Example,* the last major treatment of the New York circuit, "No book on handicapping can be written in isolation, nor can it represent solely its author's original thoughts on the subject." In that spirit, my thanks to Dr. Quirin, and also to Tom Ainslie, Tom Brohamer, Mark Cramer, Steve Davidowitz, Huey Mahl, Barry Meadow, Dick Mitchell, Dr. Howard Sartin, and William L. Scott. Special thanks to fellow handicappers Andy Beyer and James Quinn, who provided encouragement and advice during this manuscript's formative stages.

None of these well-known handicapping authors approach the game in exactly the same way. Yet all are consistent winners because, as Cramer has observed, the opposite of a profound truth often is another profound truth. Mindful of this reality, I have attempted to steer clear of absolute dos and don'ts, offering merely a discussion through example races of what works for me.

My heartfelt appreciation as well to Len Ragozin, Len Friedman, and Bob Beinish of *The Sheets,* and to Jerry Brown of *Thoro-graph,* for their cooperation in bringing form-cycle analysis through the use of performance ratings into the mainstream. As always, the game's most innovative minds are happy to share their insights with anyone interested enough to ask.

Thanks also to Charles Hayward of Little, Brown and Company, Jack Farnsworth, publisher of the *Daily Racing Form,* and Katherine Wilkins, vice president of marketing for *DRF,* who supported this project from the get-go, and to my editor, Catherine Crawford, who really knows her stuff.

Since I wasn't voted "Most Likely to Write a Book" while attending the School of Tough Beats, thanks to all the players who requested I actually do so. What follows is the result of your enthusiasm.

Last, but certainly not least, thanks to my wife, Robin, who holds Team Litfin together while I go about the business of being a degenerate horseplayer, so to speak.

INTRODUCTION

THERE NEVER was a better place and time to be twelve years old than New York City in 1970. Besides rooting for the Mets, Jets, and Knicks, I was feverishly testing my brand-new Kel-co class calculator on the races at Aqueduct. To my delight, the magical slide rule showed a profit for a month's worth of results.

The world would soon be mine.

On Saturdays I took the "A" train to the races (in those days a seventh-grader could ride the subway alone). Once in a while I forgot about seventh grade altogether and headed for the track on a weekday, hoping to parlay my lunch money into a new baseball glove or a coveted back issue of *Superman*. Once in a while I even got lucky and made a score. I'll never forget boxing Ferly and Lucie Honey in an exacta (shortly after exactas had come into existence) and listening to my pocket transistor radio in Spanish class as Harvey Pack came on with his *Pack at the Track Report:*

"The winner, OTB letter G, Ferly. Thirty-nine dollars, sixteen-eighty, and nine-twenty. Second . . ."

I held my breath: please be J, please be J, please be . . .

"J, Lucie Honey. Six-forty, four-twenty. The G-J exacta returns two hundred sixty-three dollars and eighty cents."

YES! ONE TIME! YES!

I don't remember much from Spanish 101, but that payoff remains a vivid memory to this day. Not $263.20 . . . not $263.40 . . . but *$263.80.* I can still visualize the way that glorious G-J exacta looked in black Magic Marker on the result board of the Seventy-second Street OTB, as I bounded in to collect what seemed like all the money in the world.

Inevitably, I gave back that $263.80 . . . and then some. A pattern developed where I'd arrive at the track with a thick roll of $1 bills and leave with barely enough for a pretzel and a subway token home. My Kel-co calculator had hit the skids, and a frightening realization had slapped me in the face:

Life wasn't going to be so simple after all.

In the months and years that followed, I tried every calculator, gadget, system, and mail-order hustle known to mankind, and every single one of them picked winners. Finally, it dawned on me that any system will pick *some* winners, but none will pick enough of them to show a profit in the long run.

So, what works? Everything works sometimes, nothing works all the time. A synergistic combination of class, form, speed, pace, and trainers is the way to go. This book offers opinions, observations, and techniques to aid in evaluating a race's possibilities from different angles, so that handicappers have the wherewithal to bet on improving horses and against those showing signs of decline. By the very definition of the pari-mutuel system, such tactics guarantee fair-value odds and long-term profits, provided any sensible program of money management is utilized.

Importantly, there hasn't been a comprehensive look at New York racing since Quirin's *Handicapping by Example,* which was published in 1986. Had Rip Van Winkle been a horseplayer, he'd be in for a rude awakening in the mid-1990s, for the game scarcely resembles what it was only a decade or so ago. Many of the blue-blooded stables are all but extinct due to attrition and changes in tax law; much of America's best bloodstock was whisked away by foreign interests after the bottom fell out of the breeding industry in the late 1980s; foal crops are diminishing annually to the point where small fields of overraced cripples are prevalent, even on major circuits.

Not only are there fewer horses, there are fewer people. Many casual fans have been lured away by the casinos — which do a far superior job of cultivating and maintaining their clientele — so that the percentage of knowledgeable and profit-motivated players is higher now than ever, making it more difficult than ever to find overlays. Difficult, but certainly not impossible.

The examples in this book — and there are many — were not chosen to make me look like a genius. In some instances I collected on the winner, in others the bet was lost but the horse ran well enough (or poorly enough) to prove a point; some results made more sense after the fact. The examples were carefully chosen to illustrate real-life situations, nuances, and strategies, and to point out trends that can reasonably be expected to continue. Alert readers with sharp memories and/or a file of old *Daily Racing Forms* may take umbrage that views expressed herein differ at times from my prerace analyses. For this, I make no apologies; this book is designed for the player who understands the crucial difference between selecting contenders the night before (in my case, forty-eight hours before!) and betting real money with a minute to post after odds, track conditions, late scratches, and prerace warm-ups have been evaluated.

Any rational player knows that the handicapping process does not end once the preliminary work of identifying contenders is completed. I have been the handicapping analyst on the New York circuit for the *Daily Racing Form* since 1991, and since then there have been countless times when I've made a selection I'd like to take back; this happens for a number of reasons: a key late scratch leaves one speed horse alone on the lead, or a sudden thunderstorm washes a race off the grass, or a track bias has strongly influenced the results of the day's earlier races . . . et cetera. We public handicappers do the best we can, but due to deadline constraints we can only work with preliminary information; winning at the track requires horseplayers to think on their feet, evaluating late-breaking data and relating it to the odds being offered on the toteboard. No matter what any system-seller ever tells you, no system that boasts "no judgment required" will ever work. That's what handicapping is — making judgments, and being right often enough to come out ahead. And no matter how much you learn, the game is always changing, and there is always more that you can do to improve your game. I've been playing the races in New York since the days of the Miracle Mets, which translates to a bit more than a quarter of a century. I've found that respecting these realities and being willing to adapt and change with the times has helped me to develop a reputation for consistency and dependability through the first four years or so of what I hope will be a long and productive career as both a public handicapper and a winning player.

That's what this book is about. How far you want to take this material is a matter of personal choice. Though some time and effort is required to take an edge on a consistent basis, the game should, above all else, be a source of enjoyment. If you're not having fun with your handicapping routine, inevitably it will be reflected by red ink on the bottom line. Don't feel compelled to master every technique described within these covers. If you're into "fun with numbers," be the best figure player on your block; if you enjoy researching trainer patterns, come up with a few that no one else has. It's okay to specialize — plenty of people win that way.

Winning is up to you. The edges are here, and they have pointed the way to some solid plays for me season after season. You may not strike it rich, but after digesting these contents and incorporating what you think is relevant to your own style, you'll probably be a better player than you were before. After all, one inspired play in the right race at the right time can transform a near miss into a memorable score.

Ultimately, that's the nature of the game. Anyone who remembers Ron Swoboda, Joe Namath, and Willis Reed would agree.

Dave Litfin
Belmont Park, 1995

Dave Litfin's Expert Handicapping

ONE

CONDITION ANALYSIS – SPEED FIGURES

WHEN I WENT TO AQUEDUCT or Belmont Park during my formative years, I would often skip over a few of the four basic food groups at lunchtime in order to save a couple of extra bucks for the daily double. Meanwhile, handicappers armed with a good set of speed figures were dining on champagne and caviar. In those days, speed figures weren't common knowledge, as they are now, and class was the factor that most bettors paid attention to. Claiming prices and purse values were widely regarded as the proper tools for gauging horses' intrinsic abilities, but speed handicappers operated from a much different and more scientific perspective and thus evaluated horses' moves up and down the class hierarchy much more precisely. By developing "par times" for each class — the normal final running times usually associated with each type of horse — a handful of speed handicappers could measure the speed/resiliency of the racetrack on a given day and make adjustments to the raw final times based on how much faster or slower than normal the times for the day were.

Speed handicapping seems elementary in the 1990s, but back then no one had heard of this approach. For the few speed handicappers who were around, cashing in on high-priced winners was like shooting ducks in a barrel; they knew, based on their adjusted final-time figures, exactly at what level of competition virtually any horse could be expected to perform well; often, it had little or nothing to do with a horse's supposed "class." It was a tremendous edge, the likes of which will never be seen at a racetrack again.

When Andrew Beyer's *Picking Winners* brought speed handicapping to the mainstream in 1975, figures became "the Way, the Truth, and the Light" for thousands upon thousands of players. But in *Beyer On Speed*, published in 1993, the author writes that "The increasing sophistication of the American bettors was making the use of figures less and less profitable."

Such is the nature of pari-mutuel wagering. Top-figure horses that went off at 4–1 in the good old days now routinely go postward at half that price, thanks to the popularity of speed figures. Accepting short odds on these propositions no longer constitutes a wagering advantage. Even when a horse runs a clearly superior figure to today's rivals, there is no guarantee it will reproduce an effort of the same quality next time out; horses run the same figure back-to-back only about one-third of the time.

Thankfully, two edges are available as matters presently stand:

1) Most bettors are lazy and have gotten into the habit of using speed figures as a crutch to avoid a thoughtful analysis of form cycles. A thoroughbred's current form is constantly in a state of improvement or decline. These days it is not enough merely to have an idea of how fast a horse ran in its most recent races; we must have some means of projecting whether today's performance will be better or worse than the ones that preceded it.

2) There are figure patterns that portend short- and long-term improvement and decline in form. Handicappers familiar with these patterns are in a position to bet on overlays (horses going postward at odds greater than their true chances of winning) and steer clear of underlays (horses offered at odds less than their actual winning chances).

Long before *Picking Winners* was published, Len Ragozin was making a living at the track with speed figures refined from a basic approach devised by his father, Harry Ragozin, back in the late 1940s. Today, Len Ragozin's figures — *The Sheets* — have acquired a reputation for their almost fanatical accuracy. They sell for $35 per day and exert the single most powerful influence on the toteboard in New York, not to mention the fact that many stables use *The Sheets* as a basis for buying and selling horses. Ragozin recalls how *The Sheets* got started:

> This didn't start out as a business, it was just figures for me and my father to bet and claim horses. Len Friedman, who is my partner

> now, came to me and said, "I have confidence in what you're doing, but when it comes to betting, you don't have time to do it right. How about this? You stay home and do the figures, and I'll go out to the track and bet."
>
> So here's this guy with extra-wide size thirteen feet who can't get shoes that fit, so he's out there in sneakers that have holes in them looking like a bum, and he's up at the hundred dollar window with these funny-looking cards. So naturally people said, "What are those? Can we get in on this?" That's how I got clients.

When Jerry Brown, a Ragozin associate, struck out on his own in 1982 to launch a similarly designed figure service called *Thoro-graph,* more people than ever were armed with stacks of 5″ × 8″ sheets detailing the career speed-figure histories of every horse in every race. Proof that *The Sheets* and *Thoro-graph* continue to filter into the mainstream came during the Triple Crown series of 1994, when each camp wrote articles for the *Daily Racing Form* — something that would've been unheard of twenty, ten, or even five years ago.

For the sake of simplicity, I sometimes refer to *The Sheets* and *Thoro-graph* simply as "sheets" and *Beyer Speed Figures* as "BSF" or "Beyer."

The sheets differ from Beyer in a number of ways:

- A horse's sheet contains its entire history, beginning with figures earned as a two-year-old; they are placed in the left-most of four vertical columns. Figures for three-year-olds are in the column just left of center. Four-year-old figures are just right of center. Five-year-old figures are in the right-most column. Each column begins with January at the bottom and ends with December at the top. A horse's most recent race, therefore, is always at the top of the column farthest to the right.
- Sheet-style figures include adjustments for ground loss on turns: horses that run wide are credited for having run farther. Because of this feature, sheet numbers are sensitive to track biases.
- The sheets also include adjustments for wind velocity and direction and for the amount of weight carried, the theory being that these are things that can be accurately measured.

• *The Sheets* and *Thoro-graph* employ their own clockers, who time races from the starting gate so as to include the "run-up" to the timing pole — the point where official timing of a race begins; run-up distances may vary, usually depending upon the proximity of a turn to the start of the race.

• On sheets, the lower the number, the faster the race. Theoretically, a champion runs a 0 (zero) on its best day; the figures measure how far a horse's effort was from a championship performance. Typically, Grade 1 races are run in the neighborhood of 5, give or take a point or two; good allowance runners and high-priced older claimers generally run in the range of 10; maiden claimers in New York usually run in the mid to upper 20s.

• Plus and minus signs to the right of a figure on *The Sheets* indicate a quarter of a point slower or faster, respectively. A figure of 8+ is read as 8¼; a figure of 8− is read as 7¾. A quotation mark following the number indicates half a point: 8″ is read as 8½. *Thoro-graph* uses superscript figures to indicate quarter- and half-points: 8^1 is read as 8¼; 8^2 is read as 8½; 8^3 is read as 8¾.

• The figures are arranged graphically, with the faster figures shifted to the left and the slower ones to the right. This makes patterns easier to spot, as Ragozin explains:

> If you're trying to analyze how horses come into and out of form, you will get to a point where you say, "Hey, I've seen that kind of pattern before." Even though you may have seen it before in a very high-class horse, and you're now looking at a very low-class horse, so that the numbers are entirely different, the way a healthy horse runs in and out on the sheets is the same. The combination of accurate ratings and a graphical presentation not only makes it possible to make meaningful judgments, they make it a lot of fun.

Even if you never use sheets, the form-cycle principles brought to light by Len Ragozin, Len Friedman, and Jerry Brown are universal; they can be applied by players using the Beyer figures published in the *Form* or any other reasonably accurate set of homemade figures. As will become apparent in this chapter, patterns on specific horses often, though not always, show up in the same way on Beyer as they do on the sheets; when the sheets and

Beyer show the same basic pattern for a horse, handicappers are correct in assigning more weight to the pattern's overall predictive strength, whether positive or negative.

The Beyer figures are based on the more traditional "higher number is better" scale. The highest Beyer figures will be in the 120s, and these rarified figures are earned by horses with championship potential; for example, Black Tie Affair earned a 120 winning the 1991 Breeders' Cup Classic. A figure of 110 wins most stakes races for older horses. A figure of 100 wins lesser-quality stakes and allowance races on the major circuits such as New York and California. A figure of 90 wins an average $25,000 claiming race; a figure of 80 wins an average $14,000 claimer in New York, which is the lowest level at which previous winners compete.

EXPLOSIVE HORSES

Three-year-olds that have recently run a figure equal to or slightly superior to their best two-year-old figures are strong candidates to improve again in the near future, especially if the slight "forward move" occurred soon after a return from a layoff.

If we think of thoroughbreds in human terms, a two-year-old is equivalent to a teenager, still growing and learning how to go about things; as the horse matures and grows stronger, it is logical to expect better performances as part of its normal, healthy course of development. By the same token, maturing horses that are unable to run as fast as they did in the earliest stages of their careers are exhibiting a negative sign of development.

Once a three-year-old runs the key figure — a figure equal to or slightly better than its best performance as a two-year-old — it is likely to feel the effects of that exertion, and it may require a short period of time to recover before it makes a second forward move. This period of time is approximately five weeks, but this is only a general average and is stated merely as a guideline. Some horses will throw in an "off" race if entered back quickly and then make the move in the second start following the key figure; others may return two or three weeks after the key figure and improve again right away.

The central point is this: once a three-year-old equals or slightly exceeds its best two-year-old figure, handicappers can expect it to improve again sometime in the near future. Often, these horses are entered in races in which others have already run higher figures, and they go off at generous odds.

Lightly raced four-year-olds that have recently equaled or slightly surpassed their top three-year-old figures can be similarly evaluated, particularly if they were unraced or had only a few starts at age two.

In either case, once the breakthrough figure is delivered, handicappers should be prejudiced in favor of these horses during the coming weeks.

The first time this really sank into my consciousness was at Saratoga in August of 1992. The sixth race on August 19 appeared inscrutable to most speed handicappers, but Bob Beinish, who leads instructional seminars for *The Sheets* while also serving as their customer relations representative, offered an unshakable opinion: "Everything is in place for Lochrima to run the best race of his life today," he said.

6 START 6 FURLONGS SARATOGA FINISH

6 FURLONGS. **(1.08) MAIDEN SPECIAL WEIGHT. Purse $24,000. 3-year-olds and upward foaled in New York state and approved by the New York state-bred registry. Weight: 3-year-olds 117 lbs. Older 122 lbs.**

Mick — B. c. 3(Mar), by Nostrum—Little Prema, by Cloudy Dawn — Lifetime 3 0 0 0 $1,560 — 1992 3 M 0 0 $1,560 — 1991 0 M 0 0
MAPLE E (61 9 3 10 .15) — Br.—Freeman Mr-Mrs W C (NY) — 117 — Wet 1 0 0 0
Own.—Freeman Willard C — Tr.—Freeman Willard C (6 1 2 1 .17)

19Jly92- 5Bel	fst	1⅛	:47	1:13^{1}	1:51^{2}	3↑S Md Sp Wt	54	6	4	4^{5½}	1^{hd}	3^{1½}	4^{9¼}	Davis R G	116	4.10	63-28	NiceShot116^{8¼}Concur116^{no}Who'sBelievble122	Bid, tired	9
1Jly92- 9Bel	my	7f	:22^{4}	:46	1:24^{1}	3↑S Md Sp Wt	49	8	7	8^{3¾}	5^{3½}	7^{7½}	6^{10¼}	Davis R G	116	8.30	73-14	CumberlandBlues116^{no}WlkTheWlk116^{2}Cp112	Four wide	10
22May92- 9Bel	fst	6½f	:22^{1}	:45^{2}	1:17^{3}	3↑S Md Sp Wt	50	8	13	13^{18}	10^{12}	8^{6½}	7^{9½}	Madrid A Jr	115	29.00	75-11	Mr.Lee115^{3½}AppreciteIt115^{1¾}OntheDockt115	No threat	14

LATEST WORKOUTS Aug 14 Sar 4f fst :48^{3} H — Aug 7 Sar 4f fst :47^{4} H — Jly 29 Sar 4f fst :52 B — Jly 15 Bel 5f fst 1:00^{3} H

Pago's Whim — B. c. 3(Mar), by Sir Wimborne—Ima Pago, by Pago Pago — Lifetime 1 0 0 0 $1,440 — 1992 1 M 0 0 $1,440 — 1991 0 M 0 0
SMITH M E (98 20 17 13 .20) — Br.—Dominguez Mr-Mrs R (NY) — 117
Own.—New Kan Stables — Tr.—O'Brien Colum (3 0 0 0 .00)

30Jly92- 9Sar	fst	6f	:22^{2}	:46	1:11	3↑S Md Sp Wt	50	8	8	5^{4½}	2^{2}	2^{5}	4^{11¼}	Maple E	116	21.30	78-06	Appreciate It116^{9} Bordagaray116^{nk}Concur116	Bid tired	12

LATEST WORKOUTS Aug 13 Sar tr.t 5f fst 1:03 B — Jly 19 Bel 5f fst 1:00^{4} H — Jly 13 Bel 4f fst :50^{4} B — Jly 7 Bel 4f fst :51 H

Lochrima — B. c. 3(Apr), by Carodanz—Cheval Fou, by Instrument Landing — Lifetime 5 0 0 0 — 1992 2 M 0 0 — 1991 3 M 0 0
CARR D (49 2 8 4 .04) — Br.—Santangelo George L (NY) — 117 — Wet 1 0 0 0
Own.—Santangelo George L — Tr.—Pascuma James J Jr (8 1 0 0 .13)

25Jly92- 9Bel	fst	6½f	:22^{3}	:45^{3}	1:18	3↑ Md 32500	38	4	3	5^{2}	7^{8}	8^{10}	8^{13¼}	Davis R G	114	14.70	70-15	TokenofPower114^{nk}Quintessentilly118^{nk}Strts112	Faded	10
8Jly92- 9Bel	fst	7f	:23^{1}	:46^{2}	1:25	3↑S Md Sp Wt	46	7	1	2^{hd}	2^{1}	4^{8}	5^{6¾}	Davis R G	116	11.40	72-16	ExpnsvCrm116½WlkThWlk116^{1¾}Cncr116	Speed, gv way	9
22Nov91- 4Aqu	sly	7f	:22^{2}	:45^{4}	1:23^{4}	Md 45000	24	10	1	2^{1½}	3^{3}	7^{12}	8^{27½}	Verge M E	114	7.60	56-21	PyforPly118^{6¾}LordWllstn114^{1¼}Jcksnprt118	Speed tired	10
14Nov91- 4Aqu	fst	1	:47^{3}	1:13	1:38^{1}	Md 45000	46	10	1	1^{1}	2^{hd}	3^{nk}	5^{5¾}	Verge M E	114	28.40	65-12	DoverCost114^{nk}Jessie'sd'Accord114^{2¼}AirTrety114	Tired	11
5Nov91- 3Aqu	fst	6f	:23^{2}	:48^{2}	1:14^{4}	Md 45000	31	6	9	6^{3½}	6^{4}	7^{4¾}	8^{8¾}	Verge M E	114	11.40	58-26	Cast Out114½ Del Farno118^{1½} Terrorthorn118	No threat	11

LATEST WORKOUTS Aug 4 Bel 4f fst :48 H — Jly 21 Aqu ⊡ 4f fst :49^{1} B — Jly 6 Aqu ⊡ 3f my :37^{2} B

Super Sibling — Ch. g. 6, by Fratello Ed—Superb Holme, by Superbity — Lifetime 52 0 5 6 $37,450 — 122
SANTIAGO A (8 0 1 0 .00) — Br.—Deluke Dominick J (NY)
Own.—Roe Loraine M — Tr.—Roe Lorraine M (1 0 0 0 .00)

1992	7	M	0 2	$4,770
1991	26	M	3 2	$20,820
Turf	3	0	0 0	
Wet	6	0	2 1	$8,820

27Jly92- 7Pha fst 6f	:222	:461	1:124	3↑Md Sp Wt	50	9 10	63¾	33½	32½	34½	Dentici A	Lb	122	36.80	72-17	True Justice1223 Rudy'sBoy1151½SuperSibling122	Wide	10
26Jun92- 6Pha fst 7f	:221	:452	1:244	3↑Md Sp Wt	58	4 8	76¾	66	55½	56	Dentici A	Lb	122	39.00	77-20	BlstOfIc114nkTruJustic1221½MjorMcGrth122	No threat	11
15Jun92- 6Pha fst 6f	:222	:462	1:121	3↑Md Sp Wt	39	5 6	87¾	99	710	712¾	Dentici A	b	122	25.40	67-19	CmpltThPss1148MjrMcGrth122nkPrsdntsHp114	Outrun	9
5Apr92- 2Aqu fst 6f	:232	:48	1:133	3↑Md 30000	47	4 11	119½	99	57½	49	Martinez R R5	b	115	24.90	64-25	Clrwy1135¾SntPhllp1112VctorosBnnr111	Brk slow, wide	11
20Jan92- 2Aqu fst 170	⊡:492	1:152	1:472	Md 30000	54	5 1	11	2hd	22	65½	Dentici A	b	118	13.20	62-32	Sir Ciao118½ Dr.Bartolo1221½SpaDancer118	Speed, tired	8
13Jan92- 3Aqu fst 6f	⊡:23	:471	1:131	Md 30000	48	2 9	811	89½	78	49¾	Dentici A	b	118	22.10	67-27	Kuetch1224SeaportTown122½SpaDncer118	Broke slowly	9
4Jan92- 2Aqu sly 6f	⊡:234	:482	1:133	Md 30000	49	9 3	51¾	53¼	55	38¼	Dentici A	b	118	20.10	67-24	AftertheDeluge1224¼SpDncer1184SuperSibling118	Wide	9
20Dec91- 9Aqu fst 6f	⊡:23	:472	1:13	3↑ⓈMd Sp Wt	45	9 7	95¾	105½	811	810¾	Dentici A	b	122	19.90	67-21	Convert1201½ Idasjack1201½ After theDeluge120	Outrun	12
15Dec91- 1Aqu fst 6f	⊡:23	:47	1:131	3↑Md 30000	42	2 5	42	34	46½	49¼	Dentici A	b	118	6.00	68-19	GunnryOfficr1166VlidMn116½AdmthK.116	Saved ground	7
28Nov91- 5Aqu fst 6f	:223	:462	1:13	3↑ⓈMd Sp Wt	48	1 6	65¼	47	36½	35	Dentici A	b	122	10.60	71-19	Frln'sFr1133½Al'sIcCstl1221½SprSblng122	Brk slw, wide	6

Gallant Pip — Dk. b. or br. c. 3(May), by Star Gallant—Pipparoo, by Rock Talk — Lifetime 0 0 0 0 — 1991 0 M 0 0 — 117
DAVIS R G (70 9 10 7 .13) — Br.—Irving Paparo (N.Y.)
Own.—Irving Papano — Tr.—Schettino Dominick (2 0 0 1 .00)
LATEST WORKOUTS Aug 11 Sar 5f fst 1:003 H — Aug 5 Sar 4f gd :50 Bg — Jly 26 Sar 4f fst :483 H — Jly 20 Bel 3f fst :354 Bg

Winlocs Getzaround — B. c. 3(Jun), by Cormorant—Midwest Lake, by Dawn Flight — Lifetime 0 0 0 0 — 1991 0 M 0 0 — 117
PEZUA J M (49 3 3 2 .06) — Br.—Raymond A. Roncari (N.Y.)
Own.—Scrips R Farm — Tr.—Miceli Michael (5 0 0 0 .00)
LATEST WORKOUTS Aug 13 Bel tr.t 4f fst :513 B — Aug 7 Bel 5f fst 1:042 Bg — Jly 26 Bel 5f fst 1:04 B — Jly 15 Bel 3f fst :37 B

Look's Like Bob — Ch. g. 3(Apr), by Hello Gorgeous—Tax Exempt, by Val de l'Orne — Lifetime 10 0 2 2 $17,770 — 117
DAY P (82 11 15 12 .13) — Br.—CBF Corporation (NY)
Own.—Bartow Robert C — Tr.—Dunham Bob G (3 0 0 1 .00)

1992	10	M	2 2	$17,770
1991	0	M	0 0	
Turf	1	0	0 0	
Wet	3	0	1 0	$5,810

30Jly92- 9Sar fst 6f	:222	:46	1:11	3↑ⓈMd Sp Wt	47	10 3	77¼	44	36½	512¼	Nelson D	b	116	10.80	77-06	AppreciateIt1169Bordgry116nkConcur116	Flattened out	12
19Jly92- 5Bel fst 1⅛	:47	1:131	1:512	3↑ⓈMd Sp Wt	23	4 2	25	3nk	58	728½	Rojas R I	b	116	4.30	43-28	NiceShot1168¼Concur116noWho'sBelivbl122	Bumped st	9
28Jun92- 9Bel fst 1 1/16	:463	1:12	1:433	3↑ⓈMd Sp Wt	56	2 5	43	42	36	39¾	Rojas R I	b	114	3.80	74-11	BlzonSong1143¼NcShot1146¼Look'sLkBb114	No threat	10
7Jun92- 1Bel gd 1⅛	:464	1:112	1:514	3↑ⓈMd Sp Wt	65	4 3	32	2hd	2hd	21¾	Rojas R I	b	114	5.40	68-22	GrnGltor1141¾Look'sLikBob114nkC.C.Shrp115	Held 2nd	8
29May92- 9Bel fm 1 1/16	Ⓣ:451	1:10	1:42	3↑ⓈMd Sp Wt	38	2 12	75	83	915	924¼	Rojas R I	b	115	9.40	62-14	Lonnegan1151¼Trilingul1172¼SinktheShip115	Wide turn	12
18May92- 4Bel gd 1 1/16	:47	1:114	1:434	3↑ⓈMd Sp Wt	64	1 4	32	3nk	2hd	33½	Rojas R I	b	115	11.80	79-13	DuelZone12423¾TeddyC.115¾Look'sLikBob115	Bid, wknd	9
9May92- 1Bel my 1	:461	1:11	1:371	3↑Md 35000	48	2 3	3nk	42½	57½	610¼	Rojas R I	b	115	2.90	73-14	BrothrBrkfld115¾Dn'tThwrtM1156Clb120	Dueled inside	6
20Apr92- 9Aqu my 1⅛	:48	1:131	1:54	3↑ⓈMd Sp Wt	62	7 1	11	13	2½	23	Rojas R I	b	115	21.50	63-25	Ptrot'sThndr1153Look'sLkBob1152¼DlZn124	Held place	11
29Mar92- 9Aqu fst 1	:471	1:132	1:41	3↑ⓈMd Sp Wt	49	9 3	31½	54	99	78¼	Madrid A Jr	b	115	14.20	49-33	T.V.Lnding124¾StockinPly115¾Tlcompote115	Used early	11
20Mar92- 6Suf my 6f	:221	:464	1:141	Md Sp Wt	25	4 6	78	810	810	99½	Lozano J M	Bb	122	11.70	66-20	AngryRection1222JoeyStwrt1221¾UmbrtoRx122	Outrun	11

LATEST WORKOUTS Aug 9 Sar 4f gd :53 B — ●Jly 8 Aqu ⊡ 5f fst 1:023 B

Newyork Appeal — B. c. 3(Mar), by Proud Appeal—Cool Answer, by Victorian Era — Lifetime 1 0 0 0 — 117
ANTLEY C W (100 21 15 13 .21) — Br.—Jet M Farm & McMahon Anne C (NY)
Own.—Ran-Dom Stable — Tr.—Sciacca Gary (18 3 4 2 .17)

1992	1	M	0	0
1991	0	M	0	0

[illegible]92- 9Bel fst 6f	:223	:462	1:12	3↑ⓈMd Sp Wt	46	1 8	1hd	31	53½	57	Bailey J D		116	*1.80	73-14	Drmnthdyy1221ChppsT1163½Fbn'sChc122	Dueled inside	12

[LAT]EST WORKOUTS Aug 7 Sar 4f fst :48 B — Jly 13 Bel 3f fst :361 H — Jly 8 Bel 5f fst 1:00 H — Jly 2 Bel 5f fst 1:003 H

This was a bold statement, considering that every other horse in the field that had already started had run a figure equal to or superior to Lochrima's best race, whether one chose to consult the sheets or Beyer figures.

But Lochrima exhibited what Beinish regarded as the quintessential explosive pattern: the colt had run a 27½ in his second career start and had slightly exceeded that number by running a 26¾ in his first start as a three-year-old. Lochrima had regressed slightly to a 28½ when run back on about two weeks' rest in his second start of the year, but it had now been six weeks since the key figure of 26¾. Beinish was expecting another forward move, and perhaps a more significant one:

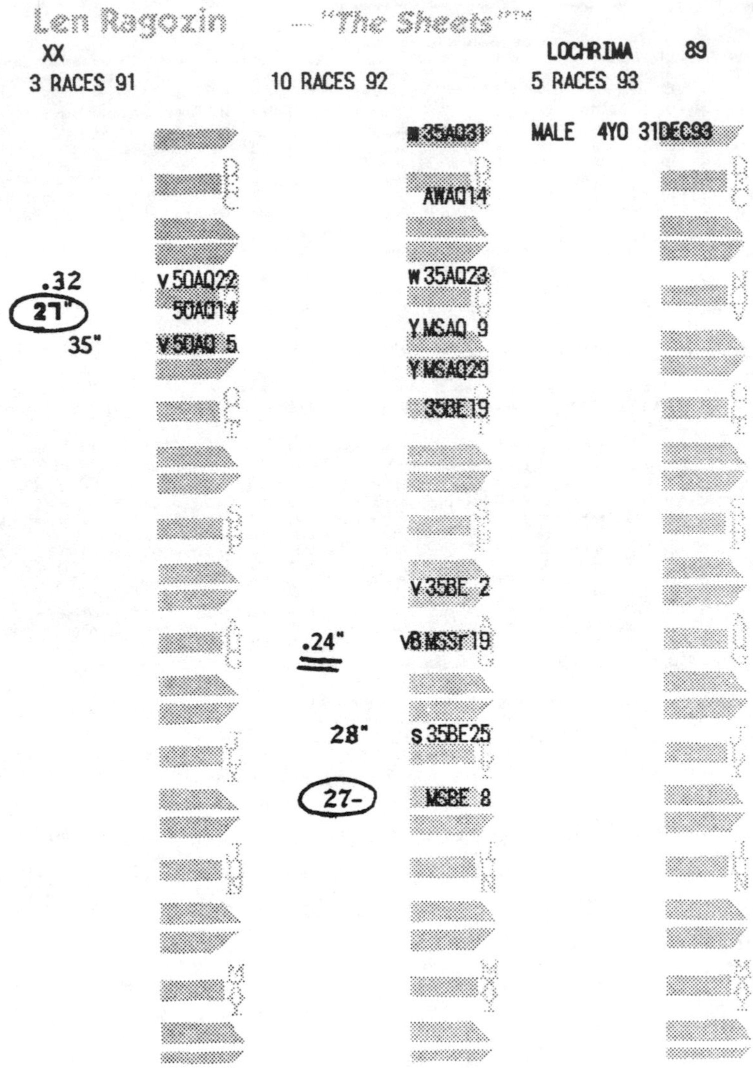

Note that the pattern is also present in the Beyer figures found in Lochrima's past performances: he ran a 46 second time out as a two-year-old and equaled that figure in his return as a three-year-old.

Beinish's argument convinced me that Lochrima was a contender, and when he flashed at an inviting 20–1 on the board, I bet him to win along with a pair of exactas using him underneath 6–5 favorite Newyork Appeal and first-time starter Gallant Pip, who was attracting substantial tote action at 3–1.

The anticipated improvement was indeed forthcoming, as Lochrima improved to a 24″ on the sheets and a Beyer figure of 58. Unfortunately for Beinish and me, Lochrima was carried extremely wide after forcing the early pace, came on again once he had straightened out for the stretch run, but wound up third, beaten by about a length.

It makes for a great example but a painful memory:

SIXTH RACE
Saratoga
AUGUST 19, 1992

6 FURLONGS. (1.08) MAIDEN SPECIAL WEIGHT. Purse $24,000. 3-year-olds and upward foaled in New York state and approved by the New York state-bred registry. Weight: 3-year-olds 117 lbs. Older 122 lbs.

Value of race $24,000; value to winner $14,400; second $5,280; third $2,880; fourth $1,440. Mutuel pool $280,064. Exacta Pool $486,902

Last Raced	Horse	M/Eqt.	A.	Wt	PP	St	¼	½	Str	Fin	Jockey	Odds $1
22Jly92 ^{9}Bel^{5}	Newyork Appeal		3	117	7	2	$4^{2\frac{1}{2}}$	3^{hd}	$2^{1\frac{1}{2}}$	1^{hd}	Antley C W	1.20
	Gallant Pip	b	3	117	4	6	$3^{\frac{1}{2}}$	$1^{\frac{1}{2}}$	$1^{\frac{1}{2}}$	$2^{\frac{3}{4}}$	Davis R G	3.20
25Jly92 ^{9}Bel^{8}	Lochrima	b	3	117	2	1	2^{1}	4^{2}	$4^{1\frac{1}{2}}$	$3^{3\frac{1}{4}}$	Carr D	20.00
27Jly92 ^{7}Pha^{3}	Super Sibling	b	6	122	3	7	5^{hd}	$5^{1\frac{1}{2}}$	5^{2}	$4^{\frac{1}{2}}$	Santiago A	13.60
	Winlocs Getzaround	b	3	117	5	5	$6^{1\frac{1}{2}}$	$6^{\frac{1}{2}}$	6^{1}	5^{nk}	Pezua J M	27.60
30Jly92 ^{9}Sar^{4}	Pago's Whim		3	117	1	3	1^{1}	$2^{\frac{1}{2}}$	$3^{\frac{1}{2}}$	6^{5}	Smith M E	3.40
30Jly92 ^{9}Sar^{5}	Look's Like Bob	b	3	117	6	4	7	7	7	7	Day P	5.30

OFF AT 3:46 Start good for all but SUPER SIBLING, Won driving. Time, :21^{3}, :45^{2}, :58^{2}, 1:12^{1} Track muddy.

$2 Mutuel Prices:				
	8–(I)–NEWYORK APPEAL	4.40	3.00	2.80
	5–(F)–GALLANT PIP		4.20	3.60
	3–(D)–LOCHRIMA			5.20
	$2 EXACTA 8–5 PAID $17.20			

B. c, (Mar), by Proud Appeal—Cool Answer, by Victorian Era. Trainer Sciacca Gary. Bred by Jet M Farm & McMahon Anne C (NY).

NEWYORK APPEAL, well placed for a half, angled between horses rallying into the stretch then finished determinedly to wear down GALLANT PIP in the final strides. GALLANT PIP never far back while saving ground, rallied along the rail to gain the lead at the top of the stretch, continued on the front into deep stretch but couldn't hold the winner safe. LOCHRIMA forced the early pace from outside, was carried six wide at the top of the stretch then finished willingly to gain a share. SUPER SIBLING, failed to seriously threaten after getting off toa slow start. WINLOCS GETZAROUND never reached contention while racing wide throughout. PAGO'S WHIM set the early pace along the inside then drifted wide while tiring on the turn. LOOK'S LIKE BOB was never a factor while racing wide.

Owners— 1, Ran-Dom Stable; 2, Irving Papano; 3, Santangelo George L; 4, Roe Loraine M; 5, Scrips R Farm; 6, New Kan Stables; 7, Bartow Robert C.

Trainers— 1, Sciacca Gary; 2, Schettino Dominick; 3, Pascuma James J Jr; 4, Roe Lorraine M; 5, Miceli Michael; 6, O'Brien Colum; 7, Dunham Bob G.

Scratched—Silver Crash; Mick (19Jly92 ^{5}Bel^{4}).

Noteworthy is that Lochrima's improved effort was delivered over a muddy track, even though he had apparently disliked slop at Aqueduct the previous autumn. This brings up two points: First, no two racetracks have the same consistency when wet; because a horse handles or doesn't handle a particular wet track doesn't necessarily mean it will run the same way over another. There are many horses that have, for example, run well on wet Saratoga tracks throughout their careers while failing to run as well on any other wet surfaces. Second, horses exhibiting an explosive pattern are indicating they are in excellent overall condition and "sitting on a big race." Horses that are in good condition are likeliest to perform well, no matter the circumstances; horses that are not in good condition have a strong tendency to use adverse circumstances such as wet tracks as an excuse not to perform to their true capabilities.

The same might be said of people.

A three-year-old that equals or slightly surpasses its best two-year-old figure may throw in an "off" race immediately afterward, as did Lochrima, but that is not always the case. If the horse has been given a few weeks off since running the key figure, it may very well deliver another forward move with no intervening race in between.

Russian Bride — Dk. b. or br. f. 3(Feb), by Saratoga Six—Aurania, by Judger

MIGLIORE R (97 16 12 13 .16) — Br.—Eaton Lee (Ky)

Own.—Kentucky Blue Stable — Tr.—Jolley Leroy (7 1 0 1 .14) — **116**

Lifetime						
11 3 2 1	1993	5	2	1	1	$70,936
$89,736	1992	6	1	1	0	$18,800
	Wet	2	2	0	0	$27,600

29Apr93-	8CD	fst	7f		:224	:462	1:241	ⒻLa Troienne	70	3	10	94	105¾	66¾	68½	Santos J A	b	113	5.40e	80-08	TrvrsCty116hdAdddAsst1131½Blld113	Sluggish brushed	10
10Apr93-	8Spt	fst	1 1/16		:473	1:123	1:45	ⒻN J Clb Oak	73	3	3	32½	32½	34	38½	Bourque C C	b	115	4.30	82-11	TruAffr1203¾Boots'nJck1224¾RssnBrd115	Bore out turn	7
21Mar93-	8Aqu	gd	1 1/16	⊡	:483	1:132	1:44	ⒻComely	(12) 88	4	4	42½	2½	2½	22	Migliore R	b	113	10.50	83-25	PrivtLight1122RussinBrid1131½TruAffir118	Good effort	6
21Mar93-Grade II																							
17Feb93-	7Aqu	fst	6f	⊡	:23	:463	1:112	ⒻAlw 27000	70	1	8	52	2hd	11	16¾	Bravo J	b	116	6.80	86-09	RussinBrd1166¾HghBrgr1161ThThTth116	Drifted, drvng	8
14Jan93-	6Aqu	my	6f	⊡	:23	:464	1:131	ⒻClm 50000	70	2	6	21	22	2hd	12¾	Migliore R	b	116	2.90	77-19	RussinBrid1162¾PromisdRlc1181½TrckCtyGrl111	Driving	8
14Jan93-Claimed from Kentucky Blue Stables, Jolley Leroy Trainer																							
26Dec92-	2Aqu	fst	6f	⊡	:231	:472	1:132	ⒻClm 35000	62	11	1	31	32	23½	21½	Migliore R	b	116	5.00	74-20	PnmJne1021½RussinBrid1164TnksforLunch116	2nd best	11
18Dec92-	7Aqu	gd	6f	⊡	:231	:47	1:12	ⒻAlw 27000	46	6	1	2½	33½	69½	615½	Davis R G	b	116	6.10	67-18	NiceCrne1166½Woodmn'sGirl1093½Incinrt116	Weakened	6
19Nov92-	7Aqu	fst	7f		:23	:463	1:242	ⒻAlw 27000	47	7	1	52	43	912	919¼	Migliore R		116	3.10e	64-16	TouchOfLove1?13½InHrGlory1185Mgroux116	Wide,tired	9
3Oct92-	8Bel	fst	6f		:222	:452	1:104	ⒻPrsnl Ensign	74	8	7	77	88	811	59	Krone J A		116	10.70	77-17	MssdthStorm1164¼FmlyEntrprz118¾TyWn118	No factor	8
3Jly92-	8Bel	fst	5½f		:22	:451	1:042	ⒻAstoria	58	7	8	53½	54	56½	58	Cruguet J		112	4.70	85-11	DstnctHbt1122½D'Accrdrss1193TryInThSk116	Four wide	8
3Jly92-Grade III																							

LATEST WORKOUTS May 29 Bel 4f fst :512 B May 22 Bel 6f fst 1:134 H May 13 Bel Ⓣ 5f fm 1:03 B (d) Apr 20 Kee 4f fst :492 B

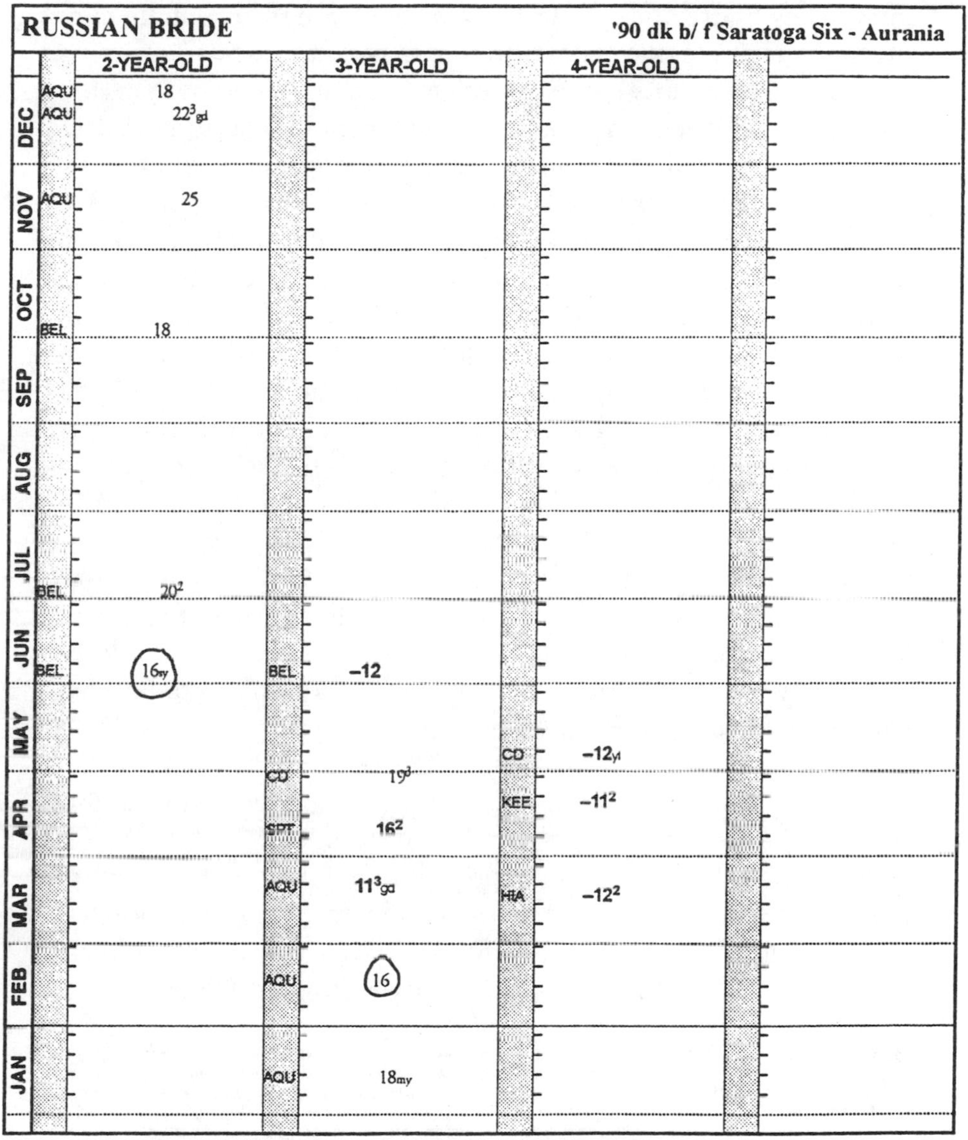

Russian Bride's *Thoro-graph* sheet indicated an explosive pattern when she was entered in the Grade 2 Comely Stakes for three-year-old fillies at Aqueduct on March 21, 1993. She was unable to get back to her debut figure of 16 until her eighth start, when she recorded another 16 in winning a preliminary allowance on February 17. Significantly, there had been several gaps between her races at age two, but the key figure, the second 16, had been earned during the midst of regular racing, as it was her fifth start in two months. The combination of more regularly spaced racing and the return to her previous top figure suggested that whatever had been holding Russian Bride back during her two-year-old year was no longer a problem.

Nearly five weeks had elapsed when Russian Bride was stretched to two turns for the first time in the Comely, a race that lured only six participants. Handicappers were faced with this decision: the filly needed to improve again in order to contend with 3–5 favorite True Affair and 3–1 second choice Private Light. Was she capable of doing so? If so, how should she be bet?

At 10–1, it was worthwhile to assume Russian Bride had been given enough time to recover from her breakthrough effort. A cautious player might have bet her to win, while also keying her underneath the two favorites in exactas. This type of place bet is a sound conservative strategy insofar as explosive-pattern horses are concerned, since handicappers are usually betting them to improve against rivals that have already run superior figures. The explosive horse may improve enough to beat one of its heretofore faster rivals but may be defeated by another. By using the exacta as a place bet, as noted author Mark Cramer has suggested, the win bet is protected while still offering the chance for a good return should the overlay run a big race but finish second.

In this case Russian Bride improved to a new top of 12 right off her key figure of 16, but was outkicked in the final furlong by Private Light and finished second. The win bet was lost, but the exacta saver in a short field paid a grossly inflated $90.80.

EIGHTH RACE
Aqueduct
MARCH 21, 1993

1 $\frac{1}{16}$ MILES.(InnerDirt). (1.41) 44th Running THE COMELY. Grade II. Purse $100,000 Added. Fillies. 3–year–olds. By subscription of $200 each which should accompany the nomination; $800 to pass the entry box; $800 to start with $100,000 added. The added money and all fees to be divided 60% to the winner, 22% to second, 12% to third and 6% to fourth. Weight: 121 lbs. Non–winners of two races of $75,000, allowed 3 lbs. Of a race of $50,000, 5 lbs. Of a race of $35,000, 7 lbs. Of two races other than maiden or claiming, 9 lbs. Starters to be named at the closing time of entries. Trophies will be presented to the winning owner, trainer and jockey. The New York Racing Association Inc. reserves the right to transfer this race to the Inner Track at a distance of six furlongs. Nominations closed Wednesday, March 3, 1993, with 17 nominations.

Value of race $113,800; value to winner $68,280; second $25,036; third $13,656; fourth $6,828. Mutuel pool $177,072, Minus show pool $1,895.55. Exacta Pool $367,636

Last Raced	Horse	M/Eqt.	A.Wt	PP	St	¼	½	¾	Str	Fin	Jockey	Odds $1
6Mar93 ^{7}Aqu^{2}	Private Light		3 112	2	2	6	5^{1}	5^{6}	3^{16}	1^{2}	Davis R G	3.00
17Feb93 ^{7}Aqu^{1}	Russian Bride	b	3 113	4	6	$4^{\frac{1}{2}}$	$4^{2\frac{1}{2}}$	$2^{\frac{1}{2}}$	2^{hd}	$2^{1\frac{1}{2}}$	Migliore R	10.50
6Mar93 ^{7}Aqu^{1}	True Affair		3 118	5	4	$3^{2\frac{1}{2}}$	$3^{1\frac{1}{2}}$	$1^{\frac{1}{2}}$	$1^{\frac{1}{2}}$	3^{19}	Bravo J	.60
6Mar93 ^{7}Aqu^{3}	Cosmic Speed Queen		3 112	1	1	5^{1}	6	6	6	4^{2}	Chavez J F	16.60
3Mar93 ^{7}Aqu^{1}	Saucy Charmer		3 112	3	5	$2^{\frac{1}{2}}$	$2^{\frac{1}{2}}$	$4^{\frac{1}{2}}$	$4^{1\frac{1}{2}}$	$5^{1\frac{1}{4}}$	Smith M E	4.20
4Mar93 ^{5}Aqu^{3}	She's Landing	b	3 114	6	3	1^{3}	$1^{\frac{1}{2}}$	$3^{\frac{1}{2}}$	5^{1}	6	Antley C W	26.00

OFF AT 4:10 Start good, Won driving. Time, :24 , :48^3, 1:13^2, 1:38 , 1:44 Track good.

$2 Mutuel Prices:				
	2-(B)-PRIVATE LIGHT	8.00	4.60	2.10
	4-(D)-RUSSIAN BRIDE		7.80	2.10
	5-(E)-TRUE AFFAIR			2.10
	$2 EXACTA 2–4 PAID $90.80			

B. f, (Mar), by Private Account—Illuminating, by Majestic Light. Trainer McGaughey Claude III. Bred by Ogden Mills Phipps (Ky).

PRIVATE LIGHT, outrun for five furlongs, angled out while gaining midway on the turn, rallied five wide into the stretch then closed determinedly in the middle of the track to win going away. RUSSIAN BRIDE, reserved for five furlongs, moved up while four wide on the turn, made a run between horses to challenge in midstretch but couldn't stay with the winner through the final sixteenth. TRUE AFFAIR, rated just behind the leaders while four wide for five furlongs, surged to the front midway on the turn, continued on the lead into midstretch then weakened in the final eighth. COSMIC SPEED QUEEN was never a factor. SAUCY CHARMER raced in close contention between horses for six furlongs and lacked a further response. SHE'S LANDING sprinted clear in the early stages, set the pace along the rail for nearly six furlongs and gave way.

Owners— 1, Phipps Ogden Mills; 2, Kentucky Blue Stables; 3, Winbound Farms; 4, R Kay Stable; 5, Heatherwood Farm; 6, Asteriglo Stable.

Trainers— 1, McGaughey Claude III; 2, Jolley Leroy; 3, Contessa Gary C; 4, Araya Rene A; 5, Schosberg Richard; 6, Martin Gregory F.

Overweight: Russian Bride 1 pound; She's Landing 2.

Scratched—Ensign Joanne (10Mar93 ^{4}Aqu^2).

Two weeks after the Comely, a similar situation presented itself, this time in a stakes race for three-year-old colts — the Grade 2 Gotham.

Examine the past performances of the eight contestants, paying particular attention to their *Beyer Speed Figures:*

9 START 1 MILE AQUEDUCT FINISH

1 MILE. **(1.32^2) 41st Running THE GOTHAM (Grade II). Purse $200,000. 3-year-olds. By subscription of $400 each which should accompany the nomination; $1,600 to pass the entry box, $1,600 to start. The Purse to be divided 60% to the winner, 22% to second, 12% to third and 6% to fourth. Weight, 126 lbs. Non-winners of a race of $100,000 at a mile or over in 1993 allowed 3 lbs. Of two races of $100,000 at anytime, 5 lbs. Of a race of $50,000, 8 lbs. Of a race other than Maiden or Claiming at a mile or over, 12 lbs. Starters to be named at the closing time of entries. Trophies will be presented to the winning owner, trainer and jockey. Closed Wednesday, March 10 with 40 Nominations.**

Castelli Street — Dk. b. or br. c. 3(May), by Leo Castelli—Power Street, by Balance of Power — Lifetime 6 2 2 1 $41,702 — 1993 1 1 0 0 $10,500 — 1992 5 1 2 1 $31,202

CASTILLO H JR (—) — Br.—Edwards Robert L (NJ) — **114**

Own.—Castelli Stables — Tr.—Anderson William D (2 0 0 0 .00) — Wet 1 0 1 0 $3,366

25Mar93- 6GS gd 6f :22 :45^3 1:11^2 [S]Alw 17500 **74** 5 3 4^4 4^{1½} 2^{hd} 1^{2¼} Migliore R 116 *.40 85–19 CstelliStret116^{2¼}WoodnShips116^{½}Bb'sHonor111 Driving 6

5Dec92- 9Med fst 1 :48 1:13^4 1:40^1 Duel Site **77** 1 4 4^1 3^2 3^{3½} 3^{¾} Gryder A T 113 5.00 78–24 DprtnCld120^{hd}BrtsBbbltr113^{¾}CstllStrt113 Finished well 7

19Nov92- 7Med fst 6f :22^3 :46^1 1:10^4 [S]Md Sp Wt **63** 6 2 2^1 2^1 1^{2½} 1^{5¼} Gryder A T 118 *.30 89–11 CstelliStreet118^{5¼}MedievlLord118^{5¾}OddsLss118 Driving 9

30Oct92- 6Aqu fst 1 :47^4 1:13^1 1:38^2 Md Sp Wt **75** 1 5 3^1 3^{nk} 2^{2½} 2^{5¾} Gryder A T 118 4.70 64–31 ColonlAffr118^{5¾}CstllStrt118^{3½}BullInthHthr118 Good try 9

21Oct92- 8Aqu fst 7f :23 :46^2 1:24 Cowdin **70** 5 5 7^4 7^{4¾} 8^{7½} 4^{9½} Gryder A T 122 34.80 75–18 Wallenda122^{¾}WildZone122^{7}DarienDecon122 Saved grnd 10

21Oct92-Grade II

9Oct92- 7Med sly 6f :22 :45^1 1:11^2 [S]Md Sp Wt **58** 1 11 6^8 5^{6½} 3^{2½} 2^{1½} Castillo H Jr 118 5.50 84–11 Mnnett118^{1½}CstelliStreet118^{5}SvvySmmy118 Slow start 12

LATEST WORKOUTS ●Mar 20 GS 6f fst 1:13^2 H ●Mar 8 GS 5f fst 1:00^2 H ●Mar 2 GS 6f fst 1:14 H ●Feb 24 GS 5f fst 1:00 Hg

Rohwer — Ch. c. 3(Apr), by Vanlandingham—Rabe's Joy, by King of the Sea — Lifetime 15 3 3 5 $134,451 — 1993 6 1 1 2 $56,203 — 1992 9 2 2 3 $78,248

MADRID A JR (46 6 7 4 .13) — Br.—Loblolly-Betz-Guscotts-Needham (Ky) — **114**

Own.—Garren Murray M — Tr.—Garren Murray M (13 1 0 3 .08) — Wet 2 1 0 0 $16,020

7Mar93- 7Aqu fst 1$\frac{1}{16}$ [•]:47^1 1:10^4 1:42^1 Seattle Slew **77** 4 4 4^3 4^3 3^{7½} 3^{10¼} Chavez J F 117 2.40 84–10 Lord Beer117^{nk} Ozan117^{10} Rohwer117 Lacked rally 5

20Feb93- 8Aqu fst 1$\frac{1}{16}$ [•]:48^3 1:13^1 1:45^1 Whirlaway **92** 3 2 3^{1½} 1^{½} 2^{hd} 2^3 Chavez J F 114 24.90 76–24 Prairie Bayou117^3 Rohwer114^3 Slews Gold114 2nd best 5

3Feb93- 6Aqu fst 170 [•]:49^2 1:14^1 1:43^4 Alw 29000 **85** 5 1 1^{hd} 1^{hd} 1^2 1^4 Davis R G 117 *1.40 83–22 Rohwer117^{4}MangoMan117^{4½}DmHndsome112 Mild drive 7

24Jan93- 8Aqu fst 170 [•]:48 1:12^2 1:42^4 Count Fleet **77** 4 1 1^{hd} 4^4 4^{6½} 3^{8½} Davis R G 117 17.30 79–24 PririeByou117^{3}SlewsGold117^{5½}Rohwr117 Dueled, wknd 6

9Jan93- 7Aqu fst 1$\frac{1}{16}$ [•]:49 1:14^2 1:45^1 Alw 29000 **70** 6 2 2^{½} 2^{hd} 4^6 7^{9½} Chavez J F 117 5.80 69–20 SlewsGold117^{1}HannibalLecter117^{6}SkyDr.117 Used early 8

2Jan93- 7Aqu fst 6f [•]:22^2 :46^2 1:11^3 Alw 27000 **61** 11 10 9^{12} 9^{9¼} 9^{11} 8^{11} Bisono C V^5 b 112 *2.30 74–18 Tough Heart119^{1½} Birdie's Fly117^{4½} Miter119 Outrun 12

23Dec92- 7Aqu fst 1$\frac{1}{16}$ [•]:46^4 1:11^3 1:45 Alw 29000 **83** 4 5 4^{4½} 4^5 3^{5½} 3^{5¾} Chavez J F 117 *1.10 77–22 Bert'sBubbletor117^{2}SlwsGold117^{3¾}Rohwr117 Mild rally 8

10Dec92- 7Aqu fst 170 [•]:48^1 1:13^4 1:44^1 Alw 29000 **76** 6 3 2^2 2^1 3^3 4^{7½} Carr D 117 *.80 76–21 GulphGorg119^{4½}StllitSignl117^{3}Brd'sFly117 Lacked rally 9

5Dec92- 8Aqu fst 1$\frac{1}{16}$ [•]:47^1 1:12^1 1:44^3 Nashua **88** 2 2 5^2 4^{2½} 3^{6½} 2^{6½} Chavez J F 114 35.70 78–22 Dalhart114^{6½} Rohwer114^2 Peace Baby114 Second best 11

5Dec92-Grade III

27Nov92- 8Aqu my 6f :22^2 :46 1:10^3 Alw 27000 **68** 6 2 4^{2½} 6^5 5^7 4^9 Chavez J F 117 *1.10 79–22 InsurdWinnr117^{3½}Birdi'sFly117^{4}VrgnRpds117 No threat 6

LATEST WORKOUTS Mar 31 Bel tr.t 3f fst :36 B ●Mar 27 Bel tr.t 5f fst :59^1 H Mar 23 Bel tr.t 5f fst 1:00^2 H Mar 5 Bel tr.t 4f my :50 B

Itaka

B. c. 3(Mar), by Jade Hunter—Americanrevelation, by Foolish Pleasure
Br.—Brophy B Giles (NY)
Tr.—Johnson Philip G (1 0 0 0 .00)

SMITH M E (43 7 5 8 .16)
Own.—Brophy Stable

114

Lifetime 8 1 1 3 $28,630 — 1993 3 0 0 1 $3,760 — 1992 5 1 1 2 $24,870 — Wet 1 0 0 0

28Feb93- 6GP	fst	7f	:23^1	:46^2	1:23^1	Alw 22000	89	1	5	1^1	1^1	2^2	3^4	Fires E	b	117	6.90	83–19	JackLivingston120^{2}FightforLove112^{2}Itak117	Weakened	7
21Jan93- 8GP	fst	7f	:22^1	:45^1	1:23^2	Alw 21600	73	2	9	5^{1¾}	5^{2½}	3^5	4^{3½}	Gonzalez M A	b	112	5.30	82–15	FrvrWhrl115^{1¼}ChntngGshk115^{2}LvngVcrsl114	Late rally	11
9Jan93-10Crc	sly	1⅛	:48^1	1:12^3	1:53^4	Trop Pk Dby	66	5	4	4^4	6^{6¾}	9^{20}	8^{14¼}	Bailey J D		112	9.30	76–15	SummrSt112^{1¾}Ducd'Sligovil112½SilvrofSlvr122	Faltered	10
9Jan93-Grade III																					
15Dec92- 7Crc	fst	1$\frac{1}{16}$	:48^3	1:13^3	1:48^1	Alw 16600	79	1	5	5^{2¾}	3^{1½}	2^{1½}	3^1	Santos J A		115	1.70	85–13	Kassec110^{no} Duc d'Sligovil115^1 Itaka115	Good effort	5
18Nov92- 6Aqu	fst	7f	:23	:46^3	1:24^3	Alw 27000	80	3	9	6^3	7^{3¾}	5^{4½}	3^3	Davis R G		119	15.70	79–16	Apprentice119^{no} Slew's Gold117^3 Itaka119	Late gain	9
22Oct92- 3Aqu	fst	6½f	:23^3	:48	1:18^4	ⓈMd Sp Wt	86	5	7	4^2	2^{hd}	1½	1^{1¼}	Smith M E		118	*.60	84–18	Itk118^{1¼}KoluctooJmmyAl118^{3¼}BoldDor118	Brk slw, drv	7
7Oct92- 6Bel	fst	6f	:22^3	:46^2	1:10^4	ⓈMd Sp Wt	63	10	13	3^2	2^1	2^6	2^{11½}	Smith M E		118	*1.30	74–16	RushChirmnBill118^{11½}Itk118^{6½}BoldDor118	Broke poorly	13
13Aug92- 4Sar	fst	6f	:22^4	:46^3	1:11^4	ⓈMd Sp Wt	53	4	13	6^{4¼}	4^2	6^{2½}	6^{6¾}	Cruguet J		118	2.90	78–13	LodBrthr118^{nk}BlmGn118^{5¼}MgcMdc118	Broke slw, wide	13

LATEST WORKOUTS Mar 31 Bel tr.t 3f fst :36^2 B ●Mar 20 Crc 6f sly 1:13^2 H (d) Mar 16 Crc 3f fst :37^1 B ●Mar 12 Crc 6f fst 1:14 H

As Indicated

Ch. g. 3(May), by Czaravich—Our Nice Sue, by Our Michael
Br.—Perkins Margot I (Ky)
Tr.—Schosberg Richard (9 4 1 0 .44)

BISONO C V (47 5 6 7 .11)
Own.—Heatherwood Farm

114

Lifetime 4 3 0 0 $62,400 — 1993 3 2 0 0 $48,120 — 1992 1 1 0 0 $14,280 — Wet 1 1 0 0 $14,280

20Feb93- 6Aqu	fst	6f	⊡:23^3	:47^1	1:11^1	Swift	—	1	5	—	—	—	—	Bisono C V		120	*1.50	— —	LyLk120½FghtngDddy114^{no}Frmnthfr120	Wheeled,1st rdr	5
31Jan93- 7Aqu	fst	6f	⊡:22^3	:45^3	1:10^4	Sly Fox	100	7	1	1^2	1^{hd}	1½	1no	Bisono C V		117	*1.70	89–16	AsIndicted117^{no}LzyLuke117^{3}Frmonthefrewy117	Driving	7
16Jan93- 7Aqu	fst	6f	⊡:22^4	:45^4	1:10^2	Alw 27000	85	6	2	2½	2^1	2½	1^{1¼}	Bisono C V^5		112	5.00	91–13	AsIndicted112^{1¼}Birdie'sFly117^{6½}OnTheBridl117	Driving	8
25Nov92- 6Grd	my	4½f	:22^4	:47^3	:54	Md Sp Wt	71	2	3		1^{1½}	1^{hd}	1½	Sabourin R B		120	*1.45	82–35	AsIndictd120½SlutThSunris115^{4½}StllrOccson115	Driving	6

LATEST WORKOUTS Mar 29 Bel tr.t 5f my 1:01 B Mar 23 Bel tr.t 5f fst :59^3 H ●Mar 16 Bel tr.t 6f fst 1:14^3 B Mar 8 Bel tr.t 4f fst :47^2 B

Ozan

B. c. 3(Feb), by Cox's Ridge—Kiva, by Tom Rolfe
Br.—Alexander Helen & Four A Stable Syn (Ky)
Tr.—Bohannan Thomas (—)

SAMYN J L (18 3 3 2 .17)
Own.—Loblolly Stable

118

Lifetime 8 2 3 1 $61,014 — 1993 4 1 2 0 $35,484 — 1992 4 1 1 1 $25,530 — Wet 2 1 0 1 $19,900

7Mar93- 7Aqu	fst	1$\frac{1}{16}$	⊡:47^1	1:10^4	1:42^1	Seattle Slew	95	5	5	2^1	2^1	2^{1½}	2^{nk}	Samyn J L		117	*1.30	94–10	Lord Beer117^{nk} Ozan117^{10} Rohwer117	Second best	5
25Feb93- 6Aqu	fst	1$\frac{1}{16}$	⊡:47^4	1:12^3	1:45	Alw 29000	86	5	6	5^{4½}	3^2	1½	1^{3½}	Samyn J L		117	3.70	80–20	Ozan117^{3½} Shower of Silver117^{hd} Iron Gavel117	Driving	8
25Jan93- 7Aqu	fst	1^{70}	⊡:47^3	1:13	1:43^3	Alw 29000	79	5	7	6^8	4^3	2^5	2^6	Samyn J L		117	8.20	78–27	HannibalLecter117^{6}Ozan117½MangoMn117	Up for place	9
9Jan93- 7Aqu	fst	1$\frac{1}{16}$	⊡:49	1:14^2	1:45^1	Alw 29000	72	3	6	6^{2¼}	6^{4¼}	7^{6½}	6^{8¼}	Samyn J L		117	3.30	71–20	Slews Gold117^1 Hannibal Lecter117^{6}SkyDr.117	No rally	8
20Dec92-10Lrl	my	1⅛	:48^4	1:13^4	1:52^4	Inner Harbor	78	4	5	5^{3¾}	5^{3½}	4^3	3^{3½}	Samyn J L		113	*1.50e	72–32	JorgeofMexico113^{no}PrairieByou122^{3½}Ozn113	Rank wide	9
5Dec92- 9Med	fst	1	:48	1:13^4	1:40^1	Duel Site	63	7	6	7^{3¾}	7^{5¼}	5^7	5^{8¼}	Samyn J L		113	2.20	71–24	DprtngClod120^{hd}Brt'sBbbltr113¾CstllStrt113	No factor	7
6Nov92- 9Aqu	my	7f	:23^4	:47^4	1:25^3	Md Sp Wt	64	5	5	4^{1¼}	3½	3^{nk}	1^{1¼}	Samyn J L		118	3.60	77–18	Ozan118^{1¼} Halostrada118^{hd} Majesty's Darby118	Driving	9
26Oct92- 5Aqu	fst	6f	:22^3	:46^1	1:11	Md Sp Wt	79	3	2	5^{1¾}	4^{1½}	3^2	2^2	Samyn J L		118	22.60	84–14	Apprentice118^2 Ozan118^{1¼} InFirstLight118	Up for place	5

LATEST WORKOUTS Apr 1 Bel tr.t 4f sly :52^1 B Mar 27 Bel tr.t 5f fst 1:01^1 H Mar 20 Bel tr.t 4f fst :47^1 H Feb 18 Bel tr.t 4f fst :48^1 H

Hickory Lake

Ch. g. 3(Mar), by Meadowlake—Belle Courante, by Cougar II
Br.—Windfields Farm (Ont-C)
Tr.—Klesaris Robert P (11 2 3 1 .18)

MIGLIORE R (42 9 7 4 .21)
Own.—New Showtime Stable

114

Lifetime 5 1 0 1 $20,080 — 1993 4 1 0 1 $19,380 — 1992 1 M 0 0 $700

8Mar93- 1Aqu	fst	6f	⊡:22^2	:45^2	1:09^2	Alw 27000	78	5	2	1½	1^{hd}	2^3	3^6	Antley C W	b	117	*1.30	90–11	KngRucks117^{2½}Tkn'Nms117^{3½}HckoryLk117	Speed, tired	7
25Feb93- 6Aqu	fst	1$\frac{1}{16}$	⊡:47^4	1:12^3	1:45	Alw 29000	80	7	1	1^{1½}	1½	2½	4^{3½}	Migliore R	b	117	2.40	76–20	Ozan117^{3½}ShowerofSilver117^{hd}IronGavel117	Dueled, trd	8
28Jan93- 5Aqu	fst	6f	⊡:23	:46^4	1:11^4	Md Sp Wt	81	3	5	1^{1½}	1^1	1^{2½}	1^4	Bravo J	b	122	*.60	84–18	Hickory Lake122^{4}JessC'sWhirl122^{4}Pilfer122	Ridden out	7
7Jan93- 6Aqu	fst	6f	⊡:22	:44^3	1:10^1	Md Sp Wt	70	9	7	5^{6¾}	5^4	4^{4¼}	5^{3¼}	McCauley W H		122	6.40	89–11	GoldenPro122^{nk}PalcePiper122^{1½}ClssicLunch122	Evenly	9
17Nov92- 1Med	fst	6f	:22^3	:46^1	1:11^2	Md Sp Wt	35	3	5	5^{1½}	5^{2¼}	3^1	4^7	Wilson R		118	*.30	79–11	Thswrthdys118^{4½}PhnFntsy118^{2¼}NskrPrnc118	Four wide	8

LATEST WORKOUTS ●Mar 19 Bel tr.t 5f fst 1:00^4 H Feb 18 Bel tr.t 4f fst :49^1 H Feb 12 Bel tr.t 5f fst 1:04^3 B

Fighting Daddy

Ch. c. 3(May), by Fight Over—Daddyslittleangel, by Rare Performer
Br.—Gallagher Mrs James H (Fla)
Tr.—Toner James J (4 1 1 1 .25)

DAVIS R G (56 10 8 13 .18)
Own.—Kimran Stables

114

Lifetime 8 3 2 0 $57,748 — 1993 2 1 1 0 $34,548 — 1992 6 2 1 0 $23,200

20Feb93- 6Aqu	fst	6f	⊡:23^3	:47^1	1:11^1	Swift	93	3	3	4^2	4^{1½}	3½	2½	Davis R G	b	114	9.50	86–20	LzyLuk120½FightingDddy114^{no}Frmonthfrwy120	Gamely	5
27Jan93- 7Aqu	fst	6f	⊡:23^4	:47^4	1:12^2	Alw 27000	87	6	5	4^{1½}	2^{hd}	1½	1^{3½}	Davis R G	b	117	*1.40	81–25	Fighting Daddy117^{3½} Zoom By117^{hd}LostPan117	Driving	7
21Dec92- 4Aqu	fst	6f	⊡:22^3	:45^3	1:10^4	Clm 75000	82	6	1	4^4	4^3	2^3	2^{2¼}	Davis R G	b	112	9.60	87–14	GldCndT114^{2¼}FhtnDdd112^{2½}OnThBrdl116	Gained place	6
10Dec92- 7Aqu	fst	1^{70}	⊡:48^1	1:13^4	1:44^1	Alw 29000	63	1	1	1^2	1^1	5^5	7^{15¼}	Migliore R	b	117	8.40	69–21	GulphGorg119^{4½}StllitSgnl117^{3}Brd'sFly117	Used in pace	9
15Nov92- 7Crc	fst	7f	:22	:45^3	1:26^4	Clm 50000	67	4	1	3^2	1^{1½}	1^5	1^2	Gonzalez M A	Lb	118	*1.50	81–13	FightingDddy118^{2}Dr.RossHop114½FlyBirdFly114	Driving	6
25Oct92- 3Crc	fst	6f	:22	:45^4	1:12^4	Md 40000	72	6	1	1^2	1^5	1^5	1^{4½}	Gonzalez M A	Lb	118	*1.90	87–17	FightingDddy118^{4½}SurelyModst118^{4}GrtEstt114	Driving	9
3Oct92- 6Crc	fst	7f	:22	:45^2	1:27	Md Sp Wt	47	10	1	1^4	1^5	2½	5^8	Gonzalez M A	b	118	14.10	72–15	BdFrGld118^{1½}LsGldnKht118^{1½}NrthrWtss118	Weakened	10
28Aug92- 6Crc	fst	6f	:22^1	:46^2	1:13^2	Md 35000	43	6	5	4^6	5^{11}	5^{10}	5^{8½}	Alferez J O		116	10.10	75–20	Crafty Chris111^3 Desert Cowboy113^{2}Truthski113	Faded	11

LATEST WORKOUTS Mar 27 Bel tr.t 5f fst :59^2 H Mar 19 Bel tr.t 6f fst 1:16^2 H Mar 10 Bel tr.t 4f fst :47^3 H Mar 3 Bel tr.t 6f fst 1:14^4 H

Strolling Along

Dk. b. or br. c. 3(Apr), by Danzig—Cadillacing, by Alydar
Br.—Phipps Ogden (Ky)
Tr.—McGaughey Claude III (7 1 2 2 .14)

ANTLEY C W (56 8 17 9 .14)
Own.—Phipps Ogden

121

Lifetime 7 2 2 0 $157,140 — 1992 7 2 2 0 $157,140

31Oct92- 8GP	fst	1$\frac{1}{16}$	:46	1:10^2	1:43^2	Br Cp Juv	67	7	7	7^{2½}	7^5	9^{10}	8^{11¾}	Antley C W	b	122	20.40	83–03	GildedTime122¾It'sli'lknownfct122½RivrSpcil122	5 wide	13
31Oct92-Grade I																					
10Oct92- 7Bel	gd	1	:44^3	1:09	1:34^4	Champagne	62	9	4	4^{3½}	4^{2½}	5^8	5^{19½}	Antley C W		122	*2.30	76–04	SeHero122^{5¾}ScrtOdds122^{5¾}PrssCrd122	Lacked respnse	10
10Oct92-Grade I																					
19Sep92- 6Bel	fst	7f	:22^1	:45	1:23^3	Futurity	88	4	7	7^{5½}	3^4	1^{hd}	1^2	Antley C W		122	*1.50	86–11	StrolingAlong122^{2}FghtforLov122^{1}Cponostro122	Driving	9
19Sep92-Grade I																					
30Aug92- 8Sar	fst	6½f	:22^2	:45	1:15^3	Hopeful	89	1	3	3^{1½}	4^{2½}	3^3	2^{3¾}	Antley C W		122	5.10	93–08	GrtNvgtr122^{3¾}StrllngAlng122¾EnglndEpcts122	Fin. well	8
30Aug92-Grade I																					
30Jly92- 8Sar	fst	6f	:21^3	:44^4	1:10^2	Sar Spec'l	87	1	10	2^{1½}	2½	1^1	2no	Antley C W		117	1.80	92–06	TctclAdntg117^{no}StrllngAln117^{5¼}MCl117	Brk sl; gamely	10
30Jly92-Grade II																					
13Jly92- 5Bel	fst	5½f	:22^1	:45^2	1:03	Md Sp Wt	94	7	3	2^4	2^4	2^{1½}	1^{2½}	Antley C W		118	10.30	100–10	StrolingAlong118^{2½}DvlshlyYors118^{8½}Dr.Alfs118	Driving	10
26Jun92- 3Bel	fst	5½f	:22^2	:45^3	1:04^3	Md Sp Wt	50	5	7	8^{6½}	8^5	6^{6½}	5^{5½}	Antley C W		118	*.80	86–07	KissinKrs118^{hd}GrmlnGry118^{no}InsurdWnnr118	Late gain	9

LATEST WORKOUTS ●Mar 27 Bel tr.t 6f fst 1:10^4 H Mar 22 Bel tr.t 6f fst 1:16^2 B Mar 17 Bel tr.t 5f gd 1:03^3 B Mar 10 Bel tr.t 4f fst :46^4 B

Three horses, Fighting Daddy, Ozan, and Itaka, were emerging from career-best performances according to the BSF. Fighting Daddy had just run three consecutive new tops, moving 10 points to an 82, 5 points to an 87, and 6 points to a 93. Ozan had just moved twice, from 79 to 86, followed by a 9-point gain to 95. Once horses have made two or three forward moves in succession, the likelihood of their making yet another forward move is diminished. Neither Fighting Daddy nor Ozan was a good bet to show improvement in the Gotham; in fact, they would probably run something less than their best.

Itaka had also run a new top in his most recent start, but with a notable difference: although the jump appeared significant at first glance — an 89 as opposed to a 73 the start prior — the new top is properly evaluated in light of his best previous effort. Itaka's previous top was the 86 he recorded as a two-year-old in his third start; the 3-point forward move from an 86 to an 89 on the Beyer scale was only a slight move, equivalent to roughly a point in sheet figures, and it represented Itaka's first move past his best two-year-old figure. Moreover, it had been nearly five weeks since the move.

Itaka was ready to explode.

Recognition of Itaka's pattern and the realization that he'd be a huge price spurred a late-night search for corroborating evidence:

- Itaka was the kind of horse sure to be overlooked by class-conscious players, since he was a New York–bred still eligible for a preliminary allowance, but he had in fact been meeting some of the best three-year-olds in Florida earlier in the year. In his first try around two turns, he was beaten a length by Duc d'Sligovil, who had since won a nonwinners-of-two allowance and repeated in a division of the Fountain of Youth by open lengths. The two colts in front of him February 28 were Jack Livingston, who had broken his maiden by eight lengths in his debut earlier that month, and Fight for Love, who had finished second in Belmont's Grade 1 Futurity the previous autumn.
- Itaka's best races had come around one turn at Aqueduct when ridden by Mike Smith, and he was returning to the Big A along with a switch back to Smith.

• Itaka, never a bullet from the gate to begin with, had been compromised by inside posts in his two most recent races at Gulfstream. Nevertheless, he recovered from a slow start first time in blinkers January 21 and raced close up to the fastest pace he had yet encountered; after the early rush-up to gain a contending position, he lost ground to midstretch but then made a second move to finish third, earning a "Late rally" comment. On February 28 he rushed up from the rail to set the pace for a half and held third behind two highly regarded colts.

• Since his last start, Itaka had twice worked bullets at six furlongs at Calder; according to the clocker's comments in the work tabs, he had "finished well" March 12 and March 20.

Itaka's past performances on the eve of the Gotham reminded me of that old hair-color commercial: "The closer you get, the better she looks." When I arrived at the track on the morning of April 3, the first thing I did was check *The Sheets* and *Thoro-graph* to see if Itaka's pattern was as explosive on their numbers as it appeared on the Beyer figures. It was:

BEL p74 ITAKA 90 race 7

5 RACES 92 7 RACES 93

19 AWCR15

16 s AWAQPGJ

14+ vwS MSAQPGJ

17" vS MSBEPGJ

MALE 3YO 16SEP93

21" vS$ MSSrPGJ

11+ Yws AWBEPGJ

9" v AWBEPGJ

'24- V AWBEPGJ

^9+ vs AWAQPGJ

13+ Y AWGP28

18- AWGP21

r.24 AWCR 9

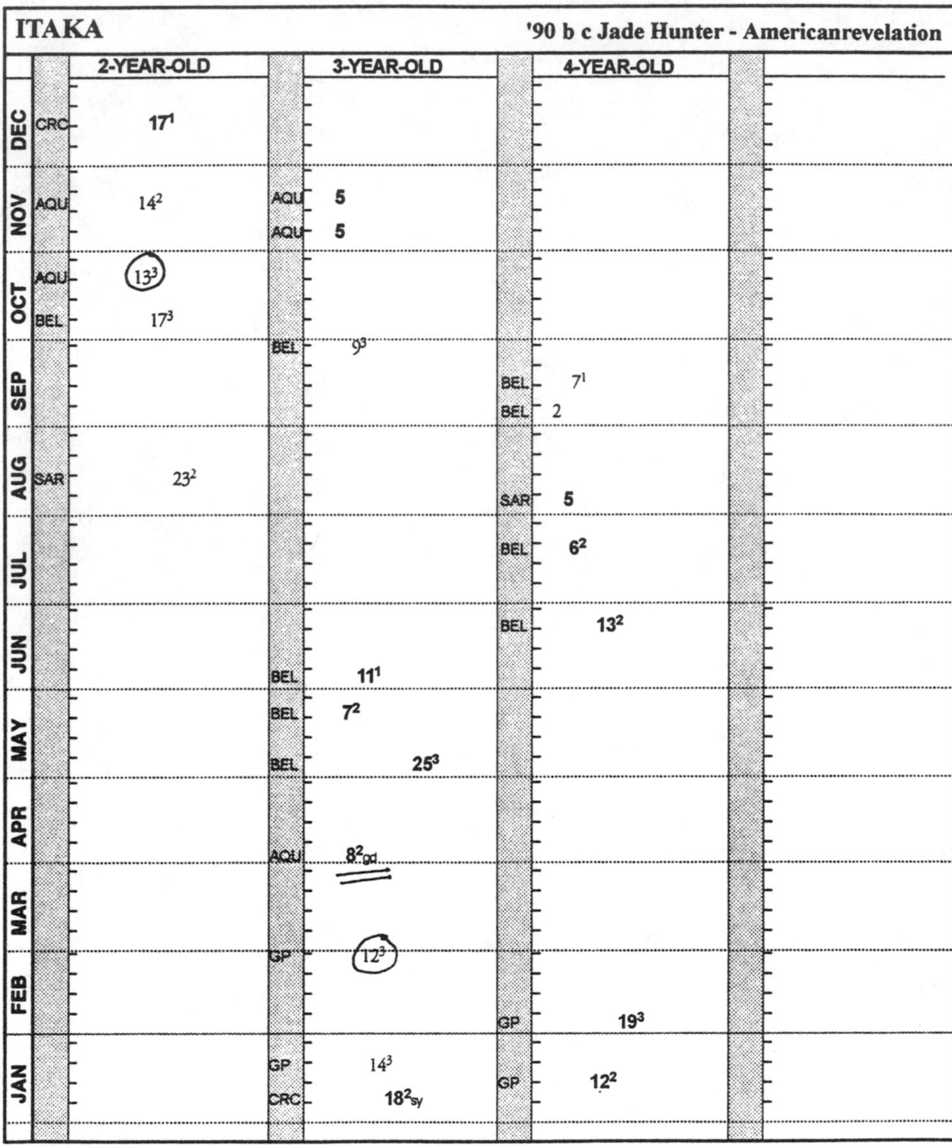

On both sheets, Itaka had broken his maiden with a 14 and had slightly surpassed it with a 13 in his most recent start. Given nearly five weeks since the breakthrough figure and odds of 14–1, there was no reason to wait for an intervening "off" race: Itaka was likely to run the best figure of his life and didn't need to improve all that much to rate a solid chance of upsetting the three betting choices — Strolling Along, Ozan, and As Indicated.

Strolling Along was giving weight to the field under the Gotham's allowance conditions, and his training schedule had been altered when the Bay Shore Stakes, his scheduled return, was canceled due to inclement weather in mid-March. What's more, Strolling Along had run a Beyer of 94, breaking his maiden second time out but had not been able to reproduce that figure in five subsequent starts.

Ozan was shortening up after a series of two-turn routes and, as previously mentioned, had just run two consecutive tops.

As Indicated's Beyer of 100 in the Sly Fox was tops in the field, but he had wheeled at the start of the Swift and thrown his rider and was now stretching beyond six furlongs for the first time.

How to bet Itaka? Assuming a $1,500 bankroll and a wagering unit of 5 percent, $75 could be played in a conservative fashion while still allowing the chance for a nice score:

$50 win: Itaka
$10 exacta part wheel: Strolling Along, As Indicated / Itaka
$5 exacta: Ozan / Itaka

As often happens, Itaka did indeed improve to a new top, running a Beyer of 100 — a move of 11 points, and a 9¼ on *The Sheets* — a move of 4 points (as mentioned, 3 points on Beyer is roughly equivalent to a point on sheets). Alas, As Indicated proved unfazed by early-pace pressure, as had been his trademark in three prior victories, and held off the fast-closing Itaka by a neck.

A straight $75 win bet would've been lost. A bet of $50 win backed up by $25 to place would've returned $125 for a net profit of $50 — a small consolation for predicting such a big effort at 14–1. But by betting $50 to win along with three exacta savers using Itaka underneath the three logical contenders, $528 was returned, for a net profit of $453.

NINTH RACE
Aqueduct
APRIL 3, 1993

1 MILE. (1.322) 41st Running THE GOTHAM (Grade II). Purse $200,000. 3-year-olds. By subscription of $400 each which should accompany the nomination; $1,600 to pass the entry box, $1,600 to start. The Purse to be divided 60% to the winner, 22% to second, 12% to third and 6% to fourth. Weight, 126 lbs. Non-winners of a race of $100,000 at a mile or over in 1993 allowed 3 lbs. Of two races of $100,000 at anytime, 5 lbs. Of a race of $50,000, 8 lbs. Of a race other than Maiden or Claiming at a mile or over, 12 lbs. Starters to be named at the closing time of entries. Trophies will be presented to the winning owner, trainer and jockey. Closed Wednesday, March 10 with 40 Nominations.
Value of race $200,000; value to winner $120,000; second $44,000; third $24,000; fourth $12,000. Mutuel pool $297,504. Exacta Pool $453,176 Triple Pool $521,597

Last Raced	Horse	M/Eqt.	A.	Wt	PP	St	¼	½	¾	Str	Fin	Jockey	Odds $1
20Feb93 6Aqu	As Indicated		3	114	4	4	11	1½	1hd	1hd	1nk	Bisono C V	3.80
28Feb93 6GP3	Itaka	b	3	114	3	8	7½	61½	3½	3½	21¼	Smith M E	14.00
31Oct92 8GP8	Strolling Along		3	121	8	1	31	21½	21	21	3nk	Antley C W	1.20
7Mar93 7Aqu2	Ozan	b	3	118	5	6	5hd	41	4½	4½	4nk	Samyn J L	2.70
25Mar93 6GS1	Castelli Street		3	114	1	7	2½	51	5½	56	516	Castillo H Jr	24.70
20Feb93 6Aqu2	Fighting Daddy	b	3	114	7	2	4½	3hd	62	61½	61½	Davis R G	10.00
7Mar93 7Aqu3	Rohwer		3	114	2	5	6hd	7hd	71	71	7nk	Madrid A Jr	18.40
8Mar93 1Aqu3	Hickory Lake		3	114	6	3	8	8	8	8	8	Migliore R	30.30

OFF AT 4:50 Start good, Won driving. Time, :232, :461, 1:103, 1:361 Track good.

$2 Mutuel Prices:			
5-(E)-AS INDICATED	9.60	6.20	4.20
4-(D)-ITAKA		10.00	6.60
9-(I)-STROLLING ALONG			3.40

$2 EXACTA 5-4 PAID $105.60 $2 TRIPLE 5-4-9 PAID $387.00

Ch. g, (May), by Czaravich—Our Nice Sue, by Our Michael. Trainer Schosberg Richard. Bred by Perkins Margot I (Ky).

AS INDICATED sprinted clear in the early stages, set the pace along the inside on the backstretch, dug in when challenged by STROLLING ALONG midway on the turn, battled heads apart inside that one into midstretch, shook loose nearing the sixteenth pole then was all out to hold off ITAKA in the final strides. ITAKA reserved for a half after breaking a step slowly, moved up rapidly while four wide on the turn then closed steadily in the middle of the track but could not get up. STROLLING ALONG, never far back, moved to engage AS INDICATED for the lead nearing the half mile pole, drew on even terms with the winner entering the stretch, battled gamely into deep stretch and weakened under pressure in the final sixteenth. OZAN settled in good position for five furlongs, races within striking distance while between horses on the turn, remained a factor into midstretch and finished evenly in the final eighth. CASTELLI STREET up close early, lagged behind a bit along the backstretch lodged a mild rally while saving ground on the turn but could not sustain his bid. FIGHTING DADDY raced in close contention between horses for five furlongs, steadied midway on the turn then gradually tired thereafter. ROHWER was never a factor. HICKORY LAKE trailed throughout. CASTELLI STREET and HICKORY LAKE wore mud caulks.

Owners— 1, Heatherwood Farm; 2, Brophy Stable; 3, Phipps Ogden; 4, Loblolly Stable; 5, Castelli Stables; 6, Kimran Stables; 7, Garren Murray M; 8, New Showtime Stable.

Trainers— 1, Schosberg Richard; 2, Johnson Philip G; 3, McGaughey Claude III; 4, Bohannan Thomas; 5, Anderson William D; 6, Toner James J; 7, Garren Murray M; 8, Klesaris Robert P.

Scratched—Silver Key (5Mar93 8GS1).

$2 Daily Double 4-5 Paid $176.80 Daily Double Pool $388,591

Lightly raced four-year-olds that have recently come around to their best three-year-old figures can be handled in much the same way as explosive three-year-olds; as with the explosive sophomores, some of them take a backward step after recording the key figure, while others fire with a big race right away. Examples from consecutive days at Saratoga in 1992 illustrate this point:

Clover City — B. g. 4, by Malinowski—Wegotluck, by Lyphard — Br.—Sunnyview Farm (NY) — **117**
CARR D (38 3 9 5 .08)
Own.—Stock Michael L — Tr.—Terrill William V (12 1 2 3 .08)

Lifetime							
16 1 2 0	1992	5	0	2	0	$12,760
$29,800	1991	11	1	0	0	$17,040
	Turf	6	1	2	0	$28,360

Date	Track	Cond	Dist	Fractions			Race	Fig	PP	St	1st	2nd	Str	Fin	Jockey	Eqt	Wt	Odds		Comment	Field
4Sep92-	7Bel	yl	1 1/16 [T]	:482	1:123	1:441	3↑[S]Alw 29000	83	4	4	32	41½	32	22¼	Carr D	b	117	*2.40	75-20	ShomrmSocty1172¼ClovrCty1171¼EbonyBl117 Willingly	10
28Aug92-	5Sar	fm	1⅛ (T)	:462	1:104	1:484	3↑[S]Alw 29000	83	10	5	42	5¾	33	2½	Carr D	b	117	23.30	85-11	Green Gaitor112½ Clover City1173½ TeddyC.114 Fin well	12
15Aug92-	2Sar	gd	1⅛ (T)	:472	1:112	1:501	3↑[S]Alw 29000	73	12	2	2½	2½	31½	64¼	Carr D	b	117	50.70	75-14	Complinim1141½GrnGtor1121½DulZon117 Bid, weakened	12
25Jly92-	5Bel	fst	6f	:222	:452	1:094	3↑[S]Alw 27000	52	8	7	76	64¾	69½	614¾	Carr D	b	117	57.70	76-15	FtforRoylty1176ShomrmScty1173¼EbnyBl117 No factor	8
11Jly92-	3Bel	fst	1 1/16	:472	1:113	1:42	3↑[S]Alw 29000	31	9	3	421½	55¾	931	941¾	Carr D	b	117	50.00	50-18	BlzonSong11310½RelCielo1119¾PrinceJubile111 Stopped	9
7Dec91-	3Aqu	fst	170 [•]	:483	1:14	1:44	3↑Clm 25000	—	2	3	32	119¼	—	—	Antley C W	b	115	7.80e	— —	Sothmpton-Ar1153¼PrdClrs1156¾PcExprss117 Pulled up	11
2Dec91-	4Aqu	gd	7f	:224	:464	1:25	Clm 30000	48	9	4	68	97	910	818¼	Velazquez J R	b	113	40.30	59-22	SunshinChrli1154NicAinit1172¼Kck'sforKcks117 Outrun	9
2Nov91-	4Aqu	fm	1 (T)	:474	1:123	1:374	3↑Alw 29000	63	6	5	64½	95	87½	714½	Velazquez J R	b	120	28.90	72-11	Devil'sCry117¾Punchpsser1155MdivlClssic117 No threat	9
23Oct91-	2Aqu	fm	1 1/16 (T)	:484	1:14	1:461	3↑[S]Md Sp Wt	73	5	3	3½	41	1hd	11½	Krone J A	b	119	4.00	81-15	CloverCity1191½It'sS.S.Mri119nkScoutSetter119 Driving	10
12Oct91-	9Bel	fst	7f	:223	:462	1:26	3↑Md 30000	58	6	8	64	97¾	74	65	Krone J A	b	115	15.00	69-17	Elan Beau119nkOronoColor's1152TenEyck115 No threat	13

LATEST WORKOUTS Sep 15 Bel 4f fst :492 B — Aug 26 Bel tr.t 4f fst :49 B — Aug 11 Bel 5f gd 1:013 H — Aug 4 Bel 4f fst :49 B

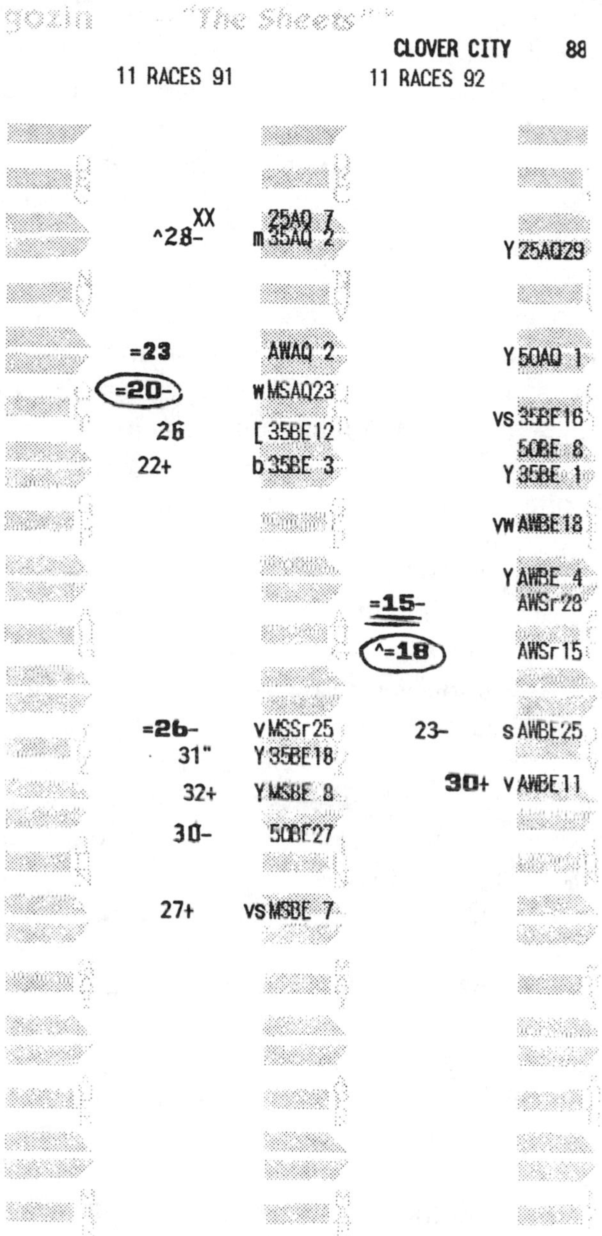
gozin "The Sheets"
CLOVER CITY 88
11 RACES 91
11 RACES 92
^28- XX
25AQ 7
m 35AQ 2
Y 25AQ29
=23
AWAQ 2
Y 50AQ 1
=20-
w MSAQ23
vs 35BE16
26
[35BE12
50BE 8
22+
b 35BE 3
Y 35BE 1
vw AWBE18
Y AWBE 4
=15-
AWSr28
^=18
AWSr15
=26-
v MSSr25
23-
s AWBE25
31"
Y 35BE18
30+
v AWBE11
32+
Y MSBE 8
30-
50BE27
27+
vs MSBE 7

Clover City improved immediately when switched to grass in the autumn of his three-year-old year, recording a Beyer of 73 and a corresponding figure of 19¾ on *The Sheets.* Returned at age four, the gelding was able to equal that figure on Beyer, and he slightly surpassed it on the sheets with an 18 when placed back on grass for the first time August 15. (Note: *The Sheets* uses an equal sign to the left of the figure to denote races run on grass, while *Thoro-graph* uses a dash.)

Since Clover City had improved first time on grass and had reproduced his best three-year-old figure at the first available grass opportunity at age four, it was conceivable he might improve again on August 28, though less than two weeks had elapsed. In this kind of situation, the odds dictate the proper strategy: had Clover City been 5–2, one might take the position that he hadn't had enough time to recover from the key figure and might take a small backward step before improving further. At 23–1, however, one can be a bit more lenient, especially when keying the explosive-line horse underneath in exactas in addition to a win wager.

In much the same way a play was fashioned for Itaka in the Gotham, available capital on Clover City might have been bet as follows: two-thirds to win and one-third keying Clover City in exactas underneath logical contenders.

Clover City improved right away — up 10 points on Beyer to an 83 and down 3¼ points on *The Sheets* to a 14¾. Again, note the approximate three-to-one relationship between Beyer and sheet-style figures. Also note the "two-move" running line on August 28, indicative of a horse in razor-sharp condition.

Once again, however, our explosive-line horse ran his eyeballs out at long odds only to be beaten for the win by a logical contender.

With $75 allotted for the race, those who bet win lost everything; those who bet $50 win and $25 place collected $247.50; those who bet $50 win and $5 exactas keying Clover City under the five contenders that looked as if they had four legs caught a $301.80 exacta two and a half times, for a return of $754.50.

FIFTH RACE
Saratoga
AUGUST 28, 1992

1 ⅛ MILES. (1.47) ALLOWANCE. Purse $29,000. 3–year–olds and upward foaled in New York State and approved by the New York State Bred Registry which have never won a race other than maiden claiming or starter. Weight, 3–year–olds 117 lbs.; older, 122 lbs. Non–winners of a race other than claiming at a mile or over since July 15 allowed 3 lbs.; of such a race since July 1, 5 lbs. (RUN ON THE MAIN TURF COURSE)

Value of race $29,000; value to winner $17,400; second $6,380; third $3,480; fourth $1,740. Mutuel pool $336,919. Exacta Pool $589,255

Last Raced	Horse	M/Eqt.A.Wt	PP	St	¼	½	¾	Str	Fin	Jockey	Odds $1
15Aug92 ^{2}Sar^{2}	Green Gaitor	3 112	7	7	7^{2}	$6^{1\frac{1}{2}}$	$6^{1\frac{1}{2}}$	1^{3}	$1\frac{1}{2}$	Cruguet J	5.10
15Aug92 ^{2}Sar^{6}	Clover City	b 4 117	10	9	$5\frac{1}{2}$	$4\frac{1}{2}$	5^{hd}	$3\frac{1}{2}$	$2^{3\frac{1}{2}}$	Carr D	23.30
15Aug92 ^{2}Sar^{12}	Teddy C.	b 3 114	5	4	9^{3}	8^{1}	$7\frac{1}{2}$	4^{1}	$3^{1\frac{3}{4}}$	Krone J A	11.40
15Aug92 ^{2}Sar^{3}	Duel Zone	b 4 117	8	12	12	10^{2}	$8^{1\frac{1}{2}}$	$6^{3\frac{1}{2}}$	4^{nk}	Perret C	6.90
15Aug92 ^{2}Sar^{4}	Winning River	b 3 112	12	11	$6^{1\frac{1}{2}}$	5^{1}	2^{hd}	2^{hd}	$5^{3\frac{1}{2}}$	Bailey J D	2.90
15Aug92 ^{2}Sar^{5}	Sudahr	b 5 117	3	3	$11\frac{1}{2}$	12	$11^{2\frac{1}{2}}$	7^{1}	6^{2}	Migliore R	20.90
15Aug92 ^{2}Sar^{7}	Lonnegan	b 3 112	1	1	$2^{1\frac{1}{2}}$	2^{1}	$1\frac{1}{2}$	5^{hd}	$7^{8\frac{1}{2}}$	Maple E	9.20
7Aug92 ^{3}Sar^{9}	Powder Cap	b 3 112	9	8	$8\frac{1}{2}$	9^{1}	$9^{1\frac{1}{2}}$	$9^{1\frac{1}{2}}$	$8\frac{3}{4}$	Antley C W	68.90
26Jly92 ^{4}Bel^{3}	Trilingual	5 117	4	2	$3^{1\frac{1}{2}}$	$3\frac{1}{2}$	4^{hd}	$8^{1\frac{1}{2}}$	9^{9}	Rojas R I	2.80
15Aug92 ^{2}Sar^{9}	Archieoffroghollow	b 4 117	6	6	10^{1}	11^{1}	$10\frac{1}{2}$	10^{8}	$10^{6\frac{3}{4}}$	McCauley W H	52.40
19Aug92 ^{2}Atl^{1}	Designated Bidder	b 3 112	2	5	1^{2}	$1\frac{1}{2}$	3^{hd}	$11^{1\frac{1}{2}}$	$11^{2\frac{1}{4}}$	Smith M E	22.30
14Aug92 ^{1}Sar^{8}	Edgewood Extra	b 3 112	11	10	4^{hd}	7^{hd}	12	12	12	Davis R G	14.40

OFF AT 3:14 Start good. Won driving. Time, :22^{1}, :46^{2}, 1:10^{4}, 1:36^{1}, 1:48^{4} [redacted]

$2 Mutuel Prices:				
	7–(G)–GREEN GAITOR	12.20	7.80	5.40
	10–(J)–CLOVER CITY		19.80	11.00
	5–(E)–TEDDY C.			6.80

$2 EXACTA 7–10 PAID $301.80

B. c, (Mar), by Talc—Our Beloved Jack, by Jackknife. Trainer Nocella Vincent R. Bred by Langsman Steven H (NY).

GREEN GAITOR, steadied between horses soon after the start, was reserved for six furlongs, rapidly gained while four wide on the turn, accelerated to the front opening a clear advantage in upper stretch then was all out to hold off CLOVER CITY in the closing strides. CLOVER CITY, rated in close contention while saving ground to the turn then closed steadily but could not get up. TEDDY C., unhurried for six furlongs raced in traffic while saving ground on the turn then rallied mildly to gain a share. DUEL ZONE outrun for six furlongs after breaking slowly failed to threaten with a mild late rally. WINNING RIVER settled just behind the early leaders while four wide, made a run from outside to challenge on the turn, remained a factor into the upper stretch then gradually tired thereafter. SUDAHR never reached contention. LONNEGAN prompted the early pace from outside, accelerated to the front nearing the far turn then faded in the drive. POWER CAP checked while drifting inward in the early stages, was never a factor. TRILINGUAL saved ground and tired. ARCHIEOFFROGHOLLOW checked between horses soon after the start and was never close thereafter. DESIGNATED BIDDER rushed up after being pinched at the start, set the pace for nearly six furlongs then gave way. EDGEWOOD EXTRA raced wide and tired.

Owners— 1, My Samsara Stables; 2, Stock Michael L; 3, Kelley Walter A; 4, Rich Jill P; 5, Corr John D; 6, Pinebourne Farm; 7, Boto Stable; 8, Krystock Paul W; 9, Armellino Frank; 10, Keegan William A Jr; 11, Graves William; 12, Deckmejian B.

Trainers— 1, Nocella Vincent R; 2, Terrill William V; 3, Dutrow Richard E; 4, Rich David C; 5, Martin Carlos F; 6, Campo John P; 7, Kelly Tim D; 8, PEITZ DAN C; 9, Blanco Louis L; 10, Forbes John H; 11, Murray Carol Ann, 12, Pascuma James J Jr.

The prestigious Whitney Handicap was essentially a three-horse race between Strike the Gold, Out of Place, and Sultry Song. None of the other starters, except for Strike the Gold's rabbit, Loach, were lower than 11–1, and none had shown anything in their recent form that would make them viable contenders.

Sultry Song's Beyer of 113 in the Hollywood Gold Cup was the top recent effort among the trio, and it also represented a slight improvement over his best figure at age three in the NYRA Mile. On *The Sheets,* Sultry Song's effort in the Gold Cup was a 5½, which equaled his best figure as a three-year-old and set the stage for improvement during the course of his four-year-old year:

8

1⅛ MILES SARATOGA START FINISH

1 ⅛ MILES. **(1.47) 65th Running THE WHITNEY HANDICAP (Grade I). Purse $250,000. 3-year-olds and upward. By subscription of $500 each which should accompany the nomination; $2,000 to pass the entry box; $2,000 to start. The purse to be divided 60% to the winner, 22% to second, 12% to third and 6% to fourth. Weights Monday, August 24. Starters to be named at the closing time of entries. Trophies will be presented to the winning owner, trainer and jockey. Closed Wednesday, August 12, with 28 nominations.**

Coupled—Strike the Gold and Loach.

Sunny Sunrise

Ch. g. 5, by Sunny's Halo—Xalapa Sunrise, by Rising Market
Br.—Koerber Mr-Mrs R (Ont-C)
Tr.—Delp Grover G (—)
ANTLEY C W (153 29 22 22 .19)
Own.—Meyerhoff Harry
113

Lifetime					
35 12 7 5	1992	10 1 3 3	$259,630
$814,403	1991	17 8 3 1	$520,893
	Turf	2 0 0 0	
	Wet	8 3 1 1	$75,553

Race	Fractions	Race	Speed	PP St 1c 2c Str Fin	Jockey		Wt	Odds		Comment line	
15Aug92- 11Lrl sly 1$\frac{1}{16}$	:464 1:112 1:423	3↑Polynes'n H	94	3 2 2½ 2½ 35 36¾	Luzzi M J	Lb	117	*1.30	93-17	HlsRsn1126½PnutButtrOnt116½SunnySnrs117	Weakened 6
15Aug92-Grade III											
18Jly92- 8Lrl fst 6f	:213 :45 1:094	3↑F Defrancis	85	9 10 109¾1012 1011 89¾	Luzzi M J	Lb	123	*3.80	82 —	Suprstrik-GB1124¾PrisinFlight114¾KingCorri117	Outrun 12
18Jly92-Grade III											
5Jly92- 10Lrl fst 1⅛	:46 1:094 1:473	3↑Baltmr BC H	106	1 1 13½ 14 11 2hd	Santos J A	L	117	3.30	102-08	ExcllntTippr112hdSunnySunrs117hdOutofPlc113	Gamely 10
5Jly92-Grade III											
16May92- 5Pim gd 6f	:224 :461 1:101	3↑Mar'lnd Bc H	86	1 5 32½ 32½ 45½ 67¾	Smith M E	L	118	*2.70	86-13	Potentility1171SmrtAlec1144BoomTowner117	Gave way 9
25Apr92- 8Spt fst 1⅛	:46 1:093 1:48	Nat Jky C H	85	2 2 21½ 2½ 411 412	Santos J A	L	119	1.30	113 —	Stalwars1151 Richman1222½ Sunny Prince113	Tired 6
25Apr92-Grade III											
12Apr92- 10Pim fst 1⅛	:462 1:104 1:491	3↑J Campel H	109	5 1 12½ 12 1hd 11¼	Smith M E	Lb	117	*.70	90-27	SunnySnrs1171¼VllyCrossng115hdMknMony108	Driving 7
12Apr92-Grade III											
7Mar92- 10GP fst 1¼	:473 1:363 2:013	3↑Gulf Park H	106	1 1 12 22 25 39½	Antley C W	Lb	114	3.60	83-14	SeaCdet1197StriketheGold1152½SunnySunrise114	Tired 6
7Mar92-Grade I											
17Feb92- 11Lrl fst 7f	:221 :444 1:214	3↑Gen George	104	11 1 33½ 31½ 11½ 22	Smith M E	Lb	123	*2.10	96-16	SnorSpdy1262SunnySnrs1232½FormlDnnr123	Faded late 12
17Feb92-Grade II											
1Feb92- 9GP fst 1⅛	:464 1:101 1:48	3↑Donn H	111	8 1 13 12 21½ 33½	Bailey J D	Lb	115	7.00	94-12	SeCdet1153OutofPlc114nkSunnySunris115	Faded inside 8
1Feb92-Grade I											
18Jan92- 10GP fst 1$\frac{1}{16}$	:474 1:11 1:433	3↑Crm Fra'ch H	110	5 1 13½ 12½ 11 2no	Bailey J D	Lb	117	*.90	94-13	PntBttrOnt114noSnnSnrs1176HnstEnsgn109	Just edged 7

LATEST WORKOUTS ●Aug 11 Lrl 4f fst :462 H Aug 5 Lrl 6f fst 1:12 H ●Jly 29 Lrl 5f fst 1:002 H ●Jly 15 Lrl 3f fst :35 H

Chief Honcho

Ch. h. 5, by Chief's Crown—Expressive Dance, by Riva Ridge
Br.—Firestone Mr-Mrs B R (Va)
Tr.—Mott William I (35 10 4 5 .29)
SMITH M E (152 31 25 19 .20)
Own.—Firestone Matthew K
116

Lifetime			
25 8 6 2	1992	3 1 0 0	$28,200
$966,607	1991	11 2 5 2	$695,660
	Wet	1 1 0 0	$18,600

Race	Fractions	Race	Speed	PP St 1c 2c Str Fin	Jockey		Wt	Odds		Comment line	
8Aug92- 8Mth fst 1⅛	:453 1:09 1:464	3↑Iselin H	89	5 9 99 910 97½ 79¼	Smith M E	Lb	117	8.80	96 —	Jolie'sHlo116hdOutofPlce1131VlleyCrossing111	No rally 11
8Aug92-Grade I											
11Jly92- 9Det fst 1⅛	:473 1:114 1:493	3↑Mich Mile	94	5 10 117½128 1211 117¼	Day P	Lb	122	*1.10	89-09	ClssicSeven113¾SunnyPrince1121½IrishSwp116	Dull try 12
11Jly92-Grade II											
18Jun92- 8Bel fst 1$\frac{1}{16}$	:461 1:102 1:41	3↑Alw 47000	107	2 3 32 2hd 2½ 1½	Krone J A	b	115	*1.00	97-03	ChiefHoncho115½ExcllntTippr1152¾KillrDillr115	Driving 4
23Nov91- 8Aqu gd 1⅜	:482 1:373 2:14	3↑Brooklyn H	104	6 3 21 2½ 22 22½	Smith M E	b	121	*.80	100-14	TimelyWrning1122½ChifHoncho1212½DRoch115	2nd best 8
23Nov91-Grade I											
2Nov91- 8CD fst 1¼	:482 1:38 2:024	3↑Br Cp Clsc	107	4 6 66 74¾ 88½ 88¾	Smith M E	LBb	126	19.70	87-09	BlackTieAffir-Ir1261¼TwilightAgend1262½Unbridled126	11
2Nov91-Grade I; 5-wide backstretch, tired											
5Oct91- 7Bel fst 1¼	:473 1:36 2:003	3↑J C Gold Cp	112	5 2 22½ 21 3½ 21¼	Smith M E	b	126	2.60	93-07	Festin-Ar1261¼ChifHoncho126nkStrikthGold121	Gamely 5
5Oct91-Grade I											
1Sep91- 11Mth fst 1⅛	:462 1:102 1:474	3↑Iselin H	111	1 7 65½ 64½ 43 3¾	Smith M E	Lb	115	4.30	98-03	BlckTAffr-Ir119nkFrmWy122½ChfHonch115	Closed well 8
1Sep91-Grade I											
3Aug91- 8Sar gd 1⅛	:472 1:111 1:48	3↑Whitney H	111	7 3 21 2½ 22½ 23¼	Smith M E	b	115	2.80	94-03	InExcess-Ir1213¼ChifHoncho1152¾KillrDillr112	2nd best 7
3Aug91-Grade I											
4Jly91- 8Bel fst 1¼	:47 1:34 1:581	3↑Suburban H	118	2 3 32 21 21 21	Smith M E	b	115	5.80	105-10	InExcess-Ir1191ChiefHoncho1156KillerDillr113	2nd best 7
4Jly91-Grade I											
8Jun91- 7Bel fst 1⅛	:442 1:084 1:463	3↑Nassau Co H	105	2 6 311 47 43½ 49½	Smith M E	b	117	10.40	86-08	Festin-Ar1167 Gervazy112nk FarmaWay123	Lacked rally 10
8Jun91-Grade II											

LATEST WORKOUTS Aug 26 Bel tr.t 5f fst 1:03 B Aug 4 Bel 5f fst 1:022 B Jly 29 Bel 6f fst 1:142 B Jly 7 Bel 6f fst 1:14 B

Sultry Song

B. c. 4, by Cox's Ridge—Sultry Sun, by Buckfinder
Br.—Live Oak Stud (Fla)
Tr.—Kelly Patrick J (27 1 3 4 .04)
BAILEY J D (125 22 19 14 .18)
Own.—Live Oak Plantation
115

Lifetime			
19 7 3 5	1992	4 1 1 1	$617,700
$1,055,276	1991	15 6 2 4	$437,576
	Turf	4 0 2 1	$67,804
	Wet	1 0 0 1	$60,000

Race	Fractions	Race	Speed	PP St 1c 2c Str Fin	Jockey		Wt	Odds		Comment line	
18Jly92- 8Bel fst 1¼	:46 1:352 2:001	3↑Suburban H	98	5 6 511 64 57 69¼	Bailey J D	b	116	1.70	81-16	PlesntTp1191½StrikthGold1191½DfnsivPly115	No factor 7
18Jly92-Grade I											
27Jun92- 4Hol fst 1¼	:461 1:344 2:001	3↑Hol Gld Cup	113	4 5 53½ 3nk 11½ 13¼	Bailey J D	b	113	9.90	96-06	SultrySong1133¼Mrquetry118hdAnotherRview120	Driving 6
27Jun92-Grade I											
6Jun92- 7Bel my 1⅛	:444 1:082 1:463	3↑Nassau Co H	108	9 5 64 63½ 3½ 31¾	Bailey J D	b	111	15.20	94-08	StrkthGold116nkPlsntTp1191½SltrySng111	Wide gamely 9
6Jun92-Grade II											
30May92- 8Pim fm 1$\frac{1}{16}$ Ⓣ	:492 1:143 1:452	Alw 35000	93	4 4 43 42½ 32 22¼	McCauley W H	b	122	*1.40	72-26	MakinMoney1142¼SultrySong1222RootBoy119	Steadied 6
2Nov91- 5CD fm 1 Ⓣ	:48 1:122 1:372	3↑Br Cp Mile	82	11 12 103½137¾141014 15¼	Bailey J D	LBb	123	16.30f	82-06	OpningVrs1261¼VldsBois-Fr126noStrofCozzn123	Outrun 14
2Nov91-Grade I											
26Oct91- 8Aqu fst 1	:444 1:083 1:333	3↑N Y R A Mile	110	5 6 62½ 52½ 51¾ 2hd	Bailey J D	b	111	10.10	94-08	Rubiano116hd Sultry Song1111 Diablo112	Gamely 15
26Oct91-Grade I											
6Oct91- 6Bel fst 1	:462 1:094 1:342	Jamaica H	108	6 3 31 3½ 2½ 1nk	Antley C W	b	113	*2.10	98-11	SultrySong113nkHonestEnsign110nkTkMOut116	Driving 7
6Oct91-Grade II											
20Sep91- 9Med fst 1⅛	:46 1:093 1:462	Pegasus H	106	4 4 43½ 32½ 35½ 35¾	Antley C W	b	114	3.90	97-07	Scan1191¾ Sea Cadet1194 Sultry Song114	Willingly 8
20Sep91-Grade I											
2Sep91- 8AP fm 1¼ Ⓣ	:464 1:364 2:011	Secretariat	100	6 7 66 64½ 41¾ 3nk	Antley C W	b	114	6.00	92-09	JackieWckie123hdOlympio126hdSultrySong114	Late bid 8
2Sep91-Grade I											
16Aug91- 8Sar gd 1⅛ Ⓣ	:473 1:111 1:49	Gallant Man	100	2 7 75¾ 87½ 63 2hd	Antley C W	b	117	13.40	85-15	Lch122hdSltrySng117hdFrstrsAllstr122	Chckd, rlld wide 10
16Aug91-Grade III											

LATEST WORKOUTS Aug 23 Sar 6f fst 1:133 H Aug 19 Sar Tr.Ⓣ 4f gd :513 B Aug 13 Sar 4f fst :48 H Aug 8 Sar 5f fst :582 H

Strike the Gold — Ch. c. 4, by Alydar—Majestic Gold, by Hatchet Man

PERRET C (76 9 10 12 .12)
Br.—Calumet Farm (Ky)
Own.—C C W Gold Stable
Tr.—Zito Nicholas P (28 1 1 4 .04)

120

Lifetime							
24 5 7 4	1992	9	2	4	1	$953,176
$2,414,426	1991	12	2	3	3	$1,443,850
	Wet	1	1	0	0	$300,000

8Aug92- 8Mth	fst	1$\frac{1}{8}$	:45^3	1:09	1:46^4	3↑Iselin H	**101**	10	11	11^{17}	11^{12}	5$^{4\frac{1}{2}}$	4$^{2\frac{1}{2}}$	Perret C		120	*1.70e	102 —	Jolie'sHlo116^{hd}OutofPlce113^{1}VllyCrossing111	Willingly	11
8Aug92-Grade I																					
18Jly92- 8Bel	fst	1$\frac{1}{4}$	:46	1:35^2	2:00^1	3↑Suburban H	**110**	4	7	7^{21}	4$^{3\frac{1}{2}}$	3$^{2\frac{1}{2}}$	2$^{1\frac{1}{2}}$	Perret C		119	*1.50e	88–16	PlsntTp119$^{1\frac{1}{2}}$StrikthGold119$^{1\frac{1}{4}}$DfnsvPly115	Rallied wide	7
18Jly92-Grade I																					
6Jun92- 7Bel	my	1$\frac{1}{8}$	:44^4	1:08^2	1:46^3	3↑Nassau Co H	**111**	5	9	9^{15}	9$^{5\frac{3}{4}}$	2$^{\frac{1}{2}}$	1^{nk}	Perret C		116	4.80	96–08	StrikthGold116^{nk}PlsntTp119$^{1\frac{1}{2}}$SultrySong111	Wide drvg	9
6Jun92-Grade II																					
9May92-10Pim	fst	1$\frac{3}{16}$	:47^3	1:11^2	1:54^4	Pim Spec H	**111**	4	7	7^{11}	7$^{8\frac{1}{4}}$	3^2	1$^{\frac{3}{4}}$	Perret C		114	6.30	88–23	StrkthGld114$^{\frac{3}{4}}$FlySFr116$^{1\frac{1}{4}}$TlghtAgnd122	Wide, driving	7
9May92-Grade I																					
4Apr92- 7Aqu	fst	1$\frac{3}{16}$	:48^1	1:12	1:55^3	3↑Thrty Six Rd	**101**	3	4	4^{13}	4^{13}	3^7	2^6	Antley C W		117	*.80	90–21	RedPine119^{6}StriketheGold117^{hd}Alyten117	Up for place	4
7Mar92-10GP	fst	1$\frac{1}{4}$	:47^3	1:36^3	2:01^3	3↑Gulf Park H	**110**	6	5	5^{18}	5^{11}	4^8	2^7	Krone J A		115	2.00	86–14	SeCdet119^{7}StrikthGold115$^{2\frac{1}{2}}$SunnySunris114	4 wide str	6
7Mar92-Grade I																					
17Feb92-10GP	fst	1$\frac{1}{8}$	:47^2	1:11^2	1:49^2	3↑Broward H	**107**	3	6	6^{14}	5^8	4^4	3^1	Krone J A		117	*.80	89–21	HnstEnsgn109^{no}PntBttrOnt114^{1}StrkthGld117	4 wide str	7
17Feb92-Grade III																					
1Feb92- 9GP	fst	1$\frac{1}{8}$	:46^4	1:10^1	1:48	3↑Donn H	**104**	6	8	8^{18}	8^{15}	7^{11}	6^7	Antley C W		116	*1.30	90–12	SeCdet115^{3}OutofPlc114^{nk}SunnySunris115	Vry wide str	8
1Feb92-Grade I																					
8Jan92- 7GP	fst	7f	:23^4	:46^2	1:24^1	Alw 22900	**99**	11	9	12^{14}	9^{11}	5^5	2$^{\frac{3}{4}}$	Antley C W		120	*.70	84–16	ByShrk112$^{\frac{3}{4}}$StriketheGold120$^{\frac{1}{2}}$PerfctFit114	Wide bckstr	12
2Nov91- 8CD	fst	1$\frac{1}{4}$	:48^2	1:38	2:02^4	3↑Br Cp Class	**113**	10	9	9^{15}	9$^{7\frac{3}{4}}$	6^7	5$^{4\frac{1}{2}}$	Valenzuela P A	B	122	6.20	91–09	BlackTieAffir-Ir126$^{1\frac{1}{4}}$TwilightAgend126$^{2\frac{1}{2}}$Unbridled126		11
2Nov91-Grade I; 7-wide in stretch, late rally																					

LATEST WORKOUTS Aug 21 Sar 5f fst 1:00^3 B   Aug 5 Sar 4f gd :51^2 B   Jly 31 Sar 5f fst 1:00^1 H   Jly 25 Sar 4f fst :51^1 B

Len Ragozin — "The Sheets"™
XX
STRIKE THE GOLD
3 RACES 90
12 RACES 91
13 RACES 92
12" vw[MSAQ15
18+ vMSAQ31
22+ bvsMSBE11
5 VAWCD 2
7+ YAWBE 5
6" AWBE15
7+ vAWSr17
6+ VAWSr28
5 VAWBE 8
11+ YAWPI18
5 vwAWCD 4
^5 wAWKE13
8- AWGP16
11+ AWGP23
18- YsAWGP26
vAWGP31
AWBE10
AWBE19
vAWSr29
7" vAWMT 8
5 vAWBE18
.5 vwAWBE 6
'7- wAWPI 9
9+ SAWAQ 4
8- AWGP 7
7+ vAWGP17
8 vAWGP 1
9- vAWGP 8

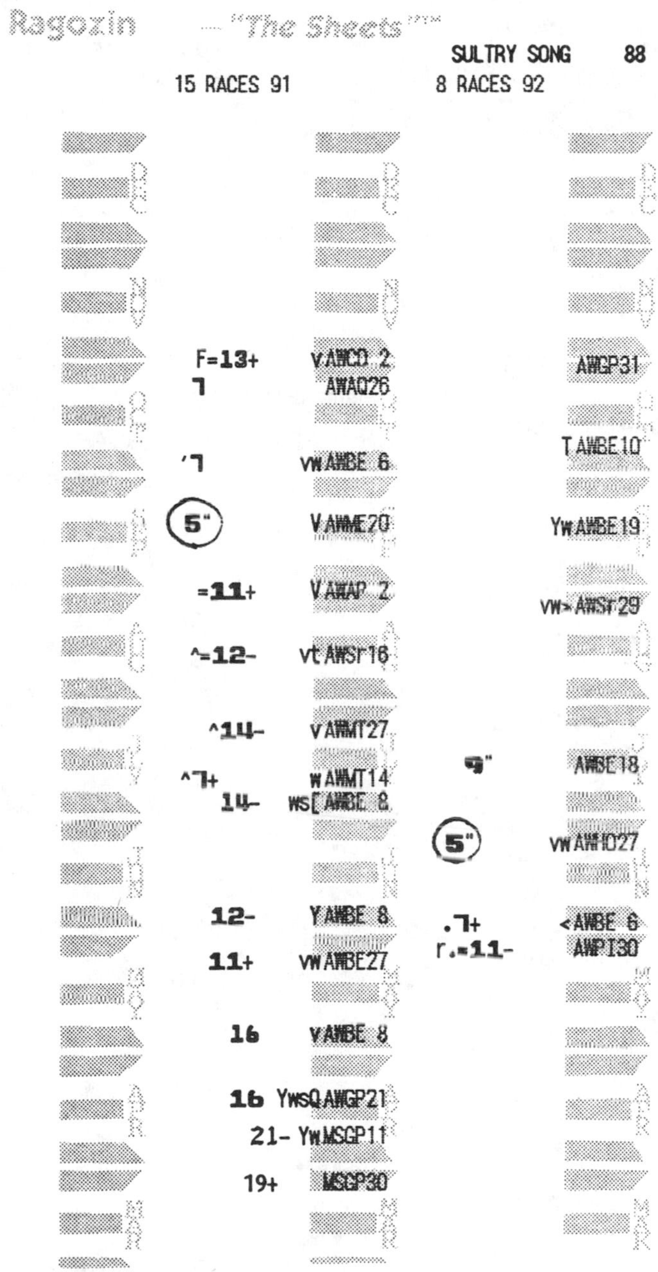
Ragozin
"The Sheets"™
SULTRY SONG 88
15 RACES 91
8 RACES 92
F=13+ vAWCD 2
7 AWAQ26
AWGP31
TAWBE10
'7 vwAWBE 6
5" VAWME20
YwAWBE19
=11+ VAWAP 2
vw>AWSr29
^=12- vtAWSr16
^14- vAWMT27
9" AWBE18
^7+ wAWMT14
14- ws[AWBE 8
5" vwAWHO27
12- YAWBE 8
.7+ <AWBE 6
r.=11- AWPI30
11+ vwAWBE27
16 vAWBE 8
16 YwsQAWGP21
21- YwMSGP11
19+ MSGP30

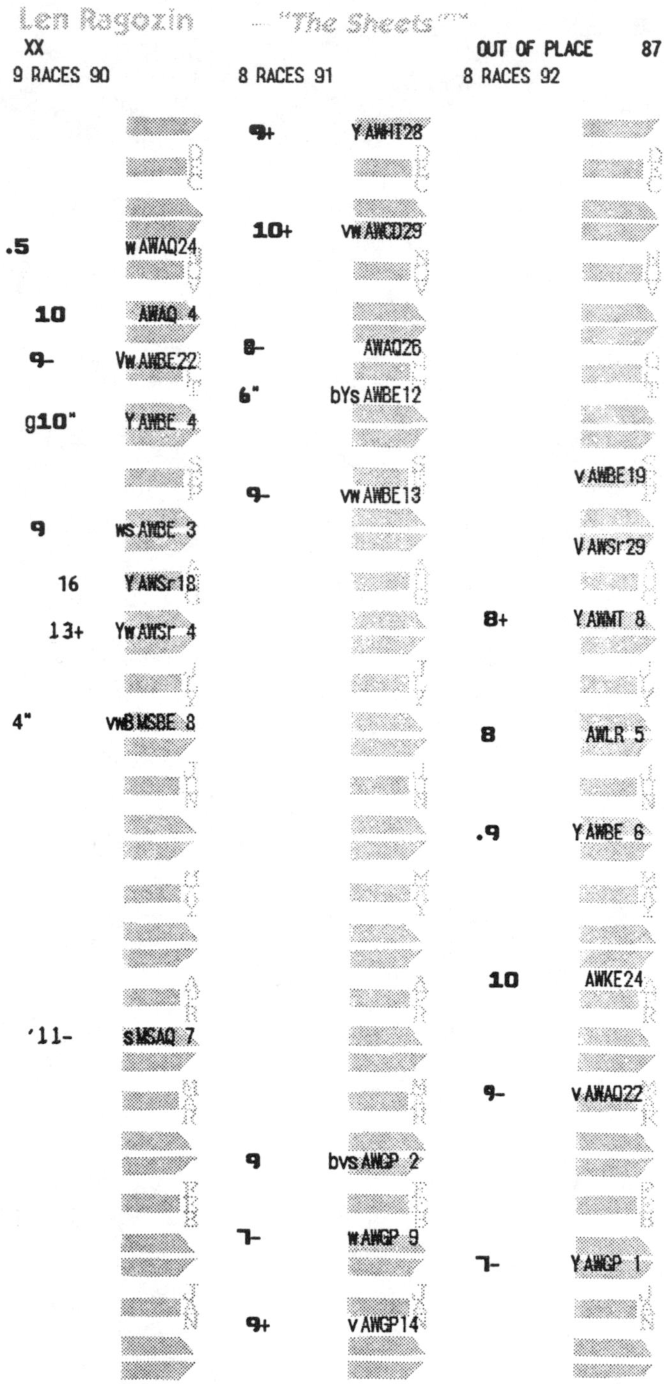
Len Ragozin — "The Sheets"™
XX
OUT OF PLACE 87
9 RACES 90
8 RACES 91
8 RACES 92
9+ YAWHI28
.5 wAWAQ24
10+ vwAWCD29
10 AWAQ 4
8- AWAQ26
9- VwAWBE22
6" bYsAWBE12
g10" YAWBE 4
vAWBE19
9- vwAWBE13
9 wsAWBE 3
VAWSr29
16 YAWSr18
8+ YAWMT 8
13+ YwAWSr 4
4" vwBMSBE 8
8 AWLR 5
.9 YAWBE 6
10 AWKE24
'11- sMSAQ 7
9- vAWAQ22
9 bvsAWGP 2
7- wAWGP 9
7- YAWGP 1
9+ vAWGP14

Sultry Song threw in a subpar effort in the Suburban Handicap at 17–10 immediately following the Gold Cup, but this was readily explained due to extraordinary circumstances: the colt had shipped three thousand miles to win the Gold Cup with a peak performance, and there had been an earthquake measuring 7.4 on the Richter scale the very next morning. Sultry Song had then shipped three thousand miles back to New York and gone into the Suburban on three weeks' rest. Understandably, the combined stress of a peak race, an earthquake, and six thousand frequent-flier miles took their toll in the Suburban, as Sultry Song beat one horse.

For the Whitney, however, Sultry Song had been given five additional weeks to recover and showed an encouraging workout line that included a speed-sharpening five furlongs in :58⅖, a breeze on the grass, and, four days later, a six-furlong move of 1:13⅗, which was accomplished, according to the *Form*'s work tab, with a final half-mile in :47⅘. As an added bonus, the track program noted Sultry Song would be racing with an "aluminum pad off," suggesting that whatever Sultry Song's foot ailments were, they had abated.

If Sultry Song rebounded to his Gold Cup effort, as was probable, he was faster than Out of Place and on par with Strike the Gold's career best. Given a relatively short price of 3–1, but with only two horses to be concerned with, a more aggressive betting approach was the preferred tack for the Whitney, once again assuming a betting unit per race of $75:

$25 win: Sultry Song

$25 exacta part wheel: Sultry Song / Out of Place, Strike the Gold

At 3–1, there was no room to hedge with Sultry Song. When 3–1 plays lose, handicappers must chalk them up as minor setbacks and move on; when they win, an attempt should be made to maximize returns. By keying Sultry Song on top in exactas with the only two conceivable contenders, a very predictable $33.40 exacta was cashed along with an $8.80 win mutuel:

EIGHTH RACE
Saratoga
AUGUST 29, 1992

1 ⅛ MILES. (1.47) 65th Running THE WHITNEY HANDICAP (Grade I). Purse $250,000. 3-year-olds and upward. By subscription of $500 each which should accompany the nomination; $2,000 to pass the entry box; $2,000 to start. The purse to be divided 60% to the winner, 22% to second, 12% to third and 6% to fourth. Weights Monday, August 24. Starters to be named at the closing time of entries. Trophies will be presented to the winning owner, trainer and jockey. Closed Wednesday, August 12, with 28 nominations.

Value of race $250,000; value to winner $150,000; second $55,000; third $30,000; fourth $15,000. Mutuel pool $539,840. Exacta Pool $583,174 Triple Pool $517,715

Last Raced	Horse	M/Eqt.	A.	Wt	PP	St	¼	½	¾	Str	Fin	Jockey	Odds $1
18Jly92 ^{8}Bel^{6}	Sultry Song	b	4	115	3	7	5^{3}	5^{4}	4^{2}	1^{hd}	1no	Bailey J D	3.40
8Aug92 ^{8}Mth^{2}	Out of Place		5	115	6	3	$6^{3\frac{1}{2}}$	6^{7}	$5^{\frac{1}{2}}$	$2^{2\frac{1}{2}}$	2^{4}	McCauley W H	2.80
8Aug92 ^{8}Mth^{7}	Chief Honcho	b	5	116	2	2	$4^{\frac{1}{2}}$	4^{hd}	6^{3}	3^{hd}	$3^{\frac{1}{2}}$	Smith M E	13.00
8Aug92 ^{8}Mth^{5}	Lost Mountain		4	114	5	6	7^{2}	7^{1}	8^{3}	4^{1}	4^{4}	Day P	11.40
8Aug92 ^{8}Mth^{4}	Strike the Gold		4	120	4	9	9	9	$7^{1\frac{1}{2}}$	6^{1}	5^{2}	Perret C	a-1.60
9Aug92 ^{6}Sar^{3}	Killer Diller	b	5	111	8	8	8^{2}	8^{hd}	9	7^{2}	$6^{\frac{1}{2}}$	Davis R G	37.00
9Aug92 ^{6}Sar^{1}	Key Contender	b	4	110	7	4	3^{5}	3^{3}	1^{hd}	$5^{\frac{1}{2}}$	$7^{1\frac{1}{4}}$	Krone J A	10.10
15Aug92 ^{11}Lrl^{3}	Sunny Sunrise	b	5	113	1	1	$2^{1\frac{1}{2}}$	$2^{\frac{1}{2}}$	3^{1}	8^{3}	8^{6}	Antley C W	13.60
8Aug92 ^{8}Mth^{6}	Loach		4	110	9	5	1^{hd}	1^{2}	2^{2}	9	9	Rojas R I	a-1.60

a-Coupled: Strike the Gold and Loach.

OFF AT 5:13 Start good. Won driving. Time, :23 , :45^{4}, 1:10 , 1:34^{4}, 1:47^{1} Track fast.

$2 Mutuel Prices:			
4-(D)-SULTRY SONG	8.80	4.60	4.40
7-(G)-OUT OF PLACE		4.00	3.60
3-(C)-CHIEF HONCHO			7.00

$2 EXACTA 4-7 PAID $33.40 $2 TRIPLE 4-7-3 PAID $308.00

B. c, by Cox's Ridge—Sultry Sun, by Buckfinder. Trainer Kelly Patrick J. Bred by Live Oak Stud (Fla).

SULTRY SONG, in hand early while four wide along the backstretch, worked his way forward from outside on the turn, surged to the front between horses in upper stretch, dueled heads apart inside out of place through the lane and outgamed that one while drifting out through the final eighth. OUT OF PLACE, reserved for five furlongs while saving ground, angled to the outside leaving the furlong marker but couldn't get by that one whilke clearly second best. CHIEF HONCHO rated in good position while saving ground, swung out while gaining on the turn raced in closed contention between horses into upper stretch then lacked a strong closing response. LOST MOUNTAIN, raced well back for six furlongs, rapidly gained on the turn, angled to the inside while making a threatening move in upper stretch but couldn't sustain his bid. STRIKE THE GOLD trailing along the backstretch, made a strong run while five wide to reach contention on the turn then flattened out. KILLER DILLER never reached contention. KEY CONTENDER stalked the early leaders from outside, surged to the front midway on the turn, then faded at the top of the stretch. SUNNY SUNRISE steadied inside LOACH leaving the first turn prompted the pace slightly off the rail for six furlongs then gave way leaving the far turn. LOACH set the pace along the inside for six furlongs and tired from his early set the pace along the inside for six furlongs and tired from his early efforts. LOACH and KEY CONTENDER wore mud caulks.

Owners— 1, Live Oak Plantation; 2, Phipps Cynthia; 3, Firestone Matthew K; 4, Loblolly Stable; 5, C C W Gold Stable; 6, Schwartz Barry K; 7, Rokeby Stables; 8, Meyerhoff Harry; 9, C C W Gold Stable.

Trainers— 1, Kelly Patrick J; 2, McGaughey Claude III; 3, Mott William I; 4, Bohannan Thomas; 5, Zito Nicholas P; 6, Alexander Frank A; 7, Miller Mack; 8, Delp Grover G; 9, Zito Nicholas P.

Scratched—Devil His Due (22Aug92 ^{7}Sar^{2}).

Before we leave the Whitney, alert readers may pose a legitimate question regarding Strike the Gold's line as it appeared on *The Sheets:* Couldn't his line be interpreted as explosive, since his recent 5s equaled his best performances at age three?

The answer is no, the reason being that Strike the Gold has now established a level by running 5s on numerous occasions without ever breaking through to something better. There is nothing *wrong* with his line; in fact, it exemplifies a consistently hard-hitting horse that is presently performing to its maximum capabilities. If one had to describe Strike the Gold's line, it would be that of a forging horse.

FORGING HORSES

Len Friedman is annually the featured speaker at *The Sheets* seminars held in New York for the Kentucky Derby and Breeders' Cup races. At a mid-1980s seminar on form cycles, he explained the difference between explosive and forging horses this way:

> To me, the ones that are really explosive have made one small move through their two-year-old top. In other words, they've just made one move past their two-year-old top — and not a big move: a point, a point and a half at the most. The difference between explosive and forging horses is this: the explosive ones I'm looking to play with just about any excuse at all sometime around four to eight weeks from when they hit that number. In a lot of cases I'd be willing to play the horse directly off that number if it's had a month off and I was getting good odds. Forging horses are the ones "looping" around to better numbers, but I would want to see some kind of intervening pattern on those horses which indicates to me the horse is still going forward in its development.

Simply stated, handicappers can evaluate older, more heavily raced horses that have recently come back around to their best figures as they might evaluate their younger counterparts, with an important new wrinkle: more caution should be exercised. Before playing this type of horse to improve again or run back to its top figure, handicappers should be looking for a bit more time between peak efforts along with some evidence that the horse is presently headed in the right direction.

The fifth race at Saratoga on August 17, 1992, was a $25,000 claiming sprint run in the mud, and it drew nine fillies and mares aged four to six. The race appeared wide open. Finger Lakes–shipper Magestic Willowa was a lukewarm favorite at 5–2, with six others going postward at odds ranging from 4–1 to 8–1. One of them, Bug's Chubbs, had a forging line on Beyer as well as on *The Sheets:*

5 START 6 FURLONGS SARATOGA FINISH

6 FURLONGS. **(1.08) CLAIMING. Purse $18,000. Fillies and mares, 3-year-olds and upward. Weights, 3-year-olds, 117 lbs.; older, 122 lbs. Non-winners of two races since July 15 allowed 3 lbs. Of a race since then, 5 lbs. Claiming price $25,000; for each $2,500 to $20,000, 2 lbs. (Races when entered to be claimed for $18,000 or less not considered.0**

Makin' Honey

Ro. f. 4, by Drone—Red Sash, by Go Marching
CRUGUET J (45 4 5 5 .09) $20,000 Br.—Santangelo George L (NY)
Own.—Lumot Stable Tr.—DiMauro Stephen (12 0 1 2 .00) 113
Lifetime 17 2 2 0 $46,656 | 1992 10 0 0 0 $3,096 | 1991 7 2 2 0 $43,560 | Turf 4 0 0 0 $150 | Wet 3 1 0 0 $16,680

21Jly92-10FL gd 1 :491 1:151 1:422 3↑ⒻAlw 6900 39 5 6 65½ 710 712 612¾ McCarthy M J b 116 8.10 59-29 WndswptAl116nkStckyRd1191¾Qn'sShllng108 No threat 8
12Jly92- 8FL fst 6f :22 :452 1:12 3↑ⒻAlw 6900 40 3 8 711 814 711 614 Nicol P A Jr b 116 3.00 72-19 Pssptnzy114noFstCrr11511Ashley'sObsession116 Outrun 8
21Jun92-10FL fst 6f :224 :46 1:124 3↑ⒻAlw 7000 51 6 6 64¼ 68 57 46½ Nicol P A Jr b 116 3.80 75-20 RomnGirl119½WindsweptAli1192LstRflction116 No rally 9
29May92- 7Bel fm 1 Ⓣ:454 1:101 1:35 ⒻClm 35000 54 9 6 63¾ 97 94¾ 915 Pezua J M b 117 19.90 72-14 Jolie Britt122hd Oriane1172 Final Road117 Outrun 9
21May92- 5Bel fst 7f :231 :463 1:242 ⒻClm 25000 55 5 3 32 31 43 48¼ Cruguet J 117 12.60 74-16 SblWy1173Crl'sCommnd1175Undrnsurd117 Lacked rally 5
11May92- 4Bel my 6f :221 :452 1:111 ⒻClm 25000 69 1 7 45 32 31 42½ Pezua J M 117 34.60 81-10 FondRomance1152SablWy115½FinlRod113 Lacked rally 7
9Apr92- 9Aqu fst 7f :223 :454 1:251 ⒻClm 25000 50 9 1 55 65½ 65½ 78¼ Cruguet J 117 24.00 71-18 OneThird1172LostinFlight117hdSprklingHnnh112 Faded 9
27Mar92- 4Aqu my 1 :461 1:112 1:37 ⒻClm 25000 48 7 8 88½ 87 88¼ 816¼ McCauley W H 117 7.30 61-23 ThrthtChrms1173¼WrldClssPr1153½BrttnErn117 Outrun 8
8Mar92- 5GP fst 7f :231 :463 1:234 ⒻClm 40000 47 2 6 74¾ 75¼ 79¾ 618½ Douglas R R 113 34.60 68-12 Butter Cream116½ StarYum1161½Solly'sFolly116 Outrun 7
9Feb92- 6GP fm *1⅛ Ⓣ 1:512 + ⒻClm 50000 48 1 4 38 1018 1126 1127¼ Cruguet J 116 49.90 — — PleasantReef1141KlassyIndividul120noAreis116 Faltered 11
LATEST WORKOUTS ●Aug 14 Sar 4f fst :472 H Aug 7 Sar 4f fst :50 B

Brave Grecian

Dk. b. or br. f. 4, by Brave Shot-GB—Greek Nixy, by Snow Knight
SMITH M E (82 17 15 12 .21) $20,000 Br.—Schickedanz Gustav (Ont-C)
Own.—Kimran Stable Tr.—Toner James J (7 0 1 0 .00) 113
Lifetime 21 3 1 3 $42,085 | 1992 11 2 0 1 $19,140 | 1991 9 1 1 2 $22,945 | Wet 4 2 0 0 $19,500

8Jly92- 3Bel fst 6f :22 :451 1:103 ⒻClm 12000 70 6 4 12½ 12½ 11½ 33¼ Davis R G b 113 10.80 84-16 TnCrk113¾MlHghGlry1172½BrvGrcn113 Svd Gnd, wknd 8
17Jun92- 2Bel fst 6f :223 :454 1:112 ⒻClm 12000 62 4 1 1½ 1hd 2½ 44 Davis R G b 113 4.40 79-16 NrthrnWlly1172½Plythbgbys106¾TnCrk113 Used in pace 8
28May92- 5Bel fst 6f :221 :452 1:104 ⒻClm 14000 63 2 3 21 2½ 32½ 55 Bailey J D 117 5.90 81-14 Plthbbs1101½BrdfrdB1133ChttsDrm113 Frcd pace tired 9
9May92- 9Bel gd 6f :214 :444 1:092 ⒻClm 17500 60 3 2 42½ 72¼ 65½ 510 Gryder A T 117 6.50 83-07 Crli'sCommnd1171½EvrlstingStr1175LuckyNck117 Tired 9
17Apr92- 2Aqu sly 6f :214 :45 1:103 ⒻClm 14000 72 1 5 11 1½ 12 14¾ Gryder A T 117 2.70 88-13 BraveGrecian1174¾Hagster1171½LurenMellis109 Driving 7
10Apr92- 3Aqu fst 7f :223 :453 1:25 ⒻClm 17500 53 8 1 2hd 1hd 32 610 Velazquez J R b 117 8.00 70-18 FinlRod1171½SolidAngel117¾IceSociety112 Dueled tired 8
27Mar92- 4Aqu my 1 :461 1:112 1:37 ⒻClm 22500 61 2 3 2hd 22 54½ 79¼ BrocklbnkGV5 b 110 24.60 68-23 ThrttCrs1173¼WrldClssPr1153½BrttEr117 Saved ground 8
18Mar92- 1Aqu fst 7f :23 :472 1:254 ⒻClm 25000 59 3 6 76 86¾ 74¾ 55¾ BrocklbnkGV5 b 112 35.10 70-23 SocilDelim117nkMisteV117noSwtn'SssyGl117 Saved grd 8
5Feb92- 3Aqu fst 6f ⊡:232 :472 1:121 ⒻClm 20000 53 5 2 2½ 3½ 58½ 515¼ Gryder A T b 115 28.40 67-22 NoCst1124½MssRdmndLn113noSwtn'SssyGl117 Used up 6
26Jan92- 3Aqu fst 6f ⊡:232 :47 1:122 ⒻClm 25000 61 6 4 43½ 85 89 89¼ Gryder A T b 119 8.40 72-22 MdstGl117noStn'SssyGl1172½ChfMstrss117 Brief speed 8
LATEST WORKOUTS Aug 11 Sar 5f fst :593 H Aug 3 Sar 5f fst 1:002 H Jly 26 Bel 5f fst 1:03 B Jly 18 Bel tr.t 4f fst :51 B

Mile High Glory

Ch. m. 6, by On To Glory—Too Nice, by Nice Catch
MIGLIORE R (47 7 5 7 .15) $20,000 Br.—October House Farm (Fla)
Own.—Hauman Eugene E Tr.—Hushion Michael E (10 2 3 2 .20) 113
Lifetime 27 8 3 2 $78,500 | 1992 7 1 2 0 $15,320 | 1991 6 1 0 1 $10,470 | Wet 5 3 0 0 $26,700

27Jly92- 1Bel my 6f :22 :45 1:10 ⒻClm 20000 60 4 4 57 55 56 513¼ Migliore R b 113 2.60 77-11 CrlsCmmnd1178¾FndRmnc115¾SrtNCrft110 In tght brk 9
8Jly92- 3Bel fst 6f :22 :451 1:103 ⒻClm 14000 76 4 1 22½ 22½ 21½ 2¾ Migliore R b 117 *1.70 86-16 TownCrek113¾MilHighGlory1172½BrvGrcin113 Good try 8
6May92- 2Bel fst 6f :221 :451 1:094 ⒻClm 35000 66 5 3 31½ 41 64½ 710 Nelson D b 117 *2.20 81-09 MjstcTrc117¾EphtcStl1172Undrsrd114 Lacked response 8
13Apr92- 9Aqu gd 6f :222 :452 1:09 3↑ⒻAlw 28000 91 3 1 11 11 1½ 23 Migliore R b 119 4.90 93-08 KombtKt1193MilHighGlory1193½StolnButy113 2nd best 8
2Mar92- 6Aqu fst 6f ⊡:231 :47 1:131 ⒻClm c-30000 55 8 2 3nk 3nk 66½ 811½ Migliore R b 114 3.60 65-30 MssRdndLn115noUndrsrd115¾ShsAShr117 Used in pace 8
22Feb92- 5Pha fst 6f :221 :452 1:113 ⒻClm 17000 78 3 1 1hd 1½ 14 13 Lloyd J S Lb 114 2.30 83-20 MlHghGlry1143R'sRndvs1141¾TlcKnsscrt116 Easy score 7
2Jan92- 5SA fst 6f :211 :44 1:094 ⒻClm 25000 41 8 5 2½ 42½ 710 816¼ McCarron C J LBb 115 *2.10 71-11 Tiaradancer1142½ Chalk Box1172 Chip's De Mere114 9
2Jan92-Wide, not urged late
10Nov91- 6BM fst 6f :221 :45 1:101 3↑ⒻClm c-16000 82 7 3 1hd 12 15 14 Boulanger G LBb 116 *2.50 85-16 MlHhGlr1164ImLttlNppr118noDltnPrncss116 Ridden out 8
20Oct91- 1SA fst 6f :212 :442 1:112 3↑ⒻClm c-10000 65 6 2 2½ 11½ 11 4nk Oldham D W LBb 115 3.70 79-16 Mbltt-Br115nkBntM116noSsOfRc-Ir115 Drifted out lane 11
1May91- 8LaD fst 6f :222 :46 1:113 3↑ⒻClm 25000 58 1 9 98¼ 89¾ 87¾ 78¾ Bourque K Lb 117 6.00 80-14 Wild Win1143 Twinkle City117½ FlakyLady117 Steadied 9
LATEST WORKOUTS Aug 8 Bel 4f fst :474 H ●Jly 19 Bel 4f fst :463 H

Treegees

Ch. f. 4, by Geiger Counter—Gable's Girl, by Screen King
KRONE J A (72 12 8 12 .17) $22,500 Br.—Howard & Ross (Ont-C)
Own.—Heatherwood Farm Tr.—Schosberg Richard (12 4 3 1 .33) 115
Lifetime 19 5 3 2 $60,006 | 1992 1 0 0 0 | 1991 18 5 3 2 $60,006 | Turf 1 0 0 0 | Wet 1 0 0 0

7Aug92- 2Sar fst 7f :222 :451 1:231 3↑ⒻClm 25000 67 1 11 85¼ 54½ 75½ 67½ Krone J A b 117 5.70 81-10 NorthernWilly113nkBoots1175AbovThSlt115 Wide, tired 12
14Nov91- 5Aqu fst 6f :22 :451 1:101 ⒻClm 25000 65 8 9 84¾ 67 47 36¼ Santos J A b 116 4.90 84-10 MissThiti1163½SlickDelivery1162¾Treegees116 Late gain 11
30Oct91- 3Aqu fst 7f :231 :472 1:254 ⒻClm 32500 66 6 5 53 41½ 45 67¾ Cordero A Jr b 114 10.30 65-25 MjesticTrick1163MissRdmondLn1161½Shimiss116 Faded 8
5Oct91- 6WO gd 7f :224 :461 1:253 ⒻClm 25000 62 7 10 95½ 76½ 57½ 53¾ David D J b 114 2.55e 81-14 HulRucks1141½KnKt111½HrdwoodFlo114 Saved ground 10
25Sep91- 5WO fst 6½f :223 :462 1:194 ⒻClm 20000 66 2 8 52 31½ 3½ 14 David D J b 116 4.30 76-18 Treegees1164 Petagaom1141½ Maine Shore114 In hand 11
15Sep91- 7WO fst 7f :221 :443 1:243 ⒻClm 25000 74 5 3 54 53½ 42½ 32½ David D J b 114 3.15 87-10 Commmorss108hdLvlyRlty1142½Trgs114 Closed willingly 7
4Sep91- 3WO fst 6f :222 :454 1:121 ⒻClm 20000 73 4 2 52¾ 31½ 3nk 1hd David D J b 114 *1.70 84-20 Treegees114hdShmrockSue1152¾SuleDuNord114 Driving 6
15Aug91- 3WO fst 6½f :222 :453 1:182 ⒻClm 20000 74 5 6 53 2hd 11½ 1no David D J b 114 2.75 83-10 Treegees114noGldCompny1083½DncOnthSnd117 Driving 6
7Aug91- 1WO fst 6f :223 :454 1:123 ⒻClm 25000 68 3 8 63¾ 44½ 31½ 2¾ David D J b 114 3.35 81-15 MoonHlo114¾Treeges114nkDncOnthSnd117 Closed well 9
25Jly91- 3WO fst 6f :224 :46 1:112 ⒻClm 20000 67 2 8 64¼ 66 56¼ 23 David D J b 114 *1.85 85-16 RefinedndBold1143Treegees114nkStrLikeTr109 Wide str 8
LATEST WORKOUTS Aug 5 Sar 3f gd :362 H Jly 30 Sar 5f fst 1:011 H Jly 23 Bel 4f fst :481 H Jly 17 Bel 4f fst :484 H

Fond Romance

B. f. 4, by Fappiano—Indian Romance, by Raja Baba
SANTAGATA N (1 0 0 1 .00) $25,000 Br.—Farish W S & Hudson E J (Ky)
Own.—Williams Michael D Tr.—Imperio Joseph (6 0 0 1 .00) 117
Lifetime 25 4 5 3 $78,120 | 1992 16 3 3 2 $59,560 | 1991 8 1 2 1 $17,120 | Turf 1 0 0 0 | Wet 4 1 1 1 $17,400

10Aug92- 3Sar fst 1⅛ :472 1:12 1:501 3↑ⒻClm 25000 47 1 4 53 42½ 610 620¼ Smith M E b 117 3.10 66-09 RdTp1176PrciousPriss1155½BrttnyErn113 Saved ground 10
27Jly92- 1Bel my 6f :22 :45 1:10 ⒻClm 22500 72 3 6 68 68 66 28¾ Santagata N b 115 11.00 81-11 CrlsCmmnd1178¾FndRnc115¾SrtNCrft110 Pinched brk 9
13Jun92- 9Bel fst 7f :231 :464 1:251 ⒻClm 25000 44 9 9 83½ 116¼ 1011 914½ Bailey J D b 117 19.40 63-18 CompnyGrl117½SnnyBrb117nkNorthrnWlly117 No factor 11
1Jun92- 3Bel sly 1$\frac{1}{16}$:471 1:114 1:433 ⒻClm 35000 72 2 1 12 1½ 43 58½ Madrid A Jr b 115 7.10 75-25 FoolnSprc113noRbcc'sGl1176AbovThSlt115 Speed, tired 7
11May92- 4Bel my 6f :221 :452 1:111 ⒻClm 22500 75 3 1 2hd 1hd 1½ 12 Madrid A Jr b 115 8.60 84-10 Fond Romance1152 SabalWay115½FinalRoad113 Driving 7
7May92- 2Bel fm 1$\frac{1}{16}$ Ⓣ:461 1:094 1:414 ⒻClm 35000 57 4 9 89 78½ 912 1014¾ Madrid A Jr b 117 18.70 72-15 Asaracket1172¾ GreatPass1172½NotAScratch117 Outrun 11
22Apr92- 6Aqu my 1⅛ :48 1:122 1:514 ⒻClm 32500 76 5 5 43 32½ 33 39 Madrid A Jr b 115 17.30 68-30 LdLr1176¾SphstctdSm1172¼FndRmnc115 Flattened out 7
5Apr92- 4Aqu fst 7f :23 :472 1:263 ⒻClm 35000 61 5 4 63 62¾ 54½ 59 Madrid A Jr b 117 6.60 63-25 TnyGrsshppr117nkOrn1131¼CmpnyGrl117 Saved ground 8
22Mar92- 6Aqu fst 1 :462 1:112 1:371 ⒻAlw 31000 70 3 4 42 41 64½ 56½ Madrid A Jr b 117 9.30 69-25 TripleSox117nkFlyingCross1174Avie'sDisy117 No threat 6
9Mar92- 9Aqu fst 1$\frac{1}{16}$ ⊡:48 1:123 1:462 ⒻAlw 31000 72 6 6 63½ 64¼ 65½ 89½ Madrid A Jr b 119 7.70 66-20 Rbcc'sGl1122FlyngCross117nkFoolnSprc112 No menace 9
LATEST WORKOUTS Jly 20 Aqu ⊡ 3f fst :382 B

Company Girl

B. m. 5, by Cormorant—Talcum Blue, by Talc
BAILEY J D (73 12 14 7 .16) $25,000 Br.—Fishback J (NY)
Own.—Wickman Joseph Tr.—Lake Robert P (5 0 0 2 .00) 117
Lifetime 55 9 6 9 $266,226 | 1992 13 1 0 3 $25,320 | 1991 13 2 3 3 $49,680 | Turf 2 0 0 0 $1,740 | Wet 11 2 0 1 $36,300

Entered 15Aug92- 9 SAR
31Jly92- 5Sar sly 6f :221 :452 1:102 3+(F)Clm 32500 74 5 5 46½ 57 55 46¼ Bailey J D b 115 15.80 86-13 Approprtly117hdJoy'sJoJo1172¼HghwyQn117 No threat 6
16Jly92- 9Bel fst 7f :22 :453 1:24 (F)Clm c-25000 62 2 11 109½ 109¼ 75¾ 56¾ Davis R G b 117 8.50 77-14 MjstcFrdm117¾CrlsCmmnd1173FlmngLbrl113 No threat 11
16Jly92-Claimed from Stronach Frank, Sedlacek Michael C Trainer
28Jun92- 1Bel fst 7f :23 :461 1:23 (F)Clm 30000 71 4 5 54½ 63½ 44½ 45¾ Davis R G b 113 5.30 83-12 HdsnDncr1133AllPr1171SphstctdSm117 Bobbled break 6
13Jun92- 9Bel fst 7f :231 :464 1:251 (F)Clm 25000 75 6 7 114¾ 94¼ 52½ 1½ Davis R G b 117 7.70 78-18 CompnyGirl117½SunnyBrbi117nkNorthrnWlly117 Driving 11
17May92- 4Bel my 7f :231 :463 1:234 (F)Clm 32500 59 1 6 44 43 64½ 68½ Santos J A b 115 7.20 76-13 MjstcFrdm115hdEmphtcStl1173MjstcTrck117 No threat 6
2May92- 1Aqu fst 7f :231 :46 1:24 (F)Clm c-25000 72 5 4 52¾ 53 54 32½ Rojas R I b 117 4.70 82-07 LstnFlght117½FlyngCrss1172CmpnyGrl117 Rallied wide 7
2May92-Claimed from Sunshine Hill Farm, Ribaudo Robert Trainer
25Apr92- 5Aqu fst 7f :224 :462 1:241 (F)Clm 35000 69 3 8 84½ 86¼ 78¾ 76½ Smith M E b 117 4.60 77-15 Avie's Daisy117hd No Cost119½ SoontoSin113 Wide trip 9
5Apr92- 4Aqu fst 7f :23 :472 1:263 (F)Clm 35000 77 2 8 74½ 72¾ 42 31½ Smith M E b 117 3.50 70-25 TnyGrsshoppr117nkOrn1131½CompnyGrl117 Rallied wide 8
2Mar92- 6Aqu fst 6f [•]:231 :47 1:131 (F)Clm c-35000 73 6 6 73¾ 64¾ 55½ 44¼ Antley C W 117 5.60 73-30 MssRdmndLn115noUndrnsrd115¾Sh'sAShr117 Late gain 8
6Feb92- 1Aqu fst 6f [•]:232 :464 1:112 (F)Clm 45000 80 5 4 53½ 42½ 45½ 43¾ Antley C W 114 2.20 82-22 WldWrnng113hdEmphtcStyl117noSunnySr115 No threat 5
LATEST WORKOUTS ●Jly 8 Aqu [•] 5f fst 1:023 B Jun 23 Aqu 4f fst :481 H

Above The Salt

Ch. f. 4, by Master Derby—Salt In My Stew, by Dr Blum
DAVIS R G (62 8 10 5 .13) $22,500 Br.—Happy Hill Farm Inc (Ky)
Own.—Davis Barbara J Tr.—Moschera Gasper S (16 5 2 3 .31) 115
Lifetime 33 11 4 5 $152,200 | 1992 7 4 0 2 $54,000 | 1991 23 6 3 2 $82,680 | Wet 5 1 0 1 $10,440

7Aug92- 2Sar fst 7f :222 :451 1:231 3+(F)Clm 22500 72 3 7 75¼ 87½ 53½ 35¼ McCauley W H 115 -- 84-10 NorthrnWilly113nkBoots1175AbovThSlt115 Lacked rally 12
7Aug92-Raced for purse money only
22Jun92- 1Bel fst 1 1/16 :474 1:12 1:432 (F)Clm 20000 82 4 2 22 2hd 11½ 1nk McCauley W H 117 1.50 85-15 AbovThSlt117nkThrtyghtChrms1171½Entrust110 Driving 6
1Jun92- 3Bel sly 1 1/16 :471 1:114 1:433 (F)Clm 30000 77 6 2 22 3½ 31½ 36 Smith M E 115 *2.00 78-25 FoolnSpruc113noRbcc'sGl1176AbovThSlt115 Wide, tired 7
22May92- 4Bel fst 1 1/16 :47 1:112 1:433 (F)Clm 30000 82 3 1 2hd 11½ 12 12¼ Smith M E 113 3.60 84-16 AbovThSlt1132¼SophistctdSm1081¾Clsky117 Drew clear 7
9May92- 2Bel my 1 :46 1:102 1:354 (F)Clm 45000 60 8 3 2½ 2½ 43½ 512¼ Pezua J M 113 *2.30 79-14 Strshrl115noAWnkAndANd1135¾Av'sDs113 Dueled, tired 8
9May92-Originally scheduled on turf
25Apr92- 7Aqu fst 7f :224 :462 1:24 3+(F)Alw 27000 85 1 5 2½ 1½ 14 16 Pezua J M 119 3.20 85-15 Above TheSalt1196Viperous1103¼R.E.Darla110 Drew off 6
11Apr92- 2Aqu sly 6f :22 :453 1:113 (F)Clm 14000 75 7 8 57¾ 36 21½ 1no Smith M E 117 3.10 83-14 AbovThSlt117noWigglsLw1172BrdfordBy110 Drifted drv 8
26Dec91- 7Aqu fst 6f [•]:234 :481 1:133 (F)Clm c-25000 82 4 8 42 31 11 1½ Cordero A Jr 116 5.30e 75-24 AbThSlt116½SnnSr1163¼MssRdmndLn116 Rail trp, drvg 10
14Dec91- 2Aqu my 6f [•]:22 :464 1:113 (F)Clm 30000 71 1 6 2hd 31 67¼ 65 Garcia L I5 107 7.30 80-13 MjsticTrck1161TinyGrsshoppr114½IvD116 Used in pace 8
6Dec91- 2Aqu fst 6f [•]:222 :461 1:113 (F)Clm 17500 87 12 2 12 11½ 16 15½ Cordero A Jr 116 *1.90 85-19 AbovThSlt1165½RthrBSocil116nkKllrBuzz112 Ridden out 12
LATEST WORKOUTS Jly 27 Bel 4f my :524 B (d) Jly 19 Bel 3f fst :363 H

Magestic Willowa

Ch. m. 5, by Magesterial—Willowa, by Son Ange
WHITLEY K (1 0 0 0 .00) $25,000 Br.—Davis Jonathan H F (NY)
Own.—Perdue Edward C Tr.—Perdue Edward C (3 0 1 0 .00) 117
Lifetime 25 9 6 0 $84,975 | 1992 5 0 2 0 $3,300 | 1991 7 4 1 0 $33,180 | Wet 4 2 1 0 $16,170

1Aug92-10FL my 1 1/8 :491 1:15 1:513 3+(F)(S)Monroe 58 5 1 3nk 33 25 59 Whitley K b 115 3.90 50-40 HvnKnwsWhy1153¾AlbmAnn1171Llc'sStr115 Weakened 7
21Jly92-11FL gd 6f :221 :462 1:134 3+(F)Clm 30000 66 5 1 65½ 44½ 26 21½ Davila J R Jr b 115 *.50e 75-28 MjstcAnr1131½MstcWll1153¼LttlAbrAn112 Rallied wide 6
31May92- 9FL sly 6f :222 :462 1:111 3+(F)Handicap 47 5 6 43½ 23½ 28 217½ Gutierrez J A b 116 3.10 72-20 Tby'sTgr12017½MgstcWll1163¼LttlAmbrAnn114 2nd best 6
9Jan92- 5Aqu fst 6f [•]:224 :482 1:121 (F)Clm 35000 63 2 5 55 55 511 58½ Pezua J M b 119 12.80 73-16 Ctchmnot1171½PhntomHill117noCompnyGirl117 Outrun 6
3Jan92- 1Aqu fst 6f [•]:231 :463 1:111 (F)Clm 50000 48 6 6 74¾ 79½ 714 718 Madrid A Jr b 117 11.70 69-20 EmphaticStyle1135¾Calisty113nkWildWrning113 Outrun 7
18Dec91- 4Aqu fst 6f [•]:223 :464 1:13 3+(F)Clm 35000 81 6 1 64 64¾ 43½ 1½ Chavez J F b 119 8.20 78-25 MgstcWllw119½SxNrrws117½MdstGl117 Up final strides 6
17Nov91- 7FL gd 6f :231 :48 1:144 3+(F)Alw 7300 63 2 6 41½ 1½ 12½ 13 Nicol P A Jr b 122 *.70 72-30 MgstcWllw1273MyLdySmnn1172MkmHppy116 Drew off 6
1Nov91- 1Aqu fst 1 :472 1:124 1:38 3+(F)Clm 45000 71 1 5 54 52¾ 54½ 512 Chavez J F b 113 9.30 60-28 Embrcng1134¾DustyDonn1131½CompnyGrl113 No threat 6
20Oct91- 9FL fst 6f :22 :452 1:110 3+(F)Alw 7500 77 4 1 34 31 11 14½ Grabowski J A b 119 3.20 89-15 MgesticWillow1194¼CrftyKtie119hdSssyBb113 Drew off 7
24Aug91- 1Sar fst 6½f :231 :464 1:19 3+(F)Clm 25000 79 1 4 21½ 43 32 1nk Chavez J F b 117 6.70 80-14 MstcWll117nkMjstcFrd1141½PrdFrnd117 Lggd In, drvg 8
LATEST WORKOUTS Aug 11 FL 5f fst 1:04 B Jly 29 FL 4f fst :50T B Jly 12 FL 5f fst 1:03 H Jun 28 FL 5f fst 1:013 H

Rather Be Social

Dk. b. or br. f. 4, by Raised Socially—Rather Be Dancing, by Caro-Ir
MADRID A JR (24 4 4 2 .17) $20,000 Br.—Pollack Andrea Singer (Ky)
Own.—De Hass Stable Tr.—Tilak Ileen I (—) 113
Lifetime 48 3 8 7 $75,200 | 1992 16 1 1 2 $15,460 | 1991 25 2 7 4 $56,860 | Turf 3 0 0 0 | Wet 4 0 0 2 $4,500

26Jly92- 7Bel fst 7f :224 :454 1:233 3+(F)Alw 27000 57 7 5 86 87¼ 67 611½ Pezua J M b 117 46.80 74-16 HudsonDncr1171½ShlWy1171¾MySistrJulit113 No factor 8
19Jly92- 3Bel fst 7f :224 :461 1:244 (F)Clm 12000 68 1 5 11 13½ 16 16½ Pezua J M b 113 1.90 80-13 RthrBScl1136½TrAlBrr1132ATmThtWs113 Kept to drive 7
3Jly92- 4Bel fm 1 1/16 (T):472 1:112 1:423 (F)Clm 35000 58 6 10 1015 98 107½ 1012¼ Madrid A Jr b 117 25.50 71-15 LfOnthFrm1192¼LvndLgnd1171¾GrtR117 Took up break 10
27Jun92- 9Bel fst 7f :23 :46 1:241 (F)Clm 12000 52 11 1 62¾ 52½ 33 37½ Velazquez J R b 113 12.50 75-12 SprlngHnnh1173Plthbbs1064½RthrBScl113 Lacked rally 11
17Jun92- 2Bel fst 6f :223 :454 1:112 (F)Clm 13000 59 2 8 88 86½ 65 55½ Maple E 115 16.70 78-16 NrthrnWlly1172½Plythbgbys106¾TnCrk113 Chckd early 8
17May92- 9Bel my 7f :223 :453 1:243 (F)Clm 12000 61 4 10 63½ 88¾ 32½ 33½ Velazquez J R 113 15.40 78-13 ITool171½RoylSummit1172RthrBSocil113 Rallied inside 11
9May92- 9Bel gd 6f :214 :444 1:092 (F)Clm 15500 60 5 6 77 83¾ 76½ 610 Velazquez J R b 113 26.10 83-07 Crl'sCmmnd1171½EvrlstngStr1175LckNck117 Wide trip 9
20Apr92- 3Aqu my 6f :213 :444 1:104 (F)Clm 15500 63 5 5 79 79 65 46½ Velasquez J b 113 40.50 80-15 Ice Society117¾ Killer Buzz1175½EpicVilla117 Wide trip 7
8Apr92- 2Aqu fst 7f :232 :474 1:264 (F)Clm 12000 43 7 6 73¾ 84 97½ 911¼ Carr D b 113 28.50 60-20 KllrBuzz117½NoholmsScrtry117¾TownCrk115 Chckd trn 11
4Apr92- 2Aqu fst 1 :472 1:131 1:393 (F)Clm 13000 48 7 1 1½ 32 53¼ 76¼ Verge M E b 115 13.40 58-21 RocktBttl113nkPkboBby1191½GrbrGirl117 Dueled, tired 9
LATEST WORKOUTS Aug 13 Bel tr.t 4f fst :493 B

Bug's Chubbs

Ch. m. 5, by D'Accord—Lightning Bug, by Cornish Prince
MOJICA R JR (6 0 0 0 .00) $22,500 Br.—Free F William (NY)
Own.—Watral Michael Tr.—Brida Dennis J (9 2 1 0 .22) 115
Lifetime 30 6 3 1 $107,220 | 1992 7 0 0 0 $3,780 | 1991 14 5 2 1 $76,440 | Turf 5 0 0 0 $3,780 | Wet 2 0 0 1 $4,560

27Jly92- 4Bel yl 1 (T):463 1:113 1:374 (F)Clm 35000 72 5 3 2½ 2hd 31½ 53¾ Rodriguez RR7 b 1104 10.70 69-29 Slsflower1171LifOnthFrm1192½GrtRviw117 Dueled tired 9
27Jly92-Dead heat
28Jun92- 8Bel fm 1 1/16 (T):461 1:092 1:41 3+(F)(S)MntVrnon 63 6 1 11 11 65½ 713¾ Pezua J M b 113 41.40 77-11 Tlc'sCvntry113nkAsrckt113nkIrshActrss122 Speed, tired 9
28Jun92-Run in Divisions
15Jun92- 8Bel fm 6f (T):22 :442 1:08 3+(F)Handicap 81 5 2 2½ 2½ 32½ 44 Pezua J M b 109 18.40 98 — Dr.Vlvt113noChchBmb1093½TBDzlng109 Frcd pace tired 6
29May92- 7Bel fm 1 (T):454 1:101 1:35 (F)Clm 35000 72 7 1 11½ 11½ 2½ 45¼ Rodriguez R R b 117 14.00 82-14 Jolie Britt122hd Oriane1172 Final Road117 Tired 9
20May92- 9Bel fst 7f :224 :46 1:243 (F)Clm 16500 65 5 3 2½ 2hd 31½ 56¼ Pezua J M b 115 4.30 75-13 SprlnHnnh1171½DlThrt1172SclDlm117 Frc'd pace, tired 9
26Apr92- 4Aqu yl 1⅛ (T):50 1:15 1:542 (F)Clm 45000 59 6 3 65 76 77 612¼ Goossens L 114 15.40 59-25 IvoryTody1171½MmorBy1151HerCountss113 Done early 7
18Mar92- 1Aqu fst 7f :23 :472 1:254 (F)Clm 22500 55 4 5 54½ 76½ 86¼ 67¾ Goossens L 115 10.90 68-23 SocilDelim117nkMisteeV117noSwtn'SssyGl117 No factor 8
10Jun91- 1Bel fst 7f :233 :471 1:241 (F)Clm c-17500 21 1 5 3½ 63 914 927¼ Chavez J F b 117 *2.10 56-15 SuperbSympathy1172½[D]Annd1174¾Kirky'sGirl117 Tired 9
31May91- 3Bel fst 6f :221 :452 1:101 (F)Clm 17500 83 1 6 54½ 53 22 2nk Chavez J F b 119 *.80e 89-03 DmdSoll117nkBug'sChubbs1195¾Crfty'sWsh111 Fin fast 7
24May91- 3Bel fst 1⅛ :47 1:123 1:522 (F)Clm 22500 33 3 1 11 1hd 613 628½ Chavez J F b 115 3.70 38-31 WonnthSn1132Foxcroft119hdLostnFlght117 Speed tired 7
LATEST WORKOUTS Aug 13 Bel tr.t 4f fst :49 B Aug 6 Bel 4f fst :50 B Jly 21 Bel 3f fst :382 B

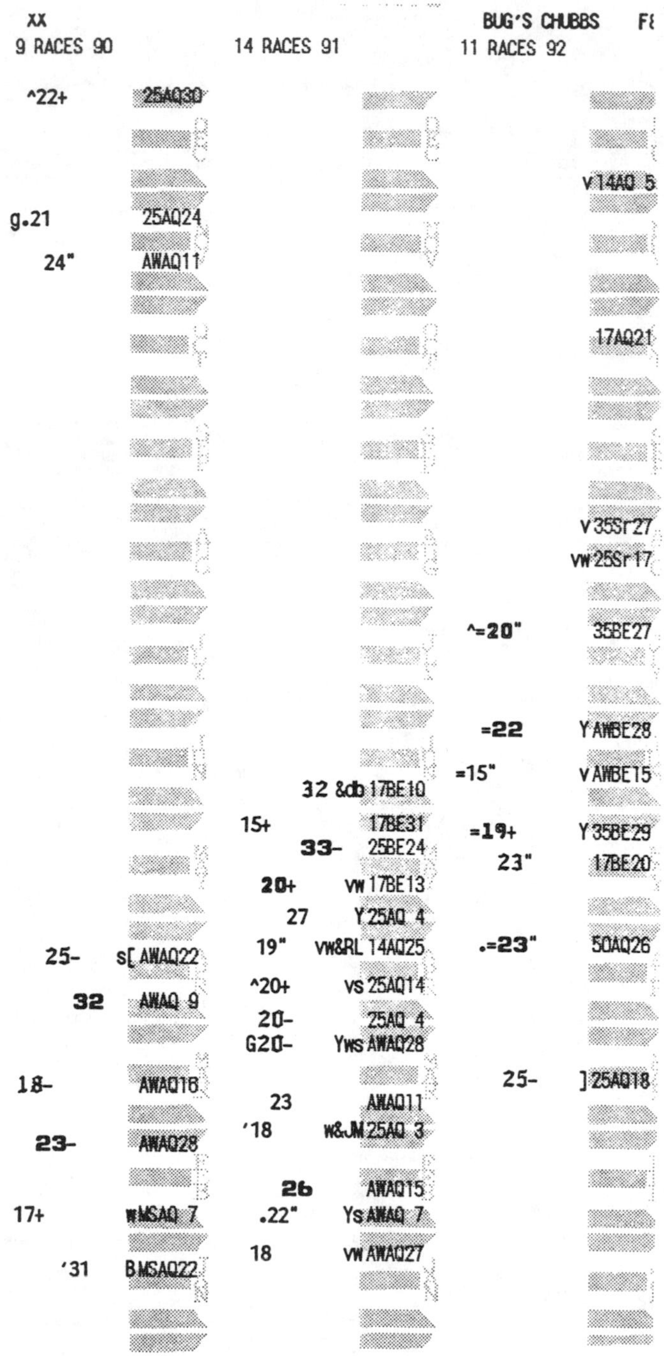
XX
9 RACES 90
^22+ 25AQ30
g.21 25AQ24
24" AWAQ11
25- s[AWAQ22
32 AWAQ 9
18- AWAQ16
23- AWAQ28
17+ wMSAQ 7
'31 BMSAQ22
14 RACES 91
32 &db 17BE10
15+ 17BE31
33- 25BE24
20+ vw 17BE13
27 Y 25AQ 4
19" vw&RL 14AQ25
^20+ vs 25AQ14
20- 25AQ 4
G20- Yws AWAQ28
23 AWAQ11
'18 w&JM 25AQ 3
26 AWAQ15
.22" Ys AWAQ 7
18 vw AWAQ27
BUG'S CHUBBS
11 RACES 92
v 14AQ 5
17AQ21
v 35Sr27
vw 25Sr17
^=20" 35BE27
=22 Y AWBE28
=15" v AWBE15
=19+ Y 35BE29
23" 17BE20
.=23" 50AQ26
25-] 25AQ18

Bug's Chubbs, Magestic Willowa, and Mile High Glory were the only fillies in the race showing a Beyer higher than 80. Magestic Willowa, at 5–2, was being grossly overbet; although she had defeated $35,000 claimers at Aqueduct in December, her last five races had been slow; there was nothing in her recent form to suggest she was anywhere near what she'd been in the late summer and autumn of 1991.

Mile High Glory's past performances were indicative of an "ouchy" horse: notice the frequent layoffs and short campaigns.

Bug's Chubbs also had an "ouchy-looking" line at age four. Although she had run figures on *The Sheets* in the range of 18 to 20 on a consistent basis to begin her four-year-old year, she'd been unable to get past the 17¼ recorded in the second start of her life. When she finally broke through with a 15¼ on May 31, she fell apart a race later and went to the shelf for nine months.

What made Bug's Chubbs so interesting was her series of performances since returning from the layoff as a five-year-old. She had "forged" right down to another 15 in five consecutive starts, improving a little bit each time out. This pattern is also evident in her Beyer figures, which ascended from 55 to 59 to 65 to 72 and finally to the 81, the figure that essentially matched her best effort prior to the layoff. The forging line was all the more impressive because her return races had come at four different distances over four different surfaces; moreover, she had not merely been "sucked along" toward the middle or rear of the pack: she had either set or forced progressively faster fractions on May 20, May 29, and June 15.

By August 17, Bug's Chubbs had developed a nice "intervening pattern" since running her 15 on *The Sheets* — a 22 followed by a 20½. The 15 hadn't knocked her for a loop as it had the year before; she had felt the effects of that race in her two subsequent starts, but she had not fallen apart, especially in light of her most recent race, which involved a hard pace duel at a mile over yielding turf.

Now, Bug's Chubbs was dropping in claiming price, switching from a double-bug to a journeyman rider, and had the look of a horse that had been "legged up" in pace duels on turf at longer distances. Two months had elapsed since her return to top form on June 15, and if she ran a figure even approaching that level, she figured to beat this field.

Further, she was ideally situated in the outside post. In a one-turn race containing cheap early speed, the outside is a great spot for a pace presser, because the rider has some options: if no one wants the lead, he can angle over and take the initiative; if the pace is hotly contested, he can stalk the duel from close range without having to hustle up to avoid being shuffled back toward the inside.

After tracking the leaders through the first quarter, Bug's Chubbs contested the lead on the turn, drew clear into the stretch, and held off Company Girl's typical too little, too late rally to win by half a length at $14.40.

FIFTH RACE
Saratoga
AUGUST 17, 1992

6 FURLONGS. (1.08) CLAIMING. Purse $18,000. Fillies and mares, 3–year–olds and upward. Weights, 3–year–olds, 117 lbs.; older, 122 lbs. Non–winners of two races since July 15 allowed 3 lbs. Of a race since then, 5 lbs. Claiming price $25,000; for each $2,500 to $20,000, 2 lbs. (Races when entered to be claimed for $18,000 or less not considered.)

Value of race $18,000; value to winner $10,800; second $3,960; third $2,160; fourth $1,080. Mutuel pool $315,548. Exacta Pool $587,966

Last Raced	Horse	M/Eqt.	A.	Wt	PP	St	¼	½	Str	Fin	Jockey	Cl'g Pr	Odds $1
27Jly92 ^{4}Bel^{5}	Bug's Chubbs	b	5	115	9	2	4^{3}	2½	$1^{1½}$	1½	Mojica R Jr	22500	6.20
31Jly92 ^{5}Sar^{4}	Company Girl	b	5	117	6	8	8^{2}	8½	6^{hd}	$2^{2½}$	Bailey J D	25000	5.60
26Jly92 ^{7}Bel^{6}	Rather Be Social	b	4	113	8	1	7^{4}	4½	3½	$3^{1¼}$	Madrid A Jr	20000	32.70
1Aug92^{10}FL^{5}	Magestic Willowa	b	5	117	7	3	6^{hd}	7^{1}	7^{2}	4^{hd}	Whitley K	25000	2.50
10Aug92 ^{3}Sar^{6}	Fond Romance	b	4	117	5	5	5½	6^{1}	5½	5^{5}	Santagata N	25000	6.20
21Jly92^{10}FL^{6}	Makin' Honey	b	4	113	1	9	9	9	8½	6½	Cruguet J	20000	28.90
8Jly92 ^{3}Bel^{3}	Brave Grecian-	b	4	113	2	7	1½	1^{hd}	$2^{1½}$	7^{4}	Smith M E	20000	6.20
27Jly92 ^{1}Bel^{5}	Mile High Glory	b	6	113	3	6	3^{1}	5^{hd}	9	8^{2}	Migliore R	20000	4.10
7Aug92 ^{2}Sar^{6}	Treegees	b	4	115	4	4	2½	3^{3}	4^{1}	9	Velazquez JR	22500	8.70

OFF AT 3:18 Start good Won driving Time, :21^{4}, :45^{2}, :57^{4}, 1:10^{4} Track muddy.

$2 Mutuel Prices:			
10–(J)–BUG'S CHUBBS	14.40	6.80	6.40
6–(F)–COMPANY GIRL		6.60	4.60
9–(I)–RATHER BE SOCIAL			7.00

$2 EXACTA 10–6 PAID $113.40

Ch. m, by D'Accord—Lightning Bug, by Cornish Prince. Trainer Brida Dennis J. Bred by Free F William (NY).

BUG'S CHUBBS stalked the leaders from outside for a half, surged to the front in upper stretch, opened a clear lead in midstretch then was all out to hold off COMPANY GIRL in the closing strides. COMPANY GIRL, outrun for a half, circled five wide entering the stretch then finding her best stride unleashed a strong late run but could not get up. RATHER BE SOCIAL, reserved early worked her way forward from outside on the turn then rallied mildly to gain a share. MAJESTIC WILLOWA unhurried for a half, failed to threaten while improving her position through the lane. FOND ROMANCE was never a serious threat. MAKIN' HONEY never reached contention. BRAVE GRECIAN set the pace along the inside to the top of the stretch and gradually tired thereafter. MILE HIGH GLORY showed only brief speed. TREEGEES was used up forcing the early pace. MILE HIGH GLORY wore mud caulks. ABOVE THE SALT WAS ORDERED SCRATCHED AT THE GATE BY THE STEWARDS ON THE ADVICE OF THE TRACK VETERINARIAN. ALL MONIES WAGERED ON ABOVE THE SALT IN THE PICK THREE, EXACTA AND MUTUEL POOLS WERE REFUNDED.

Owners— 1, Watral Michael; 2, Wickman Joseph; 3, De Hass Stable; 4, Perdue Edward C; 5, Williams Michael D; 6, Lumot Stable; 7, Kimran Stable; 8, Hauman Eugene E; 9, Heatherwood Farm.

Trainers— 1, Brida Dennis J; 2, Lake Robert P; 3, Tilak Ileen I; 4, Perdue Edward C; 5, Imperio Joseph; 6, DiMauro Stephen; 7, Toner James J; 8, Hushion Michael E; 9, Schosberg Richard.

Company Girl was claimed by Stronach Frank; trainer, Sedlacek Michael C.

Scratched—Above The Salt (7Aug92 ^{2}Sar^{3}).

The Grade 2 Ladies Handicap at Aqueduct on November 27, 1993, offered a fabulous betting opportunity for those with an awareness of forging horses.

The 6–5 favorite was Turnback The Alarm, who was giving anywhere from eight to eleven pounds to the field. This seemed reasonable, since she was a four-time Grade 1 winner meeting eight rivals that had managed a combined total of one graded stakes win — Silky Feather's Grade 3 victory in the Fair Grounds Oaks eight months ago.

My first inclination was to concede the race to the favorite and try to find another horse to use in exactas in the second slot. As I looked through the past performances of the others, it became apparent that most of them were evenly matched in terms of Beyer figures, running in the high 80s to low 90s. Fadetta had run a 97 when a gaining second in the Rare Perfume on October 10, but she had never been beyond a mile and had drawn the extreme outside post — never a good place to be in a two-turn route at Aqueduct. At 5–2 she was a contender, but an unappetizing betting prospect.

One thing that struck me about the field in general was that, for the most part, these fillies had been through long campaigns as November came to a close: Bold as Silver had raced fifteen times without a break; Avie's Daisy was making her eighteenth start; Silky Feather, Star Guest, Miss Pocket Court, and In Her Glory had also been heavily raced.

Groovy Feeling was quite obviously the freshest horse in the field, having returned from a June-to-October layoff three starts ago.

In fact, Groovy Feeling had run a Beyer of 92 in her October 11 return, a figure that matched her best races from earlier in the year. On *The Sheets* and *Thoro-graph*, the pattern was also evident: Groovy Feeling had received a 12 on *The Sheets*, essentially matching the 12¼ she had run on March 11; she had received a 9½ on *Thoro-graph*, matching her best figures from earlier in the year.

That Groovy Feeling had returned from her layoff with a career-best effort was an extremely positive sign, and so was the intervening pattern in a pair of grass races at the Meadowlands and at Laurel. She had bounced from the comeback effort, but the second grass race had been as good as the first one according to Beyer, and slightly faster according to both sheet makers. It had now been nearly seven weeks since Groovy Feeling's return effort, and there was a good chance she was now ready for another forward move.

Aqueduct

7

1¼ MILES. **(1:591) 123rd Running of THE LADIES HANDICAP. (Grade II) Purse $200,000. Fillies and mares, 3-year-olds and upward. By subscription of $400 each which should accompany the nomination; $1,600 to pass the entry box; $1,600 to start. The purse to be divided 60% to the winner, 22% to second, 12% to third and 6% to fourth. Weights Monday, November 22. Starters to be named at the closing time of entries. Trophies will be presented to the winning owner, trainer and jockey. Closed Wednesday, November 10, with 18 nominations.**

1¼ MILES — START — FINISH

1 Groovy Feeling

Own: Donaldson Robert P
MCCAULEY W H (51 7 16 4 .14)

Ro. f. 4
Sire: Groovy (Norcliffe)
Dam: Millie and Me (Wise Exchange)
Br: Clay Catesby W (Ky)
Tr: Ferriola Peter (43 8 10 4 .19)

111

Lifetime Record: 23 7 4 1 $153,487											
1993	11	2	3	1	$79,962	Turf	2	1	0	0	$18,840
1992	12	5	1	0	$73,525	Wet	2	0	0	0	$1,155
Aqu	3	2	0	0	$65,607	Dist	0	0	0	0	

13Nov93-6Lrl	yl	1 Ⓣ	:241 :49 1:144 1:402	3↑ⒻAlw 28000N$Y	80	9	4	53¾	88½	76¼	52¾	Verge M E	L 122	5.20	65-32	Ellin B.117¾ Grab The Green1171½ Nashly117nk	No threat	9
28Oct93-9Med	gd	1 1/16 Ⓣ	:231 :472 1:121 1:451	3↑ⒻAlw 30000N$mY	80	5	3	41¾	61¾	33½	1no	Verge M E	L 115 f	4.10	73-27	Groovy Feeling115no Charlotte Augusta117¾ Lovely Bid1123¾	Driving	7
11Oct93-6Lrl	fst	7f	:233 :47 1:112 1:241	3↑ⒻAlw 25000R	92	1	1	76	79	34	21¼	Prado E S	L 117	10.70	87-18	Mixed Appeal1191¼ Groovy Feeling1171½ Lip Sing1225¼	Closed	7
20Jun93-8Pha	fst	1	:231 :463 1:114 1:383	3↑ⒻAlw 25000N$Y	73	1	5	52½	64½	48	46¼	Colton R E	L 116	*1.50	79-15	After The Glitter1194½ Meetmenow111½ Quinyan1161¼	No rally	7
30May93-7Mth	fst	1 1/16	:23 :47 1:12 1:451	3↑ⒻAlw 30000N$mY	82	1	3	33	33½	35	36½	Bravo J	L 117	3.70	72-24	Fall Semester1175½ Fran's Folly1171 Groovy Feeling1171¾	Tired late	9
1May93-11Spt	fst	1⅛	:472 1:113 1:364 1:491	3↑ⒻSixty Sls H-G3	76	8	7	64	54	810	811½	Baird E T	L 114 b	22.50	83-11	Pleasant Baby1121¾ Miss Jealski113nk Steff Graf1151¼	Wide, tired	9
17Apr93-8GS	fst	1 1/16	:232 :464 1:114 1:444	3↑ⒻBetsy Ross HG3	80	1	4	63	52½	58½	56½	Black A S	L 116 f	1.70	84-15	Femma1194¾ Arlenes Money114½ Fall Semester118no	Even effort	10
25Mar93-8Aqu	fst	1⅛ [•]	:473 1:124 1:383 1:512	ⒻAlw 47000N$mY	92	2	2	21½	21	11½	12¼	Smith M E	122 f	2.70	86-21	Groovy Feeling1222¼ Maxamount1152¼ Lady Lear1151	Driving	5
11Mar93-8Lrl	fst	1 1/16	:233 :47 1:114 1:44	ⒻAlw 25000N$Y	91	3	4	43	42½	32½	2hd	Wilson R	L 119	*1.90	90-26	Gallant Stinger114hd Groovy Feeling1196½ Dress Optional1147	Closed	6
20Feb93-9Lrl	fst	1⅛	:484 1:13 1:38 1:504	3↑ⒻSquan Song H50k	89	7	4	42½	75¾	46	22	Wilson R	L 114	3.20	82-23	Gammy's Alden1122 Groovy Feeling114nk Dress Optional113½	Wide turns	7

WORKOUTS: ●Nov 8 Pha 5f fst 1:002 B *1/20* ●Oct 23 Pha 6f fst 1:141 H *1/4* Oct 4 Pha 4f fst :482 B *3/8* Sep 27 Pha 6f my 1:143 B *1/1*

2 Bold as Silver

Own: Amherst Stable
LEON F (75 5 8 15 .07)

Gr. f. 3 (Mar)
Sire: Nasty and Bold (Naskra)
Dam: Silver Judy (Silver Series)
Br: Amherst Stable (Fla)
Tr: Johnson Philip G (25 5 3 2 .20)

110

Lifetime Record: 15 3 3 2 $85,320											
1993	15	3	3	2	$85,320	Turf	4	0	0	0	$3,420
1992	0	M	0	0		Wet	2	1	1	0	$22,660
Aqu	2	1	1	0	$28,880	Dist	0	0	0	0	

17Nov93-7Aqu	fst	1⅛ ⊗	:502 1:152 1:404 1:533	3↑ⒻAlw 32000N2X	86	3	3	31	1½	12½	15	Leon F5	110	*.60	68-26	Bold As Silver1105 Chambolle115½ Home By Ten1172	Ridden out	6
24Oct93-5Aqu	fst	1⅛	:501 1:144 1:40 1:523	3↑ⒻAlw 44000N$mY	89	3	2	1½	1½	2½	2¾	Leon F5	109	8.90	72-30	In Her Glory114¾ Bold As Silver1099 Winning The Day1165½	Gamely	5
9Oct93-2Bel	fst	7f	:234 :473 1:122 1:251	3↑ⒻAlw 28000N1X	83	6	3	42½	31	1hd	1nk	Leon F5	109	3.10	77-23	Bold As Silver109nk Regal Solution114¾ Shady Willow1176	Wide, driving	6
23Sep93-5Bel	my	7f	:223 :462 1:121 1:252	3↑ⒻAlw 28000N1X	79	3	6	75¾	63	3nk	2¾	Chavez J F	113	5.70	75-26	Pleasant Courtney108¾ Bold As Silver1131¾ Stormbow1134¾	Rallied inside	8
8Sep93-6Bel	fst	1 1/16	:232 :462 1:104 1:433	3↑ⒻAlw 30000N1X	70	6	8	83¾	62	42	32¾	Chavez J F	113	5.70	81-12	Nine Keys1132½ My Girl Rodes113nk Bold As Silver1131¼	Late gain	8
22Aug93-8Sar	fm	1 3/16 Ⓣ	:473 1:114 1:361 1:542	3↑ⒻAlw 28500N1X	69	2	1	1½	1½	73¼	810	Chavez J F	112	17.50	86-13	Northern Emerald1123 Running On E1141¼ Russian Tango1121¼	Used up	10
9Aug93-6Sar	fst	6f	:22 :45 :571 1:10	3↑ⒻAlw 26500N1X	74	5	9	98¼	77½	53	54½	Santos J A	112	12.40	87-08	Strawberry'sLass1121¼ ReglSolution1122 LdyAshford114¾	Saved ground	10
24Jly93-6Bel	fst	1	:24 :472 1:114 1:371	3↑ⒻAlw 28500N1X	80	3	3	31	41¼	31½	23½	Chavez J F	111	2.70	78-16	Sakiyah1133½ Bold As Silver111hd Fleeting Ways1115	Up for place	5
11Jly93-5Bel	fst	1 1/16	:242 :481 1:13 1:433	3↑ⒻAlw 28500N1X	73	1	2	31½	32	33	31	Pezua J M	111	9.20	83-16	Imah114nk Splendid Launch111¾ Bold As Silver1114	Willingly	7
28Jun93-4Bel	fm	1¼ [T]	:492 1:14 1:381 2:021	ⒻClm 75000	75	1	5	55	64	64	64¾	Samyn J L	111	5.60	74-16	Wonder Wave1112½ Doc's Josephine111nk This Ain'tKansas1131¼	No factor	7

WORKOUTS: Nov 14 Bel tr.t 4f fst :482 H *2/16* Nov 10 Bel tr.t 4f fst :484 B *5/31* Nov 3 Bel tr.t 4f fst :50 B *25/55* Oct 4 Bel tr.t 3f fst :354 H *2/14* Sep 3 Bel tr.t 3f fst :361 B *3/7*

3 Avie's Daisy

Own: Paraneck Stable
CRUGUET J (50 8 4 7 .16)

Ch. m. 5
Sire: Lord Avie (Lord Gaylord)
Dam: My Little Molly (Golden Eagle II)
Br: Jilerlane Stables (Md)
Tr: Wilson Ronald (12 1 3 0 .08)

113

Lifetime Record: 58 9 11 9 $300,440											
1993	17	3	4	1	$127,510	Turf	4	0	0	0	
1992	20	3	4	6	$107,320	Wet	9	3	2	2	$83,860
Aqu	33	8	9	5	$235,940	Dist	0	0	0	0	

20Nov93-9Med	fst	1 1/16	:232 :464 1:113 1:45	3↑ⒻCastle Forbe40k	81	2	8	79¾	77	63¾	53¼	Cruguet J	122 b	7.70	80-20	After The Glitter1191 Cozzene's Wish1171 Femma113nk	Some gain	9
30Oct93-7Aqu	my	1 ⊗	:232 :471 1:134 1:411	3↑ⒻAlw 44000N$mY	86	6	6	46½	33	3½	13	McCauley W H	117 fb	5.50	58-33	Avie's Daisy1173 Poolesta117½ Bless Our Home1174½	Wide, driving	7
24Oct93-6Aqu	fst	7f	:231 :46 1:102 1:23	3↑ⒻAlw 40000N$Y	89	6	7	76¼	75¼	52¾	44¼	Migliore R	117 b	6.70	85-10	Noble's Honey1173½ MissCloverAppeal117no EndlessDesire119¾	No threat	7
7Oct93-8Bel	fst	1 1/16	:243 :481 1:122 1:434	3↑ⒻAlw 44000N$mY	86	1	4	43½	42½	42½	44¾	Migliore R	117 b	7.30	78-22	Testy Trestle1192 Chinese Empress1172½ RegalVictress117nk	Lacked rally	6
1Oct93-8Bel	fst	1 1/16	:222 :451 1:10 1:442	3↑ⒻHandicap48k	81	2	4	411	48	37	28½	Migliore R	114 b	9.10	71-25	Vivano1228½ Avie's Daisy114¾ Concorde's Gold1204	Late gain	4
4Sep93-9Tim	fst	1 1/16	:231 :473 1:134 1:48	3↑ⒻAlma North H40k	64	2	6	64¾	57	58	411	Douglas F G	113 b	5.00	60-33	[D]Jazzy One115hd Darinka1134 Starlight Surprise1117	No threat	7
Placed third through disqualification.																		
23Aug93-6Sar	fm	1 1/16 [T]	:25 :501 1:141 1:44	3↑ⒻAlw 46000N$Ym	59	4	6	75½	78½	79	814	Leon F5	112 b	45.30	65-16	Irish Actress1171¼ Park Dream117nk Her Favorite117nk	Outrun	8
12Jly93-8Bel	fst	1 1/16	:24 :473 1:113 1:421	3↑ⒻAlw 46000N$Y	79	5	5	54	52¼	52¼	46¾	Migliore R	116 fb	7.00	84-10	[D]Lizeality116no Queen Of Triumph116¾ Nannerl1206	No threat	6
3Jly93-6Bel	sf	1¼ [T]	:484 1:14 1:394 2:052	3↑ⒻAlw 46000N$Y	18	5	7	56	710	729	738	Pezua J M	119 fb	23.20	25-33	Royal Pageant11712 Low Tolerance119½ Ginny Dare1222¼	Outrun	7
5Jun93-3Bel	fst	1	:224 :451 1:094 1:363	3↑ⒻAlw 46000N$mY	81	2	7	77½	55	54½	58½	Migliore R	119 b	9.40	76-15	Shared Interest1173½ Spinning Round1172 S. S. Sparkle1221¾	No threat	7

4 Silky Feather

Own: Powell Stanton P
MIGLIORE R (117 15 13 22 .13)

Dk. b or br f. 3 (Apr)
Sire: Personal Flag (Private Account)
Dam: Fleur de Soie (Graustark)
Br: E. C. Johnston Jr. (NY)
Tr: Violette Richard Jr (10 3 1 2 .30)

113

Lifetime Record: 16 3 3 5 $222,776											
1993	12	3	2	4	$217,800	Turf	1	0	0	1	$4,080
1992	4	M	1	1	$4,976	Wet	1	0	1	0	$7,480
Aqu	1	0	1	0	$7,480	Dist	2	0	0	2	$54,000

27Oct93-6Aqu	wf	1⅛ ⊗	:502 1:161 1:414 1:542	3↑ⒻAlw 34000N3X	90	2	3	23	22	21	2¾	Migliore R	114	*.60	63-39	MissPocketCourt117¾ SilkyFether11421 HurryUpMry1141½	Pinched break	4
8Oct93-6Bel	fm	1¼ [T]	:474 1:12 1:364 2:014	3↑ⒻAlw 34000N3X	80	5	2	12	1½	2½	34	Bailey J D	114 b	2.30	77-18	Belle Nuit114¾ Said Privately1163¼ Silky Feather1148½	Bid, weakened	6
4Sep93-8Bel	fst	1⅛	:442 1:09 1:342 1:471	ⒻGazelle H-G1	89	8	6	718	610	45½	27½	Migliore R	117 b	10.30	85-11	Dispute1207½ Silky Feather117hd In Her Glory112no	Rallied inside	8
14Aug93-9Sar	fst	1¼	:464 1:112 1:371 2:032	ⒻAlabama-G1	93	7	5	59	41¼	41½	33¼	Migliore R	121 b	30.90	84-20	SkyBeauty1211½ FuturePretense1211¾ SilkyFether1211½	Drifted, weakened	8
11Jly93-8Bel	fst	1¼	:47 1:103 1:353 2:012	ⒻC C A Oaks-G1	92	3	3	33½	32	43	32½	Migliore R	121 b	20.60	81-16	Sky Beauty121½ Future Pretense1212 Silky Feather1213	Lacked rally	5
6Jun93-9Bel	fst	1⅛	:464 1:11 1:361 1:493	ⒻMthr Gse-G1	88	2	4	42½	44	35	38½	Migliore R	121 b	25.40	72-21	Sky Beauty1215 Dispute1213½ Silky Feather1215	No factor	4
8May93-8Bel	fst	1	:224 :453 1:10 1:352	ⒻAcorn-G1	82	5	6	65	54	56½	413½	Migliore R	121 b	29.90	77-17	Sky Beauty1215¼ Educated Risk1212½ In Her Glory1215¾	No threat	6
28Mar93-9FG	fst	1 1/16	:224 :461 1:11 1:434	ⒻF G Oaks-G3	87	2	5	511	56	32	12¾	Perrodin E J	L 113 b	39.80	95-09	Silky Feather1132¾ She's A Little Shy1212 Sum Runner1215	Driving	7
13Mar93-6OP	fst	1 1/16	:232 :482 1:142 1:47	ⒻAlw 23000N2L	74	1	3	31½	21½	1½	11½	Borel C H	L 115 b	7.60	66-23	Silky Feather1151½ Dancing Mahmoud112nk Lady Tasso115nk	Driving	8
17Feb93-6OP	fst	1 1/16	:232 :471 1:121 1:443	ⒻAlw 22000N2L	66	6	2	31½	48	510	512¾	Day P	L 120 b	4.00	65-17	Mari's Key112¾ Highest Rank1153 Zilla Peel1126	Tired	6

WORKOUTS: Nov 21 Bel 1 fst 1:381 H *1/3* Nov 16 Bel 5f fst 1:012 B *11/19* Oct 23 Bel 5f fst :594 H *5/58* Sep 30 Bel 6f fst 1:133 H *3/9* ●Aug 29 Sar 5f fst :593 H *1/15*

5 Star Guest

Own: Powhatan
DAVIS R G (175 35 29 27 .20)
B. f. 3 (Apr)
Sire: Assert (Be My Guest)
Dam: Violet (Chieftain)
Br: Raymond R. Guest (Ky)
Tr: Whiteley David A (10 2 1 2 .20)
111

Lifetime Record:	16 4 3 6	$105,579			
1993	14 4 2 6	$101,479	Turf	6 1 2 3	$39,014
1992	2 M 1 0	$4,100	Wet	3 1 0 1	$24,480
Aqu	2 1 0 0	$20,640	Dist	0 0 0 0	

12Nov93-6Aqu yl 1⅛ Ⓣ :484 1:143 1:404 1:532 3+ ⒻAlw 34000N3X 91 4 6 75 43 1hd 1¾ Migliore R 117 7.80 76-26 Star Guest117¾ Blazing Kadie1152 Dana's Wedding1155 Wide, driving 10
5Nov93-6Aqu sly 1⅛ ⊗ :484 1:132 1:392 1:523 3+ ⒻAlw 32000N2X 88 2 2 22½ 21 1hd 1¾ Migliore R 115 2.70 73-30 Star Guest115¾ Cannon Opera11510 Home By Ten1174 Driving 9
14Oct93-2Bel fst 1 :223 :453 1:101 1:353 3+ ⒻAlw 32000N2X 90 5 5 52½ 31½ 22 24 Antley C W 114 13.50 86-22 Link River1194 Star Guest1146¾ Saratoga Bid1144 Second best 6
26Sep93-9Bel sly 1 ⊗ :224 :461 1:112 1:382 3+ ⒻAlw 32000N2X 54 6 6 55 44½ 39 311¼ Perret C 113 *2.10 65-22 Tiffany Hall1128 R. E. Darla1173¼ Star Guest1132 Wide trip 6
10Jly93-7Bel fm 1¼ Ⓣ :502 1:152 1:393 2:031 3+ ⒻAlw 30500N2X 77 1 5 76 51½ 45 32¼ Smith M E 113 *1.60 72-19 Hurry Up Marya1141¼ Tiffany Hall117¾ Star Guest1132 Lacked room 7
26Jun93-7Bel fst 1 1/16 :232 :471 1:122 1:443 3+ ⒻAlw 30500N2X 75 2 4 43½ 32 35¼ 311¼ Smith M E 112 2.30 68-29 Gravette110¾ Standard Equipment11410 Star Guest1126 No rally 6
5Jun93-4Bel fm 1 1/16 Ⓣ :233 :464 1:101 1:411 ⒻTanya50k 82 7 7 77½ 63¾ 63¼ 31 Desormeaux K J 116 3.90 89-13 Missymooiloveyou116nk Shannie'sDncer121¾ StrGuest1161¾ Belated rally 7
22May93-3Bel fst 1⅛ :47 1:12 1:372 1:50 ⒻAlw 30500N2X 79 7 6 67½ 64 53½ 56¾ Bailey J D 121 5.60 72-15 TestyTrestle1164½ StndrdEquipment116no DefensSpnding116¾ Four wide 8
10May93-6Bel fst 1 1/16 :23 :461 1:111 1:443 ⒻAlw 28500N1X 77 7 7 73½ 3½ 12½ 15 Bailey J D 116 *2.10 79-19 Star Guest1165 Life's Walk1162½ Lovely Lyric116no Drew off 7
21Mar93-6GP fst 1 1/16 :24 :482 1:134 1:473 ⒻAlw 26500N1X 58 3 6 74½ 34 45 45½ Vasquez J 115 *.90 66-20 Future Starlet114½ Miss Kitty Fox1134 Nicely Wild1121 Faded 8
WORKOUTS: Nov 21 Bel 4f fst :483 H *8/16* Nov 4 Bel 3f fst :374 B *17/19* Oct 11 Bel 4f fst :51 B *29/39* Oct 5 Bel 4f fst :492 B *29/58* Sep 25 Bel 4f fst :491 B *30/93* Sep 20 Bel 4f gd :494 B *21/51*

6 Turnback The Alarm

Own: Valley View Farm
CARR D (50 2 5 4 .04)
Ro. f. 4
Sire: Darn That Alarm (Jig Time)
Dam: Boomie's Girl E (Figonero)
Br: Burke Walter J (Fla)
Tr: Terrill William V (34 1 2 5 .03)
121

Lifetime Record:	21 8 5 4	$916,504			
1993	7 3 0 2	$350,820	Turf	0 0 0 0	
1992	5 3 1 1	$336,496	Wet	3 1 0 1	$63,000
Aqu	5 1 3 0	$121,456	Dist	1 1 0 0	$150,000

6Nov93-3Aqu sly 1⅛ :471 1:124 1:381 1:51 3+ Stuyvsnt H-G3 96 6 2 2hd 2hd 42½ 44½ Davis R G 118 2.70 76-20 Michelle Can Pass115nk Key Contender1151½ Primitive Hall1132¾ Tired 8
16Oct93-5Bel fst 1⅛ :452 1:091 1:34 1:471 3+ ⒻBeldame-G1 101 2 2 21½ 31 42½ 43¾ Antley C W 123 1.50 89-12 Dispute1191¾ Shared Interest123nk Vivano1231¾ Lacked response 6
19Sep93-8Bel my 1 1/16 :232 :464 1:103 1:414 3+ ⒻRuffian H-G1 97 4 2 21 21 33 35½ Antley C W 123 2.50 87-16 Shared Interest1142½ Dispute1153 Turnback The Alarm1232½ Drifted, tired 5
5Sep93-8Bel fst 1 :233 :462 1:104 1:36 3+ ⒻGo For Wand-G1 96 2 1 11 1½ 11 11½ Antley C W 123 1.20 88-14 Turnback The Alarm1231½ Nannerl116hd November Snow1161 Driving 4
12Jun93-8Bel fst 1⅛ :461 1:102 1:351 1:48 3+ ⒻHempstead H-G1 100 3 2 22 1½ 11½ 11½ Antley C W 119 *1.40 89-12 TurnbckThAlrm1191½ Dputtion117no You'dBSurprisd11214 Drifted, driving 6
22May93-8Bel fst 1 1/16 :223 :452 1:101 1:43 3+ ⒻShuvee H-G1 93 1 3 2½ 1½ 1hd 1¾ Antley C W 117 *1.70 87-15 TurnbackTheAlarm117¾ SharedInterest1132 Vivno112nk Drifted, driving 9
8May93-1Bel fst 6f :221 :452 :571 1:10 3+ ⒻAlw 40000N$Y 92 3 3 2½ 31 31½ 31¾ Antley C W 119 *.40 88-17 Makin Faces1211 Lady Sage119¾ Turnback The Alarm1192½ Lacked rally 5
11Jly92-8Bel fst 1¼ :50 1:133 1:38 2:032 ⒻC C A Oaks-G1 92 6 3 32 1hd 1½ 11½ Antley C W 121 *1.40 74-18 Turnback The Alarm1211½ Easy Now121 Pleasant Stage121 Driving 6
7Jun92-8Bel fst 1⅛ :452 1:093 1:352 1:484 ⒻMothr Goose-G1 95 1 5 53½ 41 1hd 12¼ Antley C W 121 7.20 85-22 TurnbackTheAlrm1212¼ EsyNow1211¾ QueenofTriumph121 Wide driving 7
23May92-8Bel fst 1 :224 :453 1:10 1:35 ⒻAcorn-G1 91 1 1 1½ 11 2hd 33½ Antley C W 121 b 3.40 91-07 ProspectorsDelite1212 PlsntStg1211½ TurnbckThAlrm121 Speed, wknd 12
WORKOUTS: Nov 20 Bel tr.t 6f fst 1:131 B *1/2* ●Nov 13 Bel 5f fst :584 H *1/24* Nov 1 Aqu 5f my 1:024 B (d) *1/1* ●Oct 25 Bel 5f fst :592 H *1/22* ●Oct 12 Bel 4f fst :481 H *1/28* ●Oct 7 Bel 5f fst :594 H *1/26*

7 Miss Pocket Court

Own: Hauman Eugene E
BRAVO J (31 7 7 3 .23)
B. f. 4
Sire: Court Trial (In Reality)
Dam: Pocket Power (Full Pocket)
Br: Mangurian Mr-Mrs H T Jr (Fla)
Tr: Hushion Michael E (28 9 4 2 .32)
110

Lifetime Record:	46 9 7 11	$146,414			
1993	15 5 1 4	$89,230	Turf	12 2 0 4	$37,500
1992	20 3 4 5	$43,685	Wet	5 1 1 1	$23,710
Aqu	1 1 0 0	$20,400	Dist	1 1 0 0	$12,000

Entered 25Nov93- 7 AQU
27Oct93-6Aqu wf 1⅛ ⊗ :502 1:161 1:414 1:542 3+ ⒻAlw 34000N3X 91 4 1 13 12 11 1¾ Lovato F Jr 117 f 1.40 64-39 Miss Pocket Court117¾ Silky Feather11421 Hurry Up Marya1141½ Driving 4
1Oct93-4Bel fst 1 1/16 :23 :461 1:111 1:442 3+ ⒻClm c-50000 85 2 3 3nk 1hd 11 21 Alvarado F T 117 2.70 79-25 Fran's Folly1151 Miss Pocket Court1172¾ Huckster Rose1135½ Gamely 6
Claimed from Miron Stephen E, Debonis Robert Trainer
12Sep93-1Bel fst 1¼ ⊗ :49 1:132 1:39 2:033 3+ ⒻClm 35000 91 3 1 11 11½ 16 116 Alvarado F T 117 *1.60 73-17 Miss Pocket Court11716 Pushia1173 Won Scent1173 Mild drive 6
3Sep93-9Bel fst 1 :233 :462 1:111 1:361 3+ ⒻClm 35000 79 2 10 64½ 52½ 34 38¼ Alvarado F T 117 6.70 79-15 Butter Cream1178 Pontificate113nk Miss Pocket Court1174½ Mild rally 11
14Aug93-4Sar fm 1⅛ Ⓣ :472 1:112 1:36 1:48 3+ ⒻClm 47500 72 10 9 86 98½ 93 85½ Alvarado F T 115 28.70 84-14 Home By Ten1131½ Fashion Miss119nk Turkolady117hd No factor 11
26Jly93-2Bel fm 1¼ Ⓣ :493 1:134 1:38 2:02 ⒻClm c-35000 76 4 2 2hd 2hd 21 34½ Smith M E 117 *1.50 76-12 Bold Ryna1173½ Ivory Today1171 Miss Pocket Court1172 Forced pace 10
Claimed from West Point Stable, Reid Mark J Trainer
1Jly93-6Bel fm 1¼ Ⓣ :501 1:141 1:374 2:024 ⒻClm 50000 79 5 4 33½ 33 33½ 42½ Smith M E 117 3.00 74-16 High Talent117½ Stephen's Joy113nk Insurprise1151½ Lacked rally 9
10Jun93-2Bel gd 1⅜ Ⓣ :471 1:132 1:382 2:15 ⒻClm c-35000 84 8 7 85 42 1hd 1hd Smith M E 117 3.40 76-19 Miss Pocket Court117hd Stephen's Joy1175¼ Sweet N' Saxy1175 Driving 9
Claimed from Miron Stephen E, Debonis Robert Trainer
21May93-2Bel fm 1¼ Ⓣ :484 1:132 1:373 2:022 ⒻClm 35000 82 10 11 97½ 41½ 2½ 37 Smith M E 117 3.00 76-20 Turkolady1171¾ Stephen's Joy119hd Miss Pocket Court1174 Bid, hung 12
1May93-6Hia fm 1⅛ Ⓣ 1:483 3+ ⒻAlw 17000N3X 78 4 6 614 512 45½ 42½ Douglas R R L 120 2.90 93-02 Pleasant Reef117hd Bounding Buldly1207 Hopeful Angel117no Late rally 10
WORKOUTS: Nov 22 Bel tr.t 1 fst 1:442 B *1/1* Nov 12 Bel 5f fst 1:012 H *8/20* Nov 5 Bel tr.t 4f gd :49 B *10/32* Oct 23 Bel 7f fst 1:33 B *4/5* Sep 25 Bel tr.t 4f fst :48 B *3/61*

8 In Her Glory

Own: Bask Stable
BAILEY J D (53 11 10 6 .21)
Dk. b or br f. 3 (Apr)
Sire: Miswaki (Mr. Prospector)
Dam: Forever Waving (Hoist the Flag)
Br: Foxfield (Ky)
Tr: Schulhofer Flint S (27 3 3 8 .11)
111

Lifetime Record:	14 5 1 3	$149,484			
1993	12 4 0 3	$129,144	Turf	1 0 0 0	
1992	2 1 1 0	$20,340	Wet	0 0 0 0	
Aqu	4 3 1 0	$75,480	Dist	0 0 0 0	

24Oct93-5Aqu fst 1⅛ :501 1:144 1:40 1:523 3+ ⒻAlw 44000N$mY 90 4 4 47 42½ 1½ 1¾ Santos J A 114 *.40 73-30 In Her Glory114¾ Bold As Silver1099 Winning The Day1165½ Driving 5
10Oct93-7Bel fst 1 :231 :461 1:103 1:353 ⒻRare PerfumeG2 95 5 5 53 42 42 52¼ Maple E 112 10.90 87-09 Sky Beauty1241¾ Fadetta112nk For All Seasons114nk Lacked rally 6
4Sep93-8Bel fst 1⅛ :442 1:09 1:342 1:471 ⒻGazelle H-G1 89 7 7 516 47 35 37¼ Maple E 112 32.90 85-11 Dispute1207¼ Silky Feather117hd In Her Glory112no Willingly 8
14Aug93-7Sar fm 1 1/16 Ⓣ :242 :49 1:124 1:43 3+ ⒻAlw 46000N$mY 74 3 4 31½ 42½ 67 69¼ Smith M E 113 6.30 75-14 Terre Haute117no Far Out Beast119no Chinese Empress1193 Gave way 6
26Jun93-10Mth fst 170 :231 :474 1:114 1:414 ⒻPost-Deb-G2 77 4 5 64 87¾ 811 615 Krone J A 115 4.90 76-25 Jacody1195½ Sheila's Revenge1132½ Future Pretense1131 Gave way 9
4Jun93-6Bel fst 7f :214 :442 1:091 1:224 ⒻGoodbye Halo45k 88 2 3 43½ 44½ 44½ 44 Krone J A 121 *1.40 85-17 Ophidian1162 Lilly's Moment118½ Maison De Reve1181½ Lacked rally 4
8May93-8Bel fst 1 :224 :453 1:10 1:352 ⒻAcorn-G1 92 4 4 31½ 32 34½ 37¾ Krone J A 121 7.30 83-17 Sky Beauty1215½ Educated Risk1212½ In Her Glory1215¾ Lacked rally 6
8Apr93-8Aqu fst 7f :224 :444 1:092 1:224 ⒻGarlnd Rose45k 93 1 6 54½ 35½ 22½ 11½ Maple E 118 *.70 90-18 In Her Glory1181½ Fighting Jet11810 Saucy Charmer116no Driving 6
20Mar93-10Tam fst 1 1/16 :233 :48 1:123 1:453 ⒻFla Oaks100k 76 3 11 73 11 2hd 43 Ferrer J C 114 *1.70 92-07 Star Jolie1112 Hollywood Wildcat121nk Jacody113¾ Weakened late 11
28Feb93-10GP fst 170 :232 :474 1:13 1:42 ⒻDvna Dale-G3 88 6 3 34 41½ 32½ 36 Krone J A 112 3.70 85-18 Lunar Spook1185 Boots 'n Jackie1211 In Her Glory1123 Rallied inside 7
WORKOUTS: Nov 19 Bel 5f fst 1:01 B *8/24* Nov 13 Bel 4f fst :483 H *6/23* Nov 8 Bel 4f fst :474 H *3/27* Nov 2 Bel 4f fst :48 B *5/20* Oct 18 Bel 4f fst :482 B *8/28* ●Oct 4 Bel 5f fst 1:001 H *1/18*

9 Fadetta

Own: Mohammed Al Maktoum
PERRET C (27 5 1 4 .19)
Dk. b or br f. 3 (Mar)
Sire: Fappiano (Mr. Prospector)
Dam: Glorious Natalie (Reflected Glory)
Br: Brereton C. Jones & Halo Farms (Ky)
Tr: Mott William I (27 7 3 5 .26)
111

Lifetime Record:	5 3 2 0	$81,610		
1993	4 2 2 0	$66,010	Turf	0 0 0 0
1992	1 1 0 0	$15,600	Wet	0 0 0 0
Aqu	1 1 0 0	$15,600	Dist	0 0 0 0

10Oct93-7Bel fst 1 :231 :461 1:103 1:353 ⒻRare PerfumeG2 97 1 6 612 63 52½ 21¾ Perret C 112 5.80 88-09 Sky Beauty1241¾ Fadetta112nk For All Seasons114nk Late gain 6
5Sep93-6Bel fst 1 :233 :47 1:113 1:364 3+ ⒻAlw 32000N2X 85 5 6 41½ 2½ 1½ 11¼ Smith M E 113 *1.00 84-14 Fadetta1131¼ Sakiyah1131¼ Imah1137 Driving 6
20Aug93-5Sar gd 7f :222 :453 1:103 1:234 3+ ⒻAlw 26500N1X 87 7 4 76 43 11½ 12¾ Smith M E 113 *.70 86-15 Fadetta1132¾ Nine Keys1147 Splendid Launch1125 Wide, ridden out 7
29Jly93-6Sar fst 7f :223 :453 1:102 1:231 3+ ⒻAlw 26500N1X 80 6 6 43 42½ 41½ 21 Smith M E 113 *1.20 88-10 Devilishly Lucky1121 Fadetta113nk Regal Solution1113½ Wide turn 10
29Oct92-4Aqu fst 1 :231 :463 1:114 1:373 ⒻMd Sp Wt 77 4 6 64 3nk 11 14 Smith M E 117 2.40 74-24 Fadetta1174 Cherub1171½ Irving's Girl117 Slow st, drvg 7
WORKOUTS: Nov 23 Bel tr.t 5f fst 1:02 B *3/15* Nov 16 Bel 7f fst 1:264 B *1/1* Nov 10 Bel 5f fst 1:011 B *13/34* Nov 4 Bel 7f fst 1:313 B *3/3* Oct 29 Bel 5f fst 1:043 B *22/26* Oct 23 Bel 4f fst :502 B *64/86*

Len Ragozin — "The Sheets"™

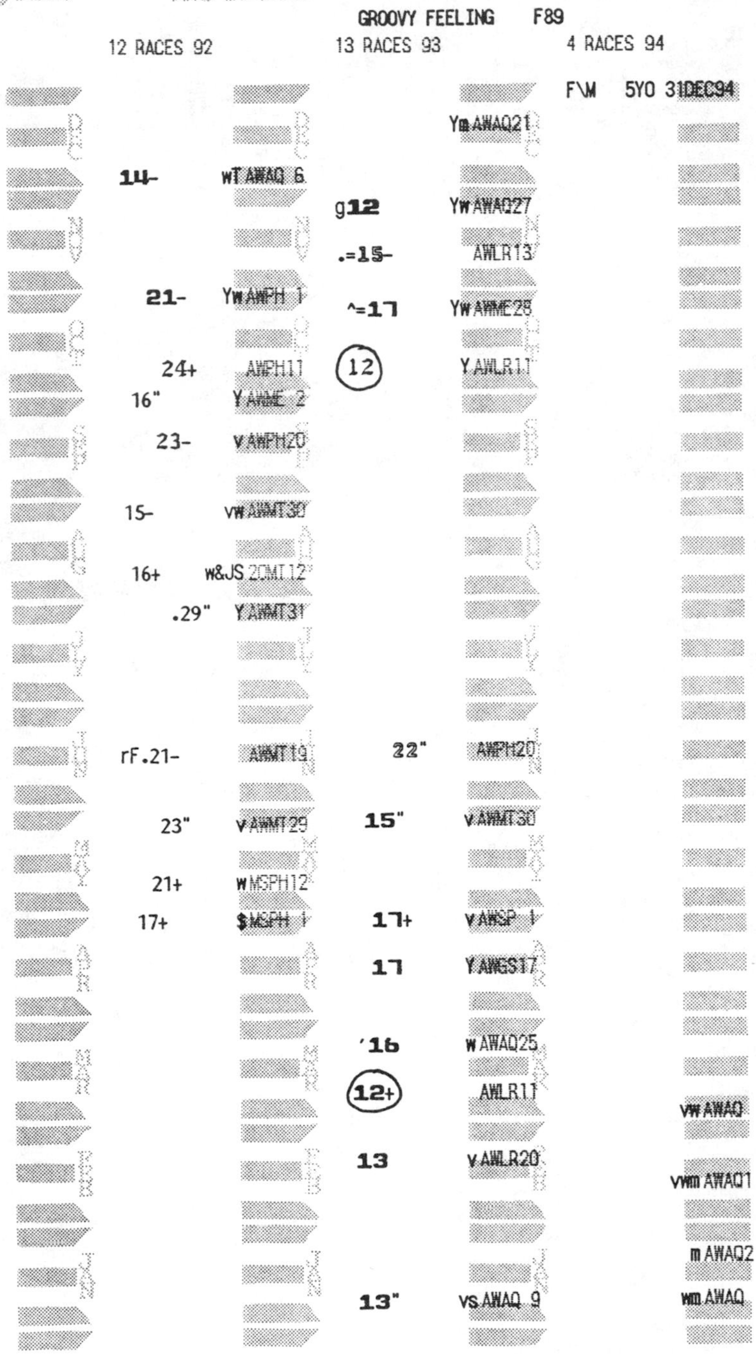
GROOVY FEELING F89
12 RACES 92
13 RACES 93
4 RACES 94
F\M 5YO 31DEC94
14- wT AWAQ 6
21- YwAWPH 1
24+ AWPH11
16" YAWME 2
23- vAWPH20
15- vwAWMT30
16+ w&JS 2CMI12
.29" YAWMT31
rF.21- AWMT19
23" vAWMT29
21+ wMSPH12
17+ $MSPH 1
YmAWAQ21
g12 YwAWAQ27
.=15- AWLR13
^=17 YwAWME28
12 YAWLR11
22" AWPH20
15" vAWMT30
17+ vAWSP 1
17 YAWGS17
'16 wAWAQ25
12+ AWLR11
13 vAWLR20
13" vsAWAQ 9
vwAWAQ
vwm AWAQ1
m AWAQ2
wm AWAQ

Consider some other evidence that Groovy Feeling was headed in the right direction:

- Trailing by nine lengths in her comeback race after the opening half-mile, she made up 7¾ lengths through a final three-eighths run in :37⅕, giving her an extrapolated final fraction of approximately :35⅗.
- Placed on grass for the first time October 28, she bounced to a Beyer of 80 but still won by a nose despite losing ground from the prestretch call to the stretch call.
- Running over yielding turf at Laurel on November 13, Groovy Feeling displayed a two-move running line, racing within four lengths of the lead after a half, dropping eight and a half lengths off the lead after three-quarters, then gaining in position and in lengths at the stretch call and again at the finish to wind up fifth, beaten by less than three lengths. After having just one horse beaten after a slow half in :49, she closed with a final quarter in roughly :24⅖ while carrying 122 pounds over the yielding course — five pounds more than the first three finishers.
- After matching her career-best figure on October 11, she had followed with long bullet workouts on October 23 and November 8.
- She had drawn the rail and was in receipt of a trainer change to Peter Ferriola, who was perennially among the leaders in New York.

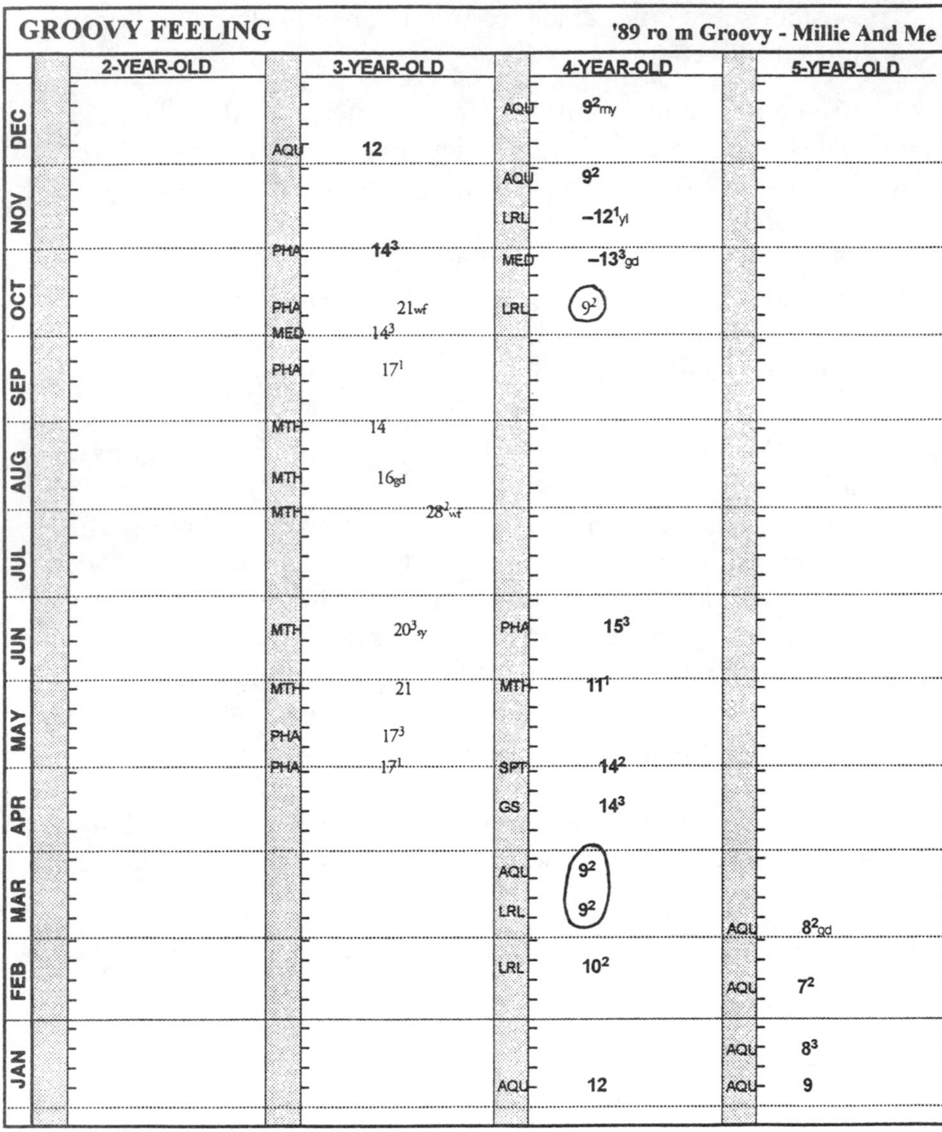

There was no question that the classiest and fastest horse in the race, at least to this point, was Turnback The Alarm. But Groovy Feeling had a conditioning edge over most of the other battle-worn fillies in this field, and she was 12–1, which are generous odds on a horse who handicaps as the second-best in the field.

Our usual $75-per-play was divided as follows: $50 to win on

Groovy Feeling along with a $25 exacta, Turnback The Alarm over Groovy Feeling. Those with a more aggressive betting approach might have taken advantage of a $116 exacta, combining a fresh horse in peak condition with the legitimate class of the field.

SEVENTH RACE
Aqueduct
NOVEMBER 27, 1993

1¼ MILES. (1.59¹) 123rd Running of THE LADIES HANDICAP. Purse $200,000. Fillies and mares, 3-year-olds and upward. By subscription of $400 each which should accompany the nomination; $1,600 to pass the entry box; $1,600 to start. The purse to be divided 60% to the winner, 22% to second, 12% to third and 6% to fourth. Weights Monday, November 22. Starters to be named at the closing time of entries. Trophies will be presented to the winning owner, trainer and jockey. Closed Wednesday, November 10, with 18 nominations.

Value of Race: $200,000 Winner $120,000; second $44,000; third $24,000; fourth $12,000. Mutuel Pool $287,374.00 Exacta Pool $464,110.00 Triple Pool $303,873.00

Last Raced	Horse	M/Eqt.	A.Wt	PP	¼	½	¾	1	Str	Fin	Jockey	Odds $1
13Nov93 6Lrl5	Groovy Feeling		4 111	1	11½	11	11½	11	13	13	McCauley W H	12.00
6Nov93 3Aqu4	Turnback The Alarm		4 121	6	3½	3½	31½	21½	21	2½	Carr D	1.20
20Nov93 9Med5	Avie's Daisy	b	5 113	3	61½	5hd	69	4hd	3½	31½	Cruguet J	28.40
24Oct93 5Aqu1	In Her Glory		3 112	8	43	42	4hd	62	51½	41	Bailey J D	8.30
10Oct93 7Bel2	Fadetta		3 112	9	9	9	81½	73½	6½	5hd	Perret C	2.50
17Nov93 7Aqu1	Bold as Silver		3 110	2	5hd	64	5hd	3hd	41	66	Leon F	36.10
27Oct93 6Aqu1	Miss Pocket Court	f	4 110	7	21	21	2hd	51	79	710½	Bravo J	21.70
12Nov93 8Aqu1	Star Guest		3 111	5	7½	83½	72	816	8	8	Davis R G	20.00
27Oct93 6Aqu2	Silky Feather		3 113	4	83½	7½	9	9	—	—	Migliore R	5.70

Silky Feather: Eased

OFF AT 3:25 Start Good. Won driving. Time, :24, :49, 1:13³, 1:39¹, 2:05⁴ Track fast.

$2 Mutuel Prices:			
1-(A)-GROOVY FEELING	26.00	8.20	8.00
6-(F)-TURNBACK THE ALARM		3.40	3.20
3-(C)-AVIE'S DAISY			8.20

$2 EXACTA 1-6 PAID $116.40 $2 TRIPLE 1-6-3 PAID $1,298.00

Ro. f, by Groovy–Millie and Me, by Wise Exchange. Trainer Ferriola Peter. Bred by Clay Catesby W (Ky).

GROOVY FEELING sprinted clear in the early stages, raced uncontested on the lead to the turn, then edged away under steady right hand encouragement. TURNBACK THE ALARM settled just behind the early leaders while saving ground, angled out while launching her bid on the turn, drifted out in midstretch, then outfinished AVIE'S DAISY for the place. AVIE'S DAISY reserved for six furlongs, split horses while advancing on the turn, then rallied mildly to gain a share. IN HER GLORY raced within striking distance from outside to the turn and lacked a strong closing response. FADETTA far back early, closed the gap a bit on the turn, then lacked a further response. BOLD AS SILVER made a run along the rail to reach contention on the turn and flattened out. MISS POCKET COURT forced the pace to reach contention on the turn, flattened out. STAR GUEST never reached contention. SILKY FEATHER steadied at the start, was never close and was eased in the stretch. MISS POCKET COURT wore mud caulks.

Owners— 1, Donaldson Robert P; 2, Valley View Farm; 3, Paraneck Stable; 4, Bask Stable; 5, Mohammed Al Maktoum; 6, Amherst Stable; 7, Hauman Eugene E; 8, Powhatan; 9, Powell Stanton P

Trainers—1, Ferriola Peter; 2, Terrill William V; 3, Wilson Ronald; 4, Schulhofer Flint S; 5, Mott William I; 6, Johnson Philip G; 7, Hushion Michael E; 8, Whiteley David A; 9, Violette Richard Jr

Overweight: In Her Glory (1), Fadetta (1).

Our final example of explosive and/or forging patterns is Freezing Fun, who combined a little of both when he broke his maiden at Saratoga on August 5, 1992:

9 START 6 FURLONGS SARATOGA FINISH

6 FURLONGS. (1.08) **MAIDEN SPECIAL WEIGHT. Purse $24,000. 3-year-olds and upward. Weights, 3-year-olds 117 lbs. Older 122 lbs.**

Coupled—Russian Tea Room and Slaymaker; Revolt and Al's Jewel.

Ripaway B. c. 4, by Kick—Lizzy's Gal, by Rambunctious
BROCKLEBANK G V (3 0 0 1 .00) Br.—Amiel Jack Estate of (NY)
Own.—Shevy Michael J Tr.—Shevy Michael J (—) **122**
Lifetime 0 0 0 0 1992 0 M 0 0 1991 0 M 0 0
LATEST WORKOUTS ●Jly 22 Sar Ⓣ 4f fm :49² H (d) Jly 17 Sar tr.t 4f gd :52⁴ B Jly 9 Sar tr.t 3f sly :38⁴ Bg Jun 13 Sar tr.t 3f fst :39² B

Russian Tea Room

Ch. c. 3(Apr), by Alydar—Tea At Five, by Olden Times
Br.—Wooden Horse Investments, Inc. (Ky)
Tr.—Alexander Frank A (4 2 1 0 .50)
DAVIS R G (23 1 4 2 .04)
Own.—Dogwood Stable
117
Lifetime 0 0 0 0 — 1991 0 M 0 0
LATEST WORKOUTS Aug 2 Sar 3f fst :37 B — Jly 19 Bel 5f fst 1:02 Hg — Jly 7 Bel 4f fst :494 B — Jun 29 Bel 4f fst :513 B

Trumpet Tongued

Ch. g. 3(Mar), by Dixieland Band—Confirmation Class, by Affirmed
Br.—Meadowhill (Ky)
Tr.—Terrill William V (7 0 0 2 .00)
CARR D (13 0 0 2 .00)
Own.—Rosenthal Mrs M
117
Lifetime 9 0 2 2 $20,560 — 1992 7 M 2 2 $19,120 — 1991 2 M 0 0 $1,440 — Turf 2 0 0 0 — Wet 2 0 2 0 $11,440

29Jly92- 6Sar fst 1 :473 1:113 1:364 3↑Md Sp Wt 80 4 2 21 2½ 2½ 33¾ Carr D b 116 8.00 — — PtrtStr1163½PrnntPrspct116nkTrptTd116 Bid, weakened 8
16Jly92- 7Bel fst 7f :221 :444 1:233 Md Sp Wt 70 1 2 1½ 2hd 31½ 44½ Carr D b 122 21.20 81–14 Ashrf122nkPrnntPrspct1222¾PrtTrsrr122 Dueled inside 10
21Jun92- 2Bel fst 1⅛ :464 1:114 1:423 3↑Md Sp Wt 63 2 5 2hd 2hd 36½ 317¾ Carr D b 114 3.20 71–19 LookAhd11411½InWlk1146¼TrmptTngd114 Dueled, tired 7
21Jun92-originally scheduled on turf
25May92- 2Bel fm 1 Ⓣ:453 1:093 1:34 3↑Md Sp Wt 66 8 1 11 1hd 45½ 712¼ Carr D b 115 4.00 80–14 RylMntnInn1154½Nlsn'sNvy115nkStpRyll115 Speed tired 12
6May92- 3Bel fm 1⅛ Ⓣ:471 1:111 1:432 3↑Md Sp Wt 74 5 6 63 51½ 41¾ 54¼ Carr D b 115 6.20 75–17 FrenchBullt124nkAllgdVlntin124noPrsonlDrw115 4-wide 12
22Apr92- 4Aqu sly 1⅛ :481 1:132 1:54 3↑Md Sp Wt 69 4 2 2hd 1½ 22 26¾ Carr D b 115 *.50e 59–30 Homstnd1156¾TrmptTngd1156Dn'tThwrtM115 2nd best 6
22Apr92-Originally scheduled on turf
11Apr92- 6Aqu sly 1 :471 1:121 1:372 Md Sp Wt 74 6 2 1½ 1hd 2½ 23¼ Carr D b 122 23.00 72–22 Rplton1223¼TrmptTongd1221PrsnlDrw122 Dueled, wknd 7
18Aug91- 9Sar fst 5f :22 :452 :581 Md Sp Wt 40 7 4 21 4¾ 66½ 710 Santos J A b 118 9.90 83–12 AmericnChnce118nkStepRoylly1182FreightBill118 Tired 10
5Aug91- 5Sar fst 5f :212 :454 :584 Md Sp Wt 50 8 3 56½ 53½ 3nk 46½ Santos J A 118 19.40 83–10 SmlnAndDncn1182½Prfrncs1182WthIt118 Saved ground 9
LATEST WORKOUTS Jly 23 Bel 4f fst :482 B — Jly 10 Bel 4f fst :48 B — Jun 15 Bel 4f fst :474 H — Jun 10 Bel 4f fst :482 B

Revolt

Dk. b. or br. c. 3(May), by Valid Appeal—Blend of Poetry, by Iron Constitution
Br.—Harry T. Mangurian, Jr. (Fla)
Tr.—Dutrow Richard E (3 0 1 0 .00)
KRONE J A (21 3 3 3 .14)
Own.—Kinsman Stable
117
Lifetime 0 0 0 0 — 1991 0 M 0 0
LATEST WORKOUTS ●Jly 26 Aqu ⊡ 5f fst 1:02 B — Jly 18 Aqu ⊡ 4f fst :474 Hg — Jun 22 Aqu 4f fst :492 B — Jun 15 Aqu 4f fst :52 B

Rise to Rule

B. c. 3(Mar), by Fappiano—Heroic Heart, by Hoist the Flag
Br.—Mellon Paul (Va)
Tr.—Miller Mack (4 2 1 0 .50)
BAILEY J D (21 6 3 1 .29)
Own.—Rokeby Stables
117
Lifetime 1 0 1 0 $5,280 — 1991 1 M 1 0 $5,280

28Nov91- 7Aqu fst 6f :222 :462 1:114 Md Sp Wt 74 3 6 54½ 32 32½ 2½ Bailey J D 118 *.90 81–19 Songrider118½RisetoRule1184½BaldSmile118 Fin. strong 7
LATEST WORKOUTS Aug 2 Sar 4f fst :463 H — Jly 28 Sar tr.t 6f fst 1:172 B — ●Jly 22 Bel 4f fst :472 Hg — Jly 18 Bel 5f fst 1:001 H

Skinman

B. c. 3(May), by Cozzene—Bold Brat, by Boldnesian
Br.—Cox Edward A Jr (Ky)
Tr.—Gleaves Philip A (5 1 1 0 .20)
DAY P (32 4 4 5 .13)
Own.—Due Process Stable
117
Lifetime 4 0 1 2 $14,126 — 1991 4 M 1 2 $14,126 — Turf 2 0 1 0 $10,616

4Oct91- 7Med fst 170 :474 1:124 1:423 Md Sp Wt 56 4 4 52¼ 44 38 38¾ Migliore R b 118 2.90 76–14 Bull Terrier1187¼ Gin AtSea1181½Skinman118 Mild rally 9
21Sep91-11Pim yl 1 Ⓣ:471 1:123 1:393 Vanland'm 57 2 5 54½ 45 411 519½ Chavez S N b 110 26.30 61–27 OldrBtSmrtr11313SntEdrd1122¼SpfDlght112 Weakened 7
7Sep91-11Pim fm 5f Ⓣ:224 :463 :591 Jet Pilot 64 3 6 43½ 42½ 45½ 35½ Chavez S N b 110 6.40 81–13 LckyVrgnn1112½ⒹConCollctor1193Sknmn110 Mild rally 7
7Sep91-Placed second through disqualification
23Jly91- 2Lrl fst 5½f :23 :473 1:063 Md Sp Wt 43 7 7 53 42½ 33 34 Castaneda M 120 *.80 82–16 Meliss'sBst1203½ThrdsMcCoy120½Skinmn120 Weakened 7
LATEST WORKOUTS Aug 3 Sar 6f fst 1:132 H — ●Jly 27 Sar 7f fst 1:291 B — ●Jly 18 Sar tr.t 5f fst 1:05 B — Jly 10 Sar tr.t 4f fst :51 B

Lets Go Mambo

Dk. b. or br. g. 3(Apr), by Mogambo—Go Getter, by Buckfinder
Br.—Sunnyview Farm (NY)
Tr.—Brida Dennis J (6 1 1 0 .17)
LABOCETTA F JR (—)
Own.—Watral Michael
117
Lifetime 0 0 0 0 — 1992 0 M 0 0 — 1991 0 M 0 0
LATEST WORKOUTS Jly 31 Sar tr.t 5f fst 1:032 B — Jly 22 Sar tr.t 4f fst :52 B — Jly 17 Sar tr.t 4f gd :494 H — Jly 3 Bel 5f fst 1:013 H

Sassy Debutante

B. f. 3(May), by Debussy—The Happy Clam, by Pontoise
Br.—Mr. and Mrs. Brian Mandrych & Diane (N.Y.)
Tr.—Monserrate Felix (—)
HERNANDEZ R C (—)
Own.—Cracky Stable
112
Lifetime 0 0 0 0 — 1991 0 M 0 0
LATEST WORKOUTS Aug 2 FL 4f fst :53 B — Jun 28 FL 4f fst :522 B

Squantum Point

B. g. 5, by Sauce Boat—Morning Watch, by Hoist the Flag
Br.—Cheston George (Ky)
Tr.—Watters Sidney Jr (—)
MAPLE E (17 1 1 3 .06)
Own.—Brookmeade Stable
122
Lifetime 10 0 3 2 $19,220 — 1991 6 M 2 1 $10,040 — 1990 4 M 1 1 $9,180 — Wet 1 0 1 0 $3,080

11Aug91- 2Sar fst 6f :22 :45 1:093 3↑Md Sp Wt 67 6 3 21½ 41½ 43 810¾ Mojica R Jr 122 6.40 85–09 BombStopper1175CrmelKing1171Previled117 Gave way 14
1Aug91- 5Sar fst 7f :23 :463 1:241 3↑Md Sp Wt 79 5 1 32 41½ 3½ 21¾ Mojica R Jr5 117 3.90 82–09 GntLp1171¾SquntmPont1171PC'sGlory117 Up for place 8
18Jun91- 1Pim sly 6f :234 :473 1:133 3↑Md 50000 65 7 1 1hd 1½ 2hd 2¾ Fenwick C C III5 117 2.40 76–17 BridgeDefendr113¾SquntumPoint117nkNuRvu114 Sharp 7
4Jun91- 1Pim fst 6f :234 :471 1:123 3↑Md 50000 63 2 1 2hd 1hd 1hd 32 Fenwick C C III5 117 2.80 80–14 SlukiDwn1131¾BridgDfndr113nkSquntumPoint117 Tired 7
11May91- 8Pim fst 6f :23 :454 1:111 3↑Md Sp Wt 62 7 3 53½ 44 56 56¾ Fenwick C C III5 117 19.20 82–12 TracyRoad115½UnclePhil1141RagtimeBet114 Weakened 8
27Apr91-12Pim fst 6f :224 :453 1:12 3↑Md Sp Wt 46 10 4 21½ 22½ 35 88½ FenwickCCIII5 b 117 7.60 76–14 MistrMusic1081UnclPhil113½PcfulLughtr114 Weakened 10
6May90- 6Aqu fst 6f :23 :47 1:112 Md Sp Wt 50 1 2 1hd 2½ 43 711½ Bruin J E b 122 *2.30 71–22 CamdenHrbor1224Udino1222SolrSplendor122 Gave way 7
19Apr90- 5Aqu fst 6f :221 :452 1:113 3↑Md Sp Wt 78 4 2 2½ 2hd 2hd 21¼ Bruin J E b 115 2.90 81–20 PlmBr1151¼SqntmPnt1154KyNtSpkr115 Best of others 7
9Apr90- 6Aqu fst 7f :222 :451 1:241 3↑Md Sp Wt 63 6 3 1hd 11½ 32 34 Bruin J E b 115 16.30 77–17 MghtyDstnct124½MgcEgl1243½SqntmPnt115 Weakened 9
9Mar90- 7Aqu fst 6f ⊡:223 :461 1:114 Md Sp Wt 56 2 9 811 713 912 613¼ Bruin J E 122 19.00 74–13 Fleecd1224HollywoodSuccss1226¾Bnkr'sBby122 Outrun 9
LATEST WORKOUTS Jly 30 Sar 5f fst 1:03 B — ●Jly 15 Pim 5f fst 1:003 H — Jun 27 Pim 4f fst :49 B

Freezing Fun

B. c. 3(Feb), by It's Freezing—Ain't We Got Fun, by Raise a Native

Lifetime 1992 3 M 1 1 $8,160 — 7 0 2 2 — 1991 4 M 1 1 $7,040 — $15,200

MADRID A JR (14 2 1 1 .14)

Br.—Tannenbaum Howard (Ky)

Own.—Austin Dale H

Tr.—Schosberg Richard (1 0 0 1 .00) **117**

16Jly92- 7Bel fst 7f :22^1 :44^4 1:23^3 Md Sp Wt 18 **65** 6 5 5$^{8\frac12}$ 5$^{7\frac12}$ 5$^{5\frac12}$ 5$^{6\frac34}$ Madrid A Jr b 122 7.60 79-14 Ashrf122^{nk}PrnntPrspct122$^{2\frac34}$PrtTrsrr122 Saved ground 10

3Jly92- 1Bel fst 7f :22^4 :46 1:23^4 3+Md Sp Wt 14 **80** 2 2 1$^{\frac12}$ 1^{hd} 1^{hd} 2$^{1\frac12}$ Madrid A Jr b 116 4.80 83-11 MustBeWr116$^{1\frac12}$FrzingFun116$^{1\frac34}$SfDpositBox116 Gamely 10

14Jun92- 6Bel fst 6f :22^3 :46^1 1:11^1 Md Sp Wt **72** 2 3 2$^{\frac12}$ 1^{hd} 3$^{\frac12}$ 3$^{2\frac12}$ Madrid A Jr b 122 7.80 81-16 I'mEscpin122$^{2\frac12}$GroovyAttr122^{hd}FrzngFun122 Bid, wknd 9

9Oct91- 2Bel fst 7f :23^2 :47^1 1:24^3 Md Sp Wt **53** 1 8 7$^{4\frac12}$ 8$^{4\frac12}$ 8$^{5\frac12}$ 8^{12} Chavez J F b 118 4.40 69-25 Offbeat118^4 All MyTricks118$^{1\frac34}$EasternBrave118 Outrun 9

29Sep91- 4Bel fst 1 :46^3 1:11^3 1:36^4 Md Sp Wt **59** 3 3 4^3 4$^{2\frac12}$ 4^9 5$^{14\frac12}$ Chavez J F b 118 10.20 71-18 Onlokr118^{10}HrrythHt118^{1}DsrtPrspctr118 Saved ground 14

16Sep91- 4Bel fst 7f :23 :46^3 1:23^4 Md Sp Wt **74** 4 3 1$^{\frac12}$ 1$^{\frac12}$ 2$^{\frac12}$ 2$^{\frac12}$ Chavez J F b 118 21.10 84-15 SnppyLndng118$^{\frac12}$FrzngFn118$^{3\frac12}$DsrtProspctr118 Gamely 7

6Aug91-10Mth fst 6f :22^2 :46^3 1:13^3 Md Sp Wt **36** 2 8 8$^{4\frac34}$ 8$^{5\frac34}$ 4$^{5\frac12}$ 3$^{3\frac12}$ Ferrer J C b 118 13.50 69-24 Erk'sChoc118$^{1\frac34}$WldDnc118$^{1\frac34}$FrzngFun118 Finished well 11

LATEST WORKOUTS Jly 31 Sar 4f fst :47^1 H Jun 28 Bel 4f fst :47^1 H Jun 10 Bel 4f fst :48^1 H

Al's Jewel

B. c. 3(Feb), by Alleged—Nalee's Fantasy, by Graustark

Lifetime 1991 1 M 0 0 — 1 0 0 0 — Turf 1 0 0 0

ANTLEY C W (27 4 7 5 .15)

Br.—Firman Pamela H-Humphrey G W-Louise (Ky)

Own.—Kelley Walter A

Tr.—Dutrow Richard E (3 0 1 0 .00) **117**

19Jly91- 5Bel fm 7f Ⓣ:22^4 :45^4 1:22^3 Md Sp Wt **12** 8 11 12^{22}12^{22}12^{19}12$^{34\frac12}$ Antley C W b 118 10.10 58-08 PrdiseCreek118^{11}ForeverFighting118^{hd}JyGe118 Outrun 12

LATEST WORKOUTS Aug 3 Sar 6f fst 1:18 B Jly 26 Aqu ⊡ 6f fst 1:17^1 B

Slaymaker

Dk. b. or br. c. 3(Mar), by Seattle Slew—Sulemeif, by Northern Dancer

Lifetime 1992 1 M 0 1 $1,620 — 1 0 0 1 — 1991 0 M 0 0 — $1,620

SMITH M E (29 6 3 6 .21)

Br.—W. S. Farish (Ky)

Own.—Dogwood Stables

Tr.—Vestal Peter M (2 0 0 1 .00) **117**

16Jly92- 3EIP fst 6f :22^3 :46 1:12^1 3+Md Sp Wt 19 **63** 7 7 5$^{1\frac12}$ 3$^{1\frac12}$ 3$^{1\frac12}$ 3^{nk} Kutz D 118 *.70 86-14 RichrdA.118^{hd}TffnyGlss118^{hd}Slymkr118 Greenly stretch 8

LATEST WORKOUTS Aug 2 Sar 4f fst :50^2 B ●Jly 13 CD 4f fst :48 H Jly 8 CD 5f fst 1:03 B ●Jun 26 CD 5f fst 1:01^2 Bg

Also Eligible (Not in Post Position Order):

Panchito

Ch. c. 3(May), by Pancho Villa—Carlisle Jim, by Hagley

Lifetime 1991 0 M 0 0 — 0 0 0 0

BROCKLEBANK G V (3 0 0 1 .00)

Br.—Victor Heerman, Jr. (Ky)

Own.—Collier Reginald B

Tr.—Kelly Tim D (2 0 0 0 .00) **117**

LATEST WORKOUTS Jly 29 Sar 5f fst 1:03 B Jly 24 Bel 4f sly :49^3 B Jly 17 Bel 3f fst :37^1 Hg Jly 3 Bel 5f fst 1:05 B

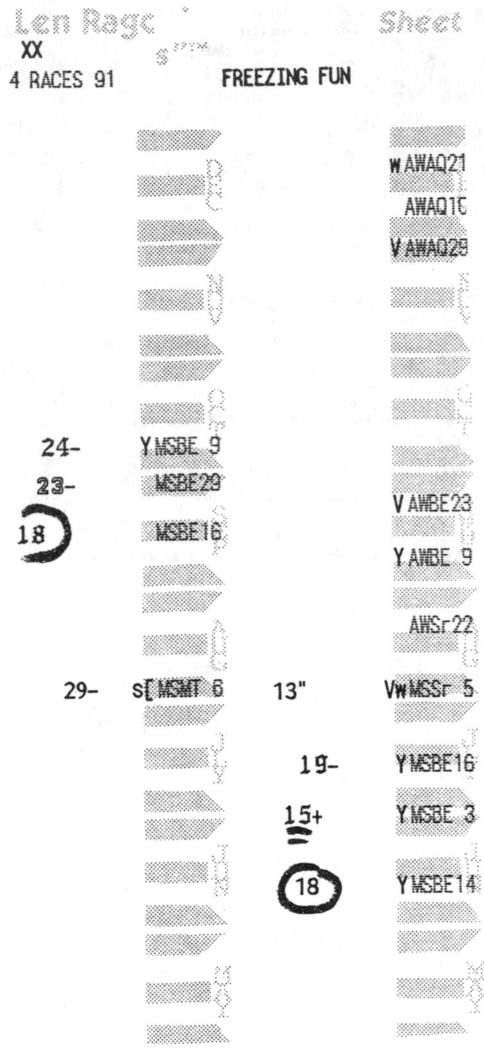

Len Ragozin Sheet
XX
4 RACES 91
FREEZING FUN
wAWAQ21
AWAQ16
VAWAQ29
24- YMSBE 9
23- MSBE29
VAWBE23
18 MSBE16
YAWBE 9
AWSr22
29- s[MSMT 6
13" VwMSSr 5
19- YMSBE16
15+ YMSBE 3
18 YMSBE14

None of the first-time starters attracted any significant toteboard action. The four contenders in terms of figures were Trumpet Tongued, Rise to Rule, Freezing Fun, and Squantum Point. The latter was still a maiden at the age of five, had not been postward in fifty-one weeks, and could be eliminated without much further ado.

Rise to Rule had run a Beyer of 74 when a fast-closing second in his debut, but was making his first start in eight months and was seriously overbet at 4–5 because of his "designer barn" connections, Rokeby Stables and Mack Miller.

This left Trumpet Tongued at 7–2 and Freezing Fun at 6–1. Both had run a Beyer of 80 recently; were that all the information handicappers had to go on, the play would be Freezing Fun at the longer odds. But there *was* more to go on: Trumpet Tongued had recorded his career-best figure last time out, whether one consulted Beyer or the sheets, and that effort had come barely a week ago, affording him but a few days of precious recovery time.

Freezing Fun, on the other hand, had run his 80 nearly five weeks ago, and he stood a much better chance of running back to that figure in this race. Notice he delivered the 80 off an explosive line: his best figure as a two-year-old was the 74 earned in his second start, and he had essentially matched it with a 72 in his seasonal debut June 14. The same pattern was evident on *The Sheets:* Freezing Fun had run an 18 second time out, had returned with a matching 18 in his first start as a three-year-old, and had then made a 2¾-point forward move to the 15¼ of July 3.

He ran into a well-meant first-time starter named Must Be War in that race, however, and settled for second at odds of 9–2. Predictably, he bounced when run back on fewer than two weeks' rest July 16, falling back to a figure of 18¾ on the sheets and a Beyer of 65.

Freezing Fun, by definition, could no longer be termed explosive once he had made that 2¾-point move. He was best classified as a forging horse who was still eligible to improve under the right circumstances.

By the time August 5 rolled around, circumstances were right, because time was on Freezing Fun's side. It had been nearly five weeks since his initial move of July 3, and three weeks since his most recent start — sufficient time to recover. Moreover, Freezing Fun had worked a handy four furlongs in :47⅕ five days before the move to a 15¼, and he had been sent out for an identical :47⅕ workout five days before this race, which fueled the belief that another 15¼ or possibly something even better would be forthcoming.

It was. Freezing Fun circled the field with a decisive move on the turn and won by an expanding margin of five and a quarter lengths, improving again on *The Sheets* to a 13½ — a forward move of 1¾ points from his previous best.

NINTH RACE
Saratoga
AUGUST 5, 1992

6 FURLONGS. (1.08) MAIDEN SPECIAL WEIGHT. Purse $24,000. 3–year–olds and upward. Weights, 3–year–olds 117 lbs. Older 122 lbs.

Value of race $24,000; value to winner $14,400; second $5,280; third $2,880; fourth $1,440. Mutuel pool $281,562. Exacta Pool $370,182 Triple Pool $601,119

Last Raced	Horse	M/Eqt.	A.	Wt	PP	St	¼	½	Str	Fin	Jockey	Odds $1
16Jly92 ^{7}Bel^{5}	12 Freezing Fun 5-4T	b	3	117	9	3	7^{5}	3^{hd}	1^{1}	$1^{5\frac{1}{4}}$	Madrid A Jr	6.90
29Jly92 ^{6}Sar^{3}	19 Trumpet Tongued RT	b	3	117	3	2	$1^{\frac{1}{2}}$	1^{hd}	2^{1}	2^{nk}	Carr D	3.90
28Nov91 ^{7}Aqu^{2}	18 Rise to Rule 2-3T		3	117	5	6	6^{1}	$6^{1\frac{1}{2}}$	5^{2}	$3^{1\frac{1}{2}}$	Bailey J D	.90
11Aug91 ^{2}Sar^{8}	17 Squantum Point 4-3T gelding	b	[illegible]	[illegible]	[illegible]	[illegible]	$4^{\frac{1}{2}}$	4^{1}	4^{1}	$4^{\frac{1}{2}}$	Maple E	15.20
	20 Revolt 2T		3	117	4	8	$2^{\frac{1}{2}}$	2^{hd}	$3^{\frac{1}{2}}$	5^{8}	Krone J A	7.30
	27 Russian Tea Room Slog RT gelding		[illegible]	[illegible]	[illegible]	[illegible]	$5^{\frac{1}{2}}$	$5^{\frac{1}{2}}$	$6^{1\frac{1}{2}}$	$6^{2\frac{1}{4}}$	Davis R G	10.10
	Lets Go Mambo 3T		3	117	6	7	3^{1}	7^{3}	7^{4}	$7^{8\frac{1}{2}}$	Laboccetta F Jr	23.00
	Panchito 2T	b	3	117	10	5	$9^{\frac{1}{2}}$	9^{4}	9^{14}	$8^{\frac{1}{2}}$	Brocklebank G V	36.10
	Ripaway Slog RT gelding		[illegible]	[illegible]	1	10	8^{3}	$8^{2\frac{1}{2}}$	$8^{\frac{1}{2}}$	9^{30}	Mojica R Jr	74.40
	Sassy Debutante RT		3	114	7	4	10	10	10	10	Roque E	87.50

OFF AT 5:32 Start Good. Won Driving. Time, :22^{2}, :45^{4}, :57^{4}, 1:10^{2} Track fast.

$2 Mutuel Prices:			
9–(J)–FREEZING FUN	15.80	6.20	3.00
3–(C)–TRUMPET TONGUED		4.60	2.60
5–(E)–RISE TO RULE			2.40

$2 EXACTA 9–3 PAID $57.00 $2 TRIPLE 9–3–5 PAID $117.00

Thus far as a three-year-old, Freezing Fun has continued to forge ahead to better figures. This brings up an important point, as anyone familiar with Horatio Luro's famous analogy about "squeezing the lemon dry" knows: Each time a horse like Freezing Fun makes a forward move to a new top figure, the likelihood that it will make another move has been correspondingly diminished, for there is only so much juice to each lemon. The first small forward moves of a horse's career are so predictive of better things to come because, after all, the chances for further development are much greater in the early stages of a horse's career.

It is probably not sheer coincidence that several of the preceding example races illustrating explosive and forging patterns took place at Saratoga, which offers the most competitive racing in the United States. Because the competition is so fierce, it only stands to reason that a horse must be in excellent physical condition to win there. At Saratoga, heavily bet horses with established, obvious form annually encounter rivals primed to achieve peak condition during the month of August. Often, these "hot condition" horses are overlooked.

Perhaps this has something to do with the venerable racetrack's "Graveyard of Favorites" mystique.

THE RECOVERY LINE

Statistical studies have identified horses making their third start back from a layoff as likely candidates for improvement. But the majority among the increasingly sophisticated handicapping community are well aware of this fact, and as a result, such horses seldom catch anyone by surprise. It is not foreordained, however, that horses must return to top form the third time back; returnees with attractive patterns making their fifth, sixth, or even seventh starts back from layoffs improve on a consistent basis as well. It stands to reason that handicappers with some means of anticipating the likeliest ones are in position to find overlays once the crowd has abandoned ship.

Explosive and forging principles can be applied effectively to horses that have had a few starts since returning from a layoff. The pattern is slightly different, but the basic premise is similar:

First time back, the horse runs a figure several points slower than its previous best. This initial exertion knocks it off form for a few races, but the horse then signals impending improvement by "circling back around" to equal or slightly surpass the initial comeback figure.

Permit had developed such a pattern — a "recovery line" as termed by Len Friedman — when he was entered in Aqueduct's fifth race on November 18, 1992:

5 6½ FURLONGS AQUEDUCT

6 ½ FURLONGS. **(1.15) ALLOWANCE. Purse $28,000. 3-year-olds and upward which have never won two races other than Maiden, Claiming or Starter. Weight: 3-year-olds 120 lbs. Older 122 lbs. Non-winners of a race other than Maiden or Claiming since November 1 allowed 3 lbs. Of such a race since October 15, 5 lbs.**

Hope Us

B. g. 4, by Tridessus—Hope At Last, by Cutlass
Br.—Burbank Lindsey D (Fla)
Tr.—Ferriola Peter (67 17 9 13 .25)
MADRID A JR (70 5 12 4 .07)
Own.—Jewel-E Stable
117
Lifetime 47 6 6 9 $95,532
1992 14 3 4 0 $33,650
1991 17 1 1 4 $29,940
Turf 2 0 0 0
Wet 7 0 0 1 $5,927

8Nov92- 7Aqu fst 1 :472 1:114 1:364 3↑Alw 31000 84 7 5 63 61¾ 42½ 41½ Frost G C5 112 3.50e 76-24 CrnshsCrnr117nkOpnntr117½PrrssMtn115 Improved pos 9
26Oct92- 4Aqu fst 6f :221 :453 1:102 3↑Clm 30000 94 1 4 44 42½ 2hd 12¾ Frost G C5 108 10.10 89-14 Hope Us1082¾ Reappeal1172 Talc's Bid117 Driving 6
12Oct92- 4Bel my 1 :464 1:11 1:363 3↑Clm c-17500 65 5 5 53½ 56 511 413¾ Gryder A T 119 7.20 73-17 LstSong1129¾Archtkton1131¼CghtLookng117 No threat 9
12Oct92-Claimed from D J Stable, Contessa Gary C Trainer
19Sep92- 5Med fst 1 1/16 :471 1:114 1:434 3↑Clm 16000 87 1 2 33 3½ 1hd 1hd Gryder A T L 115 2.80 88-17 Hope Us115hd Callisto115¾ Twice The Star115 Driving 6
1Sep92- 2Mth fst 1 1/16 :482 1:131 1:451 3↑Clm 16000 88 4 3 42½ 53½ 41¼ 22 Gryder A T L 115 4.40 81-23 TwiceTheStar1172HopeUs115noCllisto117 Stead nr 5/16 8
19Aug92- 7Mth gd 1 :472 1:123 1:381 3↑Clm 16000 77 8 7 78¼ 75¾ 66½ 78½ Bravo J L 115 2.90 72-28 TwcThStr115hdBndthBck1176½HowlngSccss117 No rally 8
7Aug92- 8Mth fst 1 1/16 :454 1:10 1:421 3↑Clm c-12500 85 3 4 411 34½ 23 21¾ Marquez C H Jr 115 2.60 96-10 Sur Lanvin1151¾ Hope Us1158Judge'sPride113 Good try 7
7Aug92-Claimed from Worswick Ronald J, Cash Russell J Trainer
28Jly92- 2Mth fst 6f :22 :454 1:112 3↑Clm 12500 69 1 8 912 911 88¾ 46 Marquez C H Jr 116 10.00 78-17 MkLck1165MjorMcClod117¾LoylRjb109 Wide into lane 9
9Jly92- 7Crc fst 6½f :223 :46 1:18 3↑Clm 18000 72 4 3 45 67½ 56 56½ Douglas R R 113 13.50 88-07 Wish Tonite1122½ Wannamoisett114½SirAlf116 Faltered 6
26Jun92- 2Crc gd 7f :224 :462 1:26 3↑Clm 14000 80 1 5 33½ 42½ 2hd 2hd Douglas R R 116 4.20 85-08 PetitCeC112hdHopUs116noWnnmoisttt116 Rallied 5 wide 7
LATEST WORKOUTS ●Oct 22 Aqu 4f fst :461 H

Uncas Chief

B. c. 3(Mar), by Ogygian—Lido Isle, by Far North
Br.—Foxfield (Ky)
Tr.—Reid Mark J (12 2 1 3 .17)
SMITH M E (110 21 14 17 .19)
Own.—Prew Brian M
115
Lifetime 10 2 1 1 $43,108
1992 10 2 1 1 $43,108
1991 0 M 0 0
Turf 3 0 0 0 $1,860
Wet 2 0 0 0

19Aug92- 9Sar my 7f :221 :443 1:233 3↑Alw 28000 51 7 5 3½ 3½ 106 1015¼ Antley C W b 113 9.10 72-17 Keratoid112nkBorderCat112½Prioritizer112 Forced pace 10
22Jly92- 7Bel fm 1 1/16 Ⓣ:463 1:10 1:40 3↑Alw 31000 82 4 3 31½ 42 43¼ 69¼ Krone J A b 111 24.10 87-15 PrdisCrk1132¾VictoryCross1176TmbrCt111 Lacked rally 9
27Jun92- 5Bel fm 1 Ⓣ:462 1:094 1:34 3↑Alw 31000 85 3 3 32½ 42½ 43 44¼ Krone J A 109 17.40 88-11 Kr'sCln109hdVctryCrss1173ShrthGlry117 Lugged in str 9
6Jun92- 5Bel my 1⅛ :45 1:09 1:482 Colin 54 1 5 63½ 98¼ 1019 1029¼ Krone J A 115 35.90 58-08 Spekerphon1223¼BrklyFitz1151¼BigSur122 Broke slowly 10
6Jun92-Grade III
6May92- 6Bel fm 1¼ 🅃:491 1:373 2:021 3↑Alw 31000 75 2 6 66 31 54 67 Krone J A 112 10.00 72-17 ProSrv119nkMchoPrcos119nkExplsvRl119 Flattened out 8
18Apr92- 6Aqu gd 1⅛ :471 1:11 1:491 Cahill Road 86 2 5 43 45 46½ 48 Smith M E 117 3.70e 82-10 AlSbin117nkJustfortherecord1174¾JyG117 Saved ground 8
5Apr92- 6Aqu fst 1⅛ :491 1:142 1:524 3↑Alw 29000 84 5 2 21 2hd 12 11½ Krone J A 110 *.80 72-30 UncsChief1101½PrderGold1164¾MyFrindBrni124 Driving 7
13Mar92- 7Aqu fst 1⅛ :482 1:13 1:523 Alw 29000 85 5 5 31 2½ 2½ 22 Gryder A T 119 2.90 71-32 CorruptConcl1172UncsChf1191½HopforGold117 Gamely 7
29Feb92- 3GP fst 1⅛ :474 1:131 1:521 Md Sp Wt 78 3 3 42 31½ 31 11 Krone J A 120 *.70 76-16 UncsChif1201NorthrnDcison1201PrsdntGs120 Clear late 10
12Feb92- 4GP fst 1 1/16 :474 1:131 1:45 Md Sp Wt 68 6 4 62¼ 63¼ 44½ 36½ Krone J A 120 10.40 80-13 JstLkPrfct1204½ImprlGld1202UncsChf120 Lugged in str 10
LATEST WORKOUTS Nov 10 Bel 5f fst 1:011 B Nov 2 Bel 4f fst :493 B Oct 26 Bel 5f fst 1:013 H Oct 19 Bel 4f fst :483 B

Crafty Coventry

Ch. c. 3(May), by Crafty Prospector—Kate Coventry, by Viceregal
Br.—CBF Corporation (NY)
Tr.—Lundy Sarah A (4 0 0 1 .00)
MIGLIORE R (80 9 8 7 .11)
Own.—Edwards James F
115
Lifetime 13 2 1 6 $117,236
1992 9 1 1 4 $78,972
1991 4 1 0 2 $38,264
Turf 5 0 0 2 $17,766
Wet 3 0 1 1 $36,240

23Oct92- 8Aqu fm 1⅛ Ⓣ:483 1:121 1:491 3↑ⓈA T Cole H 75 8 8 88½ 88 810 816¼ Madrid A Jr 111 18.00 81-07 Forlibend1151¾EbonyMagic1141½Fourstardve120 Outrun 8
20Sep92- 5Bel fm 1 1/16 🅃:46 1:093 1:403 Torsion 88 3 4 45 42 21 32 Madrid A Jr 115 5.90 93-13 FrghtBll1171¾BnrLght119nkCrftCvntr115 Bid, weakened 4
14Sep92- 4Bel gd 1 1/16 🅃:473 1:114 1:433 Clm 100000 78 5 5 43½ 4¾ 31 44¾ Migliore R b 122 *1.20 75-14 Plmos114nkBllOfRghts1184¼StrghtForwrd112 Four wide 7
20Aug92- 5Sar gd 1 1/16 Ⓣ:461 1:093 1:404 3↑Alw 31000 91 1 4 54½ 52¾ 24 33¾ Migliore R b 112 11.90 86-17 Ghz1142Crnshw'sCrnr1191¾CrftyCvntry112 Lacked rally 7
5Aug92- 8Sar fst 1⅛ :474 1:113 1:494 ⓈAlbany H 84 7 3 31½ 31 2hd 44½ Migliore R b 114 16.70 83-12 OtfthRlm1141¾ⒹMntrlMrt122½BllOfRghts114 Chck late 9
5Aug92-Placed third through disqualification
18Jly92-10FL sly 1⅛ :464 1:13 1:532 ⓈNy Derby 92 7 6 58 55 22½ 22½ Nicol P A Jr b 112 85.30 78-21 MontrlMrty1192½CrftyCvntry11210OtfthRlm119 Rallied 10
26Jun92- 5Bel fst 6f :223 :443 1:091 3↑Alw 28000 82 4 3 47 33 21½ 34 Migliore R b 113 25.20 90-07 Corx1171Mephistophels1133CrftyCovntry113 Bid, wknd 5
17May92- 8Bel my 1 :453 1:10 1:352 ⓈMike Lee H 38 12 6 52½ 63½ 1115 1228¾ Migliore R b 113 35.70 64-23 MontrlMrty1182½Dtox1132¾RoylCormrnt112 Done early 12
23Apr92- 9Aqu gd 6f :224 :463 1:113 3↑ⓈAlw 27000 77 3 1 41½ 52 11 1hd Migliore R 113 4.30 83-12 CrftyCoventry113hdRlCilo1112¾KnightOnCll110 Driving 11
4Nov91- 8Aqu fm 1 Ⓣ:462 1:122 1:373 ⓈDmonRnyon 74 6 8 911 63¾ 64½ 42 Migliore R 117 11.20 86-11 MontrelMrty117noBudgetCrisis1171¾JyGe122 Late gain 11
LATEST WORKOUTS Nov 14 Bel tr.t 4f fst :483 H Oct 20 Bel 5f fst 1:022 B Oct 14 Bel 7f fst 1:294 B Oct 6 Bel 5f fst 1:004 B

Rockford

Ch. c. 3(Feb), by Bucksplasher—Dedicated to B F, by Master Derby
Br.—Turesdale B A & Pamela (Fla)
Tr.—Toner James J (9 1 1 1 .11)
DAVIS R G (96 17 9 11 .18)
Own.—Kimram Stable
115
Lifetime 27 5 4 2 $83,116
1992 16 3 2 1 $57,658
1991 11 2 2 1 $25,458
Wet 9 4 1 1 $49,131

2Nov92- 5Aqu fst 6f :223 :452 1:101 Clm 45000 90 3 1 1½ 1½ 11½ 12½ Davis R G b 113 5.00 90-18 Rockford1132½CaseStudy117½OceanSplsh117 Drfted drv 7
11Oct92- 2Bel gd 6f :221 :451 1:103 Clm 50000 80 1 1 1½ 1hd 2½ 42¾ Bailey J D b 117 14.20 84-18 PerlssPrformr117nkYros1171½GotchLst117 Dueled, tired 8
27Sep92- 2Bel my 6f :22 :444 1:092 Clm 70000 39 3 2 2hd 44 611 620½ Bailey J D b 113 *1.10 72-14 Hwk'sFlm1142½GtchLst1131¾LrdWllstn113 Dueled, tired 6
11Sep92- 1Bel sly 6f :22 :444 1:101 Clm 70000 87 1 1 2hd 1½ 12 21¼ Davis R G b 113 3.30 88-10 BnAl'sRllh1171½Rockford1133RoscommnPrd113 Gamely 6
11Sep92-Originally scheduled on turf
30Aug92- 4Sar fst 6f :221 :45 1:09 3↑Alw 28000 58 4 4 72¾ 53 66 615¾ Bailey J D b 112 15.70 83-08 BorderCat1129CseStudy1121TheGretM.B.112 No factor 7
25Jun92- 1Bel my 6f :22 :45 1:10 Clm 50000 88 5 2 1½ 11½ 13½ 13 Bailey J D b 117 3.40 90-09 Rockford1173RomanChorus117nkPayforPlay117 Driving 7
13Jun92- 3Bel fst 6f :221 :453 1:103 Clm 70000 73 3 2 2½ 2hd 53¼ 69¼ Bailey J D b 113 6.10 78-18 IrshDmn113½PrlssPrfrmr1133RmnChrs115 Dueled, tired 6
1Jun92- 6Bel sly 6f :22 :444 1:093 3↑Alw 28000 48 4 5 43½ 56 59 519¼ McMahon H I7 b 105 *1.00 73-13 Tlc'sBd1174LItrLIt1175¼RchrdOfEnglnd112 Broke slow 5
1Jun92-Awarded fourth purse money
10May92- 5Bel sly 6f :221 :444 1:092 Clm 50000 98 7 2 1hd 1½ 12 13 Bailey J D b 117 5.40 93-12 Rockford1173AlienShore1134HighestLevl106 Drew clear 8
27Apr92- 5Aqu fst 6f :213 :441 1:101 Clm 70000 63 4 7 31 44½ 59 613 Santos J A b 114 6.70 77-14 UnrelMot1137¼LitheFntsy1131¼WinningForce115 Faded 7
LATEST WORKOUTS Nov 12 Bel tr.t 4f fst :501 B ●Oct 29 Bel 3f fst :342 H ●Oct 23 Bel tr.t 5f fst 1:014 H Oct 7 Bel tr.t 4f fst :49 B

Midnight Sunny Ch. g. 4, by Sunny North—Glorious Evening, by Jig Time
CORPES M A (5 0 0 0 .00) Br.—Big C Farms (Fla)
Own.—Fabjac Stables Tr.—Marti Carlos (2 0 0 0 .00) 117
Lifetime 28 6 8 3 $86,997 | 1992 5 2 2 0 $22,420 | 1991 11 2 3 3 $40,720 | Turf 1 0 0 0 | Wet 4 2 2 0 $24,230

6Nov92- 2Aqu my 7f :23 :461 1:253 3↑Clm c-14000 15 76 6 1 2½ 1hd 1hd 1hd Velazquez J R b 117 *1.30 77-18 MdnghtSnny117hdMrThnElt113¾TwrOfTrsrs119 Driving 7
6Nov92-Claimed from Andy Mart Stable, Figueroa Carlos R Jr Trainer
12Oct92- 1Bel my 6f :22 :45 1:084 3↑Clm 25000 81 3 2 21 2hd 23 27½ Velazquez J R b 117 4.00 88-09 Wrgod1157½MidnightSunny117nkAncintSuc110 2nd best 6
21Sep92- 9Bel fst 6f :221 :452 1:11 3↑Clm 14000 87 3 9 21 1hd 1½ 13 Velazquez J R b 117 *2.40 85-18 MidnightSunny1173NobleOffic115hdWlkonir119 Driving 9
2Sep92- 2Bel fst 6f :22 :451 1:102 3↑Clm 14000 81 4 2 31½ 1½ 1½ 2½ Velazquez J R b 117 3.10 87-15 NobleOffice113½MidnightSunny117¾Wlkonir117 Gamely 10
10Jly92- 1Bel fst 6f :222 :45 1:094 Clm c-35000 73 2 1 32 44 78½ 710½ Santos J A b 117 10.80 80-11 Reappeal1172¾ Talc's Bid1171 Two Eagles117 Tired 7
10Jly92-Claimed from Maynard Robert, Kimmel John C Trainer
23Nov91- 5Aqu gd 6f :22 :451 1:101 3↑Alw 28000 88 1 7 1½ 1hd 1hd 41½ Santos J A b 115 15.70 88-14 SllsCrr115noCrrsPlsr1151½RdHtRd115 Dueled weakened 8
31Oct91- 8Aqu fst 6f :223 :461 1:104 3↑Alw 28000 74 4 2 42 42 66 68¾ Velazquez J R b 114 11.00 78-19 ShiningBid114¾RedHotRed1141¾MichelMunyk114 Tired 8
7Oct91- 7Bel fst 6f :222 :451 1:10 3↑Alw 28000 87 1 1 2½ 1hd 31 32¾ Santos J A b 114 6.90 87-11 SngsAccnt114¾ShllsChrmr1142MdnhtSnn114 Weakened 7
16Aug91- 5Sar fst 7f :222 :443 1:222 Clm 72500 86 5 3 3½ 33½ 31 34¾ Santos J A b 115 *2.10 88-11 DvddDcd1174Pnn'sBck113¾MdnghtSnn115 Lacked rally 7
7Aug91- 1Sar fst 6f :222 :453 1:094 Clm 50000 97 3 4 1½ 11 11½ 12 Santos J A b 117 6.30 95-09 MidnightSunny1172FortyHells1133Chels'sPt113 Driving 7
LATEST WORKOUTS Oct 27 Aqu 3f fst :363 H

Permit B. c. 3(Apr), by Imperial Fling—Logiealmond, by Master Derby
ROMERO R P (71 6 10 8 .08) Br.—Shields Joseph V Jr (Fla)
Own.—Shields Joseph V Jr Tr.—Galluscio Dominic G (11 0 2 2 .00) 115
Lifetime 18 3 5 1 $73,976 | 1992 15 3 3 0 $66,576 | 1991 3 M 2 1 $7,400 | Wet 4 0 0 0 $4,836

8Nov92- 1Aqu fst 1 :47 1:113 1:37 Clm 50000 13 79 8 1 1hd 1½ 1½ 2¾ Romero R P 117 9.40 76-24 Danzig's Dance117¾ Permit117no WildDante106 Gamely 9
25Oct92- 9Aqu fst 7f :23 :464 1:25 3↑Alw 28000 75 10 1 2½ 1½ 3½ 95¼ Krone J A b 114 8.30 75-19 RomnChors114hdAncntSc117½BoldlyDn116 Dueled, tired 11
10Oct92- 1Bel my 6f :22 :442 1:082 Gulch 72 6 5 56 58 58½ 412¼ Migliore R b 115 24.40 86 — Detox1153¾ Belong to Me1225½ BorderCat119 No threat 6
27Sep92- 2Bel my 6f :22 :444 1:092 Clm 75000 79 6 3 54 34 35½ 45 Migliore R b 117 5.70 88-14 Hwk'sFlm1142¾GolchLst1131¾LordWllstn113 Lk'd rally 6
19Aug92- 9Sar my 7f :221 :443 1:233 3↑Alw 28000 59 6 3 2hd 2½ 94½ 811¾ Migliore R b 113 10.00 75-17 Keratoid112nkBorderCat112½Prioritizer112 Steadied str 10
19Aug92-Placed seventh through disqualification
7Aug92- 9Sar fst 6f :214 :443 1:10 3↑Alw 28000 72 10 4 62 41¾ 42 86¼ Migliore R b 113 5.30 88-10 RnsGrsn1121½RchrdOfEnlnd112hdMnR112 Flattened out 11
6Jun92- 2Bel my 1⅛ :451 1:092 1:413 3↑Affirmed 91 2 1 13 12 22½ 68 Pezua J M b 109 22.50 86-08 MchllCnPss1195Isn'tThtSpcl115hdFrllW115 Speed, tired 8
21May92- 4Bel fst 7f :222 :453 1:223 Clm 70000 95 3 4 23 1hd 12½ 12¾ Migliore R b 113 14.40 91-16 Permit1132¾ Polonium1132½ Roman Chorus113 Driving 7
29Mar92- 1Aqu fst [illegible] Alw 28000 61 3 2 2hd 3½ 49½ 415¾ Migliore R b 117 2.80 78-17 BlongtoM1178¾RomnChors1172TrDtch117 Dueled inside 4
21Mar92- 8Aqu gd 7f :22 :443 1:213 Bay Shore [illegible] Rojas R I b 114 60.30 80-11 ThreePet1143¼Goldwler117noBstDcortd114 Bobbled brk 10
21Mar92-Grade II
LATEST WORKOUTS Nov 6 Bel 3f sly :363 B Nov 2 Bel tr.t 4f fst :49 B Oct 20 Bel 4f fst :50 B Oct 7 Bel 4f fst :503 B

Real Cielo Ch. c. 3(Mar), by Conquistador Cielo—Lady Calpurnia, by Proudest Roman
BAILEY J D (70 14 15 15 .20) Br.—Stephens Lucille E (NY)
Own.—Stephens Lucille E Tr.—Stephens Woodford C (3 0 0 0 .00) 115
Lifetime 20 3 6 0 $93,920 | 1992 15 2 6 0 $79,240 | 1991 5 1 0 0 $14,680 | Turf 2 0 0 0 $180 | Wet 4 1 1 0 $25,240

6Nov92- 1Aqu my 6f :221 :452 1:10 3↑Alw 28000 23 53 1 4 55 55 54½ 415½ Migliore R 115 2.20 75-18 Prepornt1153½StrtFight1152CrriedInterst120 No threat 5
25Oct92- 9Aqu fst 7f :23 :464 1:25 3↑Alw 28000 14 82 1 11 64½ 52½ 52 41¾ Perret C 114 *2.60 78-19 RomnChors114hdAncntSc117½BldlyDn116 Broke slowly 11
15Oct92- 8Bel fst 6f :223 :453 1:101 3↑Alw 28000 82 6 5 53 5¾ 2hd 21 Maple E 114 2.90 88-15 DcisionMkr1171RlCilo114noBnAl'sRullh114 Up for place 7
8Oct92- 7Bel fst 1 :46 1:11 1:363 3↑Alw 31000 88 6 6 52¾ 41½ 21 22¼ Maple E 114 5.30 85-13 PrivtTrsurr1142¼RlCilo1141½SprklingSky114 Rlld inside 8
27Sep92- 8Bel sly 7f :224 :46 1:240 [illegible] 73 3 9 86½ 62½ 72¾ 76¼ Maple E 111 3.80 76-14 ArgylLk113nkWhAlng110noMjsty'sTm114 Steadied early 9
10Sep92- 8Bel sly 7f :224 :454 1:224 3↑Alw 28000 87 1 6 65½ 33 23 22¼ Maple E 111 *1.50 87-17 CseStudy1132¾RlCilo1131¼RomnChorus113 Up for place 7
27Aug92- 3Sar gd 7f :23 :454 1:23 Clm 75000 91 6 2 64¾ 33 1hd 13 Maple E 112 5.70 90-12 RelCielo112[illegible] Wide drv 6
10Aug92- 1Sar fst 1 :454 1:102 1:362 Clm 70000 86 3 4 43 41½ 32 4nk Antley C W 115 10.50 — — BurdrCt117nkRomnChrs113hdWdnWgn117 Carried wide 6
1Aug92- 1Sar my 1 :453 1:104 1:381 3↑ⓈAlw 29000 76 2 3 22½ 21 2½ 1¾ Maple E 112 *.60 — — RelCielo112¾Drminthdywy1173InnrTruth117 Hard drive 8
[illegible] fst 6f :224 :462 1:103 3↑ⓈAlw 27000 74 7 7 52½ 3½ 52¼ 41¾ Maple E 111 *.70 85-15 JinglIc1111TmmyTwo106¾MorThnElt117 Checked, wide 7
LATEST WORKOUTS Nov 14 Bel 4f fst [illegible] Nov 1 Bel 4f sly :503 B Oct 23 Bel 4f fst :482 B Oct 13 Bel 4f fst :483 B

On Beyer, it appeared as though it would take a figure in the range of 90 to win this race. Hope Us, the 8–5 favorite, had run a 94 at six furlongs on October 26; Rockford had run a 90 last out; Uncas Chief, Midnight Sunny, and Real Cielo regularly ran in the mid-80s.

Permit had run figures of 95 and 91 in May and June before going to the shelf for two months. Those figures were good enough to make him a contender at 6–1, but what were his chances of running back to that level today?

Conditions for such a recovery were good, judging from his pattern on Beyer and *Thoro-graph:* Permit recorded a Beyer of 79 making his first start in five weeks, regressed to a 72 and a 75, but then ran the telltale 79 on November 8. His *Thoro-graph* sheet revealed a nearly identical cycle — a 13½, which was three and a half points off his career best of 10, followed by a pair of 16s and the key figure of 13¼ on November 8, a figure that indicated Permit was now very likely to improve:

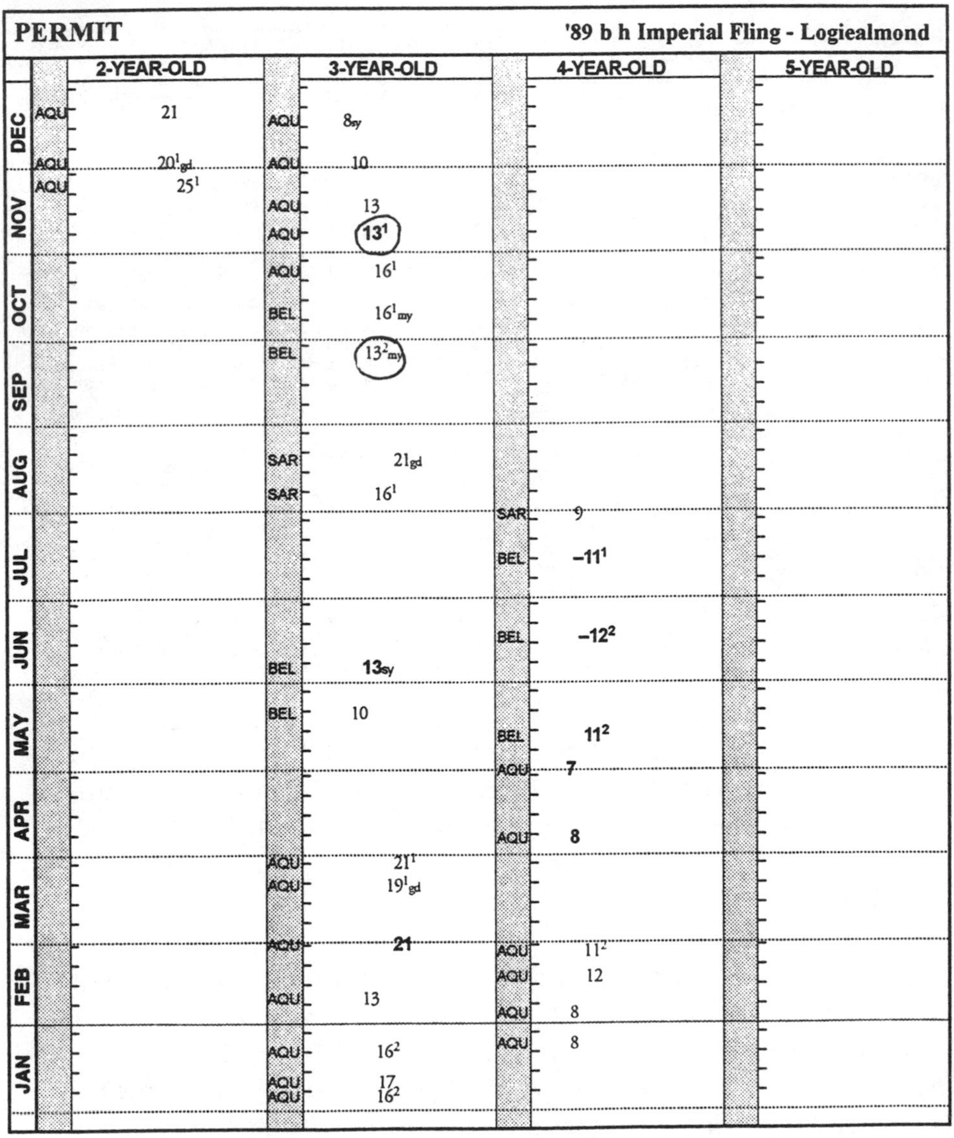

PERMIT
'89 b h Imperial Fling - Logiealmond
2-YEAR-OLD
3-YEAR-OLD
4-YEAR-OLD
5-YEAR-OLD
DEC
NOV
OCT
SEP
AUG
JUL
JUN
MAY
APR
MAR
FEB
JAN

Off this line, Permit ran another 13, which was good enough to win the race, and then went on to a productive winter campaign, winning several more times at ascending class levels while working his way to three consecutive 8s and ultimately a 7 in late April:

FIFTH RACE
Aqueduct
NOVEMBER 18, 1992

6 ½ FURLONGS. (1.15) ALLOWANCE. Purse $28,000. 3–year–olds and upward which have never won two races other than Maiden, Claiming or Starter. Weight: 3–year–olds 120 lbs. Older 122 lbs. Non–winners of a race other than Maiden or Claiming since November 1 allowed 3 lbs. Of such a race since October 15, 5 lbs.

Value of race $28,000; value to winner $16,800; second $6,160; third $3,360; fourth $1,680. Mutuel pool $172,403. Exacta Pool $348,582

Last Raced	Horse	M/Eqt.	A.	Wt	PP	St	¼	½	Str	Fin	Jockey	Odds $1
8Nov92 ^{1}Aqu^{2}	Permit		3	115	6	1	$3^{1\frac{1}{2}}$	$2^{1\frac{1}{2}}$	$2^{2\frac{1}{2}}$	1^{1}	Romero R P	6.40
2Nov92 ^{5}Aqu^{1}	Rockford	b	3	115	4	6	$1^{\frac{1}{2}}$	$1^{\frac{1}{2}}$	1^{hd}	$2^{1\frac{3}{4}}$	Davis R G	4.30
6Nov92 ^{1}Aqu^{4}	Real Cielo		3	115	7	3	$5^{\frac{1}{2}}$	4^{1}	$3^{\frac{1}{2}}$	$3^{\frac{3}{4}}$	Bailey J D	2.70
23Oct92 ^{8}Aqu^{8}	Crafty Coventry		3	115	3	4	7	$6^{\frac{1}{2}}$	4^{2}	$4^{1\frac{1}{2}}$	Migliore R	5.00
8Nov92 ^{7}Aqu^{4}	Hope Us		4	117	1	5	$6^{\frac{1}{2}}$	7	5^{hd}	$5^{2\frac{1}{2}}$	Madrid A Jr	1.60
6Nov92 ^{2}Aqu^{1}	Midnight Sunny	b	4	117	5	2	$4^{\frac{1}{2}}$	$5^{\frac{1}{2}}$	6^{6}	6^{15}	Corpes M A	26.80
19Aug92 ^{9}Sar^{10}	Uncas Chief	b	3	115	2	7	2^{1}	$3^{\frac{1}{2}}$	7	7	Smith M E	22.20

OFF AT 2:17 Start good for all but UNCAS CHIEF and ROCKFORD, Won driving. Time, :23^{4}, :47^{1}, 1:11^{3}, 1:18^{1} Track fast.

$2 Mutuel Prices:			
6–(F)–PERMIT	14.80	7.40	4.20
4–(D)–ROCKFORD		6.00	3.80
7–(G)–REAL CIELO			2.80

$2 EXACTA 6–4 PAID $67.80

B. c, (Apr), by Imperial Fling—Logiealmond, by Master Derby. Trainer Galluscio Dominic G. Bred by Shields Joseph V Jr (Fla).

PERMIT, well place early, made a run three wide to challenge on the turn, battled outside ROCKFORD into midstretch then edged clear under brisk urging. ROCKFORD, infractious in the gate prior to the start, broke slowly then stumbled leaving the gate, checked slightly between horses then rushed up to duel for the early advantage; shook off UNCAS CHIEF on the turn, battled gamely inside the winner through the lane then yielded grudgingly. REAL CIELO, reserved early, lodged a mild rally from outside on the turn but couldn't gain on the top two through the lane. CRAFTY COVENTRY, outrun for a half, failed to threaten with a mild late rally from outside. HOPE US saved ground to no avail. MIDNIGHT SUNNY was never a factor. UNCAS CHIEF rushed up along the rail after breaking slowly, dueled along the inside to the turn then gave way. UNCAS CHIEF wore two bar shoes. MIDNIGHT SUNNY raced with an aluminum pad on.

Owners— 1, Shields Joseph V Jr; 2, Kimram Stable; 3, Stephens Lucille E; 4, Edwards James F; 5, Jewel-E Stable; 6, Fabjac Stables; 7, Prew Brian M.

Trainers— 1, Galluscio Dominic G; 2, Toner James J; 3, Stephens Woodford C; 4, Lundy Sarah A; 5, Ferriola Peter; 6, Marti Carlos; 7, Reid Mark J.

A month after Permit's win of November 18, another recovery-line opportunity presented itself in the form of World Contender.

World Contender ran an 11 in October of his three-year-old season and went to the shelf for nearly a year two starts later. He ran a 14½ in his second start back, circled back around to a 14 three starts later (winning for a $12,000 tag on December 9), and then improved to an 11½, scoring a repeat victory off a double jump up the claiming ladder at 7–1.

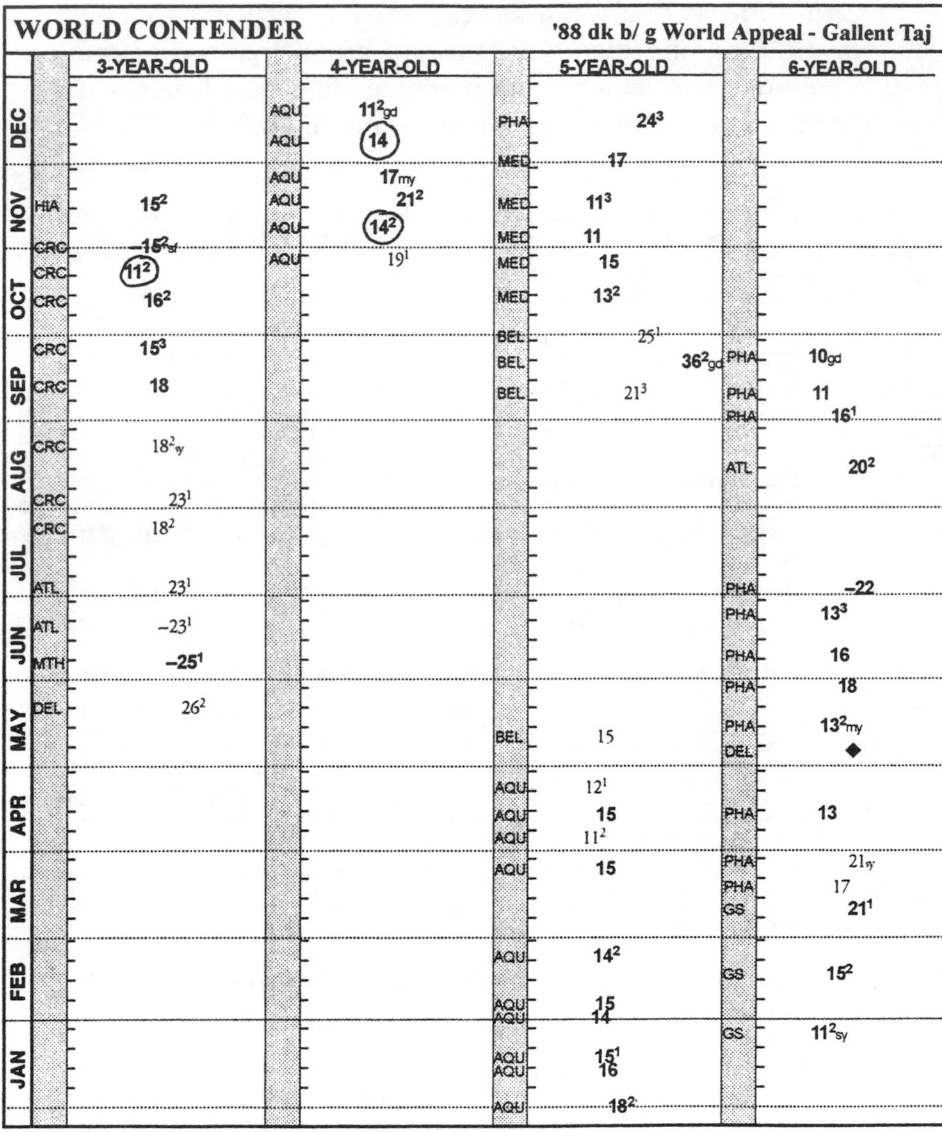

THE BOUNCE

One of the main tenets of form-cycle analysis holds that comparing a horse to itself is as important as comparing it with the rest of the field. This was Len Ragozin's first major contribution to handicapping theory.

When a three-year-old with an explosive pattern along the lines of, say, Itaka in the Gotham Stakes is going off at a big price, I will not hesitate to bet it right off a career-best figure, provided the breakthrough move was a small one and the horse hasn't been entered back on unusually short rest. Conversely, there should be no hesitation in taking a position against overbet horses that have just run a number that figures to set them back. Although even the most casual handicappers are by now aware of the bounce phenomenon, most still rate a horse solely on its most recent race, with little regard to the havoc a sudden overexertion might wreak.

Horses that have just run a speed figure many lengths superior to anything they've previously run are eligible to be muscle-sore and physically drained from the effort; if they are run back too soon, they often show these ill effects with a subpar performance, and this is known as "bouncing" off a big figure. Statistically speaking, sprinters are more susceptible to a bounce than routers; fillies are likelier to bounce than colts; cheap horses are likelier to bounce than their classier counterparts.

As a cheap filly claiming sprinter, For the Queen had three strikes against her when she backed up badly through the stretch as the 5–2 favorite on July 23:

1 For the Queen PP - 1
Own: Joques Farm
SANTOS J A (47 7 5 6 .15)

B. m. 5
Sire: Bellevue the Queen (Believe It)
Dam: Danzitup (Danzig)
Br: duPont Mrs Richard C (Md)
Tr: Moschera Gasper S (7 1 2 1 .14)

117

Lifetime Record:	10	3	1	0	$35,130						
1993	2	0	1	0	$3,850	Turf	0	0	0	0	
1992	3	1	0	0	$11,990	Wet	1	0	0	0	$180
Sar	0	0	0	0		Dist	0	0	0	0	

Entered 6Aug93- 2 SAR

23Jly93- 9Bel fst	7f	:231	:463	1:114	1:25		ⒻClm c-22500	54	1	3	11	1hd	53½	511¼	Rojas R I	115	*2.60	67-17	Jackie P.1191½ All Too Well1122 Fortune Wand1152½	Used in pace 9
Claimed from Bohemia Stable, Jerkens H Allen Trainer																				
12Jly93- 2Bel fst	6f	:223	:452	:572	1:094		ⒻClm 25000	77	7	7	32	21	21	22½	Rojas R I	117	3.50	88-10	BiddyMullign1172½ ForTheQueen1172 GettingAroundtoIt117no	Held place 7
21Aug92- 6Lrl fst	6f	:224	:461	:582	1:102	3↑	ⒻAlw 20800	44	7	4	53½	44	68	615¾	Chavez S N	117	2.90e	73-16	Rollicking Dolly1125¾ Salute theGirl1132¾ StarlightSurprise114	Fell back 7
6Jun92-10Mth my	6f	:213	:443	:572	1:11	3↑	ⒻAlw 18000	51	5	2	23	42¾	55½	510	Wilson R	116	1.70	76-12	Sister Mac116¾ No White116nk Special Vice116	Outrun 6
5Jan92- 9Lrl fst	1 1/16	:233	:473	1:122	1:442		ⒻAlw 19000	85	3	1	1½	13	15	17	Saumell L	114	*1.70	91-17	For the Queen1147 Alanna1142 Herman's Match119	Driving 6
6Dec91- 6Lrl fst	6f	:221	:454	:583	1:111	3↑	Alw 16500	76	7	4	43	31½	11½	12	Wilson R	115	4.50	85-21	For the Queen1152 Desert Victress1152 Chrisappeal120	Driving 7
16Nov91- 8Lrl fst	6f	:22	:454	:59	1:12		ⒻAlw 16500	48	3	7	717	729	714	47	Wilson R	115	7.40	74-16	WinnstyPrincess1155 PerfectEscpe1151½ HerAssets117	Stumbled badly 7
1Nov91- 8Lrl fst	6½f	:223	:454	1:11	1:173		ⒻClm 25000	55	5	3	42½	43½	69½	810	Wilson R	114	6.50	79-19	Ameri Allen1144 Graceful Lil114¾ Saucy Bird114	Gave way 9
10May91- 8Pim fst	6f	:23	:462	:59	1:114		ⒻAlw 16500	67	1	3	2hd	1hd	2hd	55	Wilson R	113	2.90	81-15	Gold Rusher1142½ Graceful Lil112½ Cafe West114	Weakened 6
19Mar91- 4Pim fst	6f	:233	:48	1:01	1:133	3↑	ⒻMd 50000	65	4	4	42	64½	52¾	1hd	Wilson R	114	3.40	77-22	For the Queen114hd Maid of Glory109nk Creole114	Driving 8

WORKOUTS: Jly 10 Bel tr.t 4f fst :49 B 5/28 Jly 7 Bel 5f fst 1:002 H 6/33 Jun 30 Bel 6f fst 1:144 B 5/7 Jun 16 Bel tr.t 5f fst 1:053 B 4/4 Jun 11 Bel tr.t 4f fst :482 H 3/18

For the Queen is not exactly the Lou Gehrig of racing. Despite the fact that she was five years of age, her entire history is on display in these past performances because she'd only made it to the races ten times. She ran twice in the spring at age three and was laid off until November; she raced four times between November and January but was then shelved again for five months; she returned on June 6, didn't race again until late August, then vanished for nearly eleven more months before surfacing on July 12. For the Queen's profile is that of a horse unable to withstand the rigors of normal training — a horse with obvious problems. When she ran a 77 Beyer after nearly eleven months of inactivity, handicappers should've expected that effort to take a toll. Quite predictably, it did.

One of the most reliable bounce candidates is the European import that has just run a big race first time in the United States.

Lovely Bird was the even-money favorite in Aqueduct's third race on November 17 on the basis of a second-place finish in her U.S. unveiling:

8 Lovely Bird
PP - 9
Own: Brody Jerome
MIGLIORE R (84 14 10 18 .17)

Ch. f. 3 (Mar)
Sire: Arctic Tern (Sea-Bird)
Dam: Swift Gal (Little Current)
Br: Gallagher's Stud (NY)
Tr: Hushion Michael E (20 8 3 1 .40)

120

Lifetime Record :	3 M 2 1	$8,453		
1993	1 M 1 0	$5,500	Turf	0 0 0 0
1992	2 M 1 1	$2,953	Wet	0 0 0 0
Aqu	1 0 1 0	$5,500	Dist	0 0 0 0

23Oct93- 5Aqu fst 6f :23^{1} :47 :59^{2} 1:12^{1} 3↑ Ⓕ Md Sp Wt 75 5 5 5$^{2\frac{1}{4}}$ 3$^{1\frac{1}{2}}$ 3^{2} 2$^{1\frac{1}{4}}$ Migliore R 119 f 3.60 80-22 Prospect Pleases119$^{1\frac{1}{4}}$ LovelyBird119^{nk} ChangeTheTune119^{6} Good effort 7

20Oct92 ♦ Chester(GB) yl *6f Ⓣ LH 1:22^{3} Ⓕ Alw 10500 2$^{\frac{3}{4}}$ Roberts M 120 3.00 Hung Parliament128$^{\frac{3}{4}}$ Lovely Bird120$^{1\frac{1}{2}}$ Heathyards Gem128^{20} 6
Tr: Michael Bell Queensferry Graduation Stakes *Well placed,led ovr 2f out,drifted right 1f out,one-paced to line*

2Oct92 ♦ Goodwood(GB) gd 6f Ⓣ Str 1:15^{4} Ⓕ Maiden 9100 3^{6} Hills M 123 4.00 Bright Spells123^{2} Ballet Shoes123^{4} Lovely Bird123$^{1\frac{1}{2}}$ 10
Isle of Wight Maiden Stakes *Always prominent, clear run 2f out, outpaced final furlong*

WORKOUTS: Nov 10 Bel 5f fst 1:00^{4} H *8/34* Oct 15 Bel tr.t 5f fst 1:03^{2} B *6/7* Oct 8 Bel 5f fst 1:01^{1} H *5/26* Sep 25 Bel tr.t 5f fst 1:03 B *18/30* Sep 9 Bel 4f fst :48^{4} Bg *10/48* Sep 1 Bel 4f fst :47^{4} H *8/40*

9 Manila Lila
PP - 10
Own: Wilson Charles T Jr
ALVARADO F T (85 7 13 10 .08)

B. f. 3 (Mar)
Sire: Manila (Lyphard)
Dam: Verbality (Verbatim)
Br: Brant Peter & Wilson Charles Jr (Ky)
Tr: Hernandez Ramon M (15 1 1 2 .07)

120

Lifetime Record :	5 M 2 1	$17,380			
1993	4 M 2 1	$15,940	Turf	0 0 0 0	
1992	1 M 0 0	$1,440	Wet	0 0 0 0	
Aqu	2 0 1 0	$7,440	Dist	1 0 1 0	$5,940

4Nov93- 9Aqu fst 1 :23^{2} :46^{4} 1:12^{3} 1:39^{4} 3↑ Ⓕ Md Sp Wt 69 5 12 9$^{7\frac{3}{4}}$ 7$^{4\frac{1}{4}}$ 3$^{1\frac{1}{2}}$ 2^{nk} Alvarado F T 120 f 5.20 65-32 Key To The Peace113^{nk} Manila Lila120^{nk} Turk's Flirt120$^{5\frac{3}{4}}$ Gamely 12

23Oct93- 5Aqu fst 6f :23^{1} :47 :59^{2} 1:12^{1} 3↑ Ⓕ Md Sp Wt 59 6 4 7$^{4\frac{1}{4}}$ 6^{5} 4^{8} 4$^{7\frac{1}{2}}$ Alvarado F T 119 3.90 73-22 Prospect Pleases119$^{1\frac{1}{4}}$ Lovely Bird119^{nk} Change The Tune119^{6} No threat 7

29Sep93- 5Bel fst 6f :23^{1} :47^{3} :59^{2} 1:11^{2} 3↑ Ⓕ Md Sp Wt 58 4 4 6$^{3\frac{3}{4}}$ 3^{2} 4$^{5\frac{1}{2}}$ 3$^{11\frac{1}{2}}$ Alvarado F T 118 f 4.20 71-19 Option Contract118^{11} Slip Lane118$^{\frac{1}{2}}$ Manila Lila118^{2} Four wide 7

6Sep93- 1Bel fst 6f :22^{4} :46^{2} :58^{3} 1:11^{2} 3↑ Ⓕ Md Sp Wt 59 7 5 3$^{1\frac{1}{2}}$ 2^{1} 2^{5} 2$^{7\frac{3}{4}}$ Sweeney K H 118 f 17.20 75-19 Gambler's Guaranty118$^{7\frac{3}{4}}$ Manila Lila118^{hd} Spike Heel118$^{1\frac{3}{4}}$ Held place 7

16Sep92- 7Bel fst 6f :22 :45^{3} :58^{2} 1:11^{4} Ⓕ Md Sp Wt 61 1 7 10^{11} 6$^{7\frac{1}{2}}$ 4^{4} 4$^{5\frac{1}{2}}$ Santiago A 117 35.10 75-18 Statuette117^{3} Black Medic117$^{2\frac{1}{2}}$ Raise a Carter117 Mild rally 11

WORKOUTS: Oct 11 Bel tr.t 4f fst :51 B *10/17* Sep 2 Bel tr.t 5f fst 1:04^{3} B *5/5* Aug 20 Sar 5f fst 1:02 Hg *18/24*

Lovely Bird is the kind of horse that attracts heavy support because the analysis seems easy: she ran a Beyer of 75 first time out, and none of her opponents has ever run a figure that matches it; where do we bet?

But if something looks too good to be true from a cursory glance at the past performances, then it probably is. Lovely Bird had been idle for a full year — presumably due to injury — and was hard-pressed to try for the win on October 23. It was probable she'd be muscle-sore following that stressful exertion, and she was now being asked to stretch from six furlongs to the unchartered waters of a flat mile.

Manila Lila, meanwhile, had finished six lengths behind Lovely

Bird when they met on October 23, but she had since defeated several of today's rivals with an improved Beyer of 69 when stretched to a mile on November 4. Manila Lila had now raced three times at six furlongs and once at a mile since she had returned from *her* layoff, which gave her ample conditioning foundation; she figured to run at least as well in her second attempt at the mile.

Manila Lila won by four widening lengths at 9–1, while Lovely Bird expired after pressing the early pace and beat one horse:

THIRD RACE **1 MILE. (1.32²) MAIDEN SPECIAL WEIGHT. Purse $27,000. Fillies and mares, 3-year-olds and upward. Weights: 3-year-olds, 120 lbs. Older, 122 lbs.**

Aqueduct

NOVEMBER 17, 1993

Value of Race: $27,000 Winner $16,200; second $5,940; third $3,240; fourth $1,620. Mutuel Pool $150,793.00 Exacta Pool $390,370.00

Last Raced	Horse	M/Eqt.	A.	Wt	PP	St	¼	½	¾	Str	Fin	Jockey	Odds $1
4Nov93 9Aqu2	Manila Lila	b	3	120	7	2	5½	6½	52	1hd	14	Alvarado F T	9.10
4Nov93 9Aqu5	Caro's Beauty		3	120	5	3	14	13	11½	22½	21½	Chavez J F	8.10
21Oct93 1Aqu2	Spike Heel		3	120	8	1	8	8	61	3hd	34	Smith M E	7.70
14Jly93 6Bel4	Cherub		3	120	2	7	2½	21	21	4½	4nk	Santos J A	7.90
4Nov93 9Aqu3	Turk's Flirt		3	120	4	5	4½	41½	3hd	51½	52	Bravo J	4.40
4Nov93 9Aqu4	Pigeon Pea	b	3	120	3	6	7hd	71	7½	61	64	Davis R G	13.90
23Oct93 5Aqu2	Lovely Bird	f	3	120	6	4	31	3hd	4½	74	75½	Migliore R	1.00
7Oct93 3Bel9	Kazumina	bf	3	115	1	8	6hd	5½	8	8	8	Leon F5	44.00

OFF AT 1:23 Start Good. Won driving. Time, :231, :47, 1:122, 1:383 Track fast.

$2 Mutuel Prices:			
9–(J)–MANILA LILA	20.20	8.40	4.00
6–(G)–CARO'S BEAUTY		10.40	6.00
10–(K)–SPIKE HEEL			4.80

$2 EXACTA 9–6 PAID $185.40

B. f, (Mar), by Manila–Verbality, by Verbatim. Trainer Hernandez Ramon M. Bred by Brant Peter & Wilson Charles Jr (Ky).

MANILA LILA reserved for five furlongs, launched a rally four wide on the turn, then wore down CARO'S BEAUTY to win going away. CARO'S BEAUTY sprinted clear along the backstretch, raced uncontested on the lead into the stretch, yielded to the winner in midstretch then held well for the place. SPIKE HEEL trailed for a half, then closed late from outside to best the others. CHERUB away a bit slowly, moved up along the inside, made a run to threaten on the turn but couldn't sustain her rally. TURK'S FLIRT settled just behind the early leaders, waited briefly for room while saving ground on the turn, angled out in upper stretch then lacked the needed response when called upon. PIGEON PEA was never a factor. LOVELY BIRD stalked the leaders from outside to the turn and lacked a further response. KAZUMINA was never a factor after breaking slowly, CARO'S BEAUTY, LOVELY BIRD and KAZUMINA wore mud caulks.

Owners— 1, Wilson Charles T Jr; 2, Jayaraman Kalarikkal K; 3, Bethel Cross Farm; 4, Andrews Edwin C; 5, Dennis Vicky G; 6, Vliettown; 7, Brody Jerome; 8, Hannah Gerald E

Trainers—1, Hernandez Ramon M; 2, Zito Nicholas P; 3, Bush Thomas M; 4, Arnold George R II; 5, Kelly Patrick J; 6, Kelly Michael J; 7, Hushion Michael E; 8, Terracciano Neal

Scratched— Tell Capote (4Nov93 9AQU6), Silly's Philly (21Oct93 1AQU4), Turkey Wing (5Nov93 3AQU4)

Even seasoned stakes-class runners that have been racing regularly abroad are not immune to the Eurobounce. George Augustus was racing competitively in Germany in late summer, shipped over for the Turf Classic, and rallied mildly for third with a Beyer of 106. On the strength of that performance he was installed at 7–5 in the

Laurel Turf Cup two weeks later against five rivals that had been running considerably lower figures. He bounced a dozen points and finished a nonthreatening third:

George Augustus
Own: Darley Stud Mgmt Co Ltd

B. h. 5
Sire: El Gran Senor (Northern Dancer)
Dam: Surely Georgie's (Alleged)
Br: Mrs George G Proskauer (Ky)
Tr: Oxx John M (—)

122

Lifetime Record:	21 7 2 5	$559,379			
1993	7 1 1 3	$244,193	Turf	21 7 2 5	$559,379
1992	3 1 0 0	$80,832	Wet	0 0 0 0	
Bel	0 0 0 0		Dist	0 0 0 0	

24Oct93-10Lrl	gd	1½ ⓣ	:521 1:182 2:082 2:322 3+	Lrl Turf CupG3	94	2 6 67 56 45½ 32½	Roberts M	123 b	*1.40	85-16	Square Cut1191¾ Wesaam119¾ George Augustus1231¼	Slow start	6
9Oct93-7Bel	fm	1½ ⓣ	:512 1:163 2:044 2:281 3+	Turf ClassicG1	106	4 5 54 52¾ 42½ 32¾	Bailey J D	126 b	17.40	78-19	Apple Tree1262¼ Solar Splendor126½ George Augustus1261	Mild gain	5
5Sep93♦ BadenBaden(Ger)	gd	*1½ ⓣLH	2:281 3+	Stk 316000 Grosser Preis von Baden-G1		36¼	Roberts M	132	3.30	— —	Lando121nk Platini1326 George Augustus1323	Chased in 4th, lacked rally, one-paced last quarter	7
15Aug93♦ Gelsenkrchn(Ger)	sf	*1½ ⓣLH	2:36 3+	Stk 237000 Aral-Pokal-G1		1nk	Roberts M	132 b	13.50	— —	DGeorge Augustus132nk Monsun119hd Shrewd Idea119¾	Improved 4f out, led 150y out, lugged in late. DQ'd, placed 2nd	11
1Aug93♦ Munich(Ger)	sf	*1¼ ⓣLH	2:09 3+	Stk 292000 Bayerisches Zuchtrennen-G1		44½	Reid J	132 b	2.20	— —	Market Booster1281¾ Komtur1192 Hondo Mondo132¾	Reserved in 6th, lacked room 2f out, angled out, finished well	7
15Jun93♦ Ascot(GB)	yl	1¼ ⓣRH	2:083 3+	Stk 147000 Prince of Wales's Stakes-G2		41¼	Roberts M	131 b	*5.00	— —	Placerville116nk Urban Sea126¾ Emperor Jones116nk	Held up in 9th, rallied ovr 2f out, no late response under pressure	11
15May93♦ Curragh(Ire)	yl	1¼ ⓣRH	2:112 4+	Stk 75500 Tattersalls Gold Cup-G2		1no	Roberts M	127 b	12.00	— —	George Augustus127no Ezzoud1243½ Approach The Bench1242	Held up, rallied 2f out, lacked room 1f out, led near line	7
3Oct92♦ Hoppegarten(Ger)	gd	*1¼ ⓣRH	2:004 3+	Stk 366000 Prix Zino Davidoff-G3		67½	Reid J	133 b	*1.40	— —	Perpendicular1331¼ Arastou1203½ Goofalik133hd	Unhurried early, progress into 5th 3f out, one-paced late	11
20Sep92♦ Frankfurt(Ger)	gd	*1¼ ⓣLH	2:082 3+	Stk 134000 Team Trophy der Volksbanken-G2		12½	Reid J	129 b	2.70	— —	George Augustus1292½ Hell Driver129no Natiello1172	Mid-pack, 4th 3f out, rallied to lead 1f out, drew clear	7
14Mar92-11GP	fm	1⅛ ⓣ	:231 :47 1:103 1:402+ 3+	Ft Laudrl H 100k	91	1 11 1212 108¾ 109¼ 95¾	Bailey J D	115 b	4.20	— —	Now Listen1142 Slew The Slewor116no Stage Colony114	8 wide str	12

WORKOUTS: Oct 7 Bel ⓣ 4f fm :523 B (d) 17/17

At Belmont a week earlier, Brazany was favored in the Lawrence Realization off his U.S. debut — a fast-closing third at the Grade 1 level. Brazany's Beyer of 103 was superior to anything his rivals in the Realization had ever run, but it was Strolling Along, the second-best horse on figures, who won at 9–2, as Brazany took a 14-point nosedive to an 89:

Brazany
Own: Paulson Madeleine

B. c. 3 (Mar)
Sire: Strawberry Road (Whiskey Road)
Dam: Waffle's Lake (Kings Lake)
Br: Allen E Paulson (Ky)
Tr: Mott William I (—)

122

Lifetime Record:	9 1 1 3	$84,659			
1993	6 1 0 2	$71,031	Turf	9 1 1 3	$84,659
1992	3 M 1 1	$13,628	Wet	0 0 0 0	
Bel	0 0 0 0		Dist	0 0 0 0	

16Oct93-3Bel	sf	1½ ⓣ	:501 1:162 2:064 2:323	Lawrence ReaG3	89	1 5 52½ 52 73½ 75	Smith M E	113	*2.30	54-29	Strolling Along114¾ Scattered Steps1131 Noble Sheba114½	No late bid	12
29Aug93-8AP	sf	1¼ ⓣ	:481 1:134 1:404 2:083	Secretariat-G1	103	4 13 109¼ 611 56½ 31¼	Desormeaux K J	114	18.70	53-40	Awad1201¼ Explosive Red123no Brazany1141¼	Late bid	14
6Jun93♦ San Siro(Ity) Tr: Francois Boulin	gd	*1 ⓣRH	1:391 3+	Stk 120000 Premio Emilio Turati-G2		43¾	St-Martin E	119	8.70	— —	Culture Vulture126nk Prospective Ruler1291 Ventiquattrofogli1192½	5th into stretch 3f out, lacked rally	9
25Apr93♦ Longchamp(Fr)	sf	*1⅝ ⓣRH	2:182	Stk 80200 Prix Greffulhe-G2		57¾	Asmussen C	128	7.50	— —	Hunting Hawk1281½ Bigstone1281½ Talloires128¾	Chased in 5th, no rally, never a factor	6
16Mar93♦ Saint-Cloud(Fr)	gd	*1⅝ ⓣLH	2:201	Stk 37100 Prix Maurice Caillault(Listed)		32	Asmussen C	123	*1.50	— —	Fantastic Dream123½ Sawasdee1271½ Brazany1231½	Led to final 16th, outfinished	5
3Mar93♦ Evry(Fr)	sf	*1 ⓣLH	1:47	Maiden 30100 Prix de l'Ile aux Paveurs		12½	St-Martin E	128	3.50	— —	Brazany1282½ Demidoff1231½ St Edmond128nk	Settled towards rear, wide rally 2f out, led final furlong, driving	13
8Dec92♦ Saint-Cloud(Fr)	hy	*1 ⓣLH	1:57	Maiden 31600 Prix Prompt		22½	Head F	128	5.00	— —	Regency1282½ Brazany1281½ Extra Point1286	4th halfway, 6th 2f out, rallied into 2nd, never catching winner	15
11Nov92♦ Saint-Cloud(Fr)	hy	*1¼ ⓣLH	2:311	Maiden 31500 Prix Maurepas (Div 1)		31¼	Head F	128	5.70	— —	Epaphos128nk Cimarron Creek1281 Brazany1282	Unhurried in 7th, rallied 1f out, bid for lead 100y out, outfinished	12
26Aug92♦ Deauville(Fr)	hy	*1 ⓣRH	1:561	Mdn (FT)35000 Prix de Bonneville		515½	Head F	128	3.20	— —	Appliance1242½ Irish Prospector1282 River Erne1243	Close up in 4th, led briefly halfway, weakened 3f out	7

WORKOUTS: Oct 12 Bel ⓣ 5f fm 1:022 B (d) 1/2 Oct 7 Bel ⓣ 7f fm 1:334 B (d) 5/5 Aug 27 AP ⓣ 5f fm 1:07 B 1/1

Stagecraft returned from a fifty-week layoff with a sharp race in a classified allowance in his U.S. debut but bounced a dozen points as the odds-on choice in the Tidal Handicap:

Stagecraft-GB B. h. 6, by Sadler's Wells—Bella Colora, by Bellypha-Ir
Br.—Meon Valley Stud (GB)
Own.—Darley Stud Management Tr.—Mott William I (35 11 7 4 .31) **115**
Lifetime 16 5 3 6 $414,916 | 1993 2 1 0 1 $62,640 | 1992 3 0 1 1 $21,580 | Turf 16 5 3 6 $414,916

13Feb93-10GP fm 1⅛ Ⓣ:472 1:104 1:474 + 3↑Can Turf 103 10 3 34 33½ 32 1nk Bailey J D 112 3.90 93-12 Stagecraft-GB112nk Roman Envoy121½ Carterista114 10
13Feb93-Altered course upper stretch. Fully extended
30Jan93- 8GP fm *1⅛ Ⓣ 1:534 + Alw 29000 95 4 10 106¼ 62¼ 32 3nk Bailey J D 122 *1.10 77-23 ImALIDI112nkPdgnsPrms114hdStgcrft-GB122 Late rally 10
15Nov92- 8CD yl 1⅛ Ⓣ:483 1:122 1:491 3↑River City H 102 1 4 32 42 31½ 3½ Day P LB 114 3.70 89-10 Cozzn'sPrnc117noLotsPol118½Stgcrft-GB114 Hung late 8
19Oct92- 8Bel gd 1⅜ T:47 1:371 2:143 3↑Tidal H 89 7 5 42½ 31½ 53 77½ Bailey J D b 122 *.80 70-23 Rssr1142½HnrRjn1113TmfrLghtnng110 Lacked response 11
19Oct92-Grade II
7Oct92- 7Bel fm 1 1/16 T:473 1:11 1:404 3↑Alw 47000 101 5 5 42 42 22½ 2½ Bailey J D b 115 *.80 93-13 Thakib115½Stgecrft-GB1153¼WildCtrct115 Rallied wide 6
19Oct91♦2Newmarket(Eng) gd 1¼ 2:014 Ⓣ DubaiChampionStks(Gr1) 75¾ Cauthen S 129 12.00 — — Tel Quel 124½ Cruachan 124½ In The Groove126 Evenly 12
5Oct91♦3Longchamp(Fra) yl*1 3/16 2:04 Ⓣ Prix Dollar(Gr1) 3¾ Cauthen S 130 *.90 — — Wiorno121¾ Muroto128hd Stagecraft130 Prom, no gain 7
14Sep91♦3Leopardst'n(Ire) gd 1¼ 2:064 Ⓣ IrishChampionStk(Gr1) 36 Cauthen S 132 5.00 — — SvDncr1234 EnvrnmntFrnd1232 Stgcrft132 Bid,no gain 7
20Aug91♦3York(Eng) gd*1¼ 2:16 Ⓣ JuddmonteInternat'l(Gr1) 35½ Cauthen S 132 *.80 — — Trmon1322 QustForFm1323½ Stgcrft132 Rated,mild bid 6
6Jly91♦4Sandown(Eng) gd 1¼ 2:073 Ⓣ Coral-EclipseStks(Gr1) 2hd Cauthen S 133 *2.00 — — EnrnmntFrnd122hd Stcrft1337 Snlmr133 Led str,missed 7
LATEST WORKOUTS Mar 3 GP Ⓣ 4f fm :50 B (d) Feb 25 GP 5f fst 1:033 B Feb 10 GP Ⓣ 4f fm :532 B (d) Jan 27 GP 5f gd 1:03 B

When today's conditions are similar to those that previously have produced a bounce, play devil's advocate if the horse is a short price and assume history will repeat itself:

12 Fairy Garden PP - 2 B. m. 5
Sire: Lyphard (Northern Dancer)
Dam: Possible Mate (King's Bishop)
Own: Payson Virginia Kraft Br: Evans Edward P (Va)
PINCAY L JR (90 11 15 15 .12) Tr: Attfield Roger L (—) **L 123**
Lifetime Record: 28 9 2 2 $462,809
1993 7 4 0 0 $286,622 | Turf 27 9 2 2 $462,809
1992 11 4 0 1 $128,646 | Wet 0 0 0 0
SA Ⓣ 0 0 0 0 | Dist Ⓣ 2 1 0 0 $120,000

11Sep93- 8Bel sf 1¼ T :492 1:142 1:391 2:034 3↑ⒻFlowr Bwl H-G1 82 5 4 44 32½ 55½ 57¼ Smith M E 120 f 3.60 64-24 FarOutBeast111½ Dahlia'sDremer110½ LdyBlessington1183¾ Lacked rally 10
27Aug93- 8Sar fm 1⅜ Ⓣ :493 1:304 2:022 2:392 3↑Seneca H-G3 103 4 6 63 53½ 31 12½ Smith M E 114 f 3.80 97-12 Fairy Garden1142½ Summer Ensign115no Dr. Kiernan1202 Going away 9
31Jly93- 8WO fm 1⅛ Ⓣ :443 1:084 1:334 1:462 3↑ⒻWO Bd BC H-G2C 80 3 6 812 813 88½ 77 Seymour D J L 120 f 2.15 80 13 MyrtleIrene1151 ProminentFether114no DnceForDonn113no Showed little 8
14Jly93- 7Atl fm 1 3/16 Ⓣ :493 1:134 1:384 1:574 3↑ⒻMatchmaker-G2 91 6 7 44 32 2½ 1nk Smith M E L 120 f *1.00 71-21 FairyGrden120nk SrtogSource118hd Logn'sMist1183 Betw horses, driving 8
22Apr93- 8Kee fm 1⅛ Ⓣ :491 1:133 1:381 1:503 ⒻBewitch-G3 89 7 6 55 64 64¼ 42 Ramos W S L 122 f 2.80 82-16 Miss Lenora112nk Hero's Love117½ Radiant Ring1191½ 8
Wide,backstretch, no late threat
31Mar93-10GP fm 1½ Ⓣ :463 1:111 2:013 2:253 3↑ⒻOrchid H-G2 104 8 7 54½ 44½ 11½ 15 Ramos W S L 115 8.20 92-12 Fairy Garden1155 Rougeur115no Trampoli1151¾ Ridden out 14
10Mar93- 9GP fm 1⅜ Ⓣ :493 1:153 1:392 2:143 3↑ⒻVery One H50k 99 8 6 65½ 42 11 11 Ramos W S L 113 6.90 96-07 Fairy Garden1131 Trampoli1152¾ Tango Charlie1142 11
Ducked out twice from left handed whip driving
1Nov92- 7GP fm 1½ Ⓣ :492 1:144 2:031 2:267 + 3↑ⒻGaily Gly 250k 89 11 5 84½ 83½ 83¾ 83¾ Krone J A L 113 *3.80 85 — Rougeur1121½ Good To Dance-Ir1131½ Indian Chris-Br113 Steadied str 13
4Oct92- 8Bel fm 1⅜ T :491 1:134 1:38 2:133 3↑ⒻAthenia H-G3 97 2 3 42 41¾ 31½ 1hd Krone J A 112 6.00 83-17 Fairy Garden112hd Passagere du Soir-GB117¾ Seewillo113 Driving 5
12Sep92- 8Bel yl 1¼ T :474 1:12 1:367 2:01 3↑ⒻFlwr Bowl H-G1 90 8 5 56½ 53½ 65 66¾ Gryder A T 112 21.00 78-20 Christiecat1161½ Ratings1144½ Plenty Of Grace115 Lacked rally 9
WORKOUTS: Nov 3 WO tr.t 5f fst 1:03 B 7/17 Oct 20 WO 5f fst 1:023 B 13/23 Oct 14 WO Ⓣ 5f fm :59 H (d) 1/2 ●Oct 7 WO tr.t T 7f fm 1:264 H (d) 1/8 Sep 30 WO tr.t Ⓣ 6f gd 1:153 B (d) 2/5 Sep 22 WO tr.t Ⓣ 4f fm :492 B (

Fairy Garden bounced from a 104 to an 89 in the April 22 Bewitch when shortened in distance and saddled with seven more pounds than her most recent start. She finally climbed back to that level with a 103, beating males in the Seneca several months later, but bounced 21 points in the Flower Bowl . . . when shortened in distance and saddled with six additional pounds.

Wait for the Wind firmly established a "performance bounce" pattern during his five-year-old season. After running a career-best Beyer of 109, he turned in one of his worst races ever when brought back in three weeks for a Grade 3 stake. Two races removed from a freshening, Wait for the Wind uncorked a 105 at Saratoga on July 31, only to bounce to a 94 when brought back three weeks later at odds on.

Wait for the Wind rebounded with another 100-plus figure on

September 11. When he returned three weeks later and was installed at even money in a classified allowance on October 11, I was eager to bet against him — even more so after seeing his sheet:

Belmont Park

7 *7 Furlongs.* (1:20²) ALLOWANCE. Purse $40,000. 3-year-olds and upward, which have not won two races of $20,000 since November 1, 1992. Weights: 3-year-olds, 118 lbs. Older, 122 lbs. Non-winners of two races of $17,000 since July 1, allowed 3 lbs. Of such a race since then, 5 lbs. (Maiden, claiming, starter and restricted races not considered.)

7 START — 7 FURLONGS — FINISH

Coupled – Jacksonport and Roman Chorus

Jacksonport
Own: Garren Murray M
CHAVEZ J F (144 33 18 14 .23)

Dk. b or br c. 4
Sire: Vigors (Grey Dawn II)
Dam: On the Brink (Cox's Ridge)
Br: Loblolly Stable (Ky)
Tr: Garren Murray M (24 3 2 4 .13)

117

Lifetime Record: 54 7 6 10 $317,397
1993 19 0 2 4 $62,992 Turf 9 0 0 0 $1,860
1992 32 6 4 5 $244,025 Wet 5 1 0 2 $25,320
Bel 15 3 1 2 $86,800 Dist 3 1 0 1 $21,360

24Sep93- 8Bel gd 1 1/16 :232 :47 1:112 1:43 3↑ Handicap48k 78 5 2 31 41½ 55 516¼ Rojas R I 111 b 8.40 71-27 Brunswick1252 Sand Lizard1192½ Federal Funds1122½ Done early 6

16Sep93- 8Bel sly 1 1/16 ⊗ :222 :444 1:09 1:402 3↑ Alw 42000N$mY 80 5 5 511 59 311 319¼ Velasquez J 117 b 4.30 81-17 Say Dance1178¾ Binary Light11710 Jacksonport1174 No threat 5

8Sep93- 8Bel fst 1 1/16 :233 :47 1:103 1:41 3↑ Handicap46k 94 6 2 31 3½ 22 33¼ Velasquez J 114 b 5.20e 93-12 Liver Stand1153 Roman Chorus114¼ Jacksonport114nk Weakened 6

28Aug93- 8Sar fst 1⅛ :464 1:101 1:343 1:472 3↑ Whitney H-G1 89 1 1 14 2½ 56¼ 515¼ Rojas R I 107 b 32.10 84-06 Brunswick1123½ West By West115¾ Devil His Due1227½ Used in pace 7

12Aug93- 7Sar fst 1⅛ :473 1:114 1:364 1:493 3↑ Upset 50k 74 4 2 32 42 73¼ 912½ Rojas R I 117 b 23.90 75-13 Sand Lizard122¾ Supermec117nk Michelle Can Pass1171 Gave way 9

4Aug93- 5Sar fst 1⅛ :49 1:124 1:371 1:493 3↑ Alw 46000N$Y 82 5 5 42½ 3½ 23 37¼ Rojas R I 117 b 6.80 80-09 Baron De Vaux1176¼ Berkley Fitz1221 Jacksonport1171 Bid, tired 5

23Jly93- 8Bel fst 1 :232 :463 1:111 1:361 3↑ Handicap46k 78 3 3 31½ 42 44¼ 512¾ Chavez J F 111 b 4.00e 74-19 Federal Funds1102¾ Roman Chorus109¾ Dalhart1137 Gave way 6

4Jly93- 9Bel fst 1¼ :471 1:11 1:352 2:011 3↑ Suburban H-G1 103 7 3 21 42½ 41 54¼ Chavez J F 109 b 27.40 81-15 Devil His Due1211½ Pure Rumor110¾ WestByWest1162 Forced pace, tired 8

20Jun93- 6Bel fst 1⅛ :453 1:093 1:352 1:484 3↑ Handicap46k 81 2 5 53½ 55 46¼ 413¾ Chavez J F 113 b 10.10 71-15 Berkley Fitz1143 Key Contender1164¾ Bill Of Rights1226 No threat 6

6Jun93- 8Bel gd 1¼ Ⓣ :481 1:12 1:353 1:584 3↑ ET ManhattanG2 66 3 2 41½ 76¾ 715 822¾ Pezua J M 112 b 51.80 73-14 Star Of Cozzene118¾ Lure1247 Solar Splendor1122½ Done early 8

WORKOUTS: Aug 23 Sar 5f fst 1:011 H 7/20 Jly 31 Sar 3f fst :351 H 3/35 Jly 19 Bel 4f fst :492 H 29/77 ●Jly 2 Bel tr.t 4f fst :48 B 1/11

Game Wager
Own: Hauman Eugene E
MIGLIORE R (76 8 9 9 .11)

B. g. 5
Sire: Pass the Line (Pas Seul)
Dam: Miami Game (Crozier)
Br: Hooper Fred W (Fla)
Tr: Hushion Michael E (21 2 1 5 .10)

119

Lifetime Record: 50 15 4 6 $241,775
1993 9 5 1 0 $86,855 Turf 4 1 0 0 $10,895
1992 19 7 1 4 $113,590 Wet 5 1 1 1 $20,250
Bel 12 6 1 2 $104,650 Dist 13 6 1 1 $77,400

18Sep93- 4Bel sly 6f :222 :451 :57 1:092 3↑ Fall Hwgt H-G2 67 3 9 910 99½ 99¾ 916¼ Migliore R 129 f 7.70e 77-14 FlySoFree135½ DemalootDemashoot1261½ TkeMeOut1343 Bumped break 10

30Aug93- 6Sar fst 6f :222 :45 :564 1:09 3↑ Alw 40000N$Y 103 3 5 67 62 4½ 12½ Migliore R 117 f *1.60 97-06 Game Wager1172½ Strikany112no Detox1173½ Going away 6

19Aug93- 1Sar fst 6f :221 :444 :562 1:081 3↑ Clm 70000 101 7 4 64½ 43 42½ 11 Migliore R 115 f 2.30e 101-06 Game Wager1151 Quickest Blade113nk Reappeal108nk Driving 7

7Aug93- 2Sar gd 7f :224 :452 1:093 1:214 3↑ Clm 70000 99 1 4 42 53 1hd 1nk Migliore R 113 f 3.70 96-08 Game Wager113nk Senor Cielo1131½ Roman Chorus1138 Wide, driving 6

21Jly93- 8Bel fst 6f :224 :46 :574 1:10 3↑ Handicap40k 99 3 5 43½ 2½ 1hd 2½ Krone J A 110 f 4.00 89-14 Regal Conquest111½ Game Wager1107 Shining Bid118nk Sharp try 6

25Jun93- 6Bel fm 1 1/16 Ⓣ :24 :47 1:104 1:413 Clm 50000 92 8 1 11 1½ 12½ 12¼ Migliore R 117 f 3.50 88-09 DH Karmani117 DH Game Wager1172 Hudlam's Sidekick117nk Gamely 8

7Jun93- 2Bel fm 1 1/16 Ⓣ :223 :464 1:11 1:414 Clm 50000 92 5 4 2½ 1½ 11 2no Migliore R 117 f 10.50 87-19 Summer Senate113no D Game Wager1172 Hair House1133 Drifted in str 8

Disqualified and placed 6th

24May93- 6Bel fst 7f :222 :452 1:101 1:223 Clm 75000 85 4 7 64 72¾ 64¼ 49 Migliore R 113 f 2.60e 81-22 Look Ahead1161½ Drummond Lane1167½ Maraud106nk No threat 8

12May93- 2Bel fst 6f :223 :46 :58 1:101 Clm 35000 95 4 6 64½ 63 11½ 11¾ Migliore R 117 3.40 89-17 Game Wager1171¾ Two Eagles1175 Rockford1121½ Wide, drv 8

3Dec92- 5Aqu fst 6f ⊡ :231 :463 :581 1:103 3↑ Clm 50000 77 1 7 77 65 68 612¾ Migliore R 117 4.40 77-20 Fabersham1145 Jolies Appeal1171¾ Track Rebel117nk No factor 7

WORKOUTS: Sep 13 Bel 4f fst :51 B 35/43 Jly 16 Bel 3f fst :36 H 3/14

Roman Chorus
Own: Garren Murray M
CHAVEZ J F (144 33 18 14 .23)

Dk. b or br g. 4
Sire: General Assembly (Secretariat)
Dam: Musical Lark (Cure the Blues)
Br: Firestone Mr-Mrs B R (Ky)
Tr: Garren Murray M (24 3 2 4 .13)

119

Lifetime Record: 70 9 11 11 $265,966
1993 26 4 5 4 $114,000 Turf 2 0 0 0
1992 37 3 6 7 $129,406 Wet 13 0 3 2 $33,430
Bel 24 4 6 4 $109,790 Dist 15 3 2 4 $78,360

18Sep93- 4Bel sly 6f :222 :451 :57 1:092 3↑ Fall Hwgt H-G2 84 6 5 88¼ 77½ 76 89¾ Alvarado F T 127 b 41.50 83-14 Fly So Free135½ Demaloot Demashoot1261½ Take Me Out1343 No factor 10

8Sep93- 8Bel fst 1 1/16 :233 :47 1:103 1:41 3↑ Handicap46k 95 1 5 53½ 52½ 42½ 23 Chavez J F 114 b 5.20e 94-12 Liver Stand1153 Roman Chorus114¼ Jacksonport114nk Up for place 6

28Aug93- 6Sar fst 1⅛ :47 1:11 1:36 1:492 3↑ Alw 46000N$Y 82 2 5 65 64½ 55 47¼ Alvarado F T 117 b 6.40 82-06 Prospector's Flag1121½ Key Contender1175½ Say Dance117nk No threat 6

19Aug93- 8Sar fst 7f :221 :442 1:084 1:213 3↑ Alw 29500N3X 98 5 5 56 46½ 31½ 1nk Chavez J F 117 b 8.90 97-06 Roman Chorus117nk Strikany1122½ Offbeat119hd Driving 7

7Aug93- 2Sar gd 7f :224 :452 1:093 1:214 3↑ Clm 70000 96 5 2 54 42½ 3½ 31½ Chavez J F 113 b 7.20 94-08 Game Wager113nk Senor Cielo1131½ Roman Chorus1138 Bid, weakened 6

31Jly93- 5Sar fst 7f :23 :452 1:091 1:212 3↑ Alw 40000N$Y 84 6 2 41½ 54 44½ 410 Rojas R I 117 b 5.20 88-08 Brunswick117nk Wait For The Wind1176 Permit1193¾ No threat 6

23Jly93- 8Bel fst 1 :232 :463 1:111 1:361 3↑ Handicap46k 97 6 6 64¾ 53 32½ 22¾ Rojas R I 109 b 4.00e 84-19 Federal Funds1102¾ Roman Chorus109¾ Dalhart1137 Rallied wide 6

15Jly93- 6Bel fst 7f :224 :46 1:094 1:213 3↑ Alw 40000N$Y 90 2 5 45½ 42 22½ 34½ Chavez J F 117 b 5.60 91-10 Curbex1174½ Lost Mountain117no Roman Chorus1175½ Willingly 6

7Jly93- 6Bel fst 7f :232 :46 1:101 1:223 Clm 45000 98 6 4 53½ 42½ 2hd 11¼ Chavez J F 113 b 8.70 90-13 Roman Chorus1131¼ Frozen Runway117no I'll Take A Stand115nk Driving 7

28Jun93- 3Bel fst 1 1/16 :232 :464 1:113 1:434 Clm 30000 95 3 6 42½ 51½ 1½ 15½ Chavez J F 113 b 6.30 83-20 Roman Chorus1135½ Runaway Storm117hd Cool As Crystal1171½ Driving 7

WORKOUTS: Aug 6 Sar 3f fst :39 B 14/15

Farewell Wave
Own: Rokeby Stables
BAILEY J D (99 12 19 11 .12)

Ch. g. 7
Sire: Topsider (Northern Dancer)
Dam: Farewell Letter (Arts and Letters)
Br: Mellon Paul (Va)
Tr: Miller MacKenzie (9 0 3 0 .00)

117

Lifetime Record: 45 12 9 6 $419,753
1993 6 2 0 1 $53,148 Turf 4 0 0 1 $10,551
1992 5 1 0 1 $37,110 Wet 7 2 2 1 $58,312
Bel 25 8 5 3 $255,184 Dist 13 4 5 1 $110,028

5Aug93- 8Sar fst 7f :223 :444 1:09 1:212 3↑ Handicap40k 96 6 7 85 66½ 62¾ 64½ Bailey J D 116 fb 9.50 93-15 Harlan111hd Take Me Out1221½ Williamstown1151 No threat 8

10Jly93- 6Bel fst 1 1/16 :232 :463 1:104 1:413 3↑ Alw 46000N$mY 81 6 5 63½ 62¾ 53¾ 56 McCauley W H 122 fb 3.80 88-06 Dry Bean111hd Berkley Fitz122nk Excellent Tipper1174 No threat 6

28Jun93- 8Bel fst 1 1/16 :233 :463 1:111 1:442 3↑ Alw 46000N$mY 96 3 3 32½ 2½ 11 11¾ Bailey J D 117 fb 4.00 80-20 Farewell Wave1171¾ Alyten1174½ Sylva Honda1171¼ Driving 6

22May93- 6Bel fst 1 :233 :47 1:11 1:354 3↑ Alw 46000N$mY 86 3 6 52½ 32½ 32½ 37¼ Bailey J D 117 fb 4.10 82-15 Sand Lizard117nk Sylva Honda1177 Farewell Wave1171¼ Lacked rally 6

30Apr93- 6CD fst 7f :23 :462 1:112 1:24 3↑ Alw 28000N$Y 100 3 7 65 64½ 21 1½ Bailey J D L 117 b 2.60 90-09 Farewell Wave117½ Soar On Wings1191½ Speedy Cure115nk Driving inside 8

10Apr93- 6Kee fst 7f :221 :442 1:084 1:211 Alw 27600N$Y 99 5 10 66 65¾ 55½ 54¼ Bailey J D L 113 fb 3.70 99-20 Wait For The Wind1151½ Speedy Cure113hd Waki Warrior1182½ No rally 10

3Sep92- 8Bel my 1 1/16 :23 :46 1:101 1:412 3↑ Handicap 91 4 4 62½ 52½ 53½ 56 Bailey J D 114 b 4.30 89-13 Isn't That Special115hd Majesterian112no Crackedbell117 No threat 6

10Aug92- 8Sar fst 1⅛ :464 1:111 1:353 1:482 3↑ Upset 52k 94 1 4 44½ 43 42½ 41¾ Bailey J D 115 b 3.40 93-09 Tank's Number112hd Isn't That Special115no Alyten115 Chckd early 5

10Jly92- 8Bel fst 1 1/16 :232 :463 1:102 1:422 3↑ Handicap 83 3 4 42½ 55 55½ 47¼ Bailey J D 116 b 3.30 82-14 Isn't That Special115½ Lost Mountain122½ Fighting Fantasy114 Outrun 5

6Jun92- 2Bel my 1 1/16 :223 :451 1:092 1:413 3↑ Affirmed 54k 96 5 8 86¾ 63½ 63¾ 35 Bailey J D 115 b *1.50 89-08 MichelleCanPass1195 Isn'tThatSpecial115hd FarewellWve115 Wide trip 8

WORKOUTS: ●Sep 29 Bel 3f fst :344 H 1/19 Sep 25 Bel 4f fst :471 H 2/95 ●Sep 20 Bel 6f gd 1:15 B 1/4 Sep 15 Bel 6f fst 1:173 B 3/4 Sep 8 Bel 5f fst 1:004 H 13/39 Sep 1 Bel 4f fst :483 B 16/40

Wait for the Wind

Own: Team Valor Stables

B. h. 5
Sire: Cure the Blues (Stop the Music)
Dam: Ivor's Fire (Sir Ivor)
Br: Semple Lindsay (Ky)
Tr: Hennig Mark (15 3 5 3 .20)

SMITH M E (145 37 23 22 .26)

119

Lifetime Record:	18	6	6	1	$153,320						
1993	8	3	2	0	$73,480	Turf	1	0	0	0	$2,700
1992	4	2	0	1	$39,240	Wet	1	0	0	1	$3,240
Bel	1	1	0	0	$24,000	Dist	6	3	2	0	$73,250

11Sep93-4Bel	gd	7f	:224	:453	1:093	1:22	3↑ Alw 40000N$Y	* 101	2	4	2½	2hd	1½	13½	Smith M E	117	*2.20	93-11	Wait For The Wind1173½ Shining Bid1175½ Agincourt117¾	Drew off	6
20Aug93-8Sar	gd	7f	:223	:453	1:10	1:223	3↑ Alw 40000N$Y	94	1	5	42½	31½	21½	23	Smith M E	117	*.70	89-15	Late Guest1173 Wait For The Wind1179 Birdie's Fly1124	Broke slowly	5
31Jly93-5Sar	fst	7f	:23	:452	1:091	1:212	3↑ Alw 40000N$Y	105	1	5	1½	11½	11	2nk	Smith M E	117	*2.00	98-08	Brunswick117nk Wait For The Wind1176 Permit1193¾	Gamely	6
19Jun93-8CD	fst	1	:222	:45	1:093	1:352	3↑ Alw 32000N$mY	87	6	5	62½	55¼	45½	57¼	Romero R P	L 117	3.70	95-06	Approach117hd Scudan1195 Trans Caribbean115hd	Flatten out	8
1May93-6CD	fst	7f	:221	:444	1:09	1:22	CD Bd B C H-G3	86	6	6	65	75	119¾	119	Sellers S J	L 113	7.40	91-01	Callide Valley1161 Furiously117hd Ojai110nk	Brief speed	11
10Apr93-6Kee	fst	7f	:221	:442	1:084	1:211	Alw 27600N$Y	109	3	2	33	33½	11	11¼	Sellers S J	L 115	4.10	103-20	Wait ForTheWind1151¼ SpeedyCure113hd WakiWarrior1182½	Sharp, up rail	10
4Mar93-9GP	fst	7f	:232	:463	1:11	1:231	Alw 24000N3X	98	3	4	1½	11	12	1hd	Sellers S J	L 113	3.90	87-20	Wait For The Wind113hd Binalong1144 Look Ahead113½	Fully extended	8
18Feb93-8GP	fst	6½f	:231	:452	1:11	1:173	Alw 23000N3X	89	2	6	32½	32½	32½	52¼	Guidry M	L 113	5.60	87-18	Lordly Ruckus113hd Ever So True1121¼ Regal Kris112¾	Weakened	11
14Apr92-8Aqu	fst	1	:232	:461	1:10	1:351	3↑ Alw 31000	94	3	2	2hd	1hd	11	11¼	Antley C W	121	*.40	86-20	Wait for the Wind1211¼ Peace Won1192¼ Roman Chorus110	Driving	6
26Mar92-6Aqu	fst	1	:233	:462	1:104	1:354	Alw 29000	99	6	2	2½	1hd	17	112	Smith M E	117	*.40	83-21	Wait for theWind11712 ChenangoValley1125 CarmelKing117	Ridden out	6

WORKOUTS: Sep 21 Bel tr.t 4f gd :502 B 51/88 Sep 7 Bel 4f fst :51 B 28/30 ●Sep 1 Bel 4f fst :47 H 1/40 Aug 16 Sar 4f fst :472 H 3/34 Aug 10 Sar 4f fst :533 B 29/29 Jly 25 Sar 5f fst 1:002 H 2/7

Shining Bid

Own: Matz Deborah A

Dk. b or br h. 5
Sire: Loustrous Bid (Illustrious)
Dam: Caro's Miss (Caro-Ir)
Br: Paxson Mrs H D (Ky)
Tr: Morgan Jack B (2 0 1 0 .00)

MAPLE E (42 5 10 5 .12)

117

Lifetime Record:	41	6	ˬ	8	$239,280						
1993	6	0	1	2	$18,400	Turf	2	0	0	0	
1992	11	2	2	0	$124,072	Wet	7	3	0	0	$104,280
Bel	13	1	2	2	$106,392	Dist	10	0	3	1	$35,512

23Sep93-8Bel	my	6f	:223	:46	:582	1:11	3↑ Alw 40000N$Y	76	7	7	52½	62¼	73¾	78½	Maple E	117	3.30	76-26	Regal Conquest119no Senor Cielo1171 Fabersham117nk	No threat	7
11Sep93-4Bel	gd	7f	:224	:453	1:093	1:22	3↑ Alw 40000N$Y	93	5	2	31½	31	2½	23½	Santos J A	117	9.10	89-11	Wait For The Wind1173½ Shining Bid1175½ Agincourt117¾	Bid, weakened	6
2Aug93-8Sar	sly	6f	:214	:443	:564	1:091	3↑ A PhenomenonG3	79	1	6	55½	55½	64½	511	Maple E	115	10.50	85-11	Gold Spring1191¼ Friendly Lover122nk Detox1154½	Saved ground	7
21Jly93-8Bel	fst	6f	:224	:46	:574	1:10	3↑ Handicap40k	81	4	2	31	1½	31	37½	Maple E	118	2.10	82-14	Regal Conquest111½ Game Wager1107 Shining Bid118nk	Bid, tired	6
6May93-8Bel	fst	7f	:224	:452	1:084	1:21	3↑ Alw 40000N$Y	94	4	2	1½	11	32	34¾	Maple E	117	5.80	93-08	Fly So Free1173½ Majesterian1171½ Shining Bid1171	Speed, tired	5
9Apr93-8Aqu	fst	6f	:224	:45	:57	1:09	3↑ Bold Ruler-G3	86	5	6	42	54½	74¾	78	Maple E	119	13.80	89-12	Slerp119hd Argyle Lake1211½ Big Jewel121nk	Tired	8
25Oct92-8Aqu	fst	6f	:221	:454	:571	1:10	3↑ Boojum H-G3	94	6	4	54	4¾	42½	56	Bailey J D	113	7.30	85-19	Belong to Me1123½ Diablo117nk Fast Turn108	4-wide	9
16Aug92-8Sar	my	7f	:221	:451	1:10	1:222	3↑ Forego H-G2	83	2	8	1hd	1½	43	713¼	Maple E	113	4.80	81-14	Rubiano1243¼ Drummond Lane1151¼ Diablo114	Dueled inside	8
3Aug92-8Sar	fst	6f	:221	:443	:562	1:083	3↑ A Phenmenon-G3	83	7	6	62	63¾	75¼	710	Maple E	122	5.40	91-08	For Really115nk Burn Fair115nk Drummond Lane122	Steadied 1/2 pl	9
18Jly92-7Bel	fst	7f	:224	:453	1:092	1:213	3↑ Tom Fool-G2	100	1	7	12	1½	3½	43½	Maple E	121	7.50	92-12	Rublano1261 Take Me Out1191½ Arrowtown119	Set pace	8

WORKOUTS: Sep 7 Bel 6f fst 1:15 B 8/12 Sep 3 Bel 4f fst :484 B 19/46 Aug 27 Bel tr.t 5f fst 1:04 B 15/20 Jly 31 Bel 4f fst :514 B 41/41 ●Jly 17 Bel 5f fst :583 H 1/35 Jly 11 Bel 4f fst :473 B 3/35

Agincourt

Own: Perez Robert

B. c. 4
Sire: [illegible]
Dam: Conquistador Blue (Conquistador Cielo)
Br: Heins & McGee Mmes (Ky)
Tr: Zito Nicholas P (37 5 2 6 .14)

ANTLEY C W (76 15 11 14 .20)

117

Lifetime Record:	21	4	0	4	$338,483						
[illegible]	[illegible]	[illegible]	[illegible]	[illegible]	[illegible]	Turf	[illegible]	[illegible]	[illegible]	[illegible]	
1992	11	2	0	3	$223,193	Wet	2	1	0	0	$8,700
Bel	7	2	0	1	$200,340	Dist	5	1	0	2	$92,868

23Sep93-8Bel	my	6f	:223	:46	:582	1:11	3↑ Alw 40000N$Y	95	3	3	21	2hd	1hd	41½	Antley C W	117	8.60	84-26	Regal Conquest119no Senor Cielo1171 Fabersham117nk	Dueled, weakened	7
11Sep93-4Bel	gd	7f	:224	:453	1:093	1:22	3↑ Alw 40000N$Y	81	1	3	1½	1hd	33	39	Antley C W	117	11.30	84-11	Wait For The Wind1173½ Shining Bid1175½ Agincourt117¾	Dueled, tired	6
30Aug93-6Sar	fst	6f	:222	:45	:564	1:09	3↑ Alw 40000N$Y	66	5	3	2hd	31	54¾	514	Chavez J F	117	10.70	83-06	Game Wager1172½ Strikany112no Detox1173½	Dueled, tired	6
6Mar93-8GP	fst	6½f	:214	:442	1:083	1:15	Alw 31000NC	82	5	5	45	68½	710	612¼	Sellers S J	L 122	16.80	90-09	Alydeed1224¾ Fly So Free114no Cold Digger1131	Faltered	7
19Feb93-7GP	fst	7f	:22	:45	1:094	1:23	Alw 24000N4X	77	7	1	33½	43	68½	611¼	Sellers S J	120	5.00	77-17	Birdonthewire1201 TropiclGentlemn1151 ToughAndRuggd1172½	Faltered	7
16Oct92-10Med	fst	1⅛	:461	1:094	1:352	1:48	3↑ Med Cup H-G1	86	2	1	1½	3½	1011	1013¼	Gryder A T	111	17.90	79-13	Sea Cadet1201¾ Valley Crossing1114 American Chance109	Used in pace	10
25Sep92-10Med	fst	1⅛	:46	1:103	1:354	1:49	Pegasus H-G1	100	10	6	58	22	32½	32½	Solis A	115	9.80	84-17	Scuffleburg1111½ Nines Wild1131 Agincourt115	Willingly	11
7Sep92-8Bel	fst	1	:23	:452	1:091	1:341	Jerome H-G1	92	5	3	31½	32	[illegible]	[illegible]	Antley C W	117	19.50	91-08	Furiously113¾ Colony Light1111¾ Dixie Brass122	Tired	6
22Aug92-8Sar	fst	7f	:212	:434	1:081	1:212	Kngs Bishop-G2	96	10	1	76	75	63½	34½	Antley C W	122	6.20	94 —	Salt Lake1173 Binalong1151½ Agincourt122	Rlld 6-wide	10
2Aug92-8Sar	fst	1⅛	:461	1:092	1:342	1:472	Jim Dandy-G2	89	5	3	33	44	44½	512¼	Chavez J F	123	15.20	88 —	Thunder Rumble117½ Dixie Brass120[illegible]	Saved ground	[illegible]

WORKOUTS: Aug 17 Sar tr.t 4f fst :512 B 12/17 Aug 1 Sar 4f fst :491 B 13/30

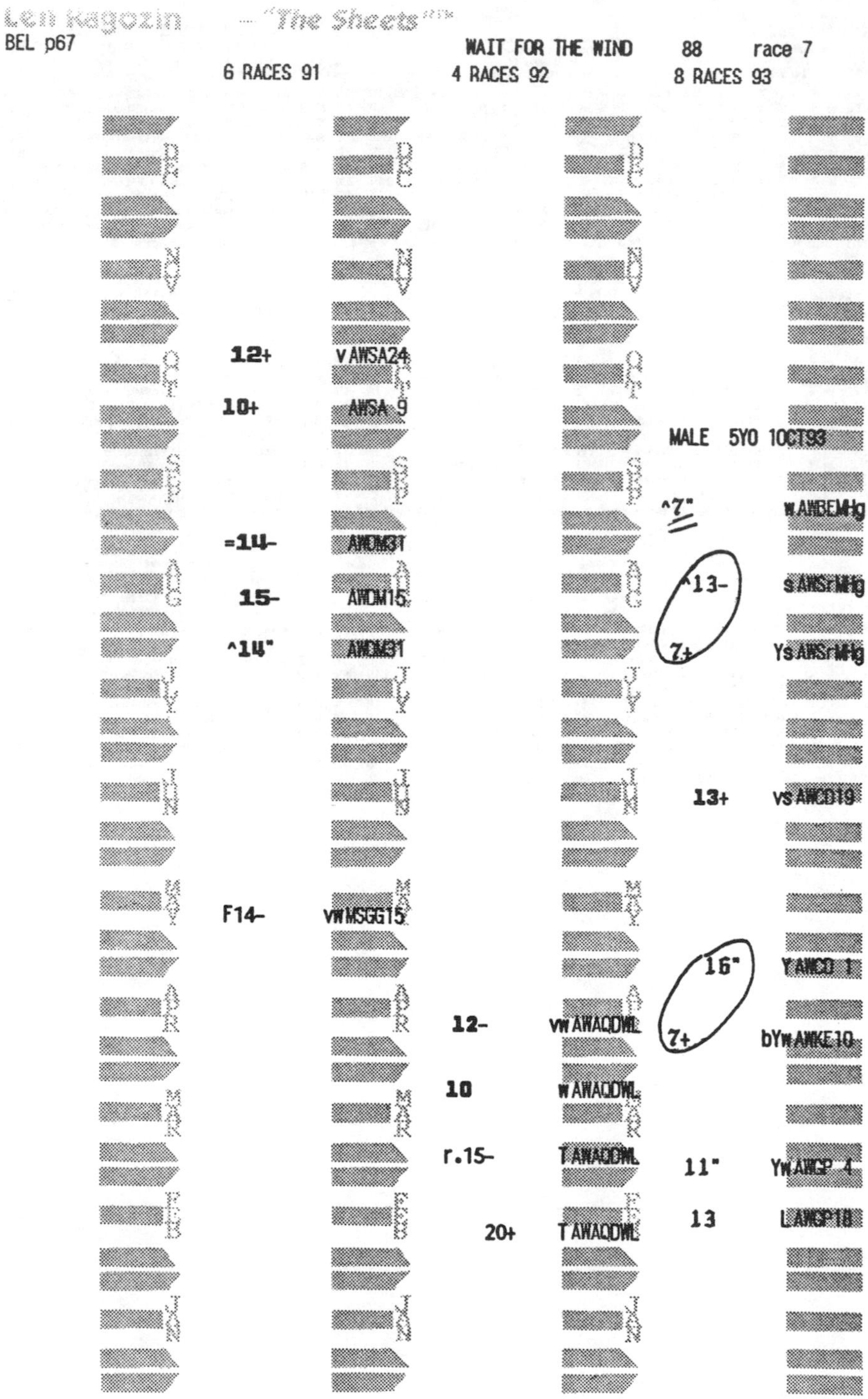
Len Ragozin — "The Sheets"
BEL p67
WAIT FOR THE WIND 88 race 7
6 RACES 91
4 RACES 92
8 RACES 93
DEC
NOV
OCT
SEP
AUG
JLY
JUN
MAY
APR
MAR
FEB
JAN
12+ vAWSA24
10+ AWSA 9
=14- AWDM31
15- AWDM15
^14" AWDM31
F14- vwMSGG15
12- vwAWAQDWL
10 wAWAQDWL
r.15- TAWAQDWL
20+ TAWAQDWL
MALE 5YO 1OCT93
^7" wAWBEMHg
^13- sAWSrMHg
7+ YsAWSrMHg
13+ vsAWCD19
16" YAWCD 1
7+ bYwAWKE10
11" YwAWGP 4
13 LAWGP18

Clearly, Wait for the Wind's "breaking point" on Beyer was a figure exceeding 100. On *The Sheets,* his corresponding breaking point was a 7¼ or a 7½. The numerical pattern was strengthened by the fact that he was repeating the same time interval between races as he had for the two bounces earlier in the season.

Handicappers who opted for a win bet on Game Wager cannot be faulted, for it appeared that if Wait for the Wind did not perform well — as was highly probable — then the consistent Game Wager figured to win if he ran back to any of four consecutive races from July 21 through August 30 — figures ranging from 99 to 103. His most recent race, a Grade 2 in the slop under 129 pounds in which he was bumped at the start, was a complete throw-out. Unfortunately, those who bet Game Wager to win had no way of knowing that the gelding, whose best sprint races always featured a strong closing punch, would be caught up dueling between horses in a four-way skirmish. Game Wager fought off all the early challenges, but was overtaken in deep stretch by the fresh closer Roman Chorus.

SEVENTH RACE
Belmont
OCTOBER 1, 1993

7 FURLONGS. (1.20^{2}) ALLOWANCE. Purse $40,000. 3–year–olds and upward which have not won two races of $20,000 since November 1, 1992. Weight, 3–year–olds, 118 lbs. Older, 122 lbs. Non–winners of two races of $17,000 since July 1 allowed 3 lbs. Of such a race since then, 5 lbs. (Maiden, claiming, starter and restricted races not considered).

Value of race $40,000; value to winner $24,000; second $8,800; third $4,800; fourth $2,400. Mutuel pool $217,617. Exacta Pool $460,387

Last Raced	Horse	M/Eqt.	A.	Wt	PP	St	¼	½	Str	Fin	Jockey	Odds $1
18Sep93 ^{4}Bel^{8}	Roman Chorus	b	4	119	3	4	$6^{\frac{1}{2}}$	6^{2}	$4^{1\frac{1}{2}}$	1^{3}	Chavez J F	a-6.20
18Sep93 ^{4}Bel^{9}	Game Wager		5	119	2	3	2^{hd}	$2^{\frac{1}{2}}$	$1^{\frac{1}{2}}$	$2^{\frac{1}{2}}$	Migliore R	2.70
24Sep93 ^{8}Bel^{5}	Jacksonport	b	4	117	1	7	$1^{\frac{1}{2}}$	1^{hd}	$2^{\frac{1}{2}}$	3^{1}	Alvarado F T	a 6.20
5Aug93 ^{8}Sar^{6}	Farewell Wave	b	7	117	4	6	7	7	$5^{\frac{1}{2}}$	4no	Bailey J D	6.20
23Sep93 ^{8}Bel^{7}	Shining Bid		5	117	6	5	5^{1}	5^{hd}	$3^{\frac{1}{2}}$	$5^{8\frac{1}{2}}$	Maple E	17.40
23Sep93 ^{8}Bel^{4}	Agincourt		4	117	7	2	3^{hd}	3^{hd}	$6^{1\frac{1}{2}}$	$6^{3\frac{1}{2}}$	Antley C W	7.10
11Sep93 ^{4}Bel^{1}	Wait for the Wind		5	119	5	1	4^{4}	4^{2}	7	7	Smith M E	1.00

a–Coupled: Roman Chorus and Jacksonport.

OFF AT 3:56 Start good, Won driving. Time, :22^{3}, :45^{2}, 1:11 , 1:24 Track fast.

$2 Mutuel Prices:

1–(C)–ROMAN CHORUS (a–entry)	14.40	5.40	5.80
2–(B)–GAME WAGER		4.20	4.60
1–(A)–JACKSONPORT (a–entry)	14.40	5.40	5.80

$2 EXACTA 1–2 PAID $62.20

Dk. b. or br. g, by General Assembly—Musical Lark, by Cure the Blues. Trainer Garren Murray M. Bred by Firestone Mr–Mrs B R (Ky).

ROMAN CHORUS unhurried early, checked briefly on the turn, angled out entering the stretch, then unleased a strong late run to win going away. GAME WAGER dueled for the lead between horses into deep stretch but couldn't hold the winner safe. JACKSONPORT rushed up along the inside after breaking slowly, battled inside GAME WAGER into the stretch and weakened in the final eighth. FAREWELL WAVE bobbled at the break, trailed for a half, circled five wide into the stretch then rallied belatedly in the middle of the track. SHINING BID reserved for a half while four wide, made a run to reach contention in upper stretch but couldn't sustain his bid. AGINCOURT stalked the pace while four wide into upper stretch and tired. WAIT FOR THE WIND raced in close contention between horses for a half, then gave way on the turn. All but SHINING BID and WAIT FOR THE WIND wore mud caulks.

Owners— 1, Garren Murray M; 2, Hauman Eugene E; 3, Garren Murray M; 4, Rokeby Stables; 5, Matz Deborah A; 6, Perez Robert; 7, Team Valor Stables.

Trainers— 1, Garren Murray M; 2, Hushion Michael E; 3, Garren Murray M; 4, Miller MacKenzie; 5, Morgan Jack B; 6, Zito Nicholas P; 7, Hennig Mark.

This brings up a point about vulnerable favorites: when the favorite is deemed to be worth playing against, the chances for exceptional returns can be maximized in exactas by eliminating it *from two positions.* An even-money shot such as Wait for the Wind usually accounts for an even larger percentage of the exacta pool, so that when a logical result occurs, the payoffs are generous.

In this particular race, it might have been feasible to key the ultra-reliable Game Wager in exactas first and second with everyone except Wait for the Wind. There were four other betting interests: for $16, Game Wager could have been boxed with everyone except the vulnerable Wait for the Wind. The result was an exacta worth $62.20, which yielded nearly 3–1 on what was effectively a win/place bet on a 5–2 shot.

The exacta bestows its greatest value when you can bet on two separate opinions in the same race instead of the same opinion twice.

In the 1992 Travers Stakes, Thunder Rumble and Dixie Brass were the top-figure contenders, assuming one or both could run back to their Jim Dandy performances:

Dixie Brass
PEZUA J M (56 3 4 3 .05)
Own.—Watral Michael

Dk. b. or br. c. 3(Mar), by Dixieland Band—Petite Diable, by Sham
Br.—Rooker John W (Ky)
Tr.—Brida Dennis J (16 3 2 1 .19)

126

Lifetime							
10 6 1 1	1992	6	3	1	1	$479,763
$542,763	1991	4	3	0	0	$63,000
	Wet	2	2	0	0	$68,040

2Aug92- 8Sar	fst	$1\frac{1}{8}$	:46^{1}	1:09^{2}	1:47^{2}	Jim Dandy	109	1	1	1^{1}	1^{1}	1^{1}	2$^{\frac{1}{2}}$	Pezua J M	126	2.80	99 — ThundrRumbl117$^{\frac{1}{2}}$DixiBrss126$^{7\frac{1}{2}}$DvlHsDu126	Drftd, gmly	8
2Aug92-Grade II																			
25May92- 8Bel	fst	1	:44^{4}	1:08^{2}	1:33^{3}	3↑ Metropoln	111	6	1	1$^{\frac{1}{2}}$	1$^{1\frac{1}{2}}$	1^{1}	1$^{2\frac{1}{4}}$	Pezua J M	107	4.50	102-05 DixieBrass107$^{2\frac{1}{4}}$PleasantTp119$^{1\frac{3}{4}}$InExcess-Ir121	Driving	11
25May92-Grade I																			
6May92- 8Bel	fst	1	:44^{2}	1:08^{4}	1:33^{3}	Withers	108	3	1	1^{2}	1$^{1\frac{1}{2}}$	1^{3}	1$^{8\frac{1}{4}}$	Pezua J M	126	7.50	102 — DixiBrss126$^{8\frac{1}{4}}$BigSur126^{3}Suprstrik-GB126	Wide,driving	8
6May92-Grade II																			
18Apr92- 7Aqu	gd	6f	:22	:44^{2}	1:09^{1}	Best Turn	87	4	6	2$^{\frac{1}{2}}$	4$^{1\frac{1}{2}}$	4$^{3\frac{1}{2}}$	4$^{3\frac{1}{2}}$	Migliore R	122	*1.40	91-05 BlongtoM115^{2}NinsWld117$^{1\frac{1}{2}}$RomnChorus115	Brk slowly	6
18Apr92-Grade III																			
28Mar92- 8GS	gd	1	:48^{1}	1:13^{2}	1:39	Cherry Hill	96	5	2	2^{hd}	1^{1}	2$^{\frac{1}{2}}$	3$^{1\frac{3}{4}}$	Mojica R Jr	117	*.80	84-19 PieinYourEye115^{no}SurelySix115$^{1\frac{3}{4}}$DixiBrss117	Bid, tired	7
28Mar92-Grade III																			
7Mar92- 8Aqu	sly	6f	⊡:22	:45	1:10^{2}	Swift	106	8	1	2^{hd}	1^{1}	1^{2}	1$^{3\frac{1}{4}}$	Mojica R Jr	120	2.70	91-17 DixieBrss120$^{3\frac{1}{4}}$AmericnChnce120$^{2\frac{1}{4}}$GoldnPhs114	Driving	8
19Dec91- 8Aqu	fst	6f	⊡:22^{3}	:47^{1}	1:13^{2}	Copelan Stk	88	7	5	1$^{1\frac{1}{2}}$	1^{1}	1$^{1\frac{1}{2}}$	1$^{3\frac{1}{4}}$	Mojica R Jr	117	*1.20	76-29 DixBrss117$^{3\frac{1}{4}}$TruDutch117^{no}SlngOnApryr115	Ridden out	9
18Nov91- 1Aqu	fst	6f	:22	:45^{1}	1:10^{3}	Alw 27000	91	1	4	2$^{1\frac{1}{2}}$	2^{1}	1^{hd}	1no	Mojica R Jr	117	2.90	88-18 DixieBrss117^{no}BstDcortd119$^{5\frac{1}{2}}$Chpito119	Drifted, drvng	5
23Oct91- 8Aqu	fst	7f	:21^{4}	:44	1:22^{3}	Cowdin	72	2	5	4$^{2\frac{1}{2}}$	4^{4}	9$^{9\frac{1}{2}}$	8$^{11\frac{3}{4}}$	Migliore R	122	7.30	77-13 Salt Lake122$^{6\frac{1}{2}}$MontrealMarty122^{nk}Offbeat122	Bmpd st	9
23Oct91-Grade II																			
25Sep91- 4Bel	sly	6f	:22^{1}	:45^{1}	1:10^{1}	Md Sp Wt	98	3	3	1$^{1\frac{1}{2}}$	1$^{2\frac{1}{2}}$	1^{7}	1^{11}	Mojica R Jr^{5}	113	28.90	89-14 DixieBrass113^{11}Chapito118^{no}Meniscus118	Kept to drive	12

LATEST WORKOUTS ●Aug 18 Sar tr.t 4f gd :47^{4} B ●Jly 29 Sar 4f fst :46^{2} B Jly 25 Sar tr.t 1 fst 1:46^{4} B ●Jly 19 Sar tr.t 5f fst 1:02^{3} H

Thunder Rumble
MCCAULEY W H (41 6 6 5 .15)
Own.—Braeburn Farm

Dk. b. or br. c. 3(Mar), by Thunder Puddles—Lyphette, by Lyphard
Br.—Widmer Konrad (NY)
Tr.—O'Connell Richard (9 1 0 3 .11)

126

Lifetime							
8 5 0 1	1992	6	4	0	1	$250,902
$265,302	1991	2	1	0	0	$14,400
	Turf	2	0	0	0	

2Aug92- 8Sar	fst	$1\frac{1}{8}$	:46^{1}	1:09^{2}	1:47^{2}	Jim Dandy	110	3	2	2^{1}	2^{1}	2^{1}	1$^{\frac{1}{2}}$	McCauley W H	117	24.90	100 — ThundrRumbl117$^{\frac{1}{2}}$DxBrss126$^{7\frac{1}{2}}$DvlHsD126	Bmp brk drvg	8
2Aug92-Grade II																			
11Jly92- 7Bel	fm	$1\frac{1}{16}$	Ⓣ:48	1:11^{1}	1:41	3↑ Alw 37000	86	7	2	2^{1}	3^{2}	6$^{6\frac{1}{4}}$	7$^{7\frac{1}{4}}$	McCauley W H	112	3.70	84-12 Now Listen117$^{1\frac{1}{2}}$ Ogle117^{1} Sir Salima117	Tired	8
13Mar92- 8Aqu	fst	$1\frac{1}{8}$	:46^{3}	1:11^{4}	1:51^{2}	Gate Dancer	98	4	4	3$^{6\frac{1}{2}}$	3^{3}	1$^{1\frac{1}{2}}$	1^{5}	McCauley W H	119	*.80	79-32 ThndrRmbl119^{5}StpOtFrnt117^{nk}Jcksnprt117	Ridden out	8
15Feb92- 8Aqu	fst	$1\frac{1}{16}$	⊡:48^{1}	1:13	1:44^{1}	Whirlaway	84	5	2	1$^{\frac{1}{2}}$	2^{hd}	3^{5}	3^{9}	McCauley W H	126	*.90	78-26 DrUnrht119$^{5\frac{1}{2}}$TnsNmbr117$^{3\frac{1}{2}}$ThndrRbl126	Dueled, tired	10
26Jan92- 8Aqu	fst	1^{70}	⊡:47^{1}	1:13	1:43	Count Fleet	91	2	1	1^{hd}	1^{hd}	1^{2}	1^{2}	McCauley W H	123	*2.50	90-17 ThunderRumble123^{2}Dr.Unright119^{3}PlceLine119	Driving	7
12Jan92- 8Aqu	fst	$1\frac{1}{16}$	⊡:48^{1}	1:13^{1}	1:46^{4}	Ⓢ Montauk	91	7	4	3^{2}	2^{1}	1$^{1\frac{1}{2}}$	1^{4}	McCauley W H	117	*2.30e	74-24 Thunder Rumble117^{4}Prioritizer117^{2}JayGee123	Drew off	10
23Dec91- 6Aqu	fst	6f	⊡:23^{2}	:47	1:11^{3}	Md Sp Wt	94	4	5	1$^{1\frac{1}{2}}$	1^{1}	1^{7}	1$^{12\frac{3}{4}}$	McCauley W H	118	4.30	85-18 ThundrRumbl118$^{12\frac{3}{4}}$Dlfild118^{2}CllHmNtty118	Ridden out	12
24Oct91- 4Aqu	fm	1	Ⓣ:49	1:14^{3}	1:40^{2}	Ⓢ Md Sp Wt	30	1	2	8^{6}	9^{7}	8^{15}	7^{20}	Smith M E	118	*1.50	54-17 PowdrCp118$^{2\frac{1}{2}}$A.J.Wrbcks118^{1}StrtYorHrt118	Bolted trn	9

LATEST WORKOUTS ●Aug 17 Sar 5f gd :59^{1} H ●Aug 11 Sar 5f fst :58^{4} H ●Jly 26 Bel 6f fst 1:11 H Jly 19 Bel 4f fst :48^{1} B

Dixie Brass was making his second start back from a layoff and stretching out in distance for the Travers. He had already bounced when stretched out for the second race of a form cycle on two previous occasions. After winning his career debut with a Beyer of 98 at six furlongs, he plummeted 26 points when asked to go seven furlongs a month later; after winning the Swift with a figure of 106 in his debut at age three, he bounced 10 points when stretched to a mile in the Cherry Hill.

A bounce stretching to a mile and a quarter second time back from another layoff seemed inevitable for Dixie Brass.

Thunder Rumble was also relatively fresh, but he owned substantially more route experience and had shown more consistency than Dixie Brass prior to his layoff, running in the 90s in four of five starts on dirt.

His figure of 110 in the Jim Dandy represented a substantial forward move beyond his previous capabilities; it was possible he would bounce in the Travers, but there was evidence suggesting he might "pair up" with another strong figure:

- Dixie Brass had not been back to the track for a workout for more than two weeks following the Jim Dandy and had breezed only once at four furlongs in the week leading to the Travers. Meanwhile, Thunder Rumble worked a total of ten furlongs, and if the Jim Dandy had taken the starch out of him, it wasn't evident from his sparkling :58⅘ and :59⅕ trials. Often, an improved race followed by sharp works is a sign of peaking form.
- The odds justified the risk. Dixie Brass was likelier to bounce and was 7–2, while Thunder Rumble, who continued to tear up the track in the mornings, was 7–1, as the crowd expressed its opinion that his Jim Dandy had been a fluke.

In situations in which a horse is fresh from a career-best figure and can win with a repeat of that effort, handicappers must weigh the odds along with any corroborating evidence (in this case, workouts) and race particulars before determining whether a bet is justified. The particulars in the Travers were that Dixie Brass, the other high-figure horse, had exhibited strong bounce tendencies second time back from a layoff when stretched out in distance; he could be eliminated from consideration as the second choice at 7–2, which opened up possibilities in the exacta:

SEVENTH RACE
Saratoga
AUGUST 22, 1992

1 ¼ MILES. (2.00) 123rd Running THE TRAVERS (Grade I). Purse $1,000,000 Guaranteed. 3-year-olds. By subscription of $1,500 each which should accompany the nomination; $3,000 to pass the entry box; $7,500 to start. The purse to be divided 60% to the winner, 22% to second, 12% to third, and 6% to fourth. Weight, 126 lbs. Starters to be named at the closing time of entries. The winner shall have its name inscribed on the Man o'War Cup and a gold plated replica will be presented to the winning owner. Trophies will also be presented to the winning trainer and jockey. Closed Wednesday, August 5 with 22 nominations.
Value of race $1,000,000; value to winner $600,000; second $220,000; third $120,000; fourth $60,000. Mutuel pool $1,429,699. Exacta Pool $1,183,044 Triple Pool $1,015,519

Last Raced	Horse	M/Eqt.A.Wt	PP	¼	½	¾	1	Str	Fin	Jockey	Odds $1
2Aug92 ^{8}Sar^{1}	Thunder Rumble	3 126	10	4^{hd}	5^{hd}	5^{hd}	4^{1}	$1^{1\frac{1}{2}}$	$1^{4\frac{1}{2}}$	McCauley W H	7.60
2Aug92 ^{8}Sar^{3}	Devil His Due	3 126	7	$9^{2\frac{1}{2}}$	$9^{1\frac{1}{2}}$	9^{4}	$7^{\frac{1}{2}}$	$3^{1\frac{1}{2}}$	$2^{4\frac{1}{2}}$	Maple E	5.40
2Aug92^{10}Mth^{9}	Dance Floor	3 126	8	$6^{1\frac{1}{2}}$	7^{3}	$7^{\frac{1}{2}}$	5^{1}	$4^{1\frac{1}{2}}$	3^{nk}	Antley C W	23.60
2Aug92 ^{8}Sar^{2}	Dixie Brass	3 126	1	$1^{1\frac{1}{2}}$	1^{2}	1^{1}	$1^{\frac{1}{2}}$	$2^{1\frac{1}{2}}$	4^{5}	Pezua J M	3.90
10Aug92 ^{8}Sar^{1}	Tank's Number	3 126	3	5^{hd}	$6^{\frac{1}{2}}$	3^{hd}	$6^{\frac{1}{2}}$	6^{1}	$5^{\frac{3}{4}}$	Bailey J D	25.10
2Aug92 ^{8}Sar^{4}	Furiously	3 126	6	7^{2}	$4^{\frac{1}{2}}$	4^{1}	$2^{\frac{1}{2}}$	$5^{\frac{1}{2}}$	$6^{1\frac{1}{2}}$	Smith M E	6.90
2Aug92^{10}Mth^{5}	Lee n Otto	3 126	9	$8^{1\frac{1}{2}}$	$8^{2\frac{1}{2}}$	$8^{2\frac{1}{2}}$	8^{2}	7^{1}	7^{8}	Migliore R	81.60
26Jly92 ^{8}FE^{2}	Alydeed	3 126	5	$3^{\frac{1}{2}}$	3^{1}	$2^{\frac{1}{2}}$	3^{hd}	8^{8}	8^{3}	Perret C	1.70
8Aug92 ^{9}Aks^{1}	Hold Old Blue	b 3 126	4	2^{1}	2^{hd}	6^{3}	9^{8}	9^{1}	$9^{4\frac{1}{4}}$	Day P	26.80
25Jly92 ^{8}Hol^{1}	Bien Bien	b 3 126	2	10	10	10	10	10	10	McCarron C J	8.00

OFF AT 5:09 Start good for all but BIEN BIEN, Won driving. Time, :23 , :46^{4}, 1:10^{3}, 1:35^{2}, 2:00^{4} Track fast.

$2 Mutuel Prices:			
10–(J)–THUNDER RUMBLE	17.20	7.80	5.40
7–(G)–DEVIL HIS DUE		6.20	4.80
8–(H)–DANCE FLOOR			6.80

$2 EXACTA 10–7 PAID $105.00 $2 TRIPLE 10–7–8 PAID $1,973.00

Dk. b. or br. c, (Mar), by Thunder Puddles—Lyphette, by Lyphard. Trainer O'Connell Richard. Bred by Widmer Konrad (NY).

THUNDER RUMBLE, moved up steadily from outside to contest the pace while four wide approaching the first turn, bumped with DANCE FLOOR while angling in a bit leaving the first turn, tucked in behind the leaders between horses along the backstretch, waited patiently while gaining a bit midway on the turn, was taken to the outside on the turn, circled four wide to challenge at the top of the stretch, accelerated to the front opening a clear advantage in midstretch then steadily increased his margin under strong right hand encouragement. DEVIL HIS DUE, raced

Thunder Rumble ran back to his Jim Dandy figure, while Devil His Due — my top pick in the *Form* on the basis of a terrific prep in the Jim Dandy followed by good workouts for Allen Jerkens — finished well to go clear for the place in deep stretch. The exacta combining two very legitimate contenders was worth $105, and was obtainable by merely throwing out a second choice who had bounce written all over him.

One of the main differences between dirt racing and grass racing is that grass horses, generally speaking, run to their figures with much more consistency. The grass is a much kinder surface to run on, and seldom are there the kind of suicidal early fractions that might cause an early-pace type to simply "chuck it" in the stretch.

Horses *do* bounce on the grass but usually in not nearly so pronounced a fashion as their dirt-racing brethren.

The sixth race at Saratoga on August 17 was the first division of the Yaddo Stakes for New York–bred fillies. The Yaddo looked like a three-horse race between Irish Actress at 4–5, Her Favorite at 3–1, and Cazzy B. at 6–1.

6 TURF COURSE 1 1/8 MILES SARATOGA START FINISH

1 1/8 MILES. (Turf). (1.45 2) 13th Running THE YADDO (1st Division). Purse $75,000 Added. Fillies and mares, 3-year-olds and upward foaled in New York State and approved by the New York State-Bred Registry. By subscription of $200 each which should accompany the nomination; $800 to pass the entry box; $800 to start with $75,000 added. The added money and all fees to be divided 60% to the winner, 22% to second, 12% to third and 6% to fourth. Weights, 3-year-olds, 116 lbs.; older, 121 lbs. Winners of two races of $30,000 at a mile or over in 1992 an additional 3 lbs. Non-winners of a race of $50,000 at any distance allowed 3 lbs.; of such a race of $30,000, 5 lbs.; of two races of $20,000 at a mile or over, 7 lbs.; of such a race, 9 lbs. Starters to be named at the closing time of entries. A perpetual trophy will be on display in the Winner's Circle. The New York Racing Association Inc. reserves the right to transfer this race to the main course. Closed Wednesday, July 29, with 38 nominations.

Coupled—Tiffany's Taylor and Irish Actress.

Asaracket — B. f. 4, by Protection Racket—Asamara, by Handsome Kid
CARR D (43 2 6 3 .05) — Br.—Big Apple Farms Inc (NY)
Own.—Slifstern Sherry — 18 Tr.—Destasio Richard A (13 1 0 1 .08) — **112**
Lifetime 20 3 4 1 $84,612 | 1992 12 2 3 1 $63,732 | 1991 4 1 1 0 $20,880 | Turf 5 1 1 1 $33,272 | Wet 2 0 1 0 $6,600

3Aug92- 5Sar fm 1 1/8 [T]:483 1:124 1:491 3+(F)Alw 31000 18 81 1 4 32 42 52 52½ Carr D b 117 3.60e 90-04 OrbtnSl117½[DH]PrncnBllrn117[DH]JstAbtDn117 In traffic 7
28Jun92- 8Bel fm 1 1/16 (T):461 1:092 1:41 3+(F)[S]MntVrnon 87 8 2 21 21 2hd 2nk Carr D b 113 20.40 91-11 Tlc'sCoventry113nkAsrcket113nkIrishActress122 Gamely 9
28Jun92-Run in Divisions
10Jun92- 4Bel fm 1 (T):452 1:094 1:342 3+(F)Alw 31000 74 6 6 64 84¾ 87 510¼ Smith M E b 117 *2.10 80-19 Mckymckenn1097Bltr110nkAnothrSnppr113 Chckd early 9
20May92- 7Bel fm 1 1/16 (T):47 1:11 1:413 3+(F)Alw 31000 85 1 1 11½ 11 2½ 33½ Gryder A T b 119 8.50 84-14 ChrlottAgst1191¾GldnGn1191¾Asrckt119 Bid, weakened 12
7May92- 2Bel fm 1 1/16 (T):461 1:094 1:414 (F)Clm 35000 83 9 1 1½ 11 13 12¾ Gryder A T b 117 21.30 87-15 Asaracket1172¾ GreatPass1172½NotAScratch117 Driving 11
22Apr92- 6Aqu my 1 1/8 :48 1:122 1:514 (F)Clm 32500 71 3 4 53½ 65½ 58½ 411½ Gryder A T b 115 12.60 65-30 LdyLr1176¾SophstctdSm1172½FndRmnc115 4 wide turn 7
6Apr92- 3Aqu fst 1 :47 1:123 1:384 (F)Clm 25000 76 5 2 11 1hd 2hd 23¾ Gryder A T b 117 15.00 64-35 Ballynoe1173¾Asaracket117nkWorldClassPro115 Gamely 8
16Mar92- 3Aqu fst 1 1/8 :484 1:143 1:541 (F)Clm 22500 79 1 1 15 12 11½ 21¼ Antley C W b 115 4.90e 64-32 Lady Lear1131¼ Asaracket1153½ Ballynoe115 Sharp try 8
4Mar92- 2Aqu fst 1 1/16 [•]:494 1:154 1:493 (F)Clm 22500 63 2 4 55½ 68 611 413 Antley C W b 117 5.40 47-37 Rebecc'sGl1126¾LostinFlight117nkMisteV113 No threat 6
13Feb92- 6Aqu fst 1 1/16 [•]:501 1:153 1:483 (F)[S]Alw 29000 80 4 1 12½ 12½ 19 113 Gryder A T b 117 5.30 65-29 Asrcket11713TitnsBll1171½BInYourBonnt117 Mild drive 6
LATEST WORKOUTS Aug 11 Sar (T) 4f fm :482 H Jly 29 Sar (T) 4f fm :514 B Jly 22 Bel 4f fst :51 B Jly 15 Bel tr.t 4f fst :50 B

Her Favorite — B. f. 4, by Poison Ivory—Duke's Dilemma, by Amber Duke
MAPLE E (54 8 3 7 .15) — Br.—Waller Thomas M (NY)
Own.—Tanrackin Farm — 13 Tr.—Freyer Donna J (1 0 0 0 .00) — **118**
Lifetime 10 3 1 2 $91,955 | 1992 5 3 0 1 $82,275 | 1991 5 M 1 1 $9,680 | Turf 7 3 1 2 $91,115 | Wet 1 0 0 0

18Jly92- 5Bel gd 1 1/16 [T]:482 1:13 1:434 3+(F)Alw 31000 89 2 5 42 21 1½ 11½ Maple E 119 2.00 79-22 HerFvorite1191½Puzl-Ir1172¾FutureQuestion113 Driving 8
28Jun92- 6Bel fm 1 1/16 (T):461 1:091 1:40 3+(F)[S]MntVrnon 93 7 8 76 41½ 1½ 11¾ Maple E 113 19.50 96-11 HrFvorit1131¾IrishLinnt1194½MdmJuml113 Wide, drvng 9
28Jun92-Run in Divisions
4Jun92- 2Bel fm 1 1/16 (T):45 1:10 1:421 3+(F)Alw 29000 81 7 6 44½ 2½ 3½ 32½ Maple E 119 10.90 82-13 FrenchStel1111¼HombyTn1111¼HrFvorit119 Wide, tired 12
24May92- 5Bel fm 1 1/4 [T]:493 1:382 2:032 3+(F)Alw 29000 73 2 6 76 63 31 52 Lidberg D W 124 14.10 71-21 PrfctGm115noNotAScrtch119hdVtArol115 Took up late 9
2May92- 9Aqu fm 1 1/16 (T):492 1:134 1:46 3+(F)Md Sp Wt 79 6 5 57 42 1½ 11 Lidberg D W 124 8.10 81-14 HerFvorite1241WinningTrip1151¾Herto'Mine115 Driving 10
15Nov91- 1Aqu fm 1 1/8 (T):494 1:15 1:533 3+(F)Md Sp Wt 77 7 4 46 42½ 21½ 2½ Samyn J L 120 5.90e 77-11 SlYGrbo120½HerFvorite120¾QueenoftheTide120 Gamely 9
7Nov91- 2Aqu fst 6f :232 :473 1:124 3+(F)[S]Md Sp Wt 37 1 11 105½ 95¾ 68 712¼ Samyn J L 120 *2.50e 65-19 RodBlock1204½CountryMouse122¾RoylLd120 No factor 13
18Oct91- 5Bel my 6f :222 :454 1:12 3+(F)[S]Md Sp Wt 37 6 7 77½ 68 77¼ 68½ Lovato F Jr 119 6.40 71-13 Wild Fun119hd Asaracket119noStickyRide119 No factor 9
10Oct91- 6Bel fm 1 1/16 [T]:471 1:111 1:422 3+(F)Md Sp Wt 76 6 7 67 56 38½ 37¼ Lovato F Jr 119 15.60 79-14 FiveDrems1196¼Kristening119¾HerFvorite119 Impr. pos. 10
3Oct91- 4Bel fst 6f :223 :461 1:12 3+(F)Md 45000 50 3 9 917 98¼ 67 45½ Lovato F Jr 115 45.90 74-16 MnstnGm1102½NtAScrtch1151RlShnnns118 No menace 9
LATEST WORKOUTS Aug 11 Sar 5f fst 1:012 B Aug 6 Sar 4f fst :50 B Aug 2 Sar 5f fst 1:014 H Jly 15 Bel tr.t 4f fst :494 B

Cazzy B. — B. m. 5, by Cormorant—Terra Verta, by Jabneh
ANTLEY C W (87 15 14 11 .17) — Br.—Freight Dispatch Inc (NY)
Own.—Dutch Acres Farms — 12 Tr.—Walsh Thomas M (3 0 2 0 .00) — **112**
Lifetime 31 4 7 7 $182,627 | 1992 7 0 2 2 $30,839 | 1991 12 1 2 3 $68,138 | Turf 27 4 7 6 $173,897 | Wet 2 0 0 1 $8,730

5Aug92- 1Sar gd 1 1/16 (T):48 1:114 1:423 3+(F)Clm 80000 89 6 3 2½ 1hd 1½ 2no McCauley W H 114 5.00 81-16 Belle of Amherst120no Cazzy B.114hd Scant112 Gamely 8
20Jly92- 8Bel fm 1 1/16 (T):47 1:104 1:403 3+(F)Alw 47000 88 2 3 42 42 45 46¼ McCauley W H 115 8.30 87-15 Scq-GB1153½SnrTppy1152½Tlc'sCvntry115 Lacked rally 8
28Jun92- 6Bel fm 1 1/16 (T):461 1:091 1:40 3+(F)[S]MntVrnon 81 5 5 45 53 44 46½ Perret C 113 4.60 89-11 HerFvorite1131¾IrishLinnt1194½MdmJuml113 Four wide 9
28Jun92-Run in Divisions
21Jun92- 5Bel yl 1 (T):47 1:111 1:362 (F)Clm 90000 87 2 5 53½ 21 21½ 2½ McCauley W H 118 2.70 79-23 BrightSunshine113½CazzyB.1181¾Starswhirl114 2nd best 8
8Jun92- 8Bel fm 1 1/16 (T):474 1:12 1:442 3+(F)Alw 47000 90 6 2 2½ 2hd 3½ 31½ McCauley W H 115 6.20 72-33 Routilnte-Ir115¾MonicFye115¾CzzyB.115 Bid, weakened 7
25May92- 7Bel fm 1 3/8 [T]:50 1:374 2:143 3+(F)SummerGust 81 7 6 63½ 41½ 76½ 811½ McCarron C J 119 19.10 66-14 Sardniy-Ir1212PlentyOfGrce119noVirginMichel119 Tired 9
6May92- 1Bel fm 1 (T):452 1:091 1:34 (F)Clm 100000 86 3 6 64½ 64 42 37 McCauley W H 122 12.80 85-17 BllofAmhrst118hdChrlttAgst1227CzzyB.122 Improvd pos 7
18Oct91- 1Bel my 1 1/16 :471 1:114 1:44 3+(F)Clm 75000 54 2 4 34½ 44 511 517¼ Bailey J D 117 3.50 65-23 Joy'sJoJo114½SugrHillChick1138½KlssyIndvdul113 Tired 5
18Oct91-Originally scheduled on turf
7Oct91- 6Bel gd 1 (T):471 1:112 1:353 3+(F)Alw 47000 81 1 8 55 52½ 54½ 59¼ Bailey J D 115 4.90 75-17 ToThLighthous1152¾Lrycl115½IrishActrss115 No threat 8
23Sep91- 8Bel gd 1 1/16 [T]:472 1:112 1:413 3+(F)Handicap 93 6 4 42½ 51¼ 36 27 Bailey J D 113 8.70 83-20 Le Famo1207 CazzyB.113¾SlewofPearls117 Up for place 7
LATEST WORKOUTS •Jly 31 Bel 5f fst 1:02 H Jun 18 Bel [T] 3f fm :38 B (d)

Sassa Blue

Ro. f. 4, by Sassafras-Fr—Stone of Blue, by Stonewalk
Br.—Empire State Breeding Assoc & Kevi (NY)
Tr.—Sciacca Gary (15 3 2 2 .20)
KRONE J A (72 12 8 12 .17)
Own.—Kevmar Stable
112
Lifetime 28 4 4 3 $98,520
1992 10 3 0 2 $54,960
1991 18 1 4 1 $43,560
Turf 8 1 1 1 $24,520
Wet 3 0 1 1 $9,900

31Jly92- 7Sar sly 1 :46 1:11 1:364 3↑ⒻAlw 33000 86 3 3 34 33 2½ 34¼ Chavez J F b 119 6.70 — — Miss Otis117¾ Tiara Miss1173½ Sassa Blue119 Bid, tired 5
31Jly92-Originally scheduled on turf
6Jly92- 6Bel gd 1 :464 1:111 1:36 3↑ⒻAlw 31000 86 1 2 11 1hd 2hd 1¾ Chavez J F b 117 5.70 90-11 SssBl117¾ThrtghtChrms1175½Sh'sAcdmc117 Stiff drive 6
6Jly92-Originally scheduled on turf
30May92- 4Bel fm 1 1/16 [T]:473 1:112 1:431 ⒻClm 45000 81 5 1 12 11 2½ 32½ Chavez J F b 113 10.70 79-13 I'mSoAgrebl1192½SpphirSkis113noSssBlu113 Drft, wknd 8
18May92- 9Bel gd 1 1/16 Ⓣ:463 1:111 1:433 ⒻClm 35000 81 4 3 34 3½ 1½ 1¾ Chavez J F b 117 26.20 78-26 SassaBlue117¾SapphireSkies117hdMamorBy117 Driving 11
21Apr92- 9Aqu my 6f :22 :451 1:104 ⒻClm 25000 64 4 4 64½ 54 54 59½ Rojas R I b 117 26.50 77-17 ModstGlw117noWgglsLw1155½MssTht113 Saved ground 9
9Apr92- 9Aqu fst 7f :223 :454 1:251 ⒻClm 25000 47 3 9 33½ 55 86¼ 89¼ Rojas R I b 117 14.00 70-18 OnThrd1172LstnFlght117hdSprlnHnnh112 Broke slowly 9
25Mar92- 4Aqu fst 6f :222 :453 1:103 ⒻClm 32500 72 7 4 52½ 3½ 64 56 Rojas R I b 115 21.70 82-13 NoCost1171½Undrinsurd1151¾VldDlt112 Four wide tired 7
3Feb92- 3Aqu fst 170 [•]:482 1:134 1:433 ⒻClm 35000 51 5 3 33 56 720 625¾ Smith M E b 117 8.70 61-19 AmPossibl1176TnyGrsshoppr115¾Entrust117 Done early 7
20Jan92- 4Aqu fst 6f [•]:233 :48 1:14 Ⓕ[S]Alw 27000 65 5 1 2½ 1hd 1hd 13 Chavez J F b 117 *1.30 73-23 Sassa Blue1173MissBlanca1171OneRealLady117 Driving 6
6Jan92- 9Aqu fst 6f [•]:23 :464 1:123 ⒻAlw 27000 69 1 8 63¾ 62¾ 72¾ 54¼ Howard D L b 117 10.40 76-21 SpyLedrLdy1171LongTrm117¾MjsticTrick117 Even trip 9
LATEST WORKOUTS Aug 14 Sar Ⓣ 4f fm :482 H (d) ●Jly 28 Sar Ⓣ 4f fm :474 H Jly 21 Bel 4f fst :48 H Jly 2 Bel 4f fst :47 H

Heaven Knows Why

B. f. 4, by Star de Naskra—Heaven Knows, by Quadrangle
Br.—Payson Virginia Kraft (NY)
Tr.—Bond Harold James (6 1 1 0 .17)
BAILEY J D (73 12 14 7 .16)
Own.—Payson Virginia Kraft
112
Lifetime 10 4 1 0 $127,320
1992 2 1 0 0 $17,100
1991 8 3 1 0 $110,220
Wet 1 1 0 0 $17,100

1Aug92-10FL my 1 1/16 :491 1:15 1:513 3↑Ⓕ[S]Monroe 72 7 3 2hd 12 15 13¾ Zoppo B L b 115 2.00e 59-40 HevnKnowsWhy1153¾AlbmAnn1171Lilc'sStr115 Driving 7
3Jun92- 8Bel fst 7f :224 :454 1:232 3↑Ⓕ[S]HydePrkH 70 6 2 31 31½ 76¾ 712 Migliore R b 114 31.40 75-12 SrtogDw114nkMssIronSmk114¾Bn'sMmnt112 Gave way 7
3Nov91- 8Aqu fst 6f :22 :453 1:112 Ⓕ[S]SchnctdyH 65 10 12 117¾117 87 610 Smith M E b 116 6.50 74-18 Ben'sMoment110¾MistyAmour1133HeyBbLulu114 Wide 14
12Oct91- 3Bel fst 6f :222 :453 1:094 3↑ⒻAlw 30000 78 4 3 31½ 31½ 45½ 57½ Migliore R b 114 4.40 83-17 MkinFces1191½ReglVictress1172¾She'sAShker114 Tired 6
31Aug91- 8Bel fst 1⅛ :464 1:104 1:472 ⒻGazelle H 46 1 1 17 31 816 829½ Migliore R b 113 20.30 62-08 VersillsTrty123½GrndGirlfrind1151¾Immrs112 Gave way 8
31Aug91-Grade I
21Jly91- 8FL fst 1 1/16 :464 1:113 1:462 Ⓕ[S]Ny Oaks 78 10 2 1hd 11½ 12 11½ Migliore R b 113 *2.20e 85-15 HvnKnowsWhy1131½Sh'sAShkr1101½FirlWild109 Driving 13
1Jly91- 9Bel fst 7f :222 :452 1:24 3↑Ⓕ[S]Alw 27000 83 12 2 12 12 12½ 17 Migliore R b 113 8.30 84-15 HvnKnwsWhy1137RllysDgh117¾CxngLdy111 Ridden out 14
13Jun91- 9Bel fst 6f :222 :46 1:111 3↑Ⓕ[S]Md Sp Wt 72 4 3 22½ 1hd 11½ 12½ Bailey J D b 114 *1.10 84-05 HnKnsWh1142½BgEDrm1144CmprmsdCrn114 Mild drive 14
17Mar91- 3GP fst 6f :214 :451 1:114 ⒻMd Sp Wt 61 4 3 44 44½ 47 57½ Fires E b 120 2.50 78-13 SantaCatalin1203Husmn1201Frn'sChrissy120 No threat 7
25Feb91- 4GP fst 6f :22 :45 1:112 ⒻMd Sp Wt 60 4 2 2hd 21 23 25¾ Perret C b 120 *1.40 82-11 CrprtFnd1205¾HvnKnwsWhy1202MssRslt115 Weakened 11
LATEST WORKOUTS ●Aug 14 Sar tr.t 5f fst 1:024 H ●Aug 8 Sar tr.t 5f fst 1:012 H ●Jly 28 Sar tr.t 6f fst 1:153 H Jly 22 Sar tr.t 6f fst 1:144 H

R. E. Darla

Dk. b. or br. f. 3(Mar), by Onyxly—Freshest Rose, by Night Invader
Br.—Mantia Royal (NY)
Tr.—Hargrave Kenneth (3 0 0 1 .00)
CRUGUET J (45 4 5 5 .09)
Own.—Trotta Gerald T
107
Lifetime 28 2 4 7 $82,420
1992 21 2 4 6 $79,540
1991 7 M 0 1 $2,880
Turf 4 0 1 0 $6,380
Wet 2 1 0 1 $21,240

1Aug92- 2Sar fm 1 1/16 Ⓣ:464 1:11 1:423 ⒻClm 75000 75 7 8 86½ 85¾ 74 56¼ Carr D b 111 15.10 74-18 Bltr111noNorcliffeDncer1143BuckSomeBll117 No threat 8
23Jly92- 5Bel sly 1 1/16 :46 1:11 1:444 ⒻClm 85000 73 2 3 35½ 33 35½ 35½ Cruguet J b 115 3.50 72-23 HckstrRs1115½HlbysBrtFlt111nkR.E.Drl115 Lacked rally 4
23Jly92-Originally scheduled on turf
10Jly92- 4Bel fst 1 1/16 :464 1:113 1:422 ⒻClm 75000 77 5 3 33 33½ 34 29¾ Cruguet J b 111 8.40 80-14 BuckSomeBelle1149¾R.E.Drl1111½NoblGirl111 Mild rally 7
10Jly92-Originally scheduled on turf
28Jun92- 2Bel fst 6½f :222 :453 1:171 ⒻClm c-20000 69 9 11 98¼105¼ 66 32¼ Carr D 114 9.30 85-12 RosofEr114noFortntChrmr1162¾R.E.Drl114 Rallied wide 11
28Jun92-Claimed from Pomerantz Lawrence J, Dimauro Stephen L Trainer
20Jun92- 5Bel my 1¼ :494 1:40 2:053 3↑Ⓕ[S]Alw 29000 61 3 6 64½ 3½ 2½ 1¾ Carr D 109 3.00 63-18 R.E.Darla109¾Watw1171½RevengeTime109 Wide, driving 6
20Jun92-Originally Scheduled on Turf
15Jun92- 7Bel fst 1 :47 1:121 1:374 3↑Ⓕ[S]Alw 29000 65 6 6 75 31½ 41½ 42½ Krone J A 109 2.90e 79-21 GirlishSecrts111nkHilbysBritFlit109nkGil'sGl113 4-Wide 10
7Jun92- 9Bel fst 6f :22 :452 1:111 3↑Ⓕ[S]Alw 27000 59 13 13 109½ 95¾ 53½ 52¾ Krone J A 109 5.90 81-14 RegalDisply1171½StpleQueen1111½WildFun110 Wide trip 14
30May92- 5Bel fm 1 1/16 Ⓣ:453 1:092 1:42 3↑Ⓕ[S]Alw 29000 70 4 11 129 118¾105½ 94½ Madrid A Jr 110 *1.30 81-13 [DH]Thtmfdnslf110nk[DH]ShrMDrs110nkDRb115 No factor 12

Tiffany's Taylor

B. f. 3(Feb), by Titanic—Tiffany Dream, by Blue Ensign
Br.—Giardina Jay A (NY)
Tr.—O'Brien Leo (21 3 3 1 .14)
SANTIAGO A (5 0 1 0 .00)
Own.—Maher Teresa M
107
Lifetime 12 3 2 0 $59,240
1992 9 2 1 0 $39,560
1991 3 1 1 0 $19,680
Turf 4 0 1 0 $8,960
Wet 3 0 1 0 $5,280

10Aug92- 5Sar fm 1 [T]:48 1:122 1:364 ⒻClm 80000 85 7 7 51¾ 3½ 3nk 2¾ Chavez J F 113 10.50 94-11 MissGarland115¾Tiffany'sTaylor1132Baltr111 Wide trip 7
16Jly92- 8Bel fst 1 1/16 :46 1:094 1:412 3↑Alw 47000 78 5 5 64 65 64½ 612½ Nunez A 104 13.60 82-13 ACalltoRise1151¾HeavyRin1154½ProServe115 No factor 7
16Jly92-Originally scheduled on turf
18Jun92- 5Bel fm 1 1/16 [T]:464 1:112 1:423 ⒻClm 90000 77 7 7 75 72¾ 53¾ 42¼ Davis R G 117 2.20e 83-11 AplchSnst113½RscnClln111hdWndsptWns121 Late gain 8
10Jun92- 7Bel fm 1 Ⓣ:472 1:113 1:353 3↑ⒻAlw 31000 81 7 7 83½ 82¾ 63¾ 55¼ Velazquez J R 110 27.10 79-19 Rffinierte-Ir1173Orine117nkSecretHze-Gb117 No threat 9
10May92- 6Bel sly 1¼ :474 1:382 2:044 3↑ⒻAlw 31000 61 3 2 33 32½ 54 612¼ Velazquez J R 110 17.30 55-26 LadyLear1194KathyMcGee1192PlaybytheRules114 Tired 7
10May92-Originally scheduled on turf
29Apr92- 3Aqu gd 1⅛ Ⓣ:49 1:141 1:513 3↑ⒻAlw 31000 75 10 3 43½ 93¾105¾ 89¼ Santiago A 113 10.10 76-15 AShkQn1193PrncngBllrn119noTpAppl-Fr119 Wide tired 10
11Apr92- 7Aqu sly 1 :461 1:111 1:372 ⒻAmerigoLdy 52 8 8 68 56 69½ 615½ Santiago A 116 2.90 60-22 CrouslMdnss1162½EnMnMny1142ShrdMgc116 No factor 8
29Mar92- 2Aqu fst 1 :484 1:152 1:40 3↑Ⓕ[S]Alw 29000 81 1 3 62¾ 51½ 14 18 Santiago A 113 *.90e 62-33 Tiffny'sTylor1138KtieBlum111nkKyl'sKrm112 Mild drive 8
14Mar92- 3Aqu fst 6f :233 :47 1:121 ⒻClm 50000 85 5 4 21 31 12 15¼ Santiago A 116 7.70 80-23 Tiffany'sTylor1165¼Kte'sCollege1161½Kersey116 Driving 6
4Sep91- 8Bel fst 6f :22 :46 1:111 Ⓕ[S]Mohawk 57 1 5 69 64¼ 46½ 510 Smith M E 113 4.20 74-16 LtstScndl1143½MssIronQull1124½SyHyPl113 Saved grnd 8
LATEST WORKOUTS Jly 31 Sar Ⓣ 3f gd :373 H (d) Jly 29 Sar 3f fst :354 H Jly 25 Sar tr.t 4f fst :503 H Jly 14 Bel 4f fst :474 H

Whozini

Gr. f. 4, by Jacques Who—Danger Zone, by Zoning
Br.—Rich Jill P (NY)
Tr.—Rich David C (2 0 0 0 .00)
CARLE J D (5 0 0 0 .00)
Own.—Rich Jill P
112
Lifetime 7 2 1 0 $38,280
1992 4 2 0 0 $33,000
1991 3 M 1 0 $5,280
Turf 3 2 0 0 $33,000
Wet 1 0 1 0 $5,280

26Jly92- 9Bel fm 1 1/16 Ⓣ:471 1:114 1:43 3↑Ⓕ[S]Alw 29000 83 9 5 53½ 2hd 1hd 12 Carle J D 119 5.70 81-24 Whozn1192Phlp1111¾RoscommnClln111 Drifted driving 12
3Jly92- 9Bel fm 1 1/16 Ⓣ:461 1:104 1:424 3↑Ⓕ[S]Md Sp Wt 82 6 6 53½ 1½ 19 110 Carle J D 122 9.40 82-15 Whozini12210 Raja Fair1164¾ Carabid116 Kept to drive 10
13Jun92- 5Bel fm 1 Ⓣ:464 1:111 1:354 3↑ⒻMd Sp Wt 56 2 8 86 96¾ 713 610¾ Carle J D 122 101.60 72-13 Insurprise1142½Kte'sPride114¾Herto'Mine114 No threat 12
13Jun92-Placed fifth through disqualification
21May92- 9Bel fst 6½f :231 :474 1:194 3↑Ⓕ[S]Md Sp Wt 25 4 7 52½ 73¼ 88¼ 810¾ Maple E 124 58.20 63-16 WhsprHll1151½RbccLrn1152CrbAm115 Lacked room trn 14
24Jly91- 9Sar fst 7f :222 :453 1:263 3↑Ⓕ[S]Md Sp Wt 31 10 3 75½109½117¾1013 Carr D 116 20.70 59-14 Freedom'sWave1163Romanllure1221½Gllntin116 Outrun 12
5Jly91- 9Bel sly 6f :221 :454 1:103 3↑Ⓕ[S]Md Sp Wt 40 3 7 914 79½ 613 216 Carr D 116 54.20 71-12 Shimissee11616 Whozini1163Gallantina116 Up for place 14
26Jun91- 6Bel fst 7f :221 :461 1:261 3↑Ⓕ[S]Md Sp Wt 31 12 7 12161114 810 813¼ Santiago A 114 111.50 60-16 ForElan1141MisteeVee1224½QuickJenny114 Never close 13
LATEST WORKOUTS Aug 13 Sar tr.t 3f fst :363 H Aug 8 Sar tr.t 5f fst 1:033 B ●Jly 23 Sar tr.t 4f fst :493 H Jly 13 Sar tr.t 4f fst :494 H

Irish Actress Dk. b. or br. m. 5, by Seattle Song—Dianette, by Thorn

SMITH M E (82 17 15 12 .21) Br.—Delaney Austin (NY)

Own.—Delaney Austin Tr.—O'Brien Leo (21 3 3 1 .14)

121

Lifetime								
35 9 8 4	1992	6	3	0	1	$122,004
$404,699	1991	13	3	3	2	$157,329
	Turf	24	7	6	3	$327,273
	Wet	2	1	0	0	$16,200

2Aug92- 7Sar	fm	1 1/16	[T]:45	$1{:}08^4$	$1{:}41^2$	3↑ⒻHandicap	94	7	7	7^{16}	7^6	$5^{2\frac12}$	$1^{\frac12}$	Smith M E	b	116	2.90	98-04	Irish Actress116½ Le Famo118nk Aurora115	Driving	7
17Jly92- 8Bel	yl	1 1/16	[T]:47^3	$1{:}12^1$	$1{:}44^1$	3↑ⒻHandicap	93	5	4	4^6	$4^{3\frac12}$	$4^{\frac34}$	1^{hd}	Smith M E	b	115	*1.40	77-29	IrshActrss115hdVrnMchl1143Rtlnt-Ir116	Chk, alt crs, dr	5
28Jun92- 8Bel	fm	1 1/16	Ⓣ:46^1	$1{:}09^2$	1:41	3↑Ⓕ[S]MntVrnon	86	7	7	7^6	5^2	$3^{\frac12}$	$3^{\frac12}$	Velazquez J R	b	122	*1.90	90-11	Tlc'sCvntry113nkAsrckt113nkIrshActrss122	Std, alt crse	9
28Jun92-Run in Divisions																					
17May92- 7Bel	yl	1	Ⓣ:48^1	$1{:}12^4$	$1{:}37^3$	3↑ⒻAlw 47000	87	3	6	6^6	$6^{3\frac14}$	$6^{4\frac34}$	$5^{5\frac34}$	McMahon H I7	b	110	5.70	68-26	LeFmo1191¼DncingDvltt119¾MmorisOfPm117	No threat	6
4May92- 6Aqu	fm	1⅛	Ⓣ:46^3	$1{:}11^1$	$1{:}49^1$	3↑[S]Kingston	94	9	5	$5^{8\frac12}$	$3^{2\frac12}$	1^1	1^{nk}	Velazquez J R	b	121	*1.00	97-07	Irish Actress121nk Koala Road1176 Jay Gee109	All out	10
4May92-Run in Divisons																					
23Apr92- 8Aqu	sf	1 1/16	Ⓣ:50^1	$1{:}15^2$	1:48	3↑ⒻAlw 47000	87	6	6	$6^{8\frac12}$	$5^{5\frac12}$	4^5	4^6	Maple E	b	117	6.50	65-29	Shref1171VirginMichl119noQunOfSvns117	Flattened out	6
22Nov91- 8Aqu	sly	1⅛	:49^2	$1{:}13^4$	1:52	3↑ⒻHandicap	—	6	4	4^2	4^4	6^{13}	—	Smith M E	b	116	2.80	— —	QueenOfSevens109nkJcuzziBoogie120½Violetr110	Eased	6
22Nov91-Originally scheduled on turf																					
14Nov91- 7Aqu	fm	1 1/16	Ⓣ:49	$1{:}13^2$	1:45	3↑ⒻAlw 47000	98	8	6	6^4	$6^{1\frac12}$	$5^{1\frac34}$	1^1	Smith M E	b	115	*1.20	87-13	IrishActress1151QuenOfSvns115½Lrycl115	Blocked,drvg	8
25Oct91- 8Aqu	fm	1⅛	Ⓣ:48^2	1:12	$1{:}50^1$	3↑[S]A T Cole H	98	7	9	$8^{6\frac34}$	$8^{3\frac34}$	$5^{1\frac14}$	2^{nk}	Smith M E	b	113	3.70e	95-09	Kt'sVlntin116nkIrshActrss1131½MrcoAurlo109	Sharp try	9

LATEST WORKOUTS Jly 11 Bel 4f fst :49^3 B   Jun 24 Bel 4f gd :47^3 H   Jun 18 Bel [T] 5f fm 1:02 B (d)

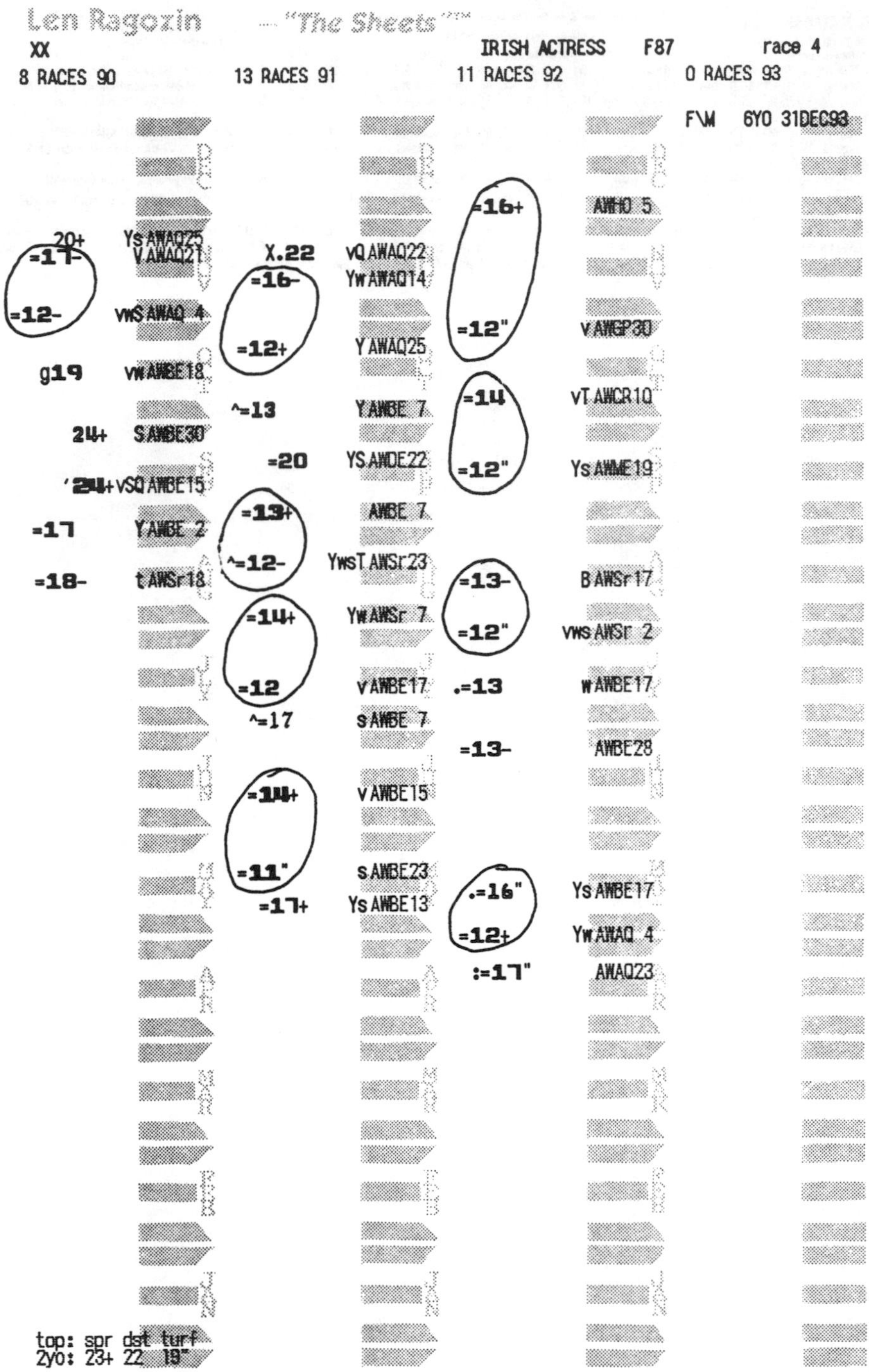
Len Ragozin ... "The Sheets"™
XX
IRISH ACTRESS F87 race 4
8 RACES 90
13 RACES 91
11 RACES 92
0 RACES 93
F\M 6YO 31DEC93
20+ YsAWAQ25
=17- VAWAQ21
=12- vwSAWAQ 4
g19 vwAWBE18
24+ SAWBE30
'24+vSQAWBE15
=17 YAWBE 2
=18- tAWSr18
X.22 vQAWAQ22
=16- YwAWAQ14
=12+ YAWAQ25
^=13 YAWBE 7
=20 YSAWDE22
=13+ AWBE 7
^=12- YwsTAWSr23
=14+ YwAWSr 7
=12 vAWBE17
^=17 sAWBE 7
=14+ vAWBE15
=11" sAWBE23
=17+ YsAWBE13
=16+ AWHO 5
=12" vAWGP30
=14 vTAWCR10
=12" YsAWME19
=13- BAWSr17
=12" vwsAWSr 2
.=13 wAWBE17
=13- AWBE28
.=16" YsAWBE17
=12+ YwAWAQ 4
:=17" AWAQ23
top: spr dst turf
2yo: 23+ 22 19"

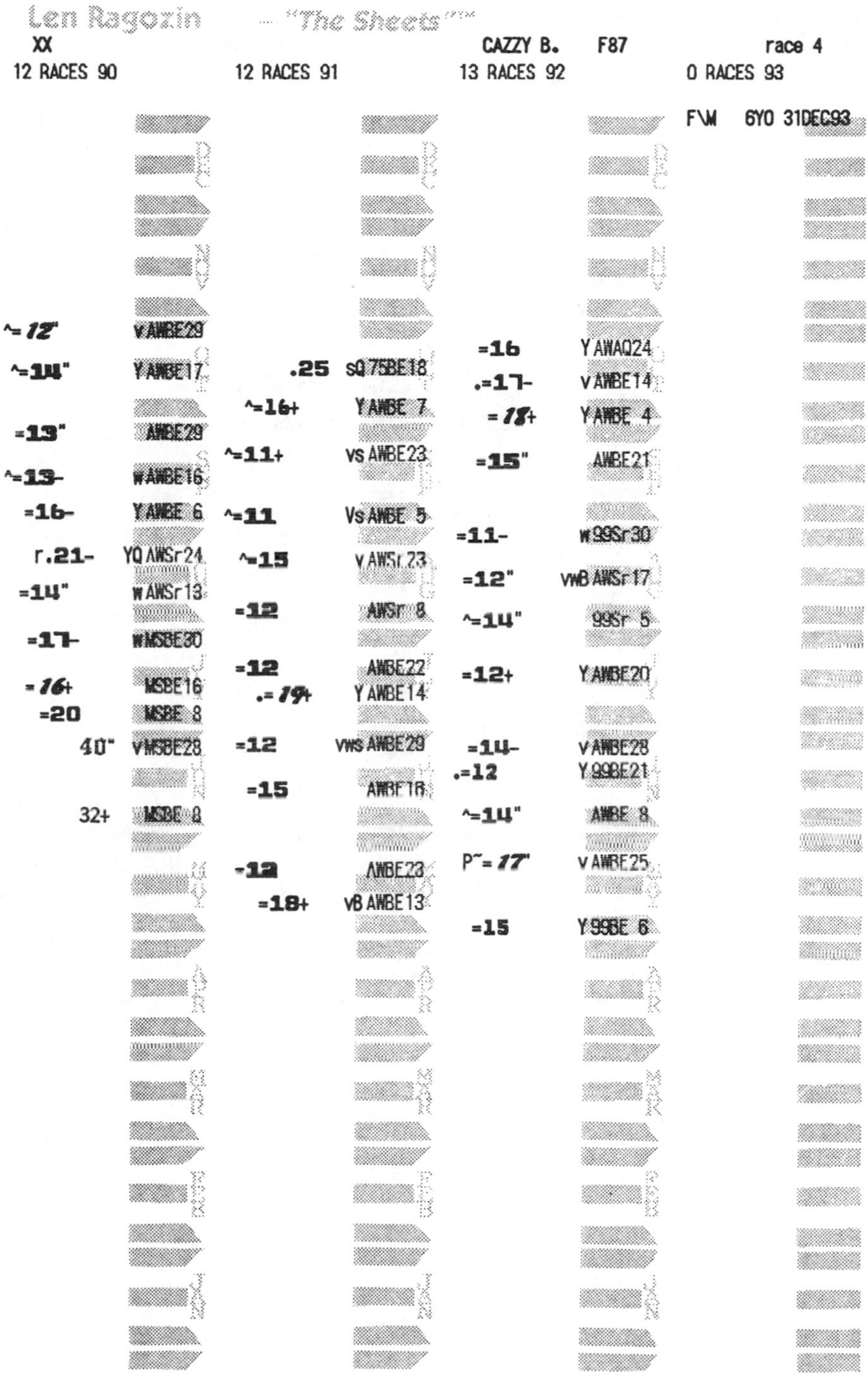
Len Ragozin — "The Sheets"™
XX
CAZZY B. F87
race 4
12 RACES 90
12 RACES 91
13 RACES 92
0 RACES 93
F\M 6YO 31DEC93
^=12" vAWBE29
^=14" YAWBE17
=13" AWBE29
^=13- wAWBE16
=16- YAWBE 6
r.21- YQAWSr24
=14" wAWSr13
=17- wMSBE30
=16+ MSBE16
=20 MSBE 8
40" vMSBE28
32+ MSBE 8
.25 sQ75BE18
^=16+ YAWBE 7
^=11+ VsAWBE23
^=11 VsAWBE 5
^=15 vAWSr23
=12 AWSr 8
=12 AWBE22
.=19+ YAWBE14
=12 vwsAWBE29
=15 AWBE16
=12 AWBE23
=18+ vBAWBE13
=16 YAWAQ24
.=17- vAWBE14
=18+ YAWBE 4
=15" AWBE21
=11- w99Sr30
=12" vwBAWSr17
^=14" 99Sr 5
=12+ YAWBE20
=14- vAWBE28
.=12 Y99BE21
^=14" AWBE 8
P~=17" vAWBE25
=15 Y99BE 6

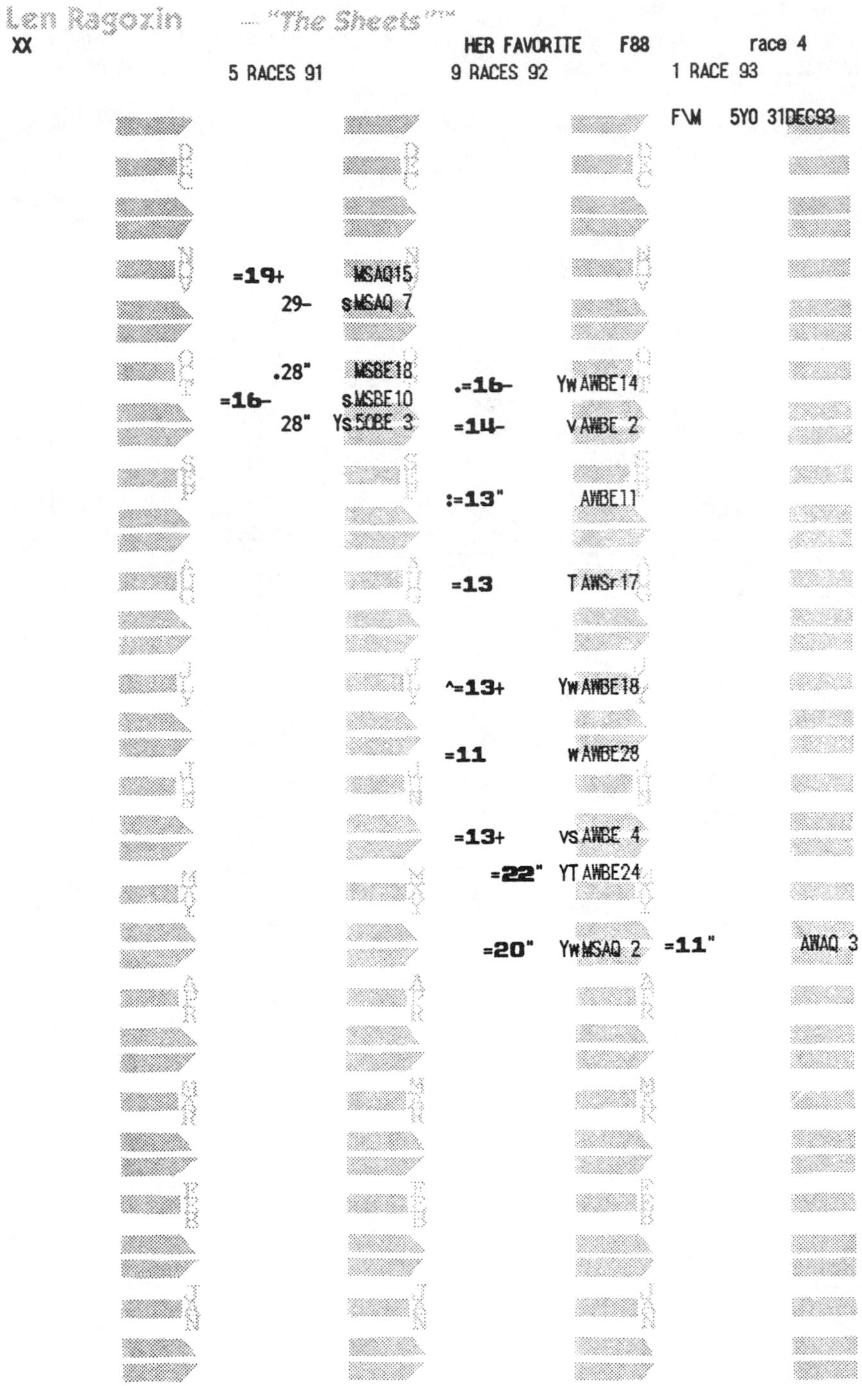

Len Ragozin — "The Sheets"™

XX HER FAVORITE F88 race 4

5 RACES 91 9 RACES 92 1 RACE 93

F\M 5YO 31DEC93

=19+ MSAQ15

29- sMSAQ 7

.28" MSBE18 .=16- YwAWBE14

=16- sMSBE10

28" Ys50BE 3 =14- vAWBE 2

:=13" AWBE11

=13 TAWSr17

^=13+ YwAWBE18

=11 wAWBE28

=13+ vsAWBE 4

=22" YTAWBE24

=20" YwMSAQ 2 =11" AWAQ 3

Irish Actress was always tough in stakes restricted to New York–breds: she was a fast-closing second against males in the Ashley T. Cole the previous autumn, she had returned to beat males by a neck in the Kingston in her second start of the year, and she had probably been best when forced to take up sharply in the stretch of the Mount Vernon on June 28. Since then, she had won back-to-back overnight handicaps against open company and had overcome an outside post similar to today's in her last victory.

A look at *The Sheets* for Irish Actress, Her Favorite, and Cazzy B. showed they were closely matched. This brought up an interesting angle on the Yaddo: If one were to make an odds line on the three contenders, which one would be favored to run a 12?

Perhaps Her Favorite or Cazzy B., but certainly not Irish Actress! The knock on Irish Actress was this: she had just run a 12½ on August 2, and on six previous occasions she had bounced after a similar figure. Usually the bounce wasn't much, mind you, but she had never run 12s back-to-back. If she failed to pair up again, she was on equal footing with Cazzy B. and Her Favorite.

Her Favorite was lightly raced and rapidly improving, was fresh from the three best races of her life, and had been given a month off for the Yaddo. Cazzy B.'s last four races had produced figures of 12, 13¾, 12¼, and 14½, and a projection could be made for at least a 12 and possibly an 11, since the five-year-old mare's sheet revealed improvement in late summer and early fall of her two previous campaigns.

I thought the race was a toss-up among the trio, and odds of 6–1 on Cazzy B. made her an obvious overlay. Taking an aggressive approach, I bet $40 to win on Cazzy B., a $25 Cazzy B./Her Favorite exacta, and a $10 exacta Her Favorite/Cazzy B.

The race unfolded perfectly except for one thing: Cazzy B. drifted out under a left-handed whip, carrying Her Favorite well past the middle of the course, and the order of finish was reversed. What would've been a touchdown resulted in a return of only $252, but the pattern on Irish Actress had been valid.

SIXTH RACE
Saratoga
AUGUST 17, 1992

1 ⅛ MILES.(Turf). (1.45^{2}) 13th Running THE YADDO (1st Division). Purse $75,000 Added. Fillies and mares, 3-year-olds and upward foaled in New York State and approved by the New York State-Bred Registry. By subscription of $200 each which should accompany the nomination; $800 to pass the entry box; $800 to start with $75,000 added. The added money and all fees to be divided 60% to the winner, 22% to second, 12% to third and 6% to fourth. Weights, 3-year-olds, 116 lbs.; older, 121 lbs. Winners of two races of $30,000 at a mile or over in 1992 an additional 3 lbs. Non-winners of a race of $50,000 at any distance allowed 3 lbs.; of such a race of $30,000, 5 lbs.; of two races of $20,000 at a mile or over, 7 lbs.; of such a race, 9 lbs. Starters to be named at the closing time of entries. A perpetual trophy will be on display in the Winner's Circle. The New York Racing Association Inc. reserves the right to transfer this race to the main course. Closed Wednesday, July 29, with 38 nominations.
Value of race $93,200; value to winner $55,920; second $20,504; third $11,184; fourth $5,592. Mutuel pool $318,965. Exacta Pool $557,692 Triple Pool $270,140

Last Raced	Horse	M/Eqt.	A.	Wt	PP	St	¼	½	¾	Str	Fin	Jockey	Odds $1
5Aug92 ^{1}Sar^{2}	[D]Cazzy B.		5	114	3	4	$4^{1\frac{1}{2}}$	4^{1}	$3^{1\frac{1}{2}}$	1^{hd}	1^{nk}	Antley C W	6.40
18Jly92 ^{5}Bel^{1}	Her Favorite		4	118	2	2	$6^{\frac{1}{2}}$	5^{2}	$4^{1\frac{1}{2}}$	3^{1}	$2^{3\frac{1}{2}}$	Maple E	3.40
2Aug92 ^{7}Sar^{1}	Irish Actress	b	5	121	8	7	7^{1}	7^{hd}	5^{2}	5^{2}	$3^{\frac{3}{4}}$	Smith M E	.80
31Jly92 ^{7}Sar^{3}	Sassa Blue	b	4	112	4	3	$1^{\frac{1}{2}}$	$1^{1\frac{1}{2}}$	$1^{1\frac{1}{2}}$	2^{hd}	$4^{\frac{3}{4}}$	Samyn J L	17.90
3Aug92 ^{5}Sar^{5}	Asaracket	b	4	112	1	1	$2^{1\frac{1}{2}}$	$2^{2\frac{1}{2}}$	$2^{\frac{1}{2}}$	$4^{\frac{1}{2}}$	5^{4}	Carr D	10.30
26Jly92 ^{9}Bel^{1}	Whozini		4	112	7	6	5^{hd}	6^{1}	6^{1}	$6^{1\frac{1}{2}}$	6^{2}	Carle J D	18.30
1Aug92 ^{2}Sar^{5}	R. E. Darla	b	3	109	6	8	8	8	8	7^{12}	7^{22}	Cruguet J	38.60
1Aug92 ^{10}FL^{1}	Heaven Knows Why	b	4	121	5	5	$3^{1\frac{1}{2}}$	3^{1}	$7^{\frac{1}{2}}$	8	8	Bailey J D	12.40

[D]-Cazzy B. Disqualified and placed second.

OFF AT 3:51 Start Good, Won driving. Time, :24 , :47^{2}, 1:10^{4}, 1:35 , 1:47^{2} Course firm.

$2 Mutuel Prices:			
3-(C)-HER FAVORITE	8.80	4.80	3.00
4-(D)-CAZZY B.		4.20	3.00
1-(A)-IRISH ACTRESS			2.40

$2 EXACTA 3-4 PAID $50.40 $2 TRIPLE 3-4-1 PAID $94.00

Her Favorite—B. f, by Poison Ivory—Duke's Dilemma, by Amber Duke. Trainer Freyer Donna J. Bred by Waller Thomas M (NY).

CAZZY B. well placed early angled to the outside along the backstretch gradually worked her way forward on the turn, overtook SASSA BLUE, to gain a narrow advantage in midstretch, drifted out under left hand whipping to brush with her favorite inside the furlong marker, battled heads apart with that one while continuing to drift through the lane and prevailed in a hard drive. Following a stewards inquiry as well as a claim of foul lodged by the rider of her favorite, CAZZY B. was disqualified from first and placed second for interference in the stretch. HER FAVORITE, raced in good position while saving ground for six furlongs, angled out on the turn, circled four wide rallying into the stretch, drew along side CAZZY B. to challenge in midstretch then was carried out by that one through the final eighth of a mile. IRISH ACTRESS, reserved for a half, worked her way into contention on the turn, lodged a mild rally while between horses in upper stretch but couldn't sustain her bid. SASSA BLUE set the pace along the inside into midstretch and weakened from her early efforts. ASRACKET raced in close contention while slightly off the rail for six furlongs then tired. WHOZINI was never a serious threat. R. E. DARLA never reached contention. HEAVEN KNOWS WHY faded after going five furlongs.

Owners— 1, Dutch Acres Farms; 2, Tanrackin Farm; 3, Delaney Austin; 4, Kevmar Stable; 5, Slifstern Sherry; 6, Rich Jill P; 7, Trotta Gerald T; 8, Payson Virginia Kraft.

Trainers— 1, Walsh Thomas M; 2, Freyer Donna J; 3, O'Brien Leo; 4, Sciacca Gary; 5, Destasio Richard A; 6, Rich David C; 7, Hargrave Kenneth; 8, Bond Harold James.

Corrected weight: Heaven Knows Why 121 pounds. **Overweight:** Cazzy B. 2 pounds; R. E. Darla 2.

Scratched—Cady Hill Fun (3Aug92 ^{2}Sar^{3}); Tiffany's Taylor (10Aug92 ^{5}Sar^{2}).

Incidentally, Cazzy B.'s pattern of improvement in late summer proved valid as well. After the Yaddo, she returned in a high-priced claimer on August 30 and won, paying $7.80. Her figure that day was a career best of 10¾.

PAIR-UPS

A common pattern occurs when a horse runs the same figure in back-to-back starts. This can be a positive or negative development, depending on how the first of the paired figures is evaluated.

Committee Chairman
Own: Vogel Marcus
NO RIDER (—)

Ch. c. 3 (Feb)
Sire: Believe It (In Reality)
Dam: After School (Arts and Letters)
Br: Marcus Vogel & Hortense Vogel (Ky)
Tr: Barrera Luis (8 1 1 2 .13)

116

Lifetime Record:	12 3 2 2	$70,240			
1993	10 3 2 1	$67,360	Turf	1 0 0 0	
1992	2 M 0 1	$2,880	Wet	3 1 1 0	$25,610
Bel (T)	0 0 0 0		Dist (T)	0 0 0 0	

22Sep93-8Bel my 1⅛ :47 1:112 1:36 1:49 3+ Alw 32000N2X 94 1 4 32½ 2hd 21 22½ McCauley W H 115 f 5.20 82-22 DAllMyTricks1122½ CommittChrmn1152½ SlwsGold1135¼ Checked 1/8 pole 7
Placed first through disqualification.
9Sep93-7Bel fst 1 1/16 :232 :461 1:11 1:431 3+ Alw 32000N2X 90 5 5 56 43 31½ 22½ McCauley W H 118 f 6.80 83-23 AllGone1132½ CommitteeChairman118¾ ChrmingBuck1175 Finished well 7
21Aug93-1Sar fst 1⅛ :46 1:111 1:37 1:501 3+ Alw 28500N1X 87 1 5 814 68 21 13 McCauley W H 112 f 4.40 85-10 Committee Chairman1123 Islanders Cure112½ Zeus Energy1121¼ Driving 9
7Aug93-10Sar gd 1⅛ (T) :471 1:113 1:372 1:494 3+ Alw 28500N1X 70 12 9 117½ 116¾ 115½ 1011 McCauley W H 113 f 20.10 69-27 Sentimental Moi1153½ Eridge113nk Nobiz Like Showbiz114¾ No factor 12
26Jly93-6Bel fst 7f :23 :461 1:11 1:241 3+ Alw 26500N1X 81 6 6 63 53 31 3½ McCauley W H 116 f 12.40 82-18 Crsey'sPl111nk Here'sNoh114hd CommitteChirmn116nk Lacked room 1/8 pl 8
18Jly93-7Bel fst 6f :223 :454 :581 1:11 3+ Md Sp Wt 75 4 2 42½ 54 21 12 McCauley W H 116 f 9.70 85-09 Committee Chairman1162 Roger Rocket116¾ Dixie Reef1166 Driving 7
3Jly93-5Bel my 1 1/16 :224 :461 1:111 1:43 3+ Md Sp Wt 74 3 4 41¼ 3½ 21½ 24¾ McCauley W H 116 fb 9.10 82-11 MineD'or1164¾ CommitteeChairman1163 FourStrTom1162½ Rallied inside 7
2Feb93-3GP fst 7f :231 :464 1:122 1:26 Md Sp Wt 40 9 10 52¼ 51¼ 78¼ 108¾ Ferrer J C 120 b 3.00 64-22 Run Dance120½ Blue Beacon1202½ Wild Edition120nk Stopped wide 11
23Jan93-3GP fst 7f :23 :464 1:121 1:25 Md Sp Wt 56 1 8 52½ 72½ 87¼ 67¼ Ferrer J C 120 b 23.40 71-16 Country Store120no Marco Bay1201 L's Golden Knight1202¾ 12
Checked on the turn, tight quarters
16Jan93-6GP sly 7f :224 :461 1:113 1:242 Md Sp Wt 64 10 2 4¾ 2½ 3½ 48½ Ferrer J C 120 b 18.40 72-21 DreadMeNot1205 StopAndListen1202 SayCheeseGeorge1151½ Weakened 10
WORKOUTS: Oct 8 Bel tr.t 5f fst 1:011 H 2/6 Sep 29 Bel tr.t 4f fst :49 B 13/51 ●Sep 16 Bel tr.t 4f fst :47 H 1/10 Sep 3 Bel tr.t 6f fst 1:18 B 2/2 Aug 27 Sar tr.t 4f fst :50 B 2/12 Aug 14 Sar 4f fst :463 H 3/23

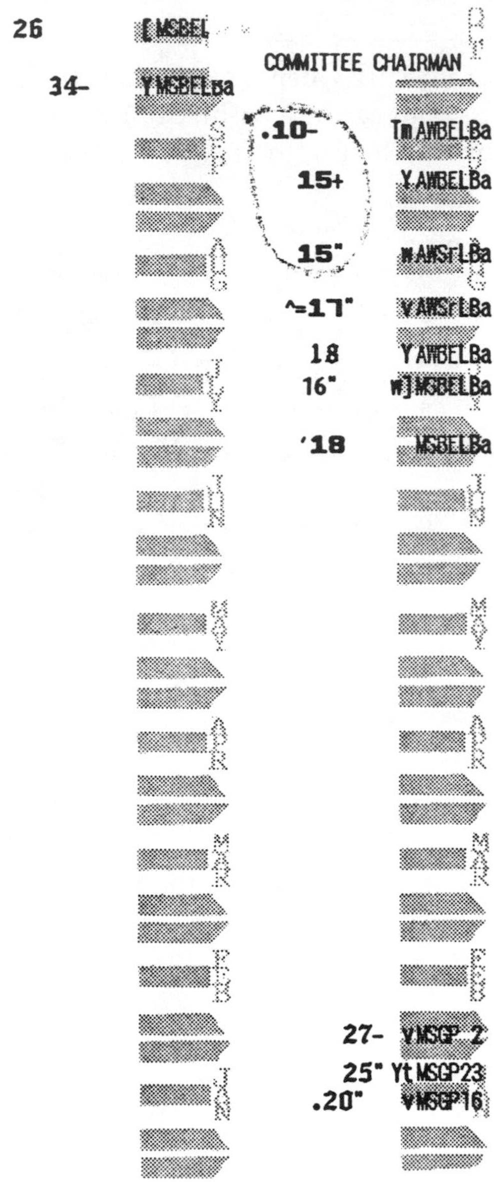

Committee Chairman paired 15s (15½ and 15¼) on *The Sheets* while essentially pairing Beyers of 87 and 90 on August 21 and September 9.

Whether the 15s are a positive or negative development depends upon an assessment of the first 15.

In the case of Committee Chairman, the first 15 continues a solid forging pattern. The colt improved six points, running a 20 first time out at age three, but the effort knocked him off form to a 25, a 27, and ultimately to the sidelines. The 18 first time back July 3 was a 2-point improvement on his previous best, made all the more impressive because it was his first route start. Another small improvement of 1½ points followed the return race, when Committee Chairman broke his maiden. Whereas the 20 had precipitated the colt's undoing in January, the move to 16½ indicated the 18 first time back hadn't bothered him. When he came down another point to 15½ three starts later, Committee Chairman was announcing that the 16½ hadn't been overly stressful either.

That initial 15½ from Committee Chairman was a strong indication of a forging horse moving to better figures with a series of small improvements. Therefore, he only reinforced the analysis by pairing up.

When a forging, lightly raced horse such as Committee Chairman pairs small improvements to a new lifetime top, one should be prejudiced in favor of continued development in upcoming races whenever the odds are generous, relative to specific circumstances: if Committee Chairman is entered off the 15s in a race in which he'll have to run an 8 to contend for the win, you'd better get tremendous odds; but if he's 5–1 in a race in which a 14 looks good enough, you'd probably want to consider a wager on that possibility.

Committee Chairman did run a new lifetime top right off the pair, paying $12.40 when moved up through a disqualification on September 22.

When a pair represents a substantial improvement to a new lifetime top, however, handicappers should take a negative viewpoint and expect the horse to react with a bounce next time out.

Case in point, Thunder Rumble, who was favored in the Woodward Stakes after his smashing Travers victory:

8

1⅛ MILES. **(1.452) 39th Running THE WOODWARD (Grade I). Purse $500,000 Guaranteed. 3-year-olds and upward. By subscription of $1,000 each which should accompany the nomination; $4,000 to pass the entry box; $4,000 to start. The purse to be divided 60% to the winner, 22% to second, 12% to third and 6% to fourth. Weight for age: 3-year-olds, 121 lbs.; older, 126 lbs. Starters to be named at the closing time of entries. The estate of Mrs. William Woodward, Sr. to add the Woodward Challenge Cup to be won three times, not necessarily consecutively, by the same owner before becoming his or her property. The owner of the winner will also receive a trophy for permanent possession and trophies will be presented to the winning trainer and jockey. Closed Wednesday, September 2, with 20 nominations.**

Sultry Song

BAILEY J D (53 12 9 7 .23)
Own.—Live Oak Plantation
B. c. 4, by Cox's Ridge—Sultry Sun, by Buckfinder
Br.—Live Oak Stud (Fla)
Tr.—Kelly Patrick J (10 1 1 0 .10)
126

Lifetime						
20 8 3 5	1992	5	2	1	1	$767,700
$1,205,276	1991	15	6	2	4	$437,576
	Turf	4	0	2	1	$67,804
	Wet	1	0	0	1	$60,000

29Aug92- 8Sar fst 1⅛ :454 1:10 1:471 3↑Whitney H 112 3 5 55½ 43 1hd 1no Bailey J D b 115 3.40 101 — SltrySong115noOtofPlc1154ChfHoncho116 Drifted, drvg 9
29Aug92-Grade I
18Jly92- 8Bel fst 1¼ :46 1:352 2:001 3↑Suburban H 98 5 6 511 64 57 69¼ Bailey J D b 116 1.70 81-16 PlesntTp1191½StrikthGold1191¼DfnsivPly115 No factor 7
18Jly92-Grade I
27Jun92- 4Hol fst 1¼ :461 1:344 2:001 3↑Hol Gld Cup 113 4 5 53½ 3nk 11½ 13½ Bailey J D b 113 9.90 96-06 SultrySong1133½Mrquetry118hdAnotherRviw120 Driving 6
27Jun92-Grade I
6Jun92- 7Bel my 1⅛ :444 1:082 1:463 3↑Nassau Co H 108 9 5 64 63¼ 3½ 31¾ Bailey J D b 111 15.20 94-08 StrkthGold116nkPlsntTp1191½SltrySng111 Wide gamely 9
6Jun92-Grade II
30May92- 8Pim fm 1 1/16 Ⓣ:492 1:143 1:452 Alw 35000 93 4 4 43 42¼ 32 22¼ McCauley W H b 122 *1.40 72-26 MakinMoney1142¼SultrySong1222RootBoy119 Steadied 6
2Nov91- 5CD fm 1 Ⓣ:48 1:122 1:372 3↑Br Cp Mile 82 11 12 103¼ 137¾ 1410 1415¼ Bailey J D LBb 123 16.30f 82-06 OpningVrs1261½VldsBois-Fr126noStrofCozzn123 Outrun 14
2Nov91-Grade I
26Oct91- 8Aqu fst 1 :444 1:083 1:333 3↑N Y R A Mile 110 5 6 62¼ 52¼ 51¾ 2hd Bailey J D b 111 10.10 94-08 Rubiano116hd Sultry Song1111 Diablo112 Gamely 15
26Oct91-Grade I
6Oct91- 6Bel fst 1 :462 1:094 1:342 Jamaica H 108 6 3 31 3½ 2½ 1nk Antley C W b 113 *2.10 98-11 SultrySong113nkHonestEnsign110nkTkMOut116 Driving 7
6Oct91-Grade II
20Sep91- 9Med fst 1⅛ :46 1:093 1:462 Pegasus H 106 4 4 43¼ 32½ 35½ 35¾ Antley C W b 114 3.90 97-07 Scan1191¾ Sea Cadet1194 Sultry Song114 Willingly 8
20Sep91-Grade I
2Sep91- 8AP fm 1¼ Ⓣ:464 1:364 2:011 Secretariat 100 6 7 66 64¼ 41¾ 3nk Antley C W b 114 6.00 92-09 JackieWckie123hdOlympio126hdSultrySong114 Late bid 8
2Sep91-Grade I

LATEST WORKOUTS Sep 15 Bel 5f fst :594 B — Sep 10 Bel 5f fst 1:03 B — Sep 6 Bel 4f fst :503 B — Aug 23 Sar 6f fst 1:133 H

Strike the Gold

PERRET C (12 2 2 1 .17)
Own.—C C W Gold Stable
Ch. c. 4, by Alydar—Majestic Gold, by Hatchet Man
Br.—Calumet Farm (Ky)
Tr.—Zito Nicholas P (12 2 0 0 .17)
126

Lifetime						
25 5 7 4	1992	10	2	4	1	$1,603,176
$3,164,426	1991	12	2	3	3	$1,443,850
	Wet	1	1	0	0	$300,000

29Aug92- 8Sar fst 1⅛ :454 1:10 1:471 3↑Whitney H 98 4 9 918 78½ 64¼ 58½ Perret C 120 *1.60e 92 — SltrySong115noOtfPlc1154ChfHnch116 Wide, flttnd out 9
29Aug92-Grade I
8Aug92- 8Mth fst 1⅛ :453 1:09 1:464 3↑Iselin H 101 10 11 1117 1112 54½ 42½ Perret C 120 *1.70e 102 — Jolie'sHlo116hdOutofPlce1131VllyCrossing111 Willingly 11
8Aug92-Grade I
18Jly92- 8Bel fst 1¼ :46 1:352 2:001 3↑Suburban H 110 4 7 721 43½ 32½ 21½ Perret C 119 *1.50e 88-16 PlsntTp1191½StrikthGold1191½DfnsvPly115 Rallied wide 7
18Jly92-Grade I
6Jun92- 7Bel my 1⅛ :444 1:082 1:463 3↑Nassau Co H 111 5 9 915 95¾ 2½ 1nk Perret C 116 4.80 96-08 StrikthGold116nkPlsntTp1191½SultrySong111 Wide drvg 9
6Jun92-Grade II
9May92-10Pim fst 1 3/16 :473 1:112 1:544 Pim Specl H 111 4 7 711 78¼ 32 1¾ Perret C 114 6.30 88-23 StrkthGld114¾FlySFr1161½TlghtAgnd122 Wide, driving 7
9May92-Grade I
4Apr92- 7Aqu fst 1 3/16 :481 1:12 1:553 3↑Thrty Six Rd 101 3 4 413 413 37 26 Antley C W 117 *.80 90-21 RedPine1196StriketheGold117hdAlyten117 Up for place 4
7Mar92-10GP fst 1¼ :473 1:363 2:013 3↑Gulf Park H 110 6 5 518 511 48 27 Krone J A 115 2.00 86-14 SeCdet1197StrikthGold1152½SunnySunris114 4 wide str 6
7Mar92-Grade I
17Feb92-10GP fst 1⅛ :472 1:112 1:492 3↑Broward H 107 3 6 614 58 44 31 Krone J A 117 *.80 89-21 HnstEnsgn109noPntBttrOnt1141StrkthGld117 4 wide str 7
17Feb92-Grade III
1Feb92- 9GP fst 1⅛ :464 1:101 1:48 3↑Donn H 104 6 8 818 815 711 67 Antley C W 116 *1.30 90-12 SeCdet1153OutofPlc114nkSunnySunris115 Vry wide str 8
1Feb92-Grade I
8Jan92- 7GP fst 7f :234 :462 1:241 Alw 22900 99 11 9 1214 911 55 2¾ Antley C W 120 *.70 84-16 ByShrk112¾StriketheGold120½PerfctFit114 Wide bckstr 12

LATEST WORKOUTS Sep 13 Bel 5f fst 1:012 B — Sep 6 Bel 3f fst :364 H — Aug 21 Sar 5f fst 1:003 B — Aug 5 Sar 4f gd :512 B

Pleasant Tap

DELAHOUSSAYE E (—)
Own.—Buckland Farm
B. h. 5, by Pleasant Colony—Never Knock, by Stage Door Johnny
Br.—Evans T M (Va)
Tr.—Speckert Christopher (—)
126

Lifetime						
29 8 7 5	1992	7	3	3	0	$739,914
$1,501,169	1991	8	1	1	3	$470,000
	Turf	3	0	1	0	$20,000
	Wet	1	0	1	0	$110,000

18Jly92- 8Bel fst 1¼ :46 1:352 2:001 3↑Suburban H 112 2 5 39 32 1hd 11½ Delahoussaye E 119 2.00 90-16 PlsntTp1191½StrthGld1191½DfnsvPl115 Ducked out,drvg 7
18Jly92-Grade I
6Jun92- 7Bel my 1⅛ :444 1:082 1:463 3↑Nassau Co H 111 7 8 815 75¼ 51½ 2nk Delahoussaye E 119 5.30 96-08 StrkthGld116nkPlsntTp1191½SltrSng111 Sted, blckd trn 9
6Jun92-Grade II
25May92- 8Bel fst 1 :444 1:082 1:333 3↑Metropoln H 107 10 11 117¼ 87 43 22¼ Delahoussaye E 119 6.70 100-05 DixiBrss1072¼PlsntTp1191¾InExcss-Ir121 Rallied, inside 11
25May92-Grade I
2May92- 7CD fst 7f :224 :452 1:221 C Downs H 104 5 6 82½ 73½ 42 1no Delahoussaye E B 120 *.80 99-02 PlesntTp120noTkMOut1202CntrllRod113 Brsh wire drvg 9
2May92-Grade III
12Apr92- 8Kee fst 7f :222 :451 1:222 3↑Comwth B C 105 3 6 66½ 64½ 2hd 12½ Delahoussaye E B 116 *.90 97-12 PlsntTp1162½ToFrdm115noRnOnthBnk118 Driving clear 6
12Apr92-Grade III
20Feb92- 8SA fst 6f :22 :443 1:084 Alw 50000 100 3 4 54 55½ 54 21¼ Delahoussaye E B 121 *1.80 91-16 Rushmore1151¼ DH ValintPete117 DH PlesntTp121 Rallied 5
20Feb92-Dead heat
11Jan92- 8SA fst 7f :221 :441 1:211 Sn Carlos H 93 1 6 712 711 69 66¼ Delahoussaye E Bb 119 *1.90 91-11 AnswrDo1201½Individulist115hdMdiPln116 Broke slowly 7
11Jan92-Grade II
30Nov91- 8Hol fm 1⅛ Ⓣ:472 1:111 1:454 3↑Citation H 97 3 6 76½ 73½ 74¼ 85¾ Flores D R b 116 20.40 95-07 Fly Till Dawn1191¾ BestPal119nkWolf-Ch119 No mishap 8
30Nov91-Grade II; Run in divisions
2Nov91- 2CD fst 6f :21 :442 1:091 3↑Br Cp Sprnt 105 7 8 1113 1110 63¼ 23 Delahoussaye E Bb 126 8.80 98-02 SheikhAlbadou-GB1243PleasantTp126½RobynDncer126 11
2Nov91-Grade I; 8-wide stretch, rugged in

LATEST WORKOUTS Sep 14 Bel 5f fst 1:02 B — Sep 8 Bel 7f fst 1:243 H — Sep 2 Bel 1 fst 1:393 B — Aug 24 Sar tr.t 5f fst 1:031 B

Thunder Rumble Dk. b. or br. c. 3(Mar), by Thunder Puddles—Lyphette, by Lyphard
MCCAULEY W H (48 14 6 3 .29) Br.—Widmer Konrad (NY)
Own.—Braeburn Farm Tr.—O'Connell Richard (9 1 0 0 .11)
121
Lifetime 9 6 0 1 $865,302 | 1992 7 5 0 1 $850,902 | 1991 2 1 0 0 $14,400 | Turf 2 0 0 0

22Aug92- 7Sar fst 1¼ :464 1:352 2:004 Travers 109 10 4 53½ 41 11½ 14½ McCauley W H 126 7.60 100 — Thunder Rumble1264½ DevilHisDue1264½DanceFloor126 10
22Aug92-Grade I; Bumped early, wide, driving
2Aug92- 8Sar fst 1⅛ :461 1:092 1:472 Jim Dandy 110 3 2 21 21 21 1½ McCauley W H 117 24.90 100 — ThundrRumbl117½DxBrss1267½DvlHsD126 Bmp brk drvg 8
2Aug92-Grade II
11Jly92- 7Bel fm 1 1/16 Ⓣ:48 1:111 1:41 3↑Alw 37000 86 7 2 21 32 66¼ 77¼ McCauley W H 112 3.70 84-12 Now Listen1171½ Ogle1171 Sir Salima117 Tired 8
13Mar92- 8Aqu fst 1⅛ :463 1:114 1:512 Gate Dancer 98 4 4 36½ 33 11½ 15 McCauley W H 119 *.80 79-32 ThndrRmbl1195StpOtFrnt117nkJcksnprt117 Ridden out 8
15Feb92- 8Aqu fst 1 1/16 ⊡:481 1:13 1:441 Whirlaway 84 5 2 1½ 2hd 35 39 McCauley W H 126 *.90 78-26 DrUnrht1195½TnsNmbr1173½ThndrRbl126 Dueled, tired 10
26Jan92- 8Aqu fst 170 ⊡:471 1:13 1:43 Count Fleet 91 2 1 1hd 1hd 12 12 McCauley W H 123 *2.50 90-17 ThunderRumble1232Dr.Unright1193PlceLine119 Driving 7
12Jan92- 8Aqu fst 1 1/16 ⊡:481 1:131 1:464 Ⓢ Montauk 91 7 4 32 21 11½ 14 McCauley W H 117 *2.30e 74-24 Thunder Rumble1174Prioritizer1172JayGee123 Drew off 10
23Dec91- 6Aqu fst 6f ⊡:232 :47 1:113 Md Sp Wt 94 4 5 11½ 11 17 112¾ McCauley W H 118 4.30 85-18 ThundrRumbl11812¾Dlfild1182CllHmNtty118 Ridden out 12
24Oct91- 4Aqu fm 1 Ⓣ:49 1:143 1:402 Ⓢ Md Sp Wt 30 1 2 86 97 815 720 Smith M E 118 *1.50 54-17 PowdrCp1182½A.J.Wrbcks1181StrtYorHrt118 Bolted trn 9
LATEST WORKOUTS Sep 14 Bel 5f fst :594 H Sep 7 Bel tr.t 5f fst 1:014 B Aug 31 Sar 4f fst :50 B ●Aug 17 Sar 5f gd :591 H

Out of Place Ch. h. 5, by Cox's Ridge—Arabian Dancer, by Damascus
ANTLEY C W (19 3 1 2 .16) Br.—Phipps Cynthia (Ky)
Own.—Phipps Cynthia Tr.—McGaughey Claude III (12 6 1 3 .50)
126
Lifetime 24 8 6 6 $673,450 | 1992 7 0 4 2 $370,056 | 1991 8 3 1 1 $168,670 | Wet 2 1 0 0 $60,000

29Aug92- 8Sar fst 1⅛ :454 1:10 1:471 3↑Whitney H 112 6 6 69½ 55 2hd 2no McCauley W H 115 2.80 101 — SultrySong115noOutofPlce1154ChiefHoncho116 Gamely 9
29Aug92-Grade I
8Aug92- 8Mth fst 1⅛ :453 1:09 1:464 3↑Iselin H 105 4 6 65½ 44½ 21 2hd McCauley W H 113 8.10 105 — Jolie'sHlo116hdOutofPlce1131VlleyCrossing111 Gamely 11
8Aug92-Grade I
5Jly92-10Lrl fst 1⅛ :46 1:094 1:473 3↑Baltmr BcH 106 7 7 77 57 33 3nk McCauley W H 113 *2.40 102-08 EcllntTppr112hdSnnSrs117hdOtfPlc113 Altered crse 1/8 10
5Jly92-Grade III
6Jun92- 7Bel my 1⅛ :444 1:082 1:463 3↑Nassau CoH 103 6 7 53 42 41 44½ McCauley W H 114 12.40 91-08 StrikthGold116nkPlsntTp1191½SultrySong111 Bid wknd 9
6Jun92-Grade II
24Apr92- 8Kee fst 1⅛ :482 1:121 1:494 Ben Ali 97 3 4 42 32 33 35 McCauley W H B 119 *1.30 81-14 DH ProfitKey1135DH Loch1175OutofPlc119 Lacked room 6
24Apr92-Grade III
22Mar92- 8Aqu fst 1 :47 1:103 1:344 3↑Wstchstr H 107 6 3 4¾ 31½ 21 2no McCauley W H 115 1.40 88-25 Rubiano117no Out of Place1152 Wild Away111 Gamely 6
22Mar92-Grade III
1Feb92- 9GP fst 1⅛ :464 1:101 1:48 3↑Donn H 111 2 5 44½ 43 42½ 23 McCauley W H 114 36.00 94-12 SeCdet1153OutofPlce114nkSunnySunrise115 Up for 2nd 8
1Feb92-Grade I
28Dec91-10Hia fst 1¼ :49 1:374 2:022 3↑Widener H 109 6 3 42¼ 62¾ 53½ 53¼ McCauley W H 118 4.00 82-21 SportsVw1161¾Alytn113nkPnutButtrOnt114 Dropped bk 11
29Nov91- 9CD fst 1⅛ :484 1:134 1:521 3↑Clark 94 9 7 74¾ 62¾ 3nk 1hd McCauley W H Bb 119 *1.80 87-22 OutofPlace119hdEchelon'sIceMan110¾BritishBnker111 11
29Nov91-Grade III; Split toes driving hard
26Oct91- 8Aqu fst 1 :444 1:083 1:333 3↑N Y R A Mile 108 14 11 84 83½ 41½ 41¼ McCauley W H 112 7.50 93-08 Rubiano116hd Sultry Song1111 Diablo112 Good effort 15
26Oct91-Grade I
LATEST WORKOUTS Sep 17 Bel 4f fst :502 B Sep 13 Bel 5f fst 1:004 H Sep 8 Bel 4f fst :48 B Aug 27 Sar tr.t 4f fst :49 H

Thunder Rumble dominated in the Travers with a monstrous performance, winning by an expanding four and a half lengths despite being bumped early and forced to race wide around both turns. His figure of 109 paired his Jim Dandy — a figure that the crowd had originally perceived to be a fluke. This opinion was reflected by their tepid support of Thunder Rumble in the Travers, but when he delivered the goods again, many of the skeptics were won over, and they drove his price down to 8–5 for his first try against older stakes horses in the Woodward.

The remaining skeptics reasoned, "If one big jump to a new top didn't make Thunder Rumble bounce, then the second one will." Indeed, the pair of 110/109 was a dozen points faster than any route figures Thunder Rumble had previously recorded; one had to wonder what was left of his reserves after the doubled-up stress at Saratoga. At 8–5, the percentage play was to exclude him from consideration in the Woodward on the assumption that he was due for a negative reaction.

The winner was Sultry Song, who was coming in off a figure

similar to Thunder Rumble's — a 112 earned in the Whitney Handicap. Their best figures were nearly identical, but there were key differences in the way these colts arrived at them. As I discussed earlier, Sultry Song had laid the groundwork for a top-notch four-year-old campaign in his third start of the year by getting back to his best three-year-old figure in the Hollywood Gold Cup. His 112 in the Whitney was a continuation of a solid forging line, and he qualified as the stakes overlay of the New York season when allowed to go off at better than 8–1. The exacta combining Sultry Song with the remarkably consistent Pleasant Tap — the eventual 1992 Eclipse winner as best older horse — paid $47.20.

EIGHTH RACE
Belmont
SEPTEMBER 19, 1992

1 ⅛ MILES. (1.45^{2}) 39th Running THE WOODWARD (Grade I). Purse $500,000 Guaranteed. 3-year-olds and upward. By subscription of $1,000 each which should accompany the nomination; $4,000 to pass the entry box; $4,000 to start. The purse to be divided 60% to the winner, 22% to second, 12% to third and 6% to fourth. Weight for age: 3-year-olds, 121 lbs.; older, 126 lbs. Starters to be named at the closing time of entries. The estate of Mrs. William Woodward, Sr. to add the Woodward Challenge Cup to be won three times, not necessarily consecutively, by the same owner before becoming his or her property. The owner of the winner will also receive a trophy for permanent possession and trophies will be presented to the winning trainer and jockey. Closed Wednesday, September 2, with 20 nominations. Value of race $500,000; value to winner $300,000; second $110,000; third $60,000; fourth $30,000. Mutuel pool $555,264. Exacta Pool $596,156 Triple Pool $477,349

Last Raced	Horse	M/Eqt.A.Wt	PP	St	¼	½	¾	Str	Fin	Jockey	Odds $1
29Aug92 ^{8}Sar^{1}	Sultry Song	b 4 126	3	7	$3^{2\frac{1}{2}}$	$1^{\frac{1}{2}}$	$1^{\frac{1}{2}}$	$1^{1\frac{1}{2}}$	$1^{1\frac{3}{4}}$	Bailey J D	8.60
18Jly92 ^{8}Bel^{1}	Pleasant Tap	5 126	6	3	$4^{\frac{1}{2}}$	5^{hd}	6^{1}	4^{hd}	2^{hd}	Delahoussaye E	1.90
29Aug92 ^{8}Sar^{2}	Out of Place	5 126	8	1	2^{hd}	$3^{1\frac{1}{2}}$	2^{1}	2^{hd}	3no	Antley C W	9.30
29Aug92 ^{8}Sar^{5}	Strike the Gold	4 126	5	5	8	8	7^{hd}	5^{2}	4^{1}	Perret C	6.40
22Aug92 ^{7}Sar^{1}	Thunder Rumble	3 121	7	2	$1^{\frac{1}{2}}$	$2^{\frac{1}{2}}$	$3^{1\frac{1}{2}}$	$3^{\frac{1}{2}}$	$5^{1\frac{1}{4}}$	McCauley W H	1.70
29Aug92 ^{8}Sar^{4}	Lost Mountain	4 126	4	4	6^{4}	7^{4}	8	$6^{\frac{1}{2}}$	6^{2}	Day P	17.90
29Aug92 ^{8}Sar^{3}	Chief Honcho	b 5 126	2	6	5^{2}	$4^{1\frac{1}{2}}$	5^{1}	7^{1}	$7^{3\frac{3}{4}}$	Smith M E	22.00
7Sep92 ^{8}Bel^{4}	Devil His Due	b 3 121	1	8	$7^{2\frac{1}{2}}$	$6^{\frac{1}{2}}$	4^{hd}	8	8	Maple E	11.50

OFF AT 5:44 Start good Won driving Time, :23^{2}, :46^{3}, 1:10^{2}, 1:34^{4}, 1:47 Track fast.

$2 Mutuel Prices:

3-(C)-SULTRY SONG	19.20	8.20	4.40
6-(F)-PLEASANT TAP		4.20	2.60
8-(H)-OUT OF PLACE			4.20

$2 EXACTA 3-6 PAID $47.20 $2 TRIPLE 3-6-8 PAID $209.00

B. c, by Cox's Ridge—Sultry Sun, by Buckfinder. Trainer Kelly Patrick J. Bred by Live Oak Stud (Fla).

SULTRY SONG, never far back while saving ground, accelerated to the front along the backstretch, set the pace along the inside to the turn, shook off OUT OF PLACE to gain a clear advantage in upper stretch then held sway under good handling. PLEASANT TAP was rated just behind the leaders while three wide for a half, fell back slightly on the far turn, launched a rally four wide entering the stretch then finished well between horses to edge out of place for the place. OUT OF PLACE stalked the pace from outside for six furlongs, made a run outside the winner to threaten on the turn, was unable to stay with that one in upper stretch but continued on willingly to gain a share. STRIKE THE GOLD, trailed for nearly six furlongs, closed a lengthy gap while circling five wide on the turn then rallied belatedly in the middle of the track. THUNDER RUMBLE, outsprinted rivals for the early advantage, relinquished the lead along the backstretch, forced the pace between horses for six furlongs, dropped back slightly midway on the turn, followed the winners path into the stretch and lacked a strong closing response. LOST MOUNTAIN was never a serious threat. CHIEF HONCHO lodged a mild rally along the inside on the far turn and flattened out. DEVIL HIS DUE, checked while ducing in at the start, was never a factor while saving ground.

Owners— 1, Live Oak Plantation; 2, Buckland Farm; 3, Phipps Cynthia; 4, C C W Gold Stable; 5, Braeburn Farm; 6, Loblolly Stable; 7, Firestone Matthew K; 8, Lion Crest Stable.

Trainers— 1, Kelly Patrick J; 2, Speckert Christopher; 3, McGaughey Claude III; 4, Zito Nicholas P; 5, O'Connell Richard; 6, Bohannan Thomas; 7, Mott William I; 8, Jerkens H Allen.

Thunder Rumble was never the same after the Travers. After relinquishing the lead under indecisive handling in the Woodward and finishing fifth, he could only manage seventh-place finishes in the Jockey Club Gold Cup and Breeders' Cup Classic, and did not race again until the spring of 1994 due to a variety of ailments.

Examine two negative pair-ups that produced vulnerable favorites at Aqueduct in April of 1994:

Bonnie Shopper
Own: Jewel-E Stables
LUTTRELL M G (13 2 2 4 .15) $50,000

B. m. 5
Sire: Shelter Half (Tentam)
Dam: Farrago (Oxford Accent)
Br: Joe-Dan Farm (NJ)
Tr: Friedman Mitchell (2 0 1 0 .00)

112[5]

Lifetime Record: 29 9 5 10 $139,878

1994	4	3	0	0	$41,460	Turf	0 0 0 0		
1993	12	2	1	6	$41,822	Wet	1 1 0 0	$14,220	
Bel Ⓣ	0	0	0	0		Dist Ⓣ	0 0 0 0		

9Apr94-5Aqu fst	1	:224 :452 1:10 1:37	ⒻClm 80000	76	4 3 2½ 1½ 3nk 4 2½	Luttrell M G5	109 b	*1.00	80-14	Seattle Vice112½ Bold As Silver118nk Fleeting Ways1181¾	Led, tired	6
12Mar94-6Aqu fst	170 ⊡	:233 :47 1:11 1:41	ⒻClm 70000	101	3 1 1½ 12½ 17 17½	Luttrell M G5	108 b	2.20	93-20	Bonnie Shopper1087½ Seattle Vice1132¾ S. S. Sparkle1135	Mild drive	6
2Feb94-4Aqu fst	170 ⊡	:243 :493 1:134 1:414	ⒻClm 32500	101	1 1 11½ 16 114 120¼	Luttrell M G5	110 b	4.20	89-31	Bonnie Shopper11020 Galloping Proudly1172¼ Chambolle117hd	Ridden out	6
23Jan94-1Aqu fst	1 1/16 ⊡	:233 :484 1:142 1:483	ⒻClm 22500	71	1 1 11 11½ 12½ 1¾	Luttrell M G5	110 b	3.00	62-31	BonnieShopper110¾ SchwayBabySwy1175½ GllopingProudly117no	Driving	11
29Dec93-5Aqu fst	1 1/16 ⊡	:234 :491 1:152 1:483 3↑	ⒻClm 22500	70	5 2 1hd 11½ 11 32	Rojas C	115 fb	5.00	60-33	Streaming1172 Noble Girl115no Bonnie Shopper1151	Bid, tired	8
26Nov93-8Med fst	6f	:221 :451 :574 1:102 3↑	ⒻⓈGirl Power H32k	66	5 8 32½ 33 44½ 67¾	Rojas C	L 115 fb	*1.60e	81-16	Sister Dell1171½ Merri Tales1201¾ Lena's Angel1142	Tired	10
13Nov93-2Med fst	170	:23 :462 1:11 1:42 3↑	ⒻClm 22000	83	5 3 31½ 11½ 13 13	Rojas C	L 115 fb	2.70	86-14	Bonnie Shopper1153 Landing Mate1194 Dun Roamin Lady1133¾	Driving	8
21Oct93-9Med sly	6f	:221 :454 :581 1:111 3↑	ⓈAlw 23700N3X	82	6 8 51¾ 31 11 11	Rojas C	L 113 fb	8.20e	85-16	Bonnie Shopper1131 Ox1141½ Kind One115nk	Driving	9
13Oct93-3Med fst	170	:223 :463 1:12 1:422 3↑	ⒻClm 25000	82	2 2 31½ 21 1½ 2no	Rojas C	L 116 fb	*1.30e	84-15	Miss Cover Girl114no Bonnie Shopper1163¾ Quinyan1144¾	Gamely	7
28Sep93-7Med fst	6f	:22 :444 :57 1:094 3↑	ⒻClm 20000	75	1 6 52¼ 65¼ 54½ 32½	Castillo R E	116 b	6.80	89-11	PennyForJessie119½ Stticlctricity1192 BonniShoppr1164½	Saved ground	8

WORKOUTS: May 5 Bel Ⓣ 4f fm :49 H (d) 3/8 Apr 3 Bel tr.t 4f fst :50 B 20/26 Mar 9 Bel tr.t 3f fst :362 H 3/18 Mar 1 Bel tr.t 3f fst :39 B 10/10 Feb 23 Bel tr.t 3f fst :371 B 2/10 Feb 15 Bel tr.t 4f fst :524 B 29/34

Bonnie Shopper's established top effort on Beyer was in the low 80s prior to her pair-up of 101s February 2 and March 12 — figures some 20 points above her previous capabilities. The comment lines read "Ridden out" and "Mild Drive," implying she won with something in reserve; this is seldom the case after exceptionally stressful efforts in back-to-back races, and the 101s were clearly stressful efforts for a horse used to running in the low 80s. Subjected to a faster, pressured pace when shortened up to a one-turn mile April 9, Bonnie Shopper had nothing left in the tank through the stretch and faded to fourth at even money.

Jericho Blaise
Own: Koziarz Ted
SANTAGATA N (52 5 11 6 .10)

B. c. 3 (Apr)
Sire: Exuberant (What a Pleasure)
Dam: Arts and Clover (Arts and Letters)
Br: Rustlewood Farm Inc (Fla)
Tr: Koziarz Ted (1 0 0 0 .00)

110

Lifetime Record: 11 3 2 2 $57,385

1994	3	2	0	0	$33,000	Turf	0 0 0 0		
1993	8	1	2	2	$24,385	Wet	2 0 1 0	$3,200	
Bel	0	0	0	0		Dist	6 1 0 2	$21,545	

16Apr94-8Aqu sly	6f	:213 :441 :562 1:091	Best Turn-G3	53	7 1 51½ 44½ 610 719¼	Santagata N	115	*1.70	77-09	Rizzi1175 Mr. Shawklit1172¼ Memories Of Linda1151	Gave way	7
1Apr94-7Aqu fst	6½f	:221 :451 1:094 1:162	Alw 29000N2X	101	1 1 12½ 12 17 17	Santagata N	117	2.20	99-16	Jericho Blaise1177 Gold Tower117½ Memories Of Linda1176½	Ridden out	5
21Feb94-7Aqu fst	6f ⊡	:223 :454 :58 1:104	Alw 26000N1X	101	4 1 2½ 11 14 17	Santagata N	117	8.60	89-20	Jericho Blaise1177 Storm Street117¾ Jacksome1172½	Kept to task	6
2Dec93-7Med fst	6f	:221 :45 :573 1:10	Alw 23500N1X	71	8 3 3½ 21 21½ 33½	Thomas D B	L 117	10.10	87-15	MedowFlight117hd Lynn'sNotebook1173½ JerichoBlis1175½	Finished evenly	8
24Nov93-9Med fst	1	:23 :47 1:13 1:391	Princeton40k	61	6 5 54½ 4½ 41 48¾	Velasquez J	L 114	7.00	71-25	Personal Merit1157 Natural Fact1171½ SladyRoberto113nk	Finished evenly	9
3Nov93-1Med fst	1	:233 :471 1:121 1:384	Md Sp Wt	72	8 3 11½ 15 15 13¾	Bravo J	L 118	3.20	82-17	Jericho Blaise1183¾ Barge In1182 Pleasant Dancer1182	Driving	9
21Oct93-6Med sly	1	:231 :463 1:121 1:39	Md Sp Wt	63	7 2 3½ 21½ 24 26¾	Bravo J	L 118	*1.50	74-19	Dinner Affair1136¾ Jericho Blaise1184¾ SashaSashaSasha1181¼	Best of rest	7
9Oct93-5Med fst	6f	:222 :462 :592 1:131	Md Sp Wt	55	1 8 74½ 64¾ 52½ 41½	Nelson D	L 118	2.50	74-25	Powerful Patch1181½ Settle Quick118hd Drop Em118no	Finished well	9
5Sep93-1Mth fst	6f	:22 :452 :574 1:10	Md Sp Wt	45	6 4 63¾ 54½ 59 418	Castillo H Jr	118	9.90	71-15	Slip Mahoney1183¾ Storm Street1185¾ Solly's Honor1188½	No rally	8
25Aug93-7Mth fst	6f	:212 :45 :573 1:11	Md Sp Wt	62	4 5 42 51¾ 35½ 39	Castillo H Jr	118	5.40	75-19	Hold My Tongue1183 Palance1186 Jericho Blaise1183¾	Mild rally	8

WORKOUTS: ●May 14 Mth 5f fst :594 H 1/15 May 4 Bel 4f fst :482 B 10/56 Apr 12 Bel tr.t 3f fst :35 H 2/17 Mar 27 Bel tr.t 4f fst :483 B 4/18 Mar 23 Bel tr.t 4f fst :481 B 9/34 Mar 7 Bel tr.t 4f fst :47 H 3/58

Jericho Blaise received an eleven-week freshening after a two-year-old campaign when he consistently ran figures in the 60s and low 70s. Upon returning, he advanced through preliminary allowances with back-to-back 101s, winning each time by seven lengths. The comment line for the April 1 win reads, "Ridden out," again implying the horse won with something left. But two races in succession 30 points above a previously established top do not usually leave anything in a horse's reserves, no matter how visually impressive the races appeared. Jericho Blaise was thrown into the Grade 3 Best Turn two weeks later and finished last at 8–5.

At this point, it's important to note that at different points in a horse's career, short-term patterns such as pairs may mean different things, as *Thoro-graph*'s Jerry Brown explains: "Pairs of new tops by 2-year-olds are a positive sign; paired tops from 3-year-olds early in the season may suggest a bounce before another good race; paired tops by older horses may be too much of an 'extension' and knock them off form."

Hansel, Pine Bluff, Devil His Due, and Strike the Gold all reacted similarly to paired tops. The bounce off the pair was a prelude to a significantly faster top next time out — what Brown has coined the "Spring Three-year-old Pattern":

STRIKE THE GOLD '88 ch h Alydar - Majestic Gold

	3-YEAR-OLD	4-YEAR-OLD	5-YEAR-OLD	6-YEAR-OLD
DEC				
NOV	CD 4^2	GP 7^2		
OCT	BEL 5^1	BEL 2^2gd		
SEP	BEL 4^2wf	BEL 2^2; SAR 7^1		
AUG	SAR 7; SAR 5^1	MTH 6		
JUL		BEL 3		
JUN	BEL 4^1	BEL 2my	BEL 2	
MAY	PIM 10; CD 6	PIM 4^1	PIM 6^3	
APR	KEE 7gd	AQU 7^3	AQU 3^3	
MAR	GP 10^1	GP 6^2		
FEB	GP 10^1	GP 5; GP 8^2		
JAN	GP 16^2	GP 8^2		

PINE BLUFF '89 b h Danzig - Rowdy Angel

Month	2-YEAR-OLD		3-YEAR-OLD		4-YEAR-OLD	5-YEAR-OLD
DEC	AQU	6^2				
NOV	AQU	11				
	CD	15^3				
OCT	BEL	14^2				
SEP	BEL	14^2wf				
AUG	SAR	14^2				
JUL						
JUN	BEL	21wf				
			BEL	3^2gd		
MAY			PIM	3^2		
			CD	9^1		
APR			OP	6^2		
MAR			OP	6^2		
			OP	9		
FEB						
JAN						

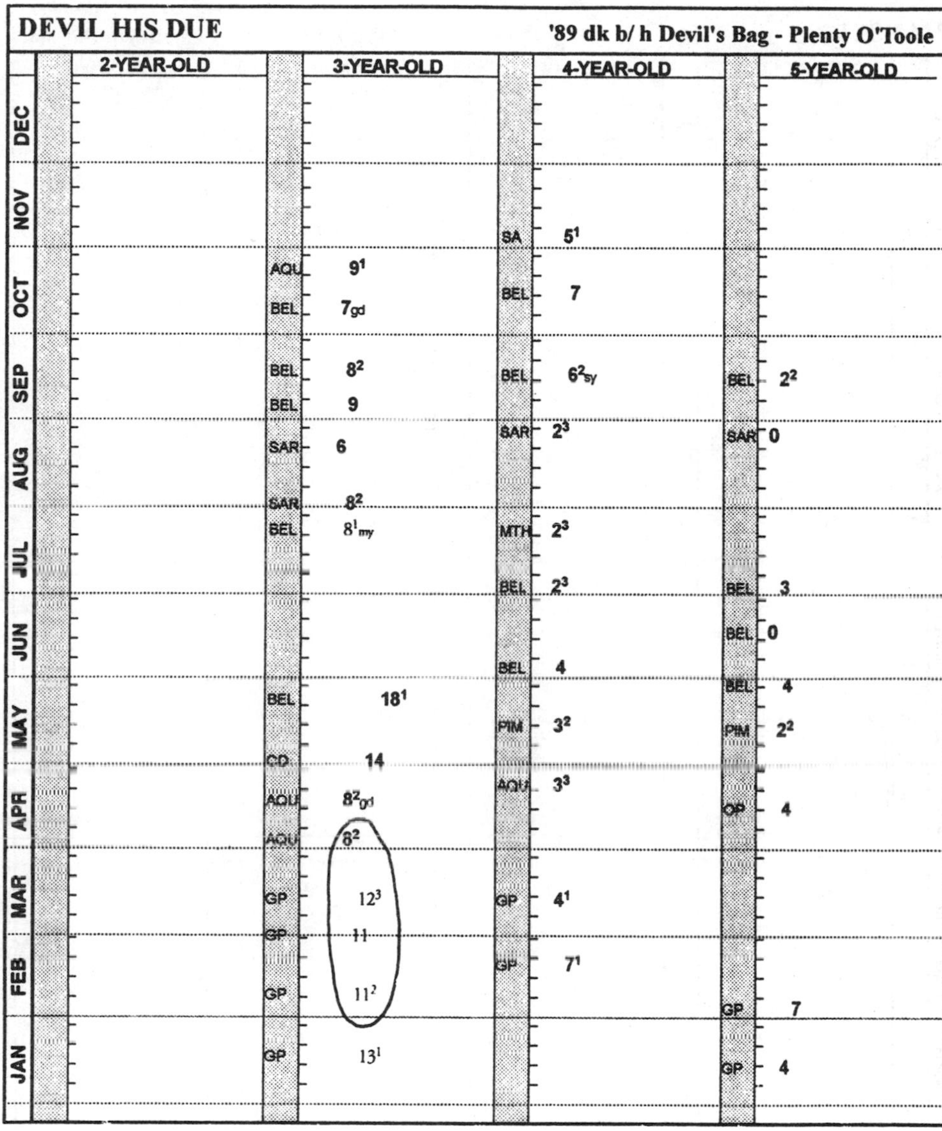
DEVIL HIS DUE
'89 dk b/ h Devil's Bag - Plenty O'Toole
2-YEAR-OLD
3-YEAR-OLD
4-YEAR-OLD
5-YEAR-OLD
DEC
NOV
OCT
SEP
AUG
JUL
JUN
MAY
APR
MAR
FEB
JAN
AQU 9¹
BEL 7gd
BEL 8²
BEL 9
SAR 6
SAR 8²
BEL 8¹my
BEL 18¹
CD 14
AQU 8²gd
AQU 8²
GP 12³
GP 11
GP 11²
GP 13¹
SA 5¹
BEL 7
BEL 6²sy
SAR 2³
MTH 2³
BEL 2³
BEL 4
PIM 3²
AQU 3³
GP 4¹
GP 7¹
BEL 2²
SAR 0
BEL 3
BEL 0
BEL 4
PIM 2²
OP 4
GP 7
GP 4

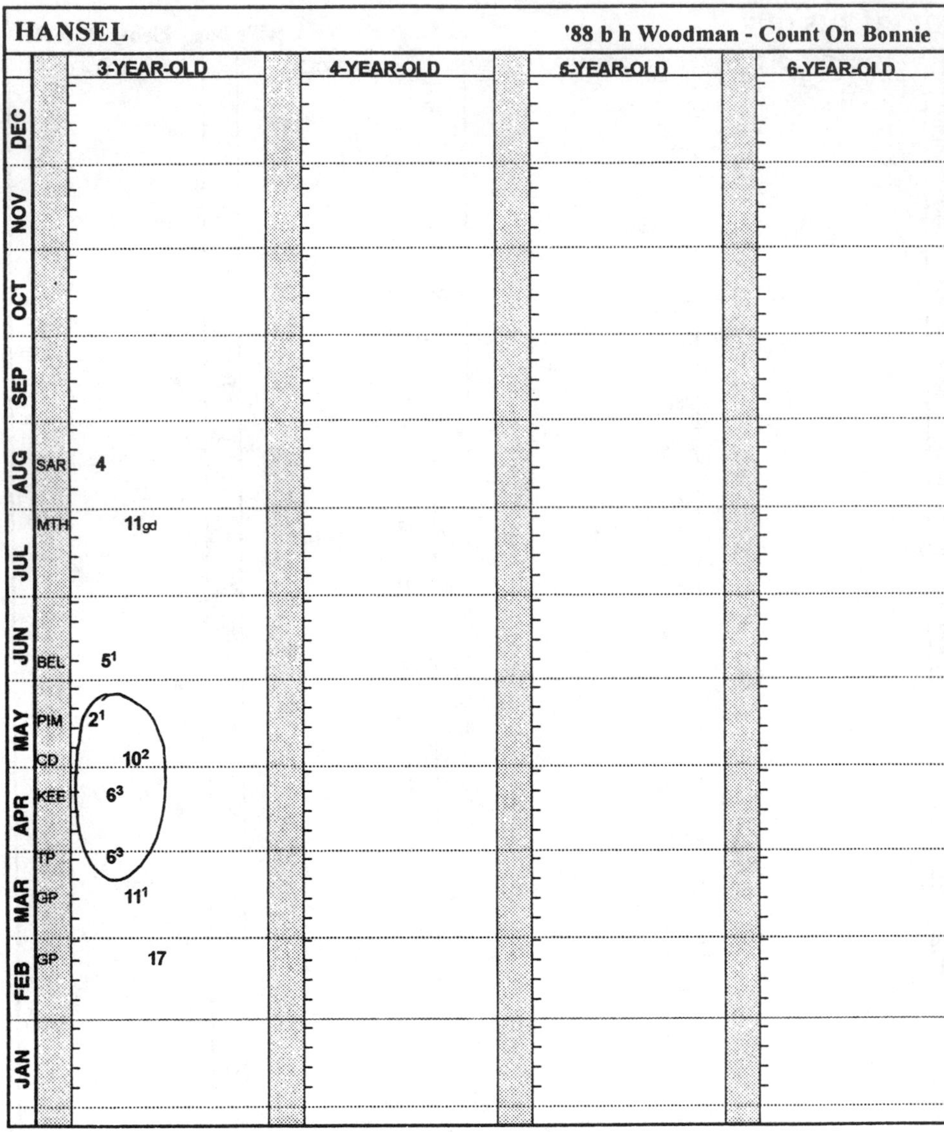
HANSEL
'88 b h Woodman - Count On Bonnie
3-YEAR-OLD
4-YEAR-OLD
5-YEAR-OLD
6-YEAR-OLD
DEC
NOV
OCT
SEP
AUG
JUL
JUN
MAY
APR
MAR
FEB
JAN
SAR 4
MTH 11gd
BEL 5^1
PIM 2^1
CD 10^2
KEE 6^3
TP 6^3
GP 11^1
GP 17

Hansel and Pine Bluff paired tops in their two final preps for the Kentucky Derby, bounced in the Derby itself, but then ran new tops to win consecutive renewals of the Preakness.

Devil His Due shows the pattern — a pair of 11s followed by a bounce to a 13 followed by an 8 in the Gotham, in which he dead-heated at 10–1 with Lure.

Strike the Gold shows the pattern "in spirit," with a 7 in the Blue Grass, a near-paired 6 to win the Derby, a bounce to 10 in the Preakness, and a new top of 4 when necked by Hansel in the Belmont.

The Kentucky Derby preps annually produce solid betting opportunities on good-priced horses. Without any kind of condition analysis, their seeming inconsistencies can drive a handicapper batty; with the benefit of such an approach, overlays on three-year-olds such as Southern Rhythm are predictable:

Southern Rhythm
Own: Heiligbrodt B & Keefer R & New W

Ch. c. 3 (Feb)
Sire: Dixieland Band (Northern Dancer)
Dam: Prospector's Queen (Mr. Prospector)
Br: Linder Bertram N (Ky)
Tr: Keefer James O (8 2 2 2 .25)

Lifetime Record :	7 4 1 0	$205,655			
1994	6 4 0 0	$201,495	Turf	0 0 0 0	
1993	1 M 1 0	$4,160	Wet	2 0 1 0	$4,160
CD	1 0 0 0		Dist	0 0 0 0	

7May94-8CD	sly	1$\frac{1}{4}$	:47^{1}	1:11^{4}	1:37^{3}	2:03^{3}	Ky Derby-G1	97	12	14	13^{13}	10^{11}	9$^{8\frac{3}{4}}$	7$^{10\frac{1}{4}}$	Gomez G K	L 126 f	20.00	84–06	Go For Gin126^{2} Strodes Creek126$^{2\frac{1}{2}}$ Blumin Affair126$^{\frac{3}{4}}$		14
Broke to the inside, 7-wide stretch																					
24Apr94-8Kee	fst	1$\frac{1}{16}$	:23^{1}	:47^{2}	1:13^{1}	1:45^{3}	Lexington-G2	104	5	7	7^{13}	5^{6}	1^{1}	1$^{2\frac{1}{2}}$	Gomez G K	L 118 f	3.80	81–19	Southern Rhythm118$^{2\frac{1}{2}}$ Soul Of The Matter118^{5} Ulises113^{8}		8
Came out, bumped 3/8s, ridden out																					
2Apr94-11TP	fst	1$\frac{1}{8}$	:46^{3}	1:11	1:36^{1}	1:49	Jim Beam-G2	84	3	6	6$^{3\frac{1}{2}}$	5$^{2\frac{3}{4}}$	5$^{6\frac{1}{2}}$	4$^{11\frac{1}{2}}$	McCarron C J	L 121	*2.40	77–19	PolarExpedition121^{nk} PowisCstle121^{7} ChimesBnd121^{4}	Bid, flattened out	11
12Mar94-9OP	fst	1	:23	:46^{2}	1:11^{3}	1:36^{4}	Southwest100k	99	4	6	6^{11}	6$^{5\frac{1}{2}}$	3$^{2\frac{1}{2}}$	1$^{2\frac{1}{2}}$	Gomez G K	L 112 f	4.50	93–20	Southern Rhythm112$^{2\frac{1}{2}}$ Dish It Out113^{hd} Polar Expedition122^{5}		6
4-wide 1/4, ridden out																					
19Feb94-8OP	fst	6f	:21^{1}	:45^{1}	:58	1:10^{3}	Alw 23000N2L	92	1	6	5^{6}	4^{4}	1$^{2\frac{1}{2}}$	1^{8}	Gomez G K	L 120 f	*.70	88–15	SothrnRhythm120^{8} Frsky'sFllow112$^{1\frac{1}{2}}$ OnTghTgr115^{1}	4-wide 1/4, handily	9
5Feb94-2OP	fst	6f	:21^{3}	:45^{2}	:58	1:10	Md Sp Wt	86	12	5	3$^{1\frac{1}{2}}$	1^{1}	1^{1}	1$^{1\frac{1}{2}}$	Day P	120 f	*1.30	91–08	Southern Rhythm120$^{1\frac{1}{2}}$ Jamiano120^{4} Cowboy's Kid120$^{1\frac{1}{2}}$	Driving	12
20Oct93-5Kee	my	6$\frac{1}{2}$f	:22	:45^{3}	1:10^{3}	1:16^{4}	Md Sp Wt	73	5	8	5$^{4\frac{1}{2}}$	5^{4}	3$^{1\frac{1}{2}}$	2^{hd}	Day P	120	2.80	92–17	JudgVonstubon120^{hd} SouthrnRhythm120^{4} DkotDnzg120^{1}	Aimed, missed	10

WORKOUTS: May 5 CD 4f fst :48^{1} B 2/25

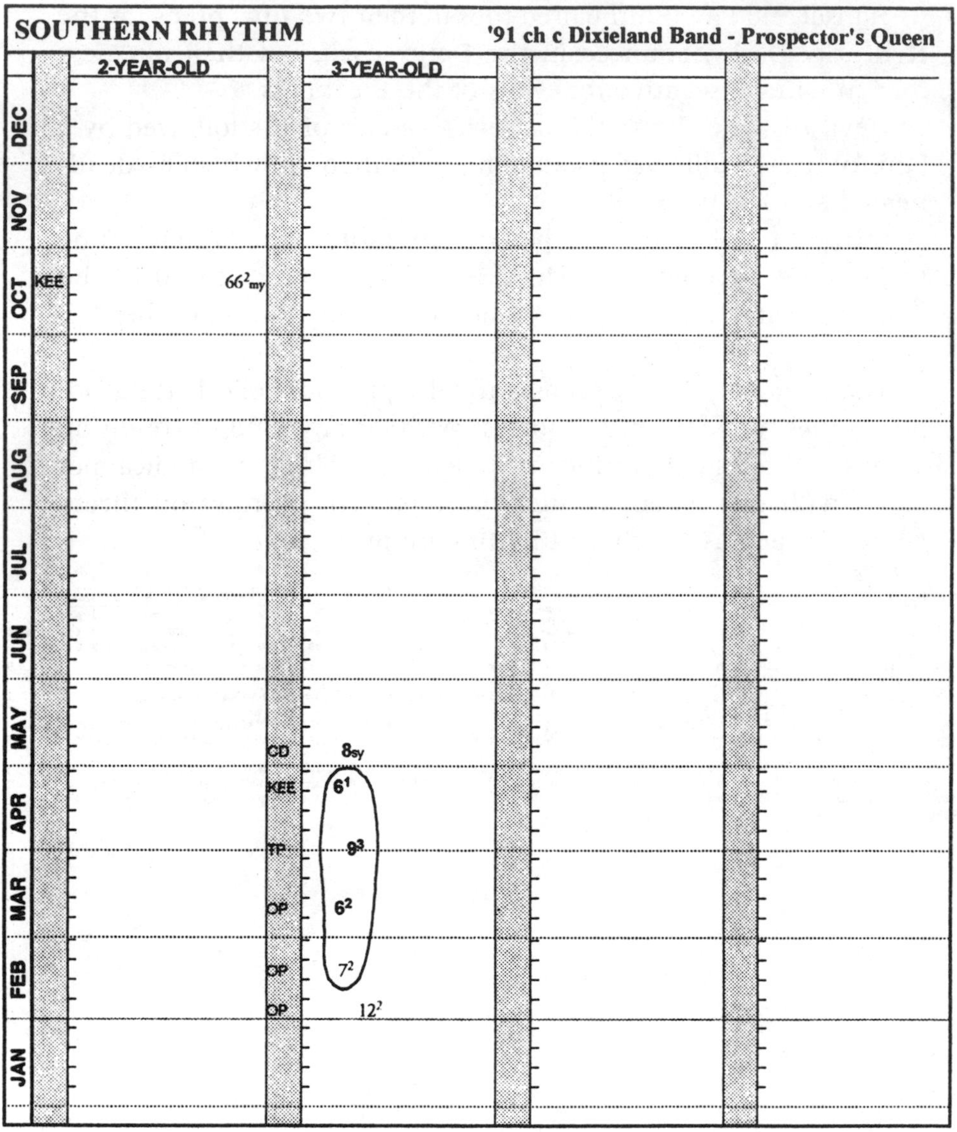

According to *Thoro-graph,* Southern Rhythm didn't pair up in his wins of February 19 and March 12, but it was fairly close: a 7½ followed by a 6½. After bouncing to a 9¾ over an inside speed-favoring track in the Jim Beam, he moved to a 6¼, winning the Lexington decisively at nearly 4–1 — the Spring Pattern in action. The pattern is similar on Beyer: two consecutive tops February 19 (a 92) and March 12 (a 99), a bounce to an 84 in the Beam, followed by a new top of 104 in the Lexington.

A FEW WORDS ABOUT THE KENTUCKY DERBY

As Jerry Brown explained in a *Daily Racing Form* article a day before the 1994 Kentucky Derby,

> Since *Thoro-graph* began making figures, there have been 12 runnings of the Derby and the winners all had certain patterns in common. For a start, every one was unraced or ran slow figures over the summer at 2, but all developed strongly to run good figures between Labor Day and the end of their juvenile campaign.
>
> Every year there is considerable hoopla about high-profile horses that do not fit this pattern (like Dehere), and every year these horses fall by the wayside as 3-year-olds, usually well before the Derby.

On the same page of that day's *Form*, Bob Beinish (of Lochnima infamy) wrote the following:

> In looking over three decades of Kentucky Derby winners a trend did start to emerge. Namely, that they just don't "bounce" like they used to. Ten or 20 years ago a horse coming off of a lifetime best race, or "top," going in to the Derby usually would bounce. The winner was often a horse cycling back to a previous good race it had run earlier. Cannonade, Seattle Slew, Affirmed and Spectacular Bid all fit this model.
>
> More recently, however, many winners won the Derby by running a brand new top after having just run a new top. Others were able to win by repeating a top they had just run. Alysheba, Winning Colors and Unbridled all ran new lifetime bests Derby Day when it looked like they were due to react. Strike the Gold and Lil E. Tee repeated tops they had just run in the race before the Derby.
>
> The catch to all this is that there were numerous horses in each race coming off tops who did bounce Derby Day.

Both Brown and Beinish had Go For Gin, the eventual winner at 9–1, on their short list of contenders. As things turned out, Go For Gin came in to the Derby off a lifetime top of 5 in the Wood Memorial, and paired up with another 5 to take the roses at Churchill Downs. His overall line on *The Sheets* is eerily reminiscent of Unbridled's:

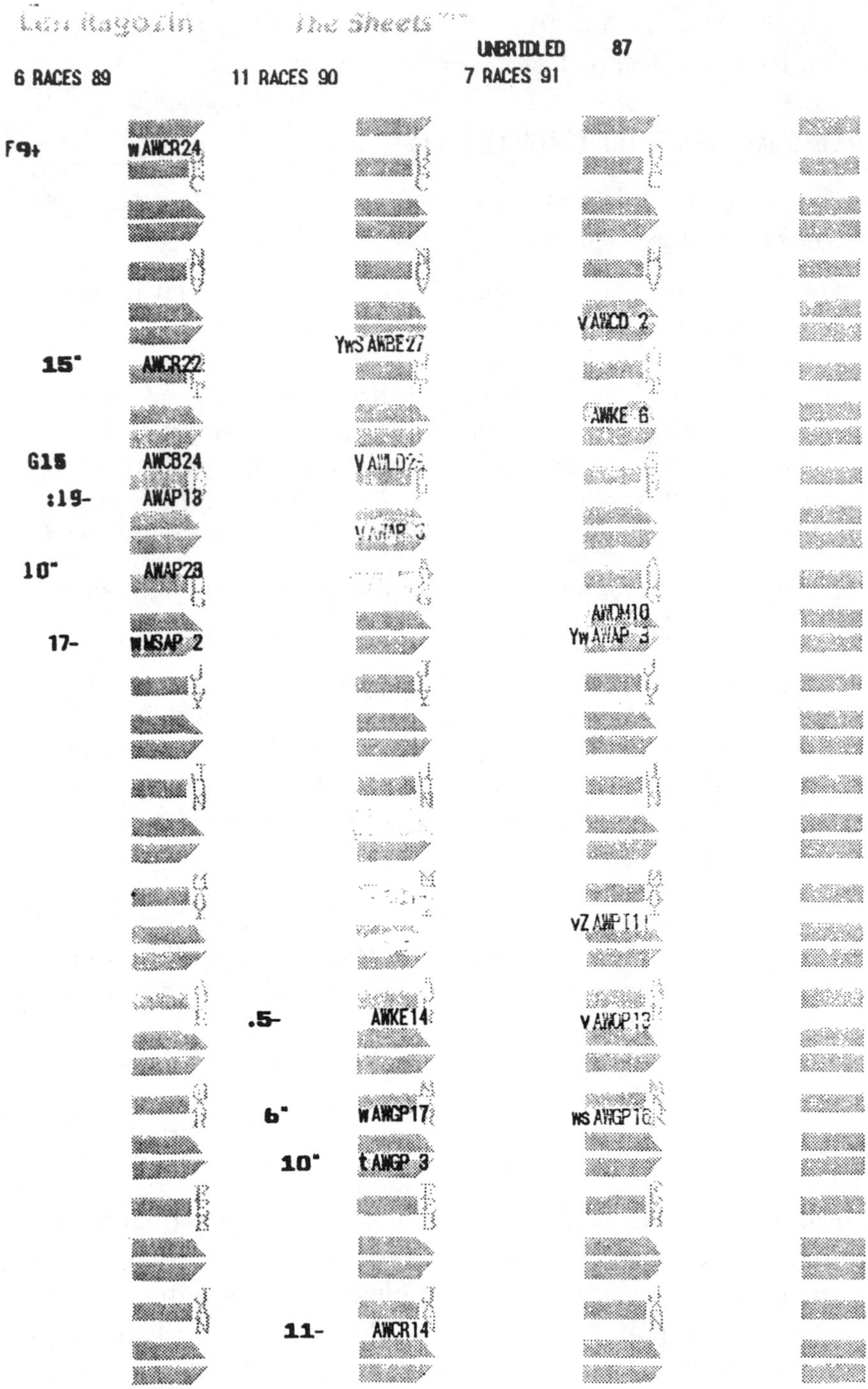
UNBRIDLED 87
6 RACES 89
11 RACES 90
7 RACES 91
F9+ wAWCR24
15" AWCR22
G15 AWCB24
:19- AWAP18
10" AWAP23
17- wMSAP 2
YwS AWBE27
VAWLD2
.5- AWKE14
6" wAWGP17
10" tAWGP 3
11- AWCR14
vAWCD 2
AWKE 6
AWDM10
YwAWAP 3
vAWOP13
wsAWGP16

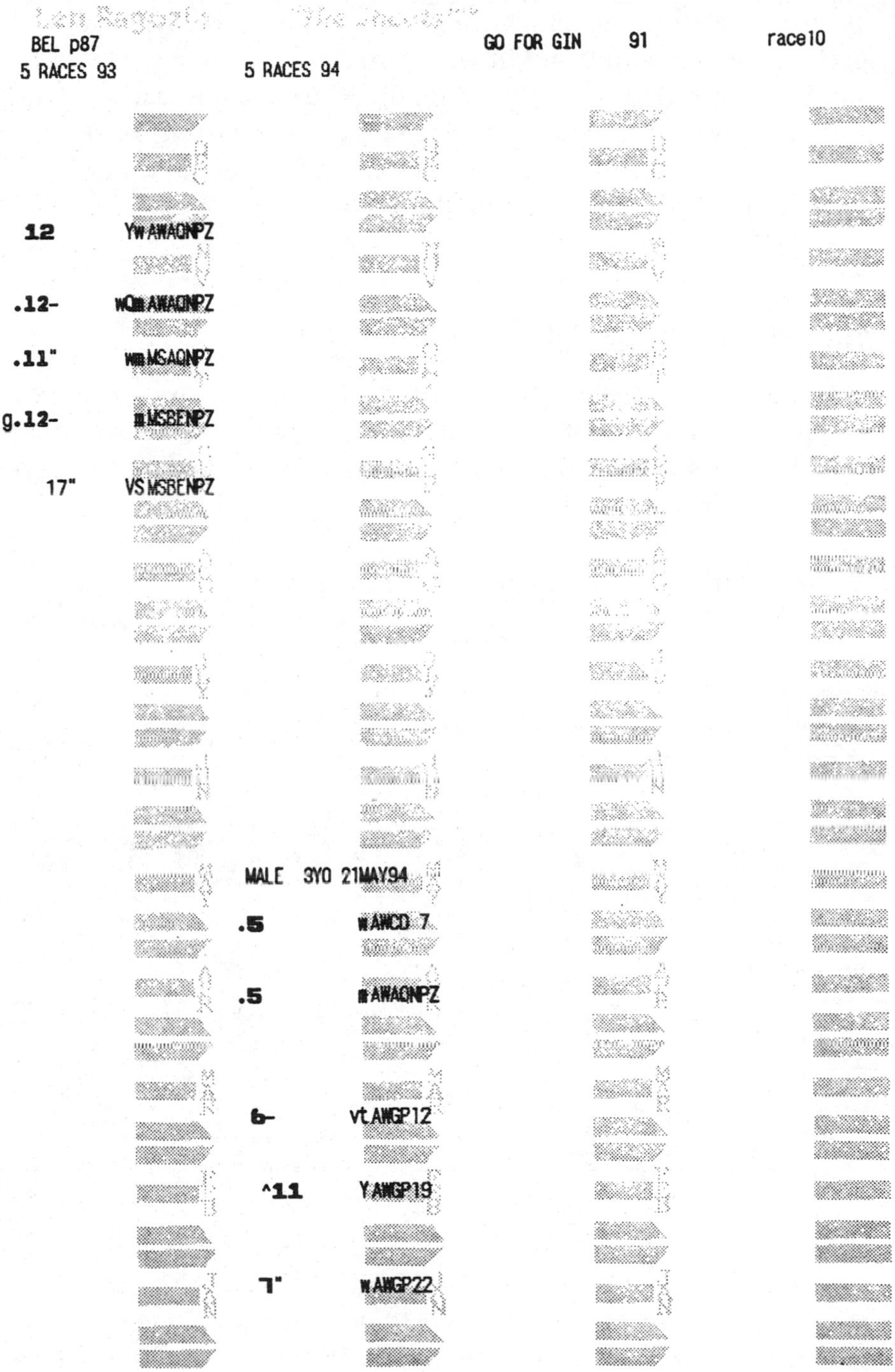

BEL p87 GO FOR GIN 91 race10

5 RACES 93 5 RACES 94

12 YwAWAQNPZ

.12- wQmAWAQNPZ

.11" wmMSAQNPZ

g.12- mMSBENPZ

17" VSMSBENPZ

MALE 3YO 21MAY94

.5 wAWCD 7

.5 mAWAQNPZ

6- vtAWGP12

^11 YAWGP19

7" wAWGP22

Note the stunning similarities from day one of their careers: each ran a 17 first time out in late summer, surged forward significantly second time out, threw in mediocre figures early in the spring, ran a new lifetime top in the range of 6 two starts before the Derby, followed with a 5 in their final Derby prep, and held that form (indeed, Unbridled ran the fastest adjusted race of his career, a 2) in Kentucky.

UTILIZING CONDITION ANALYSIS IN DAY-TO-DAY PLAY

The second race at Belmont on June 17 centered around Lovley Josephine — a 1–2 shot trained by Peter Ferriola — and Ukrainian Gal, the 8–1 second choice. The latter had been claimed from Ferriola in her most recent start:

2 START 7 FURLONGS BELMONT PARK FINISH

7 FURLONGS. **(1.20²) CLAIMING. Purse $19,500. Fillies and Mares, 4-year-old and upward. Weights, 122 lbs. Non-winners of two races since May 15, allowed 3 lbs. Of a race since then, 5 lbs. Claiming price $35,000 for each $2,500 to $30,000 2 lbs. (Races when entered to be claimed for $25,000 or less not considered).**

Ukrainian Gal — Ch. f. 4, by Malinowski—Tocatchathief, by Sail On–Sail On
CHAVEZ J F (136 25 15 11 .18) — $35,000 — Br.—Bilinski Jerry (NY) — 117
Own.—Hunt Country Valley — Tr.—Galluscio Dominic G (24 1 3 3 .04)
Lifetime 21 4 5 3 $91,360 — 1993 3 0 1 1 $9,420 — 1992 13 3 3 2 $70,340 — Turf 2 0 0 0 — Wet 2 1 1 0 $24,540

28May93- 2Bel fst 1 :463 1:11 1:373 ⒻClm c-25000 76 1 7 44 33½ 21½ 2hd Toscano P R b 117 3.20 80-16 SweetN'Saxy117hdUkrainianGl1171MggieDy115 Gamely 8
28May93-Claimed from Scuderi Vincent S, Ferriola Peter Trainer
17May93- 4Bel fst 7f :231 :464 1:254 ⒻClm 35000 67 7 1 3½ 2hd 32 45¾ Mojica R Jr b 117 4.60 68-21 FlshNumberTwo119nkAllPower1151½Tenorette113 Tired 7
12Mar93- 8Aqu fst 1 1/16 ⊡:474 1:123 1:452 ⒻAlw 33000 75 4 3 32½ 44½ 37 310¾ Mojica R Jr b 117 3.40 67-32 S.S.Sprkle112noShSidMyb11710¾UkrininGl117 Nof actor 4
25Nov92- 8Aqu my 1 :471 1:123 1:39 3+ⒻAlw 31000 76 2 3 32 31½ 1½ 12 Mojica R Jr b 115 7.00 67-29 UkrainianGl1152WitAminuteAngie115nkAldie120 Driving 6
8Nov92- 6Aqu fst 7f :224 :46 1:234 3+ⒻAlw 28000 77 5 4 65½ 64¾ 34 35½ Mojica R Jr b 115 10.00 80-19 HilbysBritFlit1152MissJzz1173¾UkrnnGl115 Lacked rally 8
1Nov92- 8Aqu fst 6f :231 :463 1:11 ⒻⓈSchnctdyH 77 2 7 65½ 64½ 55½ 56½ Mojica R Jr b 111 6.50 79-18 MssIrnS1211½MrsPMstr1191½PrcssRR112 Broke slowly 7
30Sep92- 9Bel fst 7f :222 :454 1:232 ⒻClm c-35000 70 4 9 118¾ 116¾ 45 29 McCauley W H b 118 11.20 78-19 Marilyn'sMagic1169UkrininGl118¾Kersey116 Up for 2nd 13
30Sep92-Claimed from Bilinski Jerry, Galluscio Dominic V Trainer
13Sep92-10Bel fst 7f :223 :464 1:251 3+ⒻⓈAlw 27000 65 6 8 86½ 95½ 43 1nk McCauley W H b 113 *2.60 78-12 UkrininGl113nkRomnce1181¾Jen'shot113 Chkd turn drv 11
24Aug92- 6Sar fst 6f :22 :452 1:103 3+ⒻⓈAlw 27000 65 2 7 116½ 119 83¾ 23 McCauley W H b 113 4.00 88-08 FinlCrossing1123UkrinnGl1133TmmyTwo112 Fin. strong 14
16Aug92- 7Sar gd 1⅛ Ⓣ:471 1:114 1:502 3+ⒻⓈAlw 29000 74 6 4 36½ 44 63 84½ Davis R G b 112 12.80 83-09 ScondBloom114hdRscmmnClln1121½NwYrkIss117 Faded 12
LATEST WORKOUTS May 3 Aqu 4f fst :523 B ●Apr 19 Aqu 3f fst :364 B

Lovley Josephine — B. m. 5, by Regal Embrace—Bella Bandita, by Hagley
KRONE J A (174 32 23 28 .18) — $35,000 — Br.—Whitbred Howard T (NY) — 117
Own.—Riccio James — Tr.—Ferriola Peter (68 9 13 12 .13)
Lifetime 45 9 9 9 $183,433 — 1993 8 3 2 2 $56,900 — 1992 14 3 3 4 $37,705 — Wet 4 0 1 1 $7,200

16May93- 5Bel fst 6f :221 :453 1:104 ⒻClm 45000 82 5 7 76½ 65½ 32 31¼ Krone J A b 113 *1.50 85-15 StolOn115½Bob'sLttlGl113¾LcvlyJsphn113 Rallied wide 7
5May93- 3Bel fst 6f :223 :453 1:094 ⒻClm 35000 79 2 2 54 63½ 1hd 11¼ Krone J A b 117 3.40 91-08 LovleyJosephine1171¼JckiP.117noFrOutNurs117 Driving 10
25Apr93- 2Aqu fst 7f :223 :454 1:244 ⒻClm 35000 77 1 8 33 31½ 31½ 22 Frost G C5 b 112 3.10 78-18 AllTooWll1172LoviyJospnin112¾JckiP.117 Checked turn 8
13Apr93- 1Aqu fst 1 :491 1:141 1:394 ⒻClm 35000 82 2 1 12 1½ 2hd 21¼ Frost G C5 b 112 2.50 64-35 FoolnSprc1171½LovlyJsphn112¾SwtN'Sxy117 Held place 5
27Feb93- 5Aqu fst 6f ⊡:234 :473 1:121 ⒻAlw 30000 80 3 6 63¾ 53 33½ 34¾ Frost G C5 b 114 9.10 77-18 Boots1174SfeShelter119¾LovleyJosephine114 Mild gain 6
4Feb93- 6Aqu fst 6f ⊡:233 :474 1:124 ⒻAlw 30000 73 2 5 55½ 54 56 57 Frost G C5 b 114 8.10 72-26 BlssOurHom117nkMssClovrAppl1174¾Bolg117 No threat 7
23Jan93- 5Aqu fst 6f ⊡:23 :463 1:121 ⒻAlw 30000 72 3 4 33½ 32½ 32 1nk Frost G C5 b 112 5.50 82-15 LovleyJosephine112nkBiolge117nkSnowTitle119 Driving 6
10Jan93- 4Aqu fst 6f ⊡:233 :473 1:12 ⒻClm 30000 79 5 1 3½ 2½ 1hd 1no Frost G C5 b 108 2.50 83-17 LovleyJosephin108noAllTooWll1173½NoCost117 Driving 6
10Dec92- 5Aqu fst 6f ⊡:234 :47 1:113 3+ⒻClm c-32500 73 5 4 64½ 64½ 64 48 Migliore R b 115 *1.60 77-21 Boots1136 Sharp Image115½ All Too Well117 No threat 6
10Dec92-Claimed from Schwartz Barry K, Hushion Michael E Trainer
25Nov92- 1Aqu my 7f :224 :462 1:242 3+ⒻClm 25000 86 7 2 43½ 31½ 2hd 2hd Migliore R b 117 4.00 83-18 Erhart117hd Lovley Josephine1178½ Ivi De117 Gamely 8
LATEST WORKOUTS Jun 13 Aqu 4f fst :492 B

Lovley Josephine's credentials were imposing at first glance. She had two wins and two second-place finishes from her last four starts against $35,000 down to $30,000 claimers, and she had gained in lengths at every call in a key race for $50,000 down to

$45,000 claimers on May 16. The winner, Staple Queen, had already returned to win for $80,000, and runner-up Bob's Little Gal had wired another $50,000 field next time out.

Ukrainian Gal had been a fairly effective campaigner at three, demonstrating a one-run style until claimed by Ferriola from Dominic Galluscio on September 30. Three starts after the claim, the filly won a nonwinners allowance by stalking the leaders from close range. Making her second start in nearly five months on May 17, she dueled for the early lead and was then *reclaimed* by Galluscio when dropped in for $25,000 on May 28. Whenever a horse is reclaimed, it's a big vote of confidence by a trainer who must already know the horse quite well from prior experience.

A look at *The Sheets* reveals two fillies in very different stages of their form cycles:

BEL p14 UKRAINIAN GAL F89 race 2

5 RACES 91

'33" VT AWAQDGo
g21+ Vs 35AQDGo
23+ w 35AQDGo
=21" MSAQDGo
33+ Y[MSBEDGo

13 RACES 92

.18" w AWAQPFa
16" Y AWAQPFa
17 YS AWAQPFa
16" &PF 35BEDVG
23- w AWBEDGo
19- y AWSrDGo
^=21+ v AWSrDGo
19- AWSrDGo
18" Vws 25BEDGo
24 v AWBEDGo
25- Y AWBEDGo
35+ Ys AWAQDGo
.29 Y AWAQDGo

3 RACES 93

F\M 4YO 17JUN93
16" Ys 25BEPFa
22" V 35BEPFa
19" AWAQPFa

BEL p18 LOVELY JOSEPHINE F88 race 2

3 RACES 90		20 RACES 91		14 RACES 92		8 RACES 93	
		26"	s 25AQRBa				
27	Y AWAQGSa	.21	Ys 35AQRBa	18-	m&PF 35AQMEH		
		^24+	V 35AQRBa				
				.17+	Ym 25AQMEH		
22+	v AWAQGSa						
				14"	w 35LR25		
27	YwM5BEGSa	31+&RB	35BEGSa				
		21	V 75BEGSa				
		.24-	v AWSrGSa				
		'14"	V 50SrGSa				
		16+	Vws 35BEGSa				
		23-	AWBEGSa				
						F\M	5YO 17JUN93
		16"	Vw AWBEGSa				
		21	v AWBEGSa	r.22"	v 20PI30		
				17	b 16PI22		
						15	v 50BEPFa
		20+	Y AWBEGSa	'18"	v 20PI 9		
						'15	w 35BEPFa
		20	Y[AWAQGSa				
				r21	v AWPI24	18"	Y 35AQPFa
				24-	Y AWPI12		
		28+	AWAQGSa			22-	Y 35AQPFa
				18"	w 16PI 4		
		'26+	s AWAQGSa	F21	w 8"LR22		
				1ST V.BLENGS 3/22			
		'29"	AWAQGSa	G36	14AQRBa		
		24-	v AWAQGSa	32	vs 17AQRBa	18+	Y AWAQPFa
		'32	AWAQGSa	23-	s 17AQRBa		
						g20-	Y AWAQPFa
		/22+	AWAQGSa			'20	Yw AWAQPFa
				G18"	vs 17AQRBa		
						15	vw 35AQPFa
		X35-	Ys AWAQGSa				

Ukrainian Gal has a rather nice-looking line, doesn't she? After breaking through her two-year-old top of 21½ with an 18½ in her third start back from a layoff at three, she moved down to a 16½ five races later and finished her campaign with the best four-race grouping of her life.

Although she was laid off for nearly four months, ran a 19½, and was then laid off again for two more months, the 16½ run last time out matched her best efforts of the previous fall and signaled a return to form. She had been off for three weeks since the key 16½ and had previously shown the ability to string together races of that quality or thereabouts. The reclaim was another positive sign that improved racing was soon to be forthcoming from Ukrainian Gal.

Lovley Josephine had paired 15s in her last two starts — a pair that led to a negative projection for this race.

In evaluating Lovley Josephine's entire career (one of the advantages of using sheets), the 15s essentially equaled her career top of 14½. Notice how negatively the first 14½ had affected her. After working her way down to 16s, the 14½ had knocked her for a loop — her next six starts found her unable to run anything better than a 21. She could not get back to the 14½ for well over a year. She finally threw in her next 14½ when returned from a layoff of five months. She was able to get back to a 15 three starts later but bounced to a 20 next out and then ran four more races no better than 18 before pairing 15s in her two most recent starts.

Considering that Lovley Josephine had already bounced several times following a *single* effort in the range of 15, what havoc might the stress of *consecutive* 15s wreak?

SECOND RACE
Belmont
JUNE 17, 1993

7 FURLONGS. (1.20²) CLAIMING. Purse $19,500. Fillies and Mares, 4-year-old and upward. Weights, 122 lbs. Non-winners of two races since May 15, allowed 3 lbs. Of a race since then, 5 lbs. Claiming price $35,000 for each $2,500 to $30,000 2 lbs. (Races when entered to be claimed for $25,000 or less not considered).

Value of race $19,500; value to winner $11,700; second $4,290; third $2,340; fourth $1,170. Mutuel pool $206,114. Exacta Pool $421,961 Quinella Pool $110,748

Last Raced	Horse	M/Eqt.A.Wt	PP	St	¼	½	Str	Fin	Jockey	Cl'g Pr	Odds $1
28May93 2Bel2	Ukrainian Gal	b 4 117	1	5	8	6½	1½	11½	Chavez J F	35000	8.00
3Jun93 7Bel7	Shoot the Rapids	4 117	3	2	2½	31	21	23¾	Bailey J D	35000	8.80
6Jun93 4Bel4	All Power	b 5 110	4	4	72	7½	72	3hd	Leon F5	32500	8.60
9Jun93 4Bel5	R. E. Darla	b 4 117	8	6	4½	4½	4½	4hd	Lovato F Jr	35000	21.70
16May93 5Bel3	Lovley Josephine	b 5 117	5	3	61	51	5hd	51½	Krone J A	35000	.50
20May93 7Bel8	Trust in Dixie	b 5 117	2	8	5hd	8	6½	63½	Davis R G	35000	17.40
3Jun93 6Bel3	Flight Visibility	4 117	7	1	1½	11	3hd	75	Alvarado F T	35000	13.40
10Jun93 2Bel4	Senorita Rita	b 4 110	6	7	31	2hd	8	8	Bisono C V5	32500	13.30

OFF AT 1:29 Start good Won driving Time, :23³, :46⁴, 1:12¹, 1:25 Track fast.

$2 Mutuel Prices:				
	1-(A)-UKRAINIAN GAL	18.00	8.80	8.20
	3-(C)-SHOOT THE RAPIDS		12.80	10.00
	4-(D)-ALL POWER			6.40

$2 EXACTA 1-3 PAID $165.80 $2 QUINELLA 1-3 PAID $87.20

Ch. f, by Malinowski—Tocatchathief, by Sail On-Sail On. Trainer Galluscio Dominic G. Bred by Bilinski Jerry (NY)

UKRAINIAN GAL outrun early while saving ground, circled five wide rapidly gaining on the turn, accelerated to the front a furlong out then drew clear under brisk urging. SHOOT THE RAPIDS forced the pace along the inside into upper stretch and held well for the place. ALL POWER outrun for a half, closed well from outside to gain a share. R.E. DARLA raced within striking distance while four wide entering the stretch and lacked a strong closing response. LOVLEY JOSEPHINE reserved for a half while between horses, lacked the needed response when called upon. TRUST IN DIXIE was never a factor after breaking slowly. FLIGHT VISIBILITY set the pace under pressure into upper stretch and gave way. SENORITA RITA pinched at the start, rushed up from outside, stalked the pace while three wide to the turn and tired. UKRAINIAN GAL wore mud caulks.

Owners— 1, Hunt Country Farm; 2, Macmindon Stable; 3, Corr John D; 4, Trotta Gerald T; 5, Riccio James; 6, Fried Albert Jr; 7, Hettinger William R; 8, Cee and M Stables.

Trainers— 1, Galluscio Dominic G; 2, O'Connell Richard; 3, Martin Jose; 4, Hargrave Kenneth; 5, Ferriola Peter; 6, Destasio Richard A; 7, Hernandez Ramon M; 8, Odintz Jeff.

Plenty. Lovley Josephine never entered contention at any stage of the race. Indeed, she went to the shelf immediately afterward and did not race back until the end of September:

Lovley Josephine
Own: Ferriola Ingrid
LUTTRELL M G (63 12 6 8 .19) **$35,000**

B. m. 6
Sire: Regal Embrace (Vice Regent)
Dam: Bella Bandita (Hagley)
Br: Whitbred Howard T (NY)
Tr: Ferriola Peter (30 9 6 2 .30)

112⁵

Lifetime Record:	52	9	10	10	$190,893						
1993	15	3	3	3	$64,360	Turf	0	0	0	0	
1992	14	3	3	4	$37,705	Wet	5	0	2	1	$10,940
Aqu ⊡	19	2	2	3	$49,820	Dist	29	6	6	6	$113,350

12Dec93-1Aqu	wf	6f	⊡	:22³	:46⁴	:59¹	1:11³	3+ ⒻClm 22500	73	3	7	65¾	32	2½	2nk	Luttrell M G5	110 fb	4.60	85-15	Sucyldygylord117nk LovleyJosephin110nk PrcticlSusn1136½	Checked break	7
1Dec93-4Aqu	fst	6f	⊡	:23¹	:46⁴	:59¹	1:12¹	3+ ⒻClm 22500	66	4	3	41	42	43	54	Luttrell M G5	110 fb	8.10	78-19	FortuneWand1171 OurDerDn117no GettingAroundtoit1171	Steadied turn	8
22Nov93-6Aqu	fst	6½f		:22⁴	:46¹	1:11²	1:18¹	3+ ⒻClm 22500	70	6	4	73½	75	55	48¾	Luttrell M G5	110 fb	4.50	81-22	Jen'shot117¾ Fortune Wand1196 Goblin1172	No threat	7
10Nov93-5Aqu	fst	6f		:23	:47²	:59³	1:12³	3+ ⒻClm 22500	74	8	9	85½	62¾	64½	44	Luttrell M G7	108 fb	4.10e	75-25	Jen'shot113½ Goblin1173½ Flight Visibility117no	Broke slowly, wide	9
24Oct93-9Aqu	fst	6½f		:22³	:45⁴	1:11²	1:18¹	3+ ⒻClm 17500	69	9	4	62¾	31½	22	33	Velazquez J R	117 fb	3.90	87-10	Take A Powder1122½ Goblin112½ Lovley Josephine1171¾	Willingly	10
29Sep93-4Bel	fst	7f		:22⁴	:46³	1:11⁴	1:24⁴	3+ ⒻClm 25000	60	5	5	52½	52½	53	511½	McCauley W H	117 fb	4.80	67-19	Tenorette1152½ Alice Key1106 Fortune Wand1171¼	Lacked response	7
17Jun93-2Bel	fst	7f		:23³	:46⁴	1:12¹	1:25	ⒻClm 35000	74	5	3	62½	52½	52	55½	Krone J A	117 fb	*.50	73-23	Ukrainian Gal1171½ Shoot The Rapids1173¾ All Power110hd	Lacked rally	8
16May93-5Bel	fst	6f		:22¹	:45³	:58¹	1:10⁴	ⒻClm 45000	82	5	7	76½	65½	32	31½	Krone J A	113 fb	*1.50	85-15	StapleQueen115½ Bob'sLittleGal113¾ LovleyJosephine113nk	Rallied wide	7
5May93-3Bel	fst	6f		:22³	:45³	:57³	1:09⁴	ⒻClm 35000	79	2	2	54	63½	1hd	11½	Krone J A	117 fb	3.40	91-08	Lovley Josephine1171½ Jackie P.117no Far Out Nurse1171	Driving	10
25Apr93-2Aqu	fst	7f		:22³	:45⁴	1:11	1:24⁴	ⒻClm 35000	77	1	8	33	31½	31½	22	Frost G C5	112 fb	3.10	78-18	All Too Well1172 Lovley Josephine112½ Jackie P.117½	Checked turn	8

WORKOUTS: Oct 14 Aqu 5f fst 1:04¹ B 6/7 Oct 7 Aqu 6f fst 1:16⁴ B 1/2

Ukrainian Gal ran a new top of 13½ to win, going away at an $18 mutuel, and came back to win again on July 9.

Eleven days later, another $35,000 sprint for fillies and mares presented a variation on the theme. A filly emerging from a pair-up of 15s faced a rival who was a point *faster* on her best effort.

Examine the past performances, the *Beyer Speed Figures* and *The Sheets,* for Bob's Little Gal and Marilyn's Magic. Which should be preferred?

2 START 6 FURLONGS BELMONT PARK FINISH

6 FURLONGS. (1.07^4) **CLAIMING. Purse $19,500. Fillies and Mares, 4-year-olds and upward. Weight, 3-year-olds 122 lbs. Non-winners of two races since June 1 allowed 3 lbs. Of a race since then, 5 lbs. Claiming Price $35,000, for each $2,500 to $30,000, 2 lbs. (Races when entered to be claimed for $25,000 or less not considered).**

Coupled—Goblin and Company Girl.

King's Sweetest

B. f. 4, by Rollicking—Sourest Rind, by Naskra
CHAVEZ J F (191 35 25 15 .18) — $35,000 — Br.—Bender & Bender Partnership (Md)
Own.—Bender Sondra D — Tr.—Murray Lawrence E (—) — **117**

Lifetime 17 4 2 2 $75,800 | 1993 6 0 0 1 $6,020 | 1992 10 3 2 1 $55,380 | Turf 1 0 0 0 $660 | Wet 4 0 1 0 $6,560

Date-Race	Cond	Dist	Fractions	Race	Fig	PP	St	1st	2nd	Str	Fin	Jockey	Eq	Wt	Odds	Sp-Var	Top finishers	Comment	Field
4Jun93- 6Pim	fm	5f	Ⓣ:22^3 :45^4 :57^4	3↑ⒻAlw 22300	67	2	2	$4^{3\frac12}$	$4^{5\frac12}$	$5^{5\frac14}$	$5^{7\frac14}$	Salazar A C^5	Lb	112	20.10	86-08	Jadeeda117$^{3\frac14}$SrtogClssic117^{hd}NorthernGuide117	Faded	7
18May93- 8Pim	sly	6f	:23^2 :46^4 1:12	ⒻAlw 22300	71	1	2	$3^{2\frac12}$	3^3	4^4	$4^{6\frac14}$	Salazar A C^5	Lb	112	8.10	79-23	PrincessCouldB119$\frac34$LipSing117$^{5\frac12}$DssGirl122	Weakened	7
3May93- 3Aqu	fst	6f	:22^3 :46^2 1:11^4	ⒻClm 50000	71	6	2	$4^{1\frac12}$	4^2	4^2	$4^{5\frac14}$	Bravo J	b	117	14.20	78-17	WthStrwbrrs113$^{4\frac34}$SGzr117$\frac12$GttngArondtt115	Four wide	7
3Apr93- 7Pim	fst	6f	:23^3 :47^2 1:12	ⒻAlw 25000	73	3	3	2^1	$2^{\frac12}$	$2^{1\frac12}$	$3^{5\frac12}$	Reynolds L C	Lb	119	9.60	79-22	MixedAppl117$^{1\frac34}$TrippTril114$^{3\frac34}$King'sSwtst119	Weakend	4
9Feb93- 8Pha	fst	6f	:22^2 :45^3 1:11^3	ⒻAlw 21500	61	8	4	$2^{\frac12}$	2^{hd}	3^1	$6^{4\frac34}$	Umana J L	Lb	119	9.10	78-21	Proven Pullet116$\frac12$ Laura Who116^1 Damie'sSis116	Tired	8
15Jan93- 8Aqu	my	6f	⊡:22^3 :46^1 1:11^2	ⒻAlw 41000	60	1	6	$3^{2\frac12}$	3^2	$4^{4\frac12}$	5^{11}	Chavez J F		115	13.80	75-17	Mllwlker115^{1}MissCloverAppel115$^{5\frac12}$BridjtHony110	Tired	7
30Dec92- 7Aqu	fst	6f	⊡:22^4 :45^4 1:11^1	3↑ⒻAlw 30000	83	1	2	2^{hd}	$1^{1\frac12}$	$1^{1\frac12}$	$1^{1\frac14}$	Chavez J F		115	26.40	87-12	King'sSweetest115$^{1\frac14}$LoosnUpLis117^{hd}MplLk115	Driving	7
5Jly92- 8Mth	fst	6f	:21^3 :44^3 1:11^1	ⒻCandy Eclair	61	2	8	2^{hd}	$3^{3\frac12}$	$5^{7\frac12}$	$7^{9\frac34}$	Grabowski J A	Lb	116	21.60	75-16	Rissurus116^{nk}Athnum116$^{1\frac12}$LdySumtr114	Bumped break	9
18Jun92- 7Pim	fst	1$\frac{1}{16}$	:47^1 1:11^3 1:44^1	3↑ⒻAlw 21000	54	5	5	5^2	$4^{4\frac12}$	6^{14}	$6^{18\frac34}$	Guerra W A	L	109	8.70	64-22	TwoEysFrY118^{6}On'sNtEngh111$^{1\frac12}$LngWlk118	Weakened	7
7Jun92-11Pim	fst	6f	:22^4 :46^1 1:12	ⒻAlw 17000	70	2	2	3^3	2^{hd}	1^2	1^1	Guerra W A	L	112	5.20	85-15	Kng'sStst112^{1}OpsIAm120$^{3\frac14}$MssWhtO107	Drifted, drvng	6

LATEST WORKOUTS Jun 23 Lrl 4f fst :48 B ●May 31 Lrl 4f fst :48 H May 17 Lrl 3f gd :37^4 B

Goblin

Ro. f. 4, by What Luck—Bridal Gown, by Ballacashtal
KRONE J A (211 39 25 33 .18) — $35,000 — Br.—Bissett Joan B (NY)
Own.—Riccio James — Tr.—Ferriola Peter (77 13 14 12 .17) — **117**

Lifetime 19 5 2 1 $63,050 | 1993 11 3 1 1 $34,740 | 1992 8 2 1 0 $28,310 | Turf 1 0 0 0 | Wet 2 0 1 0 $4,830

Date-Race	Cond	Dist	Fractions	Race	Fig	PP	St	1st	2nd	Str	Fin	Jockey	Eq	Wt	Odds	Sp-Var	Top finishers	Comment	Field
3Jun93- 2Bel	fst	6f	:22^4 :46^1 1:11	ⒻClm 17500	81	5	2	2^1	2^1	$1^{\frac12}$	1^{nk}	Krone J A		117	2.70	85-13	Goblin117^{nk} All Too Well117^3 Regal Display117	Driving	8
19May93- 1Bel	gd	1$\frac{1}{16}$	:45^4 1:11 1:44^2	ⒻClm 25000	70	5	2	$2^{\frac12}$	$2^{\frac12}$	3^1	$3^{2\frac12}$	Krone J A		117	4.10	77-18	FlyingCross117$^{2\frac12}$Rebecca'sGl115^{hd}Goblin117	Weakened	8
30Apr93- 1Aqu	fst	6f	:22^4 :46^1 1:12^2	ⒻClm c-17500	58	6	5	$4^{1\frac12}$	3^3	4^4	$4^{7\frac14}$	Migliore R		117	*2.50	73-16	FlyngCross117$^{2\frac34}$TrggrMoos113^{no}AlcKy117	Lacked rally	7
30Apr93-Claimed from Zimmerman Mitchell, Dimauro Stephen L Trainer																			
1Apr93- 2Aqu	sly	1	:47^3 1:13^2 1:39^1	ⒻClm 16500	68	6	5	$7^{2\frac12}$	$4^{1\frac12}$	2^2	$2^{3\frac34}$	Migliore R		115	2.90	64-33	Orine117$^{3\frac34}$Goblin115^{3}SomedySometim108	Rallied wide	7
25Mar93- 9Aqu	fst	1$\frac{1}{16}$	⊡:48^4 1:14 1:46^1	ⒻClm 14000	72	8	5	$3^{\frac12}$	$1^{\frac12}$	1^1	$1^{2\frac14}$	Santagata N		117	4.50	74-21	Goblin117$^{2\frac14}$SaratogaApril117^{hd}Rosalt119	Wide, driving	9
20Mar93- 5Aqu	fst	6f	⊡:22^3 :46^1 1:12	ⒻClm 17500	66	3	7	6^3	$5^{2\frac12}$	$6^{3\frac14}$	$5^{3\frac12}$	Santagata N		117	14.20	79-14	AngelTop117$\frac12$WildFun117$\frac12$ReglDisply117	Saved ground	9
4Mar93- 3Aqu	fst	6f	⊡:24^2 :48^1 1:13	ⒻClm 17500	66	6	1	$2^{\frac12}$	$4^{1\frac34}$	4^4	$4^{3\frac34}$	Santagata N		119	5.30	74-24	Tenorette117$\frac12$ Angel Top117$^{1\frac34}$ Catch Chati117	Tired	6
18Feb93- 2Aqu	fst	6f	⊡:22^3 :46 1:11	ⒻClm 17500	68	5	8	$7^{6\frac12}$	$6^{4\frac12}$	4^7	5^8	Migliore R		119	4.30	80-13	Lur'sScrt113^{5}AlpnMsc115$^{2\frac14}$AwsomContss112	No threat	8
8Feb93- 2Aqu	fst	6f	⊡:23^4 :47^2 1:12^3	ⒻClm 17500	71	1	7	3^1	3^2	$3^{\frac12}$	1^2	Chavez J F		117	2.90	80-24	Goblin117^{2}AlpinMusic113$^{1\frac34}$SpottdProspctor115	Driving	8
30Jan93- 2Aqu	fst	6f	⊡:23^1 :47^2 1:13^1	ⒻClm 17500	69	5	4	$2^{\frac12}$	$2^{\frac12}$	2^{hd}	4^1	Chavez J F	b	117	8.90	76-23	GnrlWhoosh113^{hd}AlcKy115^{nk}AwsmCntss112	Bid wkned	7

LATEST WORKOUTS Jun 18 Aqu 4f fst :50 B

Bridjet Honey

Ch. m. 5, by Northjet-Ir—Honeymoon Bridge, by Blushing Groom-Fr
ANTLEY C W (196 18 30 30 .09) — $32,500 — Br.—Hobeau Farm Inc (Fla)
Own.—Stronach Frank H — Tr.—Sedlacek Michael C (25 0 3 4 .00) — **115**

Lifetime 23 5 2 3 $117,580 | 1993 9 1 1 1 $31,280 | 1992 12 4 1 2 $86,300 | Turf 3 0 1 0 $5,390 | Wet 5 1 1 1 $35,540

Date-Race	Cond	Dist	Fractions	Race	Fig	PP	St	1st	2nd	Str	Fin	Jockey	Eq	Wt	Odds	Sp-Var	Top finishers	Comment	Field
13Jun93- 2Bel	fm	1	Ⓣ:45^1 1:09^4 1:35^1	ⒻClm 35000	55	9	4	$6^{4\frac34}$	$6^{5\frac12}$	$7^{6\frac12}$	9^{14}	Krone J A	b	117	*3.50	72-09	Insurpris117$^{1\frac14}$EskimoSong117^{1}PrttyFrm117	Wide, tired	12
19May93- 8Bel	gd	6f	Ⓣ:21^4 :45^3 1:11^1	3↑ⒻAlw 33500	60	4	5	$3^{\frac12}$	$5^{1\frac34}$	$7^{4\frac34}$	$7^{12\frac14}$	Krone J A		119	7.70	68-20	LightsofMrf119^{1}Poolst-Ir119$\frac34$Kt'sCollg119	Brief speed	7
5May93- 5Bel	fm	1$\frac{1}{16}$	Ⓣ:46^4 1:11 1:43^3	ⒻClm 45000	80	2	1	1^1	1^1	$1^{\frac12}$	$2^{3\frac14}$	Bravo J	b	113	7.90	75-22	HomebyTen113$^{3\frac14}$BridjtHony113$^{2\frac12}$Mxmount117	2nd best	10
14Apr93- 1Aqu	fst	6f	:22 :45 1:10^3	ⒻClm c-35000	69	2	3	$1^{\frac12}$	$1^{\frac12}$	$3^{1\frac12}$	$4^{6\frac12}$	Maple E	b	117	*.90	82-14	GttngArondtot114$^{4\frac14}$AnglTp113^{2}Lr'sScrt113	Speed tired	6
14Apr93-Claimed from Hobeau Farm, Jerkens H Allen Trainer																			
2Apr93- 8Aqu	my	6f	:22^1 :45^3 1:11^1	3↑ⒻAlw 40000	84	3	2	$2^{\frac12}$	$2^{\frac12}$	2^3	$4^{4\frac12}$	Mojica R Jr	b	115	3.40	81-20	StrtgcRwrd115^{1}CompnyGrl110$^{1\frac34}$MrrTls115	Forced pace	6
6Mar93- 4Aqu	my	6f	⊡:22^3 :45^2 1:10^1	ⒻClm 75000	92	5	2	1^1	$1^{\frac12}$	1^{hd}	1^{hd}	Mojica R Jr	b	112	7.70	92-09	BridjetHoney112^{hd}SfeShltr112^{3}StrtgicRwrd118	Driving	7
4Feb93- 8Aqu	fst	6f	⊡:23^3 :47^2 1:12^3	ⒻAlw 41000	66	6	4	1^1	$2^{\frac12}$	$3^{3\frac12}$	$5^{10\frac12}$	Bisono C V^5	b	110	*1.90	69-26	QuietDram115$^{1\frac12}$MerriTles115^{1}CompnyGirl110	Gave way	6
15Jan93- 8Aqu	my	6f	⊡:22^3 :46^1 1:11^2	ⒻAlw 41000	72	2	7	6^7	$6^{3\frac12}$	$5^{5\frac12}$	$3^{6\frac14}$	Bisono C V^5	b	110	6.10	80-17	Mlllr115^{1}MssClvrAppl115$^{5\frac14}$BrdjtHn110	Hesitated break	7
2Jan93- 6Aqu	fst	6f	⊡:23^3 :47^3 1:12	ⒻHandicap	73	4	5	5^2	$4^{1\frac14}$	$6^{2\frac14}$	$6^{4\frac34}$	Marquez C HJr	b	112	9.70	78-18	MakinFces118^{2}Squirm122^{2}StrongEmbrce111	No factor	7
19Dec92- 1Aqu	fst	6f	⊡:22 :45 1:09^2	3↑ⒻAlw 30000	94	3	4	1^1	1^1	$1^{2\frac12}$	1^2	Bisono C V^5	b	112	4.90	96-05	BrdjtHony112^{2}FlyToThMn117$^{1\frac34}$MssClvrAppl115	Driving	6

LATEST WORKOUTS ●Jun 24 Aqu 3f fst :36 H Jun 9 Aqu 4f fst :49^3 B May 31 Aqu 4f fst :50^1 B May 13 Aqu Ⓣ 5f fm 1:03^2 H

Bob's Little Gal

B. f. 4, by Barrera—Sun Moment, by Honest Moment
SMITH M E (227 55 31 30 .24) — $35,000 — Br.—Bronzine R (Fla)
Own.—Lamcresse Stable — Tr.—Barbara Robert (43 9 6 3 .21) — **117**

Lifetime 14 4 5 2 $86,870 | 1993 2 1 1 0 $17,630 | 1992 11 3 4 2 $69,240 | Wet 4 2 0 1 $26,040

Date-Race	Cond	Dist	Fractions	Race	Fig	PP	St	1st	2nd	Str	Fin	Jockey	Eq	Wt	Odds	Sp-Var	Top finishers	Comment	Field
27May93- 4Bel	fst	6f	:22^2 :45^3 1:10^2	ⒻClm 45000	89	7	2	$2^{\frac12}$	1^1	1^2	$1^{1\frac14}$	Smith M E	b	113	*1.30	88-16	Bob'sLttlGl113$^{1\frac14}$Mrlyn'sMgc113$^{2\frac12}$CmpnyGrl113	Driving	7
16May93- 5Bel	fst	6f	:22^1 :45^3 1:10^4	ⒻClm 45000	84	7	1	$1^{2\frac12}$	1^3	$1^{\frac12}$	$2^{\frac12}$	Smith M E	b	113	3.10	85-15	StpleQuen115$\frac12$Bob'sLittlGl113$\frac34$LovlyJosphin113	Gamely	7
13Dec92- 7Aqu	my	6f	⊡:23^2 :47^3 1:12	3↑ⒻAlw 28000	45	2	1	3^2	$3^{1\frac12}$	$5^{6\frac12}$	$5^{16\frac34}$	Lydon P J^5	b	110	3.70	66-18	BlssOurHom115^{4}MssCovrGrl115$^{3\frac14}$TllMrg117	Done early	5
2Dec92- 7Aqu	fst	6f	⊡:22^4 :46 1:10^3	3↑ⒻAlw 28000	68	5	4	5^4	4^2	6^7	$6^{11\frac12}$	Lydon P J^5	b	112	4.10	78-17	PrincessRoRo115$^{1\frac14}$StrtgicRwrd115^{1}Erhrt117	No factor	8
13Nov92- 8Aqu	gd	6f	:22^1 :45^2 1:10^4	3↑ⒻAlw 27000	86	8	1	2^{hd}	1^1	1^3	1^3	Lydon P J	b	115	3.10	87-17	Bob'sLttlGl115^{3}GstofHonr115^{nk}FrtntChrmr115	Driving	8
22Oct92- 4Aqu	fst	6f	:23^3 :47^1 1:12^1	3↑ⒻAlw 27000	79	3	1	$1^{\frac12}$	1^1	2^{hd}	$3^{2\frac14}$	Lydon P J^5	b	114	3.70	78-18	PtchyFrost114^{2}SblWy112^{nk}Bob'sLttlGl114	Speed, wknd	6
26Sep92- 3Bel	sly	6f	:22^1 :45^3 1:10^1	ⒻClm 70000	87	4	2	$1^{1\frac12}$	$1^{\frac12}$	$1^{1\frac12}$	1no	Smith M E	b	112	2.90	89-14	BbsLttlGl112^{no}MssClrAppl116$^{4\frac12}$ApplnMsIrn113	Driving	7
28Aug92- 3Sar	fst	6f	:22^2 :45^4 1:10^2	3↑ⒻAlw 27000	80	4	3	1^1	$1^{\frac12}$	$1^{\frac12}$	2^{nk}	Krone J A	b	112	2.80	92-08	MySstrJlt112^{nk}Bob'sLttlGl112^{2}Ksskwn117	Couldn't last	7
16Aug92- 6Sar	my	7f	:23^2 :46^2 1:24^1	3↑ⒻAlw 27000	73	5	2	2^1	2^1	$3^{1\frac12}$	$3^{3\frac14}$	Carr D		112	*1.50	81-14	DDp112^{1}AlphRscl117$^{2\frac12}$BbsLttlGl112	Drifted, weakened	7
5Aug92- 6Sar	fst	6f	:22^1 :45^3 1:10^3	3↑ⒻAlw 27000	79	3	3	$1^{1\frac12}$	$1^{\frac12}$	$1^{\frac12}$	$2^{1\frac14}$	Carr D		112	3.10	90-07	UOtbenPictures112$^{1\frac14}$Bob'sLittlGl112$\frac34$Trid112	Sharp try	10

LATEST WORKOUTS May 8 Bel 5f fst 1:01^2 B

Marilyn's Magic

Ch. f. 4, by Shananie—Vincesca, by Darby Creek Road
BISONO C V (141 14 11 11 .10) $35,000 Br.—Campbell Gilbert G (Fla)
Own.—Davis Barbara J Tr.—Moschera Gasper S (72 13 7 11 .18) 112⁵
Lifetime 26 8 4 3 $100,434 | 1993 7 1 4 0 $23,310 | 1992 14 6 0 1 $67,184 | Turf 2 0 0 0 $480 | Wet 4 2 1 0 $26,120

6Jun93- 4Bel fst 6f :22³ :45⁴ 1:10⁴ ⒻClm 35000 13 87 1 1 1hd 2hd 2½ 2² Smith M E 117 18.10 84–20 AlpineMusic1102Marilyn'sMgic1174Viperous117 Gamely 6
27May93- 4Bel fst 6f :22² :45³ 1:10² ⒻClm 45000 86 13 3 3½ 32 22 21¾ Migliore R 113 3.00 87–16 BbsLttlGl1131¼MrlnsMc1132¾CmpnGrl113 Finished well 7
16May93- 5Bel fst 6f :22¹ :45³ 1:10⁴ ⒻClm 45000 81 1 6 66 77 53½ 41½ Migliore R 113 5.10 84–15 StplQn115½Bob'sLttlGl113½LovlyJsphn113 Belated rally 7
5May93- 3Bel fst 6f :22³ :45³ 1:09⁴ ⒻClm c-35000 60 4 4 32½ 53 64¾ 67¼ Maple E 117 *1.80 83–08 LovlyJosphin1171½JckiP.117noFrOutNurs117 Done early 10
5May93-Claimed from Campbell Gilbert, Allard Edward T Trainer
20Feb93- 8Suf gd 6f :22 :46 1:13³ ⒻAlw 13000 76 6 1 2½ 2½ 32 21¾ Gambardella C LB 119 *.70 80–18 NftyOprtr1171¾Mrln'sMgc119nkFEpsd114 Forced out tn 7
7Feb93- 8Suf fst 6f :22 :46 1:13¹ ⒻAlw 13000 74 3 3 2½ 2½ 15 13½ Gambardella C LB 122 *.30 84–19 Mrlyn'sMgc1223¼PcflPnr1132¾SprtdFlyr113 Ridden out 7
23Jan93- 8Suf sly 6f :22² :47 1:14 ⒻAlw 13000 76 6 1 11 11 15 21¾ Gambardella C LB 114 *1.50 79–23 GentleDer1161¾Mrilyn'sMgic1145FoxyEpisode113 Failed 9
28Nov92- 7Med fst 6f :22¹ :45² 1:10¹ ⒻWm Parker 73 5 1 1hd 32 87¾ 65¼ Santagata N L 113 8.60 87–11 Squirm121¾ Cool Number114no LightsofMarfa116 Tired 10
13Nov92- 7Aqu gd 6f :21⁴ :45¹ 1:10¹ ⒻClm 85000 82 5 1 52½ 4¾ 53½ 54¾ Smith M E 115 3.20 85–17 MssClrAppl111nkStrtgcRrd1152½PrfctLss121 Four wide 5
17Oct92- 2Bel fst 6f :22³ :45⁴ 1:10⁴ ⒻClm 50000 90 1 2 21 2hd 1hd 11¾ Maple E 116 *2.60 86–23 Mrlyn'sMgc1161¾BddyMllgn1121¾FnlCrssng116 Driving 10
LATEST WORKOUTS Apr 30 Suf 4f fst :52³ B

Company Girl

B. m. 6, by Cormorant—Talcum Blue, by Talc
ALVARADO F T (92 12 13 14 .13) $35,000 Br.—Fishback J (NY)
Own.—Scuderi Vincent S Tr.—Ferriola Peter (77 13 14 12 .17) 117
Lifetime 70 10 11 12 $322,536 | 1993 7 0 3 3 $34,110 | 1992 21 2 2 3 $47,520 | Turf 5 1 0 0 $14,940 | Wet 15 2 2 1 $49,060

27May93- 4Bel fst 6f :22² :45³ 1:10² ⒻClm 45000 13 79 5 6 56½ 55 35 33¾ Alvarado F T b 113 5.20 84–16 Bb'sLttlGl1131¼Mrlyn'sMgc1132¾CmpnGrl113 Four wide 7
17May93- 1Bel fst 6f :22² :45 1:10² ⒻClm 70000 81 7 6 66½ 610 69 45 McCauley W H b 113 8.70e 83–21 RaiseHeck1172Meghn'sToy1132MerriTles117 No factor 7
24Apr93- 6Aqu fst 7f :22³ :45² 1:23⁴ 3↑ⒻAlw 40000 86 5 2 63½ 63¾ 53 22¼ Frost G C5 b 114 3.90 83–13 RchForClvr1192¼CompnyGrl1143Kt'sCollg119 Late gain 6
2Apr93- 8Aqu my 6f :22¹ :45³ 1:11¹ 3↑ⒻAlw 40000 92 4 6 68½ 65 33½ 21 Frost G C5 b 110 10.90 85–20 StrtgcRwrd1151CmpnyGrl1101¾MrrTls115 Broke slowly 6
4Feb93- 8Aqu fst 6f ⊡:23³ :47² 1:12³ ⒻAlw 41000 86 1 6 63 54 43½ 32½ Frost G C5 b 110 4.50 77–26 QuietDrm1151¾MrriTls1151CompnyGirl110 Broke slowly 6
29Jan93- 4Aqu fst 6f ⊡:23 :47¹ 1:12² ⒻClm 45000 81 1 6 64 63 42 32 Frost G C5 b 108 *2.60 79–24 Boots113¾ Super Style1171¼ CompanyGirl108 Mild gain 7
7Jan93- 4Aqu fst 6f ⊡:22² :45² 1:10¹ ⒻClm 45000 79 6 7 76½ 74½ 41½ 2¾ McCauley W H b 113 3.90e 91–11 HppyDppl113¾CmpnGrl113noChchBmb117 Up for place 9
14Dec92- 3Aqu gd 6f ⊡:23³ :47 1:12² 3↑ⒻClm c-25000 73 1 6 68½ 66 55¾ 44½ Vasquez M O b 117 3.50 76–17 Flowrforlxndr115¾EmphticStyl1172EpicVII117 Mild gain 6
14Dec92-Claimed from Stronach Frank, Sedlacek Michael C Trainer
4Dec92- 3Aqu fst 6f ⊡:23 :46² 1:12¹ 3↑ⒻClm 25000 71 5 6 78½ 55½ 46 21¾ Vasquez M O b 117 17.10 80–13 Shrplmg1151¾CmpnyGrl1172½LsnUpLs117 Sted 3/8 pole 7
25Nov92- 1Aqu my 7f :22⁴ :46² 1:24² 3↑ⒻClm 25000 60 5 6 66 77 711 612¼ Santagata N b 117 13.00 71–18 Erhart117hd Lovley Josephine1178¼ Ivi De117 No threat 8
LATEST WORKOUTS Jun 24 Aqu 4f fst :48⁴ B ●Jun 14 Aqu 3f fst :37¹ B Jun 8 Aqu 4f fst :49² B May 8 Aqu 5f fst 1:03¹ B

Saucyladygaylord

Dk. b. or br. f. 4, by Lord Gaylord—Lady Sauce Boat, by Sauce Boat
LOVATO F JR (19 2 0 2 .11) $35,000 Br.—Reynolds David P (Md)
Own.—Reynolds David P Tr.—Kelly Timothy D (27 2 5 2 .07) 117
Lifetime 18 6 3 1 $77,160 | 1993 5 2 1 0 $35,880 | 1992 11 4 1 1 $38,000 | Wet 1 1 0 0 $9,000

27May93- 4Bel fst 6f :22² :45³ 1:10² ⒻClm 50000 19 59 2 5 46 44½ 56 411¾ Lovato F Jr b 117 9.60 76–16 BbsLttlGl1131¼MrlnsMgc1132¾CmpnGrl113 Lacked rally 7
21Apr93- 6Aqu fst 6f :22¹ :45³ 1:11 3↑ⒻAlw 27500 78 4 6 65½ 53½ 52¾ 44¼ Lovato F Jr b 119 10.00 83–17 GttingAroundtoit119½SintI'mNot1192¼Trq119 Mild gain 7
18Feb93- 7Aqu fst 6f ⊡:23 :46³ 1:11³ ⒻAlw 27000 79 2 8 64 52 1hd 12¾ Lovato F Jr b 117 *.80 85–13 Scyldyglrd1172¾Vprs117nkBrstngUp117 Pnchd brk, wide 8
27Jan93- 6Aqu fst 6f ⊡:23³ :47⁴ 1:13² ⒻAlw 27000 76 2 4 52½ 52½ 41½ 2½ Lovato F Jr b 117 *1.30 75–25 Kumr112½Sucyldygylord1172SlsSprkn122 Finished well 7
17Jan93- 9Aqu fst 6f ⊡:22 :45 1:10³ ⒻClm 20000 86 8 5 55 55½ 32 11¾ Lovato F Jr b 113 6.90 90–15 Sucyldygylord1131¾JzzLegend112nkPhonQun115 Driving 10
5Dec92- 2Aqu fst 6f ⊡:23² :47² 1:12³ ⒻClm 17500 81 8 2 31½ 1hd 13 12¼ Lovato F Jr b 116 4.20 80–23 Scyldygylrd1162¼DshngBrrnss1143¼GrndCch107 Driving 9
9Nov92- 9Aqu fst 6f :22² :46² 1:11⁴ ⒻClm 17500 70 10 8 55¾ 42 2½ 31¼ Lidberg D W b 116 15.80 81–23 DshngBronss116hdTnrtt1181½Scyldygylrd116 Bid, wknd 12
11Oct92- 1Bel gd 6f :23¹ :46³ 1:12² ⒻClm 17500 63 2 4 41¾ 31 3nk 1nk Lidberg D W 116 4.00 78–18 Scyldygylord116nkTnortt1141¼AwsomLontss107 Driving 6
18Jly92- 9Bel fst 6f :23 :46² 1:12 ⒻClm 17500 54 7 8 53¾ 41 41¾ 64¼ Perret C b 116 2.80 76–12 [illegible] Flattened out 11
8May92- 2Bel fst 6f :22³ :45⁴ 1:11³ ⒻClm 17500 58 2 6 43 21 22½ 2½ Lidberg D W b 118 *2.40 81–13 KyChnc113½Scyldygylrd1181¾BrNEvl116 Bumped 1/16 pl 8
LATEST WORKOUTS Jun 12 Bel 4f fst :52 B May 18 Bel 5f fst 1:02³ B May 9 Bel 3f fst :36⁴ B May 1 Bel tr.t 3f fst :37² B

Biddy Mulligan

Ch. f. 4, by Geiger Counter—Cailin Deas, by It's Freezing
DAVIS R G (226 30 34 28 .13) $30,000 Br.—Byrne Michael C (Ont-C)
Own.—Vigliarolo Frank J Tr.—DiAngelo Joseph T (3 0 0 0 .00) 113
Lifetime 35 9 6 3 $164,526 | 1993 9 2 0 0 $34,503 | 1992 20 6 4 1 $107,813 | Turf 2 0 0 0 $330 | Wet 7 4 1 0 $65,038

22Jun93- 8Mth fst 6f :22 :45³ 1:11³ 3↑ⒻClm 35000 48 3 4 21½ 55 59½ 614¾ Marquez C HJr Lb 114 33.20 66–27 EvrDncng1141¾CrftyBll1161¾StrsKnockot107 Gave way 7
27May93- 4Bel fst 6f :22² :45³ 1:10² ⒻClm 50000 51 6 1 1½ 21 46 514¾ Chavez J F b 117 9.60 73–16 Bb'sLttlGl1131¼MrlnsMgc1132¾CmpnGrl113 Speed,tired 7
24Apr93- 2Grd fst 4½f :22¹ :46 :52¹ Clm 50000 60 1 3 55 56 56 Walls M K b 119 2.10 83–14 Cool Shot118¾StarDetector1183Dr.Adagio113 Faded rail 5
17Apr93-10Grd fst 4½f :21³ :45² :52 ⒻAlw 38100 73 3 1 2½ 53¾ 55¾ Attard L b 113 7.05 84–21 ContssStff1151¾MyrtlIrn119½MoonMst121 Inside speed 5
1Apr93- 7Grd sly 4½f :22⁴ :47 :53¹ ⒻAlw 27600 86 3 1 12 13 13 Walls M K b 122 2.00 84–18 BddyMllgn1223MplLk1192½FlshCncrd116 Much the best 5
27Mar93- 7Grd my 4½f :22² :46¹ :52² ⒻClm 50000 82 3 2 1½ 2hd 1no Walls M K b 116 2.20 88–16 BddMlln116noMssCls1183¾BlElctr116 Very game inside 7
5Mar93- 9GP fm 1 Ⓣ 1:36 ⒻHandicap 73 10 1 14 2hd 910 911¼ Ramos W S b 112 109.20 89 — KlssyIndivdul114nkExplosvKt1171½SoSmug113 Stopped 10
11Feb93- 7GP fst 6f :21⁴ :44³ 1:10² ⒻClm 55000 64 5 1 21 44½ 49 410¼ Penna D b 114 11.40 79–16 Ever Dancing1165 Patti L.116nk Daimon112 Faded 5
28Jan93- 7GP fst 6½f :22³ :45⁴ 1:16² ⒻClm 60000 59 2 5 1½ 22½ 611 616¼ Penna D Lb 116 10.90 78–19 Lady Sonata1162¼ Dazzling Affair1203 ButterCream116 6
28Jan93-Broken in air at start, rushed, stopped
22Dec92- 8Aqu fst 6f ⊡:22³ :46 1:10³ 3↑ⒻHandicap 65 6 1 3nk 63½ 67½ 612¼ Chavez J F b 110 7.10 77–16 LdySge1135ChristinCzrin1161¾DzzleMJoli119 Weakened 6
LATEST WORKOUTS Jun 11 Bel tr.t 5f fst 1:02 B ●May 23 Bel 5f fst :59¹ H May 13 Bel tr.t 5f fst 1:03³ B

Shoot the Rapids

B. f. 4, by Little Missouri—Slipping Away, by Sensitive Prince
BAILEY J D (144 24 28 21 .17) $35,000 Br.—Live Oak Stud (Fla)
Own.—Macmindon Stable Tr.—O'Connell Richard (23 1 4 3 .04) 117
Lifetime 8 2 3 0 $46,156 | 1993 2 0 1 0 $4,290 | 1992 5 2 1 0 $38,126 | Wet 1 0 1 0 $11,726

17Jun93- 2Bel fst 7f :23³ :46⁴ 1:25 ⒻClm 35000 83 3 2 2½ 31 2½ 21¼ Bailey J D 117 8.80 76–23 UkrininGl1171¼ShoottheRpids1173¾AllPower110 Gamely 8
3Jun93- 7Bel fst 6f :22⁴ :46¹ 1:10² 3↑ⒻAlw 27500 49 2 6 63½ 73½ 77 715¼ Bailey J D 117 25.80 73–13 AxeCreek109½JillMiner1095LittlAnni0113 Stumbled brk 7
3May92- 7Aqu fst 1 :47 1:12³ 1:38³ 3↑ⒻAlw 31000 54 6 6 62¾ 74 78 616 Velazquez J R 110 4.30 53–28 Sunny Sara1191¾ Kersey1105½ Miss Jazz119 No threat 7
28Mar92- 8Aqu fst 1 :46² 1:11² 1:37¹ ⒻComely 49 5 5 53½ 69 615 624 Velazquez J R 112 12.10 52–31 SrtogDw1141CityDnc112½LookingforWn114 Stmbld brk 7
28Mar92-Grade II
7Mar92- 7Aqu my 1⅛ ⊡:47⁴ 1:13 1:47 ⒻPlankton 78 4 1 1½ 11½ 2hd 22 Velazquez J R 116 2.30 71–24 CityDnce1142ShoottheRpids1165ShredMgic116 Gamely 6
17Feb92- 7Aqu fst 1⅛ ⊡:47¹ 1:11⁴ 1:45² ⒻAlw 29000 76 2 1 1½ 11 12½ 14 Velazquez J R 116 3.10 81–13 ShoottheRapids1164ArtGllery116¾Notonebid109 Driving 6
9Jan92- 3Aqu fst 170 ⊡:49 1:14⁴ 1:45³ ⒻMd 50000 73 2 1 11½ 11 15 112 Nelson D 121 *.70 77–26 ShtthRpds12112EndrnDncr1173¼CclcGrl117 Ridden out 7
23Dec91- 3Aqu fst 6f ⊡:23¹ :47 1:13⁴ ⒻMd 75000 65 5 6 53 25 25 2¾ Nelson D 117 5.20 73–18 HexAppel113¾ShoottheRpids1174¾BsbllCrd113 2nd best 9
LATEST WORKOUTS Jun 14 Bel 4f fst :47⁴ H May 31 Bel 4f fst :48¹ H ●May 25 Bel 5f fst 1:00¹ H May 20 Bel 5f gd 1:02⁴ H

BEL p15 MARILYN'S MAGIC

5 RACES 91		14 RACES 92		7 RACES 93	
		18–	vL AWWEETA		
		.^13+	V 99AQETA		
		11–	bw 50BEETA		
^=28+	Y AWWEETA	11+	w 35BEETA		
^25+	AWRK15	26–	Y AWMTKJJ		
=32+	Y AWAT31				
18–	w MSAT22	25	Y AWRK22		
		17'	AWRK 8		
28–	Y MSMTETA				
				F\M	4YO 28JUN93
		.22	vL AWMTETA	15	35BEGSM
				15–	50BEGSM
		.14	vw 75BEETA	16–	50BEGSM
		F24+	v AWPH 3	'21"	Y&GM 35BEETA
		21"	w AWSU13		
		37"	AWPH 4		
		19–	w AWSU25		
		.17+	Vw AWSU 7		
				^18	Vt AWSU20
				../18–	w AWSU 7
				.19	Y AWSU23

recovery time

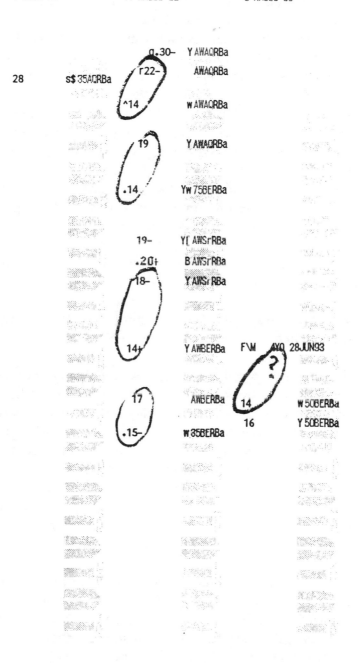

BEL p14				BOB'S LITTLE GAL	
1 RACE 91		11 RACES 92		2 RACES 93	
		q.30–	Y AWAQRBa		
		r22–	AWAQRBa		
28	s$35AQRBa				
		^14	w AWAQRBa		
		19	Y AWAQRBa		
		.14	Yw 75BERBa		
		19–	Y[AWSrRBa		
		.20+	B AWSrRBa		
		18–	Y AWSr RBa		
		14+	Y AWBERBa	F\M 4YO	28JUN93
		17	AWBERBa	14	W 50BERBa
				16	Y 50BERBa
		.15–	w 35BERBa		

On Beyer, Bob's Little Gal ran an 87 September 26 and bounced to a 79; she ran an 86 on November 13 and bounced to a 68. For this race, she is emerging from a figure of 89.

On *The Sheets,* the pattern is identical. Not only has Bob's Little Gal bounced off 14s on four previous occasions, but the strain of those 14s has taken a greater toll each time: the 14¾ was followed by a 17; the 14¼ was followed by a 17¾; the 14 was followed by a 19; the next 14 was followed by a 22. For this race, she emerges from another 14 and, according to her well-established pattern, whatever is coming today is not likely to be good. In fact, it projects to be slower than a 22!

Might the argument be made that Bob's Little Gal returned from a layoff and ran a 14 second time back — a figure that equaled her best race as a three-year-old? Wouldn't that indicate an explosive line?

No. The level of 14 is too well established, as are the negative reactions to them. Clearly, 14 represents the *breaking point* in terms of racing-related stress for Bob's Little Gal.

Now to Marilyn's Magic: Why are her paired 15s determined to be positive, whereas Lovley Josephine's paired 15s in the previous example were negative?

To begin with, Marilyn's Magic is a four-year-old and has not been nearly so heavily raced as the five-year-old Lovley Josephine. Additionally, the 15s for Lovley Josephine were strenuous efforts that equaled her well-established top. Marilyn's Magic, on the other hand, had paired up 11s last fall and had still managed to run a 13¼ in her next race. Therefore, when she paired the 15s, she was still four points away from her top; the 15s were not seriously stressful efforts on her part, as they had been for Lovley Josephine. Marilyn's Magic had some "room" to work with — something better to run back to today if in good condition.

Marilyn's Magic gave every indication of improving condition; in fact, she exhibited a variation of the recovery line. To wit:

The paired 11s followed by a 13 caused a bounce to 18 in a minor stakes at the Meadowlands, and she was shelved for nearly two months. She returned with three races at Suffolk that were well off her Belmont form of October, went to the shelf for another ten weeks, and returned with her worst performance in some time, when claimed May 5. But her three races following the claim indicated that Gasper Moschera, annually among the leading trainers in New York, had found the filly's "hole card" and fixed whatever was wrong. Her Beyer 81/*The Sheets* 15¾ first time off the claim on May 16 was the best race she had run in six months, and her running line that day showed a "change of pace," as the early-pace type suddenly closed strongly through the final stages of this race. The pair-up (86/87 on Beyer, 15s on *The Sheets*) was another small forward move, made more impressive because the races were closely spaced.

The majority of figure players on hand — whether Beyer or sheet oriented — took their analysis no further than to say, "Bob's Little Gal beat Marilyn's Magic fair and square by a length and a quarter on May 27 . . . she must be the more likely winner again today, eh?"

A condition analysis suggested that these were two fillies headed in opposite directions:

SECOND RACE
Belmont
JUNE 28, 1993

6 FURLONGS. (1.07^4) CLAIMING. Purse $19,500. Fillies and Mares, 4-year-olds and upward Weight, 3-year-olds 122 lbs. Non-winners of two races since June 1 allowed 3 lbs. Of a race since then, 5 lbs. Claiming Price $35,000, for each $2,500 to $30,000, 2 lbs. (Races when entered to be claimed for $25,000 or less not considered).

Value of race $19,500; value to winner $11,700; second $4,290; third $2,340; fourth $1,170. Mutuel pool $174,174. Exacta Pool $348,631 Quinella Pool $99,621

Last Raced	Horse	M/Eqt.	A.	Wt	PP	St	¼	½	Str	Fin	Jockey	Cl'g Pr	Odds $1
6Jun93 ^{4}Bel^2	Marilyn's Magic		4	112	4	3	$3^{2\frac{1}{2}}$	3^3	1^1	1^7	Bisono C V^5	35000	4.00
4Jun93 ^{6}Pim^5	King's Sweetest		4	117	1	1	$2^{\frac{1}{2}}$	2^{hd}	2^2	$2^{1\frac{1}{3}}$	Chavez J F	35000	6.40
27May93 ^{4}Bel^3	Company Girl	b	6	117	5	6	5^{hd}	$4^{\frac{1}{2}}$	4^2	$3^{\frac{1}{2}}$	Alvarado F T	35000	3.50
22Jun93 ^{3}Mth^6	Biddy Mulligan	b	4	113	6	2	1^3	$1^{\frac{1}{2}}$	3^1	$4^{3\frac{1}{3}}$	Davis R G	30000	25.60
17Jun93 ^{2}Bel^2	Shoot the Rapids		4	117	7	7	6^2	5^{10}	5^{14}	5^{23}	Bailey J D	35000	3.70
13Jun93 ^{2}Bel^9	Bridjet Honey	b	5	115	2	4	7	6	6	6	Antley C W	32500	15.60
27May93 ^{4}Bel^1	Bob's Little Gal	b	4	117	3	5	$4^{2\frac{1}{2}}$	—	—	—	Smith M E	35000	1.80

Bob's Little Gal, Pulled up.

OFF AT 1:29 Start good. Won driving. Time, :22 , :45^4, :58 , 1:10^3 Track fast.

$2 Mutuel Prices:			
5-(E)-MARILYN'S MAGIC	10.00	4.80	3.20
2-(A)-KING'S SWEETEST		6.60	4.40
1-(F)-COMPANY GIRL			3.20

$2 EXACTA 5-2 PAID $62.60 $2 QUINELLA 2-5 PAID $40.00

Ch. f, by Shananie—Vincesca, by Darby Creek Road. Trainer Moschera Gasper S. Bred by Campbell Gilbert G (Fla).

MARILYN'S MAGIC settled just behind the early leader, accelerated to the front in upper stretch then drew off under good handling. KING'S SWEETEST raced just inside the winner into upper stretch but couldn't stay with that one through the final furlong. COMPANY GIRL unhurried for a half, failed to threaten while improving her position in [redacted] BIDDY MULLIGAN sprinted clear in the early stages, set the pace along the inside to the turn then tired from her ear[redacted]HE RAPIDS was never a factor. BRIDJET HONEY never reached contention. BOB'S LITTLE GAL, pulled up lame on the turn and was vanned off.

[redacted] Bender Sondra D; 3, Scuderi Vincent S; 4, Vigliarolo Frank J; 5, Macmindon Stable; 6, Stronach Frank H; 7, Lamcresse Stable.

Trainers— 1, Moschera Gasper S; 2, Murray Lawrence E; 3, Ferriola Peter; 4, DiAngelo Joseph T; 5, O'Connell Richard; 6, Sedlacek Michael C; 7, Barbara Robert.

Bridjet Honey was claimed by Ferriola Ingrid; trainer, Ferriola Peter.

Scratched—Goblin (3Jun93 ^{2}Bel^{11}); Saucyladygaylord (27May93 ^{4}Bel^4).

The chart says it all. Marilyn's Magic drew off to win by seven lengths, paying $10. Bob's Little Gal, who had been showing increasingly severe negative reactions with each passing 14, pulled up lame at 9–5 and was vanned off the track.

Len Friedman, chief betting theoretician of the *Ragozin Sheets,* was kind enough to let me draw on his seminar tapes in preparing this chapter, with the understanding that he has reservations about certain matters, as he made clear to me in a letter:

Dear Dave:

Thanks for letting me speak my piece. My main thought is that it is really not correct to suggest you can have success by applying some of these sophisticated ideas to just anybody's speed ratings. All figures are not alike, and the way the figures are made reflects to some degree the theories which the maker has about horses' development.

You have selected examples where the patterns of the *Thorograph* figures match ours — but in the majority of real-life cases, they don't. Jerry Brown has his own ideas. Even a casual glance through a full day's sheets, for example, will reveal many more immediate pair-ups and trios of matching figures on his sheets than on ours; also, races run in the slop much more often produce big lifetime tops on his figures than on ours. There are other frequent differences.

As for the Beyer figures, they don't even include weight, paths, or wind. It is no surprise to us that a recent study by Sport Stat, an independent research firm, shows 15% more return per dollar on *The Sheets* than on these competitors.

Len Ragozin and I looked at hundreds of thousands of patterns on *The Sheets* over the course of thirty years while developing conclusions about condition handicapping and pattern analysis which you draw upon. **Many of the concepts contained here will definitely not apply when using figures that are conceived differently — and, we think, less accurately — than *The Ragozin Sheets.***

Best wishes,
Len Friedman

TWO

CONDITION ANALYSIS — TRAINERS AND WORKOUTS

WHENEVER A NEW ACQUAINTANCE LEARNS that I handicap horses for a living, the conversation invariably arrives at a juncture where the question that makes all horseplayers cringe is asked:

"So, you got any good tips?"

You betcha! Why, during a typical morning's walk from my car to the press box I am informed about "hot" horses by the parking lot attendant, the security guard at the front gate, the newsstand vendor, and the elevator operator, always in that order. A day without a hot tip is like a day without sunshine.

If I had a dollar for every such horse that's finished up the track during the past several years, I'd have retired to Tahiti in the prime of my life as a wealthy man. The truth is that with rare exceptions, the only inside information worth knowing is whatever can be gleaned through personal research and attention to detail.

This means that for those who are serious about winning money during the course of a typical season's play, evenings spent watching reruns of *Roseanne* are out.

As we've seen, speed figures can often be used as a time-saving means of gaining insights into physical condition that few others share. But the contender selection process is rife with complexities that extend far beyond the realm of mere numbers. Thoroughbreds are not Formula One engines that deliver an unwavering amount of horsepower race after race; nor are they a mere series of performance ratings graphed on 5″ × 8″ sheets of paper. Thoroughbreds are living, breathing, highly strung athletes that develop meaningful preferences regarding distances, running styles, weather, track conditions, jockeys, and training methods on an individual basis. Fortunately, a sizable percentage of the betting public just doesn't get it; they embrace figures as a panacea and use them out of context relative to other vital aspects of evaluating current form and condition. In so doing, they confine themselves within the boundaries of the obvious and are thus doomed to failure according to the nature of the pari-mutuel system.

Winning handicappers eventually discover that subjective, nonmeasurable factors, such as trainers, trips, track bias, and physical appearance, are their most potent source of concealed-condition plays. It's all well and good to construct personal betting lines that alert you to a first choice being overbet and a second or third choice being underbet, but only the most accurate oddsmakers can survive this way. Betting on second or third choices deemed to offer more "value" is a seductive approach in theory, but potentially leads to lazy handicapping: "I can't separate the contenders in this race, so I'll just bet the one that's going off at the biggest price." This is a sure way to invite long and frequent losing streaks.

Instead of betting $10 each on ten of my second or third choices offering supposed value, I would much rather wait for a race *in which a serious edge is perceived* and risk the entire $100 right then and there.

"Value" is a vague term until and unless a handicapper has information about a horse that is concealed from most other bettors. In this chapter, we are concerned with finding the nonmeasurable signs of sharp current condition that give us that edge.

BASICS

As Mark Cramer has explained in several of his superb books, notably *Thoroughbred Cycles,* in racing there is continuity and there is change.

Chalk players bet on continuity: the horse has been running well in recent races and will continue to do so today.

Longshot players bet on change: the horse hasn't been running well in recent races but will turn things around today.

Handicappers get the best of both worlds by learning to uncover horses that combine continuity and change: the horse is repeating a pattern that produced a positive and dramatic reversal of form earlier in its career.

Since the races themselves are the best teachers, let's take a look at Aqueduct's Grade 2 Bed o'Roses Handicap from April 3, 1993, a one-turn mile that produced two pattern repeats — one positive and one negative. Take a moment to examine the past performances:

1 MILE. **(1.322) 37th Running THE BED O'ROSES HANDICAP (Grade II). Purse $100,000 Added. Fillies and Mares. 3-year-olds and upward. By subscription of $200 each which should accompany the nomination; $800 to pass the entry box; $800 to start with $100,000 added. The added money and all fees to be divided 60% to the winner, 22% to second; 12% to third and 6% to fourth. Weights Monday, March 29. Starters to be named at the closing time of entries. Trophies will be presented to the winning owner, trainer and jockey. Closed Wednesday, March 17, 1993, with 21 nominations.**

Haunting — Ch. m. 5, by Kris S—Untamed Spirit, by Groshawk

ANTLEY C W (56 8 17 9 .14) — Br.—Meadowbrook Farm Inc (Fla)

Own.—Silverleaf Farms Inc — Tr.—Veitch John M (—) — **113**

Lifetime 30 6 4 3 $318,549 — 1993 3 0 0 1 $25,000 — 1992 10 2 2 1 $165,015 — Turf 6 1 1 0 $38,375 — Wet 1 0 1 0 $44,000

21Mar93-10GP fst 1 1/16 :481 1:124 1:452 3+ⒻRampart H 87 1 1 31½ 32½ 21 42 Santos J A 114 12.60 81-20 GrlOnMsson112hdⒹNowDnc116hdLvMLvMNt116 Faded 8
21Mar93-Grade II; Placed third through disqualification

3Mar93- 9GP fst 170 :463 1:101 1:413 3+ⒻSabin H 85 9 5 66 56 54½ 56½ Krone J A 114 6.20 87-07 NDnc1132½SpnnngRnd115noLMLMNt117 Lckd response 10

19Feb93- 9GP fst 170 :474 1:124 1:43 ⒻAlw 35500 78 5 5 42½ 3½ 21½ 41¼ Krone J A 117 4.00 85-14 HlfTDncr114noOnStGl1121½ShrGld117 Lacked response 6

26Jun92- 8Bel fst 1 :453 1:092 1:351 3+ⒻHandicap 83 4 5 54½ 54½ 53 55 Madrid A Jr 116 5.70 89-11 Rchrd'sLss1101RglVctrss1122½HrShShklt122 No threat 7

20Jun92- 7Bel sf 1 1/16 Ⓣ:481 1:122 1:441 3+ⒻHandicap 49 3 6 65½ 67½ 623 627½ Madrid A Jr 114 8.70 50-21 MayflowerLass122¾KiwiMint1151MonicaFye117 Outrun 6

2May92- 9Spt fst 1⅛ :48 1:114 1:511 3+ⒻSxty Sils H 74 9 9 1212 1211 1212 1110¼ Madrid A Jr 114 6.90 100 — Peach of It114nk Bungalow115½ZendtoAiken113 Outrun 13
2May92-Grade III

17Apr92 8Aqu sly 1⅛ :461 1:112 1:502 3+ⒻTopflight H 91 6 11 108½ 73¼ 5¾ 2¾ Madrid A Jr 112 41.40 83-18 FirmStnc114¾Huntng112nkLdyD'Accord117 Rallied wide 14
17Apr92-Grade I

29Mar92- 7Aqu fst 1 :472 1:121 1:371 3+ⒻBed O R's H 95 7 5 52¾ 51¼ 53 53¾ Madrid A Jr 114 14.80 72-33 Nnnrl1152½EnglshChrm111noSpyLdrLd115 Lacked rally 7
29Mar92-Grade II

15Mar92- 8Aqu fst 7f :224 :463 1:243 3+ⒻDistaff H 86 6 1 54½ 52½ 33 47 Madrid A Jr 116 9.00 75-25 Nnnrl1123½Mssy'sMrg1192½Wthllprbblt117 Lacked rally 6
15Mar92-Grade II

29Feb92- 8Aqu fst 1 1/16 ⊡:483 1:134 2:001 3+ⒻNext MoveH 98 1 5 44½ 42½ 21½ 23¾ Antley C W 117 2.90 75-36 SpyLeaderLdy1123¾Hunting1171½GrecinPss115 2nd best 6
29Feb92-Grade III

LATEST WORKOUTS Mar 31 Bel tr.t 5f fst 1:003 H — Mar 11 GP 4f fst :481 H — ●Feb 26 GP 4f fst :473 H — Feb 16 GP 4f fst :482 H

Missy's Mirage — Gr. m. 5, by Stop the Music—First Mirage, by Riva Ridge

MAPLE E (3 0 1 0 .00) — Br.—Stavola J & W Inc (N.J.)

Own.—Middletown Stable — Tr.—Jerkens H Allen (11 3 2 3 .27) — **123**

Lifetime 27 14 7 1 $814,210 — 1993 1 1 0 0 $40,620 — 1992 8 5 2 0 $400,078 — Wet 3 2 1 0 $195,900

27Feb93- 7Aqu fst 6f ⊡:233 :464 1:11 3+ⒻCorrectionH 107 3 5 21 21½ 1hd 13 Maple E 121 *.30 88-18 MsssMrg1213WnCrftLd1151¾StrnEmbrc109 Ridden out 6

10Oct92- 3Bel my 7f :221 :443 1:203 3+ⒻFrst Flght 108 2 4 1hd 11 1½ 21½ Maple E 121 *.40 99 — ShredInterest1111½Missy'sMirge1214¾Nnnrl119 2nd best 5
10Oct92-Grade II

19Sep92- 4Bel fst 6f :214 :443 1:09 3+ⒻGay Matelda 111 2 2 24 2½ 2½ 1¾ Maple E 115 *.70 95-11 Missy'sMirage115¾ParisianFlight1173½Serpe122 Driving 4

29Aug92- 6Sar fst 6f :22 :442 1:084 3+Alydar 101 2 5 21 22 3½ 42 Maple E 114 *1.30 98-07 Diablo122nk For Really122nk Burn Fair115 Broke slowly 5

31May92- 8Bel sly 1⅛ :451 1:084 1:47 3+ⒻHempsteadH 109 5 1 11½ 1½ 11½ 13 Maple E 118 2.80 94-09 Mssy'sMrg1183HrbourClb110nkVrsllsTrty119 Mild drive 6
31May92-Grade I

9May92- 8Bel gd 1 1/16 :451 1:091 1:403 3+ⒻShuvee H 100 6 1 11½ 11 1½ 1no Maple E 116 3.50 99-07 Mssy'sMrg116noHrbrClb110nkVrsllsTrty119 Broke in air 6
9May92-Grade I

18Apr92- 5Aqu my 7f :23 :454 1:204 3+ⒻLife's Magic 108 4 2 11½ 12 12 11¾ Maple E 119 1.30 101-06 Missy'sMirg1191¾VrsillsTrty11713Brchn'sLss119 Driving 4

15Mar92- 8Aqu fst 7f :224 :463 1:243 3+ⒻDistaff H 94 5 3 21½ 21 2½ 23½ Maple E 119 *.30 78-25 Nnnrl1123½Missy'sMirg1192½Withllprobblty117 2nd best 6
15Mar92-Grade II

23Feb92- 8Aqu fst 6f ⊡:224 :454 1:10 3+ⒻCorrectionH 106 6 1 32 31 1½ 13 Maple E 116 *.90 93-16 Missy'sMirge1163DvilishTouch1171MkinFcs114 Driving 6

2Nov91- 7Aqu fst 7f :222 :444 1:214 3+ⒻFrst Fl't H 105 5 5 31½ 21 11½ 16½ Maple E 113 *1.50 93-12 Mssy'sMrg1136½MknFcs112hdWthllprbblty114 Drew off 10
2Nov91-Grade II

LATEST WORKOUTS ●Mar 27 Bel tr.t 1 fst 1:383 B — Mar 20 Bel tr.t 7f fst 1:293 B — ●Mar 12 Bel tr.t 3f fst :342 H — ●Mar 8 Bel tr.t 4f fst :471 H

Buck Some Belle — Dk. b. or br. f. 4, by Spend a Buck—Stanwich Miss, by Advocator

BRAVO J (55 6 7 10 .11) — Br.—Crabtree & Lyster III (Ky)

Own.—Garren Murray M — Tr.—Garren Murray M (13 1 0 3 .08) — **106**

Lifetime 24 5 3 2 $124,680 — 1993 7 1 0 0 $24,240 — 1992 14 2 3 2 $66,900 — Turf 1 0 0 1 $3,840 — Wet 2 1 1 0 $26,020

20Mar93- 7Aqu fst 6f ⊡:22 :442 1:101 ⒻHandicap 65 4 5 68¾ 611 611 512½ Bravo J b 109 8.60 79-14 WinCraftyLady1223ScenicBidder1152½CalStr109 Outrun 6

7Mar93- 8Aqu fst 1 3/16 ⊡:47 1:111 1:554 3+ⒻNext MoveH 89 6 2 2½ 2hd 2hd 55¼ Bravo J b 107 37.10 90-10 LTlrnc114¾HlbysBrtFlt1121½LdLr114 Dueled, weakened 8
7Mar93-Grade III

27Feb93- 6Aqu fst 1 1/16 ⊡:484 1:134 1:462 ⒻAlw 47000 84 3 3 41½ 44 56½ 47¾ Leon F7 b 108 7.70 65-29 Richard'sLass1223½WonScent1151½Maxmount115 Faded 6

17Feb93- 8Aqu fst 1⅛ ⊡:462 1:103 1:491 3+ⒻR Treat H 96 6 2 31 32 22½ 52 Bravo J b 109 51.70 95-10 HyBbLl116nkLTlrnc1141½HlbysBrtFlt113 Saved ground 9
17Feb93-Grade III

24Jan93- 6Aqu fst 1 1/16 ⊡:48 1:122 1:45 ⒻHandicap 76 4 3 42 43 47 411¼ Chavez J F b 110 10.90 69-24 GoldenBimmer113¾Avie'sDisy1103¾LdyLr122 Saved grd 6

10Jan93- 7Aqu fst 1⅛ ⊡:481 1:134 1:53 ⒻAlw 31000 83 7 1 1½ 1½ 14 12 Chavez J F b 117 9.00 78-32 BuckSomeBelle1172MeetthBst1222RvngTim117 Driving 8

2Jan93- 4Aqu fst 1 1/16 ⊡:481 1:131 1:461 3+ⒻClm c-45000 62 6 2 31 44 610 612¼ Madrid A Jr b 113 12.50 65-18 SheSaidMaybe113nkStreaming117nkWonScent113 Tired 7
2Jan93-Claimed from Heatherwood Farm, Schosberg Richard Trainer

20Dec92- 9Aqu gd 1 1/16 ⊡:473 1:123 1:454 ⒻClm 50000 71 8 3 3½ 31½ 35½ 35¼ Madrid A Jr b 116 3.00 74-20 BlshngMoon1074RbccLrn1111½BckSomBll116 Even trip 8

5Dec92- 6Aqu fst 1 1/16 ⊡:474 1:133 1:463 3+ⒻAlw 31000 64 2 1 11 1hd 53¼ 59 Madrid A Jr b 115 13.00 66-22 LdyJnnF.1152¾HuckstrRos1152NoblGrl115 Used in pace 10

22Nov92- 7Aqu gd 1 :452 1:104 1:371 3+ⒻAlw 31000 70 5 4 41½ 2½ 42 49½ Madrid A Jr b 115 *2.70 66-20 She'sAcdemic117¾LdyJnnF.115¾Lizlity115 Flattened out 9

LATEST WORKOUTS Mar 31 Bel tr.t 3f fst :35 H — Mar 27 Bel tr.t 5f fst :594 B — Mar 5 Bel tr.t 4f my :472 H — Feb 24 Bel tr.t 3f fst :361 H

```
Lady D'Accord            Ch. m. 6, by D'Accord—Avichi, by Damascus                    Lifetime     1993  2  0  0  0      $560
                                                                                    44  8  7 10   1992 10  2  0  3  $145,466
CHAVEZ J F (53 11 8 6 .21)      Br.—Hettinger John (NY)                              $516,818     Turf  3  0  1  0    $6,820
Own.—Akindale Farm              Tr.—Zito Nicholas P (5 0 2 2 .00)              111                Wet   8  2  1  2  $125,822
9Mar93- 9GP  fst 6½f  :224 :454 1:162      ⒻAlw 29000     75 6 3 57½ 611 65¼ 58    Sweeney K H   117 12.70 87-17 ShrdIntrst1195Jnny'sPlymt1121½DlndDrm117  No factor 6
18Feb93- 9GP fst 6½f  :224 :463 1:172      ⒻAlw 27000     71 5 6 69¾ 67 59 59¾     Sweeney K H   119  6.60 80-18 MadamBear1191CorporteFund1143¾Froze117  No threat 6
26Oct92- 8Aqu fst 1⅛  :493 1:141 1:521 3+ⒻHandicap      78 3 4 32½ 32 44½ 48     Smith M E     122  2.10 67-24 LowTolernce1112½LdyLr1181¾Mxmount120  Lacked rally 6
10Oct92- 9Bel gd 1 1/16 :462 1:102 1:413 3+ⒻAlw 47000    80 5 6 66½ 43½ 36 39¾    Smith M E     117  2.40 84-04 HeyBbLulu115¾LdyLr1179LdyD'Accord117  Lacked rally 6
25Sep92- 8Bel fst 1   :47  1:112 1:361 3+ⒻHandicap      87 1 7 62½ 2hd 32 36½    Smith M E     119 *1.30 83-15 Coxwld108¾HyBbLl1115½LdyD'Accrd119  Bid, weakened 7
23Aug92- 8Sar fst 1⅛  :483 1:114 1:474 3+ⒻJohn Morris   72 6 7 73¾ 55½ 56½ 520¾  Antley C W    114  8.90 77-02 QuickMschf1136¾VrsllsTrty122½ShrdIntrst111  No threat 7
        23Aug92-Grade I
1Aug92- 6Sar gd 1     :453 1:101 1:361 3+ⒻHandicap      97 4 8 84¾ 31 1½ 13      Smith M E     122  2.70 — — LdyD'Accord1223DncColony1201½MssKrryC.111  Driving 8
31May92- 8Bel sly 1⅛  :451 1:084 1:47  3+ⒻHempsteadH    80 4 6 66 55½ 58½ 517    Perret C      114  5.60 77-09 Mssy'sMrg1183HrbourClb110nkVrsllsTrty119  No threat 6
        31May92-Grade I
9May92- 8Bel gd 1 1/16 :451 1:091 1:403 3+ⒻShuvee H     83 2 6 65 42½ 48 49¾     Chavez J F    116  5.80 89-07 Mssy'sMrg116noHrbourClb110nkVrsllsTrty119  No threat 6
        9May92-Grade I
17Apr92- 8Aqu sly 1⅛  :461 1:112 1:502 3+ⒻTopflight H   90 13 13 1312 136¾ 61½ 31  Chavez J F  117  4.50 83-18 FrmStnc114¾Huntng112nkLdyD'Accord117  Blckd, chckd 14
        17Apr92-Grade I
LATEST WORKOUTS   ●Mar 28 Bel tr.t 5f my 1:00 H   Mar 21 GP 5f gd 1:00 H   Feb 28 GP 5f fst 1:021 B   Feb 13 GP 5f fst 1:013 H

Golden Bimmer     Dk. b. or br. f. 4, by Gold Meridian—Song of Peace, by Hold Your Peace     Lifetime     1993  4  3  1  0   $80,840
                                                                                    27 12  4  2   1992 16  7  3  1  $147,160
MIGLIORE R (42 9 7 4 .21)       Br.—Mar-Ro-Mar Investments (Fla)                     $246,800
Own.—Hauman Eugene E            Tr.—Hushion Michael E (24 8 3 4 .33)           111                Wet   3  3  0  0   $56,360
22Mar93- 8Aqu fst 1 1/16 ⊡:483 1:124 1:441   ⒻHandicap     95 3 1 11 12½ 16 12½    Migliore R   b 116  *.60 84-23 GoldnBimmr1162½Avi'sDisy113noBlRy114  Taken in hand 6
15Feb93- 4Aqu gd 170 ⊡:482 1:13 1:414        ⒻClm c-90000  86 1 1 11 1hd 2½ 22     Smith M E    b 118  *.40 91-12 HighwyQuen1122GoldnBimmr118noClsky112  Weakened 5
        15Feb93-Claimed from Joques Farm, Moschera Gasper S Trainer
24Jan93- 6Aqu fst 1 1/16 ⊡:48 1:122 1:45     ⒻHandicap     95 2 1 11 11 11 1¾      Smith M E    b 113 *1.70 80-24 GoldenBimmer113¾Avie'sDaisy1103¾LadyLer122  Driving 6
18Jan93- 7Aqu fst 170 ⊡:482 1:132 1:424      ⒻClm 72500    91 3 1 11 1½ 13 14½     Smith M E    b 115  2.50 88-17 GoldenBimmer1154½HighwyQuen1131¼Clsky117  Driving 8
30Dec92- 5Aqu fst 170 ⊡:472 1:112 1:402 3+ⒻHandicap      93 5 1 2½ 23 25½ 37½    Samyn J L    b 110  1.30e 95-09 Rchrd'sLss1207½FrOtNrs113noGldnBmmr110  Weakened 6
22Dec92- 8Aqu fst 6f ⊡:223 :46 1:103 3+ⒻHandicap        79 1 5 62¾ 52½ 53½ 47    Samyn J L    b 111  7.80 83-16 LdySge1135ChristinCzrin1161¾DzzleMeJolie119  No rally 6
6Dec92- 7Aqu fst 1 1/16 ⊡:482 1:132 1:463    ⒻShy Dawn     80 2 1 1hd 2hd 21 56    Migliore R   b 118 *2.20 69-31 GroovyFlng1162Nbl'sHny1183PrfctGm116  Dueled inside 7
13Nov92- 7Aqu gd 6f  :214 :451 1:101         ⒻClm 90000    82 4 2 31 3½ 43 44½     McCauley W H b 117  *.80 85-17 MssClrAppl111nkStrtcRrd1152½PrfctLss121  Lacked rally 5
22Oct92- 6Aqu fst 6½f :23 :463 1:173 3+ⒻAlw 41000        88 2 6 1½ 12 2½ 45½     McCauley W H b 114  3.00 84-18 Bn'sMomnt1221¾ChrstnCzrn1151½RglVctrss119  Used up 6
6Jun92- 4Bel my 1 1/16 :46 1:102 1:424       ⒻTanya Stk    92 2 1 12 14 110 116    McCauley W H b 116  *.70 88-08 GoldnBmmr11616SwtWll114½Bwm114  Bobld brk,handly 5
        6Jun92-Originally scheduled on turf
LATEST WORKOUTS   Mar 20 Bel tr.t 3f fst :36 H   Mar 12 Bel tr.t 7f fst 1:30 B
```

Missy's Mirage appeared to be a mortal cinch, as was reflected in her miserly odds of 3–10. She'd run Beyers of 100 or better in nine of her last ten races, winning seven stakes, whereas none of her four rivals had *ever* run a figure higher than the mid-90s. How could she possibly lose?

The key was her performance in the Distaff Handicap over Aqueduct's main track on March 15, 1992 — a race in which she recorded a Beyer of 94, the lowest figure showing in her record. Notice that the Distaff, in which she was clearly defeated despite appearing a mortal cinch at odds of 3–10, had been her second start back from a layoff following an emphatic six-length score in the Correction, and that she had given the winner, Nannerl, seven pounds. In this race, Missy's Mirage was again making her second start of the year, following a convincing comeback victory in the Correction, and was conceding weight to the field.

Missy's Mirage had proven to be a consistent and versatile runner, but she was about to race under the exact conditions that precipitated a 12-point bounce in speed figures the previous spring.

Were any of her rivals capable of taking advantage of her vulnerable situation?

At first glance it seemed that Missy's Mirage might bounce yet beat this field regardless. Golden Bimmer had the best recent figures of the others and had won first time off the claim by Mike Hushion, who had been winning at an extraordinary percentage during the first three months of the year. The problem with Golden Bimmer was that she did her best racing on the early lead but had grown accustomed to the leisurely fractions of two-turn inner-track routes. After four straight races in which she'd been able to clear her fields with half-mile fractions of :48 or slower, Golden Bimmer would now be matched up against Missy's Mirage, a mare accustomed to setting or forcing fractions in the range of :44⅖ to :46⅘. If Golden Bimmer attempted to outsprint Missy's Mirage for the lead, she would, in the words of Chester Cheetoh, be "deep-fried to a delicate crunch" long before she reached the stretch.

But there *was* a mare in the Bed o'Roses field who was almost certain to run a vastly improved race — Lady D'Accord.

The Bed o'Roses was to be contested over a track labeled "good," which is a euphemism for "We don't know what the heck to call it."

"Good" is the most ambiguous of all track conditions: it may be used to designate a track presently receiving rain that is in transition from fast to sloppy; or it may signify a track in the process of drying out from sloppy or muddy to fast. It may be a "floated" track (maintenance crews "float" a track with heavy, wooden raftlike boards that compress the top layer of soil and squeeze moisture up from the bottom, much like wringing out a sopping wet towel or squeezing a saturated sponge); or it may be a harrowed track.

The "good" track for the Bed o'Roses was a drying-out, freshly harrowed one. These had been the exact track conditions under which Lady D'Accord had won an overnight handicap at a mile by three lengths on August 1, 1992 — the seventh race back in her current past performance block, a race in which she ran a figure of 97.

This was a plus for Lady D'Accord, but the most compelling evidence of impending improvement was not to be found in her current past performances. Players with a back file of *Racing Forms* who were sufficiently intrigued by Lady D'Accord to investigate further might have harkened back to their *Forms* of April 17, 1992 (the earliest race date showing in her present record), to see what her past performances looked like then:

Lady D'Accord Ch. m. 5, by D'Accord—Avichi, by Damascus — Lifetime 34 7 7 7 $439,662 — 1992 2 1 0 0 $68,870 — 1991 16 2 1 6 $186,255 — Turf 3 0 1 0 $6,820 — Wet 6 2 1 1 $101,822

CHAVEZ J F (134 22 19 17 $508,472) Br.—Hettinger John (NY) **117**

Own.—Akindale Farm Tr.—Zito Nicholas P (18 3 3 0 $145,266)

29Mar92- 8Aqu fst 1 :47^1 1:12^1 1:37^4 3+ⒻBed O R H 4 7 5^{1½} 2^{hd} 1½ 1^{3¼} Chavez J F 114 3.40 73-33 LdyD'Accord114^{3¼}MyTresur112^{1¾}CrystlVous112 Wide, driving 7

29Mar92-Grade II

12Mar92- 9GP fst 7f :22^4 :46 1:23^4 ⒻAlw 29000 5 6 7^{4¾} 7^5 7^{5¾} 5^9 Fires E 117 9.30 78-18 ExclsvBrd117^{1½}Jnny'sPlymt117^{4}IvoryPrncss-Ir114 No factor 8

24Nov91- 8Aqu gd 1¼ :47^3 1:37 2:02^2 3+ⒻLadies H 6 8 6^{6½} 3^{3½} 3^{3½} 3^{6¼} Cordero A Jr 116 *1.50 83-22 Worthrtsngld113^{nk}SmmrMtn115^{6}LdyD'Accrd116 Lacked rally 8

24Nov91-Grade II

2Nov91- 4CD fst 1⅛ :47^1 1:11^4 1:50^4 3+ⒻBr Cp Dstff 3 13 11^{13}12^{10}10^{9¾}10^{10¾} Santos J A B 123 160.70 83-09 DnceSmrtly120^{1½}VersillsTrty120^{2¾}BroughtToMind123 Outrun 13

2Nov91-Grade I

6Oct91- 7Bel gd 1⅛ :46^4 1:10^4 1:48 3+ⒻBeldame 4 6 6^{6½} 6^{4¼} 4^{4½} 3^9 Santos J A 123 8.00 80-11 SharpDnce123^{no}VersillesTrety119^{9}LdyD'Accord123 No threat 6

6Oct91-Grade I

21Sep91- 8Bel fst 1$\frac{1}{16}$:46^2 1:10^3 1:41^3 3+ⒻRuffian H 2 7 7^6 7^{2¾} 4^2 3^{1¾} Perret C 113 13.80 92-14 Queena120½ Sharp Dance114^{1¼} LadyD'Accord113 Rallied wide 7

21Sep91-Grade I

7Sep91- 1Bel fst 1$\frac{1}{16}$:47^3 1:11^3 1:42^1 3+ⒻAlw 47000 4 4 4^{5½} 2^1 1½ 1^{2¼} Cordero A Jr 122 *1.50 91-12 Lady D'Accord122^{2¼} Lilac's Star122¾ TwixtAppeal115 Driving 4

21Aug91- 7Sar sly 1⅛ :46^3 1:11^3 1:50^2 3+ⒻAlw 47000 3 5 5^9 4¾ 1^3 1^{8½} Cordero A Jr 115 *1.40 85-24 LdyD'Accord115^{8½}SntgoSz115½Worthrotsngld115 Ridden out 5

8Aug91- 8Sar fm 1$\frac{3}{16}$ Ⓣ:46^4 1:10 1:54^3 3+ⒻHall Of Fame 9 8 8^8 8^{6½} 7^7 7^{8½} Bailey J D 115 13.80 88-09 Sabina122^{hd} Cazzy B.115^2 Ballykelly115 No factor 9

31Jly91- 8Sar fst 1⅛ :48^1 1:12^1 1:51 3+ⒻAlw 47000 2 2 5^{1¾} 4^3 3^{2½} 3^{1¼} Santos J A 117 3.70 81-18 Lilac'sStr112^{no}HerSheShwklit117^{1¼}LdyD'Accord117 Willingly 5

Speed Index: Last Race: +6.0 3–Race Avg.: +1.0 8–Race Avg.: +1.3 Overall Avg.: +0.4

LATEST WORKOUTS Apr 13 Bel tr.t 5f gd :59^3 H Apr 8 Bel tr.t 4f fst :52 B ●Mar 24 Bel tr.t 5f fst :59^2 H Mar 7 GP 4f fst :48^2 H

Whaddya know? Lady D'Accord was a creature of habit. Not only had she won on a wet Saratoga track the previous summer, she had won a division of the Bed o'Roses 1992 renewal. Moreover, that victory had followed a dull-looking race at Gulfstream, which had been her first start back from a winter's freshening; she had worked a bullet five furlongs on March 24, five days before the win, and she received a rider switch to Jorge Chavez.

A year later, Lady D'Accord was again shipping up after recently returning from a winter's freshening with dull-looking lines at Gulfstream . . . she had worked a bullet five furlongs on March 28, six days prior to the race . . . she was receiving a rider switch back to Chavez.

The past performances you've just seen appeared on April 17, 1992 — before the *Beyer Speed Figures* had been incorporated into the *Form*. Rummaging around for another set, we find the following:

Lady D'Accord — Ch. m. 5, by D'Accord—Avichi, by Damascus
SMITH M E (168 24 30 19 .14) — Br.—Hettinger John (NY)
Own.—Akindale Farm — Tr.—Zito Nicholas P (31 3 0 4 .10) — **117**

Lifetime						
40 8 7 9	1992	8	2	0	2	$137,006
$507,798	1991	16	2	1	6	$186,255
	Turf	3	0	1	0	$6,820
	Wet	8	2	1	2	$125,822

25Sep92- 8Bel	fst	1	:47	1:11²	1:36¹	3↑ⒻHandicap	86	1	7	6²¼	2hd	3²	3⁶¼	Smith M E		119	*1.30	83-15	Coxwld108¾HyBbLl1115½LdyD'Accrd119	Bid, weakened	7
23Aug92- 8Sar	fst	1⅛	:48³	1:11⁴	1:47⁴	3↑ⒻJohn Morris	72	6	7	7³¾	5⁵½	5⁶½	5²⁰¾	Antley C W		114	8.90	77-02	QuickMschf1136¾VrsllsTrty122½ShrdIntrst111	No threat	7
23Aug92-Grade I																					
1Aug92- 6Sar	gd	1	:45³	1:10¹	1:36¹	3↑ⒻHandicap	97	4	8	8⁴¾	3¹	1½	1³	Smith M E		122	2.70	— —	LdyD'Accord1223DncColony1201½MssKrryC.111	Driving	8
31May92- 8Bel	sly	1⅛	:45¹	1:08⁴	1:47	3↑ⒻHempsteadH	80	4	6	6⁶	5⁵½	5⁸½	5¹⁷	Perret C		114	5.60	77-09	Mssy'sMrg1183HrbourClb110nkVrsllsTrty119	No threat	6
31May92-Grade I																					
9May92- 8Bel	gd	11/16	:45¹	1:09¹	1:40³	3↑ⒻShuvee H	83	2	6	6⁵	4²½	4⁸	4⁹¾	Chavez J F		116	5.80	89-07	Mssy'sMrg116noHrbourClb110nkVrsllsTrty119	No threat	6
9May92-Grade I																					
17Apr92- 8Aqu	sly	1⅛	:46¹	1:11²	1:50²	3↑ⒻTopflight H	90	13	13	13¹²	13⁶¾	6¹¼	3¹	Chavez J F		117	4.50	83-18	FrmStnc114¾Huntng112nkLdyD'Accord117	Blckd, chckd	14
17Apr92-Grade I																					
29Mar92- 8Aqu	fst	1	:47¹	1:12¹	1:37⁴	3↑ⒻBed O R's H	96	4	7	5¹½	2hd	1½	1³¼	Chavez J F		114	3.40	73-33	LdyD'Accrd1143¼MyTrsr1121¾CrystlVs112	Wide, driving	7
29Mar92-Grade II																					
12Mar92- 9GP	fst	7f	:22⁴	:46	1:23⁴	ⒻAlw 29000	71	5	6	7⁴¾	7⁵	7⁵¾	5⁹	Fires E		117	9.30	78-18	EclsvBrd1171½Jnn'sPlmt1174IvrPrncss-Ir114	No factor	8
24Nov91- 8Aqu	gd	1¼	:47³	1:37	2:02²	3↑ⒻLadies H	90	6	8	6⁶½	3³½	3³½	3⁶¼	Cordero A Jr		116	*1.50	83-22	Wrthrtsnld113nkSmrMtn1156LdDAccrd116	Lacked rally	8
24Nov91-Grade II																					
2Nov91- 4CD	fst	1⅛	:47¹	1:11⁴	1:50⁴	3↑ⒻBr Cp Dstff	90	3	13	11¹³	12¹⁰	10⁹¾	10¹⁰¾	Santos J A	B	123	160.70	83-09	DncSmrtly1201½VrsllsTrty1202¾BroghtTMnd123	Outrun	13
2Nov91-Grade I																					

LATEST WORKOUTS Oct 7 Bel 4f fst :48¹ H Oct 2 Bel 4f fst :50¹ B ●Sep 21 Bel 5f fst :59³ H Sep 17 Bel 4f fst :49¹ B

These past performances, as they appeared on October 10, show that Lady D'Accord improved her Beyer from a 71 to a 96 in the 1992 Bed o'Roses, an improvement of 25 points. Given the fact that many of the circumstances for the 1993 Bed o'Roses were identical and that she was catching her optimal track conditions, Lady D'Accord could fairly be expected to run to the best of her capabilities, which projected to a Beyer in the upper 90s.

If Missy's Mirage, already deemed vulnerable to a bounce today, gets hooked in the early stages by Golden Bimmer, she will run that rival into the ground, but in so doing she may be softened up just enough for the stretch-running Lady D'Accord to take advantage. It seems that Lady D'Accord, on her favorite kind of footing and repeating a previously successful form cycle, may also be the beneficiary of a hotly contested early pace.

EIGHTH RACE
Aqueduct
APRIL 3, 1993

1 MILE. (1.32²) 37th Running THE BED O'ROSES HANDICAP (Grade II). Purse $100,000 Added. Fillies and Mares. 3-year-olds and upward. By subscription of $200 each which should accompany the nomination; $800 to pass the entry box; $800 to start with $100,000 added. The added money and all fees to be divided 60% to the winner, 22% to second; 12% to third and 6% to fourth. Weights Monday, March 29. Starters to be named at the closing time of entries. Trophies will be presented to the winning owner, trainer and jockey. Closed Wednesday, March 17, 1993, with 21 nominations.

Value of race $112,200; value to winner $67,320; second $24,684; third $13,464; fourth $6,732. Mutuel pool $205,633, Minus show pool $6,682.73. Exacta Pool $414,181

Last Raced	Horse	M/Eqt.	A.	Wt	PP	St	¼	½	¾	Str	Fin	Jockey	Odds $1
9Mar93 9GP5	Lady D'Accord		6	111	4	4	5	4½	3¹½	2²	1½	Chavez J F	9.20
27Feb93 7Aqu1	Missy's Mirage		5	123	2	2	2³	1²	1²	1½	2³¾	Maple E	.30
20Mar93 7Aqu5	Buck Some Belle	b	4	106	3	3	3²	3¹	2hd	3²	3⁴	Bravo J	26.20
21Mar93 10GP3	Haunting		5	114	1	5	4½	5	4⁴	4¹⁶	4	Antley C W	10.30
22Mar93 8Aqu1	Golden Bimmer	b	4	111	5	1	1½	2³	5	5	—	Migliore R	3.00

Golden Bimmer, Eased.

OFF AT 4:19 Start good, Won driving. Time, :22³, :45², 1:11 , 1:36³ Track good.

$2 Mutuel Prices:				
	4-(D)-LADY D'ACCORD	20.40	3.60	2.10
	2-(B)-MISSY'S MIRAGE		2.20	2.10
	3-(C)-BUCK SOME BELLE			2.10

$2 EXACTA 4-2 PAID $53.20

Ch. m, by D'Accord—Avichi, by Damascus. Trainer Zito Nicholas P. Bred by Hettinger John (NY).
LADY D'ACCORD trailed for nearly a half, steadily worked her way forward while three wide on the turn, drew alongside MISSY'S MIRAGE to challenge in midstretch then drew clear under intermittent urging. MISSY'S MIRAGE contested the early pace along the inside, shook off GOLDEN BIMMER to get clear along the backstretch, continued on the front while saving ground into the stretch, relinquished the lead inside the furlong marker then held well to clearly best the others. BUCK SOME BELLE settled in good position while between horses for five furlongs, edged closer while racing just inside the winner on the turn then lacked a strong closing response. HAUNTING failed to seriously threaten while saving ground. GOLDEN BIMMER battled for the lead from outside, gave way on the far turn and returned bleeding from the mouth. All but HAUNTING wore mud caulks.
Owners— 1, Akindale Farm; 2, Middletown Stable; 3, Garren Murray M; 4, Silverleaf Farms Inc; 5, Hauman Eugene E.
Trainers— 1, Zito Nicholas P; 2, Jerkens H Allen; 3, Garren Murray M; 4, Veitch John M; 5, Hushion Michael E.
Overweight: Haunting 1 pound.

$2 Pick Six (6–2–5–1–2–4) 6 Wins 7 Tickets Paid $12,713.00 5 Wins 348 Tickets Paid $85.00 Pick Six Pool $158,217

Lady D'Accord, a 9–1 shot, was paying $9 underneath Missy's Mirage as the exacta combinations flashed on the monitors, but the Lady D'Accord/Missy's Mirage exacta was hardly being touched.

A handicapper with $75 to invest in the race might conceivably do something like this:

$15 win: Lady D'Accord
$40 exacta: Lady D'Accord / Missy's Mirage
$20 exacta: Missy's Mirage / Lady D'Accord

If Lady D'Accord wins but Missy's Mirage somehow fails to finish second — extremely unlikely — the return is $150. If Lady D'Accord runs her best race but finishes second to Missy's Mirage — a very real possibility, the exacta as place bet will return $90, which beats the heck out of an odds-on place wager. If Lady D'Accord and Missy's Mirage run one-two, the return will be $150 on the win bet plus approximately $1,060 on the exacta, for a total return of over $1,200, effectively transforming Lady D'Accord from a 9–1 shot into a 15–1 shot merely by having the 3–10 favorite run second. A straight bet of $75 to win on Lady D'Accord offered a return of roughly $750 but no protection in the event she ran second to the favorite. By utilizing the exacta, her odds were improved from 9–1 to 15–1 with very little risk, and the Missy's Mirage/Lady D'Accord "tough-beat" scenario was provided for with a return of outlaid capital plus a small $15 profit — enough to drown one's sorrows at the bar.

When handicappers cash in on a horse that puts them squarely in the black for the season, the natural tendency is to watch for a similar move by the same trainer.

I didn't have to wait very long. Two weeks later, Nick Zito entered Cold Hoist in an overnight handicap on grass — his first start back from Gulfstream Park — and the result was a pace-pressing win at nearly 8–1:

Cold Hoist — B. h. 5, by Secreto—Stopped Cold, by Hoist the Flag
Br.—Calumet Farm (Ky)
Tr.—Zito Nicholas P (12 0 2 0 .00)
CHAVEZ J F (107 20 10 9 .19)
Own.—Perez Robert
117

Lifetime						
37 5 3 3	1993	4	1	0	0	$28,430
$176,437	1992	20	1	3	1	$88,657
	Turf	25	4	3	1	$131,928
	Wet	4	1	0	1	$39,879

19Apr93- 8Aqu yl 1 1/16 Ⓣ:50 1:14^3 1:47	3↑Handicap	93 5 3 2½ 2½ 2½ 1¾	Chavez J F		111	7.80	76-26	ColdHoist111¾Fourstardave122^{no}OceanDawn114	Driving	6
10Mar93- 8GP fm 1⅛ Ⓣ:47^4 1:10^3 1:47^2 +	Alw 27000	93 1 9 7^{12} 76¾ 75¼ 5^4	Ferrer J C	L	112	44.00	91-07	Aptkisc-Ir1141½GoDutch113^{hd}FlyngAmrcn117	Rlld wide	9
27Feb93- 7GP fm *1 1/16 Ⓣ 1:44^4 +	Alw 31500	87 9 10 10^{11}108¾ 68½ 67¾	Ferrer J C	L	112	54.20	85-10	ExplosiveJff112^{2}Aptkisic-Ir1141¾CourtLrk112	Mild bid	10
2Feb93- 9GP fm *1⅛ Ⓣ 1:50^2 +	Alw 30000	77 8 2 33½ 6^6 9^{14} 814½	Ferrer J C	L	112	32.70	79-09	Social Retiree1171½ BigLeap-Ir114^{no}Thakib114	Stopped	9
31Dec92- 9Crc sly 1⅛ :47^4 1:12 1:53^3	3↑Alw 20400	59 1 6 55¾ 6^{11} 7^{15} 724¼	Santos J A		114	4.30	71-14	Meena114^{no} Dr Pain112^3 This Time Tony109	No factor	7
31Dec92-Originally scheduled on turf										
7Dec92- 8Aqu fst 6f ⊡:22^4 :46^1 1:12	3↑Alw 34000	63 2 4 5^9 5^{12} 5^{14} 5^{16}	Madrid A Jr		117	24.00	67-21	ClbDNch-Ar117^{nk}Wndndrns1151½PnnsBc117	No factor	5
21Nov92- 7Aqu fst 1 :46^2 1:11 1:36^2	3↑Alw 37000	62 2 2 2½ 3^{nk} 5^4 714¾	Chavez J F		117	5.20	65-25	HonorGrds117^{4}Pncil1176¼FrghtBll117	Forced pace,tired	7
21Nov92-Originally scheduled on turf										
1Nov92 9GP fm 1 1/16 Ⓣ:46 1:08^4 1:39^1 +	3↑Steinlen H	82 9 8 9^{10}10^{11}10^{15}10^{15}	Chavez J F		110	47.80	— —	RomnEnvoy120^{4}BddngProud115^{no}FmnnWls-Ir112	Wide	10
10Oct92- 5Bel sf 1 Ⓣ:46 1:10^2 1:36^1	3↑Kelso H	92 2 6 43½ 4^4 4^6 48¾	Chavez J F		108	43.90	72-19	RomnEnvoy1172¾Lure111^{2}VldesBois-Fr118	Lacked rally	9
10Oct92-Grade III										
5Sep92- 8Bel gd 1¼ 🅃:47^2 1:35^1 2:00^1	3↑Red Smith H	94 1 3 42½ 5^2 52¼ 5^5	Chavez J F		109	18.60	84-21	Montsrrt1181½Prfrncs1102¾FirstRt-Ir111	Saved ground	7
5Sep92-Grade II										

LATEST WORKOUTS May 30 Bel 4f fst :48^1 H May 15 Bel 3f fst :36^3 B ●May 7 Bel 3f fst :35^1 H Apr 28 Bel 4f fst :48^2 H

Cold Hoist's form had been dull in late fall and early winter, but his two most recent races of February 27 and March 10 indicated improvement in terms of figures, moving from 77 to 87, and up again to a 93. The chances of a bounce from the 93 were lessened by the fact that as a four-year-old, Cold Hoist had demonstrated the ability to run similar figures back-to-back, recording a 94 on September 5 followed by a 92 on October 10. Both those races had been run over wet grass courses, and today he would be racing over a course labeled "yielding."

The recent improvement coincided with the introduction of Lasix, however, and since New York rules at the time did not allow the anti-bleeding medication, I might've passed on Cold Hoist had a search of back *Forms* not revealed the following:

Cold Hoist — B. c. 4, by Secreto—Stopped Cold, by Hoist the Flag
Br.—Calumet Farm (Ky)
Tr.—Zito Nicholas P (—)
Own.—Perez Robert
119

Lifetime						
19 4 1 2	1992	6	1	1	0	$26,610
$85,960	1991	13	3	0	2	$59,350
	Turf	12	3	1	1	$61,530
	Wet	1	1	0	0	$19,800

21Apr92- 8Aqu my 1 :45^2 1:09^3 1:36^1	3↑Alw 33000	94 2 4 46½ 4^4 2½ 1no	Madrid A Jr	119	9.60	81-32	Cold Hoist119^{no} Pension Fraud121^{1}Dr.Zoom119	All out	5
14Mar92- 9GP fm 1⅛ Ⓣ:46 1:09^4 1:46^2 +	Alw 34000	91 8 5 5^8 75¾ 52¼ 75¼	Penna D	115	26.20	— —	Buchmn115¾StonMill-GB1131½Thkb118	Bshd, luggd, std	11
7Mar92- 9GP fm *1⅛ Ⓣ 1:51 +	Alw 23000	88 5 4 3^3 31½ 3½ 33½	Antley C W	115	3.40	— —	🄳Rinka Das113½ Czar114^1 ColdHoist115	Wide b'str, str	8
7Mar92-Placed second through disqualification									
25Feb92- 9GP fm *1 Ⓣ 1:38^1 +	Alw 26000	92 8 9 96¼ 64¼ 5^4 42¼	Ramos W S	117	2.60	— —	Jodi's Sweetie117^1 🄳Winning Blazer117^1 RinkaDas117		10
25Feb92-Steadied final turn, 4 wide stretch									
9Feb92- 9GP fm *1⅛ Ⓣ 1:51^2 +	Alw 20000	89 9 4 5^6 54½ 3^3 4^2	Toribio A R	117	17.90	— —	LongTrek115^{hd}KingArthur112½AjustBlde112	4 wide bstr	11
11Jan92-10GP fm 1 1/16 Ⓣ:48^3 1:12^1 1:42^2 +	3↑Appleton H	82 1 1 1½ 1^{hd}12^{11}129¼	Sweeney K H	110	105.10	— —	RoylNnj1121¼ArchsLughtr114^{nk}NtvBoundry116	Faltered	12
11Jan92-Grade III									
22Dec91-10Hia fm 1 3/16 Ⓣ 1:54^4	3↑Bougn'vila H	82 13 2 1^{hd} 2½ 108¾1210½	Sweeney K H	109	24.90f	84-08	Buckhr111^{nk}SuperAbound1151½SilncAtDwn110	Faltered	14
16Nov91- 8Hia fst 1⅛ :45^4 1:11 1:51^2	3↑Alw 19200	59 6 2 2^5 53¾ 5^{11} 5^{14}	Guerra W A	116	5.30	66-23	ClassicSeven116^{4}Meena1164½FalconMr116	Stumbled st	7
16Nov91-Originally scheduled on turf									
12Oct91- 6Bel gd 1 Ⓣ:45^2 1:09^4 1:34^3	3↑Alw 31000	96 1 3 42½ 1^{hd} 11½ 12¼	Chavez J F	114	15.70	89-18	ColdHoist1142¼Clef117^{hd}MuchoPrecious114	Drftd, drvg	10

LATEST WORKOUTS May 2 Bel 5f fst 1:01 H Apr 11 Bel 5f sly 1:03 B Apr 1 Bel tr.t 4f fst :49 B Mar 25 Aqu 5f fst 1:00^4 H

Cold Hoist's form had been less than remarkable in Florida at the beginning of 1992, but he had improved his figures prior to shipping north, and after being given a five-week freshening, he won off the ship to Aqueduct at nearly 10–1. Cold Hoist was again returning to Aqueduct off a five-week freshening, a year later almost to the day.

Whereas Lady D'Accord caught a track condition she obviously relished, which helped to explain her upset of Missy's Mirage along with her repeat of a previously successful form pattern, track conditions didn't seem to be an overriding factor in the case of Cold Hoist's ship-in wins to Aqueduct in 1992 and 1993: he won in the slop the first time and on a wet grass course the second time. What was more important was the same change in surroundings at the exact same time of the year — a factor underestimated by the vast majority of bettors but not by a shrewd trainer like Zito.

"If you're coming from winter quarters you should have an edge," Zito explained. "All the attributes that go along with taking a horse out of winter *have* to be in your favor. Over the years, it's been made pretty clear to me that often a horse's form will improve going from a warm climate to a cooler one, but not vice versa. You take your time in Florida, you come up north with a fresh horse . . ."

As evidenced by Stephen DiMauro's handling of the mare Rae Rafko, he also understands the potency of the "change in surroundings/seasonal dynamics" factor:

Rae Rafko — Gr. m. 5, by Chief's Crown—Rambling Rhythm, by Delta Oil
DAVIS R G (279 42 42 33 .15) — Br.—Robinson William B (Ky)
Own.—DiMauro Stephen — Tr.—DiMauro Stephen (58 3 5 3 .05) — **115**

Lifetime						
27 4 4 3	1993	4	1	0	0	$18,150
$113,640	1992	13	1	2	2	$52,750
	Turf	1	0	0	0	
	Wet	4	1	2	1	$40,780

21Jun93-	6Bel	my	6½f	:222	:454	1:19	3↑ⒻAlw 29500	72	2	5	78½	78	64¼	1no	Davis R G	b	117	19.70	78–17 Rae Rafko117no PerfectLass117noNiceCrane109	Driving	7
9Jun93-	8Bel	gd	6f	:224	:453	1:11	3↑ⒻAlw 29500	41	4	3	613	617	619	520½	Davis R G	b	117	27.20	64–21 MissedtheStorm1122½ClStr117¾CelestCilo117	No factor	6
21Feb93-	8GP	fst	7f	:23	:454	1:234	ⒻAlw 23000	66	9	9	912	914	917	913½	Cruguet J	b	112	26.00	70–18 LadySonata112½ButterCrem113nkSen'sAngel117	Outrun	9
4Feb93-	5GP	fst	7f	:231	:463	1:232	ⒻAlw 22000	74	3	6	52¾	55	69	610½	Cruguet J	b	112	14.80	75–23 NDnc1152½Shmyrclss113noMssVldPch112	Showed little	7
26Nov92-	9Lrl	gd	7f	:23	:462	1:233	3↑ⒻStrght Dealh	76	3	6	610	614	616	512¾	Wilson R	b	114	18.10	76–13 StemTheTide1123¼WoodSo1172MixedAppeal114	Outrun	6
28Oct92-	8Aqu	fst	7f	:231	:46	1:231	3↑ⒻHandicap	70	3	4	65	67½	510	511	Cruguet J	b	112	10.10	78–14 StrongEmbrc111nkHyBbLl1151¼PpptShow116	No threat	6
5Oct92-	8Bel	fst	7f	:23	:462	1:242	3↑ⒻAlw 41000	74	6	1	52½	64	54	44¾	Krone J A	b	115	7.70	77–17 MrsPMnstr1123MssnPss112¾AWnAndANd115	No threat	7
19Sep92-	1Bel	fst	6½f	:23	:462	1:17	3↑ⒻAlw 41000	82	4	4	54½	42	3½	33¾	Krone J A	b	115	10.90	84–11 Ben'sMoment1152¾LiteLight1161RaeRafko115	Wide trn	6
6Sep92-	6Bel	fst	1 1/16	:463	1:111	1:434	3↑ⒻAlw 47000	81	5	6	64½	63¼	41½	31½	Cruguet J		115	5.50	81–12 FrOutNurse115nkByondSlw1151¼RRfko115	Belated rally	6
15Aug92-	1Sar	my	7f	:223	:454	1:23	3↑ⒻAlw 41000	78	2	6	621	616	57	25½	Cruguet J		115	9.50	84–09 MyNecessity1105½RRfko1151¾ForignAid115	Belated bid	6

LATEST WORKOUTS Jun 30 Bel tr.t 4f fst :512 B Jun 16 Bel tr.t 4f fst :521 H Jun 4 Bel 4f fst :49 B May 27 Bel tr.t 4f fst :511 B

Rae Rafko boasted no compelling attributes in terms of recent form when she rallied for a last-to-first victory at $41.40 in a Belmont allowance on June 21, 1993. Her races in the fall of '92 found her rallying with too little too late, and she'd never so much as entered contention in two races at Gulfstream in February. Returned from a layoff June 9, she beat one horse while twenty lengths from the winner, and seemed up against it when entered back twelve days later along with a stretch to six and a half furlongs.

But observe what Rae Rafko did in June of the previous year at Belmont:

Rae Rafko — Gr. f. 4, by Chief's Crown—Rambling Rhythm, by Delta Oil
Br.—Robinson William B (Ky)
CRUGUET J (119 17 12 14 .14)
Own.—DiMauro Stephen — Tr.—DiMauro Stephen (65 6 3 10 .09) — 115
Lifetime 15 3 2 1 $60,860 — 1992 5 1 0 0 $18,120 — 1991 9 1 2 1 $28,440 — Wet 1 0 0 1 $3,720

11Jun92-	7Bel	fst	7f	:221	:451	1:24	3↑Ⓕ Alw 28000	80	2	9	912	88¾	61¾	1nk	Cruguet J		117	23.00e	84-15	RRfko117nkEndlssDsir1142¼SoontoSin117	Wide, driving 9
30May92-	6Bel	fst	6f	:214	:442	1:09	3↑Ⓕ Alw 28000	64	2	6	718	713	715	614½	Cruguet J		119	6.30e	80-12	Lights of Marfa1159½ Ryn1121½ Perfect Lass110	Outrun 7
11Feb92-	8GP	fst	7f	:23	:462	1:243	Ⓕ Alw 21800	68	9	9	1015	1014	712	610½	Cruguet J	b	115	36.50	72-23	TriGrnMw1121Jeno1155ILikeScrts115	Pass beaten ones 10
26Jan92-	7GP	fst	170	:473	1:123	1:414	Ⓕ Alw 19000	73	7	8	714	711	49½	48¾	Cruguet J		112	11.50	83-13	Lemhi Go1133 Tiara Miss117nk Jeano117	Wide str 8
8Jan92-	2GP	fst	170	:474	1:12	1:441	Ⓕ Alw 22900	76	6	7	65½	65½	56½	63¼	Cruguet J		112	21.10	77-20	PleasntJolie120noLemhiGo1131½TriGrnMw112	Late gain 9
23Dec91-	8Aqu	fst	1⅛ ⊡	:481	1:124	1:533	3↑Ⓕ Alw 31000	52	9	7	710	911	1015	818	Migliore R		115	8.00	56-32	Maxmount1172¼RunningShine1154Dmie'sSis117	Outrun 10
13Dec91-	7Aqu	sly	1 1/16 ⊡	:481	1:131	1:454	3↑Ⓕ Alw 31000	77	6	10	1012	78½	46½	34¾	Antley C W		115	14.40	74-19	MoonstoneGem1052¾Maxamount1172ReRfko115	Rallied 10
2Dec91-	7Aqu	gd	1	:463	1:12	1:382	3↑Ⓕ Alw 31000	74	5	10	910	87¼	65	56	Migliore R		115	12.70	64-33	ⒹMnstnGm1052EprssOfR1172¼FlnCrss115	Belated rally 10
23Nov91-	3Aqu	gd	7f	:23	:461	1:232	3↑Ⓕ Alw 28000	77	2	7	710	79	75¾	48	Migliore R		115	15.90	79-14	DibleRose107hdLoveBird1152KombtKt120	Broke slowly 7
9Nov91-	7Aqu	fst	1	:47	1:122	1:382	3↑Ⓕ Alw 31000	54	4	7	79	76½	78	716	Antley C W		115	6.40	54-25	Strswhirl1151EmprssOfRom1125FlyingCross115	Outrun 7

LATEST WORKOUTS Jun 30 Bel 4f fst :511 B — Jun 27 Bel tr.t 3f fst :381 B — Jun 22 Bel tr.t 4f fst :492 B — ●May 24 Bel tr.t 5f fst 1:003 H

Exact same thing, right? Dull form toward the end of a 1991 campaign, which continued into her races at Gulfstream, followed by the freshening and the ship back to Belmont on May 30, when she beat one horse while a pole behind the winner. Entered back twelve days later along with a stretch to a slightly longer sprint, she shocked with a last-to-first victory at a $48 mutuel.

DiMauro had accomplished a similar win with Rae Rafko, albeit with a slightly different approach, in the spring of 1991 as well:

Rae Rafko — Gr. f. 3(Mar), by Chief's Crown—Rambling Rhythm, by Delta Oil
Br.—Robinson William B (Ky)
Own.—DiMauro Stephen — Tr.—DiMauro Stephen — 115
Lifetime 9 2 2 1 $42,740 — 1991 8 1 2 1 $28,440 — 1990 1 1 0 0 $14,300

13Dec91-	7Aqu	sly	1 1/16 ⊡	:481	1:131	1:454	3↑Ⓕ Alw 31000	6	10	1012	78½	46½	34¾	Antley C W		115	14.40	74-19	Moonstone Gem1052¾ Maxamount1172 RaeRafko1151	Rallied 10
2Dec91-	7Aqu	gd	1	:463	1:12	1:382	3↑Ⓕ Alw 31000	5	10	910	87¼	65	56	Migliore R		115	12.70	64-33	ⒹMnstnGm1052EmprssOfRm1172¼FlnCrss1151½	Belated rally 10
23Nov91-	3Aqu	gd	7f	:23	:461	1:232	3↑Ⓕ Alw 28000	2	7	710	79	75¾	46	Migliore R		115	15.90	79-14	Diable Rose107hdLoveBird1152KombatKate1204	Broke slowly 7
9Nov91-	7Aqu	fst	1	:47	1:122	1:382	3↑Ⓕ Alw 31000	4	7	79	76½	78	716	Antley C W		115	6.40	54-25	Starsawhirl1151EmpressOfRome1125FlyingCross115nk	Outrun 7
20Oct91-	2Bel	fst	6½f	:223	:454	1:171	3↑Ⓕ Alw 28000	4	6	75½	63¼	64½	57¾	Cruguet J		114	8.60	83-08	Shopping114½ Mezzanotte1143¾ Miss Jazz1193	Outrun, wide 7
24May91-	7Bel	fst	6f	:223	:47	1:122	Ⓕ Alw 27000	6	6	76	64	52½	1hd	Antley C W		116	1.90	78-22	Rae Rafko116hd Streaming1181Ferber'sFollies116nk	Wide drv 7
4Feb91-	7GP	fst	6f	:224	:461	1:11	Ⓕ Alw 18000	2	4	57	59	57	24¾	Antley C W		117	2.70	85-15	Foreign Aid1154¾ RaeRafko117½Ferber'sFollies1131½	Late run 5
14Jan91-	3GP	fst	6f	:222	:452	1:101	Ⓕ Alw 18000	2	10	1011	911	78½	27½	Antley C W		117	5.60	86-06	Wthllprobblty1177½RRfko117nkHghwyQun1122½	Squeezed bk 10
24Dec90-	4Hol	fst	6f	:22	:46	1:114	Ⓕ Md Sp Wt	8	6	67½	34	21½	12	Flores D R	B	118	51.40e	81-15	ReRfko1182SpecilToby1181LdyAtTheGt1182¼	Altered path 1/2 10

Speed Index: Last Race: –7.0 3–Race Avg.: –10.3 3–Race Avg.: –10.3 Overall Avg.: –6.5
LATEST WORKOUTS Nov 18 Bel 4f fst :494 B — Nov 1 Bel tr.t 6f fst 1:16 B — Oct 28 Bel tr.t 4f fst :523 B

A pair of closing efforts for second, while never a serious threat to the winner at Gulfstream, followed by a layoff and a last-to-first victory in a Belmont sprint on May 24.

Rae Rafko clearly fires her absolute best race in the spring, at

Belmont, after spending the winter months in Florida. Period. Notice that she passed four rivals in the final furlong of her '91 win; she passed *five* rivals through the final furlong in '92 and '93. It didn't matter who was riding, Antley, Cruguet, or Davis. I can almost hear DiMauro's instructions to each of them: "Don't worry about how far back you are. Just let her settle into stride, then wait, then wait some more, then turn her loose. Don't worry, *she's ready.*"

In the spring of 1993, Virginia Rapids was freshened, and he improved by leaps and bounds first time back from Gulfstream. He missed by a fast-closing head at 12–1 in the Withers, which went in track-record time. In his second race back, he improved again to a Beyer of 109, winning the Peter Pan:

Virginia Rapids
MAPLE E (55 10 11 9 .18)
Own.—Middletown Stables

Ch. c. 3(Mar), by Riverman—Virginiana, by Sir Ivor
Br.—Stavola Joseph & William Inc (NJ)
Tr.—Jerkens H Allen (22 6 2 5 .27)

126

Lifetime				
12 3 2 3				
$165,238				
1993	5 2 1 1	$138,868		
1992	7 1 1 2	$26,370		
Turf	2 1 0 0	$15,600		
Wet	2 0 0 1	$3,240		

23May93- 8Bel	fst	1⅛	:46	1:101	1:482	Peter Pan	109	1	6	610	65½	21½	11¾	Maple E		114	*1.50	87–13	Virginia Rapids1141¾ColonialAffair1174Itaka114	Driving	6
23May93-Grade II																					
5May93- 8Bel	fst	1	:441	1:081	1:323	Withers	104	4	12	1211	116¾	32½	2hd	Maple E		124	12.20	105 —	Wllmstn124hdVrnRpds1241¼Frmnthfr124	Rallied 7-wide	12
5May93-Grade II																					
27Feb93- 6GP	fst	1 1/16	:473	1:124	1:462	Alw 23000	88	4	10	911	64¼	42½	11	Penna D		112	2.90	78–22	VrgnRpds1121DrdMNt113hdThrllrChllr117	Driving 7 wd	10
13Feb93- 7GP	fst	7f	:222	:454	1:24	Alw 24000	86	3	7	810	56½	42¾	3¾	Maple E		117	*1.70	82–18	DcdSlgl114noThrllrChllr112¾VrnRpds117	Late rally wide	8
13Jan93- 9GP	fst	6f	:212	:44	1:092	Spectclr Bid	86	2	7	712	67½	45	41¼	Penna D		113	14.70	93–07	GrtNvgtr119½DmltDmsht114½HddnTrc114	Late rally wd	8
24Dec92- 7Crc	fst	6f	:22	:46	1:121	Alw 15000	83	1	7	713	711	45	2no	Penna D		120	7.80	90–15	HiddnTrick115noVirginRpds1203TrdBll110	Wide, gamely	7
27Nov92- 8Aqu	my	6f	:222	:46	1:103	Alw 27000	72	4	4	53	31½	34	37½	Lidberg D W		117	5.30	80–22	InsrdWnnr1173½Brd'sFly1174VrgnRpds117	Lacked rally	6
18Nov92- 4Aqu	fst	7f	:224	:454	1:241	Alw 27000	82	1	7	57½	43½	33½	35	Lidberg D W		117	12.80	79–16	PcBby1173ColonilAffir1192VirginiRpids117	Bumped brk	8
2Oct92- 8Bel	fm	1 1/16 Ⓣ	:464	1:111	1:423	Pilgrim	39	9	8	4¾	73½	917	1024	Cruguet J	b	113	10.80	59–15	Awad113nk Dr. Alfoos1132 Compadre113	Gave way	10
2Oct92-Grade III																					
7Sep92- 2Bel	fm	1 Ⓣ	:463	1:101	1:362	Md Sp Wt	76	3	3	11	1hd	12½	1nk	Cruguet J	b	118	*2.00	80–19	VirginiRpids118nkDlry118½ShdsofSilvr118	Drifted,drvng	12
29Aug92- 4Sar	fst	6f	:214	:444	1:104	Md Sp Wt	54	9	1	2½	2½	1hd	48½	Perret C		118	2.20	81–07	DncngHntr1185½Glnbrr1181½NorwyGry118	Dueled inside	9
16Aug92- 4Sar	my	6f	:221	:461	1:12	Md Sp Wt	62	6	6	63	41½	52	51¾	Perret C		118	4.20e	82–14	Sarabic118½MarcoBay118½SpartanLeader118	Weakened	14

LATEST WORKOUTS Jun 2 Bel tr.t 3f fst :383 B May 29 Bel tr.t 3f fst :372 B May 17 Bel 1 fst •:381 H May 2 Bel 6f fst 1:134 H

A year later, the specifics of the pattern were altered slightly, as Virginia Rapids received a tune-up when returned from a layoff at Gulfstream on March 14. He did improve sharply off his most recent numbers when again shipped north, however — to a Beyer of 107 winning the Westchester, and a 109 winning the Carter:

Virginia Rapids
Own: Middletown Stables

SAMYN J L (61 9 9 13 .15)

Ch. c. 4
Sire: Riverman (Never Bend)
Dam: Virginiana (Sir Ivor)
Br: Stavola Joseph & William Inc (NJ)
Tr: Jerkens H Allen (36 8 4 7 .22)

120

Lifetime Record: 24 6 5 3 $439,258

1994	4	2	1	0	$162,290	Turf	3 1 0 0	$15,600	
1993	13	3	3	1	$250,598	Wet	5 1 2 1	$89,584	
Bel	7	3	1	0	$252,560	Dist	4 1 1 0	$105,800	

7May94- 9Bel	fst	7f	:223	:451	1:091	1:212	3↑ Carter H-G1	109	2	10	84¾	62¾	2hd	11¼	Samyn J L	118	5.70	96-06	Virginia Rapids1181¼ Punch Line114nk Cherokee Run1193¾	Wide, driving	11
2Apr94- 8Aqu	fst	1	:233	:46	1:092	1:342	3↑ Westchstr H-G3	107	3	7	54½	34½	3½	1½	Samyn J L	116	2.80	96-16	Virginia Rapids116½ Colonial Affair121nk Cherokee Run1192¼	Driving	7
14Mar94- 8GP	fst	7f	:231	:454	1:094	1:214	Alw 40200N4X	101	4	3	52	43	22	22¾	Samyn J L	117	4.40	91-13	Evil Bear1192¾ Virginia Rapids1178 Callme Guy B1221	Best of others	7
8Jan94- 9GP	fm	1 1/16 Ⓣ	:24	:473	1:111	1:404+	3↑ Appleton H-G3	85	7	8	810	88	77½	79½	Penna D	114	10.40	82-14	ParadiseCreek1213 FourstrsAllstr117nk EliteJcblr111no	Broke awkwardly	8
4Dec93- 8Aqu	fst	1 1/16 ⊡	:234	:473	1:12	1:441	3↑ Qns County HG3	92	5	7	712	77¼	65½	42½	Bailey J D	116	*1.30	81-30	Repletion1111¼ Dibbs N' Dubbs111½ Primitive Hall113¾	Mild gain	8
25Nov93- 6Aqu	fst	7f	:232	:472	1:122	1:25	Happy Thksvg54k	95	2	8	88	74¼	3½	43½	Maple E	122	4.00	75-20	As Indicated122nk Punch Line1221½ Chief Desire1221¾	Wide, flattened out	8
30Oct93- 8Aqu	my	1⅛	:492	1:14	1:391	1:521	Discovery H-G3	93	7	6	411	45	23	26½	Maple E	118	*.90	68-33	Prospctor'sFlg1146½ VirginiRpids118nk LivingVicriously1141½	Up for place	8
10Oct93- 6Bel	fst	1	:231	:454	1:094	1:351	Jamaica H-G2	94	1	8	812	74½	63¼	66¼	Maple E	119	*2.00	86-09	Mi Cielo1162¾ Prospector's Flag1131¾ Cherokee Run120¾	No threat	8
18Sep93- 3Bel	sly	1 1/16 ⊗	:232	:462	1:103	1:421	Halo54k	109	1	4	412	48	1½	17	Maple E	117	*.60	91-15	Virginia Rapids1177 Dominant Prospect1174¾ Compadre11711	Ridden out	4
6Sep93- 8Bel	fst	1	:232	:461	1:102	1:352	Jerome H-G1	102	3	5	56½	53	4¾	41	Maple E	119	*1.10	90-12	Schossberg113hd Williamstown118½ Mi Cielo116½	Wide turn	5

WORKOUTS: May 21 Bel 5f gd 1:031 B *24/25* May 3 Bel 5f fst :59 H *3/23* ●Apr 21 Bel tr.t 3f fst :352 H *1/8* ●Mar 31 Bel tr.t 4f fst :462 H *1/33* Mar 24 Bel tr.t 7f fst 1:271 B *1/1* Mar 19 GP 3f fst :384 B *6/8*

The Florida-to–New York "wake up" is commonplace, but it is just one of an infinite number of variations on the overall theme — repetition of a pattern. Horses that are successful in a given situation eventually get a chance to compete under the same conditions once again, assuming competent handlers, and often respond at good odds.

It makes no difference whether the horse is entered in a $25,000 claimer or a Grade 1 event:

7 Diamond Anchor

Own: Finkelstein Mort
BAILEY J D (92 15 13 20 .16) $25,000

Ro. g. 8
Sire: Crafty Prospector (Mr. Prospector)
Dam: Roan Promise (Wise Exchange)
Br: Stonewall Farm (NY)
Tr: Imperio Joseph (1 1 0 0 1.00)

119

Lifetime Record: 108 17 25 14 $564,060										
1993	16	1	4	2	$34,660	Turf	1	0	0	0	
1992	18	5	2	2	$119,840	Wet	16	2	2	1	$56,259
Sar	8	3	1	0	$51,460	Dist	25	5	6	6	$153,761

6Aug93- 9Sar	fst	1⅛	:473 1:114 1:371 1:50	3+ Clm 25000	92	10	8	815	46½	3½	12½	Bailey J D	117 b	9.20	86-21	Diamond Anchor1172½ Crafty Cash119nk Ridge Road1132	Wide, driving	10
25Jly93- 1Bel	fst	1 1/16	:233 :463 1:11 1:422	Clm 25000	76	2	4	42	31	65	613½	Rojas R I	117 fb	5.10	77-10	Crafty Cash1156 Charming Buck115¾ Cool As Crystal1192	Faded	8
12Jly93- 4Bel	fst	1 1/16	:233 :471 1:11 1:42	Clm 22500	92	4	4	42	3½	3½	2nk	Rojas R I	115 fb	19.90	92-10	Freezing Fun119nk Diamond Anchor1152 Corrupt Council117nk	Sharp try	7
30Jun93- 7Bel	fst	1	:241 :473 1:114 1:363	Clm 22500	77	6	7	63½	74¼	86¼	86½	Mojica R Jr	115 fb	7.90	78-26	Kellock117nk Crafty Cash1172 Danzig's Dance117nk	No factor	9
16Jun93- 6Bel	fst	1 1/16	:234 :471 1:112 1:434	Clm c-17500	76	6	6	43	32	35½	310	Antley C W	117 b	8.00	73-21	RedScmper1174 SilingOnApryer1176 DimondAnchor1172	Flattened out	7
Claimed from Ackerley Bros Farm, Lake Robert P Trainer																		
26May93- 4Bel	fst	1 1/16	:234 :472 1:12 1:434	Clm 17500	85	2	6	67	42½	42	22	Santos J A	117 b	5.80	81-16	Charming Buck1152 DiamondAnchor1172 LeadingStar1132½	Second best	7
19May93- 4Bel	wf	1⅛	:464 1:101 1:352 1:491	Clm 25000	73	5	3	32½	44	49½	511¼	Chavez J F	117 fb	8.50	72-18	Northern Teller1136¼ Arrendajo1172¼ Beyond Tomorrow115nk	Tired	8
3May93- 1Aqu	fst	1⅛	:483 1:131 1:392 1:524	Clm 32500	74	6	2	2hd	1½	54½	59½	Leon F7	108 b	12.80	62-28	D Kellock117nk Crafty Cash1178 Shaf's First Dance117hd	Dueled, tired	6
23Apr93- 6Aqu	fst	1	:231 :47 1:172 1:371	Clm 35000	66	1	4	64	62¾	65	614¾	Maple E	117 fb	5.90	63-21	Maraud1171½ Crafty Cash1125¾ Lord Cardinal1172½	No factor	6
15Apr93- 9Aqu	fst	1	:221 :45 1:094 1:362	Clm c-25000	86	9	5	68½	66	53½	23½	Davis R G	117 fb	3.30	78-18	Count V. J.1173½ Diamond Anchor1171¾ Fiftysevenvelle1171½	Second best	9
Claimed from Schwartz Arlene, Schwartz Scott M Trainer																		
2Apr93- 7Aqu	my	1⅛	:471 1:122 1:391 1:522	Clm 35000	84	4	5	63½	63½	53½	48	Bisono C V5	112 fb	7.10	66-36	Ceiling1175¾ Don't Axe Foolish1152½ Arrendajo112no	No threat	7
25Mar93- 2Aqu	gd	1 1/16 ⊡	:233 :47 1:113 1:431	Clm 45000	79	4	6	78	85½	78½	79½	Madrid A Jr	113 fb	14.50	79-21	Pay Me Today113nk Study Hard1171¾ Cost Too Much117½	Checked brk	8

WORKOUTS: ● Jun 26 Aqu 3f fst :362 B *1/10* Apr 14 Aqu 4f fst :49 B *4/6* Mar 20 Aqu ⊡ 3f fst :371 B *2/14*

Diamond Anchor

BAILEY J D (24 5 6 4 .21) $45,000
Own.—Jaques Farm

Ro. g. 7, by Crafty Prospector—Roan Promise, by Wise Exchange
Br.—Stonewall Farm (NY)
Tr.—Moschera Gasper S (3 1 1 0 .33)

118

Lifetime						
85 16 19 11	1992	11	5	0	1	$93,540
$503,100	1991	13	2	2	1	$70,448
	Turf	1	0	0	0	
	Wet	13	2	2	0	$52,329

23Aug92- 3Sar	fst	1	:453 1:101 1:354	3+ Clm 45000	89	5	9	910	73½	71¾	1nk	Bailey J D	b 113	*1.70e	— —	DmndAnchr113nkRglShnnns1131½PnsnFrd117	Wide drv	9
8Aug92- 1Sar	fst	1⅛	:472 1:114 1:503	3+ Clm 45000	90	1	8	70½	70	31½	11¼	Bailey J D	b 113	13.00	81-16	DmondAnchor1131¼PcktStrkr117TwthTws1113	Driving	7
26Jly92- 8Bel	fst	1 1/16	:454 1:102 1:42	3+ ③EvanShipmn	61	5	5	78	97¾	812	824½	McCauley W H	b 121	18.70	67-22	Corax117hd Key Deputy1175 All Smarts117	Done early	10
6Jly92- 8Bel	fst	7f	:23 :452 1:22	3+ Handicap	69	3	4	31	56½	517	516	Antley C W	b 113	3.30e	78-12	EgleAve.1223½FrostyWish1161HertofHero111	Thru early	5
12Jun92- 2Bel	fst	1	:451 1:10 1:354	Clm 50000	82	1	6	48½	46	73¾	79	Smith M E	b 117	*1.50e	82-20	RdRl1172½AClltRs1172½HrrVnKnnchn117	Saved ground	9
30Apr92- 6Aqu	fst	1	:454 1:094 1:344	Clm c-50000	84	7	4	42	32	34	46¼	Santos J A	b 117	*1.00	82-25	PctStrr117nkIstThtSpcl1156DrssdShppr113	Lacked rally	7
30Apr92-Claimed from Bauer Robert J, Dutrow Anthony W Trainer																		
9Apr92- 1Aqu	fst	1⅛	:481 1:124 1:494	Clm 80000	90	4	2	21½	21	3nk	32	Antley C W	b 114	3.30	84-24	FrstWsh118nkMdlDncr1162¾DndAnchr114	Lacked rally	5
21Mar92- 7Aqu	gd	1	:464 1:111 1:36	Alw 47000	98	1	5	52¼	3½	22	1nk	Antley C W	b 115	5.90	82-23	DimondAnchor115nkTrckRebel1151¾ArgylLk115	Driving	5
21Feb92- 4Aqu	fst	1 1/16 ⊡	:473 1:124 1:453	Clm 47500	104	2	4	44	2½	1hd	1hd	Antley C W	b 117	2.10	80-31	DmndAnchr117hdFrstWsh1198¾Jr'sFrc113	Drftd in drvg	5
10Feb92- 5Aqu	fst	170 ⊡	:47 1:122 1:432	Clm 47500	94	4	4	35	1½	13	11	Antley C W	b 115	3.60	88-23	DimondAnchor1151TwoEgls1132½SkTm115	Drftd, drvng	8

Diamond Anchor won at $28 for Gasper Moschera with a change of scene to Saratoga in 1992, going from a mile and a sixteenth around one turn to a mile and an eighth around two turns, along with a switch to Jerry Bailey on August 8. The same track distance and rider switch produced a win at $20.40 on August 6 of the following year for Joe Imperio, who must've studied the grizzled gelding's past performances and claimed him on June 16 with Saratoga in mind.

Pistols and Roses
Own: Willis Family Stables Inc

Gr. h. 5
Sire: Darn That Alarm (Jig Time)
Dam: To Be Continued (Princely Pleasure)
Br: Alter Happy (Fla)
Tr: Gianos George (—)

Lifetime Record: 27 9 4 4 $1,529,196
1994 3 1 0 0 $182,250 Turf 0 0 0 0
1993 9 2 1 2 $517,800 Wet 1 1 0 0 $30,000
GP 8 2 1 2 $572,336 Dist 4 0 0 2 $116,000

5Feb94-8GP fst 1⅛ :464 1:104 1:364 1:503 3+ Donn H-G1 99 1 4 41½ 31½ 1½ 11½ Castillo H Jr L 113 11.10 84-12 Pistols And Roses1131½ Eequalsmcsquared113¾ Wallenda118nk Driving 11
15Jan94-9GP fst 1 1/16 :23 :462 1:103 1:43 3+ Broward H-G3 92 8 3 3½ 2hd 54 56 Ramos W S L 115 9.10 89-19 Devil His Due121nk Migrating Moon116¾ Northern Trend1113½ 8
Broke outward start, rushed, gave way
1Jan94-11Crc fst 1⅛ :491 1:131 1:382 1:514 3+ Trop Pk H-G3 91 6 7 84½ 86½ 88 88½ Ramos W S L 119 6.10 86-17 Take Me Out1151½ Migrating Moon1192½ Meena1141¾ Outrun 11
18Dec93-1Crc fst 1 1/16 :24 :474 1:123 1:46 3+ Handicap23k 92 1 2 2hd 1hd 1½ 1no Ramos W S L 121 1.30 91-10 Pistols And Roses121no Friud1154 Dash For Dotty1141½ 5
Drifted out stretch, prevailed
21Aug93-3Dmr fst 1¼ :46 1:094 1:341 1:592 3+ Pacifc Clsc-G1 90 4 4 53½ 78½ 712 718 Castillo H Jr LB 124 24.50 84 — Bertrando1243 Missionary Ridge124¾ Best Pal1242 7
Wide trip, jostled intervals early
24Jly93-11Mth fst 1⅛ :462 1:103 1:354 1:491 3+ Iselin H-G1 60 7 5 45½ 44½ 716 732½ Castillo H Jr L 116 7.30 56-15 Valley Crossing113hd Devil His Due1232½ Bertrando1198 Gave way 8
15May93-9Pim fst 1 3/16 :473 1:111 1:354 1:552 Pim Special-G1 103 4 2 22 21 2½ 33 Castillo H Jr L 114 4.30 82-18 DvilHisDu1201 VllyCrossing1122 PistolsAndRoss1143½ Gave way, drifted 6
10Apr93-8OP fst 1⅛ :464 1:102 1:353 1:483 Oaklawn H-G1 104 6 4 32 41 23 54 Castillo H Jr L 115 11.80 89-19 Jovial1171½ Lil E. Tee1231½ Best Pal1231½ 4 Wide 2nd turn 10
14Mar93-10GP fst 1¼ :452 1:094 1:351 2:011 3+ Gfstrm Pk H-G1 112 5 6 65½ 52½ 61¾ 31 Castillo H Jr L 114 10.70 94-11 Devil His Due1131 Offbeat112hd Pistols And Roses1141 Late rally 9
20Feb93-9GP fst 1⅛ :47 1:11 1:363 1:50 3+ Donn H-G1 110 6 5 33 3½ 1hd 1hd Castillo H Jr L 112 44.70 87-17 PistolsAndRoses112hd IrishSwp118hd MissionryRidge1185 Fully extended 9
WORKOUTS: Jan 30 Crc 6f fst 1:113 H 1/3 ●Jan 25 Crc 5f sly 1:003 B (d) 1/15 ●Jan 11 Crc 4f sly :48 H (d) 1/29 Dec 28 Crc 4f fst :483 H 6/36 Dec 15 Crc 3f fst :353 H 2/18 Dec 8 Crc 7f fst 1:273 H 1/1

Pistols and Roses
Own.—Willis Family Stables Inc

Gr. c. 4, by Darn That Alarm—To Be Continued, by Princely Pleasure
Br.—Alter Happy (Fla)
Tr.—Gianos George (48 5 5 4 .10)

114

Lifetime 18 7 4 2 $1,084,146
1993 3 1 1 0 $255,000
1992 9 2 2 1 $713,186
Wet 1 1 0 0 $30,000

20Feb93-9GP fst 1⅛ :47 1:11 1:50 3+ Donn H 102 6 5 33 3½ 1hd 1hd Castillo H Jr L 112 44.70 87-17 PstlsdRss112hdIrsSp118hdMssrRd-GB118 Fully extended 9
20Feb93-Grade I
30Jan93-10GP fst 1 1/16 :47 1:11 1:422 3+ Broward H 92 5 4 33½ 32½ 65 77¾ Santos J A L 114 4.90 90-13 Technology1181¼Brkrvill1171BiddingProud114 Faltered 8
30Jan93-Grade III
2Jan93-10Crc fst 1⅛ :471 1:122 1:522 3+ Trp Pk H 103 7 3 1hd 1hd 21½ 25½ Santos J A L 114 7.00 95-10 Brkrvill1145½PistolsndRoss114¾CountthTim114 Gamely 7
2Jan93-Grade III
26Nov92-10Crc fst 1 1/16 :48 1:122 1:451 3+ Thksgvg Dy H — 8 — — — — — Duarte J C L 114 7.50 — — PntBttrOnt118noCntthTm1141½Pnch113 Stmbld, lst rdr 8
31Oct92-3GP fst 1⅛ :461 1:10 1:474 3+ Sn Silence H 86 1 4 54½ 74½ 78¾ 710 Duarte J C L 115 7.50 88-03 PnutButtrOnit1151½DvilOnIc1122PinkTurtl111 Faltered 9
2Aug92-10Mth fst 1⅛ :461 1:094 1:483 Haskell H 78 7 3 22 45½ 716 718¾ Vasquez J Lb 118 9.90 78-10 Technology1201¾ Nines Wild1125¼ Scudan113 Gave way 9
2Aug92-Grade I
18Jly92-11Mth fst 1 1/16 :461 1:103 1:42 Long Branch 83 1 4 34 43 48 213¾ Vasquez J L 122 *.70 85-12 Scdn11413¾PstolsndRss122¾Mnchn'Nsh114 Awkward st 8
2May92-8CD fst 1¼ :464 1:363 2:03 Ky Derby 70 7 8 75 1114 1624 1625 Vasquez J LB 126 13.40 70-06 LilE.Tee1261CasualLies1263½DanceFloor126 Tired badly 18
2May92-Grade I
11Apr92-9Kee fst 1⅛ :471 1:112 1:49 Blue Grass 104 11 1 1½ 1hd 12 1nk Vasquez J LB 121 8.90 90-10 PstlsndRss121nkCntDSvy1212½EcsttcRd121 Ducked out 11
11Apr92-Grade II
14Mar92-10GP fst 1⅛ :46 1:104 1:503 Fla Derby 94 5 4 58½ 42½ 45 34½ Castillo H Jr L 122 3.00 79-17 Tchnology1224½DncFloor122hdPstlsndRss122 4 wide str 12
14Mar92-Grade I
LATEST WORKOUTS ●Mar 6 Crc 1 fst 1:391 H Mar 2 Crc 4f fst :483 B ●Feb 13 Crc 7f fst 1:27 H Feb 9 Crc 4f fst :484 B

To most handicappers, the 1994 Donn Handicap appeared a four-horse race between Devil His Due (8–5), Wallenda (3–1), Take Me Out (7–2), and Migrating Moon (9–2). Then again, the winner for the second straight year was Pistols and Roses ($24.20), so it must've been a matter of how you read the *Form*.

Compare the 1994 past performances of Pistols and Roses with the 1993 version and the form-pattern match should be readily apparent: a fairly effective spring campaign the previous year, a layoff from May to July, another layoff until the fall, followed by comeback efforts in the Tropical Park and Broward Handicaps.

The workout schedules also help to unravel the inner workings of this enigmatic horse — a horse George Gianos obviously understood quite well. Gianos sent him a total of eleven furlongs in two workouts between the Broward and the Donn in 1993 — a breezing four furlongs followed by a handy seven furlongs. In 1994, Pistols and Roses again worked a total of eleven furlongs between the

Broward and the Donn — a breezing five furlongs and then a handy six furlongs.

Pistols and Roses won the 1993 Donn at 44–1, and up the track that day were Barkerville and Technology, who had beaten him decisively in his two most recent races. He won again in 1994, this time at 11–1, and up the track were Take Me Out and Devil His Due, who had beaten him by lengthy margins in January. So much for the "who-has-beaten-whom?" theory as it applies to handicapping a horserace.

For both upset wins, Pistols and Roses was in receipt of a rider switch to Heriberto Castillo.

LAYOFFS

Most handicappers have familiarized themselves with any number of systems over the years, many of which begin with an elimination rule something like this: "No play on any horse that hasn't started during the past [fill in the number of your choice] days."

As a result, most of us are subliminally conditioned to regard layoffs in a negative sense, which explains the fact that many returnees win as substantial overlays. In fact, in this day and age of year-round racing and declining foal crops, a layoff is frequently an edge against battle-worn, leg-weary rivals, provided the returnee a) won as a first-time starter, b) won previously when fresh, or c) hails from a barn with a history of such moves.

Case in point, Karmani. The eight-year-old gelding hadn't been out in nearly six months when returned in a grass route at Aqueduct on May 2, 1993, and he was conceding substantial weight to most of his rivals after being entered for the maximum $100,000 claiming price.

Karmani was installed as the 5–2 favorite despite these apparent drawbacks. There were few, if any, serious players with a file of back *Forms* who were anxious to bet against him:

Karmani B. g. 5, by Run the Gantlet—Muskoka Weekend, by Nostrum
Br.—Eaton Hall Farm (Ont-C)
Own.—Eaton T E Tr.—Boniface J William 117
Lifetime 12 4 3 1 $50,819 | 1990 9 4 2 0 $44,648 | 1988 3 M 1 1 $6,171 | Turf 8 3 3 0 $44,028
21Oct90- 7Pen sf 1 1/16 Ⓣ 1:48⅘ 3+B C Hcppr Ch 8 4 43½ 43½ 32 25 Salvaggio M V 116 10.90 53-55 ByeUnionAve.1135Karmani1162½WhtHeDuz1124½ Second best 10
4Sep90- 9Med fm 1 1/16 Ⓣ:45⅘ 1:09⅕ 1:40⅖ 3+Alw 19000 3 3 44 65 62½ 45 Prado E S 116 34.90 90-13 Peanut Butter Onit1164 Sasquash1161Roanoke113hd Checked 9
19Aug90- 4Pim fm 1 1/16 Ⓣ:47⅘ 1:13 1:45 3+Clm 35000 7 2 21½ 21½ 1½ 1nk Miller D A Jr 117 4.20 81-19 Karmani117nkKitchener'sReward1171½RoylRock1171½ Driving 7
3Aug90- 9Pim fm 1 1/16 Ⓣ:47⅕ 1:11⅖ 1:42⅘ 3+Alw 23000 7 4 44½ 88½ 811 87¾ Miller D A Jr 119 2.90 84-08 LouiBomacino111½ArcticReality117½RegalGem117hd Fell back 8
20Jly90- 9Atl fm *1 1/16 Ⓣ:48⅖ 1:13⅖ 1:46⅖ 3+Alw 9500 10 2 22½ 21½ 1½ 11 Miller D A Jr 122 *1.00 92-08 Karmani1221 Tainer's Toy116½ Call To Colors1225½ Driving 10
29Jun90- 8Lrl fm 1 1/16 Ⓣ:46 1:10⅗ 1:41⅘ Clm 35000 6 3 33½ 43 54 23½ Miller D A Jr 119 *2.40 84-12 Natural Disaster1143½ Karmani1191 African Rid114nk Rallied 7
15Jun90- 9Lrl fm 1⅛ Ⓣ:47 1:12 1:48⅗ 3+Alw 19000 10 1 1hd 1hd 1hd 1nk Miller D A Jr 119 4.40 91-09 Krmni119nkDevil'sFortune1211½WoodyBoyWould1145 Driving 11
24May90- 8Pim fst 6f :23⅕ :46⅖ 1:11⅕ Alw 17000 7 1 63 65¾ 47 44 Nicol P A Jr 122 7.40 86-10 WingdDmon114noLittlCsino1174ThnkYouAlvn109no No threat 7
5May90- 4Del gd 6f :22⅘ :46⅘ 1:12⅘ 3+Md Sp Wt 5 1 2hd 2hd 11 17 Nicol P A Jr 122 *1.50 83-12 Karmani1227 Falon'sDream1223½PrincePhoto117¾ Ridden out 7
11Jun88- 5WO fm 1 1/16 Ⓣ:45⅗ 1:10 1:41⅘ 3+Md Sp Wt 9 3 33 32½ 22 22½ Hawley S 114 3.25 95-04 OnemoreConnection1142½Karmani1141½HngtheExpense1151½ 10
Speed Index: Last Race: +8.0 3–Race Avg.: +3.6 8–Race Avg.: –0.2 Overall Avg.: –1.1
LATEST WORKOUTS Oct 12 Lrl 4f fst :50 B

Karmani B. g. 6, by Run the Gantlet—Muskoka Weekend, by Nostrum
Br.—Eaton Hall Farm (Ont-C)
Own.—Webb Thomas Tr.—Boniface J William 119
Lifetime 16 5 5 2 $88,359 | 1991 2 1 1 0 $25,300 | 1990 11 4 3 1 $56,888 | Turf 12 4 5 1 $81,568
10May91- 9Pim fm 1 1/16 Ⓣ:473 1:112 1:411 Alw 25000 6 2 23 23 23 23½ Prado E S 122 *1.00 96-01 EternalOrage1223½Krmni122nkMuddyRudder1144 Second best 6
28Apr91- 5Aqu gd 1⅛ Ⓣ:482 1:132 1:51 3+Alw 33000 1 2 2½ 1½ 1hd 1nk Chavez J F 119 3.20 91-18 Karmani119nkThreeCoinsUp1102Passtheale1213½ Svd grd. drv 8
9Nov90- 8Aqu fm 1⅛ Ⓣ:492 1:131 1:492 3+Alw 36000 4 1 1hd 1hd 1hd 3nk Perret C 117 7.00 104-05 HighlandDevotion115nkAcademyAwrd117noKrmni1173 Gamely 7
31Oct90- 6Aqu fm 1⅜ Ⓣ:49 1:393 2:163 3+Alw 36000 5 2 21½ 21 22 22 Perret C 117 2.70 92-06 PrivateTalk1172Krmni1172HighlndDevotion1148½ Second best 7
21Oct90- 7Pen sf 1 1/16 Ⓣ 1:483 3+B C Hcppr Ch 8 4 43½ 43½ 32 25 Salvaggio M V 116 10.90 53-55 ByeUnionAve.1135Karmani1162½WhtHeDuz1124½ Second best 10
4Sep90- 9Medfm 1 1/16 Ⓣ:454 1:091 1:402 3+Alw 19000 3 3 44 65 62½ 45 Prado E S 116 34.90 90-13 Peanut Butter Onit1164 Sasquash1161Roanoke113hd Checked 9
19Aug90- 4Pim fm 1 1/16 Ⓣ:474 1:13 1:45 3+Clm 35000 7 2 21½ 21½ 1½ 1nk Miller D A Jr 117 4.20 81-19 Karmani117nkKitchener'sReward1171½RoylRock1171½ Driving 7
3Aug90- 9Pim fm 1 1/16 Ⓣ:471 1:112 1:424 3+Alw 23000 7 4 44½ 88½ 811 87¾ Miller D A Jr 119 2.90 84-08 LouiBomacino111½ArcticReality117½RegalGem117hd Fell back 8
20Jly90- 9Atl fm *1 1/16 Ⓣ:482 1:132 1:462 3+Alw 9500 10 2 22½ 21½ 1½ 11 Miller D A Jr 122 *1.00 92-08 Karmani1221 Tainer's Toy116½ Call To Colors1225½ Driving 10
29Jun90- 8Lrl fm 1 1/16 Ⓣ:46 1:103 1:414 Clm 35000 6 3 33½ 43 54 23½ Miller D A Jr 119 *2.40 84-12 Natural Disaster1143½ Karmani1191 African Rid114nk Rallied 7
Speed Index: Last Race: –3.0 3–Race Avg.: +5.0 10–Race Avg.: +1.2 Overall Avg.: +1.2
LATEST WORKOUTS Apr 19 Del 3f fst :38 B

Karmani B. g. 7, by Run the Gantlet—Muskoka Weekend, by Nostrum
CHAVEZ J F (217 27 23 26 .12) Br.—Eaton Hall Farm (Ont-C)
Own.—Webb Thomas Tr.—Boniface J William (—) 117
Lifetime 30 7 8 6 $251,271 | 1992 4 1 0 1 $40,674 | 1991 12 2 4 3 $147,538 | Turf 25 6 8 5 $242,080
22Jun92- 8Bel gd 1¼ Ⓣ:491 1:381 2:014 3+Handicap 94 2 1 1½ 1½ 1hd 32½ Chavez J F 119 3.60 79-20 Fraise114nk Husyan1142 Karmani119 Speed, weakened 8
13Jun92-11Pim fm 1 1/16 Ⓣ:46 1:104 1:423 3+Chieftain H 89 5 6 68 43½ 33½ 45½ Chavez J F 113 8.20 82-25 BrondeVux1132½Rebuff113hdEternlOrge112 Wide, hung 10
31May92- 8WO fm 1 1/16 Ⓣ:462 1:11 1:423 ⓈConnaught 89 2 2 22 2½ 56 58 McKnight J 119 7.30 83-10 Cozzn'sPrnc1231½RnbwsfrLf1262TtfRm123 Not keep up 8
31May92-Grade III-C
30Apr92- 8Aqu fm 1⅛ Ⓣ:491 1:132 1:493 3+Alw 47000 103 7 1 1½ 1½ 11 11½ Chavez J F 117 2.80 95-15 Karmani1171½ Thakib1174½ Simili-Fr117 Driving 7
30Oct91- 9Mar fst 1 1/16 :482 1:132 1:451 3+Alw 40000 78 11 2 21 33½ 57½ 414¾ Reynolds L C 117 20.10 93-18 SunnySunris1176¾J.R.'sHorzon1172½Lgtur119 Weakened 10
19Oct91-11Lrl sf 1¼ Ⓣ:493 1:412 2:062 3+Bud Int'l 89 8 1 1½ 2hd 1113 1216½ Chavez J F 126 62.60 58-38 Leariva1231¾ Sillery122½ Goofalik126 Fell back 13
19Oct91-Grade I
22Sep91- 8WO fm 1¼ Ⓣ:454 1:352 2:003 3+ⓈSeagrm CpH 99 7 1 1hd 1hd 2½ 34½ McKnight J 119 12.10 93-06 Sky Classic1221¾ ⒹIzvestia1252½ Karmani119 Gave way 7
22Sep91-Grade III-C; Placed second through disqualification
8Sep91- 9Del fm *1 1/16 Ⓣ:471 1:112 1:424 3+Caesr Rodney 92 3 2 2hd 1hd 1½ 33 Colton R E 124 *.70 91-06 Bardland116½ Rebuff1242½ Karmani124 6
8Sep91-Steadied on heels to 1st turn
22Aug91- 8Sar yl 1⅜ Ⓣ:501 2:061 2:454 3+Seneca H 96 5 1 2½ 2hd 32 55½ Krone J A 116 4.00 63-31 El Senor121nk Rigamajig119no CrystalMoment113 Tired 8
22Aug91-Grade III
20Jly91- 8Bel fm 1½ Ⓣ:464 2:00 2:252 3+Swrd Dncr H 101 5 2 2½ 2hd 2hd 21 Chavez J F 113 36.90 97-09 Dr. Root1091 Karmani113nk El Senor116 Good try 7
20Jly91-Grade I

Karmani B. g. 8, by Run the Gantlet—Muskoka Weekend, by Nostrum
CHAVEZ J F (63 13 8 6 .21) $100,000 Br.—Eaton Hall Farm (Ont-C)
Own.—Webb Thomas W Tr.—Boniface J William (4 0 1 1 .00) 122
Lifetime 39 9 9 9 $326,391 | 1993 1 1 0 0 $18,900 | 1992 12 2 1 4 $96,894 | Turf 34 8 9 8 $317,200
2May93- 7Aqu fm 1 1/16 Ⓣ:48 1:113 1:432 Clm 100000 94 3 2 1½ 1hd 1½ 1½ Chavez J F 122 *2.50 94-11 Krmni122½Nelson'sNvy1222½Hudlm'sSidkick112 Driving 7
7Nov92-10Lrl sf 1½ Ⓣ:532 2:164 2:434 3+Turf Cup h 84 5 1 1hd 31 67½ 610¾ Rocco J 114 25.20 — — MsterDremer112nkBeNimble113nkTidemrk111 Gave way 10
7Nov92-Grade III
11Oct92- 6Due fm *1½ Ⓣ 2:282 3+S Houston 85 2 2 11 11 11 315¾ Colton R 115 16.00 — — Drummer Boy114¾ Plate Dancer11615Karmani115 Tired 10
19Sep92-10Pim fm 1⅛ Ⓣ:454 1:101 1:481 3+Damascus H 94 6 5 43 42½ 33 63¾ Reynolds L C 116 10.90 90-10 SocilReti.ee1151¾Rebuff115noBrondeVux114 Weakened 11
22Aug92- 9Mth gd 1⅛ Ⓣ:454 1:103 1:492 + 3+Longfelw H 81 2 1 2hd 2hd 87¾ 913½ Hutton G W 118 10.40 76-23 Futurist116hdMsterDrmr1142½SoStrling114 Stead, tired 11
22Aug92-Grade III
9Aug92- 9Pha fm *1½ Ⓣ 1:514 3+Ambler 96 2 1 11½ 12 12 11½ Vigliotti M J 118 *.80 92-11 Karmani1181½ Corinto-Ge1166 SuperModest118 Driving 7
2Aug92- 9Mth gd 1⅛ Ⓣ:482 1:13 1:51 + 3+Battlefield 95 6 2 21 21½ 1hd 23 Bravo J 119 4.70 78-21 Royal Ninja1193 Karmani119½ Ogle114 Good try 8
18Jly92-10Lrl fm 1⅛ Ⓣ:46 1:101 1:47 3+Alw 25300 98 5 1 1½ 11 2½ 3¾ Chavez S N 119 2.30 95-09 ⒹHFahrvegnuggen117ⒹHFruglDoc122¾Krmni119 Faded 7
8Jly92- 8Bel fm 1 1/16 Ⓣ:463 1:103 1:404 3+Alw 47000 99 3 1 1½ 1½ 11½ 3½ Migliore R 117 4.80 93-14 Buchman117½ So Sterling119no Karmani117 Held well 6
22Jun92- 8Bel gd 1¼ Ⓣ:491 1:381 2:014 3+Handicap 97 2 1 1½ 1½ 1hd 32½ Chavez J F 119 3.60 79-20 Fraise114nk Husyan1142 Karmani119 Speed, weakened 8
LATEST WORKOUTS Apr 19 Pim 6f fst 1:15 B ●Apr 16 Pim 6f fst 1:15 H Apr 12 Pim 4f sly :49 B

Karmani dueled from start to finish and prevailed by a half-length, a performance that was virtually inevitable in light of his lifetime history. Karmani had come back from a layoff of nearly two years to break his maiden at the advanced age of five back in

May of 1990. Although five-year-old maidens are poor percentage players in the long run, it seemed everyone at Delaware Park on the afternoon of May 5 knew that Karmani would win; they bet him down to 3–2, and the result was a seven-length win after a duel through the opening half.

In 1991 and again in 1992, Karmani launched his campaigns with front-running wins on grass at Aqueduct, each time switching to Jorge Chavez and withstanding early-pace pressure. Why should 1993 be any different?

Karmani developed a four-year pattern of winning first time back from a layoff. Sometimes, however, a pattern may manifest itself in the form of a big race *second* time back. Consider Codys Key:

Codys Key — Ro. c. 3(May), by Corridor Key—Go Thither, by Cabin
Br.—Wilkinson Jon (NJ)
Own.—Sheerin Raymond — Tr.—Contessa Gary C (107 20 17 13 .19) — 115
Lifetime 9 3 1 2 $55,477 — 1992 3 1 0 1 $15,075 — 1991 6 2 1 1 $40,402 — Wet 1 0 0 0

18Jly92-11Lrl	fst 7f	:231 :462 1:244	Cavalier Cup	72	4 5 54½ 66 55 44½	Chavez J F	L 119	6.10	78 —	Apprtontofllw1171¾Mjsty'sTrn1191½WdFx114	Mild rally	8
3Jly92-6Mth	fst 6f	:214 :444 1:104	3↑Alw 17000	88	1 6 1hd 12 1½ 12	Bravo J	L 110	8.50	87-17	CodysKy1102MjcFontn113¾BndtCrsr116	Drftd out, drvg	6
10Jun92-7Mth	fst 6f	:214 :442 1:10	3↑ⓈAlw 22500	73	1 8 52¾ 44½ 35½ 37½	Collazo L	L 109	8.80	83-18	ShdyShd1163¾CrftyGldn1163¾CdysKy109	Saved ground	9
28Dec91-9Pha	fst 6½f	:221 :451 1:164	Allegheny	58	1 4 1½ 3nk 58 611¾	Castillo R E	114	3.60	82-09	Dr.Unright1143½LuckyVirginn1215Spkrphon114	Used up	9
6Dec91-8Med	fst 1	:473 1:114 1:37	Cumberland	76	1 1 12 11½ 1½ 31¾	Bravo J	115	2.80	92-15	PlceLine115½CoinCollector1201¼CodysKy115	Weakened	6
20Nov91-7Med	fst 6f	:221 :453 1:113	ⓈAlw 18700	85	1 2 1hd 11½ 11½ 12¼	Bravo J	117	*.30	84-21	Codys Key1172¼Buono1175ⒹProof'sCharger114	Driving	8
8Nov91-9Med	fst 6f	:224 :462 1:11	ⓈNj Futurity	81	6 2 1hd 1hd 2hd 21¼	Bravo J	122	2.10	85-17	Munch n' Nosh1221¼CodysKey1223Burgio122	No match	7
8Nov91-Run in Divisions												
30Aug91-7Mth	fst 6f	:22 :453 1:112	ⓈMd Sp Wt	74	1 5 1½ 1½ 14 17	Douglas R R	118	*2.30	84-16	CodysKy1187WildBrzy1182TrickthTurn118	Kept to task	8
20Aug91-9Mth	sly 6f	:211 :443 1:112	ⓈOpen Mind	41	5 6 54¾ 58 611 714	Rivera L Jr	113	16.30	70-16	ThnksTRndy1207½StLdyJ113¾Mnchn'Nsh112	Thru early	7

LATEST WORKOUTS ●Jly 14 Mth 3f fst :35 B — Jun 24 Mth 6f fst 1:14 H — Jun 3 Mth 6f fst 1:142 H

Codys Key — Ro. c. 4, by Corridor Key—Go Thither, by Cabin
CHAVEZ J F (149 27 18 13 .18) — Br.—Wilkinson Jon (NJ)
Own.—Sheerin Raymond I — Tr.—Contessa Gary C (36 3 2 1 .08) — 111
Lifetime 14 4 2 2 $112,624 — 1993 2 1 0 0 $51,300 — 1992 6 1 1 1 $20,922 — Turf 1 0 0 0 $400 — Wet 1 0 0 0

29May93-8Bel	fst 6f	:224 :453 1:094	3↑Roseben H	95	5 1 1½ 2½ 2½ 1hd	Chavez J F	108	32.10	91-10	CodysKey108hdSunnybutcold111noSlrp118	Drvg,gamely	6
29May93-Grade III												
15May93-8Bel	fst 6f	:222 :453 1:101	3↑Handicap	50	3 7 62½ 72¾ 79¾ 720¼	Bravo J	110	18.20	69-17	FrindlyLovr1121½Curbx1142¾DrummondLn120	No factor	7
15Sep92-3Med	fst 6f	:22 :45 1:092	Clm 40000	71	6 1 12 1hd 22 47½	Bravo J	L 116	*.90	88-07	Mac'sClyde1164½MajorDanger109¾RoyleDerby116	Tired	6
22Aug92-8Atl	fst 6f	:22 :444 1:091	ⓈMckeeCityH	89	4 2 21 21 22½ 23½	Gryder A T	L 119	2.30	96-06	Dr.LouisA.1163½CodysKy119½Munchn'Nosh118	2nd best	4
2Aug92-5Mth	gd 1$\frac{1}{16}$ Ⓣ	:48 1:122 1:434	Restoration	78	9 5 45½ 54¼ 510 615¾	Bravo J	L 115	14.90	69-21	BddngProd1229½CobblstnRd117¾CxStrdst114	Gave way	9
18Jly92-11Lrl	fst 7f	:231 :462 1:244	Cavalier Cup	72	4 5 54½ 66 55 44½	Chavez J F	L 119	6.10	78-17	Apprtontofllw1171¾Mjsty'sTrn1191½WdFx114	Mild rally	8
3Jly92-6Mth	fst 6f	:214 :444 1:104	3↑Alw 17000	89	1 6 1hd 12 1½ 12	Bravo J	L 110	8.50	87-17	CodysKy1102MjcFontn113¾BndtCrsr116	Drftd out, drvg	6
10Jun92-7Mth	fst 6f	:214 :442 1:10	3↑ⓈAlw 22500	73	1 8 52¾ 44½ 35½ 37½	Collazo L	L 109	8.80	83-18	ShdyShd1163¾CrftyGldn1163¾CdysKy109	Saved ground	9
28Dec91-9Pha	fst 6½f	:221 :451 1:164	Allegheny	58	1 4 1½ 3nk 58 611¾	Castillo R E	114	3.60	82-09	Dr.Unright1143½LuckyVirginn1215Spkrphon114	Used up	9
6Dec91-8Med	fst 1	:473 1:114 1:37	Cumberland	76	1 1 12 11½ 1½ 31¾	Bravo J	115	2.80	92-15	PlceLine115½CoinCollector1201¼CodysKy115	Weakened	6

LATEST WORKOUTS ●Jun 17 Bel Ⓣ 3f fm :364 H (d) — Jun 11 Bel 5f fst 1:012 H — May 26 Mth 3f fst :364 B — May 22 Bel 3f fst :374 B

Codys Key — Ro. h. 5
Own: Sheerin Raymond T
Sire: Corridor Key (Danzig) — Dam: Go Thither (Cabin) — Br: Wilkinson Jon (NJ)
BAILEY J D (122 22 21 16 .18) — $70,000 — Tr: Contessa Gary C (19 3 3 1 .16) — 113
Lifetime Record: 25 7 2 3 $209,028
1994 6 1 0 0 $34,580 — Turf 1 0 0 0 $400
1993 7 3 0 1 $113,124 — Wet 2 0 0 0
Bel Ⓣ 0 0 0 0 — Dist Ⓣ 0 0 0 0

10Sep94-9Med	fst 6f	:222 :453 :574 1:104	3↑ⓈBold Josh H30k	83	7 4 41½ 31 32½ 54	Santos J A	L 122	1.80	83-18	Munch N' Nosh117hd Toroweap115¾ Dr. Louis A.1132	No rally	7
29Aug94-4Sar	fst 6f	:221 :452 :572 1:094	3↑Handicap50k	101	5 1 2½ 2½ 1hd 12	Chavez J F	110	7.50	92-13	Codys Key1102 Chief Desire122hd Humbugaboo1162¼	Driving	5
10Aug94-6Sar	fst 6f	:214 :45 :571 1:10	Clm 75000	82	1 2 34½ 35 41½ 46	Chavez J F	117	3.10	85-09	Golden Tent113no Fabersham1132 Mining Burrah1174	Checked 3/16 pl	5
28May94-8Bel	fst 6f	:22 :452 :572 1:093	3↑Roseben H-G3	78	8 10 87½ 95¼ 95¾ 911¼	McCauley W H	112	9.50	82-14	Boundary1132¾ Chief Desire117nk Birdonthewire1222	No factor	10
13May94-8Bel	fst 6½f	:223 :454 1:10 1:162	3↑Alw 40000N$Y	98	8 2 31½ 3nk 2½ 4nk	McCauley W H	115	5.30	91-14	Fabersham117hd Key Contender108hd Strikany119no	Weakened	8
10Apr94-5Hia	fst 6f	:214 :444 :571 1:102	Alw 21400N$Y	63	4 2 21½ 33 34 613	Ferrer J C	L 122	3.50	80-11	Concorde's Tune122nk Poulain D'or117nk Swedaus1193½	Faltered	7
18Sep93-4Bel	sly 6f	:222 :451 :57 1:092	3↑Fall Hwgt H-G2	85	9 3 43½ 54 65 79½	Chavez J F	133	9.80	83-14	Fly So Free135½ Demaloot Demashoot1261½ Take Me Out1343	Tired	10
15Aug93-9Sar	fst 7f	:221 :442 1:084 1:214	3↑Forego H-G2	93	9 3 66¼ 87¼ 75¾ 58	Alvarado F T	114	25.00	88-12	Birdonthewire1171½ Harlan1102¼ Senor Speedy1172½	Five wide	9
26Jly93-7Bel	fst 6f	:222 :451 :571 1:094	3↑Alw 40000N$Y	102	6 5 35½ 43½ 31½ 13	Chavez J F	122	*2.00	91-18	Codys Key1223 Lordofthemountain117no DH Senor Cielo117	Going away	6
4Jly93-5Bel	fst 6f	:223 :452 :571 1:091	3↑Alw 40000N$Y	100	5 2 21½ 32 2hd 1½	Chavez J F	122	3.80	94-11	Codys Key122½ Curbex1171¾ Boom Towner1174¾	Driving	6

WORKOUTS: Oct 1 Bel 4f fst :494 B *30/50* — Sep 22 Bel 4f fst :48 H *4/53* — Aug 24 Sar 5f fst 1:001 H *6/39* — Aug 7 Sar 4f fst :483 B *13/56* — ●Jly 31 Sar tr.t 5f fst 1:022 B *1/11* — Jly 25 Sar tr.t Ⓣ 6f fm 1:144 B *4/10*

Codys Key is a classic example of a horse who is "given" a race first time back. The first four victories of his career were accomplished second time back from a layoff, at ascending class levels and progressively longer odds: a maiden win August 30, 1991, as the favorite; a preliminary New Jersey–bred allowance win November 20, 1991, again as the favorite; an open allowance for nonwinners of two on July 3, 1992, at 8–1; and the Grade 3 Roseben Handicap on May 29, 1993, at 32–1.

Codys Key made a valiant attempt to make it five straight wins second time back from a layoff May 13, 1994, and I bet him to win along with some exacta savers. He finished fourth, beaten by a head, a head, and a nose for all the money at 5–1. Then, on closing day at Saratoga, Codys Key won second time back from a layoff at a $17 mutuel in a short field, and was the longest price in a Pick 6 sequence that paid more than $73,000.

Many handicappers are aware of statistical studies that are favorable toward horses making their third start back from a layoff — especially a router stretching out after a pair of sprints. These types are now overbet as a general rule, something I found out as far back as October of 1991, when I was at Penn National for my second go-round at the World Series of Handicapping:

Dual Rule — **B. g. 6, by Ruling Gold—Dual Concern, by Bob Wag**
Own.—Hamm Susan R — **Br.—Conner & Walsh (Pa)** — **Tr.—Mills Dennis R**

Lifetime 47 8 5 4 $40,638 — 1991 4 2 0 0 $3,588 — 1990 15 3 2 1 $16,252 — Turf 4 0 0 0

1Nov91- 8Pen	fst	170	:48	1:13	1:44^{1}	3↑Clm 3200	9	2	2½	2½	1^{hd}	1½	Vives J C	Lb	116	11.00	88-15	DualRule116½CraftyGeorge119^{1}¾WorldlyNews122^{no}	Held sway	9
19Oct91- 7Pen	fst	1 1/16	:48	1:15^{1}	1:50^{4}	3↑Clm 2500	2	5	4^{7}	3½	1^{2}	1^{3}	Baker C J	Lb	116	*2.40	56-32	Dual Rule116^{3} Native Ivory117½ VictoryFlyer116^{hd}	Drew away	12
11Oct91- 7Pen	sly	6f	:22^{1}	:46	1:12^{3}	3↑Clm 3000	8	9	9^{9}½	7^{5}¾	5^{3}¾	4^{2}	Baker C J	Lb	119	11.60	80-23	Mr.J.W.P.122^{1}CodOfEthcs119^{1}HnrblFrnd122^{no}	Late response	11
2Oct91- 8Pen	fst	6f	:23	:46^{3}	1:12^{1}	3↑Clm 3000	9	1	2^{2}	6^{5}	7^{7}	6^{6}¼	Baker C J	Lb	119	12.50	78-18	Johnny S.119^{1} Akomac122½ Exclusive Carry122^{1}½	Used up	9
13Oct90-12Del	sly	1 1/16	:48	1:12^{3}	1:46	3↑Clm 5000	2	3	6^{4}¾	8^{8}¼	6^{11}	5^{14}¼	Conner S E	Lb	116	3.40	68-16	Get to It111^{2}¼ Fishers Island122½ Mycroft119^{no}	Outrun	8
5Oct90- 8Pha	fst	1 1/16	:47	1:12	1:44^{1}	3↑Alw 13500	5	2	2^{hd}	3^{3}	6^{15}	6^{24}¾	Gunther S F	Lb	116	28.00	63-17	Boulabally116^{6} River Wolf117^{1}¾JohnnyCorvette116^{3}	Stopped	6
25Sep90- 4Lrl	fst	6½f	:23^{3}	:47	1:18	3↑Alw 5000s	4	3	5^{3}½	5^{10}	5^{9}	5^{12}	Conner S E	Lb	117	8.50	77-19	Rifleman-Nz117^{1}¼SyYouCn121^{1}¼BrddockHeights117^{1}¼	Outrun	6
15Sep90-11Del	fst	5½f	:22	:46^{1}	1:05^{3}	3↑Clm 5000	9	7	7^{4}¼	6^{5}¼	5^{5}¼	2^{3}¼	Conner S E	Lb	116	6.00	– –	Jay Arcane122^{3}¼ Dual Rule116½ Bow To You116^{2}	Up for 2nd	9
27Jun90- 8Del	fm	1 1/16	Ⓣ:46^{2}	1:11	1:43^{2}	3↑Alw 7600	8	4	4^{3}½	5^{5}¾	6^{7}½	8^{12}¾	Gunther S F	b	122	11.50	81-06	Lono116^{2} In This Mess106½ Key Shift111^{3}¾	Tired	11
10Jun90- 8Del	fst	170	:46^{3}	1:12	1:43	3↑Alw 5000s	4	2	2^{hd}	3^{nk}	2^{hd}	3^{4}¾	Gunther S F	b	122	3.30	88-22	Ah Men122^{4}¼ Lucite Light122½ Dual Rule122^{3}½	Faded	6
3Jun90- 9Del	fst	1 1/16	:46^{4}	1:10^{3}	1:43^{2}	3↑C Staats	1	1	1^{1}	4^{3}¾	5^{7}¾	5^{13}¼	Gunther S F	b	115	23.40	82-20	Flaming Emperor124^{hd} Evening Kris115½ LoyalPal115^{6}¾	Tired	6
21May90- 8Del	gd	1 1/16	:47	1:12	1:45	3↑Clm 12500	4	1	1^{4}	1^{5}	1^{4}	1^{6}½	Gunther S F	b	122	9.00	87-23	Dual Rule122^{6}½ Archer's Honor119^{7} Arias M.119^{4}½	Ridden out	7

LATEST WORKOUTS Sep 24 Pen 6f fst 1:16^{3} B — Sep 18 Pen 6f fst 1:18 B — ●Sep 10 Pen 4f fst :49^{1} H

Dual Rule was the quintessential router stretching out third time back: after a layoff of fifty-one weeks, the gelding returned with a flash of early speed on October 2, dropped back to sixth after a half, and continued on evenly thereafter, losing only another length or so to the lead horse. In the slop nine days later, Dual Rule showed a change of pace, running ninth after a quarter but then gaining in position *and* in lengths at each successive point of call to wind up fourth, beaten by two lengths.

Timing is everything at the World Series of Handicapping—a three-day test of handicapping ability and nerves (in no particular order) conducted on Friday and Saturday evenings, with the final card on Sunday afternoon. Had this been one of the final races on Sunday and had I been in contention for the $100,000 first prize, I probably would've bet my entire bankroll on the class-dropping Dual Rule at 2–1, even though he was being overbet (in a thirty-race contest, long-term percentages do not apply—you need a winner *now*). But Dual Rule's race was on Saturday night. My original, mythical bankroll of $1,000 was down to about $600, and though my tap-out bet brought me back to mid-pack in the field with a bankroll of $1,800, I never got closer than that.

Too bad the contest hadn't been scheduled for November 1, when Dual Rule was hiked up to $3,200 and won again, this time at 11–1.

Routers making their third start back after a pair of sprint lines as nice looking as Dual Rule's have little chance to escape the attention of today's well-informed bettors, but variations on the theme often do equally well at better odds:

8

1 1/16 MILES. (InnerDirt). (1.41³) 12th Running THE KINGS POINT HANDICAP. Purse $75,000 added. 3-year-olds and upward, foaled in New York State and approved by the New York State Bred Registry. By subscription of $150 each, which should accompany the nomination; $600 to pass the entry box, $600 to start, with $75,000 added. The added money and all fees to be divided 60% to the winner, 22% to second, 12% to third and 6% to fourth. Weights, Tuesday, February 25. Starters to be named at the closing time of entries. A trophy will be presented to the winning owner. Closed Wednesday, February 12 with 22 nominations.

Coupled—Argyle Lake and G'Day Mate.

Herr Von Kaninchen — **B. g. 7, by Delta Flag—Ave Maria, by Experte** — **Br.—Label Sydney (NY)** — **Tr.—Schaeffer Stephen W** — **114**

Own.—McNulty David P

Lifetime								
64 9 12 11	1992	3	0	0	1	$7,740
$418,664	1991	15	2	0	3	$126,507
	Turf	1	0	0	0	

Entered 28Feb92- 6 AQU

9Feb92- 8Aqu	fst	6f	⊡:22⁴	:46²	1:11¹	3↑ⓈHoli Hughs H	2	11	10¹¹	10⁷	9⁹	8⁷¾	Velasquez J	117	6.50	79–25	ArgyleLake114½NorthernCrush112²AllSmrts115¾	Broke slowly	11
25Jan92- 6Aqu	fst	6f	⊡:23²	:46³	1:11²	Handicap	5	5	5⁷	5⁶½	5²½	3¹½	Velasquez J	112	11.50	84–21	DHTrndBl1161½DHMnrllc1131½HrrVnKnch112nk	Saved ground	5
8Jan92- 8Aqu	fst	1⁷⁰	⊡:47³	1:12²	1:42³	Alw 47000	3	5	5¹¹	5¹⁰	5⁴½	4⁶	Velasquez J	115	9.90	86–30	Avasaurus122hd Wild Away1224¾ Sea Hunter1151¼	Outrun	5
28Dec91- 8Aqu	fst	1 1/16	⊡:46⁴	1:12³	1:46¹	3↑ⓈAlex M Robb	8	8	8⁹¼	8⁵¾	4⁶	4⁸¼	Velasquez J	119	16.00	69–25	StudyHrd1203¼SeHunter1222½Crr'sPlsur1122½	Pssd tired ones	8
15Dec91- 8Aqu	fst	6f	⊡:22	:45²	1:10⁴	3↑ⓈJoe Palmer	7	9	9¹³	9¹⁰	8⁶¼	6⁴	Cordero A Jr	122	9.40	85–19	Shine Please119nk Zee Best1191½ Jesuit1171¾	Slow start	9
1Dec91- 3Aqu	gd	1	:46³	1:10²	1:35⁴	3↑Clm 75000	4	4	4³½	5⁶½	4⁸	4⁷¾	Bailey J D	117	3.20	75–25	ScottishMonk1152½PocketStrkr1144¼Jokr'sFrc1171	No threat	6
1Nov91- 8Aqu	fst	6f	:22	:45	1:10¹	3↑Handicap	4	6	6¹³	6⁹	6⁶½	6¹⁰	Migliore R	115	7.10	80–17	Heart of a Hero112¾ Collegian1141¼ Senor Cielo1173¼	Outrun	6
13Oct91- 8Bel	fst	6f	:22¹	:45	1:09²	3↑Boojum H	6	9	9¹³	9⁷½	8⁷	8⁶	Migliore R	113	18.60	87–15	Sénor Speedy117nk Diablo1141½ For Really113½	No factor	9
13Oct91-Grade III																			
29Sep91- 8Bel	fst	7f	:23	:45³	1:22	3↑ⓈHudson H	1	8	7⁵½	5⁴½	4⁶½	3⁴	Cordero A Jr	118	9.40	90–13	D'Prrot1144ShinePlese110noHerrVonKninchen1182½	Willingly	8
14Sep91- 1Bel	my	6f	:22²	:45¹	1:09⁴	3↑Handicap	1	5	5¹³	5⁷¼	5⁷½	5⁹	Bailey J D	116	9.90	82–13	Kid Russell1172½ Mr. Nasty122¾ Tom Cobbley1144	Outrun	5

Speed Index: Last Race: +16.0 3–Race Avg.: +3.3 3–Race Avg.: +3.3 Overall Avg.: +2.0

LATEST WORKOUTS Feb 18 Bel tr.t 4f fst :48 H Feb 5 Bel tr.t 3f fst :37 H Jan 22 Bel tr.t 4f fst :48¹ H Jan 16 Bel tr.t 4f fst :48² B

Crafty Alfel

Ch. g. 4, by Crafty Prospector—Regal Lady Hour, by Regal And Royal
Br.—Iselin James H (NY)
Tr.—Iselin James H
Own.—Lippert Albert
111
Lifetime 17 4 2 2 $96,633
1992 3 0 1 0 $12,898
1991 12 4 1 1 $80,495

9Feb92- 8Aqu fst 6f ⊡:224 :462 1:111 3↑ⓈHoli Hughs H 7 4 33 2½ 2½ 43¼ Antley C W 113 13.70 84-25 Argyle Lake114½ NorthernCrush1122AllSmarts115¾ Bid, wknd 11
10Jan92- 8Aqu fst 6f ⊡:231 :464 1:113 Alw 34000 3 3 31 31½ 21 22 Antley C W 117 2.80 83-23 Sizzl'n Avenger1172 Crafty Alfel1172 Real Minx1178 2nd best 4
1Jan92- 7Aqu fst 6f ⊡:223 :453 1:113 Alw 34000 1 1 1½ 1hd 2hd 74 Cordero A Jr 117 *2.30 81-13 TopTheRcord117nkSizzl'nAvngr117½RlMinx1173 Used in pace 7
15Dec91- 8Aqu fst 6f ⊡:22 :452 1:104 3↑ⓈJoe Palmer 1 7 54 62¾ 52¾ 53¾ Antley C W 117 7.30 85-19 Shine Please119nk Zee Best1191½ Jesuit1171¾ No rally 9
25Nov91- 8Aqu fst 6f :221 :444 1:092 3↑Alw 41000 1 10 94½ 63½ 52½ 44¼ Antley C W 113 10.40 90-18 SvingsAccount1132¼ShinePles115½ShiningBid1131½ Mild rally 10
28Oct91- 8Aqu fst 7f :222 :453 1:241 3↑Alw 30000 2 5 36 34 21 1hd Antley C W 114 6.20 81-22 CraftyAlfel114hdTrackRebel1145SavingsAccount116nk Driving 5
13Oct91- 7FL gd 6f :212 :443 1:104 3↑ⓈProphet Wise 1 5 42½ 32½ 22 23 Nicol P A Jr 110 5.20 89-16 ArctcQun1213CrftyAlfl110½Lordofthmontn1243½ Second best 6
5Aug91- 8Sar fst 1⅛ :47 1:113 1:50 ⓈAlbany H 5 3 3½ 3nk 23½ 516 Smith M E 112 3.50 71-20 ExcellentTipper1214AmbassadorinLove1226AlyJed111no Tired 8
27Jly91- 5Sar fst 6f :221 :451 1:092 3↑Alw 30000 2 5 42½ 42½ 43½ 35½ Antley C W 113 5.40 91-09 Formal Dinner111½ Nymphist1175 CraftyAlfel113nk Four wide 7
6Jly91- 3Bel gd 1$\frac{1}{16}$:46 1:101 1:413 3↑Handicap 1 1 1½ 42½ 414 424½ Romero R P 111 4.20 69-05 FarewellWve1166Slvic11816Congeleur1132½ Attempt to wheel 4

Speed Index: Last Race: -9.0 2-Race Avg.: -17.5 2-Race Avg.: -17.5 Overall Avg.: -0.6

Packett's Landing

B. g. 6, by Bates Motel—Lightning Bug, by Cornish Prince
Br.—Free F William (NY)
Tr.—Brida Dennis J
Own.—Watral Michael
115
Lifetime 41 10 11 4 $738,128
1992 2 0 0 0 $2,820
1991 9 1 2 2 $92,582
Turf 3 0 1 0 $20,262

20Feb92- 8Aqu fst 1$\frac{1}{16}$ ⊡:462 1:121 1:463 Handicap 3 5 58½ 57 49 413½ Pezua J M 116 10.10 61-25 TwthTwst113hdRptdTstmny1224½RglCnst1159 Brk awkwardly 6
9Feb92- 8Aqu fst 6f ⊡:224 :462 1:111 3↑ⓈHoli Hughs H 8 5 54 86 1114 1117½ Chavez J F b 118 21.60 69-25 Argyle Lake114½NorthernCrush1122AllSmarts115¾ Done early 11
9Sep91- 8Bel fm 1 Ⓣ:451 1:082 1:322 3↑Handicap 1 4 56 57 514 519¾ Cruguet J b 115 14.10 80-09 KnownRngr-En1132Forstrdv1244½SftngGld1142½ Broke in air 5
23Aug91- 7Sar fst 1⅛ :48 1:114 1:49 3↑Handicap 1 4 52½ 54½ 46 49¾ Antley C W b 116 8.00 82-14 Zee Best1152 Slavic1172 Montubio-Ar1145¾ Saved ground 5
11Aug91- 9FL fst 1$\frac{1}{16}$:454 1:111 1:442 3↑Farmington H 6 4 46 33½ 32½ 44¼ Whitley K b 122 1.80 91-23 Tafara114hd Mercedes Won1174 Sea Hunter125nk Weakened 7
22Jly91- 8Bel fst 1$\frac{1}{16}$:454 1:10 1:42 3↑ⓈShipman 7 5 41 2hd 2½ 1hd Smith M E b 121 9.40 92-08 Pckett'sLnding121hdZeeBest1219½SHuntr126hd Wide, driving 8
4Jly91- 9FL fst 1$\frac{1}{16}$:46 1:111 1:451 3↑ⓈGen Vly Br H 1 3 36 33 1hd 2¾ Whitley K b 116 4.70 90-18 Sea Hunter122¾Packett'sLanding1161½ZeeBest1238½ Good try 5
23Jun91- 7Bel fst 7f :224 :45 1:204 3↑Alw 41000 1 3 21½ 21½ 33½ 36½ Migliore R b 117 8.70 93-07 Collegian1174LordMrch1172½Pckett'sLnding117¾ Lacked rally 7
8Jun91- 4Bel fst 1$\frac{1}{16}$:454 1:102 1:413 3↑Alw 47000 5 7 76¾ 64¼ 67½ 612¼ Migliore R b 117 6.60 82-08 ChllengeMyDuty1172¼Congelur1171¾SntorToB1224 No factor 8
22May91- 8Bel fst 7f :232 :463 1:224 3↑Alw 41000 6 2 31 1hd 21 24 Migliore R b 119 3.80 86-17 Trskwood1244Pcktt'sLnding1193¾SuchADilmm119no 2nd best 8

Speed Index: Last Race: -14.0 3-Race Avg.: -1.3 6-Race Avg.: -1.0 Overall Avg.: -2.0
LATEST WORKOUTS Feb 27 Bel tr.t 3f fst :354 H Feb 15 Bel tr.t 3f fst :37 B Feb 2 Bel tr.t 3f fst :371 B Jan 29 Bel tr.t 4f fst :482 B

Urgency *

B. g. 6, by Youth—Assurgent, by Damascus
Br.—Sunnyview Farm (NY)
Tr.—Klesaris Robert P
Own.—Nowierski Thomas J
110
Lifetime 50 16 7 7 $143,330
1992 2 1 0 0 $15,000
1991 26 11 6 2 $97,200
Turf 6 2 1 1 $23,606

9Feb92- 8Aqu fst 6f ⊡:224 :462 1:111 3↑ⓈHoli Hughs H 5 10 76 63½ 54 55¾ McCauley W H b 112 5.60e 81-25 Argyle Lake114½ Northern Crush1122AllSmarts115¾ Pnchd st 11
31Jan92- 3Aqu fst 1$\frac{1}{16}$ ⊡:471 1:123 1:453 Clm 50000 7 3 32½ 2½ 12½ 12 McCauley W H b 117 *1.80 80-25 Urgency1172 Jolies Appeal1171¼ Gallant Hitter113nk Driving 7
28Dec91- 1Aqu fst 1$\frac{1}{16}$ ⊡:473 1:124 1:444 3↑Clm c-32500 6 1 11½ 13 18 115½ Velasquez J b 115 *1.30 84-25 Urgncy11515½AdvncngEnsgn1134½RoylNTrbl1173½ Ridden out 7
8Dec91- 7Aqu fst 1$\frac{1}{16}$ ⊡:473 1:124 1:453 3↑Alw 47000 7 1 1½ 21 68¾ 617¼ McCauley W H b 115 4.60 63-30 ⒹMountinLore115noWildAwy1153½MinrlIc1136¾ Used in pace 7
20Nov91- 4Aqu fm 1 Ⓣ:484 1:132 1:364 3↑Clm 50000 1 1 12 1½ 11 11¾ McCauley W H b 117 *2.20 92-11 Urgency1171¾Wnderkin117½Arlen'sVlntin113nk Drifted,driving 8
15Nov91- 4Aqu fst 1 :453 1:094 1:342 3↑Clm c-25000 6 1 1½ 11½ 15 16 McCauley W H b 117 2.80 90-10 Urgency1176 Turning For Home1171 Roman Cat1176 Handily 7
4Nov91- 3Aqu fst 1⅛ :471 1:121 1:51 3↑Clm 25000 1 2 22 32 21½ 21¼ McCauley W H b 117 5.90 80-19 TwotheTwist1171¼Urgency1173GallantHitter1196 Good effort 7
26Oct91- 3Aqu fst 1⅛ :464 1:11 1:492 3↑Clm 25000 2 1 1½ 1½ 2½ 22 McCauley W H b 117 5.80 87-08 GallntHitter1152Urgency1175½A.M.Swinger115nk Second best 8
14Oct91- 3Bel fst 1$\frac{1}{16}$:464 1:12 1:44 3↑Clm 25000 3 1 1½ 1hd 3½ 52¾ McCauley W H b 117 7.80 79-22 RomanCat1191GallntHitter110hdSpceAbove115nk Speed, tired 8
7Oct91- 8Rkmmy 140 :473 1:144 1:46 3↑Alw 12500 5 1 11½ 2hd 21 23 Bermudez J E LBb 116 7.60 61-35 Pic Iron1193 Urgency116¾ Whippoorwilly122½ Weakened 7
7Oct91-Originally scheduled on turf

Speed Index: Last Race: +5.0 3-Race Avg.: +2.3 8-Race Avg.: -0.2 Overall Avg.: +0.7
LATEST WORKOUTS Jan 27 Bel tr.t 5f fst 1:023 H Jan 17 Bel tr.t 4f fst :49 B

Argyle Lake

Dk. b. or br. h. 6, by Talc—Ozona, by Verbatim
Br.—Punk William J (NY)
Tr.—Ferriola Peter
Own.—Riccio James
115
Lifetime 53 13 13 9 $472,070
1992 4 2 1 0 $76,400
1991 14 2 2 2 $110,440

22Feb92- 5Aqu fst 6f ⊡:222 :452 1:103 Alw 41000 4 4 66½ 55 64 24¾ Carr D b 115 3.20 85-16 TrckRebel1154¾ArgyleLke115nkFiftysevenvtt115no Bmpd, rlld 6
9Feb92- 8Aqu fst 6f ⊡:224 :462 1:111 3↑ⓈHoli Hughs H 1 2 65 41½ 31½ 1½ Carr D b 114 6.40e 87-25 Argyle Lake114½ Northern Crush1122 All Smarts115¾ Driving 11
5Feb92- 4Aqu fst 6f ⊡:232 :471 1:122 Clm 50000 6 6 63¾ 53½ 22½ 13¼ Carr D b 117 3.50 81-22 ArgyleLake1173¼ChinaPlesure115nkReppel115nk Wide driving 7
18Jan92- 1Aqu fst 6f ⊡:224 :461 1:113 Clm 70000 3 5 — — — — Carr D b 113 3.30 — — Six Speed117no ClubDeNoche-Ar1132¾MichelleCanPass113nk 7
18Jan92-Clipped heels, lost rider
28Dec91- 8Aqu fst 1$\frac{1}{16}$ ⊡:464 1:123 1:461 3↑ⓈAlex M Robb 5 5 55½ 63¾ 69½ 515 Carr D b 119 15.50 62-25 StudyHard1203¼SeaHunter1222½Carr'sPlesure1122½ Even trip 8
15Dec91- 8Aqu fst 6f ⊡:22 :452 1:104 3↑ⓈJoe Palmer 8 8 84¾ 84¼ 75¾ 87½ McCauley W H b 122 *1.50e 81-19 Shine Please119nk Zee Best1191½ Jesuit1171¾ Poor st, wide 9
5Dec91- 8Aqu fst 170 ⊡:471 1:12 1:431 3↑Alw 47000 4 3 34 33 33½ 22½ McCauley W H b 115 2.70 86-26 FormlDinner1132½ArgyleLk115noDr.Crrington11034 Up for 2nd 5
28Nov91- 8Aqu fst 6f :22 :444 1:091 3↑Sprt Page H 7 4 84½ 96¼ 87 711¼ McCauley W H b 112 23.20 84-19 SenorSpeedy1191Shuttleman1135½GallntStep113nk No factor 9
28Nov91-Grade III
29Sep91- 8Bel fst 7f :23 :453 1:22 3↑ⓈHudson H 4 5 54½ 75¼ 59 611 McCauley W H b 114 11.00e 83-13 D'Prrot1144ShinePls110noHrrVonKninchn1182½ Saved ground 8
9Sep91- 3Bel fst 7f :23 :452 1:224 3↑Clm 70000 3 5 42½ 66 56½ 710¼ McCauley W H b 113 10.90e 80-15 ScottishMonk108nkDrummondLane1134KingofWill1132 Faded 10

Speed Index: Last Race: -13.0 2-Race Avg.: -0.5 2-Race Avg.: -0.5 Overall Avg.: +1.0
LATEST WORKOUTS Feb 20 Aqu ⊡ 4f fst :521 B

G'Day Mate B. h. 9, by Darby Creek Road—Hagleys World, by Hagley
Br.—Chancellor Farm (NY)
Own.—Riccio James Tr.—Ferriola Peter
115 Lifetime 61 14 7 10 $541,246 | 1991 13 4 1 3 $200,157 | 1990 13 2 5 2 $69,920 | Turf 22 5 1 6 $162,929

30Nov91- 7Aqu fst 1⅛ :494 1:134 1:51 3↑Handicap 4 4 32 33 45 412¼ Cordero A Jr 116 3.20 69-27 Crackedbell119hd Zee Best1174¼ Turkey Point1228 Tired 5
11Nov91- 8Aqu sly 1⅛ :463 1:113 1:501 3↑[S]Gen Mcr H 7 8 715 68 41 11¼ McCauley W H 113 3.40e 85-22 G'Day Mate1131¼ Study Hard1095 Zee Best116no Driving 8
30Oct91- 5Aqu fst 1 :492 1:143 1:391 3↑Clm 45000 2 3 32 31 31½ 31¾ McCauley W H 113 *.80 64-41 DimondAnchor113noSylvstrSton1131¾G'DyMt1136 Stead,blckd 5
25Oct91- 4Aqu fst 1⅛ :482 1:123 1:50 3↑Clm 35000 6 7 75 43 31 3hd McCauley W H 117 *1.70 86-14 PocketStreaker117noCallonzo117noG'DyMte117½ Blocked trn 7
22Sep91- 4Bel fm 1 1/16 [T]:473 1:12 1:414 3↑Clm 45000 3 5 411 75¾ 45 58¼ McCauley W H 113 7.30 81-16 SpruceBaby1131Wanderkin1195RoyalNinj117nk Pinched start 8
22Sep91-Placed fourth through disqualification
9Sep91- 3Bel fst 7f :23 :452 1:224 3↑Clm 70000 6 7 97¼ 810 67 58¼ Toscano P R 113 10.90e 82-15 ScottishMonk108nkDrummondLn1134KngofWll1132 No threat 10
17May91- 8Bel fst 1 :464 1:11 1:361 3↑Handicap 2 5 54½ 56½ 513 521¼ Samyn J L 115 8.70 68-14 FarewellWave114noSoundofCannons1164¾Rhythm1225 Outrun 5
6May91- 8Aqu sly 1⅛ :482 1:12 1:51 3↑[S]Kingston 5 5 51¾ 55½ 44½ 49¾ McCauley W H 123 2.50 71-23 Fast 'N' Gold126hd Zee Best123¾ KoalaRoad1099 Lacked rally 5
6May91-Originally scheduled on turf
24Apr91- 8Aqu gd 1 :47 1:121 1:372 3↑Handicap 3 4 45 41 2hd 2hd Samyn J L 116 3.80 75-33 HrrVonKninchn119hdG'DyMt1167TrundBlu1223 Wide, gamely 4
23Mar91- 7Aqu gd 1⅛ :48 1:124 1:513 Alw 47000 3 6 64¾ 54½ 1½ 1no Cordero A Jr 115 2.70 78-30 G'DyMte115noPssN'Cll115¾PocketStreker1152¼ Pinched back 7

Speed Index: Last Race: –4.0 3–Race Avg.: +2.6 8–Race Avg.: 0.0 Overall Avg.: –0.6
LATEST WORKOUTS Feb 27 Aqu [•] 3f fst :383 B Feb 20 Aqu [•] 3f fst :39 B Feb 10 Aqu [•] 3f fst :381 B Feb 7 Aqu [•] 4f fst :54 B

Packett's Landing was a big price in the Kings Point Handicap, a race with five betting interests. This state of affairs was easily explained by his dismal effort against most of them, including the winner, Argyle Lake, in the six-furlong Hollie Hughes on February 9.

But Argyle Lake was primarily a sprinter, while Packett's Landing was at his best in routes, judging from the latter's win and second-place finish in two starts against New York–bred routers the previous July. The Hollie Hughes had been the first race for Packett's Landing in five months. After that race, he stretched to a route against open company and broke awkwardly on February 20. A week later, he picked up the tempo of his three-furlong workouts, going a handy :35⅘ as compared with two previous breezes of :37 and :37⅕. The Kings Point would be his first stakes opportunity against New York–bred routers since returning from the layoff, and it was almost certainly the spot that Dennis Brida had circled on his calendar weeks in advance.

EIGHTH RACE
Aqueduct
MARCH 1, 1992

1 1/16 MILES.(InnerDirt). (1.413) 12th Running THE KINGS POINT HANDICAP. Purse $75,000 added. 3-year-olds and upward, foaled in New York State and approved by the New York State-Bred Registry. By subscription of $150 each, which should accompany the nomination; $600 to pass the entry box, $600 to start, with $75,000 added. The added money and all fees to be divided 60% to the winner, 22% to second, 12% to third and 6% to fourth. Weights, Tuesday, February 25. Starters to be named at the closing time of entries. A trophy will be presented to the winning owner. Closed Wednesday, February 12 with 22 nominations.

Value of race $85,500; value to winner $51,300; second $18,810; third $10,260; fourth $5,130. Mutuel pool $313,313.

Last Raced	Horse	M/Eqt.A.Wt	PP	St	¼	½	¾	Str	Fin	Jockey	Odds $1
20Feb92 8Aqu4	Packett's Landing	b 6 115	3	3	12	12	11½	12	13¾	Pezua J M	7.80
9Feb92 8Aqu5	Urgency	b 6 112	4	4	26	25	23½	22½	2½	McCauley W H	1.50
9Feb92 8Aqu8	Herr Von Kaninchen	7 114	1	2	53	55	41	3½	3½	Smith M E	4.50
22Feb92 5Aqu2	Argyle Lake	b 6 115	5	5	45	42½	31½	48	46	Carr D	a-1.70
30Nov91 7Aqu4	G'Day Mate	9 115	6	6	6	6	6	512	5	Samyn J L	a-1.70
9Feb92 8Aqu4	Crafty Alfel	4 113	2	1	31	3½	52½	6	—	Antley C W	5.40

Crafty Alfel, Eased.
a-Coupled: Argyle Lake and G'Day Mate.

OFF AT 4:16 Start good Won driving Time, :23 2/5, :47 , 1:12 , 1:38 3/5, 1:45 2/5 Track fast.

$2 Mutuel Prices:				
	4-(C)-PACKETT'S LANDING	17.60	4.80	3.20
	5-(D)-URGENCY		3.60	2.60
	2-(A)-HERR VON KANINCHEN			3.00

B. g, by Bates Motel—Lightning Bug, by Cornish Prince. Trainer Brida Dennis J. Bred by Free F William (NY).

PACKETT'S LANDING, hustled away from the gate, outsprinted rivals for the early advantage, set a brisk pace while saving ground for five furlongs, was given a bit of a breather midway on the turn, repulsed a mild challenge from URGENCY at the top of the stretch and drew off under brisk urging. URGENCY settled just behind the winner for six furlongs, lodged a mild rally from outside to threaten on the turn but was no match for PACKETT'S LANDING while holding for the place. HERR VON KANINCHEN, outrun for six furlongs while saving ground, failed to threaten with a mild late rally along the inside. ARGYLE LAKE, allowed to settle early, lodged a mild rally from outside on the turn but couldn't sustain his bid. G'DAY MATE never reached contention. CRAFTY ALFEL faded after going five furlongs and was eased late.

Owners— 1, Watral Michael; 2, Nowierski Thomas J; 3, McNulty David P; 4, Riccio James; 5, Riccio James; 6, Lippert Albert.

Trainers— 1, Brida Dennis J; 2, Klesaris Robert P; 3, Schaeffer Stephen W; 4, Ferriola Peter; 5, Ferriola Peter; 6, Iselin James H.

Overweight: Urgency 2 pounds; Crafty Alfel 2.

$2 Daily Double 8–4 Paid $121.20 Daily Double Pool $207,025

In his remarkably insightful postrace comments (trainers usually offer vanilla-flavored quotes no matter what you ask them and no matter how their horse ran), Brida gave a handicapping lesson about stable intent: "I knew he would be fit today. He had his six furlong race — that was really just a workout. We were trying with him, but he's not a six-furlong horse. He was short for the mile-and-a-sixteenth race . . . but he needed that race. We were pointing for this race all along. He has his problems, he's older now, but he has class. It's nice to be a two-time winner of the race."

Two-time winner?

Packett's Landing — **B. g. 4, by Bates Motel—Lightning Bug, by Cornish Prince**
Br.—Free F William (NY)
Own.—Watral M — **Tr.—Brida Dennis J** — **121**

Lifetime							
27 9 9 2	1990	9	2	3	1	$173,615
$619,363	1989	16	7	5	1	$442,891
	Turf	2	0	1	0	$20,262

9Sep90- 7Bel fst 1 1/16 :45 2/5 1:09 3/5 1:40 3/5 3+ [R]Reg 7 Fin14 2 1 1½ 1^hd 2^3 2^8 Santos J A b 126 *1.20 91-11 SnshnJmm122^8Pctt'sLndng126^4Tnchn'sPrnc126^nk Held place 4
25Aug90- 7Sar sf 1 1/16 (T):48 3/5 1:13 4/5 1:46 3+ Sar Bd Cp H 5 3 3^2 8^5½ 8^11 8^20½ Rogers K L b 113 17.20 45-27 Who's to Pay113^nk Jalaajel115^6 Caltech120^2¼ Thur after 1/2 8
25Aug90-Grade III
30Jly90- 8Bel fst 1 1/16 :45 2/5 1:10 2/5 1:43 3+ [S]EvanShipman 6 3 3½ 2½ 2½ 3^1 Rogers K L b 126 *2.80 86-20 TnchnsPrnc121½HrrVnKnnchn121½PcttsLndn126^hd Weakened 8
8Jly90- 9FL fst 1 1/16 :46 2/5 1:10 3/5 1:44 1/5 3+ [S]Genesee H 5 5 5^5½ 3^4½ 2^hd 2^nk McCarthy M J b 126 *.60 97-18 HrrVonKnnchn116^nkPcktt'sLndng126^6½SHntr115^nk Top effort 7
17Jun90- 9Rkm fst 1 1/16 :47 1:11 4/5 1:45 2/5 3+ Father Day H 8 2 1^1½ 1^2 1^4 1^4¼ Migliore R b 114 7.70 92-29 Pcktt'sLnding114^4¼Lv!tB113^1¾Complct116^3¼ Slow start, drvg 9
7May90- 8Aqu yl 1 1/8 (T):49 2/5 1:14 4/5 1:54 3/5 3+ [S]Kingston 5 2 2½ 1^hd 1^hd 2^2¾ Velasquez J b 123 2.20 75-22 Kt'sVlntin119^2¾Pcktt'sLnding123^nkCtchThMoon126^no Gamely 9
14Apr90-11Pim fst 1 1/8 :46 1:10 1/5 1:50 4/5 3+ J Campel H 3 3 4^4½ 5^4 4^4½ 4^8¾ Barrera C b 112 10.40 73-23 Jet Stream114^4¾ Flaming Emperor113^nk Silano115^3¾ Wide 8
14Apr90-Grade III
4Mar90- 8Aqu fst 1 1/16 [•]:47 1/5 1:12 1/5 1:44 2/5 3+ [S]Kings Pt H 2 1 1^1½ 1^hd 1^2 1^2½ Velasquez J b 124 *1.30 86-27 Packett'sLnding124^2½Whodm122^5NovelNshu110^no Ridden out 9
10Feb90-10Lrl sly 1 1/8 :46 3/5 1:11 3/5 1:51 4/5 3+ Nat Dancer H 7 3 3½ 3^1½ 4^3 6^5½ Prado E S b 114 4.80 76-22 FlmngEmpror114^1¾Bldsk'sChc112^2¼OvrnghtHr111½ Weakened 9
30Dec89- 8Aqu fst 1 1/16 [•]:48 1/5 1:13 4/5 1:46 4/5 3+ [S]Alex M Robb 5 3 3^3 4^2 1½ 1^1 Santos J A b 124 3.60 75-31 Packett's Landing124^1 DiamondAnchor117^nkBert113^3 Driving 10

Speed Index: Last Race: (—) 3–Race Avg.: (—) 12–Race Avg.: (—) Overall Avg.: +2.6

LATEST WORKOUTS Sep 22 Sar tr.t 3f fst :36 3/5 B ●Sep 4 Sar tr.t 3f fst :36 2/5 H Aug 18 Sar 4f fst :48 2/5 H Aug 13 Sar 5f fst 1:01 1/5 H

Packett's Landing was the leading money earner in the 1992 Kings Point field by a fairly wide margin — thanks in part to a wire-to-wire victory in the same race two years before.

TRAINERS

The influence of trainers should never be underestimated by handicappers. After all, they're the ones calling the shots.

Competent trainers will do whatever they can to nurture and encourage the best qualities of their horses, often going to great lengths to orchestrate a revival of circumstances that previously led to peak condition and performance. But as with any other field of expertise, trainers bring varying amounts of competence to their profession, and we shouldn't make the mistake of assuming all of them know what they're doing, for that is hardly the case.

Furthermore, it's only natural that some trainers will, over the course of their careers, develop preferred methods of bringing their horses to peak condition. As a result, some trainers will tend to do better with specific kinds of horses: some will concentrate primarily on developing two-year-old sprinters, while others may take a more patient approach and do their best work with late-maturing types that perform to their fullest potential in route races. Some trainers will make their livings by patching up veteran claiming horses, and others will make national headlines by conditioning the highest-class horses of the day.

And within each of these categories there are subsets: one claiming trainer, for example, may excel with horses moving up the class ladder; another may win only when he drops one of his horses in class.

These trainer patterns are nothing new, although the recent mass availability of speed figures has removed them from the mainstream somewhat. Reliable trainers such as Allen Jerkens often produce patterns that hold up season after season.

Consider these excerpts from Andy Beyer's first book, *Picking Winners,* published in 1975:

> During the 1972 meeting at Saratoga Steve Davidowitz and I were astounded and confounded by the training of Allen Jerkens. . . .

> When his horses seemed to figure best, they lost. When they figured second- or third-best, they would win. . . . I took all of the *Racing Forms* from the previous season and tried to analyze his performance carefully. I listed all his winners and beaten favorites . . . there was one pattern that fit eighteen of his nineteen winners. Jerkens' winners either had raced within the last eight days, or else showed a recent workout so fast it left no doubt about their current condition. . . . In 1973 at Saratoga Jerkens was the leading trainer of the meeting again and almost all his winners fit the pattern. But there was one glaring exception. His sprinter Onion had been laid off for more than two months, showed a succession of indifferent workouts . . . but won big, setting a track record. A few days after his victory I was interviewing Jerkens for a newspaper story and couldn't resist trying to learn why Onion had contradicted his pattern.
>
> "I did a lot of homework on your training methods and thought I found a pattern that was pretty reliable," I said, "but Onion didn't fit it."
>
> "I don't have any pattern," Jerkens answered, explaining that every horse is an individual, and a good horseman has to treat him as an individual instead of operating with some preconceived formula.
>
> "I guess you're right," I conceded. "According to my research, Onion should have had a very fast workout before he ran."
>
> Jerkens said, "He did. Two days before the race, on Sunday, he worked a half-mile in forty-six flat on the training track. The clockers missed it."

In *Betting Thoroughbreds,* published in 1977, Steve Davidowitz wrote, "What does Allen Jerkens do with an improving horse? Move it up in company as soon as possible. Or stretch it out in distance . . ."

Onion, it may be remembered, stretched out following his sprint-win at Saratoga opening week to upset Secretariat in the nine-furlong Whitney Handicap.

Nearly two decades later, Jerkens continues to stretch horses out successfully, often at good mutuels. I was painfully reminded of this fact immediately after the running of Aqueduct's fifth race on December 19, 1992, when I made a prime bet on a 10–1 shot named Appointee, an explosive horse in terms of a figure pattern, only to watch in dismay as the Jerkens-trained Autoroute accelerated away from him to win decisively:

FIFTH RACE
Aqueduct
DECEMBER 19, 1992

$1\frac{1}{16}$ MILES.(InnerDirt). (1.41^{3}) CLAIMING. Purse $25,000. 3-year-olds. Weight, 122 lbs. Non-winners of two races at a mile or over since December 1 allowed 3 lbs. Of such a race since then, 5 lbs. Claiming price $50,000; for each $2,500 to $45,000 allowed 2 lbs. (Races when entered to be claimed for $40,000 or less not considered).

Value of race $25,000; value to winner $15,000; second $5,500; third $3,000; fourth $1,500. Mutuel pool $246,505. Exacta Pool $537,148

Last Raced	Horse	M/Eqt.	A.	Wt	PP	St	¼	½	¾	Str	Fin	Jockey	Cl'g Pr	Odds $1
20Oct92 ^{9}Med^{6}	Autoroute		3	115	4	2	$3^{2\frac12}$	$3^{\frac12}$	$2^{\frac12}$	2^{4}	$1^{3\frac14}$	Chavez J F	47500	6.70
30Nov92 ^{9}Aqu^{7}	Appointee	b	3	117	6	3	4^{hd}	4^{1}	$4^{1\frac12}$	1^{hd}	$2^{4\frac34}$	Bruin J E	50000	10.40
25Nov92 ^{7}Aqu^{3}	Danzig's Dance	b	3	117	10	7	6^{5}	6^{5}	5^{hd}	4^{1}	3^{nk}	Romero R P	50000	5.90
9Dec92 ^{4}Aqu^{5}	Lord Wollaston	b	3	108	9	6	$5^{1\frac12}$	5^{hd}	6^{hd}	3^{hd}	$4^{1\frac34}$	Bisono C V^{5}	45000	17.60
9Dec92 ^{4}Aqu^{1}	Complinim	b	3	113	3	8	8^{3}	$7^{\frac12}$	7^{3}	5^{hd}	$5^{1\frac14}$	Pezua J M	45000	3.20
2Nov92 ^{7}Aqu^{1}	Talc About Joe		3	113	1	1	7^{hd}	$8^{4\frac12}$	8^{6}	7^{6}	$6^{2\frac34}$	MrquezCHJr	45000	8.90
4Dec92 ^{1}Aqu^{2}	Songrider	b	3	113	11	4	2^{2}	$2^{2\frac12}$	$1^{\frac12}$	$6^{\frac12}$	$7^{1\frac14}$	Madrid A Jr	45000	7.60
7Dec92 ^{6}Aqu^{10}	High Tier	b	3	117	2	11	11	11	11	9^{3}	8^{2}	Lovato F Jr	50000	33.10
29Nov92 ^{2}Aqu^{4}	Lead Til Dawn	b	3	113	5	10	10^{5}	9^{hd}	9^{2}	$8^{\frac12}$	9^{6}	Samyn J L	45000	15.20
7Dec92 ^{6}Aqu^{6}	Norphlet	b	3	117	8	9	9^{hd}	10^{5}	10^{3}	$10^{\frac12}$	$10^{5\frac12}$	Davis R G	50000	4.00
4Dec92 ^{1}Aqu^{7}	Step Out Front	b	3	113	7	5	$1^{\frac12}$	1^{1}	3^{hd}	11	11	Velazquez JR	45000	18.00

OFF AT 2:21 Start good. Won driving. Time, :22^{4}, :46^{3}, 1:09^{4}, 1:34^{4}, 1:41 Track fast.

NEW TRACK RECORD

$2 Mutuel Prices:				
	5-(D)-AUTOROUTE	15.40	8.40	6.80
	1-(F)-APPOINTEE		10.40	7.20
	10-(K)-DANZIG'S DANCE			4.80

$2 EXACTA 5-1 PAID $133.20

Ch. c, (Feb), by Crafty Prospector—Viscera, by Viceregal. Trainer Jerkens H Allen. Bred by Mack Earle I (Fla).

AUTOROUTE away in good order to race just off the early leaders, began moving on the far turn to hold the edge into the lane, was joined by APPOINTEE with three sixteenths remaining, then drew off the final furlong to prove best. APPOINTEE saved ground, was boxed in briefly on the far turn, eased out three wide for the drive to dispute the lead with AUTOROUTE, then could not go with that one late while best of the rest. DANZIG'S DANCE rallied mildly. LORD WOLLASTON went fairly evenly. COMPLINIM had no rally. TALC ABOUT JOE was never prominent. SONGRIDER on the pace early, moved to a short and brief advantage on the far turn, then could not stay. HIGH TIER was outrun, as was LEAD TIL DAWN. NORPHLET showed little. STEP OUT FRONT sent to the front, tired badly on the far turn. AUTOROUTE and LORD WOLLASTON raced with mud caulks.

Owners— 1, Mack Earle I; 2, Greentree Stable; 3, Green Beverly; 4, Jilerlane Stable; 5, Cuomo Michael; 6, Camuti Thomas E; 7, Meyers Gerald J; 8, Atrium Racing Stable; 9, Ritzenberg Milton; 10, Ackerley Leland; 11, Watral Michael.

Trainers— 1, Jerkens H Allen; 2, Badgett William Jr; 3, Mott William I; 4, Peitz Daniel C; 5, Levine Bruce N; 6, Ferriola Peter; 7, Schosberg Richard; 8, Marini Thomas; 9, Johnstone Bruce; 10, Lake Robert P; 11, Brida Dennis J.

Complinim was claimed by Hauman Eugene E; trainer, Hushion Michael E; Norphlet was claimed by Jewel-E Stable; trainer, Ferriola Peter.

Scratched—Louie Vee (4Dec92 ^{1}Aqu^{5}).

Appointee had been by far the best of the others, nearly five lengths clear of the third-place finisher, but was no match for Autoroute, who lowered the track record for a mile and a sixteenth by three-fifths of a second. Autoroute's past performances appeared this way on the day he exploded:

Autoroute — Ch. c. 3(Feb), by Crafty Prospector—Viscera, by Viceregal
CHAVEZ J F (57 8 9 10 .14) — $47,500 — Br.—Mack Earle I (Fla)
Own.—Mack Earle I — Tr.—Jerkens H Allen (9 1 1 1 .11) — 115
Lifetime 10 2 1 1 $41,840 — 1992 10 2 1 1 $41,840 — 1991 0 M 0 0

20Oct92- 9Med	fst	6f	:221	:45	1:094	3+Alw 17000	51	1	5	1hd	31½	57½	614¼	Rojas R I	119	*1.10	80-08	The Great M. B.113¾OneBigHug1135WildDante113	Tired 6
2Oct92- 1Bel	fst	6f	:23	:461	1:103	3+Alw 27000	90	1	1	1½	11	12½	13¼	Rojas R I	114	8.00	87-22	Autoroute1143¼ Otto Beit114nk Uwillbking119	Driving 7
23Sep92- 7Bel	fst	7f	:23	:46	1:232	3+Alw 27000	71	2	2	1½	1½	31½	56	Rojas R I	113	4.90	81-14	PrvtTrsrr1181¾TrmptTngd1153½FrngFn113	Used in pace 6
22Aug92- 1Sar	fst	6f	:222	:452	1:091	3+Alw 27000	66	2	7	76½	73¾	75¾	611½	Smith M E	112	*1.50	87 —	CptnBr1123½IslndPrspct1123½FrnFn117	Broke thru gate 7
29Jly92- 7Sar	fst	6f	:221	:45	1:094	3+Alw 27000	82	3	2	1½	1½	11½	21¾	Smith M E	112	2.40	93-07	Slw'sGhost1131¾Autorot1121IslndProspct111	Weakened 7
17Jly92- 5Bel	fst	7f	:231	:46	1:23	3+Alw 27000	84	5	1	2½	1hd	2hd	32¾	Smith M E	111	8.00	86-12	Izata Fact112¾ Arrendajo1112 Autoroute111	Bid,wknd 7
3Jly92- 6Bel	fst	1$\frac{1}{16}$	:453	1:10	1:422	3+Alw 29000	73	1	1	11½	1hd	43	48½	Smith M E	111	7.70	81-13	CostTooMuch1111¾Ghzi1111¾BlueSquir111	Speed, tired 7
12Jun92- 7Bel	fst	7f	:222	:453	1:232	Alw 27000	63	6	1	3½	3½	65½	614½	Antley C W	119	*2.10	72-14	Norphlet111hdNewDel1176WinThPc117	Frcd pace, tired 6
4May92- 3Aqu	fst	6f	:221	:46	1:103	Md Sp Wt	97	9	1	2hd	1½	11½	12¾	Antley C W	122	3.70	88-11	Autorout1222¾SrtogFvr1226PromnntProspct122	Driving 9
18Jan92- 5GP	fst	6f	:221	:454	1:114	Md Sp Wt	53	9	4	1½	1½	3½	68¼	Fires E	120	14.50	76-14	Splinter Red1201 To You1203King'sCode120	Weakened 12

LATEST WORKOUTS Dec 15 Bel tr.t 1 fst 1:47 B — Dec 7 Bel tr.t 1 fst 1:462 B — Nov 29 Bel tr.t 1 fst 1:464 B — Nov 21 Bel tr.t 1 fst 1:48 B

Autoroute continued to develop as a router, repeating in a nonwinners-of-two allowance January 24, placing at the nonwinners-of-three level the start after that, and advancing through that condition on April 15. He returned to the inner track first time back from a layoff on January 5, 1994, and promptly won a classified allowance by ten lengths:

Autoroute — Own: Mack Earle I
Ch. h. 5
Sire: Crafty Prospector (Mr. Prospector)
Dam: Viscera (Viceregal)
Br: Mack Earle I (Fla)
Tr: Jerkens H Allen (25 7 3 4 .28) — 122

Lifetime Record:	15 6 2 1	$126,200			
1994	1 1 0 0	$24,000	Turf	0 0 0 0	
1993	3 2 1 0	$45,360	Wet	0 0 0 0	
Aqu ⊡	4 3 1 0	$64,860	Dist	3 2 0 0	$40,740

5Jan94- 6Aqu	fst	1$\frac{1}{16}$ ⊡	:232	:48	1:124	1:444	Alw 40000	107	1	2	2½	2hd	14	110	Leon F5	110	*1.10	81-24	Autoroute11010 Island Edition1154½ Land Grant1151¼	Driving 5
15Apr93- 8Aqu	fst	1	:233	:461	1:10	1:344 3+	Alw 32500N3X	103	4	2	1½	11	12	12	Chavez J F	117	3.00	90-18	Autoroute1172 Snappy Landing117nk Cool As Crystal1195½	Ridden out 5
20Feb93- 1Aqu	fst	1⅛ ⊡	:483	1:132	1:391	1:522	Alw 33000N3X	95	6	2	2½	2hd	2hd	2hd	Chavez J F	119	3.70	81-24	Hudlam's Sidekick117hd Autoroute119no Eastern Brave119¾	Gamely 6
24Jan93- 7Aqu	fst	1⅛ ⊡	:474	1:123	1:383	1:522	Alw 31000N2X	97	3	2	1½	1½	21½	1no	Chavez J F	117	*1.30	81-24	Autoroute117no Complinim1171¾ Hope Us112nk	Driving 8
19Dec92- 5Aqu	fst	1$\frac{1}{16}$ ⊡	:224	:463	1:094	1:41	Clm 47500	101	4	3	33½	2½	2hd	13¼	Chavez J F	115	6.70	103-05	Autoroute1153¼ Appointee1174¾ Danzig's Dance117nk	Driving 11
20Oct92- 9Med	fst	6f	:221	:45	:571	1:094 3+	Alw 17000	51	1	5	1hd	31½	57½	614¼	Rojas R I	119	*1.10	80-08	The Great M. B.113¾ One Big Hug1135 Wild Dante113	Tired 6
2Oct92- 1Bel	fst	6f	:23	:461	:58	1:103 3+	Alw 27000	92	1	1	1½	11	12½	13¼	Rojas R I	114	8.00	87-22	Autoroute1143¼ Otto Beit114nk Uwillbking119	Driving 7
23Sep92- 7Bel	fst	7f	:23	:46	1:102	1:232 3+	Alw 27000	71	2	2	1½	1½	31½	56	Rojas R I	113	4.90	81-14	PrivteTresurer1181¾ TrumpetTongued1153½ FrezingFun113	Used in pace 6
22Aug92- 1Sar	fst	6f	:222	:452	:571	1:091 3+	Alw 27000	66	2	7	76½	73¾	75¾	611½	Smith M E	112	*1.50	87 —	Captain Bear1123½ IslandProspect1123½ FreezingFun117	Broke thru gate 7
29Jly92- 7Sar	fst	6f	:221	:45	:571	1:094 3+	Alw 27000	81	3	2	1½	1½	11½	21¾	Smith M E	112	2.40	93-07	Slew's Ghost1131¾ Autoroute1121 Island Prospect111	Weakened 7

WORKOUTS: Jan 3 Bel tr.t 4f fst :50 B 17/44 Dec 24 Bel tr.t 7f fst 1:30 B 1/2 Dec 8 Bel tr.t 6f fst 1:16 B 3/9 Dec 4 Bel tr.t 4f fst :514 B 43/51 Nov 20 Bel tr.t 7f fst 1:29 B 1/2 ●Nov 17 Bel tr.t 6f fst 1:15 B 1/6

Appointee's defeat stung especially hard, for, in addition to a win bet, I had used him underneath the first three betting favorites in exacta savers, but not with Autoroute. I vowed never again to underestimate the chances of an Allen Jerkens–trained horse that was stretching out in distance. As things turned out, this outlook was not to be fully rewarded for more than a year:

Aqueduct

5 — *1$\frac{1}{16}$ MILES.* **(Inner Dirt). (1:41) ALLOWANCE. Purse $30,000. 4–year–olds and upward which have not won two races other than maiden, claiming or starter. Weight, 122 lbs. Non–winners of a race other than maiden or claiming at a mile or over since Janaury 1, allowed 3 lbs. Of such a race since December 15, 5 lbs.**

Coupled – Sailing On Aprayer and Charming Buck

Sorabosia — Own: Hackel Kenneth S
Ch. g. 4
Sire: It's Freezing (T. V. Commercial)
Dam: Majestic Empress (Majestic Prince)
Br: Driver Monica M (NY)
LEON F (139 22 19 18 .16) — Tr: Lenzini John J Jr (14 1 3 2 .07) — 112⁵

Lifetime Record:	9 2 1 0	$45,370			
1993	9 2 1 0	$45,370	Turf	0 0 0 0	
1992	0 M 0 0		Wet	1 0 1 0	$6,160
Aqu ⊡	4 0 0 0	$4,800	Dist	2 0 0 0	$1,920

26Dec93- 7Aqu	fst	1$\frac{1}{16}$ ⊡	:232	:47	1:121	1:47 3+	Alw 32000N2X	61	6	5	67½	711	718	619¼	Chavez J F	115 b	12.30	51-30	Tanako115½ Won Song115no Riskabit1173	Outrun 8
17Dec93- 7Aqu	fst	170 ⊡	:234	:474	1:124	1:432 3+	Alw 32000N2X	79	8	8	99½	84½	76¾	45¾	Chavez J F	115 b	13.40	79-27	Jim's Best Boy1171 Electrojet117nk Drawpoint1154½	Wide 9
20Nov93- 8Aqu	fst	1	:223	:454	1:113	1:384	[S]Jsph A Gimma60k	69	3	6	68	65¾	78½	715½	Chavez J F	113 b	29.70	54-45	Itaka1195½ Koluctoo Jimmy Al122½ Corma Ray113½	Bobbled break 8
23Oct93- 6Aqu	fst	1⅛	:491	1:15	1:404	1:534 3+	[S]Alw 30000N1X	73	7	4	55½	31	1½	11¼	Chavez J F	114 b	*.90	67-33	Sorabosia1141¼ Duel Zone1172¾ Twice The Debt1148	Driving 8
3Oct93- 9Bel	my	7f	:223	:462	1:122	1:251 3+	[S]Alw 28000N1X	75	11	6	89	75½	2½	2nk	Smith M E	116 b	14.20	77-23	Cinco Rey114nk Sorabosia1164 Newyork Appeal1172½	Sharp try 11
6Sep93- 6Bel	fst	7f	:23	:462	1:122	1:254 3+	[S]Md Sp Wt	66	10	5	42	41½	11	11	Perret C	118 b	8.00	74-19	Sorabosia1181 Sweet Ralph1183 Ti Dye1182½	Wide, driving 13
18Aug93- 3Sar	gd	6f	:222	:454	:58	1:102 3+	[S]Md Sp Wt	56	8	6	44	43½	43½	47½	Santos J A	117 b	7.10	83-08	Charlie Kenny Sr.117½ Ti Dye1174 Dacotah Brave1172¾	Four wide 9
21Jan93- 3Aqu	fst	6f ⊡	:234	:481	1:003	1:133	[S]Md Sp Wt	42	7	8	42½	31	34	47½	Antley C W	122 b	*.70	68-19	Current Impact1172½ Dernier's Lass1224 Sweet Ralph1221	Lacked rally 10
8Jan93- 9Aqu	fst	6f ⊡	:231	:47	:593	1:123	[S]Md Sp Wt	59	3	12	1012	99½	66½	42½	Nelson D	122	3.30	78-15	Chocolate Soldier117nk Jager1222 Son Of A Blum122no	Some gain 12

WORKOUTS: Jan 13 Aqu ⊡ 4f fst :494 H 1/1 Jan 7 Aqu ⊡ 3f fst :37 B 2/8 Dec 1 Aqu ⊡ 5f fst 1:031 B 3/5 Nov 10 Aqu 5f fst 1:043 B 3/3 Nov 3 Aqu 3f fst :382 B 2/4

Rohwer

Own: Garren Murray M

LUZZI M J (93 16 7 7 .17)

Ch. c. 4
Sire: Vanlandingham (Cox's Ridge)
Dam: Babe's Joy (King of the Sea)
Br: Guscotts & Loblolly & Needham/Betz (Ky)
Tr: Garren Murray M (27 1 3 2 .04)

117

Lifetime Record:	22	3	4	5	$141,051						
1994	1	0	1	0	$6,600	Turf	0	0	0	0	
1993	12	1	1	2	$56,203	Wet	3	1	0	0	$16,020
Aqu ⊡	13	1	3	3	$95,391	Dist	11	1	2	3	$88,791

6Jan94-5Aqu	fst	1⅛ ⊡	:483 1:134 1:403 1:532	Alw 30000N2X	87 2 2 11 11 1hd 2½	Rodriguez R R5	112	7.80	68-32	Nowsthetimetoshine117½ Rohwer112nk Charming Buck1175	Good try	6
26Dec93-7Aqu	fst	1 1/16 ⊡	:232 :47 1:121 1:47	3↑ Alw 32000N2X	74 8 2 2hd 42 58¾ 511½	Rodriguez R R5	110	25.20	58-30	Tanako115½ Won Song115no Riskabit1173	Tired	8
17Dec93-7Aqu	fst	1 70 ⊡	:234 :474 1:124 1:432	3↑ Alw 32000N2X	63 4 4 87½ 95¼ 910 914¾	Davis R G	115 f	4.30	70-27	Jim's Best Boy1171 Electrojet117nk Drawpoint1154½	Outrun	9
2Dec93-8Aqu	fst	1 1/16 ⊡	:241 :491 1:134 1:45	3↑ Alw 32000N2X	72 8 2 21 53 58½ 513¼	Luttrell M G5	110	8.80	67-23	Dancing Hunter1154½ Stop And Listen115½ Drawpoint1155½	Tired	8
24Nov93-7Aqu	fst	6f	:222 :46 1:112	3↑ Alw 30000N2X	56 7 5 66 79 710 713¾	Chavez J F	115 f	13.00	71-20	Richmond Runner1203 Lukie's Pop1151 Line Pro120½	Outrun	7
17Apr93-10Aqu	wf	1⅛	:464 1:103 1:352 1:482	Wood Mem-G1	70 4 12 1212 127¾ 119¾ 1117½	Chavez J F	126	58.90	76-05	Storm Tower1262 Tossofthecoin126¾ Marked Tree126½	Pinched brk	12
3Apr93-9Aqu	gd	1	:232 :461 1:103 1:361	Gotham-G2	64 2 6 75½ 74½ 79½ 719½	Madrid A Jr	118	18.40	63-21	As Indicated114nk Itaka1141¼ Strolling Along121nk	No factor	8
7Mar93-7Aqu	fst	1 1/16 ⊡	:241 :471 1:104 1:421	Sttle Slew50k	80 4 4 43 43 37½ 310¼	Chavez J F	117	2.40	84-10	Lord Beer117nk Ozan11710 Rohwer117½	Lacked rally	5
20Feb93-8Aqu	fst	1 1/16 ⊡	:24 :483 1:131 1:451	Whrlwy B C100k	94 3 2 31½ 1½ 2hd 23	Chavez J F	114	24.90	76-24	Prairie Bayou1173 Rohwer1143 Slews Gold1147	Second best	5
3Feb93-6Aqu	fst	1 70 ⊡	:244 :492 1:141 1:434	Alw 29000N1X	87 5 1 1hd 1hd 12 14	Davis R G	117	*1.40	83-22	Rohwer1174 Mango Man1173¾ Dam Handsome112hd	Mild drive	7

WORKOUTS: Jan 3 Bel tr.t 3f fst :36 B *2/14* Dec 24 Bel tr.t 3f fst :371 B *8/51* Dec 10 Bel tr.t 4f fst :483 B *6/54* Nov 19 Bel tr.t 5f fst 1:024 B *3/9* Nov 15 Bel tr.t 6f fst 1:17 B *2/2* ●Nov 9 Bel tr.t 5f fst 1:002 H *1/13*

Badger Bane

Own: Yanofsky Howard

RYAN K (3 0 0 1 .00)

Dk. b or br c. 4
Sire: Badger Land (Codex)
Dam: Urbane Manner (Northern Bay)
Br: Muirhead Mrs Alastair L (NC)
Tr: Yanofsky Howard (2 0 0 1 .00)

117

Lifetime Record:	23	6	6	1	$78,950						
1994	1	0	0	0		Turf	0	0	0	0	
1993	16	4	5	1	$66,080	Wet	2	1	0	0	$9,900
Aqu ⊡	1	0	0	0		Dist	13	4	4	0	$53,302

Entered 15Jan94- 8 PHA

6Jan94-5Aqu	fst	1⅛ ⊡	:483 1:134 1:403 1:532	Alw 30000N2X	76 6 6 43½ 44 56½ 57½	Ryan K	117 b	9.00	61-32	Nowsthetimetoshine117½ Rohwer112nk Charming Buck1175	No rally	6
12Dec93-8Pha	fst	1 70	:231 :464 1:12 1:422	Flintlock35k	70 2 5 69¾ 510 59¾ 511½	Ryan K	L 115 b	11.20	72-13	High Ranker115¾ Tri For The Gold1171 Quality Ruler1154½	Outrun	6
29Nov93-9Pha	gd	1 70	:231 :47 1:114 1:424	3↑ Alw 19000N2X	84 8 4 31½ 41½ 31½ 22½	Ryan K	L 118 b	*1.30	79-26	Jungle Combat1182½ Badger Bane1181½ Gan1182½	No match	9
19Nov93-9Pha	fst	1 1/16	:234 :483 1:14 1:481	3↑ Alw 19000N2X	80 1 8 84½ 75¼ 24 21¼	Ryan K	L 118 b	*.90	67-44	Mymamma'safox1161¼ Badger Bane1185½ Quoddy1221¾	Steadied 3/8	8
5Nov93-8Pha	sly	1 1/16	:24 :473 1:12 1:443	3↑ Alw 16500N1X	87 2 4 33 21 13½ 16½	Ryan K	L 112 b	2.60	86-22	BadgerBane1126½ NomadeRoyale1195½ MrExcellerator1142	Mild handling	9
11Oct93-7WO	fst	1⅛ ⊗	:482 1:13 1:382 1:513	3↑ Alw 19800N1X	82 4 4 32 31½ 34½ 36	Kabel T K	L 114 fb	3.05	82-12	Collosseum Cat1092 Irish Lies1134 Badger Bane114no	Four wide bid	7
26Sep93-8WO	gd	1 1/16	:24 :474 1:123 1:451	3↑ Alw 19800N1X	82 6 8 88 63½ 57½ 58¼	Kabel T K	L 115 fb	*2.20	82-18	Two Knotty1103 CollosseumCat111nk LordGordon1142½	Wide into stretch	9
21Aug93-11Det	fst	1 1/16	:232 :471 1:114 1:441	Piston B C45k	81 5 13 1311 119¾ 76½ 63	Villeneuve F A	L 118 fb	5.40	90-09	Image Of Prospect116hd Super D.J.115½ WisdomSeeker115½	Rated on rail	13
28Jly93-9WO	fst	1⅛	:492 1:141 1:392 1:52	3↑ Alw 23300N1X	87 6 6 56 42¾ 2nk 2hd	Kabel T K	L 115 b	*1.05	86-18	American Pro121hd Badger Bane1156 Irish Lies114½	Gamely outside	6
14Jly93-8WO	fst	1 1/16	:24 :481 1:123 1:45	3↑ Alw 23300N1X	86 2 7 69¾ 54¼ 41½ 2no	Kabel T K	L 115 b	6.80	91-14	FinesseBoy118no BadgerBane1153 BraveWelshmn113½	Game try outside	7

WORKOUTS: Jan 1 Pha 5f fst 1:041 B *11/12* Oct 23 WO 4f fst :49 H *5/23*

Sailing On Aprayer

Own: Rottkamp John R

CHAVEZ J F (163 33 30 19 .20)

Dk. b or br g. 5
Sire: Air Forbes Won (Bold Forbes)
Dam: I Believe (Believe It)
Br: O'Neill W R (Ky)
Tr: Odintz Jeff (37 10 7 6 .27)

119

Lifetime Record:	32	6	9	5	$141,348						
1993	22	5	6	3	$95,790	Turf	0	0	0	0	
1992	5	0	1	1	$12,180	Wet	2	1	0	0	$9,420
Aqu ⊡	11	2	2	3	$59,556	Dist	6	0	2	2	$24,906

23Dec93-6Aqu	fst	1⅛ ⊡	:491 1:144 1:404 1:533	3↑ Alw 30000N1X	95 1 1 1½ 1½ 17½ 15	Chavez J F	117 fb	*.50	75-36	Sailing On Aprayer1175 SelectiveSurgery1153½ Woodster1102	Ridden out	5
6Dec93-7Aqu	gd	1 1/16 ⊡	:24 :472 1:113 1:442	3↑ Alw 30000N1X	86 2 3 2½ 2hd 1hd 32	Velazquez J R	117	*1.40	81-21	Majesty'sDarby1151 Laminate1201 SailingOnApryer1171	Bid, weakened	7
22Nov93-7Aqu	fst	1⅛	:484 1:131 1:39 1:523	3↑ Alw 30000N1X	95 1 2 21½ 21½ 21½ 21½	Chavez J F	117 b	*1.90	71-34	Jim'sBestBoy1151½ SilingOnApryer1176½ HoldTheBsket1151½	Second best	7
11Nov93-6Aqu	fst	1	:233 :463 1:11 1:37	3↑ Alw 30000N1X	90 6 3 41¼ 31½ 23½ 23½	Chavez J F	117 b	3.70	75-27	HickoryLake1153½ SailingOnAprayer1173½ Jim'sBestBoy11510	Second best	7
16Oct93-9Bel	fst	1 1/16 ⊗	:232 :463 1:11 1:423	3↑ Alw 30000N1X	81 4 5 42 31 21½ 23½	Leon F5	112 b	4.50	85-12	StopAndListen1143½ SailingOnApryer1126 InASplitSecond1144½	Willingly	6
6Oct93-9Bel	fst	6½f	:224 :461 1:111 1:174	3↑ Clm c-17500	80 8 8 106¾ 53¼ 53 53½	Chavez J F	119 b	*2.50	80-19	Red Hot Red117nk Brucon115no Sports Alarm1133	Checked break, wide	10

Claimed from Miron Stephen E, Debonis Robert Trainer

26Sep93-4Bel	sly	7f	:231 :463 1:112 1:234	3↑ Clm 15500	96 1 7 1½ 12½ 18 111	Chavez J F	113 b	2.70	84-15	Sailing On Aprayer11311 Sports Alarm1152½ Unbuckled1179	Handily	7
10Sep93-4Bel	my	7f	:224 :46 1:101 1:224	3↑ Clm 20000	76 2 6 44 33 44 47½	Chavez J F	113 b	4.70	81-13	Ben Ali's Rullah1152 Clever Knave1153 Sanfran1172½	No late bid	6
16Aug93-1Sar	fst	1⅛	:473 1:121 1:381 1:512	3↑ Clm 22500	80 1 7 714 86¾ 51½ 44½	Alvarado F T	115	7.40	74-25	Charming Buck1153 Diamond Anchor119¾ Fifth Business113¾	Late gain	8
23Jly93-4Bel	fst	1⅛	:474 1:121 1:371 1:502	Clm 16500	84 1 5 31 54½ 43½ 45¼	Alvarado F T	115	6.60	72-19	Red Scamper1194 Corrupt Council119nk Ridge Road1131	Lacked rally	6

WORKOUTS: Jan 11 Aqu ⊡ 3f fst :374 B *9/16* Nov 4 Aqu 3f fst :384 B *2/2*

Le Risky

Own: Scuderi Vincent S

LOVATO F JR (77 7 9 11 .09)

Dk. b or br h. 5
Sire: Lejoli (Cornish Prince)
Dam: Frisky and Risky (Cormorant)
Br: Cuomo Michael (NY)
Tr: Ferriola Peter (40 11 6 4 .28)

117

Lifetime Record:	37	6	1	6	$114,488						
1994	1	0	0	0		Turf	2	0	0	0	
1993	18	3	1	6	$63,666	Wet	4	1	0	1	$21,086
Aqu ⊡	5	1	1	1	$24,840	Dist	7	1	0	0	$19,086

11Jan94-5Aqu	fst	6f ⊡	:224 :454 :573 1:093	Alw 28000N2X	76 6 2 62¾ 52½ 65 68½	Lovato F Jr	117 f	4.60	86-11	Won Song117½ Not For Love1174 Tali Hai117no	No factor	6
27Dec93-7Aqu	fst	6f ⊡	:224 :464 :594 1:13	3↑ Alw 30000N2X	85 2 2 55½ 42½ 32 2nk	Lovato F Jr	117 f	4.60e	78-28	Real Cielo117nk Le Risky1171½ Unreal Mot117nk	Just missed	6
2Dec93-4Aqu	fst	6f ⊡	:222 :453 :58 1:103	3↑ Clm c-25000	81 2 7 79½ 74½ 55 34¾	Davis R G	117	7.20	85-17	True Dutch1151¾ Runaway Storm1173 Le Risky1171½	Broke slowly	7

Claimed from Meadow Val Stable, Dutrow Richard E Trainer

12Nov93-1Aqu	fst	7f	:231 :47 1:121 1:243	3↑ Clm 30000	82 6 5 95¼ 93½ 32½ 35¾	Davis R G	113	20.00	75-19	Triodet1171¼ Commander Evander1174½ Le Risky1133½	Rallied inside	10
18Oct93-6Bel	fst	7f	:223 :454 1:102 1:231	3↑ Clm 32500	77 3 8 56 64 54½ 47¾	Davis R G	115 b	9.30	79-16	Nymphist117nk Peerless Performer1174 Ocean Splash1173½	No threat	8
25Sep93-1Bel	fst	7f	:23 :463 1:111 1:234	3↑ Clm 30000	81 4 3 53 41½ 24 36½	Davis R G	113 b	13.40	78-19	Clever Knave1144½ Stately Wager1171¾ Le Risky1133¼	No late bid	7
5Sep93-4Bel	fst	6f	:222 :453 :571 1:091	3↑ Clm 35000	80 4 4 65½ 62¾ 64½ 510¾	Santos J A	117 b	17.80	83-15	Top The Record1177 Red Hot Red1131¼ Dibbs N' Dubbs1171¾	No threat	8
25Aug93-5Sar	my	7f	:22 :441 1:082 1:211	3↑ Clm 35000	73 5 3 33½ 44¼ 39 312¾	Krone J A	117 b	3.90	86-08	Triodet1179 Top The Record1173¾ Le Risky1175½	Lacked rally	7
2Aug93-5WO	fst	1 1/16	:233 :47 1:112 1:45	3↑ Clm 50000	67 10 4 47 67½ 914 913¼	King R Jr	L 118 b	13.85	78-14	At First Asking1155 Major Pots118nk Imperial Colony1151¼	Wide	10
17Jly93-5WO	fst	1 1/16	:233 :471 1:121 1:46	3↑ Alw 24900N2X	67 2 3 32¾ 41¾ 56¼ 66	David D J	L 121 b	*2.00	80-15	Rodin1212 Dr. Adagio118nk Comarctic124no	4-Wide final turn	8

WORKOUTS: Dec 25 Aqu ⊡ 3f fst :364 H *1/3* Nov 23 Aqu 5f fst 1:021 H *2/7* Nov 4 Aqu 5f fst 1:014 H *1/3*

Swindle

Own: Hobeau Farm

SWEENEY K H (22 1 2 2 .05)

Dk. b or br h. 5
Sire: Private Account (Damascus)
Dam: Number (Nijinsky II)
Br: Claiborne Farm & The Gamely Corp. (Ky)
Tr: Jerkens H Allen (24 6 3 4 .25)

117

Lifetime Record:	7	2	1	3	$42,840					
1993	7	2	1	3	$42,840	Turf	0	0	0	0
1992	0	M	0	0		Wet	0	0	0	0
Aqu ⊡	1	0	0	0	$1,800	Dist	0	0	0	0

16Dec93-7Aqu	fst	6f ⊡	:223 :461 :59 1:12	3↑ Alw 30000N2X	81 1 6 45½ 47 47 45½	Sweeney K H	117 f	*2.30	77-22	Tough Heart115no Unreal Mot1173½ Danzig's Dance1172	Even trip	6
13Nov93-6Aqu	fst	7f	:232 :462 1:104 1:231	3↑ Alw 30000N2X	90 2 2 1hd 31½ 21 22¼	Sweeney K H	119 f	4.20	86-14	Ferociously1152¼ Swindle1192½ Carsey's Pal1154	Lacked room 1/4 pl	6
25Oct93-2Aqu	fst	7f	:231 :464 1:124 1:25	3↑ Alw 28000N1X	83 1 5 32 31½ 12½ 110½	Sweeney K H	117 f	3.10	79-20	Swindle11710 Snappy Fella1141¼ Graydon Pool1172¼	Bobbled break	7
14Oct93-6Bel	fst	6f	:222 :454 :58 1:102	3↑ Alw 28000N1X	76 5 5 52 31½ 32 37½	Sweeney K H	117 f	9.10	80-10	Man's Hero1143¾ Line Pro1143¾ Swindle1173½	No late bid	9
2Oct93-4Bel	fst	7f	:223 :463 1:104 1:233	3↑ Alw 28000N1X	76 2 5 31 21 32½ 38¼	Sweeney K H	117 f	11.50	77-21	Plantagenet1142½ Drawpoint1145¾ Swindle1176	Tired	6
23Jly93-1Bel	fst	6f	:224 :464 :59 1:121	3↑ Md 47500	64 5 9 63 2½ 1½ 12	Sweeney K H	120 f	*1.30	79-17	Swindle1202 Toga Times116¾ Stanchion112½	Driving	12
2Jun93-5Bel	fst	6f	:223 :461 :58 1:103	3↑ Md Sp Wt	75 2 1 2½ 2½ 33 36½	Sweeney K H	122 f	*1.70	80-12	Jason Dean114½ Splendid Buck1226 Swindle1222	Took up turn	6

WORKOUTS: Jan 11 Bel tr.t 1 fst 1:46 B *1/1* Jan 6 Bel tr.t 5f fst 1:041 B *15/29* Dec 13 Bel tr.t 4f fst :483 H *3/18* Nov 30 Bel tr.t 4f fst :483 B *14/41* Nov 11 Bel 4f fst :473 H *5/32*

Charming Buck
Own: J M Dee Stable
DAVIS R G (168 32 24 26 .19)

B. g. 7
Sire: Buckaroo (Buckpasser)
Dam: Charming Story (Hail to Reason)
Br: Mangurian Mr-Mrs H T Jr (Fla)
Tr: Odintz Jeff (37 10 7 6 .27)

117

Lifetime Record: 75 13 6 16 $216,665										
1994	1	0	0	1	$3,600	Turf	1	0	0	0
1993	23	6	2	5	$89,555	Wet	10	3	0	5 $42,300
Aqu ⊡	24	6	1	7	$97,040	Dist	24	6	2	7 $104,900

6Jan94-5Aqu	fst	1⅛ ⊡	:483 1:134 1:403 1:532	Alw 30000N2X	87	3	4	53¾	55	33½	3¾	Davis R G	117	*1.20	68-32	Nowsthetimetoshine117½ Rohwer112nk CharmingBuck1175	Finished well	6
26Dec93-7Aqu	fst	1 1/16 ⊡	:232 :47 1:121 1:47	3↑ Alw 32000N2X	87	4	7	713	58	48½	43½	Smith M E	117	5.90	66-30	Tanako115½ Won Song115no Riskabit1173	No threat	8
9Dec93-3Aqu	fst	1 1/16 ⊡	:242 :491 1:132 1:46	3↑ Clm 35000	86	3	3	52	63½	32	2nk	Smith M E	117	3.60	75-25	Kellock113nk Charming Buck1173 Red Scamper1171½	Finished well	7
2Dec93-6Aqu	fst	1 1/16 ⊡	:241 :484 1:133 1:461	3↑ Clm 25000	84	10	9	105¾	85¼	52	1½	Smith M E	117	6.50	74-23	CharmingBuck117½ Electrojet1173 DH I'llTakeAStand117	Wide, driving	10
15Nov93-4Aqu	fst	1⅛	:48 1:131 1:384 1:513	3↑ Clm 35000	76	8	6	613	48	47½	510¾	Chavez J F	117	2.60	67-24	Sylvester Stone1176¾ Kellock1171 Hugatag1122	No factor	8
27Oct93-8Aqu	wf	1⅛	:474 1:131 1:391 1:524	3↑ Alw 32000N2X	85	8	7	717	610	410	312	Chavez J F	117	2.20e	60-39	ContrctCourt1145¼ PoloDrive1176¾ ChrmingBuck117½	Improved position	8
3Oct93-5Bel	my	1 1/16	:243 :491 1:134 1:451	3↑ Clm 35000	82	1	2	21½	33½	43½	33	Chavez J F	117	1.60	73-24	CommnderEvnder115nk SttelyWger1172¾ ChrmingBuck117nk	Lacked rally	4
22Sep93-8Bel	my	1⅛	:47 1:112 1:36 1:49	3↑ Alw 32000N2X	78	6	5	65½	68½	67½	612½	Chavez J F	117	8.50	71-22	[D]All My Tricks1122¼ CommitteeChairman1152½ SlewsGold1135¼	No threat	7
9Sep93-7Bel	fst	1 1/16	:232 :461 1:11 1:431	3↑ Alw 32000N2X	89	1	6	66½	65	62¾	33¼	Chavez J F	117	7.50	83-23	All Gone1132¼ Committee Chairman118¾ Charming Buck1175	Late gain	7
27Aug93-7Sar	fst	1⅛	:483 1:122 1:364 1:492	3↑ Alw 30500N2X	86	5	4	42	75¾	74½	54½	Chavez J F	117	14.80	84-15	Compadre1121 My Mogul1121½ All Gone1122	No threat	7

Islanders Cure
Own: Rosenthal Robert D
VELAZQUEZ J R (142 25 22 20 .18)

B. g. 4
Sire: Cure the Blues (Stop the Music)
Dam: Family Name (Tumiga)
Br: Loradale & Thoroughbred Developers (Ky)
Tr: Schettino Dominick A (15 3 0 2 .20)

117

Lifetime Record: 13 2 2 1 $48,190										
1993	12	2	2	1	$48,190	Turf	1	0	0	0
1992	1	M	0	0		Wet	2	0	1	0 $7,960
Aqu ⊡	1	1	0	0	$16,800	Dist	2	0	0	1 $5,400

23Dec93-7Aqu	fst	6f ⊡	:23 :47 :594 1:131	3↑ Alw 28000N2L	78	2	5	11	12½	15	11	Velazquez J R	115 f	*1.10	77-20	Islanders Cure1151 Flaming Falcon1152 Smart Regent1201½	Driving	6
29Nov93-7Aqu	wf	7f	:222 :451 1:101 1:233	3↑ Alw 28000N1X	83	7	2	12	11	2½	26	Velazquez J R	115	5.30	80-18	In A Split Second1156 Islanders Cure1154 Active Duty117nk	Second best	9
25Oct93-6Aqu	fst	7f	:231 :461 1:12 1:252	3↑ Alw 28000N1X	65	2	1	11	12½	2hd	46¼	Leon F5	109	1.80	71-20	Drawpoint114¾ Pay Phone1141¾ Loud Brother1143¾	Speed, tired	5
11Oct93-7Bel	fm	1 1/16 [T]	:242 :471 1:104 1:42	3↑ Alw 30000N1X	65	8	1	1hd	11	53	810¾	Cruguet J	114	9.00e	75-12	Nobiz Like Showbiz114nk Palace Piper1142¼ T. Barone114½	Gave way	8
26Sep93-5Bel	sly	1 1/16	:223 :452 1:103 1:443	3↑ Alw 30000N1X	58	1	2	2½	21½	26	416½	Cruguet J	113	2.70	62-22	Maginsky Too11314 Snappy Fella1131 Seminole Canyon1131½	Tired	6
15Sep93-4Bel	fst	1 1/16	:232 :463 1:111 1:433	3↑ Alw 30000N1X	82	9	2	2½	2hd	2hd	33¾	Cruguet J	113	8.50	80-18	Danzig'sDnce117½ SeminoleCnyon1143¼ IslndersCure113nk	Bid, weakened	10
21Aug93-1Sar	fst	1⅛	:46 1:111 1:37 1:501	3↑ Alw 28500N1X	82	2	1	13	13	11	23	Cruguet J	112	8.30	82-10	Committee Chairman1123 Islanders Cure112½ Zeus Energy1121¼	Gamely	9
6Aug93-5Sar	fst	6f	:221 :45 :57 1:093	3↑ Alw 26500N1X	79	6	7	62¾	52¼	52	68	Cruguet J	112	18.00	86-07	Tantivy In G112nk Plantagenet1124 Senor Rex112½	Lacked rally	9
24Jly93-4Bel	fst	6f	:223 :454 :574 1:10	Alw 26500N1X	77	1	1	11	1hd	32	49¾	Leon F5	112	7.20	80-17	Plano Pleasure1171¾ Senor Rex1176 Not For Love1172	Used in pace	7
14Jly93-8Bel	fst	6f	:223 :452 :574 1:094	3↑ Alw 26500N1X	82	1	1	31½	4¾	2½	52	Samyn J L	111	8.40	89-10	Island Prospect1171¼ Hickory Lake112½ Senor Rex113hd	Saved ground	8

WORKOUTS: Jan 6 Bel tr.t 5f fst 1:054 B *25/29* Nov 27 Bel tr.t 5f fst 1:031 B *17/40* Nov 22 Bel tr.t 6f fst 1:164 B *2/3* Nov 12 Bel tr.t 4f fst :503 B *20/27* Nov 9 Bel tr.t 4f fst :513 B *17/17* Nov 4 Bel 3f fst :362 B *5/19*

Jessup North
Own: Edwards James F
SANTAGATA N (148 23 14 12 .16)

Ch. c. 4
Sire: Carr de Naskra (Star de Naskra)
Dam: Kiss Who (Raise a Man)
Br: CBF Corporation (NY)
Tr: O'Brien Leo (27 6 3 0 .22)

117

Lifetime Record: 14 2 3 2 $55,810										
1993	13	2	3	2	$55,810	Turf	1	0	0	0
1992	1	M	0	0		Wet	2	0	1	0 $4,760
Aqu ⊡	4	1	0	1	$20,160	Dist	1	0	0	1 $3,060

Entered 15Jan94- 1 AQU

22Dec93-6Aqu	fst	6f ⊡	:224 :464 :593 1:124	3↑ [S]Alw 28000N1X	81	6	1	2½	2hd	14	17	Velazquez J R	115 b	*1.20	79-21	Jessup North1157 Bob H.1171½ Starbatim115¾	Ridden out	7
6Dec93-9Aqu	gd	6f ⊡	:224 :461 :582 1:11	3↑ [S]Alw 28000N1X	77	1	4	2½	31½	22	31½	Velazquez J R	115 b	4.70	86-15	African Wish1151½ Money Stream120no Jessup North1152	Willingly	8
19Nov93-7Aqu	fst	6f	:232 :473 :593 1:12	3↑ [S]Alw 28000N1X	77	8	1	2hd	1hd	21	23	Velazquez J R	115 b	3.60	79-19	Loud Brother1153 Jessup North115½ Mt. Shannon1202¾	Held place	9
2Nov93-4Aqu	fst	7f	:222 :452 1:11 1:243	3↑ [S]Alw 28000N1X	67	1	5	28	312	29	29¼	Velazquez J R	115 b	8.00	72-18	Corma Ray1159¼ Jessup North115¾ Pluck With Luck117½	Up for place	7
20Oct93-7Aqu	sly	6f	:224 :463 :584 1:111	3↑ [S]Alw 28000N1X	64	2	1	1hd	32½	33½	24	Bailey J D	114 b	7.10	82-13	D'baja1144 DH Jessup North114 DH Alpstein1143½	Gamely	6
3Oct93-9Bel	my	7f	:223 :462 1:122 1:251	3↑ [S]Alw 28000N1X	56	9	7	44	65	75	69½	Bailey J D	114 b	15.20	67-23	Cinco Rey114nk Sorabosia1164 Newyork Appeal1172¼	Tired	11
4Sep93-7Bel	fst	7f	:223 :46 1:111 1:234	3↑ [S]Alw 28000N1X	52	10	1	53	75	114½	89½	Bailey J D	113 f	6.80	74-14	Barry's Man118½ Scrambling1133¾ Raise A Rumpus1142¼	Brief speed	12
9Aug93-4Sar	fm	1⅛ [T]	:472 1:12 1:363 1:484	Clm 50000	59	6	3	44½	42½	95½	913½	Bailey J D	117 b	36.50	80-05	Same Old Wish1153 T. Barone117½ Peter And1171½	Tired	12
29Jly93-5Sar	fst	7f	:23 :454 1:103 1:234	3↑ [S]Md Sp Wt	73	6	7	1hd	2½	2½	1no	Bailey J D	116 b	4.80	86-10	Jessup North116no Gifted Traven1119½ Charlie Kenny Sr.1163½	Driving	14
11Jun93-9Bel	fst	1 1/16	:234 :472 1:122 1:454	3↑ [S]Md Sp Wt	66	12	1	11	11½	2hd	34	Sweeney K H	114 b	43.00	69-29	Advanced Placement1143½ World Flag114½ Jessup North1143	Weakened	14

WORKOUTS: Jan 12 Bel tr.t 4f fst :483 H *11/70* Dec 17 Bel tr.t 4f fst :502 B *21/78* Dec 3 Bel tr.t 4f fst :491 B *10/44* Nov 14 Bel 4f fst :474 H *5/24*

The fifth race on January 17, 1994, was a nonwinners-of-two allowance for four-year-olds and up at a mile and a sixteenth (track record of 1:41 held by Autoroute). The field of nine included four that were stretching out, one of them a lightly raced horse named Swindle, trained by Allen Jerkens. To handicappers doing a routine horse-to-horse comparison, Swindle didn't look much better or worse than the other stretch-out prospects in the race. But players with the means and inclination to do a horse-to-horse comparison of Swindle and Autoroute knew that Swindle was a time bomb set to go off at exactly 1:54 P.M. on the afternoon of January 17.

Swindle's breezing mile workout in 1:46 six days before the race triggered my recollection of Autoroute, who had breezed in 1:47 a few days before crushing Appointee some thirteen months earlier. As I compared the records of the two, it was obvious there were other striking similarities between them as well:

· Each had won a preliminary allowance two starts before stretching out; each had run disappointingly as the favorite in the race immediately preceding the stretch-out.

· Each was lightly raced. Autoroute had raced ten times before his stretch-out win, Swindle had raced seven times.

· Each was relatively fresh. Autoroute had been idle for two months prior to his record-setting stretch-out, Swindle for a month.

· Each had demonstrated the ability to win off workouts when they broke their maidens second time out: Autoroute was idle from January to May, Swindle from early June to late July.

· They were stretching out at roughly the same time of the year.

· Both had shown early speed in their sprint races. Autoroute had often given up the chase at six and seven furlongs, while Swindle had lost ground through the final quarter in four of his seven starts.

Swindle didn't approach Autoroute's inner-track record of 1:41 while racing through snow showers over a dull, wet-fast surface, but he was just as impressive visually, taking charge on the far turn and widening out to win by a pole under a hand ride. Indeed, while Autoroute had earned a Beyer of 101 for his track record over a glib surface, Swindle was awarded an even better figure — 107 — for his tour de force on January 17 . . . a 17-point improvement on his previous best.

Offered 4–1 on a horse who should've been something like 6–5, I didn't bother with any exacta savers.

FIFTH RACE
Aqueduct
JANUARY 17, 1994

$1\frac{1}{16}$ MILES. (Inner Dirt)(1.41) ALLOWANCE. Purse $30,000. 4–year–olds and upward which have not won two races other than maiden, claiming or starter. Weight, 122 lbs. Non–winners of a race other than maiden or claiming at a mile or over since Janaury 1, allowed 3 lbs. Of such a race since December, 15, 5 lbs.

Value of Race: $30,000 Winner $18,000; second $6,600; third $3,600; fourth $1,800. Mutuel Pool $88,182.00 Exacta Pool $207,483.00

Last Raced	Horse	M/Eqt.	A.	Wt	PP	St	¼	½	¾	Str	Fin	Jockey	Odds $1
16Dec93 ^{7}Aqu^{4}	Swindle	f	5	117	6	5	$2^{1\frac{1}{2}}$	$2^{1\frac{1}{2}}$	$1^{\frac{1}{2}}$	1^{9}	1^{16}	Sweeney K H	4.30
6Jan94 ^{5}Aqu^{3}	Charming Buck		7	117	7	8	8^{1}	8^{2}	9	8^{4}	$2^{1\frac{1}{4}}$	Davis R G	a–0.90
26Dec93 ^{7}Aqu^{6}	Sorabosia	b	4	112	1	2	$3^{\frac{1}{2}}$	$3^{\frac{1}{2}}$	$3^{\frac{1}{2}}$	3^{4}	3^{hd}	Leon F^{5}	21.50
23Dec93 ^{7}Aqu^{1}	Islanders Cure	f	4	117	8	7	1^{2}	1^{1}	2^{8}	$2^{3\frac{1}{2}}$	4^{1}	Velazquez J R	13.90
6Jan94 ^{5}Aqu^{2}	Rohwer		4	117	2	1	7^{2}	7^{1}	$7^{1\frac{1}{2}}$	6^{hd}	5^{nk}	Luzzi M J	4.20
22Dec93 ^{6}Aqu^{1}	Jessup North	b	4	117	9	6	4^{hd}	$5^{\frac{1}{2}}$	$5^{2\frac{1}{2}}$	4^{2}	$6^{1\frac{1}{4}}$	Santagata N	23.00
6Jan94 ^{5}Aqu^{5}	Badger Bane	b	4	117	3	9	9	9	$8^{1\frac{1}{2}}$	$5^{\frac{1}{2}}$	$7^{8\frac{1}{2}}$	Ryan K	20.10
23Dec93 ^{6}Aqu^{1}	Sailing On Aprayer	b	5	119	4	3	5^{3}	4^{3}	4^{2}	$7^{\frac{1}{2}}$	$8^{2\frac{3}{4}}$	Chavez J F	a–0.90
11Jan94 ^{5}Aqu^{6}	Le Risky		5	117	5	4	6^{4}	6^{12}	$6^{2\frac{1}{2}}$	9	9	Lovato F Jr	7.20

a–Coupled: Charming Buck and Sailing On Aprayer.

OFF AT 1:54 Start Good. Won ridden out. Time, :24, :48³, 1:13³, 1:39², 1:46³ Track wet fast.

$2 Mutuel Prices:			
6–(F)–SWINDLE	10.60	4.40	3.60
1A–(G)–CHARMING BUCK (a–entry)		2.40	2.10
2–(A)–SORABOSIA			3.20

$2 EXACTA 6–1 PAID $30.20

Dk. b. or br. h, by Private Account–Number, by Nijinsky II. Trainer Jerkens H Allen. Bred by Claiborne Farm & The Gamely Corp. (Ky).

SWINDLE settled just behind the early lead, took charge on the turn then drew off under good handling. CHARMING BUCK far back for six furlongs, closed late to gain the place. SOROBOSIA raced close up while saving ground along the backstretch, dropped back on the turn, and failed to threaten thereafter. ISLANDERS CURE set the pace along the inside for six furlongs and tired in the drive. ROHWER never reached contention after stumbling badly a few strides away from the gate. JESSUP NORTH was never a factor. BADGER BANE was never close. SAILING ON APRAYER raced within striking distance to the turn and tired. LE RISKY gave way after going six furlongs. SWINDLE, SORABOSIA and LE RISKY wore mud caulks.

Owners— 1, Hobeau Farm; 2, J M Dee Stable; 3, Hackel Kenneth S; 4, Rosenthal Robert D; 5, Garren Murray M; 6, Edwards James F; 7, Yanofsky Howard; 8, Rottkamp John R; 9, Scuderi Vincent S

Trainers—1, Jerkens H Allen; 2, Odintz Jeff; 3, Lenzini John J Jr; 4, Schettino Dominick A; 5, Garren Murray M; 6, O'Brien Leo; 7, Yanofsky Howard; 8, Odintz Jeff; 9, Ferriola Peter

As a postscript, Swindle continued to race effectively in routes (as had Autoroute), winning at the nonwinners-of-three level two starts later.

RECORD KEEPING

Long-term trainer statistics are commercially available to handicappers from numerous sources, but, as Disraeli once observed, "There are three kinds of lies: Lies, damn lies, and statistics."

Comprehensive arrays of numbers, percentages, and R.O.I. (return on investment) figures are all well and good, but they fall short of providing handicappers the "feel" for a horse such as Swindle — a feeling of inner confidence that was fueled by comparing subtleties in Swindle's overall handling and development with that of his stablemate, Autoroute.

It is my firm belief that a low-tech pencil-behind-the-ear approach produces the best results insofar as developing a database where trainer analysis is concerned. The old-fashioned method of cutting and pasting the past performances of each day's winners and filing them by trainer in an expandable loose-leaf notebook provides handicappers with a database reaching back across the seasons, and one that is also as fresh and current as yesterday's results. In fact, saving winning past performances conceivably could've led to the ultimate in pattern-recognition wagering — a future book bet on Go For Gin to win the 1994 Kentucky Derby:

DAILY RACING FORM Sunday, October 31, 1993 PAGE 13

FEATURES

HANDICAPPER'S CORNER

Zito may be hiding another Derby winner

By DAVE LITFIN
Daily Racing Form handicapper

The 50,000 or so fans at Santa Anita and the millions more watching next Saturday's Breeders' Cup Juvenile will be hoping to catch a glimpse of the 1994 Kentucky Derby winner in action.

Should Dehere accelerate past his rivals as expected, he will become a huge winter-book favorite, but he will be a poor-percentage bet since no Juvenile winner, however impressive, has ever made a winning run for the roses.

Fly So Free was the winter-book choice three years ago after winning the Juvenile by three decisive lengths in front of 57,195 fans at Belmont Park, but it was a more intimate gathering of 9,673 on hand for an ordinary card at Aqueduct three weeks later who saw the Kentucky Derby winner break his maiden.

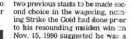

ZITO: Trains Go for Gin.

Go For Gin
Own: Condren William J
B. c. 2 (Apr)
Sire: Cormorant (His Majesty)
Dam: Never Knock (Stage Door Johnny)
Br: Pamela Darmstadt duPont (Ky)
Tr: Zito Nicholas P (5 1 1 0 .20)
0

Lifetime Record: 3 1 1 0 $22,140

1993	3	1	1	0	$22,140	Turf	0	0	0	0	
1992	0	M	0	0		Wet	2	1	1	0	$22,140
Aqu	1	1	0	0	$16,200	Dist	2	1	1	0	$22,140

21Oct93- 5Aqu sly 1 :22 :45 1:10[1] 1:35 Md Sp Wt 90 3 2 2[1] 2½ 1 1[10] Bailey J D 118 *.90 87-22 Go For Gin118[10] Retrospection118[1]¾ A Track Attack118[3] Ridden out 7
3Oct93- 2Bel sly 1 :22[4] :46 1:11[4] 1:37 Md Sp Wt 73 2 2 2 1hd 1 2¼ Bailey J D 118 1.90 79-24 Arrovente118¼ Go For Gin118[12] King Of Kolchis118[3] Bid, weakened 5
13Sep93- 5Bel fst 6f :22[1] :45 :58[2] 1:11 Md Sp Wt 70 6 11 8 8[4]½ 5 5[9]¾ Chavez J F 118 22.90 76-23 You And I118[1]½ Palance118[1]¼ Hussonet118[2]¾ Broke slowly 11
WORKOUTS: Oct 11 Bel 5f fst 1:03[2] B 34/41

Strike the Gold
Ch. c. 3(Mar), by Alydar—Majestic Gold, by Hatchet Man
Own.—Brophy B G
Br.—Calumet Farm (Ky)
Tr.—Zito Nicholas P
117
Lifetime 3 1 0 0 $17,400
1990 3 1 0 0 $17,400

15Nov90- 7Aqu fst 1 :46[1] 1:11[2] 1:3 Md Sp Wt 2 4 3[1] 1hd 1 2½ 1 8½ Smith M E b 118 4.40 74-35 Strike the Gold118[8]½ Tank Up118[3] ShiningBid118¾ Ridden out 9
31Oct90- 7Aqu fst 1 :46[4] 1:11 1:3 Md Sp Wt 4 7 7 5¾ 5 5[7] 5[11]¼ Smith M E 118 6.40 70-23 KeyContender118[4]¾ Innkeeper118[2]¾ WingdGrc118¾ Pinched bk 7
11Oct90- 5Bel fst 6f :22 :44[3] 1:0 Md Sp Wt 5 12 12[17] 10 5 8[16] 9[21]¼ Smith M E 118. 4.50 72-15 ImginryGold118[7]½ OlGrumby118[8] StndrdTm118[1]¾ Broke slowly 13
Speed Index: Last Race: -13.0 1-Race Avg.: -13.0 1-Race Avg.: -13.0 Overall Avg.: -3.6
LATEST WORKOUTS ●Jan 22 GP 3f fst :35[2] H Jan 19 GP 4f fst :49[2] Bg ●Jan 11 GP 4f fst :47[2] H ●Jan 4 GP 5f gd 1:00[4] B (d)
$73,185

Strike the Gold was a handsome colt, well-muscled, with a chestnut coat that brilliantly reflected the rays of autumn sunlight. Although he had shown enough ability in two previous starts to be made second choice in the wagering, nothing Strike the Gold had done prior to his resounding maiden win on Nov. 15, 1990 suggested he was a potential Derby winner.

In his career debut, going six furlongs at Belmont on Oct. 11, Strike the Gold, according to the Daily Racing Form chart footnote, ". . . never reached contention after breaking slowly," and passed a few tired horses to finish ninth while beaten 21 lengths.

Stretched to a mile three weeks later, Strike the Gold ". . . raced wide after being pinched back at the start," and rallied mildly to finish fifth, beaten a bit more than 11 lengths.

Third time out, in his second attempt at a mile, the Nick Zito-trained colt tracked the early leaders from fourth position and wrested command approaching the stretch to win by eight and a half widening lengths. The chart footnote read, ". . . drew off while being ridden out."

Fast forward nearly three years to an ordinary card at Aqueduct, and mark down the fifth race of Oct. 21, 1993 — a maiden special-weight for 2-year-olds won by a Nick Zito-trained colt making his third career start and second attempt at a mile.

According to the footnote, Go for Gin ". . . forced the pace from outside and drew off to a lengthy score while being ridden out."

The similarities don't end there. Like Strike the Gold, Go for Gin was no factor in his debut going six furlongs at Belmont, ". . . failing to threaten after breaking slowly" and passing a few tired horses to finish fifth, nine lengths behind eventual Cowdin Stakes winner You and I.

Given the fact he is a half-brother to 1992 Eclipse champion Pleasant Tap, who improved with maturity, it's reasonable to anticipate further development from Go for Gin.

Hey listen, the Derby is a long way off and anything can happen. All I know is that a lot of folks watching the Breeders' Cup Juvenile for clues to 3-year-old form may be disappointed. There were 6,017 fans who braved the elements to attend a rainy midweek card at Aqueduct last week, and it's just possible they saw the Derby winner break his maiden.

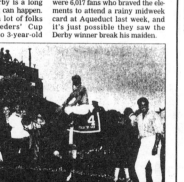

FOUR FOOTED PHOTOS

STRIKE THE GOLD: In winner's circle at Churchill Downs.

The performances of Lady D'Accord and Cold Heist in April of 1993 had heightened my respect for Nick Zito's training ability, his awareness of cycles, and his aptitude for reincarnating them. So when Go For Gin broke his maiden six months later, I found myself looking at his past performances (pp's) and thinking, "This is Strike the Gold all over again!"

So many things about their early development were the same that it was uncanny. They had both been brought out for their six-furlong debuts in late summer/early fall, and each had broken slowly before passing a few rivals. They showed improvement when stretched to a mile second time out. They broke their maidens by the length of the stretch when tried at a mile for the second time. Even their manner of victory was similar (though Strike the Gold eventually developed into a one-run closer while Go For Gin remained a free-running individual).

At the time of Go For Gin's maiden win the pattern match between the two colts was relatively obscure to all but the tiniest fraction of America's horseplayers; someone intrigued by their inescapable similarities might well have been quoted 100–1 odds at a Nevada racebook. Rest assured that the procedure of saving pp's according to trainers will uncover a steady stream of obscure (and therefore potentially lucrative) patterns.

Along with the benefits of having detailed information on a wealth of subtle topics at your fingertips, clipping the pp's also stimulates your subconscious, which subliminally examines and processes the data regarding what kinds of profiles are winning what kinds of races. This can only sharpen your intuitive skills in the long run.

Clipping the winning pp's, I like to enter the following data:

Date Distance Conditions $2 mutuel
Equipment Changes Comments

Let's look at a typical entry from Bill Mott's 1994 section:

Lahint
Own: Maktoum Al Maktoum
SMITH M E (120 23 17 16 .19)
B. c. 3 (Apr)
Sire: Woodman (Mr. Prospector)
Dam: Count On Bonnie (Dancing Count)
Br: Little Marvin Jr & Vanmeter Thomas F II (Ky)
Tr: Mott William I (26 7 4 1 .27)
111
Lifetime Record: 7 2 2 0 $72,484
1994 5 2 1 0 $67,314 Turf 0 0 0 0
1993 2 M 1 0 $5,170 Wet 0 0 0 0
Bel(T) 0 0 0 0 Dist(T) 0 0 0 0

29May94- 8Bel fst 1⅛ :453 1:101 1:354 1:49 Peter Pan-G2 91 1 5 52½ 51½ 23½ 27½ Smith M E 112 *.20e 78-17 Twining1227½ Lahint1122¾ Gash119no Broke slow, saved grnd 5
3May94- 8Bel fst 1 :23 :46 1:103 1:343 Withers-G2 88 3 8 51¾ 3nk 33 47½ Smith M E 123 5.60 82-10 Twining1235 Able Buck1231½ Presently1231 Wide, flattened out 8
12Mar94-10GP fst 1⅛ :46 1:10 1:344 1:472 Fla Derby-G1 76 9 8 86 68½ 1017 1023 McCarron C J 122 6.80 77-06 Holy Bull1225¾ Ride The Rails122no Halo's Image1221 Failed to menace 14
3Feb94- 8GP gd 1 1/16 ⊗ :233 :481 1:132 1:453 Alw 26000N2L 88 1 5 74¾ 1½ 12½ 14¼ Smith M E 122 *.90 82-20 Lahint1224¼ Bay Street Star1192½ Bai Brun1191¼ 9
Swerved inward start, steadied first turn, ridden out
4Jan94- 5GP fst 1 1/16 :24 :484 1:132 1:461 Md Sp Wt 83 7 3 32 11 12½ 12½ Smith M E 120 2.00 79-21 Lahint1202½ Signal Tap1206½ Sangre De Toro120½ 12
Steadied first turn, hand ride
3Jun93- 3Bel fst 5½f :222 :461 :584 1:051 Md Sp Wt 44 6 8 63½ 62½ 55 710 Krone J A 118 2.60 79-13 SlewGinFizz118¾ SultanOfJava1183½ PeaceNegotitions1182 Broke slowly 8
16May93- 3Bel fst 5f :223 :462 :592 Md Sp Wt 55 6 7 43 42½ 42½ 23 Smith M E 118 *.40 81-15 Gliding Arrow1183 Lahint118nk Charlie Cush118no Broke poorly 7
WORKOUTS: May 22 Bel 6f fst 1:121 H 2/21 May 13 Bel 5f fst 1:033 B 19/19 Apr 29 Bel 5f fst :593 H 11/34 Apr 22 Bel 7f fst 1:253 H 1/1 Apr 15 Bel tr.t 5f fst 1:013 H 17/41 Apr 6 GP 5f fst 1:063 B 6/6

June 9 1 1/16 (T) AlwNW2$5.80

At a glance, I am forever reminded that Lahint won on June 9, going a mile and a sixteenth in his first career start on turf. He won a nonwinners-of-two allowance, paying $5.80.

Had there been a late jockey change, I would merely have crossed out Mike Smith and written in whoever had replaced him. There was nothing in the way of an equipment change to note for Lahint, but frequently horses receive an "ON" or "OFF" for blinkers on or off; and/or a footwear notation, about the addition or removal of bar shoes, aluminum pads, and mud calks. Additionally, horses that win first time off a private purchase by new connections or off a trainer change are duly noted under the "Comments" heading:

Dominant Prospect
CHAVEZ J F (301 54 32 29 .18)
Own.—Caronia Charles A
$35,000
B. c. 3(Mar), by Fortunate Prospect—Centerfold Girl, by Decimator
Br.—Farnsworth Farm & Sucher M (Fla)
Tr.—Sciacca Gary (105 28 7 11 .27)
117
Lifetime 9 1 0 0 $13,880
1993 3 0 0 0 $1,590
1992 6 1 0 0 $12,290
Entered 23Jly93- 7 BEL
9Jly93- 4Bel fst 7f :233 :464 1:231 Clm 35000 30 4 7 31½ 31½ 79½ 724¾ Bailey J D 117 14.00 62-10 SxThrtyTwo1173½SmnlCnyn1173½TwlghtLmng117 Tired 7
14Jun93- 6Bel fst 6f :221 :453 1:103 Clm 70000 42 8 7 713 78¾ 715 721 Antley C W 113 6.00e 66-14 ChiefDesire1175InsuredWinner1133GrvlKing115 Outrun 7
3Jun93- 5Bel fst 6f :224 :454 1:101 Alw 26500 53 4 4 71½ 33 45 415½ Bailey J D 117 13.10 73 13 DiggingIn1173¾HickoryLake1173¾LostPn117 Used early 5
31Oct92- 1GP fst 170 :46 1:101 1:412 Rhythm 63 6 2 32½ 43 813 79 Bailey J D 112 48.60 85-03 DprtngCloud114nkFrySpcl116noGlorxDncr-Fr116 Faded 9
17Oct92- 7Crc fst 6f :213 :45 1:12 Alw 16000 65 3 3 3nk 2hd 31 44 Lee M A 112 4.20 87-06 Virgil Cain1122 Ziao112½ Dee Litigator113 Weakened 7
19Sep92-10Crc fst 7f :214 :444 1:243 (R)Fla Stallion 54 2 6 2½ 32 813 815¼ Alferez J O 118 24.30e 77-11 FirySpcll1182ShpsInThNght1183½GntlPtrck118 Faltered 10
19Sep92-Affirmed Division
22Aug92-11Crc fst 6f :212 :444 1:114 (R)Fla Stallion 66 6 1 3½ 45½ 57 59¾ Suckie M C 116 40.10 82-13 NotSurprising116hdGentlePtrick116¾FirySpcil116 Faded 9
22Aug92-Dr Fager Division
12Aug92- 8Crc fst 6f :22 :453 1:121 Alw 15500 54 6 5 31 54½ 54½ 59 Suckie M C 118 *2.00 81-17 ChrokRn1142½PrdOfBrkn1125AspnFrtn112 Falt 6-wd str 7
18Jly92- 3Crc fst 5½f :223 :47 1:071 Md Sp Wt 60 1 2 21½ 32 1½ 12½ Suckie M C 116 3.50 — — DnntPrspct1162½DcdSll1161IfPrspct116 Driving 5 wide 9
LATEST WORKOUTS Jly 15 Bel 4f fst :481 H Jly 5 Bel 5f fst 1:011 H Jun 28 Bel 4f fst :493 B May 29 Bel tr.t 6f fst 1:162 B

July 24 1 1/16 (T) $19.60 ON 1st Sciacca (Hertler)

It's A Runaway
Own: Caronia Charles A
CHAVEZ J F (—)
$35,000
Gr. c. 3 (Apr)
Sire: Runaway Groom (Blushing Groom-Fr)
Dam: An Affirmation (Affirmed)
Br: Dizney Donald R (Fla)
Tr: Sciacca Gary (—)
117
Lifetime Record: 19 2 2 2 $40,450
1993 10 0 1 0 $7,590 Turf 6 0 1 0 $7,310
1992 9 2 1 2 $32,860 Wet 0 0 0 0
Bel(T) 5 0 1 0 $7,310 Dist(T) 2 0 0 0 $2,580

1Aug93- 4Sar fm 1 3/16 (T) :473 1:113 1:363 1:552 Clm 35000 54 2 1 1½ 1½ 96½ 911¾ Samyn J L 117 22.60 79-09 Chiam's Connection119nk Bet Hudson1171 Show Of Heart119no Used up 12
14Jly93- 9Bel fm 1 (T) :232 :463 1:113 1:351 Clm 45000 38 10 4 52½ 5¾ 99½ 920½ Migliore R 113 16.20 65-11 HollywoodHandsome1172½ SmeOldWish1131¾ CurrentTril1174½ Wide, tired 10
27Jun93- 4Bel fm 1 1/16 (T) :25 :481 1:12 1:424 Clm 35000 67 9 3 43½ 43½ 33½ 47½ Chavez J F 117 *2.30 75-19 Cinco Rey117¾ Jim's Best Boy1174 Bet Hudson1192½ Lacked rally 10
2Jun93- 2Bel gd 1 (T) :224 :461 1:113 1:364 Clm 35000 76 1 4 1½ 1½ 2½ 24 Chavez J F 117 *2.10 74-16 Knight Course1174 It's A Runaway1173 Donnacha1179½ Second best 8
17May93- 6Bel fm 1¼ (T) :481 1:123 1:372 2:014 Clm 50000 63 5 4 43½ 62½ 53¾ 59 Santos J A 117 *2.10e 72-17 Chiam's Connection113no North Rule1131½ I'mABigShot1131½ Lacked rally 8
5May93- 2Bel fm 1 1/16 (T) :231 :461 1:11 1:433 Clm 35000 63 6 7 810 45 55½ 47½ Santos J A 117 *2.50e 71-22 North Rule1171½ I'm A Big Shot1171½ Donnacha1174½ Took up stretch 10
23Apr93- 5Aqu fst 6f :222 :454 :58 1:104 Clm 50000 51 3 4 53 65½ 77½ 712½ Migliore R 117 b 7.60e 76-15 Coming Fast1171 Mr Rocky1131¾ Miter1175 Outrun 7
10Apr93- 6Aqu fst 7f :222 :452 1:104 1:242 Clm 50000 63 3 8 55 54¾ 54¾ 66½ Davis R G 117 b 14.60 75-13 Memorable Date1131½ Miter1171¾ Bonus Award117¾ Saved ground 9
8Mar93- 4OTC fst 1 1/16 :244 :474 1:123 1:472 Obs Champion 150k 42 11 6 615 1024 1020 1024½ Castillo H Jr 122 - 70-03 Classi Envoy122¾ Lord Dearham1222 Slews Gold1221½ Broke to inside 11
Non-Wagering Event. Colts and Geldings Division
15Feb93- 8GP fst 6½f :222 :453 1:102 1:17 Alw 28000NC 56 5 7 57½ 78¾ 79¾ 714 Santos J A 114 37.70 78-13 Premier Explosion1153½ Insured Winner1121½ El Dom113hd Outrun 7
WORKOUTS: Aug 28 Sar tr.t 4f fst :493 B 2/10 ●Aug 20 Sar tr.t(T) 4f fm :48 H (d) 1/10 ●Aug 11 Sar tr.t(T) 4f fm :463 H (d) 1/14 Jly 24 Bel 4f fst :49 B 14/58 Jun 24 Bel 4f fst :484 B 19/78 Jun 18 Bel 5f fst 1:013 H 8/29

Sept. 2 1 1/16 (T) $16.20 1st Sciacca (Hertler)

Gary Sciacca emerged from obscurity in 1992 as the trainer of champion three-year-old filly Saratoga Dew. The 1993 Belmont spring-summer meeting was the meet of Sciacca's life: he won the training title by saddling thirty-one winners, including nine on grass, which paid 7–1 or better; several of those, which boasted dull-looking recent form, paid upwards of 15–1.

Dominant Prospect beat a total of one horse in three starts when returned from a layoff at Belmont, but received a trainer change from John Hertler (a fine trainer in his own right) to the streaking Sciacca for his debut on grass July 24; he raced with blinkers on and won a $35,000 claiming race on grass by nearly five lengths at a $19.60 mutuel (the class notation underneath the pp's was not necessary in this case as the claiming prices are noted in the pp's themselves; when there are restrictions in the conditions of a claiming race, however, such as "nonwinners of two," they should be noted along with the distance and footing). Five weeks later, on the final Sunday of the Saratoga meeting, Dominant Prospect won again, wiring a nonwinners-of-two allowance field at 6–1.

The second day of Belmont's spring meeting, September 2, brought about an intriguing pattern match. It's A Runaway, another three-year-old colt owned by Charles Caronia, was making his first start off a trainer change from Hertler to Sciacca and was entered in a $35,000 claimer on grass. Ordinarily, handicappers might've eliminated this colt on grounds of poor recent form, yet form hadn't seemed to matter much in Sciacca's torrid sequence of long-shot winners, a sequence that included Dominant Prospect. Moreover, It's A Runaway had twice worked bullets on grass at Saratoga, and his latest work over the deep "Oklahoma" training track had been second fastest of the morning.

It's A Runaway won in a runaway, by five and a half lengths at a $16.20 mutuel.

I do not know of a single "figure handicapper" who gave Dominant Prospect or It's A Runaway a second look. Form reversals of this nature are the domain of those who keep close tabs on trainers.

Trainer patterns are especially potent when they enable handicappers to bet against conventional wisdom:

Southern Slew Dk. b. or br. h. 5, by Slew Machine—Windy Secret, by Windy Sands
Br.—Grass R P (Ga)
Own.—Merader Maryann B Tr.—Dimitrijevic Spasoje **114**

Lifetime							
15 4 0 3	1990	11	4	0	1	$72,540
$75,780	1989	4	M	0	2	$3,240
	Turf	6	3	0	0	$61,200

21Nov90- 8Aqu	fm	1 1/16	Ⓣ:484	1:13	1:44	3↑Alw 36000	12	6	2	32½	32	1½	11½	Cruguet J	119	4.20	94-09	SouthernSlew1191½MrcoAurelio115¾C'EstLeRev1171¼	Driving	8
5Nov90- 6Aqu	fm	1 1/16	Ⓣ:474	1:12	1:431	3↑Alw 34000	14	9	1	11	1½	11½	11¼	Cruguet J	117	18.90	98 —	Southern Slew1171¼CoachDigger115½SoSterling120nk	Driving	10
15Oct90- 6Bel	fst	1 1/16	:472	1:113	1:423	3↑Alw 34000	16	6	5	53½	96¼	77½	612½	Chavez J F	117	17.00	76-19	ShtsArRngng114noPndltnRdg1142IsntThtSpcl117nk	No factor	9
15Oct90-Originally scheduled on turf																				
28Sep90- 7Bel	fm	1	Ⓣ:45	1:094	1:344	3↑Alw 31000	17	11	11	127¾	124¾	115¾	68¾	Toscano P R5	112	44.50	83-07	ScottthGrt117¾UWinIWon1133Comndownthln113nk	No threat	12
12Sep90- 7Bel	fm	1 1/16	Ⓣ:45	1:091	1:403	3↑Alw 31000	17	3	4	86	105¾	87	76¾	Chavez J F	117	22.70	91-01	C'EstLeReve1191¾Life'sSurpris113¾SprucBby117nk	No factor	11
30Jly90- 6Bel	fm	1	Ⓣ:454	1:101	1:341	3↑Alw 31000	18	7	8	812	85¾	67½	59¼	Toscano P R5	112	11.90	86-06	GoDutch1123CommissionerBrt111½DefencePolicy117¾	Outrun	9
27Apr90- 8Aqu	fm	1 1/16	Ⓣ:463	1:12	1:451	3↑Alw 32000	13	2	2	28	21½	17	13	Toscano P R5	114	11.40	88-11	Southern Slew1143 Pug's Hart1104½ Son of Talc1032	Driving	10
31Mar90- 3Aqu	sly	7f	:224	:461	1:241	Md 45000	16	7	2	44	22	1hd	15	Chavez J F	118	7.60	81-18	Southern Slew1185 Tabled1227 Squash1181¼	Driving	7
23Mar90- 9Aqu	fst	6f	:23	:48	1:132	Md 35000	22			21½	2hd	21½	34	Chavez J F	122	5.80	69-24	ThillBoy1182½RoylStright1081½SouthernSlew1222¼	Weakened	14

Speed Index: Last Race: +3.0 3–Race Avg.: –3.0 6–Race Avg.: –4.3 Overall Avg.: –4.9
LATEST WORKOUTS May 9 Bel tr.t 4f fst :481 H May 5 Bel 4f fst :483 H Apr 29 Bel 3f fst :371 B Apr 9 Crc 4f fst :53 B

Southern Slew's maiden win in the slop back on March 31, 1990, helped me to gain the second-place prize of $2,500 in one of the New York Racing Association's media handicapping contests. Southern Slew had finished third against $35,000 maiden claimers (the bottom level in New York) in his previous start, but paid $17.20 when boosted into a $50,000 down to $45,000 race, along with a stretch to seven furlongs by "Joe" Dimitrijevic.

Three years later, Polacsek returned from a layoff on May 10, finishing second in a $35,000 maiden claimer. Dimitrijevic then entered him in this spot on June 4:

3 START **1 MILE** BELMONT PARK FINISH

1 MILE. (1.323) **MAIDEN CLAIMING. Purse $14,500. 3–year–olds and upward. Weight, 3–year–olds, 114 lbs. Older, 122 lbs. Claiming price $50,000; for each $2,500 to $45,000 allowed 2 lbs.**

Polacsek B. g. 3(Apr), by Polish Navy—Ivy Road, by Dr Fager
ROJAS R I (43 3 5 3 .07) **$50,000** Br.—John Costelloe (Ky)
Own.—Nerud John A Tr.—Dimitrijevic Spasoje (4 0 1 1 .00) **114**

Lifetime							
3 0 1 0	1993	3	M	1	0	$2,920
$2,920	1992	0	M	0	0	

10May93- 3Bel	fst	6f	:221	:463	1:122	3↑Md 35000	20	60	13	13	108½	43½	21½	22	Rojas R I	115	8.00	76-16	ClssHt1112Polcsek1152½PeekAtthLdis115	Broke slowly	14
10Mar93- 6GP	fst	1 1/16	:40	1:123	1:451	Md Sp Wt		55	3	9	73	87¾	88½	912¼	Vasquez J	120	7.00	72-12	Primordil1202½BrssBer1203½DesrtOfIc120	Showed little	10
20Feb93- 3GP	fst	6f	:221	:453	1:123	Md Sp Wt		47	6	12	1217	1119	1114	99¼	Vasquez J	120	31.60	69-16	SignoirVlry1201EvlBr1201½Aplutch120	Shwd littl wd str	12

LATEST WORKOUTS May 30 Bel tr.t 3f fst :373 B May 22 Bel 5f fst 1:003 H May 1 Bel 4f fst :48 B Apr 19 Bel tr.t 4f fst :483 H

Conventional wisdom said that Polacsek was biting off more than he could chew: once a maiden has lost at the lowest level of $35,000, it is not supposed to beat a $50,000 field. But his trainer had done the same thing with Southern Slew — who hadn't merely won, but had won decisively by five lengths. Now, Polacsek was taking an identical class rise, while also stretching out from six furlongs to a longer one-turn distance. (His owner, John Nerud, trained the legendary Dr. Fager, the fastest miler of all time; his son Jan trained 1985 Breeders' Cup Mile–winner Cozzene; Nerud's well-publicized breeding philosophy is that top-class milers make the best sires; hence, the stretch to a flat mile was subtle corroborating evidence that Polacsek was well meant and would prove suited to the distance.)

Despite checking at the start and steadying sharply between horses down the backstretch, Polacsek won, paying $17.60 for Dimitrijevic — a low-profile trainer who doesn't start enough horses to develop any meaningful long-term, computer-generated statistical profiles.

Ordinarily, a horse that sits out the thirty-day jail period following a claim and then returns at a lower claiming price is downgraded by handicappers as damaged goods, and this is usually sound practice. But Gasper Moschera, annually among the leaders in New York, contradicts such "by the book" logic on a regular basis:

Emphatic Style — B. m. 5, by Crafty Prospector—Pebble Patter, by Rock Talk
GRAELL A (12 0 0 3 .00) — $14,000 Br.—Due Process Stable (NJ) — 117
Own.—Joques Farm — Tr.—Moschera Gasper S (46 7 9 11 .15)
Lifetime 51 11 11 11 $153,002 — 1992 15 2 6 4 $65,200 — 1991 22 4 4 4 $44,685 — Wet 6 1 3 2 $22,680

29Aug92- 1Sar	fst	6½f	:22	:45	1:17	3↑ⒻClm c-25000	69	7	1	4¾	31	2½	45	Chavez J F	b	117	3.30	85-07 Boots1172¾RegalDisplay1132BrittneyErin113	Wide,tired	8
29Aug92-Claimed from Bauer Robert J, Miceli Michael Trainer																				
8Aug92- 9Sar	fst	6½f	:222	:452	1:172	3↑ⒻClm 45000	69	5	9	66	64½	64¾	77¼	Chavez J F	b	113	14.50	81-07 Approprtly113nkShrpImg1171½AllToWll117	Fractious st.	9
20Jly92- 1Bel	fst	7f	:232	:47	1:234	ⒻClm c-35000	72	7	1	11	11	31	33¼	Smith M E	b	119	*1.90	82-14 SunnyBrbi117½SblWy1172¾EmphticStyl119	Speed,wknd	7
20Jly92-Claimed from Girdner Paul K, Pollard Damon Trainer																				
9Jly92- 3Bel	gd	6f	:223	:452	1:094	ⒻClm 35000	89	7	2	11	1½	1½	1hd	Smith M E	b	117	*2.30	91-14 EmphtcStyl117hdJoy'sJoJ1171½LsnUpLs113	Long drive	9
25Jun92- 2Bel	my	6f	:22	:443	1:093	ⒻClm 47500	81	8	5	31	32	23½	35¼	Krone J A	b	115	4.40	87-09 MdstGl1134StpthSng1131½EmphtcStyl115	Lacked rally	8
5Jun92- 1Bel	gd	6f	:221	:444	1:102	ⒻClm 50000	80	6	6	31	32½	31½	3nk	Krone J A	b	117	2.20	88-12 Apprprtly117nkInctng113noEmphtcStyl117	Broke slowly	6
17May92- 4Bel	my	7f	:231	:463	1:234	ⒻClm c-35000	77	4	1	11	1hd	1½	2hd	Bailey J D	b	117	*2.10	85-13 MjstcFrdom115hdEmphtcStyl1173MjstcTrck117	Gamely	6
17May92-Claimed from Hagedorn Charles G, Odintz Jeff Trainer																				
6May92- 2Bel	fst	6f	:221	:451	1:094	ⒻClm 35000	90	3	2	41½	3½	11½	2¾	Bailey J D	b	117	3.70	90-09 MjstcTrck117¾EmphtcStyl1172Undrnsurd114	Bid, wknd	8
15Apr92- 5Aqu	fst	6f	:221	:45	1:10	ⒻClm 35000	83	1	2	1½	1hd	2½	23¼	Martinez R R5	b	112	2.70	88-14 SunnySar1173¼EmphticStyle1122½AllPower117	2nd best	8

LATEST WORKOUTS Nov 9 Bel tr.t 5f fst 1:024 B Oct 30 Bel tr.t 3f fst :38 B

November 14 6½F $12 Won by 4¾

Cool as Crystal — B. g. 5, by Danzig Connection—Plenty Smart, by List
ALVARADO F T (58 7 9 9 .12) — $25,000 Br.—Foster Tilly Farms (NY) — 117
Own.—Joques Farm — Tr.—Moschera Gasper S (57 8 6 8 .14)
Lifetime 24 5 5 2 $103,120 — 1993 11 2 3 2 $60,440 — 1992 10 2 1 0 $23,000 — Wet 5 3 0 0 $34,800
Entered 17Jun93- 5 BEL

3May93- 1Aqu	fst	1⅛	:483	1:131	1:524	Clm c-35000	73	5	1	1hd	2½	44	610¼	Toscano P R	117	*1.10	62-28 ⒹKllck117nkCrftCsh1178Shf'sFrstDnc117	Dueled inside	6
3May93-Claimed from Ostman Jeffrey A, Toscano John T Jr Trainer																			
15Apr93- 8Aqu	fst	1	:461	1:10	1:344	3↑Alw 32500	99	5	1	2½	21	22	32	Toscano P R	119	10.00	88-18 Atort1171¾SnppyLndng117nkClsCrystl119	Dueled wknd	5
31Mar93- 8Aqu	fst	1⅛	:483	1:13	1:503	3↑Alw 30500	97	4	2	21	21	1hd	1¾	Toscano P R	117	3.00	83-22 CoolsCrystl117¾Htt'sMll-GB119nkSnshnMgc117	Driving	6
20Mar93- 3Aqu	fst	1⅛ ⊡	:492	1:131	1:512	Alw 31000	98	3	4	42	43	23	22¼	Rojas R I	117	4.30	84-26 BlrfTrmpts1192¼ClsCrystl117noPrdrGld117	Up for place	7
8Mar93- 7Aqu	fst	1$\frac{1}{16}$ ⊡	:481	1:12	1:424	Alw 31000	98	2	5	51¾	32	1hd	2nk	Toscano P R	117	20.60	91-11 ExoticSlw117nkCoolsCrystl1171½Crrdiogrphr117	Gamely	8
25Feb93- 7Aqu	fst	6f ⊡	:231	:464	1:11	Alw 28000	72	6	7	75½	77	66½	67¾	Toscano P R	122	11.10	80-14 ClvrKnv1171½Wnloc'sRbbtt1172BnAl'sRllh117	No factor	9
14Feb93- 4Aqu	my	6f ⊡	:223	:46	1:103	Alw 27000	94	4	1	52	32	31	11¾	Toscano P R	117	7.60	90-15 CoolsCrystl11713Oblige1173¼King'sCode112	Going away	6
28Jan93- 6Aqu	fst	1$\frac{1}{16}$ ⊡	:473	1:123	1:443	Alw 29000	86	9	3	2hd	1hd	21	37¾	Toscano P R	117	39.80	74-26 PrRmor1177¼SfProspct117½ClsCrystl117	Bid weakened	9
22Jan93- 7Aqu	my	6f ⊡	:224	:46	1:10	Alw 27000	69	6	3	32½	53¼	69	612	Toscano P R	117	6.70	81-13 A Lee Rover1174SaratogaFever1173KingValid117	Faded	10
11Jan93- 7Aqu	fst	6f ⊡	:23	:464	1:12	Alw 27000	81	5	7	86¼	64¾	63¼	52	Toscano P R	117	17.40	81-18 Sulco1121½IfiWereRidgemn117½KingVlid117	Brushed st	10
11Jan93-Placed fourth through disqualification																			

LATEST WORKOUTS Jun 4 Bel 4f fst :50 B Apr 26 Bel tr.t 4f fst :511 B

June 18 1$\frac{1}{16}$ $11.60

Line Pro
Own: Davis Barbara J
GRAELL A (11 0 2 1 .00) $25,000

Dk. b or br g. 3 (Feb)
Sire: Allen's Prospect (Mr. Prospector)
Dam: Going Line (Rambunctious)
Br: Harry L Landry (Md)
Tr: Moschera Gasper S (26 4 4 1 .15)

117

Lifetime Record:	8 2 2 2	$27,855			
1993	8 2 2 2	$27,855	Turf	0 0 0 0	
1992	0 M 0 0		Wet	1 0 1 0	$2,205
Bel	0 0 0 0		Dist	5 1 1 2	$12,690

15Aug93-10Sar fst 7f :223 :46 1:104 1:234 Clm c-35000 76 7 1 2½ 1hd 1hd 52 Krone J A 119 *1.40 84-12 Out For Gold117¾ Benny The Blade115hd The Mechanic117½ Dueled, tired 9
Claimed from Manfuso Robert T, Voss Katharine M Trainer
30Jly93-4Sar fst 6½f :214 :444 1:102 1:17 Clm 35000 85 8 1 55½ 54½ 2½ 11¾ Krone J A 117 6.80 90-09 Line Pro1171¾ Another Anton117hd Out For Gold1175 Driving 8
10Jly93-8Lrl fst 6f :221 :454 :581 1:112 3↑ Alw 16500N1X 64 3 3 43 23 25 33½ Turner T G L 110 *2.20 79-17 Mur Wick1133½ No Delay112hd Line Pro1103 Weakened 7
1Jly93-6Lrl fst 5½f :224 :461 :581 1:043 3↑ Alw 16500N1X 80 7 1 2hd 1hd 1hd 21 Turner T G L 112 3.40 95-16 Aaron's Halo1171 Line Pro1127¾ North Corridor1174 Second best 7
13Jun93-9Lrl fst 6f :221 :451 :572 1:094 Alw 16500N1X 69 3 4 34 35½ 36½ 312 Turner T G 115 19.60 79-12 Higher Strata1179½ Jessie's A Winner1152¾ Line Pro1152 Weakened 7
30May93-10Pim fst 6f :233 :464 :593 1:124 3↑ Md 25000 68 3 2 3nk 2hd 1hd 1no Turner T G 112 3.80 81-19 Line Pro112no Penalty Time1071½ Slip Through Champ11311 Driving 8
15May93-3Pim fst 6f :231 :463 :591 1:12 3↑ Md Sp Wt 46 10 4 31 43 67¾ 812 McCarron C J 115 11.30 73-09 Shuffle Off122no R. D. Golden Land1227 The Joker's Parade114½ Unruly 10
22Apr93-10Pim my 6f :233 :48 1:01 1:14 3↑ Md 18500 51 8 3 21 2hd 2hd 26¾ Turner T G 112 18.00 68-25 Talented Trick1126¾ Line Pro112nk Just For Today112no Lost whip 3/16 8
WORKOUTS: Sep 16 Bel tr.t 3f fst :374 B *3/5* Sep 12 Bel 4f fst :501 B *50/66* Aug 30 Sar tr.t 3f fst :384 B *10/12* Jly 23 Lrl 4f fst :491 B *10/15*

Sept 29 6F $6.40

Emphatic Style, Cool as Crystal, and Line Pro all showed speed but tired on the day they were claimed. All had "back-class," meaning, they had competed effectively at higher levels preceding Moschera's claim. All had been sidelined for at least six weeks and showed only a light training regimen of unspectacular, breezing works during their time away from the races. Emphatic Style and Line Pro received a switch to low-percentage rider Antonio Graell, in each instance providing him with his first winner of the meet.

Many players will not ordinarily consider a horse returning from a layoff and making its first career start on dirt:

Wajir
Own: Pin Oak Stable
PRADO E S (52 7 6 3 .13)

B. c. 4
Sire: Deputy Minister (Vice Regent)
Dam: Mandera (Vaguely Noble)
Br: Pin Oak Stud (Ky)
Tr: Dupps Kristina (2 1 0 0 .50)

119

Lifetime Record:	4 1 0 0	$16,200			
1993	4 1 0 0	$16,200	Turf	3 0 0 0	
1992	0 M 0 0		Wet	0 0 0 0	
Aqu ⊡	1 1 0 0	$16,200	Dist	1 1 0 0	$16,200

19Dec93-7Aqu fst 1⅛ ⊡ :24 :483 1:141 1:48 3↑ Md Sp Wt 70 7 6 43½ 2hd 1hd 11½ Santagata N 120 b 12.10 65-31 Wajir1201½ Seattle Ore1207 Half A Crown1204 7
Wide, lugged in stretch, driving
4Sep93-1Bel fm 1⅜ Ⓣ :502 1:161 1:41 2:18 3↑ Md Sp Wt 25 2 2 21 32½ 614 730¾ Carr D 118 h 32.70 20 36 Lcsc Majeste1181 Toasty A.12210 Lyons Hall1181 Used up 7
21Aug93-3Sar yl 1⅛ Ⓣ :49 1:14 1:391 1:511 3↑ Md Sp Wt 53 8 9 104½ 97 84½ 84½ Velazquez J R 117 65.00 63-22 Majesty's Darby117½ Rain Alert1173 Wild West1171½ Steadied early 11
24Jly93-7Bel fm 1 1/16 Ⓣ :232 :461 1:102 1:422 3↑ Md Sp Wt 36 2 12 1227 1223 1011 1017½ Alvarado F T 116 24.80 67-17 Doctor Disaster1224½ Stellar Hawk116¾ Bye And Comply116nk Never close 12
WORKOUTS: ●Jan 12 Bel tr.t 5f fst 1:001 H *1/26* Jan 1 Bel tr.t 4f fst :493 B *2/36* ●Dec 16 Bel tr.t 6f fst 1:144 H *1/4* Dec 4 Bel tr.t 3f fst :362 B *3/17* Nov 27 Bel tr.t 5f fst 1:014 H *5/40* Nov 18 Bel 5f gd 1:01 H *4/7*

Magical Afleet
Own: Gayno Stables
VELAZQUEZ J R (245 45 46 33 .18)

Ch. f. 4
Sire: Afleet (Mr. Prospector)
Dam: La Divertida (Salt Marsh)
Br: Gayno Stables (Ky)
Tr: Dupps Kristina (7 2 0 1 .29)

119

Lifetime Record:	4 1 1 1	$24,000			
1994	1 1 0 0	$15,000	Turf	3 0 1 1	$9,000
1993	3 M 1 1	$9,000	Wet	0 0 0 0	
Aqu ⊡	1 1 0 0	$15,000	Dist	0 0 0 0	

10Feb94-4Aqu fst 1⅛ ⊡ :493 1:16 1:43 1:562 ⒻMd Sp Wt 63 3 7 56 21 16 110 Velazquez J R 122 2.70 54-46 Magical Afleet12210 Lihue117nk Polish Profit122½ Took up, driving 7
12Sep93-5Bel yl 1 1/16 Ⓣ :232 :462 1:104 1:431 3↑ ⒻMd Sp Wt 69 3 5 48 45 45 24 Bailey J D 118 5.30 76-23 Arctic Aaria1184 Magical Afleet1181 Genie's Flight118½ Finished well 10
12Aug93-2Sar fm 1 1/16 Ⓣ :222 :454 1:112 1:423 3↑ ⒻMd Sp Wt 55 10 9 916 105¾ 86 711 Alvarado F T 117 3.70 70-12 New Account1171¾ Crandall1171½ Holly North1171 Wide trip 11
15Jly93-3Bel fm 1 1/16 Ⓣ :232 :471 1:113 1:422 3↑ ⒻMd Sp Wt 64 3 8 95½ 44 44 36½ Alvarado F T 116 7.30 77-15 Symphony Lady1162½ Grand It Is1164 Magical Afleet1161¾ Checked early 9
WORKOUTS: Feb 8 Bel tr.t 4f fst :49 B *5/26* Feb 2 Bel tr.t 5f fst 1:05 B *7/13* Jan 24 Bel tr.t 6f fst 1:19 B *3/8* Jan 13 Bel tr.t 5f fst 1:05 B *2/4* Jan 7 Bel tr.t 4f fst :514 B *16/23* Jan 1 Bel tr.t 3f fst :371 B *4/10*

Wajir had three starts on grass with little success from July to September, switched to a route on dirt for his first start in three and a half months, and won at 12–1 in his final start as a three-year-old for Kristina Dupps — a trainer who typically compiles only a dozen or so starts each year. Wajir's preparation for his upset win included a six-furlong work, along with two at five furlongs.

Two months later, the Dupps-trained Magical Afleet, who as a three-year-old had also raced three times on grass from July to September, returned from a similar layoff and switched from turf to a dirt route while showing a six-furlong work along with two at five furlongs. Despite taking up in the early stages, she crushed a nondescript field by ten lengths.

As well as long-term patterns (three years had elapsed between Southern Slew and Polacsek, remember), trainer handicappers become attuned to powerful short-term maneuvers:

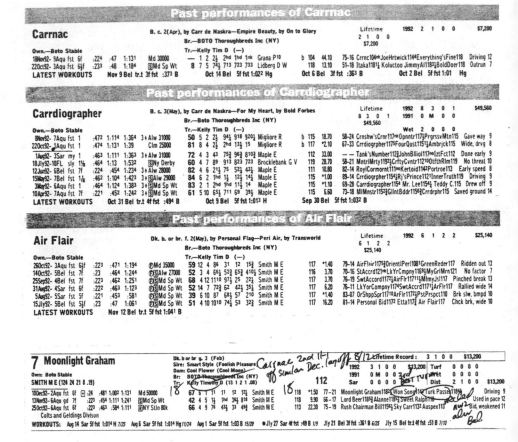

Past performances of Carrnac

Carrnac B. c. 2(Apr), by Carr de Naskra—Empire Beauty, by On to Glory
Br.—BOTO Thoroughbreds Inc (NY)
Own.—Boto Stable Tr.—Kelly Tim D (—)
Lifetime 2 1 0 0 $7,200 | 1992 2 1 0 0 $7,200

18Nov92- 9Aqu fst 6f :224 :47 1:131 Md 30000 — 1 2 2½ 2hd 1hd 1nk Grana P10 b 104 44.10 75–16 Crrnc104nkJoeHrtwick1144Everything'sFine118 Driving 12
22Oct92- 3Aqu fst 6½f :233 :48 1:184 [S]Md Sp Wt 8 7 5 74½ 713 723 733 Lidberg D W 118 13.10 51–18 Itaka1181¼ Koluctoo JimmyAl1183½BoldDoer118 Outrun 7
LATEST WORKOUTS Nov 9 Bel tr.t 3f fst :373 B Oct 14 Bel 5f fst 1:022 Hg Oct 6 Bel 3f fst :363 B Oct 2 Bel 5f fst 1:01 Hg

Past performances of Carrdiographer

Carrdiographer B. c. 3(May), by Carr de Naskra—For My Heart, by Bold Forbes
Br.—Boto Thoroughbreds Inc (NY)
Own.—Boto Stable Tr.—Kelly Tim D (—)
Lifetime 8 3 0 1 $49,560 | 1992 8 3 0 1 $49,560 | 1991 0 M 0 0 | Wet 2 0 0 0

8Nov92- 7Aqu fst 1 :472 1:114 1:364 3↑Alw 31000 50 5 2 2½ 94¼ 918 920¼ Migliore R b 115 18.70 58–24 Crnshw'sCrnr117nkOpnntr117½PrgrssvMtn115 Gave way 9
22Oct92- 1Aqu fst 1 :474 1:131 1:39 Clm 25000 81 8 4 2½ 2hd 13½ 15 Migliore R b 117 *2.10 67–33 Crrdiogrpher1175FourQust1151½Ambrjck115 Wide, drvg 8
1Aug92- 3Sar my 1 :463 1:111 1:363 3↑Alw 31000 72 4 3 43 75¾ 96¾ 810¾ Maple E 112 33.00 — — Tank'sNumber112¾JohnBlliol117noIztFct112 Done early 9
18Jly92-10FL sly 1⅛ :464 1:13 1:532 [S]Ny Derby 60 4 7 89 913 823 723 Brocklebank G V 119 28.70 58–21 MntrlMrty1192½CrftyCvntr11210OtfthRlm119 No threat 10
12Jun92- 6Bel fst 7f :224 :454 1:234 3↑Alw 28000 82 4 6 21½ 75 52¼ 43¼ Maple E 111 10.80 82–14 RoylCormornt111noKertoid1142Portroe113 Early speed 8
15May92- 7Bel fst 1 1/16 :462 1:104 1:423 3↑[S]Alw 29000 84 6 2 1hd 1½ 12¼ 14¼ Maple E 115 *1.00 89–14 Crrdiogrpher1154¼Rj'sPrince1121InnerTruth119 Driving 9
3May92- 6Aqu fst 1 :464 1:124 1:383 3↑[S]Md Sp Wt 83 2 1 2hd 1hd 11½ 14 Maple E 115 *1.10 69–28 Carrdiographer1154 Mr. Lee1154¼ Teddy C.115 Drew off 9
10Apr92- 7Aqu fst 7f :221 :452 1:242 3↑[S]Md Sp Wt 61 5 10 65½ 711 69 39½ Maple E 115 6.60 73–18 MlMnstr1152¾GllntBddr1156¾Crrdrphr115 Saved ground 14
LATEST WORKOUTS Oct 31 Bel tr.t 4f fst :494 B Oct 9 Bel 5f fst 1:013 H Sep 30 Bel 5f fst 1:032 B

Past performances of Air Flair

Air Flair Dk. b. or br. f. 2(May), by Personal Flag—Peri Air, by Transworld
Br.—Boto Thoroughbreds Inc (NY)
Own.—Boto Stable Tr.—Kelly Tim D (—)
Lifetime 6 1 2 2 $25,140 | 1992 6 1 2 2 $25,140

26Oct92- 3Aqu fst 6½f :223 :471 1:194 (F)Md 35000 59 12 4 86 31 12 15¾ Smith M E 117 *1.40 79–14 AirFlair1175¾OrientlPerl1081GreenReder117 Ridden out 13
14Oct92- 5Bel fst 7f :23 :464 1:244 (F)[S]Alw 27000 52 3 4 66¼ 52¾ 65¾ 410¼ Smith M E 116 3.70 70–16 StAccrd121nkLkYrCmpny1169½MyGrlMrn121 No factor 7
25Sep92- 4Bel fst 7f :223 :462 1:251 (F)[S]Md Sp Wt 68 4 12 1110 97½ 25 22¼ Smith M E 117 3.70 76–19 SwtAccord1172¼AirFlr11711½MlmyJsl117 Pinched break 13
31Aug92- 4Sar fst 6f :222 :463 1:123 (F)[S]Md Sp Wt 52 14 7 72¾ 62 42½ 35¼ Smith M E 117 6.20 76–11 LkYorCompny1174SwtAccrd1171½ArFlr117 Rallied wide 14
5Aug92- 5Sar fst 5f :221 :453 :581 (F)[S]Md Sp Wt 39 6 10 87 68½ 57 210 Smith M E 117 *1.40 83–07 OrShppSpr11710ArFlr1172½PstPrspct110 Brk slw, bmpd 10
15Jly92- 5Bel fst 5½f :23 :47 1:061 (F)[S]Md Sp Wt 51 4 10 1010 74¼ 53 32¾ Smith M E 117 16.20 81–14 Personal Bid1172 Etta117¾ Air Flair117 Chck brk, wide 10
LATEST WORKOUTS Nov 12 Bel tr.t 5f fst 1:041 B

7 Moonlight Graham
Own: Boto Stable
SMITH M E (124 24 21 8 .19)
Dk. b or br g. 3 (Feb)
Sire: Smart Style (Foolish Pleasure)
Dam: Cool Flower (Cool Moon)
Br: BOTO Thoroughbreds Inc (NY)
Tr: Kelly Timothy D (13 1 2 1 .08)
112
Lifetime Record: 3 1 0 0 $13,200
1992 3 1 0 0 $13,200 | Turf 0 0 0 0
1991 0 M 0 0 | Wet 0 0 0 0
Sar 0 0 0 0 | Dist 2 1 0 0 $13,200

10Dec92- 2Aqu fst 6f [•] :24 :481 1:002 1:131 Md 50000 67 6 1 11 11 12 12¼ Smith M E 118 *1.50 77–21 Moonlight Graham1182¼Won Song1142Turk Passer1184 Driving 9
13Nov92- 6Aqu gd 7f :223 :454 1:111 1:241 [S]Md Sp Wt 42 4 5 1½ 1hd 36½ 818 Smith M E 118 9.90 66–17 Lord Beer1185¾Alanne1185¼Sweet Ralph118 Used in pace 12
25Oct92- 6Aqu fst 6f :223 :463 :584 1:111 [R]NY Stln 80k 66 4 9 76 43½ 33 49¾ Smith M E 113 22.30 75–19 Rush Chairman Bill1156½Sky Carr1132 Auspex113 Bid, weakened 11
Colts and Geldings Divison
WORKOUTS: Aug 14 Sar 5f fst 1:014 H 7/25 Aug 6 Sar 5f fst 1:014 Hg 11/24 Aug 1 Sar 5f fst 1:03 B 15/20 ●Jly 27 Sar 4f fst :49 B 1/9 Jly 21 Bel 3f fst :361 B 6/25 Jly 15 Bel tr.t 4f fst :51 B 7/10

Carrnac 2nd 1-1 off similar Dec. layoff 8/12
18 18 3rd Best Turf Alw2 alw Bel.

At the 1992 Aqueduct fall meet, Tim Kelly was "automatic" when he dropped a Boto Stable–owned, lightly raced New York–bred into a claiming race for the first time following a drubbing against nonclaiming company. Three of Kelly's winners were favored and won by open lengths, but Carrnac escaped at 44–1.

Emphatic Style — B. m. 5, by Crafty Prospector—Pebble Patter, by Rock Talk
Br.—Due Process Stable (NJ)
Own.—Hagedorn Charles G — Tr.—Odintz Jeff
Lifetime 40 10 7 8 $114,202 — 1992 4 1 2 1 $26,400 — 1991 22 4 4 4 $44,685

6Feb92- 1Aqu	fst	6f	⊡:232	:464	1:112	ⒻClm 47500	2 2 11 1hd 1½ 2hd	Chavez J F	b	117	*1.10	86–22	WildWarning113hdEmphaticStyle117noSunnySar1153¾	Gamely	5
29Jan92- 6Aqu	fst	6f	⊡:23	:462	1:121	ⒻClm 47500	5 1 31 31 31½ 31	Chavez J F	b	117	*1.60	81–24	Appropritely110nkDixieRouge117¾EmphticStyle117½	Willingly	5
18Jan92- 6Aqu	fst	6f	⊡:224	:464	1:121	ⒻClm 70000	5 6 1hd 1½ 2hd 23½	Chavez J F	b	113	*2.30	78–19	Brechin'sLss1153½EmphticStyl113½BlRy113½	Dueled, held 2nd	8
3Jan92- 1Aqu	fst	6f	⊡:231	:463	1:111	ⒻClm 45000	2 3 12 15 15½ 15¾	Cordero A Jr	b	113	4.10	87–20	Emphatic Style1135¾ Calistay113nkWildWarning1132¼	Driving	7
18Dec91- 4Aqu	fst	6f	⊡:223	:464	1:13	3↑ⒻClm c-35000	3 4 31½ 31½ 33 65½	Cordero A Jr	b	117	3.50	72–25	MagesticWillow119½SiouxNrrows117½ModestGlow1172¾	Tired	6

Past performances of Catch Chati

Catch Chati — Dk. b. or br. m. 6, by Chati—Wait Till Dawn, by Cloudy Dawn
Br.—Brusaw A (NJ)
Own.—Odintz Jeff — Tr.—Odintz Jeff
Lifetime 48 8 8 13 $91,739 — 1992 4 1 1 0 $19,720 — 1991 17 4 2 4 $35,296 — Turf 4 0 0 1 $1,595

3Feb92- 7Aqu	fst	170	⊡:474	1:142	1:452	ⒻAlw 31000	4 2 2½ 1½ 1½ 2¾	Chavez J F	b	117	2.00	77–19	SunnyBarbie122¾CtchChti1175¾I'mTickledPink1172¾	2nd best	7
23Jan92- 3Aqu	fst	1 1/16	⊡:471	1:114	1:454	ⒻClm 37500	3 — — — — 511¾	Migliore R	b	115	6.00	67–24	EnglishChrm1178½Bllynoe115nkTinyGrsshoppr1193½	Fog, tired	7
10Jan92- 5Aqu	fst	1⅛	⊡:482	1:132	1:534	ⒻClm 22500	7 1 11½ 12½ 15 19¾	Chavez J F	b	115	9.30	74–28	Catch Chati1159¾ Road Block1131½ Fitfoe1152½	Ridden out	7
5Jan92- 1Aqu	my	6f	⊡:224	:462	1:12	ⒻClm c-17500	4 3 511 56½ 49½ 49¾	Bravo J		117	4.70	73–23	SouthernSooner1176½SongOfJoy1153KillrBuzz113nk	No factor	5
18Dec91 5Aqu	fst	6f	⊡:223	:47	1:14	3↑ⒻClm 14000	4 8 917 815 78¾ 1nk	Smith M E		117	5.90	73–25	CatchChati117nkLoisL.117½Crafty'sWish1124¾	Up final strides	9

LATEST WORKOUTS Dec 12 Bel tr.t 4f fst :491 B

Past performances of Rocket Battle

Rocket Battle — Ch. m. 5, by Crimson Battle—Rocketola, by Nicks Joy
Br.—Robbins B J (Ky)
Own.—Stox N Box Stable — Tr.—Odintz Jeff
Lifetime 41 9 7 3 $131,914 — 1992 4 1 2 0 $17,200 — 1991 18 5 3 2 $54,600 — Turf 1 0 0 0

3Feb92- 1Aqu	fst	170	⊡:494	1:151	1:442	ⒻClm 17500	4 1 11½ 11 12 13	Chavez J F	b	117	3.30	83–19	RocketBttle1173FoolinSpruce117nkSolidAngl1171¼	Mild drive	7
23Jan92- 5Aqu	fst	170	⊡:481	1:134	1:462	ⒻClm c-14000	1 — — — — 45¼	Lamance C	b	119	*1.50	68–24	TwentyFlags1074WorldClssPro113¾VictoriPlce115½	Fog, tired	8
10Jan92- 9Aqu	fst	1 1/16	⊡:482	1:143	1:501	ⒻClm 14000	7 1 1½ 1½ 12½ 2½	Soto J F7	b	112	3.50	56–28	SportyChrm117½RocktBttl112hdWrldClssPr113¾	Couldn't last	10
1Jan92- 9Aqu	fst	1 3/16	⊡:474	1:13	2:001	ⒻClm 14000	9 1 11½ 15 1hd 22	Soto J7	b	110	*1.30	80–23	Lady Lear1152 Rocket Battle1109½ Snofight1096½	Held 2nd	10
22Dec91- 9Aqu	fst	1 1/16	⊡:473	1:131	1:47	3↑ⒻClm 12000	9 1 13 11 17 19	Soto J F7	b	106	3.90	73–32	Rocket Battle1069 Lady Lear1133¾ Grittle115nk	Ridden out	10

LATEST WORKOUTS Dec 10 Bel tr.t 3f my :39 B

Past performances of Am Possible

Am Possible — Dk. b. or br. m. 5, by Pilot Ship—Am Impossible, by Rollicking
Br.—Troncone R J (NJ)
Own.—Gullo Giacomo — Tr.—Odintz Jeff
Lifetime 44 12 10 4 $303,963 — 1992 2 1 0 0 $13,200 — 1991 15 4 3 1 $119,561 — Turf 2 0 0 0

3Feb92- 3Aqu	fst	170	⊡:482	1:134	1:433	ⒻClm 35000	1 1 11½ 11 12½ 16	Chavez J F	b	117	*.60	87–19	AmPossible1176TinyGrsshopper115¾Entrust1171½	Ridden out	7
25Jan92- 1Aqu	fst	1¼	⊡:49	1:402	2:053	ⒻHandicap	3 1 12½ 1hd 44¼ 511	Santagata N	b	115	*1.60	83–15	Maxamount1138½ Jessi Jessi1161 Health Farm115¾	Gave way	5
30Dec91- 5Aqu	sly	170	⊡:473	1:132	1:422	3↑ⒻClm 70000	3 2 1½ 15 13½ 14¾	Chavez J F	b	113	2.80	93–18	AmPossibl1134¾SpdMnstr1154½CrftyTndron11712½	Ridden out	4
13Dec91- 3Aqu	fst	6f	⊡:22	:45	1:104	3↑ⒻClm 47500	8 6 85½ 87½ 54½ 21½	Chavez J F	b	115	8.90	87–11	Joy'sJoJo1171½AmPossible115hdCompnyGirl113nk	Belated bid	9
22Nov91- 5Aqu	sly	1⅛	:474	1:124	1:513	3↑ⒻClm c-35000	8 4 42½ 3½ 21 11	Cordero A Jr	b	117	3.00	78–28	AmPossible1171MyLady'sWim1198CullinnDimond112½	Driving	9

22Nov91-cppginally scheduled on turf

During the winter of 1991–92, Jeff Odintz saddled several winners first or second time off the claim, and all were older mares. Note that Catch Chati and Am Possible stretched from sprint to route in wiring their respective fields by lengthy margins. Emphatic

Style (here she is again!) and Rocket Battle also won convincingly. Notice the presence of Jorge Chavez everywhere.

During this period, it would have been foolhardy to consider a serious wager against any mare recently claimed by Odintz who was being ridden by Chavez.

Strawberry's Lass
Own: Perez Robert

Dk. b or br f. 3 (Jan)
Sire: Strawberry Road–Au (Whiskey Road)
Dam: Blushing Lass (Blushing Groom)
Br: Paulson Allen E (Ky)
Tr: Callejas Alfredo (7 3 0 0 .43)

122

Lifetime Record:	11 2 0 1	$36,855			
1993	9 2 0 1	$36,155	Turf	0 0 0 0	
1992	2 M 0 0	$700	Wet	2 0 0 0	$3,930
Bel	1 0 0 0	$3,180	Dist	1 0 0 0	

18Sep93–9Bel	sly	7f	:231 :464 1:11 1:232	ⓕCicada 50k	29	1	3	45½	45½	416	432½	Chavez J F		114 b	13.10	53–14	Personal Bid1185½ Sheila's Revenge1184 In Excelcis Deo11623	Outrun	4
23Aug93–7Sar	fst	7f	:222 :451 1:094 1:222 3↑	ⓕAlw 27500N2X	55	2	5	11½	3½	85¾	816	Chavez J F		117 b	10.10	77–08	In Excelcis Deo1136¾ This Ain't Kansas112no Miss Jazz117½	Used up	8
9Aug93–6Sar	fst	6f	:22 :45 :571 1:10 3↑	ⓕAlw 26500N1X	86	2	7	52½	43	31½	11¼	Chavez J F		112 b	39.80	92–08	Strawberry's Lass1121¼ Regal Solution1122 Lady Ashford114¾	Driving	10
16Jun93–7GG	fst	6f	:214 :453 :581 1:111 3↑	ⓕMd Sp Wt	69	9	1	64½	3nk	13	13	Baze R A	LB	117 b	3.30	84–13	Strawberry'sLass1173 CountryCruise117nk InyalRouge1171½	Steady drive	10
16May93–4GG	fst	6f	:214 :443 :572 1:103 3↑	ⓕMd Sp Wt	56	3	6	52½	34½	26	48	Baze G	LB	115 b	4.90	79–13	Sweet Savanna1154½ Kind And Gentle1152 CountryCruise1151½	Weakened	9
20Feb93–6SA	my	1$\frac{1}{16}$	:224 :463 1:114 1:442	ⓕMd Sp Wt	50	5	1	12	1½	57	518	Valenzuela P A	LB	117 b	3.60	64–18	Fondly Remembered1172½ Alyshena117½ Portugese Starlet1177	Faltered	7
6Feb93–9SA	fst	1	:223 :46 1:11 1:37	ⓕMd Sp Wt	47	4	2	12	43½	914	922¼	Valenzuela P A	LB	117 b	7.00	63–12	Darling Sola1173½ Fondly Remembered1175 Breezing Slew1173½		10
Checked, rank, saddle slipped																			
24Jan93–4SA	fst	6f	:214 :444 :571 1:101	ⓕMd Sp Wt	62	4	5	43	34	36½	59¼	Valenzuela P A	LB	117 b	4.30	77–15	Dash For Flash1172¾ Magical Flash1172¾ Tooty Brush1172	Bumped start	9
3Jan93–6SA	gd	6½f	:213 :451 1:11 1:173	ⓕMd Sp Wt	73	2	9	64	51¾	31½	33¼	Valenzuela P A	LB	117 b	7.20	80–15	FineImprssion1172¾ TimForAStorm117½ Strwbrry'sLss1176	Steadied 1/4	9
5Sep92–4Dmr	fst	6f	:22 :45 :571 1:091	ⓕMd Sp Wt	45	5	3	2½	43½	713	721½	Valenzuela P A		B 117	7.70	71–07	Set Them Free1176 Enchanted Spot1172 Afto117	Stopped	9

WORKOUTS: Sep 9 Bel Ⓣ 3f tf :36 B (d) *1/3* Aug 6 Sar 5f fst 1:032 Bg *20/24*

Cugar
Own: Perez Robert

B. g. 3 (Apr)
Sire: Allen's Prospect (Mr. Prospector)
Dam: Fancied (Dancing Moss)
Br: Paulson Allen E (Ky)
Tr: Callejas Alfredo (7 3 0 0 .43)

122

Lifetime Record:	10 1 3 1	$30,300			
1993	8 1 3 1	$29,700	Turf	0 0 0 0	
1992	2 M 0 0	$600	Wet	2 1 0 0	$16,200
Bel	1 1 0 0	$16,200	Dist	0 0 0 0	

18Sep93–1Bel	sly	1$\frac{1}{16}$ ⊗	:232 :463 1:121 1:451 3↑	Md Sp Wt	79	5	4	44	23	1hd	16¾	Chavez J F		118	1.90	76–15	Cugar1186¾ Hatchee1189 Lyons Hall118hd	Driving	6
1Sep93–2Dmr	fst	1$\frac{1}{16}$	:223 :47 1:121 1:433 3↑	Md 32000	85	7	9	96¼	52	1hd	2no	Desormeaux K J	LB	118	*1.10	84–16	Jutland122no Cugar11811 Reservenotachieved111½	Nipped for win	12
4Aug93–9Dmr	fst	1$\frac{1}{16}$	:231 :472 1:122 1:442 3↑	Md 32000	76	7	7	83½	43	31½	21	Valenzuela P A	LB	117	*2.30	79–24	Czar Of Maui1151 Cugar1171½ Strong1154	Good effort	11
25Jly93–2Hol	fst	1$\frac{1}{16}$	:231 :47 1:114 1:444 3↑	Md 32000	67	6	4	52¼	42½	23	2¾	Valenzuela P A	LB	117	6.10	76–19	Son Of A Bronze117¾ Cugar117hd Imperial Kid1164	4 Wide stretch	10
5Jun93–9Hol	my	1$\frac{1}{16}$	:232 :473 1:133 1:464 3↑	Md 32000	67	3	4	43½	31½	68½	613	Flores D R	LB	115	3.30	54–32	NtrlFftySx1159 I'mRnd115¾ Momonymomonymmny115nk	4 Wide stretch	10
8May93–2Hol	fst	1$\frac{1}{16}$	:224 :46 1:11 1:44 3↑	Md 32000	74	11	6	66¼	54½	54	33½	Flores D R	LB	115	19.70	77–16	Mojave Morn1172 Czar Of Maui1151½ Cugar115¾	5 Wide stretch	12
24Mar93–4SA	fst	6f	:214 :451 :58 1:11	Md 32000	47	6	6	63½	78½	78¾	612	Flores D R	LB	118	12.50	70–15	Choices11810 Intent To Assent118½ Designated Hitter118½	Outrun	12
6Mar93–6SA	fst	6f	:214 :444 :57 1:093	Md Sp Wt	29	1	6	74	109½	1113	1223½	Valenzuela P A	LB	118 b	26.70	66–10	Ltthbiggtorout1181 HrrisCounty1182 MirculousEdition118hd	No mishap	12
15Jun92–3Hol	fst	5f	:214 :451 :58	Md 80000	50	2	3	65¼	68	58	57¾	Valenzuela P A	LB	117	16.00	84–09	Gray Endeavor117hd Super Trax1176 Dr. Bryan117	Steadied 3/8	8
21May92–3Hol	fst	4½f	:221 :46 :522	Md Sp Wt	38	3	6	78		76¼	87½	Valenzuela P A		B 117	3.40	88–11	Barrett's Bullet117hd Fleet Wizard117½ Altazarr117	Outrun	10

WORKOUTS: Sep 10 Dmr 4f fst :494 H *28/36* Aug 26 Dmr 7f fst 1:283 H *12/14* Aug 15 Dmr 4f fst :483 H *18/63* Aug 1 Dmr 4f fst :484 H *12/42*

Franz
Own: Perez Robert

Ch. g. 3 (Feb)
Sire: Allen's Prospect (Mr. Prospector)
Dam: Rea (Redtop III)
Br: Allen E. Paulson (Ky)
Tr: Callejas Alfredo (7 3 0 0 .43)

122

Lifetime Record:	4 1 0 0	$17,850			
1993	4 1 0 0	$17,850	Turf	0 0 0 0	
1992	0 M 0 0		Wet	1 1 0 0	$15,000
Bel	1 1 0 0	$15,000	Dist	0 0 0 0	

27Sep93–9Bel	sly	6f	:22 :461 :584 1:121 3↑	Md Sp Wt	74	7	1	1hd	1hd	1hd	1no	Perret C		118 b	6.30	79–22	Franz118no Rise To Rule122no Eyesight118½	Hard drive	8
30Aug93–9Dmr	fst	6f	:22 :45 :573 1:103 3↑	Md 32000	70	8	3	51¾	43	45	44¾	Valenzuela P A		B 117	6.30	81–14	Maxinkuckee112½ Summer Lord1172 Duke Of Dirtywater1172½	Wide trip	11
9Aug93–4Dmr	fst	6f	:214 :451 :573 1:103 3↑	Md 40000	67	4	4	31½	31	64½	66¼	Valenzuela P A		B 117	7.50	80–09	Breathless Speed1152¾ Mydadscounteric115hd Concettino115nk	Gave way	8
30Jly93–2Dmr	fst	6½f	:22 :453 1:094 1:162 3↑	Md 50000	73	5	5	65	64	45½	45½	Valenzuela P A		117	5.10	83–13	Super Trax117hd Juiceberry1152 Copelan's Eagle1163½	Not enough late	8

WORKOUTS: Sep 15 SLR tr.t 4f fst :49 H *8/10* Sep 10 SLR tr.t 3f fst :38 H *8/9* Aug 27 Dmr 5f fst 1:001 H *14/64* Aug 20 SLR tr.t 3f fst :38 H *5/7*

In the late summer of 1993, owner Robert Perez and trainer Alfredo Callejas shipped in with a trio of three-year-olds from California, all of which had been bred by Allen Paulson.

Strawberry's Lass, the first invader, lit up the board at 40–1 on August 9 while rising in class. On September 18, Cugar, beaten repeatedly by $32,000 maiden claimers on the West Coast, ran away and hid from an off-the-turf special-weight field. Nine days later, Franz was 6–1 in a special-weight sprint, as the crowd shied away from a horse who'd lost three times in maiden claimers at descending price tags. Standard logic did not apply in the face of this short-term trend: Franz handled the rise, withstanding race-long pressure to prevail by a determined nose.

For those who care to take trainer analysis a step further, tracking beaten favorites is highly recommended. In place of the win price, note the odds. Also note finish position relative to the size of the field and beaten lengths:

```
Main Bid-Ir                 B. g. 4, by Auction Ring—Annabella, by Habitat          Lifetime      1993  4 1 0 2   $22,880
VELASQUEZ J (13 2 1 1 .15)        Br.—Samac Ltd (Ire)                                9 2 0 3      1992  3 0 0 1    $1,201
Own.—Buckram Oak Farm             Tr.—Moubarak Mohammed (3 0 1 1 .00)      121       $28,541      Turf  8 2 0 3   $28,381
29Apr93- 2Aqu gd 1 1/16 (T):47³ 1:12⁴ 1:45² 3+Alw 28500  80 9 4 4⁹ 3² 2½ 1nk Velasquez J   119 *1.00 84-11 MnBd-Ir119nkDovrCst119nkRsnblThght112   Bmpd, drvg 9
30Mar93- 8GP fm *1 1/16 (T)          1:45⁴ +   Alw 39000  79 3 4 4¹¹ 4³ 4⁴ 34½ Ramos W S     113  7.30 83-19 Starion117¹ D's Moment114³½ Main Bid-Ir113          10
      30Mar93-Crowded leaving chute, late rally
13Feb93- 8GP fm 1 1/16 (T):46² 1:11² 1:42 +  Alw 21000  81 7 7 5³¼ 3¹ 2hd 3³½ Ramos W S   113 27.80 83-12 Alfrs114²½AssrtdDnts112¹MnBd-Ir113  Lacked response 12
 2Jan93- 9Crc fst 1 :47 1:13³ 1:41⁴     Alw 16000    48 8 7 8¹⁶ 9¹⁴ 8¹³ 8²⁰ Romero R P     113 32.80 66-10 YnkAx115⁵½TrExplodng112¹½SonfScrt112  Showed little 9
      2Jan93-Originally scheduled on turf
20Aug92♦4York(Eng) gd*1         1:37 (T)Bradford&BingleyHcp        20²⁷ Dettori L  125 14.00 — — Doulb'sImge123½ Deprector135nk NoblePet122  Prom 5f 22
30Jly92♦3Goodwood(Eng) gd 1     1:36³(T)SchweppesGoldenMileHcp     14¹² Carson W   125 10.00 — — LittleBean114² Mudaffar125no PolonezPrim109  Outrun 21
27Jun92♦5Newmarket(Eng) gd 1    1:40⁴(T)HascombeStudHcp             3¹½ Dettori L  133  7.00 — — Spkr'sHous1321½ RdKit106hd MinBid133  Prom thruout 7
20ct91♦5Salisbury(Eng) gd*7f    1:29³(T)MarlboroughStks(Mdn)        1²½ Munro A    126  3.50 — — Main Bid126²½ Kayvee126⁵ JudgeandJury126  Led fnl 3f 15
19Sep91♦8Lingfield(Eng) gd 7f   1:22⁴(T)EBF Putney Stks(Mdn)       5¹²¼ Cruz A S   126  4.50 — — L'Hermin126⁸ Cstillt126²¾ Grn'sColourist126  No threat 11
LATEST WORKOUTS   Apr 24 Bel tr.t 5f fst 1:02¹ B   Apr 11 Pay tr.t 3f fst :38¹ B   Mar 16 Pay tr.t 4f fst :50² B
```

May 15 1 1/16 (T) AlwNW2 13–1 6th of 10/beaten 9L

```
Tropical Waters          B. f. 3(Feb), by Green Forest—Northern Premier, by Northern Baby   Lifetime   1993  2 1 0 0   $15,300
VELASQUEZ J (90 8 9 11 .09)       Br.—Buckram Oak Farm (Ky)                                 4 1 2 0    1992  2 M 2 0    $2,327
Own.—Buckram Oak Farm             Tr.—Moubarak Mohammed (30 2 6 5 .07)        114           $17,627    Turf  4 1 2 0   $17,627
 6Jun93- 5Bel gd 1 1/16 (T):47 1:11⁴ 1:42⁴ 3+(F)Md Sp Wt  88 6 3 3¹½ 2½ 2¹½ 1³¼ Velasquez J  114 *1.60 82-14 TropiclWtrs114³¼LittlTobin114¹½Scrtrit'sFir114  Driving 9
 2May93- 5Aqu fm 1 1/16 (T):47⁴ 1:12⁴ 1:45¹ 3+(F)Md Sp Wt  66 1 3 8⁰ 6³½ 5⁵ 5⁵¼ Velasquez J  115  2.50 80-11 Imh115¹½[DH]LittlTobin115[DH]ChcShb115  Rank, bore out 8
11Aug92♦3Yarmouth(Eng) fm*6f     1:14 (T)EBF Manshipo Stks(Mdn)       2⁴ Carson W     121 *1.00 — — LostSoldr126⁴ TropclWtrs121²½ Mm'zllAngot121  Wknd 5
20Jly92♦2Nottingham(Eng) gd*6f   1:15¹(T)EBF S & A StaplesStks(Mdn    2½ Weaver J⁵    116  4.50 — — Shiro 126½ Tropical Waters 116⁷ Bold Face126  Did, led 14
LATEST WORKOUTS   Jun 2 Bel 5f fst 1:02³ B   May 25 Bel 4f fst :48⁴ B   May 18 Bel 5f fst 1:02⁴ B   May 11 Bel 4f fst :52 B
```

June 14 1 mile (T) AlwNW1 8–5 2nd of 8/beaten 4L

```
Russian Tango            B. f. 3(Feb), by Nijinsky II—Brave Raj, by Rajab            Lifetime    1993  3 1 0 1   $18,080
KRONE J A (217 39 26 33 .18)      Br.—Warren W. Rosenthal (Ky)                        3 1 0 1     1992  0 M 0 0
Own.—Buckram Oak Farm             Tr.—Moubarak Mohammed (43 5 8 8 .12)      113       $18,080     Turf  1 1 0 0   $15,300
14Jun93- 2Bel fm 1 1/16 [T]:47¹ 1:11² 1:40² 3+(F)Md Sp Wt  92 7 3 2¹ 2hd 1²½ 1⁷ Krone J A   114 *1.60 94-11 RussinTngo114⁷RunningOnE114⁵¾SpikHl114  Ridden out 8
19Mar93- 3GP gd 7f :23 :46¹ 1:24⁴   (F)Md Sp Wt  54 11 3 6⁶ 5⁸ 4⁵¼ 4¹¹ Ramos W S   120  5.20 68-19 FuturePretense120nkOneAccount120³¾HermitgHtti120  12
      19Mar93-Drifted in on turn lacked response
24Feb93- 6GP fst 7f :22³ :46² 1:26²  (F)Md Sp Wt  57 2 8 8²½ 7⁴¼ 4⁷½ 3⁸½ Ramos W S   120  5.50 62-23 MissObsession120¹FuturePretense120⁷½RussinTngo120  12
      24Feb93-Brushed start, late rally
LATEST WORKOUTS   Jun 26 Bel 5f fst 1:01⁴ B   ●Jun 10 Bel [T] 6f gd 1:15¹ B (d)   Jun 3 Bel [T] 6f fm 1:14⁴ H (d)   May 27 Bel [T] 1 fm 1:38³ B (d)
```

July 1 1 1/16 (T) AlwNW1 3–10 2nd of 7/beaten 1L

During the spring and summer of 1993, trainer Mohammed Moubarak shipped north from Florida with a string of lightly raced and well-bred grass runners for Buckram Oak Farm and racked up several wins in maiden and/or preliminary allowance races in the span of a few weeks.

But none of Moubarak's winners, no matter how impressive, were able to repeat when hiked to the next level — a trend that should've been apparent by the time Russian Tango was installed at miserly 3–10 odds on July 1.

In late winter of 1994, the powerful Phipps/McGaughey barn saddled a pair of beaten favorites on Gulfstream Park's Florida Derby undercard:

Heavenly Prize
Own: Phipps Ogden
SMITH M E (339 70 57 38 .21)
B. f. 3 (Feb)
Sire: Seeking the Gold (Mr. Prospector)
Dam: Oh What a Dance (Nijinsky II)
Br: Phipps Ogden (Ky)
Tr: McGaughey Claude III (33 14 7 1 .42)
118
Lifetime Record: 3 2 0 1 $285,000
1993 3 2 0 1 $285,000 | Turf 0 0 0 0
1992 0 M 0 0 | Wet 0 0 0 0
GP 0 0 0 0 | Dist 1 1 0 0 $15,000

6Nov93-3SA fst 1 1/16 :232 :472 1:112 1:43 ⒻB C JuvFils-G1 90 4 4 42 32 31½ 33 Smith M E 119 *1.90 86-10 Phone Chatter119hd Sardula1193 Heavenly Prize119½ Inside bid 8
16Oct93-4Bel fst 1 :224 :451 1:10 1:352 ⒻFrizette-G1 94 5 6 62½ 2hd 12½ 17 Smith M E 119 2.40 91-12 Heavenly Prize1197 Facts Of Love1194¾ Footing1192½ Wide, driving 7
15Sep93-5Bel fst 6f :224 :462 :583 1:104 ⒻMd Sp Wt 88 4 4 52½ 2hd 12½ 19 Smith M E 117 *1.40 86-19 Heavenly Prize1179 Amy Be Happy1171¾ Vibelle117nk Ridden out 7
WORKOUTS: Mar 6 GP 3f fst :374 B 11/18 ●Feb 27 Pay 4f fst :503 B 1/6 Feb 22 Pay 4f fst :523 B 13/16 Feb 18 Pay 4f sly :582 B 4/4 Feb 14 Pay 3f sly :401 B 2/3

March 12 6F $50K Stk Even money 2nd of 13/beaten 2L

Dispute
Own: Phipps Ogden Mills
BAILEY J D (274 65 44 24 .24)
B. f. 4
Sire: Danzig (Northern Dancer)
Dam: Resolver (Reviewer)
Br: Phipps Ogden Mills (Ky)
Tr: McGaughey Claude III (33 14 7 1 .42)
122
Lifetime Record: 13 7 3 1 $789,530
1993 11 6 2 1 $750,226 | Turf 1 0 0 1 $11,196
1992 2 1 1 0 $39,304 | Wet 2 1 1 0 $58,400
GP 3 3 0 0 $148,800 | Dist 2 1 1 0 $35,704

6Nov93-4SA fst 1⅛ :464 1:11 1:36 1:481 3↑ⒻB C Distaff-G1 102 2 3 43 42 52¾ 43½ Bailey J D B 120 4.50 85-10 Hollywood Wildcat120no Paseana1232½ Re Toss1231 No late bid 8
16Oct93-5Bel fst 1⅛ :452 1:091 1:34 1:471 3↑ⒻBeldame-G1 107 6 4 43 41½ 11 11¾ Bailey J D 119 *1.40 93-12 Dispute1191¾ Shared Interest123nk Vivano1231¾ Driving 6
19Sep93-8Bel my 1 1/16 :232 :464 1:103 1:414 3↑ⒻRuffian H-G1 103 5 4 33 31½ 22 22½ Desormeaux K J 115 3.20 90-16 Shared Interest1142½ Dispute1153 Turnback The Alarm1232½ Second best 5
4Sep93-8Bel fst 1⅛ :442 1:09 1:342 1:471 ⒻGazelle H-G1 102 6 3 38 33 15 17½ Bailey J D 120 *2.00 93-11 Dispute1207½ Silky Feather117hd In Her Glory112no Mild drive 8
6Aug93-8Sar fm 1 1/16 Ⓣ :223 :46 1:10 1:412 ⒻNijana-G3 88 2 3 32 31 4¾ 3hd Bailey J D 118 2.20 87-07 Statuette114no Icy Warning114no Dispute1181¼ Brushed, gamely 8
Run In Divisions
11Jly93-8Bel fst 1¼ :47 1:101 1:353 2:012 ⒻC C A Oaks-G1 88 2 1 1½ 2hd 21½ 45½ Bailey J D 121 4.20 78-16 Sky Beauty121½ Future Pretense1212 Silky Feather1213 Tired 5
6Jun93-9Bel fst 1⅛ :464 1:11 1:361 1:493 ⒻMthr Gse-G1 94 3 1 11 1½ 22 25 Bailey J D 121 1.70 76-21 Sky Beauty1215 Dispute1213½ Silky Feather1215 No match 4
30Apr93-9CD fst 1⅛ :47 1:122 1:383 1:522 ⒻKy Oaks-G1 93 5 3 21½ 1½ 1hd 11¼ Bailey J D 121 5.10 82-17 Dispute1211¼ Eliza121nk Quinpool121nk Driving, gamely 11
13Mar93-10GP fst 1 1/16 :24 :491 1:14 1:433 ⒻBonnie Miss-G2 95 3 1 11½ 11 1½ 1¾ Bailey J D 114 2.70 92-15 Dispute114¾ Sky Beauty1143 Lunar Spook1174¾ Driving 6
12Feb93-5GP fst 170 :231 :47 1:114 1:413 ⒻAlw 30000NC 94 1 2 22½ 21 2½ 1½ Bailey J D 112 *.40 93-07 Dispute112½ Honest Princess11213 Misspitch11414 Ridden out 4
WORKOUTS: Mar 9 GP 4f fst :48 B 3/37 Mar 2 Pay 5f fst 1:06 B 5/6 Feb 25 Pay 5f fst 1:062 B 3/3 Feb 20 Pay 4f fst :532 B 3/5 Feb 15 Pay 3f fst :384 B 2/4 Feb 10 Pay 4f fst :532 B 3/5

March 12 7F $50K Stk 7–10 3rd of 9/beaten 1L

Heavenly Prize and Dispute, Grade 1 winners the previous autumn at Belmont, appeared a trifle "short" making their respective seasonal debuts in ungraded sprint stakes. Both had wintered at Payson Park and had returned off a series of slow breezes; clearly, these classy fillies were not going to be wound up to peak form for their first starts of the year. Dispute, in fact, had been saddled with high weight of 122 pounds under the allowance conditions of the $50,000 Safely Kept Stakes, while entered at a distance clearly short of her best.

On April 8 at Aqueduct, handicappers were confronted with another returnee from Phipps/McGaughey:

Aqueduct

8 *1 MILE.* (1:32²) ALLOWANCE. Purse $42,000. 3-year-olds and upward, which have not won two races of $20,000 at a mile or over since August 1. Weights: 3-year-olds, 115 lbs. Older, 124 lbs. Non-winners of a race of $21,000 at a mile or over since October 1, allowed 3 lbs. Of two races of $19,000 at a mile or over since September 1, 5 lbs. Of such a race since August 1, 7 lbs. (Maiden, claiming, starter and restricted races not considered.)

START 1 MILE FINISH

Jacksonport

Own: Garren Murray M
LUZZI M J (50 7 4 5 .14)
Dk. b or br h. 5
Sire: Vigors (Grey Dawn II)
Dam: On the Brink (Cox's Ridge)
Br: Loblolly Stable (Ky)
Tr: Garren Murray M (9 0 1 0 .00)
124

Lifetime Record: 73 8 9 15 $438,735
1994 10 1 2 1 $52,218 | Turf 9 0 0 0 $1,860
1993 28 0 3 8 $132,112 | Wet 7 1 1 2 $35,000
Aqu 17 1 2 4 $95,332 | Dist 11 2 1 2 $76,900

2Apr94- 8Aqu fst 1 :233 :46 1:092 1:342 3+ Westchstr H-G3 80 1 1 21½ 56½ 710 714 Rojas R I 108 b 15.10e 82-16 Virginia Rapids116½ Colonial Affair121nk Cherokee Run1192½ Gave way 7
23Mar94- 6Aqu fst 1⅛ :482 1:124 1:38 1:504 Alw 40000N$mY 84 3 2 2½ 31 45½ 511 Luzzi M J 119 b 6.30 71-24 Double Calvados1157 Correntino1152½ Lord Beer1191½ Gave way 5
13Mar94- 8Aqu fst 1⅛ ⊡ :473 1:111 1:361 1:492 3+ Grey Lag BCHG3 85 10 7 74¾ 84¾ 1010 913½ Mojica R Jr 109 b 12.40e 75-21 As Indicated1273½ Federal Funds110¾ Michelle Can Pass119nk Wide, tired 10
2Mar94- 6Aqu fst 1 1/16 ⊡ :234 :473 1:122 1:442 Alw 40000N$mY 96 1 1 18 14 13 21¾ Mojica R Jr 122 b *1.30e 81-25 Federal Funds1221¾ Jacksonport1225 Bill Of Rights1154 Gamely 6
25Feb94- 6Aqu fst 6f ⊡ :224 :46 :574 1:094 Handicap40k 80 4 6 65½ 62½ 63¾ 57 Luzzi M J 115 b 12.00 87-14 Preporant122nk Nymphist112nk Farmonthefreeway1125 No threat 6
21Feb94- 8Aqu fst 1⅛ ⊡ :464 1:111 1:374 1:504 3+ Stymie H-G3 85 1 6 75½ 1111 119½ 1014¾ Rydowski S R 111 b 8.50e 67-35 Koluctoo JimmyAl1114 MichelleCanPass1201½ FederalFunds111¾ Outrun 11
12Feb94- 6Aqu fst 1 1/16 ⊡ :233 :474 1:121 1:434 Alw 40000N$mY 96 2 4 33 31½ 21½ 11½ Luzzi M J 115 b *2.70 86-24 Jacksonport1151½ Commander Evander115nk Sparkling Sky1156 Driving 6
5Feb94- 6Aqu fst 1⅛ ⊡ :49 1:123 1:372 1:50 3+ Assault H-G3 88 9 6 42 43 612 916 Guerra W A 112 b 10.20e 70-28 As Indicated1245½ Autoroute1131 Michelle Can Pass121½ Stopped 9
12Jan94- 5Aqu wf 1⅛ ⊡ :491 1:141 1:394 1:53 Handicap44k 91 2 1 11 11 13½ 2no Guerra W A 114 b *1.60e 71-31 Federal Funds113no Jacksonport1141½ Sea Hunter1136½ Weakened 5
1Jan94- 8Aqu fst 1 1/16 ⊡ :24 :473 1:122 1:453 3+ Aqueduct H-G3 84 2 5 54½ 44½ 310 311½ Guerra W A 112 b 15.20 65-33 As Indicated1215 Primitive Hall1136½ Jacksonport1122½ Passed tired ones 6
WORKOUTS: Mar 31 Bel tr.t 3f fst :36 H 4/17 ●Feb 19 Bel tr.t 3f fst :352 H 1/18 ●Feb 3 Bel tr.t 3f fst :352 H 1/17 Feb 2 Bel tr.t 5f fst 1:043 B 6/13 Jan 31 Bel tr.t 4f fst :49 H 6/84 Jan 25 Bel 3f gd :372 B (d)5/14

Stormy Java

Own: Cohen Julian
SANTOS J A (17 3 3 2 .18)
Dk. b or br c. 4
Sire: Java Gold (Key to the Mint)
Dam: Ruler's Storm (Irish Ruler)
Br: Lin-Drake Farm (Fla)
Tr: Schulhofer Flint S (14 2 2 3 .14)
119

Lifetime Record: 16 4 0 3 $93,732
1994 2 0 0 0 $2,270 | Turf 2 0 0 0
1993 14 4 0 3 $91,462 | Wet 2 1 0 0 $18,600
Aqu 3 1 0 2 $24,600 | Dist 2 0 0 2 $7,500

20Feb94- 6GP fst 1 1/16 :241 :48 1:12 1:424 Alw 42000N$mY 92 6 3 33 44 54¾ 57¼ Bailey J D 119 8.90 88-17 Northern Trend115½ Scuffleburg115½ Powerful Punch1176½ 6
Faded, six wide str
20Jan94- 7GP fst 1 1/16 :231 :471 1:114 1:423 Alw 37000N$Y 82 3 4 42 42½ 45 48¾ Bailey J D 119 8.10 88-11 LivingVicriously1191 Scuffleburg1156½ DncingJon1151½ Lacked response 7
26Dec93- 6Aqu fst 1 70 ⊡ :232 :462 1:122 1:452 3+ Alw 34000N3X 89 3 3 38 32 21½ 13 Santagata N 115 5.30 75-30 Stormy Java1153 Clever Knave117¾ Committee Chairman1156½ Driving 6
9Dec93- 8Aqu fst 1 1/16 ⊡ :234 :473 1:12 1:442 Blue Swords50k 83 2 8 910 96½ 87¾ 610½ Smith M E 119 4.00 73-25 Punchl n1226½ ClssEnvoy122½ KolctooJmmyAl1192 Stead, shuffled back 9
17Nov93- 6Aqu fst 1 :231 :453 1:103 1:361 3+ Alw 34000N3X 86 6 1 2½ 3½ 32½ 34½ Santos J A 115 4.90 79-26 Repletion117¾ Contract Court1173½ Stormy Java1155½ Dueled, weakened 6
16Oct93- 6Kee sly 1 1/16 :223 :461 1:11 1:424 3+ Alw 23000N$mY 87 5 3 31 31½ 610 616½ Arguello F A Jr 115 2.50 73-04 Nelson1216½ Glenfiddich Lad1152½ Swift Sunrise1121 Tired 7
24Sep93-10Med fst 1 70 :224 :454 1:103 1:402 3+ Alw 20000N3X 84 2 7 74½ 52 42½ 32¾ Smith M E 113 *.80 91-09 A Lee Rover1161¾ Fliny1161 Stormy Java113nk Bobbled start, wide 7
28Aug93- 6Sar fst 1⅛ :47 1:11 1:36 1:492 3+ Alw 46000N$Y 82 4 3 32½ 42 44 57½ Santos J A 114 7.40 82-06 Prospector's Flag1121½ Key Contender1175½ Say Dance117nk Faded 6
3Jly93- 4Bel sf 1¼ Ⓣ :493 1:15 1:403 2:062 3+ Alw 32500N3X 41 1 1 1½ 75 718 724½ Day P 111 10.30 34-33 Hungerkill1192 Diagnostic1171½ Wesaam1173 Used up 7
21Jun93- 8Bel fm 1 1/16 Ⓣ :242 :47 1:102 1:404 3+ Alw 32500N3X 66 3 3 31½ 32 49 515½ Santos J A 113 5.00 76-14 Square Cut1171¾ Double Danger1171½ Strolling Along1138 Faded 5
WORKOUTS: ●Apr 5 Bel tr.t 4f fst :46 H 1/26 Mar 31 Bel tr.t 4f fst :481 H 3/33 Mar 25 Bel tr.t 4f fst :494 B 23/37 Mar 20 Bel tr.t 4f fst :492 B 24/36 Mar 15 GP 4f fst :483 H 9/29 Mar 10 GP 4f fst :473 H 4/37

Gold Tower

Own: Hofmann Georgia E
SAMYN J L (12 5 1 1 .42)
B. c. 3 (May)
Sire: Seeking the Gold (Mr. Prospector)
Dam: Floral Blossom (Diplomat Way)
Br: Owens Norman & Phil (Ky)
Tr: Jerkens H Allen (17 8 4 4 .35)
108

Lifetime Record: 5 2 1 1 $39,480
1994 2 0 1 0 $6,660 | Turf 0 0 0 0
1993 3 2 0 1 $32,820 | Wet 0 0 0 0
Aqu 1 0 1 0 $6,380 | Dist 0 0 0 0

1Apr94- 7Aqu fst 6½f :221 :451 1:094 1:162 Alw 29000N2X 85 5 5 58½ 58½ 48 27 Smith M E 117 *1.70 92-16 Jericho Blaise1177 Gold Tower117½ Memories Of Linda1176½ Late gain 5
13Feb94- 8GP fst 7f :214 :441 1:092 1:222 Alw 28000N2X 80 1 10 910 912 86¼ 88 Smith M E 118 3.70 85-09 Able Buck1181½ Money Of The Mind1103¾ Jac Apollo118no Mild bid 10
19Aug93- 4Sar fst 6f :214 :443 :564 1:10 Alw 26500N1X 78 2 5 57 54 31 11½ Smith M E 119 1.30 92-06 Gold Tower1191½ Arrival Time1221½ Francis Marion1172½ Wide, driving 5
31Jly93- 3Sar fst 6f :222 :46 :583 1:111 Md Sp Wt 72 1 6 76¾ 73½ 2no 11½ Smith M E 118 *2.80 86-08 Gold Tower1181½ Colonel Slade1182 Retrospection118nk Driving 8
19Jly93- 3Bel gd 5½f :221 :454 :581 1:043 Md Sp Wt 72 5 4 87½ 85½ 64½ 34½ Smith M E 118 f 5.50 88-13 Whitney Tower1183½ End Sweep118¾ Gold Tower1183 Belated rally 8
WORKOUTS: Apr 6 Bel tr.t 4f fst :482 H 9/47 Mar 24 Bel tr.t 1 fst 1:484 B 2/2 Mar 19 GP 7f fst 1:283 B 2/3 Mar 16 GP 6f fst 1:16 B 4/5 Mar 14 GP 3f fst :382 B 2/10 Mar 9 GP 3f fst :363 B 3/16

Miner's Mark

Own: Phipps Ogden
BAILEY J D (4 3 0 1 .75)
B. c. 4
Sire: Mr. Prospector (Raise a Native)
Dam: Personal Ensign (Private Account)
Br: Phipps Ogden (Ky)
Tr: McGaughey Claude III (2 1 0 1 .50)
124

Lifetime Record: 14 6 2 2 $948,250
1993 12 5 1 2 $928,570 | Turf 0 0 0 0
1992 2 1 1 0 $19,680 | Wet 3 1 1 0 $62,300
Aqu 0 0 0 0 | Dist 0 0 0 0

6Nov93- 8SA fst 1¼ :464 1:111 1:36 2:004 3+ B C Classic-G1 98 13 8 65 104¾ 1211 1211 McCarron C J B 122 19.40 80-10 Arcangues1262 Bertrando1261¾ Kissin Kris1221½ Wide, gave way 13
16Oct93- 8Bel fst 1¼ :493 1:141 1:383 2:023 3+ J C Gold CupG1 106 5 2 21 2½ 1½ 1no McCarron C J 121 8.40 78-12 Miner's Mark121no Colonial Affair1212¾ Brunswick1261½ Hard drive 5
18Sep93- 8Bel sly 1⅛ :453 1:094 1:342 1:47 3+ Woodward-G1 77 5 5 58½ 55 512 528½ McCarron C J 121 4.20 65-15 Bertrando12613 Devil His Due1263 Valley Crossing126hd No factor 6
21Aug93- 7Sar fst 1¼ :47 1:113 1:37 2:014 Travers-G1 105 8 7 76½ 31 42 33 McCarron C J 126 3.80 92-10 Sea Hero1262 Kissin Kris1261 Miner's Mark126hd 11
Broke slowly, in traffic far turn
1Aug93- 8Sar fst 1⅛ :472 1:114 1:362 1:49 Jim Dandy-G2 105 1 3 36½ 31 1hd 1nk McCarron C J 117 2.20 91-09 Minr'sMrk117nk VirginiRpids1214½ ColonilAffr1267¾ Broke outward, drvng 6
3Jly93- 8Bel my 1⅛ :454 1:093 1:344 1:473 Dwyer-G2 92 1 6 54 52½ 22 26 Bailey J D 123 *1.60 85-11 Cherokee Run1236 Miner's Mark1231½ Silver Of Silver1232¾ Up for place 6
5Jun93- 6Bel fst 1⅛ :452 1:092 1:352 1:492 Colin-G3 100 2 4 45 43½ 17 16½ Bailey J D 115 *1.20 82-15 Miner's Mark1156½ Compadre1156¾ Williamstown1222½ Driving 6
19May93- 7Bel wf 1⅛ :463 1:104 1:354 1:481 Alw 30500N2X 97 4 4 45 43½ 3nk 14½ Bailey J D 117 *.80 88-18 Miner's Mark1174½ Tactical Advantage117¾ My Mogul117¾ Ridden out 5
27Mar93- 11TP fst 1⅛ :472 1:113 1:372 1:504 Jim Beam-G2 94 5 5 44½ 64¾ 33 32¾ Bailey J D 121 3.20 76-18 Prairie Bayou121¾ Proudest Romeo1212 Miner's Mark1215 9
Off slow, no late response
9Mar93- 8GP fst 1⅛ :473 1:114 1:374 1:503 Alw 24000N1X 90 2 7 74½ 74 3½ 11 Bailey J D 112 4.70 84-13 Minr'sMrk1121 ThrillrChillr1121¾ HolySmoksAndy117nk Driving five wide 10
WORKOUTS: Apr 4 GP 5f fst 1:01 B 4/13 Mar 28 GP 4f fst :513 B 11/13 Mar 13 GP 5f fst 1:00 H 3/20 Mar 7 Pay 5f fst 1:051 B 1/2 Mar 2 Pay 5f fst 1:052 B 3/6 Feb 25 Pay 5f fst 1:06 B 2/3

Correntino

Own: Dogwood Stable
CHAVEZ J F (59 12 10 10 .20)
Dk. b or br g. 5
Sire: Lord at War-Ar (General-Fr)
Dam: La Corriente (Little Current)
Br: Wimborne Farm Inc (Ky)
Tr: O'Brien Leo (20 0 7 4 .00)
117

Lifetime Record: 36 5 10 5 $194,547
1994 4 0 2 1 $20,360 | Turf 10 1 4 1 $59,379
1993 14 1 3 3 $49,981 | Wet 4 0 0 0 $8,778
Aqu 1 0 1 0 $8,800 | Dist 2 0 1 1 $7,812

23Mar94- 6Aqu fst 1⅛ :482 1:124 1:38 1:504 Alw 40000N$mY 91 5 5 58 55 35½ 27 Chavez J F 115 b 3.80 75-24 Double Calvados1157 Correntino1152½ Lord Beer1191½ Up for place 5
27Feb94- 7Aqu fst 1 70 ⊡ :231 :464 1:114 1:414 Alw 34000N4X 99 7 6 67 63½ 42 32½ Chavez J F 117 b *1.30 87-24 Commander Evander1172 Exotic Slew117nk Correntino117nk Four wide 7
5Feb94- 6Aqu fst 1⅛ ⊡ :49 1:123 1:372 1:50 3+ Assault H-G3 96 7 7 78½ 811 712 611½ Leon F 110 18.30 75-28 As Indicated1245½ Autoroute1131 Michelle Can Pass121½ Outrun 9
9Jan94- 4Aqu fst 1 1/16 ⊡ :234 :473 1:121 1:441 Alw 34000N4X 96 1 2 43 45 33½ 2nk Chavez J F 117 *2.20 84-20 Lord Beer117nk Correntino117nk Cranshaw's Corner1173¾ Just missed 7
29Dec93- 6Aqu fst 1 1/16 ⊡ :242 :494 1:143 1:463 3+ Clm 70000 91 2 2 21 2hd 12 12½ Chavez J F 113 6.10 72-33 Correntino1132½ Cranshaw's Corner1133 Stately Wager1135 Driving 6
20Nov93- 4CD gd 1⅛ Ⓣ :48 1:134 1:402 1:534 3+ Clm 75000 86 10 6 57½ 66¼ 33 2nk Arguello F A Jr 117 6.20 63-31 Cozzemight117nk Correntino1171 Hasty Empery112nk Finished fast 10
6Nov93- 6CD fm 1⅛ Ⓣ :482 1:132 1:383 1:502 3+ Clm 75000 82 3 5 44½ 53¾ 34 36¾ Arguello F A Jr 117 7.40 73-19 First And Only1195 Just Like Perfect1191¾ Correntino1171½ No late gain 10
13Oct93- 7Kee fst 7f :22 :441 1:084 1:201 3+ Alw 23000N$Y 88 5 8 109¾ 813 75½ 68¼ Arguello F A Jr 112 17.80 100-05 Binalong1125 Star Of Rhodesia1101 Tempered Halo1102 Bumped, start 10
23Sep93- 8TP my 1 1/16 :232 :473 1:131 1:451 3+ Alw 15500N$Y 77 1 4 44 46½ 49 413½ Miller D A Jr 114 4.90 67-27 Grand Jewel1125 Return Voyage1136 Season Screen1152½ Held position 6
12Sep93- 7TP fst 6½f :231 :461 1:104 1:171 3+ Alw 16500N2Y 87 3 2 41¾ 45 44½ 32 Miller D A Jr 114 2.60 89-16 Eastern Affair119no Return Voyage1162 Correntino114nk No late response 5
WORKOUTS: Apr 4 Bel tr.t 4f fst :50 B 13/25 Mar 14 Bel tr.t 5f fst 1:023 B 8/18 Feb 25 Bel tr.t 3f fst :351 B 2/11 ●Feb 17 Bel tr.t 4f fst :492 H 1/17 Feb 1 Bel tr.t 4f fst :52 B 56/61 Jan 24 Bel tr.t 5f fst 1:043 B 11/15

Miner's Mark, overwhelmingly superior to his four rivals in terms of class and speed figures, was the best bet of the day in every newspaper's consensus box and was pounded to odds of 1–2.

There were chinks in the armor of Miner's Mark, despite the fact that the fine print in the conditions indicated the race was written expressly for him. Miner's Mark had never run at a mile, had never run at Aqueduct, had never won off a layoff, hadn't won as a first-time starter, and was saddled with top weight of 124 pounds. Most important, Miner's Mark had been a Grade 1 winner at Belmont the previous autumn, but was making his first start of the year in an ungraded race after wintering at Payson Park. Given the fact that Heavenly Prize and Dispute boasted the same factors in their records and had recently come up short, it was reasonable to assume that Miner's Mark would not run his best race on this day.

The winner at 9–2 was Stormy Java, who had an edge in conditioning after recent encounters with the graded-stakes winners Living Vicariously and Scuffleburg, not to mention the speedy Northern Trend, who had recently missed by only a neck in a Grade 3 Handicap.

Significantly, Stormy Java had worked a half-mile in :46 seconds three days before the race, the fastest of twenty-six at the distance on Belmont's training track that morning. An inspection of the *Form*'s work tab from April 5 revealed just how impressive Stormy Java's move had been:

BELMONT PARK — (Training) Track Fast

Three Furlongs		Senor Joy	:36 Hg	High Southern	:48^{2} Bg	Wild West	:48^{2} B
Aronimink	:37^{2} B	Stemming	:39^{3} B	Incinerate	:50^{4} B	Wonder Carr	:49^{1} B
Branch Water	:39 B	Whose Jacques	:39^{2} B	Inside The Beltway	:48 H	**Five Furlongs**	**:56^{1}**
Broadway And Pine	:39^{3} B	**Four Furlongs**		Iron Maiden	:47 H	Alyred	1:03^{4} B
Castigating	:39^{3} B	Babe's Mantel	:48^{2} H	Lovelines Gold	:49^{2} Bg	Charmed Prospect	1:03 B
Chief Flaherty	:37^{2} B	Buzzie	:52^{4} B	Nickel Defense	:47 H	Continued	1:01 Hg
Cosa Diavolo	:39^{2} B	Cida Zee	:49^{4} B	Party Manners	:48^{2} H	Eyes Ofa Bandit	1:02^{4} B
Dancin Duo	:37^{2} B	Crackedbell	:48 B	Poor But Honest	:48^{2} B	**Marco Bay**	**1:00 B**
Do It Fast	**:35^{4} H**	Deputy Miss	:51 B	Punchpasser	:48^{1} B	Rizzi	1:01 B
Father Shea	:37^{1} B	Eager Carnie	:50^{3} B	Stoney Wolf	:49 B	Sunshine's Word	1:00^{4} H
High Regent	:37^{1} B	Eye Catching	:48^{2} B	**Stormy Java**	**:46 H**	Vita Eterna	1:02^{4} B
Leiertim	:39^{3} B	Fancy Puddles	:50^{3} B	Taj Waki	:48^{1} H	**Six Furlongs**	**1:07^{4}**
Londolozi	:37^{2} B	Final Clearance	:47^{2} H	Thesixthofmay	:48^{1} B	Power Bolt	1:18 B
Q.'s Kids	:36 H	Gone Dancing Again	:48^{2} B	Timeless Endeavor	:50^{3} B	Slews Gold	1:15^{2} H

Additional workout: 4/4/94 track fast Classy Mirage (1M) 1:42 3/5b. STORMY JAVA (4f) did well. MARCO BAY (5f) was hard held.

Stormy Java had gone in :46 — a full second faster than the next-best time. At four furlongs, a one-second edge is noteworthy, a strong indicator of a horse sitting on a big race.

EIGHTH RACE
Aqueduct
APRIL 8, 1994

1 MILE. (1.32²) ALLOWANCE. Purse $42,000. 3-year-olds and upward, which have not won two races of $20,000 at a mile or over since August 1. Weights: 3-year-olds, 115 lbs. Older, 124 lbs. Non-winners of a race of $21,000 at a mile or over since October 1, allowed 3 lbs. Of two races of $19,000 at a mile or over since September 1, 5 lbs. Of such a race since August 1, 7 lbs. (Maiden, claiming, starter and restricted races not considered.)

Value of Race: $42,000 Winner $25,200; second $9,240; third $5,040; fourth $2,520. Mutuel Pool $131,346.00 Exacta Pool $259,288.00 Minus Show Pool $456.84

Last Raced	Horse	M/Eqt.	A.	Wt	PP	St	¼	½	¾	Str	Fin	Jockey	Odds $1
20Feb94 ^{6}GP^{5}	Stormy Java		4	119	2	4	2^{hd}	2^{3}	1^{hd}	1^{1}	1^{1}	Santos J A	4.50
6Nov93 ^{8}SA^{12}	Miner's Mark		4	124	4	2	4^{1}	5	4^{2}	$4^{2\frac{1}{2}}$	2^{hd}	Bailey J D	0.50
23Mar94 ^{6}Aqu^{2}	Correntino	b	5	117	5	1	3^{2}	3^{hd}	$3^{\frac{1}{2}}$	$2^{\frac{1}{2}}$	$3^{2\frac{1}{2}}$	Chavez J F	7.60
2Apr94 ^{8}Aqu^{7}	Jacksonport	b	5	124	1	5	$1^{\frac{1}{2}}$	1^{1}	$2^{\frac{1}{2}}$	3^{hd}	4^{2}	Luzzi M J	11.20
1Apr94 ^{7}Aqu^{2}	Gold Tower		3	110	3	3	5	4^{hd}	5	5	5	Samyn J L	4.10

OFF AT 4:07 Start Good. Won driving. Time, :24^{1}, :47^{2}, 1:11^{3}, 1:36^{1} Track fast.

$2 Mutuel Prices:			
2-(B)-STORMY JAVA	11.00	3.80	2.10
4-(D)-MINER'S MARK		2.40	2.10
5-(E)-CORRENTINO			2.10

$2 EXACTA 2-4 PAID $25.20

Dk. b. or br. c, by Java Gold–Ruler's Storm, by Irish Ruler. Trainer Schulhofer Flint S. Bred by Lin-Drake Farm (Fla).

STORMY JAVA stalked the pace from outside to the turn, surged to the front entering the stretch, opened a clear advantage in midstretch, then held sway under brisk urging. MINER'S MARK bumped at the start, raced just behind the leaders while between horses for six furlongs then outfinished CORRENTINO for the place. CORRENTINO allowed to settle early, rallied three wide to threaten in upper stretch but couldn't sustain his bid. JACKSONPORT set the pace under pressure to the turn and tired. GOLD TOWER was never a factor. JACKSONPORT and GOLD TOWER wore mud caulks.

Owners— 1, Cohen Julian; 2, Phipps Ogden; 3, Dogwood Stable; 4, Garren Murray M; 5, Hofmann Georgia E
Trainers—1, Schulhofer Flint S; 2, McGaughey Claude III; 3, O'Brien Leo; 4, Garren Murray M; 5, Jerkens H Allen
Overweight: Gold Tower (2).

WORKOUTS

One of the most important clues to a horse's form is to be found in the workout line. Thoroughbreds spend all but an hour or so of each day in their stalls, so what they accomplish during morning training hours is vital to their success in actual competition. Horses do not just arrive at the track from the farm ready to run; in order to withstand the rigors and stress of running full tilt every couple of weeks or so, they must have the proper conditioning foundation. Think of it this way: if you were going to compete in a ten-mile footrace, you wouldn't just pick yourself up off the couch after weeks of inactivity and toe up at the starting line on race day; that would invite pulled muscles, ligament strains, or worse. No, being the sensible sort that you are, you'd want to give yourself enough time to gradually get into shape, stretching and toning your muscles, building your stamina through a series of long jogs, and sharpening your speed through a series of wind sprints.

This is precisely what thoroughbreds must do; if they are asked for too much exertion too soon without the proper preparation, they are much more susceptible to injury.

How a horse is doing in the mornings can be a strong indicator of how it will do in the afternoon. One of the most notable recent examples concerned Holy Bull's dismal performance in the 1994 running of the Kentucky Derby. His twelfth-place finish at Churchill Downs might have been attributable to any number of factors, such as his 6.00 dosage index, which was well over the 4.00 guideline, or the sloppy track on the first Saturday in May. In the Derby, the long-striding gray colt broke a step slowly and was then squeezed back between horses, raced close up to the pace for half a mile, and then shockingly faded from contention.

A week later, trainer Jimmy Croll announced that Holy Bull would skip the Preakness and opt instead for the Metropolitan Mile against older horses on Memorial Day. In the *Form*'s May 15 edition, Croll explained, "There is nothing seriously wrong with Holy Bull . . . but his blood tests indicated he was just a hair off. It's mostly the time element . . . this way he'll get a few more days of rest."

Holy Bull took on some of the best older horses in training in the Met Mile and won with complete authority, earning a phenomenal Beyer figure of 122. Holy Bull was back, and he would not lose again in 1994 en route to winning the three-year-old championship and Horse of the Year honors.

Holy Bull
Own: Croll Warren A Jr
NO RIDER (–)

Gr. c. 3 (Jan)
Sire: Great Above (Minnesota Mac)
Dam: Sharon Brown (Al Hattab)
Br: Pelican Stable (Fla)
Tr: Croll Warren A Jr (1 1 0 0 1.00)

116

Lifetime Record:	10 8 0 0	$1,290,760			
1994	6 4 0 0	$955,000	Turf	0 0 0 0	
1993	4 4 0 0	$335,760	Wet	2 1 0 0	$69,360
Bel	3 3 0 0	$386,160	Dist	0 0 0 0	

30May94-8Bel	fst	1	$:22^{4}$:45 $1:09^{2}$ $1:33^{4}$	3↑ Metropltn H-G1	122	6	1	1^{1}	$1^{\frac12}$	$1^{2\frac12}$	$1^{5\frac12}$	Smith M E	112	*1.00	94-09	Holy Bull112$^{5\frac12}$ Cherokee Run118^{no} Devil His Due122^{2}	Driving	10
7May94-8CD	sly	1¼	$:47^{1}$ $1:11^{4}$ $1:37^{3}$ $2:03^{3}$	Ky Derby-G1	85	4	6	$5^{3\frac12}$	9^{9}	12^{12}	$12^{18\frac14}$	Smith M E	126	*2.20	76-06	Go For Gin126^{2} Strodes Creek126$^{2\frac12}$ Blumin Affair126$^{\frac34}$		14
Off slow, in tight start, tired badly																		
16Apr94-9Kee	fst	1⅛	$:47^{4}$ $1:12^{3}$ $1:37^{4}$ 1:50	Blue Grass-G2	113	1	1	1^{3}	1^{2}	$1^{1\frac12}$	$1^{3\frac12}$	Smith M E	121	*.60	84-26	Holy Bull121$^{3\frac12}$ Valiant Nature121^{5} Mahogany Hall121$^{2\frac14}$	Sharp, ridden out	7
12Mar94-10GP	fst	1⅛	:46 1:10 $1:34^{4}$ $1:47^{2}$	Fla Derby-G1	115	6	1	$1^{2\frac12}$	$1^{2\frac12}$	1^{5}	$1^{5\frac34}$	Smith M E	122	2.70	100-06	Holy Bull122$^{5\frac34}$ Ride The Rails122^{no} Halo's Image122^{1}	Ridden out	14
19Feb94-9GP	gd	1$\frac{1}{16}$	$:22^{4}$ $:45^{3}$ $1:10^{2}$ $1:44^{3}$	Ftn of YouthG2	57	4	1	$1^{\frac12}$	2^{1}	6^{8}	$6^{24\frac14}$	Smith M E	119	*1.30	63-19	Dehere119$^{\frac34}$ Go For Gin119$^{1\frac12}$ Ride The Rails117$^{3\frac34}$	Stopped badly	6
30Jan94-9GP	fst	7f	$:21^{3}$:44 $1:08^{1}$ $1:21^{1}$	Hutcheson-G2	108	1	4	$1^{1\frac12}$	$1^{1\frac12}$	$2^{\frac12}$	$1^{\frac34}$	Smith M E	122	*.50	97-11	Holy Bull122$^{\frac34}$ Patton113^{3} You And I119^{3}		5
Broke inward start, raced well off rail, ridden out																		
23Oct93-11Crc	fst	1$\frac{1}{16}$	:23 $:46^{2}$ $1:11^{3}$ $1:46^{1}$	[R]FS In Rlty400k	93	9	1	$1^{1\frac12}$	1^{2}	1^{4}	$1^{7\frac12}$	Smith M E	120	*.50	88-12	Holy Bull120$^{7\frac12}$ Rustic Light120^{1} Forward To Lead120$^{1\frac12}$	Ridden out	12
18Sep93-6Bel	sly	7f	$:22^{2}$ $:45^{3}$ $1:10^{1}$ $1:23^{1}$	Futurity-G1	103	2	1	1^{1}	1^{1}	$1^{2\frac12}$	$1^{\frac12}$	Smith M E	122	3.10	87-14	Holy Bull122$^{\frac12}$ Dehere122^{5} Prenup122^{8}	All out	6
2Sep93-7Bel	fst	6½f	:22 $:44^{1}$ $1:09^{4}$ 1:17	Alw 28000N2X	91	3	1	$1^{\frac12}$	1^{hd}	$1^{2\frac12}$	1^{7}	Smith M E	119	*.90	88-15	Holy Bull119^{7} Goodbye Doeny117^{3} End Sweep119$^{\frac12}$	Ridden out	6
14Aug93-7Mth	fst	5½f	$:21^{3}$ $:44^{4}$ $:57^{1}$ $1:03^{4}$	Md Sp Wt	101	1	3	1^{1}	$1^{1\frac12}$	$1^{1\frac12}$	$1^{2\frac12}$	Rivera L Jr	118	*1.10	95-17	Holy Bull118$^{2\frac12}$ Palance118$^{7\frac12}$ Hold My Tongue118^{9}	Driving	9

WORKOUTS: May 28 Mth 4f fst $:46^{4}$ Bg *2/67* ●May 22 Mth 6f fst 1:11 H *1/4* ●May 16 Mth 4f gd $:46^{4}$ H *1/6* May 6 CD 3f fst $:36^{3}$ B *2/19* May 2 CD 6f fst $1:14^{3}$ H *3/6* Apr 24 Kee 5f fst $1:02^{1}$ B *3/13*

Alert handicappers who noted Holy Bull's lackluster workouts between the Blue Grass and the Derby might've gotten a sense that all was not well with the horse — a suspicion confirmed in the paddock and during the post parade for the race when his overall demeanor appeared lethargic and listless.

"Listless? While the band was playing 'My Old Kentucky Home' and all those other horses were keyed up and jumping out of their skins, Holy Bull was *asleep,*" observed a columnist for one of New York's major daily newspapers upon Holy Bull's return to Belmont Park.

Indeed, it seemed as if Holy Bull had sleepwalked through his pre-Derby works, notably on May 2, when his six furlongs in 1:14 ⅗ was only third best of six at the distance, and on May 6, when he blew out in :36⅗, galloping out another furlong in a crawling :51 and change.

These are the works from a horse who's supposed to set the pace in the Derby?

When Holy Bull is right, he works fast, real fast. His drills leading up to the Met — a pair of handy bullets including a 1:11 on May 22, followed by a *breeze from the gate* on May 28 that was second fastest of sixty-seven at the distance — were strong indicators that Holy Bull had shaken off the effects of his pre-Derby malaise.

Horses routinely are afflicted with minor twenty-four-hour bugs and ailments, and they even react to the weather similarly to humans: they get the sniffles, run temperatures, suffer from aching feet, have muscles that stiffen up, and endure the constant bumps, jostles, and bruises during the course of normal racing and training that any human athlete would be subjected to. Is it any wonder, then, that they seldom run a race of the same quality twice in a row?

Since workouts are the principal medium through which a trainer trains, what happens in the mornings is frequently a harbinger of what will happen in the afternoons.

At the beginning of Belmont's 1992 spring meet, Bob Barbara established a strong pattern by winning with three fillies first time back from a layoff in a sprint; all boasted a handy five furlongs as their latest workout:

Bob's Little Gal B. f. 3(Mar), by Barrera—Sun Moment, by Honest Moment Lifetime 1991 1 M 0 0
CARR D (6 2 0 0 $22,800) $35,000 Br.—Bronzine R (Fla) 1 0 0 0
Own.—Barbara Robert Tr.—Barbara Robert (—) 115

27Nov91- 9Aqu fst 6f :22⁴ :47 1:12³ ⓕMd 30000 47 7 12 8⁴ 7$3\frac{1}{4}$ 7⁷ 5$8\frac{1}{2}$ Smith M E 113 *2.70 69-20 CdyHllFun117$1\frac{1}{4}$BstllBll117⁵SqoynScrb113 Broke slowly
LATEST WORKOUTS Apr 24 Bel 5f fst 1:00 Hg Apr 15 Bel 5f fst 1:00¹ H Mar 30 Bel tr.t 3f fst :37² B

May 10 6F Mdn clmg $5.40 1st by 18L

Appealing Jeanne — Gr. f. 3(Feb), by Valid Appeal—Discreet Street, by Northern Prospect
ANTLEY C W (19 6 1 2 $94,140) — Br.—Petelain Stables (Fla)
Own.—Sabine Stable — Tr.—Barbara Robert (1 1 0 0 $7,200) — **116**
Lifetime 4 1 1 1 $22,920 — 1992 2 0 0 1 $3,24[illegible] — 1991 2 1 1 0 $19,68[illegible] — Wet 1 0 0 0

22Jan92- 1Aqu fst	6f	⊡:233	:474	1:131	ⒻAlw 27000	67	3 1 1½ 2hd 1½ 3½	Santagata N	118	2.80	76-23	King'sSwtst116noLdyTrickry116½ApplingJnn118	Gamely	5
4Jan92- 1Aqu sly	6f	⊡:232	:481	1:141	ⒻAlw 27000	22	2 6 21 21½ 69½ 616¾	Santagata N	121	4.40	55-24	Biolage1162 Snow Title1164 Northern Duster116	Tired	7
26Dec91- 6Aqu fst	6f	⊡:23	:471	1:14	ⒻMd Sp Wt	74	6 2 2½ 2½ 13½ 17	Santagata N	117	*1.80	73-24	ApplingJnn1177RosColony1171DixiChms117	Ridden out	10
8Dec91- 2Aqu fst	6f	⊡:224	:47	1:13	ⒻMd Sp Wt	77	1 4 11½ 11 13 2hd	Santagata N	117	3.40	78-20	HeadBand117hdAppelingJenne1172¼Secretly117	Gamely	5

LATEST WORKOUTS May 6 Bel 5f fst 1:002 H — Apr 30 Bel 4f fst :483 H — Apr 24 Bel tr.t 3f fst :373 B

May 13 6F AlwNW1 $9.00

Makin Faces — B. f. 4, by Premiership—Political Mixup, by Political Coverup
SMITH M E (65 8 7 14 $271,732) — Br.—Powell & Robinson A & A G (Fla)
Own.—Sabine Stable — Tr.—Barbara Robert (6 2 1 1 $30,640) — **117**
Lifetime 25 7 5 6 $267,866 — 1992 4 1 0 1 $[illegible] — 1991 15 5 3 4 $159,522 — Wet 2 0 0 0

15Mar92- 8Aqu fst	7f	:224	:463	1:243	3↑ⒻDistaff H	73	3 5 11½ 11 53½ 613	Velazquez J R	113	13.50	69-25	Nnnrl1123½Missy'sMrg1192½Wthllprobblty117	Gave way	6
15Mar92-Grade II														
23Feb92- 8Aqu fst	6f	⊡:224	:454	1:10	3↑ⒻCorrectionH	96	3 3 1½ 11 2½ 34	Smith M E	114	3.60	89-16	Mss'sMrg1163DvlshTch1171MnFcs114	Speed weakened	6
2Feb92- 8Aqu fst	6f	⊡:232	:471	1:124	3↑ⒻBerlo H	97	6 1 13 12 12 11	Smith M E	113	6.60	79-27	MkinFces1131DevilishTouch117nkRlIrishHop115	Driving	6
1Jan92- 8Aqu fst	6f	⊡:223	:453	1:104	3↑ⒻInterboro H	71	5 3 2hd 2hd 66¾ 710¾	Smith M E	115	4.10	78-13	WoodSo1111¼DevilishTouch1181¼DoItWithStyl116	Tired	7
1Jan92-Grade III														
21Dec91- 7Aqu fst	6f	⊡:22	:452	1:111	3↑ⒻAlw 41000	99	7 3 11½ 13 14 11¼	Santagata N	120	2.90	87-16	MkinFces1201¼RelIrishHop1221CrftyTndroni115	Driving	7
20Nov91- 8Aqu fst	6f	:22	:452	1:103	3↑ⒻHandicap	90	3 2 1hd 1½ 1½ 3nk	Smith M E	114	3.00	88-14	ChristinaCzarin116nk[D]Serpe113noMkinFces114	Gamely	6
20Nov91-Placed second through disqualification														
2Nov91- 7Aqu fst	7f	:222	:444	1:214	3↑ⒻFrst Fl't H	91	9 1 1½ 11 21½ 26½	Velazquez J R	112	12.30	86-12	Mssy'sMrg1136½MknFcs112hdWthllprbblty114	Held 2nd	10
2Nov91-Grade II														
23Oct91- 5Aqu fst	1	:453	1:10	1:354	3↑ⒻAlw 47000	93	1 1 14 16 17 11¼	Smith M E	113	*1.30	83-19	MkinFces1131¼CrftyTendroni1155SlptThruIt114	Driving	7
12Oct91- 3Bel fst	6f	:222	:453	1:094	3↑ⒻAlw 30000	97	5 2 11 2hd 11½ 11¼	Smith M E	119	*1.40	91-17	MkinFces1191¼ReglVictress1172¾Sh'sAShkr114	Driving	6
29Sep91- 5Bel fst	7f	:233	:464	1:231	3↑ⒻAlw 28000	91	4 2 1hd 1hd 11 12¾	Smith M E	115	*1.20	88-13	MakinFces1152¾SntCtlin1132I'mTickledPink113	Driving	7

LATEST WORKOUTS ●May 14 Bel 5f fst :584 H — May 7 Bel 4f fst :483 B — May 2 Bel 3f fst :354 B

May 25 6½F Clf Alw $6.40

When the three-year-old filly Cove Hill Miss was entered first time back from a layoff in a sprint, she showed a handy five furlongs from the gate on June 4, and handicappers tracking recent trends should've expected a peak performance:

Cove Hill Miss — B. f. 3(Apr), by Fit To Fight—Key To AKita, by Key To The Mint
ROJAS R I (89 8 7 12 .09) — $30,000 Br.—Silveri Mr-Mrs J (NY)
Own.—Silveri Lucianne — Tr.—Barbara Robert (18 6 2 1 .33) — **112**
Lifetime 8 2 1 1 $34,200 — 1992 6 2 1 0 $31,320 — 1991 2 M 0 1 $2,880 — Wet 1 0 1 0 $5,280

25Mar92- 3Aqu fst	6½f	:223	:453	1:172	ⒻClm 45000	41	2 2 1½ 2½ 48½ 517¼	Velazquez J R	112	3.80	74-13	Kt'sCollg1147¾AwsomCntss112noTnrtt114	Dueled inside	5
16Mar92- 8Aqu fst	7f	:224	:462	1:243	ⒻOver All	—	5 2 32½ 75 913 —	Velazquez J R	116	51.00	— —	SrtogDew1164¾MissCoverGirl116hdGiveNotice118	Eased	9
28Feb92- 7Aqu fst	6f	⊡:222	:46	1:131	Ⓕ[S]Alw 27000	72	1 8 21½ 2hd 11 12	Velazquez J R	118	7.90	77-20	Cove Hill Miss1182R.E.Darla118nkMissMimsi118	Driving	9
22Jan92- 5Aqu fst	6f	⊡:233	:474	1:14	Ⓕ[S]Md Sp Wt	56	3 1 31½ 21½ 1½ 11½	Lidberg D W	121b	4.60	73-23	[DH]CHllMss1211½[DH]Thtfdnslf1211½TtdAccrd121	Driving	7
22Jan92-Dead heat														
13Jan92- 7Aqu fst	6f	⊡:233	:48	1:143	Ⓕ[S]Md Sp Wt	40	10 1 3½ 2½ 3½ 65½	Lidberg D W	121b	*1.20	64-27	KtBlm121nkThtfdnslf121hdTtdAccrd121	Frcd pace,tired	11
13Jan92-Dead heat														
4Jan92- 5Aqu sly	6f	⊡:232	:481	1:14	Ⓕ[S]Md Sp Wt	62	3 3 32½ 31½ 21½ 21	Lidberg D W	121	4.70	72-24	SndThnkng1211CvHllMss1215¾MssMms121	Best of rest	10
5Dec91- 9Aqu fst	6f	⊡:223	:464	1:133	Ⓕ[S]Md Sp Wt	57	3 5 53½ 51¼ 22½ 32½	Lidberg D W	117	6.90	72-22	FlghtVsblt1172½SndThnkng117noCvHllMss117	Willingly	12
21Nov91- 5Aqu fst	6f	:224	:462	1:12	ⒻMd 50000	53	10 11 74 53½ 47 69½	Lidberg D W	117	48.50	71-19	FrVll1175¼TrgrMs1171½Wrhtsnrrn113	Broke awkwardly	12

LATEST WORKOUTS Jun 4 Bel 5f fst 1:001 Hg — May 30 Bel 5f fst 1:003 H — May 21 Bel tr.t 4f fst :483 B — May 2 Bel 4f fst :483 H

June 20 6F 35–30K clmg $18.80

Cove Hill Miss wired her field at 8–1.

While many handicappers will be forced to guess about layoff horses — particularly those shipping in — handicappers with a trainer's past-performance file will have much more to go on:

San Romano
ATTARD L (—)
Own.—Stavro Steven A

Dk. b. or br. c. 3(Apr), by Cool Victor—Bye The Bye, by Balzac
Br.—Knob Hill Stables (Ont-C)
Tr.—England Phillip (1 0 1 0 .00)

111

Lifetime					
11 4 0 2	1992	3 3 0 0	$122,268
$145,128	1991	8 1 0 2	$22,860
	Turf	1 0 0 0	
	Wet	2 0 0 0	$6,180

10May92- 9WO	fst	7f	:23	:453	1:242	SQueenston	85	3	3	42¼	22½	2½	1½	Walls M K		121	*2.75	89-16	SnRomno121½GrndHooley117nkHoldingStdy115	Driving	7
10May92-Grade III-C																					
29Mar92- 9Grd	fst	6½f	:232	:47	1:184	Woodstock	84	2	2	11	11	12	12¼	Seymour D J		117	*.75	87-11	SnRomno1172¼HopforGold1152½BrURuckus117	Handily	9
22Mar92- 6Grd	fst	4½f	:22	:444	:503	SAlw 22600	83	5	1		1½	12½	14	Seymour D J		116	20.50	99-06	SnRomno1164FlyngFghtr1193Kng'sCollg119	Ridden out	7
27Oct91- 8WO	my	1⅛	:473	1:134	1:55	SCoron'tn Fy	61	3	6	66¼	65¼	41½	511	McAleney J S	b	122	12.65e	66-27	KeenFlcon1222½Loudmus1223½Benburb122	Lacked rally	9
27Oct91-Grade I-C																					
17Oct91- 3WO	fst	6½f	:223	:462	1:193	Md 60000	68	1	4	44	21½	13	15	McAleney J S	b	114	14.95	77-24	SnRomno1145SondthVctry1171AdvncWrd109	Authority	6
4Oct91- 6WO	sly	5½f	:223	:464	1:072	Md 50000	40	1	7	86¾	813	619	69	Walls M K	b	117	4.30	74-23	BoldDrcton1172½Crrgnvr117noRckrck117	Saved ground	9
1Sep91-10WO	fm	*7f T	:223	:454	1:243	Md Sp Wt	5	10	3	88½	810	1024	1029¾	Sabourin R B	b	115	21.35	70 —	DooYou1204AdvanceWord115nkKeenFlcon110	Far back	10
18Aug91- 4WO	fst	6f	:22	:451	1:114	SBull Page	53	4	9	78	79½	614	611	McAleney J S	b	115	52.60	75-15	Cool Shot1155½SteadyRise1172¾MyLastTry117	Wide str	10
2Aug91- 7WO	fst	5½f	:221	:454	1:052	SAlw 24400	28	4	6	614	612	614	614¼	Attard L	b	116	19.80	79-10	BlndRvrLck119noMplLk121¾MLstTr119	Showed nothing	6
21Jly91- 2WO	fst	6f	:224	:462	1:122	SMd Sp Wt	54	7	4	54	57½	49	36¼	Ramsammy E	b	118	*1.45e	77-15	BrveAl1182¼ChngeofFortune1184SnRomno118	Late bid	8

LATEST WORKOUTS Jly 20 WO 4f fst :48 B Jly 16 WO 4f fst :484 Hg Jly 10 WO 4f fst :512 B Jly 5 WO 4f fst :522 B

July 24 6F AlwNW4 $20.60 Dueled, drew off

Apelia
ATTARD L (—)
Own.—Stavro Steven A

Dk. b. or br. f. 3(Mar), by Cool Victor—Arbela, by Conquistador Cielo
Br.—Knob Hill Stables (Ont-C)
Tr.—England Phillip (—)

118

Lifetime			
7 4 0 1	1992	7 4 0 1	$67,214
$67,214	1991	0 M 0 0	
	Turf	1 0 0 0	
	Wet	1 0 0 1	$8,354

12Jly92- 8WO	gd	6½f T	:222	.454	1:161	FSOntDamsel	76	2	1	75	911	84½	74¾	Seymour D J		116	*1.85	86-09	DnceforDonn1162MyrtleIren116½MinTopic123	Gave way	11
12Jly92-Grade III-C																					
19Jun92- 8WO	fst	6f	:214	:444	1:101	3↑FAlw 27600	90	4	3	1½	2hd	13	13	Seymour D J		114	*1.15	94-11	Apelia1143PlatinumPws1163MemotoRun122	Ridden out	8
4Jun92- 7WO	fst	6f	:223	:462	1:112	FAlw 25900	85	4	1	22½	1½	13	13	Seymour D J		118	*.10	88-16	Apelia1183 Smaral1134½ Bad Sal115	In hand	4
27May92- 8WO	fst	6f	:222	.454	1:103	3↑Alw 22600	97	1	3	21½	11	11½	16	Seymour D J		114	1.50	92-13	Apelia1146 Blue Electron1115 NiceOccasion108	Handily	8
17May92- 9WO	fst	7f	:221	:443	1:242	FSFury	57	1	4	2hd	1hd	710	713½	Seymour D J		114	3.50	75-14	MoonMist1162½Prsnthsprng120noSngAndSwng116	Tired	9
17May92-Grade II-C																					
2May92- 9WO	sly	6f	:22	:453	1:13	FStar Shoot	66	3	2	3½	1½	1hd	36¼	Seymour D J		114	*.35e	74-20	MainTopic114nkDebra'sVictory1256Apelia114	Weakened	4
2May92-Grade II-C																					
4Apr92- 7Grd	fst	4½f	:22	:454	:514	3↑FMd Sp Wt	83	6	1		1hd	13½	17	Seymour D J		114	4.65	93-14	Apeli1147PyingGuest1113½GenuineGoer114	Wrapped up	7

LATEST WORKOUTS Aug 26 WO 4f fst :484 B ●Aug 19 WO 4f fst :463 H Aug 15 WO 4f fst :482 B ●Aug 11 WO 4f gd :48 B

When Apelia was entered in Saratoga's Gallant Bloom Stakes on August 30, most in the crowd were forced to guess about her state of readiness, since the three-year-old filly was making her first start in seven weeks and showed four workouts of half a mile; "the book" says a returnee should have at least one work at least five furlongs in length. Further, most people must have wondered, "Who is this trainer Phil England? And who is this jockey L. Attard?"

But handicappers who had a file on England noted the pp's of another Steven Stavro–owned three-year-old, San Romano, who had shipped from Woodbine off an identical layoff and scored a two-length upset at 9–1 in a nonwinners-of-four allowance at Belmont the previous month. They saw that Apelia's work pattern was identical as well: a series of workouts at four furlongs, the most recent coming four days before the race, and the second-most recent the only work termed "handily." Like her winning predecessor, Apelia was sired by Cool Victor, bred by Knob Hill Stables, and was receiving a rider switch to Attard.

Although most in the crowd were forced to guess about Apelia, the select few who were able to make this comparison knew that Apelia was a prime bet at 5–1. As San Romano had done, Apelia raced forwardly throughout and drew off to a convincing victory:

SEVENTH RACE
Saratoga
AUGUST 30, 1992

6 FURLONGS. (1.08) 1st Running THE GALLANT BLOOM. Purse $50,000 Added. Fillies. 3-year-olds. Weight: 121 lbs. Non-winners of four races other than maiden or claiming, allowed 3 lbs. Of three races other than maiden or claiming, 5 lbs. Of two races other than maiden or claiming, 7 lbs. $100 to nominate; $100 to enter and $200 to start. A trophy will be presented to the owner of the winner. Closed Monday, August 17, 1992, with 16 nominations.

Value of race $54,000; value to winner $32,400; second $11,880; third $6,480; fourth $3,240. Mutuel pool $337,874. Exacta Pool $637,917

Last Raced	Horse	M/Eqt.A.Wt	PP	St	¼	½	Str	Fin	Jockey	Odds $1
12Jly92 ^{8}WO^7	Apelia	3 118	8	2	2^1	$1^{\frac{1}{2}}$	$1^{1\frac{1}{2}}$	$1^{2\frac{3}{4}}$	Attard L	5.30
1Aug92 ^{8}Sar^3	Preach	3 116	5	4	$5^{\frac{1}{2}}$	$5^{1\frac{1}{2}}$	$4^{\frac{1}{2}}$	$2^{3\frac{1}{2}}$	Krone J A	1.30
1Aug92 ^{8}Sar^5	Fretina	3 116	7	1	8	$7^{1\frac{1}{2}}$	3^1	3^1	Davis R G	30.00
15Aug92 ^{1}Sar^1	My Necessity	3 118	1	8	$3^{\frac{1}{2}}$	2^{hd}	$2^{1\frac{1}{2}}$	$4^{\frac{1}{2}}$	Velazquez J R	17.70
3Jun92 ^{8}Bel^2	Miss Iron Smoke	3 116	6	3	4^2	4^1	5^{hd}	$5^{1\frac{3}{4}}$	Day P	2.00
2Aug92 ^{5}Sar^4	Lights of Marfa	b 3 116	4	5	$1^{\frac{1}{2}}$	3^1	$6^{1\frac{1}{2}}$	6^3	Antley C W	6.80
20Aug92 ^{8}Sar^7	Looking for a Win	3 114	2	6	6^{hd}	8	8	7^2	Maple E	34.80
15Aug92 ^{1}Sar^5	Mission Pass	3 118	3	7	$7^{1\frac{1}{2}}$	$6^{\frac{1}{2}}$	7^{hd}	8	Smith M E	19.00

OFF AT 4:36 Start good, Won driving. Time, :22 , $:44^3$, $:56^2$, $1{:}08^4$ Track fast.

$2 Mutuel Prices:				
	8–(H)–APELIA	12.60	5.00	5.00
	5–(E)–PREACH		3.00	2.60
	7–(G)–FRETINA			5.40

$2 EXACTA 8–5 PAID $38.40

Dk. b. or br. f, (Mar), by Cool Victor—Arbela, by Conquistador Cielo. Trainer England Phillip. Bred by Knob Hill Stables (Ont–C).

APELIA stalked the early pace from outside, surged to the front on the turn, opened a clear advantage in upper stretch thenheld sway under good handling. PREACH reserved for a half while five wide, closed steadily from outside to best the others. FRETINA, outrun to the top of the stretch, finished willingly along the inside to gain a share. MY NECESSITY, never far back, made a run along the inside to threaten on the turn but couldn't sustain her bid. MISS IRON SMOKE, settled just behind the leaders to the turn then lacked the needed response when called upon. LIGHTS OF MARFA set the pace slightly off the rail to the turn and tired from her early efforts. LOOKING FOR A WIN, never reached contention. MISSION PASS was never a factor. MISS IRON SMOKE wore mud caulks.

Owners— 1, Stavro Steven A; 2, Claiborne Farm; 3, Willmott Peter S; 4, Happy Hill Farm; 5, Siegel Jan; 6, Live Oak Plantation; 7, Sigel Marshall E; 8, Young William T.

Trainers— 1, England Phillip; 2, McGaughey Claude III; 3, Vestal Peter M; 4, Preger Mitchell C; 5, Jerkens H Allen; 6, Kelly Patrick J; 7, Picou James E; 8, Lukas D Wayne.

Sometimes it will be weeks before a pattern match involving workouts is uncovered, as with San Romano and Apelia. At other times, it may be just a matter of a day or two:

Enjoy The Silence
Own: Red Oak Stable

Ch. m. 5
Sire: Valid Appeal (In Reality)
Dam: Well Defined (Well Decorated)
Br: Ocala Stud Farms Inc (Fla)
Tr: Sacco Gregory D (—)

Lifetime Record :	**36**	**9**	**6**	**4**	**$206,751**						
1994	1	1	0	0	$24,000	**Turf**	4	0	0	0	$2,350
1993	18	6	2	2	$139,971	**Wet**	2	2	0	0	$36,800
HIA	4	3	1	0	$56,600	**Dist**	26	9	2	3	$189,001

17Mar94-9Hia	fst	6f		$:22^2$	$:45^4$	$:57^2$	$1{:}09^4$	3↑	ⒻGld Beauty H40k	**100**	4	2	$5^{2\frac{1}{2}}$	1^1	$1^{1\frac{1}{2}}$	$1^{1\frac{3}{4}}$	Bravo J	L 115	2.10	96-15	Enjoy The Silence115$^{1\frac{3}{4}}$ Lady Sonata115$^{7\frac{1}{2}}$ Touch Of Love110$^{2\frac{1}{2}}$	Driving	6
4Dec93-9Med	sly	6f		:22	$:44^2$	$:56^4$	$1{:}09^3$	3↑	ⒻPhoenix40k	**88**	1	5	4^2	$1^{\frac{1}{2}}$	$1^{\frac{1}{2}}$	$1^{1\frac{1}{2}}$	Smith M E	L 122	2.60	93-12	Enjoy The Silence122$^{1\frac{1}{2}}$ Saint I'm Not115$^{1\frac{1}{2}}$ Tell Margie113$^{\frac{1}{2}}$	Driving	6
13Nov93-8Med	fst	6f		$:21^3$	$:44^2$	$:56^4$	$1{:}09^4$	3↑	ⒻLvnhriseasy35k	**84**	2	8	5^6	$3^{2\frac{1}{2}}$	2^4	4^4	Santos J A	L 122	4.10	88-15	Fortunate Charmer115$^{2\frac{1}{2}}$ Bless Our Home113$^{1\frac{1}{2}}$ MerriTales113^{hd}	Slow start	8
8Oct93-9Med	fst	6f		$:21^4$	$:44^3$	$:57^1$	$1{:}10^1$	3↑	ⒻMed Bd B C HG3	**61**	2	5	4^6	$4^{6\frac{1}{2}}$	5^{10}	5^{17}	Santagata N	L 115	6.40	73-17	Raise Heck115^{nk} Miss Indy Anna119^2 Merri Tales111$^{4\frac{3}{4}}$	No menace	5
25Sep93-9Med	fst	6f		$:22^2$	$:45^1$	$:57^1$	$1{:}09^2$	3↑	ⒻMonmouth Cou40k	**95**	3	2	1^2	$1^{1\frac{1}{2}}$	1^3	$1^{2\frac{1}{4}}$	Santagata N	L 119	*1.20	94-11	Enjoy The Silence119$^{2\frac{1}{4}}$ Capture TheCrown115$^{2\frac{1}{4}}$ SilverTango113	Driving	3
10Sep93-9Med	fst	6f		$:22^2$	$:45^3$	$:57^4$	$1{:}10^3$	3↑	ⒻHydrangea35k	**81**	2	6	4^3	3^4	$3^{3\frac{1}{2}}$	4^6	Bravo J	L 119	*2.10	82-18	Dear Jane113^4 Cool Number116$^{1\frac{3}{4}}$ Bless Our Home113^{nk}	Tired, inside	7
28Aug93-7Mth	fm	5f	Ⓣ	$:21^4$	$:44^3$		$:56^3$	3↑	ⒻMth Beach35k	**47**	7	2	$5^{1\frac{1}{2}}$	7^5	7^{10}	$7^{13\frac{3}{4}}$	Ferrer J C	L 119	8.10	77-09	Lynn's A Dream113$^{\frac{1}{2}}$ SeeYuInCourt119$^{\frac{3}{4}}$ LittleGrayWolf117$^{\frac{1}{2}}$	No menace	7
8Aug93-9Mth	fst	6f		$:21^2$	$:44^2$	$:56^4$	$1{:}10^2$	3↑	ⒻNew Era35k	**92**	2	4	$3^{1\frac{1}{2}}$	2^{hd}	1^4	$1^{4\frac{1}{2}}$	Bravo J	L 119	*.60	87-22	Enjoy The Silence119$^{4\frac{1}{2}}$ KombatKate113^1 MeetHuncaMunca113^2	Driving	5
24Jly93-7Mth	fm	5f	Ⓣ	$:21^4$	$:44^3$		$:56^3$	3↑	ⒻWest Long Br35k	**87**	2	6	$7^{3\frac{3}{4}}$	$7^{2\frac{3}{4}}$	$5^{3\frac{1}{2}}$	$5^{1\frac{1}{2}}$	Squartino R A	L 117	16.80	89-09	WorldlyPossession113^{hd} Lynn'sADrem113^{hd} SeeYuInCourt117^{hd}	Late gain	8
5Jly93-8Mth	fst	6f		$:21^3$	$:44^2$	:57	$1{:}10^2$	3↑	ⒻAlw 30000N$Y	**89**	7	1	$3^{1\frac{1}{2}}$	1^{hd}	1^{hd}	$1^{1\frac{3}{4}}$	Homeister R B^5	L 114	*2.00	87-17	Enjoy The Silence114$^{1\frac{3}{4}}$ Capture TheCrown115^2 TastefulT.V.117$^{2\frac{1}{2}}$	Driving	7

WORKOUTS: Mar 12 Hia 7f fst $1{:}28^2$ Bg *2/2* Mar 7 Hia 6f fst $1{:}14^3$ H *2/6* Mar 2 Hia 5f fst 1:02 Bg *10/21* ●Feb 16 Hia 4f fst $:48^2$ Bg *1/16*

Phone Fantasy
Own: Red Oak Stable

B. c. 4
Sire: Phone Trick (Clever Trick)
Dam: April Again (Alleged)
Br: Red Oak Farm Inc (Fla)
Tr: Sacco Gregory D (—)

Lifetime Record:	11 4 2 2	$52,540			
1994	1 1 0 0	$11,200	Turf	4 2 0 1	$22,550
1993	8 3 1 2	$38,390	Wet	0 0 0 0	
HIA	3 2 0 1	$23,800	Dist	6 1 2 1	$18,790

19Mar94-6Hia fst 6f	:222	:452	:573	1:102	Alw 16000N2X	90	6	1	21½	21½	1hd	11½	Maple E	116	5.40	93-11	Phone Fantasy1161½ Gentle Patrick1161¼ Entroski115½		6
Five wide top str, driving																			
26Oct93-9Med yl 170 Ⓣ	:221	:472	1:123	1:434	3↑ Alw 20000N2X	73	4	2	31½	2½	2hd	45¼	Marquez C H Jr	113	9.60	67-30	Electric Spark1202¾ To Ridley113¾ Joviality1161¾	Weakened	9
1Sep93-6Mth fm 1 Ⓣ	:234	:472	1:123	1:382	3↑ Alw 18000N1X	84	4	1	22½	32	21½	1½	Marquez C H Jr	112	6.30	74-26	Phone Fantasy112½ Alphatero1162¾ MaginskyToo1102¼	Lost whip, driving	7
11Aug93-5Mth fm 1$\frac{1}{16}$ Ⓣ	:233	:482	1:131	1:461	Clm 22000	70	2	2	32	22½	1hd	1hd	Squartino R A	115	3.70	73-25	Phone Fantasy115hd Gerson113no Firestorming1132½	Hard drive	10
27Jun93-8Mth fst 6f	:22	:451	:573	1:104	3↑ Alw 18000N1X	57	1	4	22	53	58	512½	Marquez C H Jr	112	3.00	72-21	ClssOfHisOwn116nk MomentOfSpring1169 Thosewerthdys1101¾	Gave way	7
30May93-8Mth fm 1 Ⓣ	:231	:463	1:102	1:353	Spend a Buck35k	73	9	1	1½	2hd	1½	34	Wilson R	113	*2.00e	84-13	Go Cuervo1134 U. S. Invader115no PhoneFantasy113¾	Tried to get out 1/4	9
8May93-4Hia fst 7f	:231	:464	1:12	1:252	Md Sp Wt	68	4	4	21	1hd	1hd	1no	Toribio A R	122	2.50	82-17	Phone Fantasy122no Rue Fabert1224 David T.1224¼		8
Pushed inward, fully extended																			
28Apr93-7Hia fst 6f	:222	:46	:581	1:11	Md Sp Wt	66	3	5	23	23	25	39	Toribio A R	122	4.40	81-14	Humbugaboo1228 Rue Fabert1221 Phone Fantasy122hd	Weakened	11
6Feb93-2GP fst 6f	:221	:452	:58	1:111	Md Sp Wt	74	6	3	42½	47	36½	28	Perret C	120	6.30	77-18	JackLivingston1208 PhoneFantasy1205½ LitigtionRex120no	Best of others	10
17Nov92-1Med fst 6f	:223	:461	:59	1:112	Md Sp Wt	42	1	7	1hd	1hd	1½	24¼	Marquez C H Jr	118	3.70	82-11	Thosewerethedays1184¼ Phone Fantasy1182¼ Naskra Prince118	2nd best	8

WORKOUTS: Mar 15 Hia 4f fst :484 B 9/19 Mar 9 Hia 6f fst 1:142 Hg2/7 Mar 2 Hia 5f fst 1:02 Bg10/21 ●Feb 25 Hia 5f fst 1:01 Hg1/15 ●Feb 19 Hia 4f sly :481 H 1/7 Feb 12 Hia 3f fst :37 B 4/18

Two days after Enjoy The Silence returned with a stakes win in the early stages of Hialeah's spring meet, along came another Gregory Sacco–trained layoff prospect, Phone Fantasy.

Like Enjoy The Silence, Phone Fantasy had campaigned with a good degree of success in New Jersey prior to the layoff, and each had worked a handy six furlongs ten days prior to their comeback win. Moreover, since both had breezed five furlongs from the gate in 1:02 on March 2, the assumption could be made they had worked in company; it was to Phone Fantasy's credit that he had finished on even terms with his older stablemate, who was a proven multiple-stakes winner.

This example also underscores the fact that owners as a handicapping factor are underestimated by many bettors. Red Oak Stable happens to be the *nom de course* for John Brunetti — the president of Hialeah. No wonder his horses had been primed for peak efforts at that track!

Workouts provide clues regarding trainer intention in other ways:

November Snow
ANTLEY C W (4 1 0 0 .25)
Own.—Mack Earle I

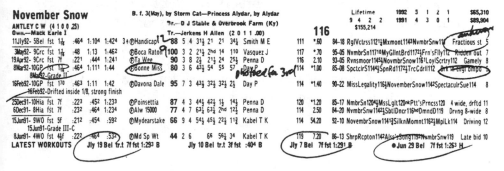

B. f. 3(May), by Storm Cat—Princess Alydar, by Alydar
Br.—D J Stable & Overbrook Farm (Ky)
Tr.—Jerkens H Allen (2 0 1 1 .00)

116

Lifetime		1992	5 1 2 1	$65,310
9 4 2 2	$155,214	1991	4 3 0 1	$89,904

11Jly92- 5Bel fst 1$\frac{1}{16}$	:464	1:104	1:424	3↑ ⒻHandicap	88	5	4	31½	21	21	34¼	Smith M E	111	*.60	84-18	RglVctrss1121¼Mxmont1143NvmbrSnw114	Fractious st	5
3May92- 9Crc fst 1$\frac{1}{16}$	:48	1:13	1:462	ⒻBoca Raton	100	3	2	21½	2hd	14	110	Vasquez J	117	*.70	95-05	NvmbrSn11710MyGllntBrd1172½Frn'sFlly112	Ridden out	7
19Apr92- 9Crc fst 7f	:221	:444	1:241	ⒻTa Wee	90	3	8	2½	21½	24	25½	Penna D	116	2.10	93-05	Rvnsmoor1145½NovmbrSnow1161LoylScrtry112	Gamely	8
8Mar92-10GP fst 1$\frac{1}{16}$	:464	1:111	1:44	ⒻBonne Miss	80	3	6	43½	54	55	57	Day P	114	*1.00	85-08	SpctclrS1144½SpnRd1172½TrcCdrll112	Brk in tngl bmpd	6
8Mar92-Grade II																		
16Feb92-10GP fst 170	:463	1:11	1:42	ⒻDavona Dale	95	7	3	43½	32½	32½	2½	Day P	114	*1.40	90-22	MissLegality116½NovemberSnow1142SpectaculrSue114		8
16Feb92-Drifted inside 1/8, strong finish																		
25Dec91-10Hia fst 7f	:223	:452	1:233	ⒻPoinsettia	87	4	3	44½	42½	1½	14½	Penna D	120	*1.20	85-17	NmbrSn1204½MssLglt120nkPtt'sPrncss120	4 wide, drftd	11
6Dec91- 8Hia fst 7f	:232	:464	1:234	ⒻAlw 15000	77	4	7	63¼	63¼	2hd	12½	Penna D	114	2.50	84-20	NvmbrSnw1142½SbtlDncr116hdDmndD119	Drvng 8-wide	8
15Jun91- 9WO fst 5f	:212	:454	:592	ⒻMydearstake	66	9	4	54½	45½	22½	11¾	Kabel T K	114	54.20	92-10	NovembrSnow1141¾SilknMomnt1162½MplLk114	Driving	12
15Jun91-Grade III-C																		
8Jun91- 4WO fst 4½f	:222	:464	:532	ⒻMd Sp Wt	44	2	6		66	56¼	34	Kabel T K	119	7.20	86-13	ShrpRcpton1142Alss'sSong1192NvmbrSnw119	Late bid	10

LATEST WORKOUTS Jly 19 Bel tr.t 7f fst 1:293 B Jly 10 Bel tr.t 3f fst :404 B Jly 7 Bel 7f fst 1:291 B ●Jun 29 Bel 7f fst 1:263 H

August 1 7F Test Stk. $11.40

When the three-year-old filly November Snow was entered in the Grade 1 Test Stakes second time back from a layoff, her workout line made it perfectly clear that the return in a mile-and-a-sixteenth route against older rivals had been designed strictly as a prep by Allen Jerkens. His filly loved seven furlongs, showing two wins, along with a second-place finish (despite breaking behind the field) in the Ta Wee from three starts at the distance. Tellingly, three of her last four workouts had been at seven furlongs. Handicappers who referred back to November Snow's pp's as they appeared for her July 11 return saw she had also worked seven furlongs on June 21, which meant four of her last five works had been at the Test distance.

Trainers sometimes telegraph positive intention with a horse by repeating a previously successful workout:

Diamond Anchor — Ro. g. 7, by Crafty Prospector—Roan Promise, by Wise Exchange
Own.—Bauer Robert J — $47,500 — Br.—Stonewall Farm (NY) — Tr.—Dutrow Anthony W — 115
Lifetime 75 11 19 10 $409,560 — 1992 1 0 0 0 — 1991 13 2 2 1 $70,448 — Turf 1 0 0 0

4Jan92- 6Aqu	sly	1-1/16	⊡:473	1:123	1:432	Alw 47000	4	4	42	45½	511	524½	Cordero A Jr	b 115	3.80	66-19	Conveyor11512PocketStrekr1171½Pnny'sBuck1151½	Even trip	5
28Dec91- 8Aqu	fst	1-1/16	⊡:464	1:123	1:461	3↑ⓈAlex M Rdb	7	6	66	73¾	79½	715¼	Velazquez J R	b 119	8.10	62-25	StudyHard1203¼SeaHunter1222½Carr'sPlesure1122½	No factor	8
16Dec91- 6Aqu	fst	1-1/8	⊡:474	1:123	1:513	3↑Clm 45000	1	3	32	1½	12½	18	Cordero A Jr	b 113	3.80	84-31	DiamondAnchor1138LethlFctor1171¾GllntHitter115nk	Driving	9
24Nov91- 1Aqu	gd	1	:47	1:111	1:353	3↑Clm 45000	1	3	31	61¾	74¼	711¾	Santos J A	b 115	3.50	72-22	Avasurus1132PocketStreker1174DngerousDwn113nk	Gave way	7
30Oct91- 5Aqu	fst	1	:492	1:143	1:391	3↑Clm 45000	5	2	21	41½	21	1no	Santos J A	b 113	9.00	66-41	DimondAnchor113noSylvesterStone1131¾G'DyMte1136	Driving	5
26Sep91- 3Bel	sly	1-1/16	:463	1:12	1:433	3↑Clm 47500	5	2	24	34	412	418¼	Antley C W	b 115	3.10	66-18	Nome1135½DngrousDwn1172¼MountinGhost11310½	Done early	5
9Sep91- 3Bel	fst	7f	:23	:452	1:224	3↑Clm 70000	4	9	63	45½	77	610¼	Santos J A	b 114	32.40	80-15	Scottish Monk108nkDrummondLane1134KingofWill1132	Tired	10
3Apr91- 3Aqu	fst	1	:452	1:091	1:342	Clm 65000	3	4	45	49	59½	516	Madrid A Jr	b 117	4.20	74-23	Scottish Monk1178 Johnny Ross1101¾ Galba115½	Outrun	5
23Mar91- 7Aqu	gd	1-1/8	:48	1:124	1:513	Alw 47000	7	7	78¼	75¾	42½	43	Madrid A Jr	b 115	6.90	75-30	G'DayMate115noPassN'Call115¾PocketStreker1152¼	Late gain	7
15Mar91- 8Aqu	sly	1	:472	1:12	1:373	Alw 37000	3	5	53¾	44½	46½	43¾	Madrid A Jr	b 117	3.10	70-35	ShtsArRngng1171½AllFlgsFln1171½DrBbbA1171	Saved ground	5

Speed Index: Last Race: -15.0 — 3-Race Avg.: -4.3 — 9-Race Avg.: -2.3 — Overall Avg.: -2.6
LATEST WORKOUTS ●Feb 1 Aqu ⊡ 5f fst 1:023 B — Dec 11 Aqu ⊡ 5f fst 1:012 H

February 10 1 and 70 yds. $9.20

Diamond Anchor, profiled earlier in this chapter for a track switch/jockey switch pattern at Saratoga, had developed a work pattern at Aqueduct earlier in his career. The predictable roan gelding won for a $47,500 tag on February 10 after having worked five furlongs on February 1. Note that his previous victory on December 16 had come on the heels of a similar five-furlong work December 11.

Diamond Anchor's pp's as they appeared for his win of October 30, 1991, showed more of the same:

Diamond Anchor — Ro. g. 6, by Crafty Prospector—Roan Promise, by Wise Exchange

Own.—Bauer Robert J — $45,000 — Br.—Stonewall Farm (NY) — Tr.—Dutrow Anthony W — 113

Lifetime 70 9 19 10 $379,560 — 1991 9 0 2 1 $40,448 — 1990 16 2 5 1 $126,560 — Turf 1 0 0 0

Date/Race	Cond	Dist	Fractions	Race	PP	St	1st	2nd	Str	Fin	Jockey		Wt	Odds	Sp-Var	Top finishers	Comment	Field
26Sep91- 3Bel	sly	1 1/16	:463 1:12 1:433	3+ Clm 47500	5	2	24	34	412	418¼	Antley C W	b	115	3.10	66-18	Nome1135½DngrousDwn1172¼MountinGhost11310½	Done early	5
9Sep91- 3Bel	fst	7f	:23 :452 1:224	3+ Clm 70000	4	9	63	45½	77	610¼	Santos J A	b	114	32.40	80-15	Scottish Monk108nkDrummondLane1134KingofWill1132	Tired	10
3Apr91- 3Aqu	fst	1	:452 1:091 1:342	Clm 65000	3	4	45	49	59½	516	Madrid A Jr	b	117	4.20	74-23	Scottish Monk1178 Johnny Ross1101¾ Galba115½	Outrun	5
23Mar91- 7Aqu	gd	1⅛	:48 1:124 1:513	Alw 47000	7	7	78¼	75¾	42½	43	Madrid A Jr	b	115	6.90	75-30	G'DayMate115noPassN'Call115¾PocketStreker1152¼	Late gain	7
15Mar91- 8Aqu	sly	1	:472 1:12 1:373	Alw 37000	3	5	53¾	44½	46½	43¾	Madrid A Jr	b	117	3.10	70-35	ShtsArRngng1171½AllFlgsFln1171¼DrBbbA1171	Saved ground	5
3Mar91- 8Aqu	fst	1 1/16 ⊡	:472 1:113 1:422	3+ ⓈKings Pt H	6	5	53	42½	21	21	Madrid A Jr	b	114	12.00	95-14	G'DyMte1111DimondAnchor1141RoughRogu1173	Second best	8
17Feb91- 7Aqu	fst	1 1/16 ⊡	:481 1:123 1:451	Alw 47000	3	3	42	54	53¼	33¾	Santagata N	b	115	5.60	78-22	TopCash1153½PocketStreaker110nkDHG'DyMte115	Fin. evenly	7
17Feb91- Dead heat																		
1Feb91- 5Aqu	fst	1 1/16 ⊡	:482 1:131 1:443	Clm c-75000	3	6	64½	74½	79¼	510	Thibeau R J Jr	b	117	*1.10	75-26	Galba117hd Congeleur1176½ Red Scamper1133	No excuse	7
14Jan91- 8Aqu	fst	1 1/16 ⊡	:471 1:11 1:432	Alw 47000	1	4	42½	31½	2hd	2¾	Cordero A Jr	b	115	4.10	90-13	SHntr115¾DmondAnchor115nkBb'sBrthrChp1101¾	Outfinished	7
29Dec90- 8Aqu	my	1 1/16 ⊡	:472 1:11 1:441	3+ ⓈAlex M Robb	7	4	45½	45½	46½	46¾	Cordero A Jr	b	119	4.20	80-22	Rough Rogue1151¼ Zee Best1223¼ Sea Hunter1262¼	Evenly	8

Speed Index: Last Race: −16.0 — 3–Race Avg.: −4.6 — 9–Race Avg.: +0.6 — Overall Avg.: +0.1

LATEST WORKOUTS — Oct 19 Aqu 5f fst 1:012 H — Oct 12 Aqu 4f fst :472 H — ●Sep 22 Aqu 4f fst :48 H — Sep 18 Aqu 4f fst :491 B

Again, his five-furlong work was the prelude to victory.

At times, the *absence* of workouts is a big key in eliminating a short-priced contender.

The ninth race at Saratoga on August 27 was a $35,000 claimer on grass at nine furlongs, and it appeared to be a two-horse race between No Holme Keys and Madame Dahar, who were cofavored at 2–1:

6 Madame Dahar PP-6 — B. f. 4 — Sire: Dahar (Lyphard) — Dam: Bold Whim (Bold Hour) — Br: Gallo Robert & Syn Dahar (Ky) — Tr: Fisher John R S (4 0 0 0 .00)

Own: Klighman Joel — BAILEY J D (143 24 17 25 .17) — $35,000 — 117

Lifetime Record: 20 5 3 5 $86,738 — 1993 4 0 0 0 $3,480 — 1992 12 5 2 4 $78,718 — Sar Ⓣ 3 0 0 1 $4,950 — Turf 17 5 3 4 $85,198 — Wet 0 0 0 0 — Dist Ⓣ 3 1 0 0 $10,398

Date/Race	Cond	Dist	Fractions	Race	Beyer	PP	St	1st	2nd	Str	Fin	Jockey	Wt	Odds	Sp-Var	Top finishers	Comment	Field
14Aug93- 4Sar	fm	1⅛ Ⓣ	:472 1:112 1:36 1:48	3+ ⒻClm 50000	77	11	1	119½	110½	72¾	63	Santos J A	117	11.10	86-14	Home By Ten1131¼ Fashion Miss119nk Turkolady117hd	No threat	11
30Jly93- 2Sar	fm	1⅜ Ⓣ	:471 1:112 1:363 1:557	3+ ⒻClm 50000	81	5	2	48	53	32½	43½	Krone J A	117	3.00	88-15	Fashion Miss1192¾ Asaracket115½ Turkolady117½	Lacked rally	9
4Jly93- 1Bel	yl	1 1/16 Ⓣ	:24 :471 1:121 1:434	ⒻClm 75000	77	4	8	812	89½	64¾	45	Krone J A	117	8.20	72-23	Herat O' Mine113nk Talk Politics117¾ Buck Some Belle1154	Mild gain	8
13Jun93- 8Mth	fm	1 1/16 Ⓣ	:233 :471 1:10 1:41	+ 3+ ⒻAlw 30000N$Y	69	1	6	67	57	68½	59	Wilson R	116	3.50	87-07	Dior's Angel1163 White Corners116hd North Again1163¾		6
Steadied early, brushed rail																		
9Nov92- 6Aqu	yl	1 1/16 Ⓣ	:244 :493 1:144 1:47	3+ ⒻAlw 47000	87	7	6	66½	63	63½	32	Antley C W	117	11.20	74-22	Chipaya-GB115hd Far Out Beast1152 Madame Dahar117	Late gain	8
10Oct92- 9Med	gd	1 1/16 Ⓣ	:237 :472 1:12 1:443	ⒻJersey Blus 35k	80	1	6	62½	31½	11½	13¼	Molina V H	114	2.40	75-17	Madame Dahar1143¼ Joy Valentine1141¼ Raven Runner116	Drew out	6
2Oct92- 8Pha	yl	1 1/16 Ⓣ	:23 :48 1:131 1:462	3+ ⒻAlw 19795	76	6	7	66	31½	1½	13	Molina V H	113	*.90	79-24	Madame Dahar1133 Sugar Nipper1131 Meetmenow118	Driving	9
18Sep92- 8Pha	fm	1⅛ Ⓣ	:491 1:133 1:384 1:513	3+ ⒻAlw 16616	81	8	6	65	42½	1hd	11¼	Molina V H	110	*1.10	86-14	Madame Dahar1101¼ Smart Caper1101¾ Regallino119	Driving	8
13Sep92- 2Bel	gd	1 1/16 Ⓣ	:234 :473 1:121 1:431	ⒻClm 50000	77	2	2	47	57	64¾	34	Day P	118	[illegible]	[illegible]	[illegible] Madame Dahar116	Late gain	7
[illegible]	fm	[illegible]	[illegible]	ⒻClm 75000	85	8	4	42	32	52½	31½	Day P	116	6.60	89-09	Kris' Dear Deby1141½ Tiffany Hall112½ Madame Dahar116	Willingly	8
1Aug92- 8Pha	yl	*1⅛ Ⓣ	1:543	ⒻMselle 26k	59	3	4	47½	411	57	512	Molina V H	120	3.00	66-22	Cozzene's Flite1201¼ My Swinger120no Toosie120	No threat	6
19Jly92- 7Mth	fm	1 1/16 Ⓣ	:24 :483 1:123 1:432	3+ ⒻAlw 18000	76	8	4	41½	31	3nk	34	Bravo J	110	6.00	83-12	Fashion Model1162 Belle of Summer1162 Madame Dahar110	Did, tired	10

WORKOUTS: Jun 8 Fai tr.t Ⓣ 5f gd 1:08 B 1/1 — May 18 Fai 5f gd 1:034 B 1/2 — May 11 Fai 4f gd :534 B 1/1

9 No Holme Keys PP-10 — Ch. m. 5 — Sire: Dewan Keys (Dewan) — Dam: Ligia M (Noholme Jr) — Br: Goodpaster Jane (Ky) — Tr: Reid Mark J (12 2 0 0 .17)

Own: Barge Marc — ANTLEY C W (93 10 11 13 .11) — $35,000 — 117

Lifetime Record: 22 9 1 3 $108,570 — 1993 2 1 0 0 $12,900 — 1992 6 4 1 0 $58,300 — Sar Ⓣ 2 2 0 0 $26,400 — Turf 14 8 1 1 $95,250 — Wet 1 1 0 0 $8,100 — Dist Ⓣ 2 2 0 0 $26,400

Date/Race	Cond	Dist	Fractions	Race	Beyer	PP	St	1st	2nd	Str	Fin	Jockey	Wt	Odds	Sp-Var	Top finishers	Comment	Field
19Jly93- 1Bel	fm	1 Ⓣ	:23 :46 1:103 1:354	ⒻClm 35000	86	3	3	31	1½	11½	12¼	Antley C W	117 fb	1.90	83-18	NoHolmeKeys1172¼ AShakyQueen119hd MissGretLuck117¾	Wide, driving	8
2Jly93- 4Bel	fm	1 1/16 Ⓣ	:241 :473 1:112 1:424	ⒻClm 35000	75	2	1	11½	1½	2hd	63¾	Antley C W	117 fb	1.10	78-17	A Shaky Queen1171½ Flight Visibility117nk Smart Holly117¾	Used in pace	8
2Oct92- 3Bel	fm	1¼ Ⓣ	:492 1:133 1:374 2:023	3+ ⒻClm 35000	85	10	1	11	11	11	11¼	Antley C W	117 b	*.70	77-15	ⒹNo Holme Keys1171¼ Ivory Today117nk Azadeh117	Bthrd rivals	11
Disqualified and placed seventh																		
2Sep92- 1Bel	fm	1¼ Ⓣ	:472 1:112 1:361 2:013	3+ ⒻClm 45000	87	5	2	2½	2hd	1½	2½	Davis R G	113 b	3.20	81-15	Gharah117½ No Holme Keys1131¼ Sharpener113	Gamely	8
23Aug92- 2Sar	fm	1⅛ Ⓣ	:48 1:103 1:351 1:473	3+ ⒻClm 35000	89	9	2	26	2hd	14	17½	Antley C W	117 b	*1.00	92-06	No Holme Keys1177½ Leading Lyndsey1172¾ Titans Belle117	Mild drive	12
29Jly92- 9Sar	fm	1⅛ Ⓣ	:464 1:104 1:353 1:482	3+ ⒻClm 35000	85	11	3	21½	2½	2½	1no	Antley C W	119 b	*2.50	88-09	No Holme Keys119no Sharpener1171½ Mamora Bay117	Driving	11
12Jly92- 4Bel	fm	1 1/16 Ⓣ	:231 :454 1:10 1:42	ⒻClm 35000	85	2	1	1½	11	12	12	Antley C W	117 b	*1.50	86-14	No Holme Keys1172 Oriane117hd Great Review117	Driving	10
23May92- 2Bel	fm	1 1/16 Ⓣ	:222 :451 1:092 1:412	ⒻClm 35000	85	5	3	3½	2½	1½	11¼	Antley C W	117 b	4.90	89-07	NoHolmeKeys1171¼ LifeOntheFrm1173½ AmdsAppel117	Lost whp, drvng	11
5Nov91- 1Med	fm	170 Ⓣ	:221 :461 1:104 1:40	ⒻClm 25000	68	8	2	2hd	1½	32	58	Jocson G J	L 114 b	4.40	85-06	Creme the Cat1092 Mt. Morna1142½ Misty Sauce114	Faded	10
19Oct91- 8Med	yl	1 1/16 Ⓣ	:224 :473 1:13 1:461	3+ ⒻAlw 17000	71	2	4	33½	37½	411	514¼	Jocson G J	L 113 b	7.20	52-38	Aunt Sigourney1166¾ Jakes Jan1165 Highland Manor113	No rally	10
14Sep91- 7Med	fm	170 Ⓣ	:224 :471 1:112 1:401	3+ ⒻAlw 16000	85	5	1	1½	1½	12½	1nk	Jocson G J5	L 105 b	2.70	92-11	No Holme Keys110nk Flight Luxe1141¾ Million Dollar Mom112	Driving	10
4Sep91- 7Med	fm	1 1/16 Ⓣ	:222 :46 1:102 1:42	3+ ⒻAlw 16000	77	10	1	1½	2½	24	37¼	Jocson G J5	L 105 b	5.20	80-11	Be Grise-Ir1165 Spectra Photo-Ir1132¼ No Holme Keys105	Weakened	11

WORKOUTS: Jun 17 Bel 4f fst :484 B 15/58 — Jun 10 Bel Ⓣ 4f gd :504 B (d) 6/8 — Jun 3 Bel 4f fst :473 H 3/33

Since returning from a layoff of seven months, Madame Dahar had recorded Beyers of 69, 77, 81, and 77. Another effort in the high 70s or low 80s would be good enough to defeat all her rivals in this field with the exception of No Holme Keys, whose figures in $35,000 grass routes the previous summer were all in the mid- to high 80s. It seemed she had recaptured that form in her second start back from a layoff by running an 86 for a convincing win on July 19. In fact, No Holme Keys owned *six* figures superior to Madame Dahar's recent efforts, and she had won both her starts at Saratoga in 1992.

"Throw No Holme Keys out," was the advice to the audience from the Wizard, a.k.a. Michael Kipness, when he and I made our weekly appearance on Harvey Pack's "Paddock Show" the morning of the race.

The Wizard had initially turned me on to horseracing by bringing a copy of *Ainslie's Complete Guide to Thoroughbred Racing* into our seventh-grade homeroom more than two decades earlier. Unlike most public handicappers (myself included), who are employed by a newspaper and therefore receive the same paycheck week after week no matter how many winners they pick, Michael's income as C.E.O., president, and founder of a selection sheet known as *The Wizard* depends almost entirely on his performance: pick seven winners a day, and sales skyrocket; draw blanks for a few days, and sales crash and burn.

Whenever the Wizard summarily dismisses the chances of an obvious contender, it means he has seen something negative about the horse's record that is not obvious to most other handicappers.

His reasoning in this case was as follows: "Every time No Holme Keys has won, she's shown a workout. The absence of a workout raises serious concerns about her readiness for today's race."

Indeed, a subsequent check of the mare's past performances from four 1992 wins revealed the following:

When No Holme Keys was brought back for a victory in her seasonal debut of May 23, 1992, her workout lines looked like this:

No Holme Keys
ANTLEY C W (56 10 2 7 $187,960)
Own.—Barge Marc

Ch. f. 4, by Dewan Keys—Ligia M, by Noholme Jr
$35,000 Br.—Mrs. Jane Goodpaster (Ky)
Tr.—Reid Mark J (8 2 0 2 $51,960)

117

Lifetime 14 4 0 3 $37,370

1991	14	4	0	3	$37,370
1990	0	M	0	0	
Turf	6	3	0	1	$24,050
Wet	1	1	0	0	$8,100

5Nov91- 1Med	fm	170	Ⓣ:461	1:104	1:40	ⒻClm 25000	68	8	2	2hd	1½	32	58	Jocson G J	Lb	114	4.40	85-06 Creme theCat1092Mt.Morna1142¾MistySauce114	Faded	10
19Oct91- 8Med	yl	1⅟₁₆	Ⓣ:473	1:13	1:461	3↑ⒻAlw 17000	71	2	4	33½	37½	412	514¼	Jocson G J	Lb	113	7.20	52-38 AuntSigourney1166¾JksJn1165HighlndMnor113	No rally	10
14Sep91- 7Med	fm	170	Ⓣ:471	1:112	1:401	3↑ⒻAlw 16000	85	5	1	1½	1½	12½	1nk	Jocson G J5	Lb	105	2.70	92-11 NoHolmKys110nkFlghtLx1141¾MllonDllrMm112	Driving	10
4Sep91- 7Med	fm	1⅟₁₆	Ⓣ:46	1:102	1:42	3↑ⒻAlw 16000	77	10	1	1½	2½	24	37¾	Jocson G J5	Lb	105	5.20	80-11 BGrs-Ir1165SpctrPhoto-Ir1132¾NHlmKys105	Weakened	11
23Aug91- 6Atl	gd	*1	Ⓣ:491	1:151	1:423	ⒻClm 22500	79	7	2	2hd	11	15	14½	Jocson G J5	Lb	107	4.00	71-29 No Holme Keys1074½BlueJewel1114½CityCat112	Driving	12
20Jly91- 5Pha	fm	1⅟₁₆	Ⓣ:483	1:142	1:473	ⒻClm 17000	64	2	5	42½	1hd	12½	1½	Molina V H	Lb	114	4.40	59-27 NoHolmKys114½MissMcCnn1102¾TwoThrtyT112	Driving	10
29Jun91- 8Pha	fst	1	:47	1:122	1:40	ⒻAlw 14000	60	6	4	43	52½	43½	45½	Jocson G J5	Lb	117	4.30	75-19 FrshSpry1161½ZnzritStorm116hdJckiP.116	Flattened out	8
12Jun91- 9Pha	fst	1⅟₁₆	:464	1:113	1:46	ⒻClm 28000	58	2	2	3nk	1hd	22	31½	Castillo R E	Lb	112	3.80	77-10 Ddjol1161½MchllsFlly115noNHlmKys112	Came in, bmpd.	5
18May91-10Pha	fst	170	:48	1:132	1:46	ⒻAlw 14000	63	4	4	41½	43	45	45½	Colton R E	L	122	8.60	60-35 Ginny Wolf1191½ Fresh Spray116no Damie'sSis116	Wide	8
6May91- 4Pha	sly	170	:472	1:131	1:45	ⒻMd Sp Wt	57	8	5	54¾	32½	22½	11¾	Colton R E	L	122	3.40	71-21 NHlmKys1221¾OnPttQn122nkFrFlsh122	Steadied.driving	9

Speed Index: Last Race: -9.0 3-Race Avg.: -5.3 6-Race Avg.: -4.8 Overall Avg.: -6.1

LATEST WORKOUTS May 19 Pha 5f sly 1:022 B May 13 Pha 4f fst :49 B May 5 Pha 5f fst :592 B Apr 28 Pha 4f fst :472 B

When she won her third straight race on August 23, 1992, her workout lines looked like this:

No Holme Keys Ch. f. 4, by Dewan Keys—Ligia M, by Noholme Jr Lifetime 1992 3 3 0 0 $39,600
ANTLEY C W (118 26 18 15 .22) $35,000 Br.—Goodpaster Jane (Ky) 17 7 0 3 1991 14 4 0 3 $37,370
Own.—Barge Marc Tr.—Reid Mark J (12 6 2 1 .50) 117 $76,970 Turf 9 6 0 1 $63,650 Wet 1 1 0 0 $8,100
29Jly92- 9Sar fm 1 1/8 ①:464 1:104 1:482 3↑ⒻClm 35000 84 11 3 21½ 2½ 2½ 1no Antley C W b 119 *2.50 88-09 NoHolmeKeys119noSharpener1171½MmorBy117 Driving 11
12Jly92- 4Bel fm 1 1/16 ①:454 1:10 1:42 ⒻClm 35000 85 2 1 1½ 11 12 12 Antley C W b 117 *1.50 86-14 No Holme Keys1172Oriane117hdGreatReview117 Driving 10
23May92- 2Bel fm 1 1/16 ①:451 1:092 1:412 ⒻClm 35000 85 5 3 3½ 2½ 1½ 11¼ Antley C W b 117 4.90 89-07 NHlKs1171¼LfOnthFr1173½AdsAppl117 Lost whp, drvng 11
5Nov91- 1Medfm 170 ①:461 1:104 1:40 ⒻClm 25000 68 8 2 2hd 1½ 32 58 Jocson G J Lb 114 4.40 85-06 Creme theCat1092Mt.Morna1142½MistySauce114 Faded 10
19Oct91- 8Medyl 1 1/16 ①:473 1:13 1:461 3↑ⒻAlw 17000 71 2 4 33½ 37½ 412 514¼ Jocson G J Lb 113 7.20 52-38 AuntSigourney1166¾JksJn1165HighlndMnor113 No rally 10
14Sep91- 7Medfm 170 ①:471 1:112 1:401 3↑ⒻAlw 16000 85 5 1 1½ 1½ 12½ 1nk Jocson G J5 Lb 105 2.70 92-11 NoHolmKys110nkFlghtLx1141¾MllonDllrMm112 Driving 10
4Sep91- 7Medfm 1 1/16 ①:46 1:102 1:42 3↑ⒻAlw 16000 77 10 1 1½ 2½ 24 37¼ Jocson G J5 Lb 105 5.20 80-11 BGrs-Ir1165SpctrPhoto-Ir1132¼NHlmKys105 Weakened 11
23Aug91- 6Atl gd *1 ①:491 1:151 1:423 ⒻClm 22500 79 7 2 2hd 11 15 14½ Jocson G J5 Lb 107 4.00 71-29 No Holme Keys1074½BlueJewel1114¼CityCat112 Driving 12
20Jly91- 5Pha fm 1 1/16 ①:483 1:142 1:473 ⒻClm 17000 64 2 5 42½ 1hd 12½ 1½ Molina V H Lb 114 4.40 69-27 NoHolmKys114½MissMcCnn1102½TwoThrtyT112 Driving 10
29Jun91- 8Pha fst 1 :47 1:122 1:40 ⒻAlw 14000 60 6 4 43 52½ 43½ 45½ Jocson G J5 Lb 117 4.30 75-19 FrshSpry1161½ZnzritStorm116hdJckiP.116 Flattened out 8
LATEST WORKOUTS Aug 20 Sar 3f fst :382 B ●Aug 12 Sar 4f fst :472 H Jly 26 Bel 3f fst :351 H Jly 8 Bel 5f fst 1:011 H

Note the workouts preceding the wins: a work July 8 followed by a win July 12; a work July 26 followed by a win July 29; a work August 20 followed by a win August 23.

When she won on October 2, 1992, her workout lines looked like this:

No Holme Keys Ch. f. 4, by Dewan Keys—Ligia M, by Noholme Jr Lifetime 1992 5 4 1 0 $58,300
ANTLEY C W (57 14 4 7 .25) $35,000 Br.—Goodpaster Jane (Ky) 19 8 1 3 1991 14 4 0 3 $37,370
Own.—Barge Marc Tr.—Reid Mark J (10 1 3 1 .10) 117 $95,670 Turf 11 7 1 1 $82,350 Wet 1 1 0 0 $8,100
2Sep92- 1Bel fm 1¼ Ⓣ:472 1:361 2:013 3↑ⒻClm 45000 87 5 2 2½ 2hd 1½ 2½ Davis R G b 113 3.20 81-15 Gharah117½ No Holme Keys1131¼ Sharpener113 Gamely 8
23Aug92- 2Sar fm 1 1/8 ①:46 1:103 1:473 3↑ⒻClm 35000 89 9 2 26 2hd 14 17½ Antley C W b 117 *1.00 92-06 NoHlmKys1177½LdngLyndsy1172¾TtnsBll117 Mild drive 12
29Jly92- 9Sar fm 1 1/8 ①:464 1:104 1:482 3↑ⒻClm 35000 85 11 3 21½ 2½ 2½ 1no Antley C W b 119 *2.50 88-09 NoHolmeKeys119noSharpener1171½MmorBy117 Driving 11
12Jly92- 4Bel fm 1 1/16 ①:454 1:10 1:42 ⒻClm 35000 85 2 1 1½ 11 12 12 Antley C W b 117 *1.50 86-14 No Holme Keys1172Oriane117hdGreatReview117 Driving 10
23May92- 2Bel fm 1 1/16 ①:451 1:092 1:412 ⒻClm 35000 85 5 3 3½ 2½ 1½ 11¼ Antley C W b 117 4.90 89-07 NHlKs1171¼LfOnthFr1173½AdsAppl117 Lost whp, drvng 11
5Nov91- 1Medfm 170 ①:461 1:104 1:40 ⒻClm 25000 68 8 2 2hd 1½ 32 58 Jocson G J Lb 114 4.40 85-06 Creme theCat1092Mt.Morna1142½MistySauce114 Faded 10
19Oct91- 8Medyl 1 1/16 ①:473 1:13 1:461 3↑ⒻAlw 17000 71 2 4 33½ 37½ 412 514¼ Jocson G J Lb 113 7.20 52-38 AuntSigourney1166¾JksJn1165HighlndMnor113 No rally 10
14Sep91- 7Medfm 170 ①:471 1:112 1:401 3↑ⒻAlw 16000 85 5 1 1½ 1½ 12½ 1nk Jocson G J5 Lb 105 2.70 92-11 NoHolmKys110nkFlghtLx1141¾MllonDllrMm112 Driving 10
4Sep91- 7Medfm 1 1/16 ①:46 1:102 1:42 3↑ⒻAlw 16000 77 10 1 1½ 2½ 24 37¼ Jocson G J5 Lb 105 5.20 80-11 BGrs-Ir1165SpctrPhoto-Ir1132¼NHlmKys105 Weakened 11
23Aug91- 6Atl gd *1 ①:491 1:151 1:423 ⒻClm 22500 79 7 2 2hd 11 15 14½ Jocson G J5 Lb 107 4.00 71-29 No Holme Keys1074½BlueJewel1114¼CityCat112 Driving 12
LATEST WORKOUTS Sep 14 Bel 4f fst :473 H Aug 20 Sar 3f fst :382 B ●Aug 12 Sar 4f fst :472 H

Note the :47⅗ work on September 14.

It is true that No Holme Keys did not have a workout leading to her half-length defeat of September 2, which was a sharp effort; but only a few days had elapsed between starts. Likewise, she had not worked before her first win of 1993, but only about two weeks had elapsed between starts.

For this race, however, No Holme Keys had been on the shelf for nearly six weeks and showed not a single workout. She had won off a layoff in the past, but always with at least two workouts as part of her training regimen. As corroborating evidence that No Holme Keys was probably not ready to race to her fullest potential, the Wizard noticed that she had worn front bandages for her two return starts in July, and referred to this comment line in the chart footnote for her win of July 19: "took the lead while drifting out on the turn."

The lack of a recent work, the addition of front bandages, and the "drifting out" comment were indicators, taken together, that

No Holme Keys was not in the kind of consistent form she'd been in the previous summer.

NINTH RACE
Saratoga
AUGUST 27, 1993

1 ⅛ MILES.(InnerTurf). (1.47³) CLAIMING. Purse $21,500. Fillies and Mares. 3-year-olds and upward. Weights: 3-year-olds, 117 lbs.; Older, 122 lbs. Non-winners of two races at a mile or over since August 1, allowed 3 lbs. Of such a race since then, 5 lbs. Claiming price $35,000. (Races when entered to be claimed for $25,000 or less not considered.)

Value of race $21,500; value to winner $12,900; second $4,730; third $2,580; fourth $1,290. Mutuel pool $332,197.

Last Raced	Horse	M/Eqt.	A.	Wt	PP	St	¼	½	¾	Str	Fin	Jockey	Cl'g Pr	Odds $1
14Aug93 4Sar6	Madame Dahar		4	117	5	7	8½	71	6½	1½	11½	Bailey J D	35000	2.30
18Aug93 5Sar8	Galloping Proudly	b	4	117	7	9	91	9hd	91	6½	2no	Bisono C V	35000	69.50
18Aug93 5Sar2	Ivory Today	b	5	117	6	6	7hd	83½	8½	71½	3nk	Krone J A	35000	5.60
19Jly93 1Bel2	A Shaky Queen	b	5	117	9	8	4hd	51½	52	41	41½	Nelson D	35000	7.90
18Aug93 5Sar5	Eskimo Song	b	4	117	3	3	61	6½	72	3½	5no	Smith M E	35000	14.30
4Aug93 7Sar7	Miss Angel Too		4	117	1	1	5½	42½	3½	5hd	65	Nicol P A Jr	35000	7.50
18Aug93 5Sar6	High Talent	b	4	117	4	4	2hd	22½	21½	2hd	73½	Migliore R	35000	15.10
18Aug93 5Sar4	Pretty Firm		4	117	10	10	10	10	10	93	81½	Santos J A	35000	18.20
19Jly93 1Bel1	No Holme Keys		5	117	8	5	11½	11½	11½	82½	97	Davis R G	35000	2.20
14Aug93 10Sar7	Take A Powder	b	5	117	2	2	31	31	41	10	10	Chavez J F	35000	31.40

OFF AT 5:27 Start good Won driving Time, :23 , :46³, 1:11 , 1:36³, 1:49⁴ Course firm.

$2 Mutuel Prices:				
	6-(F)-MADAME DAHAR	6.60	4.20	2.80
	8-(I)-GALLOPING PROUDLY		33.00	11.20
	1-(G)-IVORY TODAY			4.00

$2 EXACTA 6-8 PAID $514.80 $2 TRIPLE 6-8-1 PAID $2,070.00

B. f, by Dahar—Bold Whim, by Bold Hour. Trainer Fisher John R S. Bred by Gallo Robert & Syn Dahar (Ky).

MADAME DAHAR reserved for six furlongs while saving ground, angled four wide to launch her bid entering the stretch, accelerated to the front in midstretch, then edged clear under pressure. GALLOPING PROUDLY outrun to the turn while saving ground, split horses in midstretch then outfinished IVORY TODAY for the place. IVORY TODAY unhurried for six furlongs, angled out in upper stretch then rallied belatedly in the middle of the stretch. A SHAKY QUEEN raced in good position while saving ground to the turn, rallied between horses in upper stretch, but couldn't sustain her bid. ESKIMO SONG rated just behind the early leaders, made a strong run along the rail to threaten in midstretch then flattened out. MISS ANGEL TOO raced in close contention while slightly off the rail for six furlongs then lacked the needed response when called upon. HIGH TALENT prompted the pace slightly off the rail in upper stretch and tired in the final eighth. PRETTY FIRM never reached contention. NO HOLME KEYS was used up setting the early pace. TAKE A POWDER faded after going five furlongs.

Owners— 1, Kligman Joel; 2, Four B Mice Stable; 3, Zimmerman Mitchell; 4, Jujugen Stable; 5, Cromor Stable; 6, Kraft Payson Virginia; 7, Mariano Peter E; 8, Winbound Farms; 9, Barge Marc; 10, Odintz Jeff.

Trainers— 1, Fisher John R S; 2, Bailie Sally A; 3, DiMauro Stephen L; 4, Carroll Henry L; 5, Monaci David; 6, Bond Harold James; 7, Belfiore Thomas; 8, Contessa Gary C; 9, Reid Mark J; 10, Odintz Jeff.

Scratched—Somthingscandalous (6Aug93 2Sar1); Couloir (18Aug93 5Sar); Sweet N' Saxy (14Aug93 2Sar9).

Madame Dahar ran as expected, winning the race and paying $6.60. No Holme Keys, the slight favorite, also ran as the Wizard had expected, setting the early pace and tiring abruptly in the stretch to finish ninth, beaten by some thirteen lengths.

Finally, the significance of workouts may have to do with the type of horse under consideration. A habitual front-runner has done nothing of note when it blows out in :34, but a front-runner such as Appreciate It deserves extra credit for stamina-building workouts:

Appreciate It — **B. g. 3(May), by Cannon Shell—My Appreciation, by Exclusive Native**
Br.—Seymour John (NY)
Tr.—Hushion Michael E (—)
Own.—Cohn Seymour

Lifetime						
9 2 1 2	1992	9	2	1	2	$41,760
$41,760	1991	0	M	0	0	
	Turf	2	0	0	0	
	Wet	1	1	0	0	$16,200

21Oct92- 6Aqu	fst	6f	:22¹	:45²	1:11¹	Clm 35000	—	5	1	21	31½	32	43¼	Madrid A Jr	b	117	7.50	82-18	ClvrKnv115nk StrtFight1173EstblishdLi115	Lacked rally	9
26Sep92- 9Bel	sly	6f	:22¹	:45	1:10¹	3↑ S Alw 27000	86	3	1	12	13½	12	13	Madrid A Jr	b	113	*2.60	89-14	ApprctIt1133Drmnthdywy1172¾EbonyBlu117	Ridden out	8
4Sep92- 7Bel	yl	1 1/16 T	:48²	1:12³	1:44¹	3↑ S Alw 29000	61	2	1	11½	1hd	45	815½	Migliore R		113	14.30	61-20	ShomrmScty1172¾ClvrCty1171¼EbnyBl117	Used in pace	10
23Aug92- 9Sar	fst	6f	:22	:45	1:10¹	3↑ S Alw 27000	73	6	4	11	1hd	1½	32¾	Migliore R		119	9.80	91-07	PrincConsort1171¾EbonyBlu117½ApprctIt119	Weakened	12
30Jly92- 9Sar	fst	6f	:22²	:46	1:11	3↑ S Md Sp Wt	78	6	2	11½	12	15	19	Migliore R		116	*1.30	89-06	AppreciateIt1169Bordagaray116nkConcur116	Mild drive	12
20Jly92- 5Bel	fm	1 1/16 T	:46³	1:11¹	1:42⁴	3↑ S Alw 29000	58	2	1	11½	1½	73¼	911¼	Migliore R		113	15.90	71-15	Imprgnbl117hdPtrt'sThndr1112¼TddyC.111	Used in pace	10
15Jly92- 9Bel	fst	6f	:21⁴	:45¹	1:11²	3↑ Md 35000	69	12	1	11	13	12	33½	Migliore R		116	5.50	79-14	SgrHos1163ToknofPowr112½ApprctIt116	Speed,faltered	13
18Jun92- 2Bel	fst	6f	:22	:45⁴	1:11³	3↑ S Md Sp Wt	54	10	4	11	1½	2½	54	Brocklebank G V		114	*1.00	78-13	Dark Palette113½ Cap1121¼ Jen's Shot104	Speed,tired	12
22May92- 9Bel	fst	6½f	:22¹	:45²	1:17³	3↑ S Md Sp Wt	64	4	2	2½	1hd	11½	23½	Brocklebank G V		115	5.10	81-11	Mr. Lee1153½AppreciateIt1151¾OntheDocket115	Gamely	14

LATEST WORKOUTS Sep 22 Bel 7f fst 1:30 B Sep 18 Bel 1 fst 1:44³ B

Appreciate It blew three clear leads in the first three starts of his career. Trainer Mike Hushion, observing his gelding's obvious stamina problems, set him up for the maiden win July 30 by entering him in a turf route ten days earlier.

After Appreciate It weakened as the pace setter in his first allowance start, Hushion entered him in another turf route on September 4, breezed him a slow mile on September 18, and breezed him a slow seven furlongs on September 22. Hushion was training Appreciate It with a purpose: there was no need to drill him for speed in the mornings — Hushion already knew his horse had good speed; what his horse needed was conditioning designed to improve endurance.

With the turf route and two long stamina works under his belt, Appreciate It customarily set the pace, but did not tire in the stretch on September 26, winning "ridden out" as a lukewarm favorite at $7.20.

Similarly, a fast blowout can be significant when it appears out of character:

Mr. Baba
Own: Paxson Mrs Henry D
KRONE J A (25 3 3 6 .12)

Ch. c. 3 (Mar)
Sire: Nepal (Raja Baba)
Dam: Critical Miss (Reviewer)
Br: Paxson Mrs Henry D (NY)
Tr: Dickinson Michael W (6 2 0 0 .33)

114

Lifetime Record :	1 M 0 0		$0
1994	1 M 0 0	Turf	1 0 0 0
1993	0 M 0 0	Wet	0 0 0 0
Bel Ⓣ	0 0 0 0	Dist Ⓣ	0 0 0 0

2Apr94- 1Cam fm *1 Ⓣ 1:43¹ 3+ Md Sp Wt — 3 10 9⁵½ 10¹⁶ 10¹⁵ 10¹⁴½ Simpson A 140 - — — Grenade150¹ Island Skater144½ Paddock Dancer147¹½ Away slowly 12
WORKOUTS: May 24 Fai 3f fst :39 B 1/1 May 12 Fai 3f fst :35 Bg 1/3 May 7 Fai 6f fst 1:14³ B 2/5 May 2 Fai 6f fst 1:15¹ B 3/3

Mr. Baba made his career debut at a hunt meet on April 2, receiving the comment "Away slowly" for his tenth-place finish in a nonbetting event at Camden.

Next entered in the big leagues on June 4, Mr. Baba was 8–1 against a field of New York–breds going a mile and a sixteenth on the grass.

The workout of May 12 begged attention: :35 from the gate. Breezing.

Thirty-five breezing from the gate? Such a work strongly suggested that Mr. Baba's slowness from the gate on April 2 had been due to racing luck and was not indicative of his true early speed and/or agility.

While the :35Bg work might not have swayed a bettor by itself, it was a tip-off to look for other positives. The first came by looking back at trainer Michael Dickinson's previous meet's winner:

Matchless Dancer
Own: Prestonwood Farm
BAILEY J D (66 17 7 14 .26)

Gr. c. 4
Sire: Nijinsky II (Northern Dancer)
Dam: Matching (What Luck)
Br: Prestonwood Farms (Ky)
Tr: Dickinson Michael W (5 1 0 0 .20)

124

Lifetime Record:	7 2 2 0	$41,490			
1994	1 1 0 0	$18,000	Turf	7 2 2 0	$41,490
1993	6 1 2 0	$23,490	Wet	0 0 0 0	
Bel (T)	3 1 1 0	$25,320	Dist (T)	2 1 0 0	$19,710

11May94-6Bel	fm	1¼ (T)	:49	1:123	1:37	2:013	3+ Alw 30000N1X	96	1	5	41½	11½	16	18¾	Bailey J D	119	3.70	82-21	Matchless Dancer1198¾ Musical Storm119nk Moscow Magic1124	Driving	9
13Aug93-4Sar	fm	1½ (T)	:501	1:143	2:052	2:293	3+ Alw 28500N1X	85	6	9	816	44½	22	21¼	Smith M E	113	4.00	80-15	GroomedToWin1121¼ MatchlessDancer1133 Glenbarra1125¼	Rallied inside	9
31Jly93-4Sar	fm	1⅜ (T)	:492	1:151	1:401	2:172	3+ Alw 28500N1X	78	8	2	2½	21	43	63	Smith M E	113	*2.40	76-15	Noble Sheba111¾ No Sneaker113nk Groomed To Win112hd	Tired	10
12Jly93-7Bel	fm	1¼ (T)	:493	1:134	1:374	2:02	3+ Alw 28500N1X	86	4	5	31½	32	53	41	Smith M E	116	5.50	79-12	Dover Coast117¾ Shoaly Water117hd Jodi's The Best113nk	Mild rally	9
1Jly93-9Lrl	fm	1½ (T)	:48	1:134	2:081	2:321	3+ Md Sp Wt	80	3	7	67	43	13	17½	Pino M G	114 f	*.40	89-13	Matchless Dancer1147½ FlashGorgeous1142¾ GoForTheMagic1081¼	Driving	9
14Jun93-5Bel	fm	1⅜ (T)	:493	1:134	1:382	2:142	3+ Md Sp Wt	80	6	5	42½	31	2½	2nk	Smith M E	114	5.40	79-11	Noble Sheba114nk Matchless Dancer1144¾ Off The Cuff1225	Gamely	9
30May93-3Pim	fm	1⅜ (T)	:491	1:171	1:423	2:204	3+ Md Sp Wt	73	3	6	712	55	58	55½	Delgado A	113	5.60	— —	Gold Quoit1142¾ Heroisbreezin'112nk Class First1141	Sluggish start	8

WORKOUTS: May 7 Fai 4f fst :53 B 3/8 May 2 Fai 5f fst 1:052 B 6/8

May 29 1¼ (T) AlwNW2 $6.20

Matchless Dancer had provided Dickinson with back-to-back wins at a mile and a quarter on the grass when returned from a nine-month layoff earlier in the meet. Matchless Dancer had been fit enough to accomplish these tasks despite showing only a pair of breezing works at Fair Hill. This effectively squashed any concerns about the readiness of Mr. Baba, for, if anything, he showed substantially more Fair Hill–preparation leading up to his first start in two months: besides the unexpectedly quick :35 blowout, he had recorded two previous six-furlong moves.

The second positive indicator didn't come until race day, when track announcer Tom Durkin noted in his rundown of the scratches and late changes at twelve noon that Mr. Baba was a "new gelding."

A few hours later, Mr. Baba broke alertly and raced in a forward early position, challenged for command entering the stretch, and drew off to win by three lengths, paying $18.40.

NINTH RACE Belmont JUNE 4, 1994

1$\frac{1}{16}$ MILES. (Turf)(1.391) MAIDEN SPECIAL WEIGHT. Purse $27,000. 3-year-olds and upward foaled in New York State and approved by the New York State-Bred Registry. Weights: 3-year-olds, 114 lbs. Older, 122 lbs.

Value of Race: $27,000 Winner $16,200; second $5,940; third $3,240; fourth $1,620. Mutuel Pool $233,215.00 Exacta Pool $345,986.00 Triple Pool $575,162.00

Last Raced	Horse	M/Eqt.	A.	Wt	PP	St	¼	½	¾	Str	Fin	Jockey	Odds $1
2Apr94 1Cam10	Mr. Baba		3	114	7	4	4hd	3hd	2hd	1½	13	Krone J A	8.20
27May94 5Bel2	Watrals Sea Trip		3	114	8	9	8½	83	812	41½	21	Graell A	3.60
22Nov93 3Aqu3	Silver Safari	b	3	114	9	2	1½	11	11½	22	33	Luzzi M J	2.10
6May94 5Bel3	Wolf Shadow		4	122	6	1	52½	5½	3hd	31	4¾	Samyn J L	4.60
10May94 5Bel5	Rogersdividends	bf	3	114	3	3	61	64	52½	51½	55½	Alvarado F T	10.30
28May94 11GS3	Joyful Bundle	b	3	114	10	8	21½	22	41½	64	67½	Bailey J D	4.60
17May94 3Bel6	Grave Dancer	b	3	114	2	5	31	41	61	71½	71	Velazquez J R	46.60
24May94 5Bel5	Buck Mulligan	b	5	122	4	7	710	712	71½	820	830	Migliore R	14.70
21Jly93 5Bel9	Ricamisa		3	114	1	6	10	10	10	10	9	Leon F	48.60
27May94 3Bel5	Pickwick Punch		4	122	5	10	9½	94	92½	9½	—	Lovato F Jr	79.10

Pickwick Punch: Broke Down

OFF AT 5:33 Start Good. Won driving. Time, :22³, :45², 1:10, 1:35⁴, 1:42² Course firm.

$2 Mutuel Prices:			
7–(G)–MR. BABA	18.40	8.20	5.20
8–(H)–WATRALS SEA TRIP		5.40	3.20
9–(I)–SILVER SAFARI			3.00

$2 EXACTA 7–8 PAID $147.40 $2 TRIPLE 7–8–9 $368.00

Ch. g, (Mar), by Nepal–Critical Miss, by Reviewer. Trainer Dickinson Michael W. Bred by Paxson Mrs Henry D (NY).

MR. BABA raced in good position while saving ground, slipped through along the inside to challenge entering the stretch then drew clear under pressure. WATRALS SEA TRIP outrun for six furlongs, closed late along the rail to gain the place. SILVER SAFARI set the pace slightly off the rail into upper stretch and weakened. WOLF SHADOW lodged a rally from outside to threaten on the turn then lacked a strong closing bid. ROGERSDIVIDENDS raced within striking distance to the turn and lacked a further response. JOYFUL BUNDLE was used up forcing the early pace. GRAVE DANCER gave way after going five furlongs. BUCK MULLIGAN checked early, never reached contention. RICAMISA was outrun. PICKWICK PUNCH broke down in midstretch.

Owners— 1, Paxson Mrs Henry D; 2, Watral Michael; 3, Very Un Stable; 4, Boto Stable; 5, Walsh Mrs Thomas M; 6, Perez Robert; 7, Ahearn David E; 8, Nuesch Felix J; 9, Miller Laurence P; 10, Drakos William

Trainers—1, Dickinson Michael W; 2, Brida Dennis J; 3, O'Connell Richard; 4, Turner William H Jr; 5, Walsh Thomas M; 6, Callejas Alfredo; 7, Trimmer Richard K; 8, Destasio Richard A; 9, Campo John P; 10, Beattie Richard L

Scratched— Green Baize (10Mar94 1GP6), Landing Pad (27May94 3BEL3), Amandalynn's Star (4May94 9BEL9), Advance Warning (18May94 3BEL7), Skate For Joy, Whose Jacques (10May94 3BEL6), Coshio (19May94 9BEL2), Cool Cop (28May94 6GS7), Velvel (14May94 5BEL6), North Forty Four (14May94 5BEL7)

Learning that Mr. Baba was a new gelding turned out to be an important piece of information, going along with the trainer-pattern match and the key :35Bg workout. With lightly raced horses such as Mr. Baba, sometimes this is all a handicapper has to go on . . .

LIGHTLY RACED HORSES

Handicappers who maintain trainer and betting records are eventually struck by an inescapable conclusion: races for lightly raced horses are extremely fertile ground for overlays.

The past performances of lightly raced horses convey precious little data about innate ability or about distance, running style, and footing preferences. Yet, the majority of bettors evaluate only what these diamonds in the rough have done thus far and leave it at that, when the most profitable approach is to do just the opposite — anticipate what they're *about to do*. One of the oldest racing axioms says "Don't bet on a horse to do something it's never done before"; this may be sound advice when the odds are prohibitive, and/or a horse has had several previous chances to race effectively under similar conditions and failed, but it is *not* the way to bet lightly raced horses. Handicappers should always be on the lookout for young horses going to the turf for the first time or stretching out in distance with suitable pedigrees or returning from a layoff as three-year-olds after showing signs of promise at two.

From this overall perspective, winning mutuels are a constant source of amazement.

Successful play in maiden and preliminary-allowance races requires handicappers to have an information edge on their competition, and these days there is no excuse for being improperly equipped: past performances of a trainer's previous winners shed ample light on what to expect from a barn's subsequent runners; a file of the *Form*'s workout tabs, which often contain valuable information about "in company" works and fractional times, can be kept up-to-date with a minimal expenditure of time and energy; and there are helpful peripheral sources, notably *Maiden Stats* — "the book" on two-year-olds, published annually by Bloodstock Research — that aid tremendously toward attaining an information edge.

It is difficult to underemphasize the significance of the lightly raced horse's connections. For example, it is accepted by most bettors that first-time starters attracting little or no pari-mutuel support are poor percentage bets and should be avoided like the plague. It may be true that if you bet on *all* of them, long-term losses will be steep. But there are exceptions to every handicapping rule — longshot firsters *do* win for some owner/trainer connections. Once handicappers have developed a healthy respect and understanding of a rule, they may, through research, ultimately cash in on the horses who qualify as legitimate exceptions.

Historically speaking, a first-timer owned by John Peace and trained by George "Rusty" Arnold is worth an automatic bet — especially when dismissed on the toteboard:

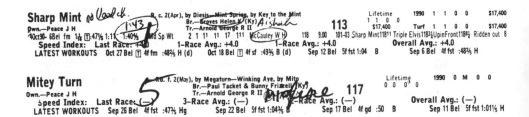

Sharp Mint B. c. 2(Apr), by Diesis—Mint Spring, by Key to the Mint
Br.—Groves Helen K (Ky)
Own.—Peace J H Tr.—Arnold George R II 113
Lifetime 1 1 0 0 $17,400 | 1990 1 1 0 0 $17,400 | Turf 1 1 0 0 $17,400
40ct90- 6Bel fm 1 1/16 [T]:47 1/5 1:11 1:40 4/5 Md Sp Wt 2 1 11 11 17 111 McCauley W H 118 9.00 101-03 Sharp Mint11811 Triple Elvis118 3/4 UpinFront118 8 1/4 Ridden out 8
Speed Index: Last Race: +4.0 1-Race Avg.: +4.0 1-Race Avg.: +4.0 Overall Avg.: +4.0
LATEST WORKOUTS Oct 27 Bel [T] 4f fm :48 2/5 H (d) Oct 18 Bel [T] 4f sf :49 3/5 B (d) Sep 12 Bel 5f fst 1:04 B Sep 6 Bel 4f fst :48 2/5 H

Mitey Turn Ro. f. 2(May), by Megaturn—Winking Aye, by Mito
Br.—Paul Tacket & Bunny Frizzell (Ky)
Own.—Peace J H Tr.—Arnold George R II 117
Lifetime 0 0 0 0 | 1990 0 M 0 0
Speed Index: Last Race: (—) 3-Race Avg.: (—) 12-Race Avg.: (—) Overall Avg.: (—)
LATEST WORKOUTS Sep 26 Bel 4f fst :47 3/5 Hg Sep 22 Bel 5f fst 1:04 3/5 B Sep 17 Bel 4f gd :50 B Sep 11 Bel 5f fst 1:01 1/5 H

FIFTH RACE 7 FURLONGS. (1.20⅘) MAIDEN SPECIAL WEIGHT. Purse $27,000. 2-year-old fillies. Weights, 117 lbs.

Belmont

OCTOBER 1, 1990

Value of race $27,000; value to winner $16,200; second $5,940; third $3,240; fourth $1,620. Mutuel pool $213,892. Exacta Pool $398,546

Last Raced	Horse	M/Eqt.A.Wt	PP	St	¼	½	Str	Fin	Jockey	Odds $1
	Mitey Turn	2 117	10	12	$10^{\frac{1}{2}}$	10^{2}	$1^{\frac{1}{2}}$	1^{4}	Migliore R	59.80
	Fabulous Climb	2 117	14	10	$11^{2\frac{1}{2}}$	12^{1}	$6^{\frac{1}{2}}$	$2^{1\frac{1}{2}}$	Perret C	13.70
	Extra Dry	2 117	5	4	$4^{\frac{1}{2}}$	$3^{\frac{1}{2}}$	$2^{\frac{1}{2}}$	$3^{\frac{1}{2}}$	Bailey J D	40.10
21Sep90 7Bel5	Trust in Dixie	2 117	7	5	$6^{1\frac{1}{2}}$	$7^{1\frac{1}{2}}$	5^{hd}	4^{3}	Samyn J L	17.00
	Belleofbasinstreet	2 110	2	14	$12^{\frac{1}{2}}$	$11^{\frac{1}{2}}$	$8^{1\frac{1}{2}}$	5^{2}	Guymon T F7	8.70
23Sep90 3Bel9	Scintillating Suzi	b 2 117	9	8	$7^{\frac{1}{2}}$	6^{hd}	3^{hd}	6^{2}	Smith M E	6.50
23Sep90 3Bel3	Miss Barkin	b 2 117	13	3	3^{1}	$2^{\frac{1}{2}}$	4^{1}	$7^{1\frac{1}{4}}$	Chavez J F	2.90
15Sep90 7Med3	Silver Ore Gold	2 117	3	7	8^{hd}	8^{1}	$7^{\frac{1}{2}}$	8^{hd}	Maple E	12.90
23Aug90 5Sar4	Rita	2 117	8	11	$13^{\frac{1}{2}}$	$13^{1\frac{1}{2}}$	10^{2}	$9^{\frac{1}{2}}$	Antley C W	2.80
	Dawn's Reality	2 117	12	13	14	14	$11^{1\frac{1}{2}}$	$10^{3\frac{1}{2}}$	Cordero A Jr	25.20
	Spy Leader Lady	2 117	6	1	2^{1}	1^{1}	$9^{\frac{1}{2}}$	11^{2}	Rojas R I	11.00
	Trim Cut	2 117	4	9	9^{4}	$9^{\frac{1}{2}}$	13^{8}	$12^{4\frac{1}{4}}$	McCauley W H	21.30
6Sep90 4Med6	Social Delima	b 2 117	11	6	$5^{\frac{1}{2}}$	5^{hd}	$12^{\frac{1}{2}}$	13^{7}	Cruguet J	28.60
20Sep90 6Med8	Sarasota Pam	b 2 117	1	2	1^{1}	$4^{\frac{1}{2}}$	14	14	Douglas R R	49.90

OFF AT 3:00 Start good, Won driving. Time, :22⅘, :46⅗, 1:12⅕, 1:24⅗ Track fast.

$2 Mutuel Prices:				
	10–(J)–MITEY TURN	121.60	61.80	23.40
	14–(N)–FABULOUS CLIMB		15.40	10.60
	5–(E)–EXTRA DRY			19.80
	$2 EXACTA 10–14 PAID $1,480.00			

Ro. f, (May), by Megaturn—Winking Aye, by Mito. Trainer Arnold George R II. Bred by Paul Tacket & Bunny Frizzell (Ky).

MITEY TURN far back for a half proved rapidly into contention while circling five wide on the turn then sustaining her rally finished full of run in the middle of the track to win going away. FABULOUS CLIMB devoid of early speed was well back for a half raced in traffic while advancing on the turn then finishing her best stride closed ground between horses late to gain the place. EXTRA DRY made a run along the rail to challenge in upper stretch but couldn't sustain her bid. TRUST IN DIXIE raced within striking distance between horses into upper stretch and lacked a strong losing bid. BELLOFBASINSTREET finished well late after breaking slowly. SCINTAILLATING SUZI lodged a mild rally from outside on the turn and flattened out. MISS BARKIN contested the pace between horses into upper stretch and lacked a further response. SILVER ORE GOLD steadied in traffic when blocked on the turn and was no threat thereafter. RITA was never close. SPY LEADER set or forced the pace slightly off the rail to the top of the stretch and gave way. SARASOTA PAM stopped after setting the early pace.

Owners— 1, Peace J H; 2, Phipps O M; 3, Beler C P; 4, Fried A Jr; 5, Amherst Stable; 6, Hooper Mrs F W; 7, Spiegel R; 8, Burning Day Farm; 9, Brushwood Stable; 10, Darby Dan Farm; 11, Olsson S; 12, Buckland Farm; 13, Brodkin A K; 14, Driscoll T G.

Trainers— 1, Arnold George R II; 2, McGaughey Claude III; 3, Sciacca Gary; 4, Destasio Richard A; 5, Johnson Philip G; 6, Picou James E; 7, Schaeffer Stephen W; 8, Kelly Tim D; 9, Stephens Woodford C; 10, Veitch John M; 11, Duncan Susan; 12, Elder Andrew; 13, Mazza John F; 14, Hills Timothy A

Darien Deacon — B. c. 2(Apr), by Deputy Minister—Try Sympathy, by Habitat — Lifetime 1 1 0 0 $14,400 — 1992 1 1 0 0 $14,400

DAY P (121 16 21 18 .13) — Br.—Callahan Peter J (Ont-C) — **122**

Own.—Andrews Edwin C — Tr.—Arnold George R II (22 2 5 3 .09)

27Jly92- 6Bel gd 6f :22¹ :45¹ 1:09³ Md Sp Wt 86 1 7 3⁵½ 4⁴ 2½ 1⁴ Krone J A 118 28.30 92-09 DrinDcon118⁴Minr'sMrk118^hdOnThBridl118 Going away 9

LATEST WORKOUTS Aug 16 Sar tr.t 5f gd 1:05³ B Aug 9 Sar tr.t 4f fst :51⁴ B Jly 25 Bel 3f gd :40 Bg Jly 21 Bel 5f fst 1:01 H

Tassie Belle — Dk. b. or br. f. 3(Apr), by Tasso—Northern Dynasty, by Northern Jove — Lifetime 2 2 0 0 $23,400 — 1992 2 2 0 0 $23,400

SAMYN J L (8 1 1 1 .13) — Br.—Kaster Nancy R & R S (Ky) — **110**

Own.—Peace John H — Tr.—Arnold George R II (2 1 0 0 .50)

18Dec92- 8Aqu gd 6f ⊡:23 :46³ 1:11³ ⒻAlw 27000 89 7 1 1¹ 1² 12½ 11¼ Samyn J L 116 *1.10 85-18 TssieBell1161¼FltingWys1185¾FightingJt116 Ridden out 7

23Oct92- 4Aqu fst 6f :22³ :46 1:11 ⒻMd 35000 80 9 1 1² 1⁵ 11² 112¾ Samyn J L 117 18.20 86-16 TssieBelle117¹²¾Notimelost113¹SssyTre115 Ridden out 12

LATEST WORKOUTS May 6 Bel 4f fst :49⁴ B Apr 30 Bel 4f fst :46⁴ H Apr 20 Pha 5f fst 1:02¹ B

None of the Peace/Arnold bombshell winners shown here exhibited any obvious signs of being ready to win first time out: their sires aren't particularly fashionable, and their workouts weren't particularly notable. Be that as it may, these horses didn't just win, they *crushed* their fields, and at a variety of distances: Mitey Turn by four lengths at seven furlongs; Sharp Mint by eleven lengths in a grass route; Tassie Belle and Tali Hai by a dozen and six lengths, respectively, going six furlongs.

Even when the owner is not John Peace, it is never wise to discount the chances of an Arnold-trained firster, no matter the odds:

Tali Hai B. g. 3(May), by Talinum—Royal Fuss, by J O Tobin
SAMYN J L (50 9 6 6 .18) Br.—Calumet Farm (Ky)
Own.—Peace John H Tr.—Arnold George R II (7 1 1 1 .14) **117**
Lifetime 1 1 0 0 $14,400 | 1993 1 1 0 0 $14,400 | 1992 0 M 0 0
18Jan93- 5Aqu fst 6f ⊡:23^{3} :47^{3} 1:12^{4} Md Sp Wt 75 4 3 4$^{2\frac{1}{4}}$ 4$^{1\frac{1}{4}}$ 1$^{\frac{1}{2}}$ 1^{6} Samyn J L 122 31.40 79-21 Tali Hai122^{6}PalacePiper122^{1}ClassicLaunch122 Drew off 7
LATEST WORKOUTS Feb 5 Bel tr.t 4f fst :49^{1} H Jan 29 Bel tr.t 4f fst :51^{4} B Jan 9 Bel tr.t 4f fst :53 B Jan 3 Bel tr.t 4f fst :48^{2} Hg

Darien Deacon (going away by four lengths) at 28–1 should've been an automatic inclusion for trainer handicappers in what happened to be the middle leg of the Pick-3s.

Claude "Shug" McGaughey, as the trainer for the blue-blooded stable of Ogden Phipps and his son, Ogden Mills Phipps, rarely starts a first-timer that goes off at anything more than two- or three-to-one. When a Phipps-owned newcomer is higher than that, it is usually a sign that this isn't "one of the ones."

But McGaughey has a few horses for other, less highly profiled owners, notably, Emory Hamilton:

Tara Roma B. f. 3(Feb), by Lyphard—Chic Shirine, by Mr Prospector
DAVIS R G (170 25 26 18 .15) Br.—Hamilton Mrs Emroy A (Ky)
Own.—Hamilton Emory A Tr.—McGaughey Claude III (34 8 9 6 .24) **111**
Lifetime 1 1 0 0 $14,100 | 1993 1 1 0 0 $14,100 | 1992 0 M 0 0
28May93- 5Bel fst 6f :22 :45^{1} 1:10^{4} ⒻMd Sp Wt 78 1 4 5^{10} 5$^{3\frac{1}{2}}$ 3$^{2\frac{1}{2}}$ 1^{nk} Davis R G 121 12.40 86-14 TaraRom121^{nk}ForllSesons121^{nk}MyGirlRodes121 Driving 7
LATEST WORKOUTS Jun 11 Bel 3f fst :39^{1} B May 27 Bel 3f fst :35^{4} H May 22 Bel 4f fst :49^{2} Hg May 16 Bel 4f fst :49^{4} B

Waldoboro B. c. 3 (Mar)
Own: Hamilton Emory A
Sire: Lyphard (Northern Dancer)
Dam: Chic Shirine (Mr. Prospector)
Br: Mrs. Emory A. Hamilton (Ky)
LUZZI M J (123 20 16 13 .16) Tr: McGaughey Claude III (17 4 2 5 .24) **111**

Lifetime Record:	1 1 0 0	$15,000		
1994	1 1 0 0	$15,000	Turf	0 0 0 0
1993	0 M 0 0		Wet	0 0 0 0
Bel	1 1 0 0	$15,000	Dist	0 0 0 0

11May94- 3Bel fst 7f :22^{4} :46^{2} 1:11^{2} 1:24 Md Sp Wt 84 11 1 1$^{\frac{1}{2}}$ 1^{1} 1$^{2\frac{1}{2}}$ 1^{3} Luzzi M J 122 21.30 83-17 Waldoboro122^{3}Pleasant Phoenix122$^{2\frac{3}{4}}$Chrys122$^{1\frac{3}{4}}$ Driving 11
WORKOUTS: May 28 Bel 5f fst :59^{3} H *2/59* May 22 Bel 4f fst :48^{3} B *28/119* May 10 Bel 3f fst :36^{1} B *12/53* May 3 Bel 5f fst 1:00 Hg *7/23* Apr 26 Bel 5f fst 1:04 B *15/17* Apr 17 Bel tr.t 5f my 1:01 Hg(d) *2/5*

"Waldoboro can't win" was the opinion of many players when he made his first career start on May 11, 1994. "He's dead on the board."

But the previous May, Waldoboro's full sister, Tara Roma, had also been "dead on the board."

Different trainers have differing methods with their young horses, as Tom Bohannan freely explained: "Mine have a tendency to run much better the second time they start. I try not to put too much pressure on them. I don't expect anything out of any horse the first time they run. I just hope they finish well."

Pine Bluff B. c. 2(May), by Danzig—Rowdy Angel, by Halo Lifetime 1991 2 1 0 0 $14,400

Br.—Loblolly Stable (Ky) 2 1 0 0

Own.—Loblolly Stable Tr.—Bohannan Thomas $14,400

16Aug91- 6Sar fst 7f :22^{1} :45^{1} 1:23^{4} Md Sp Wt 5 8 42½ 42½ 2½ 11½ Perret C 118 3.00 86-11 Pine Bluff1181½ Harry the Hat1182 Noactor1187 Wide drv 10

13Jun91- 4Bel fst 5f :21^{2} :44 :56^{1} Md Sp Wt 7 8 5^{4} 5^{4} 45½ 510¾ Smith M E 118 4.30 96-05 Lure1185 In a Walk1182¾ Money Run1183 Brk slowly 8

LATEST WORKOUTS ●Sep 1 Bel 4f fst :46 H Aug 27 Bel 5f fst 1:02^{2} B Aug 12 Sar tr.t 4f fst :50 H Aug 7 Sar tr.t 5f fst 1:05^{3} B

Past Performances of Totemic

Totemic Ch. f. 2(Feb), by Vanlandingham—Strong Totem, by Fappiano Lifetime 1991 2 1 0 0 $14,400

Br.—Loblolly Stable (Ky) 2 1 0 0

Own.—Loblolly Stable Tr.—Bohannan Thomas $14,400

31Aug91- 3Bel gd 7f :22^{2} :45^{1} 1:23^{1} ⒻMd Sp Wt 3 5 41½ 41½ 1hd 12 Krone J A 117 6.40 88-11 Totemic1172 Fateful Beauty1172¾ Sleek Stephie1172¼ Driving 7

10Jly91- 6Bel fst 5½f :22^{1} :46^{1} 1:06^{1} ⒻMd Sp Wt 6 9 84¾ 83¼ 86½ 77½ Smith M E 117 21.90 76-17 BlssOurHom117¾FuturQston1171¾PrttyMlody1171½ No factor 9

LATEST WORKOUTS Aug 23 Bel 5f fst 1:01^{1} Bg Aug 18 Bel tr.t 4f fst :48^{4} B Aug 13 Bel tr.t 4f fst :48^{2} H

Zimmerman Dk. b. or br. c. 2(Feb), by Cox's Ridge—Prove Us Royal, by Prove It Lifetime 1992 2 1 0 0 $14,400

SMITH M E (68 8 10 6 .12) Br.—Anthony John Ed & Conrad Marian L (Ky) 2 1 0 0

Own.—Loblolly Stable Tr.—Bohannan Thomas (6 1 1 2 .17) 122 $14,400

29Aug92- 9Sar fst 6f :22^{1} :45^{3} 1:10^{2} Md Sp Wt 15 83 4 5 55½ 42¼ 2hd 17 Smith M E 118 5.20 92-07 Zimmerman1187RglnRod1183Environment118 Drew off 8

6Jly92- 3Bel gd 6f :22^{2} :45^{4} 1:11 Md Sp Wt 27 41 5 5 3½ 43½ 68 711½ Perret C 118 5.50 73-12 StelliteSignl118½Wllnd1184½ShdsofSllvr118 Tired badly 9

LATEST WORKOUTS Sep 14 Bel 3f fst :35^{4} H ●Sep 8 Bel tr.t 4f fst :48 H ●Aug 25 Bel tr.t 4f fst :47^{2} H Aug 19 Bel tr.t 4f my :49^{3} H

Pine Bluff, Totemic, and Zimmerman didn't do anything more than Bohannan was expecting of them in their debuts, finishing no better than fifth and no closer than seven and a half lengths to the winner. Each received several weeks off after their debut, and showed considerably more "polish" when returned for their second start, winning decisively from off the pace.

Pine Bluff (the 1992 Preakness winner) and Totemic (also a stakes winner at age three) were stretching to seven furlongs after getting their first taste of competition in five- and five-and-a-half-furlong dashes, respectively. Very often, the way young horses run in one or two of these short sprints gives little indication of their true potential, but they can show a lot more once they've gotten their feet wet. Essentially, they are "experienced" first-time starters who haven't been well meant up to that point.

Indeed, one of the silliest notions passed down from generation to generation as handicapping gospel is that two-year-olds are among the most predictable of horses because they run to their figures.

Run to their figures?

That implies two-year-olds have already established a level of performance and will remain on a form of equine cruise control through the late summer and fall. Nothing could be farther from reality; the first few sprints these youngsters run are often just the tip of the iceberg, which means that handicappers placing too much emphasis on the few speed figures available fail to grasp the essence of a much bigger picture.

Consider the way a pair of Dogwood Stable–owned juveniles were patiently prepared for sudden development in split divisions of a maiden special weight at Saratoga on August 4, 1993.

In the first division, Bayou Bartholomew had done the expected for Loblolly and Bohannan by improving sharply second time out, missing by a nose; the half-brother to ill-fated Preakness-winner Prairie Bayou was the favorite at 8–5. Personal Escort, Caherdaniel, and Explored were the next three choices, and all had recorded a Beyer as good or better than Arrival Time's 58 and 55 from two starts at five and a half furlongs:

Saratoga

3 *7 Furlongs.* (1:20^{2}) MAIDEN SPECIAL WEIGHT. Purse $23,500. 2-year-olds. Weight, 118 lbs.

START / 7 FURLONGS / FINISH

Coupled - Strauss and Kerkorian

2 Personal Escort PP - 1
Own: Phipps Ogden Mills
BAILEY J D (28 5 4 7 .18)
B. c. 2 (May)
Sire: Mr. Prospector (Raise a Native)
Dam: Dance Number (Northern Dancer)
Br: Ogden Mills Phipps (Ky)
Tr: McGaughey Claude III (5 2 0 2 .40)
118
Lifetime Record: 1 M 0 0 $1,410
1993 1 M 0 0 $1,410 | Turf 0 0 0 0
1992 0 M 0 0 | Wet 0 0 0 0
Sar 0 0 0 0 | Dist 0 0 0 0

23Jun93- 3Bel fst 5½f :21^{4} :45^{1} :58^{1} 1:05^{2} Md Sp Wt 56 7 7 69½ 69 67½ 45½ Bailey J D 118 2.10 82-14 Gusto Z118¹¼ Wire Squire118³½ Arrival Time118¾ No threat
WORKOUTS: Aug 2 Sar tr.t 4f fst :50 B 8/14 Jly 29 Sar tr.t 4f fst :50 B 3/22 Jly 24 Bel 3f fst :37^{3} B 6/22 Jly 4 Bel 4f fst :51^{4} B 44/48 Jun 18 Bel 4f fst :48 H 4/62 Jun 11 Bel 4f fst :49^{1} Bg 24/55

1 Strauss PP - 2
Own: Condren & Cornacchia & Paulson
ALVARADO F T (12 0 0 1 .00)
Ch. c. 2 (May)
Sire: Nijinsky II (Northern Dancer)
Dam: Brorita (Caro)
Br: Allen E. Paulson (Ky)
Tr: Zito Nicholas P (7 1 0 1 .14)
118
Lifetime Record: 0 M 0 0 $0
1993 0 M 0 0 | Turf 0 0 0 0
1992 0 M 0 0 | Wet 0 0 0 0
Sar 0 0 0 0 | Dist 0 0 0 0

WORKOUTS: Aug 1 Sar 4f fst :49^{3} H 15/30 Jly 28 Sar 5f fst 1:04^{2} B 24/25 Jly 17 Bel 5f fst 1:02^{3} B 22/35 Jly 4 Bel 5f fst 1:02 H 11/19 Jun 17 Bel 5f fst 1:05 B 28/33 Jun 11 Bel 5f fst 1:04^{3} B 43/46 Jun 4 Bel 5f fst 1:04^{3} B 26/32 May 29 Bel 5f fst 1:06 Bg 33/35 May 22 Bel 4f fst :53 Bg 62/67 May 7 Bel 4f fst :52 B 44/50

3 Caherdaniel PP - 4
Own: Meriwether John W
DAVIS R G (13 2 1 0 .15)
Dk. b or br c. 2 (Apr)
Sire: Tank's Prospect (Mr. Prospector)
Dam: K. J. Ma Kate (Chieftain)
Br: Dr. W. O. Reed (Ky)
Tr: Freeman Willard C (2 0 0 1 .00)
118
Lifetime Record: 2 M 2 0 $10,340
1993 2 M 2 0 $10,340 | Turf 0 0 0 0
1992 0 M 0 0 | Wet 0 0 0 0
Sar 0 0 0 0 | Dist 0 0 0 0

19Jly93- 5Bel gd 5½f :22^{1} :45^{2} :58^{1} 1:05 Md Sp Wt 60 2 2 2hd 1hd 2² 2¾ Davis R G 118 *1.90 89-13 Rizzi118¾ Caherdaniel118¾ Solly's Honor118½ Gamely
23Jun93- 5Bel fst 5½f :22^{1} :46 :59 1:05^{4} Md Sp Wt 63 9 8 5⁴ 52¼ 3² 2nk Davis R G 118 14.70 86-14 Linkatariat118nk Caherdaniel118² Mcdee118²¼ Rallied wide
WORKOUTS: Jly 28 Sar 5f fst 1:03 B 15/25 Jly 16 Bel 4f fst :49 B 18/33 Jly 11 Bel 5f fst 1:01 H 7/22 Jly 2 Bel 5f fst 1:04 B 14/14 Jun 20 Bel 4f fst :50 B 15/35 Jun 14 Bel 3f fst :36^{3} Hg 6/20

4 Explored PP - 5
Own: Harbor View Farm
LEON F (11 1 2 2 .09)
Ch. c. 2 (Mar)
Sire: Mr. Leader (Hail to Reason)
Dam: Alyaffirm (Alydar)
Br: Harbor View Farm (Ky)
Tr: Jerkens H Allen (5 1 1 0 .20)
113^{5}
Lifetime Record: 2 M 1 0 $5,170
1993 2 M 1 0 $5,170 | Turf 0 0 0 0
1992 0 M 0 0 | Wet 0 0 0 0
Sar 1 0 0 0 | Dist 0 0 0 0

28Jly93- 5Sar fst 5f :21^{4} :45^{3} :58^{2} Md Sp Wt 52 5 6 6⁶ 63¼ 63½ 66½ Krone J A 118 *1.10 86-08 Wire Squire118½ Mcdee118½ Mobile118nk No factor
8Jly93- 5Bel fst 5f :21^{4} :45^{1} :58 Md Sp Wt 76 3 3 6⁶ 62¼ 31½ 2¾ Krone J A 118 4.50 90-09 The Jogger118¾ Explored118² Frisco Gold118² Rallied wide
WORKOUTS: Jly 4 Bel 4f fst :47^{4} Hg 7/48 Jun 30 Bel 3f fst :38^{2} Bg 17/24 Jun 23 Bel 3f fst :35^{4} H 5/42 Jun 17 Bel 3f fst :39^{4} Bg 16/17 Jun 8 Bel tr.t 5f fst 1:04^{3} B 9/11 ●Jun 4 Bel tr.t 3f fst :35^{4} H 1/11

5 Shoot Back PP - 6
Own: Voss Mrs Thomas H
MCCARRON C J (2 1 0 0 .50)
B. c. 2 (Apr)
Sire: Waquoit (Relaunch)
Dam: Miss Castle Hill (Ack Ack)
Br: Mary P. Voss (Md)
Tr: Voss Thomas H (2 0 1 0 .00)
118
Lifetime Record: 1 M 0 0 $465
1993 1 M 0 0 $465 | Turf 0 0 0 0
1992 0 M 0 0 | Wet 0 0 0 0
Sar 0 0 0 0 | Dist 0 0 0 0

15Jly93- 5Lrl fst 5f :22^{3} :46^{2} :58^{4} Md Sp Wt 45 10 8 76½ 78½ 7⁸ 59½ Guerra W A 115 11.10 89-13 Honorable Flight120¹½ Callable120⁵½ Cache And Carry120¹¾ No factor
WORKOUTS: ●Jly 12 Pim 4f fst :49 H 1/4 ●Jly 6 Pim 4f fst :48 Hg 1/23 Jun 23 Pim 4f fst :50^{1} B 7/17 Jun 16 Pim 4f fst :50^{2} B 3/7

6 Best Of Music PP-7
Own: December Hill Farm
KRONE J A (35 9 1 3 .26)

Dk. b or br c. 2 (Mar)
Sire: Stop the Music (Hail to Reason)
Dam: Best of Bubbles (Graustark)
Br: White Fox Farm (Ky)
Tr: Donk David (—)
118

Lifetime Record: 1 M 0 0 $0
1993 1 M 0 0 | Turf 0 0 0 0
1992 0 M 0 0 | Wet 0 0 0 0
Sar 0 0 0 0 | Dist 0 0 0 0

19Jly93-3Bel gd 5½f :22^1 :45^4 :58^1 1:04^3 Md Sp Wt 25 1 2 65½ 65 78¼ 815½ Krone J A 118 13.20 76-13 Whitney Tower118^{3½} End Sweep118¾ Gold Tower118^3 No factor 8

WORKOUTS: Jly 29 Sar tr.t⓪ 5f fm 1:03^2 H (d)4/6 Jly 11 Bel 4f fst :50 B 20/35 ●Jly 5 Bel 5f fst :59 H 1/39 Jun 28 Bel 5f fst 1:01^3 H 6/24 Jun 18 Bel 5f fst 1:02^1 H 15/29 Jun 13 Bel 4f fst :48^2 Hg6/44

7 Thirty Good Ones PP-8
Own: Anstu Stable
SANTOS J A (31 4 4 4 .13)

B. c. 2 (Apr)
Sire: Clever Trick (Icecapade)
Dam: Cup of Honey (Raise a Cup)
Br: Hurstland Farm Inc (Ky)
Tr: Schulhofer Flint S (9 4 2 1 .44)
118

Lifetime Record: 1 M 0 0 $0
1993 1 M 0 0 | Turf 0 0 0 0
1992 0 M 0 0 | Wet 0 0 0 0
Sar 0 0 0 0 | Dist 0 0 0 0

23Jun93-3Bel fst 5½f :21^4 :45^1 :58^1 1:05^2 Md Sp Wt 30 35 2 5 47½ 56½ 57 813¼ Sweeney K H 118 8.50 75-14 Gusto Z118^{1¼} Wire Squire118^{3½} Arrival Time118¾ Faded 9

WORKOUTS: Aug 2 Sar 3f fst :36^1 H 5/17 Jly 28 Sar 4f fst :49^1 B 10/23 Jly 23 Sar 4f fst :50 B 7/9 Jly 17 Sar tr.t 4f fst :51^2 B 2/6 Jly 12 Sar 4f fst :51 B 1/3 Jly 7 Sar 4f fst :51^2 B 3/4

8 Bayou Bartholomew PP-9
Own: Loblolly Stable
ANTLEY C W (28 1 1 3 .04)

Dk. b or br c. 2 (Mar)
Sire: Demons Begone (Elocutionist)
Dam: Whiffling (Wavering Monarch)
Br: Loblolly Stable (Ky)
Tr: Bohannan Thomas (3 0 0 1 .00)
118

Lifetime Record: 2 M 1 0 $5,170
1993 2 M 1 0 $5,170 | Turf 0 0 0 0
1992 0 M 0 0 | Wet 0 0 0 0
Sar 0 0 0 0 | Dist 0 0 0 0

8Jly93-3Bel fst 5f :22^1 :45^2 :58^1 Md Sp Wt 16 74 5 3 45 44 44 2no Perret C 118 11.30 90-09 QuickToFinish118no BayouBrtholomew118^{1½} Presently118^{2½} Strong finish 8
13Jun93-6Bel fst 5f :22 :45^3 :58^3 Md Sp Wt 46 2 1 48 58 57½ 512 Smith M E 118 4.70 76-16 Crary118^1 Fabulous Force118^4 Mr. Tyler118^1 No threat 6

WORKOUTS: Jly 24 Bel 5f fst 1:02^2 B 16/28 Jly 19 Bel 4f fst :49^3 B 34/76 Jly 4 Bel 3f fst :35 H 3/22 Jun 28 Bel 5f fst 1:01^3 H 6/24 Jun 23 Bel 4f fst :48^4 B 23/85 Jun 2 Bel 4f fst :49^2 Hg34/56

9 Arrival Time PP-10
Own: Dogwood Stable
DAY P (3 1 0 0 .33)

Ch. c. 2 (Apr)
Sire: Time for a Change (Damascus)
Dam: Stella Matutina (Bolkonski)
Br: Wakefield Farm (Ky)
Tr: Alexander Frank A (4 0 1 1 .00)
118

Lifetime Record: 2 M 0 1 $4,230
1993 2 M 0 1 $4,230 | Turf 0 0 0 0
1992 0 M 0 0 | Wet 0 0 0 0
Sar 0 0 0 0 | Dist 0 0 0 0

23Jun93-3Bel fst 5½f :21^4 :45^1 :58^1 1:05^2 Md Sp Wt 21 58 3 2 36½ 35½ 34 34¾ Davis R G 118 9.50 83-14 Gusto Z118^{1¼} Wire Squire118^{3½} Arrival Time118¾ Willingly 9
3Jun93-3Bel fst 5½f :22^2 :48^1 :58^4 1:05^1 Md Sp Wt 55 8 4 31½ 42 43½ 46¼ Smith M E 118 20.20 83-13 SlewGinFizz118¾ SultanOfJava118^{3½} PeaceNegotitions118^3 Lacked rally 8

WORKOUTS: Jly 31 Sar 4f fst :47^3 H 3/44 Jly 25 Bel 5f fst 1:00^2 H 2/18 Jly 18 Bel 5f fst 1:01^4 B 11/14 Jly 11 Bel 5f fst 1:00^1 H 3/22 Jly 4 Bel 4f fst :49^2 B 33/48 Jun 19 Bel 4f fst :47 H 2/34

Trainer handicappers wishing to get a richer account of what to expect from Arrival Time could refer back to their file on Frank Alexander's winners at Saratoga's 1992 meet:

Compadre
ANTLEY C W (—)
Own.—Dogwood Stable

B. c. 2(May), by El Gran Senor—Natania, by Naskra
Br.—Foxfield (Ky)
Tr.—Alexander Frank A (—)
118

Lifetime 0 0 0 0 1992 0 M 0 0

LATEST WORKOUTS Jly 26 Bel 4f fst :47^2 H Jly 19 Bel 5f fst 1:01^2 Hg Jly 13 Bel 5f fst 1:05 B Jly 7 Bel 3f fst :36^4 B

July 30 5F MSW $19.40

Wallenda
ANTLEY C W (9 2 1 1 .22)
Own.—Dogwood Stable

Dk. b. or br. c. 2(Apr), by Gulch—So Glad, by Liloy
Br.—Haras Santa Maria de Araras & Brant (Fla)
Tr.—Alexander Frank A (3 1 1 0 .33)
118

Lifetime 2 0 1 1 $8,160 1992 2 M 1 1 $8,160

6Jly92-3Bel gd 6f :22^2 :45^4 1:11 Md Sp Wt 69 7 6 54½ 33 22 2½ Antley C W 118 10.10 84-12 StellitSignl118½Wllnd118^{4½}ShdsofSilvr118 Wide, gamely 9
18Jun92-6Bel fst 5f :22^2 :46^1 :58^4 Md Sp Wt 52 1 1 3nk 3½ 32 34 Perret C 118 *1.50 83-13 I Like to Win118¾ Rastra118^{3¼} Wallenda118 Dueled late 8

LATEST WORKOUTS Jly 29 Sar 4f fst :47^1 H Jly 23 Bel 5f fst 1:01^3 B Jly 17 Bel 5f fst 1:01^2 B Jly 3 Bel 3f fst :36^1 B

August 2 6F MSW $9.20

Alexander had struck early with a pair of two-year-old maiden winners, which, like Arrival Time, had worked half-miles in :47 and change four days prior to winning their races. As with Arrival Time, their two preceding workouts had been at five furlongs. Additionally, Wallenda's pp's practically mirrored Arrival Time's: each had been early-pace factors first time out in shorter sprints, and they had then been taken a bit farther off the pace second time out.

Wallenda had improved significantly according to the Beyer

figures in his win, running an 81 — a jump of a dozen points from his second race, and 29 points above his debut:

Wallenda 4-1 a better
ANTLEY C W (71 11 12 10 .15)
Own.—Dogwood Stable
Dk. b. or br. c. 2(Apr), by Gulch—So Glad, by Liloy
Br.—Haras Santa Maria de Araras & Brant (Fla)
Tr.—Alexander Frank A (8 2 1 1 .25)
115
Lifetime 3 1 1 1 $22,560 | 1992 3 1 1 1 $22,560

2Aug92- 4Sar fst 6f :222 :454 1:102 Md Sp Wt (15) 81 6 2 31½ 32 1hd 12 Antley C W 118 3.60e 92-10 Wallenda1182 All Gone1184 D'Orazio118 Driving 12
6Jly92- 3Bel gd 6f :222 :454 1:11 Md Sp Wt (17) 69 7 6 54½ 33 22 2½ Antley C W 118 10.10 84-12 StellitSignl118½Wllnd1184½ShdsofSilvr118 Wide, gamely 9
18Jun92- 6Bel fst 5f :222 :461 :584 Md Sp Wt (26) 52 1 1 3nk 3½ 32 34 Perret C 118 *1.50 83-13 I Like to Win118¾ Rastra1183½ Wallenda118 Dueled late 8
LATEST WORKOUTS Aug 10 Sar 3f gd :371 B Jly 29 Sar 4f fst :471 H Jly 23 Bel 5f fst 1:013 B Jly 17 Bel 5f fst 1:012 B

Arrival Time improved 21 points by wiring this field at 9–1, earning a Beyer of 79. This was a jump of 21 points from his second start, and 24 points above his debut — roughly the same amount of development from three starts that stablemate Wallenda had shown.

3 Arrival Time
Own: Dogwood Stable
DAVIS R G (72 13 7 5 .18)
Ch. c. 2 (Apr)
Sire: Time for a Change (Damascus)
Dam: Stella Matutina (Bolkonski)
Br: Wakefield Farm (Ky)
Tr: Alexander Frank A (13 2 2 3 .15)
122

Lifetime Record: 3 1 0 1 $18,330											
1993	3	1	0	1	$18,330	Turf	0	0	0	0
1992	0	M	0	0		Wet	0	0	0	0
Sar	1	1	0	0	$14,100	Dist	0	0	0	0

4Aug93- 3Sar fst 7f :221 :451 1:101 1:231 Md Sp Wt (16) 79 9 1 12 11 11½ 11¼ Day P 118 9.00 89-09 Arrival Time1181¼ Caherdaniel1184½ Bayou Bartholomew1183 Driving 9
23Jun93- 3Bel fst 5½f :214 :451 :581 1:052 Md Sp Wt 58 3 2 36½ 35½ 34 34¾ Davis R G 118 9.50 83-14 Gusto Z1181¼ Wire Squire1183½ Arrival Time118¾ Willingly 9
3Jun93- 3Bel fst 5½f :222 :461 :584 1:051 Md Sp Wt 55 8 4 31½ 42 43½ 46½ Smith M E 118 20.20 83-13 SlewGinFizz118¾ SultanOfJava1183½ PeaceNegotiations1182 Lacked rally 8
WORKOUTS: Aug 15 Sar 4f fst :484 B 8/21 Jly 31 Sar 4f fst :473 H 3/45 Jly 25 Bel 5f fst 1:002 H 2/18 Jly 18 Bel 5f fst 1:014 B 11/14 Jly 11 Bel 5f fst 1:001 H 3/22 Jly 4 Bel 4f fst :492 B 33/48

The second division, run about an hour and a half later, was a splendid betting opportunity for players in tune with the fact that Dogwood, which had pointed its two-year-olds for the beginning of the 1992 Saratoga meet, was on the same flight path in 1993, having just won the first division at 9–1 with a maiden surging forward to new heights. What, then, might be the projection for Ridgewinder?

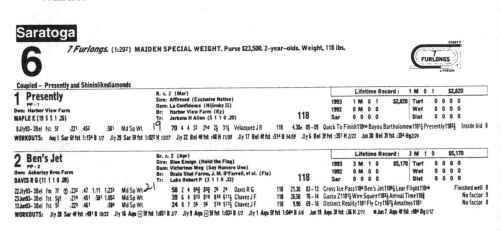

Saratoga

6 *7 Furlongs.* (1:202) MAIDEN SPECIAL WEIGHT. Purse $23,500. 2-year-olds. Weight, 118 lbs.

START 7 FURLONGS FINISH

Coupled – Presently and Shininlikediamonds

1 Presently
PP - 1
Own: Harbor View Farm
MAPLE E (19 5 5 1 .26)
B. c. 2 (Mar)
Sire: Affirmed (Exclusive Native)
Dam: La Confidence (Nijinsky II)
Br: Harbor View Farm (Ky)
Tr: Jerkens H Allen (5 1 1 0 .20)
118

Lifetime Record: 1 M 0 1 $2,820										
1993	1	M	0	1	$2,820	Turf	0	0	0	0
1992	0	M	0	0		Wet	0	0	0	0
Sar	0	0	0	0		Dist	0	0	0	0

8Jly93- 3Bel fst 5f :221 :452 :581 Md Sp Wt (19) 70 4 4 32 2hd 2½ 31¼ Velazquez J R 118 4.30e 89-09 Quick To Finish118no Bayou Bartholomew1181¼ Presently1182½ Inside bid 8
WORKOUTS: Aug 1 Sar 6f fst 1:154 B 1/2 Jly 29 Sar 5f fst 1:022 H 13/27 Jly 22 Bel 4f fst :48 H 11/59 Jly 17 Bel 4f fst :514 B 54/59 Jly 6 Bel 3f fst :351 H 2/23 Jun 30 Bel 3f fst :354 Hg2/24

2 Ben's Jet
PP - 2
Own: Ackerley Bros Farm
DAVIS R G (11 1 1 0 .09)
Gr. c. 2 (Apr)
Sire: Blue Ensign (Hoist the Flag)
Dam: Victorious Meg (Soy Numero Uno)
Br: Ocala Stud Farms, J. M. O'Farrell, et al. (Fla)
Tr: Lake Robert P (3 1 1 0 .33)
118

Lifetime Record: 3 M 1 0 $5,170										
1993	3	M	1	0	$5,170	Turf	0	0	0	0
1992	0	M	0	0		Wet	0	0	0	0
Sar	0	0	0	0		Dist	0	0	0	0

22Jly93- 3Bel fm 7f ⓣ :233 :47 1:11 1:233 Md Sp Wt (21) 58 2 4 84¾ 83¾ 26 24 Davis R G 118 21.30 83-12 Cross Ice Pass1184 Ben's Jet1186¼ Lear Flight118nk Finished well 8
23Jun93- 3Bel fst 5½f :214 :451 :581 1:052 Md Sp Wt 39 6 4 812 810 810 611½ Chavez J F 118 26.50 76-14 Gusto Z1181¼ Wire Squire1183½ Arrival Time118¾ No factor 9
13Jun93- 3Bel fst 5f :223 :461 :584 Md Sp Wt 24 8 7 56 56 510 517½ Chavez J F 118 9.90 69-16 Distinct Reality1181 Fly Cry1187½ Amathos1181 No factor 8
WORKOUTS: Jly 28 Sar 4f fst :491 B 10/23 Jly 16 Aqu ⊡ 5f fst 1:051 B 3/7 Jly 9 Aqu ⊡ 5f fst 1:033 B 1/3 Jly 1 Aqu 5f fst 1:044 B 5/6 Jun 19 Aqu 3f fst :36 H 2/11 ●Jun 7 Aqu 4f fst :484 Bg1/12

3 Ocean Code PP-3
Own: Alba Isao
MCCAULEY W H (18 2 2 4 .11)
Ch. c. 2 (Apr)
Sire: Ogygian (Damascus)
Dam: Whidah (Codex)
Br: Peter M. Brant & Edward P. Evans (Ky)
Tr: Jolley Leroy (2 0 0 0 .00)
118
Lifetime Record: 1 M 0 0 $0
1993 1 M 0 0 | Turf 0 0 0 0
1992 0 M 0 0 | Wet 0 0 0 0
Sar 0 0 0 0 | Dist 0 0 0 0
19Jly93-5Bel gd 5½f :221 :452 :581 1:05 Md Sp Wt –0 3 5 911 88¼ 816 825¼ Migliore R 118 34.20 65-13 Rizzi118¾ Caherdaniel118¾ Solly's Honor118¼ Pinched break 9
WORKOUTS: ●Aug 2 Sar tr.t 5f fst 1:014 H 1/10 ●Jly 30 Sar tr.t 5f fst 1:04 B 1/6 Jly 15 Bel 4f fst :472 H 11/47 Jly 5 Bel 4f fst :52 B 56/62 Jun 24 Bel 5f fst 1:05 B 28/34 Jun 15 Bel 5f fst 1:033 B 20/25

4 Malmo PP-4
Own: Condren & Cornacchia & Paulson
BAILEY J D (28 5 4 7 .18)
Ch. c. 2 (May)
Sire: Jade Hunter (Mr. Prospector)
Dam: Aspern (Riverman)
Br: Allen E Paulson (Ky)
Tr: Zito Nicholas P (7 1 0 1 .14)
118
Lifetime Record: 1 M 0 0 $0
1993 1 M 0 0 | Turf 0 0 0 0
1992 0 M 0 0 | Wet 0 0 0 0
Sar 0 0 0 0 | Dist 0 0 0 0
8Jly93-3Bel fst 5f :221 :452 :581 Md Sp Wt 38 1 6 810 77 68½ 611½ Bailey J D 118 21.10 78-09 Quick To Finish118no Bayou Bartholomew1181½ Presently1182½ No factor 8
WORKOUTS: Jly 31 Sar 4f fst :49 B 13/44 Jly 24 Sar 5f fst 1:014 H 8/16 Jly 17 Bel 5f fst 1:013 Hg 15/35 Jun 30 Bel 5f fst 1:012 H 8/26 Jun 23 Bel 5f fst 1:032 B 38/48 Jun 16 Bel 5f fst 1:02 B 12/19

5 Amathos PP-5
Own: Mohammed Al Maktoum
SMITH M E (35 9 7 3 .26)
B. c. 2 (May)
Sire: Cox's Ridge (Best Turn)
Dam: Amathea (Iron Ruler)
Br: Russell S. Davis (Ky)
Tr: Mott William I (13 6 2 0 .46)
118
Lifetime Record: 1 M 0 1 $2,820
1993 1 M 0 1 $2,820 | Turf 0 0 0 0
1992 0 M 0 0 | Wet 0 0 0 0
Sar 0 0 0 0 | Dist 0 0 0 0
13Jun93-3Bel fst 5f :223 :461 :584 Md Sp Wt 52 4 6 67 46 48 38½ Smith M E 118 6.50 78-16 Distinct Reality1181 Fly Cry1187½ Amathos1181 No threat 8
WORKOUTS: Aug 1 Sar 4f fst :524 B 29/30 Jly 26 Sar 5f fst 1:024 B 10/16 Jly 19 Sar 6f fst 1:184 B 2/3 Jly 13 Sar 4f fst :503 H 3/7 Jly 7 Sar 3f fst :393 B 4/6 May 29 Sar 5f fst 1:043 Bg 1/1

1A Shininlikediamonds PP-6
Own: Gainesway Stable
MCCARRON C J (2 1 0 0 .50)
B. c. 2 (Feb)
Sire: Explodent (Nearctic)
Dam: Diamond Glove (Silent Screen)
Br: Gainesway Thoroughbred Ltd (Ky)
Tr: Jerkens H Allen (5 1 1 0 .20)
118
Lifetime Record: 1 M 0 0 $0
1993 1 M 0 0 | Turf 0 0 0 0
1992 0 M 0 0 | Wet 0 0 0 0
Sar 0 0 0 0 | Dist 0 0 0 0
8Jly93-3Bel fst 5f :221 :452 :581 Md Sp Wt 24 7 5 78 89¼ 810 816¼ Sweeney K H 118 4.30e 74-09 Quick To Finish118no Bayou Bartholomew1181½ Presently1182½ Outrun 8
WORKOUTS: Jly 30 Sar 4f fst :474 Hg 6/29 Jly 22 Bel 4f fst :481 H 14/59 Jly 5 Bel 5f fst 1:03 B 30/39 Jly 2 Bel 3f fst :38 Bg 8/12 Jun 26 Bel tr.t 3f fst :38 B 7/10

6 Gone Dancing Again PP-7
Own: Valando Thomas
SANTOS J A (30 4 4 4 .13)
B. c. 2 (Mar)
Sire: Gone West (Mr. Prospector)
Dam: Now Dancer (Sovereign Dancer)
Br: Elizabeth Jones Valando (Ky)
Tr: Schulhofer Flint S (9 4 2 1 .44)
118
Lifetime Record: 0 M 0 0 $0
1993 0 M 0 0 | Turf 0 0 0 0
1992 0 M 0 0 | Wet 0 0 0 0
Sar 0 0 0 0 | Dist 0 0 0 0
WORKOUTS: Jly 29 Sar 4f fst :50 B 20/36 ●Jly 24 Sar 4f fst :481 Hg 1/24 Jly 19 Sar 4f fst :50 B 3/13 Jly 14 Sar tr.t 5f fst 1:042 B 1/2 ●Jly 8 Sar 4f fst :492 H 1/11 Jly 4 Sar 4f fst :494 B 1/3 ●Jun 23 Sar tr.t 3f fst :373 H 1/7 ●Jun 17 Sar 3f fst :364 H 1/10 ●Jun 11 Sar tr.t 3f fst :38 Bg 1/9 Jun 5 Sar 3f fst :384 Hg 2/15 ●May 30 Sar 3f fst :381 B 1/6 May 25 Sar tr.t 3f fst :374 H 1/2

7 Sophie's Friend PP-8
Own: Scheftel Stuart
KRONE J A (34 8 1 3 .24)
Dk. b or br c. 2 (May)
Sire: Wild Again (Icecapade)
Dam: Hassam (Arctic Tern)
Br: Joe Cochonour & Larry Hickox (Ky)
Tr: Veitch John M (6 0 0 1 .00)
118
Lifetime Record: 1 M 0 0 $1,410
1993 1 M 0 0 $1,410 | Turf 0 0 0 0
1992 0 M 0 0 | Wet 0 0 0 0
Sar 0 0 0 0 | Dist 0 0 0 0
19Jly93-3Bel gd 5½f :221 :454 :581 1:043 Md Sp Wt 48 6 7 76½ 75 44 47¼ Santos J A 118 13.00 85-13 Whitney Tower1183¼ End Sweep110¾ Gold Tower1184 Broke slowly, wide 8
WORKOUTS: Jly 31 Sar 5f fst 1:022 H 17/25 Jly 26 Bel 4f fst :48 H 7/14 Jly 18 Bel 3f fst :363 B 4/13 Jly 15 Bel 4f fst :462 H 4/47 Jly 9 Bel 4f fst :48 Hg 4/36 Jly 4 Bel 4f fst :482 Hg 15/48

8 Mr Blueberry PP-9
Own: Maki James
CHAVEZ J F (30 3 2 2 .10)
Dk. b or br c. 2 (Feb)
Sire: Our Native (Exclusive Native)
Dam: Determining (Decidedly)
Br: E W Thomas & Partners (Ky)
Tr: Wismer Norman (—)
118
Lifetime Record: 2 M 1 0 $3,240
1993 2 M 1 0 $3,240 | Turf 0 0 0 0
1992 0 M 0 0 | Wet 0 0 0 0
Sar 0 0 0 0 | Dist 0 0 0 0
20Jly93-3ElP fst 6f :221 :46 :582 1:11 Md Sp Wt 56 1 8 710 67½ 59¼ 27 Bruin J E L 118 4.60 84-00 Judge T C1187 Mr Blueberry118no Camptown Dancer110½ Mild gain rail 8
16Jun93-1CD fst 5½f :23 :463 :523 1:053 Md Sp Wt 18 8 12 1213 1217 1121 920 Bull M L L 119 f 35.70 74-23 Strawberry A O K.1191½ Look For Trouble11910 Busta1194 12
Broke in air, outrun
WORKOUTS: Jun 25 Kee 4f fst :503 Bg 6/9 Jun 4 Kee 4f fst :52 B 18/18 May 26 Kee 3f fst :372 Bg 3/12 Apr 23 Kee 3f fst :373 B 3/9 Apr 10 Tam 3f fst :373 B 11/23

9 Ridgewinder PP-10
Own: Dogwood Stable
DAY P (3 1 0 0 .33)
Ch. c. 2 (Feb)
Sire: Cox's Ridge (Best Turn)
Dam: Add Mint (Vigors)
Br: Betty M. Peters & Ball Peters Beitz (Ky)
Tr: Vestal Peter M (4 0 1 1 .00)
118
Lifetime Record: 2 M 0 0 $0
1993 2 M 0 0 | Turf 0 0 0 0
1992 0 M 0 0 | Wet 0 0 0 0
Sar 0 0 0 0 | Dist 0 0 0 0
16Jun93-1CD fst 5½f :23 :463 :523 1:053 Md Sp Wt 20 1 6 64½ 67½ 512 719¼ Arguello F A Jr 119 35.10 75-23 Strawberry A. O K.1191½ Look For Trouble11910 Busta1194 12
Bobbled, nearly clipped heels 1/2 pole
30May93-1CD fst 5f :223 :462 :584 Md Sp Wt 38 2 1 2hd 41½ 56¾ 610¾ Arguello F A Jr 120 8.40 88-07 FlghtFortyNn120no LookFrTrbl1206½ CmptwnDncr1202 Used early inside 11
WORKOUTS: Jly 23 CD 5f fst 1:022 B 10/25 Jly 1 CD 4f fst :481 B 6/33 Jun 13 CD 4f fst :50 B 22/55 May 25 CD 5f gd 1:022 Bg 7/27 May 18 CD 5f fst 1:023 Bg 9/28 May 11 CD 5f fst 1:022 B 5/27

Presently was the 9–5 favorite off his promising debut, in which the full brother to grass champion Flawlessly had been on or near the pace the entire way. His Beyer of 70 was clearly superior to what any of his rivals had run to date.

Gone Dancing Again, from the owner/trainer connections of 1990s juvenile champion Fly So Free, had been working bullets at Saratoga since at least May and was being solidly supported at 2–1.

Several others in the field had run faster Beyers than Ridgewinder as well, so the distance-bred colt was being ignored at 29–1 on the basis of his two poor finishes in shorter dashes at Churchill Downs for Peter Vestal, who trains Dogwood Stable's Midwestern division. The key to the race was that, in light of Dogwood's established pattern, Ridgewinder's Churchill races could be deemed irrelevant; corroborating evidence came by noting that he had flashed some speed from an inside post first time out and had then received a major trouble line in his second start, when he broke from the rail (often an intimidating post for inexperienced two-year-olds), bobbled, and nearly clipped heels approaching the far turn.

Like Arrival Time earlier in the day, Ridgewinder was now stretching out to seven furlongs, was drawn in the outside post, and was switching to Pat Day. He made an excellent appearance in the post parade and prerace warm-ups and was hovering at around 30–1 shortly before post time. A good wagering strategy in this situation would've taken into account the possibility that Ridgewinder might improve enough to win but, given that he was in against a legitimate favorite in Presently and a heavily bet unknown commodity in Gone Dancing Again, he might lose to one or both of them. If Ridgewinder finished second to either of the two, his place price would be minimal, so a win bet and a pair of exacta savers were in order:

SIXTH RACE
Saratoga
AUGUST 4, 1993

7 FURLONGS. (1.20^{2}) MAIDEN SPECIAL WEIGHT. Purse $23,500. 2-year-olds. Weight 118 lbs.

Value of race $23,500; value to winner $14,100; second $5,170; third $2,820; fourth $1,410. Mutuel pool $340,695. Exacta Pool $601,343

Last Raced	Horse	M/Eqt.A.Wt	PP	St	¼	½	Str	Fin	Jockey	Odds $1
8Jly93 ^{3}Bel^{3}	Presently	2 118	1	6	1^{hd}	1^{1}	1^{4}	$1^{4\frac{3}{4}}$	Maple E	a-1.80
16Jun93 ^{1}CD^{7}	Ridgewinder	2 118	10	1	$3^{1\frac{1}{2}}$	3^{hd}	2^{hd}	$2^{2\frac{3}{4}}$	Day P	29.50
20Jly93 ^{3}ElP^{2}	Mr. Blueberry	2 118	9	4	9^{6}	7^{1}	$4^{\frac{1}{2}}$	$3^{2\frac{1}{4}}$	Chavez J F	15.40
8Jly93 ^{3}Bel^{6}	Malmo	2 118	4	10	7^{1}	6^{hd}	9	4^{hd}	Bailey J D	32.10
13Jun93 ^{3}Bel^{3}	Amathos	2 118	5	7	$5^{\frac{1}{2}}$	$8^{\frac{1}{2}}$	$5^{\frac{1}{2}}$	5^{nk}	Smith M E	5.20
	Gone Dancing Again	2 118	7	5	4^{hd}	4^{1}	3^{1}	6no	Santos J A	2.40
22Jly93 ^{3}Bel^{2}	Ben's Jet	2 118	2	8	8^{hd}	9	$6^{\frac{1}{2}}$	7^{nk}	Davis R G	12.40
19Jly93 ^{3}Bel^{4}	Sophie's Friend	2 118	8	3	$6^{\frac{1}{2}}$	5^{hd}	8^{hd}	$8^{2\frac{1}{2}}$	Krone J A	5.00
8Jly93 ^{3}Bel^{8}	Shininlikediamonds	2 118	6	2	$2^{\frac{1}{2}}$	$2^{\frac{1}{2}}$	7^{hd}	9	McCarron C J	a-1.80
19Jly93 ^{5}Bel^{8}	Ocean Code	b 2 118	3	9	10	—	—	—	McCauley W H	26.50

Ocean Code, Pulled up.
a–Coupled: Presently and Shininlikediamonds.
OFF AT 3:37 Start good, Won ridden out. Time, :22^{4}, :45^{3}, 1:10^{1}, 1:23 Track fast.

$2 Mutuel Prices:				
	1-(A)-PRESENTLY (a-entry)	5.60	4.00	3.00
	9-(J)-RIDGEWINDER		16.80	6.60
	8-(I)-MR. BLUEBERRY			5.20
	$2 EXACTA 1-9 PAID $131.60			

B. c, (Mar), by Affirmed—La Confidence, by Nijinsky II. Trainer Jerkens H Allen. Bred by Harbor View Farm (Ky).

PRESENTLY dueled inside his entrymate along the backstretch, took charge on the turn, then drew off under mild encouragement. RIDGEWINDER raced in close contention while three wide to the turn, but was no match for the winner while clearly second best. MR BLUEBERRY outrun for a half circled five wide on the turn, then rallied mildly to gain a share. MALMO never reached contention after breaking slowly. AMATHOS up closed early while saving ground, faded leaving the far turn. GONE DANCING AGAIN made a run along the rail to threaten on the turn, then flattened out. BEN'S JET was never a factor. SOPHIE'S FRIEND raced wide and tired. SHINNINLIKEDIAMONDS forced the pace outside the winner for a half and tired. OCEAN CODE was pulled up along the backstretch. PRESENTLY, SHININLIKEDIAMODNS and MALMO wore mud caulks.

Owners— 1, Harbor View Farm; 2, Dogwood Stable; 3, Maki Jim; 4, Condren & Cornacchia & Paulson; 5, Maktoum Al Maktoum; 6, Valando Thomas; 7, Ackerley Bros Farm; 8, Scheftel Stuart; 9, Gainesway Stable; 10, Aiba Isso.

Trainers— 1, Jerkens H Allen; 2, Vestal Peter M; 3, Wismer Norman; 4, Zito Nicholas P; 5, Mott William I; 6, Schulhofer Flint S; 7, Lake Robert P; 8, Veitch John M; 9, Jerkens H Allen; 10, Jolley Leroy.

Statistically, longshots finish second approximately twice as often as they win. Ridgewinder had a clean trip from the outside post, attended the pace throughout, and, although he improved to a Beyer of 70 to outdistance the third-place finisher by nearly three lengths, he was no match for Presently.

For those with a win bet and an exacta saver, that was just fine, as the exacta returned $131.60 . . . compared to Ridgewinder's place mutuel of only $16.80.

Knowing how a stable has handled its young horses in the past can give handicappers a strong feeling of omniscience in numerous other situations, such as first time on turf:

Manila Lila
Own: Wilson Charles T Jr
ALVARADO F T (—)

B. f. 4
Sire: Manila (Lyphard)
Dam: Verbality (Verbatim)
Br: Brant Peter & Wilson Charles Jr (Ky)
Tr: Hernandez Ramon M (—)

119

Lifetime Record: 7 1 2 2 $37,180

1993	6 1 2 2	$35,740	Turf	0 0 0 0			
1992	1 M 0 0	$1,440	Wet	0 0 0 0			
Bel	3 0 1 1	$9,940	Dist	0 0 0 0			

8Dec93-7Aqu fst 1 1/16 ⊡	:241	:492	1:142	1:472	3↑ ⒻAlw 30000N2L	68	3 6	54½	42½	34	37	Alvarado F T	120	3.90	61-34	Prospect Pleases1156½ Princess Haifa115½ Manila Lila1203½	Mild gain	7
17Nov93-3Aqu fst 1	:231	:47	1:122	1:383	3↑ ⒻMd Sp Wt	69	7 5	66	53	1hd	14	Alvarado F T	120 b	9.10	71-26	Manila Lila1204 Caro's Beauty1201½ Spike Heel1204	Wide, driving	8
4Nov93-9Aqu fst 1	:232	:464	1:123	1:394	3↑ ⒻMd Sp Wt	69	5 12	97¾	74½	31½	2nk	Alvarado F T	120 f	5.20	65-32	Key To The Peace113nk Manila Lila120nk Turk's Flirt1205¾	Gamely	12
23Oct93-5Aqu fst 6f	:231	:47	:592	1:121	3↑ ⒻMd Sp Wt	59	6 4	74¼	65	48	47½	Alvarado F T	119	3.90	73-22	Prospect Pleases1191¼ Lovely Bird119nk Change The Tune1196	No threat	7
29Sep93-5Bel fst 6f	:231	:473	:592	1:112	3↑ ⒻMd Sp Wt	58	4 4	63¾	32	45½	311¼	Alvarado F T	118 f	4.20	71-19	Option Contract11811 Slip Lane118½ Manila Lila1182	Four wide	7
6Sep93-1Bel fst 6f	:224	:462	:583	1:112	3↑ ⒻMd Sp Wt	59	7 5	31½	21	25	27¾	Sweeney K H	118 f	17.20	75-19	Gambler's Guaranty1187¾ Manila Lila118hd Spike Heel1181¾	Held place	7
16Sep92-7Bel fst 6f	:22	:453	:582	1:114	ⒻMd Sp Wt	61	1 7	1011	67½	44	45½	Santiago A	117	35.10	75-18	Statuette1173 Black Medic1172¼ Raise a Carter117	Mild rally	11

Dan Kulchisky, the *Form*'s computer operator in New York, is a spot player. After watching Manila Lila go through her paces on dirt one late autumn day at Aqueduct, he mentioned that he was looking forward to betting her the first time she went to the grass.

"I'll be along for the ride when she switches to the grass next May," he advised.

While most in the crowd were scrambling around to make a bet in the next five minutes, Kulchisky had, after the seventh race on

December 8, already penciled Manila Lila in for a spot on turf *five months* down the road.

And not without good reason. Two good reasons, to be precise:

Verbasle
Dk. b. or br. f. 3(Feb), by Slewpy—Verbality, by Verbatim
Br.—Wilson Charles T Jr (Ky)
Tr.—Hernandez Ramon M
Own.—Wilson Charles T Jr
111
Lifetime 8 2 2 2 $147,988 | 1991 3 1 0 2 $24,120 | 1990 5 1 2 0 $123,868 | Turf 1 1 0 0 $17,400

Date	Race	Track/Dist	Fractions	Class	Running line	Jockey	Wt	Odds	Figs	Finish	Comment
12May91-	6Bel	fm 1 1/16 Ⓣ	:464 1:102 1:411	3+ⒻAlw 29000	11 11 1013 73¾ 32 11¼	Madrid A Jr	110	7.50	90-07	Verbasle1101¼ Crockadore1193 Shareefa1136	Wide, driving 12
13Apr91-	6Aqu	fst 1	:453 1:102 1:372	3+ⒻAlw 29000	2 1 2hd 1hd 1hd 34½	Gelpi A L Jr7	105	*1.60	71-29	Erhart1113¾ Dame de Soleil119½ Verbasle1053½	Bid, wknd 6
29Mar91-	6Aqu	fst 6f	:22 :453 1:112	ⒻAlw 27000	6 7 76½ 54½ 26 311	Madrid A Jr	116	*1.30	73-22	Raise Heck11611 Cozzinia116no Verbasle1161¾	Imp.position 7
17Nov90-	8Aqu	gd 1 1/8	:50 1:153 1:534	ⒻDemoiselle	3 7 79½ 77 64 79¼	Maple E	112	3.60	58-39	Dbutnt'sHlo1162PrivtTrsur121nkSlptThruIt1122	Broke slowly 7
17Nov90-Grade II											
27Oct90-	4Bel	fst 1 1/16	:454 1:11 1:44	ⒻBr Cp Juv F	11 11 119¼ 86 56½ 410¼	Maple E	119	37.10	72-15	MedowStr1195PrivteTrsur1191DncSmrtly1194¼	Saved ground 13
27Oct90-Grade I											
16Sep90-	8Bel	fst 7f	:222 :452 1:224	ⒻMatron	6 5 613 67½ 42½ 26	Maple E	119	10.20	84-14	MeadowStar1196Verbasle1193ClarkCottge1192¼	Gained place 6
16Sep90-Grade I											
23Aug90-	5Sar	fst 7f	224 :462 1:252	ⒻMd Sp Wt	2 13 85 43½ 22½ 1nk	Maple E	117	*2.60	78-16	Vrbsl117nkMkinFcs1172¾Plywithbgboys1173¼	Strong handling 14
2Aug90-	5Sar	fst 5f	:221 :46 :59	ⒻMd Sp Wt	7 5 22½ 23 24 21¼	Maple E	117	33.40	88-05	Teen Angel1171¼ Verbasle1178¾ His Nickel117no	Gamely 9

Speed Index: Last Race: –3.0 1–Race Avg.: –3.0 1–Race Avg.: –3.0 Overall Avg.: –4.8
LATEST WORKOUTS May 26 Bel 5f fst 1:03 B May 23 Bel Ⓣ 5f fm 1:03 B May 9 Bel Ⓣ 4f gd :52 B (d) May 4 Bel 5f fst 1:002 H

Verbal Intrigue
B. f. 3(Mar), by Dahar—Verbality, by Verbatim
Br.—Wilson Charles T Jr (Ky)
Tr.—Hernandez Ramon M (22 1 3 4 .05)
RODRIGUEZ R R (57 2 4 3 .04)
Own.—Wilson Charles T Jr
10410
Lifetime 7 1 0 0 $16,320 | 1992 3 1 0 0 $16,320 | 1991 4 M 0 0 | Turf 1 1 0 0 $15,600

Date	Race	Track/Dist	Fractions	Class	Speed	Running line	Jockey	Wt	Odds	Figs	Finish	Comment
14May92-	3Bel	fm 1 1/16 Ⓣ	:48 1:12 1:433	3+ⒻMd Sp Wt	78	5 4 41½ 43 3½ 12¼	RodriguezRR10	b 106	15.70	78-20	VerbalIntrigue1062¼Vistbhn115nkHelenGeGe115	Driving 11
29Apr92-	9Aqu	fst 6f	:223 :46 1:122	3+ⒻMd 30000	42	3 3 74¼ 64¾ 65¾ 44¾	Martinez R R5	b 109	14.00	74-15	HopforsII1051¼EndrngDncr1151¾WldDsco124	No threat 10
13Apr92-	1Aqu	gd 6f	:222 :454 1:111	3+ⒻMd 50000	47	1 6 65½ 48½ 48 56¾	Lopez C E Jr7	108	35.60	78-08	SeattleCielo1082Sncerre1152¼Hrpoon115	Saved ground 7
7Dec91-	4Aqu	fst 6f ⊡	:222 :461 1:131	ⒻMd 75000	27	4 9 1011 1013 915 716	Madrid A Jr	b 117	43.40	61-18	TriggrMoos1138Sh'sSoSmrt113nkYouArGold113	Outrun 10
29Nov91-	1Aqu	fst 1	:463 1:13 1:393	ⒻMd Sp Wt	45	3 6 68 76¾ 710 616¼	Verge M E	b 117	40.90	47-34	RoylChrter1171ShredMgic1178SleekStphi117	No factor 7
7Nov91-	6Aqu	fst 7f	:232 :472 1:252	ⒻMd Sp Wt	45	8 2 41½ 64 66 613	Verge M E	117	20.40	62-19	AplchSnst1173½ⒹSlvpln117½WyfthWrld117	Brief speed 11
23Oct91-	6Aqu	fst 6f	:222 :462 1:122	ⒻMd Sp Wt	42	4 6 916 911 98¼ 68	Verge M E	117	78.90	71-13	Ryn1172¼Slpwththnmy1172HollywodSml117	Never close 9

LATEST WORKOUTS Jun 19 Bel 4f fst :54 Bg

Manila Lila's half-sisters, Verbasle and Verbal Intrigue, raced four or five times on the dirt as two-year-olds. They had been brought back the next spring and had won at Belmont in May when placed on grass for the first time at odds of 7–1 and 15–1, respectively.

Manila Lila, also out of the mare Verbality, owned and bred by Charles T. Wilson, and trained by Ramon "Mike" Hernandez, remained in harmony with the natural order of things on May 25, when she switched to the grass and overcame traffic problems in midstretch to win going away:

Manila Lila
Own: Wilson Charles T Jr
ALVARADO F T (114 19 10 12 .17)
B. f. 4
Sire: Manila (Lyphard)
Dam: Verbality (Verbatim)
Br: Brant Peter & Wilson Charles Jr (Ky)
Tr: Hernandez Ramon M (10 3 0 0 .30)
119
Lifetime Record: 9 2 2 2 $56,860
1994 2 1 0 0 $19,680 | Turf 1 1 0 0 $18,000
1993 6 1 2 2 $35,740 | Wet 0 0 0 0
Bel Ⓣ 1 1 0 0 $18,000 | Dist Ⓣ 0 0 0 0

Date	Race	Track/Dist	Fractions	Class	Speed	Running line	Jockey	Wt	Odds	Figs	Finish	Comment
25May94-	6Bel	fm 1 1/16 Ⓣ	:242 :48 1:121 1:423	3+ⒻAlw 30000N1X	82	4 7 62¾ 61½ 51½ 11¾	Alvarado F T	121	4.10	83-12	Manila Lila1211¾ Silly's Philly121hd Insurprise1211¾	Alt crs stretch, drvg 10
3May94-	6Bel	fst 7f	:223 :454 1:101 1:231	3+ⒻAlw 28000N1X	66	2 2 44½ 34 46½ 49	Alvarado F T	119	15.00	78-14	Aly's Conquest114hd Night And Dreams1121 Tara Roma1198	Tired 6
8Dec93-	7Aqu	fst 1 1/16 ⊡	:241 :492 1:142 1:472	3+ⒻAlw 30000N2L	69	3 6 54½ 42½ 34 37	Alvarado F T	120	3.90	61-34	Prospect Pleases1156½ Princess Haifa115½ Manila Lila1203½	Mild gain 7
17Nov93-	3Aqu	fst 1	:231 :47 1:122 1:383	3+ⒻMd Sp Wt	69	7 5 66 53 1hd 14	Alvarado F T	120 b	9.10	71-26	Manila Lila1204 Caro's Beauty1201½ Spike Heel1204	Wide, driving 8
4Nov93-	9Aqu	fst 1	:232 :464 1:123 1:394	3+ⒻMd Sp Wt	69	5 12 97¾ 74½ 31½ 2nk	Alvarado F T	120 f	5.20	65-32	Key To The Peace113nk Manila Lila120nk Turk's Flirt1205¾	Gamely 12
23Oct93-	5Aqu	fst 6f	:231 :47 :592 1:121	3+ⒻMd Sp Wt	59	6 4 74½ 65 48 47½	Alvarado F T	119	3.90	73-22	Prospect Pleases1191½ Lovely Bird119nk Change The Tune1196	No threat 7
29Sep93-	5Bel	fst 6f	:231 :473 :592 1:112	3+ⒻMd Sp Wt	58	4 4 63¾ 32 45½ 311½	Alvarado F T	118 f	4.20	71-19	Option Contract11811 Slip Lane118½ Manila Lila1182	Four wide 7
6Sep93-	1Bel	fst 6f	:224 :462 :583 1:112	3+ⒻMd Sp Wt	59	7 5 31½ 21 25 27¾	Sweeney K H	118 f	17.20	75-19	Gambler's Guaranty1187¾ Manila Lila118hd Spike Heel1181¾	Held place 7
16Sep92-	7Bel	fst 6f	:22 :453 :582 1:114	ⒻMd Sp Wt	61	1 7 1011 67½ 44 45½	Santiago A	117	35.10	75-18	Statuette1173 Black Medic1172½ Raise a Carter117	Mild rally 11

WORKOUTS: Jun 11 Bel tr.t 5f fst 1:03 B 3/6 Jun 3 Bel tr.t 4f fst :512 B 3/3 May 22 Bel 5f fst 1:02 B 40/72 Apr 24 Bel tr.t 5f fst 1:024 H 2/4 Apr 18 Bel tr.t 4f fst :492 B 19/27 Apr 8 PBD 4f gd :50 B 1/2

It was a harmonius result for Kulchisky as well, who smiled for days afterward. "You know, it's not just the money," he explained. "When the same family of horses keeps winning in the same kind of spot for the same connections year after year, there's a really nice feeling of continuity to the game — the feeling that things are unfolding as they should."

That, and there's also the money.

Lightly raced, grass-bred three-year-olds such as Manila Lila may receive a prep race or two on dirt prior to the surface switch. Others, as illustrated in chapter 1, signal impending improvement by developing an explosive line. And, of course, there are others who surge ahead in their development in their first start back.

The favorite in Gulfstream Park's sixth race February 16 was Future Answer; fluctuating between 7–2 and 4–1 was Princess Joanne:

Future Answer
Own: Hooper Fred W
SELLERS S J (133 21 20 17 .16)

B. f. 3 (May)
Sire: Copelan (Tri Jet)
Dam: What a Future (Roberto)
Br: Hooper Fred W (Fla)
Tr: White William P (50 6 5 6 .12)

L 118

Lifetime Record: 9 2 2 0 $28,250

1994	2	1	1	0	$15,620	Turf	1 0 0 0		$160
1993	7	1	1	0	$12,630	Wet	3 2 0 0		$20,640
GP	2	1	1	0	$15,620	Dist	2 0 0 0		$290

30Jan94-5GP	fst	6f	:21³ :44² :57¹ 1:10⁴	ⒻAlw 24000N1X	76	4	9	4¾	5¾	2½	2½	Sellers S J	L 117 b	6.20	86-11	Red Soul117½ Future Answer1172½ Valid Miss Match117½		11
Drifted out upper str, rallied																		
12Jan94-6GP	sly	6f	:21³ :45¹ :58² 1:11⁴	ⒻClm 40000	87	4	5	64¾	3³	1½	19½	Sellers S J	L 117 b	2.00e	82-19	Future Answer1179½ Dance Thru Time115³ Lookingtoyou1172¾		8
Eight wide top str, driving																		
19Dec93-9Crc	fst	7f	:21⁴ :45² 1:12 1:26²	ⒻAlw 15000N1X	49	2	8	36½	4⁵	7⁹	710½	Douglas R R	117 b	*2.60e	72-16	K. C. Super Pet1171½ Esplendita113½ Precise Time1172½	Thru early	8
2Dec93-8Crc	fst	6f	:21⁴ :45³ :58² 1:12	ⒻAlw 15000N1X	72	10	1	52½	32½	22½	22½	Douglas R R	117 b	19.40	86-17	Shananie'sBet1172½ FutureAnswer117½ SginDubh1171½	Not good enough	10
3Nov93-9Crc	gd	*1 1/16 Ⓣ	1:46	ⒻAlw 16000N2X	32	5	4	3¹	4³	7¹³	716½	Madrid S O	117 b	10.00	[illegible]	Out The Pot120³ Long Gone Blues117nk Rubyfoo117hd	Stopped	7
16Oct93-7Crc	sly	6f	:21⁴ :45³ :58³ 1:12¹	ⒻAlw 14000N1X	61	7	2	44½	44½	4⁴	5⁶	Douglas R R	118	12.50	81-13	Shoe Band1181¾ Relic Reality1183½ Dance Thru Time115no	Faded	7
2Oct93-10Crc	gd	7f	:22¹ :45 1:11³ 1:26²	ⒻAlw 14000N1X	46	9	1	4⁶	46½	8⁹¼	610¼	Toribio A R	118	16.60	73-14	Copewithme113⁴ Betweenthisandthat115½ Sgian Dubh110½	Faded	9
17Sep93-9Crc	fst	6f	:22 :45² :58 1:11¹	ⒻAlw 14000N1X	35	2	7	41½	57½	59½	516½	Toribio A R	118	4.90	75-07	Kudos For Sweets1156½ Copewithme113hd Curvacious Cutie115nk	Faded	7
29Aug93-6Crc	sly	5½f	:22⁴ :47³ 1:00³ 1:07¹	ⒻMd Sp Wt	58	8	7	62¾	31½	2hd	1¾	Toribio A R	116	10.80	91-14	Future Answer116¾ Miss Aciss1162½ American Dawn1161½		9
Six wide top str, driving																		

WORKOUTS: Feb 11 Crc 4f fst :48 H 3/20 ●Jan 25 Crc 4f sly :48 H (d) 1/25 ●Jan 3 Crc 5f sly 1:01 H 1/20 ●Dec 14 Crc 4f fst :48 H 1/31 Nov 17 Crc 6f fst 1:01³ H 2/20

Princess Joanne
Own: Double R Stable & Kaufman Robert
BRAVO J (167 19 22 19 .11)

Ch. f. 3 (Apr)
Sire: Crafty Prospector (Mr. Prospector)
Dam: Illustrious Joanne (Illustrious)
Br: James H. Iselin (NJ)
Tr: Serpe Philip M (16 4 1 1 .25)

118

Lifetime Record: 2 1 0 0 $16,200

1993	2	1	0	0	$16,200	Turf	0 0 0 0	
1992	0	M	0	0		Wet	0 0 0 0	
GP	0	0	0	0		Dist	0 0 0 0	

13Nov93-9Med	fst	6f	:22 :45 :58³ 1:11³	ⒻⓈNJ Futy57k	52	2	7	2¹	3²	3³	46½	Bailey J D	119	*1.30	76-15	Donna Doo119⁵ Aspiring Proof119¹ Avie's Fancy119½	Tired	8
27Oct93-5Med	fst	6f	:22³ :46¹ :58³ 1:11¹	ⒻⓈMd Sp Wt	77	9	2	3¹	2hd	1¹	18¾	Bravo J	117	3.00	85-17	PrincessJoanne1178¾ Papp'sJen117½ WonderfulTonight1173¾	Going away	10

WORKOUTS: Feb 12 GP 4f fst :51¹ B 41/44 Feb 6 GP 7f fst 1:28 B 2/6 Feb 1 GP 7f sly 1:29³ B 2/3 Jan 20 GP 7f fst 1:28 B 1/3 ●Jan 11 GP 6f gd 1:14 H 1/4 Dec 29 GP 5f fst 1:01 B 3/34

Future Answer's best figure was an 87 in the slop as "first time Lasix" on January 12. Her next-best effort was a closing effort for the place spot, with a Beyer of 76 in her most recent outing. She had weakened through the stretch in both prior seven-furlong starts.

Princess Joanne had never been past six furlongs but showed three consecutive workouts at today's distance and had won off works to begin her career the previous October; she had been solidly backed for her debut and had not disappointed, winning off by eight lengths while showing the ability to race up close to the pace and blow by rivals in the stretch. Although she had faded in a New Jersey–bred Futurity sprint as the 13–10 favorite in her second and final start at two, she had already demonstrated a considerable amount of potential. Given three months to grow and mature (approximately the recovery time for commonly sustained bucked shins), she figured to run as well or better than she had in her debut:

Princess Joanne
Own: Double R Stable & Kaufman Robert
DOUGLAS R R (3 0 0 0 .00)

Ch. f. 3 (Apr)
Sire: Crafty Prospector (Mr. Prospector)
Dam: Illustrious Joanne (Illustrious)
Br: James H. Iselin (NJ)
Tr: Serpe Philip M (—)

115

Lifetime Record:	3 2 0 0	$31,800			
1994	1 1 0 0	$15,600	Turf	0 0 0 0	
1993	2 1 0 0	$16,200	Wet	0 0 0 0	
Hia	0 0 0 0		Dist	1 1 0 0	$15,600

16Feb94-6GP fst 7f :221 :451 1:094 1:221 ⒻAlw 26000N1X 96 9 2 62½ 31 12 17½ Bravo J 118 3.60 92-12 Princess Joanne1187½ Mystic Union1183¼ Future Answer1181½ Driving 9
13Nov93-9Med fst 6f :22 :45 :583 1:113 ⒻⓈNJ Futy57k 52 2 7 21 32 33 46½ Bailey J D 119 *1.30 76-15 Donna Doo1195 Aspiring Proof1191 Avie's Fancy119½ Tired 8
27Oct93-5Med fst 6f :223 :461 :583 1:111 ⒻⓈMd Sp Wt 77 9 2 31 2hd 11 18½ Bravo J 117 3.00 85-17 PrincessJoanne1178½ Papp'sJen117½ WonderfulTonight1173¾ Going away 10
WORKOUTS: Mar 15 GP 4f fst :492 B 16/29 Mar 8 GP 6f fst 1:14 H 1/3 Mar 1 GP 3f fst :39 B 16/18 Feb 12 GP 4f fst :511 B 41/44 Feb 6 GP 7f fst 1:28 B 2/6 Feb 1 GP 7f sly 1:293 B 2/3

Princess Joanne, from the same outside post where she had broken her maiden, overpowered the field with a jump to a Beyer of 96, and paid $9.20.

Less than two weeks later, trainer Phil Serpe won with Gifted Son, another three-year-old returning in a seven-furlong race at Gulfstream for his first start of the year:

Gifted Son
Own: Minassian Harry
BRAVO J (—)

B. g. 3 (Mar)
Sire: Rexson's Hope (Rexson)
Dam: Hot Times Ahead (Cutlass)
Br: Yeoman John & Jean (Fla)
Tr: Serpe Philip M (1 0 0 1 .00)

117

Lifetime Record:	4 1 1 0	$18,700		
1994	2 1 0 0	$16,800	Turf	1 0 0 0
1993	2 M 1 0	$1,900	Wet	0 0 0 0
Aqu	0 0 0 0		Dist	0 0 0 0

21Mar94-6OTC fst 1 1/16 :234 :474 1:122 1:46 3+OBSChmpnshp100k 82 3 5 53½ 65¼ 43½ 58¾ Bravo J L 122 - 91-07 ⒹPad122½ Crystal Pistol1226½ Can't Slow Down122nk Failed to menace 9
1Mar94-6GP fst 7f :214 :443 1:094 1:23 Md 75000 82 2 7 44½ 33½ 1hd 14¼ Bravo J L 120 3.10 88-12 Gifted Son1204¼ Heroic Pursuit1226 Tres Froid1204 Driving 8
23Aug93-3Sar fm 1 Ⓣ :243 :481 1:121 1:383 Md Sp Wt — 7 10 1048 — — — Migliore R 118 14.70 — 16 Sultan Of Java1184 Silver Target118hd Exclusive Casino1181½ Pulled up 10
29Jun93-5Mth fst 5f :222 :462 1:00 Md 32000 57 6 6 45 35 33½ 22¾ Bravo J 118 6.40 78-24 Private Enough1182¾ Gifted Son118nk Sonny's Bruno1182½ Fin. well 9
WORKOUTS: Apr 8 GP 6f fst 1:183 B 3/3 Apr 2 GP 5f fst 1:04 B 15/19 Mar 15 GP 7f fst 1:282 B 1/2 Mar 10 GP 4f fst :53 B 35/37 Feb 15 GP 7f fst 1:272 Hg 1/3 Feb 8 GP 5f fst 1:031 B 23/25

Gifted Son's fiasco on turf was to be disregarded in light of the pattern match. Like his stablemate, he had been worked at least twice at the distance, was also getting a switch back to Joe Bravo, and was even being bet in much the same way at 3–1. As an added bonus, he was getting Lasix for the first time. Although his second-place finish on dirt first time out indicated his ability to run well off works, that race had been against $32,000 claimers. Could he handle $75,000 company? Key-race devotees familiar with the horse he had outfinished for second money on June 29 voted yes:

Sonny's Bruno
Own: Port Sidney L
LUZZI M J (163 26 14 15 .16)

B. c. 3 (Apr)
Sire: Queen City Lad (Olden Times)
Dam: Settlers Cabin (Cabin)
Br: Arthur Hancock (Ky)
Tr: Tesher Howard M (23 5 3 6 .22)

119

Lifetime Record:	9	5	1	2	$100,826						
1994	1	1	0	0	$32,970	Turf	0	0	0	0	
1993	8	4	1	2	$67,856	Wet	2	1	0	1	$29,376
Aqu ⊡	2	1	0	1	$47,946	Dist	2	1	0	1	$47,946

22Jan94-5Aqu	fst	170 ⊡	:234	:474	1:132	1:441	Count Fleet50k	83	7	7	75	61	2 2 3/4	1 1/2	Luzzi M J	113	3.90	77-24	Sonny's Bruno113 1 1/2 Cape Verde1131 Hussonet1133	5 wide, driving	7
11Dec93-8Aqu	sly	1 1/16 ⊡	:222	:463	1:114	1:463	Nashua-G3	82	4	—	—	—	—	3 1/2	Marquez C H Jr	114	21.40	71-31	Popol'sGold114no PrsonlMrt117 1 1/2 Sonny'sBrno114 2 1/2	Snow, bid, weakened	11
19Nov93-4Aqu	fst	7f	:223	:452	1:104	1:24	Alw 30000N2X	81	3	5	714	714	66	28	Marquez C H Jr	117	12.30	76-19	Able Buck1178 Sonny's Bruno117 2 3/4 Gusto Z119 3/4	Late gain	7
31Oct93-3Aqu	sly	1	:224	:47	1:131	1:39	Clm 50000	80	1	5	5 4 1/2	2 1 1/2	2hd	1 1/2	Marquez C H Jr	117	2.80	69-36	Sonny's Bruno117 1 1/2 Francis Marion11715 Dinner Affair11314	Wide, driving	5
8Oct93-3Med	fst	6f	:221	:451	:58	1:112	Alw 17000N1X	76	6	3	5 4 3/4	5 3 1/2	3 3/4	1 3/4	Marquez C H Jr	120	2.70	84-17	Sonny's Bruno120 3/4 Mr Vincent112no Joe Casey117 5 1/2	Driving	7
25Sep93-7Bel	fst	6f	:223	:461	:582	1:111	Alw 28000N1X	62	2	2	34	53	55	4 11 1/2	Santagata N	117	15.20	73-19	Crary1175 Goodbye Doeny1176 Mobile117nk	No threat	5
8Sep93-1Bel	fst	6f	:222	:46	:583	1:113	Clm 50000	71	2	3	43	32	22	1nk	Chavez J F	117	5.60	82-17	Sonny'sBruno117nk EveningTease11619 ZelBrown1132	Lugged in, driving	5
13Jly93-1Mth	fst	6f	:223	:464	1:00	1:133	Md 32000	48	2	6	6 2 3/4	64	31	1 1/2	Squartino R A	118	*.70	71-22	Sonny'sBrn118 1 1/2 Mdln'sSnny1141 Mmnt'sGlry118 2 3/4	Stmbld start, driving	8
29Jun93-5Mth	fst	5f	:222	:462		1:00	Md 32000	56	2	4	35	46	4 5 1/2	33	Squartino R A	118	8.40	78-24	Private Enough118 2 3/4 Gifted Son118nk Sonny's Bruno118 2 1/2	Closed well	9

WORKOUTS: ●Feb 4 Bel tr.t 4f fst :482 H 1/19 Jan 17 Bel tr.t 4f fst :494 H 19/47 Jan 11 Bel tr.t 5f fst 1:05 B 13/21 Jan 6 Bel tr.t 5f fst 1:041 B 15/29 Dec 30 Bel tr.t 3f fst :361 H 2/16 Dec 24 Bel tr.t 4f fst :513 B 58/105

As maiden $32,000 fields go, Gifted Son had run in an extraordinarily tough one, with the winner going on to compete effectively in stakes.

Recognition of connection/workout patterns is a big edge in playing lightly raced horses. When this hidden information is supplemented by statistical data from peripheral sources, such as *Maiden Stats*, these races can become a handicapper's prime source of overlays.

Maiden Stats sells annually for about $100 from the Kentucky-based firm Bloodstock Research Information Services and is potentially worth many times its cover price. Resembling a phone book in size, weight, and scope, it provides an easy-to-read capsule summary on virtually every two-year-old registered in America with the Jockey Club. Naturally, each edition retains its usefulness as each crop of two-year-olds turns three on January 1, et cetera. After a couple of years, handicappers will have access to every horse's "number."

Explanations of the Statistics

SIRE INFORMATION

 # wnr - the number of winners the sire has produced.

 # str - the number of starters the sire has produced.

2yo wnr - the number of 2-year-old winners the sire has produced.

2yo str - the number of 2-year-old starters the sire has produced.

%1st - the percentage of first time starter winners the sire has produced. A sire with 15+% first time starter winners is typically considered a strong candidate to win their first start.

awd - the average winning distance of the sire's runners. An awd greater than 7.0 is typically considered a potential router.

Mud w% - the win percentage of the sire's runners in the mud. A sire with 15+% mud win percentage typically indicates a preference to an off-track.

Mud sts - the sire's runners number of starts in the mud.

Turf w% - the win percentage of the sire's runners on the turf. A sire with 15+% turf win percentage typically indicates a preference for the turf.

Turf sts - the sire's runners number of starts on the turf.

% 1stT - the percentage of first time turf winners the sire has produced. A sire with 15+% first time turf winners is typically considered a strong candidate to win their first start on the turf.

Spi - Sire Production Index. This index indicates the racing class of the sire's foals based upon relative earnings. The higher the number the better the sire.

DAM INFORMATION

prf - The dam's racing performance (ur: unraced, up: unplaced, w: winner, p: placed, sp: stakes placed, sw: stakes winner).

Dpi - Dam Production Index. This index indicates the racing class of the dam's foals based upon relative earnings. The higher the number the better the dam.

 # fls - the number of foals the dam has produced.

 # wnr - the number of winners the dam has produced.
 # str - the number of starters the dam has produced.

 # sw - the number of stakes winners the dam has produced.

2yo wnr - the number of 2-year-old winners the dam has produced.

2yo str - the number of 2-year-old starters the dam has produced.

awd - the average winning distance of the dam's runners. An awd greater than 7.0 is typically considered a potential router.

Mud w% - the win percentage of the dam's runners in the mud. A dam with 15+% mud win percentage typically indicates a preference to an off-track. Before weighing your decision on this statistic, consider the number of starts the dam's foals have made in the mud.

Mud sts - the dam's runners number of starts in the mud.

Turf wnr - the number of turf winners the dam has produced.

Turf str - the number of turf starters the dam has produced.

Dosage Index - the horse's Dosage Index.

SIBLING INFORMATION

Top Sibling - the top money earner the dam has produced.

+ - indicates the top sibling is a full brother or sister to the runner.

Earn$ - the earnings of the top sibling.

YEARLING SALES INFORMATION

Price - the public auction price as a yearling. A sales price above the sire's sales average and stud fee typically indicates the horse has a better pedigree or physical conformation.

Sire avg. - the sire's average price of yearlings sold at public auction in 1992.

Rnk - the horse's ranking in the marketplace compared to all other yearlings sold at public auction by the horse's sire in 1992. The lower the ranking versus the sire's number of yearlings sold at public auction typically indicates the horse has a better pedigree or physical conformation. The best ranking is 1.

 # sld - the total number of yearlings by the sire that were sold in 1992 at public auction.

Stud Fee - the sire's 1991 stud fee (the year the horse was conceived).

A look at Keeneland's third race of April 22, 1993, makes it easy to see how this book might come in handy:

3

4 ½ FURLONGS. **(.51) MAIDEN. SPECIAL WEIGHT. Purse $15,600 (includes $2,600 from KTDF). Fillies. 2-year-olds. Weight, 117 lbs. (Preference to fillies catalogued in 1993 Keeneland 2-year Sale.)**

Cahaba Dancer — Dk. b. or br. f. 2(Apr), by Marshua's Dancer—Country Chic, by Cox's Ridge — Lifetime 0 0 0 0 — 1993 0 M 0 0
MELANCON L (12 2 1 1 .17) — Br.—Dawahare A F (Ky)
Own.—Dawahare A F & Ellis William — Tr.—McPeek Kenneth G (10 2 0 2 .20) — 117
LATEST WORKOUTS Apr 20 Kee 3f fst :38³ Bg Apr 15 CD 4f sly :50 Bg ●Apr 4 CD 3f fst :36¹ B

Bob's Claim — Dk. b. or br. f. 2(Feb), by Claim—How's That, by Lord Avie — Lifetime 0 0 0 0 — 1993 0 M 0 0
ARGUELLO F A JR (1 0 0 0 .00) — Br.—Lake Charles III (Ky)
Own.—Dike Charles E — Tr.—Montano Angel (6 0 0 1 .00) — 117
LATEST WORKOUTS Apr 16 Kee 4f gd :50² Bg Mar 31 Kee 3f fst :37 Bg

Crafty and Evil — Ch. f. 2(Mar), by Crafty Prospector—Evil Elaine, by Medieval Man — Lifetime 0 0 0 0 — 1993 0 M 0 0
STEINER J J (9 1 0 4 .11) — Br.—Wood M L Mr-Mrs (Ky)
Own.—Siegel Jan-Mace & Samantha — Tr.—Mayberry Brian A (10 0 0 3 .00) — 117
LATEST WORKOUTS Apr 18 Kee 3f fst :37¹ B Mar 28 Kee 3f fst :37³ B

Autumn In Dixie — B. f. 2, by Dixieland Band—Autumn Olive, by Gallant Lad — Lifetime 0 0 0 0 — 1993 0 M 0 0
SELLERS S J (68 19 9 7 .28) — Br.—Cheney Mark Mr-Mrs W (Ky)
Own.—Cheney Terrell — Tr.—Wilkinson Jack R III (—) — 117
LATEST WORKOUTS Apr 18 Kee 4f fst :48² Bg Apr 10 Kee 3f my :36³ B

Normandy Belle — B. f. 2, by Fit To Fight—French Flick, by Silent Screen — Lifetime 0 0 0 0 — 1993 0 M 0 0
PERRET C (39 9 10 5 .23) — Br.—Firman Pamela Mrs H (Ky)
Own.—Humphrey G Watts Jr — Tr.—Pierce Joseph H Jr (4 1 0 1 .25) — 117

Odie West — Ch. f. 2(Apr), by Westheimer—Miss Odie, by Cannonade — Lifetime 2 0 2 0 $6,240 — 1993 2 M 2 0 $6,240
OUZTS P W (15 0 2 0 .00) — Br.—O'Neal Dr & Mrs Dave (Ky)
Own.—Lunsford Clyde — Tr.—Short Thomas (6 0 2 0 .00) — 117 — Wet 1 0 1 0 $3,120
14Apr93- 1Kee sly 4½f :22² :46² :52³ ⒻMd Sp Wt 46 3 5 5⁶½ 4⁵½ 2¹½ Ouzts P W 117 7.30 94-08 AshlsSprft117½OdWst117hdChttCd117 Bid, fully extend 10
6Apr93- 3Kee fst 4½f :22⁴ :47¹ :53⁴ ⒻMd Sp Wt 25 4 4 4⁵ 4³½ 2½ Ouzts P W 117 19.60 89-07 CityJoyc117½OdiWst117nkSpphirBds117 Swung out late 6
LATEST WORKOUTS Apr 1 KHC 4f fst :50³ Hg

Flip The Cannon — Dk. b. or br. f. 2, by Cannon Dancer—Tribute Of Gold, by Full Out — Lifetime 0 0 0 0 — 1993 0 M 0 0
NEAGLE W J (10 1 0 3 .10) — Br.—Demeritte Larry (Ky)
Own.—Demeritte Beryl — Tr.—Demeritte Larry (1 0 1 0 .00) — 117

New Fe — B. f. 2(Apr), by King Nerraw—Fefe La Canard, by Qui Native — Lifetime 0 0 0 0 — 1993 0 M 0 0
STACY A T (15 1 2 3 .07) — Br.—King Warren L (Ky)
Own.—War-Bec Farm — Tr.—King Warren L (2 0 1 0 .00) — 117
LATEST WORKOUTS Apr 20 Kee 3f fst :36 Bg Apr 14 Kee 4f fst :48² Hg Apr 11 Kee 3f fst :36² B Apr 4 Kee 3f fst :38 B

All in the field except Odie West were first-time starters. A check of Crafty and Evil's listing in *Maiden Stats* suggested she was to be taken very seriously:

	SIRE INFO								DAM INFO										SIBLING INFO	YRLG SALES INFO		
Horse	# wnr/str	2yo wnr/str	% 1st	awd	Mud wi/sts	Turf wi/sts	% 1stT	Spi	prf	Dpi	# fls	# wnr/str	# sw	2yo wnr/str	awd	Mud wi/sts	Turf wnr/str	Dosage Index	Top Sibling /Earn$	Price/Sire avg	# Rnk/sld	Stud Fee
CRAFTY AND EVIL	163/192	60/115	23	6.4	20/ 504	7/ 187	5	2.67	sw	0.08	2	0/ 1	0	0/ 1	0.0	0/ 1	0/ 1	4.45		$100k/$ 44k	1/28	15k
CRAFY BALLY	67/144	18/ 90	1	6.6	8/ 251	4/ 47	9	0.31	sp		3							2.60				
CRAFTY BOBBIE	246/323	73/198	8	7.3	14/1258	8/ 487	7	0.97	w	3.08	8	5/ 6	0	2/ 4	7.3	31/ 16	2/ 2	5.67	Trebizond /$409k			

Crafty and Evil's sire, Crafty Prospector, was shown as winning with 23 percent of his first-time starters. And among the twenty-eight Crafty Prospector yearlings sold in 1992, Crafty and Evil's $100,000 purchase price was the highest, indicating there was something about this filly's pedigree, conformation, and/or overall appearance that buyers had been willing to pay a premium for.

She won at a $21 mutuel.

Another recommended source of information is *Saratoga Scorecard,* the annual spiral-bound volume by John Angelo, which details, among other things, six-year histories of dozens of prominent trainers.

Supplementing the *Form*'s pp's with *Maiden Stats* and *Saratoga Scorecard* brought the third race at Saratoga on August 19, 1993, into much sharper focus:

Saratoga

3

5 Furlongs. (:56^4) **MAIDEN SPECIAL WEIGHT. Purse $23,500. Fillies, 2-year-olds. Weight, 117 lbs.**

1 Alarming Pride
Own: Big C Farms
ALVARADO F T (57 4 4 7 .07)

Gr. f. 2 (Apr)
Sire: Darn That Alarm (Jig Time)
Dam: Pride Goeth (Proudest Roman)
Br: Big C Farms (Fla)
Tr: Hough Stanley M (12 2 0 2 .17)

117

Lifetime Record :	0 M 0 0		$0
1993	0 M 0 0	Turf	0 0 0 0
1992	0 M 0 0	Wet	0 0 0 0
Sar	0 0 0 0	Dist	0 0 0 0

WORKOUTS: Aug 16 Sar tr.t 4f fst :49^2 B *4/16* Aug 10 Sar tr.t 5f fst 1:05 B *4/4* Aug 4 Sar 5f fst 1:01^2 Hg *14/58* Jly 29 Sar tr.t 4f fst :49^2 H *2/22* Jly 22 Bel 4f fst :48^1 Bg *14/59* Jly 15 Bel 4f fst :47^2 H *11/47* Jly 8 Bel 3f fst :36^1 B *8/24* Jun 30 Bel 3f fst :36 H *3/24*

2 Chad's Texaswonder
Own: Winbound Farms
CHAVEZ J F (102 10 10 14 .10)

B. f. 2 (Mar)
Sire: Coup de Kas (Kaskaskia)
Dam: Chad's Sister (Caracolero)
Br: Estate of B F Phillips Jr (Tex)
Tr: Contessa Gary C (15 2 2 1 .13)

117

Lifetime Record :	0 M 0 0		$0
1993	0 M 0 0	Turf	0 0 0 0
1992	0 M 0 0	Wet	0 0 0 0
Sar	0 0 0 0	Dist	0 0 0 0

WORKOUTS: ●Aug 16 Sar 3f fst :35^3 H *1/11* Aug 9 Sar 5f fst 1:00^4 Hg *5/20* Aug 4 Sar tr.t(T) 6f fm 1:18 B (d) *2/2*

3 Annie Bonnie
Own: Leachman John P
SMITH M E (119 23 20 7 .19)

Ch. f. 2 (May)
Sire: Geiger Counter (Mr. Prospector)
Dam: General Bonnie (Fuzzbuster)
Br: Paul Martyn (Ont-C)
Tr: Jolley Leroy (7 0 0 0 .00)

117

Lifetime Record :	0 M 0 0		$0
1993	0 M 0 0	Turf	0 0 0 0
1992	0 M 0 0	Wet	0 0 0 0
Sar	0 0 0 0	Dist	0 0 0 0

WORKOUTS: Aug 14 Sar 4f fst :48^2 H *8/23* Aug 9 Sar 5f fst 1:00 Hg *2/20* Aug 4 Sar 4f fst :48^1 Hg *11/47* Jly 29 Sar 4f fst :49^3 Bg *15/36* Jly 13 Bel 4f fst :51^1 B *37/42* Jly 5 Bel 4f fst :52 B *56/62* May 8 Bel 3f fst :37^3 B *31/41*

4 Roshni
Own: Shoaib Hassan
DAVIS R G (72 13 7 5 .18)

B. f. 2 (Feb)
Sire: Pancho Villa (Secretariat)
Dam: Tracy's Espoir (Silent Screen)
Br: Robert E Masterson (Ky)
Tr: Carroll Del W II (5 0 0 0 .00)

117

Lifetime Record :	0 M 0 0		$0
1993	0 M 0 0	Turf	0 0 0 0
1992	0 M 0 0	Wet	0 0 0 0
Sar	0 0 0 0	Dist	0 0 0 0

WORKOUTS: Jly 23 Bel 5f fst 1:01^1 H *9/28* Jly 19 Bel 4f fst :51^4 B *69/77* Jly 14 Bel tr.t 4f fst :52 B *2/2* Jly 4 Bel tr.t 3f fst :40^2 B *16/17*

5 April Green
Own: Buckram Oak Farm
KRONE J A (118 22 13 10 .19)

Ch. f. 2 (Feb)
Sire: Green Forest (Shecky Greene)
Dam: Laylitna (Key to the Mint)
Br: Buckram Oak Farm (Ky)
Tr: Moubarak Mohammed (14 1 0 3 .07)

117

Lifetime Record :	0 M 0 0		$0
1993	0 M 0 0	Turf	0 0 0 0
1992	0 M 0 0	Wet	0 0 0 0
Sar	0 0 0 0	Dist	0 0 0 0

WORKOUTS: Aug 10 Sar 5f fst 1:01^2 B *8/26* Aug 7 Sar tr.t 3f fst :37^2 B *4/15* Aug 4 Sar 5f fst 1:04^3 B *52/58* Jly 29 Sar 5f fst 1:03 B *16/28* Jly 22 Bel 4f fst :51 B *51/59*

6 Hope Is Real
Own: Assimakopoulos Charles
CARABALLO J C (3 0 0 1 .00)
Ch. f. 2 (Mar)
Sire: Gallapiat (Buckpasser)
Dam: Thepleasureisreal (What a Pleasure)
Br: Dale Harrison (Fla)
Tr: Assimakopoulos C (2 0 0 1 .00)
117
Lifetime Record: 1 M 0 1 $2,820
1993 1 M 0 1 $2,820 | Turf 0 0 0 0
1992 0 M 0 0 | Wet 0 0 0 0
Sar 1 0 0 1 $2,820 | Dist 1 0 0 1 $2,820
8Aug93-3Sar fst 5f :22^1 :45^3 :57^4 ©Md Sp Wt 50 2 5 3$^{1\frac{1}{2}}$ 2^1 2^4 3$^{6\frac{1}{2}}$ Caraballo J C 117 b 17.30 89-05 Shoo Baby117$^{6\frac{1}{2}}$ Nobody Picked Six117^{hd} Hope Is Real117^{no} Weakened 7
WORKOUTS: Aug 4 Rkm 4f fst :49^3 B 17/28 Jly 26 Rkm 5f fst 1:03 B 8/11 Jly 14 Rkm 5f fst 1:03 Hg4/13 Jly 7 Rkm 6f fst 1:17^1 Hg4/5 Jun 30 Rkm 5f fst 1:02^3 Hg8/11 Jun 23 Rkm 4f fst :48^3 H 3/28

7 Red Mistress
Own: Due Process Stable
BAILEY J D (106 19 14 22 .18)
Ch. f. 2 (Jan)
Sire: Deputy Minister (Vice Regent)
Dam: Wild Mistress (Secretariat)
Br: Cable Stable Ltd (Ky)
Tr: Gleaves Philip (12 1 2 1 .08)
117
Lifetime Record: 0 M 0 0 $0
1993 0 M 0 0 | Turf 0 0 0 0
1992 0 M 0 0 | Wet 0 0 0 0
Sar 0 0 0 0 | Dist 0 0 0 0
WORKOUTS: Aug 13 Sar 5f fst 1:02^1 B 6/15 ●Aug 8 Sar 4f fst :47^2 H 1/41 Aug 4 Sar 5f fst 1:02 H 20/58 Jly 31 Sar 5f fst 1:03^4 B 22/25 Jly 26 Sar 4f fst :50 Bg9/18 Jly 21 Sar 4f gd :48^2 H 1/1
Jly 16 Sar tr.t 3f fst :39^4 B 3/5 Jly 11 Sar 3f fst :39^4 B 1/2 Jly 6 Sar tr.t 3f fst :39^4 B 7/8 May 26 Sar tr.t 3f fst :38^1 H 2/9

8 The Bink
Own: Fox Ridge Farm
MAPLE E (56 10 7 6 .18)
B. f. 2 (Mar)
Sire: Seeking the Gold (Mr. Prospector)
Dam: Toll Fee (Topsider)
Br: Fox Ridge Farm, Inc. (Ky)
Tr: Kelly Patrick J (18 2 2 2 .11)
117
Lifetime Record: 0 M 0 0 $0
1993 0 M 0 0 | Turf 0 0 0 0
1992 0 M 0 0 | Wet 0 0 0 0
Sar 0 0 0 0 | Dist 0 0 0 0
WORKOUTS: Aug 15 Sar 4f fst :49^2 B 14/21 Aug 10 Sar 4f fst :49^3 B 18/25 Aug 5 Sar 3f fst :38^4 B 9/10 ●Aug 2 Sar 3f fst :35^4 Hg 1/17 Jly 28 Sar 3f fst :38 B 6/8 Jly 19 Bel 3f fst :36 Bg2/25
Jly 2 Bel 3f fst :36 Hg2/12 Jun 25 Bel 3f fst :39^2 Bg30/32

9 Illegal Appeal
Own: Miller Leverett S
LEON F (34 2 4 7 .06)
B. f. 2 (Feb)
Sire: Valid Appeal (In Reality)
Dam: Illegal Fund (Damascus)
Br: Harry T. Mangurian, Jr. (Fla)
Tr: Connors Robert F (2 0 0 0 .00)
112^5
Lifetime Record: 0 M 0 0 $0
1993 0 M 0 0 | Turf 0 0 0 0
1992 0 M 0 0 | Wet 0 0 0 0
Sar 0 0 0 0 | Dist 0 0 0 0
WORKOUTS: Aug 13 Sar 5f fst 1:04 Bg12/15 Jly 31 Sar 4f fst :50 B 27/45 Jly 20 Del 3f sly :38^3 B 1/2 Jun 28 Del 4f fst :49^1 Bg10/18

The five-furlong dash consisted of eight fillies making their debuts along with one other, Hope Is Real, who had run a promising third when unveiled earlier in the meet. Three of the firsters were taking action on the board:

Red Mistress	2–1
The Bink	5–2
Annie Bonnie	7–2
Hope Is Real	7–1

Coincidentally, Annie Bonnie was profiled in Henry Baker's weekly "Baby Talk" column in that day's edition of the *Form*. Baker noted that Annie Bonnie had worked in company with another two-year-old a week earlier, and "looked like she was leaving a launching pad when the starting gate opened." Her trainer, Hall of Famer Leroy Jolley, added that "all the racing secretary has to do is put us in a race with seven or eight others like the one we worked with and we should be in pretty good shape."

This was great inside stuff, and it helped to explain Annie Bonnie's heavy toteboard action. But *Saratoga Scorecard* noted that Jolley's record with first-time starters over the past six Saratoga meets was a dreadful 1 for 52.

"Beware the good works here," wrote Angelo. "They're like rubes dressed up in tuxedos."

Okay, so sometimes statistics are relevant: it's hard to argue with 1 for 52.

The favorite was Red Mistress, whose bullet :47$\frac{2}{5}$ workout of August 8 had been faster than forty others at the distance. But her yearling sales info from *Maiden Stats* threw up a red flag:

1 Unnamed Foals Dam's Name, Yob	# wnr/str	2yo wnr/str	% 1st	awd	Mud w%/sts	Turf w%/sts	% 1stT	Spi	prf	Dpi	# fls	# wnr/str	# sw	2yo wnr/str	awd	Mud w%/sts	Turf wnr/str	Dosage Index	Top Sibling	/Earn$	Price/Sire avg	# Rnk/sld	Stud Fee
[illegible]ad,80	84/136	22/ 63	12	7.8	17/ 101	14/ 335	8	4.53	sw	2.03	5	2/ 2	1	1/ 1	5.3	0/ 1	1/ 2	3.00	Tabdeed	/$ 35k			
e Application,78	1/ 6	1/ 5	0	8.3	0/ 1	0/ 1	0	0.38	tr	1.11	8	3/ 5	0	2/ 5	8.3	14/ 7	0/ 3	1.67	Wide Colony	/$100k	$ 8.0k/$ 12k	6/ 14	5.0k
[illegible],76									w	2.36	10	5/ 8	1	0/ 3	7.2	10/ 21	2/ 3	5.00	Cuentalamera	/$293k	$ 29k/$ 12k	1/ 5	5.0k
: Mistress,79	134/184	40/ 101	16	7.2	17/ 286	13/ 358	5	3.99	p	3.19	7	4/ 5	1	2/ 5	6.3	8/ 12	0/ 3	3.00	We Are A We	/$243k	$ 40k/$ 123k	18/ 19	50k
[illegible]Best,79	138/193	40/ 121	7	7.8	11/ 439	15/ 712	9	1.55	w	1.43	6	5/ 5	0	3/ 3	7.0	0/ 7	1/ 3	4.71	+Koorachee	/$ 88k	$ 17k/$ 7.4k	1/ 22	7.5k

Red Mistress had sold for less than a third the price of an average Deputy Minister yearling, going for $40,000 as opposed to her sire's average of $123,000. This ranked her the second-least expensive of nineteen Deputy Minister yearlings sold in 1992 — a juicy piece of info that indicated there was something about her pedigree and/or physical makeup that prospective buyers had not liked.

The other first-timer attracting support was The Bink, who had shown the required zip for a short dash with a trio of workouts ranked $\frac{1}{17}$, $\frac{2}{25}$, and $\frac{2}{12}$. The *Closer Look* noted that in addition to The Bink's past performances, this homebred was the first foal out of Toll Fee, a stakes winner of $334,000, who was in turn out of Toll Booth, a "blue hen" mare who'd produced several stakes winners, including Christiecat. Another positive was that several two-year-olds from Seeking the Gold's first crop had already won impressively earlier in the Spa meet.

With glaring negatives surrounding Annie Bonnie and Red Mistress, it seemed that The Bink was the likeliest of the trio to run well. It was also true that Hope Is Real's odds of 7–1 as the established form were looking better and better, as negative stats on Red Mistress and Annie Bonnie were brought to light.

Handicappers who fancied Hope Is Real might have bet her to win, along with an exacta saver underneath The Bink. Those who liked The Bink might've tried to improve on her 5–2 odds by keying her on top in exactas.

THIRD RACE **5 FURLONGS. (:56^{3}) MAIDEN SPECIAL WEIGHT. Purse $23,500. Fillies. 2-year-olds. Weight: 117 lbs.**

Saratoga

AUGUST 19, 1993

Value of race $23,500; value to winner $14,100; second $5,170; third $2,820; fourth $1,410. Mutuel pool $288,178. Exacta Pool $538,606

Last Raced	Horse	M/Eqt.	A.	Wt	PP	St	$\frac{3}{16}$	$\frac{3}{8}$	Str	Fin	Jockey	Odds $1
	The Bink		2	117	8	9	$3^{1\frac{1}{2}}$	1^{2}	$1^{3\frac{1}{2}}$	$1^{8\frac{1}{2}}$	Maple E	2.50
8Aug93 ^{3}Sar^{3}	Hope Is Real	b	2	117	6	2	7^{2}	$5^{\frac{1}{2}}$	$3^{\frac{1}{2}}$	$2^{2\frac{1}{2}}$	Caraballo J C	7.60
	Chad's Texaswonder		2	117	2	4	1^{hd}	$2^{\frac{1}{2}}$	$2^{\frac{1}{2}}$	3^{2}	Chavez J F	10.50
	Alarming Pride		2	117	1	1	8^{16}	8^{8}	$6^{\frac{1}{2}}$	$4^{\frac{1}{2}}$	Alvarado F T	10.60
	April Green		2	117	5	5	2^{hd}	$3^{1\frac{1}{2}}$	$4^{1\frac{1}{2}}$	$5^{\frac{3}{4}}$	Krone J A	12.10
	Roshni	b	2	117	4	6	6^{hd}	$7^{1\frac{1}{2}}$	$5^{\frac{1}{2}}$	$6^{1\frac{3}{4}}$	Davis R G	29.70
	Red Mistress		2	117	7	7	$5^{\frac{1}{2}}$	4^{hd}	$7^{\frac{1}{2}}$	$7^{1\frac{3}{4}}$	Bailey J D	2.30
	Illegal Appeal		2	112	9	8	9	9	9	$8^{2\frac{1}{4}}$	Leon F^{5}	47.30
	Annie Bonnie		2	117	3	3	$4^{\frac{1}{2}}$	$6^{\frac{1}{2}}$	8^{2}	9	Smith M E	3.90

OFF AT 2:05 Start good, Won ridden out. Time, :21^{4}, :45^{1}, :57^{2} Track fast.

$2 Mutuel Prices:				
	8-(H)-THE BINK	7.00	4.40	3.60
	6-(F)-HOPE IS REAL		6.80	4.60
	2-(B)-CHAD'S TEXASWONDER			6.80
	$2 EXACTA 8-6 PAID $79.20			

B. f, (Mar), by Seeking the Gold—Tell Fee, by Topsider. Trainer Kelly Patrick J. Bred by Fox Ridge Farm, Inc. (Ky).

THE BINK away a bit slowly, rallied boldly from outside to take charge midway on the turn, then drew off to a lengthy score while being ridden out. HOPE IS REAL checked between horses leaving the backstretch, gradually gained while four wide on the turn, then finished with good energy to best the others. CHAD'S TEXASWONDER battled for early advantage along the inside, relinguished the lead on the turn, and gradually tired thereafter. ALARMING PRIDE outrun for a half failed to threaten while improving her position through the lane. APRIL GREEN was used up forcing the early pace. ROSHNI was never a factor while saving ground. RED MISTRESS raced greenly while wide throughout. ILLEGAL APPEAL was never close. ANNIE BONNIE showed only brief speed.

Owners— 1, Fox Ridge Farm; 2, Assimakopoulos Charles; 3, Winbound Farms; 4, Big C Farms; 5, Buckram Oak Farm; 6, Shoaib Hassan; 7, Due Process Stable; 8, Miller Leverett S; 9, Leachman John P.

Trainers— 1, Kelly Patrick J; 2, Assimakopoulos C; 3, Contessa Gary C; 4, Hough Stanley M; 5, Moubarak Mohammed; 6, Carroll Del W II; 7, Gleaves Philip A; 8, Connors Robert F; 9, Jolley Leroy.

When The Bink recovered from a slow start to blow by the field around the turn, and Hope Is Real rallied to go clear for the place spot in deep stretch, both scenarios were rewarded by a robust $79.20 exacta. Red Mistress raced greenly and bore out leaving the turn, finishing seventh. Annie Bonnie flashed brief speed and wound up last.

It naturally follows that *Maiden Stats* is particularly useful for evaluating first-time-turf and first-time-slop situations. These days, however, even though the crowd has become more and more aware of successful turf breeding, they don't seem as well informed about horses that are especially well bred for distance racing. For this reason, stretch-outs often provide exceptional value.

RIDE THE RAILS									ur	2.10	13	6/ 8	2	1/ 4	6.4	5/ 19	0/ 4	1.22	Seeker's Journey	/$237k	$ 90k/$ 41k	3/38	15k
RIDE THE STATS	9/ 16	3/ 6	17	6.1	6/ 18	20/ 5	0	0.38	p		2							9.00					
RIDE TILL DAWN	23/ 43	7/ 29	7	6.7	10/ 73	19/ 42	13	0.63	ur		1							2.60					
RIDGE	253/342	60/167	12	7.6	15/ 573	10/ 698	5	3.71	ur		1							1.15					
RIDGE STEPPER	8/ 16	6/ 10	10	6.3	0/ 17	0/ 4	0	0.46	w		2							3.00					
RIDGETOWN	253/342	60/167	12	7.6	15/ 573	10/ 698	5	3.71	sw	2.98	6	3/ 4	1	2/ 3	7.3	0/ 0	3/ 3	1.25	Storm Dove	/$ 70k			
RIDGEWINDER	253/342	60/167	12	7.6	15/ 573	10/ 698	5	3.71	sw	0.00	3	1/ 2	0	0/ 1	10.0	0/ 0	1/ 2	3.00	Lady Dundee	/$ 12k	$ 70k/$ 75k	13/27	50k
RIDGEWOOD RED	10/ 12	1/ 2	0	6.3	24/ 29	14/ 14	0	0.47	p		2							5.67					
RIDGMAR	7/ 8	3/ 5	20	6.4	13/ 8	0/ 0	0	0.77	w		1							2.00					
RIFA	27/ 40	5/ 20	10	6.7	12/ 125	0/ 9	0	0.38	sp	5.55	4	2/ 3	1	1/ 1	5.6	0/ 1	1/ 1	4.60	To The Post	/$208k			
RIFAWAN	253/342	60/167	12	7.6	15/ 573	10/ 698	5	3.71	w		1							2.20					

Ridgewinder
Own: Dogwood Stable
Ch. c. 2 (Feb)
Sire: Cox's Ridge (Best Turn)
Dam: Add Mint (Vigors)
Br: Betty M. Peters & Gail Peters Beitz (Ky)
Tr: Vestal Peter M (—)
122

Lifetime Record : 3 M 1 0 $5,170
1993 3 M 1 0 $5,170 Turf 0 0 0 0
1992 0 M 0 0 Wet 0 0 0 0
GS 0 0 0 0 Dist 0 0 0 0

4Aug93-6Sar fst 7f $:22^4$ $:45^3$ $1:10^1$ 1:23 Md Sp Wt 70 10 1 3½ 3¹½ 2⁴ 2⁴¾ Day P 118 29.50 85-09 Presently118⁴¾Ridgewinder118²¾Mr Blueberry118²¼ Good effort 10

16Jun93-1CD fst 5½f :23 $:46^3$ $:52^3$ $1:05^3$ Md Sp Wt 20 1 6 6⁴½ 6⁷½ 5¹² 7¹⁸¼ Arguello F A Jr 119 35.10 75-23 Strawberry A. O K.119¹¼Look For Trouble119¹⁰Busta119⁴ 12
Bobbled, nearly clipped heels 1/2 pole

30May93-1CD fst 5f $:22^3$ $:46^2$ $:58^4$ Md Sp Wt 38 2 1 2hd 4¹¼ 5⁶¾ 6¹⁰¾ Arguello F A Jr 120 8.40 88-07 FlghtFortyNn120no LookFrTrbl120⁶½ CmptwnDncr120² Used early inside 11

WORKOUTS: Jly 23 CD 5f fst $1:02^2$ B 10/26 Jly 1 CD 4f fst $:48^1$ B 6/33 Jun 13 CD 4f fst :50 B 22/55 May 25 CD 5f gd $1:02^2$ Bg7/27 May 18 CD 5f fst $1:02^3$ Bg9/28 May 11 CD 5f fst $1:02^2$ B 5/27

A look at Ridgewinder's line from *Maiden Stats* would have served to confirm the theory that his races at five and a half furlongs gave minimal indication of his true potential. According to the Explanation of Statistics, an average winning distance over 7.0 furlongs for sire and/or dam is an indicator that the pedigree contains strong influences of stamina. Ridgewinder's sire, Cox's Ridge, gets horses with an average winning distance of 7.6 furlongs, and his dam, Add Mint, had produced one previous winner whose AWD was *10.0 furlongs.*

Because the crowd, generally speaking, is reluctant to bet on maidens stretching to a route for the first time, overlays come along frequently:

Aqueduct

5

1 MILE 70 YARDS. (Inner Dirt). ($1:39^3$) MAIDEN SPECIAL WEIGHT. Purse $25,000. 3-year-olds. Weight, 122 lbs.

Triple Fast
Own: Fried Albert A Jr
MIGLIORE R (206 39 35 27 .19)
Ch. g. 3 (May)
Sire: Affirmed (Exclusive Native)
Dam: Faster Than Fast (Raja Baba)
Br: Albert Fried, Jr. (NY)
Tr: Destasio Richard A (75 2 14 9 .03)
122

Lifetime Record : 1 M 0 0 $0
1994 1 M 0 0 Turf 0 0 0 0
1993 0 M 0 0 Wet 0 0 0 0
Aqu ⊡ 1 0 0 0 Dist 0 0 0 0

3Feb94-7Aqu fst 6f ⊡ :23 :48 $1:00^3$ 1:13 Ⓢ Md Sp Wt 33 6 12 11¹² 10⁶¾ 6¹² 5¹⁷½ Luzzi M J 122 8.80 60-23 Raja's Charter122⁹Arnoldovich122⁴½Russian Love122nk Broke slowly 12

WORKOUTS: Feb 20 Bel tr.t 4f fst $:50^3$ B 19/32 Feb 1 Bel tr.t 3f fst $:38^1$ B 19/29 Jan 23 Bel tr.t 3f fst $:37^4$ B 3/22 Jan 12 Bel tr.t 6f fst $1:16^4$ H 2/2 ●Jan 7 Bel tr.t 3f fst $:37^1$ B 1/14 Dec 31 Bel tr.t 5f fst $1:03^3$ B 8/24

Javavoom
Own: Meyers Gerald J
DAVIS R G (265 49 45 43 .18)
B. g. 3 (Feb)
Sire: Java Gold (Key to the Mint)
Dam: Kashie West (Sir Ivor)
Br: Smiser Dr & Mrs R West & Miller Mrs Mackenzie (Ky)
Tr: Schosberg Richard (60 11 14 9 .18)
122

Lifetime Record : 1 M 0 0 $0
1994 1 M 0 0 Turf 0 0 0 0
1993 0 M 0 0 Wet 0 0 0 0
Aqu ⊡ 1 0 0 0 Dist 0 0 0 0

15Feb94-5Aqu fst 6f ⊡ $:23^1$ $:46^3$ $:59^1$ $1:12^2$ Md Sp Wt 35 4 11 8³½ 8⁷ 9¹¹ 9¹⁵½ Luzzi M J 122 5.30 66-22 Cosa Diavolo122½Approximate122⁴Showiz122no Broke slowly 11

WORKOUTS: Feb 7 Bel tr.t 5f fst $1:02^1$ H 7/14 Jan 31 Bel tr.t 5f fst $1:03^4$ B 11/33 Jan 22 Bel tr.t 4f fst :52 B 40/69 Jan 12 Bel tr.t 4f fst $:48^2$ Hg10/79 Jan 6 Bel tr.t 3f fst $:37^1$ B 6/16 Dec 30 Bel tr.t 3f fst $:37^2$ B 9/16

Gash
Own: Vanderbilt Alfred G
PRADO E S (137 14 20 14 .10)
Ro. g. 3 (May)
Sire: Distinctive Pro (Mr. Prospector)
Dam: Low Cut (The Axe II)
Br: Vanderbilt Alfred G (NY)
Tr: Eppler Mary E (11 1 1 1 .09)
122

Lifetime Record : 1 M 0 0 $330
1993 1 M 0 0 $330 Turf 0 0 0 0
1992 0 M 0 0 Wet 0 0 0 0
Aqu ⊡ 0 0 0 0 Dist 1 0 0 0 $330

9Dec93-6Lrl fst 1$\frac{1}{16}$ $:23^3$ $:47^2$ $1:13^2$ $1:46^2$ Md Sp Wt 42 8 7 7⁵½ 5¹¼ 6⁹¼ 6¹⁵¼ Pino M G 120 21.80 63-29 Cashel Dancer120⁶¾Battleship Grey120²Double Ridder120¹ Very wide 8

WORKOUTS: ●Feb 22 Pim 4f sly $:48^3$ H 1/9 ●Feb 10 Pim 5f fst 1:02 B 1/6 Feb 5 Pim 4f fst $:48^3$ H 6/22 Jan 11 Pim 4f fst :49 B 2/15 Jan 1 Pim 4f fst $:49^2$ Bg2/5 Dec 24 Pim 5f fst 1:02 H 3/24

Graduate School
Own: Ackerley Bros Farm
CHAVEZ J F (285 51 46 33 .18)
B. c. 3 (May)
Sire: Bates Motel (Sir Ivor)
Dam: Never Wood (Torsion)
Br: Hutson Bruce (Ky)
Tr: Lake Robert P (51 10 6 8 .20)
122

Lifetime Record : 3 M 0 0 $1,380
1994 3 M 0 0 $1,380 Turf 0 0 0 0
1992 0 M 0 0 Wet 1 0 0 0 $1,380
Aqu ⊡ 3 0 0 0 $1,380 Dist 0 0 0 0

15Feb94-5Aqu fst 6f ⊡ $:23^1$ $:46^3$ $:59^1$ $1:12^2$ Md Sp Wt 55 6 3 10⁵ 7⁶¾ 8⁸¾ 6⁷½ Chavez J F 122 b 32.70 74-22 Cosa Diavolo122½Approximate122⁴Showiz122no No threat 11

13Jan94-5Aqu sly 6f ⊡ $:23^4$ $:49^1$ $1:02^2$ $1:16^3$ Md Sp Wt 49 1 4 3²½ 3²½ 4⁶ 4⁸¾ Chavez J F 122 12.00 52-40 Daunting Era122¾Index Fund122⁴Yes And It Counts122³½ No late bid 8

2Jan94-1Aqu fst 6f ⊡ $:23^3$:48 $1:00^3$ $1:13^2$ Md Sp Wt 44 5 5 6⁵½ 5⁹½ 5¹⁴ 6¹⁶¼ Luzzi M J 122 28.40 60-27 Prank Call122¹¾Hawaii Star122¹¹Matthew Red Dog122³ No factor 8

WORKOUTS: Feb 4 Aqu ⊡ 4f fst $:51^1$ B 5/7 Jan 31 Aqu ⊡ 6f fst 1:20 B 2/3 Dec 29 Aqu ⊡ 4f fst :50 Hg5/12 Dec 24 Aqu ⊡ 6f fst $1:19^3$ B 7/8 Dec 18 Aqu ⊡ 6f fst $1:17^3$ Bg3/4 Dec 8 Aqu ⊡ 5f fst $1:02^4$ B 6/9

Telly's Kris
Own: La Croix David
LUZZI M J (200 31 19 17 .16)

B. c. 3 (Apr)
Sire: Kris S. (Roberto)
Dam: Telferner (Tell)
Br: Meadowbrook Farms, Inc. (Fla)
Tr: Barbara Robert (42 3 6 5 .07)

122

Lifetime Record:	6 M 1 0	$10,240		
1994	2 M 1 0	$7,000	Turf	0 0 0 0
1993	4 M 0 0	$3,240	Wet	0 0 0 0
Aqu ⊡	4 0 1 0	$8,620	Dist	4 0 1 0 $8,620

4Feb94- 5Aqu fst 170 ⊡	:243	:483	1:131	1:442	Md Sp Wt	68	8	4	3nk	33	42½	46¾	Luzzi M J	122 b	3.70	69-29	Don Called117¾ Long Lane1222½ Hawaii Star122¾	Tiring, steadied	9
9Jan94- 3Aqu fst 170 ⊡	:234	:48	1:13	1:441	Md Sp Wt	72	1	5	42¾	43	22½	2nk	Luzzi M J	122 b	19.80	77-20	Final Clearance122nk Telly's Kris1225½ Don Called1171	Best of rest	7
30Dec93- 3Aqu fst 1 1/16 ⊡	:233	:482	1:144	1:50	Md Sp Wt	49	9	2	21	3½	58½	514½	Chavez J F	118 b	15.00	40-37	Concoctor1181 Final Clearance1182 Smartweed1185	Tired	10
18Dec93- 3Aqu fst 170 ⊡	:241	:482	1:14	1:444	Md Sp Wt	60	5	6	64¾	63	48	410	Chavez J F	118	7.20	68-22	Happy Fella1187½ Private Cody1181½ P P Prospect1181¼	Flattened out	10
13Nov93- 3Aqu fst 1 ⊗	:234	:472	1:124	1:392	Md Sp Wt	49	7	5	53½	53	57	47	Velazquez J R	118	10.80	60-27	Mcdee1186¼ Orpheum118hd Kerkorian118¾	Lacked rally	10
4Nov93- 5Aqu fst 7f	:23	:461	1:113	1:244	Md Sp Wt	54	8	1	54½	54½	58	512¾	Velazquez J R	118	17.20	67-17	I'm Very Irish1181½ Plutonius1188 Signal Tap118½	No factor	8

WORKOUTS: Jan 31 Bel tr.t 4f fst :522 B 62/84 Dec 2 Bel tr.t 4f fst :50 B 17/41

Top All Figure
Own: Jakubovitz Jerome R
LEON F (231 33 34 28 .14)

Ch. g. 3 (Mar)
Sire: Top Figure (Atlas)
Dam: All England (St. Chad)
Br: Hammond Mrs M S (Va)
Tr: Clement Linda (2 0 0 0 .00)

122

Lifetime Record:	2 M 0 0	$201		
1994	2 M 0 0	$201	Turf	0 0 0 0
1993	0 M 0 0		Wet	0 0 0 0
Aqu ⊡	0 0 0 0		Dist	0 0 0 0

6Feb94- 1Pen fst 5½f	:222	:464	:592	1:06	Md Sp Wt	10	3	10	910	810	67½	514	McMahon W G	120	41.00	74-20	Icanttakesnomore1202½ Am A Pal1202¾ Nineteen Footer1207½	Outrun	10
3Jan94- 3Pha fst 5½f	:223	:462	:593	1:061	Md 17500	8	8	11	1117	1121	1124	916¼	Colton R E	122 b	79.20	69-19	Hat And Shoes1222 Red Light Pappa1221½ Winter Camp1223¼	Off slow	11

WORKOUTS: Feb 3 Pen 4f fst :513 B 17/25 Dec 29 Pen 4f fst :511 Bg21/43 Dec 17 Pen 5f fst 1:053 Bg6/6 Nov 27 Pen 5f fst 1:052 B (d) 17/20

Tenochtitlan
Own: Cohn Seymour
SINDAB P JR (7 0 1 1 .00)

Dk. b or br c. 3 (Apr)
Sire: Conquistador Cielo (Mr. Prospector)
Dam: Alexandra My Love (Danzig)
Br: Dennis Gray (Ky)
Tr: Terrill William V (58 3 5 7 .05)

117[5]

Lifetime Record:	2 M 0 0	$1,380		
1994	2 M 0 0	$1,380	Turf	0 0 0 0
1993	0 M 0 0		Wet	0 0 0 0
Aqu ⊡	2 0 0 0	$1,380	Dist	0 0 0 0

15Feb94- 5Aqu fst 6f ⊡	:231	:463	:591	1:122	Md Sp Wt	48	9	4	31	43¾	75¾	810	Carr D	122 b	18.50	71-22	Cosa Diavolo122½ Approximate1224 Showiz122no	Tired	11
4Feb94- 7Aqu fst 6f ⊡	:223	:462	:592	1:123	Md Sp Wt	58	8	6	66½	75½	75¾	46½	Carr D	122	37.50	74-21	Hi Jinxer1224 Lulu's Little Boy1221½ Copper Mount122¾	No threat	10

WORKOUTS: Feb 21 Bel tr.t 4f fst :511 B 14/19 Feb 1 Bel tr.t 5f fst 1:032 B 12/20 ●Jan 21 Bel tr.t 4f fst :51 B 1/13 Jan 11 Bel tr.t 4f fst :501 B 27/57 Jan 3 Bel tr.t 4f fst :512 B 27/44 Dec 18 Bel tr.t 4f fst :51 B 65/130

The fifth race at Aqueduct on February 24, 1994, lured just six three-year-old maidens after scratches. Telly's Kris was the 11–10 favorite on the basis of his last two starts, in which he had earned the best Beyer figures by a fairly wide margin. Among the four stretching to a route for the first time was Graduate School, who had improved slightly each time out, running figures of 44, 49, and 55 in three sprints. This race was to be contested in the slop, and besides the fact that he was the only entrant with experience under such conditions, *Maiden Stats* revealed good percentages on off-tracks from both his sire and dam.

Most important, Graduate School's sire, Bates Motel, showed a high AWD of 7.4, and Graduate School was also listed as being a full brother to $732,000-earner Private School. Even if a handicapper didn't remember that Private School had won the nine-furlong Ohio Derby (and several other route stakes) as a three-year-old, merely noting his career earnings would serve to indicate an accomplished router; sprinters don't generally earn that kind of money unless they're on the order of a Groovy or a Safely Kept.

GRACES MEMORY	51/ 83	15/ 29	15	6.5	13/ 172	0/ 10	0	0.43	ur	0.10	7	1/ 4	0	0/ 2	6.0	10/ 20	0/ 0	0.00	+Apple Swift	/$ 32k			
GRACE TWEEDIE	9/ 25	7/ 21	0	6.2	18/ 17	0/ 1	0	0.69	sw	0.87	7	4/ 4	0	1/ 2	6.9	0/ 3	0/ 1	2.73	Great Karroo	/$ 32k			
GRACIE'S DANCE	3/ 6	3/ 6	33	5.6	0/ 2	0/ 0	0	1.32	sp	0.60	4	1/ 2	0	1/ 1	5.8	0/ 2	0/ 0	4.71	Cruise Dancer	/$ 13k	$ 2.0k/$ 9.3k	5/ 5	2.0k
GRACIE'S LIPS	144/ 179	59/ 120	13	6.6	14/ 491	11/ 239	5	1.08	w	0.33	8	4/ 5	0	0/ 2	5.8	8/ 26	0/ 0	11.00	Burr Tee Bee	/$ 48k	$ 1.5k/$ 4.6k	8/ 8	1.0k
GRACIEUSE	203/ 273	83/ 165	11	8.2	7/ 57	18/ 1089	18	9.89	ur	9.97	8	4/ 6	2	2/ 3	9.0	0/ 0	3/ 3	1.90	Oczy Czarnie	/$198k			
GRACIOUS GRANNY	16/ 36	13/ 27	7	6.4	20/ 15	0/ 5	0	1.77	sp	0.00	2	0/ 1	0	0/ 1	0.0	0/ 0	0/ 0	3.00					
GRACIOUS MELANIE	16/ 26	2/ 7	0	6.2	12/ 60	0/ 0	0	0.16	ur	0.00	10	0/ 1	0	0/ 1	0.0	0/ 0	0/ 0	19.00					
GRADEPOINT	48/ 86	11/ 44	4	7.3	10/ 116	2/ 65	0	0.62	ur	1.10	3	1/ 1	0	0/ 1	6.5	0/ 3	0/ 1	2.73	Sweet Seattle Miss	/$ 37k			
GRADUATE SCHOOL	134/ 177	28/ 101	7	7.4	17/ 409	9/ 425	5	2.01	sw	3.90	8	5/ 6	1	1/ 3	6.8	26/ 19	0/ 2	6.00	+Private School	/$732k	$ 28k/$ 23k	5/ 16	10k

FIFTH RACE **1 MILE 70 YARDS. (Inner Dirt)(1.39^3) MAIDEN SPECIAL WEIGHT. Purse $25,000. 3-year-olds. Weight, 122 lbs.**

Aqueduct

FEBRUARY 24, 1994

Value of Race: $25,000 Winner $15,000; second $5,500; third $3,000; fourth $1,500. Mutuel Pool $84,372.00 Exacta Pool $183,093.00

Last Raced	Horse	M/Eqt.	A.	Wt	PP	St	¼	½	¾	Str	Fin	Jockey	Odds $1
15Feb94 ^{5}Aqu^6	Graduate School	b	3	122	3	4	2^1	2^1	1^1	$1^{1\frac{1}{2}}$	$1^{1\frac{1}{2}}$	Chavez J F	6.20
9Dec93 ^{6}Lrl^6	Gash	b	3	122	2	2	4^5	$4^{1\frac{1}{2}}$	$3^{\frac{1}{2}}$	$2^{\frac{1}{2}}$	$2^{1\frac{3}{4}}$	Prado E S	3.10
15Feb94 ^{5}Aqu^8	Tenochtitlan	b	3	117	6	5	5^1	5^8	5^4	4^6	$3^{\frac{1}{2}}$	Sindab P Jr^5	4.50
4Feb94 ^{5}Aqu^4	Telly's Kris	b	3	122	4	3	3^1	3^1	$2^{\frac{1}{2}}$	$3^{1\frac{1}{2}}$	4^8	Luzzi M J	1.10
6Feb94 ^{1}Pen^5	Top All Figure		3	122	5	6	6	6	6	5^1	5^6	Leon F	30.50
15Feb94 ^{5}Aqu^9	Javavoom		3	122	1	1	1^{hd}	1^{hd}	$4^{\frac{1}{2}}$	6	6	Davis R G	5.70

OFF AT 1:58 Start Good. Won driving. Time, :23^4, :47^3, 1:13, 1:39^4, 1:44 Track sloppy.

$2 Mutuel Prices:			
4–(D)–GRADUATE SCHOOL	14.40	4.60	3.00
3–(C)–GASH		4.40	3.00
7–(G)–TENOCHTITLAN			3.80

$2 EXACTA 4–3 PAID $49.00

B. c, (May), by Bates Motel–Never Wood, by Torsion. Trainer Lake Robert P. Bred by Hutson Bruce (Ky).

GRADUATE SCHOOL dueled outside JAVAVOOM for a half, opened a clear advantage on the turn, dug in when threatened in upper stretch and held sway under brisk urging. GASH steadied between horses nearing the backstretch, was rated just behind the leaders for five furlongs, steadied while attempting to launch his bid along the inside on the turn, raced in tight along the rail in upper stretch then finished well from outside to best the others. TENOCHTITLAN was strung out six wide on the first turn, dropped back approaching the backstretch, was unhurried for five furlongs, gradually worked his way forward from outside on the turn then closed late to gain a share. TELLY'S KRIS forced the pace while four wide to the turn and tired. TOP ALL FIGURE was never a factor. JAVAVOOM set the pace under pressure to the far turn and gave way. A claim of foul lodged by the rider of GASH against the winner for interference nearing the quarter pole was disallowed. GRADUATE SCHOOL, TENOCHTITLAN and JAVAVOOM wore mud caulks.

Owners— 1, Ackerley Bros Farm; 2, Vanderbilt Alfred G; 3, Cohn Seymour; 4, La Croix David; 5, Jakubovitz Jerome R; 6, Meyers Gerald J

Trainers—1, Lake Robert P; 2, Eppler Mary E; 3, Terrill William V; 4, Barbara Robert; 5, Clement Linda; 6, Schosberg Richard

Scratched— Triple Fast (3Feb94 ^{7}AQU^5)

Graduate School didn't need to improve much at all to beat four of his rivals. If he did improve, as his pedigree suggested was likely, his only rival was the favored Telly's Kris. Anytime a candidate for improvement with only one serious rival is 6–1, feel free to get involved — especially when the race is in the slop and your 6–1 shot has been equipped with mud calks after having previously raced without them in the slop.

THREE

PACE AND TRACK BIAS

FOR INTERPRETING PAST RESULTS and projecting scenarios for upcoming races, few handicapping factors are as potentially enlightening as pace. If final-time speed figures are measurements of how fast horses have run, then pace figures are measurements of *how horses have run fast.* In other words, students of pace are concerned with how a horse has rationed its energy during the early, middle, and final stages of a race.

Some ways of using available energy are more efficient than others. For example, let's say you're going out for a one-mile run, and you want to run your absolute best time for the distance. How would you do it? There are three options: sprint out at top speed right from the start, in an attempt to go as fast as possible for as far as possible; merely jog the first three-quarters of a mile while conserving energy for an all-out sprint in the final quarter; or run the entire distance at a moderately demanding rate of speed.

The all-out sprint method will find you gasping for breath before a quarter-mile has been completed, and you will probably end up finishing the mile on your hands and knees. By jogging slowly most of the way and sprinting the last part, you will have plenty of energy left at the finish, but it will have taken you quite a long time to get there. The third option is by far the most efficient. By rationing energy at an even rate of speed, you will arrive at the finish in the fastest time possible; you'll be dog-tired, but that's because you will have finished with nothing held back in reserve. After all, there's no sense finishing a race with gas still left in the tank; if you do, you haven't run to your peak potential.

Basically, this is what pace is all about. Some races develop as in our first scenario, with everyone going hell-bent-for-leather right from the bell and finishing "on fumes." Others feature an even pace, with several quarter-mile segments run in roughly the same time. Still others feature exceptionally slow early segments and an all-out sprint to the finish line.

When analyzing how a race is likely to develop, handicappers need to evaluate the contenders in terms of who will be leading early, who will be running in midpack, and who will be rallying in the stretch. To do this, it is necessary to evaluate each contender's fractional times and corresponding beaten lengths from races run under conditions similar to today's.

PITFALLS

Unfortunately, those players of a mind to use sophisticated pace ratings are bound to encounter numerous difficulties in their practical application.

To begin with, the beaten lengths at each point of call as published in the past performances are not scientifically measured; they are merely the best estimate of a *DRF* trackman, who frenetically rattles off margins to his assistant as the field is in full flight; the horses are often tightly bunched and may be constantly changing their positions, so that by the time the trackman gets to the rear members of the field, they may have gained or lost considerable ground from the time when the first margin was called.

Plus, beaten lengths become increasingly ambiguous the farther back in the field one ventures, as no two trackmen call margins in exactly the same way. One trackman might call a third-place finisher in a typical six-furlong sprint this way:

9	8	5	2
10	8	5	3

While another trackman might call the same horse this way:

11	7	4	2
10	7	4	3

It should be readily apparent that handicappers attempting to analyze internal fractions would get a much different picture from these accounts. Both calls are roughly the same, giving a similar overall impression of a rallying third-place finish. But in the first instance, the horse is credited with a one-length gain in the second fraction and a three-length gain to the stretch call, whereas in the second instance, the same horse has gained four lengths in the second fraction and three more lengths to the stretch call.

Moreover, both calls may be absolutely correct — the discrepancy may occur because one trackman commenced his call a split second sooner or later than the other!

Since races are not run in a vacuum, the effects of wind can blow fractional times out of whack. A tailwind down the backstretch will make the opening quarter of a sprint appear much faster than it actually was, and vice versa.

Wonder Carr and Midnight Sunny appeared to be the two primary early-pace horses in a claiming sprint at Belmont on May 10. They had never met before. Which one figured to win the early duel?

Wonder Carr
Own: Hagedorn Charles G
LOVATO F JR (9 0 0 0 .00) $12,000
B. g. 5
Sire: Carr de Naskra (Star de Naskra)
Dam: Heaven Knows (Quadrangle)
Br: Payson Virginia Kraft (NY)
Tr: Hushion Michael E (6 0 1 2 .00)
113

Lifetime Record: 21 5 8 1 $30,732					
1994	3 0 2 0	$4,180	Turf	1 0 0 0	
1993	13 3 5 1	$26,612	Wet	4 1 3 0	$10,320
Bel	0 0 0 0		Dist	0 0 0 0	

22Apr94- 1Aqu	fst	6f	:22^3 :46^2 :59 1:12	Clm 10000	77 4 2 2^{hd} 2^{hd} 1^{hd} 1^{nk}	Lovato F Jr	117 fb *1.60	82-17	[D]Wonder Carr117^{nk} Bens Brother Frank113¾ Tricky Catman110^2		7
Drifted in 3/16 pl, lost whip 1/16 pl Disqualified and placed second											
14Apr94- 2Aqu	my	6f	:21^4 :45^3 :58^3 1:11^3	Clm 12500	73 4 3 41½ 2^1 2^{hd} 2^2	Lovato F Jr	117 fb 3.20	82-14	ComingFast117^2 WonderCarr117^3 NumberedAccord113^1	Bid, weakened	5
30Jan94- 7Aqu	gd	6f	[•] :22^4 :45^4 :58 1:10^3	Clm 10000	77 8 3 4^1 41½ 5^4 55½	Prado E S	117 b *2.00	84-10	Case Study1171½ Mcpine1081¾ Tony Blue1122½	Wide, tired	9
15Dec93- 1Aqu	my	6f	[•] :23 :46^2 :58^4 1:12 3↑	Clm 14000	75 1 8 44½ 32½ 33½ 23½	Velazquez J R	117 b *1.80	79-21	Nowhere Man1173½ Wonder Carr117^{nk} Red Hot Red117^7	Rail trip	8
9Dec93- 1Aqu	fst	6f	[•] :23^1 :46^3 :59 1:12^1 3↑	Clm 12500	75 5 5 3^1 1^{hd} 1^{hd} 2^{nk}	Graell A	117 b *.90	82-17	Numbered Accord108^{nk} Wonder Carr117½ Premier Flag113^4	Gamely	7
8Nov93- 1Aqu	fst	6f	:22^1 :45^2 :57^4 1:11^1 3↑	Clm c-25000	72 3 6 41½ 52½ 5^6 6^8	Nicol P A Jr	119 fb 11.80	77-22	TropicalIllusion1171½ NorthernCrush1191¾ Metternich113^5	Bumped break	6
Claimed from Payson Virginia Kraft, Bond Harold James Trainer											
23Oct93- 8FL	fst	6f	:22^4 :46 :59^4 1:12^3 3↑	Clm 20000	81 4 1 1^{hd} 2^{hd} 1^{hd} 2^{hd}	Nicol P A Jr	122 fb *1.20	83-22	Minstrel Pip112^{hd} Wonder Carr1221¾ Snake Creeps Down117½	Gamely	7
3Oct93- 8FL	gd	5½f	:22^1 :45^4 :58^4 1:05 3↑	[S]Alw 11400N2	79 5 2 1^{hd} 1½ 1^2 14½	Nicol P A Jr	122 fb *1.00	90-17	Wonder Carr1224½ Doctor E116^3 Del Rio118^{hd}	Ridden out	7
24Sep93- 7FL	gd	6f	:22^3 :45^4 :58^1 1:11 3↑	[S]Alw 10100N1	87 3 1 2^{hd} 2^{hd} 1^4 1^5	Nicol P A Jr	122 fb 3.80	91-18	Wonder Carr122^5 Priceless Peanut116^2 Zig Off115^3	Ridden out	6
18Sep93- 9FL	fst	5½f	:22^3 :45^4 :59^2 1:05^4 3↑	Alw 6400N3L	71 6 4 22½ 2^2 1^{hd} 1^{hd}	Nicol P A Jr	116 fb *.50	86-20	WonderCarr116^{hd} Timeswereygood116¾ Turk'sHero114^4	Steadied 5/8 pole	7

WORKOUTS: Apr 10 Bel tr.t 4f fst :52 B 45/48 Apr 5 Bel tr.t 4f fst :49^1 B 18/26

Midnight Sunny
Own: Wazup Stable
SANTAGATA N (18 1 3 3 .06) $14,000
Ch. g. 6
Sire: Sunny North (Northern Dancer)
Dam: Glorious Evening (Jig Time)
Br: Big C Farms (Fla)
Tr: Figueroa Carlos R Jr (1 0 1 0 .00)
117

Lifetime Record: 57 14 10 5 $172,907					
1994	6 3 0 1	$26,340	Turf	6 1 0 0	$14,190
1993	20 5 2 1	$59,570	Wet	6 2 3 0	$27,530
Bel	7 1 2 1	$17,980	Dist	4 1 0 0	$10,110

29Apr94- 1Aqu	fst	6f	:22^3 :46 :58^1 1:10^3	Clm 17500	81 4 1 1^1 2½ 3^1 43½	Santagata N	119 fb 4.70	85-11	Revolt117^{nk} Out For Gold1131½ Mr. Miami117^2	Speed, tired	5
9Apr94- 1Aqu	fst	6f	:22^1 :45^2 :57^3 1:10^1	Clm 17500	92 2 2 1½ 1^{hd} 2^{hd} 1no	Velazquez J R	119 fb 3.40	91-13	Midnight Sunny119^{no} Kakarapis1175½ Alex's Candy112^2	Came again	6
11Mar94- 2Aqu	gd	6f	[•] :23^2 :46^3 :58^3 1:10^4	Clm 22500	71 4 1 2^1 23½ 35½ 48¾	Velazquez J R	115 fb 2.30	80-17	Nowhere Man117^5 Baypark1153½ Jessup North117^{nk}	Forced pace, tired	6
2Mar94- 3Aqu	fst	6f	[•] :23^2 :46^2 :58^3 1:11^2	Clm 17500	85 5 1 1½ 2^1 2^1 1no	Velazquez J R	117 fb 2.70	86-20	Midnight Sunny117^{no} Alex's Candy1121¾ Maraud117^2	Drifted, driving	7
4Feb94- 3Aqu	fst	6f	[•] :22^3 :46^4 :58^4 1:12^1	Clm c-12500	81 1 4 2^{hd} 1^{hd} 1½ 11¾	Chavez J F	117 fb *.80	82-21	Midnight Sunny1171¾ Red Hot Red117^{nk} Brucon117^1	Driving	10
Claimed from Riccio James A, Parisella John Trainer											
1Feb94- 7Aqu	fst	6f	[•] :22^4 :46^4 :59^2 1:12^1	Clm 17500	81 2 1 2½ 2^{hd} 1^{hd} 31¾	Leon F^5	112 fb *1.40	80-19	ExplodngRnbow1191½ Strwmn117½ MdnghtSunny112^{no}	Dueled, weakened	10
29Dec93- 1Aqu	fst	6f	[•] :23^3 :47^2 :59^2 1:12^1 3↑	Clm c-12500	88 7 1 11½ 14½ 1^6 1^6	Migliore R	117 fb *.50	82-22	Midnight Sunny117^6 Prioritizer1124½ Espiocrat1087½	Driving	7
Claimed from Wazup Stable, Figueroa Carlos R Jr Trainer											
16Dec93- 9Aqu	fst	6f	[•] :22^3 :46^3 :59^2 1:12^3 3↑	Clm 17500	78 8 2 4^2 5^3 54½ 43½	Migliore R	117 fb 5.40	76-22	Mr. Miami1151½ Strawman117^2 Brucon115^{nk}	Wide	8
2Dec93- 4Aqu	fst	6f	[•] :22^2 :45^3 :58 1:10^3 3↑	Clm 22500	77 4 2 3½ 1^{hd} 22½ 46½	Velazquez J R	115 fb 19.20	84-17	True Dutch1151¾ Runaway Storm117^3 Le Risky1171½	Dueled, tired	7
24Nov93- 7Aqu	fst	6f	:22^2 :46 1:11^2 3↑	Alw 30000N2X	57 4 2 5^5 6^7 69¾ 613½	Migliore R	117 fb 12.50	71-20	Richmond Runner120^3 Lukie's Pop115^1 Line Pro120½	No factor	7

WORKOUTS: Apr 25 Aqu 4f fst :53^4 B 6/6 Apr 2 Aqu 3f fst :38^2 B 8/9

Based on their most recent races over Aqueduct's main track, one might give Midnight Sunny the early edge. But Midnight Sunny had raced with the benefit of a tailwind on the far turn April 29, and his swift fractions of April 9 had also been enhanced by a strong tailwind down the backstretch.

On the other hand, Wonder Carr had raced into a strong *headwind* down the backstretch on April 22, which had slowed things down considerably.

FOURTH RACE
Belmont
MAY 10, 1994

6½ FURLONGS. (1.14^{3}) CLAIMING. Purse $12,000. 4-year-olds and upward. Weight, 122 lbs. Non-winners of two races since April 15, allowed 3 lbs. Of a race since then, 5 lbs. Claiming price $14,000, for each $1,000 to $12,000, allowed 2 lbs. (Races when entered to be claimed for $10,000 or less not considered.)

Value of Race: $12,000 Winner $7,200; second $2,640; third $1,440; fourth $720. Mutuel Pool $190,343.00 Exacta Pool $339,292.00 Quinella Pool $101,405.00

Last Raced	Horse	M/Eqt.	A.	Wt	PP	St	¼	½	Str	Fin	Jockey	Cl'g Pr	Odds $1
22Apr94 ^{1}Aqu^{1}	Wonder Carr	bf	5	113	2	3	$2^{1\frac{1}{2}}$	$1^{\frac{1}{2}}$	1^{8}	1^{11}	Lovato F Jr	12000	11.70
23Dec93 ^{1}Aqu^{2}	Jocovitch	bf	5	113	3	12	8^{1}	7^{1}	2^{hd}	$2^{\frac{1}{2}}$	Davis R G	12000	6.70
30Apr94 ^{1}Aqu^{7}	Eastern Brave	bf	5	113	4	13	$10^{3\frac{1}{2}}$	10^{6}	7^{1}	3^{nk}	Mojica R Jr	12000	12.60
24Apr94 ^{2}Aqu^{5}	Numbered Accord	b	9	106	6	2	5^{2}	$5^{\frac{1}{2}}$	$4^{1\frac{1}{2}}$	4^{1}	Beckner D V^{7}	12000	18.40
9Apr94 ^{1}Aqu^{6}	True Dutch		5	117	8	6	$7^{1\frac{1}{2}}$	$8^{1\frac{1}{2}}$	$6^{\frac{1}{2}}$	$5^{2\frac{1}{4}}$	Alvarado F T	14000	13.50
29Apr94 ^{1}Aqu^{4}	Midnight Sunny	bf	6	117	10	4	4^{hd}	$4^{1\frac{1}{2}}$	5^{1}	$6^{1\frac{1}{4}}$	Santagata N	14000	2.60
10Apr94 ^{3}Aqu^{5}	Be Loyal	b	4	117	12	11	13	12^{2}	$10^{\frac{1}{2}}$	7^{1}	Samyn J L	14000	5.20
6Jan94 ^{1}Aqu^{6}	Aarons Classi Boy	b	4	113	13	10	12^{2}	11^{1}	$9^{\frac{1}{2}}$	8^{nk}	Frost G C	12000	77.90
17Apr94 ^{9}Aqu^{9}	Mr Sledge	b	4	110	1	5	3^{hd}	$3^{\frac{1}{2}}$	$3^{\frac{1}{2}}$	$9^{1\frac{1}{2}}$	Sindab P Jr^{7}	14000	10.20
27Apr94 ^{4}Aqu^{6}	Loud Brother	b	4	117	11	7	6^{1}	6^{1}	8^{1}	10no	Maple E	14000	11.20
21Nov93 ^{7}CD^{5}	Stayed Too Long	bf	6	110	9	8	9^{5}	9^{hd}	11^{1}	11^{9}	Mickens T J^{7}	14000	89.70
16Jly93 ^{2}Bel^{4}	Appreciate It	bf	5	112	7	1	1^{hd}	$2^{1\frac{1}{2}}$	12^{7}	$12^{2\frac{1}{2}}$	Luttrell M G^{5}	14000	4.90
4Feb94 ^{1}Aqu^{9}	Time For The Bird	bf	4	117	5	9	11^{1}	13	13	13	Heredia J J	14000	112.20

OFF AT 2:27 Start Good. Won driving. Time, :22^{3}, :45^{3}, 1:09^{4}, 1:16^{2} Track fast.

$2 Mutuel Prices:

2-(B)-WONDER CARR	25.40	11.40	7.20
3-(C)-JOCOVITCH		7.80	4.20
4-(D)-EASTERN BRAVE			8.40

$2 EXACTA 2-3 PAID $109.00 $2 QUINELLA 2-3 PAID $59.40

B. g, by Carr de Naskra–Heaven Knows, by Quadrangle. Trainer Hushion Michael E. Bred by Payson Virginia Kraft (NY).

WONDER CARR dueled along the rail for a half, shook off APPRECIATE IT leaving the turn, opened a wide gap in upper stretch then steadily increased his margin under intermittent urging. JOCOVITCH reserved for a half, finished willingly between horses to gain the place. EASTERN BRAVE outrun for a half after breaking slowly, circled five wide into the stretch then rallied belatedly in the middle of the track. NUMBERED ACCORD raced within striking distance between horses to the turn and lacked a strong closing bid. TRUE DUTCH was never a serious threat. MIDNIGHT SUNNY raced just behind the leaders from outside to the top of the stretch and lacked the needed response when called upon. BE LOYAL was never close while racing wide. AARONS CLASSI BOY never reached contention. MR SLEDGE raced up close while saving ground to the top of the stretch and gave way. LOUD BROTHER raced wide and tired. STAYED TOO LONG was outrun, as was TIME FOR THE BIRD. APPRECIATE IT was used up dueling for the early lead.

Owners— 1, Hagedorn Charles G; 2, Larkin Donald R; 3, Perroncino John S; 4, Aquilino Joseph; 5, Joques Farm; 6, Wazup Stable; 7, Hackel Kenneth S; 8, Boyan Thomas C; 9, Schifrin Lois D; 10, Fox Ridge Farm; 11, Jujugen Stable; 12, Ferriola Ingrid A; 13, Harnarain Jagatnarain

Trainers—1, Hushion Michael E; 2, Kelly Michael J; 3, Terracciano Neal; 4, Aquilino Joseph; 5, Moschera Gasper S; 6, Figueroa Carlos R Jr; 7, Lenzini John J Jr; 8, Galluscio Dominic G; 9, Shapoff Stanley R; 10, Kelly Patrick J; 11, Carroll Henry L; 12, Ferriola Peter; 13, Harnarain Jagatnarain

Scratched— Freeze Dry (4May94 ^{1}BEL^{5}), Tricky Catman (22Apr94 ^{1}AQU^{3})

Wonder Carr outsprinted Midnight Sunny in the opening stages and went on to a convincing win.

Fractional times at Aqueduct are particularly susceptible to the effects of wind. The track sits just a stone's throw from Jamaica Bay as well as John F. Kennedy International Airport, so there are no tall structures anywhere close by.

"On top of that, Aqueduct is absolutely unique," adds Len Ragozin. "It's the biggest grandstand in the country, and there are certain directions of wind where the grandstand has an airfoil effect, and so these winds are distorted. You can't use these directions for what they are, you've got to change them."

One of the basic tenets of pace handicapping is that slow early fractions favor horses racing on or close to the lead, while a fast, hotly contested pace favors off-the-pace types. This principle can be seen at work in two nine-furlong routes from Aqueduct on November 29:

SECOND RACE
Aqueduct
NOVEMBER 29, 1992

1 1/8 MILES. (1.47) CLAIMING. Purse $20,000. 3-year-olds. Weights, 122 lbs. Non-winners of two races at a mile or over since November 1 allowed 3 lbs. Of such a race since then 5 lbs. Claiming Price $25,000 for each $2,500 to $20,000, 2 lbs. (Races when enterd to be claimed for $18,000 or less not considered).

Value of race $20,000; value to winner $12,000; second $4,400; third $2,400; fourth $1,200. Mutuel pool $167,656. Exacta Pool $332,542 Quinella Pool $106,693

Last Raced	Horse	M/Eqt.	A.Wt	PP	St	¼	½	¾	Str	Fin	Jockey	Cl'g Pr	Odds $1
17Nov92 7Lrl1	Days Dwindle Down	b	3 119	4	3	$3^{1\frac{1}{2}}$	$3^{1\frac{1}{2}}$	$3^{\frac{1}{2}}$	1^{2}	$1^{1\frac{3}{4}}$	Luzzi M J	25000	1.70
22Oct92 1Aqu7	Career Luck		3 113	8	4	5^{hd}	4^{1}	$4^{1\frac{1}{2}}$	$2^{1\frac{1}{2}}$	2^{hd}	Pezua J M	20000	13.70
25Oct92 2Aqu9	Achtung		3 117	7	5	8^{2}	$7^{\frac{1}{2}}$	5^{1}	3^{1}	$3^{\frac{1}{2}}$	Carr D	25000	16.80
23Oct92 6Aqu3	Lead Til Dawn	b	3 117	6	7	9	9	9	4^{2}	4^{7}	McCuleyWH	25000	5.00
11Nov92 4Aqu11	Nake The Snake		3 117	9	9	7^{1}	8^{6}	6^{2}	5^{3}	5^{nk}	Romero R P	25000	15.60
20Nov92 6Aqu5	Except No Equal	b	3 117	2	8	4^{hd}	5^{hd}	8^{2}	7^{4}	$6^{3\frac{1}{2}}$	Smith M E	25000	3.40
6Nov92 6Aqu2	Beulah Hill Road	b	3 117	3	1	2^{hd}	2^{8}	1^{hd}	6^{1}	7^{2}	Madrid A Jr	25000	8.80
8Nov92 1Aqu7	Sunshine Magic		3 112	1	2	1^{hd}	1^{hd}	$2^{1\frac{1}{2}}$	$8^{1\frac{1}{2}}$	$8^{3\frac{1}{2}}$	Bisono C V5	25000	6.40
15Nov92 9Aqu10	Brother Brookfield	b	3 117	5	6	6^{3}	6^{hd}	7^{hd}	9	9	Davis R G	25000	24.60

OFF AT 12:55 Start good Won driving Time, :23², :46², 1:11³, 1:37 , 1:50 Track fast.

$2 Mutuel Prices:			
4-(D)-DAYS DWINDLE DOWN	5.40	4.00	3.40
9-(J)-CAREER LUCK		10.80	6.20
8-(H)-ACHTUNG			6.60

$2 EXACTA 4–9 PAID $70.60 $2 QUINELLA 4–9 PAID $51.80

B. g, (Feb), by Baldski—Nodouble Princess, by Nodouble. Trainer Gaudet Edmond D. Bred by Rosenthal Morton (Fla).

DAYS DWINDLE DOWN, well placed behind the dueling leaders, went after the front two leaving the backstretch, took over near the quarter pole and held sway under urging. CAREER LUCK, three wide early, rallied between foes in the drive and held the place. ACHTUNG swung to the inside entering the stretch, finished willingly. LEAD TIL DAWN made a run into contention from the outside on the far turn and finished willingly while farthest outside. NAKE THE SNAKE was outrun. EXCEPT NO EQUAL saved ground to no avail. BEULAH HILL ROAD engaged for command for over six furlongs and gave way. SUNSHINE MAGIC saved ground while alternating for command and stopped. BROTHER BROOKFIELD raced between foes and faded. CAREER LUCK wore mud caulks.

Owners— 1, Bailey Morris; 2, Atkins S Stephen; 3, Giorgi Vincent Jr; 4, Ritzenberg Milton; 5, Cuminale Richard P; 6, Joques Farm; 7, Pennington Cheryl D; 8, Sunshine Hill Farm; 9, Nixon Robert H A.

Trainers— 1, Gaudet Edmond D; 2, Levine Bruce N; 3, Ortiz Paulino O; 4, Johnstone Bruce; 5, Jensen Kay Erik; 6, Moschera Gasper S; 7, Rice Linda; 8, Ribaudo Robert; 9, Arnold George R II.

Days Dwindle Down was claimed by Hagedorn Charles G; trainer, Moschera Gaspar.

Scratched—With It (26Nov92 9Aqu2); Cost Too Much (25Nov92 3Aqu3).

NINTH RACE
Aqueduct
NOVEMBER 29, 1992

1 ⅛ MILES. (1.47) CLAIMING. Purse $20,000. 3-year-olds and upward. Weights, 3-year-olds 120 lbs. Older 122 lbs. Non-winners of two races at a mile or over since November 1 allowed 3 lbs. Of such a race since then 5 lbs. Claiming Price $25,000 for each $2,500 to $20,000, 2 lbs. (Races when entered to be claimed for $18,000 or less not considered).

Value of race $20,000; value to winner $12,000; second $4,400; third $2,400; fourth $1,200. Mutuel pool $210,519. Exacta Pool $306,108 Triple Pool $518,455

Last Raced	Horse	M/Eqt.	A.Wt	PP	St	¼	½	¾	Str	Fin	Jockey	Cl'g Pr	Odds $1
8Nov92 ^{3}Aqu^{2}	Commander Evander	b	4 117	4	1	$1^{1\frac{1}{2}}$	$1^{2\frac{1}{2}}$	$1^{1\frac{1}{2}}$	$1^{1\frac{1}{2}}$	1^{4}	Velazquez JR	25000	4.40
12Oct92 ^{4}Bel^{3}	Caught Looking	b	4 113	2	2	$6^{\frac{1}{2}}$	5^{hd}	2^{hd}	2^{hd}	$2^{2\frac{1}{2}}$	Santagata N	20000	9.40
9Nov92 ^{2}Aqu^{1}	Leading Star	b	4 113	5	9	9^{2}	9^{4}	8^{hd}	5^{4}	$3^{\frac{1}{2}}$	Rojas R I	20000	9.90
4Oct92 ^{2}Bel^{3}	Cantinero	b	4 117	6	6	4^{hd}	7^{hd}	5^{hd}	4^{1}	4^{1}	Samyn J L	25000	2.90
12Nov92 ^{2}Aqu^{9}	Shomrim Society	b	4 112	10	7	7^{hd}	$6^{\frac{1}{2}}$	$3^{\frac{1}{2}}$	$3^{\frac{1}{2}}$	$5^{5\frac{1}{2}}$	Bisono C V^{5}	25000	24.40
19Nov92 ^{4}Aqu^{6}	Overloaded	b	4 117	9	10	10	10	$9^{\frac{1}{2}}$	$7^{\frac{1}{2}}$	6^{hd}	Madrid A Jr	25000	8.60
1Nov92 ^{2}Aqu^{9}	Clover City	b	4 117	3	8	8^{3}	$8^{1\frac{1}{2}}$	10	$9^{\frac{1}{2}}$	7^{nk}	Carr D	25000	15.60
13Nov92 ^{9}Aqu^{6}	Barron Mohawk	b	4 117	1	3	3^{1}	3^{hd}	6^{hd}	8^{hd}	8^{nk}	Davis R G	25000	7.70
1Nov92 ^{2}Aqu^{5}	Prince Anon	b	5 117	7	5	5^{hd}	4^{hd}	4^{hd}	6^{hd}	9^{nk}	Chavez J F	25000	3.80
13Nov92 ^{1}Aqu^{5}	Nyabardi		5 112	8	4	2^{hd}	2^{hd}	7^{hd}	10	10	Frost G C^{5}	25000	17.10

OFF AT 4:13 Start good, Won driving. Time, :24^{2}, :49 , 1:12^{4}, 1:36^{4}, 1:49^{1} Track fast.

$2 Mutuel Prices:

4-(D)-COMMANDER EVANDER	10.80	5.40	4.80
2-(B)-CAUGHT LOOKING		10.80	8.80
5-(E)-LEADING STAR			6.40

$2 EXACTA 4-2 PAID $91.40 $2 TRIPLE 4-2-5 PAID $598.00

Ch. g, by Top Command—Mom's Mia, by Great Mystery. Trainer Alvarez Luis C. Bred by Fuller Peter (Ky).

COMMANDER EVANDER broke alertly, set all the pace, responded when challenged in midstretch and held sway. CAUGHT LOOKING advanced along the inside on the backstretch, came out to challenge in midstretch, was not able to battle the winner and was best of the others. LEADING STAR rallied belatedly outside. CANTINERO raced within striking distance, lacked a stretch response. SHOMRIM SOCIETY raced wide and tired. OVERLOADED was outrun. CLOVER CITY was no factor. BARRON MOHAWK tired from his early efforts. PRINCE ANON was forwardly placed while wide and gave way leaving the far turn. NYABARDI gave way after half.

Owners— 1, Last State Stable; 2, Ernesto Lee; 3, Conrad V & Giacchimo C; 4, Rory Green Stable; 5, Dee Pee Stable; 6, Clifton William L Jr; 7, Stock Michael L; 8, Clanna Stable; 9, Ran-Dom Stable; 10, Bauer Robert J.

Trainers— 1, Alvarez Luis C; 2, Duquesnay Robert L; 3, Bolton Amos E; 4, Klesaris Robert P; 5, Figueroa Carlos R Jr; 6, Bond Harold James; 7, Terrill William V; 8, Martin Carlos F; 9, Sciacca Gary; 10, Forbes John H.

Scratched—Devil's Fortune (16Oct92 ^{2}Bel^{10}).

Days Dwindle Down benefited from a quintessentially perfect trip, winning the day's second race, as Sunshine Magic and Beulah Hill Road went head-to-head through suicidal fractions of :23⅖, :46⅖, and 1:11⅗. While the battle was raging, Days Dwindle Down was ideally positioned off the duel, racing *in the clear.* At the half, note that he was eight lengths off the duelers while also a length and a half in front of the horse racing in fourth. Not surprisingly, Days Dwindle Down inherited the lead from the exhausted pace setters approaching the stretch and quickly opened up a lead, which he maintained to the wire. Also not surprisingly, he was beaten as the favorite next time out, when raised in class following the claim and unable to get the same kind of perfect circumstances.

In the ninth race, the mile fraction was almost identical to the second race — 1:36⅘ as compared to 1:37 — but the way the field got to that point made Commander Evander's victory foreordained.

Whereas the first route featured a fast and contested pace, Commander Evander had loped along unmolested through dawdling splits of :24⅖, :49, and 1:12⅘.

But even when handicappers are comparing races from the same distance run on the same day, they must proceed with extreme caution lest they be misled by data that apparently defies reality. For example, the data from two races at a mile and a sixteenth on Belmont's inner turf course May 12 seemed to fly in the face of all that pace handicappers hold sacred:

SEVENTH RACE
Belmont
MAY 12, 1994

1$\frac{1}{16}$ MILES. (Inner Turf)(1.39^{1}) ALLOWANCE. Purse $32,000. 3-year-olds and upward, foaled in New York State and approved by the New York State-bred Registry, which have not won two races other than maiden, claiming or starter. Weights: 3-year-olds, 115 lbs. Older, 124 lbs. Non-winners of a race other than claiming at a mile or over since April 15, allowed 3 lbs. Of such a race since April 1, 5 lbs.

Value of Race: $32,000 Winner $19,200; second $7,040; third $3,840; fourth $1,920. Mutuel Pool $195,573.00 Exacta Pool $465,823.00

Last Raced	Horse	M/Eqt.	A.	Wt	PP	St	¼	½	¾	Str	Fin	Jockey	Odds $1
29Apr94 7Aqu1	Alpstein	b	4	119	4	2	$4^{1/2}$	$4^{1/2}$	6^{hd}	$3^{1/2}$	$1^{1\,1/4}$	Migliore R	7.50
10Apr94 3Aqu6	Island Resort		4	119	9	8	3^{2}	2^{hd}	$2^{1/2}$	$2^{1/2}$	2^{hd}	Hernandez R	a-6.70
24Nov93 6Aqu5	Doctor Disaster		5	119	7	6	$1^{1\,1/2}$	$1^{2\,1/2}$	1^{1}	$1^{1/2}$	$3^{1\,1/4}$	Samyn J L	5.20
21Apr94 4Aqu1	Knight Course		4	124	1	1	6^{hd}	$6^{1/2}$	$3^{1/2}$	4^{hd}	$4^{1\,1/4}$	Chavez J F	0.90
27Apr94 1Aqu9	Achtung	bf	5	112	8	10	$9^{1\,1/2}$	$9^{3\,1/2}$	$7^{1/2}$	$5^{2\,1/2}$	$5^{1\,3/4}$	Beckner D V7	31.50
17Apr94 6Aqu2	Personnel Director	b	3	110	3	3	5^{hd}	5^{hd}	5^{hd}	$6^{2\,1/2}$	$6^{1\,1/4}$	Luttrell M G5	6.60
20Apr94 9Aqu7	Pago's Whim	b	5	119	6	9	10	10	10	7^{3}	7^{13}	Mojica R Jr	31.10
4May94 1Bel7	Eyes Ofa Bandit	b	4	119	2	4	$8^{2\,1/2}$	8^{1}	$9^{1\,1/2}$	8^{8}	8^{12}	Velazquez J R	27.70
26Feb94 7GS9	Ojay Smojay		4	119	5	5	7^{2}	7^{2}	$8^{1/2}$	9^{3}	$9^{12\,1/2}$	Olea R E	18.10
13Apr94 6Aqu1	Small Pack	f	4	119	10	7	$2^{1\,1/2}$	$3^{1\,1/2}$	$4^{1/2}$	10	10	Luzzi M J	a-6.70

a-Coupled: Island Resort and Small Pack.

OFF AT 3:58 Start Good. Won driving. Time, :24^{3}, :49^{2}, 1:13^{1}, 1:38^{1}, 1:44^{2} Course firm.

$2 Mutuel Prices:			
5-(D)-ALPSTEIN	17.00	7.20	5.60
1-(I)-ISLAND RESORT (a-entry)		6.00	4.00
8-(G)-DOCTOR DISASTER			4.40

$2 EXACTA 5-1 PAID $80.00

Ch. g, by Raconteur-Cunning Vixen, by Provante. Trainer Destasio Richard A. Bred by Nuesch Felix J (NY).

ALPSTEIN raced in traffic while between horses for five furlongs, dropped back slightly while blocked on the turn, angled between horses to launch his bid in upper stretch then outfinished ISLAND RESORT under brisk urging. ISLAND RESORT checked in the early stages, forced the pace between horses to the turn then finished with good energy for the place. DOCTOR DISASTER set the pace along the inside into midstretch and weakened. KNIGHT COURSE took up between horses in the early stages, angled out on the far turn, made a run to threaten at the top of the stretch then flattened out. ACHTUNG checked at the start, raced well back for five furlongs, made a strong run along the rail to threaten in midstretch but couldn't sustain his bid. PERSONNEL DIRECTOR steadied between horses in the early stages, raced within striking distance to the turn and lacked a further response. PAGO'S WHIM was never a factor. EYES OFA BANDIT never reached contention. SMALL PACK was used up trying to keep the early pace.

Owners— 1, Nuesch Felix J; 2, Denny Mary F; 3, Olson James F; 4, Nedlaw Stable; 5, Giorgi Vincent Jr; 6, Casson Helen G; 7, New Kan Stables; 8, Rosenthal Robert D; 9, Samuels Richard; 10, Sahn Robert I

Trainers—1, Destasio Richard A; 2, Levine Bruce N; 3, Brida Dennis J; 4, Kimmel John C; 5, Ortiz Paulino O; 6, Battles Jake; 7, O'Brien Colum; 8, Schettino Dominick A; 9, Samuels Richard; 10, Levine Bruce N

Scratched— My Mogul (9Oct93 5BEL4), Presence (24Apr94 2AQU6), Clover City (3May94 9BEL5), Similar Star (30Mar94 5AQU7), Cinco Rey (3May94 9BEL4), Memories Of Linda (24Apr94 8AQU2), Planetary Circle (1May94 2AQU3), Tunbridge Wells (3May94 9BEL2), Crafty Investment (20Apr94 1AQU8), Watrals Sea Trip (13Nov93 3AQU9)

FOURTH RACE
Belmont
MAY 12, 1994

1$\frac{1}{16}$ MILES. (Inner Turf)(1.39^{1}) CLAIMING. Purse $30,000. 4-year-olds and upward. Weight, 122 lbs. Non-winners of two races at a mile or over since April 1, allowed 3 lbs. Of such a race since then, 5 lbs. Claiming price $75,000, for each $2,500 to $70,000, allowed 2 lbs. (Races when entered to be claimed for $65,000 or less not considered.)

Value of Race: $30,000 Winner $18,000; second $6,600; third $3,600; fourth $1,800. Mutuel Pool $216,352.00 Exacta Pool $357,556.00 Quinella Pool $95,396.00

Last Raced	Horse	M/Eqt.	A.	Wt	PP	St	¼	½	¾	Str	Fin	Jockey	Cl'g Pr	Odds $1
8Apr94 ^{10}Hia^{1}	Royal Ninja		8	119	2	5	9	8$^{\frac{1}{2}}$	7$^{\frac{1}{2}}$	4$^{\frac{1}{2}}$	1^{nk}	Bailey J D	75000	7.70
15Mar94 ^{10}GP^{3}	Scannapieco	b	4	117	1	4	7^{1}	6^{1}	4$^{\frac{1}{2}}$	1^{hd}	2$^{2\frac{3}{4}}$	Santos J A	75000	4.00
5May94 ^{4}Bel^{4}	So Sterling	b	7	113	6	6	5^{3}	4^{2}	3^{1}	2^{hd}	3^{2}	McCauley W H	70000	7.90
5May94 ^{4}Bel^{2}	Cranshaw's Corner	bf	6	113	3	1	6^{hd}	7$^{1\frac{1}{2}}$	5^{1}	6^{3}	4$^{\frac{1}{2}}$	Smith M E	70000	3.20
21Apr94 ^{8}Aqu^{6}	Known Ranger-GB		8	114	5	2	4$^{\frac{1}{2}}$	2^{1}	2$^{1\frac{1}{2}}$	3^{1}	5^{5}	Migliore R	70000	2.40
23Apr94 ^{8}Aqu^{1}	Rohwer	f	4	108	8	7	2^{1}	3$^{\frac{1}{2}}$	6^{1}	7^{1}	6^{1}	Beckner D V^{7}	70000	a-15.30
24Mar94 ^{7}FG^{1}	Black Question	bf	5	113	4	8	8^{1}	9	8^{3}	8^{8}	7$^{\frac{3}{4}}$	Davis R G	70000	5.70
27Feb94 ^{10}GP^{5}	Best Selection		4	113	7	3	1$^{\frac{1}{2}}$	1^{2}	1^{1}	5$^{\frac{1}{2}}$	8^{9}	Velazquez J R	70000	22.00
1May94 ^{4}Aqu^{10}	Punchpasser	bf	6	106	9	9	3^{1}	5^{hd}	9	9	9	Mickens T J^{7}	70000	a-15.30

a-Coupled: Rohwer and Punchpasser.

OFF AT 2:29 Start Good. Won driving. Time, :25, :49^{1}, 1:13^{1}, 1:37^{2}, 1:43^{3} Course firm.

$2 Mutuel Prices:			
3-(B)-ROYAL NINJA	17.40	8.00	4.20
2-(A)-SCANNAPIECO		5.80	4.80
7-(G)-SO STERLING			4.80

$2 EXACTA 3-2 PAID $85.80 $2 QUINELLA 2-3 PAID $34.60

Ch. g, by Aly North–Royal Contessa, by Royal Union. Trainer Serpe Philip M. Bred by Kohr Mrs E D Jr (Fla).

ROYAL NINJA unhurried early, gradually gained while saving ground on the turn, altered course to the outside in upper stretch then finished strongly in the middle of the track to get up in the final strides. SCANNAPIECO reserved for a half while saving ground, rallied between horses on the turn, surged to the front in midstretch, continued on the lead into deep stretch but couldn't hold the winner safe. SO STERLING rated just behind the leaders while saving ground for six furlongs, made a run along the rail to challenge in midstretch but couldn't sustain his bid. CRANSHAW'S CORNER under a snug hold early, steadily gained from outside to reach contentoin on the turn then lacked a strong closing bid. KNOWN RANGER never far back, faded after going five furlongs. BLACK QUESTION was never a factor. BEST SELECTION set the pace along the inside into upper stretch and tired. PUNCHPASSER was finished early.

Owners— 1, Top Five Stable; 2, Ross Alfred S; 3, Aldila Farm; 4, G Lack Farms; 5, Miron Stephen E; 6, Garren Murray M; 7, Roussel Louie J III; 8, Minassian Harry; 9, Garren Murray M

Trainers—1, Serpe Philip M; 2, Sciacca Gary; 3, Combs Don; 4, Martin Gregory F; 5, Debonis Robert; 6, Garren Murray M; 7, Badgett William Jr; 8, Johnstone Bruce; 9, Garren Murray M

Overweight: Known Ranger-GB (1).

Scratched— Keen Falcon (24Feb94 ^{8}GP^{5}), Go Dutch (1May94 ^{4}AQU^{6}), Rocking Josh (28Apr94 ^{4}AQU^{3}), Sparkling Sky (30Apr94 ^{4}AQU^{1})

The first route was for established high-priced claimers, several of whom were stakes-placed; they had combined to win over $1,000,000 on the grass. The second route carried an inflated $32,000 purse. It was for New York–breds who had never won two races other than maiden or claiming; the field had combined for about one-tenth the earnings of the claimers.

The six-furlong split for each race was 1:13⅕, but based on how each field had arrived at that point, the early pace setters in the claimer should've held on better than the early pace setters in the allowance for state-breds. The claimers had recorded splits of :25 and :49⅕, while the New York–breds had run :24⅖ and :48⅖.

Nevertheless, just the opposite happened.

The eventual first three finishers in the *slower*-paced race had been last, seventh, and fifth, respectively, at the first call. The horses involved in the early pace had all collapsed: the horses racing first, second, and third at the first call wound up sixth, next-to-last, and last, respectively.

The eventual first three finishers in the *faster*-paced race (for horses of established lesser ability, remember) had been involved in the early running, racing first, third, and fourth, respectively, at the first call. None of the horses racing well behind the early fractions were able to make up any ground whatsoever, despite the faster fractions.

Both races were run on a course labeled "firm."

What gives?

Well, this is one of many situations where on-track players can gain a big edge. As the field loaded into the gate for the fourth race, a sudden and violent thunderstorm passed over Belmont Park from the north, bringing with it a steady wind in the range of 30 mph that was blowing directly against the field as it rounded the clubhouse turn and made its way into the backstretch. By the time the seventh race was run an hour and a half later, the sun was out and there was only a gentle zephyr of about 5 mph blowing against the field through the same stage of their race.

Unless you knew of these conditions, it was impossible to make any pace-oriented judgments about these races that coincided in any way with reality.

Turf races pose unique problems even when there are no weather-related effects clouding the picture. When the temporary rails are in place to protect the inner portions of the course, many tracks record only a final time, which is in some instances manually taken. In his "By the Numbers" column in the January 28, 1994, edition of *Daily Racing Form,* Mark Hopkins explained that Gulfstream Park, in conjunction with Teleview Patrol Service, had installed equipment designed not only to ensure accurate final times, but also to provide estimated fractional times for turf races run at "about" distances: "It is Teleview Patrol Service's attempt to provide estimations of fractional times at the 'about' turf distances that should stir continued controversy. The danger in reporting estimated adjusted fractions . . . is that it can mislead those handicappers doing any real analysis of fractional times."

Indeed, many of the fractional times reported as "official" during Gulfstream's 1994 winter meeting were hard to swallow. On February 25, two races at "about nine furlongs" were run, with the temporary rail set twenty-five feet out from the hedge. The fifth was a $40,000 claimer for fillies and mares four and up, run in 1:53⅖. The seventh was a nonwinners-of-three allowance for fillies and mares of the same age, which was run in 1:52⅗.

Fine. The allowance contained classier and faster fillies who figured to run in the neighborhood of four-fifths faster. But here's how the internal fractions were reported:

$40K claimer — :25⅕, :25⅖, :24⅗, :25, :12⅕

NW3 allowance — :23⅗, :23⅘, :24⅖, :25⅕, :15⅗

Taking these fractions at face value, the claimers ran the final furlong :03⅖ seconds faster than the allowance fillies, which is a difference of roughly seventeen lengths.

Consider the past performances of Via Borghese, one of the top grass mares in the country in 1993, as they looked after her return win at Gulfstream on February 26, 1994:

Via Borghese
Own: Parrish M E
BAILEY J D (274 65 44 24 .24)

B. m. 5
Sire: Seattle Dancer (Nijinsky II)
Dam: Angela Serra (Arctic Tern)
Br: Bedford Farms & Panama Foreign Traders (Ky)
Tr: Penna Angel Jr (22 3 3 3 .14)

L 119

Lifetime Record: 16 10 3 1 $498,294
1994 1 1 0 0 $25,200 | Turf 16 10 3 1 $498,294
1993 9 5 3 0 $404,797 | Wet 0 0 0 0
GP Ⓣ 3 3 0 0 $82,230 | Dist Ⓣ 2 2 0 0 $110,355

26Feb94- 8GP fm *1 Ⓣ :23 :46² 1:10³ 1:37 ⒻAlw 42000N$mY 97 5 7 76¼ 54½ 1½ 1nk Bailey J D L 114 *.50 95-11 Via Borghese114nk Topsa1143½ Too Loud1164 10
Steadied top str, driving inside
23Oct93-10Lrl yl 1⅛ Ⓣ :48² 1:13² 1:38³ 1:51² 3+ ⒻAll Along-G2 102 2 4 45½ 45½ 31½ 2no Velasquez J L 118 *.70 73-32 Lady Blessington116no Via Borghese118hd Logan's Mist1161¾ Gamely 5
28Aug93- 9AP gd 1 3/16 Ⓣ :49² 1:13³ 1:38 1:55³ 3+ ⒻBeverly D-G1 102 4 4 42½ 31½ 31 3nk Velasquez J L 123 7.00 88-11 DLet's Elope123no Flawlessly123nk Via Borghese123no Crowded late 7
Placed second through disqualification.
8Aug93-10Rkm fm *1⅛ Ⓣ 1:46⁴ 3+ ⒻSpcy Lvng H-G3 103 2 5 56 44½ 31 12 Velasquez J LB 121 *.70 100-08 Via Borghese1212 Ginny Dare1121 Saratoga Source1141 Driving 9
4Jly93-11Rkm fm 1 1/16 Ⓣ :23¹ :47³ 1:11⁴ 1:43 3+ ⒻRkm BC H100k 103 6 4 54 53 12½ 12¾ Velasquez J L 115 *.60 98-10 Via Borghese1152¾ Navarra1132 Miss Otis1101 Mild drive 9
19Jun93- 8Bel fm 1¼ Ⓣ :47¹ 1:11¹ 1:35 1:59 3+ ⒻNew York H-G2 101 3 3 36½ 2hd 2½ 2no Velasquez J 117 3.80 95-11 Aquilegia114no Via Borghese117¾ Ginny Dare1083 Sharp try 11
25Apr93-11Hia fm 1⅛ Ⓣ 1:48² 3+ ⒻBlk Helen H150k 87 6 4 43¾ 41¾ 64 74 Bailey J D 119 *.50 92-03 Klassy Individual113no Winnie D.1131 Captive Miss117¾ 8
Checked 1/8 pole, failed to recover
4Apr93-10Hia fm 1 1/16 Ⓣ 1:41¹ 3+ ⒻHia B C H75k 98 6 5 51¼ 41¼ 1hd 11 Ramos W S 117 *.40 106-03 Via Borghese1171 Klassy Individual1135½ Spinning Round114nk Driving 9
15Feb93-10GP fm 1⅛ Ⓣ :48³ 1:12³ 1:36³ 1:48¹ + 3+ ⒻSwnee Rvr H-G3 103 6 5 32½ 31 11 11 Bailey J D 116 *1.80 91-11 Via Borghese1161 Marshua's River1132¼ Blue Daisy114hd Driving 14
31Jan93-10GP fm 1⅛ Ⓣ :48³ 1:13 1:39 1:50 + ⒻAlw 28000N$mY 98 4 4 32 1hd 11 13 Bailey J D 112 3.10 82-19 Via Borghese1123 Klassy Individual113½ Kiwi Mint119½ Driving 12

WORKOUTS: Mar 7 GP 6f fst 1:15 B *3/4* Feb 21 GP 6f fst 1:14² B *7/22* Feb 12 GP 5f fst 1:01⁴ B *28/46* Feb 6 GP 5f fst 1:03 B *34/55* Jan 25 GP Ⓣ 4f gd :53³ B (d) *7/8* Jan 17 GP 3f fst :38 B *26/37*

At the "about" distance of one mile, Via Borghese had rallied to make up a deficit of four and a half lengths through a final fraction listed as a slow :26⅖ seconds, giving her a ballpark adjusted final-quarter time of a moderate :25⅖ seconds.

But her two wins at Gulfstream from the previous year told a much different story. Her win of February 15 was accomplished with a final furlong in :11⅗ and a final three-eighths, adjusted for one length gained, in :35⅖. Her win of January 31 was accomplished, according to the "official" fractions, with a final eighth in *:11 flat.*

Via Borghese had been capable of finishing her final furlong in well under :12 seconds at Gulfstream the previous winter; since then, she had also raced her final quarter in the ten-furlong New York Handicap in :24 flat.

Are there any pace handicappers who feel confident about rating this mare off her allowance return, in which she came home in a supposed :25⅖?

I didn't think so.

Even when turf races are accurately timed whether the rails are up or down, as is thc case at Belmont, handicappers must be alert to the following situation:

Belmont Park

8 ***1 1/16 MILES.*** **(Inner Turf). (1:39¹) ALLOWANCE. Purse $30,500. Fillies and mares, 3-year-olds and upward, which have not won two races other than maiden, claiming or starter. Weights, 3-year-olds, 116 lbs. Older, 122 lbs. Non-winners of a race other than maiden or claiming at a mile or over since July 1, allowed 3 lbs. Such a race since June 15, 5 lbs.**

Coupled – Star Jolle and Slew The Duchess

Whozini Gr. m. 5 Lifetime Record: 8 2 1 0 $38,200

Own: Rich Jill P — Sire: Jacques Who (Grey Dawn II) — Dam: Danger Zone (Zoning) — Br: Rich Jill P (NY) — Tr: Rich David C (6 1 2 2 .17)

CARLE J D (25 0 2 4 .00) **117**

1992	5 2 0 0	$33,000	Turf	4 2 0 0	$33,000
1991	3 M 1 0	$5,280	Wet	1 0 1 0	$5,280
Bel Ⓣ	3 2 0 0	$33,000	Dist Ⓣ	2 2 0 0	$33,000

17Aug92- 6Sar fm 1⅛ Ⓣ :47² 1:10⁴ 1:35 1:47² 3↑ ⒻⓈYaddo 93k 76 7 5 6⁸ 6⁷ 6³¾ 6⁹¼ Carle J D 112 18.30 84-08 ⒹCazzy B.114nk Her Favorite118³½ Irish Actress121 No threat 8

Run in divisions

26Jly92- 9Bel fm 1 1/16 Ⓣ :23³ :47¹ 1:11⁴ 1:43 3↑ ⒻⓈAlw 29000 83 9 5 5³½ 2hd 1hd 1² Carle J D 119 5.70 81-24 Whozini119² Philip111¹¾ Roscommon Colleen111 Drifted driving 12

3Jly92- 9Bel fm 1 1/16 Ⓣ :23 :46¹ 1:10⁴ 1:42⁴ 3↑ ⒻⓈMd Sp Wt 82 6 6 5³½ 1½ 1⁹ 1¹⁰ Carle J D 122 9.40 82-15 Whozini122¹⁰ Raja Fair116⁴¾ Carabid116 Kept to drive 10

13Jun92- 5Bel fm 1 Ⓣ :23³ :46⁴ 1:11¹ 1:35⁴ 3↑ ⒻMd Sp Wt 56 2 8 8⁶ 9⁶¾ 7¹³ 6¹⁰¾ Carle J D 122 101.60 72-13 Insurprise114²½ Kate's Pride114¾ Herat o' Mine114 No threat 12

Placed fifth through disqualification

21May92- 9Bel fst 6½f :23¹ :47⁴ 1:13¹ 1:19⁴ 3↑ ⒻⓈMd Sp Wt 25 4 7 5²½ 7³½ 8⁸¾ 8¹⁰¾ Maple E 124 58.20 63-16 Whisper Hello115¹½ RebeccaLauren115² CurbAmex115 Lacked room trn 14

24Jly91- 9Sar fst 7f :22² :45³ 1:12³ 1:26³ 3↑ ⒻⓈMd Sp Wt 31 10 3 7⁵½ 10⁹½ 11⁷¾ 10¹³ Carr D 116 20.70 59-14 Freedom's Wave116³ Romanallure122¹½ Gallantina116 Outrun 12

5Jly91- 9Bel sly 6f :22¹ :45⁴ 1:10³ 3↑ ⒻⓈMd Sp Wt 40 3 7 9¹⁴ 7⁹½ 6¹³ 2¹⁶ Carr D 116 54.20 71-12 Shimissee116¹⁶ Whozini116³ Gallantina116 Up for place 14

26Jun91- 6Bel fst 7f :22¹ :46¹ 1:12² 1:26¹ 3↑ ⒻⓈMd Sp Wt 31 12 7 12¹⁶ 11¹³ 8¹⁰ 8¹³½ Santiago A 114 111.50 60-16 For Elana114¹ Mistee Vee122⁴½ Quick Jenny114 Never close 13

WORKOUTS: ●Jly 14 Sar tr.t 4f fst :49⁴ H 1/6 Jly 10 Sar tr.t 4f fst :52 B 2/6 Jly 3 Sar 5f fst 1:04³ H 2/2 Jun 26 Sar tr.t 4f fst :51³ H 1/2 ●Jun 18 Sar 4f fst :51² B 1/7 Jun 12 Sar tr.t 3f fst :38⁴ B 3/4

Jiving Around Dk. b or br f. 3 (Feb) Lifetime Record: 11 2 5 1 $54,970

Own: Lightsy Thomas L — Sire: Entropy (What a Pleasure) — Dam: Jiving (Baldski) — Br: Farnsworth Farm (Fla) — Tr: Lightsy Thomas L (2 2 0 0 1.00)

VELASQUEZ J (152 14 15 20 .09) **111**

1993	6 2 2 0	$40,650	Turf	2 2 0 0	$32,400
1992	5 M 3 1	$14,320	Wet	1 0 1 0	$3,080
Bel Ⓣ	2 2 0 0	$32,400	Dist Ⓣ	1 1 0 0	$15,300

14Jun93- 4Bel fm 1 Ⓣ :23 :46¹ 1:09⁴ 1:33⁴ 3↑ ⒻAlw 28500N1X 89 2 5 4⁴ 4¹½ 1²½ 1⁴¼ Smith M E 113 8.80 93-11 Jiving Around113⁴¼ Tropical Waters114⁶ Brave And True112hd Driving 8

20May93- 5Bel gd 1 1/16 Ⓣ :23¹ :47¹ 1:12³ 1:45¹ 3↑ ⒻMd Sp Wt 85 1 3 4⁴½ 3² 2½ 1¹ Velasquez J 115 fb 10.70 70-30 Jiving Around115¹ Java Jade115⁴ Annie Money115nk Driving 10

23Apr93- 3Aqu fst 6f :22³ :46² :58³ 1:11² 3↑ ⒻMd 50000 69 2 2 2½ 2½ 1¹ 2¹ Velasquez J 115 fb 7.70 84-15 Miss Bold Appeal115¹ Jiving Around115²¾ Waving The Flag115⁴ Gamely 7

18Feb93- 5Aqu fst 6f ⊡ :23 :46⁴ :59² 1:12¹ ⒻMd Sp Wt 54 11 3 7³¾ 5² 5³ 5⁶¾ Bisono C V5 116 b 10.90 75-13 Stormbow121¹¾ Hello Hanne121¹½ Tell Capote121¹ Wide, flattened out 11

8Feb93- 5Aqu fst 6f ⊡ :23¹ :47² :59⁴ 1:12¹ ⒻMd Sp Wt 42 3 4 4¹ 3½ 4⁴½ 5¹⁴½ Bisono C V5 116 b *1.10 68-24 SaucyChrmer121² PreciselyPerfect121⁸ Mdeline'sAffir116³ Wide, tired 6

17Jan93- 5Aqu fst 6f ⊡ :22⁴ :46² :59 1:11⁴ ⒻMd Sp Wt 64 4 3 3³ 4²½ 3²½ 2² Bisono C V5 116 6.80 82-15 Saratoga Bid121² Jiving Around116¹¾ Interrupta121hd Second best 12

31Dec92- 6Aqu gd 6f ⊡ :23³ :47² :59³ 1:12² ⒻMd Sp Wt 58 6 2 4³ 3³ 2⁵ 2⁶ Velasquez J 117 2.80 75-17 Yellow Mountain117⁶ Jiving Around117⁷ Eastern Tune117³½ Best of rest 7

21Dec92- 7Aqu fst 6f ⊡ :22⁴ :46 :58³ 1:11³ ⒻMd Sp Wt 58 6 1 1½ 2hd 2½ 3⁷½ Velasquez J 117 2.30 77-14 Bright Penny117²½ Princesse Niner112⁵ Jiving Around117hd Weakened 8

23Nov92- 9Aqu my 6f :22³ :47 :59³ 1:12¹ ⒻMd 50000 57 2 4 4¹½ 3¹ 2²½ 2⁷¾ Romero R P 117 4.50 72-21 Nice Crane113⁷¾ Jiving Around117¹¾ Foolish Special117 2nd best 13

25Oct92- 4Aqu fst 7f :23³ :48 1:13⁴ 1:26⁴ ⒻMd 75000 34 5 5 1¹ 1¹ 3⁴½ 7¹⁵½ Romero R P 117 *2.70 55-19 Megaroux113⁴¾ Nicely Wild117⁴¾ Foolish Special117 Used in pace 8

WORKOUTS: ●Jly 14 Aqu ⊡ 5f fst 1:01 H 1/4 Jly 7 Aqu ⊡ 5f fst 1:01³ H 2/3 ●Jun 26 Aqu 4f fst :48 H 1/7 May 16 Aqu 3f fst :36³ H 3/5 May 4 Aqu 5f fst 1:02³ B 2/6 Mar 31 Aqu 4f fst :48 H 3/15

Home by Ten

Own: Vogel Marcus
MAPLE E (139 23 27 16 .17)

B. f. 4
Sire: Far Out East (Raja Baba)
Dam: Playful Hooky (Master Derby)
Br: Vogel Hortense & M (Ky)
Tr: Barrera Luis (20 3 5 2 .15)

117

Lifetime Record: 31 3 9 4 $114,700

1993	9	1	2	0	$32,270	Turf	20	2 8	3	$95,710
1992	14	1	6	3	$69,080	Wet	3	0 0	0	$2,920
Bel ⓣ	15	1	7	2	$68,210	Dist ⓣ	15	2 5	2	$70,320

30Jun93- 6Bel fm 1 1/16 ⓣ :243 :483 1:122 1:422 3+ ⒻAlw 30500N2X 82 8 6 74 52½ 52½ 54 Maple E 117 f 14.50 80-15 Winnetka1172 Star Jolie110¾ Statuette111no Lacked rally 9
19Jun93- 1Bel fm 1 1/16 ⓣ :234 :471 1:112 1:41 ⒻClm 85000 75 4 6 66 53 57 510¼ Smith M E 116 f 3.10 80-11 Big Big Affair113½ Miss Otis1164 At The Spa1124 No factor 6
7Jun93- 7Bel fm 1 ⓣ :24 :482 1:13 1:361 3+ ⒻAlw 30500N1X 76 1 3 31½ 31 41½ 33¾ Maple E 117 f *1.00 77-19 [D]Blue Tess1093½ I'm So Agreeable117nk Home By Ten117hd Saved ground 10
Placed second through disqualification.
29May93- 3Bel fm 1 ⓣ :232 :463 1:104 1:343 ⒻClm 80000 88 7 3 32 51½ 41 41 Maple E 114 f 4.60 88-12 Far Out Beast120¾ Cazzy B.116nk Eenie Meenie Miney118hd Stead str 7
13May93- 2Bel fm 1 ⓣ :231 :461 1:101 1:35 ⒻClm 80000 88 1 7 65½ 62¾ 3½ 2nk Maple E 114 f 7.00 87-13 French Steal122nk Home By Ten1141¾ Beyond Slew112nk Gamely 8
5May93- 5Bel fm 1 1/16 ⓣ :233 :464 1:11 1:433 ⒻClm 45000 86 8 5 64¾ 65 2½ 13¼ Maple E 113 f 8.90 78-22 Home By Ten1133¼ Bridjet Honey1132¾ Maxamount117½ Going away 10
24Mar93-11GP fm 1 1/16 ⓣ :234 :483 1:121 1:441+ ⒻClm 50000 81 3 5 52¾ 54¾ 85 106 Gonzalez M A 116 f 7.20 69-24 Whip Cream116nk Beautifully Bare1122 [D]Ballet Rouge1141½ Gave way 12
26Feb93-10GP sly 1 1/16 ⊗ :24 :474 1:123 1:46 ⒻClm 60000 69 3 5 612 68½ 44½ 46½ Maple E 116 14.00 73-24 Red Ice1145½ It Stands Alone118hd Fashion Miss1161 Late rally 8
27Jan93- 1GP fst 1 1/16 ⊗ :234 :484 1:143 1:464 ⒻClm 50000 64 4 4 33½ 31 42½ 47½ Maple E 116 11.30 68-23 Jo Lo's Joy1131 Beautifully Bare1122 Women In Uniform1124½ Faded 7
6Nov92- 5Aqu my 1 :241 :481 1:133 1:39 ⒻClm 80000 68 1 5 56 44 44 46¾ Smith M E 113 4.60 60-29 Buck Some Belle1114 Tiffany's Taylor111¾ Turkolady111 No threat 5
Originally scheduled on turf

WORKOUTS: Jun 27 Bel tr.t 3f fst :364 B 2/6 Jun 14 Bel 3f fst :362 H 3/21 Jun 5 Bel tr.t 3f fst :38 B 9/19 May 26 Bel tr.t 3f fst :37 B 5/6 May 20 Bel tr.t 3f my :373 B 5/5 May 3 Bel tr.t 3f fst :374 B 6/10

Gypsy Sweetheart

Own: Akindale Farm
CHAVEZ J F (281 51 31 27 .18)

Ch. f. 4
Sire: D'Accord (Secretariat)
Dam: Flick Your Bick (Bicker)
Br: John Hettinger (NY)
Tr: Lewis Lisa L (16 2 0 4 .13)

119

Lifetime Record: 6 2 0 0 $31,500

1993	4	1	0	0	$17,100	Turf	1	1 0	0	$17,100
1992	2	1	0	0	$14,400	Wet	2	1 0	0	$14,400
Bel ⓣ	1	1	0	0	$17,100	Dist ⓣ	1	1 0	0	$17,100

23Jun93- 6Bel gd 1 1/16 [T] :243 :483 1:131 1:433 3+ Ⓕ[S]Alw 28500N1X 80 4 5 42 32½ 21½ 13 Chavez J F 117 17.40 78-19 Gypsy Sweetheart1173 She's A Queen117nk New York Issue117no Driving 9
6Jun93- 7Bel fst 1⅛ :471 1:124 1:391 1:522 3+ Ⓕ[S]Alw 28500N1X 54 12 2 21 1½ 46 714¼ Sweeney K H 117 91.80 53-21 Belle Nuit1092 Alkris1143½ State Street Dori1092½ Bid, tired 12
12May93- 7Bel fst 6f :222 :462 :592 1:121 3+ Ⓕ[S]Alw 26500N1X 29 3 10 96¾ 97¾ 87 717¾ Santos J A 119 19.40 61-17 Kweilin119½ Tammy Two1196 Nav Flag111nk No factor 11
15Jan93- 6Aqu my 6f [•] :231 :47 :591 1:122 Ⓕ[S]Alw 27000N1X 16 2 7 42 65¼ 714 723¼ Lovato F Jr 119 *2.40 57-17 Wild Fun1173¼ Smart Holly1192 Gail's Gal1172½ Gave way 7
20Dec92- 4Aqu my 6f [•] :232 :472 :594 1:123 3+ Ⓕ[S]Md Sp Wt 75 5 3 12 11½ 12 12¾ Lovato F Jr 120 *2.60 80-15 Gypsy Sweetheart1202¾ Smart Holly1206¾ Curb Amex1201½ Driving 6
29Nov92- 1Aqu fst 7f :233 :463 1:114 1:243 3+ ⒻMd Sp Wt 49 6 1 41¾ 22 56¾ 67½ Bruin J E 120 37.60 75-11 Romantic Dinner120nk Meadow Victory1201 Turkodawn120hd Tired 7

WORKOUTS: ●Jly 4 Bel 4f fst :464 H 1/48 Jun 2 Bel 4f fst :502 B 43/56 May 23 Bel 4f fst :502 B 28/41 Apr 26 Bel tr.t 5f fst 1:022 H 2/6 Apr 20 Bel tr.t 5f fst 1:013 H 3/13 Apr 14 Bel tr.t 5f fst 1:01 H 9/31

My Girl Delana

Own: Dizney Donald R
ROJAS R I (107 6 10 11 .06)

Ch. f. 4
Sire: Bates Motel (Sir Ivor)
Dam: Schuyler (Daryl's Joy)
Br: Dizney Donald R (Fla)
Tr: Monaci David (61 3 10 9 .05)

117

Lifetime Record: 23 2 2 1 $44,065

1993	8	0	1	0	$9,805	Turf	13	2 0	0	$28,955
1992	12	2	0	1	$31,270	Wet	4	0 2	1	$13,020
Bel ⓣ	3	1	0	0	$15,600	Dist ⓣ	7	1 0	0	$12,830

8Jly93- 7Bel fm 7f ⓣ :214 :433 1:084 1:202 3+ ⒻAlw 40000N$Y 65 7 2 56 69½ 69½ 59¾ Rojas R I 115 b 15.50 93 — Lights Of Marfa117no Cazzy B.115nk Via Dei Portici1171½ No factor 7
12Jun93- 8Mth fm 1 1/16 ⓣ :23 :47 1:104 1:404+ 3+ ⒻAlw 21000N2X 74 6 7 79½ 65¾ 68 410 Ferrer J C L 117 16.80 87-08 Palace Revolt1194¾ Bantierna1211½ Ready Alarm1174 No solid bid 7
2Jun93- 7Mth fm *1⅛ ⓣ :491 1:132 1:382 1:504+ 3+ ⒻAlw 19500N3L 71 3 7 712 86½ 68 66 Rivera L Jr L 117 21.50 88-09 Sleepy Time118nk Ready Alarm1173½ Duplicity1171¾ No rally 8
7Apr93- 8Hia fm *1⅛ ⓣ 1:492 ⒻAlw 16000N3L 70 6 9 917 912 911 87 Nunez E O L 116 2.70 87-06 Hopeful Angel116nk Ready Alarm116½ R. E. Darla116hd No factor 9
25Mar93- 9GP sly 1⅛ :48 1:132 1:394 1:531 ⒻAlw 30000N2X 69 5 6 613 68½ 35 25 Krone J A L 112 3.00 66-25 Groovy Babe1135 My Girl Delana1122¾ Ready Alarm11312 Rallied wide 6
16Feb93- 9GP fm *1 1/16 ⓣ 1:451+ ⒻAlw 22000N2X 81 6 10 106½ 106¾ 62¾ 42¾ Nunez E O L 112 12.60 88-11 Miss Lenora117nk Poolesta1171½ Crystal Stepper1141½ Belated bid 10
6Feb93- 8GP fst 1⅛ ⊗ :49 1:134 1:401 1:54 ⒻAlw 22000N2X 70 5 8 88½ 56 53½ 43½ Nunez E O L 112 13.90 64-28 Joyce D.112¾ Women In Uniform115no Miss Lenora1152½ Belated bid 9
24Jan93- 9GP fm *1 1/16 ⓣ 1:454+ ⒻAlw 20000N2X 72 4 10 107¾ 64¾ 69½ 67½ Nunez E O L 112 12.30 80-12 Northern Nation1171½ Sailing Minstrel1131½ Alvear1142½ 10
Extremely wide final turn
29Oct92- 9Med fm 1 1/16 [T] :23 :47 1:111 1:422 3+ ⒻAlw 18000 72 11 12 119½ 94½ 76¾ 64¾ Rojas R I L 113 6.60 86-09 Irish Reach1132½ Alphabulous112nk Lu Lu's Lullaby113 Some gain 12
6Oct92- 8Med fm 1 1/16 [T] :231 :472 1:112 1:42 3+ ⒻAlw 16000 79 1 6 64¾ 31½ 21 1¾ Rojas R I L 111 *2.10 93-08 My Girl Delana111¾ I'm Harriet1164 Alice Dear116 Driving 10

WORKOUTS: ●Jun 26 Bel 6f fst 1:112 Hg 1/7 May 10 Bel 4f fst :48 H 5/38 Mar 17 GP 5f fst 1:002 H 2/18 Mar 2 GP 4f fst :483 H 8/30 Feb 1 GP 4f fst :482 H 4/23

Statuette

Own: Blum Peter E
DAVIS R G (325 47 47 38 .14)

B. f. 3 (Apr)
Sire: Pancho Villa (Secretariat)
Dam: Mine Only (Mr Prospector)
Br: Blum Peter E (Ky)
Tr: Destasio Richard A (75 5 3 10 .07)

111

Lifetime Record: 6 2 2 2 $81,304

1993	2	1	0	1	$20,760	Turf	3	1 1	1	$48,040
1992	4	1	2	1	$60,544	Wet	0	0 0	0	
Bel ⓣ	3	1	1	1	$48,040	Dist ⓣ	2	0 1	1	$30,940

30Jun93- 6Bel fm 1 1/16 ⓣ :243 :483 1:122 1:422 3+ ⒻAlw 30500N2X 84 2 3 42 31½ 31½ 32¾ Davis R G 111 *1.90 81-15 Winnetka1172 Star Jolie110¾ Statuette111no Saved ground 9
14Jun93- 7Bel fm 1 ⓣ :23 :453 1:092 1:342 3+ ⒻAlw 28500N1X 84 6 3 31½ 41¼ 1hd 12¾ Davis R G 111 *1.40 90-11 Statuette1112¾ Watrals Charm117nk Spectaculaire1175¼ Mild drive 7
22Oct92- 8Aqu fst 7f :231 :463 1:114 1:244 ⒻAstarita-G2 67 6 1 52 52¾ 36 312 Davis R G 119 5.70 69-18 Missed the Storm1195½ Dispute1196½ Statuette119 Lacked rally 6
10Oct92- 8Bel fm 1 1/16 ⓣ :23 :461 1:104 1:422 ⒻMiss Grillo-G3 82 1 2 2hd 1hd 2½ 21¼ Davis R G 114 6.30 82-18 Missymooiloveyou1141¼ Statuette1141¾ Port of Silver118 Rank, gamely 11
16Sep92- 7Bel fst 6f :22 :453 :582 1:114 ⒻMd Sp Wt 75 2 2 22 22 1½ 13 Davis R G 117 2.90 81-18 Statuette1173 Black Medic1172½ Raise a Carter117 Driving 11
28Aug92- 4Sar fst 6f :22 :451 :571 1:104 ⒻMd Sp Wt 67 4 6 11 1½ 2½ 23¼ Davis R G 117 14.10 87-08 True Affair1173¼ Statuette117½ Vallation117 Broke slowly 9

WORKOUTS: Jly 15 Bel [T] 4f fm :474 H (d) 2/21 Jly 8 Bel [T] 4f fm :491 B (d) 3/9 Jun 24 Bel [T] 5f fm 1:03 B (d) 8/12 Jun 10 Bel [T] 5f tf 1:02 B (d) 6/16 Jun 3 Bel [T] 6f fm 1:16 B (d) 7/10 ●May 27 Bel ⓣ 5f fm :592 H (d) 1/

Dahlia's Dreamer

Own: Paulson Mrs Allen E
KRONE J A (287 49 47 39 .17)

Ch. f. 4
Sire: Theatrical (Nureyev)
Dam: Dahlia (Vaguely Noble)
Br: Allen E Paulson (Ky)
Tr: Mott William I (75 21 9 13 .28)

117

Lifetime Record: 6 2 1 0 $31,320

1993	6	2	1	0	$31,320	Turf	4	1 0	0	$17,460
1991	0	M	0	0		Wet	1	0 1	0	$3,060
Bel ⓣ	2	0	0	0	$3,660	Dist ⓣ	1	0 0	0	$1,830

19Jun93- 6Bel fm 1 1/16 [T] :233 :462 1:104 1:413 3+ ⒻAlw 30500N2X 79 2 1 1½ 11½ 31½ 43¾ Smith M E 117 *1.70 84-11 Turkolady117¾ Belle Nuit1141 Magic Street1092 Speed, tired 6
6May93- 7Bel gd 1¼ [T] :471 1:112 1:362 2:004 3+ ⒻAlw 30500N2X 75 6 2 2½ 31 55 414¾ Bailey J D 119 *.60 71-19 La Piaf1192 Eenie Meenie Miney1194 Fast Reema1198¾ Forced pace 7
31Mar93-10GP fm 1½ ⓣ :463 1:111 2:013 2:253 3+ ⒻOrchid H-G2 95 10 1 13 13 21½ 67½ Krone J A 112 6.50 84-12 Fairy Garden1155 Rougeur115no Trampoli1151¾ Faded 14
7Mar93-11GP fm 1⅛ ⓣ :491 1:124 1:372 1:493+ ⒻAlw 23000N1X 84 5 2 2hd 11 12½ 13¼ Krone J A 117 *1.20 84-11 Dahlia's Dreamer1173¼ Sleepy Time1151 Southward1121½ Ridden out 12
16Feb93- 4GP fst 1 1/16 :242 :491 1:142 1:472 ⒻMd Sp Wt 64 10 2 2½ 1hd 12½ 15 Krone J A 120 *.50 73-24 Dahlia's Dreamer1205 Princess Blackbird1204½ NoNewTaxes120nk Driving 12
26Jan93- 4GP sly 1 1/16 :223 :473 1:134 1:482 ⒻMd Sp Wt 63 6 3 31 31½ 22 2¾ Krone J A 120 *1.60 67-28 Tsu's Thumper120¾ Dahlia's Dreamer1207½ Visioness1203 9
Crowded start, drifted out top stretch, just missed

WORKOUTS: Jly 12 Bel 5f fst 1:002 H 6/33 Jun 30 Bel 5f fst 1:013 H 11/26 Jun 14 Bel 5f fst 1:012 B 12/29 Jun 7 Bel 5f fst 1:022 H 22/49 May 30 Bel 6f fst 1:161 B 2/3 May 23 Bel 5f fst 1:03 B 27/30

Star Jolie
Own: Perlow Jeffrey
CARR D (93 5 13 8 .05)

Dk. b or br f. 3 (Mar)
Sire: John Alden (Speak John)
Dam: La Jolie (Sir Wiggle)
Br: Farnsworth Farms (Fla)
Tr: Terrill William V (78 11 8 13 .14)

111

Lifetime Record:	10 2 2 2	$96,927			
1993	9 2 2 1	$95,627	Turf	2 0 1 0	$9,947
1992	1 M 0 1	$1,300	Wet	0 0 0 0	
Bel (T)	2 0 1 0	$9,947	Dist (T)	2 0 1 0	$9,947

30Jun93-6Bel	fm	$1\frac{1}{16}$ (T)	$:24^3$	$:48^3$	$1:12^2$	$1:42^2$	3↑ (F)Alw 30500N2X	85	3	1	1^1	$1\frac{1}{2}$	1^1	2^2	Carr D	110	11.10	82-15	Winnetka117^2 Star Jolie$110\frac{3}{4}$ Statuette111^{no}	Gamely	9
5Jun93-2Bel	fm	$1\frac{1}{16}$ [T]	$:23^3$	$:46^4$	$1:10^2$	$1:40^3$	(F)Tanya 50k	83	4	3	3^3	$3^{1\frac{1}{2}}$	$4^{2\frac{1}{2}}$	$4^{4\frac{1}{2}}$	Antley C W	116	9.10	88-13	Russian Bride$116\frac{1}{2}$ Bright Penny118^4 Magic Street116^{hd}	Lacked rally	9
22May93-3Bel	fst	$1\frac{1}{8}$	:47	1:12	$1:37^2$	1:50	(F)Alw 30500N2X	81	2	4	4^5	5^3	$2^{1\frac{1}{2}}$	$4^{5\frac{1}{2}}$	Santos J A	116	2.90	74-15	TestyTrestle$116^{4\frac{1}{2}}$ StndrdEquipment116^{no} DefenseSpnding$116\frac{3}{4}$	Bid, tired	8
8May93-8Bel	fst	1	$:22^4$	$:45^3$	1:10	$1:35^2$	(F)Acorn-G1	78	3	5	$4^{2\frac{1}{2}}$	4^3	$4^{6\frac{1}{2}}$	$5^{15\frac{1}{4}}$	Santos J A	121	17.80	76-17	Sky Beauty$121^{5\frac{1}{2}}$ Educated Risk$121^{2\frac{1}{2}}$ In Her Glory$121^{5\frac{3}{4}}$	Tired	6
10Apr93-11Hia	fst	$1\frac{1}{8}$	:48	1:12	$1:37^4$	$1:51^1$	Flamingo 200k	87	7	6	5^9	7^{11}	5^6	$5^{5\frac{1}{4}}$	Nunez E O	117	8.20	83-19	Forever Whirl118^{hd} Bull Inthe Heather122^{hd} Pride Prevails118^4	Mild bid	9
20Mar93-10Tam	fst	$1\frac{1}{16}$	$:23^3$	:48	$1:12^3$	$1:45^3$	(F)Fla Oaks 100k	81	9	9	$10^{5\frac{1}{2}}$	$3^{2\frac{1}{2}}$	1^{hd}	1^2	Nunez E O	111	5.60	95-07	Star Jolie111^2 Hollywood Wildcat121^{nk} Jacody$113\frac{3}{4}$	Driving	11
25Feb93-6GP	fst	$1\frac{1}{16}$	$:23^3$	$:47^4$	1:12	$1:44^3$	(F)Alw 23000N1X	89	1	3	3^2	$2^{2\frac{1}{2}}$	2^2	$2^{2\frac{1}{2}}$	Bailey J D	112	*2.20	84-21	Sheila's Revenge$114^{2\frac{1}{2}}$ Star Jolie112^7 Star Guest$117^{4\frac{1}{4}}$	Best of others	8
24Jan93-5GP	fst	$1\frac{1}{16}$	:24	$:48^2$	$1:13^2$	$1:46^2$	(F)Alw 19000N1X	67	4	3	3^1	4^2	$4^{1\frac{3}{4}}$	$3^{4\frac{1}{4}}$	Vasquez J	114	4.30	74-24	Dream Mary$113^{3\frac{1}{2}}$ T. V. Maud$112\frac{3}{4}$ Star Jolie114^1	Lacked response	8
2Jan93-5Crc	gd	7f	$:22^3$	$:46^2$	$1:12^3$	$1:26^1$	(F)Md Sp Wt	63	3	5	5^2	$5^{1\frac{3}{4}}$	2^2	1^{nk}	Vasquez J	120	*2.40	84-14	Star Jolie120^{nk} Muffer's Pet120^3 Gana120^2	Driving	9
13Dec92-3Crc	fst	6f	:22	$:46^1$	$:59^1$	$1:12^4$	(F)Md Sp Wt	56	10	10	9^5	7^8	4^8	3^6	Vasquez J	120	11.80	81-12	Gipsy Countess120^1 Code Blum120^5 Star Jolie$120\frac{1}{2}$	Mild rally, wide	12

WORKOUTS: Jly 12 Bel 4f fst $:47^4$ H *5/44* Jly 7 Crc 5f fst $1:02^3$ B *7/20* Jly 1 Crc 4f fst $:51^2$ B *36/41* Jun 25 Bel 5f fst 1:01 H *2/16* May 31 Bel 4f fst $:51^2$ B *37/48* May 20 Bel [T] 4f tf $:48^4$ B (d)*3/7*

Dahlia's Dreamer was an absolute standout on early pace, largely thanks to her race on the inner turf course June 19, when she set fractions of :23⅗ and :46⅖.

Dahlia's Dreamer had run those fractions going a mile and a sixteenth on the inner course. As you can see by the diagram, this is a race that starts right on the clubhouse turn:

There are three possible configurations for a race on Belmont's inner-turf course at the distance of a mile and a sixteenth:

- The temporary rails are down.
- The temporary rails are set nine feet out.
- The temporary rails are set eighteen feet out.

When the rails are out, the circumference of the course is effectively *lengthened*. Thus, when the rails are down, the run-up to the timing pole is practically nonexistent — perhaps ten feet or so. When the rails are up, the field gets more run-up distance to the timing pole. So, in effect, when the rails are down, the first quarter is run around a turn from what is essentially a flat-footed start.

Nobody seems to get it. They're off, the first quarter goes up as :25⅖, and everyone from the announcer to the media to the $2 bettor in the grandstand says, "Wow, it's a slow pace!"

Not! The pace setters may well be *running hard* through that :25⅖ quarter, but since it's all turn and from a standing start, there's a limit to how fast they can go.

When the rails are *up*, and the fields get a big running start to the timing pole, they've gathered a full head of steam and the first quarters go in faster times.

From June 16–28, 1993, the temporary rails were down, which meant no run-up. The early splits for fifteen inner-course races were as follows:

:24⅘	:48⅖	
:24⅕	:45⅘	($46K overnight handicap)
:24⅘	:48⅕	
:23⅗	*:46⅖*	(Pace set by Dahlia's Dreamer)
:24⅕	:46⅘	
:24⅖	:47	(NW3 allowance males)
:24⅗	:48⅗	
:25⅖	:49⅕	($46K classified ALW males)
:25	:48⅕	
:25⅖	:48⅗	
:24	:47	
:24⅗	:47⅘	
:25⅗	:49⅕	
:25	:48⅗	
:25	:48⅕	

Dahlia's Dreamer's :23⅗ quarter-time was faster than the next-best times by several lengths, and her half-time of :46⅖ was eclipsed only by Furiously, an older male who had since broken a course record at Monmouth in winning the Oceanport Handicap.

EIGHTH RACE
Belmont
JULY 19, 1993

$1\frac{1}{16}$ MILES.(InnerTurf). (1.39^{1}) ALLOWANCE. Purse $30,500. Fillies and mares 3-year-olds and upward which have never won two races other than maiden, claiming or starter. Weight, 3-year-olds, 116 lbs. Older, 122 lbs. Non-winners of a race other than maiden or claiming at a mile or over since July 1 allowed 3 lbs. Of such a race since June 15, 5 lbs.

Value of race $30,500; value to winner $18,300; second $6,710; third $3,660; fourth $1,830. Mutuel pool $176,889. Exacta Pool $335,115

Last Raced	Horse	M/Eqt.A.Wt	PP	St	¼	½	¾	Str	Fin	Jockey	Odds $1
19Jun93 ^{6}Bel^{4}	Dahlia's Dreamer	4 117	7	6	1^{1}	$1\frac{1}{2}$	$1\frac{1}{2}$	2^{2}	1^{2}	Krone J A	3.40
30Jun93 ^{6}Bel^{3}	Statuette	3 111	6	5	$5\frac{1}{2}$	5^{hd}	$3\frac{1}{2}$	$1\frac{1}{2}$	2^{3}	Davis R G	3.50
14Jun93 ^{4}Bel^{1}	Jiving Around	3 113	2	2	3^{hd}	3^{hd}	4^{2}	3^{2}	$3^{1\frac{3}{4}}$	Velasquez J	1.60
30Jun93 ^{6}Bel^{2}	Star Jolie	3 111	8	7	$4^{2\frac{1}{2}}$	4^{1}	2^{hd}	$4\frac{1}{2}$	4no	Carr D	7.60
30Jun93 ^{6}Bel^{5}	Home by Ten	4 117	3	3	6^{hd}	7^{3}	7^{6}	$5\frac{1}{2}$	$5^{2\frac{1}{2}}$	Alvarado F T	11.80
17Aug92 ^{6}Sar^{6}	Whozini	5 117	1	1	$7^{2\frac{1}{2}}$	6^{2}	$5\frac{1}{2}$	6^{8}	6^{8}	Carle J D	27.60
23Jun93 ^{6}Bel^{1}	Gypsy Sweetheart	4 119	4	4	2^{1}	$2\frac{1}{2}$	6^{hd}	7^{3}	7^{1}	Chavez J F	7.30
8Jly93 ^{7}Bel^{5}	My Girl Delana	b 4 117	5	8	8	8	8	8	8	Rojas R I	22.80

OFF AT 4:31 Start good, Won driving. Time, :23^{2}, :46^{4}, 1:10^{4}, 1:35^{3}, 1:42^{1} Course good.

$2 Mutuel Prices:				
	7-(G)-DAHLIA'S DREAMER	8.80	4.60	2.80
	6-(F)-STATUETTE		4.60	2.60
	2-(B)-JIVING AROUND			2.80
	$2 EXACTA 7-6 PAID $40.80			

Ch. f, by Theatrical-Ir—Dahlia, by Vaguely Noble. Trainer Mott William I. Bred by Paulson Allen E (Ky).

DAHLIA'S DREAMER rushed up between horses to gain the early advantage, set the pace while racing well off the rail to the turn, relinquished the lead in upper stretch, then battled back gamely to win going away. STATUETTE settled in good position for five furlongs, rallied smartly between horses to gain the lead in upper stretch,but couldn't match strides with the winner through the final eighth. JIVING AROUND never far back, made a run along the rail to challenge at the quarter pole, but couldn't sustain her bid. STAR JOLIE rated just behind the early leaders while racing wide rallied outside the winner to threaten on the turn, then gradually tired thereafter.HOME BY TEN was never a serious threat. WHOZINI lodged a mild rally along the inside on the turn and flattened out. GYPSY SWEETHEART drifted out in the early stages, forced the pace for five furlongs and gave way. MY GIRL DELANA was pinched back at the start then trailed throughout.

Owners— 1, Paulson Madeleine; 2, Blum Peter E; 3, Lightsy Thomas L; 4, Perlow Jeffrey M; 5, Vogel Marcus; 6, Rich Jill P; 7, Akindale Farm; 8, Dizney Donald R.

Trainers— 1, Mott William I; 2, Destasio Richard A; 3, Lightsy Thomas L; 4, Terrill William V; 5, Barrera Luis; 6, Rich David C; 7, Lewis Lisa L; 8, Monaci David.

Overweight: Jiving Around 2 pounds.

Scratched—High Talent (1Jly93 6Bel1); Blazing Kadie (24Jun93 7Bel1); Java Jade (1Jly93 7Bel1); Wonder Wave (15Jly93 5Bel1); Slew the Duchess (10Jly93 7Bel6); Sweet Accord (26Jun93 7Bel4).

Dahlia's Dreamer wired her field July 19 with fractions of :23⅗ and :46⅘, which were comparable to her splits from the June 19 race. Importantly, the rails were *up* on July 19. Although Dahlia's Dreamer ran roughly the same splits as she had last time out, she had been given a full running start this time: the fractions were nearly the same, but Dahlia's Dreamer hadn't been forced to work nearly as hard to run them.

Consider the fractions for inner-course races at a mile and a sixteenth with the rails up:

:23⅘	:47⅕	
:23⅗	:46⅘	
:23⅘	:46⅗	
:23⅖	*:46⅘*	(Dahlia's Dreamer win July 19)

Even when there's no apparent reason for a screwy-looking time, it happens:

SEVENTH RACE Belmont JULY 8, 1993 — **7 FURLONGS.(Turf). (1.20²) ALLOWANCE. Purse $40,000. Fillies and Mares. 3-year-olds and upward which have not won $25,000 in 1992-93. Weights: 3-year-olds, 116 lbs.; Older, 122 lbs. Non-winners of $24,000 since June 10, allowed 3 lbs. Of $18,000 twice since April 1, 5 lbs. Of $18,000 since November 10, 7 lbs. (Highweights preferred.)**

Value of race $40,000; value to winner $24,000; second $8,800; third $4,800; fourth $2,400. Mutuel pool $187,055. Exacta Pool $403,308

Last Raced	Horse	M/Eqt.	A.Wt	PP	St	¼	½	Str	Fin	Jockey	Odds $1
24Jun93 5Bel4	Lights of Marfa	b	4 117	2	7	3½	3½	2hd	1no	Alvarado F T	4.10
13Jun93 7Bel7	Cazzy B.		6 115	4	4	67	54	46	2nk	McCauley W H	2.80
27Jun93 7Bel8	Via Dei Portici	b	4 117	1	6	22½	21½	31	31½	Velazquez J R	9.60
11Jun93 8Bel1	Rose Indien-Fr		4 122	3	3	1½	1½	11	48	Smith M E	1.40
12Jun93 8Mth4	My Girl Delana	b	4 115	7	2	51½	68	62	52¾	Rojas R I	15.50
21Jun93 6Bel1	Rae Rafko	b	5 115	5	5	7	7	7	6nk	Davis R G	16.20
30May93 9Bel7	Strategic Reward	b	4 114	6	1	42½	43	51½	7	Bisono C V5	6.40

OFF AT 3:50 Start good. Won driving. Time, :21⁴, :43³, 1:08⁴, 1:20² Course firm.
Equals Track Record

$2 Mutuel Prices:				
	2-(C)-LIGHTS OF MARFA	10.20	4.80	4.20
	4-(E)-CAZZY B.		3.60	3.40
	1-(B)-VIA DEI PORTICI			7.00
	$2 EXACTA 2-4 PAID $31.40			

Gr. f, by Marfa—Glittering Sky, by Air Forbes Won. Trainer Kelly Patrick J. Bred by Live Oak Stud (Fla).

LIGHTS OF MARFA rated just behind the early leaders, split horses in midstretch, took the lead in deep stretch, then was all out to hold off CAZZY B. in the closing strides. CAZZY B. unhurried for a half, split horses while gaining on the turn, angled out in upper stretch then closed steadily but could not get up. VIA DEI PORTICI forced the pace from outside into upper stretch, and held well to gain a share. ROSE INDIEN set the early pace under pressure while saving ground to the turn, opened a clear advantage in midstretch, then weakened in the final eighth. MY GIRL DELANA was never a factor. RAE RAFKO was never close. STRATEGIC REWARD raced within striking distance to the turn and gave way.

Owners— 1, Live Oak Plantation; 2, Dutch Acres Farms; 3, Happy Hill Farm; 4, Buckram Oak Farm; 5, Dizney Donald R; 6, DiMauro Stephen; 7, Heatherwood Farm.

Trainers— 1, Kelly Patrick J; 2, Walsh Thomas M; 3, Preger Mitchell C; 4, Moubarak Mohammed; 5, Monaci David; 6, DiMauro Stephen; 7, Schosberg Richard.

Scratched—My Necessity (25Jun93 ⁸Bel²); Kweilin (17Jun93 ⁷Bel⁶); Reach For Clever (27Jun93 ⁷Bel²).

During the 1993 season at Belmont, most of the seven-furlong grass races were clocked in supersonic times — times that appeared too fast considering the unspectacular nature of most of the fields.

When Lights of Marfa equaled the course record of 1:20⅖, which had been set the previous month by fourth-place finisher Rose Indien, there were three fillies in the win photo. Could all of them have run so well on a given day?

The fractions of the race looked like this when broken down:

:21⅘; :21⅘; :25⅕; :11⅗

According to the "official" fractions, the field blazed the opening quarter in :21⅘, reeled off another :21⅘ quarter, then seemed to slow down as if by mutual agreement, running the third quarter in *:25⅕*. The field then continued on its merry way, picking up the tempo once again with a last eighth in :11⅗.

This just doesn't make any sense. Either the third quarter was too slow, or the last eighth was too fast, but something doesn't look quite right.

As Len Ragozin (a stickler for details) declared:

> Well, you talk about insisting on rational explanations for races. I defy anybody [chuckling noticeably] to take the times of Saratoga grass races, with any kind of chart they've got or anything, and make any sense of what's going on up there in those races. It took us years. The fact of the matter is, there's quite a few races there, where they say it's being run at such-and-such a distance . . . and it isn't! It's kind of a casual meeting.

It should be noted at this point that turf races are hand-timed on Saratoga's inner grass course when the temporary rails are up. All races run over Aqueduct's ramshackle grass course are hand-timed as well, and it's hard to imagine *any* hand-times from Aqueduct being accurate, when one takes into account the angle that a clocker gets for the start of a race:

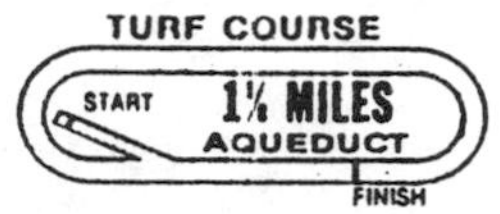

The field breaks out of a chute at what is practically a head-on angle to the stands, offering even the World's Greatest Clocker nothing close to an accurate perception of depth from that vantage point.

So, as I've made painfully clear, getting a handle on meaningful and/or accurate fractions is next to impossible in a variety of situations.

For handicappers still concerned with pace . . . what to do?

For me, the approach that works best is to look for situations that seem pretty much clear-cut. Scan the field, get an idea of the race's overall characteristics . . . and punt.

EARLY-PACE ADVANTAGES

Unchallenged early speed wins far more than its share of races at every racetrack in the country, whether we're talking about $2,500 claimers at Penn National or Grade 1 stakes races at Saratoga.

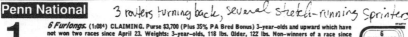

Penn National 3 routers turning back, several stretch-running sprinters

1 ***6 Furlongs.*** **(1:08⁴) CLAIMING. Purse $3,700 (Plus 35% PA Bred Bonus) 3–year–olds and upward which have not won two races since April 23. Weights: 3–year–olds, 118 lbs. Older, 122 lbs. Non–winners of a race since September 23, allowed 3 lbs. A race since August 23, 5 lbs. Claiming price $3,500, if for $3,000, allowed 3 lbs. (Races for $2,500 or less not considered in eligibility.)**

Siren's Gold
Own: Damore D Hrabovsky J & Mumma C
QUEZADA F (210 21 26 20 .10) $3,500

B. c. 4
Sire: Allen's Prospect (Mr. Prospector)
Dam: Canadian Venture (Viceregal)
Br: Standedge (Va)
Tr: Sersch Joe (67 11 15 10 .16)

L 119

Lifetime Record:	31	5	5	0	$14,214						
1993	19	3	5	0	$9,714	Turf	0	0	0	0	
1992	9	2	0	0	$4,080	Wet	4	0	0	0	$174
Pen	26	5	5	0	$13,794	Dist	23	4	5	0	$11,820

13Oct93-2Pen	fst	6f	$:22^2$	:46	$:58^3$	$1:11^2$	3↑ Clm 3500N2Y	47	6	8	$7^{6½}$	$7^{3¾}$	$5^{5½}$	$6^{7½}$	Quezada F	L 117 fb	4.20	81-13	Sevastapuff117^3 Crown Of Blue116^2 Lees Dream119^{no}	Outrun	8
3Oct93-10Pen	fst	6f	$:22^2$	$:46^1$	:59	$1:12^2$	3↑ Clm 3500N2Y	57	5	9	9^8	$8^{7½}$	$6^{6¼}$	2^4	Quezada F	L 117 fb	15.10	80-19	Alywishus117^4 Siren's Gold117^{no} Filleds Champ117½	Up for second	9
22Sep93-2Pen	fst	5½f	$:22^2$	$:46^3$	$:59^3$	$1:06^1$	3↑ Clm 2500N2Y	56	3	9	$8^{4¾}$	$7^{1½}$	$3^{2½}$	1½	Quezada F	L 117 fb	*3.80	86-14	Siren's Gold117½ Market Quest$117^{3¾}$ Jack's Babe117½	Closed well	9
10Sep93-1Pen	fst	1^{70}	$:23^1$	:48	1:15	$1:47^1$	3↑ Clm 2500N2Y	19	7	4	$4^{1¾}$	2½	8^{13}	$9^{18½}$	Cabrera S	L 117 fb	6.40	52-29	Real Silver115^3 Aristocat119^4 What's Not Fair119^4	Faltered	9
27Aug93-10Pen	fst	6f	$:22^1$	$:45^4$	$:58^3$	$1:11^4$	3↑ Clm 2500N2Y	58	1	9	$5^{3¾}$	$5^{3½}$	2^3	2^5	Quezada F	L 119 fb	11.30	82-18	Shortstop122^5 Siren's Gold119^1 Kalua's Caper117^{no}	Saved ground	9
6Aug93-5Pen	sly	6f	$:22^1$	$:46^1$	$:59^1$	$1:12^4$	3↑ Clm 3500N3Y	29	1	8	6^4	6^5	$7^{5¾}$	$8^{10½}$	Deibler C E III	L 119 fb	8.50	72-21	Aggie Social117½ Sevastapuff119¾ Brass Ones109^{hd}	Broke slowly	8
24Jly93-4Pen	fst	6f	$:22^2$	:46	:59	$1:12^1$	3↑ Clm 3500N2Y	32	6	5	4^4	$6^{5¼}$	$6^{7¾}$	6^{15}	Vazquez J J	L 122 fb	*1.60	70-19	Major Wager$119^{3¾}$ Grand Design116^1 Diesel Doctor$119^{1½}$	Stopped	6
10Jly93-9Pen	fst	5½f	:22	$:45^3$	$:58^3$	$1:05^2$	3↑ Alw 2500s	53	2	5	$5^{5½}$	$5^{4½}$	$6^{4¾}$	$7^{5½}$	Vazquez J J	L 122 fb	18.30	85-14	Eugene Eugene122^{no} Uncle Hughie120^{nk} Hunk A Gold116^2	Gave way	7
28Jun93-8Pen	fst	6f	$:21^4$	$:45^3$	$:58^4$	$1:12^2$	3↑ Clm 5000N4L	65	3	5	3^3	2^1	2^{hd}	$1^{2½}$	Vazquez J J	L 114 fb	5.50	84-16	Siren's Gold$114^{2½}$ R. D.'s Magic122½ Chilling Reign115^{no}	Driving	8
18Jun93-7Pen	fst	6f	$:21^4$	$:45^3$	$:58^2$	$1:11^3$	3↑ Clm 2500N4L	67	3	7	2^1	1^1	1½	0no↓	Vazquez J J	L 117 fb	23.30	88-14	DH D Siren's Gold117 DH Full Reserve$117^{3½}$ Devri117^{hd}	Drifted out	11

Disqualified and placed second

WORKOUTS: Aug 4 Pen 4f fst :51 Bg 16/23

Crown Of Blue

Own: Dodge Betty Lou *(Salvaggio)*
[illegible] .11) $3,500

Dk. b or br g. 6
Sire: Regal Embrace (Vice Regent)
Dam: Stone of Blue (Stonewalk)
Br: Empire State Breeding & Langan (NY)
Tr: Dodge Albert (58 6 9 10 .10)

122

Lifetime Record: 20 5 4 4 $13,722										
1993	11	2	3	3	$6,780	Turf	1	0	0	0
1992	3	1	1	1	$3,030	Wet	3	0	0	1	$382
Pen	4	1	2	0	$3,300	Dist	8	2	1	2	$5,262

13Oct93-2Pen fst 6f	:222 :46 :583 1:112 3↑ Clm 3000N2Y	58 4 6 55¾ 42 43 23 Potts C L	116 fb 13.00 86-13	Sevastapuff1173 Crown Of Blue1162 Lees Dream119no	Second best	8
2Oct93-5Pen gd 6f	:221 :463 :594 1:132 3↑ Clm 2500N2Y	55 9 4 62½ 61½ 31½ 12 Salvaggio M V	119 fb 4.70 79-22	Crown Of Blue1192 Vanish Dancer117¾ Aggie Social1192¼	Saved ground	10
24Sep93-10Pen fst 6f	:223 :463 :594 1:132 3↑ Clm 2500N2Y	50 5 7 74½ 73½ 75¾ 43¾ Salvaggio M V	122 fb *3.00 75-18	Poppy1171½ Chance Dance117½ Hush Hush Indian1221¾	Outrun	10
14Sep93-12FL fst 5½f	:222 :463 :592 1:06 3↑ Clm 3000N2Y	53 4 8 66 65¼ 55 36 Miller D R	122 fb 4.80 79-20	Freeze Over1224½ Wim Wham1161½ Crown Of Blue1221½	Finished well	8
27Aug93-1FL fst 5½f	:224 :473 1:011 1:08 3↑ Clm 3000N1Y	55 2 6 46 35 22½ 13 Miller D R	120 fb 2.60 75-20	Crown Of Blue1203 Double Pursuit1202¾ Bold Dozer1202¾	Ridden out	6
17Aug93-2FL gd 6f	:233 :48 1:012 1:14 3↑ Clm 3000N1Y	54 3 7 1hd 2hd 3½ 32¼ Miller D R	120 fb *2.00 74-22	Talc'sReward1202 RememberCrr120nk CrownOfBlue120no	Weakened late	7
4Aug93-3FL fst 5½f	:224 :472 1:01 1:073 3↑ Clm 3000N1Y	60 1 7 32 32 31 31¼ Miller D R	120 fb 4.30 76-27	[D]LordPngn120nk Z.Z.Qckfoot1201 CrownOfBl1204	Took up sharply 3/16	8
Placed second through disqualification.						
30Jly93-5Pen fst 5½f	:222 :464 1:00 1:064 3↑ Clm 2500N1Y	53 2 8 42¼ 32 42 2½ Potts C L	120 fb *2.10 82-16	Bare As Sweet115½ Crown Of Blue1202¾ Aliento1201	Late run	8
20Jly93-3FL fst 5½f	:222 :464 1:001 1:062 3↑ Clm 3000N1Y	55 2 6 63¾ 64½ 55 46 Miller D R	120 b 4.60 77-27	Cat In The Act1205½ Royal Motion113½ Talc's Reward120hd	No solid bid	7
11Jly93-3FL fst 5½f	:23 :473 1:004 1:07 3↑ Clm 3000N1Y	48 5 4 2hd 2hd 31 34¾ Miller D R	120 b 4.50 75-22	Fly Julio Fly1202¾ Smoken Wilbur1202 Crown Of Blue120hd	Weakened	9

Fishers Island

Own: Edmunds Eleanor

FORREST C W (11 1 5 1 .09) $3,000

B. g. 7
Sire: Rollicking (Rambunctious)
Dam: Jaded Origin (Shecky Greene)
Br: Bonsal F A (Md)
Tr: Edmunds Eleanor W (1 0 1 0 .00)

L 114

Lifetime Record: 62 8 11 8 $39,184											
1993	5	1	1	0	$3,720	Turf	8	0	0	2	$1,789
1992	13	2	4	2	$9,209	Wet	6	2	3	1	$9,575
Pen	17	4	4	2	$14,634	Dist	7	1	1	0	$4,253

31Aug93-5Tim fst *6½f	:231 :47 1:133 1:184 3↑ Clm 6000N2Y	47 6 2 33½ 611 611 614½ Forrest C W	L 115 b 15.30 66-18	Ba Ha Ba1171½ Loon Mountain1151 Flying Tempo1176	Fell back	6
28Jly93-7Pen fst 170	:241 :481 1:131 1:44 3↑ Clm 4500N2Y	52 7 5 44½ 55½ 98½ 99 Munar L H	L 119 b 11.50 77-20	Malcom F.1173 Huwaki119nk Saudi117½	Gave way	9
14Jly93-6Pen fst 170	:233 :472 1:124 1:43 3↑ Clm 4500N2Y	59 9 4 31½ 32 47½ 69½ Leonardi J A	L 119 b 10.60 82-20	Star Express1196¾ Northern Slugger117½ Malcom F.117hd	Tired	10
2Jly93-8Pen sly 170	:221 :464 1:141 1:453 3↑ Clm 4500N1Y	65 2 4 38 11½ 12½ 11¾ Munar L H	L 117 b 3.00 78-27	Fishers Island1171¾ Persuasive Manor1204½ Chance Dance112¾	Driving	7
21Jun93-7Pen sly 6f	:222 :454 :582 1:114 3↑ Clm c-3500N1Y	68 1 7 55 54½ 55 2no Forrest C W	L 120 b 11.70 87-15	Rapheal's Advocate120no Fishers Island1204 Kelli's Secret110¾	Late run	8
Claimed from Bonsal Frank Jr, Edmunds Eleanor W Trainer						
1Nov92-8Pen fst 170	:23 :474 1:143 1:472 3↑ Clm 4500	43 4 4 56 57½ 56¾ 57½ Leonardi J A5	L 108 b 6.30 62-36	All Trae116hd Dom Luck1193 Si's Pride116	Outrun	7
19Oct92-10Del fst 170	:233 :474 1:14 1:444 3↑ Clm 4000	50 5 1 13 1hd 76¾ 810¾ Petersen J L	L 119 b 4.40 67-29	Chapala1141½ Mighty Ken1192¾ Social Patriot110	Used in pace	10
3Oct92-2Del fst 1 1/16	:234 :48 1:122 1:46 3↑ Clm 3500	63 4 1 11½ 11 2½ 21 Petersen J L	L 118 b 7.00 81-21	Hard Trapper1191 Fishers Island118no Bluegrass Country118	Held well	7
25Sep92-4Del sly 170	:224 :47 1:134 1:453 3↑ Clm 3500	62 5 1 21½ 21½ 3nk 31½ Petersen J L	L 118 b 6.10 73-30	Always Glad114¾ Stone Pony116½ Fishers Island118	Needed late bid	8
4Sep92-9Pen fst 170	:23 :47 1:124 1:44 3↑ Clm 5000	59 6 4 411 32½ 42½ 53¼ Aviles R B	L 116 b 4.50 83-21	Northern Slugger108nk Henry John1162 Ripplewood116	Tired	8

WORKOUTS: Oct 1 Pim 4½f fst :51 B *10/11* ●Aug 5 Pen 3f fst :361 B *1/9*

Cast Out

Own: Thompson Terry E

CANARY T K (704 117 69 85 .17) *(AS=PACED RACE)* $3,500

Dk. b or br g. 4
Sire: At The Threshold (Norcliffe)
Dam: Chiasma (Chieftain)
Br: Racehorses Inc (Fla)
Tr: Thompson Harry F Jr (549 117 81 89 .21)

L 119

Lifetime Record: 24 4 2 1 $35,108											
1993	9	1	1	0	$4,673	Turf	1	0	0	0	
1992	12	2	1	1	$22,035	Wet	1	0	0	0	
Pen	2	0	0	0		Dist	6	2	1	0	$18,955

9Oct93-10Pen fst 1½	:474 1:133 1:411 2:09 3↑ Clm 3500 *(OPEN)*	50 6 6 45½ 712 815 819¼ Canary T K	L 118 fb 7.50 55-32	Native Reception1204 Southampton1201 Lucky Wilbury1161¾	Thru early	9
19Sep93-5Pim fst 1⅛	:472 1:123 1:39 1:522 3↑ Clm 5000N2Y	18 5 6 66¾ 65½ 1020 1036¾ Luzzi M J	L 117 fb 5.70 41-25	HomeJamesAlfred1172¼ TurkishReason1175 OneTwoPunch1124¼	Stopped	10
1Sep93-4Tim fst 1⅛	:494 1:161 1:44 1:573 3↑ Clm 4000N2mY	63 6 6 32 22½ 2hd 1¾ Castillo F	L 117 fb 3.40 82-28	Cast Out117¾ A Laughing Devil1172 Smart Saint1175	Driving	7
22Aug93-2Pim fst 1⅛	:48 1:124 1:384 1:521 3↑ Clm 5000N2Y	61 1 5 44 43 43½ 43½ Luzzi M J	L 117 fb *1.90 75-16	Aqua Sport1172¼ For Yourself1171½ Bates Back Again112no	Evenly	7
10Aug93-4Pim fst 170	:231 :47 1:114 1:424 3↑ Clm 6000	62 1 5 32 32 34 45¼ Luzzi M J	L 113 fb 5.60 — —	Muddy Rudder1171¼ Malcom F.117½ Island Cruise1173½	Weakened	8
24Jly93-1Lrl fst 6f	:224 :46 :58 1:101 3↑ Clm 5000	77 2 5 44 43½ 32 22 Luzzi M J	L 117 fb 15.30 87-13	Solo Jim's Memory1172 Cast Out1172¼ Tracy Road1142	Rallied	6
13Jly93-2Lrl fst 6f	:223 :462 :584 1:114 3↑ Clm 5000N2Y	53 6 8 78 57½ 46 46 Cullum W5	L 112 20.60 75-19	Village Native114¾ Flying Tempo1191½ Eighty Million1173¾	No threat	8
18Mar93-2Lrl fst 7f	:24 :474 1:132 1:262 Md 5000	5 9 8 88¾ 915 916 927½ Salazar A C7	L 108 b 38.30 49-21	Thoughtful Light1223½ Eppa109½ Sorta Wasso114½	Outrun	9
6Jan93-9Pen fst 170	:234 :482 1:132 1:442 Clm 5000N4L	19 8 7 78¼ 911 919 1029¼ Martin S D	L 117 b 8.30 55-22	Watch For Cops1176 Lees Dream1142 Miei Fratelli1243	Stopped	10
8Dec92-1Lrl fst 6f	:224 :464 :594 1:123 Clm 5000	42 4 8 811 812 810 89 Castillo F5	L 109 b 18.00 69-21	Curry Lane114no Mt. Airy Posse1121½ Blazing Finale1071	Trailed	8

WORKOUTS: Aug 4 Bow 4f fst :494 B *2/6*

Crafty North only rival close to 77

Anthony's Gold

Own: Quaker Cat Stable

VIVES J C (605 59 101 75 .10) $3,500

Dk. b or br g. 5
Sire: Fast Gold (Mr. Prospector)
Dam: Flushed (Gladwin)
Br: Harron Paul F (Pa)
Tr: Minnich Clarence H (332 29 40 42 .09)

L 117

Lifetime Record: 62 6 5 4 $43,981											
1993	21	1	3	2	$9,631	Turf	3	0	0	0	$86
1992	15	2	0	1	$9,735	Wet	11	2	2	0	$13,295
Pen	5	0	0	1	$1,071	Dist	3	0	0	0	$851

9Oct93-8Pen fst 170	:243 :492 1:153 1:473 3↑ Clm 3500N2Y	54 7 3 55½ 67½ 63¾ 63¼ Vives J C	L 117 b 9.10 65-32	Daisy Patch117½ Aristocat1141 Brushed116no	Used up	8
29Sep93-7Pen fst 170	:232 :481 1:151 1:47 3↑ Clm 3500N3Y	44 8 3 33 84 78¾ 79½ Vives J C	L 117 b 6.00 61-25	Southampton117¾ Squeeze The Breeze117¾ Bright Red1172	Gave way	9
4Sep93-8Pen fst 1 1/16	:234 :472 1:122 1:46 3↑ Clm 6250	54 4 1 2hd 42½ 55½ 57¾ Vives J C	L 116 b 14.70 80-16	Rischioso1163¾ Spring Out1161 Captain Daft1163	Gave way	5
23Aug93-7Pen fst 170	:223 :462 1:12 1:432 3↑ Clm 6250	44 4 5 57½ 78¾ 913 915¾ Vives J C	L 116 b 12.50 73-22	Easy Paces1161¾ Rischioso1166 Play Boy G116nk	Stopped	10
1Aug93-9Pen fst 170	:23 :464 1:123 1:442 3↑ Clm 6250	64 4 5 51½ 31 22 3¾ Vives J C	L 116 b 11.10 83-20	Winds Of Change116½ Spotty Brush118nk Anthony's Gold1161¼	No excuse	7
19Jly93-2Pen fm 1 1/16 (T)	1:431 3↑ Clm c-5000	46 4 10 107¾ 89¼ 712 614½ Baker C J	L 116 b 8.20 67-19	Wilkes1221¼ Salem King1168 Del Farno117no	No menace	11
Claimed from Resta Gabe, Delaney Ralph J Jr Trainer						
11Jly93-10Pha fst 170	:231 :471 1:122 1:441 3↑ Clm 5000	63 5 5 53¼ 42 43½ 43 Cecil K Y7	L 109 b 5.20 72-25	Cojaks OrBettor1161¼ CaseTheAce1191 Dancer'sLight116½	Flattened out	7
21Jun93-4Pha my 170	:222 :46 1:114 1:431 3↑ Clm 4000N1Y	70 5 6 56½ 55 1hd 14½ Cecil K Y7	L 109 b 15.00 80-26	Anthony's Gold1094½ Stay Tuned Tumaura1191½ Loader1192	Driving	8
14Jun93-3Pha fst 170	:231 :47 1:121 1:432 3↑ Clm 4000N1Y	54 7 6 78 57½ 45½ 46¼ Ryan K	L 116 b 9.40 73-18	Frigid Dancer1161¼ Encase1164½ Asian Star116½	Some gain	9
31May93-3Pha fst 170	:23 :47 1:124 1:45 3↑ Clm 4000N1Y	45 2 6 67¾ 52¼ 712 611¾ Ryan K	L 116 b 8.00 59-24	Summon Thee1163½ Rams Ace1163 Encase1162		7
Bumped, wide, gave way						

Sea Harrier

Own: Walsky Allison E

FUENTES M (34 6 7 2 .18) $3,000

B. g. 10
Sire: Lively King (Tentam)
Dam: Salati (Dancing Dervish)
Br: Peralta-Ramos Jacqueline (Md)
Tr: Walsky Michael S (156 13 23 21 .08)

L 114 *(116)*

Lifetime Record: 140 27 18 15 $119,599											
1993	16	3	4	3	$9,963	Turf	11	0	1	2	$4,055
1992	23	7	2	2	$17,442	Wet	6	1	0	1	$8,160
Pen	58	13	6	7	$39,021	Dist	83	19	13	7	$65,339

17Oct93-8Pen fst 6f	:222 :454 :584 1:122 3↑ Clm 2500	60 7 3 43½ 44½ 3½ 21 Fuentes M	L 118 fb 15.60 83-16	Ryon's King1201 Sea Harrier1181 Shortstop118½	Saved ground	10
1Oct93-6Pen fst 6f	:223 :461 :59 1:121 3↑ Clm 2500	49 5 8 85½ 33 58 67½ Potts C L	L 118 fb 5.70 77-21	Caballo1221 Lees Dream1225 Bet The Breeze1161½	Tired	9
22Sep93-8Pen fst 6f	:224 :461 :584 1:114 3↑ Clm 3000N1Y	52 1 7 74¾ 72½ 56½ 45½ Deibler C E III	L 117 fb 2.90 81-14	Lees Dream117¾ Jungle Boy1171¾ Shag Dancer1203	Outrun	7
5Sep93-4Pen fst 6f	:223 :462 :591 1:123 3↑ Clm 2500	67 1 5 52¾ 54 43 31¼ Potts C L	L 120 fb 3.40 82-16	Kan Tang Go118¾ Fatty Boy120½ Sea Harrier1203	Saved ground	6
25Aug93-7Pen fst 6f	:221 :461 :59 1:114 3↑ Clm 2500	66 7 7 67 42 2½ 13 Potts C L	L 118 fb *1.70 87-13	Sea Harrier1183 Raspberry Native1163 Schulte1162¼	Drew off	8
16Aug93-9Pen fst 6f	:22 :452 :581 1:113 3↑ Clm 3000	64 1 7 54½ 76¾ 74½ 63½ Flores J L	L 113 fb 3.50 84-20	[D]Denning Start116½ Fatty Boy1181 Steal Man Jack1161½	Outrun	9
4Aug93-5Pen fst 6f	:22 :451 :58 1:113 3↑ Clm 2500	62 6 10 98¾ 77½ 35½ 3½ Potts C L	L 118 fb 4.90 87-15	Paul's Pearl116½ Beth's Dandy116no Sea Harrier1182¾	Late rally	10
21Jly93-3Pen fst 6f	:224 :462 :592 1:121 3↑ Clm 3000N3Y	64 5 6 65¾ 64¾ 55 32½ Ortiz R O5	L 109 fb 11.10 82-20	Crafty North114½ Steal Man Jack1142 Sea Harrier1091¾	Mild rally	6
28Jun93-6Pen fst 6f	:22 :454 :584 1:124 3↑ Clm 2500N2Y	60 8 3 810 76½ 66 11¾ Ortiz R O3	L 114 fb *1.60 82-16	Sea Harrier1141¾ Tom Freda1171 Tre Figlio117nk	Ridden out	9
20Jun93-5Pen fst 6f	:22 :454 :583 1:12 3↑ Clm 2500N2Y	63 4 7 67 3½ 2hd 2no Potts C L	L 122 fb *1.70 86-13	Raspberry Native119no Sea Harrier1221 Tre Figlio117¾	Just missed	9

Lees Dream B. c. 4
Own: Tierra Farms
Sire: English Master (Master Derby)
Dam: Hunting Forbes (Air Forbes Won)
Br: Rivergreen Farm (Fla)
FLORES J L (952 131 129 134 .14) $3,000 Tr: Bellucci Bruno (549 104 71 84 .19) L 116
Lifetime Record: 38 6 6 10 $21,820
1993 12 3 2 3 $8,705 Turf 0 0 0 0
1992 22 3 4 6 $12,754 Wet 4 2 0 1 $4,870
Pen 27 6 6 8 $20,907 Dist 25 6 2 6 $15,879

13Oct93-2Pen fst 6f	:222 :46 :583 1:112 3+ Clm 3000N2Y	53 8 1 32½ 2hd 31½ 35 Flores J L	L 119 f 2.00 84-13	Sevastapuff1173 Crown Of Blue1162 Lees Dream119no	Weakened 8
1Oct93-6Pen fst 6f	:223 :461 :59 1:121 3+ Clm 2500	66 1 3 2½ 1hd 2hd 21 Flores J L	L 122 f 7.00 84-21	Caballi1221 Lees Dream1226 Bet The Breeze1161½	Second best 9
22Sep93-8Pen fst 6f	:224 :461 :584 1:114 3+ Clm 3500N1Y	66 3 5 31½ 2hd 2hd 1¾ Flores J L	L 117 f 6.80 87-14	Lees Dream117¾ Jungle Boy1171½ Shag Dancer1203	Driving 7
6Sep93-4Pen fst 6f	:223 :462 :591 1:12 3+ Clm 2500N2Y	61 7 6 52½ 21½ 2hd 14 Potts C L	L 117 f 2.80e 86-20	Lees Dream1174 Poppy117no Johnny S.1191½	Ridden out 7
27Aug93-10Pen fst 6f	:221 :454 :583 1:114 3+ Clm 2500N2Y	56 9 1 63¾ 33 43½ 46 Flores J L	L 117 f 12.80 81-18	Shortstop1225 Siren's Gold1191 Kalua's Caper117no	Weakened 9
9Aug93-6Pen fst 6f	:222 :461 :59 1:122 3+ Clm 2500N2Y	43 7 7 810 88½ 66¾ 55½ Marvin R J7	L 112 f 11.60 78-18	Scarsdale1172 Jetsdream1191 Poppy117½	No menace 10
24Jly93-5Pen fst 6f	:222 :463 :592 1:13 3+ Clm 2500N2Y	44 3 8 54¾ 73½ 67½ 98½ Flores J L	L 122 f *2.20 73-19	French Date122½ Kalua's Caper1191 DH Once Regal117	Thru early 11
12Jly93-3Pen fst 6f	:231 :471 :593 1:121 3+ Clm 3000N1Y	58 2 6 51½ 41½ 2½ 32¾ Flores J L	L 117 f *.80e 82-17	Genuino113¾ Denning Start1172 Lees Dream1171	Lacked late bid 7
5Jly93-1Pen fst 6f	:222 :454 :59 1:13 3+ Clm 3000N1Y	50 2 7 42½ 44 43½ 33½ Flores J L	L 117 f 3.10 78-21	Diesel Doctor1121 Tonto Equinas1202½ Lees Dream1172	Lacked rally 8
27Jun93-2Pen fst 6f	:223 :462 :591 1:121 3+ Clm 2500N4L	60 4 8 61 21½ 1hd 12 Flores J L	L 117 f 8.80 85-15	Lees Dream1172 Namascus1171 Down To Nothing1102	Drew clear 9

Crafty North B. h. 8
Own: Gilbert Vicki
Sire: Crafty Prospector (Mr. Prospector)
Dam: Attractive Lady (Great Sun)
Br: Aljim Farm Inc (NY)
NO RIDER ( ) $3,000 Tr: Lake Scott A (189 32 26 33 .17) L 114
Lifetime Record: 48 16 6 10 $192,461
1993 11 4 1 1 $9,545 Turf 0 0 0 0
1991 18 6 3 2 $34,952 Wet 4 1 1 1 $12,810
Pen 17 6 3 2 $16,017 Dist 31 12 4 4 $136,131

6Oct93-8Pen fst 5½f	:221 :46 :59 1:054 3+ Clm 2500	46 7 6 63½ 65½ 56½ 47 Deibler C E III	L 118 f 2.60 81-22	Beth's Dandy1161½ Shortstop1185¾ Flo's Boy Max120no	Outrun 7
28Aug93-3Pen fst 6f	:213 :444 :572 1:104 3+ Clm 4000	58 2 5 47 56½ 25 37½ Pinero F E	L 116 fb *1.10 84-17	Smile Be Happy1114 Monsignor K.1153½ Crafty North1161	Saved ground 6
14Aug93-8Pen fst 5½f	:222 :462 :59 1:054 3+ Clm 2500	75 4 2 31 2hd 11 11¾ Pinero F E	L 120 fb *1.30 88 —	Crafty North1201¾ Big Magic1181 Roman Diamond1163	Driving 7
21Jly93-3Pen fst 6f	:224 :462 :592 1:121 3+ Clm 3000N3Y	70 3 5 41 41½ 21½ 1½ Pinero F E	L 114 fb 2.60 85-20	Crafty North114½ Steal Man Jack1142 Sea Harrier1091¾	Driving 6
30Jun93-1Pen fst 5½f	:221 :461 :59 1:053 3+ Clm 3500N2Y	69 6 3 74½ 52½ 4¾ 2½ Pinero F E	L 117 fb *1.10 88-15	Just Plain Justin117½ Crafty North1172 Old Key1192	Wide,second best 7
2Jun93-7Pen fst 5½f	:222 :462 :582 1:06 3+ Clm 2500N2Y	78 4 7 53½ 31 12 16½ Pinero F E	L 122 fb 2.90 92-14	Crafty North1226½ Maclyn1154½ Schulte117nk	Easily 8
19May93-9Pen fst 6f	:222 :454 :581 1:111 3+ Clm 2500N1Y	69 5 8 52¾ 12 14 13½ Pinero F E	L 122 fb 8.40 90-12	Crafty North1223½ Sea Harrier122¾ Little Winston1221¾	Easily 8
2May93-5Pen fst 6f	:221 :451 :574 1:102 3+ Clm 2500N1Y	47 1 8 76½ 46 45½ 49 Pinero F E	L 122 b 9.50 86-12	Major Wager1223½ Xyris1222 Maclyn1223¾	Forced up 9
5Apr93-4Pen fst 6f	:222 :462 :592 1:124 Clm 2500N1Y	50 7 5 54½ 32 63½ 68¾ Vives J C	L 117 b 3.50 75-17	Schavono1171¾ Major Wager1171 Aliento117½	Bid, tired 9
27Feb93-6Pen fst 6f	:224 :463 :59 1:121 Clm 3500N3Y	44 7 5 42½ 41½ 53 66½ Potts C L	L 117 b 6.10 78-17	Sharp Society1171 Too Forever122¾ Mister Ten1171¾	Four wide 7

WORKOUTS: Oct 5 Pen 3f fst :371 B 5/11

The second night of the 1993 World Series of Handicapping at Penn National began with a six-furlong sprint for males aged three and up that had not won two races with a claiming price of more than $2,500 during the past six months.

Normally, this type of race is difficult for once-a-year visitors to get a handle on. Without detailed information about trainer patterns (beyond the rudimentary statistics published in the *Form* and the track program), trips, and/or any track biases that may have been in existence, handicappers seldom find the kind of horses that $100,000 dreams are made of.

Enter Lees Dream, a horse with such a demonstrable advantage in terms of early pace that no computer-generated pace ratings were needed to uncover it. Scanning the entrants for a glimpse of the race's overall characteristics, the following was plain to see:

Siren's Gold: Toward the rear of the field in all recent sprints. He had broken dead last in two previous starts when drawn on the rail.

Crown Of Blue: Dueled for the lead on an off track at Finger Lakes six starts back, but those were the slowest fractions in his current pp's. Well off the early leaders in five subsequent starts.

Fishers Island: Had shown speed in routes in the fall of '92, but had not been an early factor in five starts from June to August when returned from a layoff. Returning from another absence, his record at the distance, 1 for 7, indicated most of his wins had come at longer distances.

CAST OUT: Not without merit, dropping from an unrestricted $3,500 claimer; Beyer of 77 in most recent sprint six starts back was among tops in the field. Still, he hadn't been able to influence early pace going a mile and a quarter last time out, which made him unlikely to be near the early lead going six furlongs.

ANTHONY'S GOLD: Never in the money at the distance, shortening up from a series of routes where he generally raced no closer than midpack in the early stages.

SEA HARRIER: A one-run closing sprinter with no early speed at all.

LEES DREAM: Big early-speed improvement in three most recent races! After being no closer than fourth at the first call from June 27 through September 6, he won September 22 by pressing the pace, engaging in a prolonged head-to-head duel from the turn to deep stretch and edging clear. Saddled with 122 pounds next time out, he broke from the rail, dueled from start to finish, and was five lengths clear of the third-place finisher at the wire. From the extreme outside post October 13 he encountered a pace that was a bit faster than his two previous starts, but was third after a quarter, and challenged for the lead around the turn with a gain of more than two lengths on the pace.

With access to the press box, I went through the result charts to learn that Caballo, who had beaten him by a length on October 1, had returned to win an unrestricted $3,500 claimer a few days ago, and that Sevastapuff, the winner on October 13, had dropped down from $5,000 claimers. The best I could do in the way of trainer patterns was to note from the pp's that Bruno Bellucci was a high-volume guy who had won with an admirable 19 percent of his 549 starters for the year, and to recall that he'd saddled two winners the previous night.

CRAFTY NORTH: Appeared to be the only horse capable of bothering Lees Dream in the early stages, judging from close-to-the-pace win on August 14, which earned him a solid Beyer of 75. Also the field's leading money earner by a wide margin, and a winner of ten of twenty-nine starts over the past two seasons. There was a cloud surrounding his physical condition and readiness for this race, however: after winning four of five starts from May through August while racing every two to three weeks, he had been on the shelf for more than five weeks, returning on October 6 off nothing more than a solitary three-furlong breeze. Dropped to $2,500 that night, he raced toward the rear of the field early and finished a nonthreatening fourth, losing ground at each succeeding call; his Beyer of 46 was his worst figure in five months.

Horses on minor circuits such as Penn National do not stay in the barn for five weeks without a good reason — especially when the horse in question is an eight-year-old who's just won four of his last five starts.

Twenty-twenty hindsight suggests that, with my mythical $1,000 bankroll still relatively intact at $980 after the opening round of the contest, the proper strategy called for me to push all my chips to the center of the table. But for some unknown reason I couldn't do it. I wound up betting only $180, perhaps because I didn't feel like wandering around the track like some lost soul for the rest of the ten-race card, should Lees Dream somehow lose.

It was satisfying to watch the race unfold according to plan. The result went a long way toward convincing me that solid betting propositions can be found at any track, whether Belmont Park or Beulah. But even as Lees Dream flashed under the wire well in front, I felt a sickening sense of loss, for I knew that a golden opportunity to seize command of the World Series had come and gone; I had chosen to play it safe — a conditioned response to long-term play but the wrong approach to a thirty-race contest — and it would be all downhill from there.

FIRST RACE
Penn National
OCTOBER 23, 1993

6 FURLONGS. (1.08^{4}) CLAIMING. Purse $3,700 (Plus 35% PA Bred Bonus) 3-year-olds and upward which have not won two races since April 23. Weights: 3-year-olds, 118 lbs. Older, 122 lbs. Non-winners of a race since September 23, allowed 3 lbs. A race since August 23, 5 lbs. Claiming price $3,500, if for $3,000, allowed 3 lbs. (Races for $2,500 or less not considered in eligibility.)(Day 103 of a 111 Day Meet. Cloudy. 55.)

Value of Race: $3,700 Winner $2,220; second $740; third $407; fourth $222; fifth $111. Mutuel Pool $20,921.00 Exacta Pool $24,300.00

Last Raced	Horse	M/Eqt.	A.	Wt	PP	St	¼	½	Str	Fin	Jockey	Cl'g Pr	Odds $1
13Oct93 ^{2}Pen^{3}	Lees Dream	Lf	4	116	7	1	2^{hd}	1^{hd}	1^{1}	1^{3}	Flores J L	3000	2.20
13Oct93 ^{2}Pen^{6}	Siren's Gold	Lb	4	119	1	6	5^{hd}	3^{hd}	3^{hd}	2^{hd}	Quezada F	3500	12.30
13Oct93 ^{2}Pen^{2}	Crown Of Blue	bf	6	122	2	4	1^{hd}	$4^{1\frac{1}{2}}$	$2^{1\frac{1}{2}}$	3^{1}	Salvaggio M V	3500	3.20
9Oct93 ^{10}Pen^{8}	Cast Out	Lbf	4	119	4	8	$7^{\frac{1}{2}}$	5^{3}	5^{1}	4^{2}	Canary T K	3500	8.80
17Oct93 ^{8}Pen^{2}	Sea Harrier	Lbf	10	116	6	5	$6^{\frac{1}{2}}$	$6^{2\frac{1}{2}}$	6^{3}	$5^{2\frac{3}{4}}$	Fuentes M	3000	8.90
6Oct93 ^{8}Pen^{4}	Crafty North	Lbf	8	116	8	2	4^{1}	2^{hd}	4^{hd}	$6^{\frac{1}{2}}$	Deibler C E III	3000	2.90
9Oct93 ^{8}Pen^{6}	Anthony's Gold	Lb	5	117	5	7	8	7^{hd}	7^{4}	7^{10}	Vives J C	3500	15.30
31Aug93 ^{5}Tim^{6}	Fishers Island	Lb	7	114	3	3	3^{hd}	8	8	8	Forrest C W	3000	12.70

OFF AT 7:31 Start For All But CRAFTY NORTH. Won driving. Time, $:23^2$, :47, $:59^2$, $1:12^1$ Track fast.

$2 Mutuel Prices:				
	7-LEES DREAM	6.40	4.20	3.20
	1-SIREN'S GOLD		9.20	5.60
	2-CROWN OF BLUE			3.20
	$2 EXACTA 7-1 PAID $57.00			

B. c, by English Master–Hunting Forbes, by Air Forbes Won. Trainer Bellucci Bruno. Bred by Rivergreen Farm (Fla).

LEES DREAM vied for the lead between rivals to the stretch, reached the front turning for home then steadily drew away under pressure to prove best. SIREN'S GOLD rallied three-wide nearing the stretch then could not match strides with the winner and outfinished CROWN OF BLUE for second position. The latter dueled for the lead to the stretch then saved ground to no avail. CAST OUT was a factor racing in tight and steadied late. CRAFTY NORTH reared at the start then contested the pace to the stretch and weakened. FISHERS ISLAND stopped

Owners— 1, Tierra Farms; 2, Damore D Hrabovsky J & Mumma C; 3, Dodge Betty Lou; 4, Thompson Terry E; 5, Walsky Allison E; 6, Gilbert Vicki; 7, Quaker Cat Stable; 8, Edmunds Eleanor

Trainers— 1, Bellucci Bruno; 2, Sersch Joe; 3, Dodge Albert; 4, Thompson Harry F Jr; 5, Walsky Michael S; 6, Lake Scott A; 7, Minnich Clarence H; 8, Edmunds Eleanor W

Corrected weight: Sea Harrier (116) **Overweight:** Crafty North (2).

As stated, horses with an early-pace edge win $2,500 claiming sprints, and they also win more than their fair share of the classiest routes. Class may sometimes laugh at pace in Grade 1 routes, as some have said, but don't tell that to anyone who bet against Black Tie Affair in the 1991 Breeders' Cup Classic, a race he won by laying down a methodical series of :24 quarters under Jerry Bailey. And don't tell it to anyone who bet against Quick Mischief in the 1992 John A. Morris Handicap:

8 1⅛ MILES SARATOGA START FINISH

1 ⅛ MILES. **(1.47) 45th Running THE JOHN A MORRIS HANDICAP (Grade I). Purse $200,000. Fillies and mares, 3-year-olds and upward. By subscription of $400 each which should accompany the nomination: $1,600 to pass the entry box, $1,600 to start. The purse to be divided 60% to the winner, 22% to second, 12% to third and 6% to fourth. Weights Wednesday, August 19. Starters to be named at the closing time of entries. Trophies will be presented to the winning owner, trainer and jockey. Closed Wednesday, August 5 with 16 nominations.**

Quick Mischief — B. m. 6, by Distinctive Pro—Mischief Pronto, by Pronto
PERRET C (60 7 7 9 .12) — Br.—Croll W A (Fla)
Own.—Mordas Greg G — Tr.—Carlesimo Charles Jr (1 0 0 0 .00) — 113

Lifetime						
24 10 5 3	1992	4	2	1	0	$82,716
$393,712	1991	2	1	0	0	$21,000
	Turf	1	0	0	0	$1,050
	Wet	2	1	0	1	$145,745

9Aug92- 8Sar	gd	7f	$:22^1$	$:44^3$	$1:21^1$	3↑ⒻBallerin	101	6	4	$2^{1\frac12}$	4^2	$4^{1\frac12}$	$4^{\frac34}$	McCauley W H	113	4.60	98-06 Serpe116¾HrbourClub116hdNnner122	Lckd rm, boxed i	9
9Aug92-Grade I																			
4Jly92- 9Mth	gd	$1\frac{1}{16}$	$:45^4$	$1:10^2$	1:43	3↑ⒻM Pitcher H	97	3	2	2^{hd}	1^2	2^{hd}	$2^{4\frac14}$	Gryder A T	115	3.80	90-12 VrsllsTrt120¼QcMschf115¾CnsWsh113	Stmbld strt,jstl	6
4Jly92-Grade II																			
21Jun92- 9Mth	fst	5f	$:21^4$	$:44^3$	:57	3↑ⒻNauvoo Stks	102	3	4	3^1	$2^{2\frac12}$	2^1	$1^{1\frac14}$	McCauley W H	122	*1.00	96-16 QuickMschf122 1¼ChngABb122 3½DncPly122	Edged clear	6
21Jun92-Originally scheduled on turf																			
5Mar92- 8Aqu	fst	6f	⊡$:22^4$	$:46^2$	$1:11^4$	ⒻAlw 41000	94	5	2	2^1	2^{hd}	$2^{\frac12}$	1^{nk}	McCauley W H	115	*1.30	84-20 QuickMischief115nkShrpImg115 1½ChrgingFir115	Driving	6
23Jun91- 9Mth	fst	1^{70}	$:46^2$	1:11	$1:41^2$	3↑ⒻLadysSecret	49	2	5	5^2	6^7	7^{15}	$8^{23\frac12}$	Gryder A T	117	*.70	65-19 McKlts113⁴TrmptsBlr117 6¾Whnhn117	Stumbld badly st	8
8Jun91-10Mth	fst	6f	$:22^1$	$:45^2$	$1:09^4$	3↑ⒻReadytogo	104	4	2	$2^{1\frac12}$	1^{hd}	$1^{2\frac12}$	$1^{5\frac34}$	Gryder A T	113	2.30	92-15 QckMschf113 5¾InthCrl122 2½CrftyTndron119	Ridden out	5
24Nov90- 9Pha	fst	$1\frac{1}{16}$	$:46^2$	$1:11^3$	$1:45^2$	3↑ⒻWhitemrshH	98	6	2	$2^{3\frac12}$	$2^{\frac12}$	2^{hd}	$2^{\frac34}$	Vargas J L	117	*.90	81-26 Addy Bug112¾ Quick Mischief117⁴ Tia Juanita115	Hung	6
9Nov90- 9Med	fst	1⅛	$:47^4$	$1:12^3$	1:52	3↑ⒻLong LookH	86	5	2	$2^{2\frac12}$	2^1	3^2	$4^{5\frac14}$	Rojas R I	119	*1.50	70-31 BuytheFirm120 3¾SettlDwn114 1¼HppyGini116	Weakened	7
9Nov90-Grade II																			
21Oct90- 9Bel	fst	7f	$:22^2$	$:44^4$	$1:22^2$	3↑Ⓕ1st Flght H	101	4	2	$2^{\frac12}$	2^{hd}	$1^{\frac12}$	$2^{2\frac12}$	Rojas R I	115	4.90	89-18 Qun113 2½QuickMischif115¾APnnyisPnny122	Held place	5
21Oct90-Grade II																			
22Sep90- 8Bel	sly	$1\frac{1}{16}$	$:45^1$	$1:09^4$	$1:42^4$	3↑ⒻRuffian H	96	6	2	2^{hd}	$1^{\frac12}$	$1^{2\frac12}$	1^3	Rojas R I	111	7.20	88-13 QuickMischif111³PrsonlBusinss113⁴Misturin115	Driving	9
22Sep90-Grade I																			

LATEST WORKOUTS ●Aug 3 Mth 5f fst $:59^1$ H ●Jly 26 Mth 1 fst $1:41^4$ B Jly 17 Mth 5f fst $1:03^4$ B ●Jun 28 Mth 1 fst 1:44 H

Risen Colony

B. f. 4, by Pleasant Colony—Cherokee Phoenix, by Nijinsky II

MCCAULEY W H (45 6 6 5 .13)
Own.—Buckland Farm

Br.—Evans T M (Ky)
Tr.—Pearce Ross R (1 0 0 0 .00)

112

Lifetime						
24 6 3 2	1992	8	1	1	1	$102,624
$225,550	1991	15	5	2	0	$119,806
	Turf	5	2	0	0	$19,980
	Wet	1	0	0	0	$12,000

2Aug92- 7Mth	fst	170	:452 1:101 1:423	3↑Ⓕ Lorillard	74	7	8	810	59	47	52¼	Krone J A	b	113	*1.60	81–10	FllSmstr1171Concrd'sGld1191¼MllnDllrMm113	Mild bid	10
19Jly92-11Del	fst	1¼	:50 1:393 2:03	3↑Ⓕ Delaware H	87	1	3	32½	33½	36	38¾	Lidberg D W	b	113	7.00	82–21	BrllntBrss1171¾TrnRbbry1117RsnCln113	Drftd, held 3rd	6
19Jly92-Grade II																			
20Jun92-10Pim	fst	1⅛	:461 1:101 1:49	3↑Ⓕ Pim Distaffh	82	1	5	47½	56½	48½	412½	Luzzi M J	b	114	14.30	78–20	WldrnssSong121nkHrbrClb1102¼BrllntBrss117	No factor	7
25May92- 7Bel	fm	1⅜ Ⓣ	:50 1:374 2:143	3↑Ⓕ SummerGust	87	9	7	73½	63½	54	66½	Santos J A	b	121	5.80	71–14	Srdniy-Ir1212PlntyOfGrc119noVirginMichl119	5 wide tn	9
17Apr92- 8Aqu	sly	1⅛	:461 1:112 1:502	3↑Ⓕ Topflight H	90	14	14	1414	126¼	82¾	41¼	Santos J A	b	115	21.30	83–18	FirmStnce114¾Hunting112nkLdyD'Accord117	Wide trip	14
17Apr92-Grade I																			
29Feb92- 8Aqu	fst	1 3/16 ⊡	:483 1:134 2:001	3↑Ⓕ Next MoveH	94	6	4	54½	54	53½	45¼	McCauley W H	b	117	*2.30	74–36	SpyLdrLdy1123¾Hunting1171½GrcinPss115	Lacked rally	6
29Feb92-Grade III																			
8Feb92- 8Aqu	fst	1⅛ ⊡	:473 1:124 1:52	3↑Ⓕ R Treat H	94	6	3	32	2hd	22	25	McCauley W H	b	118	*1.00	78–26	GrcnPss1125RsnColny1181½TwxtAppl110	Bid, weakened	6
8Feb92-Grade III; Run in Divisions																			
25Jan92-10Lrl	fst	1 1/16	:472 1:122 1:451	3↑Ⓕ Rcg Wr'trsH	97	3	3	34½	33½	11	13½	Luzzi M J	b	116	*.90	87–22	RsnColony1163½WtforthLdy1133½GlGoldlcks114	Driving	6
28Dec91- 9GS	fst	1	:473 1:122 1:38	3↑Ⓕ Del Vlly H	97	4	2	31½	2hd	11	11½	Colton R E	b	115	1.90	89–15	RisenColony1151½GoldenLure1132½FirleWild111	Driving	8
30Nov91- 9Med	fst	1 1/16	:463 1:11 1:44	Ⓕ Honey BeeH	92	3	4	49½	31½	1hd	1½	Chavez J F	b	113	4.50	87–19	RisenColony113½WideCountry1215LongWalk114	Driving	4
30Nov91-Grade III																			

LATEST WORKOUTS ●Aug 20 Del 4f fst :49 B   Jly 12 Del 5f fst 1:012 B   Jly 6 Del 5f fst 1:023 B

Firm Stance

Ch. f. 4, by Affirmed—Du Marche, by Montparnasse II

DAY P (90 11 16 14 .12)
Own.—Gainesway Stable

Br.—Mackebee Lester P (Ky)
Tr.—Shirota Mitch (3 0 1 0 .00)

116

Lifetime						
16 7 3 0	1992	10	3	2	0	$325,788
$431,774	1991	2	2	0	0	$39,598
	Turf	3	1	1	0	$57,178
	Wet	3	2	0	0	$141,749

9Aug92- 8Sar	gd	7f	:221 :443 1:211	3↑Ⓕ Ballerina	99	5	5	87	96½	84¼	51¾	Day P		122	8.20e	97–06	Serape116¾ Harbour Club116hd Nannerl122	Rallied wide	9
9Aug92-Grade I																			
18Jly92-10RD	gd	1 1/16	:48 1:123 1:454	3↑Ⓕ Bud Brd [illegible]	92	4	2	2hd	2hd	11	11	Day P	LB	121	*.50	88–19	FrmStnc1211FppsCosyMss1213OnMmntnTm112	Driving	9
18Jly92-Originally scheduled on turf																			
28Jun92- 9CD	fm	1⅛ Ⓣ	:464 1:103 1:471	3↑Ⓕ Locst Grveh	101	3	4	55	62¼	31	2nk	Johnson P A	LB	118	*2.60	100–01	BhvingDncr117nkFirmStnc118nkOldnRijn112	Weakened	10
14Jun92- 8CD	fm	1 1/16 Ⓣ	:473 1:113 1:414	3↑Ⓕ Alw 40900	100	2	5	55½	54½	51¾	1nk	Johnson P A	LB	119	*1.50	100–05	FirmStance119nkSuperFan119¾Quilma-Ch122	5 wide str	6
1May92- 7CD	fst	1 1/16	:481 1:122 1:44	3↑Ⓕ Bud Bd CpH	91	7	3	53½	53½	44½	43¾	Day P	LB	115	4.00	90–13	Fowda1172DnceColony1141¾FitforQueen120	No late bid	7
1May92-Grade II																			
17Apr92- 8Aqu	sly	1⅛	:461 1:112 1:502	3↑Ⓕ Topflight H	92	7	4	45	83¼	4¾	1¾	Day P		114	*2.10	84–18	FrmStnc114¾Hntng112nkLdD'Accrd117	Svd grnd drvng	14
17Apr92-Grade I																			
14Mar92- 4GP	fm	1 1/16 Ⓣ	:454 1:092 1:392 +	3↑Ⓕ BckrmOkH	100	2	4	48½	711	54	43½	Day P		112	7.90	— —	GrbtheGren1193Christict117hdJuliLRouss-Ir117	Fin well	10
14Mar92-Grade III																			
23Feb92-10GP	fst	1 1/16	:472 1:12 1:433	3↑Ⓕ Rampart H	98	12	4	53½	53¼	22½	25½	Day P		111	10.50	88–19	Fit For A Queen1195½ Firm Stance1117¼ Nannerl113		12
23Feb92-Grade II; 4 wide backstretch, final turn																			
2Feb92-10GP	fst	7f	:223 :453 1:231	3↑Ⓕ S Jones H	95	7	4	41½	61¾	33½	41	Lopez R D		113	8.30	89–12	Nnnrl111hdWthliprbblty1201FtFrAQn119	Brshd svrl tms	10
2Feb92-Grade III																			
15Jan92- 9GP	fst	6f	:221 :453 1:11	3↑Ⓕ First Lady H	91	8	9	116½	99	79	53¾	Lopez R D		113	6.70	84–21	Wthllprbblt1183ChrstnCrn114½SprtfFghtr114	5 Wide str	14

LATEST WORKOUTS Aug 16 Sar tr.t 4f gd :503 B   Aug 7 Sar 3f fst :37 B   ●Aug 3 Sar tr.t 3f fst :354 H   Jly 16 CD 3f fst :383 B

Versailles Treaty

B. f. 4, by Danzig—Ten Cents a Dance, by Buckpasser

SMITH M E (118 23 19 16 .19)
Own.—Phipps Cynthia

Br.—Phipps Cynthia (Ky)
Tr.—McGaughey Claude III (17 0 7 3 .00)

122

Lifetime						
16 8 6 2	1992	4	1	1	2	$148,318
$852,154	1991	11	6	5	0	$689,636
	Wet	2	0	1	1	$35,726

4Jly92- 9Mth	gd	1 1/16	:454 1:102 1:43	3↑Ⓕ M Pitcher	104	6	5	55½	22	1hd	14½	Smith M E		120	*.40	94–12	VrsllsTrty1204½QckMschf1153½Czn'sWsh113	Ridden out	6
4Jly92-Grade II																			
31May92- 0Del	sly	1⅛	:451 1:084 1:47	3↑Ⓕ Hempstead	104	1	4	32	42	32	33¼	Smith M E		119	*1.20	91–09	Mssy'sMrg1183HrbrClb110nkVrsllsTrty119	Evenly inside	6
31May92-Grade I																			
9May92- 0Bel	gd	1 1/16	:451 1:091 1:403	3↑Ⓕ Shuvee H	100	4	4	21½	21	32	3nk	Smith M E		119	*.50	99–07	Mssy'sMrg118noHrbourClb110nkVrsllsTrty119	Willingly	6
9May92-Grade I																			
18Apr92- 5Aqu	my	7f	:23 :454 1:204	3↑Ⓕ Life's Magic	104	1	4	43½	43	22	21¾	Smith M E		117	*.60	99–06	Mssy'sMrg1191¾VrsllsTrty11713Brchn'sLss119	Willingly	4
2Nov91- 4CD	fst	1⅛	:471 1:114 1:504	3↑Ⓕ Br Cp Dstff	105	9	7	78	64	42¼	21½	Cordero A Jr		120	4.80	92–09	DncSrtl1201½VrsllsTrt1202¾BrhtTMd123	Wide, 2nd best	13
2Nov91-Grade I																			
6Oct91- 7Bel	gd	1⅛	:464 1:104 1:48	3↑Ⓕ Beldame	101	1	3	23	1hd	2hd	2no	Cordero A Jr		119	*1.20	89–11	ShrpDnce123noVersillsTrty1199LdyD'Accord123	Gamely	6
6Oct91-Grade I																			
31Aug91- 8Bel	fst	1⅛	:464 1:104 1:472	Ⓕ Gazelle H	95	7	3	57¾	2hd	11	1½	Cordero A Jr		123	*.90	92–08	VersillesTrety123½GrndGirlfrind1151¾Immrs112	Driving	8
31Aug91-Grade I																			
10Aug91- 9Sar	gd	1¼	:471 1:361 2:022	Ⓕ Alabama	96	2	3	21½	1½	12	14½	Cordero A Jr		121	*.90	92–15	VersillesTrty1214½TilForbid1211DsigntdDncr121	Driving	6
10Aug91-Grade I																			
27Jly91- 8Sar	fst	7f	:214 :441 1:224	Ⓕ Test	101	6	2	74½	53½	31	12¾	Cordero A Jr		114	5.20	91–09	VrsllsTrty1142¾Ifycldsmnw1212½ⒹZmHmmr121	Bumped	7
27Jly91-Grade I																			
24Jun91- 8Bel	fst	7f	:224 :451 1:214	3↑Ⓕ Alw 30000	93	5	2	31	42	1hd	11¾	Cordero A Jr		109	*.40	95–06	VrsllsTrt1091¾PrdKrn1174BrhtCndls117	Steadied 3/8 pl	5

LATEST WORKOUTS Aug 21 Sar tr.t 4f fst :503 B   Aug 16 Sar tr.t 4f gd :481 H   Aug 10 Sar tr.t 4f fst :502 B   Aug 3 Sar tr.t 4f fst :501 B

Shared Interest

B. f. 4, by Pleasant Colony—Surgery, by Dr Fager

KRONE J A (92 18 11 13 .20)
Own.—Evans Robert S

Br.—Folsom Robert S (N.Y.)
Tr.—Schulhofer Flint S (32 9 5 3 .28)

111

Lifetime						
9 6 1 0	1992	2	1	0	0	$27,000
$173,400	1991	7	5	1	0	$146,400
	Wet	1	1	0	0	$28,200

9Aug92- 8Sar	gd	7f	:221 :443 1:211	3↑Ⓕ Ballerina	97	2	8	43	53	63½	62¾	Krone J A		116	*1.70e	96–06	Serape116¾ Harbour Club116hd Nannerl122	Four wide	9
9Aug92-Grade I																			
19Jly92- 1Bel	fst	6½f	:222 :451 1:162	3↑Ⓕ Alw 45000	92	5	2	3½	2hd	1½	11½	Krone J A		113	1.70	91–13	ShredInterest1131½PupptShow1194MkinFcs119	Driving	5
18Oct91- 8Med	fst	1	:46 1:103 1:36	3↑Ⓕ BrlngtnCnty	92	1	3	32	3½	11	11¼	Krone J A		114	*.90	99–06	ShrdIntrst1141¼Cn'sWsh1135TxtAppl113	Boxed in, drvg	7
20Jly91-11Mth	fst	1⅛	:46 1:102 1:502	Ⓕ Mth Oaks	91	6	5	63¾	31	21	21¼	Krone J A		114	4.90	85–13	Fowda1211¼ SharedInterest1142¼NaleesPin116	Willingly	8
20Jly91-Grade II																			
6Jly91- 8Bel	gd	1¼	:462 1:343 2:002	Ⓕ C C A Oaks	82	6	3	34	43½	47½	417¼	Krone J A		121	4.60e	78–05	Lite Light1217 MeadowStar1212CarGal121	Lacked rally	6
6Jly91-Grade I																			
19Jun91- 8Bel	sly	1 1/16	:453 1:10 1:423	3↑Ⓕ Handicap	92	2	2	2hd	11	13	13	Krone J A		109	*1.20	89–11	ShredInterst1093LdyD'Accord1153Coroly116	Mild drive	5
13May91- 7Bel	fst	1 1/16	:47 1:12 1:43	3↑Ⓕ Alw 31000	104	3	3	31	2½	1hd	1nk	Krone J A		110	*.70	87–19	ShredInterst110nkGtLucky11118TopCrdit119	Long drive	5
26Apr91- 7Aqu	fst	7f	:221 :444 1:231	3↑Ⓕ Alw 27000	92	4	8	31½	22	1½	14½	Krone J A		115	*.40	86–15	ShrdIntrst1154½QcTBlm1112BldLdE.114	Broke slow, drv	9
6Apr91- 6Aqu	fst	7f	:231 :454 1:231	Ⓕ Md Sp Wt	97	3	5	2½	2½	11½	15	Smith M E		121	5.50	86–18	ShredInterest1215Husmn12110Streming121	Ridden out	6

LATEST WORKOUTS Aug 17 Sar 5f gd 1:014 B   Aug 13 Bel tr.t 3f fst :362 B   Aug 7 Sar 4f fst :494 B   Aug 2 Sar 4f fst :483 B

Lady D'Accord — Ch. m. 5, by D'Accord—Avichi, by Damascus
ANTLEY C W (118 26 18 15 .22) — Br.—Hettinger John (NY)
Own.—Akindale Farm — Tr.—Zito Nicholas P (21 1 1 2 .05) — 114

Lifetime						
38 8 7 8	1992	6	2	0	1	$131,366
$502,158	1991	16	2	1	6	$186,255
	Turf	3	0	1	0	$6,820
	Wet	8	2	1	2	$125,822

1Aug92- 6Sar gd 1 :453 1:101 1:361 3+ⒻHandicap 97 4 8 84¾ 31 1½ 13 Smith M E 122 2.70 — — LdyD'Accord1223DncColony1201½MssKrryC.111 Driving 8
31May92- 8Bel sly 1⅛ :451 1:084 1:47 3+ⒻHempsteadH 80 4 6 66 55½ 58½ 517 Perret C 114 5.60 77–09 Mssy'sMrg1183HrbourClb110nkVrsllsTrty119 No threat 6
31May92-Grade I
9May92- 8Bel gd 1$\frac{1}{16}$:451 1:091 1:403 3+ⒻShuvee H 83 2 6 65 42½ 48 49¾ Chavez J F 116 5.80 89–07 Mssy'sMrg116noHrbourClb110nkVrsllsTrty119 No threat 6
9May92-Grade I
17Apr92- 8Aqu sly 1⅛ :461 1:112 1:502 3+ⒻTopflight H 90 13 13 1312136¾ 61¼ 31 Chavez J F 117 4.50 83–18 FrmStnc114¾Huntng112nkLdyD'Accord117 Blckd, chckd 14
17Apr92-Grade I
29Mar92- 8Aqu fst 1 :471 1:121 1:374 3+ⒻBed O R's H 96 4 7 51½ 2hd 1½ 13¼ Chavez J F 114 3.40 73–33 LdyD'Accrd1143¼MyTrsr1121¾CrystlVs112 Wide, driving 7
29Mar92-Grade II
12Mar92- 9GP fst 7f :224 :46 1:234 ⒻAlw 29000 71 5 6 74¾ 75 75¾ 59 Fires E 117 9.30 78–18 EclsvBrd1171½Jnn'sPlmt1174IvrPrncss-Ir114 No factor 8
24Nov91- 8Aqu gd 1¼ :473 1:37 2:022 3+ⒻLadies H 90 6 8 66½ 33½ 33½ 36¼ Cordero A Jr 116 *1.50 83–22 Wrthrtsnld113nkSmrMtn1156LdDAccrd116 Lacked rally 8
24Nov91-Grade II
2Nov91- 4CD fst 1⅛ :471 1:114 1:504 3+ⒻBr Cp Dstff 90 3 13 11131210109¾1010¾ Santos J A B 123 160.70 83–09 DncSmrtly1201½VrsllsTrty1202¾BroghtTMnd123 Outrun 13
2Nov91-Grade I
6Oct91- 7Bel gd 1⅛ :464 1:104 1:48 3+ⒻBeldame 86 4 6 66½ 64¼ 44½ 39 Santos J A 123 8.00 80–11 ShrpDnc123noVrsillsTrty1199LdyD'Accord123 No threat 6
6Oct91-Grade I
21Sep91- 8Bel fst 1$\frac{1}{16}$:462 1:103 1:413 3+ⒻRuffian H 101 2 7 76 72¾ 42 31¾ Perret C 113 13.80 92–14 Queen120¾ShrpDnce1141½LdyD'Accord113 Rallied wide 7
21Sep91-Grade I
LATEST WORKOUTS Aug 21 Sar 3f fst :354 H Aug 16 Sar 5f my 1:01 H Aug 10 Sar 5f gd 1:02 B ●Jly 27 Sar 5f fst :594 H

Dance Colony — B. m. 5, by Pleasant Colony—Dance Review, by Northern Dancer
BAILEY J D (96 13 18 9 .14) — Br.—Evans T M (Ky)
Own.—Dinwiddle Farm — Tr.—Arnold George R II (17 2 3 3 .12) — 111

Lifetime						
22 6 5 2	1992	4	0	2	0	$53,340
$469,070	1991	2	1	0	0	$30,660
	Turf	1	0	0	0	
	Wet	6	2	1	0	$90,600

1Aug92- 6Sar gd 1 :453 1:101 1:361 3+ⒻHandicap 91 5 6 72¾ 41¼ 2½ 23 Bailey J D 120 3.90 — — LdyD'Accrd1223DncClny1201½MssKrrC.111 Second best 8
31May92- 8Bel sly 1⅛ :451 1:084 1:47 3+ⒻHempsteadH 93 6 3 42½ 31½ 44½ 49¾ Bailey J D 113 21.30 84–09 Mssy'sMrg1183HrborClb110nkVrsllsTrty119 Wide, tired 6
31May92-Grade I
1May92- 7CD fst 1$\frac{1}{16}$:481 1:122 1:44 3+ⒻBud Bd €pH 94 6 2 21 1hd 2½ 22 Stevens G L B 114 20.50 92–13 Fowd1172DnceColony1141¾FitforQuen120 Bid, 2nd best 7
1May92-Grade II
12Apr92- 7Kee fst *7f :222 :451 1:263 ⒻAlw 30000 84 7 9 44 54 42½ 55½ Bailey J D B 113 5.00 91–12 WildernessSong1212½WdddBliss113¾HrdFrz110 No rally 12
10Oct91- 1Bel fst 1$\frac{1}{16}$:48 1:122 1:434 3+ⒻHandicap 90 4 2 21½ 2hd 11 1no Smith M E 119 4.40 83–22 DncColony119noGottgttdon1164¾HrShShwklt117 All out 5
27Jun91- 8Bel fst 7f :221 :452 1:23 3+ⒻAlw 41000 85 3 5 66½ 54 51¼ 45¾ McCauley W H 117 6.10 83–15 LckyLdyLrn1172¼TxtAppl1173½LckyDlght117 No threat 7
3Nov90-11Lrl fst 1⅛ :472 1:123 1:502 ⒻA Arundel H 78 2 2 1½ 2½ 36 510¼ Miller D A Jr b 116 *2.00 79–21 McKilts1144Trumpt'sBlr1156Scrto'sGlory113 Gave way 6
11Oct90- 8Bel fst 1$\frac{1}{16}$:46 1:10 1:414 3+ⒻHandicap 90 4 2 2½ 3nk 31 35½ Cordero A Jr b 117 *2.30 87–06 Gottgttdon1131½Nskr'sRtrn1214DncColny117 Weakened 6
22Sep90-10Pha sly 1$\frac{1}{16}$:463 1:112 1:434 ⒻCotillion H 87 1 4 43 44 68 612½ Ayarza I b 117 6.00 77–16 VlyMid1195Toffeefe1151½Trumpt'sBlr116 Saved ground 8
22Sep90-Grade II
29Aug90- 8Bel fst 1⅛ :46 1:104 1:504 ⒻGazelle H 97 6 5 43 22½ 1hd 2nk McCauley W H b 116 23.80 80–26 HighlandTalk111nkDanceColony1163¾SheCn116 Gamely 7
29Aug90-Grade I
LATEST WORKOUTS Aug 21 Sar tr.t 3f fst :372 B Aug 16 Sar tr.t 5f gd 1:053 B Aug 10 Sar tr.t 5f fst 1:04 B Jly 20 Bel 4f fst :503 B

Versailles Treaty, one of the most consistent fillies a handicapper will ever encounter, was the 3–5 favorite as she emerged from a convincing win in Monmouth's Molly Pitcher. She had been first or second in all but two of her sixteen career starts, and her victories in the Test and Alabama the previous summer attested to the fact that she had no problems handling the Saratoga surface.

Quick Mischief was the second choice at 7–2, and, although she had been four lengths behind Versailles Treaty in the Molly Pitcher, there were some obvious indicators that she was capable of reversing the decision in the Morris. The Molly Pitcher had been Quick Mischief's first route start in more than a year, and she had run exceptionally well in light of the fact that she stumbled and was jostled about at the start, engaged in a head-to-head duel through a half in :45⅘, repulsed the early challengers, and held on to be well clear for the place. Versailles Treaty, meanwhile, had been allowed to relax off the early-pace duel, and swept by in the final furlong.

In the Morris, however, Quick Mischief might now be the horse with a conditioning edge. She had been beaten by less than a length in the Ballerina while pressing fractions of :22⅕ and :44⅗, and the chart footnote revealed a horrific trip:

"Quick Mischief, up close early while saving ground, was trapped along the inside on the turn and through most of the stretch, angled out in deep stretch and rallied belatedly."

Versailles Treaty had not been out since early July, showed no workouts longer than four furlongs, and would be picking up two pounds off the Molly Pitcher, while Quick Mischief would be dropping two.

Most important of all, Quick Mischief had been crying to run through those torrid Ballerina fractions but was unable to find room to maneuver until it was too late. Stretching back to two turns for the Morris, she was drawn on the rail, and appeared the dominant early-pace horse in the field. In all probability, she would be able to clear the field heading to the clubhouse turn and slow things down to a crawl.

The Morris was a classic example of how the pace dynamics of a race, along with changes in form cycles, can be key factors in the reversal of a previous result. Quick Mischief was sure to be "tighter" for this route than she had been for her initial tussle with Versailles Treaty, and she was probably going to have a much easier time controlling the fractions as well.

In the running, Quick Mischief stole away to a clear lead through dawdling splits of :24⅗ and :48⅗, which ensured she would have plenty in reserve for the final run to the wire. Indeed she did, winning by nearly seven lengths, with Versailles Treaty along to complete a $27.20 exacta:

EIGHTH RACE
Saratoga
AUGUST 23, 1992

1 ⅛ MILES. (1.47) 45th Running THE JOHN A MORRIS HANDICAP (Grade I). Purse $200,000. Fillies and mares, 3-year-olds and upward. By subscription of $400 each which should accompany the nomination: $1,600 to pass the entry box, $1,600 to start. The purse to be divided 60% to the winner, 22% to second, 12% to third and 6% to fourth. Weights Wednesday, August 19. Starters to be named at the closing time of entries. Trophies will be presented to the winning owner, trainer and jockey. Closed Wednesday, August 5 with 16 nominations.

Value of race $200,000; value to winner $120,000; second $44,000; third $24,000; fourth $12,000. Mutuel pool $336,184. Exacta Pool $452,839 Triple Pool $343,771

Last Raced	Horse	M/Eqt.	A.Wt	PP	St	¼	½	¾	Str	Fin	Jockey	Odds $1
9Aug92 ^{8}Sar^4	Quick Mischief		6 113	1	1	1½	$1^{1\frac{1}{2}}$	1^1	1^2	$1^{6\frac{3}{4}}$	Perret C	3.90
4Jly92 ^{9}Mth^1	Versailles Treaty		4 122	4	2	4^1	4^1	3^1	4^4	2½	Smith M E	.70
9Aug92 ^{8}Sar^6	Shared Interest		4 111	5	6	5½	2^{hd}	2½	2^{hd}	$3^{1\frac{1}{2}}$	Krone J A	10.40
9Aug92 ^{8}Sar^5	Firm Stance		4 116	3	3	2^{hd}	3½	4^3	3½	4^{12}	Day P	4.40
1Aug92 ^{6}Sar^1	Lady D'Accord		5 114	6	5	7	7	5^{hd}	5^2	5^6	Antley C W	8.90
1Aug92 ^{6}Sar^2	Dance Colony		5 111	7	7	6^{hd}	6^{hd}	6	6	6	Bailey J D	26.70
2Aug32 ^{7}Mth^5	Risen Colony	b	4 112	2	4	3^{hd}	5½	—	—	—	McCauley W H	43.40

Risen Colony, Pulled up.

OFF AT 5:13 Start good. Won driving. Time, :24 3, :48 3, 1:11 4, 1:35 3, 1:47 4 Track fast.

$2 Mutuel Prices:				
	1-(A)-QUICK MISCHIEF	9.80	4.20	3.60
	4-(D)-VERSAILLES TREATY		2.60	2.20
	5-(E)-SHARED INTEREST			3.40

$2 EXACTA 1-4 PAID $27.20 $2 TRIPLE 1-4-5 PAID $149.00

B. m, by Distinctive Pro—Mischief Pronto, by Pronto. Trainer Carlesimo Charles Jr. Bred by Croll W A (Fla).

QUICK MISCHIEF, sprinted clear in the early stages, was rated on the lead through moderate fractions for five furlongs, extended her margin when asked for run approaching the stretch, then drew off under steady pressure. VERSAILLES TREATY, settled just behind the winner for six furlongs, lagged behind slightly in upper stretch then finding her best stride outfinished SHARED INTEREST for the place. SHARED INTEREST bumped at the start, angled quickly to the inside, was unhurried through the opening half mile, moved up between horses along the backstretch, lodged a mild rally outside the winner to threaten on the turn, remained a factor into midstretch then lacked a strong closing bid. FIRM STANCE raced in close contention between horses along the backstretch, angled to the inside on the far turn, rallied along the rail to threaten in midstretch but couldn't sustain her bid. LADY D'ACCORD bumped with SHARED INTEREST at the start then never reached contention. DANCE COLONY, strung out five wide on the first turn, was never a factor. RISEN COLONY pulled up lane on the far turn and was vanned off.

Owners— 1, Mordas Greg G; 2, Phipps Cynthia; 3, Evans Robert S; 4, Gainesway Stable; 5, Akindale Farm; 6, Dinwiddle Farm; 7, Buckland Farm.

Trainers— 1, Carlesimo Charles Jr; 2, McGaughey Claude III; 3, Schulhofer Flint S; 4, Shirota Mitch; 5, Zito Nicholas P; 6, Arnold George R II; 7, Pearce Ross R.

LATE-PACE ADVANTAGES

Horses capable of controlling the early pace win far more than their fair share of races, but the "lone closer" enjoys a similar advantage to the "lone speed."

8 START 6 FURLONGS INNER DIRT TRACK AQUEDUCT FINISH

6 FURLONGS. **(InnerDirt). (1.08 3) HANDICAP. Purse $41,000. Fillies and Mares, 3-year-olds and upward. Weights Saturday, December 19. Declarations by 10:00 A.M. Sunday, December 20.**

Golden Bimmer — Dk. b. or br. f. 3(Feb), by Gold Meridian—Song of Peace, by Hold Your Peace
SAMYN J L (41 4 7 8 .10) — Br.—Mar-Ro-Mar Investments (Fla)
Own.—Joques Farm — Tr.—Moschera Gasper S (38 4 9 11 .11) — 111

Lifetime 21 9 3 1 $157,860 — 1992 14 7 3 0 $139,060 — 1991 7 2 0 1 $18,800 — Wet 3 3 0 0 $56,360

6Dec92- 7Aqu fst 1 1/16 ⊡:48 2 1:13 2 1:46 3 ⒻShy Dawn 75 2 1 1hd 2hd 21 56 Migliore R b 118 *2.20 69-31 GroovyFlng1162Nbl'sHny1183PrfctGm116 Dueled inside 7
13Nov92- 7Aqu gd 6f :21 4 :45 1 1:10 1 ⒻClm 90000 78 4 2 31 3½ 43 44½ McCauley W H b 117 *.80 85-17 MssClrAppl111nkStrtcRrd1152¼PrfctLss121 Lacked rally 5
22Oct92- 6Aqu fst 6½f :23 :46 3 1:17 3 3↑ⒻAlw 41000 85 2 6 1½ 12 2½ 45½ McCauley W H b 114 3.00 84-18 Bn'sMomnt1221¾ChrstnCzrn1151¼RglVctrss119 Used up 6
6Jun92- 4Bel my 1 1/16 :46 1:10 2 1:42 4 ⒻTanya Stk 92 2 1 12 14 110 116 McCauley W H b 116 *.70 88-08 GoldnBmmr11616SwtWll114½Bwm114 Bobld brk,handly 5
6Jun92-Originally scheduled on turf
24May92- 6Bel fst 6f :22 2 :45 1 1:09 3 3↑ⒻAlw 30000 91 5 5 32 31½ 31 21½ Santos J A b 113 *1.30 90-11 Miss KerryC.1211½GoldenBimmer1132Scant110 2nd best 5
14May92- 7Bel fst 7f :22 :45 1 1:22 4 ⒻAlw 28000 89 2 1 34 32 11½ 12 Santos J A b 116 *.70e 90-08 GoldnBimmr1162DixChms1164LookngforWn116 Driving 7
7May92- 8Bel fst 6f :22 :45 1:09 4 3↑ⒻAlw 28000 87 5 1 21 1½ 11 21½ Santos J A b 114 *1.50 89-13 MissKerryC.1191½GoldenBimmer1142¼Vivno112 2nd bst 8
22Apr92- 7Aqu my 6f :22 :45 1:10 ⒻClm 72500 94 5 1 21½ 1½ 13½ 15½ Santos J A b 114 *1.00 91-16 GoldnBmmr1145½NrthrnDstr112nkKrsy109 Kept to drive 6
10Apr92- 6Aqu fst 6f :22 3 :46 1:11 ⒻClm c-50000 83 3 2 11 11 13½ 15 Antley C W b 116 1.40 86-18 GoldenBimmer1165Kt'sCollg118nkBSpcil114 Ridden out 6
10Apr92-Claimed from Bauer Robert J, Forbes John H Trainer
12Mar92- 4GP fst 7f :23 :46 2 1:25 4 ⒻClm 40000 67 8 4 51½ 62¼ 31½ 1hd Krone J A Lb 116 *1.90 77-18 GldnBmmr116hdUptnSh116nkGrndCch112 Driving inside 12
LATEST WORKOUTS Dec 1 Bel tr.t 4f fst :48 1 H ●Nov 9 Bel tr.t 4f fst :47 4 H

Makin Faces — B. f. 4, by Premiership—Political Mixup, by Political Coverup
DAVIS R G (85 15 10 4 .18) — Br.—Powell & Robinson A & A G (Fla)
Own.—Sabine Stable — Tr.—Barbara Robert (9 1 1 1 .11) — 122

Lifetime 29 8 5 8 $308,368 — 1992 8 2 0 3 $89,930 — 1991 15 5 3 4 $159,522 — Turf 1 0 0 0 $260 — Wet 2 0 0 0

12Sep92- 7Med gd 5f Ⓣ:21 4 :45 :57 2 3↑ⒻAlw 26000 68 7 4 53½ 54 67¼ 77½ Carr D 115 6.10 82-10 Baby o' Mine117hd Quick Casting1154½Maxixe119 Tired 10
19Jly92- 1Bel fst 6½f :22 2 :45 1 1:16 2 3↑ⒻAlw 45000 79 4 1 1hd 3nk 32 35¼ Smith M E 119 *1.20 85-13 ShrdIntrst1131½PpptShw1194MknFcs119 Dueled, wknd 5
21Jun92- 8Bel fst 7f :22 3 :45 2 1:22 2 3↑ⒻVagrancy H 78 5 2 11 11½ 3½ 38¼ Carr D 112 4.20 84-10 Nannerl1162 Serape1156¼ Makin Faces112 Speed, tired 6
21Jun92-Grade III
25May92- 5Bel fst 6½f :22 4 :45 3 1:16 2 3↑ⒻAlw 41000 99 4 2 11 1½ 12½ 12¼ Smith M E 117 2.20 91-10 MakinFces1172¼PuppetShow119½MedowStr117 Driving 5
15Mar92- 8Aqu fst 7f :22 4 :46 3 1:24 3 3↑ⒻDistaff H 73 3 5 11½ 11 53½ 613 Velazquez J R 113 13.50 69-25 Nnnrl1123½Missy'sMrg1192¼Wthllprobblty117 Gave way 6
15Mar92-Grade II
23Feb92- 8Aqu fst 6f ⊡:22 4 :45 4 1:10 3↑ⒻCorrectionH 96 3 3 1½ 11 2½ 34 Smith M E 114 3.60 89-16 Mss'sMrg1163DvlshTch1171MnFcs114 Speed weakened 6
2Feb92- 8Aqu fst 6f ⊡:23 2 :47 1 1:12 4 3↑ⒻBerlo H 97 6 1 13 12 12 11 Smith M E 113 6.60 79-27 MkinFces1131DevilishTouch117nkRlIrishHop115 Driving 6
1Jan92- 8Aqu fst 6f ⊡:22 3 :45 3 1:10 4 3↑ⒻInterboro H 71 5 3 2hd 2hd 66¾ 710¾ Smith M E 115 4.10 78-13 WoodSo1111½DevilishTouch1181½DoItWithStyl116 Tired 7
1Jan92-Grade III
21Dec91- 7Aqu fst 6f ⊡:22 :45 2 1:11 1 3↑ⒻAlw 41000 99 7 3 11½ 13 14 11¼ Santagata N 120 2.90 87-16 MkinFces1201¼RelIrishHop1221CrftyTndroni115 Driving 7
20Nov91- 8Aqu fst 6f :22 :45 2 1:10 3 3↑ⒻHandicap 90 3 2 1hd 1½ 1½ 3nk Smith M E 114 3.00 88-14 ChristinaCzarin116nk⊡Serpe113noMkinFces114 Gamely 6
20Nov91-Placed second through disqualification
LATEST WORKOUTS ●Dec 15 Bel tr.t 5f fst 1:00 4 H Nov 29 Bel tr.t 5f fst 1:00 1 H ●Nov 20 Bel 4f fst :46 2 H ●Nov 14 Bel tr.t 3f fst :35 4 H

Lady Sage — B. f. 3(Feb), by Lord Gaylord—Foxcroft Finale, by Real Value
Br.—David P. Reynolds (Md)
SANTAGATA N (56 7 4 5 .13)
Own.—Reynolds David P
Tr.—Kelly Tim (—)
113
Lifetime 9 4 2 2 $74,360 | 1992 9 4 2 2 $74,360 | 1991 0 M 0 0 | Wet 1 1 0 0 $9,300

15Nov92- 5Aqu	fst	7f	:231	:463	1:234	ⒻAladancer	80	1	3	54	53½	53½	57	Perret C		121	6.70	79-19	Mrs. P Minister121hd Squirm121½ Preach121	4 wide	5
30Oct92- 5Aqu	fst	6f	:23	:463	1:113	3↑ⒻAlw 30000	87	3	5	61½	21½	1½	12½	Rodriguez R R7		1064	3.90	83-17	DHLadySage1062½DHPrech1142½LightsofMrf114	Driving	6
30Oct92-Dead heat																					
26Sep92-10Pim	gd	1 1/16	:46	1:104	1:443	ⒻOaks	79	7	5	76½	67	35	35¾	Pino M G	L	114	3.50	75-18	Deputation1142¾SingingRing1143LadySage114	Steadied	7
8Aug92- 5Sar	fst	6f	:222	:453	1:102	3↑ⒻAlw 28000	85	5	5	53	4¾	1hd	1½	Maple E		112	*1.80	92-07	LadySage112½StrategicReward1121½EpicVill119	Driving	7
17Jly92- 7Bel	fst	6f	:231	:46	1:10	3↑ⒻAlw 28000	90	2	3	41½	41	32	31¾	Perret C		113	*.70	88-12	MyNecessity111hdStrtgicRwrd1111¾LdySg113	Mild rally	6
27Jun92- 3Bel	fst	6f	:222	:451	1:092	ⒻAlw 27000	96	3	2	42½	3½	1hd	14	Perret C		121	3.00	93-12	LadySge1214Bob'sLittleGl116½S.S.Sprkle116	Drew clear	6
20Jun92- 5Mth	my	6f	:221	:45	1:103	3↑ⒻMd Sp Wt	75	7	2	44	2hd	1½	11¾	Lidberg D W		115	*.60	88-13	LadySage1151¾Roxaneka115noPstEFgioli115	Drew clear	8
23Apr92- 5Kee	fst	6f	:221	:46	1:094	ⒻMd Sp Wt	97	1	1	11½	11	1hd	2½	Lopez R D	LB	121	2.80	93-09	HrbrSprngs121½LdS12118DnsClb121	Exchngd bmps 2nd	11
8Apr92- 3Kee	fst	6½f	:223	:47	1:181	ⒻMd Sp Wt	63	10	4	51¼	1hd	1hd	22½	Lopez R D	LB	121	56.40	83-09	SvthD1212½LdySg1216½GdnghtLvng121	Dueled 2nd best	11

LATEST WORKOUTS Dec 14 Bel tr.t 5f my 1:031 B Dec 5 Bel tr.t 4f fst :493 B Nov 28 Bel tr.t 4f fst :493 B ● Nov 9 Bel tr.t 5f fst 1:001 H

Christina Czarina — B. f. 4, by Czaravich—Christines Pixie, by Mr Prospector
Br.—Stavola M J (NJ)
BRUIN J E (49 3 5 6 .06)
Own.—Lorraine & Cindy Stable
Tr.—Jerkens H Allen (14 4 2 1 .29)
116
Lifetime 32 7 10 5 $278,121 | 1992 9 0 3 3 $46,486 | 1991 18 5 5 2 $165,622 | Turf 3 0 3 0 $17,000 | Wet 3 0 0 1 $12,626

14Dec92- 7Aqu	gd	6f	⊡:23	:462	1:104	3↑ⒻAlw 41000	79	3	4	42½	32½	31½	33½	Bruin J E		115	*1.20e	85-17	StrngEmbrc1171¾Mllwlkr1081¾ChrstnCzrn115	Willingly	7
19Nov92- 8Aqu	fst	6f	:223	:46	1:11	3↑ⒻAlw 41000	85	2	4	22	23	31½	32¼	Cruguet J		115	*1.50	84-16	WnCrftyLdy1151½PpptSh115¾ChrstnCzrn115	Weakened	5
22Oct92- 6Aqu	fst	6½f	:23	:463	1:173	3↑ⒻAlw 41000	94	1	1	33½	32	1½	21¾	Cruguet J		115	1.90	88-18	Bn'sMomnt1221¾ChrstnCzrn1151½RglVctrss119	2nd best	6
9Oct92- 9Med	sly	6f	:213	:441	1:092	3↑ⒻBud Brds H	86	3	4	54	44	42½	41¾	Cruguet J		113	10.60	94-11	WoodS1151HrbrClb116noPnchlnPtty109	Some late gain	6
9Oct92-Grade III																					
19Sep92- 8Med	fm	5f	Ⓣ:224	:453	:573	3↑ⒻⓈHandicap	90	1	6	42½	42¼	31	21	Cruguet J		122	*1.60	88-11	JzzLgnd1121ChristinCzrin1221½MissKrryC.119	Willingly	7
4Mar92- 9GP	fst	6f	:214	:444	1:101	3↑ⒻHeather H	77	9	2	44	44½	77¼	95¾	Cruguet J	L	111	4.40	86-14	ChangeABabe1141½Illeria112nkShanJuliet110	4 wide str	10
21Feb92- 9GP	sly	6f	:213	:453	1:11	ⒻHandicap	88	5	4	44	43½	31½	32½	Cruguet J	L	112	*2.00	85-19	GnPrppsDrm1132Hprct112½ChrstnCrn112	Brshd ins 7/16	7
2Feb92-10GP	fst	7f	:223	:453	1:231	3↑ⒻS Jones H	82	9	1	31	31	42¾	67	Cruguet J		113	9.10	83-12	Nnnerl111hdWithllprobbility1201FitForAQueen119	Tired	10
2Feb92-Grade III																					
15Jan92- 9GP	fst	6f	:221	:453	1:11	3↑ⒻFirst Lady H	92	3	10	42	43½	33	23	Cruguet J		114	12.90	85-21	Wthllprbblty1183ChrstnCrn114½SprtfFghtr114	Willingly	14
20Nov91- 8Aqu	fst	6f	:22	:452	1:103	3↑ⒻHandicap	91	6	1	41¾	31	2½	1nk	Cruguet J		116	7.50	88-14	ChristinaCzarin116nkDSerpe113noMkinFces114	Driving	6

LATEST WORKOUTS Dec 4 Bel tr.t 6f fst 1:19 B Nov 29 Bel tr.t 4f fst :51 B Nov 16 Bel tr.t 4f fst :481 H Nov 10 Bel tr.t 6f fst 1:192 B

Dazzle Me Jolie — B. f. 4, by Carr de Naskra—Mawgrit, by Hoist The Flag
Br.—Riordan M (Ky)
MADRID A JR (55 6 6 3 .11)
Own.—Stanzione Jolie
Tr.—Thompson J Willard (3 1 0 2 .33)
119
Lifetime 18 7 4 3 $250,046 | 1992 4 0 1 1 $10,250 | 1991 13 6 3 2 $230,496 | Turf 2 0 0 0 $350 | Wet 1 0 0 0 $1,620

10Nov92- 9Med	fst	6f	:22	:45	1:093	3↑ⒻAlw 24000	80	5	1	2hd	11	1hd	31	Santagata N		115	2.70	94-09	CrftyBelle115½SuperStyle115½DzzleMeJoli115	Stead, str	7
29Aug92- 5Mth	fst	6f	:214	:452	1:114	3↑ⒻAlw 27000	94	5	1	21½	31½	31	2hd	Wilson R		115	*1.50	82-16	DltWthStyl115hdDzzlMJl115hdNvrMyLv115	Just missed	6
19Aug92- 9Mth	fst	6f	:213	:444	1:104	3↑ⒻAlw 27000	78	4	5	611	59½	56½	44¾	Wilson R		115	*1.20	82-20	Ranch Ragout122½ Femma115¾ Patti L.115	Jostled	6
25Jly92- 8Mth	gd	5f	Ⓣ:213	:444	:571	3↑ⒻW L GBrnch	65	4	3	42	53½	64	78½	Wilson R		113	3.90	79-12	FifthndJiggr1193¾DncPly119¾SYuInCourt107	Gave way	7
5Oct91- 8Bel	fst	1	:452	1:094	1:353	ⒻRare Prfme	102	7	4	2½	2hd	12	12¾	Santos J A		115	10.70	92-07	DlMJl1152¾GrndGrlfrnd112noWdCntry124	Drifted drvng	9
5Oct91-Grade II																					
21Sep91- 5Bel	fst	1	:464	1:112	1:36	3↑ⒻAlw 47000	93	7	1	1½	1hd	1½	31¼	Santos J A		114	*1.10	83-14	TrnRobbry119hdLlc'sStr1171¼DzzlMJol114	Drifted, tired	7
31Aug91- 8Mth	fst	6f	:214	:45	1:101	ⒻDrly Precios	94	5	2	3nk	11	11½	11¼	Vargas J L		122	*.80	90-12	DazzleMeJolie1221¼FarOutNurse1131¾RyLdy113	Driving	6
27Jly91- 9Mth	gd	6f	:213	:443	1:102	ⒻBlu Sprklr	95	4	4	41	42½	31	1hd	Vargas J L		121	*.90	89-11	DzzlMJol121hdSlvrSymphony1134PrvtApplus112	Got up	8
7Jly91- 8Mth	gd	6f	:213	:443	1:101	ⒻCandyeclair	99	6	5	2½	1hd	1½	12½	Vargas J L		119	2.90	90-16	DzlMJl1192½SlvrSymphny1133½FrOtNrs113	Edged clear	10
16Jun91-10Mth	fm	1	Ⓣ:462	1:103	1:353	ⒻRevidere	78	1	1	2½	2hd	74¼	710¼	Wilson R		121	*2.10	85-06	FishngEs114hdJns'sWrld1182¼ThKnghtsQn112	Gave way	9

LATEST WORKOUTS Dec 1 Aqu 5f fst 1:01 H Nov 24 Aqu 4f fst :503 B Nov 7 Aqu 3f fst :371 B ● Oct 30 Aqu 3f fst :364 B

Biddy Mulligan — Ch. f. 3(May), by Geiger Counter—Cailin Deas, by It's Freezing
Br.—Byrne M C (Ont-C)
CHAVEZ J F (73 12 13 12 .16)
Own.—Vigliarolo Frank
Tr.—McGaughey Claude III (9 1 1 3 .11)
109
Lifetime 25 7 6 3 $130,023 | 1992 19 6 4 1 $107,813 | 1991 6 1 2 2 $22,210 | Turf 1 0 0 0 | Wet 5 2 1 0 $34,078

6Dec92- 5Aqu	fst	6f	⊡:23	:47	1:124	3↑ⒻAlw 30000	77	6	1	1½	2hd	31	43¾	Chavez J F	b	117	2.30	75-20	DMssClrAppl1152DcRlr1171½SssBl117	Dueled, weakened	8
6Dec92-Placed third through disqualification																					
20Nov92- 7Aqu	fst	6f	:224	:461	1:102	3↑ⒻAlw 28000	92	7	1	1½	1½	12	12½	Chavez J F	b	115	13.80	89-19	BiddyMullign1152½EnjoyThSlnc115½SnowTtl115	Driving	10
3Nov92- 3Aqu	sly	6f	:23	:471	1:114	ⒻClm 45000	79	3	1	11½	1½	1½	22	Chavez J F	b	112	5.00	80-21	MrriTls1142BiddyMullign112¾MssCovrGrl116	Weakened	7
17Oct92- 2Bel	fst	6f	:223	:454	1:104	ⒻClm 45000	84	2	1	11	1hd	2hd	21¾	Chavez J F	b	112	29.00	84-23	Mrlyn'sMgc1161¾BddMllgn1121¾FnlCrssng116	Sharp try	10
5Oct92- 9Bel	fst	6f	:222	:461	1:114	ⒻClm 25000	74	2	1	1½	1½	13	14½	Chavez J F	b	116	3.60	81-17	BiddyMullign1164½OnDumplng1161½GrndCch114	Driving	9
17Sep92- 8Med	fst	6f	:214	:453	1:10	ⒻClm 25000	32	4	4	2½	41¾	68½	619¼	Rojas R I	Lb	115	5.80	74-12	CshTwenty1137½PlsMilly1121½MyGllntQun112	Gave way	6
6Sep92- 1Bel	fst	6f	:221	:46	1:113	ⒻClm 35000	60	3	1	1hd	2hd	32½	59½	Antley C W	b	116	*2.50	72-15	FrtntChrmr1161¼Krs1165½GttngArndtt116	Dueled, tired	6
27Aug92- 9Sar	fst	7f	:22	:444	1:24	ⒻClm 35000	75	10	2	11	12½	17½	21¼	Antley C W	b	116	8.80	84-12	CountryLk1141¼BddyMllgn1162BmnBo116	Couldn't last	10
21Jly92- 9Mth	fst	6f	:22	:452	1:111	3↑ⒻAlw 17000	41	8	1	2½	45	812	815	Santagata N	L	112	4.60	70-18	CherokeVil1071¼YouthfulSis1101½CoolNumbr112	Faded	8
11Jly92- 9Bel	fst	6f	:221	:451	1:101	ⒻClm 35000	65	8	1	11	1hd	42½	47¼	Velazquez J R		116	11.80	82-11	ApplngMsIrn1163¾NrthrnDstr116noFrtntChrmr114	Tired	12

LATEST WORKOUTS ● Dec 1 Bel tr.t 5f fst 1:003 H ● Nov 14 Bel tr.t 5f fst 1:00 H

The feature at Aqueduct on December 22 was an overnight handicap at six furlongs, and a field of six went to the post after scratches. Golden Bimmer, Makin Faces, Dazzle Me Jolie, and Biddy Mulligan could all be classified as early-pace types, while Christina Czarina was a pace presser who had been blanked from nine starts during the year.

Lady Sage was the closer who figured to be the prime beneficiary of a hotly contested early pace. She was shortening back to her best distance and was also getting a substantial weight concession from Makin Faces and Dazzle Me Jolie, two fillies who hadn't done much racing over the past several months. At 4–1, Lady Sage figured to have all the best of it:

EIGHTH RACE
Aqueduct
DECEMBER 22, 1992

6 FURLONGS.(InnerDirt). (1.08^3) HANDICAP. Purse $41,000. Fillies and Mares, 3-year-olds and upward. Weights Saturday, December 19. Declarations by 10:00 A.M. Sunday, December 20.

Value of race $41,000; value to winner $24,600; second $9,020; third $4,920; fourth $2,460. Mutuel pool $470,155. Exacta Pool $284,844

Last Raced	Horse	M/Eqt.A.Wt	PP	St	¼	½	Str	Fin	Jockey	Odds $1
15Nov92 ^{5}Aqu^5	Lady Sage	3 113	3	6	4½	3^{1½}	1^2	1^5	Santagata N	4.20
14Dec92 ^{7}Aqu^3	Christina Czarina	4 116	4	3	5½	4^{hd}	4½	2^{1¾}	Bruin J E	3.30
10Nov92 ^{9}Med^3	Dazzle Me Jolie	4 119	5	2	2^{hd}	2½	3^1	3^{nk}	Madrid A Jr	2.70
6Dec92 ^{7}Aqu^5	Golden Bimmer	b 3 111	1	5	6	5^1	5^4	4^{hd}	Samyn J L	7.80
12Sep92 ^{7}Med^7	Makin Faces	4 122	2	4	1^{hd}	1½	2^{hd}	5^{5½}	Davis R G	2.50
6Dec92 ^{5}Aqu^3	Biddy Mulligan	b 3 110	6	1	3^{1½}	6	6	6	Chavez J F	7.10

OFF AT 3:37. Start good. Won driving. Time, :22^3, :46 , :58 , 1:10^3 Track fast.

$2 Mutuel Prices:			
4-(D)-LADY SAGE	10.40	4.60	2.80
5-(E)-CHRISTINA CZARINA		4.40	2.60
6-(G)-DAZZLE ME JOLIE			2.40

$2 EXACTA 4–5 PAID $45.00

B. f, (Feb), by Lord Gaylord—Foxcroft Finale, by Real Value. Trainer Kelly Timothy D. Bred by David P. Reynolds (Md).

LADY SAGE always prominent, eased out three wide approaching the stretch, then closed determinedly to take a clear lead a furlong out and prove best under good handling. CHRISTINA CZARINA offered a good closing response four wide to be clear for the place. DAZZLE ME JOLIE dueled on the front outside of MAKIN FACES then weakened in the lane. GOLDEN BIMMER failed to mount a solid bid. MAKIN FACES battled on the pace while saving ground to the stretch, then weakened. BIDDY MULLIGAN with the leaders early three wide, weakened on the turn. LADY SAGE and CHRISTINA CZARINA raced with mud caulks.

Owners— 1, Reynolds David P; 2, Lorraine & Cindy Stable; 3, Stanzione Jolie; 4, Joques Farm; 5, Sabine Stable; 6, Vigliarolo Frank.

Trainers— 1, Kelly Timothy D; 2, Jerkens H Allen; 3, Thompson J Willard; 4, Moschera Gasper S; 5, Barbara Robert; 6, McGaughey Claude III.

Overweight: Biddy Mulligan 1 pound.

Scratched—Damie's Sis (28Nov92 ^{9}Med^3); Win Crafty Lady (14Dec92 ^{7}Aqu^4); Mallwalker (14Dec92 ^{7}Aqu^2).

Here's another example. It's August 31 at Saratoga, and the sixth race is a preliminary allowance at seven furlongs with a field of seven three-year-olds. Find the dominant closer:

6

7 FURLONGS. **(1.20 2) ALLOWANCE. Purse $27,000. 3–year–olds and upward which have never won a race other than Maiden, Claiming or Starter. Weights, 3–year–olds 117 lbs. Older 122 lbs. Non–winners of a race other than Claiming since August 1 allowed 3 lbs. Of such a race since July 15, 5 lbs.**

Otto Beit

Dk. b. or br. g. 3(May), by Rock'n Rollick—Sorry Ange, by Son Ange

Lifetime 17 4 3 4 $50,135 — 1992 10 2 2 2 $36,645 — 1991 7 2 1 2 $13,490 — Wet 1 0 0 0 $1,320

BAILEY J D (136 23 20 15 .17) — Br.—Houghton Mrs R B (Pa) — **112**

Own.—Thor John — Tr.—Moschera Gasper S (35 11 5 4 .31)

14Aug92- 1Sar fst 1 :464 1:121 1:381 Clm c-35000 62 8 5 53½ 41¼ 41½ 57 Krone J A 117 *2.40 – – DrwCrd113nkAllMyTricks113hdRmblAwy117 Stmbld brk 9

14Aug92-Claimed from Dweck Raymond, Forbes John H Trainer

1Aug92- 9Sar gd 7f :224 :46 1:223 Clm 45000 78 1 7 1hd 2½ 41½ 33 Krone J A 113 7.10 89-04 PerlssPrformr115½Hwk'sFlm1142½OttoBit113 Weakened 9

20Jly92- 3Bel fst 6f :222 :451 1:101 Clm 45000 84 1 3 31 22 21½ 42 Krone J A 113 5.80 87-14 ProprBondr117½UnrlMt113½EstblshdL113 Saved ground 7

19Jun92- 6Bel gd 6f :222 :45 1:092 3↑Alw 29000 77 4 4 32 52¼ 64¾ 56¼ Krone J A 109 6.40 87-14 StrtFght1092AdmrlsHoly117¾PrncConsrt117 Done early 7

25May92- 1Bel fst 1 :47 1:113 1:363 Clm 45000 80 5 4 43 32 3½ 1nk Krone J A 113 4.70 87-05 OttBt113nkCstTMch117nkHwk'sFlm117 Pinched brk, wd 7

10May92- 5Bel sly 6f :221 :444 1:092 Clm 50000 73 6 8 66 87 67 49½ Krone J A 117 3.10 83-12 Rockford1173AlienShore1134HighestLevel106 Wide trip 8

11Apr92-12Pha fst 6f :22 :451 1:103 ⓈAlw 19575 80 8 5 42¾ 21 22½ 22 Jocson G J L 116 *.70 86-13 LordAtLaw1162OttoBeit1168½Readyn'Rollic116 2nd best 8

2Apr92- 9Aqu fst 7f :223 :453 1:24 Clm 35000 90 6 1 21½ 2hd 1½ 22½ Krone J A 117 4.30 82-19 Scudbuster1172½ Otto Beit1176 Yaros117 Second best 10

3Mar92- 3GP fst 6f :22 :453 1:112 Clm 25000 72 1 4 31½ 31½ 4¾ 1½ Krone J A L 112 3.40 86-13 OttBt112½WhskChsr116nkBctYJc114 Came out,lckd rm 7

16Feb92- 4GP fst 7f :222 :451 1:252 Clm c-15000 63 9 4 32 43½ 41 31½ Penna D L 116 3.70 77-16 Majestic Tai116hd Sweet Baby Glen1151½ Otto Beit116 12

16Feb92-Steadied twice stretch, brushed inside 1/8

LATEST WORKOUTS Jly 28 Bel 4f fst :50 B — Jly 17 Mth 4f fst :53 B — Jly 10 Mth 3f fst :39 B

Count New York

Ch. g. 3(Jun), by Cutlass—Mrs Bridges, by Bold Effort

Lifetime 2 1 1 0 $12,800 — 1992 2 1 1 0 $12,800 — 1991 0 M 0 0

BRAVO J A (—) — Br.—Robert Bantivoglio (Fla) — **114**

Own.—Bantivoglio Robert T — Tr.—Tammaro John J III (—)

23Aug92- 6Mth fst 6f :213 :443 1:101 3↑Alw 17500 83 3 4 44 42½ 23½ 21 Homeister RBJr5 108 *1.40 89-14 ClrPtrc1131CntNYr1082½BtnYdM111 Bumped brk wide 8

28Jly92- 5Mth fst 6f :224 :463 1:112 3↑Md Sp Wt 83 1 5 2hd 2hd 11½ 12 Marquez C H Jr 116 5.30 84-17 CntNYr1162ChnlsTtnc1164½DncnChs111 Good handling 9

LATEST WORKOUTS Aug 19 Mth 5f gd 1:01 H — Aug 11 Mth 4f fst :48 H — Aug 4 Mth 5f fst 1:024 B — Jly 22 Mth 5f fst 1:031 B

Ambassador Six

B. c. 3(Feb), by Saratoga Six—Diplomette, by Sr Diplomat

Lifetime 2 1 0 1 $11,670 — 1992 2 1 0 1 $11,670 — 1991 0 M 0 0

SMITH M E (165 33 28 20 .20) — Br.—Fares Farm, Inc. (Ky) — **114**

Own.—Fares Farm — Tr.—Hauswald Philip M (1 0 1 0 .00)

16Jly92- 6EIP fst 6f :224 :464 1:123 3↑Md Sp Wt 60 7 4 2hd 2hd 12½ 11¾ Melancon L B 118 *1.00 84-14 AmbassadorSix1181¾MtBird1181LoclPub118 Swrv in str 9

9Feb92- 4GP fst 6f :22 :452 1:101 Md Sp Wt 86 2 6 53 55 32 32 Fires E 120 23.20 90-09 DlHsD120noDntSllthFr1202AbssdrS120 Willingly inside 11

LATEST WORKOUTS Aug 25 Sar 4f fst :493 B — Aug 14 Sar 4f fst :502 B — Jly 14 CD 3f fst :372 B — Jly 7 CD 5f fst 1:023 B

Clever Knave

Dk. b. or br. c. 3(Apr), by Clever Trick—Face Nord, by Northjet

Lifetime 2 1 0 0 $5,340 — 1992 2 1 0 0 $5,340 — 1991 0 M 0 0

VELAZQUEZ J R (73 2 8 9 .03) — Br.—George Strawbridge (Ky) — **112**

Own.—C'Est Tout Sta — Tr.—Daggett Michael H (19 0 2 4 .00)

14Aug92- 1Sar fst 1 :464 1:121 1:381 Clm c-30000 71 5 3 31½ 3nk 11 42 Perret C 113 7.10 – – DrwCrd113nkAllMyTrcks113hdRmblAy117 Bid weakened 9

14Aug92-Claimed from Dogwood Stables Inc, Vestal Peter M Trainer

19Jly92- 7AP gd 6½f :22 :454 1:19 3↑Md 10000 70 4 8 23 1hd 1½ 14½ Silva C H 115 6.10 76-21 ClevrKnv1154½BcusH'sGry1153¾KingWhl115 Ridden out 12

LATEST WORKOUTS Aug 24 Sar 4f fst :51 B — Aug 12 Sar 3f fst :353 H — Aug 6 Sar 5f fst 1:012 H — Jly 7 CD 4f fst :534 B

Spancil Hill

Ch. c. 3(Apr), by Alydar—Paddy's Princess, by St Paddy

Lifetime 8 1 1 2 $31,100 — 1992 8 1 1 2 $31,100 — 1991 0 M 0 0 — Turf 1 0 0 0 — Wet 2 0 0 1 $5,220

MIGLIORE R (95 15 9 12 .16) — Br.—Kingston Park Stud Inc (Ky) — **112**

Own.—Nedlaw Stable — Tr.—Kimmel John C (11 1 1 2 .09)

19Aug92- 7Sar my 1 :473 1:114 1:362 3↑Alw 29000 82 2 2 32 31½ 42 45¼ Migliore R 113 5.60 – – ClnLht1121½PrtPrspct1171½PrlssPrfrr112 Lacked a rally 6

6Aug92- 5Sar fst 1⅛ :463 1:112 1:50 3↑Alw 29000 73 3 2 2½ 2hd 32 39½ Day P 112 3.10 77-13 BlueSquir1126HrrythHt1124½SpncilHill112 Forced pace 6

19Jly92- 6Bel gd 1 1/16 Ⓣ:481 1:122 1:421 3↑Alw 29000 63 2 2 21 3½ 86½ 818¼ Migliore R 113 11.40 67-19 CobblstonRd1111½LkAhd113¾AndrwSn111 Forced pace 8

2Jly92- 5Bel fst 1 :463 1:111 1:37 Alw 29000 83 5 4 41½ 3½ 2½ 21¼ Migliore R 117 5.20 84-17 SrvsEmRght1171¼SpnclHll117nkSothld122 Up for place 6

20Jun92- 4Bel my 1 :451 1:094 1:352 Alw 29000 79 1 1 11½ 1½ 2hd 32 Antley C W b 117 2.80 91-18 EstrnBrv117¾PrsidntGs1171½SpncilHll117 Bid weakened 7

4Jun92- 6Bel fst 7f :222 :444 1:22 3↑Alw 27000 51 2 2 1hd 23 514 424½ Migliore R b 111 11.00 69-11 Frosly10911½CobblstnRd1117OcnSplsh109 Dueled, tired 6

13May92- 4Bel fst 7f :222 :45 1:23 Md Sp Wt 73 9 1 2hd 1½ 15 13¾ Migliore R b 122 12.00 89-07 Spancil Hill1223¾ Emerald Fable122nk Croon122 Driving 10

24Apr92- 6Aqu fst 7f :222 :461 1:233 Md Sp Wt 63 8 8 710 68½ 68 714 Santos J A 122 3.90 73-19 Wisconsin1225½Dnzig'sDnc1224VldHmlock122 No factor 9

LATEST WORKOUTS Aug 3 Sar 4f fst :51 B — ●Jly 28 Sar 5f fst 1:01 H

Southold

Dk. b. or br. c. 3(Mar), by Seattle Slew—Logetta, by Forli

Lifetime 9 1 1 2 $26,890 — 1992 9 1 1 2 $26,890 — 1991 0 M 0 0 — Turf 1 0 0 0 — Wet 2 0 0 0

ROJAS R I (62 4 3 5 .06) — Br.—Amerivest TB 2 & Wooden Horse Inv (Ky) — **112**

Own.—C C W Gold Stable — Tr.—Zito Nicholas P (29 1 1 4 .03)

19Aug92- 7Sar my 1 :473 1:114 1:362 3↑Alw 29000 45 3 4 54½ 64½ 67½ 625½ Smith M E 112 10.80 – – ClnLht1121½PrnntPrspct1171½PrlssPrfrr112 Wide tired 6

6Aug92- 5Sar fst 1⅛ :463 1:112 1:50 3↑Alw 29000 59 2 1 1½ 1hd 64½ 618 Pezua J M b 112 7.70 69-13 BluSquir1125HrrythHt1124½SpncilHill112 Dueled inside 6

11Jly92- 6Bel fm 1¼ Ⓣ:504 1:393 2:032 3↑Alw 29000 66 10 2 21 2hd 918 916½ Perret C 111 9.80 36-11 ThQnsPrnc114hdCrnshsCrnr1221TmfrLhtnn117 Stopped 10

2Jly92- 5Bel fst 1 :463 1:111 1:37 Alw 29000 82 3 1 1hd 2½ 31 31½ Pezua J M b 122 12.80 83-17 SrvsEmRght1171½SpnclHll117nkSthld122 Bid, weakened 6

12Jun92- 3Bel fst 1 :464 1:12 1:38 Md Sp Wt 78 1 1 1hd 3nk 1½ 11½ Pezua J M b 122 8.90 80-20 Sothold1221½LookAhd1222¾PromnntProspct122 Driving 9

16May92- 2Pim gd 1 1/16 :483 1:131 1:45 3↑Md Sp Wt 73 8 2 1hd 1hd 22½ 33¼ Perret C 113 *2.70 76-18 TimeKiller1141¾FrazzledAct1121½Southold113 Gave way 9

11Apr92- 6Aqu sly 1 :471 1:121 1:372 Md Sp Wt 61 5 3 41½ 65¼ 68 510¼ Gryder A T 122 7.40 65-22 Repletion1223¼TrumpetTongud1221PrsonlDrw122 Tired 7

28Mar92- 7Aqu fst 1 :47 1:131 1:384 Md Sp Wt 71 3 1 1½ 1½ 21 23½ Smith M E 122 4.30 64-31 Electrojet1223½Southold122nkPrsonlDrw122 Held place 7

1Mar92- 4GP fst 7f :223 :452 1:233 Md Sp Wt 51 7 11 3½ 911 911 613½ Sellers S J 120 2.60e 74-10 Dignitas1203 To You1202 Devil Storm120 Brief speed 12

LATEST WORKOUTS Jly 31 Sar 5f fst 1:004 H — Jly 25 Sar 5f fst 1:01 H — Jly 20 Bel 5f fst 1:023 B

Offbeat — B. c. 3(May), by Fappiano—Dance Number, by Northern Dancer
Br.—Phipps O M (Ky)
Tr.—McGaughey Claude III (23 1 8 5 .04)
ANTLEY C W (168 34 24 23 .20)
Own.—Phipps Ogden Mills
112

Lifetime						
9 1 1 3	1992	3	0	0	1	$5,100
$136,924	1991	6	1	1	2	$131,824
	Turf	1	0	0	0	

Entered 30Aug92- 6 SAR

25Jly92- 6Bel	fst 1	$:46^{1}$	1:10	1:35	Alw 29000	80	2	4	5^{2}	$5^{1\frac{3}{4}}$	3^{4}	$3^{7\frac{1}{2}}$	Antley C W	117	2.30	88-09	Ghazi117$^{1\frac{1}{4}}$ Sulaco117^{6} Offbeat117	Lacked rally 8
18Jun92- 7Bel	fm $1\frac{1}{16}$ Ⓣ	$:46^{1}$	1:10	$1:40^{2}$	3↑Alw 29000	64	7	7	10^{12}	$11^{9\frac{3}{4}}$	11^{13}	$9^{18\frac{1}{2}}$	Antley C W	113	4.50	75-11	Paradise Creek112^{4} Scuffleburg113^{6}Alfaares117	Outrun 11
27May92- 6Bel	fst 7f	$:22^{2}$	$:45^{2}$	$1:22^{3}$	3↑Alw 27000	76	2	5	$5^{4\frac{1}{2}}$	$5^{2\frac{1}{2}}$	$4^{3\frac{1}{2}}$	$4^{8\frac{3}{4}}$	Antley C W	114	*1.00	82-13	RnsGrmsmn113$^{1\frac{3}{4}}$AdrlsHl119^{5}Wscnsn112	Saved ground 7
16Nov91- 8Aqu	fst $1\frac{1}{8}$	$:47^{2}$	$1:12^{1}$	$1:50^{4}$	Remsen	85	4	5	$7^{4\frac{1}{2}}$	$6^{4\frac{1}{2}}$	3^{3}	$2^{4\frac{3}{4}}$	McCauley W H	113	2.00e	77-23	PineBluff113$^{4\frac{3}{4}}$Offbeat113$^{1\frac{1}{4}}$CheapShdes122	Up for 2nd 8
16Nov91-Grade II																		
2Nov91- 6CD	fst $1\frac{1}{16}$	$:46^{3}$	1:12	$1:44^{3}$	Br Cp Juv	86	13	14	13^{12}	$10^{8\frac{3}{4}}$	5^{11}	$4^{8\frac{1}{2}}$	Smith M E	122	18.50f	83-09	Arazi122^{5}Bertrando122$^{3\frac{1}{2}}$SnppyLnding122	Wide stretch 14
2Nov91-Grade I																		
23Oct91- 8Aqu	fst 7f	$:21^{4}$	:44	$1:22^{3}$	Cowdin	82	7	7	9^{13}	8^{11}	$5^{7\frac{1}{2}}$	$3^{6\frac{3}{4}}$	Cordero A Jr	122	3.40	82-13	SaltLake122$^{6\frac{1}{2}}$MontrealMarty122^{nk}Offbeat122	Mild gain 9
23Oct91-Grade II																		
9Oct91- 2Bel	fst 7f	$:23^{2}$	$:47^{1}$	$1:24^{3}$	Md Sp Wt	78	7	5	$6^{3\frac{1}{2}}$	$4^{1\frac{1}{2}}$	2^{hd}	1^{4}	Cordero A Jr	118	*2.70	81-25	Offbet118^{4}AllMyTricks118$^{1\frac{3}{4}}$EsternBrve118	Wide, drvng 9
11Sep91- 7Bel	fst 1	$:48^{3}$	$1:13^{2}$	$1:38^{2}$	Md Sp Wt	63	4	6	4^{2}	$6^{3\frac{1}{2}}$	4^{4}	3^{6}	Cordero A Jr	118	3.10	72-22	NstyBusiness118^{2}DitchPlins118^{4}Offbet118	Lacked rally 8
16Aug91- 6Sar	fst 7f	$:22^{1}$	$:45^{1}$	$1:23^{4}$	Md Sp Wt	49	4	9	$10^{6\frac{1}{2}}$	$9^{7\frac{1}{4}}$	$8^{9\frac{1}{2}}$	$6^{12\frac{1}{2}}$	Cordero A Jr	118	3.50	73-11	Pine Bluff118$^{1\frac{1}{2}}$ Harry theHat118^{2}Noactor118	Brk slwly 10

LATEST WORKOUTS Aug 29 Sar tr.t 3f fst :38 B Aug 21 Sar tr.t 4f fst $:49^{4}$ B Aug 17 Sar tr.t 3f fst :38 B Aug 6 Sar tr.t 4f fst $:51^{4}$ B

Several of the contenders were evenly matched in terms of Beyer figures, but Count New York, Ambassador Six, Clever Knave, Spancil Hill, and Southold had all done their best racing on or near the early lead. Otto Beit, the only multiple winner in the field, had raced primarily against claimers and could best be classified as a pace-pressing type who was probably ill-equipped to handle this kind of a pace.

This left Offbeat, who was shortening up from a pair of longer races while making his fourth start back from a layoff. Offbeat had broken his maiden at seven furlongs with a strong off-the-pace rally the previous autumn, had rallied from last to finish third in the Cowdin Stakes (run over a speed-biased surface) two weeks later, and had then rallied for fourth in the Breeders' Cup Juvenile when stretched to two turns for the first time. In his final start at two, he came from well off the pace to finish second behind Pine Bluff, who had gone on to win the Preakness Stakes as a three-year-old. Offbeat's speed figures were as good as any others in the field, and he enjoyed a tactical edge as the lone true closer:

SIXTH RACE
Saratoga
AUGUST 31, 1992

7 FURLONGS. (1.20^{2}) ALLOWANCE. Purse $27,000. 3-year-olds and upward which have never won a race other than Maiden, Claiming or Starter. Weights, 3-year-olds 117 lbs. Older 122 lbs. Non-winners of a race other than Claiming since August 1 allowed 3 lbs. Of such a race since July 15, 5 lbs.

Value of race $27,000; value to winner $16,200; second $5,940; third $3,240; fourth $1,620. Mutuel pool $314,560. Exacta Pool $591,327

Last Raced	Horse	M/Eqt.	A.	Wt	PP	St	¼	½	Str	Fin	Jockey	Odds $1
25Jly92 ^{6}Bel^{3}	Offbeat		3	112	7	1	7	$6^{2\frac{1}{2}}$	$3^{1\frac{1}{2}}$	$1^{4\frac{1}{2}}$	Antley C W	2.20
23Aug92 ^{6}Mth^{2}	Count New York	b	3	114	2	5	2^{hd}	$2^{\frac{1}{2}}$	1^{hd}	$2^{4\frac{1}{4}}$	Bravo J	2.80
16Jly92 ^{6}ElP^{1}	Ambassador Six	b	3	114	3	6	$6^{2\frac{1}{2}}$	$5^{1\frac{1}{2}}$	$5^{\frac{1}{2}}$	3^{nk}	Smith M E	3.10
19Aug92 ^{7}Sar^{4}	Spancil Hill	b	3	112	5	3	3^{hd}	1^{1}	2^{hd}	4^{3}	Migliore R	4.50
14Aug92 ^{1}Sar^{5}	Otto Beit	b	3	112	1	7	1^{hd}	3^{1}	$4^{\frac{1}{2}}$	5^{8}	Bailey J D	6.30
14Aug92 ^{1}Sar^{4}	Clever Knave		3	112	4	4	4^{3}	$4^{2\frac{1}{2}}$	6^{4}	6^{5}	Velazquez J R	23.00
19Aug92 ^{7}Sar^{6}	Southold	b	3	112	6	2	$5^{\frac{1}{2}}$	7	7	7	Rojas R I	24.40

OFF AT 3:48. Start good. Won driving. Time, $:22^{1}$, $:44^{2}$, $1:10^{1}$, $1:23^{2}$ Track fast.

$2 Mutuel Prices:

7–(G)–OFFBEAT	6.40	3.60	2.80
2–(B)–COUNT NEW YORK		3.80	3.00
3–(C)–AMBASSADOR SIX			3.20

$2 EXACTA 7–2 PAID $30.20

B. c, (May), by Fappiano—Dance Number, by Northern Dancer. Trainer McGaughey Claude III. Bred by Phipps O M (Ky).

OFFBEAT outrun early, launched a rally while four wide on the turn then wore down COUNT NEW YORK to win going away. COUNT NEW YORK forced the pace between horses to the turn, surged to the front gaining a brief lead in midstretch but couldn't stay with the winner through the final eighth. AMBASSADOR SIX unable to keep pace for a half, angled out in upper stretch then lacked a strong closing response. SPACEL HILL set or forced the pace between horses into midstretch and tired. OTTO BEIT rushed up along the inside after breaking slowly, then gave way after dueling for a half mile. CLEVER KNAVE dueled for the early lead between horses dropped back on the far turn and failed to threaten thereafter. SOUTHOLD was never a factor.

Owners— 1, Phipps Ogden Mills; 2, Bantivoglio Robert T; 3, Fares Farm; 4, Nedlaw Stable; 5, Thor John; 6, C'Est Tout Sta; 7, C C W Gold Stable.

Trainers— 1, McGaughey Claude III; 2, Tammaro John J III; 3, Hauswald Philip M; 4, Kimmel John C; 5, Moschera Gasper S; 6, Daggett Michael H; 7, Zito Nicholas P.

A look at the positions and beaten lengths from the result chart shows that an intense four-way speed duel developed, as might have been expected. Otto Beit, Count New York, Spancil Hill, and Clever Knave were heads apart through a quarter in :22⅕, and Spancil Hill was able to get clear only midway on the turn by running another :22⅕ quarter, with Count New York in hot pursuit.

While all this in-fighting was going on, Offbeat galloped along under a relaxed hold, angled out for clear sailing on the turn, reached even terms a furlong out, and roared off to win by four and a half widening lengths.

MIDRACE ADVANTAGES

The second fraction in sprints is run around a turn and is often called the "hidden fraction," because horses with superior "turn times" often go unnoticed by the crowd. That must've been the case when Patchy Frost was allowed to go postward at better than 5–1 in the fourth at Belmont on October 22:

4 — 6 FURLONGS AQUEDUCT (START / FINISH)

6 FURLONGS. **(1.08) ALLOWANCE. Purse $27,000. Fillies and Mares. 3-year–olds and upward which have never won a race other than Maiden, Claiming or Starter. Weights: 3year–olds, 119 lbs.; oldaer, 122 lbs. Non–winners of a race other than claiming since October 1 allowed 3 lbs.; of such a race since September 15, 5 lbs.**

Patchy Frost — B. f. 3(May), by Storm Cat—Consequential, by Dr Fager — Lifetime 3 1 0 0 $15,605 — 1992 3 1 0 0 $15,605; 1991 0 M 0 0
BAILEY J D (—) — Br.—William Strong & Overbrook Farm (Ky)
Own.—Young William T — Tr.—Lukas D Wayne (—) — 114

9Sep92- 7Bel fst 6½f :22^{2} :45^{2} 1:16^{3} 3↑ⒻAlw 27000 61 3 6 2½ 2½ 5^{5} 6^{11} Smith M E 118 2.10 79–15 ViaDeiPortici113¾SablWy117^{4}GoingAshore113 Used up 7
23Aug92- 1Sar fst 6f :22 :45^{2} 1:09^{4} 3↑ⒻMd Sp Wt 84 8 2 45½ 1½ 1½ 1^{6} Smith M E 117 3.20 95–07 PtchyFrost117^{6}ShsSprkin117^{6}¼GustofHonor117 Driving 9
19Jun92- 5CD fst 6½f :23 :46^{4} 1:19^{1} 3↑ⒻMd Sp Wt 56 7 1 41¾ 3½ 31½ 44½ Woods C R Jr B 112 *2.10 79–10 NwThngs112^{3}GoldnStrk112^{1}RckCrk112 Flatten out late 12
LATEST WORKOUTS Oct 1 Bel 5f fst 1:02^{1} H Sep 21 Bel 4f fst :50^{2} B Sep 5 Bel 4f fst :49^{4} B

Jode — Dk. b. or br. f. 3(Apr), by Danzig—Belle de Jour, by Speak John — Lifetime 1 1 0 0 $9,421 — 1992 0 0 0 0; 1991 1 1 0 0 $9,421; Turf 1 1 0 0 $9,421
SMITH M E (—) — Br.—DWD Corp (Fla)
Own.—Maktoum al Maktoum — Tr.—Mott William I (—) — 114

15Jun91♦7York(Eng) gd 6f 1:14^{1} ⓉEBF Duchess ofKentSt(Mdn) 12½ Eddery Pat 121 *1.50 — — Jod1212½ ChngingTims126^{1} SilvoAlfrdo126 Rated, drvg 9
LATEST WORKOUTS Oct 16 Bel 4f fst :49 B Oct 7 Bel 5f fst :59^{4} H Sep 17 Sar tr.t 4f fst :51 B

Bob's Little Gal — B. f. 3(Mar), by Barrera—Sun Moment, by Honest Moment
LYDON P J (—) — Br.—Bronzine R (Fla) — 1095
Own.—Lamcresse Stable — Tr.—Barbara Robert (—)
Lifetime 8 2 4 1 $49,800 — 1992 7 2 4 1 $49,800 — 1991 1 M 0 0 — Wet 3 2 0 1 $26,040

26Sep92- 3Bel sly 6f	:221 :453 1:101	ⒻClm 70000	86 4 2 11½ 1½ 11½ 1no	Smith M E	b 112	2.90	89-14	BbsLttlGl112noMssClrAppl1164½ApplnMsIrn113	Driving	7
28Aug92- 3Sar fst 6f	:222 :454 1:102	3↑ⒻAlw 27000	80 4 3 11 1½ 1½ 2nk	Krone J A	b 112	2.80	92-08	MySstrJlt112nkBob'sLttlGl1122Ksskwn117	Couldn't last	7
16Aug92- 6Sar my 7f	:232 :462 1:241	3↑ⒻAlw 27000	73 5 2 21 21 31½ 33½	Carr D	112	*1.50	81-14	DDp1121AlphRscl1172½BbsLttlGl112	Drifted, weakened	7
5Aug92- 6Sar fst 6f	:221 :453 1:103	3↑ⒻAlw 27000	79 3 3 11½ 1½ 1½ 21¼	Carr D	112	3.10	90-07	UOtbenPictures1121¼Bob'sLittlGl112¾Trid112	Sharp try	10
27Jun92- 3Bel fst 6f	:222 :451 1:092	ⒻAlw 27000	86 5 1 21 2½ 2hd 24	Carr D	116	*2.20	89-12	LadySge1214Bob'sLittleGl116½S.S.Sprkle116	Held place	6
29May92- 6Bel fst 6f	:222 :452 1:101	3↑ⒻAlw 27000	81 2 4 11 1hd 21 21¾	Carr D	110	*1.80	87-13	MyNecssity1101¾Bob'sLittlGl1103SpicyScrt110	2nd best	5
10May92- 9Bel sly 6f	:222 :453 1:10	3↑ⒻMd 35000	89 9 2 11½ 14 110 118½	Carr D	115	*1.70	90-12	Bb'sLttlGl11518½SftlySpkng108hdSssDds115	Ridden out	12
27Nov91- 9Aqu fst 6f	:224 :47 1:123	ⒻMd 30000	47 7 12 84 73¼ 77 58½	Smith M E	113	*2.70	69-20	CdyHllFun1171¼BstllBll1175SqoyhScrb113	Broke slowly	14

LATEST WORKOUTS Sep 20 Bel 4f fst :494 B

Sabal Way — B. f. 4, by Proud Appeal—Virgin Reef, by Unconscious
STEWART J F (—) — Br.—Hough Stanley M (Fla) — 1125
Own.—Saks Martin — Tr.—Ferriola Peter (—)
Lifetime 14 2 4 3 $55,710 — 1992 12 1 4 3 $41,310 — 1991 2 1 0 0 $14,400 — Turf 1 0 0 0 — Wet 4 0 1 2 $10,590

12Oct92- 6Bel my 7f	:23 :463 1:233	3↑ⒻAlw 27000	76 1 6 31½ 2½ 32½ 35½	McCauley W H	b 117	2.30	80-09	FlyTThMn1175½ShdyWll117noSblWy117	Bid, weakened	6
9Sep92- 7Bel fst 6½f	:222 :452 1:163	3↑ⒻAlw 27000	85 7 1 63 42 23 2¾	Carr D	b 117	4.10	89-15	ViDeiPortici113¾SblWy1174GoingAshor113	Rallied wide	7
26Jly92- 7Bel fst 7f	:224 :454 1:233	3↑ⒻAlw 27000	79 2 7 63 74¾ 43 21¼	Carr D	b 117	*1.60	85-16	HudsonDncer1171¼SblWy1171¾MySistrJulit113	Fin well	8
20Jly92- 1Bel fst 7f	:232 :47 1:234	ⒻClm c-35000	78 5 4 43 41½ 21 2½	Carr D	117	2.90	84-14	SunnyBrbi117½SblWy1172¾EmphticStyl119	Rallied wide	7
20Jly92-Claimed from Hough Stanley M, Hough Stanley M Trainer										
4Jly92- 6Bel sly 7f	:224 :461 1:231	3↑ⒻAlw 27000	69 3 5 44 53½ 45 36¾	Santos J A	117	3.70	81-14	EpicVilla1174HudsonDancer1172¾SablWy117	Four wide	6
15Jun92- 1Bel fst 7f	:232 :464 1:23	3↑ⒻAlw 27000	77 4 6 21 22 33½ 34½	Maple E	117	5.40	84-10	BlessOurHome113¾Bravely1194SablWy117	Broke slowly	6
5Jun92- 1Bel gd 6f	:221 :444 1:102	ⒻClm 45000	72 1 4 63½ 55 64½ 53½	Carr D	113	5.50	84-12	Apprprtly117nkInctng113noEmphtcStl117	Saved ground	6
21May92- 5Bel fst 7f	:231 :463 1:242	ⒻClm 25000	73 2 2 53¾ 51¼ 1½ 13	Carr D	117	3.30	82-16	SblWy1173Crl'sCommnd1175Undrnsrd117	Wide driving	5
11May92- 4Bel my 6f	:221 :452 1:111	ⒻClm 22500	70 4 3 68 65½ 63½ 22	Carr D	115	3.80	82-10	Fond Romance1152SabalWay115½FinalRoad113	Fin well	7
10Apr92- 8Crc fst 170	:474 1:134 1:454	3↑ⒻAlw 16000	56 6 4 33 67½ 612 613¾	Ferrer J C	L 120	3.40	75-16	Joyce D.1108 P J Floral1121 Grant Jima120	Faltered	6

LATEST WORKOUTS Sep 4 Aqu ⊡ 3f my :372 B (d) Aug 25 Aqu ⊡ 4f fst :49 B

Shady Willow — Gr. f. 4, by Dom Alaric-Fr—Grise Petite, by Dancer's Image
ANTLEY C W (—) — Br.—Fuller Peter (Ont-C) — 117
Own.—Girdner Paul — Tr.—Pollard Damon (—)
Lifetime 29 2 11 4 $88,448 — 1992 11 1 5 1 $43,494 — 1991 15 1 5 3 $40,808 — Turf 2 0 0 0 — Wet 3 0 2 0 $10,680

12Oct92- 6Bel my 7f	:23 :463 1:233	3↑ⒻAlw 27000	76 5 3 41½ 31 22½ 25½	Antley C W	b 117	6.40	80-09	FlyToTheMoon1175½ShdyWllw117noSblWy117	Held place	6
16Sep92- 5Bel fst 1	:462 1:114 1:374	3↑ⒻAlw 29000	74 5 4 3½ 2½ 21 22½	Smith M E	b 117	2.80	79-19	Strmng1172½ShdyWllow1172TrstnDx117	Bid, weakened	7
29Aug92- 5Sar gd 1⅛ Ⓣ	:493 1:134 1:52	3↑ⒻAlw 29000	62 5 10 1011 910108¾1014¼	Krone J A	117	9.30	65-19	Herto'Mine114¾MissRiverCoins1194Trmontt112	Outrun	10
21Aug92- 3Sar fst 1	:472 1:12 1:371	3↑ⒻClm c-25000	80 3 2 22 2½ 1½ 11¼	Smith M E	b 117	*1.80	— —	ShdyWllw1171¼FlnSprc1175DnyFthrs117	Check 1/2, drv	8
21Aug92-Claimed from Pat's Bonto Farm, Moschera Gasper S Trainer										
29Jly92- 3WO fst 1 1/16	:483 1:13 1:471	3↑ⒻAlw 26800	72 1 3 54 46½ 45 22½	Kabel T K	b 116	1.45	75-25	MntsIntHrs1112½ShdWll116hdVdctrss116	Game for 2nd	5
22Jly92- 8WO fst 7f	:224 :454 1:252	3↑ⒻAlw 24400	71 4 6 45½ 67¾ 54½ 3½	Kabel T K	b 116	3.10	83-18	StarryVal113½Smaral114noShdyWillow116	Good energy	8
9Jly92- 7WO fst 1 1/16	:482 1:124 1:462	3↑ⒻAlw 34000	76 1 4 42½ 43¼ 42½ 21	Baird G R	b 112	17.30	81-23	PrmrQstn1121ShdyWllw1121½PltnmPws122	Closed well	4
1Jly92- 4WO fm 1 1/16 Ⓣ	:464 1:101 1:413	3↑ⒻⓇVictoriana	72 2 10 1011 910101210 10	Baird G R	b 113	68.70	86-04	ContryStg117½HopForABrz1172AGlForGordo119	Outrun	10
13Jun92- 8CD fst 1 1/16	:492 1:142 1:46	3↑ⒻAlw 32500	66 6 4 43 32 54¼ 67¼	Sarvis D A	LBb 112	21.00	77-18	SingForFree1082AnotherMomnt1112BurgrQun112	Tired	9
2Jun92- 2CD fst 1 1/16	:484 1:15 1:472	3↑ⒻAlw 29650	68 4 6 54½ 41¼ 21½ 23	Sarvis D A	LBb 112	4.90	74-22	Norma1113ShadyWillow1122½DisyLove119	Second best	6

LATEST WORKOUTS Oct 8 Bel 4f fst :50 B

Neo-Classical-GB — B. f. 3(Mar), by Primo Dominie—Musical Sally, by The Minstrel
VELAZQUEZ J R (—) — Br.—Lord Dundas (GB) — 114
Own.—Sugar Maple Farm — Tr.—Johnson Philip G (—)
Lifetime 5 1 2 1 $8,868 — 1992 1 0 0 0 — 1991 4 1 2 1 $8,868 — Turf 5 1 2 1 $8,868

14Apr92♦6Newmarket(Eng) gd 7f	1:262	Ⓣ ChrisBlackwellHcp	1515¼	Holland D	130	16.00	— —	BewreofAgnts130no SpnishMinr1282 Showgi127	Led 3f	15
25Jun91♦1Yarmouth(Eng) gd*7f	1:31	Ⓣ ⒻE.B.F.Stakes(Mdn)	16	Eddery P	123	*.90	— —	Neo-Classicl1236 SlightRisk1238 Arvid123	Led thruout	5
14Jun91♦1York(Eng) gd 6f	1:122	Ⓣ ⒻUniv.ofYorkTurfClubStk	23	Cauthen S	120	2.75	— —	Twafeaj1203 Neo-Classicl1202 MyJerseyPerl129	Led 4f	6
27May91♦6Leicester(Eng) gd 6f	1:151	Ⓣ ⒻLioness Stks(Mdn)	21½	Hills R	123	*1.75	— —	LastExit1231½ Neo-Clssicl1231½ SpecilGllery123	Led 5f	13
17May91♦1Newbury(Eng) gd 6f	1:152	Ⓣ ⒻHatherden Stks(Mdn)	36½	Cauthen S	123	5.00	— —	CultrVltr1233½ AtmosphrcBls1233 No-Clsscl123	Evenly	8

LATEST WORKOUTS Oct 19 Bel tr.t 3f fst :361 H Oct 14 Bel tr.t 5f fst 1:033 B Oct 5 Bel tr.t 4f fst :492 B Sep 30 Bel tr.t 3f fst :36 H

The favorite in this preliminary allowance for fillies was Jode, a half-sister to 1985 Kentucky Derby–winner Spend A Buck. The Danzig filly had won clearly in her debut more than sixteen months ago, but had to be regarded as something of an unknown quantity making her U.S. debut off a sparse and irregularly spaced workout line.

The second choice was Bob's Little Gal, a one-dimensional speedster who had been defeated at odds of 3–1 or less in five previous attempts at the condition. She had recorded turn times of :23⅖ in her three most recent starts at six furlongs — times that are obtained by subtracting the quarter-mile from the half-mile time, and adjusting by a fifth of a second for each length lost or gained.

In Bob's Little Gal's most recent race, for example, she set the pace of :22⅕ and :45⅗, running her second quarter in :23⅖ (:45⅗ minus :22⅕ equals :23⅖, with no adjustment for beaten lengths necessary).

The third choice, Sabal Way, had also been tried and found wanting on numerous occasions at the preliminary allowance level; like Bob's Little Gal, she had finished in the money in all recent attempts, but remained eligible for the condition nevertheless. Her turn times in two starts since returning from a layoff were :23⅖ on October 12 (:46⅗ minus :23 equals :23⅗, minus another ⅕ for her one-length gain equals :23⅖) and :22⅘ on September 9 (:45⅖ minus :22⅖ equals :23, minus ⅕ for her one-length gain equals :22⅘).

Fourth choice was Patchy Frost. Although she had been beaten by more than ten lengths by Sabal Way on September 9, the race represented the first time she had ever had two races so closely spaced. Her maiden win at Saratoga had come off a two-month layoff, and her Beyer of 84 that day was comparable to the best figures recorded by Sabal Way and Bob's Little Gal. For this race, Patchy Frost had been given six weeks off, and, judging from her maiden performance, it seemed reasonable to assume she preferred her races spaced well apart.

In breaking her maiden, Patchy Frost recorded a :22⅖ turn time, gaining five and a half lengths through a second quarter that had been run in :23⅖. This was a significantly faster turn time than Bob's Little Gal (I'm always picking on her, aren't I?) and Sabal Way were accustomed to. For that matter, it was also faster than what Shady Willow (yet another in the field to have finished in the money on several occasions without breaking through this most basic allowance condition) was used to.

At 5–1, Patchy Frost was a bargain price for a horse with such a potential edge in the second fraction, mainly due to the presence of Jode, who was attracting all the money. A reasonable play into the race might've been a win bet on Patchy Frost along with an exacta saver using her underneath the unknown commodity. As things turned out, the saver proved unnecessary:

FOURTH RACE
Aqueduct
OCTOBER 22, 1992

6 FURLONGS. (1.08) ALLOWANCE. Purse $27,000. Fillies and Mares. 3-year-olds and upward which have never won a race other than Maiden, Claiming or Starter. Weights: 3year-olds, 119 lbs.; oldaer, 122 lbs. Non-winners of a race other than claiming since October 1 allowed 3 lbs.; of such a race since September 15, 5 lbs.

Value of race $27,000; value to winner $16,200; second $5,940; third $3,240; fourth $1,620. Mutuel pool $145,258. Exacta Pool $298,585 Quinella Pool $71,168

Last Raced	Horse	M/Eqt.A.Wt	PP	St	¼	½	Str	Fin	Jockey	Odds $1
9Sep92 7Bel6	Patchy Frost	3 114	1	3	2½	2½	1hd	12	Bailey J D	5.70
12Oct92 6Bel3	Sabal Way	b 4 112	4	4	5½	42½	3½	2nk	Stewart J F Jr5	4.80
26Sep92 3Bel1	Bob's Little Gal	b 3 114	3	1	1½	11	22	35	Lydon P J5	3.70
15Jun91 7Eng1	Jode	3 114	2	6	3hd	31	49	49	Smith M E	.90
12Oct92 6Bel2	Shady Willow	b 4 117	5	2	6	6	6	5½	Antley C W	9.00
14Apr92 6Eng15	Neo-Classical-GB	3 114	6	5	4½	5½	51	6	Velazquez J R	13.30

OFF AT 1:53 Start good. Won driving. Time, :23³, :47¹, :59³, 1:12¹ Track fast.

$2 Mutuel Prices:

1-(A)-PATCHY FROST	13.40	7.40	3.20
5-(E)-SABAL WAY		5.00	2.80
4-(D)-BOB'S LITTLE GAL			2.60

$2 EXACTA 1-5 PAID $73.60 $2 QUINELLA 1-5 PAID $35.20

B. f, (May), by Storm Cat—Consequential, by Dr Fager. Trainer Lukas D Wayne. Bred by William Strong & Overbrook Farm (Ky).

PATCHY FROST forced the pace from outside into upper stretch, took command a furlong out then edged clear under pressure. SABAL WAY checked slightly between horses nearing the far turn, swung four wide to launch her bid at the top of the stretch then outfinished BOB'S LITTLE GAL for the place. BOB'S LITTLE GAL set the pace along the inside into midstretch and weakened in the final eighth. JODE, away slowly, raced in close contention while saving ground to the turn and lacked a strong closing bid. SHADY WILLOW never reached contention. NEO CLASSICAL was finished before going a half.

Owners— 1, Young William T; 2, Saks Martin; 3, Lamcresse Stable; 4, Maktoum al Maktoum; 5, Girdner Paul; 6, Sugar Maple Farm.

Trainers— 1, Lukas D Wayne; 2, Ferriola Peter; 3, Barbara Robert; 4, Mott William I; 5, Pollard Damon; 6, Johnson Philip G.

Overweight: Bob's Little Gal 5 pounds.

Scratched—Mama Warbucks (26Sep92 8Med6); Kersey (17Oct92 2Bel4).

Handicappers desiring to utilize sophisticated pace-rating methods and/or learn more about the intricacies of pace should consult Tom Brohamer's *Modern Pace Handicapping*. The book is quite technical and by no means an easy read, but it remains the definitive work on the subject, although geared primarily to the Santa Anita/Hollywood Park circuit, where speed and position are the essence of the game, and where track-surface variants do not generally vary as wildly as they do in New York.

New York players may find, as I have, that attempting to get too precise with pace ratings is more trouble than it's worth, due to the circumstances detailed earlier in this chapter, along with one other major fly in the ointment: the jockeys. Countless times, the pace for a New York race — whether a sprint or a route, on grass or dirt — takes on a frustratingly European flavor, as everyone plays the "waiting game" through the opening fractions. The cynical phrase "the better the race, the slower the pace" never rang truer than in the Grade 2 Forego Handicap — supposedly the kind of race in which handicappers might've expected torrid fractions — when the fractions were absurdly slow:

NINTH RACE
Saratoga
AUGUST 24, 1994

7 FURLONGS. (1.20²) 15th Running of THE FOREGO HANDICAP. Purse $100,000 Added. Grade II. 3-year-olds and upward. By subscription of $100 each which should accompany the nomination; $500 to pass the entry box, $500 to start with $100,000 added. The added money and all fees to be divided 60% to the winner, 22% to second, 12% to third and 6% to fourth. Weights Friday, August 19. Starters to be named at the closing time of entries. Trophies will be presented to the winning owner, trainer and jockey. Closed with 25 nominations.

Value of Race: $110,000 Winner $66,000; second $24,200; third $13,200; fourth $6,600. Mutuel Pool $422,546.00 Exacta Pool $474,120.00 Triple Pool $403,776.00

Last Raced	Horse	M/Eqt.	A.	Wt	PP	St	¼	½	Str	Fin	Jockey	Odds $1
16Jly94 ^{9}ElP^{1}	American Chance		5	113	7	2	3½	4½	2^{1}	1^{1}	Day P	7.10
1Aug94 ^{7}Sar^{1}	Evil Bear		4	114	5	1	1½	1^{1}	1½	2¾	Lopez C	9.40
11Jun94 ^{9}Bel^{2}	Go For Gin		3	117	6	3	4$1\frac{1}{2}$	3^{hd}	3^{hd}	3^{3}	McCarron C J	1.80
12Aug94 ^{6}Sar^{1}	Harlan	b	5	113	3	6	6^{hd}	7	5½	4^{nk}	Smith M E	6.70
7Aug94 ^{8}Sar^{3}	I Can't Believe		6	112	2	4	2½	2^{1}	4$1\frac{1}{2}$	5^{nk}	Maple E	8.90
30Jly94 ^{8}Sar^{5}	Kyoko		4	112	4	5	5^{hd}	5½	6^{1}	6^{nk}	Bailey J D	30.50
26Jun94 ^{7}Bel^{1}	Virginia Rapids		4	123	1	7	7	6½	7	7	Samyn J L	1.60

OFF AT 5:15 Start Good. Won driving. Time, $:23^{4}$, $:47^{3}$, 1:11, $1:22^{3}$ Track fast.

$2 Mutuel Prices:			
8–(H)–AMERICAN CHANCE	16.20	7.80	6.20
6–(F)–EVIL BEAR		11.00	8.60
7–(G)–GO FOR GIN			3.60

$2 EXACTA 8–6 PAID $110.00 $2 TRIPLE 8–6–7 PAID $399.00

Dk. b. or br. h, by Cure The Blues–American Dance, by Seattle Slew. Trainer Carroll David. Bred by Firestone Mr & Mrs B R (Ky).

AMERICAN CHANCE settled just behind the early leaders, rallied three wide while between horses on the turn, made a run to challenge in midstretch then drew clear through the final seventy yards. EVIL BEAR set a moderate pace along the inside into the stretch, continued on the front into deep stretch but couldn't hold the winner safe. GO FOR GIN raced in close contention while between horses for a half, dropped back slightly while in traffic on the turn, then finished with good energy along the inside to gain a share. HARLAN checked at the start, steadied between horses on the turn, then failed to threaten thereafter. I CAN'T BELIEVE raced in close contention along the inside to the top of the stretch and tired. KYOKO made a run four wide to reach contention on the turn and flattened out. VIRGINIA RAPIDS raced in traffic while trapped along the rail to the turn then lacked the needed response when called upon.

Owners— 1, Gunther John D; 2, Sabini Joseph C; 3, Condren William & Cornacchia Joseph; 4, Young William T; 5, Brnjas John; 6, Perez Robert; 7, Middletown Stables

Trainers—1, Carroll David; 2, Reid Robert E Jr; 3, Zito Nicholas P; 4, Lukas D Wayne; 5, Passero Frank A Jr; 6, Callejas Alfredo; 7, Jerkens H Allen

Overweight: Harlan (2), Kyoko (4).

Scratched— Devil On Ice (30Jly94 ^{8}SAR^{1})

The fractional line of :23⅘; :47⅗; 1:11; and 1:22⅗ broke down as follows: :23⅘; :23⅘; :23⅖; and :11⅗, rendering the chances of any horse more than a length or so from the early lead virtually nil. By way of comparison, the day's previous dirt race was a sprint for $35,000 claimers, and they cut fractions of :22⅖ and :45⅖. Handicappers who tried to get a handle on the pace of the Forego saw all their calculations fly out the window as soon as the little pinheads (as Andy Beyer fondly refers to them) went out in that ridiculously slow opening quarter. Try calculating *that* in advance!

Nevertheless, for all the pitfalls that can develop insofar as pace ratings are concerned, handicappers must always respect the chances of a horse that owns *clear-cut advantages* (whether early, midrace, or late). Such horses will strongly affect the outcome of their race at the very least.

The best way for New York players to incorporate pace into their handicapping routine is to begin the contender selection process with these four questions:

1) What are the race conditions, and what type of runner is favored by them?
2) Who is the likely favorite?
3) How is the race likely to be run — are there any horses that figure to be helped or hindered by the pace match-up? That is to say, does one horse enjoy a *demonstrable* edge in terms of early, midrace, or late pace, or does the favorite appear to be at a disadvantage in regard to the probable pace?
4) What type of running style has been most successful at today's distance?

THE TRACK PROFILE/EVALUATING TRACK BIAS

A universal technique that can yield an edge in terms of pace analysis is the compilation of an accurate track profile. A track profile is merely a record, kept separately by distance and surface, of the types of running styles that have been winning at your track.

Along with saving result charts, back issues of the *Form*, and winning past performances arranged according to trainer (along with their beaten favorites), maintaining a track profile can provide a vital edge, and it takes only minutes a day. A typical entry for a day's six-furlong races might look like this:

Date/Race	Winner (# field)	1st Call	2nd Call	Str	Fin	Mutue
1-27-3	Nag o'Mine(6)	5^{8}	4^{5}	3^{2}	1^{nk}	$27.8
1-27-6	Banana Nose(11)	10^{8}	7^{6}	4^{3}	1^{2}	$15.4
1-27-7	Iseldomwin(7)	6^{9}	3^{3}	2^{1}	1^{3}	$22.0

The data is obtained by extracting the winner's beaten lengths from the result chart. The first entry shows that Nag o'Mine won the third race on January 27. In a six-horse field, Nag o'Mine raced fifth, eight lengths from the lead after the opening quarter (the first call); she raced fourth, five lengths from the lead after a half-mile (the second call); she raced third, two lengths from the lead at the stretch call; and she won by a neck, paying $27.80.

Including the field size will help you get a better overall picture of the race. A horse who rallies to win after racing fifth of six in the early stages takes on more of a stretch-running "feel" than would a horse who rallied from fifth in a field of fourteen. In the former instance, the winner had only one rival beaten early; in the latter instance, it had nine rivals beaten early.

I recommend including the mutuel because a series of short-priced, front-running winners yields no concrete evidence that a speed-favoring bias existed; if all the winners were *expected* to run well, it may have been nothing more than coincidence that they happened to be front-runners. If, on the other hand, the day's winners at a given distance all won on the lead, and paid high average mutuels, then the chances increase that a bias was helping these horses to run better than the crowd thought they would.

A good tip-off that a bias, particularly a speed-favoring bias, was in existence, is a series of abnormally high winning margins. That's why I like to include the winner's margin.

Track profiles are helpful in illuminating day-to-day biases, but their greatest significance involves subtler, long-term trends that often manifest themselves according to distance. It helps to know, for example, that of the last twenty races at a given distance, the vast majority of the winners have shown a common running style, even though a bias may not be recognized by players who fail to maintain a profile. When a race has been handicapped down to two or three contenders, and only one fits the current profile, that contender may own a decisive tactical edge, and so may the profile keeper.

The track profile yields its most powerful edge when the typical winner's running style suddenly shifts due to weather conditions, track maintenance, or some other reason. During the 1993 Saratoga meeting, speed more than held its own at seven furlongs during the early part of August; of seventeen such races contested during that period, a dozen were won by horses who either set the pace or raced in second position at the first call. But from mid to late August, the next seventeen seven-furlong races yielded the astounding total of fifteen winners that raced fifth or farther back at the first call. Handicappers who recognized the bias shift profited in the short term by betting the closers when all those around them were still betting the speed, and they also profited in the long term by properly evaluating seven-furlong performances when these horses raced back at later dates.

FOUR

NEGATIVES

THERE IS ONLY ONE REASON to bet money on the outcome of a horserace: an edge is perceived.

There are only two situations that constitute an edge: a legitimate contender is underbet; or a horse with no special redeeming qualities is overbet.

Through the first three chapters I discussed ways to isolate contenders from the first situation — those horses going postward at odds greater than their true chances of winning.

Situation number two is vastly underrated as a source of value, and that is what I will be dealing with here. The percentages shift to the side of the player whenever one of the favorites in a race can be eliminated — particularly in New York, The Home of the Overbet Favorite.

In terms of exotic wagers, such as the exacta and trifecta, a negative opinion about a favorite often proves even more valuable because you're eliminating the horse *from two or more wagering positions.* When you can make a case for a short-priced horse to finish worse than second in an exacta race, or out of the money altogether in a trifecta, you're laying the groundwork for a big score.

As I explained earlier, negative patterns in terms of speed figures and training maneuvers often bring overbet horses to light, but there are several other situations that also deserve your attention.

DISADVANTAGED BY THE PROBABLE PACE

A horse is advantaged by the pace when its running style is unique to the field, that is, the only early speed, the only presser, or the only closer. Conversely, a horse is disadvantaged when it is one of several in the race with a similar style.

From time to time, a reliable elimination scenario occurs when a lightly raced horse that has been dominating rivals of questionable ability is now taking a step up in class and is suddenly faced with genuine pace pressure for the first time; when a stretch to a longer distance is also involved, the combination is usually lethal.

8 SARATOGA — 7 FURLONGS (SARATOGA; START; FINISH)

7 FURLONGS. (1.20²) 80th Running THE TEST (Grade I). Purse $150,000 Added. Fillies. 3-year-olds. By subscription of $300 each, which should accompany the nomination; $1,200 to pass the entry box; $1,200 to start, with $150,000 added. The added money and all fees to be divided 60% to the winner, 22% to second, 12% to third and 6% to fourth. Weight, 121 lbs. Winners of two races of $50,000 since April 15, 3 lbs. additional. Non-winners of a race of $50,000 in 1991, allowed 3 lbs. Of a race of $35,000 since April 15, 5 lbs. Of a race of $25,000 in 1991, 7 lbs. Starters to be named at the closing time of entries. Trophies will be presented to the winning owner, trainer and jockey. Nominations Closed Wednesday, July 10. Closed with 22 nominations.

Ifyoucouldseemenow — B. f. 3(Apr), by Tunerup—Real Jenny, by Valid Appeal — Br.—Cane Norman E (Fla) — Tr.—Mayberry Brian A — 121 — Lifetime 12 5 2 4 $258,575 — 1991 7 2 1 3 $176,275 — 1990 5 3 1 1 $82,300
Own.—Siegel Jan
8Jun91- 6Hol fst 1 1/16 :47 1:112 1:43 ⒻPrincess 6 3 3 3/4 31 2hd 2nk Pedroza M A B 118 *1.60 86-14 Wngt116nkIfycldsmnw1184FppsCsyMss1174 Bump'd often, lt 7
8Jun91-Grade II
25May91- 8Hol fst 7f :213 :44 1:214 ⒻRailbird 6 2 4 2 1/2 4 2 1/2 3 2 1/2 3 1 1/2 Pedroza M A B 122 *.80 94-11 Szzqcut119hdZmHmmr1171 1/2Ifyocoldsmnow1225 1/4 Mild lt. gain 6
25May91-Grade II
3May91- 9CD fst 1 1/8 :464 1:12 1:494 ⒻKy Oaks 3 5 512 6 2 1/2 5 7 1/2 7 17 1/2 Pedroza M A B 121 4.50e 67-03 LitLight121noWithllprobbity121nkTlForbd121 1/4 Brief turn rally 10
3May91-Grade I
17Apr91- 8Kee fst *7f 1:27 ⒻBeaumont 2 3 5 3/4 3nk 14 14 Pedroza M A B 122 1.90 95-07 Ifyoucouldsmnow1224VrsilsTrty1142 1/2EvrLdy1147 Ridden out 6
7Apr91-Grade III
16Mar91- 8SA fst 1 1/16 :46 1:121 1:422 ⒻS A Oaks 4 2 2 1/2 2hd 11 3 3/4 Pedroza M A B 117 1.50e 87-15 LiteLight1171GrdenGl1172 1/2Ifyoucouldsmnow1171 1/4 Weakened 5
16Mar91-Grade I
9Feb91- 8SA fst 7f :223 :46 1:233 ⒻS Ynez B Cp 5 1 3 2 1/2 31 31 3nk Pedroza M A B 121 *.90 85-15 Brazen121hd Fowda116hd Ifyoucouldseemenow1211 1/4 Gamely 5
9Feb91-Grade II
5Jan91- 8SA fst 6f :212 :443 1:093 ⒻPsdna Br Cp 1 4 21 2 1/2 12 14 Pedroza M A B 118 1.70 88-17 Ifyoucouldseemenow1184Brazen1182Cuddles1212 1/2 Ridden out 5
28Nov90- 8Hol fst 6 1/2f :213 :442 1:161 ⒻMcsn Br Cp 1 5 3 1/2 1hd 11 1/2 11 1/2 Pedroza M A B 115 9.10 94-06 Ifyoucouldseemenow1151 1/2Cuddls115hdFrOutNurs1153 Driving 11
4Oct90- 7SA fst 6 1/2f :213 :443 1:161 ⒻAlw 32000 10 1 2 1/2 2hd 11 1/2 12 Pedroza M A B 118 6.50 89-11 Ifyoucouldsmnow1182SrtogSuccss115noNicAssy1184 1/2 Driving 10
13Sep90- 10Fpx fst 6 1/2f :213 :452 1:173 ⒻBsls & Bws 5 1 4 3/4 4 2 1/2 3 3/4 23 Pedroza M A B 114 2.80 86-10 Brzn1143Ifyoucouldsmnow1142SrtogSuccss1143 Finished well 9
Speed Index: Last Race: +5.0 3–Race Avg.: +2.3 7–Race Avg.: +1.1 Overall Avg.: 0.0
LATEST WORKOUTS Jly 22 Sar 4f fst :48 H

Classy Women — B. f. 3(Feb), by Relaunch—Aironica, by Proud Clarion — Br.—Winchell Verne H (Ky) — Tr.—Vienna Darrell — 114 — Lifetime 2 2 0 0 $33,000 — 1991 2 2 0 0 $33,000 — 1990 0 M 0 0 — Turf 1 1 0 0 $17,000
Own.—Herrick W
6Jly91- 7Hol fm 5 1/2f ⓣ:212 :433 1:01 3+ⒻAlw 32000 6 2 23 2 3 1/2 12 15 1/4 Valenzuela P A B 116 *2.30 — — ClssyWomn1165 1/4Bdmnton1161 1/2CommttDcsn116 3/4 Ridden out 8
21Jun91- 6Hol fst 6f :213 :442 1:094 3+ⒻMd Sp Wt 2 3 2 1/2 12 15 14 1/4 Valenzuela P A LB 116 3.50 91-11 ClssyWomn1164 1/4PollyPrton1163VsblGold1162 Lugged in lane 10
Speed Index: Last Race: +2.0 1–Race Avg.: +2.0 1–Race Avg.: +2.0 Overall Avg.: +2.0
LATEST WORKOUTS Jly 3 Hol 3f fst :37 B Jun 28 Hol 3f fst :381 B Jun 18 Hol 4f fst :521 H Jun 13 Hol 6f fst 1:134 H

Zama Hummer — Dk. b. or br. f. 3(Apr), by Knights Choice—Press to Test, by Saltville — Br.—Roe Timothy K (Wash) — Tr.—Dutton Jerry — 121 — Lifetime 6 4 1 0 $139,055 — 1991 4 3 1 0 $132,160 — 1990 2 1 0 0 $6,895
Own.—Roe Tim K
4Jly91- 7Bel fst 6f :213 :443 1:094 ⒻPrioress 10 8 109 1/4 9 5 1/2 3 2 1/2 12 1/4 Stevens G L 114 4.20 91-11 ZmHummr1142 1/4Mssy'sMrg114nkDvlshTouch1182 1/4 Going away 10
4Jly91-Grade II
25May91- 8Hol fst 7f :213 :44 1:214 ⒻRailbird 1 6 2hd 1hd 1hd 2hd Solis A B 117 18.70 95-11 Szqct119hdZmHmmr1171 1/2Ifyocldsmnw1225 1/4 Light brush 1/16 6
25May91-Grade II
25Apr91- 5Hol fst 6f :221 :452 1:093 3+ⒻAlw 36000 5 3 2 1/2 2hd 1hd 13 McCarron C J B 115 2.90 92-10 ZmHummer1153PerkySlew1131 1/2GinRummyJudy1191 1/4 All out 6
31Mar91- 7SA fst 6 1/2f :212 :444 1:161 ⒻAlw 32000 1 4 22 21 1/2 11 1/2 11 3/4 Solis A B 119 12.20 89-14 ZamHummer1191 3/4ImpertinentLdy1193ChiefAppel1195 Driving 8
4Aug90- 9Lga fst 6 1/2f :214 :443 1:172 ⒻMrcr Grls 8 5 7 3 1/2 8 7 1/2 5 5 3/4 5 4 1/2 Gonsalves F A 114 2.50 88-15 CdetteStevens1124 1/2GylWrmng1123Ldy'sExcus1183 Late rally 8
17Jun90- 4Lga fst 5f :222 :452 :581 ⒻMd Sp Wt 7 2 1hd 13 15 15 Boulanger G 115 *.90 94-15 ZmHummer1155Doin'thePuylup1152Peterhof'sPte1183 Easily 9
Speed Index: Last Race: +2.0 3–Race Avg.: +3.3 6–Race Avg.: +2.8 Overall Avg.: +2.8
LATEST WORKOUTS Jly 24 Sar 4f fst :474 B ●Jly 18 Sar 5f fst :593 H ●Jly 12 Bel 3f fst :352 B Jun 27 SA 6f fst 1:382 H

Withallprobability — B. f. 3(Mar), by Mr Prospector—Solomoff, by Northern Dancer — Br.—Farish W S (Ky) — Tr.—Lukas D Wayne — 127 — Lifetime 7 4 2 0 $306,633 — 1991 6 3 2 0 $292,820 — 1990 1 1 0 0 $13,813
Own.—Evans Edward
25May91- 8Bel fst 1 :462 1:113 1:372 ⒻAcorn 6 3 5 1 1/2 64 6 8 1/2 6 18 3/4 Perret C 121 2.00 64-17 MeadowStr1216VersillesTrety1212 1/2DzzleMeJoli1212 3/4 Gave way 6
25May91-Grade I
3May91- 9CD fst 1 1/8 :464 1:12 1:494 ⒻKy Oaks 9 1 18 1hd 24 210 Day P B 121 2.10 94-03 LitLight121noWithllprobbility121nkTlForbd121 1/4 Saved second 10
3May91-Grade I
14Apr91- 9OP gd 1 1/16 :481 1:122 1:414 ⒻFantasy 7 1 11 1/2 1hd 22 22 Perret C 121 1.00 91-08 LiteLight1212Withllprobbility121noNicesPin1212 Game effort 8
14Apr91-Grade II
16Mar91- 10GP fst 1 1/16 :464 1:111 1:431 ⒻBonnie Miss 5 1 11 11 12 1/2 12 1/2 Perret C 117 *.30 97-17 Wthllprobblty1172 1/2FncyRbbons1172 1/2OtIstng1141 1/4 Ridden out 6
16Mar91-Grade II
7Feb91- 9GP fst 7f :221 :444 1:222 ⒻForward 4 2 2hd 2hd 11 1/2 14 1/2 Perret C 114 *.70 94-10 Withllprobbility1144 1/2PrivteTrsur1181 1/2FrOutNurs112 1/2 Handily 8
7Feb91-Grade II
14Jan91- 3GP fst 6f :222 :452 1:101 ⒻAlw 18000 5 3 12 11 1/2 14 17 1/2 Perret C 117 *.40 94-06 Withllprobbility1177 1/2ReRfko117nkHighwyQueen1122 1/2 Handily 10
23Nov90- 3CD my 6f :214 :46 1:112 ⒻMd Sp Wt 4 4 1 1/2 1 1/2 1 1/2 13 Day P B 120 *.90 89-16 Withllprobbility1203ProspectSouth1205Adios1206 Ridden out 12
Speed Index: Last Race: +4.0 3–Race Avg.: +3.0 3–Race Avg.: +3.0 Overall Avg.: 0.0
LATEST WORKOUTS Jly 22 Sar tr.t 5f fst 1:034 B Jly 16 Bel 5f fst 1:01 B Jly 9 Bel 5f fst 1:013 B Jly 2 Bel 4f fst :482 B

Devilish Touch — Dk. b. or br. f. 3(May), by Devil's Bag—Velvet Touch, by Restless Native
Own.—Burning Tree Farm — Br.—Clay R N & Clifton Beth Hipp (Ky) — Tr.—Garcia Carlos A — 118
Lifetime 6 4 1 1 $191,331 — 1991 2 1 0 1 $52,982 — 1990 4 3 1 0 $138,339
4Jly91- 7Bel fst 6f :21³ :44³ 1:09⁴ ⒻPrioress 1 2 2hd 1hd 1½ 3²½ Perret C 118 *2.60 88-11 ZmHmmr114²½Missy'sMrg114nkDvlshTch118²½ Bid Weakened 10
4Jly91-Grade II
1Jun91- 8Mth fst 6f :21³ :45² 1:11 ⒻMsWodford 4 3 2½ 1½ 14 1½ Perret C 121 *.60 86-15 DevilishTouch1211½FarOutNurse114⁴Lur'sSecret112¹⁶ Driving
29Oct90- 7Bel fst 6½f :22¹ :45 1:18 ⒻAstarita 5 2 3½ 2½ 1½ 1³½ Perret C 116 1.00 87-15 DevilishTouch116³½MkinFces112hdMissy'sMirge112²½ Driving
29Oct90-Grade II
6Oct90- 8Med fst 6f :22² :45⁴ 1:10² ⒻBlm Fld Col 5 3 2½ 1½ 1³½ 17 Perret C 120 1.40 90-14 DevilishTouch1207PrayerfulMiss117nkRellyQuick120³ Handily 5
16Aug90- 8Sar fst 6f :22 :45¹ 1:11² ⒻAdirondack 3 7 1² 1½ 1½ 2¹½ Santos J A 119 *.90 86-11 RellyQuick1141½DevilishTouch1191½Frbr'sFollis114½ Good try 9
16Aug90-Grade II
21Jly90- 6Lrl fst 5½f :22¹ :45³ 1:05² ⒻToddler Bc 2 7 1³½ 1³½ 15 1⁴½ Rocco J 112 *1.30 90-15 DevilishTouch112⁴½Prongle110½GlGoldilocks110hd Ridden out 8
Speed Index: Last Race: -1.0 3-Race Avg.: +0.6 6-Race Avg.: +2.6 Overall Avg.: +2.6
LATEST WORKOUTS ●Jly 19 Lrl 6f fst 1:12 H ●Jly 13 Lrl 4f fst :46³ H Jly 2 Lrl 4f fst :48 H ●Jun 25 Lrl 5f fst 1:01 B

Versailles Treaty — B. f. 3(Apr), by Danzig—Ten Cents a Dance, by Buckpasser
Own.—Phipps Cynthia — Br.—Phipps Cynthia (Ky) — Tr.—McGaughey Claude III — 114
Lifetime 7 4 3 0 $120,956 — 1991 6 3 3 0 $104,756 — 1990 1 1 0 0 $16,200
24Jun91- 8Bel fst 7f :22⁴ :45¹ 1:21⁴ 3+ⒻAlw 30000 5 2 31 42 1hd 1¹½ Cordero A Jr 109 *.40 95-06 VrsllsTrty1091½ProudKrn117⁴BrghtCadls117nk Steadied 3/8 pl 5
25May91- 8Bel fst 1 :46² 1:11³ 1:37² ⒻAcorn 2 5 31 31 2² 26 Cordero A Jr 121 5.30e 77-17 MedowStr1216VersillsTrty121²½DzzlMJoli121²½ Saved ground 6
25May91-Grade I
3May91- 8Aqu fst 1 :47¹ 1:12³ 1:39 3+ⒻAlw 31000 5 4 41½ 41 2hd 1²½ Cordero A Jr 113 *.50 67-34 Versailles Treaty113²½ Frederick Fair110¾ Kirky's Girl119½ 7
3May91-Blocked turn, steadied 3/16, ridden out
7Apr91- 8Kee fst *7f 1:27 ⒻBeaumont 4 5 4nk ½ 24 24 Bailey J D B 114 *1.10 91-07 Ifycldsmnw122⁴VrsllsTrty114²½EvrLdy114⁷ Wide backstretch 6
7Apr91-Grade III
22Feb91- 7GP fst 7f :22² :45³ 1:23² ⒻAlw 17000 4 4 51½ 41 1²½ 17 Bailey J D 115 *1.30 89-14 VersillesTrety1157SisterSlev115½FlowingMlody1151½ Handily 8
28Jan91- 8GP fst 7f :22¹ :45¹ 1:24⁴ ⒻAlw 21400 4 4 31 31 1hd 2¹½ Bailey J D 115 *.30 80-14 SpnshBlld1121½VrsllsTrty115nkHomr'sHonyBn114½ Weakened 8
21Nov90- 3Aqu fst 7f :23² :47³ 1:25² ⒻMd Sp Wt 6 2 53½ 31½ 14½ 19 Bailey J D 117 *1.20 75-21 Versailles Treaty1179 Trust in Dixie117¾ El Fox117³ Handily 7
Speed Index: Last Race: +1.0 3-Race Avg.: +0.6 5-Race Avg.: -1.6 Overall Avg.: -1.8
LATEST WORKOUTS Jly 24 Sar tr.t 4f fst :50³ B ●Jly 18 Bel 5f fst :59¹ H Jly 11 Bel 4f fst :48 B Jly 5 Bel 3f gd :39³ B

Aurora — B. f. 3(May), by Danzig—Althea, by Alydar
Own.—Groves Helen K — Br.—Alexander-Aykroyd-Groves (Ky) — Tr.—Schulhofer Flint S — 114
Lifetime 2 2 0 0 $31,200 — 1991 2 2 0 0 $31,200 — 1990 0 M 0 0
6Jly91- 5Bel gd 6f :22² :45 1:09 3+ⒻAlw 28000 3 1 11 11 1²½ 15 Bailey J D 116 *.10 95-09 Aurora1165 Kinklets117²½ All Too Well1111½ Ridden out 5
24Jun91- 1Bel fst 6f :22 :44⁴ 1:08² ⒻMd Sp Wt 1 1 1½ 11 1³ 17½ Bailey J D 121 *.80 98-06 Aurora1217½ Little Wolf Girl1116½MissInsync1216 Ridden out 7
Speed Index: Last Race: +4.0 2-Race Avg.: +4.0 2-Race Avg.: +4.0 Overall Avg.: +4.0
LATEST WORKOUTS ●Jly 21 Sar 6f fst 1:12⁴ B Jly 15 Bel 4f fst :49³ B Jly 2 Bel 4f fst :49¹ B Jun 21 Bel 4f fst :47 H

The Test Stake's 1991 renewal is one of the oldest examples in this book, and it predates the arrival of the *Beyer Speed Figures* to the *Form*. The past performances contain the *Thoro-graph* ratings just to the left of the running lines, and you can see that Aurora had paired 7s in winning her first two starts rather impressively.

Aurora's first two wins were so impressive that stories detailing her early days as a foal appeared in the racing pages of a couple of newspapers on Saturday, July 27, as the regally bred daughter of Danzig took on six more experienced rivals who had yet to approach her figures.

Now, it is one thing for a *two-year-old* to take a jump from preliminary allowance to Grade 1 — in fact, the best two-year-olds from top connections may at times move directly to a Grade 1 stake immediately after a maiden win; the best of them handle the rise, because *all* the entrants are relatively light on experience. But a *three-year-old* moving from maiden or preliminary allowance to a Grade 1 stake is a horse of a different color — they are conceding a wealth of experience. When the lightly raced three-year-old is also a front-runner stretching out in distance against a field containing several with a similar running style, it is faced with several considerable obstacles and should not be regarded as anything more than a marginal contender. When the horse is heavily favored, handicappers take an edge by betting against it.

Aurora's two wins had been accomplished wire-to-wire after getting clear through half-mile fractions of :44⅘ and :45. A check of the company line for her win of July 6 revealed that the runner-up, Kinklets, had been, in boxing parlance, a cream puff:

Kinklets — Gr. f. 4, by Drone—Julia Jane, by Mr Prospector
Br.—Shehan William R (NJ)
Tr.—Klesaris Robert P
117
Own.—Lamarca Stable

Lifetime 34 3 10 4 $108,600 | 1991 11 2 3 3 $57,820 | 1990 21 1 7 1 $49,880 | Turf 1 0 0 0

26Jun91- 3Bel	fst	7f	:224	:461	1:241	(F)Clm c-32[illegible]	8	3	52½	4nk	1½	31½	Krone J A	b	117	*2.50	81-16	CiaoCiaoBambin1171½GteAppel117nkKinklets1171½	Bid, wknd	9
14Jun91- 3Bel	fst	6f	:222	:452	1:093	(F)Clm 35000	1	1	42½	53¾	33½	32¾	Krone J A	b	119	5.30	89-11	SouthrnSoonr1171½Embrcing1171½Knklts119nk	Altered course	7
20May91- 2Bel	fst	6f	:224	:47	1:121	3+(F)Clm 35000	5	4	42½	51¼	12	1¾	Krone J A	b	119	*1.60e	79-16	Kinklets119¾ Mineral Bath1192¼ I'm SoAgreeable1191	Driving	9
29Apr91- 3Aqu	fst	6½f	:223	:454	1:174	3+(F)Alw 28000	2	3	42	53½	45	55½	Krone J A	b	121	3.90	83-17	WArW119½ChristinCzrn1103½WthStrwbrrs1191¼	Saved ground	7
18Apr91- 7Aqu	gd	6f	:222	:462	1:111	3+(F)Alw 28000	8	8	42½	33½	37½	49¼	Mojica R Jr5	b	119	6.80	76-21	HyBbLulu1159RisHck115nkWithStrwbrris119no	Flattened out	9
6Apr91- 7Aqu	fst	7f	:224	:454	1:241	3+(F)Alw 28000	4	2	31	21	21½	21¾	Pincay L Jr	b	124	3.20	79-18	Underinsurd1121¾Kinklts1244¾UnitndConqur114¾	Second best	7
26Mar91- 7Aqu	fst	6f	:221	:46	1:10	(F)Alw 27000	6	6	42¾	41¼	2hd	13½	Krone J A	b	117	*2.20	91-17	Kinklets1173½ Guard Room117hd Alwaysinlove1171¼	Driving	9
15Mar91- 7Aqu	sly	7f	:233	:48	1:254	(F)Alw 27000	3	6	41¼	1hd	23½	49	Cordero A Jr	b	117	*1.80	64-28	Mineral Bath1173 Lois L.1105½ WindCharmer112½	Pinched bk	6
6Mar91- 8Aqu	fst	6f	[•]:224	:462	1:113	(F)Alw 27000	6	2	2½	2½	21½	2¾	Cordero A Jr	b	117	*1.30	84-19	Kindawild117¾ Kinklets1171¾ Tributary117¾	Held place	6
13Feb91- 6Aqu	fst	6f	[•]:224	:462	1:12	(F)Alw 27000	1	4	32	31½	22	22¼	Cordero A Jr	b	117	1.80e	81-20	Underinsurd1172¼Kinklts1174BountifulMorning112nk	2nd best	8

Kinklets would never be confused with a graded-stakes horse. She had won just three of thirty-four starts while finishing second on no less than ten occasions, and seemed the type destined never to advance through the most basic allowance condition.

For the Test Stakes, Aurora would not be in the gate with any tomato cans like Kinklets. Four in the field had won or placed in graded stakes at the Test's seven furlongs. Moreover, Aurora would not hold a one-length advantage on this field if she ran a half-mile similar to the ones she'd run at Belmont: Classy Women had broken her maiden in faster splits; Zama Hummer had lost a photo in the seven-furlong Railbird after dueling the entire way in :21⅗ and :44; Withallprobability had won the Grade 2 Forward Gal after dueling through a :44⅘ half; and Devilish Touch, a four-time stakes winner, had run faster splits than Aurora as the pace setter in Belmont's Prioress only two days before Aurora's allowance win.

The race was ripe for a closer, and, predictably, Aurora wilted under the intense pace pressure and finished off the board, with Versailles Treaty and Ifyoucouldseemenow — the only entrants to have shown any closing ability — along for a one-two finish and a nice exacta.

EIGHTH RACE
Saratoga
JULY 27, 1991

7 FURLONGS. (1.20²) 66th Running THE TEST (Grade I). Purse $150,000 Added. Fillies. 3-year-olds. By subscription of $300 each, which should accompany the nomination; $1,200 to pass the entry box; $1,200 to start, with $150,000 added. The added money and all fees to be divided 60% to the winner, 22% to second, 12% to third and 6% to fourth. Weight, 121 lbs. Winners of two races of $50,000 since April 15, 3 lbs. additional. Non-winners of a race of $50,000 in 1991, allowed 3 lbs. Of a race of $35,000 since April 15, 5 lbs. Of a race of $25,000 in 1991, 7 lbs. Starters to be named at the closing time of entries. Trophies will be presented to the winning owner, trainer and jockey. Nominations Closed Wednesday, July 10. Closed with 22 nominations.

Value of race $173,400; value to winner $104,040; second $38,148; third $20,808; fourth $10,404. Mutuel pool $412,041. Exacta Pool $488,917 Triple Pool $270,392

Last Raced	Horse	M/Eqt.A.Wt	PP	St	¼	½	Str	Fin	Jockey	Odds $1
24Jun91 ^{8}Bel^{1}	Versailles Treaty	3 114	6	2	7	5^{1}	3^{hd}	$1^{2\frac{3}{4}}$	Cordero A Jr	5.20
8Jun91 ^{6}Hol^{2}	Ifyoucouldseemenow	3 121	1	7	$5^{\frac{1}{2}}$	6^{5}	$5^{2\frac{1}{2}}$	$2^{2\frac{1}{2}}$	Pedroza M A	7.80
4Jly91 ^{7}Bel^{1}	[D]Zama Hummer	3 121	3	5	$3^{\frac{1}{2}}$	4^{2}	2^{hd}	$3^{3\frac{3}{4}}$	Antley C W	3.50
6Jly91 ^{7}Hol^{1}	Classy Women	3 114	2	6	2^{1}	2^{1}	1^{1}	4^{4}	Valenzuela P A	9.30
6Jly91 ^{5}Bel^{1}	Aurora	3 114	7	1	$1^{\frac{1}{2}}$	1^{hd}	$4^{\frac{1}{2}}$	5no	Santos J A	1.00
4Jly91 ^{7}Bel^{3}	Devilish Touch	3 118	5	3	4^{1}	$3^{\frac{1}{2}}$	$6^{3\frac{1}{2}}$	$6^{4\frac{1}{2}}$	Castaneda K	22.10
25May91 ^{8}Bel^{6}	Withallprobability	3 127	4	4	6^{1}	7	7	7	Smith M E	9.80

[D]-Zama Hummer Disqualified and placed sixth.

OFF AT 5:06 Start Good, Won driving. Time, :21⁴, :44¹, 1:09³, 1:22⁴ Track fast.

$2 Mutuel Prices:

6-(F)-VERSAILLES TREATY	12.40	5.40	4.40
1-(A)-IFYOUCOULDSEEMENOW		8.20	4.20
2-(B)-CLASSY WOMEN			6.00

$2 EXACTA 6-1 PAID $92.40 $2 TRIPLE 6-1-2 PAID $687.00

B. f, (Apr), by Danzig—Ten Cents a Dance, by Buckpasser. Trainer McGaughey Claude III. Bred by Phipps Cynthia (Ky).

VERSAILLES TREATY, trailed early while saving ground, steadily worked her way forward along the inside leaving the backstretch, swung to the outside while gaining on the turn, was bumped off stride while sandwiched between horses rallying from wide into the stretch, then unleashed a strong late run outside the leaders to win going away. IFYOUCOULDSEEMENOW, unable to keep pace early while racing well off the rail, circled five wide to reach contention on the turn, was bumped by VERSAILLES TREATY at the top of the stretch then finished with good energy in the middle of the track top gain the place. ZAMA HUMER, settled in good position just behind the early speed duel, swerved out for room soundly bumping DEVILISH TOUCH and causing a chain reaction while rallying into the stretch, battled between horses into midstretch then weakened in the final eighth. CLASSY WOMEN alternated for the lead inside AURORA to the top of the stretch, shook off that open to gain a clear advantage in midstretch then tired from her early efforts. AURORA set the pace under pressure from outside into upper stretch then gave way. DEVILISH TOUCH, well placed just behind the early leaders, launched a rally between horses on the turn took up sharply when knocked off stride causing the rider to come out of his irons at the top of the stretch failed to seriously threaten thereafter. WITHALLPROBABILITY never reached contention. Following a stewards inquiry into the incident at the quarter pole SAMA HUMMER was disqualified from third and placed sixth for bothering several horses at the top of the stretch.

Owners— 1, Phipps Cynthia; 2, Siegel Jan; 3, Roe Tim K; 4, Herrick W; 5, Groves Helen K; 6, Burning Tree Farm; 7, Evans Edward.

Trainers— 1, McGaughey Claude III; 2, Mayberry Brian A; 3, Dutton Jerry; 4, Vienna Darrell; 5, Schulhofer Flint S; 6, Garcia Carlos A; 7, Lukas D Wayne.

A similar situation occurred in the 1993 running of the Grade 2 Withers Stakes. Jess C's Whirl had dominated six rivals in the ungraded Cryptoclearance Stakes at Aqueduct a month earlier, recording a Beyer of 109, which was substantially superior to his opponents in the Withers.

8 START 1 MILE BELMONT PARK FINISH

1 MILE. **(1.33) 118th Running THE WITHERS Grade II Purse $100,000 added. 3-year-olds. By subscription of $200 each which should accompany the nomination: $800 to pass the entry box; $800 to start with $100,000 added. The added money and all fees to be divided 60% to the winner, 22% to second, 12% to third and 6% to fourth. Weight, 124 lbs. Starters to be named at the closing time of entries. Trophies will be presented to the winning owner, trainer and jockey. Closed Wednesday, April 21 with 40 nominations.**

Tactical Advantage

Ch. c. 3(May), by Forty Niner—Twitchet, by Roberto
Br.—Hidaway Farm (Ky)
Tr.—Schulhofer Flint S (—)
SANTOS J A (—)
Own.—Teinowitz Phillip
124

Lifetime 5 2 1 0 $135,710
1993 1 0 1 0 $6,710
1992 4 2 0 0 $129,000

12Apr93- 7Aqu fst 1 :464 1:12 1:371 3↑Alw 30500 86 4 3 33 42 3nk 23 Santos J A 114 *.20 75-29 RnwyStorm1143TctclAdvntg1141½Prrtzr112 Broke slow 6
10Oct92- 7Bel gd 1 :443 1:09 1:344 Champagne 73 6 9 97¼ 87 48 414 Delahoussaye E 122 2.90e 82-04 Sea Hero1225¾ SecretOdds1225¾PressCard122 In traffic 10
10Oct92-Grade I
30Aug92- 8Sar fst 6½f :222 :45 1:153 Hopeful 86 7 2 52½ 53½ 54 45 Krone J A 122 5.00 92-08 GrtNgtr1223¾StrllngAlng122¾EnglndEpcts122 Wide trip 8
30Aug92-Grade I
30Jly92- 8Sar fst 6f :213 :444 1:102 Sar Spec'l 87 3 3 42½ 41½ 21 1no Krone J A 117 *1.30 92-06 TctclAdnt117noStrllnAln1175¾MCl117 Bumpd st., drvng 10
30Jly92-Grade II
26Jun92- 4Bel fst 5½f :222 :452 1:033 Md Sp Wt 81 6 1 1½ 1hd 13 15 Santos J A 118 *1.40 97-07 TcticlAdvntge1185OnTheBridl118noDr.Alfoos118 Driving 9

LATEST WORKOUTS Apr 30 Bel 4f fst :472 H Apr 25 Bel 5f fst 1:004 H Apr 20 Bel 4f fst :48 B Apr 8 Bel tr.t 4f fst :474 H

Duc d'Sligovil

Gr. c. 3(Apr), by Sezyou—Peppermint Day, by Al Hattab
Br.—Scott J D (Fla)
Tr.—McNeill Jeremy (—)
KRONE J A (—)
Own.—McNeill Roy
124

Lifetime 12 3 4 3 $213,249
1993 5 2 1 0 $179,094
1992 7 1 3 3 $34,155
Wet 2 0 1 0 $20,000

17Apr93-10Aqu fst 1⅛ :464 1:103 1:482 Wood Mem 94 2 5 42 3½ 21½ 43¼ Krone J A b 126 15.80 91-05 StormTower1262Tossofthcoin126¾MrkdTr126 Bid, wknd 12
17Apr93-Grade I
20Mar93-10GP sly 1⅛ :47 1:114 1:511 Fla. Derby 84 7 4 43 41½ 63¼ 76¼ Krone J A b 122 9.40 75-14 BullIntheHether1222StormTower122hdWllend122 Faded 13
20Mar93-Grade I
27Feb93- 8GP fst 1$\frac{1}{16}$:482 1:131 1:45 Ftn O Youth 94 5 2 2hd 1½ 14 12¼ Krone J A b 112 4.30 85-22 Ducd'Slgovl1122¼BllInthHthr113¼SlvrofSlvr122 Driving 9
27Feb93-Grade II; Run in Divisions
13Feb93- 7GP fst 7f :222 :454 1:24 Alw 24000 88 8 1 1hd 11½ 12½ 1no Perret C b 114 2.10 83-18 DcdSlgl114noThrllrChllr112¾VrnRpds117 Fully extended 8
9Jan93-10Crc sly 1⅛ :481 1:123 1:534 Trop Pk Dby 86 10 2 21½ 1hd 1hd 21¾ Lee M A 112 12.80 88-15 SummrSt1121¾Ducd'Sligovil112¼SilvrofSilvr122 Gamely 10
9Jan93-Grade III
15Dec92- 7Crc fst 1$\frac{1}{16}$:483 1:133 1:481 Alw 16600 81 5 1 1hd 1½ 11½ 2no Gonzalez M A 115 *1.50 86-13 Kassec110no Duc d'Sligovil1151 Itaka115 Sharp try 5
26Nov92- 9Crc fst 1$\frac{1}{16}$:48 1:132 1:48 Alw 15000 74 6 1 1hd 1hd 1hd 32 Gonzalez M A 116 *.90 85-08 Zio112noSnImgintion1162Ducd'Sligovl116 Lugged in str 8
4Oct92-10Crc fst 170 :471 1:122 1:432 Foolish Plsr 86 7 1 1½ 2hd 1hd 3¾ Gonzalez M A 112 7.00 95-04 It'sllnnfct117¼ThtsOrBc112nkDcdSlgl112 Yld. grudgngly 7
19Sep92- 7Crc fst 6f :22 :451 1:113 Alw 14000 66 2 3 2hd 2hd 33 35 Douglas R R 118 *.40 88-11 HiddenTrick1125ElDom112hdDucd'Sligovil118 Late rally 6
6Sep92-10Crc fst 7f :23 :461 1:25 Trnbrry Isle 77 4 1 1hd 1hd 1hd 2½ Douglas R R 112 2.00 89-12 NotSrprsng116¼Dcd'Slgvl1123Dtsppl112 Yld. grudgingly 5

LATEST WORKOUTS ●Apr 30 Aqu 4f fst :47 H ●Apr 10 Crc 1 sly 1:443 B (d) Apr 3 Crc 5f fst 1:02 B ●Mar 15 Crc 6f fst 1:13 H

Farmonthefreeway

B. g. 3(May), by Talc—Screened, by Alydar
Br.—Werblin David A (NY)
Tr.—O'Connell Richard (—)
MIGLIORE R (—)
Own.—Very Un Stable
124

Lifetime 11 5 1 3 $207,981
1993 6 3 0 3 $147,972
1992 5 2 1 0 $60,009

17Apr93- 9Aqu fst 6f :214 :442 1:084 Best Turn 103 4 7 75 75¼ 31½ 12 Migliore R b 119 2.60 98-12 Frmonthefreewy1192LzyLuke1221½WonSong115 Driving 8
17Apr93-Grade III
28Mar93- 8Aqu gd 6f ⊡:224 :453 1:093 ⓈD Clinton H 99 1 7 31 11 12½ 15½ Migliore R b 121 *1.00 95-15 Frmonthfrwy1215½Prspctr'sFlg1103ChfMstr110 Driving 8
20Feb93- 6Aqu fst 6f ⊡:233 :471 1:111 Swift 95 2 4 31½ 31 2½ 3½ Smith M E b 120 2.20 86-20 LzyLk120½FghtngDddy114noFrmonthfrwy120 Sharp try 5
10Feb93- 8Aqu fst 6f ⊡:224 :461 1:104 Who Dr Who 96 6 5 42½ 1hd 13½ 15½ Smith M E b 119 *.60 89-16 Frmonthefreewy1195½TliHi1171¼StolenZl119 Ridden out 6
31Jan93- 7Aqu fst 6f ⊡:223 :453 1:104 Sly Fox 93 6 3 44½ 41¾ 34 33 Smith M E b 117 4.20 86-16 AsIndctd117noLzyLuk1173Frmonthfrwy117 Lacked rally 7
9Jan93- 1Aqu fst 170 ⊡:482 1:132 1:422 Clm 100000 80 7 5 62½ 55 47½ 36¼ Bisono C V5 117 2.80 84-20 Tnko1221¾Yeckley1144½Frmonthefreewy117 Belated bid 7
20Dec92- 8Aqu gd 1$\frac{1}{16}$ ⊡:471 1:123 1:452 ⓈBongard 78 1 4 42 32 31½ 43 Nelson D 117 8.20 78-20 OvrthBrn1221ClssEn1132RshChrmnBll122 Saved ground 9
5Dec92- 8Aqu fst 1$\frac{1}{16}$ ⊡:471 1:121 1:443 Nashua 75 11 6 65½ 74¾ 69½ 614 Nelson D 114 25.60 71-22 Dalhart1146½Rohwer1142PeaceBby114 Lacked response 11
5Dec92-Grade III
7Nov92- 7Aqu fst 1 :46 1:104 1:363 ⓈDmonRnyon 71 8 4 52½ 41½ 25 26 Nelson D 119 *1.50 73-13 OverthBrink1176Frmonthfrwy1192BoldDor117 2nd best 10
7Nov92-Originally scheduled on turf
28Oct92- 6Aqu fst 6f :22 :451 1:111 Alw 29000 80 3 4 31 21½ 2½ 1½ Nelson D 117 *1.60 85-14 Frmonthefrewy117½JdCrving117nkSlw'sGold117 Driving 8

LATEST WORKOUTS ●May 1 Bel 5f fst :591 H Apr 14 Bel tr.t 4f fst :483 H Apr 7 Bel tr.t 4f fst :483 B Mar 23 Bel tr.t 4f fst :483 H

Virginia Rapids

Ch. c. 3(Mar), by Riverman—Virginiana, by Sir Ivor
Br.—Stabola Joseph & William Inc (NJ)
Tr.—Jerkens H Allen (—)
MAPLE E (—)
Own.—Middletown Stables
124

Lifetime 10 2 1 3 $47,078
1993 3 1 0 1 $20,708
1992 7 1 1 2 $26,370
Turf 2 1 0 0 $15,600
Wet 2 0 0 1 $3,240

27Feb93- 6GP fst 1$\frac{1}{16}$:473 1:124 1:462 Alw 23000 88 4 10 911 64¼ 42½ 11 Penna D 112 2.90 78-22 VrgnRpds1121DrdMNt113hdThrllrChllr117 Driving 7 wd 10
13Feb93- 7GP fst 7f :222 :454 1:24 Alw 24000 86 3 7 810 56½ 42¾ 3¾ Maple E 117 *1.70 82-18 DcdSlgl114noThrllrChllr112¾VrnRpds117 Late rally wide 8
13Jan93- 9GP fst 6f :212 :44 1:092 Spectclr Bid 86 2 7 712 67½ 45 41¼ Penna D 113 14.70 93-07 GrtNvgtr119¾DmltDmsht114½HddnTrc114 Late rally wd 8
24Dec92- 7Crc fst 6f :22 :46 1:121 Alw 15000 83 1 7 713 711 45 2no Penna D 120 7.80 90-15 HiddnTrick115noVirginRpds1203TrdBll110 Wide, gamely 7
27Nov92- 8Aqu my 6f :222 :46 1:103 Alw 27000 72 4 4 53 31½ 34 37½ Lidberg D W 117 5.30 80-22 InsrdWnnr1173½Brd'sFly1174VrgnRpds117 Lacked rally 6
18Nov92- 4Aqu fst 7f :224 :454 1:241 Alw 27000 82 1 7 57½ 43½ 33½ 35 Lidberg D W 117 12.80 79-16 PcBby1173ColonilAffir1192VirginiRpids117 Bumped brk 8
2Oct92- 8Bel fm 1$\frac{1}{16}$ Ⓣ:464 1:111 1:423 Pilgrim 39 9 8 4¾ 73½ 917 1024 Cruguet J b 113 10.80 59-15 Awad113nk Dr. Alfoos1132 Compadre113 Gave way 10
2Oct92-Grade III
7Sep92- 2Bel fm 1 Ⓣ:463 1:101 1:362 Md Sp Wt 76 3 3 11 1hd 12½ 1nk Cruguet J b 118 *2.00 80-19 VirginiRpids118nkDlry118½ShdsofSilvr118 Drifted,drvng 12
29Aug92- 4Sar fst 6f :214 :444 1:104 Md Sp Wt 54 9 1 2½ 2½ 1hd 48½ Perret C 118 2.20 81-07 DncngHntr1185¼Glnbrr1181¼NorwyGry118 Dueled inside 9
16Aug92- 4Sar my 6f :221 :461 1:12 Md Sp Wt 62 6 6 63 41½ 52 51¾ Perret C 118 4.20e 82-14 Sarabic118½MarcoBay118½SpartanLeader118 Weakened 14

LATEST WORKOUTS May 2 Bel 6f fst 1:134 H Apr 28 Bel 7f fst 1:281 B ●Apr 20 Bel tr.t 5f fst 1:003 H ●Apr 8 Bel tr.t 4f fst :472 H

Lazy Luke

CHAVEZ J F (—)
Own.—Someday Farm

Ch. g. 3(Apr), by Pancho Villa—Quickening Dawn, by To The Quick
Br.—Freeman-Betz Partnership & Needham (Ky)
Tr.—Camac Robert W (—)
124

Lifetime 7 3 3 1 $123,365 | 1993 3 1 2 0 $81,280 | 1992 4 2 1 1 $42,085 | Wet 1 0 1 0 $2,900

17Apr93- 9Aqu fst 6f :214 :442 1:084 Best Turn 98 1 8 2½ 22 2½ 22 Chavez J F b 122 2.80 96-12 Frmonthefreewy1192LzyLuke1221½WonSong115 Gamely 8
17Apr93-Grade III
20Feb93- 6Aqu fst 6f ⊡:233 :471 1:111 Swift 96 4 2 1½ 11 1½ 1½ Antley C W b 120 1.70 87-20 LyLk120½FghtngDddy114noFrmnthfr120 Drifted,driving 5
31Jan93- 7Aqu fst 6f ⊡:223 :453 1:104 Sly Fox 101 5 2 22 2hd 2½ 2no Antley C W b 117 2.90 89-16 AsIndicted117noLzyLuke1173Frmonthefrwy117 Gamely 7
26Dec92- 9Pha fst 6½f :22 :444 1:16 Allegheny 86 9 2 2hd 1½ 14 1½ Molina V H b 114 18.60 98-11 Lazy Luke114½ Marked Tree1143½ Cee K'o114 Driving 9
13Dec92- 9Pha my 6f :221 :461 1:123 Alw 14500 74 4 4 2½ 11 2hd 2nk Umana J L5 117 1.40 78-27 Yeckley116nk Lazy Luke11711½MaginskyToo116 Gamely 5
1Dec92- 8Pha fst 6f :222 :453 1:12 Alw 14500 73 3 5 2hd 1hd 2hd 31½ Capanas S b 122 2.20 79-22 Tom Tylor1161¼ Stu!m116nk LazyLuke122 Bumped rival 7
20Nov92- 6Pha fst 6f :222 :46 1:131 Md Sp Wt 63 6 4 41¼ 1hd 15 17½ Capanas S b 121 8.20 75-23 LLk1217½InvstmntBnkr1212½FlmngFlght121 Drew clear 9

LATEST WORKOUTS May 1 Pha 5f fst 1:033 B | Apr 28 Pha 5f fst 1:052 B | Apr 13 Pha 5f fst 1:021 B | ●Apr 8 Pha 4f fst :501 B

Strolling Along

SMITH M E (—)
Own.—Phipps Ogden

Dk. b. or br. c. 3(Apr), by Danzig—Cadillacing, by Alydar
Br.—Phipps Ogden (Ky)
Tr.—McGaughey Claude III (—)
124

Lifetime 8 2 2 1 $181,140 | 1993 1 0 0 1 $24,000 | 1992 7 2 2 0 $157,140

3Apr93- 9Aqu gd 1 :461 1:103 1:361 Gotham 97 8 3 2½ 2hd 2hd 31½ Antley C W 121 *1.20 81-21 AsIndicated114nkItak1141¼StrollingAlong121 Bid wknd 8
3Apr93-Grade II
31Oct92- 8GP fst 1$\frac{1}{16}$:46 1:102 1:432 Br Cp Juv 67 7 7 72½ 75 910 811¾ Antley C W b 122 20.40 83-03 GildedTime122¾It'sli'lknownfct122¾RivrSpcil122 5 wide 13
31Oct92-Grade I
10Oct92- 7Bel gd 1 :443 1:09 1:344 Champagne 62 9 4 43½ 42½ 58 519½ Antley C W 122 *2.30 76-04 SeHero1225¾ScrtOdds1225¾PrssCrd122 Lacked respnse 10
10Oct92-Grade I
19Sep92- 6Bel fst 7f :221 :45 1:233 Futurity 88 4 7 75½ 34 1hd 12 Antley C W 122 *1.50 86-11 StrolngAlong1222FghtforLov1221Cponostro122 Driving 9
19Sep92-Grade I
30Aug92- 8Sar fst 6½f :222 :45 1:153 Hopeful 89 1 3 31½ 42½ 33 23¾ Antley C W 122 5.10 93-08 GrtNvgtr1223¾StrlingAlng122¾EnglndEpcts122 Fin. well 8
30Aug92-Grade I
30Jly92- 8Sar fst 6f :213 :444 1:102 Sar Spec'l 87 1 10 21½ 2½ 11 2no Antley C W 117 1.80 92-06 TctclAdntg117noStrllngAln1175¼MCl117 Brk sl; gamely 10
30Jly92-Grade II
13Jly92- 5Bel fst 5½f :221 :452 1:03 Md Sp Wt 94 7 3 24 24 21½ 12½ Antley C W 118 10.30 100 10 StrollngAlong1182½DvlshlyYors1184¼Dr.Alfs118 Driving 10
26Jun92- 3Bel fst 5½f :222 :453 1:043 Md Sp Wt 50 5 7 86½ 85 66½ 55½ Antley C W 118 *.80 86-07 KissinKrs118hdGrmlnGry118noInsurdWnnr118 Late gain 9

LATEST WORKOUTS ●Apr 28 Bel 5f fst 1:00 H | Apr 24 Bel 5f fst 1:032 B | Apr 15 Bel tr.t 4f fst :49 B | Apr 2 Bel tr.t 3f my :382 B (d)

Montbrook

LADNER C J III (—)
Own.—Cohen Israel

Dk. b. or br. c. 3(Feb), by Buckaroo—Secret Papers, by Jet Diplomacy
Br.—Ocala Stud Farms Inc (Fla)
Tr.—Gaudet Edmond D (—)
124

Lifetime 4 2 0 1 $48,468 | 1993 4 2 0 1 $48,468 | 1992 0 M 0 0

17Apr93- 9Aqu fst 6f :214 :442 1:084 Best Turn 91 7 2 1½ 12 1½ 44½ Ladner C J III 117 6.40 93-12 Frmonthefrwy1192LzyLuk1221½WonSong115 Spd, wknd 8
17Apr93-Grade III
25Mar93- 8Pim fst 6f :23 :462 1:12 Hirsch Jacb 92 7 6 11 11½ 12½ 13½ Luzzi M J 114 *.60e 85-20 Mntbr1143½WthtDssnt122nkMhtG114 Lugged in, drvng 7
18Feb93- 7Lrl fst 7f :224 :454 1:26 Alw 17100 78 4 2 14 16 13 31½ Ladner C J III 120 *.50 77-24 Smrt'nTgh1201½Mr.Rdctv117nkMntbrk120 Lugged in 1/8 8
11Feb93- 7Lrl fst 6f :231 :463 1:104 Md Sp Wt 97 10 4 11 14 17 113½ Ladner C J III 120 *1.00 86-23 Montbrook12013½ThJokr'sPrd120hdCrmpton120 Driving 13

LATEST WORKOUTS Apr 29 Lrl 7f fst 1:273 H | ●Apr 9 Lrl 4f fst :46 H | ●Mar 19 Lrl 4f fst :463 H

Tanako

VELAZQUEZ J R (—)
Own.—Loblolly Stable

B. c. 3(May), by Vanlandingham—Lady From Hell, by Bravest Roman
Br.—Loblolly Stable (Ky)
Tr.—Bohannan Thomas (—)
124

Lifetime 6 3 0 1 $49,980 | 1993 4 2 0 0 $36,300 | 1992 2 1 0 1 $13,680

16Apr93- 8Aqu fst 1 :454 1:094 1:354 Alw 28500 92 7 3 32½ 31½ 2½ 11 Velazquez J R 117 2.10 85-19 Tanako1171 Birdie's Fly117nk Stormy Java119 Driving 7
21Feb93- 9OP fst 1 :46 1:112 1:37 Old Rosebud 74 7 10 109¾ 107 1011 99¾ Miller D A Jr 113 *1.20e 82-24 Mr.Scrooge1121¼ProudstRomo112hdFoxtrl117 Checked 10
30Jan93- 9OP fst 1 :481 1:112 1:373 Alw 22000 64 10 9 99¾ 89 77 710¾ Day P 120 *.60e 78-19 EnchntngFutr108hdIvoryPrk1147¼MrkdTr111 No threat 10
9Jan93- 1Aqu fst 170 ⊡:482 1:132 1:422 Clm 100000 91 3 2 21 21 2hd 11¾ Velazquez J R 122 *2.40 90-20 Tanako1221¾Yeckley1144½Farmonthefreewy117 Driving 7
29Nov92- 5Aqu fst 1 :46 1:11 1:364 Clm 75000 74 7 6 61¼ 71 41½ 3¾ Velazquez J R 117 *2.30 77-15 JorgeofMexico115½StolnZl117nkTnko117 Stead, late bid 9
29Oct92- 3Aqu fst 7f :232 :462 1:241 Md 75000 80 6 1 41½ 2½ 1hd 12 Velazquez J R 118 10.70 84-14 Tanako1182 Dynamic Duke114¾ PalacePiper107 Driving 6

LATEST WORKOUTS Apr 27 Bel 4f gd :501 B | Apr 7 OP 6f fst 1:143 H | Mar 31 OP 5f fst 1:02 B | Mar 25 OP 5f fst 1:024 B

Williamstown

PERRET C (—)
Own.—Willmott Peter S

Dk. b. or br. c. 3(Mar), by Seattle Slew—Winter Sparkle, by Northjet-Ir
Br.—Equus Breeders (Ky)
Tr.—Vestal Peter M (—)
124

Lifetime 12 4 3 1 $135,191 | 1993 2 0 0 1 $15,474 | 1992 10 4 3 0 $119,717 | Wet 2 1 1 0 $48,030

18Apr93- 8Kee fst 1$\frac{1}{16}$:492 1:132 1:433 Lexington 88 4 3 31½ 2hd 3nk 41½ Kutz D 115 8.40 84-24 GrndJwl118½ElBkn1131TrthofItAll118 Bid flattened out 9
18Apr93-Grade II
6Apr93- 8Kee gd 7f :222 :45 1:211 Lafayette 89 2 6 32 41½ 41 36½ Kutz D 121 3.50 96-07 ChrokRn1183½PovrtySlw1123Wllmstwn121 A/C 1/8 pole 8
6Apr93-Grade III
12Dec92- 9TP my 6½f :223 :46 1:18 Tp Prevue 92 7 4 11½ 1½ 1½ 1nk Kutz D 122 *1.00 90-15 Wllstn122nkAntrRd1227ShGrtn116 Bumped pole gamly 7
28Nov92-10CD fst 1$\frac{1}{16}$:473 1:124 1:453 B & W J Clb 77 7 4 31 1½ 1hd 55¾ Kutz D 121 17.30e 80-16 Wild Gale116nk MiCielo1165ShoalCreek121 Bid flatered 11
28Nov92-Grade III
8Nov92- 8CD fst 1 :443 1:102 1:372 Iroquois 80 3 11 94½ 62¾ 44 64¾ Kutz D 121 4.90e 85-16 SholCrk1141SwMill116½DmlootDmshoot116 Flatten out 13
8Nov92-Grade III
16Oct92- 8Kee my 7f :214 :442 1:241 Fort Springs 76 4 6 11 12½ 12½ 2nk Kutz D 121 1.80 88-11 AntrmRd.116nkWllmstwn1212½ArtrP116 Soundly jltd st. 8
3Oct92-12Tdn fst 6f :221 :454 1:12 Youthful B C 80 3 8 1hd 12 11½ 11¾ Kutz D 116 *1.20 85-12 Wllmstown1161¾Spltwndwcp1163Mr.Gngstr122 In hand 9
30Aug92- 1Sar fst 7f :231 :46 1:24 Alw 27000 76 2 6 42 42 31 1¾ Day P 117 3.80 85-08 Wllmstown117¾Stllrton117nkDr.Alfs122 Stmbld brk, drv 6
20Aug92- 3Sar fst 6f :22 :452 1:11 Alw 27000 74 2 7 33½ 21½ 1½ 2¾ Day P b 117 *1.20 88-14 KissinKris117¾Wllmstown117noUntdProspct117 Gamely 7
6Aug92- 7Sar fst 6f :214 :452 1:101 Alw 27000 73 2 8 1½ 1½ 21 25 Day P 119 *1.00e 88-14 SawMill1175Willimstown1191¾KissinKris117 Held place 8

LATEST WORKOUTS ●Apr 30 CD 5f gd 1:00 H | Apr 4 Kee 3f fst :363 B | ●Mar 28 OP 6f fst 1:102 Hg | ●Mar 22 OP 6f gd 1:133 H

Blushing Julian — Ch. c. 3(Apr), by Mt Livermore—Slanted, by Sir Wimborne
Br.—Rosemont Farm Inc (Ky)
PETERSON J L (—) Tr.—Arnone Michael J (—) **124**
Own.—Gambone John
Lifetime 4 2 1 0 $26,280 | 1993 4 2 1 0 $26,280 | 1992 0 M 0 0 | Wet 1 0 0 0 $3,900

2Apr93- 8GS my 1$\frac{1}{16}$	:47^2	1:12	1:45	Garden St	88	6 1 1½ 1½ 2^{hd} 4^{nk}	Black A S	Lb 115	*1.00	90-13	TrfrthGld117^{nk}Tn'Nms115^{hd}PrmrCmmndr115	Game try	8
2Apr93-Grade III													
23Mar93- 5Pha fst 6f	:22	:45	1:10^4	Alw 14539	85	5 5 1^1 1^5 1^8 1^{6¾}	Black A S	Lb 119	*.30	87-21	BlushngJuln119^{6¾}AnothrHuy111^{4½}LnMrr116	Ridden out	6
30Jan93- 9Pha fst 7f	:45	1:10^3	1:23^4	Patriot	87	5 1 1^2 1^1 2^{hd} 2¾	Black A S	b 115	*.90	86-18	Chip'sDancer115¾BlushingJulian115^{3½}TrifortheGold119		9
30Jan93-Swerved backstretch, in tight early stretch													
3Jan93- 6Pha fst 7f	:22^1	:44^3	1:23^2	Md Sp Wt	81	7 2 1^5 1^4 1^{2½} 1^{4½}	Black A S	b 122	*1.20	90-15	BlshngJln122^{4½}Qlbsh122^{10½}WOOffcr122	Impressive win	12

LATEST WORKOUTS ●Apr 28 Pha 6f fst 1:11^4 B ●Apr 20 Pha 5f fst :59^2 H ●Mar 21 Pha 3f fst :34 B ●Mar 7 Pha 5f fst :58^3 H

Prospector's Flag — Dk. b. or br. c. 3(Jan), by Personal Flag—Sugar Gold, by Mr Prospector
Br.—Hettinger James (NY)
BAILEY J D (—) Tr.—Zito Nicholas P (—) **124**
Own.—Akindale Farm
Lifetime 7 2 2 0 $53,054 | 1993 5 1 1 0 $33,374 | 1992 2 1 1 0 $19,680 | Turf 1 0 0 0 $230

16Apr93- 7Aqu fst 1	:46	1:10^3	1:37	3+ⓈAlw 28500	84	3 4 2½ 1^1 1^4 1^{3¾}	Antley C W	110	*.60	79-19	Prospctor'sFlg110^{3¾}MyMgl107^{10}Lchrm119	Steadied brk	5
28Mar93- 8Aqu gd 6f ⊡:22^4	:45^3	1:09^3		ⓈD Clinton H	85	7 1 2½ 2^1 2^{2½} 2^{5½}	Chavez J F	110	14.40	89-15	Frmnthfrwy121^{5½}Prspctr'sFlg110^{3}ChfMstr110	2nd best	8
6Mar93- 5GP fm 1$\frac{1}{16}$ Ⓣ:46^4	1:11^2	1:41^3	+	Alw 23000	65	4 3 4^2 3^{2½} 6^{7¾} 8^{13¼}	Santos J A	115	37.20	76-04	Halissee120^{4½}GatorSpirit117^{hd}Scannapieco113	Faltered	12
13Feb93- 7GP fst 7f	:22^2	:45^4	1:24	Alw 24000	61	6 8 7^9 6^{7½} 7^{9¼} 7^{12½}	Romero R P	117	40.10	70-18	Ducd'Slgovl114^{no}ThrllrChllr112¾VrgnRpds117	No factor	8
21Jan93- 8GP fst 7f	:22^1	:45^1	1:23^2	Alw 21600	37	9 5 1^{hd} 4^2 11^{16}11^{20¾}	Perret C	117	8.30	65-15	FrvrWhrl115^{1½}ChntngGshk115^{2}LvngVcrsly114	Stopped	11
9Dec92- 5Aqu fst 6f ⊡:23^2	:48	1:13^3		ⓈMd Sp Wt	71	10 4 3^{2½} 2^{hd} 1^5 1^{5½}	Romero R P	118	2.00	75-20	Prospector's Flag118^{5½} Jager118^{nk}DaringFly118	Driving	12
21Nov92- 4Aqu fst 7f	:22^3	:46^2	1:25^1	Md Sp Wt	52	8 1 4^{1½} 4^{1½} 2^4 2^7	Romero R P	118	7.50	72-16	Hlstrd118^{7}Prspctr'sFlg118^{2¾}HghlPrchd118	Rallied wide	8

LATEST WORKOUTS Apr 30 Bel 5f fst 1:00^1 H Apr 24 Bel 5f fst 1:00^4 H Apr 6 Bel tr.t 4f fst :47^2 H Mar 21 GP 5f gd 1:00^3 H

Jess C's Whirl — Dk. b. or br. c. 3(Mar), by Island Whirl—Proud Woman, by Proudest Roman
Br.—Oleck Thoroughbred Farm Inc (Fla)
ANTLEY C W (—) Tr.—Forbes John H (—) **124**
Own.—Oleck Theodore
Lifetime 4 2 2 0 $54,900 | 1993 4 2 2 0 $54,900 | 1992 0 M 0 0

3Apr93- 7Aqu gd 7f	:22^3	:45^2	1:22^2	Cryptoclrnc	109	2 6 1½ 1^2 1^7 1^{10}	Antley C W	115	*1.40	92-14	JssC'sWhrl115^{10}WnSng117^{2¾}Nsthtmtshn117	Mild drive	7
22Mar93- 6Aqu fst 6f ⊡:23^1	:46^1	1:10^2		Alw 27000	95	2 7 1½ 1^1 1^2 2^{nk}	Lidberg D W	119	*1.20	91-17	Nsthttshn117^{nk}JssCsWhrl119^{3½}TnNs117	Fract, brk slow	7
17Feb93- 5Aqu fst 6f ⊡:22^1	:45	1:09^4		Md Sp Wt	93	4 2 1½ 1^{1½} 1^4 1^{3¾}	Lidberg D W	122	2.40	94-09	Jess C's Whirl122^{3¾} Bandaid Bob122^3 Pilfer122	Driving	8
28Jan93- 5Aqu fst 6f ⊡:23	:46^4	1:11^4		Md Sp Wt	72	1 7 2^{1½} 2^1 2^{2½} 2^4	Lidberg D W	122	4.00	80-18	HickoryLke122^{4}JessC'sWhirl122^{4}Pilfr122	Brk slw, gmly	7

LATEST WORKOUTS May 2 Bel 4f fst :49^4 B ●Apr 25 Bel 6f fst 1:10^2 H ●Apr 19 Bel tr.t 5f fst 1:00 H Apr 12 Bel tr.t 5f fst 1:00^3 H

Itaka — B. c. 3(Mar), by Jade Hunter—Americanrevelation, by Foolish Pleasure
Br.—Brophy B Giles (NY)
DAVIS R G (—) Tr.—Johnson Philip G (—) **124**
Own.—Brophy Stable
Lifetime 9 1 2 3 $72,630 | 1993 4 0 1 1 $47,760 | 1992 5 1 1 2 $24,870 | Wet 1 0 0 0

3Apr93- 9Aqu gd 1	:46^1	1:10^3	1:36^1	Gotham	100	3 7 6^4 3^1 3^1 2^{nk}	Smith M E	b 114	14.00	83-21	AsIndicted114^{nk}Itk114^{1¼}StrollingAlong121	Rallied wide	8
3Apr93-Grade II													
28Feb93- 6GP fst 7f	:23^1	:46^2	1:23^1	Alw 22000	91	1 5 1^1 1^1 2^2 3^4	Fires E	b 117	6.90	83-19	JackLivingston120^{2}FightforLove112^{2}Itak117	Weakened	7
21Jan93- 8GP fst 7f	:22^1	:45^1	1:23^2	Alw 21600	74	2 9 5^{1¾} 5^{2½} 3^5 4^{3½}	Gonzalez M A	b 112	5.30	82-15	FrvrWhrl115^{1½}ChntngGshk115^{2}LvngVcrsl114	Late rally	11
9Jan93-10Crc sly 1⅛	:48^1	1:12^3	1:53^4	Trop Pk Dby	66	5 4 4^4 6^{6¾} 9^{20} 8^{14¼}	Bailey J D	112	9.30	76-15	SummrSt112^{1¾}Ducd'Sligovil112½SilvrofSlvr122	Faltered	10
9Jan93-Grade III													
15Dec92- 7Crc fst 1$\frac{1}{16}$	:48^3	1:13^3	1:48^1	Alw 16600	79	1 5 5^{2¾} 3^{1½} 2^{1½} 3^1	Santos J A	115	1.70	85-13	Kassec110^{no} Duc d'Sligovil115^1 Itaka115	Good effort	5
18Nov92- 6Aqu fst 7f	:23	:46^3	1:24^3	Alw 27000	80	3 9 6^3 7^{3¼} 5^{4½} 3^3	Davis R G	119	15.70	79-16	Apprentice119^{no} Slew's Gold117^3 Itaka119	Late gain	9
22Oct92- 3Aqu fst 6½f	:23^3	:48	1:18^4	ⓈMd Sp Wt	86	5 7 4^2 2^{hd} 1½ 1^{1¼}	Smith M E	118	*.60	84-18	Itk118^{1¼}KoluctooJmmyAl118^{3½}BoldDor118	Brk slw, drv	7
7Oct92- 6Bel fst 6f	:22^3	:46^2	1:10^4	ⓈMd Sp Wt	63	10 13 3^2 2^1 2^6 2^{11½}	Smith M E	118	*1.30	74-16	RushChirmnBill118^{11½}Itk118^{6½}BoldDor118	Broke poorly	13
13Aug92- 4Sar fst 6f	:22^4	:46^3	1:11^4	ⓈMd Sp Wt	53	4 13 6^{4¼} 4^2 6^{2½} 6^{6¾}	Cruguet J	118	2.90	78-13	LodBrthr118^{nk}BlmGn118^{5¼}MgcMdc118	Broke slw, wide	13

LATEST WORKOUTS ●Apr 30 Bel tr.t 5f fst 1:00^2 H ●Apr 25 Bel tr.t 6f fst 1:17^4 B ●Apr 20 Bel tr.t 4f fst :47^2 H Apr 13 Bel tr.t 4f fst :49^4 B

The problem with Jess C's Whirl was that he had run his 109 by dominating overmatched horses through a half-mile in :45⅖ and racing unchallenged through the stretch. In four previous starts, Jess C's Whirl had never run a half-mile faster than :45, but in the Withers he would be facing three horses — Lazy Luke, Montbrook, and Blushing Julian — who had at least that much early speed, and possibly more. After all, a look at the quarter-mile times showed that Jess C's Whirl had never run faster than :22⅕, and had run that fast only once, whereas Lazy Luke had been just a half-length off the :21⅘ quarter set by Montbrook, despite breaking flat-footed in the Best Turn, and Blushing Julian had wired his most recent sprint field with a :22 quarter. To make matters worse, Jess C's Whirl was not an especially sharp breaker.

The basic point is this: you didn't have to be a rocket scientist to scan the likely pace scenario of the Withers and conclude that Jess C's Whirl, who was stretching out another furlong and facing several rivals with high early speed, really had his work cut out for him.

Accepting odds of 2–1 on such a proposition was not a good idea; the way the race shaped up, it made sense to look for a horse with rateable, positional speed that might enjoy Belmont's sweeping turn. There were several possibilities in the full field, and no matter which was fancied, the odds were guaranteed to be an overlay due to all the action on Jess C's Whirl. The eventual winner was Williamstown, who looked this way on *The Sheets:*

SAR p71 WILLIAMSTOWN 90 race 8

10 RACES 92 5 RACES 93

12+ Ywt AWTP12
17" AWCD28
17" Y AWCD 8
.17" t AWKE16
22- w AWTD 3
21- YwT] AWSrPMV
17" AWSrPMV
19- Y AWSrPMV
21 Yw MSEL14
26" Y[MSCD21

'4" vw AWBEPMV
14 v AWKE18
11 Yt AWKE 6

A textbook example of an explosive line: the colt had worked his way down to a 12¼ in his final start as a two-year-old and had broken through that level *slightly* by running an 11 in his first start at age three. Williamstown then reacted in the Lexington Stakes when brought back on less than two weeks of rest, but the effort was promising: he had still run a reasonably good figure after contending for the lead at the stretch call, while making his first route start in nearly five months. Importantly, Williamstown was now a month removed from his breakthrough figure of 11, and was approaching the desired time frame for another forward move (as detailed in chapter 1). The bullet work over a "good" track on April 30, along with the colt's previously demonstrated ability on wet tracks, served as additional positive indicators, since the Withers would be run under showery and "wet fast" conditions.

Favored by the pace match-ups and approaching peak physical condition, Williamstown was a clear overlay at 10–1 against the vulnerable favorite, Jess C's Whirl. He ran a new top of 4½ — a huge forward move — and returned $23.60 to his scattered backers while establishing a track record.

EIGHTH RACE
Belmont
MAY 5, 1993

1 MILE. (1.33) 118th Running THE WITHERS Grade II Purse $100,000 added. 3-year-olds. By subscription of $200 each which should accompany the nomination: $800 to pass the entry box; $800 to start with $100,000 added. The added money and all fees to be divided 60% to the winner, 22% to second, 12% to third and 6% to fourth. Weight, 124 lbs. Starters to be named at the closing time of entries. Trophies will be presented to the winning owner, trainer and jockey. Closed Wednesday, April 21 with 40 nominations.
Value of race $128,000; value to winner $76,800; second $28,160; third $15,360; fourth $7,680. Mutuel pool $292,061. Exacta Pool $456,309

Last Raced	Horse	M/Eqt.	A.Wt	PP	St	¼	½	¾	Str	Fin	Jockey	Odds $1
18Apr93 ^{8}Kee^{4}	Williamstown		3 124	9	5	$3\frac{1}{2}$	$5\frac{1}{2}$	$4\frac{1}{2}$	$1\frac{1}{2}$	1^{hd}	Perret C	10.80
27Feb93 ^{6}GP^{1}	Virginia Rapids		3 124	4	12	12	12	11^{4}	3^{hd}	$2^{1\frac{1}{4}}$	Maple E	12.20
17Apr93 ^{9}Aqu^{1}	Farmonthefreeway	b	3 124	3	11	11^{8}	11^{4}	$8\frac{1}{2}$	$4^{1\frac{1}{2}}$	3^{2}	Migliore R	7.70
17Apr93 ^{9}Aqu^{4}	Montbrook		3 124	7	4	$1^{1\frac{1}{2}}$	1^{1}	1^{1}	2^{2}	$4^{4\frac{1}{2}}$	Ladner C J III	85.10
17Apr93 ^{9}Aqu^{2}	Lazy Luke	b	3 124	5	8	10^{1}	$10^{1\frac{1}{2}}$	7^{hd}	$7\frac{1}{2}$	5^{nk}	Chavez J F	33.50
17Apr93 ^{10}Aqu^{4}	Duc d'Sligovil	b	3 124	2	10	$7\frac{1}{2}$	9^{hd}	$10^{1\frac{1}{2}}$	$8^{1\frac{1}{2}}$	6^{nk}	Krone J A	5.90
2Apr93 ^{8}GS^{4}	Blushing Julian	b	3 124	10	1	2^{hd}	$3^{1\frac{1}{2}}$	2^{hd}	$5^{1\frac{1}{2}}$	$7\frac{1}{2}$	Petersen J L	48.70
16Apr93 ^{8}Aqu^{1}	Tanako		3 124	8	6	$6\frac{1}{2}$	8^{hd}	$9\frac{1}{2}$	$9\frac{1}{2}$	$8^{2\frac{1}{2}}$	Velazquez J R	32.90
12Apr93 ^{7}Aqu^{2}	Tactical Advantage		3 124	1	7	$4\frac{1}{2}$	4^{hd}	$6\frac{1}{2}$	6^{hd}	$9^{2\frac{1}{2}}$	Santos J A	9.20
3Apr93 ^{9}Aqu^{3}	Strolling Along		3 124	6	9	$9\frac{1}{2}$	6^{1}	5^{1}	10^{2}	10^{3}	Smith M E	3.10
3Apr93 ^{7}Aqu^{1}	Jess C's Whirl		3 124	11	2	$5\frac{1}{2}$	2^{1}	3^{1}	11^{16}	11^{20}	Antley C W	2.40
3Apr93 ^{9}Aqu^{2}	Itaka	b	3 124	12	3	8^{hd}	7^{hd}	12	12	12	Davis R G	12.90

OFF AT 4:33 Start good, Won driving. Time, :22 , :44^{1}, 1:08^{1}, 1:32^{3} Track fast.

New Track Record

$2 Mutuel Prices:				
	9-(I)-WILLIAMSTOWN	23.60	9.80	6.00
	4-(D)-VIRGINIA RAPIDS		11.00	6.40
	3-(C)-FARMONTHEFREEWAY			4.40
	$2 EXACTA 9-4 PAID $281.00			

Dk. b. or br. c, (Mar), by Seattle Slew—Winter Sparkle, by Northjet-Ir. Trainer Vestal Peter M. Bred by Equus Breeders (Ky).

WILLIAMSTOWN rated in good position between horses along the backstretch, remained well placed just behind the leaders approaching the quarter pole, charged past MONTBROOK to gain the lead in midstretch then was all out to hold off VIRGINIA RAPIDS in the final strides. VIRGINIA RAPIDS, taken in hand early, raced far back while trailing for nearly five furlongs, gradually gained on the turn, was forced to circle seven wide entering the stretch then finished fastest in the middle of the track but could not get up. FARMONTHEFREEWAY devoid of early speed, was unhurried while saving ground along the backstretch, swung four wide midway on the turn, advanced six wide, into the stretch, made a run to threaten in midstretch and held well to gain a share. MONTBROOK outsprinted rivals for the early advantage, set a rapid pace while slightly off the rail to the top of the stretch, relinguished the lead to the winner in midstretch then weakened from his early efforts. LAZY LUKE reserved for a half, raced in close quarters between horses on the far turn then failed to threaten while improving his position through the stretch. DUC D'SLIGOVIL was never a factor and returned bleeding. BLUSING JILIAN raced in close contention between horses into upper stretch and tired. TANAKO was never a factor while between horses. TACTICAL ADVANTAGE raced just inside the winner while saving ground for five furlongs then lacked a further response. STROLLING ALONG in hand early, steadied worked his way forward while five wide entering the stretch, then lacked the needed response when called upon. JESS C'S WHIRL never far back, moved up to contest the pace nearing the half mile pole, remained a factor while four wide to the turn then gave way. ITAKA raced within distance while five wide to the far turn then faltered. VIRGINIA RAPIDS and JESS C'S WHIRL wore mud caulks.

Owners— 1, Willmott Peter S; 2, Middletown Stables; 3, Very Un Stable; 4, Cohen Israel; 5, Someday Farm; 6, McNeill Roy; 7, Gambone John; 8, Loblolly Stable; 9, Teinowitz Phillip; 10, Phipps Ogden; 11, Oleck Theodore; 12, Brophy Stable.

Trainers— 1, Vestal Peter M; 2, Jerkens H Allen; 3, O'Connell Richard; 4, Gaudet Edmond D; 5, Camac Robert W; 6, McNeill Jeremy; 7, Arnone Michael J; 8, Bohannan Thomas; 9, Schulhofer Flint S; 10, McGaughey Claude III; 11, Forbes John H; 12, Johnson Philip G.

Scratched—Prospector's Flag (16Apr93 7Aqu1).

UNSUITED TO THE FOOTING

One of the most basic, yet often overlooked, factors is the surface underfoot. Horses are affected by the circumstances of their races: the pace, the run for position leaving the gate, their form cycles, and, most significantly, the surface on which they're running.

Halissee

Own: Lotis M & Merud J A

Gr. c. 4
Sire: Cozzene (Caro-Ire)
Dam: Hedonic (Fappiano)
Br: Nerud John A Trust (Ky)
Tr: Mott William I (—)

122

Lifetime Record:	12	5	1	1	$200,180						
1994	1	0	0	0	$350	Turf	8	5	1	1	$199,630
1993	6	4	0	0	$158,510	Wet	1	0	0	0	$350
Sar	1	0	0	0		Dist	1	0	0	0	

11Jan94-9GP	sly	1 1/16	⊗	:231	:463	1:114	1:453	Alw 35000N$Y	63	4	5	615	512	412	518½	Perret C	115	2.40	63-27	Conveyor1151½ Danc'n Jake11913 Always Silver1153¾	Showed little	6
13Jun93-8Bel	fm	1 1/16	Ⓣ	:244	:481	1:12	1:404	Hill Prince-G3	95	4	1	1hd	1hd	12½	12½	Krone J A	121	*.40	92-09	Halissee1212½ Proud Shot117½ Logroller1143	Lugged in, driving	5
15May93-10Bel	fm	1	Ⓣ	:23	:454	1:102	1:341	Saranac-G3	95	4	2	2hd	1½	12½	13	Krone J A	114	*.80	91-12	Halissee1143 Forest Wind1172 Compadre1143	Drew off	9
31Mar93-6GP	fm	1 1/16	Ⓣ	:224	:47	1:104	1:414+	Alw 30000N2X	93	3	3	31½	22½	11	13	Perret C	117	*1.50	87-12	Halissee1173 Forest Wind117½ Palashall1201½	Driving	9
6Mar93-5GP	fm	1 1/16	Ⓣ	:224	:464	1:112	1:413+	Alw 23000N1X	88	8	5	52	11½	14	14½	Perret C	120	*2.00	88-04	Halissee1204½ Gator Spirit117hd Scannapieco1131	Ridden out	12
10Feb93-10GP	fm	*1 1/16	Ⓣ				1:47 +	Alw 21000N1X	66	10	2	21	31½	64½	78½	Perret C	120	*1.20	74-17	Timely Threat1153½ Compadre1121½ Satellite Signal1142	Faltered	10
27Jan93-7GP	fst	1 1/16	⊗	:234	:473	1:224	1:463	Alw 20000N2X	58	7	4	44½	42½	58½	612½	Perret C	115	2.90	64-23	Proud Shot117½ Midnight Cookie1121½ Halo Of Merit1151	Faded	8
18Oct92-11Lrl	fm	1 1/16	Ⓣ	:232	:474	1:133	1:452	Laurel Fty-G3	75	1	3	52	32	23	33½	Gryder A T	122	*3.20	72-25	Lord of the Bay1223 Glorieux Dancer-Fr122nk Halissee122	Needed more	11
5Oct92-3Bel	fm	1 1/16	Ⓣ	:233	:464	1:11	1:414	Md Sp Wt	86	11	3	3½	2hd	1½	11	Smith M E	118	*.60	87-12	Halissee1181 A In Sociology1182¾ Cozze Mike118	Driving	12
7Sep92-5Bel	fm	1	Ⓣ	:23	:462	1:102	1:352	Md Sp Wt	78	11	2	2½	2hd	2½	22½	Madrid A Jr	118	5.00	83-19	Sea Hero1182½ Halissee1182½ Awad118	2nd best	11
2Aug92-4Sar	fst	6f		:222	:454	:58	1:102	Md Sp Wt	62	9	5	73½	64	64½	67½	Davis R G	118	34.00	84-10	Wallenda1182 All Gone118 D'orazio118	Wide trip	12
13Jly92-5Bel	fst	5½f		:221	:462		1:03	Md Sp Wt	40	2	9	810	810	811	610¾	Perret C	118	16.40	81-10	Strolling Along1182½ Devilishly Yours1188½ Dr. Alfoos118	Broke slowly	10

Halissee was a distinct underlay at Gulfstream Park on January 11, when his scheduled allowance on the grass was rained off to a sloppy main track. Although Halissee was a Grade 3 winner on grass, he had never finished better than sixth in three previous starts on dirt, and he was making his first start in seven months.

There is just no reason to accept 2–1 in this kind of situation, especially in light of the fact that among his opponents January 11 were Conveyor, Say Dance, and Lord of the Bay — mudlarks who had each recorded a career-best Beyer in the slop — in addition to Danc'n Jake, who was one for one on a wet track, and Always Silver, who had won a $50,000 stake in the mud two starts back.

Halissee was the second choice in the race, and he failed to handle the footing, finishing far back.

GRADED-STAKES WINNERS PREPPING IN ALLOWANCE RACES

Handicappers must always read between the lines for a clue to a stable's intentions, and when it comes to graded-stakes winners returning from a layoff in allowance races, the intent should be fairly clear: the allowance race is a prep designed to sharpen the horse for a future, richer spot.

Turnback The Alarm — Ro. f. 4, by Darn That Alarm—Boomie's Girl E, by Figonero
ANTLEY C W (57 5 8 13 .09)
Own.—Valley View Farm
Br.—Burke Walter J (Fla)
Tr.—Terrill William V (15 2 1 2 .13)
117

Lifetime	1993	1	0	0 1	$4,800
15 5 5 3	1992	5	3	1 1	$336,496
$570,484	Wet	1	1	0 0	$31,980

8May93- 1Bel	fst	6f	:221	:452	1:10	3+ⒻAlw 40000	93	3	3	2½	31	31½	31¾	Antley C W		119	*.40	88–17 MkinFcs1211LdySg119¾TurnbckThAlrm119	Lacked rally	5
11Jly92- 8Bel	fst	1¼	:50	1:38	2:032	ⒻC C A Oaks	92	6	3	32	1hd	1½	11¼	Antley C W		121	*1.40	74–18 TurnbckTheAlrm1211¼EsyNow1211¼PlsntStg121	Driving	6
11Jly92-Grade I																				
7Jun92- 8Bel	fst	1⅛	:452	1:093	1:484	ⒻMothrGoose	95	1	5	53½	41	1hd	12¼	Antley C W		121	7.20	85–22 TrnbcThAlrm1212¼EsN1211¾QnfTrmph121	Wide driving	7
7Jun92-Grade I																				
23May92- 8Bel	fst	1	:453	1:10	1:35	ⒻAcorn	91	1	1	1½	11	2hd	33½	Antley C W	b	121	3.40	91–07 PrspctrsDlt1212PlsntSt1211½TrbcThAlr121	Speed, wknd	12
23May92-Grade I																				
2May92- 7Aqu	fst	7f	:214	:434	1:214	ⒻFamily Style	103	1	5	2½	21	21½	2nk	Carr D		118	2.80	96–07 AmrcnRl121nkTrnbckThAlrm11816LkngfrWn116	Gamely	5
18Apr92- 3Aqu	my	6f	:213	:442	1:10	ⒻAlthea	84	3	1	32	32½	2hd	11¾	Antley C W		116	*.60	91–06 TrnbcThAlr1161¾MssCrGrl1161½TddsTpT116	Mild drive	5
8Dec91- 8Aqu	fst	1 1/16 ⊡	:483	1:132	1:463	ⒻTempted	82	5	1	1hd	2hd	2½	23	Santos J A	b	121	*.70	72–30 Dputton1143TurnbckThAlrm1213BlssOrHom114	Gamely	9
8Dec91 Grade III; Stumbled start, dueled, tired																				
17Nov91- 8Aqu	fst	1⅛	:47	1:122	1:52	ⒻDemoiselle	91	2	1	1½	2hd	1hd	2¾	Santos J A	b	116	7.90	75–32 StolnButy113¾TurnbckThAlrm116nkEsyNow116	Gamely	6
17Nov91-Grade II																				
13Oct91-11Crc	fst	1 1/16	:474	1:14	1:49	ⒻⓇFlaStallion	54	10	5	42	43½	610	610¾	Santos J A		120	*1.60	67–17 MissJlski120½RunforBby120nkSubtlDncr120	Bmpd in str	15
13Oct91-My Dear Girl Division																				
28Sep91-10Crc	fst	170	:47	1:144	1:472	ⒻGardenia Bc	57	2	4	44½	21	32	21	Carr D		116	*1.40	75–15 PttsPrcss1131TrbcTAlr1161ApplTGlr112	Lost whip gamely	8

LATEST WORKOUTS May 20 Bel 4f gd :48 B May 17 Bel 1 fst 1:394 H May 16 Bel 3f fst :37 B May 1 Bel 4f fst :474 B

Turnback The Alarm had been among the leaders of the three-year-old filly division in 1992, winning the Mother Goose and the Coaching Club American Oaks, but she had sustained a fracture to her right hind leg while training toward the Alabama Stakes in August, an injury that required surgery and months of recuperation. Entered in a six-furlong classified allowance in her return from a ten-month layoff on May 8, the roan filly was hammered to odds of 2–5. Handicappers reading between the lines might have surmised that Turnback The Alarm would not be at tops for this relatively meager purse and was using this race as a prep for an eventual return to a stakes route. Sure enough, Turnback The Alarm pressed the pace but lacked the needed response in the stretch and finished third behind sprint-specialist Makin Faces. Two weeks later, Turnback The Alarm returned in the spot for which she had been intended all along — the Grade 1 Shuvee at a mile and a sixteenth — and won at $5.40:

EIGHTH RACE
Belmont
MAY 22, 1993

1 $\frac{1}{16}$ MILES. (1.40^{2}) 18th Running THE SHUVEE HANDICAP (Grade I). Purse $150,000. Fillies and Mares, 3-year-olds and upward. By subscription of $300 each which should accompany the nomination; $1,200 to pass the entry box; $1,200 to start. The purse to be divided 60% to the winner, 22% to second, 12% to third and 6% to fourth. Weights Monday, May 17. Starters to be named at the closing time of entries. Trophies will be presented to the winning owner, trainer and jockey. Closed Wednesday, May 5, with 20 nominations.
Value of race $150,000; value to winner $90,000; second $33,000; third $18,000; fourth $9,000. Mutuel pool $320,125. Exacta Pool $516,305

Last Raced	Horse	M/Eqt.A.Wt	PP	St	¼	½	¾	Str	Fin	Jockey	Odds $1
8May93 ^{1}Bel^{3}	Turnback The Alarm	4 117	1	6	$3^{1\frac{1}{2}}$	$2^{\frac{1}{2}}$	$1^{\frac{1}{2}}$	1^{hd}	$1^{\frac{3}{4}}$	Antley C W	*1.70
30Apr93 ^{8}Aqu^{2}	Shared Interest	5 113	8	3	2^{hd}	3^{2}	2^{1}	2^{2}	2^{2}	Bailey J D	a-1.70
3May93 ^{5}Aqu^{4}	Vivano	4 112	3	7	$4^{2\frac{1}{2}}$	$4^{1\frac{1}{2}}$	$4^{\frac{1}{2}}$	5^{1}	3^{nk}	Smith M E	7.60
16Apr93 ^{9}OP^{4}	Queen of Triumph	4 113	6	2	5^{1}	6^{1}	$3^{\frac{1}{2}}$	$3^{\frac{1}{2}}$	4^{1}	Perret C	b-7.80
30Apr93 ^{8}Aqu^{1}	S. S. Sparkle	b 4 110	4	5	$7^{\frac{1}{2}}$	5^{hd}	7^{1}	$4^{\frac{1}{2}}$	5no	Madrid A Jr	9.60
27Mar93 ^{9}GP^{2}	Nannerl	6 117	5	8	8^{3}	7^{1}	6^{hd}	6^{hd}	6^{hd}	Krone J A	a-1.70
1May93 ^{5}CD^{6}	Jeano	5 113	7	1	9	9	9	7^{1}	7^{2}	Davis R G	8.40
3Apr93 ^{8}Aqu^{4}	Haunting	5 114	2	9	$6^{\frac{1}{2}}$	8^{3}	8^{hd}	8^{8}	8^{22}	Santos J A	18.80
16Apr93 ^{9}OP^{9}	Richard's Lass	5 111	9	4	1^{1}	$1^{\frac{1}{2}}$	5^{hd}	9	9	Chavez J F	b-7.80

***—Actual Betting Favorite.**
a-Coupled: Shared Interest and Nannerl; b-Queen of Triumph and Richard's Lass.
OFF AT 4:44 Start good. Won driving. Time, :22^{3}, :45^{2}, 1:10^{1}, 1:36^{1}, 1:43 Track fast.

$2 Mutuel Prices:				
	3-(A)-TURNBACK THE ALARM	5.40	2.80	2.20
	1-(H)-SHARED INTEREST (a-entry)		2.60	2.20
	5-(C)-VIVANO			2.80

$2 EXACTA 3-1 PAID $13.20

Ro. f, by Darn That Alarm—Boomie's Girl E, by Figonero. Trainer Terrill William V. Bred by Burke Walter J (Fla).

TURNBACK THE ALARM forced the early pace between horses, moved up to engage RICHARD'S LASS for the lead on the far turn, shook off that one leaving the three-eighths pole, dug in when challenged by SHARED INTEREST midway on the turn, drifted out a bit while battling heads apart for the lead in midstretch then turned back SHARED INTEREST under brisk urging. SHARED INTEREST stalked the pace while three wide along the backstretch, drew along side the winner to challenge on the turn, dueled heads apart from outside into deep stretch but couldn't stay with TURNBACK THE ALARM through the final seventy yards. VIVANO settled in good position for six furlongs, launched a rally four wide on the turn then finished willingly to gain a share. QUEEN OF TRIUMPH reserved early, made a run between horses to threaten on the turn but couldn't sustain her bid. S. S. SPARKLE unhurried early, moved into contention while slightly off the rail on the turn then lacked a strong closing response. NANNERL outrun for five furlongs, circled five wide into the stretch and lacked the needed response when called upon. JEANO never reached contention. HAUNTING was never a factor. RICHARD'S LASS was used up setting the early pace.

Owners— 1, Valley View Farm; 2, Evans Robert S; 3, Port Sidney L; 4, Perez Robert; 5, Heatherwood Farm; 6, Marablue Farm; 7, Smith Bentley; 8, Hutson David; 9, Perez Robert.

Trainers— 1, Terrill William V; 2, Schulhofer Flint S; 3, Pascuma James J Jr; 4, Callejas Alfredo; 5, Schosberg Richard; 6, Schulhofer Flint S; 7, Nafzger Carl A; 8, Veitch John M; 9, Callejas Alfredo.

Overweight: Queen of Triumph 2 pounds; S. S. Sparkle 1; Haunting 3.

The eighth race at Gulfstream on March 4 contained some interesting subplots:

Gulfstream Park

8

1 1/16 MILES. (1:40¹) ALLOWANCE. Purse $44,000 (plus $3,000 FOA). 4-year-olds and upward which have not won $15,000 twice at one mile or over since July 30, 1993, other than maiden, claiming or starter. Weight, 122 lbs. Non-winners of $20,000 at one mile or over since October 30, 1993, allowed 3 lbs. $12,500 twice at one mile or over since September 30, 5 lbs. $15,000 at one mile or over since July 30, 7 lbs. (Maiden, claiming and starter races not considered.)

1 1/16 MILES
START ▲ ▲ FINISH

Dancing Jon
Own: Cowan Marjorie & I
BAILEY J D (238 61 37 18 .26)

Dk. b or br h. 6
Sire: Gate Dancer (Sovereign Dancer)
Dam: Love From Mom (Mr Prospector)
Br: Cowan Mr & Mrs I M (Fla)
Tr: Sonnier J Bert (39 6 9 5 .15)

L 117

Lifetime Record: 29 5 5 6 $150,392
1994 3 0 0 2 $10,230 | Turf 7 0 2 0 $11,070
1993 14 2 2 1 $52,817 | Wet 1 1 0 0 $8,400
GP 3 0 0 3 $11,380 | Dist 6 1 0 3 $49,010

3Feb94- 9GP gd 1 1/16 :234 :474 1:12 1:44 Alw 39000N$mY 90 1 6 512 59½ 45 36¼ Douglas R R L 119 fb 12.80 84-20 Conveyor1224 Mythical Hunter1192½ Dancing Jon1194 6
Seven wide top str, late rally
20Jan94- 7GP fst 1 1/16 :231 :471 1:114 1:423 Alw 37000N$Y 83 2 7 714 76¾ 56 37½ Sellers S J L 115 fb 30.40 90-11 Living Vicariously1191 Scuffleburg1156¼ Dancing Jon1151½ 7
Seven wide str, late rally
6Jan94- 8GP gd *1⅛ Ⓣ :484 1:151 1:39 1:51 + Alw 35000N$mY 56 4 10 1020 1015 1016 1020 Sellers S J L 119 fb 31.20 70-17 Ghazi1152¾ Glenfiddich Lad115nk Jodi's Sweetie1151½ Never close 10
18Dec93- 1Crc fst 1 1/16 :24 :474 1:123 1:46 3+ Handicap23k 83 2 4 412 46 44 45½ Sellers S J L 113 fb 18.50 86-10 PistolsAndRoses121no Friud1154 DshForDotty1141½ Lacked late response 5
4Dec93-10Crc fst 1 1/16 :234 :481 1:124 1:463 3+ Handicap23k 93 4 4 48 35½ 35 43¾ Guidry M L 114 fb 8.80 84-16 Meena1182½ Sportin' Jack110¾ Dash For Dotty116½ Lacked response 7
20Nov93- 7Haw fst 1¼ :473 1:112 1:363 2:02 3+ Bud Haw G C-G2 89 4 7 712 78¾ 710 713½ Silva C H L 113 fb 28.80 86-13 Evanescent115nk Marquetry123no Valley Crossing1171½ No factor 7
6Nov93- 3Haw fst 1 1/16 :232 :461 1:104 1:431 3+ Alw 21000R 93 2 6 610 55½ 31½ 34¼ Razo E Jr L 122 fb 4.50 93-11 Stalwars122¾ Likely Target1153¾ Dancing Jon1223 Even finish 6
23Oct93-10Haw fm 1 Ⓣ :24 :473 1:12 1:371 3+ HawthBud B CG3 67 8 7 98¼ 87½ 97½ 912¾ Razo E Jr L 114 fb 15.90 70-21 Lord Sreva109hd Words Of War1142½ Rin Tin Bid112¾ No factor 10
4Oct93- 8AP fst 1 :222 :451 1:103 1:363 3+ Alw 27500R 98 3 6 612 52½ 2½ 1¾ Guidry M L 113 fb 5.50 83-23 Dancing Jon113¾ Gee Can He Dance1132½ Dr Pain1199½ 4 Wide turn 6
11Sep93- 9AP fst 1 :224 :45 1:10 1:344 3+ Equips Ml H-G3 86 1 9 913 99½ 610 613½ Pettinger D R L 111 fb 5.20 79-18 Split Run1147 Gee Can He Dance1143 Danc'n Jake114hd Wide rally 11
WORKOUTS: Mar 1 GP 4f fst :49 B 14/30 Feb 21 GP 4f fst :512 B 55/59 Jan 30 GP 3f fst :36 H 2/11 Dec 11 GP 3f fst :383 B 19/31

Seattle Morn
Own: Drey Alan
FIRES E (186 25 20 14 .13)

Ch. c. 4
Sire: Grey Dawn II (Herbager)
Dam: Tilting (Seattle Slew)
Br: Ringler Mr & Mrs David V (Ky)
Tr: Ebert Dennis W (26 7 2 3 .27)

L 117

Lifetime Record: 21 4 5 3 $217,134
1994 4 1 1 0 $25,520 | Turf 3 0 0 0 $9,000
1993 13 2 2 3 $189,813 | Wet 2 0 2 0 $14,610
GP 5 2 1 0 $38,720 | Dist 6 2 1 1 $44,698

24Feb94- 7GP fst 1 1/16 :23 :46 1:101 1:423 Alw 31000N3X 95 8 1 12 1½ 1hd 1nk Fires E L 117 5.30 97-12 Seattle Morn117nk Stop AndListen1193½ DreadMeNot1194½ Fully extended 8
4Feb94- 8GP gd 1 1/16 :242 :493 1:141 1:46 Alw 30000N3X 76 7 5 52½ 74¾ 76½ 710½ Fires E L 117 3.60 69-30 Aggressive Chief1171½ Jack's Hope1122¾ Devoted Glory1171½ Stopped 7
20Jan94- 9GP fst 1 1/16 :231 :47 1:104 1:424 Alw 28000N3X 94 8 1 11 2hd 2hd 2nk Fires E L 117 b 5.70 96-11 I Like To Win110nk Seattle Morn117¾ Marco Ray1173¾ Gamely 8
8Jan94- 7GP fst 6f :214 :443 :561 1:084 Alw 26000N3X 79 7 1 3½ 32½ 35½ 47¾ Fires E L 117 b 9.00 89-12 K S Fury1227 Evil Bear1174 Sans Souci Slew1171½ Gave way 7
11Dec93- 8Haw fst 170 :24 :484 1:122 1:414 3+ Sun Beau40k 86 1 1 22 24 23 32¾ Razo E Jr L 114 fb 16.10 89-19 Jan Artic1222½ Higgler111½ Seattle Morn114no Inside bid 7
6Nov93- 5Haw fm 1 Ⓣ :224 :454 1:111 1:351 3+ R F Carey H100k 47 12 2 21 52¾ 1216 1222½ Razo E Jr L 114 fb 43.60 71-10 High Habitation1143 Beau Fasa114nk Glenfiddich Lad114¾ Wide, tired 12
18Oct93- 7Haw fst 170 ⊗ :231 :471 1:121 1:413 Alw 19000N1T 85 4 3 3nk 2hd 1½ 11¾ Sibille R L 117 fb *1.10 93-09 Seattle Morn1171¾ Big Twister1172½ Spartan Leader1147½ Wide rally 7
9Oct93- 9Haw gd 1⅛ Ⓣ :46 1:103 1:364 1:501 Haw Derby-G3 78 11 4 46½ 46 77¾ 411 Guidry M L 113 fb 28.80 61-26 Snake Eyes1223½ Lt. Pinkerton1173 F L Bent1154½ Lacked rally 12
19Sep93- 5AP fst 6½f :221 :454 1:111 1:174 3+ Alw 21500N2X 47 7 2 41½ 21 32 33 Diaz J L L 112 fb 2.30 79-20 Cobar116nk Rut1152¾ Seattle Morn1121½ Led briefly 7
10Jly93- 8AP fm 1⅛ Ⓣ :471 1:11 1:364 1:494 Round Table-G3 71 10 1 1½ 2½ 107½ 1210 Sibille R L 115 26.10 78-13 Snake Eyes120nk Lt. Pinkerton118nk Lykatill Hil123½ Gave way rail 12
WORKOUTS: Feb 22 GP 4f fst :48 H 4/47 Feb 13 GP 6f fst 1:141 H 2/8 Jan 29 GP 4f fst :49 B 8/75 Jan 17 GP 5f fst 1:02 B 33/61 Jan 5 GP 3f fst :38 B 27/43

Royal n Gold
Own: Stempler Mel
RIVERA L JR (77 8 8 10 .10)

Ch. h. 5
Sire: Fountain of Gold (Mr. Prospector)
Dam: That Royal Touch (Ace of Aces)
Br: Saurbier Marvin R (Fla)
Tr: Lotti Gene A Jr (9 4 2 0 .44)

L 115

Lifetime Record: 21 8 4 1 $116,125
1994 4 3 1 0 $48,500 | Turf 0 0 0 0
1993 14 4 2 1 $55,815 | Wet 2 0 1 0 $4,740
GP 4 3 1 0 $48,500 | Dist 7 4 1 0 $56,325

25Feb94- 9GP fst 1 1/16 :231 :462 1:101 1:43 Alw 34000N4X 87 6 1 11½ 12½ 12 2no Rivera L Jr L 117 fb 1.80 95-10 JttngAlong117no RoylNGold1171¾ LostDutchmn117¾ Gave way grudgingly 6
13Feb94- 1GP fst 1 1/16 :231 :463 1:103 1:422 Clm 75000 91 4 1 11½ 11½ 11 11½ Rivera L Jr L 115 fb *1.30 98-09 Royal N Gold1151½ Daniel's Boy115½ Danc'n Jake1173½ Driving 6
15Jan94- 3GP gd 1⅛ :481 1:123 1:372 1:501 Clm 40000 96 6 1 11 11½ 12 11½ Rivera L Jr L 117 fb *1.70 86-19 Royal N Gold1171½ Patriot Strike1179½ Golden Eskimo1173½ Driving 7
4Jan94-11GP fst 1 1/16 :23 :463 1:122 1:453 Clm 25000 88 4 4 42 12½ 14½ 11¾ Rivera L Jr L 117 fb 3.40 87-21 Royal N Gold1171¾ Morambo117¾ Exploding Dawn1191½ Driving 11
12Dec93- 4Crc fst 6f :214 :454 :581 1:111 3+ Clm 32000 86 4 1 2½ 1hd 2½ 23¼ Rivera L Jr L 117 fb 3.20 89-16 Doyouseewhatisee1163¼ RoylNGold1172¾ JunkBondKing117¾ Second best 7
1Dec93- 3Crc fst 6f :221 :451 :574 1:111 3+ Clm 25000 88 4 4 1½ 1hd 21½ 31½ Rivera L Jr L 117 fb *2.30 91-10 Barbs Ike110nk Waheed1151 Royal N Gold1171½ Weakened 7
28Oct93- 7Med fst 170 :233 :463 1:11 1:403 3+ Alw 22000N4X 78 4 2 21½ 21 46 69¼ Leon F5 L 111 fb 2.70 84-18 Bert's Bubbleator113nk Local Problem1164¾ Palace Line1162½ Tired 6
16Oct93- 8Med fst 170 :24 :473 1:12 1:414 3+ Clm 40000 70 3 5 2½ 1hd 55 59¾ Vega A L 115 fb *1.40 77-19 ⒹIsland Edition1151¼ Red Ritual110¾ Fling1154¾ Bid, tired 6
23Sep93- 4Pim fst 1 1/16 :232 :47 1:104 1:424 3+ Clm 25000 91 6 1 11 11 1hd 1¾ Delgado A L 117 fb *2.60 91-19 Royal N Gold117¾ Ebonizer1176¾ Chiffonade115¾ Driving 8
7Aug93- 5Pha my 1 :232 :462 1:111 1:373 3+ Clm 50000 76 4 1 1hd 2hd 33 57½ Vega A L 119 fb 2.90 83-17 Brukabookie112nk My Sentiment120nk Just Alice1076¾ Dueled, tired 5
'ORKOUTS: Feb 23 Hia 4f fst :483 H 3/14 Feb 4 Hia 4f fst :503 B 14/23 Dec 31 Hia 3f fst :362 H 2/13 Dec 26 Hia 7f fst 1:311 B 1/1 Dec 20 Hia 3f fst :361 H 2/2

Summer Set
Own: Pugh C N Jr & Smith E
CASTANEDA M (103 4 5 11 .04)

B. g. 4
Sire: Singular (Nodouble)
Dam: Illgotten Gains (Search for Gold)
Br: Johnston W E & Smith George A (Ohio)
Tr: Azpurua Manuel J (24 0 1 4 .00)

115

Lifetime Record: 24 5 5 2 $139,033
1993 11 3 0 1 $97,723 | Turf 0 0 0 0
1992 13 2 5 1 $41,310 | Wet 4 1 0 1 $68,183
GP 1 0 0 0 | Dist 12 4 0 1 $53,313

23Oct93-14Tdn fst 1¼ :463 1:113 1:371 2:033 3+ ⓈEndrnc Chp H150k 49 4 1 11 911 1115 1124½ D'Amico A J LB 117 8.80e 83-07 Numerically1171 Cozzemight1225¾ Tis Andy's Turn1222½ Pace,stopped 12
4Sep93-13RD fst 1¼ :484 1:143 1:403 2:083 3+ ⓈGov Buck C H100k 70 9 4 43½ 68 811 913 Cooksey P J LB 116 7.80 55-29 Skip Larue1142 Erland's Point115nk Dashing Devil1181 Nothing left 14
20Aug93-13RD fst 170 :241 :481 1:122 1:432 Alw 12000NC 95 5 1 12 1½ 12½ 15 Cooksey P J LB 116 1.90 89-20 Summer Set1165 Erland's Point116½ Party Native12217 Ridden out 5
31Jly93-12Tdn fst 1 1/16 :231 :471 1:121 1:45 ⓈForest Cty H30k 75 4 4 5¾ 54 48½ 411 Lovato A J LB 120 2.60 82-18 Numerically1151 Erland's Point1195½ Reggies TimeEx1204¾ Flattened-out 8
4Jly93-12Tdn sly 1⅛ :47 1:113 1:381 1:513 ⓈClv Gld Cp H100k 85 3 5 54½ 54 56¾ 44¾ Neagle J E B 123 2.50 86-15 Dashing Devil122¾ Reggies Time Ex1191½ Sham Topper1152½ Evenly 8
19Jun93-13Tdn fst 1⅛ :473 1:113 1:364 1:492 Ohio Derby-G2 88 5 1 1½ 21 34½ 78 Martinez W B 120 31.40 94-06 Forever Whirl1222½ Boundlessly120nk Mighty Avanti1141 Pace-gave way 10
5Jun93-11Tdn my 1 1/16 :234 :481 1:13 1:442 Blk Gld BC H40k 90 2 1 11 1½ 2hd 31½ Neagle J E B 120 2.30 95-19 Truth Of It All1211½ Reggies Time Ex115no Summer Set1207½ Good ;try 4
8May93-12Tdn fst 1 1/16 :231 :471 1:112 1:443 ⓈSum Slvr Cup30k 87 3 1 1hd 2hd 2hd 11 Neagle J E B 122 *2.20 95-11 SummerSet1221 ReggisTimEx1182¾ DshingDvil1191½ Gamely, hand ridden 10
13Mar93-12TP fr 1 1/16 :23 :471 1:141 1:493 J Battaglia100k 55 6 1 32 21½ 58 515¾ Lopez R D 121 4.20 43-37 Fafa Lemos112¾ Over Jack Mountain11512 Beyond His Years1132 Tired 9
27Feb93-10GP fst 1 1/16 :233 :48 1:123 1:444 Fntn of Yth-G2 76 9 3 32 33 69¾ 711½ Gonzalez M A 117 15.50 74-22 Storm Tower1133 Great Navigator1171 Kissin Kris1172 Faltered 9
Run in divisions

Pure Rumor
Own: Lazy F Ranch
DAVIS R G (1 0 0 0 .00)

B. h. 5
Sire: Private Account (Damascus)
Dam: Rumor (Alleged)
Br: Mrs. Martha F. Gerry (Ky)
Tr: Penna Angel Jr (16 3 3 3 .19)

115

Lifetime Record:	13 4 5 1	$170,250			
1993	5 3 2 0	$135,680	Turf	5 0 1 1	$10,400
1992	8 1 3 1	$34,570	Wet	1 0 1 0	$5,720
GP	0 0 0 0		Dist	5 4 1 0	$81,750

4Jly93-9Bel	fst	1¼	:471 1:11 1:352 2:011	3↑ Suburban H-G1	107	8	6	66	63	31	2½	Davis R G	110 b	7.40	83-15	DevilHisDue1211½ PureRumor110¾ WestByWst1162	Broke slowly, rallied	8
7Jun93-8Bel	fst	1 1/16	:231 :464 1:113 1:432	3↑ Handicap46k	100	1	4	42½	3nk	11	13½	Santagata N	112 b	*1.60	85-22	Pure Rumor1123½ Key Contender11413 Sylva Honda113	Driving	4
26May93-8Bel	fst	1 1/16	:241 :472 1:114 1:422	3↑ Alw 30500N2X	100	4	3	32	31	11½	15	Santagata N	119 b	2.70	90-16	Pure Rumor1195 Tanako1121½ Very Personal1116	Drew off	6
28Jan93-6Aqu	fst	1 1/16 ⊡	:233 :473 1:123 1:443	Alw 29000N1X	99	5	8	64¾	42	11	17¼	Santagata N	117 b	*1.10	82-26	PureRumor1177¼ SafeProspect117½ CoolAsCrystl1173	Lugged in, driving	9
6Jan93-7Aqu	gd	1⅛ ⊡	:482 1:121 1:364 1:491	Alw 29000N1X	93	4	1	1hd	1½	11	2¾	Santagata N	122 b	3.30	96-13	Choko117¾ Pure Rumor1226¾ All My Tricks1172¼	Gamely	7
22Dec92-1Aqu	fst	170 ⊡	:24 :483 1:132 1:423	3↑ Md Sp Wt	89	8	2	2hd	11	13½	18	Santagata N	120 b	*.90	92-09	Pure Rumor1208 Flying Colonel1205½ All Canadian1202	Ridden out	8
12Oct92-3Bel	my	1¼	:481 1:124 1:374 2:031	3↑ Md Sp Wt	81	7	2	2½	21½	21	24½	Santagata N	119 b	2.90	70-17	Appointee1194½ Pure Rumor11915 Off The Cuff119	2nd best	7
Originally scheduled on turf																		
29Sep92-1Med	fst	1 1/16	:24 :474 1:123 1:433	3↑ Md Sp Wt	81	9	7	43½	31½	2hd	21¼	Santagata N	116	*2.00	88-11	Crijinsky1161¼ Pure Rumor1166 Ack Classy116	Hung hld 1st trn	9
Originally scheduled on turf																		
10Aug92-6Sar	fm	1⅝ Ⓣ	:491 1:141 2:043 2:421	3↑ Md Sp Wt	50	3	8	84¾	63	910	918½	Smith M E	117 b	3.50e	65-11	Roberto's Grace1173 Muy Mogambo1171½ Off The Cuff117	Wide outrun	11
??Aug92-6Sar	fm	1⅛ Ⓣ	:464 1:103 1:353 1:48	3↑ Md Sp Wt	78	2	6	77½	76½	53	32¼	Day P	117 b	2.50	88-04	Annuities117hd Roberto's Grace1172¼ Pure Rumor117	Late gain	12

WORKOUTS: Mar 1 GP 5f fst 1:003 H 4/21 Feb 21 GP 6f fst 1:143 B 8/22 Feb 12 GP 5f fst 1:014 B 28/46 Feb 6 GP 5f fst 1:03 B 34/55 Jan 29 GP 4f fst :492 B 29/75 Jan 23 GP 4f fst :533 B 29/31

Baron Mathew
Own: Crown Stable
DOUGLAS R R (223 19 37 35 .09)

Ch. g. 6
Sire: Naskra (Nasram)
Dam: Switch Ur Kingdom (Key To The Kingdom)
Br: Forest Retreat Farms Inc (Fla)
Tr: Blengs Vincent L (61 7 11 5 .11)

L 115

Lifetime Record:	35 9 5 10	$236,836			
1994	3 0 1 2	$12,070	Turf	8 2 1 0	$25,800
1993	11 3 0 3	$132,301	Wet	2 1 0 1	$11,855
GP	12 2 2 4	$51,510	Dist	12 6 2 3	$97,880

6Feb94-10GP	fst	170	:241 :471 1:102 1:39	Alw 39000N$Y	84	6	6	64¾	44½	36½	313	Douglas R R	L 117 f	*1.80	93-12	Blacksburg1225 Jodi's Sweetie1158 Baron Mathew1173	Late rally	7
26Jan94-9GP	fst	7f	:221 :442 1:084 1:213	Clm 80000	92	3	3	46½	46½	41¼	21¾	Douglas R R	L 117 f	*3.00	93-12	Cold Digger1171¾ Baron Mathew1171½ Oh My Blue Boy110no	Rallied	6
4Jan94-4GP	gd	6f	:22 :451 :58 1:11	Clm 62500	86	1	9	910	78½	55½	32¾	Douglas R R	L 117 f	20.30	83-14	Gallant Step1152½ Imaging117nk Baron Mathew117hd	Out late, rallied	10
31Jly93-9Lrl	fst	1⅛	:481 1:12 1:362 1:482	3↑ Broad Brush50k	83	3	2	31½	33	45½	610¾	Elliott S	L 113 b	5.40	85-17	Frottage1123½ Gala Spinaway1141½ Ibex111nk	Gave way	6
10Jly93-6Bel	fst	1 1/16	:232 :463 1:104 1:413	3↑ Alw 46000N$mY	58	5	6	53½	52½	66¾	619	Bisono C V5	117 f	3.20	75-06	Dry Bean111hd Berkley Fitz122nk Excellent Tipper1174	No factor	6
19Jun93-9Lrl	fst	1⅛	:464 1:104 1:36 1:484	3↑ Bltmr B C H-G3	95	3	6	66½	44	21½	36	Luzzi M J	L 115 f	4.10	88-19	Sunny Sunrise120hd Snappy Landing1146 Baron Mathew1155	Gave way	6
22May93-14Suf	fst	1⅛	:474 1:122 1:382 1:51	3↑ Suf Bud B C100k	99	10	8	63½	42½	2hd	11¾	Prado E S	LB 112 f	7.50	99-14	Baron Mathew1121¾ Snappy Landing1143½ Alyten116nk	Driving	10
2May93-8Pim	fm	1 1/16 Ⓣ	:23 :461 1:10 1:412	Alw 30000NC	78	5	5	48	56½	64¾	610¾	Prado E S	L 122 f	2.80	83-09	Reggae114¾ Rebuff114¾ Gilded Youth1145	Weakened	8
11Apr93-9Hia	fst	1⅛	:493 1:133 1:38 1:504	Calle Ocho25k	93	3	5	54	32	41½	32	Douglas R R	L 117 f	1.90	88-19	Northern Trend1131½ Dr Pain113½ Baron Mathew117no	Late rally six wide	5
??Mar93-8GP	fm	1 1/16 Ⓣ	:234 :474 1:113 1:414+	Handicap55k	95	7	4	57½	67½	43½	54¼	Perret C	L 114 f	17.60	83-12	Paradise Creek1221 Sylva Honda1131 Flying American1112	Faded	7

WORKOUTS: Mar 2 GP 3f fst :374 B 8/14 Feb 23 GP 5f fst 1:01 B 5/30 Feb 15 GP 3f fst :36 B 4/34 ●Jan 24 GP 3f fst :36 H 1/7 ●Jan 20 GP 3f fst :353 H 1/39 Jan 15 GP 3f gd :38 B (d) 16/30

West by West
Own: Peace John H
SAMYN J L (73 5 2 6 .07)

B. h. 5
Sire: Gone West (Mr. Prospector)
Dam: West Turn (Cox's Ridge)
Br: Peace John H (Ky)
Tr: Arnold George R II (7 1 0 0 .14)

L 115

Lifetime Record:	21 8 2 4	$748,713			
1993	9 4 1 2	$427,735	Turf	0 0 0 0	
1992	9 3 1 1	$265,050	Wet	2 0 0 0	$6,900
GP	2 1 0 1	$12,930	Dist	5 3 0 1	$71,965

18Sep93-8Bel	sly	1⅛	:453 1:094 1:342 1:47	3↑ Woodward-G1	67	2	4	35½	45	614	634½	Samyn J L	126 b	4.50	59-15	Bertrando12613 Devil His Due1263 Valley Crossing126hd	Tired	6
28Aug93-8Sar	fst	1⅛	:464 1:101 1:343 1:472	3↑ Whitney H-G1	109	2	3	45	63	31½	23½	Samyn J L	115	2.30e	95-06	Brunswick1123½ West By West115¾ Devil His Due1227½	Rallied inside	7
4Jly93-9Bel	fst	1¼	:471 1:11 1:352 2:011	3↑ Suburban H-G1	106	1	4	53	21	2½	32¼	Samyn J L	116 b	2.70	83-15	Devil His Due1211½ Pure Rumor110¾ West By West1162	Bid, weakened	8
5Jun93-8Bel	fst	1⅛	:462 1:103 1:35 1:472	3↑ Nassau C H-G1	113	8	3	2½	2½	11½	1¾	Samyn J L	114 b	4.20	92-15	West By West114¾ Valley Crossing1121 Strike The Gold1173½	Driving	8
13May93-8Bel	fst	1 1/16	:23 :46 1:101 1:404	3↑ Alw 46000N$mY	109	5	4	43	31	11	11	Samyn J L	117 b	*.60	98-02	West By West1171 Berkley Fitz11714 Fabersham117½	Driving	7
24Apr93-9Spl	fst	1⅛	:462 1:093 1:353 1:492	Nl Jky Clb HG3	96	5	4	42¾	35	53¾	42	Samyn J L	L 118 b	4.10	91-07	Stalwars118nk Count The Time115½ Richman1191¼	Bore out turn	8
7Apr93-7Kee	fst	1 1/16	:24 :48 1:12 1:414	Alw 30000N$mY	107	4	4	11	2hd	2hd	1¾	Day P	L 118 b	*.60	95-21	West By West118¾ Flying Continental1213 Dual Elements1184		6
Brushed, 1/8 pole, driving																		
14Mar93-9FG	fst	1⅛	:481 1:13 1:372 1:491	New Orlns H-G3	96	6	8	85¾	96	54	34¾	Samyn J L	L 119 b	*1.50	93-14	Latin American1123½ Delafield1151¼ West By West119¾	Hit gate	12
??Feb93-10FG	fst	1 1/16	:251 :49 1:13 1:434	Whrlway H30k	98	2	2	21	21	21½	13¼	Samyn J L	L 117 b	*.80	95-16	West By West1173¼ Place Dancer112¾ Genuine Meaning113nk	Driving	5
21Nov92-8Aqu	fst	1⅜	:494 1:143 1:392 2:164	3↑ Brooklyn H-G1	99	1	6	54	52¼	21	47¾	Samyn J L	111 b	8.20	78-25	ChiefHoncho1175½ [D]LostMountin1141 VlleyCrossing113	Flattened out	11

WORKOUTS: Mar 1 Pay 5f fst 1:06 B 1/2 Feb 24 Pay 5f fst 1:052 B 4/5 Feb 17 Pay 5f sly 1:044 B 1/3 Feb 11 Pay 4f fst :512 B 8/18 ●Feb 5 Pay 4f fst :50 B 1/15

A quick perusal of the *Beyer Speed Figures* suggested a two-horse race between West by West and Pure Rumor. The former had won the Grade 1 Nassau County Handicap and more than $400,000 in a fine 1993 campaign that saw him run five figures in the 106 to 113 range. Pure Rumor had won four of his last six starts, finished second in the Grade 1 Suburban Handicap most recently, and showed ascending figures of 99, 100, 100, and, finally, a 107 in the Suburban. Naturally, West by West and Pure Rumor were the betting choices at 6–5 and 2–1, respectively, against four opponents who had never run a figure higher than the mid-90s.

But there was a problem: West by West and Pure Rumor were returning from layoffs, and although both previously had shown the ability to win when fresh, there was reason for skepticism regarding intent in one case (West by West) and readiness in the other (Pure Rumor).

West by West was a Grade 1 winner, and it was highly unlikely that his connections intended to have him primed for an all-out try in a $44,000 allowance, when so many richer races were on the horizon; indeed, to do so would be amateurish.

Pure Rumor, meanwhile, was a major question mark in terms of physical condition. He had been sidelined for eight months, after X rays following the Suburban revealed a stress fracture of his left foreleg. This was not "inside information" that the general public didn't know about: Pure Rumor's injury was detailed in John Piesen's prerace story, which appeared on the front page of the day's *Form*, with trainer Angel Penna quoted as saying, "I've never trained a horse who had a stress fracture like he did, so I'm not sure what to expect."

If the trainer didn't know what to expect, handicappers projecting a representative speed figure and an immediate return to top form were being recklessly optimistic in taking 2–1.

With clouds over the two betting choices, what were the prospects of their four rivals? Players who handicapped the race the night before were anticipating a suicidal speed duel between Seattle Morn and Royal n Gold, but the complexion of the race changed dramatically when Royal n Gold scratched in the morning. A revised look at the fractions of the most recent two-turn routes of the four remaining entrants, adjusted with the ballpark "one length equals a fifth of a second," showed that Seattle Morn had a significant edge as the lone early speed:

Dancing Jon	:50	1:13⅕
Summer Set	:48⅕	1:12
Baron Mathew	:48⅕	1:11⅖
Seattle Morn	*:46*	*1:10⅕*

Seattle Morn was the clear early leader, but this fact alone does not qualify a horse as an automatic bet; the horse should also satisfy questions concerning bias, midrace pressure, class, and, of course, condition. In terms of bias, Seattle Morn had an edge, because the Gulfstream surface had been playing to speed all winter long, and the earlier route races on the card had continued the trend, with Gallant Guest winning the first route on the card by laying second through the opening half, taking over on the far turn, and drawing off; the next dirt route went to 9–2 shot Weshtrum, who led past every pole, with the exacta completed by a 10–1 shot who chased in second the entire trip. In terms of condition and ability to handle midrace pressure, Seattle Morn was fresh from a nonwinners-of-three–allowance win, in which he had overcome the outside post to gain a clear lead and held stubbornly through a prolonged drive; he had held on with similar resolve, also from an extreme outside post, in his previous fast track route on January 20.

Speed figure fanatics with tunnel vision saw only that the two favorites were the horses with the best figures — as almost always is the case. A more comprehensive look at the race's dynamics revealed two favorites unlikely to produce their best efforts, a key late scratch, and a razor-sharp colt stepping to the next level who was now left with a tremendous tactical advantage in terms of the probable pace. Seattle Morn sprinted clear early, maintained a daylight advantage through six furlongs in 1:11 (slower than his two previous good races at the meeting against lesser company), and had enough in reserve to repulse a challenge in midstretch from Dancing Jon. That was the only challenge that ever came; Pure Rumor showed nothing close to his pre–stress fracture form, finishing last, while West by West trailed early and offered a belated rally for third.

EIGHTH RACE
Gulfstream
MARCH 4, 1994

$1\frac{1}{16}$ MILES. (1.40^{1}) ALLOWANCE. Purse $44,000 (plus $3,000 FOA). 4–year–olds and upward which have not won $15,000 twice at one mile or over since July 30, 1993 other than maiden, claiming, or starter. Weight, 122 lbs. Non–winners of $20,000 at one mile or over since October 30, 1993, allowed 3 lbs. $12,500 twice at one mile or over since September 30, 5 lbs. $15,000 at one mile or over since July 30, 7 lbs. (Maiden, claiming and starter races not considered.)

Value of Race: $44,000 Winner $26,400; second $8,800; third $5,720; fourth $2,200; fifth $440; sixth $440. Mutuel Pool $278,208.00 Perfecta Pool $373,294.00 Trifecta Pool $324,772.00

Last Raced	Horse	M/Eqt.	A.	Wt	PP	St	¼	½	¾	Str	Fin	Jockey	Odds $1
24Feb94 ^{7}GP^{1}	Seattle Morn	L	4	117	2	2	$1^{1\frac{1}{2}}$	1^{1}	1^{1}	1^{hd}	$1^{1\frac{1}{2}}$	Fires E	3.20
3Feb94 ^{9}GP^{3}	Dancing Jon	Lbf	6	117	1	1	5^{hd}	3^{hd}	3^{hd}	2^{2}	$2^{3\frac{1}{4}}$	Bailey J D	7.20
18Sep93 ^{8}Bel^{6}	West by West	Lb	5	115	6	6	6	$5^{1\frac{1}{2}}$	$4^{1\frac{1}{2}}$	4^{hd}	$3^{1\frac{3}{4}}$	Samyn J L	1.30
6Feb94 ^{10}GP^{3}	Baron Mathew	Lf	6	115	5	4	$3^{\frac{1}{2}}$	4^{hd}	$5^{1\frac{1}{2}}$	3^{hd}	4no	Douglas R R	9.10
23Oct93 ^{14}Tdn^{11}	Summer Set		4	115	3	3	2^{4}	2^{5}	$2^{\frac{1}{2}}$	5^{5}	5^{6}	Castaneda M	58.90
4Jly93 ^{9}Bel^{2}	Pure Rumor	b	5	115	4	5	$4^{\frac{1}{2}}$	6	6	6	6	Maple E	2.10

OFF AT 4:15 Start Good. Won driving. Time, :23^{2}, :46^{3}, 1:11, 1:36^{1}, 1:42^{2} Track fast.

$2 Mutuel Prices:

2–SEATTLE MORN	8.40	4.60	2.60
1–DANCING JON		5.40	2.60
7–WEST BY WEST			2.40

$2 PERFECTA 2 & 1 PAID $47.60 $2 TRIFECTA 2–1–7 PAID $155.60

Ch. c, by Grey Dawn II–Tilting, by Seattle Slew. Trainer Ebert Dennis W. Bred by Ringler Mr & Mrs David V (Ky).

SEATTLE MORN sprinted to an early lead, set the pace, inside, while under good rating, then, under strong urging in the drive, held DANCING JON safe. The latter void of early foot, moved into a forward position down the backstretch, challenged for the lead midstretch but could not overtake the top one in the drive. WEST BY WEST trailed the field early, made a run on the final turn then closed with a belated bid in the drive. BARON MATHEW, a forward factor early, weakened. SUMMER SET raced closest to the pace from the beginning then faltered. PURE RUMOR, within striking distance early, stopped.

Owners— 1, Drey Alan; 2, Cowan Irving & Marjorie; 3, Peace John H; 4, Crown Stable; 5, Pugh C N Jr & Smith G; 6, Lazy F Ranch
Trainers—1, Ebert Dennis W; 2, Sonnier J Bert; 3, Arnold George R II; 4, Blengs Vincent L; 5, Azpurua Manuel J; 6, Penna Angel Jr
Scratched— Royal N Gold (25Feb94 ^{9}GP^{2})

Notably, West by West got the tune-up his connections had been looking for. He came out of the allowance race to win the Grade 3 Widener Handicap in his next start:

West by West
Own: Peace John H
SAMYN J L (24 9 2 1 .38)

B. h. 5
Sire: Gone West (Mr. Prospector)
Dam: West Turn (Cox's Ridge)
Br: Peace John H (Ky)
Tr: Arnold George R II (5 2 0 0 .40)

116

Lifetime Record:	23 9 2 5	$874,433			
1994	2 1 0 1	$125,720	Turf	0 0 0 0	
1993	9 4 1 2	$427,735	Wet	2 0 0 0	$6,900
Aqu	3 0 1 0	$161,000	Dist	7 2 2 1	$556,500

27Mar94-11Hia fst 1⅛ :464 1:104 1:363 1:494 3↑ Widener H-G3	109	5	5	6¾	5¾	4½	1nk	Samyn J L	L 114 b	5.00	95-13	West By West114nk Migrating Moon1141½ Pistols And Roses115nk		8
Seven wide top str, driving														
4Mar94-8GP fst 1 1/16 :232 :463 1:11 1:422 Alw 44000N$mY	92	6	6	56¼	41½	42¼	34¾	Samyn J L	L 115 b	*1.30	93-14	Seattle Morn1171½ Dancing Jon1173½ West By West1151¾	Belated bid	6
18Sep93-8Bel sly 1⅛ :453 1:094 1:342 1:47 3↑ Woodward-G1	67	2	4	35½	45	614	634½	Samyn J L	126 b	4.50	59-15	Bertrando12613 Devil His Due1263 Valley Crossing126hd	Tired	6
28Aug93-8Sar fst 1⅛ :464 1:101 1:343 1:472 3↑ Whitney H-G1	109	2	3	45	63	31½	23½	Samyn J L	115	2.30e	95-06	Brunswick1123½ West By West115¾ Devil His Due1227½	Rallied inside	7
4Jly93-9Bel fst 1¼ :471 1:11 1:352 2:011 3↑ Suburban H-G1	106	1	4	53	21	2½	32½	Samyn J L	116 b	2.70	83-15	Devil His Due1211½ Pure Rumor110¾ West By West1162	Bid, weakened	8
5Jun93-8Bel fst 1⅛ :462 1:103 1:35 1:472 3↑ Nassau C H-G1	113	8	3	2½	2½	11½	1¾	Samyn J L	114 b	4.20	92-15	West By West114¾ Valley Crossing1121 Strike The Gold1173½	Driving	8
13May93-8Bel fst 1 1/16 :23 :46 1:101 1:404 3↑ Alw 46000N$mY	109	5	4	43	31	11	11	Samyn J L	117 b	*.60	98-02	West By West1171 Berkley Fitz11714 Fabersham117½	Driving	7
24Apr93-9Spt fst 1⅛ :462 1:093 1:353 1:492 Nl Jky Clb HG3	96	5	4	42¾	35	53¾	42	Samyn J L	L 118 b	4.10	91-07	Stalwars118nk Count The Time115½ Richman1191½	Bore out turn	8
7Apr93-7Kee fst 1 1/16 :24 :48 1:12 1:414 Alw 29000N$mY	107	4	4	11	2hd	2hd	1¾	Day P	L 118 b	*.60	95-21	West By West118¾ Flying Continental1213 Dual Elements1184		6
Brushed, 1/8 pole, driving														
14Mar93-9FG fst 1⅛ :481 1:13 1:372 1:491 New Orlns H-G3	96	6	8	85¾	96	54	34¾	Samyn J L	L 119 b	*1.50	93-14	Latin American1123½ Delafield1151½ West By West119¾	Hit gate	12

WORKOUTS: Apr 21 Bel 4f fst :483 B 9/33 Apr 15 Bel tr.t 6f fst 1:152 B 9/14 Apr 9 Bel tr.t 5f fst 1:012 B 21/39 Mar 23 Pay 5f fst 1:042 B 6/9 Mar 17 Pay 5f fst 1:054 B 2/6 Mar 12 Pay 4f fst :51 B 2/15

CHRONIC MONEY-BURNERS

As with favorites unsuited to the class demands, the footing, or the probable pace, handicappers can take an edge by avoiding habitual nonwinners, particularly the kind that show just enough in their races to attract continued support at the windows.

Mr Sledge
Own: Schifrin Lois D
NO RIDER (—)

Gr. c. 3 (Apr)
Sire: Premiership (Exclusive Native)
Dam: Laughing Ruler (Iron Ruler)
Br: Fernung Earle E (Fla)
Tr: Shapoff Stanley R (30 0 9 4 .00)

122

Lifetime Record:	19 M 7 6	$33,920			
1993	9 M 4 4	$19,080	Turf	0 0 0 0	
1992	10 M 3 2	$14,840	Wet	0 0 0 0	
Aqu	11 0 4 4	$21,900	Dist	3 0 2 1	$8,270

26May93-2Bel fst 7f :223 :453 1:11 1:243 3↑ Md 30000	75	7	2	23	21½	21½	31¼	Santagata N	113 b	*1.60	79-22	Run Lo Run120no Westbridge1151½ Mr Sledge11310	Bid, weakened	8
14May93-3Bel fst 6½f :22 :453 1:103 1:171 3↑ Md 47500	68	4	5	54½	51½	43½	310	Santagata N	113 b	7.40	77-18	Air1152 Shootthemessenger1158 Mr Sledge1131	Lacked rally	9
29Apr93-1Aqu fst 1 :23 :467 1.113 1.381 3↑ Md 45000	75	8	5	21	21	23	27	Santagata N	113 b	*2.50	66-35	Islanders Cure1157 Mr Sledge1137 Camelot North106¾	Second best	8
10Apr93-3Aqu fst 7f :232 :462 1:102 1:232 3↑ Md 45000	74	1	6	2½	2½	21½	27	Santagata N	113 b	2.00	80-13	Turk Passer1157 Mr Sledge11313 Sail Clear1[illegible]	Second best	5
21Mar93-9Aqu gd 6f ⊡ :224 :454 :581 1:111 Md 35000	74	9	7	72¾	31	22	2¾	Santagata N	122 b	*2.00	86-13	Alex K.111¾ Mr Sledge1221½ Camelot North1176½	Second best	12
11Mar93-1Aqu fst 6f ⊡ :231 :464 :592 1:124 Md 50000	64	2	4	32	23	23	34	Santagata N	122 b	*1.10	75-19	Mr Rocky1182 Run Galtee Run1182 Mr Sledge1226½	Saved ground	6
25Feb93-3Aqu fst 6f ⊡ :233 :471 :592 1:12 Md 50000	70	5	2	33	32½	32½	23½	Santagata N	122 b	6.10	79-14	Shot Doctor1223½ Mr Sledge1223 Mr Rocky1186	Second best	6
11Feb93-5Aqu fst 6f ⊡ :233 :471 :591 1:12 Md 50000	68	9	3	53	31	32	33¾	Santagata N	122	5.90	79-16	Nowsthetimetoshine1181 ShotDoctor1222¾ MrSledge1222	Bid, weakened	9
8Jan93-2Aqu fst 6f ⊡ :23 :464 :59 1:114 Md 50000	70	4	7	73½	41	31	42¼	Santagata N	122	7.50	82-15	Five Star General1222 Allentown118hd Stack Um Up118no	No late bid	11
19Dec92-4Aqu fst 6f ⊡ :223 :453 :58 1:101 Md 50000	64	3	9	82¾	43	33	37	Romero R P	118	5.70	85-05	Won Song1145½ Gravel Ridge1181¾ Mr Sledge118no	Mild rally	11

WORKOUTS: ●May 8 Bel tr.t 4f fst :49 B 1/16 Apr 26 Bel tr.t 4f fst :492 B 8/16 Apr 19 Bel tr.t 4f fst :481 H 5/33 Apr 7 Bel tr.t 4f fst :491 B 12/22 Mar 31 Bel tr.t 4f fst :481 H 11/55 Mar 7 Bel tr.t 4f gd :471 H 2/23

Mr Sledge burned up hundreds of thousands of dollars in the win pool through his first nineteen starts, finishing second seven times and third six times. Handicappers who picked up early on the sucker profile of Mr Sledge were able to bet against him at odds of 8–5, 5–2, 2–1, 2–1, and 11–10 from mid-March to late May.

Always Ashley B. g. 7, by Rallying Cry—Foolish Leader, by Mr Leader
CHAVEZ J F (205 39 27 15 .19) $13,000 Br.—Lostritto Joseph A (NY)
Own.—Odintz Jeff Tr.—Odintz Jeff (50 5 6 7 .10) 115

Lifetime	1993	12	0	2	3	$15,040
65 3 10 15	1992	21	0	2	7	$37,920
$145,980	Turf	1	0	0	0	
	Wet	2	0	0	1	$2,160

10Jun93- 9Bel	fst	6f	:232	:464	1:12	Clm 13000 21	62	8	11	1211	107¾	85¾	88¼	Bisono C V5	b 110	10.00	72-17	JolsAppl1171½TknfPwr1171¼NwyrkAppl115	Checked brk	12
21May93- 9Bel	fst	6f	:221	:461	1:11	Clm 14000	71	3	5	88½	74	55	46¼	Chavez J F	b 117	3.10	79-20	WillCojack1172JoliesAppeal1151¼Reappel117	Mild gain	8
3May93- 2Aqu	fst	6f	:231	:471	1:122	Clm 14000	70	7	6	32	51¾	5¾	32	Toscano P R	b 117	*1.80	78-17	SportsAlrm1172SecrtAlrt113hdAlwysAshly117	Mild rally	8
26Apr93- 6Aqu	fst	7f	:224	:46	1:243	3↑Alw 27500	69	5	3	62	53	64	59¼	Chavez J F	b 119	9.40	72-21	Prioritizr1192ChfDsr1122¾Bob'sCormornt113	Four wide	7
18Apr93- 2Aqu	fst	6f	:222	:453	1:102	Clm 17500	83	3	1	33	32½	32	22	Chavez J F	b 117	3.50	88-15	OldWys1172AlwysAshley1174Letumcelebrt117	Willingly	4
25Mar93- 7Aqu	fst	6f	⊡:231	:461	1:104	Alw 28000	84	6	7	83¼	85	54½	64½	Frost G C5	b 112	14.40	84-17	EpldngRnb1172BlnCt117nkMdnhtSnn117	Saved ground	9
3Mar93- 2Aqu	fst	6f	⊡:224	:454	1:113	Clm 17500	84	1	8	85¼	85½	54	41¾	Chavez J F	b 117	6.00	83-19	PyforPly1171½OttBt117nkI'mAPckpckt112	Broke slowly	8
19Feb93- 3Aqu	fst	6f	⊡:232	:47	1:123	Clm 17500	76	6	9	65	65½	53½	42¾	Chavez J F	b 117	*2.70	77-23	I'mAPickpocket1101½DlRio117nkPrmirFlg113	Mild gain	10
10Feb93- 1Aqu	fst	6f	⊡:222	:454	1:111	Clm 17500	86	5	2	48	44	41½	21¾	Chavez J F	b 117	6.00	85-16	EsyGoingA.J.1121¾AlwysAshly1173ScrtAlrt115	2nd best	6
31Jan93- 9Aqu	fst	6f	⊡:224	:462	1:112	Clm 17500	69	2	10	87¼	76	78½	49	Chavez J F	b 117	5.60	77-16	WlkingStrt1171¾EsyGongA.J.1125¾Tlc'sBd117	Five wide	11

LATEST WORKOUTS Jun 23 Aqu 3f fst :363 H

Always Ashley has raced sixty-five times in his career, winning on just three occasions. He hasn't won since at least 1991, so why would any player have been interested in this hapless gelding as a win proposition on February 19, when he was 27–10, or on May 3, when he was 9–5, or on May 21, when he was 3–1?

If you want to use horses like Mr Sledge and Always Ashley *underneath* a bona fide contender in exactas, fine. But don't waste any money using horses with this type of profile in the win slot.

BASEMENT-LEVEL CLAIMERS

Basement-level claimers, by definition, are for the worst horses on the circuit. Form is fleeting and erratic in these events — a state of affairs attributable to two factors: the horses don't have much ability; and they suffer from various infirmities that flare up and abate on short notice.

It makes little sense to assume that just because a basement-level claimer recently delivered a strong performance, it is ready to do so again today, especially when any negative signs are present.

Brave Grecian
Own: Davis Barbara J
Dk. b or br m. 5
Sire: Brave Shot-GB (Bold Bidder)
Dam: Greek Nixy (Snow Knight)
Br: Schickedanz Gustav (Ont-C)
Tr: Moschera Gasper S (8 2 1 0 .25)
122

Lifetime Record: 33 8 2 4 $95,415										
1993	6 2 1 1	$20,450	Turf	0	0	0	0	
1992	17 5 0 1	$52,020	Wet	9	5	0	0	$51,300
Bel	10 4 0 2	$35,640	Dist	1	0	0	0	

2Sep93- 4Bel	fst	6f	:222	:454	:581	1:11	3↑Ⓕ Clm 14000	56	5	4	67	63¼	75½	510¼	Smith M E	117 fb	*.60	75-15	Dance On The Sand1172½ Miss Tahiti1174 Take A Powder1172½	No factor	7
24Jly93- 2Bel	fst	6f	:223	:462	:583	1:112	Ⓕ Clm 15500	82	8	7	62¾	3½	12	17½	Smith M E	113 fb	*2.30	83-17	Brave Grecian1137½ Alice Key1101¾ Jen'shot1173½	Wide, driving	8
10Jly93- 9Bel	fst	6f	:223	:454	:58	1:104	Ⓕ Clm 13000	65	6	2	43	31	32½	34	Graell A	117 fb	*1.50	82-08	Killer Buzz113½ Miss Tahiti1173½ Brave Grecian117nk	Flattened out	6
18Jun93- 2Bel	fst	6f	:222	:462	:591	1:123	Ⓕ Clm 14000	73	4	3	33½	32	22	1¾	Graell A	117 fb	5.00	77-18	Brave Grecian117¾ Miss Tahiti1131½ Holiday Gala1152½	Driving	9
23Apr93- 2Aqu	fst	6f	:23	:464	:584	1:112	Ⓕ Clm 12000	70	3	1	2hd	1½	13	2nk	Graell A	113 fb	3.80	85-15	Majestic Trick110nk Brave Grecian1132¾ Creme Countess1131¾	Gamely	8
22Jan93- 9Aqu	my	6f	⊡:223	:46	:583	1:121	Ⓕ Clm 14000	55	2	4	44½	54½	55	56	Graell A	117 b	*1.50	76-13	One Dumpling1121½ Laura's Secret1081½ Town Creek1151¾	Evenly	10
4Dec92- 3Aqu	fst	6f	⊡:23	:462	:584	1:121	3↑Ⓕ Clm 25000	64	7	2	21	31½	33	44½	Migliore R	117 b	4.40	77-13	Sharp Image1151¾ Company Girl1172½ Loosen UpLisa117nk	Finished evenly	7
23Nov92- 7Aqu	my	6f	:224	:464	:591	1:122	3↑Ⓕ Alw 27000	87	1	1	1hd	11	12½	13¾	Migliore R	117 b	*1.50	79-21	Brave Grecian1173¾ Sabal Way1174 Silvaplana115	Driving	6
2Nov92- 9Aqu	fst	6f	:221	:453	:582	1:114	3↑Ⓕ Clm c-14000	—	12	1	11	2hd	1315	—	Migliore R	117 b	*1.10	— 18	Town Creek1171 Betsy Bell115nk Mean Missy113	Gave way, eased	13
Claimed from Havman Eugene, Hushion Michael E Trainer																					
28Sep92- 9Bel	my	6f	:222	:453	:573	1:103	3↑Ⓕ Clm c-14000	81	4	1	12	13	12½	14	Davis R G	119 b	*.80	87-11	Brave Grecian1194 Rather Be Social1132½ Tiny Grasshopper117	Driving	5
Claimed from Kimran Stable, Toner James J Trainer																					

WORKOUTS: Aug 29 Sar tr.t 4f fst :50 B 6/23 Jun 13 Bel 5f fst 1:032 B 20/22 May 30 Bel tr.t 4f fst :49 B 5/18 Apr 16 Bel tr.t 4f fst :484 B 7/23

Brave Grecian was an overpowering winner on July 24 against a field of $17,500–$15,500 fillies, which is one step up from the basement level in New York. She recorded a Beyer of 82 — good enough to make her the favorite against a typical field of $25,000 sprinters, and competitive in some of the easier $35,000 spots. Had Gasper Moschera entered Brave Grecian two weeks later for $25,000 or $35,000, handicappers might've assumed she was razor-sharp and capable of handling the class rise in her present form. But Moschera didn't run Brave Grecian at all during the Saratoga meet, and she showed only one slow breeze at half a mile in the nearly six weeks that elapsed between starts, and she was *dropped* in class to $14,000 on September 2.

While there are no hard and fast rules in this game, here is one generally worth following: play devil's advocate with horses dropping in class after a big win. Moschera has been among the top claiming trainers in New York over the past decade, and he doesn't make it a practice to give anything away to rival trainers in the cutthroat claiming game; when he offered Brave Grecian for $14,000 off a six-week layoff and showing only one work, he was telling us that something was bothering his mare and that she would not run nearly as well as she had against a better class of fillies in her last start. At odds of 3–5, she finished a well-beaten fifth.

SUSPICIOUS DROPS

Betting against suspicious class-droppers needn't be confined to the basement level. When the overall record suggests rapid decline, handicappers should take a negative view of the animal. Claiming races were invented to bring together horses of similar abilities; run a horse worth $10,000 in a $5,000 claimer and you'll win the purse, but someone will surely claim your horse; run a horse worth $10,000 in a $20,000 claimer and no one will claim your horse, but you won't win any purse money, either. Operate on the theory that at the racetrack, as anywhere else, there is no such thing as a free lunch; in other words, nobody is giving anything away.

Twilight Looming
Own: Hackel Kenneth S
CHAVEZ J F (177 39 22 23 .22) $16,500

B. g. 3 (Mar)
Sire: Ogygian (Damascus)
Dam: Fun Forever (Never Bend)
Br: William H Floyd (Ky)
Tr: Galluscio Dominic G (20 3 5 3 .15)

115

Lifetime Record:	5 2 0 1	$43,316			
1993	4 2 0 1	$43,316	Turf	0 0 0 0	
1992	1 M 0 0		Wet	0 0 0 0	
Bel	2 0 0 1	$2,340	Dist	3 1 0 0	$22,243

12Aug93-10Sar fst 6f :22^2 :45^3 :57^4 1:10^2 Clm 25000 47 6 9 9$4\frac{3}{4}$ 9$4\frac{1}{2}$ 11$7\frac{1}{2}$ 12$14\frac{1}{4}$ Nelson D 117 *2.60 76-11 Super Forbes117^4 Carrnac113^{hd} Lost Pan117$1\frac{1}{2}$ No excuse 12
9Jly93-4Bel fst 7f :23^3 :46^4 1:10^4 1:23^1 Clm c-35000 68 2 6 1^{hd} 2^{hd} 3^2 3$6\frac{3}{4}$ Bisono C V5 117 2.40 80-10 SixThirtyTwo117$3\frac{1}{2}$ SminolCnyon117$3\frac{1}{4}$ TwilightLoomng117^{no} Dueled, tired 7
Claimed from Lukas D Wayne, Lukas D Wayne Trainer
20Jun93-3CD fst 6f :21^2 :45^2 :58^2 1:11^3 3↑ Alw 24000N1X 78 7 7 6^4 6$5\frac{1}{4}$ 3$1\frac{1}{2}$ 1^2 Romero R P L 113 *1.00 88-14 Twilight Looming113^2 Running Total115^1 Del Hil Man115$\frac{1}{2}$ 7
Awaited room split foes, 1-16
10Jun93-1CD fst 6½f :22^3 :46^2 1:11^3 1:18^1 3↑ Md Sp Wt 79 6 4 2^{hd} 1$1\frac{1}{2}$ 1$1\frac{1}{2}$ 1$3\frac{1}{2}$ Romero R P L 113 7.00 90-11 TwilightLooming113$3\frac{1}{2}$ VictoryTrl113$\frac{1}{2}$ [DH] OcoSundown113 Steady drive 11
17Sep92-5Bel fst 6f :22^3 :46^1 :58^1 1:11 Md Sp Wt 34 13 14 9$7\frac{1}{2}$ 10$5\frac{3}{4}$ 10^{13} 9$18\frac{3}{4}$ Solis A 118 42.40 66-18 Living Vicariously118$\frac{3}{4}$ Man's Hero118^{no} Digging In118 Broke slowly 14

WORKOUTS: Oct 4 Bel 5f fst 1:06 B *18/18* Sep 30 Bel 4f fst :47^4 H *2/69* Sep 25 Bel 3f fst :36 H *3/29* Sep 12 Bel 3f fst :39 B *26/27* Aug 6 Sar 5f fst 1:03 B *16/24*

Twilight Looming returned as a three-year-old to break his maiden impressively at Churchill Downs, dueling for the early lead and pulling away by three and a half lengths against special-weight rivals. Just ten days later, he demonstrated versatility by coming from off the pace and splitting rivals to win by two, despite being forced to await racing room in the stretch. At this point, Wayne Lukas looked to have a promising young horse, and the next logical spot would've been a nonwinners-of-two allowance. But instead, Lukas elected to put the horse up for sale in a $35,000 claimer at Belmont on July 9.

Reading between the lines, the unspoken message from Lukas was something like this: "I know his record looks pretty good, but I don't have any further use for him."

Twilight Looming's form declined on July 9, just as Lukas had suggested it would, as he weakened to finish nearly seven lengths behind at odds of 2–1. He was claimed from the race, and the negative profile grew even stronger on August 12, when, in his first start for new connections, he was offered for $25,000.

The crowd didn't read the signals, and saw only a horse with recent ability taking a drop in class. But Lukas had already given up on the horse by dropping him in for $35,000, and now his new connections were giving up on him too, offering him for $10,000 less than what they'd paid barely a month ago.

Twilight Looming finished last as the 5–2 favorite. He was then dropped to $16,500 on October 7, and finished fourth as the third choice in the wagering.

Importantly, handicappers could've anticipated Twilight Looming's decline as soon as Lukas gave him up and taken a position against him at short odds in three successive spots.

On October 15, 1992, The Great Carl was sixty cents to the dollar in a $35,000 claiming sprint, and Lord Cardinal was 60–1. Make a case for the longshot:

5

7 FURLONGS. **(1.20[2]) CLAIMING. Purse $20,000. 3-year-olds and upward. Weight: 3-year-olds 119 lbs., older 122 lbs. Non-winners of two races since September 15 allowed 3 lbs., of a race since then 5 lbs. Claiming Price $35,000. For each $2,500 to $30,000, 2 lbs. (Races when entered to be claimed for $25,000 or less not considered).**

The Great Carl — B. h. 5, by Star Choice—Dear Annie, by Impressive
ANTLEY C W (108 27 8 14 .25) — $35,000 — Br.—Clark William G (Ky)
Own.—Hackel Kenneth — Tr.—Lenzini John J Jr (4 0 0 0 .00) — 117

Lifetime							
40 8 5 9	1992	8	2	1	0	$58,076
$243,683	1991	13	2	1	7	$95,154
	Turf	20	2	2	5	$98,175
	Wet	3	1	1	0	$32,660

9Sep92- 9Med	fst	170	:452	1:094	1:391	3↑Alw 26000	85	7	1	1hd	1hd	2hd	45½	Nelson D	b	115	*.90	96–08	Cold Digger1151¾ Link1153¼ Regal Conquest115	Tired	7
22Aug92- 5Sar	fst	6f	:214	:441	1:082	3↑Alw 41000	88	5	2	1hd	2hd	21½	57½	Nelson D	b	119	5.60	94 —	SnrSpd1151¼SngsAccnt1152½FrmlDnnr115	Dueled inside	7
5Aug92- 3Sar	fst	7f	:222	:45	1:213	3↑Clm c-50000	104	5	2	2½	2½	1½	13	Perret C	b	117	3.00	97–07	TheGreatCarl1173GameWger1133¼Nymphist117	Driving	7
5Aug92-Claimed from Dogwood Stable, Vestal Peter M Trainer																					
4Jly92- 8FP	sly	1 1/16	:464	1:12	1:44	3↑Cardinal H	90	3	4	410	47	32½	45¼	Bruin J E		118	2.90	79–24	Jarrar1182FoundBuck115½OiltoReson113	Flattened out	7
14Jun92- 9RD	fm	1 1/16	Ⓣ:462	1:10	1:421	3↑Black Swan	83	9	8	74¼	43¾	63¾	65½	Sipus E J Jr	B	121	3.90	87–07	StrmyDp121nkRglAffr114nkHvnlyLgcy115	Lacked close	9
24May92- 8AP	sly	1	:46	1:111	1:371	3↑Equipoise M	102	2	6	54½	53½	2½	2½	Day P		113	*2.30e	79–25	KatahulCounty114½TheGretCrl1133Stlwrs116	4 wide trn	9
24May92-Grade III																					
10May92- 9CD	fst	1	:462	1:112	1:363	3↑Alw 39450	95	1	6	52¼	31½	11	13½	Bruin J E	B	115	2.70	94–06	ThGrtCrl1153½GunsofClo1125BgCourg115	Driving, clear	8
8Apr92- 9Kee	fm	1	Ⓣ:47	1:111	1:351	Alw 28800	82	2	4	41½	1hd	2hd	75	Bruin J E	B	114	8.20	98 —	Mxgrm111hdTkThtStp1121LrdJhn117	Wide backstretch	9
14Dec91- 9Haw	fst	170	:471	1:123	1:451	3↑Sun Beau	85	5	6	86	66	43	32½	Silva C H	b	115	*1.60	67–32	RnforYorHny1131¼WllfSlnc1111¼ThGrtCrl115	Mild rally	14
9Nov91- 7Haw	gd	1	Ⓣ:48	1:134	1:383	3↑R Carey H	98	1	5	55	46½	31½	34	Silva C H		118	12.10	71–25	SlewtheSlewor1141½Jljl1182½ThGrtCrl118	Mild wide bid	9

LATEST WORKOUTS Oct 6 Aqu 3f fst :372 B Aug 17 Sar tr.t 4f fst :493 H

Lord Cardinal — B. c. 4, by Deputy Minister—Katie Cochran, by Roberto
DAVIS R G (175 22 22 24 .13) — $32,500 — Br.—Ledyard Lewis C (Pa)
Own.—Barge Marc — Tr.—Reid Mark J (17 1 3 2 .06) — 115

Lifetime							
12 1 0 1	1992	5	0	0	1	$3,840
$24,180	1991	7	1	0	0	$20,340
	Turf	9	1	0	1	$22,980
	Wet	1	0	0	0	

28Sep92- 5Bel	sly	1 1/16	:464	1:11	1:432	3↑Clm c-25000	13	6	6	914	922	929	943¾	Antley C W	117	14.60	41–22	QckCommndr117hd[D]HdOrphn1084PcktStrkr119	Outrun	9
28Sep92-Claimed from Peace John H, Arnold George R II Trainer																				
21Sep92- 3Bel	fm	1 1/16	[T]:47	1:101	1:402	3↑Clm 35000	81	6	6	84¼	84¼	56½	66¾	Antley C W	117	5.90	89–11	Shs1173¾TurtleBech117¾CommissionerBrt117	No threat	10
4Sep92- 9Bel	yl	1	Ⓣ:461	1:11	1:362	3↑Clm 35000	74	11	7	94¼	83¼	44½	47	Antley C W	117	11.40	73–20	SthrnSl1172[D]Dr.Brtl1172TrnngFrHm119	Took up 1/2 pl	12
4Sep92-Placed third through disqualification																				
21Aug92- 5Sar	fm	1⅛	[T]:474	1:12	1:49	3↑Clm 35000	70	12	9	64	85½	108	1011	Davis R G	117	8.50	83–09	GldnExplsv117nkPrnc'sCv1173½A.M.Swngr117	Wide trip	12
9Aug92- 1Sar	gd	6f	:222	:45	1:092	3↑Clm 35000	77	5	7	74¼	66½	46½	47¼	Davis R G	117	29.50	90–06	LuckyTent115¾SunnyndPlesnt1176ShinPls113	No threat	7
13Oct91- 7Bel	fm	1⅜	[T]:464	1:363	2:142	3↑Alw 29000	83	8	5	65	42½	31	51¾	Smith M E	114	*1.50	77–20	Jill'sTank1141ExplosiveRule114nkCrownSalute107	Tired	8
8Sep91- 8Pim	fm	1 1/16	Ⓣ:462	1:103	1:43	Marylnd Turf	82	13	11	1210	812	68	58¾	Krone J A	117	7.40	81–10	Scttsll1171½SbtlStp1221½BbthBrd117	Passed tired ones	13
25Aug91- 6Sar	fm	1 1/16	[T]:481	1:122	1:431	3↑Alw 29000	82	4	5	67	76¼	53	42	Day P	112	5.40	90–13	GoldnExplosv112nkPnchpssr1171½MdvlClssc117	Lt rally	9
14Aug91- 7Sar	fm	1 1/16	Ⓣ:453	1:10	1:421	3↑Alw 29000	83	1	4	513	76	64	53	Smith M E	112	10.70	82–09	Wtmotl1121DoblDngr114nkGldnExplsv113	Saved ground	10
29Jly91- 7Sar	fm	1 1/16	[T]:47	1:113	1:421	3↑Alw 29000	64	3	4	53¼	41½	55½	514½	Krone J A	111	*1.20	82–04	Shasa112nkSpruceBaby1178LordofFlnders113	No threat	9

LATEST WORKOUTS Oct 8 Bel 4f fst :481 H Aug 18 Sar tr.t 4f gd :501 B

The Great Carl came within half a length of winning a Grade 3 stake in his third start of the season but was entered for a $50,000 tag and claimed just three starts later. After succumbing in a pair of speed duels against allowance horses, The Great Carl is now being dropped to $35,000 by John Lenzini. The Great Carl had whipped a $50,000 field by three lengths only three starts ago, so why wouldn't Lenzini enter him at the level from which he'd claimed him? Why take a $15,000 loss on the horse so quickly?

It should be obvious that Lenzini believes The Great Carl is not as good as he was a couple of months ago; the horse may be well meant, but Lenzini is probably hoping that someone will take the horse off his hands and cut his losses.

Lord Cardinal is not nearly as accomplished as The Great Carl, but, then again, he is not heading in the wrong direction either. In fact, he's only had three dirt races in his career, the two most recent of which came in the slop, and one over a "good" track at Saratoga in his first start of the year. He was claimed from the slop race, and the race is a throw-out, as he failed to handle the footing and was basically eased after dropping back early.

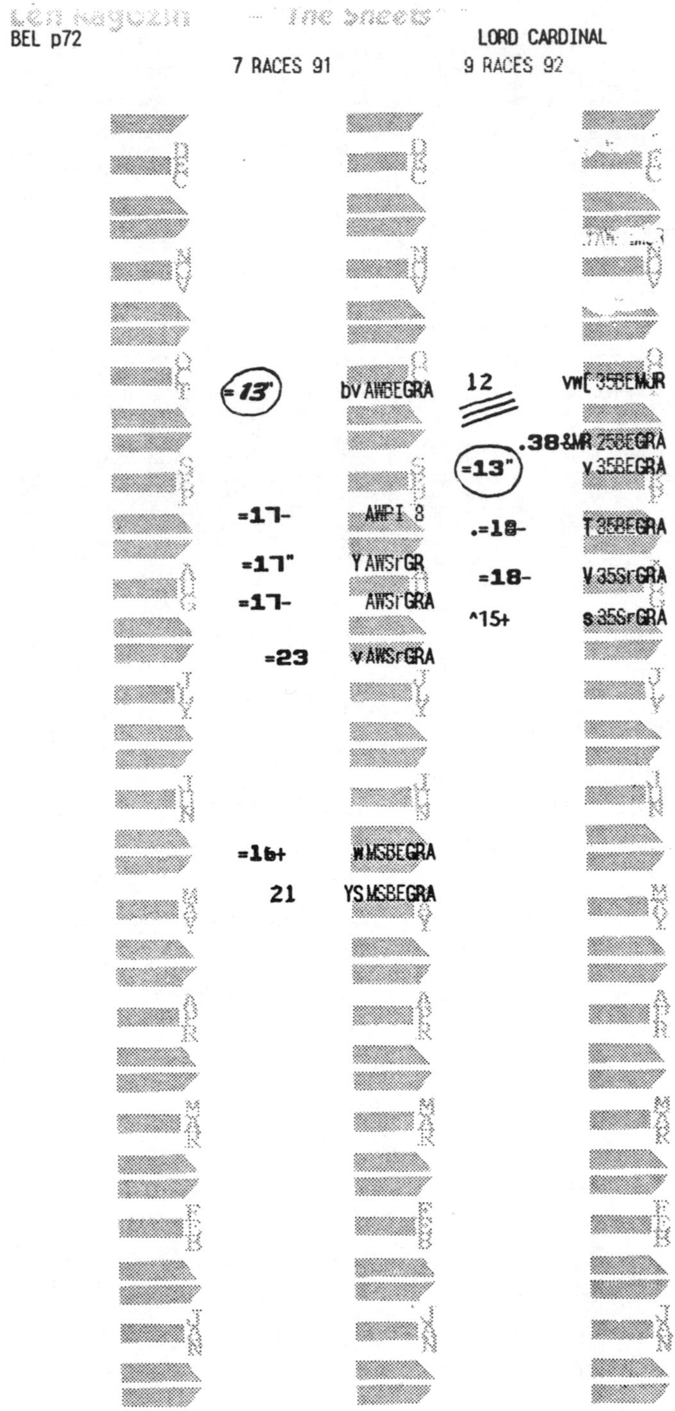
Len Ragozin — "The Sheets"
BEL p72
LORD CARDINAL
7 RACES 91
9 RACES 92
=13"
bv AWBEGRA
12
vw[35BEMJR
.38 &MR 25BEGRA
=13"
y 35BEGRA
=17-
AWPI 8
.=18-
T 35BEGRA
=17"
Y AWSrGR
=18-
V 35SrGRA
=17-
AWSrGRA
^15+
s 35SrGRA
=23
v AWSrGRA
=16+
w MSBEGRA
21
YS MSBEGRA

The 38 in the slop should be forgiven in light of the explosive line. The lightly raced colt closed out his three-year-old season by running a 13½, the best race of his career to date; in his fourth start at age four, he returned to that level with another 13½, which set him up nicely for a forward move.

The move was only a small one, down to a 12, but it was enough to catch The Great Carl by a nose at $122.20:

FIFTH RACE
Belmont
OCTOBER 15, 1992

7 FURLONGS. (1.20²) CLAIMING. Purse $20,000. 3-year-olds and upward. Weight: 3-year-olds 119 lbs., older 122 lbs. Non-winners of two races since September 15 allowed 3 lbs., of a race since then 5 lbs. Claiming Price $35,000. For each $2,500 to $30,000, 2 lbs. (Races when entered to be claimed for $25,000 or less not considered).

Value of race $20,000; value to winner $12,000; second $4,400; third $2,400; fourth $1,200. Mutuel pool $178,487. Exacta Pool $399,467

Last Raced	Horse	M/Eqt.	A.	Wt	PP	St	¼	½	Str	Fin	Jockey	Cl'g Pr	Odds $1
28Sep92 5Bel9	Lord Cardinal	b	4	115	9	2	31	3hd	21	1no	Davis R G	32500	60.10
9Sep92 9Med4	The Great Carl	b	5	117	1	7	1½	1½	11½	2nk	Antley C W	35000	.60
7Oct92 1Bel4	Eastern Brave	b	3	114	5	6	72	75	4hd	31¼	Maple E	35000	27.40
4Oct92 1Bel4	Stately Wager		4	117	4	4	6½	6hd	5½	46½	Chavez J F	35000	5.10
5Oct92 1Bel3	Curbex		4	117	2	1	2½	2hd	62½	5½	Carr D	35000	10.00
27Sep92 6Bel4	Fabersham	b	4	117	7	5	4½	43	3hd	63¼	Smith M E	35000	6.40
27Sep92 9Rkm4	Won the Laurel	b	4	117	6	9	9	9	82½	7hd	Duys D C	35000	17.20
27Sep92 8Bel9	Kellock	b	4	117	3	8	54	5½	71½	89	Migliore R	35000	11.30
23Oct89 8Aqu6	Activado-Ur		7	106	8	3	81	8½	9	9	RodriguzRR7	30000	28.30

OFF AT 3:01 Start good Won driving Time, :23¹, :46 , 1:10 , 1:22⁴ Track fast.

$2 Mutuel Prices:				
	9-(I)-LORD CARDINAL	122.20	24.80	15.20
	1-(A)-THE GREAT CARL		3.00	3.00
	5-(E)-EASTERN BRAVE			9.60

$2 EXACTA 9-1 PAID $394.80

B. c, by Deputy Minister—Katie Cochran, by Roberto. Trainer Reid Mark J. Bred by Ledyard Lewis C (Pa).

LORD CARDINAL forced the pace between horses while three wide into upper stretch and outgamed THE GREAT CARL under brisk urging. THE GREAT CARL, rushed up along the rail after breaking a step slowly, dueled along the inside for a half, opened a clear lead in midstretch, continued on the front into deep stretch and yielded grudgingly. EASTERN BRAVE, in tight at the start, raced well back for a half then rallied strongly along the inside but could not get up. STATELY WAGER, reserved for a half, circled four wide entering the stretch then rallied mildly in the middle of the track. CURBEX dueled between horses to the top of the stretch and tired. FABERSHAM raced in close contention while four wide to the turn then lacked a further response. WON THE LAUREL was never close after being pinched back at the start. KELLOCK, saved ground and tired. ACTIVADO was outrun.

Owners— 1, Barge Marc; 2, Hackel Kenneth; 3, Brophy Stable; 4, Cohen Robert B; 5, Pascuma Michael J; 6, Ken-Mort Stable; 7, Heubeck Harriet C; 8, Hauman Eugene E; 9, D'Amelio Frank O.

Trainers— 1, Reid Mark J; 2, Lenzini John J Jr; 3, Johnson Philip G; 4, Shapoff Stanley R; 5, Pascuma Warren J; 6, Skiffington Thomas J; 7, Grusmark Karl M; 8, Hushion Michael E; 9, D'Amelio Frank O.

The Great Carl was claimed by Joques Farm; trainer, Moschera Gasper S; Eastern Brave was claimed by Perroncino John; trainer, Terracciano Neal; Curbex was claimed by Jewel-E Stable; trainer, Ferriola Peter; Won the Laurel was claimed by Russo August; trainer, Hebert William.

There are situations when precipitous class drops should be evaluated a bit differently:

Easy Spender
Own: Corr John D
PRADO E S (38 5 4 1 .13) **$25,000**

Dk. b or br g. 4
Sire: Spend a Buck (Buckaroo)
Dam: Magic Lass (Damascus)
Br: Firestone Mr & Mrs B R (Fla)
Tr: Martin Jose (16 4 2 2 .25)

117

Lifetime Record :	19	7	0	0	$79,920						
1993	14	5	0	0	$57,900	Turf	3	1	0	0	$14,700
1992	5	2	0	0	$22,020	Wet	5	1	0	0	$10,620
Aqu ⊡	5	2	0	0	$23,820	Dist	0	0	0	0	

21Dec93- 9Aqu	my	1 1/16 ⊡	:241	:481	1:131	1:473	Clm 17500	89	6	1	11	13	17	111½	Santagata N	117 f	*2.90	67-38	Easy Spender11711 Cinnomen Bay117¾ Stack Um Up1082	Handily	9
29Nov93- 7Aqu	wf	7f	:222	:451	1:101	1:233	3↑ Alw 28000N1X	67	4	3	54½	34	46½	513½	Santagata N	115	14.20	72-18	In A Split Second1156 IslandersCure1154 ActiveDuty117nk	Saved ground	9
21Nov93- 9Aqu	fst	7f	:23	:461	1:114	1:252	Clm 25000	83	2	7	2½	1½	11½	11	Santagata N	117 f	7.90	77-20	Easy Spender1171 Bates Return119½ Pal's Memory1174¾	Driving	9
23Oct93- 1Aqu	fst	1	:233	:464	1:122	1:372	Clm 35000	45	1	1	1½	52¾	610	625	Leon F5	112 b	10.30	52-33	Tanako1172¾ Wet Reel1171¼ Six Thirty Two1174	Used in pace	6
14Oct93- 6Bel	fst	6f	:222	:454	:58	1:102	3↑ Alw 28000N1X	52	6	4	62½	73¾	68	717	Velazquez J R	114 fb	26.30	71-10	Man's Hero1143¾ Line Pro1143¾ Swindle1173¼	Checked 3/8 pl	9
3Oct93- 4Bel	my	1 1/16 ⊗	:231	:472	1:131	1:461	3↑ Alw 30000N1X	29	6	2	1½	53½	512	529	Velasquez J	114 fb	5.20	42-24	Track Beau114¾ In A Split Second1142¼ Baron Von Blixen11411	Gave way	6
30Sep93- 6Bel	fst	1⅛	:471	1:12	1:38	1:513	Clm c-25000	81	6	1	12½	12½	14	15	Migliore R	117 fb	*1.60	71-25	Easy Spender1175 Aarons Classi Boy1152¼ World Game1152	Driving	6
Claimed from Hauman Eugene E, Hushion Michael E Trainer																					
21Aug93- 1Sar	fst	1⅛	:46	1:111	1:37	1:501	3↑ Alw 28500N1X	68	7	2	23	23	56	511¾	Bailey J D	112 fb	*1.00e	73-10	CommitteeChairman1123 IslandersCure112½ ZeusEnergy1121¼	Gave way	9
9Aug93- 4Sar	fm	1⅛ Ⓣ	:472	1:12	1:363	1:484	Clm c-50000	56	8	1	1hd	2½	53	1015	Smith M E	117 b	*2.00	79-05	Same Old Wish1153 T. Barone117½ Peter And1171½	Bumped break, tired	12
Claimed from Mott William I, Mott William I Trainer																					
4Jly93- 6Bel	yl	1 1/16 Ⓣ	:24	:472	1:112	1:431	3↑ Alw 28500N1X	73	3	1	1½	1hd	52½	69¾	Smith M E	111 b	3.40	70-23	Talb1172 Threeharvardavenue1172¾ Palace Piper1132	Speed, tired	9

WORKOUTS: ●Jan 3 Bel tr.t 4f fst :472 H 1/44 Dec 17 Bel tr.t 4f fst :491 B 6/78 Nov 17 Bel tr.t 4f fst :483 H 6/32 Nov 12 Bel tr.t 5f fst 1:02 B 5/9

Easy Spender won for $25,000 on November 21, and was entered for $17,500 two starts later, winning by nearly a dozen lengths as a lukewarm choice at nearly 3–1. At the time, Easy Spender was closing out his three-year-old season. All three-year-olds become four-year-olds on January 1, at which time they must compete against older claiming horses. Typically, a three-year-old who can compete successfully for $35,000 against its own age group will require a drop to $17,500 to be effective against older horses. Easy Spender had one last chance to race against three-year-olds on December 21, and trainer Jose Martin was well aware that whoever claimed him that day would be forced to run him against older horses for the rest of his career. This was a case of a horse taking a *well-meant* drop in class.

FAVORITES THAT OPEN WELL ABOVE THEIR MORNING-LINE ODDS

In *Kinky Handicapping,* respected handicapping author Mark Cramer refers to favorites opening above their morning-line odds as "The Kiss of Death." The morning-line odds found in the track program are an educated estimate of how the wagering is expected to go; a horse expected to be favored will usually be listed at odds higher than what he'll actually close at, so as to encourage betting. When a morning-line favorite opens above those already inflated odds, says Cramer, it is not a good sign. Random checks of his theory in New York during the winter and early spring of 1994 suggest he wasn't exaggerating.

During the early part of April, for example, the following horses opened well above their morning-line odds, and ran miserably:

Horse	Morning Line	Open	Close	Finish
Glory's Winner	2–1	9–2	8–5	Last of 8
Sturdy Dancer	8–5	5–2	6–5	4th by 17
He's Spectacular	5–2	9–2	8–5	Last of 7
Facetious Buck	5–2	7–1	5–2	7th by 19
Wild Child	5–2	6–1	7–2	5th by 7
Sovereign Shield	3–1	6–1	9–2	Eased

When a horse's published record is good enough to merit favoritism on the morning line, and its virtues are readily apparent to even the most casual handicapper, it's a bad sign when the horse fails to attract strong support during the early stages of the betting. Inevitably, this type of horse gets bet down in the closing minutes by those believing they have found the "value" in the race. In actuality, all they have found is the Kiss of Death.

FIVE

ANGLES

THE MOST SUCCESSFUL PLAYERS do not handicap races the night before, come up with two or three solid selections, and merely show up at the track or simulcast outlet to bet on them. The process just isn't as mechanical as that.

An intensive handicapping session should not be geared toward finding winners, but, rather, toward accumulating and organizing pertinent data relative to the contenders, how the races figure to be run, and how they figure to be bet by the crowd. As each post time nears, additional factors, such as weather, track bias, late scratches, and physical appearance, are weighted against the odds, and the intuitive process takes over.

Intuition guides decision making, but for this creative and artistic process to flow smoothly, a handicapper must do his homework and have a thorough understanding of each race, even if it is only to realize, "I don't understand this race, therefore I won't bet on it."

What follows, then, is an informal and loosely organized discussion about angles that might trigger an inspired moment for handicappers and cause them to dig deeper into a horse's past performances.

FIRST TIME FOR A TAG

Whenever a horse is dropping to a claiming race for the first time and it is the only entrant with that distinction, it deserves close inspection, for its connections are now taking a risk that their runner will be claimed away from them. If the horse has shown some ability against nonclaiming competition and is now entered for a fairly high price — $50,000 or so — it may own a class edge.

Heavy Rain
Own: McDonald James C

Dk. b or br g. 6
Sire: Wild Again (Icecapade)
Dam: Rain Chaser (Ben Adhem)
Br: Calumet Farm (Fla)
Tr: Lukas D Wayne (11 5 1 0 .45)

122

Lifetime Record: 48 7 6 5 $239,371											
1994	1	1	0	0	$12,600	Turf	29	5	4	1	$148,993
1993	9	0	1	3	$24,543	Wet	3	1	1	1	$36,240
GP ⓣ	1	1	0	0	$12,600	Dist ⓣ	2	1	0	0	$21,600

23Jan94-10GP	fm	*1⅜ ⓣ	:51	1:18	1:44^{1}	2:20^{3}	Clm 40000	89	1	5	7$^{3\frac{1}{4}}$	5$^{2\frac{1}{2}}$	2$^{\frac{1}{2}}$	1^{hd}	Bailey J D	L 117	4.90	71-23	Heavy Rain117^{hd} Caveat's Image117$^{2\frac{3}{4}}$ WonTheLaurel117$^{1\frac{1}{2}}$	Fully extended	10
26Dec93-10Lrl	fst	1¼	:49^{1}	1:13^{4}	1:38^{3}	2:03^{2}	3↑ Congrssnal H75k	82	9	6	6^{5}	7$^{9\frac{1}{2}}$	8^{14}	8^{15}	Chavez S N	L 108	62.80	75-23	Northern Launch114$^{2\frac{1}{4}}$ Greatsilverfleet112$^{2\frac{3}{4}}$ Ameri Valay115$^{2\frac{1}{4}}$	Gave way	9
16Dec93-8Pha	fst	1⅛	:48^{3}	1:14^{2}	1:41^{2}	1:55^{1}	3↑ Alw 25000R	84	3	7	7^{12}	7^{10}	4$^{9\frac{1}{2}}$	3$^{10\frac{1}{4}}$	Molina V H	L 116	8.60	52-43	Northern Launch116$^{4\frac{3}{4}}$ Accession116$^{5\frac{1}{2}}$ Heavy Rain116^{3}	No factor	7
19Nov93-8Aqu	yl	1⅛ ⓣ	:50^{1}	1:15	1:40^{1}	1:51^{3}	3↑ Alw 44000N$mY	81	1	7	7$^{5\frac{1}{2}}$	6$^{5\frac{1}{2}}$	6$^{2\frac{3}{4}}$	5^{6}	Velazquez J R	117	18.20	79-15	Daarik117$^{1\frac{1}{2}}$ Pride Of Summer117^{2} Bisbalense117$^{\frac{1}{2}}$	Saved ground	10
8Nov93-8Aqu	fst	1	:23^{4}	:46^{2}	1:10^{2}	1:36	3↑ Alw 44000N$mY	53	7	9	8^{10}	9^{10}	9^{16}	9$^{25\frac{1}{4}}$	Samyn J L	117	40.90	59-25	Itaka115$^{6\frac{3}{4}}$ Nymphist117$^{\frac{3}{4}}$ Farewell Wave110^{nk}	Outrun	9
3Jly93-7Bel	sf	1⅜ ⓣ	:50^{2}	1:14^{3}	1:40	2:17^{3}	3↑ Bwlng Grn H-G2	88	4	8	8$^{6\frac{1}{2}}$	7$^{4\frac{1}{4}}$	5^{5}	4^{10}	Samyn J L	109	30.60	69-33	Dr. Kiernan114^{4} Spectacular Tide111^{3} Lomitas117^{3}	Checked early	9
13Jun93-5Bel	fm	1½ ⓣ	:48	1:12^{3}	2:00^{4}	2:25^{1}	3↑ Handicap46k	93	3	8	7$^{5\frac{1}{2}}$	5^{2}	3$^{1\frac{1}{2}}$	3^{2}	Krone J A	118	6.10	94-09	Dr. Kiernan114^{2} Wanderkin113^{no} Heavy Rain118$^{\frac{1}{2}}$	Willingly	10
29May93-9Pim	fm	1½ ⓣ	:47^{1}	1:12^{2}	2:02^{4}	2:28	3↑ Riggs H75k	101	1	12	8$^{9\frac{3}{4}}$	7^{4}	7$^{3\frac{3}{4}}$	5$^{2\frac{1}{2}}$	Moorefield W T	L 110	43.00	120 —	Gary Gumbo115^{1} Futurist119$^{1\frac{1}{4}}$ Rebuff114^{no}	Willingly	12
15May93-8GS	fm	1$\frac{1}{16}$ ⓣ	:23^{2}	:46^{2}	1:11	1:42^{2}	3↑ Handicap20k	90	2	8	8^{13}	7^{8}	5$^{2\frac{3}{4}}$	2$^{1\frac{1}{2}}$	Torres C A	L 115	7.00	100-04	Royal Ninja119$^{1\frac{1}{2}}$ Heavy Rain115^{hd} New Identity110$^{1\frac{1}{4}}$	Up for place	8
3May93-11Del	fst	1	:24^{1}	:48	1:13^{3}	1:39^{3}	3↑ Alw 9300N1Y	72	6	6	5^{6}	2^{hd}	2^{hd}	3$^{2\frac{1}{4}}$	Torres C A	L 114	*1.30	83-22	Midas113$^{\frac{3}{4}}$ Slewpy Slew116$^{1\frac{1}{2}}$ Heavy Rain114$^{5\frac{3}{4}}$	Held well	6

WORKOUTS: Jan 18 GP 4f sly :49^{1} B *3/21* Jan 11 GP 4f gd :51 B *35/38*

When Wayne Lukas dropped Twilight Looming in for a tag, it was a strong negative signal, because the horse was lightly raced and had just won two in a row.

Lukas dropped Heavy Rain to a claimer for the first time on January 23 at Gulfstream, but this was a positive drop, because the horse had recently demonstrated that it *needed* softer company. Those who were unwilling to excuse Heavy Rain's poor recent finishes dismissed him a bit too early in the handicapping process. While it's true the gelding had been beaten by more than fifty-six lengths in four combined starts since the layoff, note the conditions under which they were run: three dirt races and one over yielding turf. His three races over firm turf in 1993 corresponded with his best Beyer figures, and the presence of Jerry Bailey was an additional signal that Lukas, who had won with five of his first eleven starts at the Gulfstream meet, was spotting the horse for a win. This is the class drop/jockey switch angle popularized by Mark Cramer. At odds of 9–2, Heavy Rain was a reasonable class-angle play.

FIRST TRY AGAINST RESTRICTED CLAIMERS

By now, handicappers are well aware that the drop from maiden special-weight to maiden-claiming is the most powerful class drop in all of racing. As a result, such horses routinely return lower mutuels than they did a few years ago. The same principles apply with horses dropping from open to restricted claimers, but the public hasn't made as strong a connection with this move. These claiming races, restricted to those horses that have never won two races in their careers, are a staple of the Racing Secretary's condition book from late fall to early spring. Often, recent form and beaten lengths have little to do with the outcome, especially when one entrant is dropping down to the nonwinners-of-two-lifetime condition for the first time.

Halo Habit
Own: Paxson Mrs Henry D

Dk. b or br g. 5
Sire: Halo (Hail to Reason)
Dam: Force o' Habit (Habitony)
Br: Paxson Mrs H D (Ky)
Tr: Windridge Marianne (3 1 0 0 .33)

122

Lifetime Record:	12	2	1	1	$28,780						
1994	1	1	0	0	$8,400	Turf	1	0	0	0	$450
1993	6	1	0	0	$10,900	Wet	3	1	0	1	$12,600
Aqu ⊡	4	1	1	0	$13,680	Dist	3	2	0	0	$18,850

12Jan94-4Aqu	wf	1⅛ ⊡	:474	1:13	1:40	1:531	Clm 25000N2L	88	9	1	11	11	11	14	Luzzi M J	117 fb	7.10	70–31	Halo Habit1174 Majesty's Man1173 Precisely David113no	Driving	11
23Dec93-6Aqu	fst	1⅛ ⊡	:491	1:144	1:404	1:533	3+ Alw 30000N1X	67	3	3	32	31	511	517¾	Davis R G	117 fb	13.40	57–36	Sailing On Aprayer1175 Selective Surgery1159½ Woodster1102	Tired	5
30May93-10GG	fm	1⅜ Ⓣ	:493	1:144	1:391	2:174	Clm 20000	78	3	1	11	1hd	41	54½	Baze R A	LB 117 fb	5.10	75–13	Jetskier117no Worry Free117½ Speak Firm1172	Gave way	7
17Apr93-5SA	fst	1 1/16	:231	:472	1:113	1:424	Clm 25000	75	2	3	31½	42	47	713½	Almeida G F	LB 115 b	29.80	76–16	Tank's Spirit1197 Bold Current1151¾ Skylaunch116nk	Wide trip	10
3Apr93-1SA	fst	1 1/16	:224	:46	1:104	1:432	Alw 36000N2L	76	2	3	44½	35½	58½	67¼	Almeida G F	LB 117 b	15.60	80–12	Private Policy1172½ Bad Boy Butch117½ L'honorable120¾	No mishap	9
3Mar93-2SA	fst	1⅛	:472	1:123	1:381	1:513	Md 40000	85	6	2	2hd	2hd	11½	1¾	Almeida G F	LB 120 b	10.10	72–22	Halo Habit120¾ Crimson Leaf1183½ Call Me Wild1181½	4 Wide 1st turn	11
18Feb93-6SA	sly	1 1/16	:23	:47	1:12	1:432	Md 40000	61	3	7	86¼	97¾	811	616¼	Walls M K	LB 119 b	6.20e	71–15	Lend The Gold1193½ Crimson Leaf1172¾ Buck Tide118½	Lugged out	9
28Nov92-3Hol	fst	1 1/16	:224	:46	1:101	1:42	3+ Md Sp Wt	50	6	6	75¾	67½	715	723½	Steiner J J	B 118 b	*.70	68–14	Great1212 Please Pause Paul118nk Fort Valley1182	No rally	9
24Oct92-6SA	my	1	:23	:471	1:13	1:402	3+ Md Sp Wt	73	8	6	65¾	64½	56	37¼	Castro J M	B 117 b	5.20	58–32	Mr. Coconuts1175 Please Pause Paul1172¼ Halo Habit117	5 wide stretch	8
8Oct92-6SA	fst	6f	:214	:444	:57	1:093	3+ Md Sp Wt	71	1	7	96¼	85½	86	73½	Castro J M	B 117 b	51.50	84–12	Altanero117½ Atlantian1171½ Alythree117	4-wide stretch	9

WORKOUTS: Jan 6 Bel tr.t 5f fst 1:03 B *6/29* Jan 1 Bel tr.t 3f fst :382 B *8/10* Dec 19 Bel tr.t 4f my :514 B *2/4* Nov 13 Bel 4f fst :483 H *6/23* Nov 8 Bel 4f fst :491 H *12/27* Nov 2 Bel 4f fst :522 B *20/20*

Halo Habit typified the desired profile in his win at 7–1 on January 12 — a horse who has never lost against restricted claimers. The gelding had shown early speed on grass and dirt in two starts against open claimers in California prior to a layoff of seven months, and had returned December 23 showing speed through the opening six furlongs of an allowance route. Dropped in with nonwinners-of-two-races-lifetime claimers on January 12, he wired the field by four lengths. Note the recurring form pattern as well: Halo Habit's maiden victory was also accomplished second time back from a layoff at nine furlongs.

The crowd usually overbets last-out finish positions and beaten lengths, so overlays are frequent in these restricted claiming races on horses that have been losing to tougher opponents. Prior to Halo Habit's win, several previous restricted claiming races at Aqueduct's winter meet were garnered by horses that had been well beaten in tougher company in their most recent starts:

Winner	Class prior race	Beaten lengths
Dream Prosperous	Open $35K clmg	9
Five Star General	Allowance	3
La Vie Dansant	Allowance	13
Bronto Bill	Allowance	3
Pucker Lips	Open $50K clmg	7
Sand Kicker	Open $16K clmg	15
Back Bay Brittany	Allowance	8

In restricted claiming races, the old adage "class will tell" often proves the key.

FOR WHOM WAS THE RACE WRITTEN?

As I mentioned earlier, one of the first things to do in the handicapping process is to read the fine print of the conditions and compare them to the records of the horses. Sometimes, it will be readily apparent that the race was written by the Racing Secretary with one horse specifically in mind:

Incinerate
Own: Hobeau Farm
LEON F (63 8 5 6 .13)

Ch. f. 4
Sire: Groovy (Norcliffe)
Dam: Horsafire (Hold Your Peace)
Br: Elcee H Stable (Fla)
Tr: Jerkens H Allen (35 8 4 7 .23)

121

Lifetime Record:	32 6 4 6	$141,870			
1994	4 3 1 0	$56,560	Turf	3 0 0 0	$400
1993	17 2 2 3	$52,610	Wet	3 0 0 2	$6,060
Bel	12 1 1 2	$28,100	Dist	0 0 0 0	

22Mar94-6Aqu	fst	7f		$:23^2$	$:47^3$	$1:12^3$	$1:25^3$		ⒻAlw 30000N3X	83	5	2	4^4	$4^{2\frac{1}{2}}$	$3^{3\frac{1}{2}}$	1^{nk}	Leon F	119 b	1.70	76-26	Incinerate119^{nk} Cala Star$117^{1\frac{3}{4}}$ Sassa Blue117^5	Blckd, alt crs, drvg	5
19Feb94-7Aqu	fst	6f	⊡	$:23^1$	$:46^2$	$:59$	$1:11^3$		ⒻAlw 28000N2X	82	7	6	$7^{6\frac{1}{2}}$	$6^{4\frac{1}{2}}$	$5^{1\frac{1}{2}}$	1^1	Leon F	117 b	*1.10e	85-14	Incinerate117^1 Personal Girl$117^{\frac{3}{4}}$ Obligated Sue117^4	Wide, driving	7
3Feb94-6Aqu	fst	6f	⊡	$:22^3$	$:46^2$	$:59^2$	$1:13$		ⒻAlw 28000N2X	78	2	8	$8^{8\frac{3}{4}}$	$8^{5\frac{1}{2}}$	$4^{5\frac{1}{2}}$	$2^{\frac{1}{2}}$	Leon F5	114 b	3.10e	77-23	Tuesday Edition$112^{\frac{1}{2}}$ Incinerate114^2 Figi Bidders117^{nk}	Gamely	8
2Jan94-2Aqu	fst	6f	⊡	$:23^3$	$:48^2$	$1:01^2$	$1:14^1$		ⒻAlw 26000N1X	74	2	8	$8^{7\frac{3}{4}}$	$6^{5\frac{1}{2}}$	$3^{2\frac{1}{2}}$	1^{hd}	Leon F5	112 b	2.30e	72-27	Incinerate112^{hd} Our Dear Dana117^5 Auila117^7	Up final strides	8
13Nov93-9Aqu	fst	7f		$:23^1$	$:46^4$	$1:11^3$	$1:24^3$		ⒻClm 35000	64	9	2	7^4	$6^{2\frac{1}{2}}$	4^7	$4^{6\frac{3}{4}}$	Maple E	116 b	4.40	74-14	Megaroux116^4 Track City Girl$109^{3\frac{1}{2}}$ Meadow Quick116^{nk}	Four wide	9
29Oct93-8Aqu	fst	7f		$:22^3$	$:46$	$1:11^1$	$1:24^3$	3↑	ⒻAlw 28000N1X	72	2	8	8^8	$7^{5\frac{1}{4}}$	3^5	2^5	Maple E	114 b	4.50	76-16	Fleeting Ways114^5 Incinerate$114^{5\frac{1}{2}}$ Splendid Launch114^2	Checked break	8
20Oct93-2Aqu	sly	1		$:24^1$	$:48$	$1:13^1$	$1:38^2$		ⒻClm 45000	69	3	4	$4^{1\frac{1}{2}}$	$4^{1\frac{3}{4}}$	$4^{3\frac{1}{2}}$	$3^{6\frac{1}{4}}$	Samyn J L	112 b	13.00	66-29	Alkris$118^{1\frac{1}{4}}$ Gail On The Run114^5 Incinerate$112^{1\frac{1}{2}}$	No late bid	6
9Oct93-2Bel	fst	7f		$:23^1$	$:47^3$	$1:12^4$	$1:25^1$	3↑	ⒻAlw 28000N1X	68	2	2	3^2	$4^{1\frac{1}{2}}$	4^3	4^7	Samyn J L	114 b	9.20	70-23	Bold As Silver109^{nk} Regal Solution$114^{\frac{3}{4}}$ Shady Willow117^6	Lacked rally	6
23Sep93-5Bel	my	7f		$:22^3$	$:46^2$	$1:12^1$	$1:25^2$	3↑	ⒻAlw 28000N1X	65	2	7	$8^{8\frac{1}{4}}$	$8^{6\frac{1}{4}}$	$5^{2\frac{3}{4}}$	$5^{7\frac{1}{2}}$	Samyn J L	113 b	12.90	68-26	Pleasant Courtney$100^{\frac{3}{4}}$ Bold As Silver$113^{1\frac{3}{4}}$ Stormbow$113^{4\frac{3}{4}}$	No factor	8
11Sep93-2Bel	gd	7f		$:23^1$	$:46^3$	$1:10^4$	$1:22^3$	3↑	ⒻAlw 28000N1X	72	3	5	5^6	$5^{3\frac{3}{4}}$	$5^{5\frac{1}{4}}$	$4^{9\frac{1}{2}}$	Samyn J L	113 b	4.60	80-11	For All Seasons113^9 Regal Solution113^{hd} Fleeting Ways$113^{\frac{1}{2}}$	No threat	6

WORKOUTS: ●May 14 Bel tr.t 4f fst $:48^1$ H 1/13 May 7 Bel tr.t 6f fst 1:18 B 1/1 Apr 29 Bel tr.t 4f fst $:48^3$ H 4/20 Apr 23 Bel 4f fst :49 B 19/39 Apr 5 Bel tr.t 4f fst $:50^4$ B 24/26 Mar 12 Bel tr.t 4f fst $:50^4$ B 30/34

Handicappers had to respect the chances of Incinerate when she returned from a two-month layoff on May 29. She had returned from a similar absence with a victory at the beginning of the year, and had turned into one of the most improved fillies in New York, advancing quickly through the nonwinners allowance conditions.

Incinerate's recent and regularly spaced workouts included a bullet :48⅕ over the training track May 14, which was a tip-off that she would again run well off the layoff. But the clincher was the fine print in the conditions:

6½ Furlongs. **(1:14³) ALLOWANCE. Purse $40,000. Fillies and mares, 3-year-olds and upward which have not won $8,500 twice since February 20. Weights: 3-year-olds, 115 lbs. Older, 124 lbs. Non-winners of $25,000 since August 1, allowed 3 lbs. (Maiden, claiming, starter and restricted races not considered.)**

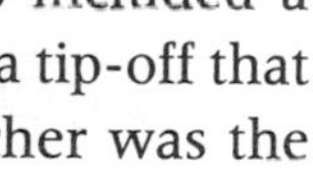

The race was for fillies and mares aged three and up that had not won $8,500 twice since *February 20.* A scan of Incinerate's past performances showed a win on March 22 and a second win on *February 19.*

Incinerate's second win came *24 hours* prior to the cutoff date.

Coincidence? Hardly. Incinerate won a race written especially for her, and paid $11.60 in a six-horse field.

Less than a week later, Distinct Reality recorded the best Beyer figure of his career in winning a six-furlong classified allowance on June 2. Could the performance have been anticipated?

Belmont Park

8 *6 Furlongs.* (1:07^4) **ALLOWANCE. Purse $40,000. 3–year–olds and upward which have not won three races of $7,800 since July 5, 1993. Weights: 3–year–olds, 114 lbs. Older, 122 lbs. Non–winners of a race of $20,000 since March 1, allowed 2 lbs. Of such a race since August 1, 4 lbs. (Maiden, claiming, starter and restricted races not considered.)**

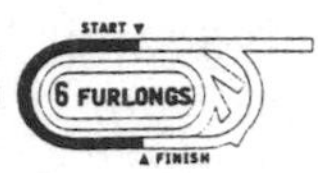

Distinct Reality
Own: Can Am Stables
LUZZI M J (119 18 15 13 .15)

Dk. b or br c. 3 (Apr)
Sire: Distinctive Pro (Mr. Prospector)
Dam: Cornish Art (Cornish Prince)
Br: Rankin R Alex & Wright Louis (Ky)
Tr: Hough Stanley M (19 4 4 2 .21)

112

Lifetime Record:	11	4	3	1	$177,277						
1994	3	0	2	0	$26,177	Turf	2	1	1	0	$27,650
1993	8	4	1	1	$151,100	Wet	0	0	0	0	
Bel	2	2	0	0	$81,570	Dist	6	1	2	1	$67,657

15May94-9Pim fst	6f		:22^2	:45^3	:58^2	1:11^2	Hrsch Jacobs54k	**86**	3	7	7^{6½}	6^{4½}	3^{nk}	2^{nk}	Pino M G	114	3.40	90-11	Foxie G114^{nk} Distinct Reality114^{¾} Spartan's Hero1141^{½}	Wide, lugged in	7	
26Feb94-5GP fst	7f		:22^1	:44^3	1:09^2	1:21^4	Alw 40000N$Y	**40**	6	2	3^{nk}	2^{hd}	5^{8¾}	6^{26¼}	Bailey J D	115	*1.00	68-13	Road Rush1152^{¾} Rustic Light1151^{½} Meadow Flight115^6		6	
Six wide top str, stopped																						
5Jan94-8GP fst	6f		:23	:46^2	:58^3	1:10^1	Spec Bid BC74k	**87**	3	4	2^{hd}	2^{hd}	2^{1½}	2^{3¾}	Bailey J D	119 b	2.10	86-14	Halo'sImage1143^{¾} DistinctReality119^{nk} SenorConquistdor1131^{¼}	Weakened	7	
4Dec93-7Aqu fst	6f	⊡	:22^1	:45	:57^4	1:10^4	Perpetuate54k	**61**	3	7	4^{2½}	4^3	6^{5¼}	6^{11}	Bailey J D	122	*1.00	78-16	Rizzi117^{nk} End Sweep1197^{½} Mr. Flintlock119^{nk}	Tired	7	
29Oct93-8Med fst	6f		:22^2	:45^2	:57^4	1:10^3	Comet35k	**88**	3	2	1^{hd}	2^{hd}	1^1	1^{5¾}	Bailey J D	120	*1.50	88-18	Distinct Reality1205^{¾} Storm Street1131^{¾} Bermuda Cedar113^1	Driving	5	
9Oct93-9Med fm	1	Ⓣ	:22	:45^4	1:10^1	1:36	World Appl35k	**80**	3	3	4^{5½}	3^{4½}	2^{2½}	2^{1¼}	Bravo J	120	*1.50	92-11	Shananie's Boss1121^{¼} Distinct Reality1204^{¾} British Raj1159^{½}	Best of rest	11	
25Sep93-8Med yl	5f	Ⓣ	:22^1	:46^4		1:00	Littl Lion35k	**70**	3	5	3^{1½}	2^{1½}	2^1	1^{nk}	Bailey J D	120	2.50	77-23	Distinct Reality120^{nk} Shananie's Boss113^2 Three Timer120^{nk}	Driving	8	
13Aug93-8Sar fst	6f		:22^1	:45^4	:58^1	1:10^2	Sanford-G3	**63**	1	2	1^{hd}	1^{hd}	3^{1½}	3^{10½}	Bailey J D	122	9.20	79-07	Dehere122^5 Prenup1155^{½} Distinct Reality1222^{¾}	Dueled, tired	6	
29Jly93-9Sar fst	6f		:21^4	:45	:57^2	1:09^4	Sar Special-G2	**68**	9	2	2^{½}	2^{½}	2^{½}	4^8	Bailey J D	122	3.00	85-10	Dehere117^{nk} Slew Gin Fizz117^2 Whitney Tower1175^{¾}	Bid, tired	9	
5Jly93-9Bel fst	5½f		:21^1	:44^4	:57^4	1:04^3	Tremont B C-G3	**76**	4	2	3^{3½}	3^{2½}	2^{hd}	1^2	Bailey J D	115	8.40	92-09	Distinct Reality115^2 Gusto Z1151^{½} Slew Gin Fizz1153^{½}	Driving	7	

WORKOUTS: May 31 Bel 4f fst :52^2 B *22/24* ●May 25 Bel 4f fst :46^2 H *1/35* ●May 10 Bel 6f fst 1:10^2 H *1/16* May 4 Bel 4f fst :48^3 B *13/56* Apr 29 Bel 5f fst :58^4 H *6/34* Apr 23 Bel 5f fst :59^3 H *4/41*

The race was for those that had not won three races of $7,800 since July 5, 1993. Whaddya know? — Distinct Reality's third win back had come in Belmont's Tremont Stakes (he was two for two over the track) on *July 5, 1993*.

The colt won by a length and a quarter, earning a Beyer of 107 and paying $8.60 in a six-horse field.

EIGHTH RACE
Belmont
JUNE 2, 1994

6 FURLONGS. (1.07^4) ALLOWANCE. Purse $40,000. 3–year–olds and upward which have not won three races of $7,800 since July 5, 1993. Weights: 3–year–olds, 114 lbs. Older, 122 lbs. Non–winners of a race of $20,000 since March 1, allowed 2 lbs. Of such a race since August 1, 4 lbs. (Maiden, claiming, starter and restricted races not considered.)

Value of Race: $40,000 Winner $24,000; second $8,800; third $4,800; fourth $2,400. Mutuel Pool $166,852.00 Exacta Pool $299,170.00

Last Raced	Horse	M/Eqt.	A.	Wt	PP	St	¼	½	Str	Fin	Jockey	Odds $1
15May94 ^{9}Pim^2	Distinct Reality		3	112	2	1	2^{½}	2^{hd}	1^{½}	1^{1¼}	Luzzi M J	3.30
6Nov93 ^{9}SA^5	Harlan	b	5	120	5	3	3^2	3^2	2^{½}	2^{3½}	Bailey J D	2.90
15May94 ^{9}Bel^2	Golden Tent	bf	5	118	4	6	5^4	4^{1½}	4^2	3^{2½}	Migliore R	a-5.10
19May94 ^{7}Bel^1	Lukie's Pop	f	4	118	1	4	1^1	1^{½}	3^1	4^{½}	Chavez J F	1.30
17Mar94 ^{9}OP^1	Zimmerman		4	118	3	5	6	6	6	5^1	Smith M E	6.30
5Mar94 ^{7}Aqu^3	Peerless Performer	f	5	118	6	2	4^1	5^2	5^{hd}	6	Lovato F Jr	a-5.10

a–Coupled: Golden Tent and Peerless Performer.

OFF AT 4:29 Start Good. Won driving. Time, :22^2, :45, :56^4, 1:09 Track fast.

$2 Mutuel Prices:	3–(B)–DISTINCT REALITY	8.60	3.20	3.20
	5–(E)–HARLAN		4.00	2.60
	1–(D)–GOLDEN TENT (a–entry)			2.80
	$2 EXACTA 3–5 PAID $36.00			

Dk. b. or br. c, (Apr), by Distinctive Pro–Cornish Art, by Cornish Prince. Trainer Hough Stanley M. Bred by Rankin R Alex & Wright Louis (Ky).

DISTINCT REALITY forced the pace between horses for a half, surged to the front in upper stretch then turned back HARLAN under brisk urging. HARLAN stalked the leaders while three wide into upper stretch, made a run to threaten in midstretch but was no match for the winner. GOLDEN TENT broke in the air slightly at the start, was unhurried early, swung out on the turn, then lacked a strong closing bid. LUKIE'S POP set the pace along the inside into upper stretch and tired. ZIMMERMAN never reached contention. PEERLESS PERFORMER faded after going a half. GOLDEN TENT and PEERLESS PERFORMER wore mud caulks.

Owners— 1, Can-Am Stable; 2, Young William T; 3, Hauman Eugene E; 4, Joadea Stables; 5, Loblolly Stable; 6, Hagedorn Charles G

Trainers—1, Hough Stanley M; 2, Lukas D Wayne; 3, Hushion Michael E; 4, Armstrong Dale; 5, Bohannan Thomas; 6, Moschera Gasper S

FIRST TRY AGAINST OLDER

Care is required in evaluating claiming races at the beginning of the year. January 1 is the universal birthday for thoroughbreds, and newly turned four-year-olds are facing their elders for the first time. Even though all thoroughbreds have a "birthday" on January 1, they were not all born on the same day, or even the same time of the year; some were actually foaled in January, but others were foaled in February, March, April, and even May. The "late foals" born in the spring may be four-year-olds on paper come New Year's Day, but they are actually still three. Usually, these horses are at a disadvantage early in their four-year-old campaigns when forced to compete against more seasoned and fully matured rivals.

3

6 FURLONGS. **(InnerDirt). (1.08^3) CLAIMING. Purse $18,000. 4-year-olds and upward. Weight, 122 lbs. Non-winners of two races since December 1 allowed 3 lbs. Of a race since then, 5 lbs. Claiming price $25,000 for each $2,500 to $20,000, 2 lbs. (Races when entered to be claimed for $18,000 or less not considered.)**

Maximum Leader — **Dk. b. or br. g. 5, by Irish Tower—Conversion Rate, by Buckfinder**

ROSARIO V (14 1 0 1 .07) — **$25,000** **Br.—Butler Gregory E (Ky)**

Own.—R Kay Stable — **Tr.—Araya Rene A (11 1 2 1 .09)** — **107^{10}**

Lifetime							
44 9 9 1	1992	19	4	4	0	$74,760
$156,460	1991	18	4	4	1	$69,260
	Turf	2	0	0	0	
	Wet	8	1	1	1	$19,860

20Dec92- 2Aqu	my	1^{70}	⊡:47^1	1:12^3	1:43^3	3↑Clm 20000	76	3	2	2½	2^{hd}	2^{hd}	44¾	Chavez J F	b	113	6.30	82–23	WorldContndr1151½CosmicBll117^{2}LstSong117	Bid, tired	7
13Dec92- 9Aqu	my	6f	⊡:23	:46^3	1:11^4	3↑Clm 17500	80	3	7	67½	6^7	5^6	2^2	Velasquez J	b	117	11.50	82–18	RghtJb117^{2}MxmmLdr117^{hd}MjrMccllm112	Up for place	8
3Dec92- 9Aqu	fst	6f	⊡:22^4	:46^2	1:11^2	3↑Clm 17500	68	9	6	83¾	64¼	75½	7^{10}	Velasquez J	b	117	5.50	76–20	TruendBlue1175¼Kllock117^{1}RcingSplndor113	Wide trip	10
11Nov92- 2Aqu	fst	7f	:22^1	:45	1:23^1	3↑Clm 25000	49	1	5	1½	1½	78½	816½	Davis R G	b	117	8.40	72–15	Fbershm1173¼MnilHemp115^{hd}ShinePls117	Used in pace	10
28Oct92- 9Aqu	fst	6f	:22^1	:45	1:11	3↑Clm 14000	78	2	6	1^{hd}	12½	1^6	1^2	Antley C W	b	117	5.00	86–14	MmmLdr117^{2}CmmndrEvndr117^{3}MjrMccllm117	Driving	11
9Oct92- 2Bel	sly	6f	:22^2	:46	1:11^1	3↑Clm 14000	54	1	1	1^1	2^{hd}	32½	69¼	Maple E	b	117	2.50	75–16	I'veGotMine115^{4}BlitzthePss1171¼Espo117	Used in pace	7
26Sep92- 2Bel	sly	6½f	:22^2	:45^4	1:18	3↑Clm 17500	54	5	4	1½	2^{hd}	42½	59¼	Rosario H D^7	b	110	7.00	74–14	CapWhite1171¾Talc'sBid117^{nk}Calibeau117	Dueled, tired	7
17Sep92- 2Bel	fst	6f	:22^2	:46^1	1:10^4	3↑Clm 17500	69	6	6	4^5	42¼	33½	56¼	Pezua J M	b	117	3.30	80–18	RcngSplndr117^{nk}Wrgd1132¼RdScmpr119	Saved ground	7
5Aug92- 8Del	fm	5f	Ⓣ:21^4	:46^1	:58	3↑Clm 20000	40	1	9	9^{11}	99¾	7^{14}	813½	Castaneda K	b	116	4.70	80–06	Greenvill108¾SugrGuy122^{3}LoudPlid106	Showed nothing	9
20Jun92- 1Bel	my	6f	:22^2	:45	1:09^4	Clm c-25000	28	3	3	2^{hd}	3½	8^{11}	9^{25}	McCauley W H	b	117	*2.00	66–07	Convert1172½ Mine Fire117^{no} Kellock115	Dueled tired	9

20Jun92-Claimed from Jewel-E Stable, Ferriola Peter Trainer

LATEST WORKOUTS Dec 10 Bel tr.t 5f fst 1:02^2 B Nov 25 Bel tr.t 3f my :36^1 H Nov 16 Bel tr.t 4f fst :48^2 H Nov 9 Bel tr.t 3f fst :37^1 B

Crafty Mana — Ch. h. 7, by Crafty Prospector—Indian Lightning, by Navajo
SANTAGATA N (99 13 7 12 .13) — $25,000 — Br.—[illegible] s Stable (Fla) — 117
Own.—Ruggieroo Carl P — Tr.—[illegible]perio Joseph (18 0 1 2 .00) — 1—NE

	Lifetime					
44 15 3 9	1992	8	2	2	2	$30,840
$140,284	1991	16	6	1	2	$70,920
	Turf	1	0	0	0	$348
	Wet	6	2	0	0	$8,740

6Dec92- 9Aqu	fst	6f	⊡$:22^4$	$:46^4$	1:12	3↑Clm 14000	82	10	3	$4^{1½}$	3^{nk}	1^1	$2^{1¾}$	Santagata N	b	117	5.90	81–20	MjorMccllm112^{1¾}CrftyMn117^{1¾}TwrOfTrsrs117	Wide bid	11
9Mar92- 3Aqu	fst	6f	⊡$:22^3$	$:45^4$	$1:11^2$	Clm 14000	77	2	5	$4^{1½}$	$4^{1¼}$	1^2	$1^{1¼}$	Santagata N	b	119	*.90	86–16	CraftyMn119^{1¼}IrishChili115^{4½}Thorium110	Wide, driving	7
23Feb92- 5Aqu	fst	6f	⊡$:22^4$	$:46^1$	$1:10^4$	Clm 25000	85	8	1	4^{nk}	$5^{1¼}$	$3^{2½}$	$5^{6¼}$	Santagata N	b	119	6.50	83–16	LordSuc117^{1½}FghtngAffr115^{3½}TooTru117	In tight 3/8 pl	10
14Feb92- 5Aqu	fst	6f	⊡:23	$:46^2$	$1:11^4$	Clm 32500	82	1	5	$3^{1½}$	$3^{2½}$	$3^{5½}$	$5^{3½}$	Santagata N	b	117	5.90	80–23	Penny'sBuck117^{1¾}FortyHlls113^{½}RipplingDl119	Sted late	9
3Feb92- 6Aqu	fst	6f	⊡:23	:47	$1:12^2$	Clm 30000	92	8	2	4^1	$3^{1½}$	1^2	$1^{½}$	Santagata N	b	113	*2.40	81–23	CraftyMn113^{½}Mrchtime114^{½}FightingAffir117	Wide drvg	8
22Jan92- 6Aqu	fst	6f	⊡$:22^4$	$:45^4$	1:11	Clm 30000	91	2	8	$2^{1½}$	2^1	2^3	$2^{2¾}$	Santagata N	b	113	7.30	85–23	RoyalEagle117^{2¾}CraftyMan113^{3}LeftyPriolo115	2nd best	9
12Jan92- 3Aqu	fst	6f	⊡$:22^3$	$:45^4$	$1:11^3$	Clm c-22500	83	6	3	4^2	$3^{½}$	$4^{3½}$	$4^{5½}$	Santagata N		115	2.80	79–23	RvrPtrot115^{nk}[D]LordSuc117^{4½}FghtngAffr117	Four wide	9
12Jan92-Placed third through disqualification																					
1Jan92- 5Aqu	fst	6f	⊡$:22^2$	$:45^1$	$1:10^3$	Clm 22500	90	3	4	$3^{4½}$	$5^{7½}$	4^5	$3^{3½}$	Lydon P J		109^6	2.50	86–13	BunaLite117^{2½}AllSilver117^1[DH]RiverPtriot117	Mild rally	7
1Jan92-Dead heat																					
8Dec91- 3Aqu	fst	6f	⊡$:22^3$	:46	$1:11^2$	3↑Clm c-17500	100	8	1	$3^{1½}$	2^{hd}	1^1	$1^{4½}$	Santagata N		119	2.60	86–20	CrftyMn119^{4½}CrmelPie117^{2½}HppyKentuckin108	Driving	8
28Nov91- 2Aqu	fst	6f	$:22^2$	$:45^3$	$1:10^2$	3↑Clm 17500	96	1	3	2^1	2^{hd}	1^1	$1^{1½}$	Santagata N		117	4.20	89–19	CrftyMn117^{1½}HppyKntuckn112^{1¾}RomnRport117	Driving	9

LATEST WORKOUTS Nov 16 Aqu 5f fst 1:02 B

Songrider — B. g. 4, by Skywalker—Kilts Girl, by Royal Saxon
MADRID A JR (91 8 9 11 .09) — $25,000 — Br.—Loradale (Ky) — 117
Own.—Meyers Gerald J — Tr.—Schosberg Richard (23 2 3 4 .09)

	Lifetime					
15 3 2 2	1992	12	2	2	2	$48,820
$64,480	1991	3	1	0	0	$15,660
	Wet	1	0	0	0	

19Dec92- 5Aqu	fst	1$\frac{1}{16}$	⊡$:46^3$	$1:09^4$	1:41	Clm 45000	71	11	2	2^1	$1^{½}$	$6^{5¼}$	7^{14}	Madrid A Jr	b	113	7.60	89–05	Autoroute115^{3½}Appointe117^{4¾}Dnzig'sDnc117	Weakened	11
4Dec92- 1Aqu	fst	6f	⊡:23	:46	$1:11^2$	Clm 50000	77	2	4	3^2	4^2	3^4	$2^{1½}$	Madrid A Jr	b	117	7.60	84–13	ExplosiveOn113^{1½}Songridr117^{nk}WildDnt113	Up for 2nd	7
5Nov92- 6Aqu	sly	1	:47	$1:12^2$	$1:38^2$	Clm 75000	73	2	3	$3^{½}$	$3^{1½}$	$5^{7½}$	$6^{11¾}$	Davis R G	b	112	10.30	58–30	Yaros116^{5¼} Doc Janas112^{nk} Sparkling Sky113	Used up	6
5Nov92-Originally scheduled on turf																					
11Oct92- 8Bel	gd	1	:45	$1:09^1$	$1:34^1$	Jamaica H	63	6	2	2^3	$5^{3½}$	7^9	7^{20}	Davis R G	b	110	39.00	79–09	West by West112^{5¾} Offbeat111^{no} Portroe111	Gave way	7
11Oct92-Grade II																					
2Oct92- 6Bel	fst	7f	$:22^3$	:46	$1:24^1$	3↑Alw 28000	82	6	2	3^2	2^{hd}	3^{nk}	$3^{4¾}$	Perret C	b	114	8.90	78–22	LookAhed119^{1¾}RomnChorus114^{3}Songridr114	Bid, wknd	8
6Jly92- 7Bel	gd	1$\frac{1}{16}$	$:45^1$	$1:09^3$	$1:42^3$	3↑Alw 31000	90	7	2	$2^{½}$	1^{hd}	1^{hd}	3^{nk}	Perret C	b	116	5.20	89–11	TigerTiger111^{nk}ShretheGlory117^{hd}Songrider116	Gamely	7
6Jly92-Originally scheduled on turf																					
25Jun92- 6Bel	gd	1$\frac{1}{16}$	$:47^3$	1:12	$1:43^2$	3↑Alw 29000	85	6	1	1^{hd}	1^{hd}	1^2	1^7	Krone J A	b	109	2.00	85–18	Songridr109^{7}TtonPrinc117^{no}MsmircShdow109	Drew off	6
13Jun92- 3Bel	fst	6f	$:22^1$	$:45^3$	$1:10^3$	Clm 75000	80	1	1	$1^{½}$	1^{hd}	3^2	$4^{6¼}$	Krone J A	b	117	*1.30	81–18	IrshDmn113^{½}PrlssPrfrmr113^{3}RnChrs115	Dueled inside	6
22May92- 7Bel	fst	7f	$:22^3$	$:45^2$	$1:22^3$	Alw 27000	87	1	7	$1^{½}$	$1^{½}$	2^{hd}	$2^{1½}$	Krone J A	b	117	*2.40	89–11	Kertoid117^{1½}Songridr117^{nk}CobblstonRod117	Held place	9
14May92- 1Bel	fst	6f	$:22^3$	$:45^1$	$1:09^1$	Clm 35000	90	1	1	1^1	2^{hd}	$1^{2½}$	$1^{5½}$	Krone J A	b	117	6.70	94–08	Songrider117^{5½} Mashriq110^{2}FleetRomeo117	Drew clear	8

LATEST WORKOUTS Dec 16 Bel tr.t 4f fst :49^1 B — Nov 28 Bel tr.t 5f fst 1:00^4 H — Nov 21 Bel tr.t 4f fst :49^1 B — Nov 2 Bel tr.t 4f fst :50^2 B

Songrider was the 3–2 favorite in a six-furlong, $25,000 sprint on January 2, 1993, because the crowd placed too much emphasis on the drop from the $50,000–$45,000 level. Songrider had raced against three-year-olds in his three most recent starts against claimers but was now meeting older claiming rivals for the first time in his career.

His overall profile was that of a horse in decline: earlier in his three-year-old season, Songrider had recorded Beyers in the mid-80s or higher in four of five starts but had tailed off noticeably since his return from a three-month layoff, running figures of 82, 63, 73, 77, and 71.

Crafty Mana was the third choice at 9–2, as the crowd shied away due to the class rise from the $14,000 level. But Crafty Mana was a proven and experienced performer, having won more than a third of forty-four career starts, including three wins on Aqueduct's inner track the previous winter, when he rose successfully from $17,500 to the $35,000–$30,000 level. The seven-year-old had received a useful tightener on December 6 while making his first start in nine months, racing wide, offering a sustained rally to get the lead in midstretch, and finishing second for $14,000. Crafty Mana's back figures over the surface were rivaled only by Songrider, who appeared a long way removed from the form he had shown several months ago. The double jump was a sign of confidence on the part of the trainer, who had won twice with the horse after claiming him at last year's winter meet, and it turned out to be a shrewd maneuver, as Crafty Mana drove clear, paying $11. Songrider faded to fifth after forcing the pace.

THIRD RACE
Aqueduct
JANUARY 2, 1993

6 FURLONGS.(InnerDirt). (1.08^3) CLAIMING. Purse $18,000. 4-year-olds and upward. Weight, 122 lbs. Non-winners of two races since December 1 allowed 3 lbs. Of a race since then, 5 lbs. Claiming price $25,000 for each $2,500 to $20,000, 2 lbs. (Races when entered to be claimed for $18,000 or less not considered.)

Value of race $18,000; value to winner $10,800; second $3,960; third $2,160; fourth $1,080. Mutuel pool $242,703. Exacta Pool $570,085

Last Raced	Horse	M/Eqt.	A.	Wt	PP	St	¼	½	Str	Fin	Jockey	Cl'g Pr	Odds $1
6Dec92 ^{9}Aqu^2	Crafty Mana	b	7	117	2	3	2^2	2^2	$1^{1½}$	1^2	Santagata N	25000	4.50
27Dec92 ^{9}Aqu^4	Otto Beit	b	4	115	5	5	$5^{½}$	$4^{½}$	3^{hd}	2no	Graell A	22500	7.70
17Dec92 ^{1}Aqu^3	Star Kalibur	b	5	117	7	6	$6^{½}$	$5^{1½}$	$4^{2½}$	$3^{2½}$	Bravo J	25000	3.50
26Dec92 ^{1}Aqu^3	Right Jab	b	5	115	8	1	1^2	1^1	2^{hd}	4^{nk}	Bruin J E	22500	19.20
19Dec92 ^{5}Aqu^7	Songrider	b	4	117	3	4	$3^{2½}$	3^{hd}	$5^{4½}$	5^4	Madrid A Jr	25000	1.50
20Dec92 ^{2}Aqu^4	Maximum Leader	b	5	107	1	7	8^2	$8^{½}$	6^1	$6^{1½}$	Rosario V^{10}	25000	16.40
26Nov92 ^{9}Aqu^2	With It	b	4	117	9	2	4^1	6^2	8^3	7^2	Richards G G	25000	27.40
23Dec92 ^{9}Aqu^1	Jet Craft	b	4	108	4	8	$7^{½}$	7^{hd}	$7^{½}$	$8^{1¼}$	Bisono C V^5	20000	10.60
25Nov92 ^{3}Aqu^8	Four Quest	b	4	117	6	9	9	9	9	9	Chavez J F	25000	14.40

OFF AT 1:24 Start good, Won driving. Time, :23 , :46^3, :58^4, 1:11^3 Track fast.

$2 Mutuel Prices:				
	2-(B)-CRAFTY MANA	**11.00**	**6.00**	**4.60**
	5-(E)-OTTO BEIT		**7.00**	**4.60**
	7-(G)-STAR KALIBUR			**3.60**
	$2 EXACTA 2-5 PAID $80.40			

Ch. h, by Crafty Prospector—Indian Lightning, by Navajo. Trainer Imperio Joseph. Bred by Due Process Stable (Fla).

CRAFTY MANA stalked RIGHT JAB on the front, moved to challenge that one turning for home, drove clear a furlong out and held sway under good handling. OTTO BEIT saved ground and finished well to gain the place. STAR KALIBUR was moving well at the finish and just missed the place. RIGHT JAB made the pace to upper stretch, then gave way when headed. SONGRIDER raced in easy striking position but had no rally. MAXIMUM LEADER was never prominent. WITH IT raced wide. JET CRAFT failed to menace. FOUR QUEST was outrun.

Owners— 1, Ruggieroo Carl P; 2, Thor John; 3, Buckley John F; 4, Abramowitz Darren E; 5, Meyers Gerald J; 6, R Kay Stable; 7, Flying Zee Stable; 8, Giammattei Joseph L; 9, Two Sisters Stable.

Trainers— 1, Imperio Joseph; 2, Moschera Gasper S; 3, Dandy Ronald J; 4, Jerkens Steven T; 5, Schosberg Richard; 6, Araya Rene A; 7, Martin Carlos F; 8, Bottazzi Patrick L; 9, Pascuma James J Jr.

Star Kalibur was claimed by Murphy Karen; trainer, Hushion Michael E.

Along the same lines: Two days earlier, trainer Mike Hushion demonstrated why he is so effective with recent claims:

Appealing Tracy — **Dk. b. or br. c. 4, by Valid Appeal—Tracy Lou, by Avatar**
MIGLIORE R (57 17 14 10 .30) — **Br.—Mangurian Mr-Mrs H T Jr (Fla)**
Own.—Quad Star Stable — **Tr.—Hushion Michael E (23 9 5 1 .39)** — **119**

Lifetime								
11 4 0 2	1993	1	1	0	0	$16,800
$54,300	1992	9	3	0	2	$36,420
	Turf	3	0	0	1	$2,400

1Jan93- 6Aqu	fst	6f	⊡:23^1	:46^3	1:11	Alw 28000	90	5	6	$7^{4½}$	$7^{3¼}$	$3^{½}$	$1^{3½}$	Migliore R	b	117	3.00	88–16	ApplingTrcy117^{3½}Chnl'sTitnic117^{nk}OcnSplsh117 Driving	8
16Nov92- 2Aqu	fst	7f	:22^2	:45^1	1:22^4	Clm c-50000	67	3	4	$6^{7¼}$	$6^{4½}$	$4^{6½}$	$5^{11¾}$	Chavez J F	b	117	3.00	79–09	Norphlet117^{nk}CoolQuaker112^{2}EsternBrve113 Four wide	8
16Nov92-Claimed from Kinsman Stable, Domino Carl J Trainer																				
25Oct92- 1Aqu	fst	6½f	:22^3	:46^1	1:17^4	Clm 35000	90	3	5	$7^{4¾}$	$6^{4½}$	3^1	1^2	Chavez J F	b	117	5.10	89–19	ApplnTrc117^{2}EsGnAJ117^{4½}SshMc117 Stmbld bk,wd,drv	7
6Sep92- 9Crc	fst	1$\frac{1}{16}$	:48^4	1:13^1	1:45^1	3↑Alw 16000	76	7	3	$3^{1½}$	$2^{1½}$	2^6	$3^{11½}$	Vasquez J	b	116	*2.10	89–04	ThisTimTony111^{10}Akrm118^{1½}ApplingTrcy116 Weakened	7
29Aug92-11Crc	fm	*1⅛ Ⓣ			1:44^4	Manalapan H	63	11	5	6^8	$8^{6¾}$	11^{21}	$11^{18¾}$	Morales C E	b	110	76.70	80–02	SilverConquest112^{nk}Crtrist115^{2½}SidBr112 Wide ent trip	11
15Aug92- 4Crc	fst	1	:47^2	1:12^4	1:40^1	3↑Alw 16600	83	4	3	$3^{4½}$	2^1	2^{hd}	$1^{1½}$	Lee M A	b	111	*2.10	94–04	ApplngTrc111^{1½}Grhm'sCrcr112^{5½}PttCC116 Drvg 4 wide	8
1Aug92- 6Crc	fm	1$\frac{1}{16}$ Ⓣ	:48^4	1:12^2	1:42^1	3↑Alw 16600	77	4	2	$4^{1½}$	4^3	$4^{5½}$	3^2	Lee M A		111	2.30	87–08	Our Man116½ Starion115^{1½} Appealing Tracy111 Rallied	10
17Jly92- 9Crc	fm	*1$\frac{1}{16}$ Ⓣ			1:44^3	3↑Alw 16600	82	2	4	$4^{1½}$	$7^{5¼}$	5^4	$4^{2½}$	Nunez E O		111	7.40	86–14	TmForClss116^{1½}AnmlsLvU.116^{1}BrnzSprc112 10 wide str	8
5Jly92- 8Crc	fst	7f	:21^4	:45	1:25^1	3↑Alw 15500	72	1	8	6^5	$7^{5¼}$	$6^{7¼}$	$6^{4½}$	Vasquez J		115	*1.10	84–06	Bull Gator116^{1½} Petit CeeCee116^{1½}Tragna112 No threat	9
20Jun92- 3Crc	fst	6½f	:22^4	:46^1	1:18^2	3↑Md Sp Wt	85	5	2	2^1	$2^{1½}$	1^2	1^8	Vasquez J		115	2.40e	93–07	ApplngTrcy115^{8}Kowlsk115^{1½}WthPrms115 Convincingly	7

LATEST WORKOUTS **Jan 17 Bel tr.t 6f fst 1:19^2 B** **Dec 10 Bel tr.t 5f fst 1:04^1 B** **Dec 4 Bel tr.t 5f fst 1:05 B**

Appealing Tracy was making his first start as a four-year-old, but was not meeting any older rivals in his nonwinners-of-two allowance sprint on New Year's Day; his seven opponents were *all* newly turned four-year-olds like himself. For these newly turned fours, a nonwinners allowance is often an easier spot than a basement-level $14,000 claimer . . . especially in the dead of winter. There were several things to like about Appealing Tracy:

- Seldom will you see a three-year-old claimed for $50,000 late in the year, as Appealing Tracy was. Three-year-olds racing for a $50,000 tag against their own age late in the year usually require a significant drop to compete effectively with older claimers. Hushion took this horse because he was still eligible for the nonwinners-of-two and nonwinners-of-three allowance races — the kind that often come up light on talent during the winter months.
- The layoff was a positive sign, because Appealing Tracy had broken his maiden when returned for his first start of 1992 on June 20 and had also won first time back from a seven-week absence on October 25, despite stumbling at the start.
- Unlike several of his rivals on January 1, Appealing Tracy had not developed into a chronic also-ran in the nonwinners-allowance ranks. From seven career starts on dirt, he had won three times; two of the four defeats had come from difficult post positions — the extreme outside in a two-turn route at Calder on September 6, and the treacherous inside post going one turn in a Calder sprint on July 5.

FIRST TIME BACK AT LEVEL OF CLAIM

Trainers claim horses because they believe they can win with them, so it makes sense to monitor closely the movements of recent claims and give them the benefit of the doubt when it seems as though the trainer is doing things with a specific purpose. Sometimes it may take a few starts for trainer and horse to become familiar with each other:

Clever Knave Dk. b. or br. c. 3(Apr), by Clever Trick—Face Nord, by Northjet
Br.—George Strawbridge (Ky)
Own.—C'Est Tout Stable Tr.—Daggett Michael H (—)

Lifetime 6 2 0 0 $18,840 | 1992 6 2 0 0 $18,840 | 1991 0 M 0 0 | Turf 1 0 0 0

21Oct92- 6Aqu	fst	6f	:221	:452	1:111	Clm 32500	—	2	7	31½	21½	21½	1nk	Nelson D	115	23.90	85–18	CleverKnve115nkStrtFight1173EstblishedLie115	Driving	9	
8Oct92- 2Bel	fm	1 1/16 Ⓣ	:471	1:111	1:413	Clm 35000	50	7	3	41½	51¼	118	1119½	Velazquez J R	117	2.60e	68–06	LeadTilDwn1173¾Lonnegn1101¾FunEscort117	Gave way	12	
12Sep92- 2Bel	fst	1 1/16	:462	1:103	1:424	Clm 45000	74	7	3	32	3½	42	44¾	Velazquez J R	113	18.20	83–14	LordWollston113¾LouieV1173¾EirPowr113	Lacked rally	7	
12Sep92-Originally scheduled on turf																					
31Aug92- 6Sar	fst	7f	:221	:442	1:232	3↑Alw 27000	49	4	4	4nk	42½	62¾	620	Velazquez J R	112	23.00	68–11	Offbet1124½CountNewYork1144½AmbssdorSix114	Tired	7	
14Aug92- 1Sar	fst	1	:464	1:121	1:381	Clm c-30000	71	5	3	31½	3nk	11	42	Perret C	113	7.10	— —	DrwCrd113nkAllMyTrcks113hdRmblAy117	Bid weakened	9	
14Aug92-Claimed from Dogwood Stables Inc, Vestal Peter M Trainer																					
19Jly92- 7AP	gd	6½f	:22	:454	1:19	3↑Md 10000	70	4	8	23	1hd	1½	14½	Silva C H	115	6.10	76–21	ClevrKnv1154½BcusH'sGry1153¾KingWhl115	Ridden out	12	

LATEST WORKOUTS ●Oct 17 Bel tr.t 4f fst :471 H Sep 30 Bel 5f fst 1:021 B Sep 21 Bel tr.t 4f fst :50 B Aug 24 Sar 4f fst :51 B

What was there to like about Clever Knave when he shocked a field of $35,000–$30,000 sprinters at nearly 24–1 on October 21?

The horse became interesting on August 14, when he was claimed from his first race on the New York circuit. Usually, trainers like to have at least a passing familiarity with a horse they're about to invest in; when a shipper (read: unknown commodity) is claimed the first time it hits the local circuit — especially one such as Clever Knave who shows only a single race — it bears watching.

The display of determination shown by Clever Knave when he paid $49.80 was hard to predict off a cursory glance at his recent finish positions and beaten lengths, but horses that light up the board this way nearly always require a second, more probing analysis. Mike Daggett claimed the horse out of a race in which he blew a clear lead in midstretch, and then watched him "spit the bit" in a seven-furlong allowance on August 31 after engaging in an early four-way duel for the lead (fourth by a neck at the first call), finishing twenty lengths up the track.

It was time to work on the colt's stamina, was it not? Twelve days later, Daggett entered Clever Knave in a turf route, only to see it rained off to the main track; he offered an improved effort nevertheless, pressing the pace and finishing fourth, beaten by less than five lengths. On October 8, Clever Knave did start on grass and pressed the pace for six furlongs before doing a steady fade through the final five-sixteenths of a mile. Nine days later, with two recent route races under his belt, Clever Knave was asked for a speed-sharpening workout and responded with a bullet half-mile on the training track in :47⅕ — by far his most impressive recent workout; a check of the *Form*'s work tab from October 17 revealed that the next-fastest work at the distance on the training track had been :48⅖, more than a second slower than Clever Knave's move.

On October 21, Clever Knave was making his second start back at the level of the claim by Daggett — but it was his first start on *dirt* back at the $35,000 level. Handicappers intrigued by Daggett's purposeful training regimen might've given the colt one shot for $35,000 on dirt. After being "legged up" in routes on dirt and on the turf, Clever Knave was again an early-pace factor but did not tire in the stretch this time, surging late to win by a neck.

OUT OF JAIL, UP IN CLASS

If a horse is entered within thirty days after being claimed, eligibility rules in New York require it to run for a claiming price 25 percent higher than what the new connections paid for it. During this thirty-day period, the horse is said to be "in jail." Once the thirty days are up, the horse is "out of jail" and can now be entered in whatever spot the new barn chooses. As a general rule, horses that do not run during the jail period and return below their original claiming price are poor percentage plays. Why would you buy something for, say, $35,000, not use it for a month, and then offer it for sale for $25,000? You wouldn't, unless you knew that your purchase was no longer worth what you paid for it. (Remember, there *are* exceptions to any rule, as we saw with Gasper Moschera's freshly claimed drop-down winners in chapter 2.)

By the same token, horses that sit out the jail period and return shortly thereafter at a *higher* price often prove to be very interesting propositions. The horse is out of jail and eligible to run for the same amount (or less) that it was claimed for; the rise in class is a sign of the new stable's confidence.

Calskey
CHAVEZ J F (81 14 13 14 .17)
Own.—Nahama Benjamin

B. f. 4, by Silent Cal—Do Re Me, by Gallant Knave
Br.—Mullins Joan S (Pa)
Tr.—Levine Bruce N (10 3 4 2 .30)

115

Lifetime						
34 10 4 1	1992	18	7	0	1	$82,524
$134,139	1991	16	3	4	0	$51,615
	Turf	12	2	0	0	$26,121
	Wet	5	2	0	0	$25,605

9Dec92-	1Aqu	fst	$1\frac{1}{16}$	[·]:48	1:14	$1:46^{1}$		(F)Clm 45000	87	6	8	8^{13}	5^{2}	$1\frac{1}{2}$	1^{2}	Chavez J F	b	113	6.10	77-26	Calskey113^{2} National Spirit$113^{5\frac{1}{4}}$ Erhart117	Driving 8
26Nov92-	1Aqu	sly	$1\frac{1}{8}$	$:47^{3}$	$1:12^{3}$	$1:51^{4}$	3↑	(F)Clm 30000	79	5	7	$7^{8\frac{1}{2}}$	$5^{2\frac{1}{2}}$	$1^{1\frac{1}{2}}$	1^{4}	Chavez J F	b	113	11.90	77-20	Calskey113^{4} Triple Sox117^{2} WonScent117	Wide driving 8
14Oct92-	4Bel	fst	1	$:46^{2}$	$1:11^{2}$	1:37	3↑	(F)Clm c-17500	84	7	8	7^{6}	4^{2}	2^{1}	$1^{1\frac{1}{2}}$	McMahon H I^{7}	b	110	5.30	92-20	Calskey$110^{1\frac{1}{2}}$WorldClassPro117^{9}Rebecca'sGl117	Driving 9
14Oct92-Claimed from Gold n Oats Stable, Klesaris Robert P Trainer																						
2Oct92-	3Bel	fm	$1\frac{1}{4}$	[T]$:49^{2}$	$1:37^{4}$	$2:02^{3}$	3↑	(F)Clm 35000	78	5	10	$10^{8\frac{3}{4}}$	$9^{4\frac{1}{2}}$	8^{6}	8^{5}	McCauley W H	b	117	29.70	72-15	[D]NoHolmeKeys$117^{1\frac{1}{2}}$IvoryTody117^{nk}Azdh117	No threat 11
29Aug92-	2Sar	gd	$1\frac{3}{8}$	[T]$:49^{3}$	$1:40^{1}$	$2:19^{3}$	3↑	(F)Clm c-35000	64	7	8	$7^{3\frac{1}{4}}$	$8^{7\frac{1}{2}}$	$10^{9\frac{3}{4}}$	$10^{14\frac{3}{4}}$	Krone J A	b	117	7.90	57-19	Stphn'sJy117^{no}CllnnDmnd$117^{1\frac{1}{2}}$Q.E.Sl117	Outrun, wide 10
29Aug92-Claimed from Girdner Paul K, Pollard Damon Trainer																						
10Aug92-	2Sar	fm	$1\frac{3}{8}$	[T]:48	$1:39^{1}$	$2:17^{1}$	3↑	(F)Clm 35000	75	9	9	$10^{6\frac{1}{2}}$	$5^{3\frac{1}{2}}$	$6^{3\frac{1}{4}}$	$4^{8\frac{1}{2}}$	Smith M E	b	119	5.30	76-11	City Cat$117^{6\frac{1}{2}}$ Stephen's Joy$117^{1\frac{1}{2}}$ Q. E. Slew117	4 wide 10
2Aug92-	3Sar	fm	$1\frac{1}{8}$	[T]$:46^{1}$	1:11	$1:49^{1}$	3↑	(F)Clm 45000	73	8	11	11^{21}	$11^{9\frac{3}{4}}$	$10^{7\frac{1}{4}}$	$8^{6\frac{1}{2}}$	Migliore R	b	113	28.10	86-04	Embractania113^{nk} Ivory Today$119^{\frac{1}{2}}$ Oriane113	Outrun 11
22Jly92-	1Bel	fm	$1\frac{3}{8}$	[T]$:47^{1}$	$1:37^{2}$	$2:15^{3}$		(F)Clm 35000	80	7	7	9^{8}	3^{1}	$1\frac{1}{2}$	1^{3}	Smith M E	b	117	4.20	73-15	Clskey117^{3}NotAScrtch$117^{\frac{1}{2}}$KthyMcGe117	Wide, driving 10
12Jly92-	4Bel	fm	$1\frac{1}{16}$	(T)$:45^{4}$	1:10	1:42		(F)Clm 35000	80	8	9	$9^{9\frac{1}{4}}$	$9^{8\frac{3}{4}}$	$6^{5\frac{3}{4}}$	$4^{2\frac{3}{4}}$	Smith M E	b	117	33.00	83-14	NoHolmeKeys117^{2}Orine117^{hd}GretRviw117	Outside rally 10
17Jun92-	6Bel	fm	$1\frac{1}{4}$	[T]$:47^{3}$	$1:37^{1}$	$2:01^{4}$	•	(F)Clm 45000	61	7	6	6^{16}	$8^{4\frac{1}{4}}$	$7^{8\frac{1}{2}}$	$8^{14\frac{1}{2}}$	Davis R G	b	113	14.90	66-18	QueenoftheTide$113^{1\frac{3}{4}}$IvoryTody$113^{2\frac{1}{2}}$LdyLer117	Outrun 9

LATEST WORKOUTS Nov 7 Aqu 4f fst $:48^{4}$ H

Bruce Levine claimed Calskey for $17,500 on October 14 and put her away for six weeks. By the time November 26 rolled around, he could've entered Calskey for $17,500, or even for $14,000 if he had thought that's where she would be competitive. Instead, Levine *double-jumped* Calskey into a $35,000–$30,000 spot, thus implying to handicappers who read between the lines two positive things:

1) "I'm handling this horse patiently because she's a proven performer who's earned her keep all her life [see career record upper right-hand corner of pp's]."

2) "After being so patient with this horse, I'm not willing to lose her to a claim by someone else for anything less than $30,000, because that's how good I think she is now."

Calskey justified Levine's confidence, winning by four expanding lengths at nearly 12–1. She then came right back to beat a $50,000–$45,000 field by two lengths at better than 6–1.

When a trainer has just shown you a successful move of this nature, he merits considerable respect when he does it again in the near future:

Giant Leap
Own: Trombly Wayne
VELAZQUEZ J R (85 15 15 8 .23) **$32,500**
Dk. b or br g. 6
Sire: Conquistador Cielo (Mr. Prospector)
Dam: Leap of the Heart (Nijinsky II)
Br: Mellon Paul (Va)
Tr: Klesaris Robert P (10 3 0 2 .30)
115

Lifetime Record:	35	6	6	8	$112,185						
1994	6	1	2	0	$16,170	Turf	1	0	0	0	
1993	17	3	4	2	[illegible]	Wet	7	1	4	2	$29,070
Aqu	3	2	0	1	$30,840	Dist	12	4	1	3	$30,765

7Apr94-4Aqu	my	7f	:23 :461 1:112 1:241	Clm 25000	84	4 2	21½ 1½ 1½ 11½	Velazquez J R	117 fb	2.80	83-23	Giant Leap1171½ The Mechanic1146 Sea Baba1134¼	Driving	6
6Mar94-11GP	fst	1 1/16	:232 :463 1:104 1:431	Clm c-16000	78	7 5	52¼ 31½ 35½ 44¼	Santos J A	L 117 fb	*1.80	89-06	Sammy From Miami1173½ Major Manila117hd Paraco117¾	Faded	12
Claimed from Zim Pom Stable, Blengs Vincent L Trainer														
24Feb94-5GP	fst	1 1/16	:233 :47 1:111 1:434	Clm 18000	83	8 4	22½ 21½ 23½ 24	Santos J A	L 115 fb	2.70	89-12	Country Town1154 Giant Leap1153½ Freebie One117nk	Second best	11
3Feb94-3GP	my	1 1/16	:23 :471 1:123 1:444	Clm 16000	83	8 6	65½ 42 23 22¼	Douglas R R	L 117 fb	3.80	84-23	Concorde's Revenge1172¼ Giant Leap1174½ Jeffrey Who1173	Best of rest	9
23Jan94-11GP	fst	7f	:223 :451 1:094 1:221	Clm 20000	76	7 10	84 72 65 57½	Bailey J D	L 119 fb	*2.60	84-08	Silent Generation1101¼ Colonel Mosby1172¼ Perfect Star1171¼		11
Eight wide str, belated bid														
8Jan94-5GP	fst	7f	:22 :443 1:092 1:222	Clm 25000	81	4 6	98 77 56½ 55¾	Douglas R R	L 117 fb	4.90	85-09	Good Scout1192½ Waheed1111¼ Syndicate's Pal117¾	Saved ground	11
15Dec93-7Crc	fst	7f	:23 :47 1:124 1:254 3↑	Clm 20000	82	2 7	63½ 52¼ 1hd 11½	Douglas R R	L 119 fb	*2.10	86-21	Giant Leap1191½ Legal Freight1153½ Waheed117nk	4 wide, clear	7
16Nov93-9Lrl	fst	6f	:22 :464 :574 1:103 3↑	Alw 18000N2X	85	4 7	710 77 44 41½	Klinger C O	L 117 fb	3.50	87-16	Roy's Delight120no Crumpton115no Ragtime Dancing1171¼	No threat	7
17Oct93-4Lrl	fst	7f	:233 :471 1:121 1:25 3↑	Clm 18500	81	4 4	74½ 52¼ 2hd 1hd	Klinger C O	L 119 fb	3.10	84-18	Giant Leap119hd Cruel Cavalier1171¾ Sleek N Graceful117½	Wide, driving	7
1Oct93-1Pim	fst	6f	:23 :462 :59 1:112	Clm 14500	88	1 1	31½ 52 53 1¾	Luzzi M J	L 117 fb	*1.50	88-13	Giant Leap117¾ Roger Jon1131 Me No Sissy1171¼	Steadied 1/4, driving	7

WORKOUTS: Mar 4 GP 3f fst :37 B *2/13* Feb 22 GP 3f fst :37 B *8/23* Feb 15 GP 3f fst :362 B *10/34* Feb 1 GP 3f sly :362 H *3/8* Jan 19 GP 4f gd :48 B *2/19*

Ken's Landing
Own: Lazer Two Stable
MIGLIORE R (62 10 14 7 .16) **$70,000**
Ch. g. 3 (May)
Sire: Prosperous (Mr. Prospector)
Dam: Fay Goldberg (Superbity)
Br: Kennedy Louis J (Fla)
Tr: Klesaris Robert P (5 1 1 1 .20)
113

Lifetime Record:	11	3	3	2	$50,021						
1994	4	2	0	1	$27,860	Turf	0	0	0	0	
1993	7	1	3	1	$22,161	Wet	0	0	0	0	
Bel	1	1	0	0	$14,400	Dist	4	3	0	0	$33,970

5May94-6Bel	fst	6f	:22 :452 :58 1:11	Clm 50000	79	1 4	78¼ 52 1½ 13½	Migliore R	117 f	6.30	86-18	Ken's Landing1173½ Cape Verde1101½ Index Fund117¾	Wide, driving	7
15Mar94-3GP	fst	6f	:22 :453 :582 1:112	Clm c-32000	73	4 4	56¼ 45 22 12½	Chapman K L5	112 f	4.10	84-15	Ken's Landing1122½ Fortunate Move117no Powerful Patch117nk	Driving	9
Claimed from Kimran Stable, Toner James J Trainer														
21Feb94-5GP	fst	7f	:221 :452 1:102 1:232	Clm 25000	78	4 8	31½ 11 13 31	Chapman K L5	112 f	6.20	85-13	Grateful Appeal119nk Talktomylawyer117¾ Ken'sLanding1122¼	Weakened	10
21Jan94-7GP	fst	6f	:22 :451 :572 1:101	Clm 50000	51	3 8	64½ 88¼ 812 1012¾	Santos J A	117	14.70	77-11	Ultimate Don117nk Maudlin's Sunny117¾ Honest Colors1172½	Stopped	10
28Nov93-7Grd	gd	6½f	:241 :473 1:134 1:204	Alw 18000N2L	72	3 3	34 34½ 32½ 2hd	David D J	119	*1.20	77-23	All My Effort119hd Ken's Landing1193 Groveland1171½	Stalked duel turn	5
20Nov93-9Grd	fst	1	:23 :471 1:124 1:411	Alw 31000NC	60	3 4	42½ 32 56½ 410	Montpellier C	116	9.10	62-25	YongeCstlefield1245 WinterRenegde1161½ BoldShot1153½	Two path turns	7
12Nov93-8Grd	fst	6½f	:231 :472 1:134 1:204	Clm 37500	66	2 7	68¼ 33½ 34 21½	David D J	118	4.95	75-25	Top End1221½ Ken's Landing1183 J J Liberty1161¾		7
Clumsy early, closed steadily														
28Oct93-6Grd	fst	7f	:23 :47 1:13 1:263	Clm 47500	57	5 8	65¼ 74¾ 43½ 33½	Duross A C5	111	13.15	81-15	BldAndAmzng1221 JJLbrty1162¼ Kn'sLndng111¾	Rallied between horses	8
15Oct93-6WO	fst	6f	:23 :464 1:124	Md 24000	61	4 7	51½ 33 2½ 12¾	David D J	120	3.05	81-15	Kn'sLnding1202¾ SpnishSky1201¼ SingsoloSundy1122	Stalked pace battle	9
24Sep93-3WO	fst	7f	:231 :463 1:122 1:254	Md 37500	50	4 8	32½ 22 32½ 55¼	King R Jr	119	5.50	77-14	Saint Penny1222¼ Catch The Native1222 Play With A Leader119½		10
Hit rail top of stretch														

WORKOUTS: May 4 Bel tr.t 3f fst :38 B *14/22* Mar 10 GP 5f fst 1:00 H *2/18* Mar 2 GP 4f fst :48 H *2/42*

Bob Klesaris claimed Giant Leap for $16,000 out of a race at Gulfstream Park on March 6 and freshened him up during the jail period. Scarcely twenty-four hours after Giant Leap was out of jail (and eligible to race for $17,500 or even $14,000), Klesaris showed confidence by entering him for $25,000, and the result was a $7.60 win by a length and a half.

A month later, the Klesaris-trained Ken's Landing showed the same profile: claimed from a race at Gulfstream, freshened during the jail period, and entered back at a higher level. Result: a decisive score at better than 6–1.

RECLAIMED

Anytime a trainer reclaims a horse formerly in his possession, he is telling you point blank, "I know this horse pretty well, and I liked him enough when I had him to take a chance on him again."

8 1⅜ MILES AQUEDUCT START FINISH

1 ⅜ MILES. **(2.14) HANDICAP. Purse $47,000. 3–year–olds and upward. Weights Friday, November 20. Declarations by 10:00 a.m., Saturday, November 21. Closing Friday, November 20. Closed with 11 nominations.**

Coupled—Bold Blazer and Convertible.

Captive Tune — **B. g. 4, by Fappiano—Captive Spirit, by Affirmed**
Br.—North Ridge Farm (Ky)
Tr.—Toner James J (10 1 2 1 .10)
VELAZQUEZ J R (85 12 10 11 .14)
Own.—Steelbinder Arthur
112

Lifetime		1992	17	2	3	5	$73,760
34 4 4 8		1991	14	2	1	2	$24,744
$99,564		Turf	11	0	1	3	$16,278
		Wet	2	1	0	1	$18,806

18Nov92- 1Aqu	fst	1⅛	:47^4	1:12^3	1:50^3	3↑Clm c-45000	**92**	3 8 7^{6½} 7^{3¼} 1^{½} 1no	Smith M E	b 113	3.70	83–26 CptvTn113^{no}SttlWgr114^{3}GnMcCn113	Pnchd brk wd drv	9
18Nov92-Claimed from Joques Farm, Moschera Gasper S Trainer														
7Nov92- 1Aqu	gd	1⅜	:48	1:37^4	2:15	3↑Clm c-35000	**86**	6 5 4^{3½} 2^{2½} 2^{1½} 2^{2¼}	Davis R G	b 117	2.00	93–13 Ceiling117^{2¼}CptivTun117^{12}CommissionrBrt117	2nd best	6
7Nov92-Claimed from Steelbinder G. Arthur; Toner James J. Trainer; Originally scheduled on turf														
29Oct92- 7Aqu	fst	1⅛	:47^2	1:11	1:49^4	3↑Alw 31000	**79**	6 5 3^2 4^{5½} 4^9 5^{9½}	Velazquez J R	b 117	16.20	77–24 Yaros114^3 Blazon Song114^2 Electrojet116	Tired	8
8Oct92- 6Bel	fm	1⅜	(T):49	1:36^4	2:13^3	3↑Clm 50000	**68**	5 7 7^{6½} 7^{5½} 7^{7¾} 7^{21}	Samyn J L	b 117	9.70	78–06 Critic'sCornr113^{½}Dvl'sCry119^{7}HghlndDvoton117	Outrun	7
25Sep92- 5Bel	fm	1¼	[T]:49^2	1:37	2:00^4	3↑Alw 31000	**83**	2 6 6^{3¼} 6^{3½} 6^6 6^8	Krone J A	b 117	7.30	78–10 EbonyMgc117^{½}Crnshw'sCornr117^{4}TmbrCt113	No factor	7
9Sep92- 4Bel	fm	1¼	[T]:48^2	1:36^2	2:00^2	3↑Alw 31000	**85**	4 5 5^4 5^{3¾} 4^7 3^7	Bailey J D	b 117	4.50	81–10 Dignostic117^{4½}TimberCt113^{2½}CptivTun117	Checked brk	9
10Aug92- 7Sar	fm	1⅜	[T]:47^3	1:37	2:15^1	3↑Alw 31000	**93**	7 4 5^5 5^{5½} 6^{3½} 4^{3¾}	Antley C W	b 117	9.80	90–11 Key Deputy117^{3}PowerBolt117^{½}TimberCat112	No threat	7
2Aug92- 6Sar	fm	$1\frac{3}{16}$	(T):47^2	1:11^4	1:54^1	3↑Alw 31000	**85**	5 10 11^{14} 11^{6¾} 10^{5½} 7^6	Antley C W	b 117	14.30	91–04 ShrethGlory117^{nk}King'sGnt117^{½}Puchinito117	No factor	11
7Jun92- 7Bel	yl	1¼	[T]:48	1:37^1	2:02^2	3↑Manhattan H	**61**	11 11 11^{13} 11^{11} 11^{23} 11^{31¼}	Carr D	b 109	85.40	47–22 SkyClassic123^{3}RomnEnvoy111^{1¼}LegerCt-Ar116	Outrun	11
7Jun92-Grade II														

LATEST WORKOUTS **Oct 22 Bel 4f fst :47^3 H**

Captive Tune was claimed away from Jimmy Toner on November 7 for $35,000, but he wasted no time in reclaiming the gelding, and in fact took a $10,000 loss on the transaction when he put up $45,000 of owner Arthur Steelbinder's money to claim him back just eleven days later.

Unspoken message from Toner: "I'm paying ten thousand more than I lost him for because I know how sharp he is right now, and I'll get that ten grand back in no time."

Well, what's five days in the grand scheme of things? Toner entered Captive Tune in a $47,000 overnight handicap on November 23, and the result was a win by four and three-quarter lengths at a mutuel of $14. The winner's share for Steelbinder and Toner amounted to $28,200 — a quick return on their investment.

TURF-TO-DIRT

The turf-to-dirt switch has been involved in a number of stakes upsets by lightly raced horses in recent seasons. For example, the exacta of Sea Hero and Secret Odds in the 1992 Champagne Stakes, which was run over a drying-out track listed as "good," was worth $515. They were the only turf-to-dirt horses in the field:

Sea Hero — B. c. 3(Mar), by Polish Navy—Glowing Tribute, by Graustark
Br.—Mellon Paul (Va)
Own.—Rokeby Stables — Tr.—Schulhofer Flint S (19 5 3 4 .26) — **117**
Lifetime 7 3 1 0 $339,720 — 1992 7 3 1 0 $339,720 — Turf 2 2 0 0 $33,000

31Oct92- 8GP	fst	$1\frac{1}{16}$	:46 1:10^2 1:43^2	Br Cp Juv	72	6	6	$6^{2\frac12}$	$6^{3\frac12}$	$8^{7\frac34}$	$7^{8\frac34}$	Bailey J D		122	2.40	86-03	GilddTim122¾It'sli'lknownfct122½RvrSpcl122	No excuse 13
31Oct92-Grade I																		
10Oct92- 7Bel	gd	1	:44^3 1:09 1:34^4	Champagne	99	1	5	3^2	2^{hd}	$1^{\frac12}$	$1^{5\frac34}$	Bailey J D	b	122	8.80	96-04	SeaHero122$^{5\frac34}$SecretOdds122$^{5\frac34}$PressCard122	Drew away 10
10Oct92-Grade I																		
21Sep92- 7Bel	fm	1	Ⓣ:45^3 1:09^3 1:34^3	Alw 29000	86	7	4	$4^{2\frac12}$	$3^{\frac12}$	$1^{1\frac12}$	$1^{3\frac34}$	Bailey J D	b	122	*.70	89-11	Sea Hero122$^{3\frac34}$ SimilarStar117¾Compadre117	Mild drive 7
7Sep92- 5Bel	fm	1	Ⓣ:46^2 1:10^2 1:35^2	Md Sp Wt	83	1	5	$3^{1\frac12}$	$3^{\frac12}$	$1^{\frac12}$	$1^{2\frac14}$	Bailey J D		118	*.90	85-19	Sea Hero118$^{2\frac14}$ Halissee118$^{2\frac12}$ Awad118	Driving 11
21Aug92- 6Sar	fst	7f	:23 :46 1:24	Md Sp Wt	69	4	8	$7^{4\frac12}$	$6^{4\frac12}$	$4^{2\frac12}$	$2^{1\frac14}$	Madrid A Jr		118	3.00	84-14	ThrillerChiller118$^{1\frac14}$SeHero118^{nk}AllGon118	Rallied wide 10
2Aug92- 4Sar	fst	6f	:22^2 :45^4 1:10^2	Md Sp Wt	63	5	3	$8^{3\frac34}$	8^6	$7^{5\frac12}$	$5^{7\frac14}$	Madrid A Jr		118	6.80	85-10	Wallenda118^2 All Gone118^4 D'Orazio118	Stead sharply 12
13Jly92- 5Bel	fst	5½f	:22^1 :45^2 1:03	Md Sp Wt	56	5	6	6^8	6^8	4^8	$4^{13\frac14}$	Bailey J D		118	*1.30	87-10	StrollngAlng118$^{2\frac12}$DvlshlyYrs118$^{8\frac12}$Dr.Alfs118	No threat 10

LATEST WORKOUTS ●Feb 5 Hia 4f fst :47 H — Jan 31 Hia 5f fst 1:00^3 H — Jan 26 Hia 4f sly :48^4 B — Jan 21 Hia 6f fst 1:14 H

Secret Odds — B. c. 2(Apr), by Secreto—Clever Miss, by Kaskaskia
STEVENS G L (—)
Br.—Bender Howard M & Sondra (Md)
Own.—Bender Sondra D — Tr.—Murray Lawrence E (—) — **122**
Lifetime 6 2 2 0 $154,815 — 1992 6 2 2 0 $154,815 — Turf 1 0 1 0 $11,515

10Oct92- 7Bel	gd	1	:44^3 1:09 1:34^4	Champagne	86	4	1	$1^{\frac12}$	1^{hd}	$2^{\frac12}$	$2^{5\frac34}$	Desormeaux K J		122	31.70	90-04	Sea Hero122$^{5\frac34}$ Secret Odds122$^{5\frac34}$ PressCard122	Gamely 10
10Oct92-Grade I																		
13Sep92-11Pim	fm	1	Ⓣ:47 1:11^4 1:38	Vanland'm	75	8	1	1^3	$1^{\frac12}$	$2^{1\frac12}$	2^8	Reynolds L C		111	2.60	70-27	Storm Flight110^{8}SecretOdds111$^{2\frac12}$Qizilbash115	2nd best 11
30Aug92- 8Sar	fst	6½f	:22^2 :45 1:15^3	Hopeful	59	2	6	4^2	$3^{1\frac12}$	$8^{7\frac12}$	$8^{16\frac12}$	Migliore R		122	17.10	80-08	GrtNtr122$^{3\frac34}$StrllnAln122¾EnlndEpcts122	Chkd brk, sted 8
30Aug92-Grade I																		
2Aug92- 9Lrl	fst	6f	:22^1 :45^4 1:11^1	Ⓢ Rollicking	87	2	1	1^1	1^4	$1^{3\frac12}$	$1^{7\frac12}$	Reynolds L C		113	*.30	86-19	ScrtOdds113$^{7\frac12}$TkngRsks113^{15}BckystownPk113	Handily 6
17Jly92- 8Lrl	fst	5½f	:22^3 :46 1:04^2	Md Sp Wt	93	6	1	1^2	1^2	1^4	1^9	Reynolds L C		120	2.20	97-15	ScrtOdds120^{9}WildAboutHrry120$^{8\frac12}$TkingRisks120	Easily 8
25Jun92- 5Pim	fst	5f	:22^2 :46^1 :58^2	Md Sp Wt	29	12	12	5^4	4^7	4^9	$8^{13\frac14}$	Reynolds L C		120	*3.30	83-13	GlRoyl120½DownHomDoctor120^{6}½Gclimb120	Sluggish st 12

LATEST WORKOUTS ●Oct 25 GP 5f fst :58 H — ●Oct 4 Lrl 4f fst :47^1 H — ●Sep 24 Lrl 4f fst :46^1 H — ●Sep 9 Lrl 4f fst :47^3 H

Valiant Nature broke his maiden on the grass at Hollywood Park second time out and then stretched out to upset Breeders' Cup Juvenile–winner Brocco in the Hollywood Futurity a month later:

2 Valiant Nature PP - 2
Own: V H W Stables
PINCAY L JR (—)
B. c. 3 (Mar)
Sire: His Majesty (Ribot)
Dam: Premium Win (Lyphard)
Br: Winchell Verne H (Ky)
Tr: McAnally Ronald (—) — **126**

Lifetime Record:	5 2 1 1	$421,500			
1994	2 0 1 1	$130,000	Turf	1 1 0 0	$16,500
1993	3 2 0 0	$291,500	Wet	1 0 0 1	$30,000
CD	0 0 0 0		Dist	0 0 0 0	

16Apr94- 9Kee	fst	1⅛	:47^4 1:12^3 1:37^4 1:50	Blue Grass-G2	107	6	2	2^3	2^2	$2^{1\frac12}$	$2^{3\frac12}$	Pincay L Jr		121	3.60	80-26	HolyBull121$^{3\frac12}$ ValiantNature121^5 MahognyHll121$^{2\frac12}$	Bid 1/4 pole, 2nd best 7
20Mar94- 4SA	my	$1\frac{1}{16}$	:23^4 :47^3 1:12^1 1:44^3	San Felipe-G2	102	5	1	1^2	1^1	2^{hd}	$3^{2\frac12}$	Pincay L Jr	B	119	1.30	70-33	Soul Of The Matter116$^{2\frac12}$ Brocco119^{hd} Valiant Nature119^{16}	Outfinished 5
19Dec93- 8Hol	fst	$1\frac{1}{16}$	:23^1 :46^1 1:09^3 1:40^3	Hol Futy-G1	106	2	1	1^3	$1^{1\frac12}$	1^2	$1^{\frac34}$	Pincay L Jr	B	121	16.00	98-12	Valiant Nature121¾ Brocco121$^{2\frac12}$ Flying Sensation121½	Speed, held 6
17Nov93- 4Hol	fm	1 Ⓣ	:46^3 1:11^1 1:36^1	Md Sp Wt	78	4	1	1^{hd}	$1^{1\frac12}$	$1^{1\frac12}$	$1^{3\frac12}$	Pincay L Jr	B	118	*2.50	84-14	Valiant Nature118$^{3\frac12}$ Saltgrass118$^{3\frac12}$ Unrivaled118^1	Ducked in 1/16 9
Quarter time unavailable																		
10Oct93- 9SA	fst	6f	:21^4 :44^3 :57 1:09^4	Md Sp Wt	47	6	7	$6^{4\frac12}$	$8^{7\frac14}$	8^9	$10^{14\frac14}$	Pincay L Jr	B	117	13.20	74-16	Sky Kid117^{hd} Gracious Ghost117^5 Al's River Cat117$^{1\frac12}$	Lugged out late 11

WORKOUTS: ●May 2 CD 6f fst 1:14 H 1/6 Apr 25 Kee 4f fst :48 B 2/17 ●Apr 14 Kee 4f fst :48 H 1/65 Apr 8 SA 1 fst 1:37^3 H 1/3 Apr 3 SA 6f fst 1:13^3 B 4/21 Mar 29 SA 4f fst :48^1 B 23/50

Brought back for his three-year-old debut in the San Felipe, Valiant Nature was second choice to Brocco, but neither was a match for Soul Of The Matter, a turf-to-dirt horse who handled the exceptionally tiring track and came from ten lengths behind to win going away at 6–1:

```
3 Soul Of The Matter                    Dk. b or br c. 3 (Apr)                              Lifetime Record :   5 3 0 2   $178,250
                                        Sire: Private Terms (Private Account)          1994   3 2 0 1   $147,850 | Turf   1 0 0 *1    $9,000
                                        Dam: Soul Light (T. V. Commercial)             1993   2 1 0 1    $30,400 | Wet    1 1 0 0  $118,500
Own: Bacharach Burt                     Br: Blue Seas Music Inc (WV)          L 118    Kee    0 0 0 0            | Dist   1 1 0 0  $118,500
DESORMEAUX K J (—)                      Tr: Mandella Richard (1 1 0 0 1.00)

20Mar94-4SA  my  1 1/16   :234 :473 1:121 1:443  San Felipe-G2    106 4 5 510 58 32 12¼ Desormeaux K J B 116  6.30 72-33 SoulOfTheMatter1162¼ Brocco119hd ValiantNature11916 Wide, strong rally 5
 5Mar94-1SA  fm  1  ⓣ :222 :46  1:103 1:351  Pirate Cove61k    91 4 6 76½ 65 54 32  Desormeaux K J B 115  2.90 87-07 Eagle Eyed113¾ Majestic Style1141¼ Soul Of The Matter1152  8
     Lacked room 2nd turn & 1/8
 9Jan94-3SA  fst 6½f     :213 :441 1:084 1:152  Alw 37000N1X      96 3 4 54¾ 44 22½ 11½ Desormeaux K J B 120  *.50 95-08 Soul OfTheMatter1201½ Rotsaluck1171 Pollock'sLuck1203½ Drifted in 1/16 6
26Nov93-11Hol fst 7f     :22  :443 1:081 1:21   H Prevue BC-G3    96 2 5 41½ 41½ 21½ 31½ McCarron C J  B 115  2.00 97-09 Individual Style1211½ Egayant117nk Soul Of The Matter1151½  6
     Drifted in, checked 1/8
30Oct93-6SA  fst 6½f     :212 :444 1:094 1:161  Md Sp Wt          88 6 5 54 31 2hd 14  Desormeaux K J B 117  3.60 90-12 SoulOfTheMatter1174 Al'sRiverCat1173½ Elaine'sLove1173 Clear, driving 7
WORKOUTS: Apr 17 SA 7f fst 1:274 B 2/7  Apr 6 SA 4f fst :49 B 21/31  Mar 31 SA ⓣ 4f fm :503 H (d) 1/1  Mar 17 SA ⓣ 4f fm :492 H (d) 1/2  Mar 4 SA ⓣ 3f fm :371 H (d) 2/2  Feb 27 SA ⓣ 6f fm 1:17 H (d) 1/1
```

The turf-to-dirt angle on tiring muddy tracks first came to my attention at Saratoga on the afternoon of August 8, 1990. The main track was labeled "muddy" early in the day and upgraded to "good" for the last four races; it was the kind of gummy and "holding" mud that had many horses gasping for breath by the far turn, and the day's races were dominated by horses that had last raced on the turf. In the opener, a Rockingham shipper named Pic Iron, who had finished second on grass at her home base three weeks earlier, won at $8.40. The early daily double was completed by Cosmic Belle, a filly who had finished eighth on grass just four days earlier but who rallied from eleventh position to win, going away by four lengths at $39. In the third, Valid Delta, dead last in a $35,000 grass route on July 21, wired $50,000 sprinters at $41. In the seventh, Seattle Colony, eighth on grass last time out, won an allowance sprint as the longest shot in the field at $26.80. The nightcap went to turf-to-dirt Totem Zone, who wired her field by eight lengths at $12.60. There seemed to be no track bias involved. Pic Iron, Valid Delta, and Totem Zone won on the front end, but Cosmic Belle and Seattle Colony were stone-cold closers.

This angle continues to get winners at the Spa, as it did in back-to-back divisions of a maiden special-weight sprint for New York–breds on August 18, 1993. Overnight rains rendered the track a sea of mud during training hours, but by noon the sun was shining and the track was in that nebulous state between muddy and good — exactly the conditions that were present August 8, 1990. Sure enough, Seminole Spirt and Charlie Kenny Sr., who were each turning back in distance after a longer race on the grass, survived prolonged stretch duels to win by half a length:

Seminole Spirt
Own: Bomze Diane K
NO RIDER (—)
Dk. b or br c. 2 (Apr)
Sire: Compliance (Northern Dancer)
Dam: Hello Poppy (Hasty Flyer)
Br: Michael Spielman (NY)
Tr: O'Brien Leo (—)
112

Lifetime Record: 5 1 1 0 $22,090							
1993	5 1 1 0	$22,090	Turf	0 0 0 0			
1992	0 M 0 0		Wet	0 0 0 0			
GS	0 0 0 0		Dist	2 0 1 0	$6,580		

18Aug93- 2Sar gd 6f :224 :463 :59 1:112 SMd Sp Wt 58 12 1 4¾ 2hd 2½ 1½ Smith M E 118 b 6.70 85-08 Seminole Spirt118½ Background Artist1182¾ Boldly Brave1181½ Driving 13
22Jly93- 3Bel fm 7f Ⓣ :233 :47 1:11 1:233 Md Sp Wt 36 1 7 72¾ 63 710 514¼ Nelson D 118 b 11.40 73-12 Cross Ice Pass1184 Ben's Jet1186¼ Lear Flight118nk Steadied turn 8
25Jun93- 3Bel fst 6f :224 :471 1:002 1:143 SMd Sp Wt 40 3 2 54 65 63¾ 42½ Smith M E 118 b 2.60e 64-22 Private Deal118nk Silver Safari118¾ Legasus1181½ Mild rally 10
14Jun93- 3Bel fst 5½f :224 :463 :591 1:06 SMd Sp Wt 52 4 5 43 23 35 26 Smith M E 118 2.80 79-14 CraftyHrold1186 SeminoleSpirt118hd BckgroundArtist118½ Up for place 9
16May93- 3Bel fst 5f :223 :462 :592 Md Sp Wt 54 1 1 31 31½ 32½ 43¼ Carr D 118 7.20e 81-15 Gliding Arrow1183 Lahint118nk Charlie Cush118no Lacked rally 7
WORKOUTS: Jly 18 Bel 4f fst :523 B 28/30 Jun 24 Bel 3f fst :363 B 2/20 Jun 13 Bel 3f fst :37 B 3/14 Jun 1 Bel 5f gd 1:042 B 4/6 May 25 Bel 3f fst :383 B 17/20 May 13 Bel 3f fst :37 Bg 8/15

Charlie Kenny Sr.
Own: Kenny Charles F
NO RIDER (—)
B. g. 3 (May)
Sire: Titanic (Alydar)
Dam: Kenny's Melissa (Nehoc's Bullet)
Br: Kenny Charles F (NY)
Tr: Kenny Charles F (—)
111

Lifetime Record: 6 1 0 3 $22,620					
1993	4 1 0 2	$19,740	Turf	1 0 0 0	
1992	2 M 0 1	$2,880	Wet	1 0 0 1	$2,880
GS	0 0 0 0		Dist	0 0 0 0	

18Aug93- 3Sar gd 6f :222 :454 :58 1:102 3+ SMd Sp Wt 75 5 2 32 31 1hd 1½ Krone J A 117 2.90 90-08 Charlie Kenny Sr.117½ Ti Dye1174 Dacotah Brave1172¾ Driving 9
13Aug93- 2Sar fm 1 1/16 Ⓣ :233 :481 1:131 1:44 3+ Md Sp Wt 47 10 8 83¼ 93¾ 105½ 1013¼ Mojica R Jr 117 18.80 66-15 All Known1173 Delray117¾ Perhaps Grass1172 Wide, outrun 10
29Jly93- 5Sar fst 7f :23 :454 1:103 1:234 3+ SMd Sp Wt 52 13 1 72½ 42½ 33½ 39½ Mojica R Jr 116 5.60 76-10 Jessup North116no Gifted Traven1119½ Charlie Kenny Sr.1163½ Lacked rally 14
19Jly93- 9Bel gd 6f :221 :454 :581 1:112 3+ SMd Sp Wt 59 6 3 2½ 22 2½ 31½ Mojica R Jr 116 7.60 81-13 Pro On Ice1161½ Lake116hd Charlie Kenny Sr.1161½ Willingly 14
7Oct92- 6Bel fst 6f :223 :462 :582 1:104 SMd Sp Wt 30 11 4 42 54½ 412 524¼ Madrid A Jr 118 18.30 62-16 Rush Chairman Bill11811 Itaka1186½ Bold Doer118 Tired 13
27Sep92- 9Bel sly 6f :222 :462 :58 1:114 SMd Sp Wt 42 2 2 44 32½ 34½ 37¾ Madrid A Jr 118 40.00 73-14 Gravel King1187 Mt. Shannon118¾ Charlie Kenny Sr.118 Lacked rally 14
WORKOUTS: Jly 10 Sar tr.t 5f fst 1:032 H 1/1 Jly 1 Sar tr.t 5f fst 1:023 H 1/2 Jun 23 Sar tr.t 5f fst 1:042 B 2/5 ●Jun 18 Sar 4f fst :512 B 1/7 Jun 9 Sar tr.t 4f gd :534 B 2/2 ●Jun 3 Sar 4f fst :494 H 1/7

The success of the turf-to-dirt/turnback-in-distance combination is not limited to Saratoga. Examine the field for the sixth race at Gulfstream Park on March 2, 1994:

Gulfstream Park

6 *7 Furlongs.* (1:204) MAIDEN CLAIMING. Purse $20,000 (plus $1,800 FOA). Fillies, 3-year-olds. Weight, 121 lbs. Claiming price $80,000; if for $75,000, allowed 2 lbs. (Registered Florida breds preferred.)

START 7 FURLONGS FINISH

Ballpoint
Own: Kramer J & Samuels D
VALLES E S (73 5 3 9 .07) $75,000
Gr. f. 3 (Feb)
Sire: Tilt Up (Olden Times)
Dam: Grise Petite (Dancer's Image)
Br: Dreyfuss Donald & Liebeskind Harvey & Partners (Fla)
Tr: Spatz Ronald B (20 0 1 3 .00)
L 119

Lifetime Record: 4 M 0 2 $4,050					
1994	2 M 0 1	$2,620	Turf	0 0 0 0	
1993	2 M 0 1	$1,430	Wet	1 0 0 0	$130
GP	2 0 0 1	$2,620	Dist	0 0 0 0	

16Feb94- 5GP fst 6f :223 :46 :583 1:113 ⒻMd 75000 56 7 4 33½ 43½ 45½ 33 Sellers S J L 119 fb 6.30 80-12 Biddy Mason119hd Crypto Jack1123 Ballpoint1192 [illegible]
Angled out upper str, late rally
29Jan94- 6GP fst 6f :214 :444 :571 1:101 ⒻMd Sp Wt 55 5 8 64¾ 47 49½ 612¼ Valles E S L 120 fb 38.10 78-10 Delightful Dec120¾ Say It With Roses1152 Our Miz Waki120nk 10
Bumped start, through early
29Aug93- 6Crc sly 5½f :224 :473 1:003 1:071 ⒻMd Sp Wt [illegible] Douglas R R 116 f 4.30 77-14 Future Answer116¾ Miss Aciss116¾ American Dawn1161½ Showed little 9
15Aug93- 6Crc fst 5½f :224 :47 [illegible] ⒻMd Sp Wt 48 1 6 2hd 7hd 21½ 36¾ Douglas R R 116 f 17.70 88-16 Copewithme116¾ Silver Maggie116¾ Ballpoint116nk Weakened 11
WORKOUTS: Feb 12 Crc 4f fst :503 Bg 34/45 Jan 26 Crc 4f sly :49 B (d) 6/16 Jan 20 Crc 5f fst 1:042 Bg 19/20 Jan 14 Crc 4f sly :49 B (d) 4/27 Jan 8 Crc 5f fst 1:04 B 26/34 Dec 30 Crc 3f fst :39 B 11/12

Via Wood
Own: Penna Ellnor
BAILEY J D (231 59 35 18 .26) $75,000
B. f. 3 (May)
Sire: Tapping Wood (Roberto)
Dam: Vianca (Nonparrell)
Br: Claim Ehnthell (Fla)
Tr: Penna Angel Jr (15 3 3 3 .20)
L 119

Lifetime Record: 1 M 0 1 $1,700				
1994	1 M 0 1	$1,700	Turf	0 0 0 0
1993	0 M 0 0		Wet	0 0 0 0
GP	1 0 0 1	$1,700	Dist	0 0 0 0

11Feb94- 5GP fst 6f :22 :45 :58 1:12 ⒻMd 50000 51 11 1 106 78½ 54½ 31½ Bailey J D 121 14.90 80-12 Celtic Twang121½ Sonesta Miss121¾ Via Wood1211 Rallied 12
WORKOUTS: Feb 26 GP 3f fst :362 Bg 7/18 Feb 21 GP 5f fst 1:04 B 52/58 Feb 6 GP 5f fst 1:02 B 21/55 Feb 5 GP 3f fst :39 Bg 33/40 Jan 29 GP 5f fst 1:03 B 53/70 Jan 23 GP 5f fst 1:01 B 14/52

Satellite Dish
Own: Tatta Ann & Zerreli F
SAMYN J L (71 5 2 6 .07) $75,000
B. f. 3 (Apr)
Sire: Blushing John (Blushing Groom)
Dam: Lilac Garden (Roberto)
Br: Foxfield (Ky)
Tr: Nesky Kenneth A (3 0 0 0 .00)
L 119

Lifetime Record: 0 M 0 0 $0			
1994	0 M 0 0	Turf	0 0 0 0
1993	0 M 0 0	Wet	0 0 0 0
GP	0 0 0 0	Dist	0 0 0 0

WORKOUTS: Feb 21 GP 4f fst :49 B 18/60 Feb 20 GP 5f fst 1:033 B 22/29 Feb 10 GP 6f fst 1:141 H 6/7 Jan 29 GP 5f fst 1:02 Bg 36/70 Jan 22 GP 5f fst 1:012 B 24/53 Jan 16 GP 4f fst :483 B 23/89
Jan 11 GP 3f gd :363 B 9/26 Jan 6 GP 3f fst :383 B 22/28 Dec 31 GP 3f fst :36 H 2/30 Oct 23 Aqu 4f fst :494 Hg 5/15 Oct 18 Aqu 6f fst 1:172 B 1/1 Oct 11 Aqu 5f fst 1:03 B 4/6

Royal Cozzene
Own: Kupferberg Max & Saul J
SANTOS J A (219 29 36 32 .13) $80,000
Gr. f. 3 (Jun)
Sire: Cozzene (Caro)
Dam: Metropolitan Lady (Apalachee)
Br: Ray Corbett (NY)
Tr: Margotta Anthony Jr (7 0 1 1 .00)
121

Lifetime Record: 4 M 0 0 $1,690					
1994	1 M 0 0	$190	Turf	1 0 0 0	
1993	3 M 0 0	$1,500	Wet	1 0 0 0	
GP	1 0 0 0	$190	Dist	1 0 0 0	$1,500

9Jan94- 6GP gd 6f :221 :454 :582 1:11 ⒻMd Sp Wt 38 5 10 98¾ 1016 812 814½ Santos J A 120 38.30 72-13 NightAndDrms1202¼ DrndAlrmng1201½ Mynmspnm1201½ Failed to menace 12
14Nov93- 8Aqu yl 1 Ⓣ :233 :492 1:16 1:41 ⒻSEast View60k 16 11 11 119½ 108½ 1016 1026½ Sanders J L 112 38.00 44-29 Great Triumph1184 Casa Eire1183 All For Fitness1163 Outrun 11
9Oct93- 1Bel fst 7f :234 :482 1:134 1:271 ⒻMd Sp Wt 22 5 5 52 42 48½ 419 Sanders J L 117 17.40 48-23 Sky Flasher1173 Something Light11714 S. M. Fran1172 Checked break 5
26Sep93- 2Bel sly 6½f :231 :473 1:131 1:194 ⒻMd 72500 11 5 4 520 512 511 524 Sanders J L 115 14.60 50-15 Rock The Nest1175 Miner's Inch1139 Believe In Doris1085½ Outrun 5
WORKOUTS: Feb 20 GP 7f fst 1:303 B 2/2 ●Feb 5 GP 3f fst :36 H 1/40 Jan 21 GP 6f fst 1:15 B 9/15 Dec 31 GP 3f fst :38 B 18/30 Dec 24 GP 5f fst 1:053 B 61/63 Dec 5 GP 3f fst :37 B 4/20

Cozigoldi
Own: Cresci Dorothy
BRAVO J (234 33 34 25 .14) $80,000
Dk. b or br f. 3 (Mar)
Sire: Cozzene (Caro)
Dam: Big Goldie (Big Spruce)
Br: Cresci Mrs Dorothy E (Ky)
Tr: Contessa Gary C (19 3 3 0 .16)
L 121

Lifetime Record: 1 M 0 0 $230					
1994	1 M 0 0	$230	Turf	0 0 0 0	
1993	0 M 0 0		Wet	0 0 0 0	
GP	1 0 0 0	$230	Dist	1 0 0 0	$230

6Feb94- 6GP fst 7f :223 :452 1:104 1:233 ⒻMd Sp Wt 52 9 1 84¾ 84¾ 45½ 610 Bravo J L 121 25.10 75-11 LottaDncing1213½ CodeOfOld1214½ BlushingMggie1211½ Six wide str, tired 10
WORKOUTS: Feb 28 Hia 3f fst :373 B 5/6 Feb 19 Hia 4f sly :513 B 7/7 Feb 1 Hia 5f sly 1:014 H 1/2 Jan 21 Hia 3f fst :373 Bg 7/12 Jan 15 Hia 7f fst 1:291 H 2/3 Jan 7 Hia 5f fst 1:044 B 11/11

Fortone
Own: Martorana Anthony
DUARTE J C (12 0 1 3 .00) $75,000
Ch. f. 3 (Mar)
Sire: Lord Avie (Lord Gaylord)
Dam: Intrepid Trek (Damascus)
Br: Harvey Liebeskind & Donald Dreyfuss (Fla)
Tr: Triola Robert (5 0 0 0 .00)
L 119

Lifetime Record: 6 M 1 3 $8,850											
1994	2 M	0	0	$1,350	Turf	1	0	0	0	$250
1993	4 M	1	3	$7,500	Wet	0	0	0	0	
GP	1	0 0	0	$1,100	Dist	1	0	0	1	$1,560

13Feb94- 5GP fm *1⅛ ① :48 1:12³ 1:37⁴ 1:51³+ ⒻMd Sp Wt 60 10 5 710 75¾ 58¼ 57 Duarte J C L 121 9.80 80-06 Wild Wild Life1212¼ Pridefully121nk Eurostar1212 Belated bid 10
16Jan94- 6GP fst 1 1/16 :23³ :48 1:13 1:45² ⒻMd Sp Wt 61 1 4 65 31½ 32½ 44¼ Duarte J C L 120 *2.50 79-12 Here's My Neffer1202½ Slew Lake120no Northern Advance1201¾ 10
Six wide top str, weakened
29Dec93- 3Crc fst 1 1/16 :23⁴ :48⁴ 1:14³ 1:47⁴ ⒻMd Sp Wt 60 4 4 43 47½ 311 28½ Duarte J C L 119 *1.40 73-19 Polish Symphony1198½ Fortone1192½ Teewinot11916 Second best 7
30Nov93- 3Crc fst 1 1/16 :24¹ :49 1:14² 1:49³ ⒻMd Sp Wt 63 6 4 22½ 21½ 21½ 32¼ Duarte J C 118 11.50 71-19 Tasso Bee1182 Northern Advance118nk Fortone11810 Not good enough 6
21Nov93- 6Crc fst 7f :23¹ :46² 1:11⁴ 1:25 ⒻMd Sp Wt 55 3 4 32½ 611 412 311 Castaneda M 119 8.30 79-10 Chalynn1193½ Tasso Bee1197½ Fortone1192¼ Passed tired ones 8
31Oct93- 6Crc fst 5½f :22² :46⁴ :59⁴ 1:06³ ⒻMd Sp Wt 44 11 10 107¾ 911 78¼ 37¼ Castaneda M 118 13.50 87-11 Dixie Blue1186 Chalynn1181¼ Fortone1181¼ 12
Seven wide top str, late rally
WORKOUTS: Feb 5 Crc 5f fst 1:02¹ B 24/50 Dec 17 Crc 4f fst :48³ H 3/24 Dec 11 Crc 5f fst 1:05 B 45/52

K T Island
Own: Cass Stable
SMITH M E (283 55 49 33 .19) $80,000
B. f. 3 (Apr)
Sire: Island Whirl (Pago Pago)
Dam: Beat the Chief (Chieftain)
Br: Samara Farm (Fla)
Tr: Sanders Gregory E (25 2 3 3 .08)
121

Lifetime Record: 1 M 0 0 $680										
1994	1 M	0	0	$680	Turf	0	0	0	0
1993	0 M	0	0		Wet	0	0	0	0
GP	1	0 0	0	$680	Dist	0	0	0	0

11Feb94- 5GP fst 6f :22 :45 :58 1:12 ⒻMd 50000 48 12 2 41½ 2hd 21 42¼ Smith M E 121 *1.00 79-12 Celtic Twang121½ Sonesta Miss121¾ Via Wood1211 Weakened 12
WORKOUTS: Feb 28 GP 3f fst :36 B 4/16 Feb 22 GP 4f fst :48 H 4/47 Feb 8 GP 5f fst 1:00 H 4/25 ●Jan 29 Crc 5f gd 1:01 Hg 1/54 ●Jan 25 Crc 3f sly :35² Hg(d) 1/11 ●Jan 3 Crc 3f sly :36 H 1/14

Crypto Jack
Own: Postime '93
SELLERS S J (198 27 29 29 .14) $75,000
Dk. b or br f. 3 (Apr)
Sire: Cryptoclearance (Fappiano)
Dam: Speed Trap (Accipiter)
Br: St Francis Farm (Fla)
Tr: Donovan L William (35 1 4 4 .03)
119

Lifetime Record: 3 M 1 1 $5,615										
1994	1 M	1	0	$3,600	Turf	0	0	0	0
1993	2 M	0	1	$2,015	Wet	0	0	0	0
GP	1	0 1	0	$3,600	Dist	0	0	0	0

16Feb94- 5GP fst 6f :22³ :46 :58³ 1:11³ ⒻMd 75000 64 1 6 43¾ 32 21½ 2hd Chapman K L7 112 7.70 83-12 Biddy Mason119hd Crypto Jack1123 Ballpoint1192 Rallied inside 9
30Jly93- 5Lrl fst 5½f :23 :47² 1:00 1:06² ⒻMd Sp Wt 45 7 5 76 88 78½ 68 Turner T G 119 9.70 79-15 Shang Valay1191 Another Dessa1194¼ Rabba Jabba Doo1191½ Wide 10
17Jly93- 4Lrl fst 5½f :23¹ :47⁴ 1:00 1:06¹ ⒻMd Sp Wt 45 3 8 79 68½ 46½ 310 Saumell L 119 *2.40 78-19 Fashion Maven1197 Whats The Point1193 Crypto Jack1193¼ Wide 8
WORKOUTS: Feb 10 GP 5f fst 1:01 H 8/20 Jan 29 GP 5f fst 1:01 Bg 5/70 Jan 22 GP 5f fst 1:01 Bg 10/53 Jan 17 GP 5f fst 1:01 B 7/61 Jan 11 GP 5f gd 1:01² B 6/32 Jan 5 GP 4f fst :51¹ B 57/65

The three-year-old fillies in this high-priced maiden claimer at seven furlongs lacked any significant experience on sloppy tracks, but more important, four of the eight entrants had never been beyond six furlongs, and one of the two who had raced at the distance (Royal Cozzene) had not been postward in nearly two months. These fillies were all eligible to get the "staggers" in the seventh and deciding furlong, and it appeared that Fortone enjoyed an edge in terms of "bottom," that is, a conditioning foundation that would give her more stamina in the latter stages of the race.

Fortone had shown some speed on dirt at Calder back in November, and she had shown a midrace move while racing six wide approaching the stretch in her most recent start on dirt — a route at a mile and a sixteenth. Following that race, Fortone broke from the extreme outside post, going nine furlongs on the grass February 13, offering a "belated bid" according to the comment line. Shortening up after a series of four route races, the latest on grass, Fortone was meeting several rivals who had never been this far; if he uncorked the kind of move in this sprint that he'd shown January 16, he would be surging past leg-weary rivals in the stretch.

The drop from special-weight to claimer was an added bonus:

SIXTH RACE
Gulfstream
MARCH 2, 1994

7 FURLONGS. (1.20³) MAIDEN CLAIMING. Purse $20,000 (plus $1,800 FOA). Fillies, 3–year–olds. Weight, 121 lbs. Claiming price $80,000; if for $75,000, allowed 2 lbs. (Registered Florida breds preferred.)

Value of Race: $21,800 Winner $13,800; second $3,800; third $2,400; fourth $1,000; fifth $200; sixth $200; seventh $200; eighth $200. Mutuel Pool $218,880.00 Perfecta Pool $219,269.00 Trifecta Pool $202,390.00

Last Raced	Horse	M/Eqt.	A.	Wt	PP	St	¼	½	Str	Fin	Jockey	Cl'g Pr	Odds $1
13Feb94 5GP5	Fortone	Lb	3	119	6	1	$3^{\frac{1}{2}}$	2^1	1^{hd}	$1^{2\frac{1}{4}}$	Duarte J C	75000	7.70
16Feb94 5GP2	Crypto Jack	b	3	119	8	3	4^1	3^{hd}	$3^{1\frac{1}{2}}$	$2^{3\frac{1}{2}}$	Sellers S J	75000	2.30
11Feb94 5GP4	K T Island		3	121	7	2	$1^{1\frac{1}{2}}$	$1^{\frac{1}{2}}$	2^3	$3^{\frac{1}{2}}$	Smith M E	80000	3.90
11Feb94 5GP3	Via Wood	L	3	119	2	5	5^{hd}	$5^{2\frac{1}{2}}$	5^2	$4^{\frac{3}{4}}$	Bailey J D	75000	2.50
	Satellite Dish	L	3	119	3	6	7^5	7^6	6^6	$5^{\frac{3}{4}}$	Samyn J L	75000	22.20
16Feb94 5GP3	Ballpoint	Lbf	3	119	1	7	2^{hd}	4^{hd}	4^{hd}	$6^{9\frac{1}{4}}$	Valles E S	75000	11.20
6Feb94 6GP6	Cozigoldi	L	3	121	5	4	6^1	6^{hd}	$7^{3\frac{1}{2}}$	$7^{1\frac{1}{2}}$	Bravo J	80000	4.60
9Jan94 6GP8	Royal Cozzene		3	121	4	8	8	8	8	8	Santos J A	80000	52.60

OFF AT 3:16 Start Good. Won driving. Time, :22¹, :45, 1:10⁴, 1:24⁴ Track sloppy.

$2 Mutuel Prices:				
	6–FORTONE	17.40	5.60	3.60
	8–CRYPTO JACK		3.40	2.60
	7–K T ISLAND			3.20

$2 PERFECTA 6 & 8 PAID $62.80 $2 TRIFECTA 6–8–7 PAID $323.60

Ch. f, (Mar), by Lord Avie–Intrepid Trek, by Damascus. Trainer Triola Robert. Bred by Dreyfuss D & Liebeskind H (Fla).

FORTONE, a forward factor early, made a run to challenge for the lead leaving the backstretch, gained a slim lead midstretch then, under left handed urging, proved best. CRYPTO JACK, within striking distance early, moved into a forward position leaving the backstretch, rallied in the drive to take down the place. K T ISLAND sprinted to an early lead, set the pace until midstretch then weakened. VIA WOOD reserved early then closed with a belated bid. SATELLITE DISH void of early foot, made a mild late bid. BALLPOINT raced closest to the pace early then faded. COZIGOLDI, a forward factor early, tired. ROYAL COZZENE was outrun.

Owners— 1, Martorana Anthony; 2, Postime '93; 3, Cass Stable; 4, Penna Elinor; 5, Tatta Ann & Zerreli F; 6, Kramer J & Samuels D; 7, Cresci Dorothy; 8, Kupferberg Max & Saul

Trainers—1, Triola Robert; 2, Donovan L William; 3, Sanders Gregory E; 4, Penna Angel Jr; 5, Nesky Kenneth A; 6, Spatz Ronald B; 7, Contessa Gary C; 8, Margotta Anthony Jr

WON PACE DUEL, LOST THE RACE

The general betting public, as we know, overbets good last-out finish positions and beaten lengths, but often overlooks horses moving from unfavorable to favorable pace scenarios.

One angle that regularly produces overlays is the horse that recently won a pace duel but lost the race to a closer.

Examine the chart of Keeneland's Queen Elizabeth, noting the positions of the horses after the opening quarter-mile:

EIGHTH RACE
Keeneland
OCTOBER 30, 1993

1⅛ MILES. (Turf)(1.47^{2}) 10th Running of THE QUEEN ELIZABETH II CHALLENGE CUP. (GRADE I) Purse $200,000. Fillies, 3-year-olds. By invitation with no nomination or starting fees. The owner of the winner to receive $124,000 with $40,000 to second, $20,000 to third, $10,000 to fourth and $6,000 to fifth. Weight, 121 lbs. The Keeneland Association will invite a representative field of fillies to compete. The field will be drawn by the closing day of entries. A gold julep cup will be presented to the owner of the winner. Winning trainer and jockey to receive a silver julep cup.

Value of Race: $200,000 Winner $124,000; second $40,000; third $20,000; fourth $10,000; fifth $6,000. Mutuel Pool $220,762.00 Exacta Pool $156,599.00 Quinella Pool $42,380.00

Last Raced	Horse	M/Eqt.	A.Wt	PP	St	¼	½	¾	Str	Fin	Jockey	Odds $1
11Oct93 ^{9}Lrl^{4}	Tribulation		3 121	6	4	$5^{1/2}$	6^{4}	$6^{1 1/2}$	1^{hd}	1^{2}	Samyn J L	21.40
11Oct93 ^{7}SA^{1}	Miami Sands-IR	L	3 121	4	7	7^{1}	7^{1}	9	5^{1}	$2^{1/2}$	Pincay L Jr	7.70
2Oct93 ^{11}LaD^{1}	Possibly Perfect		3 121	5	3	3^{hd}	2^{hd}	$4^{1/2}$	2^{hd}	3^{3}	Day P	2.40
3Oct93 Lch^{5}	Marillette		3 121	9	9	9	9	7^{hd}	$6^{1/2}$	4^{2}	McCarron C J	13.60
13Oct93 ^{8}Kee^{1}	Weekend Madness-IR		3 121	1	1	1^{hd}	1^{1}	$1^{1 1/2}$	3^{hd}	$5^{1/2}$	Woods C R Jr	9.40
11Sep93 ^{8}Dmr^{3}	Amal Hayati	Lb	3 121	2	2	6^{4}	4^{hd}	3^{hd}	$4^{1/2}$	6^{nk}	Sellers S J	10.30
3Oct93 Lch^{4}	Ajfan		3 121	7	5	2^{hd}	3^{1}	2^{hd}	$7^{1 1/2}$	7^{2}	Martinez W	17.20
3Oct93 ^{8}Bel^{2}	Kirov Premiere-GB		3 121	3	8	$8^{1 1/2}$	8^{1}	8^{hd}	8^{4}	8^{6}	Bailey J D	*2.40
10Oct93 Mil^{3}	Nicer-IR		3 121	8	6	4^{1}	5^{hd}	5^{1}	9	9	Holland D	6.00

***—Actual Betting Favorite.**

OFF AT 4:41 Start Good. Won driving. Time, :24^{1}, :48^{4}, 1:13^{4}, 1:40^{3}, 1:53^{3} Course yielding.

$2 Mutuel Prices:				
	6–TRIBULATION	44.80	17.60	6.80
	4–MIAMI SANDS-IR		8.80	5.00
	5–POSSIBLY PERFECT			3.20

$2 EXACTA 6–4 PAID $409.00 $2 QUINELLA 4–6 PAID $137.80

B. f, (Mar), by Danzig–Graceful Touch, by His Majesty. Trainer Toner James J. Bred by Mr. & Mrs. J. Phillips, A. Seelbind (Ky).

TRIBULATION, in hand soon after the start while racing in behind the leaders and saving ground, remained in hand around the second turn while appearing full of run, came out to advance from between rivals six-wide into the stretch, reached the front a furlong out and was kept to left-handed urging in the drive to edge clear. MIAMI SANDS, unhurried for six furlongs, edged up inside nearing the stretch, lacked room behind a wall of horses while checked lightly in the upper stretch, angled out to find room by following the winner and was second best. POSSIBLY PERFECT prompted the pace from the start while racing outside of WEEKEND MADNESS, was on even terms for the lead in the upper stretch and came up empty. MARILLETTE was sluggish to start and angled inside to save ground, was unhurried for six furlongs, also lacked room while along the inside into the stretch, was checked lightly when the rider sought an opening and could not threaten when clear. WEEKEND MADNESS gained the lead at once, made the pace under constant pressure, held on well until the eighth pole and faltered. AMAL HAYATI, well-placed from the start while rated along in behind the leaders, tired when the test came a furlong out. AJFAN prompted the pace for six furlongs and weakened. KIROV PREMIERE, unhurried and saving ground early, eased off the inside on the backstretch, had to come eight wide as the field bunched into the stretch and had no rally. NICER raced forwardly although four wide for six furlongs and tired.

Owners— 1, Seelbinder G Art & Phillips James W; 2, Pabst Henry; 3, Blue Vista Inc; 4, Darley Stud Management; 5, New Phoenix Stable; 6, Al Khalifa Abdullah & Rashid; 7, Shadwell Stable; 8, Team Valor; 9, Corbett Mrs Catherine

Trainers— 1, Toner James J; 2, Cross Richard J; 3, Frankel Robert; 4, Gosden John H M; 5, Kessinger Burk Jr; 6, Lukas D Wayne; 7, Jones Harry Thomson; 8, Hennig Mark; 9, Hills Barry W

Scratched— Statuette (4Oct93 ^{8}BEL^{4})

Weekend Madness had the lead by a head over Ajfan, who was a head in front of Possibly Perfect, who was in turn a head in front of Nicer. The pace was hotly contested at this point, with four fillies heads apart battling for the lead. Of the four who were setting and forcing the early pace, Possibly Perfect fared the best at the finish, defeating the other three by open lengths, though unable to withstand the late surges of Tribulation and Miami Sands. Possibly Perfect "won" the pace duel, but lost the race in a fine effort.

Two weeks later, Possibly Perfect returned in the Grade 1 Yellow Ribbon Stakes at Santa Anita, and found herself in a much more favorable pace scenario:

EIGHTH RACE
Santa Anita
NOVEMBER 14, 1993

1¼ MILES. (Turf)(1.57^2) 25th Running of THE YELLOW RIBBON STAKES (Grade I Invitational). Purse $400,000. Fillies and mares, 3-year-olds and upward (Weight for Age). By invitation, with no nomiantion or starting fees. The winner to receive $240,000, with $80,000 to second, $8,000 to third, $24,000 to fourth and $8,000 to fifth. Weights: 3-year-olds, 118 lbs; Older, 122 lbs. The Oak Tree Raceing Association will invite a representative field of fillies and mares to compete. The field will be drawn by the closing time of entries. A trophy will be presented to the owner of the winner. Closed Thursday, November 4, with 13 nominations.

Value of Race: $400,000 Winner $240,000; second $80,000; third $48,000; fourth $24,000; fifth $8,000. Mutuel Pool $467,026.00 Exacta Pool $405,854.00 Quinella Pool $69,518.00

Last Raced	Horse	M/Eqt.	A.	Wt	PP	¼	½	¾	1	Str	Fin	Jockey	Odds $1
30Oct93 ^{8}Kee^{3}	Possibly Perfect	B	3	118	11	1^{1}	1^{1}	1^{1}	1^{hd}	1^{1}	$1^{1\frac{1}{4}}$	Nakatani C S	16.60
30Oct93 ^{8}Kee^{1}	Tribulation	B	3	118	12	2^{hd}	3^{1}	$2^{\frac{1}{2}}$	2^{1}	2^{2}	2^{hd}	Samyn J L	f-8.50
24Oct93 ^{8}SA^{1}	Miatuschka	LB	5	122	2	$3^{1\frac{1}{2}}$	2^{hd}	$5^{1\frac{1}{2}}$	4^{1}	$3^{1\frac{1}{2}}$	3no	Black C A	21.50
3Oct93 Lch^{1}	Verveine	B	4	122	13	10^{1}	10^{2}	$10^{\frac{1}{2}}$	$10^{1\frac{1}{2}}$	$5^{\frac{1}{2}}$	$4^{2\frac{1}{2}}$	Smith M E	6.70
17Oct93 ^{4}WO^{1}	Hero's Love	LBb	5	122	8	$11^{1\frac{1}{2}}$	$12^{\frac{1}{2}}$	$12^{\frac{1}{2}}$	$11^{1\frac{1}{2}}$	9^{2}	$5^{\frac{1}{2}}$	Fires E	12.10
2Oct93 New^{4}	Lyphard's Delta	B	3	118	5	9^{1}	$8^{\frac{1}{2}}$	6^{hd}	$8^{1\frac{1}{2}}$	7^{hd}	6no	Stevens G L	31.60
30Oct93 ^{8}Kee^{2}	Miami Sands-IR	LB	3	118	7	$12^{\frac{1}{2}}$	11^{1}	13	13	10^{1}	7^{nk}	Pincay L Jr	14.00
17Oct93 ^{8}Bel^{2}	Bright Generation-Ir	LB	3	118	1	$8^{1\frac{1}{2}}$	4^{hd}	$3^{\frac{1}{2}}$	$6^{\frac{1}{2}}$	$6^{\frac{1}{2}}$	8^{hd}	Delahoussaye E	8.30
3Oct93 Lch^{10}	Market Booster	LB	4	122	4	7^{hd}	7^{hd}	8^{2}	$5^{\frac{1}{2}}$	$8^{\frac{1}{2}}$	9^{nk}	Kinane M J	f-8.50
10Oct93 ^{8}SA^{3}	Let's Elope-NZ	LBb	6	122	6	4^{hd}	5^{1}	4^{hd}	$3^{\frac{1}{2}}$	$4^{1\frac{1}{2}}$	$10^{1\frac{1}{4}}$	Valenzuela P A	1.30
23Oct93 ^{10}Lrl^{1}	Lady Blessington-FR	LB	5	122	10	13	13	$11^{1\frac{1}{2}}$	$12^{\frac{1}{2}}$	11^{2}	$11^{3\frac{1}{2}}$	Bailey J D	12.20
24Oct93 ^{8}SA^{6}	Campagnarde-Ar	LB	6	122	9	6^{hd}	9^{3}	9^{1}	9^{hd}	$12^{\frac{1}{2}}$	12^{6}	Solis A	47.00
3Oct93 ^{8}LaD^{2}	Revasser	Bb	4	122	3	$5^{1\frac{1}{2}}$	$6^{1\frac{1}{2}}$	$7^{\frac{1}{2}}$	$7^{1\frac{1}{2}}$	13	13	Desormeaux K J	21.70

f–Mutuel Field: Tribulation and Market Booster.

OFF AT 4:16 Start Good. Won driving. Time, :24^{3}, :50, 1:14^{4}, 1:38^{2}, 2:02^{4} Course firm.

$2 Mutuel Prices:				
	10–POSSIBLY PERFECT	35.20	14.60	9.20
	13–TRIBULATION (f-field)		9.40	6.00
	2–MIATUSCHKA			9.60

$2 EXACTA 10–12 PAID $303.40 $2 QUINELLA 10–12 PAID $120.80

B. f, (May), by Northern Baby–Avasand, by Avatar. Trainer Frankel Robert. Bred by Mr. & Mrs. Robert Witt (Ky).

POSSIBLY PERFECT sprinted quickly to the early lead, was well rated while setting the pace along the rail, responded gamely when challenged leaving the second turn to inch away again and proved best under a hard hand ride. TRIBULATION stalked the pace outside MIATUSCHKA to the second turn, but outside the winner on that bend but could not match strides through the drive while gamely holding second. MIATUSCHKA forced the early pace inside, raced between rivals on the backstretch, a bit off the rail on the second turn, swung out for the drive and finished with interest. VERVEINE, unhurried to the second turn, moved up slightly off the rail on that turn, swung far out in upper stretch and finished well. HERO'S LOVE saved ground well off the pace to the second turn, angled out to come wide into the lane and had a mild late bid. LYPHARD'S DELTA, bumped, squeezed back and steadied at the start, saved ground off the early pace, moved up inside leaving the backstretch, steadied briefly in midstretch and lacked the needed late kick. MIAMI SANDS, slow to begin, came far wide into the stretch. BRIGHT GENERATION, off a step slowly, bid inside leaving the backstretch and steadily weakened thereafter. MARKET BOOSTER, bumped hard at the start, moved up between rivals into and through the second turn, then lacked a further response. LET'S ELOPE was well placed outside rivals to the stretch but did not rally. LADY BLESSINGTON had a mild bid outside on the backstretch and lacked a further response. CAMPAGNARDE lacked a rally outside. REVASSER, bumped hard and turned sideways after the start, was taken outside on the backstretch, came wide into the lane, steadied midstretch and quit.

Owners— 1, Blue Vista Inc; 2, Phillips & Seelbinder; 3, Bollinger & Jackson & Ramirez; 4, Wildenstein Daniel; 5, Stronach Frank; 6, Palides Investment N V; 7, Pabst Henry; 8, Salman Fahad; 9, Moyglare Stud; 10, Marks Dennis & Margaret; 11, Team Valor & Sengupta & Thomas; 12, Paulson Allen E; 13, Juddmonte Farms

Trainers— 1, Frankel Robert; 2, Toner James J; 3, Jackson Bruce L; 4, Lellouche Elie; 5, Vella Daniel J; 6, Frankel Robert; 7, Cross Richard J; 8, Drysdale Neil; 9, Weld Dermot K; 10, McAnally Ronald; 11, Hennig Mark; 12, Whittingham Charles; 13, Frankel Robert

Instead of dueling with three other rivals out of the gate, Possibly Perfect sprinted to the lead, rated along through an easy half-mile in :50 seconds while conserving energy, and had plenty left for the final stages, winning at 16–1.

When reading through the charts on your circuit, take note of early fractions that were contested by several horses and award a gold star to the early-pace combatant that fares the best, even if it eventually finishes well behind an opportunistic off-the-pace winner; when these pace-duel "winners" find an easier early-pace scenario, they have a way of surprising the crowd.

NEVER ASSUME

Result charts sometimes reveal that a horse performed quite differently from what is suggested by the condensed past performances. Indeed, the chart of Gulfstream Park's second race on February 27 proved the key to finding the winner of Aqueduct's third on April 22.

Aqueduct

3

7 Furlongs. (1:20^1) **MAIDEN SPECIAL WEIGHT. Purse $24,000. Fillies and mares, 3-year-olds and upward.**
Weights: 3-year-olds, 115 lbs. Older, 124 lbs.

Social Ease
Own: Sullimar Stable
LUZZI M J (105 15 10 11 .14)
Ch. f. 3 (Feb)
Sire: Dr. Carter (Caro)
Dam: Grasiosa (Cougar II)
Br: Frances A. Genter Stable (Ky)
Tr: Johnson Philip G (10 3 2 0 .30)
115
Lifetime Record: 0 M 0 0 $0
1994 0 M 0 0 | Turf 0 0 0 0
1993 0 M 0 0 | Wet 0 0 0 0
Aqu 0 0 0 0 | Dist 0 0 0 0
WORKOUTS: Apr 20 Bel 3f fst :36^3 Hg *3/13* Apr 15 Bel tr.t 4f fst :49 B *33/82* Apr 10 Cam 4f fst :50 B *1/1*

Patelin's Legacy
Own: Buckland Farm
MICKENS T J (50 3 3 7 .06)
Dk. b or br f. 3 (May)
Sire: Cherokee Colony (Pleasant Colony)
Dam: Patelin (Cornish Prince)
Br: T. M. Evans (Va)
Tr: Campo John P (15 2 1 0 .13)
108^7
Lifetime Record: 2 M 0 0 $0
1994 2 M 0 0 | Turf 0 0 0 0
1993 0 M 0 0 | Wet 0 0 0 0
Aqu 0 0 0 0 | Dist 0 0 0 0
27Feb94- 5Aqu fst 6f ⊡ :24 :49^2 1:01^4 1:14^3 ⒻMd Sp Wt 36 4 3 1½ 2^{hd} 5^{1½} 5^{6¾} Alvarado F T 121 12.40 63-22 Something Light121^{nk} Lancette121^{hd} Northern Evening121^{no} Dueled, tired 5
3Feb94- 2Aqu fst 6f ⊡ :22^4 :47 1:00^1 1:14^1 ⒻMd Sp Wt 46 3 9 7^5 7^{7½} 8^{6¾} 7^7 Alvarado F T 121 30.90 65-23 Lawyerette121^{nk} Very Careless121^{1¼} Lancette121½ No menace 12
WORKOUTS: Apr 16 Bel tr.t 4f fst :49^4 H *33/74* Apr 6 Bel tr.t 4f fst :49^1 B *24/48* Mar 25 Bel tr.t 4f fst :48^2 H *4/37* Mar 19 Bel tr.t 4f fst :51 B *36/42* Mar 9 Bel tr.t 4f fst :48 Hg *6/25* Feb 16 Bel tr.t 3f fst :39 B *19/21*

Basic Assumption
Own: Matz Michael
ALVARADO F T (68 7 12 9 .10)
B. f. 3 (May)
Sire: Known Fact (In Reality)
Dam: Parisian Honey (Honey Jay)
Br: Audley Farm Inc (Va)
Tr: Arnold George R II (4 1 0 0 .25)
115
Lifetime Record: 1 M 0 0 $240
1994 1 M 0 0 $240 | Turf 0 0 0 0
1993 0 M 0 0 | Wet 0 0 0 0
Aqu 0 0 0 0 | Dist 0 0 0 0
27Feb94- 2GP fst 6f :22^2 :45^2 :58^1 1:11 ⒻMd Sp Wt 56 12 1 8^{7½} 7^{10} 7^{11} 5^{9½} Sellers S J 121 14.60 76-13 Daylight Dreamer121^{6½} Park Valley121^{nk} Southern Crown121^3 Belated bid 12
WORKOUTS: ●Apr 20 Bel 4f fst :47^3 H *1/27* Apr 15 Bel tr.t 5f fst 1:00^3 H *7/41* Apr 9 Bel tr.t 5f fst 1:02^3 B *28/39* ●Feb 22 Pay 3f fst :38 B *1/7* Feb 17 Pay 5f sly 1:05^3 B *2/3* Feb 12 Pay 3f fst :39^1 Bg *5/9*

Very Careless
Own: Char-Mari Stable
DAVIS R G (127 30 21 20 .24)
Ch. f. 3 (Feb)
Sire: Ogygian (Damascus)
Dam: Madruga (Irish River)
Br: Arriola Joseph (Ky)
Tr: Gross George F (3 0 0 2 .00)
115
Lifetime Record: 5 M 3 0 $15,300
1994 4 M 2 0 $11,500 | Turf 0 0 0 0
1993 1 M 1 0 $3,800 | Wet 0 0 0 0
Aqu 1 0 0 0 | Dist 0 0 0 0
9Apr94- 3Aqu fst 6f :22^1 :45^3 :58^2 1:12^2 ⒻMd Sp Wt 50 4 2 2½ 2^2 4^5 7^{4½} Thomas D B 121 7.40 75-13 Rythym Bid121^{2¾} Jade Bird121^{nk} Stop Right Here121^{1¼} Forced pace, tired 10
3Feb94- 2Aqu fst 6f ⊡ :22^4 :47 1:00^1 1:14^1 ⒻMd Sp Wt 62 9 3 1^{1½} 1^{1½} 1½ 2^{nk} Davis R G 121 1.70 72-23 Lawyerette121^{nk} Very Careless121^{1¼} Lancette121½ Gamely 12
23Jan94- 7Aqu fst 6f ⊡ :23 :47 1:00 1:13^3 ⒻMd Sp Wt 53 11 2 4^3 7^{5½} 6^6 4^{5¼} Davis R G 121 4.40 70-23 Royal Revels116^1 Lady Lou S.121^2 Amy Be Happy121^{2¼} Lacked rally 12
1Jan94- 5Aqu fst 6f ⊡ :23^1 :47^3 1:00^4 1:14^2 ⒻMd Sp Wt 59 5 2 1^1 1^1 1^{2½} 2^{nk} Davis R G 121 *.90 71-27 ForcingBid116^{nk} VeryCrelss121^{nk} StrlingPound121^2 Caught deep stretch 9
3Dec93- 7Med fst 6f :22^4 :46 :58^4 1:11^3 ⒻMd Sp Wt 59 2 6 1½ 1^1 1^{1½} 2^{nk} Bravo J 117 *2.40 83-14 LittleBarbie117^{nk} VeryCareless117^{1¾} MnilFlight117^{2¼} Caught, final strides 9
WORKOUTS: Apr 5 GS 4f fst :48^2 B *4/12* Mar 18 GS 5f fst 1:01^3 B *4/16* Mar 12 GS 3f fst :36^4 B *6/29*

Perfect Probe
Own: Evans Edward P
SANTOS J A (35 5 8 8 .14)
Dk. b or br f. 4
Sire: Mr Prospector (Raise a Native)
Dam: Sangue (Lyphard)
Br: Third Kirsmith Racing Associates (Va)
Tr: Clement Christophe (6 0 0 1 .00)
124
Lifetime Record: 5 M 0 2 $10,650
1994 1 M 0 1 $4,800 | Turf 0 0 0 0
1992 4 M 0 1 $5,850 | Wet 1 0 0 1 $3,900
Aqu 0 0 0 0 | Dist 0 0 0 0
17Mar94- 3SA fst 6f :21^2 :44 :56^3 1:09^1 ⒻMd Sp Wt 62 5 1 1^{1½} 1^1 1^{hd} 3^{10½} Desormeaux K J LB 121 b 2.30 80-11 Run To Reign116^{6½} Mythical Bird121^4 Perfect Probe121^{3½} Weakened 6
25Oct92- 3SA sl 6f :22^2 :47^1 1:00^3 1:14^2 ⒻMd Sp Wt 67 2 4 1^{1½} 1^{hd} 1½ 3^2 McCarron C J B 117 b 4.70 62-32 Nijivision117^{1½} Dash For Flash117½ Perfect Probe117 Weakened a bit 7
11Oct92- 9SA fst 6f :21^3 :45^1 :58 1:11 ⒻMd Sp Wt 69 11 6 6^{2½} 4^{1½} 2^{1½} 4^{2¾} Nakatani C S B 117 b 14.90 78-16 Afto117^{no} Nijivision117 Enchanted Spot117 Rough start, wide 12
13Sep92- 9Dmr fst 6f :22 :45^1 :58^1 1:11^2 ⒻMd Sp Wt 49 12 1 3^{nk} 1^{hd} 6^2 9^{7½} Nakatani C S B 118 b 5.20 75-14 Turkstand118^{1½} Running Renee118^{1½} Heir D' Mint118 Steadied 1/8 12
30Aug92- 6Dmr fst 6f :22^1 :45^2 :58^1 1:10^4 ⒻMd Sp Wt 34 2 8 8^{11} 8^{11} 8^{12} 7^{17¾} Desormeaux K J B 117 6.40 67-12 Stellar Affair117^{2¾} Alyshena117½ Dash For Flash117 8
Hesitated start, raced green
WORKOUTS: Apr 15 Bel tr.t 4f fst :49^1 B *38/82* Mar 14 Hol 3f fst :36^2 H *4/17* Mar 9 Hol 6f fst 1:13^4 H *5/18* Mar 4 Hol 6f fst 1:13^4 H *3/12* ●Feb 26 Hol 4f fst :47 H *1/11* Feb 21 Hol 6f fst 1:13 H *1/3*

Grandmother
Own: Harbor View Farm
ROSARIO V (4 1 0 0 .25)

B. f. 3 (May)
Sire: Gulch (Mr. Prospector)
Dam: Deal With Love (Secretariat)
Br: Jacobs Ethel D & Wolfson Mr & Mrs Louis E (Ky)
Tr: Jerkens H Allen (35 11 6 8 .31)

1087

Lifetime Record:	1 M 0 0	$0		
1994	1 M 0 0		Turf	0 0 0 0
1993	0 M 0 0		Wet	0 0 0 0
Aqu	1 0 0 0		Dist	0 0 0 0

9Apr94- 3Aqu fst 6f :221 :453 :582 1:122 ⒻMd Sp Wt 50 2 10 74¾ 75¼ 67 64½ Rosario V7 114 12.20 76-13 Rythym Bid1212¾ Jade Bird121nk Stop Right Here1211¼ Broke slowly 10
WORKOUTS: Apr 15 Bel tr.t 5f fst 1:014 H 19/41 Apr 4 Bel tr.t 3f fst :37 B 3/10 Mar 31 Bel tr.t 3f fst :362 B 6/17 Mar 25 Bel tr.t 5f fst 1:032 B 13/16 Mar 11 GP 5f fst 1:02 B 11/26 Mar 1 GP 4f fst :48 Hg5/30

Continued
Own: Burning Day Farm
LEON F (64 8 7 8 .13)

Ch. f. 3 (Feb)
Sire: Forty Niner (Mr. Prospector)
Dam: Chain Bracelet (Lyphard)
Br: Paliafito James L (Ky)
Tr: Carroll Del W II (7 0 0 1 .00)

115

Lifetime Record:	1 M 0 0	$240			
1994	1 M 0 0	$240	Turf	0 0 0 0	
1993	0 M 0 0		Wet	0 0 0 0	
Aqu	0 0 0 0		Dist	1 0 0 0	$240

19Feb94- 5GP gd 7f :222 :46 1:113 1:25 ⒻMd Sp Wt 53 8 4 85½ 44 58 511½ Sellers S J L 121 b 2.00 66-20 Brand Loyalty1216½ Swiss Candy1211¼ Sonnet1212¼ 9
Eight wide top str, mild bid
WORKOUTS: Apr 15 Bel tr.t 6f fst 1:14 H 5/14 Apr 5 Bel tr.t 5f fst 1:01 Hg3/8 Mar 25 Bel tr.t 4f fst :483 H 6/37 Mar 15 GP 4f fst :482 H 8/29 Mar 9 GP 5f fst 1:01 B 3/23 Feb 12 GP 5f fst 1:01 Bg16/46

The race cried out for a horse with some closing punch. The likely pace setters, Very Careless and Perfect Probe, were stretching beyond six furlongs for the first time. Very Careless had blown clear leads on three occasions, and had returned from a layoff April 9 with the worst performance of her career in terms of figures. Perfect Probe had set blistering fractions on March 17, but that had been her first start in nearly a year and a half, and she showed only one workout in the five weeks that had elapsed since then.

None of the other entrants had gained any appreciable ground in the late stages of their previous races. None, that is, except Basic Assumption, whose strong run through the final quarter of her debut was camouflaged to anyone without access to a chart of the race:

SECOND RACE
Gulfstream
FEBRUARY 27, 1994

6 FURLONGS. (1.074) MAIDEN SPECIAL WEIGHT. Purse $24,000 (plus $2,000 FOA). Fillies, 3-year-olds. Weight, 121 lbs.

Value of Race: $24,000 Winner $14,400; second $4,320; third $2,400; fourth $960; fifth $240; sixth $240; seventh $240; eighth $240; ninth $240; tenth $240; eleventh $240; twelfth $240. Mutuel Pool $125,611.00 Perfecta Pool $131,900.00 Trifecta Pool $115,034.00

Last Raced	Horse	M/Eqt.	A.	Wt	PP	St	¼	½	Str	Fin	Jockey	Odds $1
	Daylight Dreamer		3	121	6	4	1hd	1hd	14	16¼	Perret C	3.40
20Jly93 5Mth6	Park Valley	Lb	3	121	8	3	23½	24	22	2nk	Bravo J	4.50
	Southern Crown	L	3	121	1	6	3hd	44	43	33	Castillo H Jr	9.10
23Jan94 6GP10	Lill's Cutlass		3	116	5	5	51½	5½	61½	4no	Chapman K L5	55.10
	Basic Assumption		3	121	12	1	8hd	72½	73½	51½	Sellers S J	14.60
11Aug93 5Det5	Sweet Lady Gate		3	121	7	8	7½	61	5½	6hd	Rodriguez P A	64.20
	Token Of Esteem		3	121	2	9	41½	31	3hd	77	Bailey J D	1.40
	Jazzability		3	121	3	10	102	8hd	8½	8hd	Hernandez R	14.90
	Pretty Smart		3	121	9	7	114	102½	92½	93	Ramos W S	54.30
	Crypto Lass		3	121	4	12	12	12	115	101¼	Barton D M	33.90
	Branch Water		3	121	10	11	9hd	92	10½	118	Maple E	10.90
	Tour Eiffel	bf	3	121	11	2	6hd	111½	12	12	Madrid S O	74.80

OFF AT 1:29 Start Good. Won ridden out. Time, :222, :452, :581, 1:11 Track fast.

$2 Mutuel Prices:

6–DAYLIGHT DREAMER	8.80	4.80	4.20
8–PARK VALLEY		4.40	4.20
1–SOUTHERN CROWN			5.40

$2 PERFECTA 6 & 8 PAID $50.80 $2 TRIFECTA 6–8–1 PAID $393.80

B. f, (May), by Seattle Slew–Sleep On It, by Buckpasser. Trainer Nafzger Carl A. Bred by Burning Daylight Farms Inc (Va).

DAYLIGHT DREAMER sprinted to an early lead, set the pace, inside, while under under pressure from PARK VALLEY, settled in the stretch with a clear advantage, then, under a strong hand ride, won very convincingly. PARK VALLEY vied for the early lead on the outside of DAYLIGHT DREAMER early then was no match for the winner in the drive and held on gamely for the place. SOUTHERN CROWN, a forward factor early, came into the stretch six wide, then closed with a good late rally just missing the place. LILL'S CUTLASS reserved early, then closed with a belated bid. BASIC ASSUMPTION unhurried early while racing wide, then made a mild late bid wide in the stretch. SWEET LADY GATE failed to seriously menace. TOKEN OF ESTEEM bounced around at the start was forward factor until in the stretch then weakened. JAZZABILITY was no threat while being seven wide in the stretch. PRETTY SMART showed little. CRYPTO LASS was no factor. BRANCH WATER was never close. TOUR EIFFEL reserved early then stopped.

Owners— 1, Burning Daylight Farms Inc; 2, Ballet Stable; 3, Robsham E Paul; 4, Hall Floyd & Larry; 5, Vintage Stables; 6, McMaster Marilyn & Roland; 7, Evans Edward P & Overbrook Farm; 8, Sullimar Stable; 9, Aitken Louis F; 10, Circle 7 Stable Inc; 11, Live Oak Plantation; 12, La Isla Stable

Trainers— 1, Nafzger Carl A; 2, Jennings Lawrence Jr; 3, Generazio Frank Jr; 4, Hirsch Alan; 5, Arnold George R II; 6, Gianos George; 7, Lukas D Wayne; 8, Johnson Philip G; 9, Vanier Harvey L; 10, Shirota Mitch; 11, Kelly Patrick J; 12, Mills Randy

Scratched— Code Of Old (6Feb94 6GP2), K T Island (11Feb94 5GP4)

Handicappers looking only at Basic Assumption's running line in the past performances might've assumed she had raced evenly, for she was seven and a half lengths behind at the quarter, ten lengths behind at the half, eleven behind at the stretch call, and she wound up beaten by nine and a half lengths. But the chart shows that the winner, Daylight Dreamer, drew away from the field after going head-and-head for the lead through the opening half. Therefore, had Basic Assumption actually been running "evenly," she would've lost roughly six lengths' worth of ground in the final quarter as the winner opened up.

But Basic Assumption *gained* half a length in the final quarter. *She was keeping pace with Daylight Dreamer in the stretch.* Suppose we were to say that Daylight Dreamer hadn't been in the race: what would Basic Assumption's running line look like if we eliminated Daylight Dreamer's margins relative to the rest of the field? It would look like this:

	¼	½	str	fin
Basic Assumption	7 7¼	6 9¾	6 7	4 3¼

Had Daylight Dreamer not been in this race, Park Valley would've won wire-to-wire, and Basic Assumption's revised running line, shown above, would indicate a solid closing response in her career debut, as she gained six and a half lengths on Park Valley through the final quarter.

Basic Assumption's move (from post 12 on a notoriously inside-biased track) was well hidden, and her two most recent workouts hinted that she was being "set down" for this race. Note that her works at Payson Park leading up to the February 27 debut were all termed "breezing," but the last two works, which had come within the past week, were termed "handily," and showed sharply improved speed, especially the bullet :47⅗ — best of twenty-seven at the distance.

The race was over by midstretch:

THIRD RACE **7 FURLONGS. (1.20¹) MAIDEN SPECIAL WEIGHT. Purse $24,000. Fillies and mares, 3-year-olds and upward. Weights: 3-year-olds, 115 lbs. Older, 124 lbs.**

Aqueduct

APRIL 22, 1994

Value of Race: $24,000 Winner $14,400; second $5,280; third $2,880; fourth $1,440. Mutuel Pool $167,550.00 Exacta Pool $383,967.00

Last Raced	Horse	M/Eqt.	A.	Wt	PP	St	¼	½	Str	Fin	Jockey	Odds $1
27Feb94 ²GP⁵	Basic Assumption		3	115	3	5	$4^{\frac{1}{2}}$	$4^{2\frac{1}{2}}$	$1^{1\frac{1}{2}}$	$1^{7\frac{3}{4}}$	Alvarado F T	2.20
19Feb94 ⁵GP⁵	Continued	b	3	115	7	1	6^{hd}	3^{1}	4^{8}	2^{nk}	Leon F	3.90
17Mar94 ³SA³	Perfect Probe	b	4	124	5	3	$2^{1\frac{1}{2}}$	2^{1}	2^{hd}	$3^{1\frac{1}{2}}$	Santos J A	1.90
9Apr94 ³Aqu⁷	Very Careless		3	115	4	4	$1^{\frac{1}{2}}$	$1^{\frac{1}{2}}$	3^{1}	4^{9}	Davis R G	8.40
9Apr94 ³Aqu⁶	Grandmother		3	108	6	2	7	5^{1}	5^{6}	5^{12}	Rosario V⁷	4.80
27Feb94 ⁵Aqu⁵	Patelin's Legacy	b	3	108	2	6	3^{hd}	$6^{\frac{1}{2}}$	6^{hd}	$6^{\frac{3}{4}}$	Mickens T J⁷	46.10
	Social Ease		3	115	1	7	$5^{1\frac{1}{2}}$	7	7	7	Luzzi M J	18.40

OFF AT 1:54 Start Good. Won driving. Time, :23³, :47¹, 1:12³, 1:25¹ Track fast.

$2 Mutuel Prices:				
	3-(C)-BASIC ASSUMPTION	6.40	4.00	2.40
	7-(G)-CONTINUED		4.20	2.60
	5-(E)-PERFECT PROBE			2.60

$2 EXACTA 3-7 PAID $24.60

B. f, (May), by Known Fact-Parisian Honey, by Honey Jay. Trainer Arnold George R II. Bred by Audley Farm Inc (Va).

BASIC ASSUMPTION reserved for a half, launched a rally three wide on the turn, charged to the front in midstretch, then drew off under mild encouragement. CONTINUED gradually gained while four wide on the turn, checked while lugging in nearing the furlong marker then outfinished PERFECT PROBE for the place. PERFECT PROBE forced the pace from outside to the turn, gained a brief lead in upper stretch then weakened in the final eighth. VERY CARELESS set the pace along the inside to the top of the stretch and tired. GRANDMOTHER was never a factor. PATELIN'S LEGACY showed only brief speed. SOCIAL EASE away slowly, bumped with GRANDMOTHER at the half mile pole and was never close thereafter. GRANDMOTHER wore mud caulks.

Owners— 1, Matz Michael; 2, Burning Day Farm; 3, Evans Edward P; 4, Char-Mari Stable; 5, Harbor View Farm; 6, Buckland Farm; 7, Sullimar Stable

Trainers—1, Arnold George R II; 2, Carroll Del W II; 3, Clement Christophe; 4, Gross George F; 5, Jerkens H Allen; 6, Campo John P; 7, Johnson Philip G

WEIGHT AND INTENT

The significance of weight remains one of the most perplexing and controversial subjects in handicapping, and unless you have a doctorate in physics, the effect of a few pounds on or off the back of a thoroughbred who weighs in at roughly half a ton will remain one of life's mysteries. What *is* worth considering, though, is that many trainers are weight-conscious and therefore try to find races where their horse gets the maximum-weight allowance under the conditions. To be sure, a few pounds off can't possibly hurt.

An example of using the conditions of a race in conjunction with weight occurs when a horse is moving up to face tougher company soon after a victory against lesser-quality rivals. The horse may well be tired after the all-out effort to win and be penalized for the win by adding extra pounds as it steps up in class. The weight disadvantage and a bounce combine to produce a less-than-optimal performance. Often, however, the horse will "bounce back" in its second attempt at the new, higher level once it is no longer forced to carry excess baggage.

Mr Sledge
Own: Schifrin Lois D

Gr. c. 4
Sire: Premiership (Exclusive Native)
Dam: Laughing Ruler (Iron Ruler)
Br: Fernung Earle E (Fla)
Tr: Shapoff Stanley R (39 5 3 1 .13)

122

Lifetime Record:	23	2	7	6	$48,500						
1994	3	1	0	0	$8,580	Turf	0	0	0	0	
1993	10	1	4	4	$25,080	Wet	0	0	0	0	
Aqu ⊡	11	2	2	3	$27,080	Dist	1	0	0	0	$900

16Feb94-7Aqu	fst	6f	⊡	$:22^{4}$	$:47^{3}$	1:00	$1:12^{3}$	Clm 20000N2L	85	7	5	$6^{4\frac{1}{2}}$	1^{hd}	1^{3}	1^{2}	Santagata N	113 b	8.60	80-25	Mr Sledge113[2] Saratoga Ridge108[hd] Alpstein117[8]	Driving	12
3Feb94-1Aqu	fst	6f	⊡	$:22^{4}$	$:46^{1}$	$:59^{2}$	$1:12^{2}$	Clm 25000	66	7	5	6^{3}	$6^{4\frac{1}{4}}$	$6^{4\frac{1}{2}}$	$7^{7\frac{1}{4}}$	Santagata N	117 b	27.50	74-23	I'm No Quacker115[¾] Danzig'sDance117[1] Gallapiat'sMoment112[3]	Evenly	9
5Jan94-7Aqu	fst	6f	⊡	$:22^{2}$	$:46^{3}$	$:59^{3}$	$1:12^{3}$	Clm 25000N2L	61	3	6	4^{4}	$4^{3\frac{1}{4}}$	2^{3}	4^{8}	Santagata N	122 b	6.30	72-26	Sand Kicker113[1] Mt. Shannon117[6] Be Loyal115[1]	Flattened out	10
16Dec93-3Aqu	fst	6f	⊡	$:23^{3}$	$:48^{3}$	$1:01^{2}$	$1:14^{3}$	3↑ Md 25000	59	2	4	$4^{1\frac{1}{2}}$	$1^{\frac{1}{2}}$	$1^{3\frac{1}{2}}$	$1^{5\frac{3}{4}}$	Santagata N	120 b	*1.20	70-22	Mr Sledge120[5¾] Run Galtee Run120[nk] Pilfer120[7½]	Driving	6
26May93-2Bel	fst	7f		$:22^{3}$	$:45^{3}$	1:11	$1:24^{3}$	3↑ Md 30000	75	7	2	2^{3}	$2^{1\frac{1}{2}}$	$2^{1\frac{1}{2}}$	$3^{1\frac{1}{4}}$	Santagata N	113 b	*1.60	79-22	Run Eo Run120[no] Westbridge115[1¼] Mr Sledge113[10]	Bid, weakened	8
14May93-3Bel	fst	6½f		:22	$:45^{3}$	$1:10^{3}$	$1:17^{1}$	3↑ Md 47500	68	4	5	$5^{4\frac{1}{2}}$	$5^{1\frac{1}{2}}$	$4^{3\frac{1}{2}}$	3^{10}	Santagata N	113 b	7.40	77-18	Air115[2] Shootthemessenger115[8] Mr Sledge113[1]	Lacked rally	9
29Apr93-1Aqu	fst	1		:23	$:46^{2}$	$1:11^{3}$	$1:38^{1}$	3↑ Md 45000	75	8	5	2^{1}	2^{1}	2^{3}	2^{7}	Santagata N	113 b	*2.50	66-35	Islanders Cure115[7] Mr Sledge113[7] Camelot North106[¾]	Second best	8
10Apr93-3Aqu	fst	7f		$:23^{2}$	$:46^{2}$	$1:10^{2}$	$1:23^{2}$	3↑ Md 45000	74	1	5	$2^{\frac{1}{2}}$	$2^{\frac{1}{2}}$	$2^{3\frac{1}{2}}$	2^{7}	Santagata N	113 b	2.00	80-13	Turk Passer115[7] Mr Sledge113[13] Sail Clear106[1]	Second best	5
21Mar93-9Aqu	gd	6f	⊡	$:22^{4}$	$:45^{4}$	$:58^{1}$	$1:11^{1}$	Md 35000	74	9	7	$7^{2\frac{3}{4}}$	3^{1}	2^{2}	$2^{\frac{3}{4}}$	Santagata N	122 b	*2.00	86-13	Alex K.111[¾] Mr Sledge122[1½] Camelot North117[6½]	Second best	12
11Mar93-1Aqu	fst	6f	⊡	$:23^{1}$	$:46^{4}$	$:59^{2}$	$1:12^{4}$	Md 50000	64	2	4	3^{2}	2^{3}	2^{3}	3^{4}	Santagata N	122 b	*1.10	75-19	Mr Rocky118[2] Run Galtee Run118[2] Mr Sledge122[6½]	Saved ground	6

WORKOUTS: Feb 1 Bel tr.t 5f fst $1:02^{4}$ B *5/28* Jan 24 Bel tr.t 4f fst :50 B *17/42* Jan 1 Bel tr.t 4f fst :51 B *29/36*

Remember Mr Sledge from my earlier discussion regarding "chronic money-burners?" Well, he returned from a layoff on December 16 and finally broke his maiden. Now, we might consider him as a possible contender in a claiming race restricted to nonwinners of two races lifetime, provided conditions were favorable. But conditions were anything but favorable for Mr Sledge in the start immediately following his maiden win. The fine print in the conditions that afternoon read, "Weight 122 pounds. Nonwinners of a race since December 15 allowed three pounds; of a race since December 1, allowed five pounds."

Mr Sledge had won a day *after* the cutoff date of December 15, and thus was saddled with the maximum 122 pounds, conceding from five to sixteen pounds to the field. He ran surprisingly well under the circumstances, rallying to second position in midstretch before "flattening out," under his impost, according to the comment line.

A month later, Mr Sledge was again entered for $25,000, but this was a much tougher spot — an unrestricted race open to all comers.

On February 16, Mr Sledge was back for another try against nonwinners-of-two lifetime claimers, but with an important difference from January 5: instead of carrying 122 pounds, he was only required to carry 113, because the conditions read, "Weight 122 pounds. Nonwinners of a race since February 1 allowed three pounds; of a race since January 15, allowed five pounds."

Mr Sledge now fulfilled the date requirements for all the weight allowances, his victory coming a month prior to the cutoff dates. Moreover, trainer Skippy Shapoff elected to enter Mr Sledge for the minimum $20,000 claiming price instead of the top price of $25,000, which meant he would receive an additional four pounds off.

Question: In which restricted $25,000 claimer do you think Mr Sledge was more well meant — the January 5 race under 122 pounds with no weight allowance, or the February 16 race getting the full weight allowance plus an additional four pounds because he's entered for only $20,000?

If you said February 16, go directly to the cashier's window and collect the $19.20 mutuel.

Here's another example where the stable's intent was obvious:

Viola D. — B. f. 3(Mar), by Turkoman—Mom's Mia, by Great Mystery

MAPLE E (63 10 14 9 .16) — $50,000 — Br.—Fuller Peter & Jayeff B Stables (Ky) — **116**

Own.—Fuller Peter D — Tr. Allard Edward T (1 0 0 0 .00)

Lifetime								
15	3	2	3	1993	7	3	1	0	$19,560
$40,010				1992	8	1	1	3	$20,450
				Turf	2	0	0	0	$115
				Wet	4	1	1	1	$10,400

12May93- 8Suf	gd	*1 Ⓣ			1:431	3↑ⒻAlw 11500	48	5	1	1½	34	55	69½	Gambardella C	Bb	114	*.70	85-12 SilvrDollrTwo116½Johnrys'gl1031Victori'sPrmr116	Tired	8
17Apr93- 5Suf	sly	1	:482	1:141	1:42	3↑ⒻAlw 11000	65	2	1	14	14½	16	17	Gambardella C	LBb	114	*.60	74-33 Viola D.1147IDemand1161¾GranvilleMoss117	Ridden out	7
9Apr93- 4Aqu	fst	1⅛	:50	1:144	1:533	ⒻClm 50000	62	3	1	11½	1hd	1hd	2hd	Maple E	b	116	5.00	68-29 ThsAn'tKnss114hdVID.1162¼MssSmrt113	Drifted gamely	7
3Mar93- 8Suf	gd	6f	:224	:472	1:142	ⒻAlw 10500	43	4	6	54	44	47	47	Vargas J L	Bb	122	4.90	71-20 Shnn'sDncr1162¾MollyW1161TwofKm119	Flattened out	6
5Feb93- 8Suf	fst	1	:484	1:144	1:444	ⒻAlw 10000	55	5	2	22	31	22	11½	Gambardella C	Bb	116	*.80	60-38 Viola D.1161½ Passel1169½JulieApple116	Rallied outside	7
23Jan93- 8GS	fst	1	:474	1:132	1:392	ⒻJersey Belle	52	2	4	21	75¼	77¼	616½	Santagata N	b	114	8.00	68-23 Sntimntldmona1156¼ClvrClvr1147¾GrbThGlory114	Tired	8
10Jan93- 9Pha	fst	170	:464	1:121	1:43	ⒻAlw 18755	36	6	3	33	45	510	417	Romero J A	b	116	2.30	64-18 Smart Devil1115 R M's Girl1161½ Kneeling122	Wide	8
12Dec92- 9Pha	sly	1 1/16	:483	1:15	1:494	ⒻVillager	50	4	4	31½	32	77½	611½	Castillo R E	b	114	9.50	48-39 CtoLdy114nkFstivFinnish1143Dshroo114	Bore out early	8
21Nov92- 8Med	fst	1	:461	1:104	1:383	ⒻGuttenberg	52	1	3	32½	37½	413	310¾	Santagata N		113	8.20	77-19 Concorde'sFinale1158¼Dshroo1152ViolD.113	Saved grnd	10
5Nov92- 6Med	sly	1	:471	1:13	1:384	ⒻAlw 15000	62	5	4	36	22	23	23	Santagata N		117	*2.00	83-16 ActngProud1173VolD.1179Jssc'sTwoStp113	Best of rest	7

LATEST WORKOUTS ●Jun 6 Mth 5f fst 1:024 B — Jun 1 Mth 5f sly 1:04 B — May 24 Suf 4f fst :481 H — May 8 Suf 5f fst 1:024 H

Viola D. was out of her element sprinting six furlongs on March 3 and was conceding six pounds to the first two finishers. In all probability, the sprint race was designed as a "bridge" between her route win of February 5 and her narrow loss in a $50,000 claimer at Aqueduct on April 9, and if she had to lug top weight of 122 pounds, so much the better for conditioning purposes. Without the sprint, Viola D. would've come in to Aqueduct off a two-month layoff; with the sprint serving as a sharpener, she nearly wired the field at 5–1 off the stretchout, and then returned to Suffolk, where she advanced through the next allowance condition — this time carrying 114 pounds (at her best distance) instead of the 122 she'd carried in her previous attempt at the new class level.

ENTRIES

Result charts are extraordinarily useful in finding pace-duel winners (Possibly Perfect), hidden moves (Basic Assumption), and shifts to more favorable conditions in terms of weight (Mr Sledge), and they are also a key tool in evaluating another aspect of stable intent: entries.

When a trainer enters two horses in a race, it's important to analyze how the race was run, and how the entrymates fared in relation to each other. When one-half of the entry wins, and the other half changes its usual style of running dramatically, handicappers can reasonably expect the "change of pace" horse to improve sharply when entered back on its own.

Siri — Ch. f. 4, by Thunder Puddles—Ambitious Flowers, by Bold Ambition
BISONO C V (71 11 8 7 .15) — $25,000 — Br.—Bronfman Mrs Georgiana W (NY)
Own.—My Kid's Stable — Tr.—Destasio Richard A (10 1 1 0 .10) — 114^5

Lifetime						
12 2 0 2	1993	1	0	0	0	
$43,560	1992	11	2	0	2	$43,560
	Turf	5	1	0	1	$18,240
	Wet	1	0	0	0	

8Jan93-	5Aqu	fst	1⅛	[•]	$:48^2$	1:13	$1:51^2$		ⒻClm 35000	72	2	5	5^5	$6^{5\frac{1}{2}}$	5^{10}	$5^{11\frac{1}{4}}$	Bisono C V^5	b	114	8.40	75–14	$FoolinSpruc119^6Kris'DrDby117^3SwtN'Sxy114$	No factor 6
19Dec92-	6Aqu	fst	1 1/16	[•]	$:47^4$	$1:12^2$	$1:44^3$	3↑	Ⓕ[S]Alw 29000	66	8	7	$6^{3\frac{1}{2}}$	5^2	1^{hd}	1^2	Bisono C V^5	b	110	5.60	85–05	$Siri110^2GllopingProudly115^{\frac{3}{4}}TitnsBell117$	Lck rm, drvng 10
4Dec92-	7Aqu	fst	1 1/16	[•]	$:49^3$	$1:14^4$	$1:47^3$	3↑	Ⓕ[S]Alw 29000	55	12	2	2^1	3^2	$4^{3\frac{1}{2}}$	4^7	Gryder A T	b	115	6.10e	63–27	$IrshIntrn115^{1\frac{1}{4}}EsttsPrcss115^{2\frac{1}{4}}GllpPrdl115$	Forced pace 12
13Nov92-	5Aqu	gd	1⅛		$:47^3$	$1:12^1$	$1:51^4$		ⒻClm 45000	72	2	5	$5^{3\frac{1}{2}}$	5^4	$4^{8\frac{1}{2}}$	$4^{7\frac{1}{2}}$	Bisono C V^5	b	107	31.70	69–22	$HuckstrRos112^5BoundingBlivr114^{\frac{1}{2}}SuprSz116$	No threat 8
13Nov92-Originally scheduled on turf																							
25Oct92-	5Aqu	gd	1⅛	(T)	$:49^3$	$1:15^1$	$1:53^3$	3↑	Ⓕ[S]Alw 29000	60	7	5	$5^{2\frac{1}{2}}$	$6^{3\frac{1}{2}}$	$8^{9\frac{1}{4}}$	$8^{11\frac{1}{2}}$	Bisono C V^5	b	109	4.20	63–21	$Los'Grl117^{1\frac{1}{4}}TtnsBll117^{1\frac{1}{4}}NwYorkIssu114$	Steadied early 11
20Sep92-	2Bel	fm	1 1/16	[T]	$:47^3$	1:12	$1:42^4$		ⒻClm 35000	75	1	6	4^2	4^1	$4^{1\frac{1}{2}}$	$3^{\frac{1}{2}}$	McCauley W H	b	116	6.90	83–13	$SenoritRit116^{\frac{1}{2}}Thtimofdonslif116^{no}Siri116$	Checked brk 10
12Sep92-	6Bel	yl	1 1/16	(T)	$:46^4$	$1:11^4$	$1:44^1$	3↑	Ⓕ[S]Alw 29000	70	2	8	$7^{7\frac{1}{2}}$	$6^{4\frac{1}{2}}$	$8^{3\frac{3}{4}}$	$7^{6\frac{1}{2}}$	McCauley W H		113	3.20e	68–20	$HvnlyHoofr113^{1\frac{3}{4}}IrishIntrn113^{\frac{1}{2}}TlkPolitics118$	No threat 10
14Aug92-	5Sar	fm	1 3/16	(T)	$:47^4$	$1:12^3$	$1:56^1$	3↑	ⒻAlw 29000	63	4	9	10^8	$10^{7\frac{1}{4}}$	5^6	$5^{12\frac{1}{4}}$	McCauley W H		117	5.90	75–12	$MorDynmc112^1MssRvrCns122^{\frac{1}{2}}Trmntt113$	Bumpd early 10
27Jly92-	3Bel	yl	1¼	[T]	$:48^2$	$1:40^4$	$2:06^1$	3↑	Ⓕ[S]Md Sp Wt	65	3	9	$7^{5\frac{3}{4}}$	$4^{1\frac{1}{2}}$	1^3	$1^{7\frac{1}{2}}$	McCauley W H		116	2.60	59–29	$Siri116^{7\frac{1}{2}}$ Victoria $Lane116^{no}$ Carabid116	Pnch bk, sted 9
18Jly92-	2Bel	fst	1		$:47^4$	$1:13^1$	$1:38^3$	3↑	Ⓕ[S]Md Sp Wt	48	7	5	3^2	2^{hd}	4^3	$3^{8\frac{3}{4}}$	Davis R G		116	*1.50	68–16	$GllopingProudly109^{1\frac{1}{4}}Doc'sTlcGirl116^{7\frac{1}{2}}Sir116$	Wide trip 7

LATEST WORKOUTS Jan 3 Bel tr.t 4f fst :52 B Dec 15 Bel tr.t 4f fst :52 B

When Siri was allowed to get away at 5–1 in her win of December 19, it was probably because the crowd shied away from her most recent outing: a low Beyer of 55 and a fourth-place finish, beaten by seven lengths on December 4. But note that Siri was part of an entry that day, and the habitual off-the-pace runner displayed surprising early speed from post 12.

A check of the chart reveals that the prime beneficiary of Siri's sudden early-speed tactics was her entrymate, Irish Intern:

SEVENTH RACE
Aqueduct
DECEMBER 4, 1992

1 1/16 MILES.(InnerDirt). (1.413) ALLOWANCE. Purse $29,000. Fillies and Mares, 3-year-olds and upward foaled in New York State and approved by the New York State-bred Registry which have never won a race other than Maiden, Claiming or Starter. Weight: 3-year-olds 120 lbs., older 122 lbs. Non-winners of a race other than Claiming at a mile or over since November 15 allowed 3 lbs., of such a race since November 1, 5 lbs.

Value of race $29,000; value to winner $17,400; second $6,380; third $3,480; fourth $1,740. Mutuel pool $200,227. Exacta Pool $422,652

Last Raced	Horse	M/Eqt.A.Wt	PP	St	¼	½	¾	Str	Fin	Jockey	Odds $1
22Oct92 2Aqu9	Irish Intern	b 3 115	10	11	12	101	6½	2½	11¼	Davis R G	a-6.10
15Nov92 6Aqu3	Estates Princess	3 115	3	4	1½	11	11	1hd	22¼	Velasquez J	5.70
15Nov92 6Aqu6	Galloping Proudly	3 115	4	5	41	41½	21	33	33½	Romero R P	4.30
13Nov92 5Aqu4	Siri	b 3 115	12	10	21	2½	31	42	43	Gryder A T	a-6.10
20Nov92 1Aqu1	That's Ravishing	Bb 3 115	11	9	102	9hd	112	91½	5nk	McCauley W H	24.60
15Nov92 6Aqu8	Titans Belle	4 117	8	8	8½	11hd	12	101	6hd	Mojica R Jr	29.60
5Nov92 8Aqu2	She's a Queen	3 115	1	1	5½	5hd	71½	71½	7¾	Santagata N	2.70
15Nov92 6Aqu12	New York Issue	3 115	6	7	112	12	10hd	8½	8nk	Smith M E	43.40
15Nov92 6Aqu10	Doc's Talc Girl	3 110	2	2	31	3½	5½	5hd	91	Frost G C5	42.20
15Nov92 6Aqu2	Essen 'N Fressen	b 3 115	9	12	92½	62½	4½	6hd	103	Rojas R I	2.80
24Nov92 8Med5	Nine Whitney Place	3 115	7	6	7½	7½	81½	112	114½	Chavez J F	13.60
15Nov92 6Aqu13	Raggedy Frass	3 115	5	3	62½	82	9½	12	12	Bruin J E	62.50

a-Coupled: Irish Intern and Siri.

OFF AT 3:10 Start good, Won driving. Time, :244, :493, 1:144, 1:404, 1:473 Track fast.

$2 Mutuel Prices:				
	1-(K)-IRISH INTERN (a-entry)	14.20	6.40	4.40
	4-(C)-ESTATES PRINCESS		7.20	6.20
	5-(E)-GALLOPING PROUDLY			4.60
	$2 EXACTA 1–4 PAID $93.60			

B. f, (Apr), by Dr Blum—Erin's Slew, by Seattle Slew. Trainer Destasio Richard A. Bred by Fried Albert Jr (NY).

IRISH INTERN trailed early after breaking a bit slowly, rapidly worked her way forward while four wide on the turn then finished determinedly in the middle of the track to wear down ESTATES PRINCESS. The latter set the pace along the inside into midstretch and yielded grudgingly. GALLOPING PROUDLY well placed for a half rallied slightly off the rail to threaten on the turn, remained a factor into midstretch then weakened in the final eighth. SIRI forced the pace from outside for nearly six furlongs and tired. THAT'S RAVISHING was never a factor. TITANS BELLE passed only tiring horses. SHE'S A QUEEN faded after going six furlongs. NEW YORK ISSU was never close. DOC'S TALC GIRL was used up trying to keep the early pace. ESSEN 'N FRESSEN far back early after breaking poorly made a sustained run five wide to reach contention on the turn then flattened out. NINE WHITNEY PLACE failed to threaten. RAGGEDY FRASS was finished early. ESSEN 'N FRESSEN wore mud caulks.

Owners— 1, Fried Albert Jr; 2, Lucy Grace Stables; 3, Four B Mice Stable; 4, My Kid's Stable; 5, Schwarz Arlene; 6, Kershaw Warren E; 7, Konrad Diana U; 8, Meittinis Louis N; 9, Mt View Manor Farm; 10, Dee Pee Stables; 11, McRich Stables; 12, Bomze Richard.

Trainers— 1, Destasio Richard A; 2, Ortiz Paulino O; 3, Bailie Sally A; 4, Destasio Richard A; 5, Schwartz Scott M; 6, O'Brien Colum; 7, Groeschel Arthur; 8, Meittinis Louis N; 9, Hernandez Ramon M; 10, Figueroa Carlos R Jr; 11, Hirsch William J Jr; 12, O'Brien Leo.

Scratched—Nuzzle (16Nov92 1Aqu1); Gypsyfortuneteller (15Nov92 6Aqu4).

Estates Princess set the pace and might've gone all the way had Siri not been hustled out to apply some early pressure, effectively acting as a "rabbit" to set up the stretch charge of her mate.

Here's another example:

Southern Slew — Dk. b. or br. h. 7, by Slew Machine—Windy Secret, by Windy Sands

SMITH M E (212 50 29 29 .24) — $50,000 — Br.—Grass R P (Ga)

Own.—Mercader Maryann B — Tr.—Badgett William Jr (29 9 8 2 .31) — 119

Lifetime: 33 11 1 4 — $181,610

1993	4	3	1	0	$43,490
1992	7	3	0	1	$47,340
Turf	21	10	1	1	$165,530
Wet	2	1	0	0	$9,000

24May93- 1Bel	fm	1 1/16	[T]:463	1:10	1:40	Clm 75000	92	3	3	43½	41½	21	12½	Smith M E		112	2.10	96-07	SothrnSlw1122½WhtAbotMchl112nkHppyTrls114	Driving	5
13May93- 4Bel	fm	1 1/16	[T]:481	1:114	1:413	Clm 50000	87	3	1	62¾	63¼	25	23¾	Smith M E		117	*1.00e	84-13	KnwnRngr-En1173¾SthrnSl117nkWndrkn113	Up for 2nd	9
28Mar93- 3FG	fm	*1 1/16	(T):47	1:112	1:434	Clm 35000	92	1	4	44½	42¼	12½	12¼	Martin E Jr	L	117	*.70	101-04	SouthernSlew1172¼FirstChllenge1172¾Vrolet115	Driving	12
10Mar93- 7FG	fm	*1 1/16	(T):49	1:131	1:45	Clm 35000	93	5	3	44½	32	2hd	12	Martin E Jr	L	117	2.50	95-10	SouthernSlw1172KiltrtnCross1152Aptuto-Ch117	Driving	6
1Nov92- 2Aqu	fm	1⅛	(T):49	1:14	1:51	3↑Clm 50000	88	7	2	21	2hd	12	12	Davis R G		117	3.20	88-10	Southern Slew1172RinTinBid117nkBestOffer117	Driving	9
19Oct92- 3Bel	gd	1 1/16	[T]:502	1:144	1:44	3↑Clm 45000	93	3	2	2½	2½	11½	16	Smith M E		113	10.20	78-23	SothrnSlw1136HghlndDvotn1141TrnngFrHm113	Driving	10
9Oct92- 5Bel	sly	1 1/16	:46	1:102	1:424	3↑Clm 35000	69	3	7	63	33	36½	512¾	Smith M E		117	4.90	75-12	ShrpMint1178FnlDstnton1172¾Ft'NFsty117	Chckd 3/8 pl	11
9Oct92-Originally scheduled on turf																					
4Sep92- 9Bel	yl	1	(T):461	1:11	1:362	3↑Clm 35000	87	10	3	2hd	2hd	1½	12	Smith M E		117	3.70	80-20	SothrnSlw1172[D]Dr.Brtolo1172TrnngForHom119	Driving	12
30Jly92- 4Sar	fm	1 1/16	(T):464	1:102	1:401	3↑Clm 35000	87	4	7	74½	56½	36½	38	Smith M E		117	4.00	85-05	EbonyMgc1176GorgPhlps-Ir1172SthrnSlw117	Late gain	12
9Jly92- 2Bel	gd	1 1/16	:463	1:111	1:43	Clm 50000	62	2	2	32	32½	46½	410¼	Antley C W		117	4.00	77-25	St.Vvn-Ar113¾GoldnExplosv1173TrnngForHm117	Tired	6
9Jly92-Originally scheduled on turf																					

LATEST WORKOUTS Jun 17 Bel 4f fst :494 B Jun 7 Bel 4f fst :502 B May 22 Bel 4f fst :512 B May 10 Bel 4f fst :492 B

Southern Slew was part of an even-money entry when returned from a freshening on May 13, the comment line reading, "Up for 2nd."

There's only so much space in a comment line, but the chart of the race tells the whole story:

FOURTH RACE
Belmont
MAY 13, 1993

1 $\frac{1}{16}$ MILES.(InnerTurf). (1.39^1) CLAIMING. Purse $24,500. 4-year-olds and upward. Weight, 122 lbs. Non-winners of two races since April 15 allowed 3 lbs. Of such a race since then, 5 lbs. Claiming price $50,000; for each $2,500 to $45,000 allowed 2lbs. (Races when entered to be claimed for $40,000 or less not considered).

Value of race $24,500; value to winner $14,700; second $5,390; third $2,940; fourth $1,470. Mutuel pool $186,100. Exacta Pool $377,945 Quinella Pool $89,455

Last Raced	Horse	M/Eqt.A.Wt	PP	St	1/4	1/2	3/4	Str	Fin	Jockey	Cl'g Pr	Odds $1
5Mar93 ^{9}FG^3	Known Ranger-En	7 117	6	7	2^1	1^1	$1^{1\frac{1}{2}}$	1^5	$1^{3\frac{3}{4}}$	Santos J A	50000	a-1.00
28Mar93 ^{3}FG^1	Southern Slew	7 117	3	4	1^{hd}	6^1	6^{hd}	2^1	2^{nk}	Smith M E	50000	a-1.00
3May93 ^{8}Aqu^7	Wanderkin	b 10 113	4	3	8^2	8^2	8^1	4^{hd}	$3^{2\frac{3}{4}}$	Antley C W	45000	18.50
1May93 ^{4}Aqu^4	Scudbuster	b 4 113	1	1	$7^{1\frac{1}{2}}$	7^2	$7^{1\frac{1}{2}}$	5^{hd}	4no	Samyn J L	45000	11.70
1May93 ^{4}Aqu^1	Won the Laurel	b 5 113	2	2	9	9	9	8^8	$5^{1\frac{1}{2}}$	McCuleyWH	45000	3.40
3May93 ^{8}Aqu^2	Beau Canari	7 113	5	5	$4^{\frac{1}{2}}$	$2^{\frac{1}{2}}$	3^{hd}	3^{hd}	6^1	Pezua J M	45000	5.20
1May93 ^{7}Aqu^4	Now Is The Hour	b 6 113	8	8	5^{hd}	3^{hd}	$2^{\frac{1}{2}}$	$6^{\frac{1}{2}}$	7^5	Velasquez J	45000	12.10
3May93 ^{8}Aqu	Kate's Valentine	8 117	7	6	6^1	5^1	5^1	$7^{\frac{1}{2}}$	8^9	Madrid A Jr	50000	8.90
26Apr93 ^{7}Aqu^{10}	Scout Setter	b 5 113	9	9	3^1	4^{hd}	4^{hd}	9	9	Santagata N	45000	48.90

a-Coupled: Known Ranger-En and Southern Slew.

OFF AT 2:33 Start good, Won driving. Time, :25 , :48^1, 1:11^4, 1:35^2, 1:41^3 Course firm.

$2 Mutuel Prices:				
	1-(F)-KNOWN RANGER-EN (a-entry)	4.00	3.60	2.80
	1-(C)-SOUTHERN SLEW (a-entry)	4.00	3.60	2.80
	4-(D)-WANDERKIN			9.00

$2 EXACTA 1-4 PAID $63.00 $2 QUINELLA 1-4 PAID $49.00

Dk. b. or br. g, by Known Fact—Home On The Range, by Habitat. Trainer Badgett William Jr. Bred by Cliveden Stud (Eng).

KNOWN RANGER took the lead along the backstretch, extended his margin entering the stretch then drew off under intermittent urging. SOUTHERN SLEW sprinted to the front soon after the start, relinquished the lead to his entrymate in the early stages, dropped back steadily nearing the far turn, was unhurried to the turn, slipped through along the rail rallying in the stretch then finished with good energy for the place.WANDERKIN far back for six furlongs, launched a rally between horses entering the stretch then closed steadily to gain a share. SCUDBUSTER, reserved for six furlongs, improved his position with a mild late rally. WON THE LAUREL trailed to the the turn, angled wide at the top of the stretch then rallied belatedly. BEAU CANARI raced in close contention along the inside to the turn and lacked a strong closing bid. NOW IS THE HOUR never far back, made a run between horses to threaten on the turn but couldn't sustain his rally. KATE'S VALENTINE faded after going six furlongs. SCOUT SETTER, up close early, gave way on the turn.

Owners— 1, Roussel Louie J III; 2, Mercader Maryann B; 3, Poma Stable; 4, Cohn Seymour; 5, Russo August F; 6, Regan John N; 7, Marx Joseph A; 8, Edwards James F; 9, Foss Monte.

Trainers— 1, Badgett William Jr; 2, Badgett William Jr; 3, Meittinis Louis N; 4, Terrill William V; 5, Hebert William; 6, Brida Dennis J; 7, Alvarez Luis C; 8, Lundy Sarah A; 9, Daggett Michael H.

The winner was Southern Slew's entrymate, Known Ranger. It doesn't appear from Southern Slew's running line and footnote comment that he had any interest in hooking up with his mate in a taxing duel that might've been detrimental to both in terms of future condition.

The footnote states that Southern Slew ". . . sprinted to the front soon after the start, relinquished the lead to his entrymate in the early stages, dropped back steadily nearing the far turn, was unhurried to the turn, slipped through along the rail rallying into the stretch, then finished with good energy for the place."

Ridden more aggressively just eleven days later when on his own, Southern Slew had little trouble handling a rise in class to $75,000, winning by two and a half lengths at $6.20 in a short field.

My all-time favorite example of this entry maneuver is the tag-team of Kiri's Clown and A In Sociology:

Belmont Park

7 *1 1/16 MILES.* (Inner Turf). (1:391) HANDICAP. Purse $48,000. 3-year-olds and upward. Weights Wednesday, May 18. Declarations by 10:00 A.M. Thursday, May 19. Closed Wednesday, May 18, with 19 nominations.

Coupled - Kiri's Clown and Same Old Wish

Sand Lizard
Own: Loblolly Stable
CHAVEZ J F (71 7 14 8 .10)

Gr. g. 5
Sire: Temperence Hill (Stop the Music)
Dam: Amyark (Caro-IR)
Br: Loblolly Stable (Ky)
Tr: Bohannan Thomas (2 0 0 1 .00)

111

Lifetime Record:	18 6 2 4	$214,793			
1994	4 0 1 2	$16,780	Turf	2 1 0 0	$27,600
1993	14 6 1 2	$198,013	Wet	3 1 0 1	$17,500
Bel ⓣ	2 1 0 0	$27,600	Dist ⓣ	0 0 0 0	

7May94-7Bel	fst	1 1/16		:224 :444 1:084 1:403	3↑ Alw 44000N$mY	96	3	5	33½	22	24	37	Velazquez J R	115 b	*1.70	92-12	Blare Of Trumpets1157 Jacksonport108no Sand Lizard1151¼	No late bid	6
9Apr94-8OP	wf	1 1/16		:233 :471 1:112 1:442	Alw 43000N3Y	96	9	5	33	33	33	3¾	Gomez G K	115 b	*1.50	78-22	Nelson115¾ Capitalimprovement121hd Sand Lizard1156	Willingly	10
26Mar94-9OP	sly	1 1/16		:223 :453 1:111 1:433	Razorback H-G2	83	4	7	57	57¾	610	716½	Martinez J R Jr	114 b	8.50	67-17	Prize Fight1132½ Brother Brown1201½ Country Store1134	4-wide 2nd turn	8
12Mar94-8OP	fst	1 1/16		:231 :464 1:113 1:433	Alw 36000N1Y	96	1	5	41¾	41½	3½	2½	Day P	115 b	*.90	82-20	Cruel Cavalier115½ Sand Lizard1152½ Meena1214½	Gamely	8
9Oct93-9Pha	fst	1⅛		:482 1:12 1:37 1:501	3↑ Norristown HG3	93	6	4	31	3½	2½	31	Carr D	117 b	2.40	86-18	Primitive Hall109¾ Gala Spinaway116nk Sand Lizard1171¾	Hung	7
24Sep93-8Bel	gd	1 1/16		:232 :47 1:112 1:43	3↑ Handicap48k	104	4	4	41½	1hd	2½	22	Davis R G	119 b	2.60	85-27	Brunswick1252 Sand Lizard1192½ Federal Funds1122½	Second best	6
28Aug93-8Sar	fst	1⅛		:464 1:101 1:343 1:472	3↑ Whitney H-G1	86	4	6	65½	74	68½	617¼	Santos J A	114 b	8.20	82-06	Brunswick1123½ West By West115¾ Devil HisDue1227½	Steadied, wide turn	7
12Aug93-7Sar	fst	1⅛		:473 1:114 1:364 1:493	3↑ Upset53k	95	1	4	53	52	1hd	1¾	Santos J A	122 b	3.00	88-13	SandLizrd122¾ Supermec117nk MichelleCnPss1171	Std, blocked, driving	9
24Jly93-8Bel	fm	1¼	[T]	:482 1:121 1:361 2:001	3↑ Handicap46k	95	4	3	32	31	41½	52¾	Santos J A	115	2.60	86-17	Thakib117nk Square Cut1161½ Wild Acclaim1141	Lacked rally	6
5Jly93-8Bel	gd	1¼	[T]	:49 1:124 1:364 2:013	3↑ Alw 46000N$mY	95	6	2	2½	31½	3½	1nk	Santos J A	117	5.40	82-16	Sand Lizard117nk Zero For Conduct1171 Binary Light117hd	Driving	7

WORKOUTS: May 2 Bel 4f fst :474 H 6/30 Apr 27 Bel 4f fst :471 H 3/31 Mar 22 OP 4f fst :484 B 3/19 ●Mar 3 OP 4f fst :48 H 1/46 Feb 23 OP 5f sly 1:03 B 7/18

Correntino
Own: Dogwood Stable
LEON F (46 4 3 5 .09)

Dk. b or br g. 5
Sire: Lord at War-Ar (General-Fr)
Dam: La Corriente (Little Current)
Br: Wimborne Farm Inc (Ky)
Tr: O'Brien Leo (25 6 2 2 .24)

110

Lifetime Record:	37 5 10 6	$199,587			
1994	5 0 2 2	$25,400	Turf	10 1 4 1	$59,379
1993	14 1 3 3	$49,981	Wet	4 0 0 0	$8,778
Bel ⓣ	0 0 0 0		Dist ⓣ	4 1 1 0	$26,216

6Apr94-8Aqu	fst	1		:241 :472 1:113 1:361	3↑ Alw 42000N$Y	93	5	3	34	3½	21	31	Chavez J F	117 b	7.60	86-24	Stormy Java1191 Miner's Mark124hd Correntino1172½	Bid, weakened	6
23Mar94-6Aqu	fst	1⅛		:482 1:124 1:38 1:504	Alw 40000N$mY	91	5	3	38	33	33½	27	Chavez J F	115 b	3.80	75-24	Double Calvados1157 Correntino1152½ Lord Beer1191½	Up for place	5
27Feb94-7Aqu	fst	170	⊡	:231 :464 1:114 1:414	Alw 34000N4X	99	7	6	67	63½	42	32¾	Chavez J F	117 b	*1.30	87-24	Commander Evander1172 Exotic Slew117nk Correntino117nk	Four wide	7
5Feb94-6Aqu	fst	1⅛	⊡	:49 1:123 1:372 1:50	3↑ Assault H-G3	96	7	7	78½	811	712	611¼	Leon F	110	18.30	75-28	As Indicated1245½ Autoroute1131 Michelle Can Pass121½	Outrun	9
9Jan94-4Aqu	fst	1 1/16	⊡	:234 :473 1:121 1:441	Alw 34000N4X	96	1	2	43	45	33½	2nk	Chavez J F	117	*2.20	84-20	Lord Beer117nk Correntino117nk Cranshaw's Corner1173¾	Just missed	7
29Dec93-6Aqu	fst	1 1/16	⊡	:242 :494 1:143 1:463	3↑ Clm 70000	91	2	2	21	2hd	12	12½	Chavez J F	113	6.10	72-33	Correntino1132½ Cranshaw's Corner1133 Stately Wager1136	Driving	6
20Nov93-4CD	gd	1⅛	ⓣ	:48 1:134 1:402 1:534	3↑ Clm 75000	86	10	6	57½	66¼	33	2nk	Arguello F A Jr	117	6.20	63-31	Cozzemight117nk Correntino1171 Hasty Empery112nk	Finished fast	10
6Nov93-6CD	fm	1⅛	ⓣ	:482 1:132 1:383 1:502	3↑ Clm 75000	82	3	5	44½	53¼	34	36¾	Arguello F A Jr	117	7.40	73-19	First And Only1195 Just Like Perfect1191¾ Correntino1171½	No late gain	10
13Oct93-7Kee	fst	7f		:22 :441 1:084 1:201	3↑ Alw 28175N$Y	88	5	8	109¾	813	75¼	68¼	Arguello F A Jr	112	17.80	100-05	Binalong1125 Star Of Rhodesia1101 Tempered Halo1102	Bumped, start	10
23Sep93-8TP	my	1 1/16		:232 :473 1:131 1:451	3↑ Alw 27900N$Y	77	1	4	44	46½	49	413½	Miller D A Jr	114	4.90	67-27	Grand Jewel1125 Return Voyage1136 Season Screen1152½	Held position	6

WORKOUTS: ●May 1 Bel 6f fst 1:134 H 1/4 Apr 23 Bel 5f fst 1:021 B 28/41 Apr 4 Bel tr.t 4f fst :50 B 13/25 Mar 14 Bel tr.t 5f fst 1:023 B 8/18 Feb 25 Bel tr.t 3f fst :351 B 2/11

Kiri's Clown
Own: Cobble View Stable
LUZZI M J (83 11 13 10 .13)

Dk. b or br h. 5
Sire: Foolish Pleasure (What a Pleasure)
Dam: Kiri (Kris)
Br: Landon & Sullivan Mary A (Fla)
Tr: Johnson Philip G (21 4 2 3 .19)

116

Lifetime Record:	26 9 3 3	$243,156			
1994	1 0 0 0		Turf	24 9 3 3	$243,156
1993	7 2 1 2	$80,332	Wet	0 0 0 0	
Bel ⓣ	11 4 1 2	$100,304	Dist ⓣ	13 4 1 2	$120,526

7May94-8Bel	fm	1 1/16	[T]	:241 :464 1:102 1:404	3↑ Alw 44000N$mY	80	3	3	32	2½	43	58	Luzzi M J	115	*.90e	84-13	A In Sociology115hd Dover Coast1152½ Ocean Wave115½	Bid, tired	8
6Aug93-7Sar	fm	1⅛	[T]	:464 1:101 1:35 1:47	3↑ Alw 46000N$mY	101	1	1	11	11½	12	1¾	Davis R G	117	5.40	103-07	Kiri's Clown117¾ Majesty's Time119nk Ganges1191½	Driving	10
31May93-9Mth	fm	1	ⓣ	:243 :48 1:103 1:341	3↑ Red Bank H-G3	91	6	4	31	3½	62¾	55½	Santagata N	L 116	4.60	89-07	Adam Smith116nk Fourstars Allstar1161½ Rinka Das1151¼	Tired	8
16May93-7Bel	fm	1 1/16	ⓣ	:233 :462 1:10 1:40	3↑ Handicap46k	99	3	2	2½	1hd	21	3½	Davis R G	118	*.90	95-13	Rinka Das113½ Maxigroom119no Kiri's Clown1183½	Weakened	4
1May93-9Aqu	fm	1 1/16	ⓣ	:232 :473 1:112 1:421	3↑ FT Marcy H-G3	98	5	9	74	3½	1hd	22	Davis R G	114	4.20	98-06	Adam Smith1122 Kiri's Clown1141 Casino Magistrate113no	Second best	11
4Apr93-7Kee	fm	1	ⓣ	:23 :454 1:102 1:342	Alw 27360N$Y	98	1	5	56½	54	34½	34¼	Guidry M	112	8.00	94-08	Lure1234 Rocket Fuel118nk Kiri's Clown112½	No late response	7
13Feb93-10GP	fm	1⅛	ⓣ	:472 1:104 1:351 1:474+	3↑ Cndn Turf H-G2	101	3	8	810	79½	54	72¼	Gonzalez M A	L 114	9.60	91-12	Stagecraft112nk Roman Envoy121½ Carterista114no	No threat	10
30Jan93-9GP	fm	*1 1/16	ⓣ	1:474+	Alw 33500N$YmT	102	9	7	73	84¼	41¾	1½	Gonzalez M A	L 117	8.10	78-23	Kiri's Clown117½ Flying American117½ Carterista1193	Driving	10
21Oct92-7Aqu	fm	1	ⓣ	:232 :472 1:122 1:36	3↑ Alw 47000	101	6	4	42	41¼	11½	13	Bailey J D	112	*1.40	96-13	Kiri's Clown1123 Turkey Point115nk So Sterling117	Driving	6
3Oct92-5Bel	fm	1 1/16	[T]	:23 :463 1:104 1:402	3↑ Alw 33000	100	5	5	54¼	2½	18	15½	Bailey J D	114	*1.10	96-06	Kiri's Clown1145½ King's Gent1195 Pro Serve117	Driving	8

WORKOUTS: May 14 Bel 4f fst :464 H 2/48 May 3 Bel tr.t 4f fst :483 H 3/7 Apr 27 Bel tr.t 7f fst 1:253 H 1/2 Apr 21 Bel tr.t 6f fst 1:123 H 1/1 Apr 15 Bel tr.t 5f fst 1:004 H 10/41

River Majesty

Own: McNall Bruce P

SMITH M E (48 12 4 7 .25)

B. h. 5
Sire: Majestic Light (Majestic Prince)
Dam: Pier (Riverman)
Br: Tanz Meryl Ann (Ky)
Tr: Clement Christophe (13 3 2 1 .23)

121

Lifetime Record: 27 6 5 3 $234,692											
1994	1	0	0	1	$5,520	Turf	27	6	5	3	$234,692
1993	10	4	2	0	$143,970	Wet	0	0	0	0	
Bel ⓣ	2	2	0	0	$42,000	Dist ⓣ	5	3	0	1	$72,770

21Apr94-8Aqu yl 1 1/16 ⓣ :243 :501 1:151 1:464 3+ Handicap46k 99 5 6 63 31½ 31½ 31¼ Samyn J L 122 *1.70 74-28 Personal Draw1141¼ Irish Linnet115no River Majesty122½ Bid, weakened 6
2Nov93-8Aqu sf 1⅛ ⓣ :49 1:142 1:41 1:542 3+ Knickrbkr H-G3 98 2 4 48 42 3½ 12 Smith M E 115 3.00 71-29 River Majesty1152 Daarik114hd Home Of The Free118nk Driving 6
15Oct93-8Med yl 1 1/16 ⓣ :241 :493 1:144 1:464 3+ John Henry40k 92 2 5 59½ 57½ 23 1nk Smith M E L 119 *1.70 65-34 River Majesty119nk Sylva Honda1133 Ogle113¾ Up, final stride 8
24Sep93-6Bel yl 1 1/16 ⓣ :234 :474 1:123 1:443 3+ Alw 36000N4X 97 3 7 65 53 11½ 14 Smith M E 119 2.40e 73-37 River Majesty1194 Mukddaam117nk Palace Line117¾ Wide, ridden out 7
3Sep93-8Bel fm 1 1/16 [T] :244 :473 1:111 1:411 3+ Alw 34000N3X 94 3 3 38 44½ 3½ 12 Smith M E 117 3.60 90-10 RiverMjesty1172 HppyTrils1171 PrimitiveHll117nk Saved ground, driving 6
29Jly93-8Sar fm 1⅜ ⓣ :48 1:123 1:363 1:542 3+ Alw 32500N3X 87 6 7 512 42½ 33 54 Smith M E 117 3.50 92-14 Lyphard Legend1172 Pride Of Summer1171½ Wesaam117nk Flattened out 9
4Jly93-6AP gd 1⅜ ⓣ :484 1:13 1:38 1:564 3+ Sts n Stps HG3 94 1 10 109½ 98¾ 77 63 Ramos W S L 114 11.40 79-19 Little Bro Lantis1142½ Stark South119nk Coaxing Matt115no Late rally 12
29May93-7Hol gd 1 1/16 ⓣ :241 :472 1:104 1:40 Alw 50000N3X 96 6 3 34 52½ 53½ 53 Black C A LB 115 3.30 93-07 Man From Eldorado116nk Nine Carat115hd Nutley1151½ 4 Wide stretch 6
9May93-8Hol fm 1⅛ ⓣ :463 1:094 1:33 1:45 3+ John Henry HG2 92 4 5 64 62½ 64¾ 65 Black C A LB 113 16.20 94-04 Leger Cat115hd Rainbow Corner114no Jahafil1161½ Troubled trip 8
28Mar93-8SA yl 1⅛ ⓣ :472 1:123 1:373 1:50 Mrmonts H79k 103 1 4 43½ 31½ 1hd 2hd Black C A LB 115 5.00 69-31 Never Black118hd River Majesty1155 Barraq1165½ Gamely 5

WORKOUTS: May 12 Bel [T] 5f fm 1:024 B (d) 7/17 May 3 Bel 5f fst 1:013 B 11/23 Apr 18 Bel tr.t 4f fst :492 B 19/27 Apr 4 Pay 5f fst 1:05 B 3/3 Mar 28 Pay 4f fst :531 B 5/5 Mar 22 Pay 4f fst :52 B 4/10

Same Old Wish

Own: L S I Gold Stable

MAPLE E (29 2 4 4 .07)

B. g. 4
Sire: Lyphard's Wish (Lyphard)
Dam: Olden Roberta (Roberto)
Br: Tucker Paula J (Fla)
Tr: Johnson Philip G (21 4 2 3 .19)

111

Lifetime Record: 17 5 1 2 $99,244											
1993	11	4	1	0	$75,744	Turf	14	5	1	1	$96,024
1992	6	1	0	2	$23,500	Wet	1	0	0	1	$3,120
Bel ⓣ	8	2	1	1	$42,440	Dist ⓣ	9	3	0	1	$53,550

4Nov93-7Aqu yl 1⅛ ⓣ :484 1:144 1:411 1:534 3+ Alw 32000N2X 90 8 9 812 52¾ 2hd 1no Maple E 117 b 1.80 74-26 [D]Same Old Wish117no Sentimental Moi1151¾ Impregnable1172 10
Came in, drifted out str, driving Disqualified and placed 4th
8Oct93-9Bel fm 1¼ [T] :494 1:134 1:382 2:023 3+ Alw 30000N1X 89 7 2 21 21 2hd 1hd Maple E 114 b *1.00 77-18 SameOldWish114hd TheWildIrishman1162½ ChmpgneAffir1141½ Hard drive 10
11Sep93-9Med yl 1⅜ ⓣ :48 1:13 1:372 2:143 Rutgers H-G3 89 11 5 55½ 62½ 3½ 53¾ Santos J A 113 b 6.80 97-07 KirovPremiere1111½ SentimentlMoi111hd ScatteredStps1121¾ Needed more 12
23Aug93-2Sar fm 1 1/16 ⓣ :243 :491 1:13 1:422 Clm 75000 91 4 5 42 41 1hd 12¼ Maple E 112 b 2.90 82-16 Same Old Wish1122¼ Tali Hai1141½ Flying Cherub116½ Driving 9
9Aug93-4Sar fm 1⅛ [T] :472 1:12 1:363 1:484 Clm 47500 89 3 4 32 32 1½ 13 Maple E 115 b 6.90 94-05 Same Old Wish1153 T. Barone117½ Peter And1171½ Driving 12
14Jly93-9Bel fm 1 ⓣ :232 :463 1:113 1:351 Clm 45000 77 7 9 63½ 2½ 2hd 22¼ Maple E 113 b 5.60 83-11 Hollywood Handsome1172¼ Same Old Wish1131¾ CurrentTrial1174½ Gamely 10
5Jly93-2Bel gd 1 1/16 ⓣ :231 :452 1:104 1:423 Clm 35000 82 6 4 41½ 31 2½ 16 Maple E 117 b *2.10 83-16 Same Old Wish1176 Class Hat1172 Donnacha1171 Perfect trip 10
18Jun93-6Bel fm 1 1/16 ⓣ :233 :464 1:104 1:404 Clm 45000 69 8 4 2½ 21 45 49½ Maple E 113 13.60 82-16 Easy Spender1173½ T. Barone113½ Five Star General1135½ Forced pace 12
4Jun93-5Bel fm 1 1/16 ⓣ :23 :461 1:102 1:421 Clm 50000 67 9 6 86½ 84½ 63½ 66¾ Pezua J M 117 17.30 78-18 Die Laughing1171 Zoom By117½ I'm A Big Shot1154½ Four wide 10
10May93-4Bel fm 1 1/16 ⓣ :23 :461 1:102 1:40 3+ Alw 28500N1X 53 4 7 810 74½ 1012 1021¾ Antley C W 113 8.80 74-11 Llandaff1106 Irish Harbour1105½ Trilingual119nk Outrun 11

WORKOUTS: ●May 15 Bel tr.t 3f fst :35 H 1/19 May 10 Bel 1 fst 1:391 B 1/2 ●May 3 Bel tr.t 3f fst :35 H 1/7 Apr 27 Bel tr.t 6f fst 1:133 H 1/1 Apr 21 Bel tr.t 7f fst 1:283 B 1/1 Apr 15 Bel tr.t 6f fst 1:131 H 2/14

Farmonthefreeway

Own: Very Un Stable

VELAZQUEZ J R (62 8 10 10 .13)

B. g. 4
Sire: Talc (Rock Talk)
Dam: Screened (Alydar)
Br: Werblin David (NY)
Tr: O'Connell Richard (10 1 0 3 .10)

111

Lifetime Record: 26 5 3 10 $293,495											
1994	6	0	0	3	$20,526	Turf	1	0	0	0	$2,760
1993	15	3	2	7	$212,960	Wet	6	1	1	4	$103,794
Bel ⓣ	0	0	0	0		Dist ⓣ	1	0	0	0	$2,760

21Apr94-8Aqu yl 1 1/16 ⓣ :243 :501 1:151 1:464 3+ Handicap46k 98 4 2 31 52½ 53 41¾ Velazquez J R 113 8.00 73-28 Personal Draw1141¼ Irish Linnet115no River Majesty122½ No threat 6
20Mar94-7Aqu fst 6f ⊡ :23 :462 :584 1:112 Alw 36000N$Y 90 1 5 56 54½ 44 32¾ Velazquez J R 115 2.40 83-21 Won Song1151½ Nowhere Man1151½ Farmonthefreeway115no Broke slowly 5
25Feb94-6Aqu fst 6f ⊡ :224 :46 :574 1:094 Handicap40k 97 3 5 42½ 41 2hd 3½ Velazquez J R 112 10.80 93-14 Preporant122nk Nymphist112nk Farmonthefreeway1125 Bid, weakened 6
10Feb94-6Aqu fst 6f ⊡ :242 :48 1:00 1:122 Alw 36000N$Y 82 6 3 2½ 2½ 24 45 Velazquez J R 115 b 12.10 76-30 Senor Cielo1154½ Memorized110½ The Great M. B.115no Weakened 7
30Jan94-6Aqu gd 6f ⊡ :223 :46 :574 1:093 3+ Sptng Plt H83k 75 8 3 52 85 87¼ 911½ Velazquez J R 110 b 19.70 83-10 Chief Desire114no Strikany1121¾ Secret Odds1151½ Steadied 3/8 pl 10
17Jan94-6Aqu wf 6f ⊡ :222 :461 :584 1:12 3+ [S]Hol Hughes H54k 90 3 6 44½ 21 32 35½ Velazquez J R 113 b 21.60 77-24 Fbershm1173¾ ToughHert1111¾ Frmonthefrewy1132 Altered course 1/8 pl 7
30Dec93-7Aqu fst 6f ⊡ :234 :48 1:00 1:122 3+ Handicap44k 56 2 5 63¾ 64¾ 69½ 616¼ Migliore R 114 fb 7.30 64-24 Crafty Alfel1193 Fabersham115½ Preporant121nk Trailed 6
5Dec93-8Aqu sly 6f ⊡ :22 :453 :573 1:093 3+ [S]Joe Palmer67k 78 1 5 511 47 45½ 313¼ Migliore R 120 b 6.20 82-18 Preporant1228¾ Burn Fair1174½ Farmonthefreeway1201 No factor 5
13Nov93-7Aqu fst 6f :222 :454 :574 1:10 3+ Handicap44k 79 5 7 66½ 52½ 43½ 48 Migliore R 114 fb 4.20 84-14 Fabersham115hd Storm Boot1165 Plantagenet1133 Broke slowly 7
31Oct93-5Aqu sly 7f :231 :463 1:104 1:23 3+ Handicap44k 84 5 1 43 32 23½ 36¼ Migliore R 114 fb 1.50 83-18 Shining Bid1166 Liver Stand116nk Farmonthefreeway1141 No late bid 6

WORKOUTS: May 10 Bel 5f fst :59 H 2/45 Apr 15 Bel tr.t 4f fst :50 B 57/82 Apr 10 Bel tr.t 4f fst :513 B 44/48 Mar 13 Bel tr.t 3f fst :36 B 5/19

Daarik (Ire)

Own: Shadwell Stable

DAVIS R G (62 8 4 14 .13)

B. h. 7
Sire: Diesis-GB (Sharpen Up-GB)
Dam: Bay Street (Gundy)
Br: Dick D M (Ire)
Tr: Skiffington Thomas J (8 1 1 3 .13)

118

Lifetime Record: 40 14 4 5 $385,524											
1994	5	2	1	0	$79,580	Turf	40	14	4	5	$385,524
1993	7	2	1	4	$105,414	Wet	0	0	0	0	
Bel ⓣ	9	3	0	2	$96,060	Dist ⓣ	14	3	0	3	$90,190

24Apr94-7Kee fm 1⅛ ⓣ :471 1:12 1:37 1:49 Alw 28000NC 97 2 2 32½ 32½ 2hd 1no Day P L 120 b 2.30 92-13 Daarik120no Jodi's Sweetie1135½ Canabird1111½ 7
Exchanged brushes stretch, all out
13Mar94-10GP fm 1½ ⓣ :492 1:131 2:01 2:243 3+ Pan Amrcn H-G2 89 10 9 811 66 58¼ 58 Perret C L 113 b 8.50 89-09 Fraise124¾ Summer Ensign113hd Fairy Garden115¾ 10
Six wide top str belated bid
26Feb94-10GP fm *1⅛ ⓣ :48 1:113 1:354 1:494+ Alw 45000N$mY 81 4 8 711 76 68 710¼ Bailey J D L 119 b *1.60 86-11 Flying American115nk Social Retiree1153½ Bidding Proud1222 No threat 9
28Jan94-7GP gd *1⅛ ⓣ :493 1:142 1:383 1:514+ Alw 38000N$mY 103 4 5 56 42½ 2hd 1nk Bailey J D L 119 b *1.10 86-20 Daarik119nk Flying American1195 Spectacular Tide117nk Fully extended 8
2Jan94-7Crc fm 1½ ⓣ :48 1:113 2:023 2:274 3+ WL McKnght HG2 102 7 8 77½ 32½ 22 21¼ Bailey J D L 113 b 5.40 90-17 Cobblestone Road1131½ Daarik1131¾ Fraise1261 12
Broke in, steadied, gamely
11Dec93-10Crc fm *1⅛ ⓣ 1:444 3+ Trpcl Turf HG3 96 11 11 1115 1110 79½ 3½ Penna D L 114 b 6.90 95-22 Carterista121nk Rinka Das113hd Daarik114¾ 12
Steadied early, full of run inside
19Nov93-8Aqu yl 1⅛ ⓣ :501 1:15 1:401 1:513 3+ Alw 44000N$mY 94 9 8 86½ 75½ 41½ 11½ Bailey J D 117 b *1.00 85-15 Daarik1171½ Pride Of Summer1172 Bisbalense117½ Driving 10
2Nov93-8Aqu sf 1⅛ ⓣ :49 1:142 1:41 1:542 3+ Knickrbkr H-G3 94 6 6 615 611 53½ 22 Santos J A 114 b 2.40 69-29 River Majesty1152 Daarik114hd Home Of The Free118nk Rallied 6
16Oct93-6Bel sf 1 ⓣ :224 :454 1:103 1:354 3+ Kelso H-G3 93 3 10 109½ 86½ 45 38¼ Perret C 112 b 19.00 75-29 Lure1253½ Paradise Creek1205 Daarik112½ Late gain 10
2Oct93-1Bel yl 1 1/16 ⓣ :242 :481 1:123 1:432 3+ Clm 75000 100 4 5 54 31½ 1hd 12 Bailey J D 117 b *1.20 79-28 Daarik1172 Known Ranger1152¾ Ebony Magic113nk Driving 8

WORKOUTS: May 12 Bel [T] 5f fm 1:033 B (d) 11/17 May 6 Bel 4f fst :523 B 21/21 Apr 21 Kee ⓣ 5f fm 1:033 B (d) 6/7 Apr 14 GP 5f fst 1:04 B 6/7 Apr 8 GP 4f fst :502 B 4/14 Apr 4 GP 3f fst :383 B 5/7

Nijinsky's Gold

Own: Powell Stanton P

SANTOS J A (65 10 15 11 .15)

Ro. g. 5
Sire: Lot o' Gold (Lothario)
Dam: Super Jamie (Nijinsky II)
Br: Oechsner George D III (La)
Tr: Violette Richard Jr (3 0 1 0 .00)

119

Lifetime Record: 31 7 5 6 $246,136											
1994	5	0	0	3	$32,430	Turf	16	5	0	4	$141,209
1993	11	3	1	1	$83,251	Wet	1	0	1	0	$23,260
Bel ⓣ	0	0	0	0		Dist ⓣ	7	2	0	2	$57,598

1May94-8Aqu fm 1 1/16 ⓣ :231 :472 1:111 1:422 3+ Ft Marcy H-G3 100 6 6 66 62¾ 31½ 32¼ Samyn J L 113 b 5.00 95-07 Adam Smith118nk Halissee1132 Nijinsky's Gold1132 Late gain 7
26Mar94-11Hia fm 1 1/16 ⓣ 1:393 3+ Royal Palm H50k 102 9 7 88½ 54 42 32¼ Samyn J L L 113 b 6.80 103-03 Social Retiree1141½ Bidding Proud1151 Nijinsky's Gold113¾ Rallied 12
6Mar94-9GP fst 1¼ :46 1:093 1:34 2:002 3+ Gulfstr Pk HG1 99 2 5 47 55 53½ 86½ Samyn J L L 112 fb 61.40 92-06 Scuffleburg113hd Migrating Moon114½ Wallenda117¾ Tired 10
29Jan94-9GP fm 1⅛ ⓣ :472 1:111 1:343 1:474+ 3+ Canadn Trf HG2 98 8 5 56¾ 32½ 42 34 Santos J A L 113 b 12.50 89-11 Paradise Creek1233½ Glenfiddich Lad113¾ Nijinsky's Gold113nk 8
Bid wide, not good enough
8Jan94-9GP fm 1 1/16 ⓣ :24 :473 1:111 1:404+ 3+ Appleton H-G3 99 3 7 76 75 54½ 43½ Samyn J L L 113 b 19.30 89-14 Paradise Creek1213 Fourstars Allstar117nk Elite Jeblar111no 8
Steadied chute, rallied
4Dec93-7FG gd 1 1/16 ⊗ :231 :464 1:121 1:442 3+ [S]La Turf100k 100 9 10 1015 68½ 23 21½ Bourque K L 115 b 5.80 90-12 Dixie Poker Ace1131½ Nijinsky's Gold1159 Zarbycat1172½ 10
Trailed, 6 wide rally, 2nd best
8Oct93-9LaD gd *1 1/16 ⓣ :234 :483 1:122 1:422 3+ Alw 15000N$Y 95 7 5 52 21½ 2hd 11 Ardoin R L 115 b *1.20 93-07 Nijinsky's Gold1151 Apart1211 Justin N.1186 Driving 7
11Sep93-9AP fst 1 :224 :45 1:10 1:344 3+ Equips Ml H-G3 78 11 11 1123 1118 1018 817½ Perrodin E J L 113 29.80 75-18 Split Run1147 Gee Can He Dance1143 Danc'n Jake114hd Mild rally 11
28Aug93-11AP gd 1 1/16 ⓣ :24 :492 1:134 1:431 3+ Newbury H75k 90 2 6 56½ 65½ 53 62¼ Gomez G K L 114 b 5.00 86-11 MagesterilCheer112hd GeeCnHeDnce1131 Mr.LightTres1131½ 4 Wide turn 9
30Jly93-8AP fm 1 ⓣ :241 :464 1:104 1:351 3+ Mister Gus32k 98 4 8 713 711 33 1½ Gomez G K L 115 b 3.40 99-07 Nijinsky'sGold115½ FritzBarthold1172½ PlateDncer115nk Wide throughout 9

WORKOUTS: May 15 Bel 6f fst 1:171 B 4/5 Apr 24 Bel 7f fst 1:312 B 1/1 ●Apr 16 Bel tr.t 5f my :594 H 1/30 Feb 21 PBD 5f gd 1:02 B 1/3

Kiri's Clown returned from a nine-month layoff at Belmont on May 7 as part of an odds-on entry, and recorded the lowest Beyer showing in his past performances. Handicappers seeking a clearer picture regarding the purpose of that race referred back to the May 7 chart, and knew it was nothing more than a prep:

EIGHTH RACE
Belmont
MAY 7, 1994

$1\frac{1}{16}$ MILES. (Inner Turf)(1.39^{1}) ALLOWANCE. Purse $44,000. 3-year-olds and upward which have not won a race of $20,000 at a mile or over since September 1, 1993. Weights: 3-year-olds, 115 lbs. Older, 124 lbs. Non-winners of a race of $18,000 at a mile or over since March 1, allowed 3 lbs. Of such a race since January 15, 5 lbs. Of such a race since December 1, 7 lbs. (Maiden, claiming, starter and restricted races not considered.)

Value of Race: $44,000 Winner $26,400; second $9,680; third $5,280; fourth $2,640. Mutuel Pool $325,284.00 Exacta Pool $683,046.00

Last Raced	Horse	M/Eqt.	A.Wt	PP	St	¼	½	¾	Str	Fin	Jockey	Odds $1
16Oct93 ^{6}Bel^{4}	A In Sociology		4 115	8	5	1^{1}	$1^{1\frac{1}{2}}$	$1^{\frac{1}{2}}$	1^{2}	1^{hd}	Samyn J L	a-0.90
13Mar94 ^{5}GP^{9}	Dover Coast	b	5 115	2	4	6^{2}	5^{1}	5^{6}	$2^{\frac{1}{2}}$	$2^{2\frac{1}{2}}$	Santagata N	23.70
26Mar94 ^{11}Hia^{6}	Ocean Wave		4 115	5	7	7^{1}	$7^{1\frac{1}{2}}$	$6^{1\frac{1}{2}}$	$5^{\frac{1}{2}}$	$3^{\frac{1}{2}}$	Davis R G	5.80
12Dec93 ST^{12}	Fourstardave		9 115	4	3	$4^{\frac{1}{2}}$	4^{2}	$4^{\frac{1}{2}}$	$3^{\frac{1}{2}}$	4^{5}	Migliore R	4.10
6Aug93 ^{7}Sar^{1}	Kiri's Clown		5 115	3	2	$3^{\frac{1}{2}}$	$3^{\frac{1}{2}}$	2^{1}	4^{2}	5^{1}	Luzzi M J	a-0.90
22Dec93 ^{8}Crc^{6}	Casino Magistrate		5 115	1	1	2^{2}	$2^{\frac{1}{2}}$	$3^{\frac{1}{2}}$	6^{6}	6^{4}	Velazquez J R	13.40
10Apr94 ^{11}Hia^{7}	Smarginato-IR		4 115	7	8	8	8	8	7^{3}	7^{16}	Santos J A	3.90
15Apr94 ^{8}Aqu^{8}	Akiko	f	5 115	6	6	$5^{1\frac{1}{2}}$	6^{4}	7^{1}	8	8	Cruguet J	26.30

a-Coupled: A In Sociology and Kiri's Clown.

OFF AT 3:56 Start Good. Won driving. Time, :24^{1}, :46^{4}, 1:10^{2}, 1:34^{2}, 1:40^{4} Course firm.

$2 Mutuel Prices:			
1A-(H)-A IN SOCIOLOGY (a-entry)	3.80	2.60	2.20
3-(B)-DOVER COAST		9.40	3.60
5-(E)-OCEAN WAVE			2.80

$2 EXACTA 1-3 PAID $56.00

B. c, by Ends Well-Social Class, by What a Pleasure. Trainer Johnson Philip G. Bred by R I C Stables (NY).

A IN SOCIOLOGY sprinted clear in the early stages, shook off a mild challenge from his entrymate on the turn, opened a clear advantage then was all out to hold off DOVER COAST in the final strides. DOVER COAST unhurried for five furlongs while saving ground, swung four wide on the turn then closed steadily but could not get up. OCEAN WAVE far back for six furlongs, rallied belatedly to gain a share. FOURSTARDAVE raced in good position along the inside to the top of the stretch and lacked a strong closing bid. KIRI'S CLOWN never far back, made a run from outside to challenge on the turn then flattened out. SMARGINATO never reached contention. AKIKO was finished early. CASINO MAGISTRATE checked along the inside on the first turn, forced the pace from outside for five furlongs and tired.

Owners— 1, Ronca Frederick E; 2, Charvi Stable; 3, Royal Lines Stable; 4, Bomze Richard; 5, Cobble View Stable; 6, Blue Goose Stable; 7, Port Sidney L; 8, Sommer Viola

Trainers—1, Johnson Philip G; 2, Sciacca Gary; 3, Hough Stanley M; 4, O'Brien Leo; 5, Johnson Philip G; 6, Kelly Thomas J; 7, Clement Christophe; 8, Martin Frank

Scratched— Rocking Josh (28Apr94 ^{4}AQU^{3})

A In Sociology, according to the footnote, "sprinted clear in the early stages, *shook off a mild challenge from his entrymate* on the turn, opened a clear advantage . . ."

Trainer Phil Johnson accomplished two things with his two runners, both of whom were making their first starts of the year: He won the purse with A In Sociology; and he got a good tightener into Kiri's Clown.

On May 21, Kiri's Clown was coupled with another Johnson-trained runner, but this time it was *his* turn to go for the lead. He had several other factors working for him as well:

• A check of the pace match-ups showed that Kiri's Clown was the only legitimate early speed in the race.

• He was four for eleven on Belmont grass, including a narrow loss by half a length in a similar overnight handicap four races back, a race in which he battled on the front end under pressure throughout.

• Johnson had demonstrated at the previous year's spring meeting that he was very effective with grass horses making their second start back from a layoff:

Far Out Beast B. m. 6, by Far Out East—Dragoness-, by Formidable
DAVIS R G (84 7 14 13 .08) $95,000 Br.—Cobbleview Stable-Sullivan Mary A (Ky)
Own.—Sullimar Stable Tr.—Johnson Philip G (26 2 1 4 .08) 120
Lifetime 30 6 9 3 $200.030 | 1993 1 0 0 u | 1992 10 1 4 1 $73,810 | Turf 25 5 7 3 $184,570

13May93- 2Bel	fm	1	Ⓣ:461	1:101	1:35	ⒻClm 100000 13	83	4 2	2½	2½	2hd	52½	Davis R G	b	122	*2.70	84-13	FrnchStl122nkHombyTn1141½ByondSlw112	Forced pace 8
9Nov92- 6Aqu	yl	1 1/16	Ⓣ:493	1:144	1:47	3+ⒻAlw 47000	91	2 2	32½	42	21	2hd	Krone J A	b	115	*1.10	76-22	Chipaya-GB115hdFarOutBeast1152MdmeDhr117	Gamely 8
16Oct92- 9Med	fm	1 1/16	Ⓣ:464	1:103	1:414	3+ⒻIndian King	92	6 10	1011	85¼	64¼	21½	Krone J A	b	113	*2.50	87-11	GilddSt1221½FrOutBst1131½Routilnt-Ir113	Up for place 14
5Oct92- 5Bel	fm	1 1/16	[T]:481	1:114	1:412	ⒻClm 85000	92	1 4	41½	41½	2½	11½	Krone J A	b	116	*.70	91-12	FarOutBeast1161½MonicaFye1161½MissGrlnd113	Driving 5
19Sep92- 9Med	fm	1 1/16	Ⓣ:473	1:104	1:411	3+ⒻViolet H	92	5 5	52¼	52½	54	52½	Samyn J L	b	112	6.40	89-10	HghlndCrstl116hdIrshActrss116¾Nvrr109	Lacked fin bid 7
6Sep92- 9Mth	fm	1⅛	Ⓣ:471	1:113	1:484	+ 3+ⒻQnChrlotH	98	5 3	35	32	1½	2no	Santagata N	b	112	2.40	92-14	Seewillo111noFarOutBeast1129¼Forldiesonly113	Gamely 5
6Sep92-Grade III																			
14Aug92- 7Sar	fm	1 3/16	Ⓣ:482	1:113	1:533	3+ⒻHandicap	90	5 3	21	2½	2½	33	Cruguet J	b	111	3.60	97-12	LeFamo1222BethBelieves1131FarOutBest111	Bid, wknd 6
5Aug92- 1Sar	gd	1 1/16	Ⓣ:48	1:114	1:423	3+ⒻClm 90000	90	2 5	31	2hd	2½	4nk	Krone J A	b	118	*.60e	81-16	BelleofAmherst120noCzzyB.114hdScnt112	Bmpd weaknd 8
11Jly92- 1Bel	fm	1 1/16	[T]:474	1:114	1:414	3+ⒻAlw 47000	96	5 5	54	51¾	32	2¾	Krone J A	b	115	11.80	88-11	DncingDevlette115¾FrOutBest1151¾Ristn-GB115	Rallied 7
21Jun92- 5Bel	yl	1	Ⓣ:47	1:111	1:362	ⒻClm 90000	81	6 3	22	41¼	43½	43½	Velazquez J R	b	118	*2.20	76-23	BrghtSunshn113½CzzyB.1181¾Strswhrl114	Bid weakened 8

LATEST WORKOUTS May 22 Bel tr.t 5f fst 1:032 B ●May 7 Bel tr.t 5f fst 1:012 H May 1 Bel tr.t 5f fst 1:023 B Apr 25 Bel tr.t 4f fst :484 B

May 29 1m (T) $100–$75K clmg $6.80 R. Davis

Insurprise B. f. 4, by Greinton-GB—Setting Trick, by Tom Rolfe
SAMYN J L (67 10 7 13 .15) $35,000 Br.—Isaacs Harry Z (Va)
Own.—Twelve Oaks Stable Tr.—Johnson Philip G (42 5 2 4 .12) 117
Lifetime 11 1 0 0 $18,090 | 1993 1 0 0 0 | 1992 8 1 0 0 $18,090 | Turf 10 1 0 0 $18,090 | Wet 1 0 0 0

5May93- 5Bel	fm	1 1/16	Ⓣ:464	1:11	1:433	ⒻClm 50000	63	3 2	21	21	55½	813½	Bisono C V5	112	17.40	64-22	HomebyTen1133½BridjtHony1132½Mxmount117	Used up 10
1Oct92- 5Bel	fm	1 1/16	[T]:472	1:12	1:43	ⒻClm 50000	78	7 2	21½	1hd	31	43½	Samyn J L	116b	6.60	79-18	NoblGrl116¾HvnlyHfr1141½RscmmnClln112	Forced pace 7
1Oct92-Dead heat																		
18Sep92- 8Bel	fm	1 1/16	[T]:461	1:094	1:411	3+ⒻAlw 29000	70	5 5	511	49	56½	58¼	Carr D	113	17.30	84-12	MissGrlnd1132HombyTn113nkDvil'sMstrss113	No threat 8
2Sep92- 7Bel	fm	1	Ⓣ:45	1:092	1:344	3+ⒻAlw 29000	76	1 4	415	46½	42	53¾	Davis R G	113	*1.60e	84-15	JoyofLf-Ir1132ColdSplsh1131½HombyTn113	Stead early 8
1Aug92- 2Sar	fm	1 1/16	Ⓣ:464	1:11	1:423	ⒻClm 80000	65	6 2	2hd	3nk	52½	810¾	Day P	113	16.00	70-18	Bltr111noNrclffDncr1143BckSmBll117	Forced pace,wide 8
19Jly92- 9Bel	gd	7f	Ⓣ:221	:453	1:232	3+ⒻAlw 27000	60	10 6	88	53½	99¾	1012¼	Krone J A	111	4.00	76-12	West Virginia1111 Gidget1113 Salsflower117	Gave way 11
29Jun92- 8Bel	fm	1 1/16	Ⓣ:463	1:10	1:413	3+ⒻAlw 29000	71	5 1	44	33½	32½	45¼	Krone J A	111	3.50	83-14	Turkoldy112¾MissGrlnd109½FiveDrems117	Lacked rally 10
13Jun92- 5Bel	fm	1	Ⓣ:464	1:111	1:354	3+ⒻMd Sp Wt	76	10 4	41½	2hd	1hd	12¼	Krone J A	114	2.50e	83-13	Insurprise1142¼Kte'sPrid114¾Hrto'Min114	Wide driving 12
24May92- 3Bel	fm	1 1/16	Ⓣ:474	1:113	1:422	3+ⒻMd Sp Wt	70	8 1	1hd	1½	2hd	62½	Cruguet J	115	9.50	81-21	ForstKy115nkGoldfAtmn1152Ts'sThmpr115	Speed tired 12
28Oct91- 7Aqu	fm	1 1/16	Ⓣ:481	1:14	1:453	ⒻMd Sp Wt	55	3 2	2hd	2½	68	716½	Velazquez J R	117	4.70	67-19	Chinese Empress1175½LaLupe117½FrenchSteal117	Tired 10

LATEST WORKOUTS Jun 9 Bel tr.t 5f fst 1:033 B Jun 4 Bel tr.t 3f fst :381 B May 27 Bel tr.t 4f fst :473 H May 20 Bel tr.t 4f my :494 B

June 13 1m (T) $35K clmg $15.20 J. L. Samyn

Like Far Out Beast and Insurprise, Kiri's Clown was making his second start back, after forcing the pace and fading through the stretch in his return. As the race developed, Kiri's Clown was stalked through the opening six furlongs by his entrymate Same Old Wish (who, trip handicappers will tell you, exhibited no apparent sense of urgency in the proceedings as they hit the far turn), opened up a clear lead coming to midstretch, and won decisively at 3–1.

A In Sociology and Kiri's Clown reenacted the same scenario again at Saratoga:

Saratoga

9

1½ MILES. **(Inner Turf). (2:254) 20th Running of THE SWORD DANCER INVITATIONAL HANDICAP. Purse $250,000. Grade I. 3-year-olds and upward. Invitation only by Saturday, July 16, with no subscription fees. The purse to be divided 60% to the winner, 22% to second, 12% to third and 6% to fourth. The New York Racing Association Inc. will select a field of (14) invitees by Saturday, July 16. The assignment of weights for these invitees will be published on Wednesday, July 20. The Owners and/or Trainers of these (14) selected horses will be required to notify The New York Racing Association Inc. of their intention of running or not, no later than Saturday, July 23. A list of the Alternates and their weight assignments will be published on Monday, July 15. The New York Racing Association Inc. reserves the right to reassign weight to any horse after the weights have been published. Starters to be named at the closing time of entries. Trophies will be presented to the winning owner, trainer and jockey. This race will be limited to 14 Starters and Alternates (Highweights preferred). The New York Racing Association Inc. reserves the right to transfer this race to the Main Track.**

Coupled – Solar Splendor and Binary Light; Pescagani and Royal Mountain Inn

---

3 Kiri's Clown PP-1
Own: Cobble View Stable
LUZZI M J (27 6 3 4 .22)

Dk. b or br h. 5
Sire: Foolish Pleasure (What a Pleasure)
Dam: Kiri*GB (Kris)
Br: Landon & Sullivan Mary A (Fla)
Tr: Johnson Philip G (5 1 0 0 .20)

112

Lifetime Record: 31 11 3 3 $391,956
1994 6 2 0 0 $148,800 | Turf 29 11 3 3 $391,956
1993 7 2 1 2 $80,332 | Wet 0 0 0 0
Sar ⓣ 3 2 0 0 $46,800 | Dist ⓣ 0 0 0 0

25Jly94-8Sar fm 1 1/16 ⓣ :232 :464 1:104 1:411 3+ Daryl'sJoyH-G3 92 9 4 42½ 32 54 55¼ Luzzi M J 114 4.70e 82-15 A In Sociology115nk Namaqualand1132 Fourstars Allstar120nk Tired 9
14Jly94-8Bel fm 1¼ ⓣ :463 1:104 1:342 1:583 3+ Handicap48k 87 2 2 22 22 23½ 54¼ Luzzi M J 121 *2.20 92-05 Pescagani1163½ Heavy Rain113¾ Bisbalense114nk Tired 7
19Jun94-9Rkm fm *1⅛ ⓣ 1:463 3+ NH Sweeps H-G3 103 1 1 1hd 1½ 13 1¾ Luzzi M J LB 113 8.70 101-09 Kiri's Clown113¾ RiverMajesty115hd FourstarsAllstar1203 Inside, driving 8
10Jun94-6Bel fm 7f ⓣ :222 :442 1:074 1:20 3+ Jaipur-G3 72 7 1 42 31½ 75½ 716 Luzzi M J 114 4.30 86 — Nijinsky'sGold114nk DominntProspect1144½ HomeOfTheFr1222 Gave way 7
Run in divisions
21May94-7Bel yl 1 1/16 ⓣ :252 :493 1:134 1:441 3+ Handicap48k 104 2 1 11 1½ 11½ 12 Luzzi M J 116 3.00e 75-25 Kiri's Clown1162 River Majesty121½ Daarik118¾ Driving 7
7May94-8Bel fm 1 1/16 ⓣ :241 :464 1:102 1:404 3+ Alw 44000N$mY 80 3 3 32 2½ 43 58 Luzzi M J 115 *.90e 84-13 A In Sociology115hd Dover Coast1157½ Ocean Wave115½ Bid, tired 8
6Aug93-7Sar fm 1⅛ ⓣ :464 1:101 1:35 1:47 3+ Alw 46000N$mY 101 1 1 11 11½ 12 1¾ Davis R G 117 5.40 103-07 Kiri's Clown117¾ Majesty's Time119nk Ganges1191½ Driving 10
31May93-9Mth fm 1 ⓣ :243 :48 1:103 1:341 3+ Red Bank H-G3 91 6 4 31 3½ 62¾ 55¼ Santagata N L 116 4.60 89-07 Adam Smith116nk Fourstars Allstar1161½ Rinka Das1151½ Tired 8
16May93-7Bel fm 1 1/16 ⓣ :233 :462 1:10 1:40 3+ Handicap46k 99 3 2 2½ 1hd 21 3¾ Davis R G 118 *.90 95-13 Rinka Das113¾ Maxigroom119no Kiri's Clown1181½ Weakened 4
1May93-9Aqu fm 1 1/16 ⓣ :237 :471 1:112 1:421 3+ FT Marcy H-G3 98 5 9 74 3½ 1hd 22 Davis R G 114 4.20 98-06 Adam Smith1122 Kiri's Clown1141 Casino Magistrate113no Second best 11
WORKOUTS: Jly 12 Bel 4f fst :494 B 30/60 Jly 7 Bel 6f fst 1:142 H 4/6 Jly 2 Bel 5f fst 1:01 H 5/19 Jun 27 Bel 4f fst :494 B 16/32 Jun 9 Bel ⓣ 3f fm :353 B (d)2/5 Jun 4 Bel 5f fst :594 H 4/20

---

4 L'Hermine (GB) PP-2
Own: Four Fifths Stable
DAVIS R G (22 1 4 3 .05)

Dk. b or br h. 5
Sire: Slip Anchor (Shirley Heights)
Dam: Mondialite*Fr (Habitat)
Br: Kura C (GB)
Tr: Walden W Elliott (—)

110

Lifetime Record: 24 6 1 3 $161,178
1994 10 4 0 1 $135,533 | Turf 22 5 1 3 $147,101
1993 3 1 0 0 $14,915 | Wet 0 0 0 0
Sar ⓣ 0 0 0 0 | Dist ⓣ 2 0 0 0 $1,500

4Jly94-9AP fm 1⅜ ⓣ :472 1:11 1:36 1:543 3+ Strs&StrpsH-G3 95 3 6 54¾ 42½ 22 52½ Melancon L J L 111 b 8.60 91-08 Marastani113¾ [D]Kazabaiyn114½ Snake Eyes117¾ Checked stretch 12
Placed 4th through disqualification.
11Jun94-11CD fm 1⅛ ⓣ :48 1:112 1:353 1:481 3+ Louisville H108k 100 3 5 55½ 55 43½ 1nk Melancon L L 110 b 4.50 90-11 L'hermine110nk Llandaff1161½ Snake Eyes118¾ 5
Bumped start, driving
30May94-8CD fm 1 1/16 ⓣ :232 :47 1:12 1:472 3+ Alw 37110N$Y 97 6 6 69 17½ 1hd 11 Sellers S J L 123 b 2.10 94-09 L'hermine1234 Stylish Senor118¾ Jesse Come Home116½ Driving clear 7
12May94-8CD fm 1⅛ ⓣ :481 1:124 1:37 1:49 Clm 50000 93 3 5 53½ 53½ 31½ 1no Day P L 118 b *1.00 86-11 L'hermine118no Kiltartan Cross1124 Polish Blue116½ 10
23Apr94-7Kee fm 1⅛ ⓣ :47 1:11 1:35 1:474 Alw 31410N$Y 88 4 3 53½ 54 43 31½ Day P L 112 b 4.90 96-07 Llandaff1211½ Franchise Player112nk L'hermine1121½ No late response 8
10Apr94-11Hia fm 1⅜ ⓣ 1:533 3+ BougnvileaH-G3 90 6 6 84¾ 84¾ 73½ 63 Nunez E O L 110 42.60 98-08 Awad116nk Flying American1144 Summer Ensign1141½ Failed to menace 14
12Mar94-12GP fm 1½ ⓣ :481 1:122 2.021 2:251 Hcp 50000s 93 4 5 44½ 41½ 52¾ 42¾ McCarron C J L 115 7.10 92-02 Heavy Rain1161¾ Dinner In Rio114nk Eternal Orage117nk Belated bid 8
5Mar94-9GP fm 1⅜ ⓣ :492 1:14 1:38 2:143 Alw 35600N3X 82 5 4 53½ 79 76¾ 67¼ Santos J A L 119 4.30 85-10 Turk Passer1174¾ Telegrapher117nk Boss Man Jarett117nk Tired 10
13Feb94-9GP fm *1⅛ ⓣ :464 1:103 1:352 1.49 + Alw 31000N3X 100 7 5 54 53½ 21½ 1¾ Santos J A L 117 58.00 100-06 L'hermine117¾ Turk Passer1173½ Dominant Prospect1174½ Driving 10
23Jan94-10GP fm *1⅜ ⓣ :51 1:18 1:441 2:203 Clm 40000 — 8 — — — — — Perret C L 117 19.30 — 23 Heavy Rain117hd Caveat's Image1172¾ Won The Laurel1171½ Refused 10
WORKOUTS: Jly 26 OD 5f fst 1.023 B 10/24 Jly 20 CD 4f fst :513 B 32/36 Jun 29 CD ⓣ 4f fm :522 B (d)4/7 Jun 22 CD ⓣ 4f yl :531 B (d)4/4

---

5 Glanville PP-3
Own: Perez Robert
CHAVEZ J F (27 2 1 2 .07)

B. h. 5
Sire: Shahrastani (Nijinsky II)
Dam: Jury's Choice (Advocator)
Br: Princess Stud (Ky)
Tr: Callejas Alfredo (9 0 0 1 .00)

109

Lifetime Record: 27 1 8 7 $135,510
1994 6 0 2 2 $26,689 | Turf 27 1 8 7 $135,510
1993 10 1 2 3 $44,472 | Wet 0 0 0 0
Sar ⓣ 0 0 0 0 | Dist ⓣ 12 1 4 2 $67,671

12Jly94-8Bel fm 1⅜ ⓣ :502 1:142 1:382 2:144 3+ Alw 32000N2X 84 7 2 2½ 1½ 1½ 34¼ Chavez J F 117 b 3.90 89-08 Champagne Affair1172½ [D]Shoal Creek1172 Glanville1171 Weakened 7
Placed second through disqualification.
2Jly94-7Bel fm 1⅜ ⓣ :50 1:14 1:37 2:131 3+ BowlingGrnH-G2 78 6 6 66½ 67½ 610 616½ Maple E 112 b 14.00 72-15 Turk Passer1102¾ Sea Hero117nk Fraise124nk Broke slowly 6
22May94 ♦ Longchamp(Fr) sf *1 11/16 ⓣRH 3:274 4+ Prix Vicomtesse Vigier-G2 Stk 146000 52¼ Boeuf D 123 b 10.00 Molesnes120nk Epaphos127nk Infrasonic1231½ 7
Tr: Jean-Marie Beguigne
Unhurried in 6th, brief effort 2f out, one-paced late. Raintrap 4th
29Apr94 ♦ Saint-Cloud(Fr) gd *1 11/16 ⓣLH 3:114 4+ Prix de Barbeville-G3 Stk 60000 31 Boeuf D 121 b 9.00 Pinot128¾ Molesnes118nk Glanville121nk 7
Tracked in 3rd, 4th 1f out, in tight, finished well
28Mar94 ♦ M-Laffitte(Fr) hy *1 11/16 ⓣRH 3:354 4+ Prix Right Royal (Listed) Stk 36700 21 Jarnet T 123 b 6.00 Always Earnest1231 Glanville1232 La Pointe1201 9
Well placed in 3rd, 6th 3f out, bid 2f out, chased winner home
11Mar94 ♦ M-Laffitte(Fr) hy *1⅞ ⓣRH 3:32 4+ Prix Karaway Alw 29300 32½ Boeuf D 123 b *2.50 Sharp Imposter1231 Pontiac Brave1231½ Glanville1232½ 10
Tracked in 3rd, lacked room on rail over 1f out, unable to recover
29Nov93 ♦ Saint-Cloud(Fr) fr *1½ ⓣLH 2:451 3+ Prix Denisy (Listed) Stk 35500 67¾ Guillot S 128 b 19.00 Beefeater1261½ Amal1242 La Pointe1242 9
Close up in 3rd, weakened through final furlong
12Nov93 ♦ Marseille-PV(Fr) gd *1 11/16 ⓣLH 3+ Prix Henri Cabassu (Listed) Stk 35800 23 Boeuf D 129 b *1.50 Table Mountain1213 Glanville129¾ One Lap To Go1226 9
Tracked leader, led 10f to 1f out, held 2nd. Time not taken
26Oct93 ♦ M-Laffitte(Fr) hy *1½ ⓣRH 2:352 3+ Prix Scaramouche (Listed) Stk 35800 58½ Jarnet T 128 b 7.70 Dariyoun128no Bikasaite1284 Hurtevent1234 8
Unhurried in 5th, lacked rally
26Sep93 ♦ La Teste(Fr) sf *1½ ⓣRH 4+ Grand Prix du Sud-Ouest (Lstd) Stk 89900 33¾ Jarnet T 123 b - Manhattan River1203½ Little Wassl128nk Glanville1231 9
Well placed in 4th, 3rd halfway, no late response. Time not taken
WORKOUTS: Jly 18 Bel 4f fst :483 Hg26/84 Jun 29 Bel 5f fst 1:02 H 15/28

1 Solar Splendor
PP - 4
Own: Live Oak Plantation
MAPLE E (12 0 0 5 .00)

Ch. g. 7
Sire: Majestic Light (Majestic Prince)
Dam: Sultry Sun (Buckfinder)
Br: Live Oak Stud (Fla)
Tr: Kelly Patrick J (3 0 0 1 .00)

112

Lifetime Record:	35	10	3	6	$1,359,868						
1994	3	0	1	0	$35,640	Turf	32	9	3	5	$1,342,228
1993	6	1	1	1	$153,200	Wet	0	0	0	0	
Sar Ⓣ	6	2	0	1	$135,690	Dist Ⓣ	5	1	1	1	$470,000

2Jly94-7Bel fm 1⅜ [T] :50 1:14 1:37 2:131 3↑ BowlingGrnH-G2 85 4 2 2½ 2½ 3¾ 512¾ McCauley W H 115 3.00 76-15 Turk Passer1102¾ Sea Hero117nk Fraise124nk Tired 6

11Jun94-7Bel fm 1¼ [T] :462 1:10 1:334 1:573 3↑ ET ManhattanG1 100 6 4 43½ 2½ 23 26¾ McCauley W H 112 4.90e 95-02 ParadiseCreek1246¾ SolarSplendor112½ RiverMjesty1137 Bid, weakened 7

30May94-7Bel fm 1 1/16 Ⓣ :23 :46 1:10 1:394 3↑ Alw 44000N$mY 81 5 4 32 31 43 410¾ McCauley W H 119 6.30 88-12 Fourstars Allstar119nk Sea Hero1195 Roman Envoy11?5½ Lacked rally 6

6Nov93-7SA fm 1½ Ⓣ :483 1:122 2:012 2:25 3↑ B C Turf-G1 79 11 3 33 53 1416 1417¾ McCauley W H LB 126 59.80f 75-04 Kotashaan126½ Bien Bien1261½ Luazur126¾ Nothing left 14

9Oct93-7Bel fm 1½ Ⓣ :512 1:163 2:044 2:281 3↑ Turf ClassicG1 107 2 1 11½ 11½ 11 22¼ McCauley W H 126 7.40 79-19 Apple Tree1262¼ Solar Splendor126½ George Augustus1261 Gamely 5

6Sep93-5Bel fm 1 1/16 [T] :243 :47 1:093 1:404 3↑ Alw 42000N$Y 101 3 5 612 59¼ 27 11 Maple E 117 4.30 92-11 Solar Splendor1171 Blacksburg1191½ Daarik117hd Driving 7

21Aug93-9Sar fm 1⅛ Ⓣ :464 1:094 1:331 1:452 3↑ B Baruch H-G2 80 3 3 32½ 53½ 57½ 512¼ McCauley W H 114 11.70 89-07 Furiously1191 Star Of Cozzene123no Royal Mountain Inn1143 Done early 5

3Jly93-7Bel sf 1⅜ Ⓣ :502 1:143 1:40 2:173 3↑ Bwlng Grn H-G2 81 9 2 2½ 2hd 44½ 614 McCauley W H 117 4.70 65-33 Dr. Kiernan1144 Spectacular Tide1113 Lomitas1173 Bid, tired 9

6Jun93-8Bel gd 1¼ [T] :481 1:12 1:353 1:584 3↑ ET ManhattanG2 99 8 1 1hd 1hd 21 37¾ McCauley W H 112 6.70e 88-14 Star Of Cozzene118¾ Lure1247 Solar Splendor1122¼ Speed, weakened 8

10Oct92-9GP fm 1½ Ⓣ :474 1:112 2:00 2:24 3↑ B C Turf-G1 — 8 1 41¾ 99¾ 1021 — McCauley W H L 126 10.40 — — Fraise126no Sky Classic1262 Quest For Fame1261 Bobbled, eased 10

WORKOUTS: Jly 25 Sar tr.t Ⓣ 4f fm :47 H 2/25 Jly 14 Bel [T] 4f fm :471 H (d)4/14 Jun 29 Bel 4f fst :492 B 20/52 Jun 23 Bel [T] 4f fm :49 B (d)6/14 Jun 8 Bel 4f fst :484 B 31/66 May 24 Bel 4f fst :484 B 21/51

6 Fraise
PP - 5
Own: Paulson Madeleine
SMITH M E (30 5 7 5 .17)

B. h. 6
Sire: Strawberry Road (Whiskey Road)
Dam: Zalataia (Dictus)
Br: Paulson Allen E (Ky)
Tr: Mott William I (13 1 2 2 .08)

123

Lifetime Record:	29	10	5	5	$2,520,105						
1994	4	1	1	2	$254,500	Turf	27	10	5	5	$2,520,105
1993	5	2	0	1	$627,000	Wet	1	0	0	0	
Sar Ⓣ	1	1	0	0	$150,000	Dist Ⓣ	12	5	3	1	$2,203,500

2Jly94-7Bel fm 1⅜ [T] :50 1:14 1:37 2:131 3↑ BowlingGrnH-G2 102 3 4 43 32 43½ 33 Smith M E 124 b *1.30 85-15 Turk Passer1102¾ Sea Hero117nk Fraise124nk No late bid 6

30Apr94-11Hia gd 1½ Ⓣ 2:30 3↑ HiaTurfCupH-G3 108 6 2 21 2hd 1hd 21½ Smith M E L 124 b *.40 77-18 Awad1161½ Fraise1241½ Flying American1131 6
Raced outside entire trip, drifted out each turn, second best

13Mar94-10GP fm 1½ Ⓣ :492 1:131 2:01 2:243 3↑ Pan Amrcn H-G2 104 7 2 21 1hd 1hd 1¾ Smith M E L 124 b *1.10 97-09 Fraise124¾ Summer Ensign113hd Fairy Garden115¾ 10
Brushed approaching eighth pole, driving

2Jan94-7Crc fm 1½ Ⓣ :48 1:113 2:023 2:274 3↑ WL McKnght HG2 99 11 7 45½ 53½ 34 33 McCarron C J L 126 b *.50 88-17 Cobblestone Road1131½ Daarik1131¾ Fraise1261 12
5 wide stretch, lacked needed rally

12Dec93-8Hol yl 1½ Ⓣ :484 1:134 2:061 2:321 3↑ Hol Turf Cp-G1 111 4 6 32 32½ 11½ 16 McCarron C J LB 126 b *1.40 63-37 Fraise1266 Know Heights126½ Explosive Red12219 Clearly best 6

6Nov93-7SA fm 1½ Ⓣ :483 1:122 2:012 2:25 3↑ B C Turf-G1 106 1 10 107 85½ 63½ 42¼ Valenzuela P A LB 126 b 14.10 90-04 Kotashaan126½ Bien Bien1261½ Luazur126¾ Blocked far turn 14

9Oct93-7Bel fm 1½ Ⓣ :512 1:163 2:044 2:281 3↑ Turf ClassicG1 102 3 3 31½ 31½ 53 55 Valenzuela P A 126 b 3.30 76-19 Apple Tree1262¼ Solar Splendor126½ George Augustus1261 Rank, tired 5

18Apr93-4SA fm *1¾ Ⓣ :473 1:593 2:224 2:45 San Jn Cp H-G1 106 3 4 33 31½ 21½ 31½ Valenzuela P A LB 123 b 1.80e 106-12 Kotashaan121no Bien Bien1191½ Fraise12310 Not enough late 5

27Mar93-11GP gd *1½ Ⓣ 2:324 3↑ Pan Amrcn H-G2 107 5 8 64¼ 2hd 2hd 1nk Valenzuela P A L 124 b *1.20 77-29 Fraise124nk Stagecraft117hd Futurist1145¾ Fully extended 8

13Dec92-8Hol fm 1½ Ⓣ :502 1:16 2:06 2:311 3↑ Hol Turf Cp-G1 105 6 5 42 31½ 31½ 1no Valenzuela P A LB 126 b *.70 68-32 [D]Fraise126no Bien Bien1221½ Trishyde1191¾ 6
Steadied 3/8, bumped foe twice late; Disqualified and placed second

WORKOUTS: Jly 29 Bel 7f fst 1:28 B 1/2 Jly 11 Bel 5f fst 1:06 B 18/18 Jun 29 Bel 5f fst 1:023 B 17/28 Jun 23 Bel [T] 6f fm 1:19 B (d)5/7 Jun 16 Bel [T] 6f fm 1:183 B (d)6/7

2 Pescagani
PP - 6
Own: Drecchie Vincent
KRONE J A (21 2 4 2 .10)

Dk. b or br c. 4
Sire: Caveat (Cannonade)
Dam: Nan's Pest (Pesty Nanette)
Br: Jenkins Richard H (Md)
Tr: Tagg Barclay (1 1 0 0 1.00)

111

Lifetime Record:	22	7	3	2	$232,272						
1994	9	3	1	0	$103,999	Turf	12	4	2	1	$156,826
1993	13	4	2	2	$128,273	Wet	3	1	0	0	$36,356
Sar Ⓣ	0	0	0	0		Dist Ⓣ	1	1	0	0	$45,000

14Jly94-8Bel fm 1¼ [T] :463 1:104 1:342 1:583 3↑ Handicap48k 97 6 1 12 12 13½ 13½ Krone J A 116 b 5.00 97-05 Pescagani1163½ Heavy Rain113¾ Bisbalense114nk Driving 7

18Jun94-11Lrl fm 1 1/16 Ⓣ :234 :483 1:134 1:441 3↑ Chieftain H55k 84 7 2 22 21 21½ 54½ Prado E S L 117 b *1.70 76-19 Marry Me Do1131½ Bold Print108½ Oscar Max113¾ Gave way 7

28May94-10Pim fm 1½ Ⓣ :484 1:133 2:031 2:292 3↑ Riggs H75k 95 7 1 1½ 14 14 11½ Johnston M T L 115 b 9.10 93-11 Pescagani1151½ Asserche1182¼ Master Dreamer112nk Driving 13

3May94-6Pim gd 1 1/16 Ⓣ :231 :472 1:103 1:41 3↑ Alw 25000N2Y 93 5 1 1½ 13 13 2no Wilson R L 124 b *1.40 96-04 Dancing Douglas119no Pescagani1243¾ Up In Front1192¼ Drifted late 6

23Apr94-8Pim fst 1⅛ :461 1:101 1:36 1:492 3↑ [S]Jennings H100k 88 4 9 919 918 713 713¼ Miller D A Jr L 115 b 22.50 85-16 Taking Risks1143 Frottage117nk Tidal Surge1125 Outrun 9

27Mar94-8Hia fm *1 1/16 Ⓣ 1:411 Alw 20000N$mY 89 3 9 914 96 55½ 42¼ Sellers S J L 119 b 7.90 94-08 Dr. Alfoos1131 Royal Ninja114¾ Rocket Fuel119½ 9
Eight wide top str, belated bid

11Mar94-7GP fm *1 1/16 Ⓣ :234 :47 1:111 1:422+ Alw 36000N4X 99 7 2 1hd 1hd 13 1½ Sellers S J L 117 b 11.30 105-01 Pescagani117½ Namaqualand1173½ Ivor The Perfect117½ Fully extended 10

10Feb94-7GP fst 7f :221 :443 1:082 1:21 Alw 40000N$Y 68 4 7 74¼ 54½ 78½ 712½ Smith M E L 122 b 14.80 85-06 American Chance119nk Loach1152 Concorde's Future1152 No factor 7

5Jan94-9GP gd *1⅛ Ⓣ :483 1:133 1:40 1:531+ Alw 31700N4X 77 1 1 11½ 1½ 44½ 69 Santos J A L 117 b *2.10 70-23 [D]Pidgeon'sPromise117nk Scnnpieco1193½ SilvrConqust1171¾ Used on lead 8

4Dec93-10Lrl sly 1⅛ :484 1:133 1:383 1:511 Annapolis55k 76 1 3 31 33½ 35½ 415 Wilson R L 119 b 3.10 67-35 Greatsilverfleet1155 Lead Me To Gold1155½ Raglan Road1154¾ Weakened 8

WORKOUTS: ● Jly 8 Lrl 4f fst :48 H 1/17 Jly 2 Lrl 4f fst :481 H 5/37 Jun 14 Lrl Ⓣ 5f fm 1:013 B (d)2/4 May 17 Lrl 5f fst 1:034 B 10/13

7 Square Cut
PP - 7
Own: Wachtel Edwin H
PERRET C (11 3 3 1 .27)

B. g. 5
Sire: Assert (Be My Guest)
Dam: Diamondsareagirls (Diamonds Are Trump)
Br: Benjamin Arthur Racing (Md)
Tr: Devereux Joseph A (—)

111

Lifetime Record:	32	8	4	5	$403,629						
1994	9	2	0	1	$119,625	Turf	29	8	4	5	$403,354
1993	16	4	3	3	$255,694	Wet	0	0	0	0	
Sar Ⓣ	2	0	1	0	$51,248	Dist Ⓣ	4	1	1	0	$164,000

4Jly94-9Hol fm 1 1/16 Ⓣ :23 :462 1:093 1:393+ Clm 125000 97 9 1 1½ 2hd 21½ 45½ Valenzuela F H LB 116 b 15.60 92-05 Approach The Bench1171½ Sinag1191½ The Tender Track1192¾ Weakened 9

18Jun94-7GG fm 1⅜ Ⓣ :471 1:114 1:364 2:15 3↑ GoldenGateH-G2 74 7 1 2hd 2hd 713 817½ Valenzuela F H LB 116 b 36.80 77-12 Alex The Great118½ Fanmore117no Emerald Jig113hd Stopped 8

14May94-8GG fm 1⅛ Ⓣ :471 1:103 1:352 1:473 3↑ RollingGrnH-G3 90 5 3 3½ 2½ 54¾ 57½ Boulanger G LB 116 b 11.00 96-07 Blues Traveller1121½ Gothland117¾ Emerald Jig1143 Gave way 7

25Apr94-8SA gd 1¼ Ⓣ :491 1:142 1:382 2:03 [R]SanJacinto H111k 100 1 1 11½ 11½ 11½ 13½ Valenzuela F H LB 115 b 3.30 72-33 Square Cut1153½ Memento Mori1133 Samourzakan116½ Driving 8

20Mar94-8SA gd 1⅛ Ⓣ :493 1:14 1:381 1:501 Cedar Key H61k 99 3 1 14 12½ 12 13½ Valenzuela F H LB 114 b 7.10 68-25 Square Cut1143½ Turkish Blazor115hd Bossanova1182 Clearly best 6

19Feb94-5SA gd 1 Ⓣ :231 :464 1:111 1:361 Clm 100000 91 5 5 57 53½ 52¼ 31¾ Antley C W LB 116 b 6.60 82-16 Fax News1161½ Nominator115½ Square Cut1163½ 6
Squeezed start, 4 wide 2nd turn

6Feb94-11TuP fm 1 1/16 Ⓣ :24 :474 1:122 1:45 3↑ TuP Bud BC H108k 51 9 3 45 1111 1219 1221¾ Castro J M L 115 b 14.70 66-10 [DH]Megan's Interco122 [DH]Ranger1182½ Siebe1151½ 12
Gave way; not urged late

23Jan94-2SA fm 1 Ⓣ :223 :46 1:102 1:343 Clm 100000 94 4 9 914 85 75½ 42¾ Antley C W LB 116 b 14.80 89-08 Southern Wish114no Echo Of Yesterday1161¾ Gogarty1171 10
Awkward start, very wide

1Jan94-8SA fm 1⅛ Ⓣ :472 1:11 1:36 1:483 S Gabriel H-G2 39 4 5 77½ 811 821 829½ Antley C W LB 115 33.40 46-24 Earl Of Barking118no Fanmore1165 Navarone119½ Done early 8

12Dec93-8Hol yl 1½ Ⓣ :484 1:134 2:061 2:321 3↑ Hol Turf Cp-G1 23 5 3 53 610 623 648¾ Antley C W LB 126 23.90 — 37 Fraise1266 Know Heights126½ Explosive Red12219 Done early 6

WORKOUTS: Jly 24 SA 5f fst 1:004 H 6/19 Jly 17 SA 6f fst 1:142 H 9/9 Jun 30 SA 3f fst :36 H 4/15 Jun 16 GG Ⓣ 3f fm :362 H 1/2 Jun 3 Hol Ⓣ 5f fm 1:002 H (d)3/8 May 26 Hol Ⓣ 5f fm 1:023 H (d)6/7

8 Sea Hero
PP - 8

Own: Rokeby Stables

BAILEY J D (31 7 5 4 .23)

B. c. 4
Sire: Polish Navy (Danzig)
Dam: Glowing Tribute (Graustark)
Br: Mellon Paul (Va)
Tr: Miller MacKenzie (4 0 1 0 .00)

117

Lifetime Record:	20	6	3	3	$2,920,590						
1994	4	1	2	1	$96,680	Turf	5	2	2	1	$79,970
1993	9	2	0	2	$2,484,190	Wet	1	1	0	0	$24,000
Sar Ⓣ	0	0	0	0		Dist Ⓣ	0	0	0	0	

2Jly94-7Bel	fm	1⅜ [T]	:50	1:14	1:37	2:131	3+ BowlingGrnH-G2	102	1	3	32	43½	23	22¾	Luzzi M J	117	2.20	85-15	Turk Passer1102¾ Sea Hero117nk Fraise124nk	Checked 3/8 pl	6
18Jun94-8Bel	fst	1⅛	:46	1:092	1:342	1:463	3+ Brooklyn H-G2	100	4	3	47	36½	35	39½	Bailey J D	119	2.10	88-12	Devil His Due1208½ Wallenda1181½ Sea Hero1194	Bobbled break	7
30May94-7Bel	fm	1 1/16 Ⓣ	:23	:46	1:10	1:394	3+ Alw 44000N$mY	104	2	2	22	21	11	2nk	Bailey J D	119	*.70	99-12	Fourstars Allstar119nk Sea Hero1195 Roman Envoy1195½	Gamely	6
17May94-8Bel	my	7f ⊗	:231	:461	1:102	1:223	3+ Alw 40000N$Y	105	4	1	33	21	11	11½	Bailey J D	119	*1.70	90-17	Sea Hero1191½ Rocking Josh1152½ Dominant Prospect1151	Mild drive	5
19Sep93-8WO	fst	1⅛	:474	1:112	1:362	1:491	Mlsn Mlln-G2	102	3	6	54	55	36½	35½	Bailey J D	L 126	2.05	95-04	Peteski1214½ Cheery Knight117¾ Sea Hero1262½	Gave best stretch	6
21Aug93-7Sar	fst	1¼	:47	1:113	1:37	2:014	Travers-G1	109	7	8	810	41½	1½	12	Bailey J D	126	6.70	95-10	Sea Hero1262 Kissin Kris1261 Miner's Mark126hd	Wide, bumped, driving	11
1Aug93-8Sar	fst	1⅛	:472	1:114	1:362	1:49	Jim Dandy-G2	93	4	6	68	53	44	47½	Bailey J D	126	5.50	83-09	Miner's Mark117nk Virginia Rapids1214½ Colonial Affair1262¾	Lacked rally	6
5Jun93-9Bel	gd	1½	:484	1:132	2:024	2:294	Belmont-G1	86	10	5	65	810	713	715	Bailey J D	126	3.20	66-15	Colonial Affair1262½ Kissin Kris126¾ Wild Gale1262	Finished far turn	13
15May93-10Pim	fst	1 3/16	:464	1:111	1:37	1:563	Preakness-G1	85	9	9	107¾	74½	75¾	58½	Bailey J D	126	4.30	70-18	PrairieBayou126½ CherokeeRun1267 ElBakan126nk	Lacked late response	12
1May93-8CD	fst	1¼	:463	1:111	1:364	2:022	Ky Derby-G1	105	6	13	129½	73½	11	12½	Bailey J D	L 126	12.90	100-07	Sea Hero1262½ Prairie Bayou126hd Wild Gale126nk	Driving inside	19

WORKOUTS: ●Jly 28 Sar tr.t 3f my :372 B 1/5 Jly 23 Sar 7f sly 1:274 B 1/1 Jly 16 Bel 5f fst 1:011 B 12/40 Jly 9 Bel 4f gd :473 B 2/16 Jun 29 Bel 4f fst :48 B 2/52 Jun 25 Bel 4f fst :483 B 9/43

9 Majesty's Darby
PP - 9

Own: Phillips James W

SAMYN J L (15 3 1 1 .20)

Ch. g. 4
Sire: His Majesty (Ribot)
Dam: Darby Trail (Roberto)
Br: Phillips Mr & Mrs James W (Ky)
Tr: Toner James J (7 0 1 2 .00)

109

Lifetime Record:	18	4	2	3	$107,239						
1994	7	2	1	2	$62,659	Turf	7	3	0	1	$67,489
1993	9	2	1	0	$41,700	Wet	3	0	0	1	$4,380
Sar Ⓣ	2	1	0	0	$15,300	Dist Ⓣ	1	0	0	0	

4Jly94-10Lrl	yl	1¼ Ⓣ	:503	1:162	1:424	2:063	3+ Ft McHenry H114k	91	4	9	910	85½	84¾	32¼	Samyn J L	110 b	7.20	59-43	Dinner In Rio112¾ Binary Light1121½ Majesty's Darby110no	Rallied	9
7Jun94-8Bel	gd	1¼ [T]	:494	1:133	1:39	2:03	3+ Alw 34000N3X	93	6	7	714	63½	62½	1hd	Samyn J L	119 b	*1.80	75-25	Majesty's Darby119hd No Sneaker1191¾ Ocean Wave119½	Driving	7
28May94-10Pim	fm	1½ Ⓣ	:484	1:133	2:031	2:292	3+ Riggs H75k	86	2	13	1314	1113	89	65¼	Salazar A C	111 b	22.10	88-11	Pescagani1151½ Asserche1182½ Master Dreamer112nk	No threat	13
4May94-4Bel	fm	1¼ [T]	:484	1:122	1:363	2:01	3+ Alw 32000N2X	96	5	7	74½	64	31	11½	Samyn J L	119 b	5.90	85-15	Majesty's Darby1191½ Noble Sheba1194¾ Peter And119no	Driving	7
3Mar94-9GP	fst	1¼	:471	1:114	1:364	2:033	Alw 31000N2X	84	4	6	612	54¾	54½	33¼	Smith M E	119 b	2.60	80-21	Primordial119no Vandeventer1223¼ Majesty's Darby1193¼	Late rally	7
2Feb94-8GP	sly	1¼ ⊗	:491	1:143	1:401	2:054	3+ Noble Dncr H50k	72	5	5	55½	58½	58	519½	Samyn J L	110 b	12.80	53-32	Strolling Along116hd Cobblestone Road1134¾ Friud1142	Outrun	5
15Jan94-5GP	fst	1⅛	:501	1:141	1:384	1:512	Alw 28700N2X	84	5	5	63¾	54½	42½	21½	Samyn J L	122 b	5.50	79-19	Stop And Listen1191½ Majesty's Darby122no Laminate1222	Rallied	7
6Dec93-7Aqu	gd	1 1/16 ⊡	:24	:472	1:113	1:442	3+ Alw 30000N1X	89	6	6	510	46	32	11	Samyn J L	115 b	15.80	83-21	Majesty's Darby1151 Laminate1201 Sailing On Aprayer1171	Driving	7
22Nov93-7Aqu	fst	1⅛	:484	1:131	1:39	1:523	3+ Alw 30000N1X	82	5	5	53	34	36½	49½	Samyn J L	115 b	5.50	63-34	Jim'sBestBoy1151½ SilingOnApryer1176½ HoldTheBskt1151½	Flattened out	7
14Nov93-6Aqu	fst	1 ⊗	:231	:463	1:113	1:373	3+ Alw 30000N1X	79	1	8	65	42½	34	22	Maple E	115 b	21.60	74-27	RestlessDoctor1172 Majesty'sDarby1151¾ TheWildIrishmn1154	Late gain	8

WORKOUTS: Jly 25 Sar tr.t Ⓣ 4f fm :48 B 13/25 Jun 29 Bel 5f fst 1:03 B 22/28 Jun 23 Bel [T] 6f fm 1:184 B (d) 4/7 ●Jun 16 Bel [T] 4f fm :48 H (d) 1/8 May 21 Bel tr.t 6f gd 1:143 H 1/2 May 14 Bel 3f fst :364 B 10/23

10 Alex The Great (GB)
PP - 10

Own: Vistas Stables

VALENZUELA P A (—)

Ch. h. 5
Sire: Bairn (Northern Baby)
Dam: Another Pageant (Welsh Pageant)
Br: Hesmonds Stud Ltd (GB)
Tr: Rash Rodney (—)

118

Lifetime Record:	19	4	5	5	$370,559						
1994	6	2	1	2	$290,875	Turf	18	4	4	5	$362,760
1993	8	1	2	2	$46,350	Wet	0	0	0	0	
Sar Ⓣ	0	0	0	0		Dist Ⓣ	2	0	1	0	$6,810

18Jun94-7GG	fm	1⅜ Ⓣ	:471	1:114	1:364	2:15	3+ GoldenGateH-G2	105	4	5	510	43½	1hd	1½	Valenzuela P A	LB 118 b	6.50	94-12	Alex The Great118½ Fanmore117no Emerald Jig113hd	Rallied wide	8
24Apr94-8SA	fm	*1¾ Ⓣ	:47	1:594	2:243	2:463	SanJuanCapH-G1	102	8	8	76½	65½	45	32¾	Antley C W	LB 114 b	19.40	89-08	Bien Bien122¾ Grand Flotilla1162 Alex The Great1141½	Wide into lane	9
3Apr94-8SA	fm	1⅛ Ⓣ	:473	1:113	1:362	1:482	[R]MiramontesH85k	100	8	10	813	85¾	1hd	12½	Antley C W	LB 114 b	9.70	77-21	AlexTheGreat1142½ Vegieman114no KingdomOfSpain1151½	4 wide into lane	11
26Feb94-8SA	fm	1¼ Ⓣ	:472	1:112	1:36	2:003	[R]S Marino H82k	98	1	3	34½	42	31	32½	Antley C W	LB 114 b	9.40	82-16	Semillon1162½ Memento Mori114no Alex The Great1141¾	Rail trip	7
10Feb94-8SA	gd	1⅛ Ⓣ	:47	1:112	1:364	1:49	Alw 44000N3L	101	3	6	69¾	51½	3½	21	Antley C W	LB 116 b	6.50	73-26	Semillon1161 Alex The Great1163½ Pricelessly1172	Off very slow	7
5Dec93-3Hol	fm	1¼ Ⓣ	:473	1:122	1:363	2:012	3+ Alw 32000N2L	96	3	7	76½	12½	14	16½	Antley C W	LB 121 b	1.60	87-14	Alex The Great1216½ Wise Words1182½ Don't Tell Frank115¾		7

Off step slow, 5 wide 3 1/2, ridden out

11Nov93-8SA	gd	1¼ ⊗	:483	1:113	1:383	2:041	3+ Alw 34000N2L	91	1	6	53	31	21	21¾	Pincay L Jr	LB 122 b	*1.20	72-24	Piccolo1171¾ Alex The Great1226½ Natural Fifty Six1152½	Bid, outfinished	7
14Oct93-7SA	fm	1⅛ Ⓣ	:471	1:11	1:354	1:482	3+ Alw 34000N2L	87	8	6	42½	2hd	1½	27	Pincay L Jr	LB 122 b	3.00	75-23	Swiss Mirage1227 Alex The Great1221 Wise Words1181¼	4 Wide 1st turn	8
1Sep93-8Dmr	fm	1⅛ Ⓣ	:482	1:123	1:363	1:49	3+ Alw 38000N2L	89	3	7	77½	62¾	23½	31	Pincay L Jr	LB 122	4.80	90-09	Passo Geno119¾ Arinthod118hd Alex The Great1227½	Off slowly, wide	7
4Aug93-5Dmr	fm	1⅛ Ⓣ	:493	1:141	1:382	1:50	3+ Alw 36000N2L	73	4	8	83½	82¾	94½	64½	Gonzalez S5	LB 117	9.90	78-07	Kingdom Of Spain122½ Passo Geno119nk Tidy Colony122½	Troubled trip	10

WORKOUTS: Jly 21 Hol 1 fst 1:401 H (d) 1/3 Jly 15 Hol Ⓣ 1 fm 1:40 H (d) 1/3 Jly 8 Hol Ⓣ 6f fm 1:144 H (d) 1/2 Jun 26 Hol 3f fst :39 H 44/46 Jun 15 Hol 4f fst :532 H 42/43 Jun 8 Hol Ⓣ 1 fm 1:414 H (d) 3/4

11 Turk Passer
PP - 11

Own: Laveen & Shanley & Weiss

VELAZQUEZ J R (16 2 2 3 .13)

Dk. b or br g. 4
Sire: Turkoman (Alydar)
Dam: Insilca (Buckpasser)
Br: The Oaks Horse Farm Corp. (Fla)
Tr: Margotta Anthony Jr (4 0 2 1 .00)

113

Lifetime Record:	18	5	3	3	$196,490						
1994	7	2	2	1	$138,180	Turf	6	2	2	1	$137,900
1993	10	3	1	1	$56,630	Wet	4	1	0	0	$19,300
Sar Ⓣ	0	0	0	0		Dist Ⓣ	1	0	0	0	$12,000

2Jly94-7Bel	fm	1⅜ [T]	:50	1:14	1:37	2:131	3+ BowlingGrnH-G2	107	5	1	1½	1½	13	12¾	Velazquez J R	110	31.00	88-15	Turk Passer1102¾ Sea Hero117nk Fraise124nk	Driving	6
2Jun94-7Bel	fm	1¼ [T]	:481	1:122	1:37	2:001	3+ Alw 36000N4X	94	3	4	31½	31	33½	33½	Krone J A	119	*1.40	86-13	Sentimental Moi1191¾ Correntino1191½ Turk Passer1193	No late bid	8
30Apr94-11Hia	gd	1½ Ⓣ				2:30	3+ HiaTurfCupH-G3	103	3	4	31	41¾	44½	44¾	Castaneda M	L 113	7.90	74-18	Awad1161½ Fraise1241½ Flying American1131	Lacked response	6
8Apr94-10Hia	fm	*1 3/16 Ⓣ				1:561	[R]Alw 18800N$mY	94	7	9	825	719	53½	2nk	Castaneda M	L 114	*1.90	91-18	Royal Ninja114nk Turk Passer114no Drummer Boy1141	Rallied	10
5Mar94-9GP	fm	1⅜ Ⓣ	:492	1:14	1:38	2:143	Alw 35600N3X	96	8	3	42	23½	11½	14¾	Sellers S J	L 117	*1.40	93-10	Turk Passer1174¾ Telegrapher117nk Boss Man Jarett117nk	Driving	10
13Feb94-9GP	fm	*1⅛ Ⓣ	:464	1:103	1:352	1:49	+ Alw 31000N3X	98	4	6	77½	77	33½	2¾	Sellers S J	L 117	6.20	99-06	L'hermine117¾ Turk Passer1173½ Dominant Prospect1174½	Rallied	10
11Jan94-8GP	sly	7f	:214	:444	1:101	1:232	Alw 28000N4X	74	7	4	69½	610	58½	510¾	Bailey J D	117	15.00	75-20	Sweet Beast1176 Never Round117no Jetting Along122hd	Failed to menace	9
8Nov93-8Aqu	fst	1	:234	:462	1:102	1:36	3+ Alw 44000N$mY	72	5	3	75¾	76½	711	614¾	Bailey J D	120	2.70	68-25	Itaka1156¾ Nymphist117¾ Farewell Wave110nk	Wide trip	9
30Oct93-8Aqu	my	1⅛	:492	1:14	1:391	1:521	Discovery H-G3	63	5	3	512	715	815	724¾	Alvarado F T	114	8.60	50-33	Prospector'sFlag1146½ VirginiRpids118nk LivingVicriously1141½	Done early	8
9Oct93-5Bel	fst	1 1/16	:234	:471	1:114	1:432	3+ Alw 32000N2X	101	1	6	62½	3½	1½	14	Bailey J D	114	*1.60	85-15	Turk Passer1144 All My Tricks1123½ Slews Gold1141½	Driving	7

WORKOUTS: Jly 25 Sar 3f fst :373 B 15/34 Jly 14 Bel [T] 5f fm 1:003 H (d) 4/20 Jun 23 Bel [T] 5f fm 1:031 B (d) 13/17 Jun 16 Bel 5f fst 1:02 B 15/27 May 28 Bel 5f fst 1:01 Hg 12/61

12 Noble Sheba
PP - 12

Own: Valando Thomas

SANTOS J A (31 7 3 6 .23)

Ch. c. 4
Sire: Alysheba (Alydar)
Dam: Farewell Partner (Northern Dancer)
Br: Wilson Ralph Jr (Ky)
Tr: Schulhofer Flint S (8 2 1 0 .25)

110

Lifetime Record:	17	4	5	2	$121,986						
1994	4	2	1	1	$50,480	Turf	14	4	4	2	$116,236
1993	10	2	4	1	$71,366	Wet	1	0	0	0	
Sar Ⓣ	2	1	0	0	$17,100	Dist Ⓣ	1	0	0	1	$15,096

28Jun94-8Bel	fm	1⅜ [T]	:482	1:123	1:364	2:14	3+ Alw 34000N3X	94	2	2	21	1½	1½	11½	Santos J A	119 b	2.80	84-12	Noble Sheba1191½ Jodi's The Best1192 Laminate1192½	Driving	6
17Jun94-7Bel	fm	1¼ [T]	:481	1:113	1:354	1:594	3+ Alw 32000N2X	95	1	5	56	51½	1½	11½	Santos J A	119 b	3.20	91-10	Noble Sheba1191½ Moscow Magic1112 Grateful Appeal111hd	Driving	9
29May94-4Bel	fm	1¼ [T]	:504	1:151	1:392	2:023	3+ Alw 32000N2X	88	1	3	44	41	43	33½	Santos J A	121 b	2.30	73-19	MatchlessDancer124no ChampagneAffair1213½ NobleSheba1211¾	Mild rally	10
4May94-4Bel	fm	1¼ [T]	:484	1:122	1:363	2:01	3+ Alw 32000N2X	93	2	3	32	32½	2½	21½	Santos J A	119 b	*2.20	84-15	Majesty's Darby1191½ Noble Sheba1194¾ Peter And119no	Good effort	7
16Oct93-3Bel	sf	1½ Ⓣ	:501	1:162	2:064	2:323	Lawrence ReaG3	95	11	4	42	41½	31½	31¾	Santos J A	114 b	41.90	57-29	Strolling Along114¾ Scattered Steps1131 Noble Sheba114½	Willingly	12
24Sep93-7Bel	yl	1¼ [T]	:501	1:153	1:413	2:072	3+ Alw 32000N2X	90	8	5	65½	3½	1hd	2no	Santos J A	114 b	28.10	53-37	Dover Coast117no Noble Sheba114nk Who's Believable1171¾	Gamely	12
5Sep93-7Bel	fm	1¼ [T]	:493	1:134	1:381	2:021	3+ Alw 32000N2X	76	2	8	87	93½	85	86½	Santos J A	113 b	14.10	72-19	Groomed To Win1152½ Hugatag1171 Cap White117nk	No factor	9
19Aug93-7Sar	gd	1⅝ Ⓣ	:49	1:134	2:034	2:402	3+ Alw 30500N2X	76	2	5	42½	63	52½	57¾	Maple E	114 b	7.20	85-07	Caveat'sImage1142 CpWhite112½ Who'sBelievble1171	Lacked response	7
31Jly93-4Sar	fm	1⅜ [T]	:492	1:151	1:401	2:172	3+ Alw 28500N1X	84	9	3	32½	32	2½	1¾	Maple E	111 b	9.60	79-15	Noble Sheba111¾ No Sneaker113nk Groomed To Win112hd	Driving	10
12Jly93-7Bel	fm	1¼ [T]	:493	1:134	1:374	2:02	3+ Alw 28500N1X	71	2	9	911	97½	96	97¾	Maple E	113 b	9.60	72-12	Dover Coast117¾ Shoaly Water117hd Jodi's The Best113nk	Outrun	9

WORKOUTS: Jly 25 Sar tr.t Ⓣ 5f fm 1:02 B 13/17 Jly 18 Sar 4f fst :483 H 4/9 Jly 11 Bel 4f fst :50 B 29/39 Jly 6 Bel 4f fst :493 B 42/75 Jun 25 Bel 4f fst :50 B 26/43 Jun 11 Bel 4f fst :504 B 27/37

2b Royal Mountain Inn PP-13
Own: Steadfast Stable
KRONE J A (21 2 4 2 .10)
Ro. g. 5
Sire: Vigors (Grey Dawn II)
Dam: Highland Mills (Pia Star)
Br: Rowand George E (Ky)
Tr: Tagg Barclay (1 1 0 0 1.00)
115

Lifetime Record:	11 6 0 3	$182,194			
1994	1 1 0 0	$26,400	Turf	9 6 0 2	$180,254
1993	7 4 0 2	$138,254	Wet	0 0 0 0	
Sar ⓣ	1 0 0 1	$14,064	Dist ⓣ	0 0 0 0	

9Jly94-7Bel fm 1 1/16 ⓣ :23 :452 1:091 1:394 3+ Alw 44000N$mY 106 5 5 64¼ 31 1½ 13 Krone J A 117 2.70 99-19 Royal Mountain Inn1173 River Majesty117¾ Say Dance1221 Driving 7
11Aug93-9Sar fm 1⅛ ⓣ :464 1:094 1:331 1:452 3+ B Baruch H-G2 106 2 4 43 31½ 31 31 Krone J A 114 3.10 101-07 Furiously1191 Star Of Cozzene123no Royal Mountain Inn1143 Willingly 5
18Jly93-8Bel fm 1¼ Ⓣ :48 1:113 1:353 1:594 3+ Red Smith H-G2 106 5 3 39 22½ 12 13 Krone J A 110 *1.60 91-11 RoyalMountainInn1103 SpectacularTide1132 ShreTheGlory111¾ Driving 8
12Jun93-6Bel fm 1 ⓣ :224 :45 1:092 1:332 3+ Alw 36500N4X 109 4 4 33 31 13 16 Krone J A 117 2.10 95-15 Royal Mountain Inn1176 Big Leap1175 Up In Front1171 Ridden out 8
15May93-7Bel fm 1 1/16 ⓣ :23 :461 1:10 1:40 3+ Alw 30500N2X 102 9 3 34 2½ 11 12¼ Krone J A 119 *1.70 96-12 Royal Mountain Inn1192¼ World Order1195¼ Grady's Star121nk Driving 10
10Apr93-5Hia fm *1 1/16 ⓣ 1:424 Alw 15000N1X 87 1 10 1112 97¾ 42¾ 11¼ Penna D 116 *1.00 93-07 Royal Mountain Inn1161¼ Assorted Donuts1163¼ Ozama116½ Driving 12
31Mar93-4GP fm 1⅛ ⓣ :481 1:113 1:362 1:484+ Alw 30000N2X 87 5 3 31½ 42½ 31 31½ Santos J A 114 *2.50 86-12 OcenDwn1121½ ThreePicSuit114hd RoylMountinInn114½ Lacked response 11
4Mar93-6GP fm *1 1/16 ⓣ 1:432+ Alw 23000N1X 78 5 5 64 62¾ 45½ 56½ Santos J A 114 3.60 93 — Free Flyer1123¾ Tiffany's Bid1121 Electric Spark113nk Failed to menace 10
25May92-2Bel fm 1 ⓣ :223 :453 1:093 1:34 3+ Md Sp Wt 89 10 3 31½ 2hd 13 14¼ Smith M E 115 2.70 92-14 Royal Mountain Inn1154¼ Nelson's Navy115nk Step Royally115 Drew off 12
5May92-7Pim fst 6f :23 :461 :583 1:11 3+ Md Sp Wt 70 4 4 47½ 45 35 36½ Desormeaux K J 114 5.10 83-13 The Beak1164¼ Aegean Valley1142 Royal MountainInn114 Flattened out 8
WORKOUTS: Jly 22 Lrl 4f fst :50 B 10/15 Jly 7 Lrl 4f fst :481 H 4/19 ●Jun 21 Lrl 4f fst :471 Hg 1/22 Jun 14 Lrl ⓣ 1 fm 1:433 B (d) 1/1 Jun 7 Lrl ⓣ 5f fm :593 H (d) 3/6 ●Jun 2 Lrl 4f fst :473 H 1/16

1a Binary Light PP-14
Own: Live Oak Plantation
LEON F (5 0 0 1 .00)
Ch. h. 5
Sire: Bionic Light (Majestic Light)
Dam: Dial Zero (Gumme)
Br: Live Oak Stud (Fla)
Tr: Kelly Patrick J (3 0 0 1 .00)
109

Lifetime Record:	46 5 6 6	$330,252			
1994	4 0 1 0	$36,390	Turf	38 4 4 6	$254,292
1993	16 0 4 2	$86,836	Wet	3 1 2 0	$75,960
Sar ⓣ	4 0 0 1	$6,240	Dist ⓣ	0 0 0 0	

14Jly94-8Bel fm 1¼ Ⓣ :463 1:104 1:342 1:583 3+ Handicap48k 76 5 5 59 45½ 67 69½ Davis R G 115 4.20 87-05 Pescagani1163½ Heavy Rain113¾ Bisbalense114nk Flattened out 7
4Jly94-10Lrl yl 1¼ ⓣ :503 1:162 1:424 2:063 3+ Ft McHenry H114k 94 3 7 77½ 41 3½ 2¾ Delgado A L 112 13.40 60-43 Dinner In Rio112¾ Binary Light1121½ Majesty's Darby110no Wide, rallied 9
11Jun94-7Bel fm 1¼ Ⓣ :462 1:10 1:334 1:573 3+ ET ManhattanG1 84 7 6 613 46 410 414¼ Davis R G 112 4.90e 88-02 Paradise Creek1246¾ Solar Splendor112½ River Majesty1137 No threat 7
20May94-11Pim fm 1⅛ ⓣ :484 1:131 1:364 1:482 3+ ET Dixie H-G2 85 5 5 54¼ 54¾ 56 57½ Davis R G L 115 26.10 85-14 Paradise Creek124¾ Lure1245½ Astudillo115½ Trailed 5
4Dec93-8Aqu fst 1 1/16 ⊡ :234 :473 1:12 1:441 3+ Qns County HG3 90 4 4 48 55½ 76 63½ Davis R G 110 11.20 80-30 Repletion1111½ Dibbs N' Dubbs111½ Primitive Hall113¾ Lacked rally 8
2Nov93-8Aqu sf 1⅛ ⓣ :49 1:142 1:41 1:542 3+ Knickrbkr H-G3 83 5 5 512 57- 68 67 Samyn J L 110 7.30 64-29 River Majesty1152 Daarik114hd Home Of The Free118nk Outrun 6
18Oct93-8Bel sf 1⅜ Ⓣ :47 1:134 1:392 2:174 3+ Tidal H-G2 92 7 4 46½ 52¼ 33 23¼ Samyn J L 110 5.30 59-35 MioRobertino1103¼ BinaryLight1102 MgesterilCheer116no Steadied 3/8 pl 7
2Oct93-10Pim fm 1 ⓣ :233 :463 1:093 1:351 3+ Damascus H113k 72 7 3 33 68½ 713 715 Turner T G L 111 18.70 77-19 Cleone1134 Adam Smith118½ Square Cut1142¼ Fell back 8
26Sep93-6Bel sly 1 1/16 ⊗ :23 :46 1:103 1:42 3+ Handicap48k 103 4 3 32 21½ 22½ 23¼ McCauley W H 113 3.00 89-22 Lech1183¼ Binary Light1139¼ Lost Mountain1163 Second best 5
16Sep93-8Bel sly 1 1/16 ⊗ :222 :444 1:09 1:402 3+ Alw 42000N$mY 99 3 4 37½ 34½ 25 28¾ Antley C W 117 8.00 91-17 Say Dance1178¾ Binary Light11710 Jacksonport1174 Second best 5
WORKOUTS: ●Jly 27 Sar tr.t ⓣ 4f sf :512 B 2/11 Jly 21 Sar 3f fst :37 H 7/8 Jun 30 Bel Ⓣ 4f fm :501 B (d) 6/9 Jun 23 Bel Ⓣ 4f fm :49 B (d) 6/14 Jun 8 Bel 4f fst :472 H 6/66 Jun 2 Bel Ⓣ 4f fm :49 B (d) 10/15

The Grade 1 Sword Dancer Handicap appeared quite an ambitious spot for Kiri's Clown on the surface of things, but a closer inspection suggested he had a big shot to have a strong impact on the outcome.

In his most recent race, the Daryl's Joy on July 25, Kiri's Clown had once again been coupled with A In Sociology, who went wire to wire in lasting by a neck, while Kiri's Clown broke from the extreme outside post and was content to lay well off the pace his entrymate was establishing.

In the Sword Dancer, Kiri's Clown would be running on his own, and the late scratches of Pescagani and Solar Splendor brightened his prospects for getting the early lead. Instead of breaking from a difficult outside post as he had in the Daryl's Joy, he would be breaking from the coveted rail in a race that began in close proximity to the first of *three* turns. A ground-saving trip was assured, and especially noteworthy was the fact that Kiri's Clown had won both of his Saratoga grass races prior to the Daryl's Joy, including a *course-record performance on the inner course in wire-to-wire fashion* at the 1993 meeting.

So, we have a horse being wheeled back on four days' rest after a no-try from the extreme outside behind his winning entrymate; we have a horse who owns a record time over the course; we have a horse running on a "good" course who shows a career best Beyer on "yielding" ground; and we have a horse with positional speed who's guaranteed to save ground on all three turns.

Did I mention that we're being offered 15–1?

There were three conceivable threats who might be able to run down Kiri's Clown: Fraise, the 1992 Sword Dancer–winner; the enigmatic Sea Hero, who had run fairly well despite trouble in the recent Bowling Green Handicap; and Alex The Great, an improving shipper from California possessed of a potent closing kick.

The bet was $75, assuming 5 percent of a $1,500 bankroll, apportioned as follows:

$45 win

$10 exactas: Alex The Great, Sea Hero, Fraise over Kiri's Clown.

NINTH RACE
Saratoga
JULY 30, 1994

1½ MILES. (Inner Turf)(2.25^{4}) 20th Running of THE SWORD DANCER INVITATIONAL HANDICAP. Purse $250,000. Grade I. 3-year-olds and upward. Invitation only by Saturday, July 16, with no subscription fees. The purse to be divided 60% to the winner, 22% to second, 12% to third and 6% to fourth. The New York Racing Association Inc. will select a field of (14) invitees by Saturday, July 16. The assignment of weights for these invitees will be published on Wednesday, July 20. The Owners and/or Trainers of these (14) selected horses will be required to notify The New York Racing Association Inc. of their intention of running or not, no later than Saturday, July 23. A list of the Alternates and their weight assignments will be published on Monday, July 15. The New York Racing Association Inc. reserves the right to reassign weight to any horse after the weights have been published. Starters to be named at the closing time of entries. Trophies will be presented to the winning owner, trainer and jockey. This race will be limited to 14 Starters and Alternates (Highweights preferred). The New York Racing Association Inc. reserves the right to transfer this race to the Main Track.

Value of Race: $250,000 Winner $150,000; second $55,000; third $30,000; fourth $15,000. Mutuel Pool $533,623.00 Exacta Pool $559,404.00 Triple Pool $548,889.00

Last Raced	Horse	M/Eqt.	A.	Wt	PP	¼	½	1	1¼	Str	Fin	Jockey	Odds $1
10Jun94 7GG1	Alex The Great-GB	b	5	118	8	8^{1}	$8^{1\frac{1}{2}}$	6^{hd}	3^{2}	2^{3}	$1^{\frac{3}{4}}$	Valenzuela P A	3.20
25Jly94 8Sar5	Kiri's Clown		5	112	1	$1^{\frac{1}{2}}$	1^{1}	$1^{\frac{1}{2}}$	$1^{\frac{1}{2}}$	$1^{\frac{1}{2}}$	2^{2}	Luzzi M J	15.30
4Jly94 9AP5	L'Hermine-GB	b	5	112	2	4^{1}	$4^{1\frac{1}{2}}$	$3^{\frac{1}{2}}$	$5^{\frac{1}{2}}$	5^{4}	3^{hd}	Davis R G	14.20
2Jly94 7Bel3	Fraise	b	6	123	4	9^{hd}	$9^{\frac{1}{2}}$	$8^{\frac{1}{2}}$	$6^{\frac{1}{2}}$	4^{hd}	4^{4}	Smith M E	1.50
4Jly94 9Hol4	Square Cut	b	5	112	5	2^{4}	2^{8}	2^{9}	2^{2}	$3^{\frac{1}{2}}$	$5^{3\frac{1}{2}}$	Perret C	44.60
4Jly94 10Lrl3	Majesty's Darby	b	4	110	7	10	10	$9^{\frac{1}{2}}$	7^{3}	$6^{\frac{1}{2}}$	6^{7}	Samyn J L	23.90
2Jly94 7Bel2	Sea Hero		4	117	6	$7^{1\frac{1}{2}}$	$7^{1\frac{1}{2}}$	$4^{\frac{1}{2}}$	4^{hd}	7^{12}	7^{10}	Bailey J D	3.30
28Jun94 8Bel1	Noble Sheba		4	114	10	5^{2}	$5^{\frac{1}{2}}$	7^{1}	8^{3}	8^{3}	$8^{1\frac{1}{2}}$	Santos J A	22.60
2Jly94 7Bel1	Turk Passer		4	113	9	6^{hd}	6^{1}	10	9^{hd}	9^{4}	9^{15}	Velazquez J R	9.80
12Jly94 8Bel3	Glanville	b	5	109	3	$3^{1\frac{1}{2}}$	$3^{\frac{1}{2}}$	$5^{\frac{1}{2}}$	10	10	10	Chavez J F	64.00

OFF AT 5:30 Start Good. Won driving. Time, :23^{1}, :46^{2}, 1:11^{4}, 1:37, 2:02^{3}, 2:28^{3} Course good.

$2 Mutuel Prices:			
10–(J)–ALEX THE GREAT–GB	8.40	5.00	4.60
3–(A)–KIRI'S CLOWN		13.20	9.60
4–(B)–L'HERMINE–GB			7.80

$2 EXACTA 10–3 PAID $137.00 $2 TRIPLE 10–3–4 PAID $1,646.00

Ch. h, by Bairn–Another Pageant, by Welsh Pageant. Trainer Rash Rodney. Bred by Hesmonds Stud Ltd (GB).

ALEX THE GREAT checked slightly soon after the start, raced well back for a mile, launched a rally three wide on the far turn, rapidly closed the gap approaching the stretch, then wore down KIRI'S CLOWN in the final sixteenth. KIRI'S CLOWN took the lead soon after the start, set the pace under pressure to the top of the stretch, shook off SQUARE CUT to get clear in upper stretch, continued on the front into deep stretch but couldn't hold the winner safe. L'HERMINE settled in good position while saving ground to the turn then finished willingly to gain a share. FRAISE checked slightly in the early stages, was outrun for seven furlongs, gradually gained while four wide leaving the quarter pole then failed to threaten with a mild rally in the middle of the track. SQUARE CUT forced the pace from outside to the top of the stretch and weakened. MAJESTY'S DARBY was never a factor while three wide. SEA HERO raced just inside the winner while between horses to the turn and lacked a further response. NOBLE SHEBA raced wide and tired. TURK PASSER never reached contention. GLANVILLE faded after going a mile.

Owners— 1, Vistas Stables; 2, Cobble VIew Stable; 3, Four Fifths Stable; 4, Paulson Madeleine; 5, Wachtel Edwin H; 6, Phillips James W; 7, Rokeby Stables; 8, Valando Thomas; 9, Shanley Michael; 10, Perez Robert

Trainers—1, Rash Rodney; 2, Johnson Philip G; 3, Walden W Elliott; 4, Mott William I; 5, Devereux Joseph A; 6, Toner James J; 7, Miller Mackenzie; 8, Schulhofer Flint S; 9, Margotta Anthony Jr; 10, Callejas Alfredo

Overweight: L'Hermine-GB (2), Square Cut (1), Majesty's Darby (1), Noble Sheba (4).

Scratched— Solar Splendor (2Jly94 7BEL5), Pescagani (14Jly94 8BEL1), Royal Mountain Inn (9Jly94 7BEL1), Binary Light (14Jly94 8BEL6)

Despite being hounded by Square Cut through demanding early splits of :23⅕ and :46⅖, Kiri's Clown held tenaciously in the stretch, running the race of his career to finish second behind Alex The Great, two lengths clear for the place.

The win bet was lost, a fact of life we must accept when betting on longshots, since they will run second twice as often as they win. The $30 invested in exactas-as-place-bet saved the day, however, with a $10 ticket on the $137 combination, good for a return of $685, which was just slightly less than what would've been collected on the win bet had Kiri's Clown managed to hold on. Had the $30 been bet to place, the return would only have been $198.

A FINAL WORD

THIS IS USUALLY the "Putting It All Together" section of a handicapping tome, where the author leads you by the hand through an amazingly profitable day at the racetrack, a day when you cash in on eight winning exactas.

The truth is, those days are few and far between. Indeed, most days are a wash, with handicappers finding they've merely traded money with the track for a few hours, winning a little, losing a little.

The trick to amassing profits over the long haul is this:

When you lose, lose a little. When you win, win a little . . . but sometimes win **BIG.**

Such an approach requires patience. The proper way to bet on thoroughbreds — the proper way to speculate on *anything,* including stocks, bonds, mutual funds, et cetera — is to bet a little when losing, and to escalate bets when ahead. Human nature is not quite so logical, however. Most of us have a tendency to become overly conservative when winning, and to throw caution to the wind when in the midst of a losing streak.

To avoid such self-made disasters, handicappers should make a promise to themselves never to relax their standards in what constitutes a worthwhile investment of risk capital. The inherent structure of pari-mutuel wagering rewards those who can see things beyond the obvious and unerringly punishes those who want something for nothing.

As a public handicapper I attend the races five days a week, fifty-two weeks a year, so I can't afford to get careless. Neither should you, no matter what level of involvement with racing your lifestyle permits. To me, the fun is in the digging, the unearthing of a piece of information that few others have found. Usually, these insights come through one of the following five avenues:

1) An interpretation of speed figures leading to a firm judgment about a horse's impending improvement.

2) An insight into a trainer's "modus operandi," leading to the conclusion that his/her horse is about to run a better race than would be apparent through a less-informed read of its past performances.

3) A horse moving from an unfavorable to a favorable pace match-up.

4) An angle that "triggers" a more detailed analysis of a horse that might at first have been overlooked.

5) A strong negative opinion about a short-priced horse, developed from either a poor speed-figure pattern, a poor trainer pattern, or a switch from a favorable to an unfavorable pace match-up.

Uncovering these opportunities doesn't require any God-given gift, such as musicians who are born with perfect pitch. But it does require, besides a well-capitalized bankroll, an investment of something even more precious: time.

If you have the time to do the necessary research and the time to stop and think for a while about the not-so-obvious factors that might prove the key to a given race, you've already taken an edge on nine out of ten fellow horseplayers. It is my sincere hope that thoughtful horseplayers will find some of the ideas and procedures set forth in this book worthy of merit and incorporate them into their overall approach to the game.

Remember, it takes only one insight or nugget of information in the right race at the right time to make the difference between a near miss and a memorable score.

Wouldn't you agree?